ANTIQUES
PRICE GUIDE **2009**

Miller's Antiques Price Guide 2009
By Judith Miller

First American edition published in 2008
by Miller's, a division of Mitchell Beazley,
imprints of Octopus Publishing Group Ltd,
2-4 Heron Quays, London E14 4JP
Miller's is a registered trademark of
Octopus Publishing Group Ltd

An Hachette Livre Company
www.octopusbooks.co.uk

ISBN 978 1 84533 455 0

A CIP record for this book is available
from the Library of Congress

Set in Frutiger

Colour reproduction by Fine Arts, China
Printed and bound in China by C&C Offset Printing Co., Ltd.

Distributed in the United States and Canada by
Sterling Publishing Co., Inc.,
387 Park Avenue South, New York, NY 10016-8810

Publishing Manager Julie Brooke
Editors Sara Sturgess, Stephen Wells
Editorial Assistant Katy Armstrong
Digital Asset Co-ordinator John Parton
Design and DTP Tim and Ali Scrivens, TJ Graphics;
additional design by Jeremy Tilston, The Oak Studio
Photographers Graham Rae, Elizabeth Field,
John McKenzie, Dave Pincott
Indexer Hilary Bird
Production Manager Peter Hunt
Jacket Design Tim Foster, Juliette Norsworthy

ANTIQUES
PRICE GUIDE **2009**

Judith Miller

MILLER'S

CONTENTS

LIST OF CONSULTANTS

CERAMICS
Judith Miller

FURNITURE
Sebastian Clarke
Samuel T. Freeman & Co.
1808 Chestnut Street
Philadelphia
Pennsylvania 19103

CLOCKS
Chris Jussel
Samuel T. Freeman & Co.
1808 Chestnut Street
Philadelphia
Pennsylvania 19103

MODERN
John Sollo
Rago Arts & Auction Center
333 North Main Street
Lambertville
New Jersey 08530

ORIENTAL
Robert Waterhouse
Samuel T. Freeman & Co.
1808 Chestnut Street
Philadelphia
Pennsylvania 19103

FOLK ART
Ron Pook
Pook & Pook Inc
463 East Lancaster Avenue
Downingtown
Pennsylvania 19335

ARTS & CRAFTS
David Rago
Rago Arts & Auction Center
333 North Main Street
Lambertville
New Jersey 08530

HOW TO USE THIS BOOK

Running head Indicates the sub-category of the main heading.

The introduction Gives key facts about the factory, maker or style, along with stylistic identification points, value tips and advice on fakes.

Caption The description of the item illustrated, including when relevant, the period, the maker or factory, medium, the year it was made, dimensions and condition. Many captions have **footnotes** which explain terminology or give identification or valuation information.

The price range These give a ball park figure of what you should pay for a similar item. The great joy of antiques is that there is not a recommended retail price. The ranges are based on actual prices, either what a dealer will take or the full auction price. They are expressed in US$ (even for Canadian antiques). Canadian readers should refer to lastest conversion rates at http://finance.yahoo.com.

Page tab This appears on every page and identifies the main category heading as identified in the Contents List on pages 4-5.

A closer look Does exactly that. This is where we show identifying aspects of a factory or maker, point out rare colors or shapes, and explain why a particular piece is so desirable.

The object The antiques are shown in fulll color. This is a vital aid to identification and valuation. With many objects, a slight color variation can signify a large price differential.

Sorce code Every item has been specially photographed at an auction house, a dealer, an antiques market or a private collection. These are credited by code at the end of the caption, and can be checked against the Key to Illustrations on pages 683-684.

INTRODUCTION

It has been a very exciting year for me returning home to Miller's in time for our 30th Anniversary edition. Miller's is still the only global name in antiques and collectibles and we are publishing now in more countries and being translated into even more languages. This mirrors the world of Antiques itself. When we published the first Miller's Antiques Price Guide in 1978 (with black and white slightly fuzzy images) the antiques world was more national if not regional. The Internet has changed all that. It has provided a global market place and has seen prices for say a Lalique 'Poissons' vase sell for similar sums in Sydney, Edinburgh, Chicago and Hong Kong. Knowing what you are looking at has never been more relevant. Being able to spot the genuine article from the fake; the high quality handcrafted from the mass produced; the rare from the common has become the vital tools of the antiques and collectibles hunter. Our buying patterns and tastes may have changed but our need for authoritative price guides is a constant.

We are surrounded by the prophets of doom and gloom. The end of the antiques world has been predicted many times over the thirty years I have been producing Price Guides. This year is no different. Yes, some dealers' shops have closed but the dealers tend to reappear at antiques fairs or centers. Good specialist dealers and auction houses adapt and make the most of new opportunities. Many are taking advantage of the Internet boom and trading online where they can reach a global marketplace. Many people have prophesized the end of antique shops and the bricks and mortar auction. They see a world of cyber bidding and buying. While I absolutely accept that this has become an important part of our business, I believe there will always be the place for the thrill of finding a new treasure trove in an antiques shop you have just discovered and the silent joy when a much desired object is 'knocked down' to you, at auction, for less than your limit.

Another exciting development in October 2008 is the launch of our Miller's website – millersantiquesguide.com. This has been in the planning stage for well over a year and we aim to provide a site for everyone who loves the world of antiques and collectibles. It will attract the committed expert and the inquiring novice. You can search tens of thousands of antiques and collectibles from around the world – with full captions and price ranges. We include easy-to-understand extra information, including top tips and special features to look for. You also have access to fully illustrated articles from myself and the Miller's team of experts, including many names from the Antiques Roadshow, both in the UK and the US. As a global brand, Miller's team of experts travels the world to bring you the best of antiques and collectibles. What's selling where? Where are the hidden treasures? Spot trends as they happen. If you are travelling to Budapest, Buenos Aires or Buffalo find out where to shop. The best dealers and auctioneers can be tracked down through our dealer and auctioneer locator linked to Google maps. We will keep you up-to-date with all the antiques news. You will be able to view videos that will help you get more out of antiques as we walk you through all aspects of buying, selling, identifying and valuing. This is an incredibly exciting development for Miller's in its 30th year. We may be involved in treasures from the past but we also embrace the technology of the future.

Judith Miller.

A red enamel and gilt metal singing bird box, ivory cover carved with a bird. RGA

A Daum etched and enameled glass thistle vase, in autumnal palette. DRA

A rare Chinese Kangxi period blue and white bowl, decorated with prunus WW

PORCELAIN

THE PORCELAIN MARKET

The economy may be in turmoil but the antiques market, although a little lackluster, has remained reasonably steady while the ceramic year has been very much the curate's egg: good in parts. Anything rare, early and of excellent quality has sold strongly but middle range ceramics have not fared as well and any damage has severely affected the value of these wares.

Berlin plaques must have an impressed KPM mark. As always, attractive, romantic, scantily dressed young women fetch a premium, but well-painted groups of figures are also selling well.

The market for English blue and white is still strong for well painted early examples with collectors paying top dollar for anything dated. Rare shapes such as egg cups are particularly in demand. Later transfer printed wares are not doing as well, particularly if they feature common patterns.

Early Chelsea still demands a premium and the market can accept damage. Dry-edge Derby figures remain rare and desirable, but later figures are less easy to sell unless they are of exceptional quality. Late 18thC/early 19thC pieces with fine quality painting and gilding, like the botanical painting of Quaker Pegg, have risen in value steadily.

Although often summarily dismissed there are many fine pieces of Dresden, often painted by Hausmaler, to be found. Prices for Meissen remain very strong, particularly for pieces from 1720-50 and the work of J. G. Höroldt, C. F. Höroldt and J.J. Kandler. Some Samson work is now being collected in its own right – particularly desirable are the imitation Kakiemon ware and Chinese copies with elaborate gilt-bronze mounts. The market for good quality 18thC Sèvres remains very buoyant, as there is global demand for the high quality painting and gilding.

BERLIN

A late 19thC KPM oval porcelain plaque, painted with a young beauty wearing a diaphanous dress, impressed 'KPM' and sceptre mark, framed and signed 'Wagner'.

6.75in (17cm) high

$3,600-4,400   **FRE**

A late 19thC Berlin porcelain plaque, depicting 'Psyche in Moonlight', nude with a diaphanous cloth across her lap, mounted in a green plush and gilt frame.

5.75in (14.5cm) high

$3,000-4,000   **FRE**

A late 19thC KPM porcelain plaque, painted with a young maiden, impressed 'KPM' and sceptre.

The KPM mark denotes the Berlin porcelain factory.

7.75in (19.5cm) high

$5,600-6,400   **FRE**

MILLER'S COMPARES

An early 20thC Berlin porcelain roundel, depicting Lady Devonshire within a cobalt border, gilt details, signed 'Ullmer', in a giltwood frame.

Plaque 11.5in (29cm) diam

$800-1,000   **FRE**

A late 19thC KPM porcelain oval plaque, depicting a profile portrait of a young brunette beauty.

Plaque 8.5in (21.5cm) wide

$10,000-12,000   **FRE**

A late 19thC Berlin porcelain plaque, of a young maiden illuminated by a chamberstick, painted with 'Good Night'.

7in (28cm) high

$3,000-4,000   **FRE**

A 19thC Berlin porcelain plaque, depicting a young woman wearing a white head-covering and garland of leaves, her hands clasped to her chin, impressed mark '311C' and bearing paper label, framed.

Plaque 5in (12.5cm) wide

$3,000-5,000   **FRE**

The most desirable Berlin plaques on the market today usually feature a beautiful girl, such as the one shown above right. The further off the shoulder her clothes, the more suggestively they drape, and the more flesh that can be seen, the greater the value is likely to be. Collectors look for exceptional painting, with even skin tone and painstakingly detailed face, hair and breasts. Folds in clothing and other fabric should be realistic. The plaque shown here on the right has all of these, plus the artist has painted a crown of beautifully rendered flowers in her hair.

The stiff formality of plaques bearing historical portraits inspired by the English painter Thomas Gainsborough, such as the one on the left, are no longer as desirable. Equally unpopular in today's market are plaques painted with religious scenes.

A late 19thC Berlin painted porcelain plaque, painted with 'Springtime' after Jules Frederic Ballavoine, inscribed verso, framed.

7.5in (19cm) high

$700-900 FRE

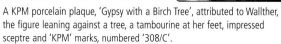

A KPM porcelain plaque, 'Gypsy with a Birch Tree', attributed to Wallther, the figure leaning against a tree, a tambourine at her feet, impressed sceptre and 'KPM' marks, numbered '308/C'.

8in (20.5cm) high

$7,000-9,000 FRE

A late 19th/early 20thC KPM porcelain plaque, depicting a winged nymph by a pool, gazing at her reflection, impressed 'KPM' and sceptre marks, framed.

8.75in (22cm) high

$4,000-5,000 FRE

A late 19thC Berlin porcelain plaque, signed indistinctly, depicting Marie Antoinette, picking roses from a garden, framed.

9in (22.75cm) high

$3,000-4,000 FRE

A late 19thC Berlin porcelain plaque, depicting Queen Louise walking down the steps of a palace, after Richter, framed.

9.5in (24cm) high

$4,000-5,000 FRE

A Berlin porcelain plaque, 'Le Coupe Enchantee', after Georges Achille-Fould, depicting a young beauty seated on the edge of a table and raising a glass of wine, stamped 'Made in Germany', framed.

Plaque 5.5in (14cm) wide

$800-1,200 FRE

A 19thC KPM porcelain plaque, depicting a young beauty in Renaissance costume holding a basket of fruit, impressed 'KPM' and sceptre marks, framed.

Plaque 7.5in (19cm) wide

$7,000-8,000 FRE

A KPM artist signed hand painted porcelain plaque, depicting an Odalisque, verso impressed 'KPM' beneath the sceptre and signed lower right 'S. Miriam', the rectangular plaque in a vintage carved and molded gilt-wood frame.

c1900

The plaque 15.75in (40cm) high

$20,000-30,000 JACK

A late 19thC KPM porcelain plaque, finely painted with the 'Fruit sellers' after Murillo, with a giltwood & gesso frame, impressed 'KPM' and sceptre mark.

12in (30.5cm) high

$16,000-20,000 FRE

A late 19thC KPM porcelain plaque, depicting a mother holding her young child, impressed 'KPM' and sceptre mark, framed.

9.75in (25cm) high

$6,000-7,000 FRE

A late 19thC large Berlin porcelain plaque, finely painted with a Tyrolean tavern scene, after Franz von Defregger, signed 'Defregger', dated and framed.

1877   *14.5in (37cm) high*

$8,500-9,500   **FRE**

A late 19thC Berlin porcelain plaque, painted with a tavern scene, framed.

9.5in (24cm) wide

$3,600-4,400   **FRE**

A late 19thC pair of KPM porcelain plaques, painted with bust length portraits of a young Gypsy boy and his companion, impressed 'KPM' and sceptre.

9.75in (25cm) high

$7,000-8,000   **FRE**

After Gerrit Dou, 'The Prayer of the Spinner', a KPM porcelain plaque, depicting an old woman praying over her meal, in a Dutch interior, in a giltwood frame.

11in (28cm) high

$10,000-14,000   **FRE**

A late 19thC KPM porcelain plaque, depicting two young women whispering by candlelight, in the manner of Godfried Schalcken, impressed 'KPM' and sceptre marks.

7in (18cm) high

$2,000-3,000   **FRE**

A 19thC KPM porcelain plaque, painted with 'Meleager and Atlanta' after Peter Paul Rubens, in a giltwood & gesso frame, impressed 'KPM' & sceptre mark.

12in (30.5cm) wide

$12,000-16,000   **FRE**

A late 19th/early 20thC KPM porcelain plaque, 'Repenting Magdalena', depicting Magdalena with her eyes cast upward, printed sceptre and KPM marks, partial paper label, framed.

7.5in (19cm) wide

$4,000-6,000   **FRE**

After Gabriel Cornelius Ritter Von Max, 'The Vision', a KPM porcelain plaque, painted with a profile portrait of a young woman with long brown hair, her eyes downcast and hands clasped at her breast, a floral wreath appearing above her, impressed 'KPM' and factory marks, framed.

A KPM porcelain plaque, 'Jesus and John the Baptist', depicted as children, with Jesus reclining asleep in John's lap, a grazing sheep to the right, impressed 'KPM' and sceptre marks, in a giltwood frame.

Plaque 8in (20cm) wide

$7,000-8,000 FRE

Plaque 9.5in (24cm) high

$5,000-7,000 FRE

A late 19thC 'Berlin'-style porcelain plaque, finely painted with a bust-length portrait of an elderly gentleman, after Balthazar Denner, impressed spurious 'KPM' and sceptre mark.

A late 19thC Berlin porcelain cabinet plate, decorated with a portrait of 'Blanche', within a gilt and cobalt border, signed 'Herner', pseudo blue beehive mark.

A late 19thC KPM Art Nouveau porcelain vase, with a painted reserve depicting a bust length portrait of a young beauty inscribed 'Orientalin', enriched with gilt, blue sceptre mark.

9.5in (24cm) high

$1,800-2,400 FRE

9.75in (24.5cm) diam

$400-600 FRE

19.25in (49cm) high

$8,000-9,000 FRE

A 19thC KPM porcelain and gilt bronze mounted bijouterie box, painted throughout, with crown finial, lined interior, and angel's mask motifs, raised on Rococo scroll feet, underglaze blue sceptre mark.

10.5in (26.5cm) wide

$5,600-6,400 FRE

A pair of Berlin brûles parfum and covers, painted with scenes of courting couples and flowers, blue sceptre marks.

c1880 *7in (17.5cm) high*

$500-600 WW

PORCELAIN

ESSENTIAL REFERENCE: BOW

Founded in mid-18thC at Stratford Langthorne, Essex. Bow was one of the first two porcelain factories in England.

Blue and white wares are divided into three periods:

● Early period 1749–54, thickly potted, glaze often blue/green.
● Middle period 1755–65, darker blue, thinly potted, relatively heavy.
● Late period 1765–76, marked deterioration in quality.
● Early polychrome wares decorated in 'famille rose' colors.
● In 1775 the factory was acquired by W. Dewsbury. All Bow molds and tools moved to the Derby porcelain factory.

A rare early Bow white glazed teapot and cover, the globular body with applied flowering prunus, unmarked, damages and restoration.

c1750-55   7.5in (19cm) high

$1,000-1,600   WW

A rare Bow white glazed piggin, with applied prunus decoration, damages, the handle restored.

c1752-55   3in (8cm) high

$1,000-1,200   WW

A small Bow 'Jumping Boy' pattern blue and white plate, the border with Chinese emblems and flowers on hatched bands, a small restored chip at 12 o'clock.

c1760   6.5in (16.5cm) diam

$1,200-1,600   WW

A Bow pickle dish, decorated in blue with a variation of the Worcester Pickle Leaf Vine pattern, minor wear and damages.

c1765   3.75in (9.5cm) high

$300-500   WW

A small Bow blue and white mug, painted with pine trees and rockwork flanked by huts, beneath a hatched border.

c1765   3.5in (9cm) high

$2,000-2,400   WW

A Bow figure of Ceres, emblematic of Earth, holding a cornucopia, a lion resting at her feet, minor damages.

c1758   (7.5in) 19cm high

$1,600-2,400   WW

A Bow figure of a dancer or gallant, in expansive pose before a tree stump on a molded base, unmarked, damages and restoration.

c1756-58   7.25in (18.5cm) high

$1,000-1,400   WW

A Bow model of a flower girl, after Boucher, with blooms in her apron and a basket of grapes on her arm, barefoot on a shallow molded base, incised 'AF' repairer's mark.

c1758   6in (15cm) high

$1,000-1,400   WW

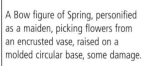

A Bow figure of Spring, personified as a maiden, picking flowers from an encrusted vase, raised on a molded circular base, some damage.

c1760-65   9.5in (24cm) high

$1,000-1,400   WW

A Bow figure of a sportsman, holding a gun in his left hand, a dog seated beside him, applied flowers to the base, unmarked, restored.

c1756-60   5in (13cm) high

$1,400-2,000   **WW**

CLOSER LOOK: BOW CANDLESTICKS

After c1755 Bow figures were well colored and in characteristic colors which were dominated by: milky, deep sky-blue; rich egg-yolk yellow; and deep purplish puce.

Elaborate and overpowering treestump supports with floral bocage are typical of Bow figures after c1760.

Figures were slip-molded which made a heavier body and necessitated careful construction so they did not collapse in the kiln.

After c1760 bases were modeled in the Rococo style and raised on high scroll feet.

A pair of Bow peacock candlesticks, each bird before flowering bocage, on a scrollwork base, red anchor and dagger mark, and blue cross mark to one, 'G' mark to the other, damages and restoration.

c1760   11in (28cm) high

$8,000-10,000   **WW**

A pair of Bow frill vases and covers, with applied mask handles, painted with butterflies and insects amidst large applied flowers, the shoulders and necks pierced, the finials molded as a bird tucking its head under one wing, damages and restoration.

c1760-70   11.75in (30cm) high

$1,400-2,000   **WW**

A pair of Bow vases, with orange blossoms, with applied mask handles, red anchor and dagger marks, damages and restoration.

c1770   7.25in (18.5cm) high

$2,000-3,000   **WW**

One of a rare pair of Bow eggcups, painted with stylized flowers in polychrome enamels, unmarked, one with a small rim chip.

c1750-55   2.75in (7cm) high

$7,000-9,000 PAIR   **WW**

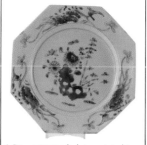

A Bow octagonal plate, painted in polychrome enamels with peony, bamboo and insects above blue rockwork, unmarked, minor wear and damages, paper label for the E & J Handley Collection.

c1753   9.25in (23.5cm) diam

$1,000-1,400   **WW**

A Bow octagonal plate, painted in polychrome enamels with peony and an insect, unmarked, some damages, paper label for the E & J Handley Collection.

c1755   9in (23cm) diam

$800-1,000   **WW**

A rare Bow reticulated oval basket and cover, applied with blue and puce flowers, the handle modeled as a bird with its head tucked under one wing, standing on a branch, impressed 'T' mark, some restoration to the bird finial.

c1760-65   6.25in (16cm) high

$7,000-9,000   **WW**

PORCELAIN

A Caughley caddy spoon, printed in blue with a pagoda on an island and two small sailing boats.

c1780   4in (10.5cm) high

$1,200-1,600   **WW**

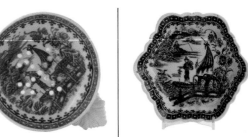

A Caughley strainer, printed in blue, with the 'Fisherman' or 'Pleasure Boat' pattern, the center pierced with a cross-shaped pattern of holes, unmarked.

c1780-1790   3.75in (9.5cm) high

$300-400   **WW**

A Caughley teapot stand, printed with the 'Fisherman' or 'Pleasure Boat' pattern, unmarked, a tiny rim flake.

c1780   6in (15cm) high

$200-240   **WW**

A Caughley heart shaped dish, painted in blue with the 'Weir' pattern within a Greek key and paneled diaper border between gilt bands.

c1790   10.75in (27cm) wide

$600-700   **NEA**

A late 18thC Caughley sauceboat, cover and ladle, painted in blue and gold with flower sprigs and border patterns, 'S' mark to the base, minor faults and the cover a poor fit.

                    6.75in (17cm) high

$500-600   **WW**

ESSENTIAL REFERENCE: CHELSEA

The factory's early history is very vague but it may have acquired the knowledge of porcelain manufacture in 1742.

Triangle Period 1745–49:
- Wares scarce and costly.
- Mainly undecorated.
- Body comparatively thick, slightly chalky with 'glassy' glaze.

Raised Anchor Period 1749–52:
- Paste now improved.
- Mostly restrained decoration, either Kakiemon or sparse floral work.
- Most collectible ware of this and the Red Anchor period was fable decorated.
- Creamy, waxy appearance of glaze virtually indistinguishable from Red Anchor glaze.

Red Anchor Period 1752–56:
- Significant Meissen influence.
- Glaze now slightly opaque and paste smoother.
- Figures unsurpassed by any other English factory.
- Chelsea 'toys' are rare and expensive.

Gold Anchor Period 1757–69:
- Rococo influence, rich gilding and characteristic mazarine blue.
- Decoration quite florid in style, especially in comparison to earlier painting.
- Influenced by Sèvres.
- Thick glaze can craze.

A Chelsea model of a child, seated on a flared plinth, holding a globe, marked around the equator with the hours of the day, red anchor mark to the back of the base, restoration to the extremities.

c1755-60   5in (12.5cm) high

$3,600-4,400   **WW**

A rare Chelsea model of Cupid in disguise as a moneylender, wearing a black cloak and hat, standing on a gilt-decorated base, unmarked, restored.

c1755-60   4.5in (11.5cm) high

$1,200-1,800   **WW**

A Chelsea model of a recumbent sheep, red anchor mark to the front of the base, restoration to the base and faint body cracks.

c1755   4in (10cm) high

$4,400-5,600   **WW**

A Chelsea fable group, 'The Cock and the Jewell', with a cockerel and hens before flowering bocage, a jeweled necklace at their feet, raised and titled on a scrollwork base, unmarked, damages and restoration.

c1760   8.75in (22cm) high

$5,000-6,000   **WW**

CLOSER LOOK: CHELSEA GOLD ANCHOR MODEL

A pair of Chelsea sweetmeat figures, modeled as bun-sellers, each beside a deep square-section basket, raised on scrollwork bases with applied flowers, gold anchor marks, some damage and restoration to both.

c1760-1765   9.5in (24cm) high

$2,000-3,000   **WW**

Figures made at Chelsea during the gold anchor period were often inspired by prints, the subjects of which the modelers embellished. Groups were often swamped by floral bocage.

The figures portrayed tend to have disproportionately small heads.

The bases were high, pierced and scrolled, heightened with gilding and applied flowers. Unlike most other Rococo bases, Chelsea bases were usually symmetrical.

Models tended to be extensively covered in high-quality gilding.

A Chelsea sweetmeat figure, modeled as a dandy in a long pink coat, lifting the lid on an oval basket, a dog seated beneath, raised on a scrollwork base, gold anchor mark, damages and restoration.

c1760-65   7.75in (19.5cm) high

$1,000-1,400   **WW**

A rare Chelsea model of Hercules slaying the Lernaean Hydra, assisted by his nephew, Iolaus, who seals the neck stumps with a red hot brand, the bocage hung with the golden apples of the Hesperides, raised on a scrolled base, gold anchor mark, damages and restoration.

c1760-65   13.75in (35cm) high

$50,000-60,000   **WW**

A pair of Chelsea figures of sportsmen, one holding a gun, the other holding a dead game bird with a spaniel at his feet, both on floral scrolled bases, gold anchor marks, damages and restoration.

c1765   8.25in (21cm) high

$8,000-10,000   **WW**

A Chelsea fable candlestick, 'The Fox and the Goat', the goat's head protruding from the well shaft, the fox perched on the edge dispensing his wisdom to "Never trust the advice of a man in difficulties", gold anchor mark, some restoration.

c1765-1770   10.5in (27cm) high

$1,000-1,400   **WW**

A pair of Chelsea figures of Summer and Winter, personified as a young girl with a lap full of flowers, and as a man wrapped against the cold and smoking a pipe, on scrollwork bases, gold anchor mark to one, damage and restoration.

c1765   5.25in (13.5cm) high

$3,600-4,400   **WW**

PORCELAIN

A 19thC Chelsea scent bottle with floral stopper, formed as a theatrical with a sword standing before a flower encrusted pillar, the base bearing the title 'Fidelle en Amitie'.

3.25in (8cm) high

$2,000-3,000 WW

A Chelsea plate, painted in the 'Warren Hastings' pattern, with panels of animals from 'Aesop's fables' to the molded border, red anchor mark, restored.

c1753 *9.5in (24cm) high*

$2,000-3,000 WW

A Chelsea plate with ogee edge, painted in the Kakiemon palette with the 'Flying Fox' and 'Rooting Squirrel' pattern, unmarked.

c1753 *8.75in (22.5cm) high*

$2,000-3,000 WW

A Chelsea Rococo molded plate, painted with panels of flowers within purple scrolling borders, red anchor mark, small rim chip.

c1755 *8.25in (21cm) high*

$800-1,200 WW

A Chelsea rectangular octagonal dish, with molded rim, painted with flowers, butterflies and insects, unmarked, some wear to the enamels.

c1755 *12.5in (32cm) high*

$1,300-1,500 WW

A Rococo-molded Chelsea plate, the border painted with four pairs of colorful birds, the well with flower sprays and sprigs, a red anchor mark, faint rim cracks.

c1755 *9in (23cm) high*

$600-1,000 WW

A pair of Chelsea molded plates, painted with flowers in polychrome enamels, red anchor marks, one heavily restored.

c1755 *8.5in (21.5cm) high*

$440-560 WW

A Chelsea dish, modeled as a large pink peony, the stalk forming the handle, some restoration.

c1755-60 *8.25in (21cm) diam*

$4,000-6,000 WW

A Chelsea silver-shaped botanical dish, painted with a floral specimen in polychrome enamels, red anchor mark, cracked and riveted.

c1755-60 *8in (20.5cm) diam*

$800-1,200 WW

A Chelsea plate, the well painted with flowers in polychrome enamels, the molded rim with yellow birds in pairs, gold anchor mark.

c1760-65 *8.5in (21.5cm) high*

$1,000-1,400 WW

A Chelsea plate, painted with pomegranates amidst scattered insects, the rim with panels of exotic birds on a dark blue ground, gold anchor mark, some restoration to the rim.

c1765 *8.25in (21cm) high*

$1,400-1,800 WW

A Chelsea dish, with reticulated border, painted with flower sprays, gold anchor mark, some wear and minor damages.

c1765-69 *8in (20.5cm) high*

$700-800 WW

A pair of Chelsea cinquefoil lobed plates, painted with butterflies and gilt flowers, the rims with turquoise panels within gilt scrolls, gold anchor marks, probably refired, peppering and specking to the glaze.

c1765 *9.25in (23.5cm) diam*

$800-1,200 WW

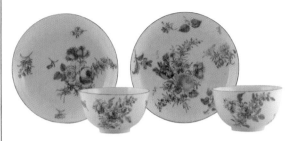

A good pair of Chelsea tea bowls and saucers, finely painted with sprays of flowers in polychrome enamels, brown line rims, red anchor marks.

c1755

$5,000-6,000 WW

A Chelsea two-handled cup and saucer, the pine-cone molding painted with gilt arrowheads on a puce ground beneath a gilded border of insects and flowers, gold anchor marks, some wear to the gilding.

c1765 *6in (15cm) high*

$3,600-4,400 WW

A pair of Chelsea Rococo molded tripod stands, hung with bunches of grapes, the acanthus leaf scrolls picked out in puce, green and gilt, one with an anchor mark in puce.

c1752-58 *5in (12.5cm) high*

$2,400-3,000 WW

A pair of Chelsea strawberry-molded sauceboats, the interiors with botanical specimens, flowers and insects, the handles formed as stalks, red anchor marks, both damaged and repaired.

c1754-56 *6.75in (17cm) high*

$2,800-3,600 WW

A Chelsea basket, painted with fruit and insects, with pierced and molded rim, gold anchor mark, minor chips to the foot rim and wear to the enamel.

c1765 *8.25in (21cm) high*

$1,400-1,800 WW

A rare Chelsea white glazed bowl, with applied prunus decoration, unmarked, broken and repaired.

c1749-52 *8in (20cm) high*

$2,000-3,000 WW

A rare Chelsea wine cooler, painted with polychrome flower sprays, the sides molded with bullrushes emerging from a shell motif, red anchor mark, restored.

c1755 *10.25in (26cm) high*

$1,600-2,400 WW

A set of six Coalport plates, the wells painted with flowers, the rims molded with grapevines and gilded with scrolling motifs, one with a printed 'Society of Arts' mark.

c1820   *8in (20.5cm) diam*

$1,200-1,800   **WW**

An early 19thC Coalport plate, painted in the manner of William Billingsley with panels of flowers on a scale blue ground, unmarked.

8.5in (21.5cm) high

$200-400   **WW**

A molded Coalport plate, brightly painted with flowers and with gilt details to the border.

c1820   *9.25in (23.5cm) diam*

$200-400   **WW**

An early 20thC Coalport plate, the center painted with a still life of fruit, signed 'Howard', within a raised gilt and pale yellow border.

10.5in (27cm) high

$600-800   **WW**

A pair of Coalport plates, naturalistically painted with birds and butterflies, on a pale green ground, one with a printed mark, some wear to the gilding.

c1870   *9.5in (24cm) diam*

$400-600   **WW**

A pair of Coalport two-handled vases, each ovoid body painted with birds amongst trees and flowers beneath a fluted waisted neck enriched with gilding, set with scroll and leaf molded handles, raised on a circular foot, with gilt ampersand marks.

c1860   *12in (33cm) high*

$7,000-8,000   **SOTH**

An early 19thC Coalport campana vase, with gilt loop handles, each side painted with figures and buildings in a rural setting, the white ground gilded with garlands and foliate scrolls, tiny faults.

9.75in (24.5cm) high

$500-700   **WW**

A pair of Coalport ovoid vases and covers, painted by John Randall, with colorful exotic birds amidst fruit and flowers, molded with gilt rope swags, unmarked, some restoration.

c1870   13.5in (34cm) high

$1,800-2,400   **WW**

A pair of late 19thC Coalport vases and covers, with colorful birds to one side, flowers and fruit to the other, on a blue-scale ground, printed factory marks and pattern numbers in gilt, restoration to both.

15.5in (39.5cm) high

$1,000-1,400   **WW**

A Coalport part tea service, comprising a teapot and cover, sugar bowl and cover, six cups and eight saucers, decorated with colorful flowers on pale yellow bands, enriched with gilding, pattern number 996, some damages.

c1825

$600-800   **WW**

A Coalport letter rack, molded with leaves and painted with a basket of flowers, unmarked, damages and restoration.

c1825   7.75in (19.5cm) high

$640-760   **WW**

A mid-19thC large Coalport parian ware centerpiece, designed as a central support modeled as three symbolic angels, each holding their own attribute, their wings supporting a turquoise glazed and ivy gilded bowl with foliate and scroll pierced rim, all raised on a tri-partite plinth base, with conforming turquoise and gilt decoration, unmarked.

20.75in (53cm) high

$2,000-3,000   **HALL**

A limited edition Coalport model, 'The Pheasant', printed marks, no. 107 of 750, with a wood stand and reference sheet.

c1979   11in (30cm) high

$200-400   **WW**

DAVENPORT

A 19thC Davenport mug, printed with the Royal coat of arms for Queen Victoria and the legend 'Imperial Measure', printed mark, minor damages.

5in (12.5cm) high

$200-300   **WW**

A Davenport spiral molded vase, painted with a figure with four sheep before a house, the reverse with a panel of flowers on a cerise ground, with a richly gilded neck, handles and foot, unmarked.

c1835   8in (20.5cm) high

$300-400   **WW**

An unusual Davenport pink lusterware tea service, comprising teapot and cover, sugar bowl and cover, milk jug and cover, butter dish and cover, ten teacups and ten saucers, printed in black with a variant of the 'Swiss Pastime' pattern, black printed marks, minor faults.

c1835

$800-1,200   **WW**

A fine Davenport porcelain plate, lavishly painted with roses, hollyhocks, phlox and Morning Glory, the border gilded, impressed factory mark.

c1820   9.25in (23.5cm) diam.

$2,000-2,400   **WW**

ESSENTIAL REFERENCE: DERBY

The first porcelain factory in Derby, England was possibly started by André Planché and was operating experimentally by 1750.

Early period 1750-56
- Early soft paste is fine-grained and grayish and almost has the appearance of hard paste porcelain. Grayish white glaze.
- Figures are known as 'dry-edge' because the glaze was wiped off the edge of the bases to prevent them sticking in the kiln.

Later period 1756-69
- In 1756, William Dewsbury, John Heath and André Planché started what became the first Derby Porcelain Factory.
- Restrained decoration, with much of the body left plain, in the Meissen style.
- Excellent body, sometimes with faintly bluish appearance.

Chelsea-Derby 1770-84
- In 1770, Dewsbury bought the Chelsea factory and ran it until 1784 in conjunction with Derby.
- Chelsea-Derby figures made at Derby.
- Unglazed white biscuit figures. Move away from the academic Meissen style towards the more fashionable French taste.
- 1770s: body of silky appearance and bluish-white tone.
- 1780s: body very smooth with white glaze. Painting on such pieces is superb, especially the landscapes of Jockey Hill and Zachariah Boreman.
- 1780s and 1790s: noted for exceptional botanical painting by 'Quaker' Pegg and John Brewer.
- Around 1800 the body degenerated, becoming somewhat thicker, and glaze tended to crack and allow discoloration.
- Products made at both factories bore the same mark – an anchor and the letter D.

Crown Derby 1784-1811
- Factory adopted a crowned D as its mark.
- Earlier styles continued to be made. Other products included Neoclassical tablewares, sometimes painted with naturalistic flowers, by William Billingsley and others. Statuettes produced after models by Jean-Jacques Spängler and Pierre Stephan.

Bloor Derby 1811-45
- Period of steady decline in which factory lost all individuality.

Royal Crown Derby
- Established in 1876. The factory remains active today.

A rare Derby dry-edge figure of a long-haired Cupid, seated on a cushion and holding a garland of flowers, unmarked, damaged, paper label for 'Frances L. Dickson collection' with handwritten note connecting it to the Glaisher Collection.

c1750   *3.5in (9cm) high*

$4,000-5,000   **WW**

A Derby figure of a dancing shepherdess, holding her skirt in her right hand with flowers in her left, a sheep recumbent at her feet, the base applied with flowers, some restoration.

c1754   *6.5in (16.5cm) high*

$700-800   **WW**

A Derby model of Neptune, standing before a dolphin on a tall base of shells and seaweed, gold anchor mark, some damages.

c1758-65   *9.75in (25cm) high*

$1,400-2,000   **WW**

A Derby model of lovers, the young gardener seated and holding a spade, his companion standing with a basket of flowers on her hip, some good restoration.

c1760-65   *6in (15cm) high*

$2,000-3,000   **WW**

A pair of Derby sweetmeat figures, each beside a rectangular box before tall flowering bocage, raised on a molded circular base, damages and restoration.

c1765   *8.75in (22cm) high*

$1,400-2,000   **WW**

A large Derby model of Athena, resting her shield in her left hand, her right hand raised above her head, standing on a molded circular base, damage and restoration.

c1765   *13in (33.5cm) high*

$600-800   **WW**

A Derby group of Spring and Winter, as a young girl with a basket of flowers and a sportsman with a gun and satchel, incised '68', losses and restoration.

c1760-70   *9.25in (23.5cm) high*

$1,300-1,500   **WW**

A large Derby model of Athena, her shield in her left hand, resting upon a stack of books atop of which sits an owl, some damage and restoration.

c1765   15.25in (38.5cm) high

$800-1,000   **WW**

A Derby model of a musician, playing a tambourine and blowing on a pipe, leant on a blossom encrusted tree stump, restored.

c1765   10.5in (27cm) high

$500-700   **WW**

A pair of Derby shepherds, the girl gathering flowers in her apron, with a sheep at her feet, the young man holding a pipe with a dog at his side, both on scroll bases, both figures restored.

c1765   7.5in (19cm) high

$1,000-1,200   **WW**

A Derby model of Neptune, his mantle billowing in the wind, standing beside a dolphin on a shell and scrollwork base, one arm broken and repaired.

c1765-69   8.25in (21cm) high

$700-900   **WW**

A pair of Derby figures of Spring and Summer, personified as children, Spring with a floral crown and a basket of flowers on his lap, Summer with a diadem of corn, holding a cornsheaf, both on scrollwork bases, some restoration to one figure.

c1765-70   5.5in (14cm) high

$900-1,100   **WW**

A Derby model of the Four Seasons, personified as four figures around an obelisk, holding flowers, fruit and corn, damages and restoration.

c1760-1770   9.5in (24.5cm) high

$1,200-1,800   **WW**

A pair of 18thC Derby figures of the Dresden shepherds, the woman collecting flowers in her apron wearing a white jacket and pink flower sprigged skirt, with a tree trunk and lamb at her feet, the man with a fruit basket, wearing a green and yellow cloak, a white polychrome flower sprigged coat and red gilt flower sprigged breeches, with a dog and a tree trunk by his feet, on Rococo bases.

9.75in (25cm) high

$2,000-2,400   **L&T**

A pair of Derby figures of musicians, he with a flageolet and tambourine, she with a triangle, both stood before flowering bocage on scrollwork bases, some restoration to both.

c1770   8.5in (21.5cm) high

$600-1,000   **WW**

A Derby candlestick, with two playful lambs beneath flowering bocage, raised on a scrollwork and shell base, some restoration.

c1765-1770   *8.75in (22.5cm) high*

$500-700   **WW**

A Derby candlestick figure, modeled as a young lady carrying flowers in her apron, and standing before a leafy flowering tree, some restoration.

c1770   *10.5in (26.5cm) high*

$800-1,000   **WW**

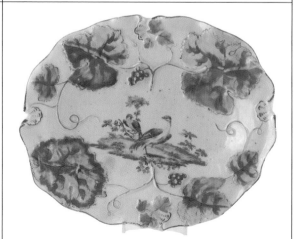

A Derby model of two goldfinches, feeding a nest of three chicks on floral bocage, raised on a scrollwork base, unmarked, restored.

c1765-70   *8in (20cm) high*

$800-1,000   **WW**

A Derby oval dish, painted with a large apple surrounded by various insects and butterflies, unmarked, wear to the enamels.

c1755-60   *9in (23cm) diam*

$900-1,100   **WW**

A Derby dish, molded with leaves and grapes, picked out in polychrome enamels, the well painted with two birds, unmarked, minor faults.

c1758   *10.5in (27cm) diam*

$1,600-2,000   **WW**

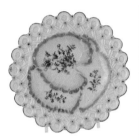

A Derby plate, molded with three geranium leaves to the center, the rim with a geometric flower-studded design, painted with flower sprays in polychrome enamels, unmarked, chip to the foot rim, the enamels worn.

c1758-1760   7.25in (18.5cm) diam
$900-1,100   **WW**

A Derby leaf molded dish, painted with flower sprays, each leaf edged in green enamel, the stalk forming a handle, unmarked, minor damages.

c1760-65   6.5in (16.5cm) diam
$1,000-1,400   **WW**

A late 18thC Derby plate, with a spiral fluted border and painted with a rose, a puce factory mark above pattern number 65, small restored rim chip.

                    9in (23cm) diam
$200-400   **WW**

A Derby Animal service plate, painted to the center by John Brewer, with two donkeys in a landscape, crown and crossed baton mark, dots and 'D' in purple and pattern 268.

c1795-1800   8.75in (22.5cm) diam
$800-1,000   **NEA**

A Derby Rococo molded flower vase, each side painted with an exotic bird before a flowering tree, unmarked, damages and restoration.

c1765   8.75in (22.5cm) high
$800-1,000   **WW**

A Derby Rococo vase, painted with birds and flowers, with applied flower heads, unmarked, small chips.

c1765   9in (23cm) high
$1,000-1,600   **WW**

One of a pair of Derby third quarter 18thC painted 'frill' covered vases, the pierced domed cover with bird finial over an inverted baluster-form body painted with insects, with pierced trellis motif at the shoulder and encrusted with masks and floral garlands, on a spreading foot, unmarked.

                  11.5in (29cm) high
$700-900 PAIR   **FRE**

CLOSER LOOK: DERBY CAMPANA VASE

William Pegg's painting is considered to be on a par with the best botanical still life painters of his day. His flowers have a three-dimensional quality and intensity.

Other artists of the time tended to paint in the center or at random. Pegg painted across the entire surface.

Unlike most of his contemporaries, Pegg painted largely from nature rather than copying from botanical magazines of the period.

Named, signed pieces by Pegg are rare and desirable.

A Derby two-handled vase of elongated campana form, painted in the manner of Quaker Pegg, with a broad band of summer flowers including a passion flower, tulip and roses, against a black background, set with scroll and leaf molded loop handles, raised on a socle foot and square base, red painted factory mark and number 24.

William 'Quaker' Pegg was the leading flower painter of his day. Born in 1775 he worked at the Derby factory for two short periods, the first from 1796 to 1801, and the second from 1813 to 1820. In 1800 he joined The Society of Friends and went on to develop a religious mania that resulted in him rejecting his own work as religious idolatry.

c1815   12.5in (32cm) high
$16,000-20,000   **SOTH**

PORCELAIN

A pair of Derby cos lettuce sauceboats, painted and applied with flowers, unmarked.

c1756   *7.75in (20cm) high*

$1,000-1,600   **WW**

A Derby cylindrical butter-tub and cover, painted with birds and flowers, a molded strawberry knop to the cover, raised on three claw feet, unmarked, damage and restoration, the handles missing.

c1760   *4.5in (11.5cm) high*

$800-1,200   **WW**

A Derby silver-shaped cream jug, decorated in blue with a Chinese pagoda, unmarked, minor damages.

c1770   *4.75in (12cm) high*

$500-600   **WW**

A pair of early 19thC Derby models of a young man and woman, after Meissen, both seated, on pierced and gilded bases, incised model number marks, some restoration, the object in the man's hand replaced.

         6.75in (17cm) high

$700-900   **WW**

A pair of Derby models, one of a man fitting a lady's shoe, the other of a gentleman having his shoe shone, each on pierced circular bases, imprinted and incised marks, some restoration.

c1820   *7in (18cm) high*

$400-600   **WW**

One of a set of four Derby cornucopia wall pockets, modeled en rocaille and painted in colored enamels with panels of exotic birds, one damaged with old repairs.

c1765   *Tallest 9.75in (24.5cm) high*

$12,000-16,000 THE SET   **DN**

An early 19thC Derby bone china figure of Napoleon, standing beside a plinth inscribed with his birthday and date of death, raised on a square base, crowned 'D' mark in iron red, restored.

         7.75in (20cm) high

$400-600   **WW**

A pair of Derby Mansion House dwarfs, based on a drawing by Jacques Callot, the first example holding a staff and wearing a hat bearing an advertisement form 'Mr. Curious' dog & monkey act', inscribed 'No. 227', the other example wearing a hat advertising a 'poultry sale', inscribed 'No. 227', both with crowned 'D' marks.

c1820   *the tallest 6.75in (17cm) high*

$1,200-1,600   **FRE**

A pair of early 19thC Derby two-handled vases, painted with flowers and gilt foliate motifs on a white ground, crowned 'D' and crossed batons marks in iron red, some restoration.

9in (23cm) high

$1,400-2,000 WW

A garniture of three Derby campana vases, painted with panels of flowers on a dark blue ground, highlighted with foliate bands of gilding, the handles of each vase formed as a snake, printed 'Bloor Derby' marks, some damages and restoration.

c1825 *8.25in (21cm) high*

$600-800 WW

A Derby bute-shaped teacup and saucer, painted with landscape panels in the manner of Jockey Hill, on a yellow ground, titled 'On the Coast of Sussex' and 'Near Rochester', some wear to the enamels.

c1800

$500-700 WW

A pair of early 19thC Derby cups and saucers, painted with rural scenes of Britain on a lavish blue and gilt ground, crowned crossed batons mark and each piece titled in iron red, some wear to the gilding

$400-500 WW

An early 19thC Derby porter mug, painted with a panel of flowers on a green ground, beneath a gilt scrolling foliate border, partial red printed mark to the base, rim crack.

6.75in (17cm) high

$300-400 WW

An early 19thC Derby porter mug, painted in the manner of Robert Brewer with Chatsworth Hall, on dark blue ground, crowned crossed batons and 'D' mark in iron red, titled to the base, restored.

7in (17.5cm) high

$300-500 WW

An early 19thC Derby botanical plate, painted in pattern number '141' with Caparis Spinosa, the caper shrub, titled to the base, painted crowned crossed batons mark in blue.

8.75in (22cm) diam.

$400-600 WW

A Derby plate, the well painted with an octagonal panel of buildings behind a waterfall, probably by George Robertson, the border with stylized gilt foliage on an orange ground, titled 'Near Keswick, Cumberland', iron red factory mark.

c1812 *8.75in (22cm) diam*

$400-600 WW

A Derby bourdalou, painted with sprigged decoration in blue, green and gilt, unmarked. some wear.

c1800 *9.75in (24.5cm) high*

$800-1,200 WW

A Derby oval sauce tureen and cover, painted with a variation of the 'Kylin' pattern, a blue seal mark, a chip beneath the foot rim.

7.75in (19.5cm) high

$600-1,000 WW

An early 19thC porcelain rectangular plaque, probably painted by Thomas Steele on a Derby blank, with a still-life of fruit spilling over a tabletop, in a gilt and black frame, restored.

12.5in (32cm) high

$800-1,000 WW

A Derby oval coffee pot, each side painted with a panel of flowers in the manner of William Billingsley, on a pale tangerine ground decorated with gilt foliage, unmarked, wear to the gilding.

c1800 *10in (25.5cm) high*

$600-1,000 WW

A Bloor Derby porcelain figure, 'The Tailor's Wife', on a naturalistic base, with gilt scrolled decoration, incised 'N62'.

c1820 *9.25in (23.5cm) high*

$1,300-1,500 SWO

A pair of first half 19thC Bloor Derby figures of Shakespeare and Milton, standing leaning on pedestals, each holding a scroll containing lines from 'The Tempest' and 'Paradise Lost', printed iron red marks.

10.25in (26cm) high

$1,200-2,000 WW

A Bloor Derby rectangular bowl, painted with a panel of birds in the manner of Richard Dodson within a blue gilt border, on an oval base, printed mark in iron red, damages.

c1830 *11.5in (29cm) wide*

$400-500 WW

A large early 19thC Bloor Derby two-handled vase and cover, painted with flowers in the manner of William 'Quaker' Pegg, the handles rising from rams' heads, crowned 'D' mark in iron red, damaged and riveted.

14.5in (37cm) high

$1,600-2,400 WW

A Royal Crown Derby ovoid jug, richly decorated in raised enamels, turquoise jeweling and gilding on a dark blue ground, printed and incised marks, date code for 1893.

7.25in (18.5cm)

$300-500 WW

A Royal Crown Derby urnular vase, painted and signed by W. E. J. Dean, with a castle in a river landscape, within a gilt shaped oval frame reserved on a cobalt blue ground, the rim molded with egg-and-dart edged in gilt, gilt scroll acanthus molded handles, painted marks in red, date code for 1920.

5in (13cm) high

$1,000-1,200   **NEA**

A Royal Crown Derby figure of Olga, wearing a long red fur-lined coat and pulling at the lead of a large dog, printed mark in iron red with date code for 1933.

6.5in (16.5cm) high

$300-500   **WW**

DRESDEN

A pair of late 19th/early 20thC Dresden vases and covers, of ovoid form, decorated with alternating panels of painted flowers reserved on a gilt ground and figural landscape scenes, the borders with scrolling gilt and stylized flower-heads on a white ground, blue painted mark.

21.75in (55cm) high

$1,800-2,400   **L&T**

A large pair of early 20thC Dresden centerpieces, each with a pierced basket on a tall column around which three figures stand, cross and 'T' marks, minor faults.

19.75in (50cm) high

$1,000-1,600   **WW**

A pair of late 19thC Dresden gilt-metal mounted vases and covers, each of ovoid form, the cover with rose-head finial and pierced panels, the body with twin scroll handles, both with painted landscape panels raised on four gilt-metal scroll feet.

16.5in (42cm) high

$4,800-5,600   **L&T**

A pair of 20thC Dresden urn-shaped vases, painted with mythological and classical scenes on a gilt blue ground, crowned 'D' marks.

105in (26.5cm) high

$800-1,000   **WW**

A late 19thC Dresden porcelain cabinet plate, signed 'Klem', blue underglaze Dresden Richard Klem mark, frame.

9.5in (24cm) diam

$700-900   **FRE**

PORCELAIN

A Frankenthal coffee cup, painted with two soldiers with spears in a landscape above Rococo scrolls, the base with impressed marks and an underglaze blue lion rampant, the gilt rim rubbed.

c1760

$600-800   **WW**

A Frankenthal teacup and saucer, painted with scenes of allegorical figures and flowers, bordered in purple and gilt, painted underglaze crowned 'CT' marks in blue and incised marks.

c1770   *5.5in (14cm) high*

$1,400-2,000   **WW**

An 18thC Frankenthal porcelain vase, with four women holding baskets of flowers.

14in (35.5cm) high

$2,000-3,000   **POOK**

A Frankenthal figure of a young woman, probably modeled by J. F. Lück, wearing a neckerchief and hat, and peddling a basket of fruit, painted and incised marks.

c1760   *5.5in (13.5cm) high*

$4,400-4,800   **WW**

FÜRSTENBURG

A Fürstenburg figure of a girl playing the lute, modeled by C.C. Schubert, restored, 'F' in underglaze blue.

c1775   *7in (18cm) high*

$800-1,000   **SOTA**

A late 18thC Fürstenburg figure allegorical for Winter, after the model by Desoches from 1773.

7.5in (19cm) high

$800-1,000   **SOTA**

A late 18thC Fürstenburg figure of a Putto in disguise, modeled wearing a bonnet and fan, fan, sleeves, arm and wings restored.

5.5in (14cm) high

$600-800   **SOTA**

A set of ten 18thC Fürstenburg porcelain cameo plates, each centrally painted with a portrait bust medallion depicting and inscribed with Greek scholars, underglaze blue marks.

9.5in (24cm) diam

$4,000-6,000 THE SET   **L&T**

ESSENTIAL REFERENCE: MEISSEN

Founded in Germany c1710, Meissen was the first porcelain factory in Europe.

- First wares: director, J. F. Böttger's fine, extremely hard red stoneware, with engraved designs and lacquer painting. Stoneware superseded by white hard paste, discovered by Böttger and Tschirnhaus c1709.
- 1720–50: enameling on Meissen unsurpassed. Löwenfink: bold, flamboyant chinoiserie or Japonnaise subjects, often derived from the engravings of Petruschenk, particularly on Augustus Rex wares. J. G. Höroldt: elaborate miniature chinoiserie figure subjects. C. F. Höroldt: European and Levantine quay scenes.
- Crossed swords factory mark used from 1723.
- In late 1720s, a glassier, harder looking paste introduced.
- Best figures are from the late 1730s and early 1740s, especially the great Commedia dell'Arte figures/groups. Finest Meissen figures by J. J. Kändler (chief modeler from 1733).
- Other modelers include Paul Reinicke and J. F. Eberlein.
- Extensive range of dinner services, tea and coffee services, candlesticks and other useful/decorative wears. Kändler designed the factory's most famous service, known as the 'Swan' service.
- The naturalistic flower subjects of the 1740s gradually became less realistic and moved towards the *manier Blumen* of the 1750s/60s.
- 1763: complete reorganisation of factory as Rococo fell out of fashion. Less-ornate Louis XVI style tablewares produced.
- The early 19thC saw the mass production of popular styles including the Biedermeier and early Neoclassical styles.
- Mid-19thC onwards: mass production of revived Rococo style, using 18thC molds.
- 1920s and 1930s: Art Deco figures modeled by Paul Scheurich and Max Esser.
- Factory still active.

A Meissen figure of Vulcan, modeled as a bearded blacksmith, forging an arrowhead on his anvil, crossed swords mark to the back of the base, damages and restoration.
c1740-50   4.5in (11.5cm) high
$1,000-1,600   **WW**

A mid-18thC Meissen figural group of a young couple, crossed swords mark, minor losses to the hands.

4.25in (10.5cm) high
$1,800-2,400   **WW**

CLOSER LOOK: MEISSEN FIGURE

Johann Joachim Kandler arrived at Meissen in 1731 and dramatically improved the quality of the factory's figures. From 1740 until his death in 1775 his figures were the most admired part of Meissen's output.

The figures were modeled separately and then assembled. Some figures show so much movement they appear lifelike.

The modeling of faces is usually severe but with subtle coloring. Hair is usually finely executed with black or dark brown brush strokes. The bright enamel colors are typical of 18thC Meissen.

Early bases were mounds with applied flowers, but by the 1740s these became heavier and decorated with Rococo scrolls.

A mid-18thC Meissen white glazed figure of Cupid, a bow and quiver of arrows on his back, raised on a square base with applied flowers, crossed swords mark, damages and losses.

5in (12.5cm) high
$340-440   **WW**

A Meissen model of a pastry seller, holding a basket overflowing with cakes and buns, a cross swords mark to the back of the base, minor damage.
c1755   7.75in (19.5cm) high
$5,000-6,000   **WW**

A mid-18thC Meissen porcelain figure, 'Caliope', modeled by J. J. Kandler (1706-1775), the figure seated under a tree and writing music, a putto playing the lute to her right, books and pipes to her feet, incised 'Caliope' at the rear of the base and applied with flowering branches, traces of cross swords in blue.

9.5in (24cm) high
$7,000-10,000   **FRE**

PORCELAIN

A Meissen figure of an Native American woman, wearing a skirt and cloak of colorful feathers, holding a bow and arrow, with a quiver of arrows by her side, faint mark to the base, losses, restoration.

c1760   6in (15.5cm) high

$1,800-2,000   **WW**

A mid-18thC and 19thC Meissen figure of Cupid, in disguise as a wig-maker, and a Berlin-style figure of Cupid disguised as a girl, both marked in underglaze blue, damages and restoration.

3.5in (9cm) high

$700-900   **WW**

A late 18thC Meissen scent bottle, modeled as a man holding a dog, which looks over his shoulder, the dog's head forming the stopper, blue crossed swords mark, the dog's tail restored.

3.25in (8.5cm) high

$1,000-1,400   **WW**

A late 18th/early 19thC Meissen figure of a lady hunter, holding a gun with a small dog at her feet, crossed swords mark with a star beneath the hilts, restoration to the barrel of the gun.

5.5in (13.5cm) high

$800-1,200   **WW**

An 18thC Meissen model of a sheep, standing four square on a leaf-encrusted base, unmarked, damages.

2.5in (6.5cm) high

$600-1,000   **WW**

A mid-18thC Meissen lamb, lying on a molded base, its head turned to dexter and a pink ribbon tied in a bow around its neck, faint mark to the base.

2.75in (7cm) high

$800-1,200   **WW**

A rare Meissen Hausmaler plate, painted in the manner of Franz Ferdinand Mayer with figures and a donkey in a landscape scene, the rim with flower sprays, acanthus leaf scrolls and a bird on a branch, the reverse with a crossed swords mark, and incised marks to the foot rim, a small restored rim chip and a little wear to the gilding.

A Meissen Böttger porcelain saucer, decorated with applied sprigs of leaves and flowers, unmarked, some good restoration.

c1715-20   5.25in (13.5cm) diam

$1,200-1,600   **WW**

Hausmaler is German for 'home painter' and refers to an artist who decorated porcelain in his own studio, independently of factory supervision. The decoration of Hausmaler pieces varies in quality but can be of a very high standard, as in this case.

c1745   8.75in (22.5cm) diam

$6,000-8,000   **WW**

A Meissen saucer, painted with figures on horseback in a rural landscape scene on a gilt ground, crossed swords mark and gilt 'D', some wear to the gilding.

c1740   *5in (13cm) diam*

$800-1,200   **WW**

A Meissen saucer, the center painted with a harbour scene, and with four figures, within an elaborate gilt-edged panel, the reverse with crossed swords marks and a dot between the hilts '43' impressed and 'VII' in gilt.

c1760   *5.25in (13.5cm) diam*

$400-500   **WW**

An 18thC Meissen plate with molded osier border, painted with flower sprays, crossed swords mark. *Osier is a molded pattern that simulates basket weave.*

     9.5in (24cm) diam

$360-440   **WW**

A mid-18thC molded Meissen dish, painted with flower sprays in polychrome enamels, gilt decoration to the rim, crossed swords mark in blue.

     11.5in (29.5cm) diam

$500-700   **WW**

A small 18th/19thC Meissen dish, painted probably outside the factory, with the 'Rock and Bird' pattern, crossed swords mark with a star above the hilts, a small rim crack.

     6in (15cm) diam

$240-300   **WW**

A rare Meissen teabowl, painted with two panels of ships at sea in ornate gilt cartouches, divided by sprays of indianische Blumen, the base marked in gilt 'VII'.

c1735-40   *3in (8cm) diam*

$2,400-3,000   **WW**

An early Meissen bowl, probably decorated in the Augsburg workshop of Seuter, painted with Goldchinesen in various pursuits within exotic landscapes, above scrolling foliate designs, unmarked, a restored rim chip and haircrack, wear to the interior gilding.

c1720-25   *6.75in (17cm) high*

$2,600-2,800   **WW**

A pair of 18thC Meissen Kakiemon cups, crossed swords mark in blue.

c1735

$2,000-3,000   **JN**

A Meissen bowl, painted with figures in a landscape, crossed swords mark, broken and repaired.

c1740   *4.25in (11cm) diam*

$400-500   **WW**

PORCELAIN

An early Meissen teapot and cover, painted in blue with a bird and flowering prunus above rockwork, crossed swords mark with 'W' between the hilts, incised 'X' near the foot rim, a small restored rim chip to the cover.

c1735   *7in (17.5cm) high*

$3,600-4,400   **WW**

A Meissen coffee pot and cover, with a clip handle, painted with Deutsche Blumen, crossed swords and incised marks, some damage and metal repair to the spout.

c1750   *9in (23cm) high*

$500-700   **WW**

An unusual 18thC Meissen porcelain and ormolu casket and cover, the burgundy ground with floral painted panels, surmounted by a lemon, supported on a finely cast ormolu swept case.

8.5in (21.5cm) high

$800-1,200   **JN**

A Meissen figure of a lady, seated by a table with a bible in her hand and spinning a wheel on a table beside her, crossed swords and incised marks to base.

c1860   *6.25in (16cm) high*

$1,400-1,800   **SWO**

A 19thC Meissen porcelain allegorical figure group, modeled as three scantily clad putti, each engaged in a different activity representing Sculpture, underglaze blue crossed swords mark.

8.25in (21cm) high

$1,600-2,000   **FRE**

A 19thC Meissen porcelain figure group, modeled as pair of boys in 19thC dress assisting a young girl as she walks on a pair of stilts, underglaze blue crossed swords mark.

8.75in (22cm) high

$1,400-2,000   **FRE**

A 19thC Meissen group of five children, playing the lute, piccolo and harp and one conducting, set on a naturalistic base with gilt decoration, cross swords mark in blue, incised 'B24'.

6.75in (17cm) high

$600-800   **JN**

A pair of Meissen groups, a Classical young lady standing beside a pedestal with a cupid and dog at her side and a Classical young lady standing beside a tree trunk, two cupids and a dog at her feet, cross sword mark in blue.

11in (28cm) high

$2,400-3,000   **JN**

A Meissen model of a flower girl, standing holding a basket of flowers under one arm, after a model by Acier and Schönheit, crossed swords mark and incised 'C68', minor damages.

c1880   *7.75in (19.5cm) high*

$900-1,100   **WW**

A Meissen model of a young girl, as the personification of Touch, seated by a table on which stands a parrot in a cage, from a model called 'Sentiment' by Johann Schönheit, crossed swords mark and incised 'E4'.

c1880   *5.75in (14.5cm) high*

$1,400-2,000   **WW**

A Meissen model of a young girl, as the personification of Sight, seated at her dressing table and looking at her reflection in a mirror, from an earlier model by Johann Schönheit, crossed swords mark and 'E3' incised.

c1880   *5.75in (14.5cm) high*

$1,400-2,000   **WW**

A 19thC Meissen model of 'Les Amies', with a young lady consoling her friend, before a plinth with an urn and Cupid's instruments of love, the oval base with billing doves and a discarded love letter, incised and faint crossed swords marks, minor damage.

9.5in (24cm) high

$1,600-2,000   **WW**

A large late 19thC Meissen allegorical figure group, emblematic of Geography, comprising a maiden standing before a globe, a tablet in her hand and attended by four putti with various devices, behind her a seated putto, beneath a palm tree, blue crossed swords and incised marks.

16in (40cm) high

$12,000-16,000   **FRE**

A 19thC Meissen porcelain figure group, 'Parcae', after a model by J. J. Kandler, modeled as Chronus assisting the three fates Atropos, Clotho and Lachesis as they spin, measure and cut the thread of Life, and accompanied by a putto, on a stepped shaped base, blue crossed swords marks, incised 'N33' and impressed '137' and '57'.

15in (38cm) high

$8,000-12,000   **FRE**

A 19thC Meissen figure of a young boy, smartly dressed in a pink tunic and breeches holding a flower wreath on a gilt scrolled base, unmarked.

5in (12.5cm) high

$600-800   **JN**

A 19thC Meissen Putti standing by an urn, holding a wreath and flowers, a quire of arrows by his side, the base inscribed 'Je les Courrone', crossed swords mark in blue, incised 'J3, 25, 14'.

5in (12.5cm) high

$800-1,200   **JN**

A pair of late 19thC Meissen figural condiments, modeled as a man and female in traditional costume, each holding a flower encrusted covered ewer, blue crossed swords marks.

Highest 7.25in (18.5cm) high

$2,400-3,600   **FRE**

A 19thC Meissen figural group of Ceres, the goddess of agriculture, gathering sheaves of corn with three putti, one with a basket of apples on his head, crossed swords mark, incised and painted numbers, damages.

7.75in (19.5cm) high

$1,200-1,600   **WW**

PORCELAIN

A pair of 19thC Meissen figural Season groups, after the models by J.J. Kändler, depicting Summer and Autumn, each modeled with Classical figures seated on billowing Rococo clouds, supporting a plaque painted with figures on horseback, raised on shaped bases applied with flowers and grapes, crossed swords marks, some losses and restoration.

13in (33cm) high

$6,000-10,000   WW

A pair of 19thC Meissen porcelain sweetmeat dishes, each reclining figure in 19thC costume supporting a floral encrusted bowl, raised on a scrolled base, gilt details, underglazed blue crossed swords mark.

12in (30.5cm) long

$3,000-4,000   FRE

A late 19th/early 20thC Meissen porcelain figure, modeled as a shepherdess holding a lamb on her hip, underglaze blue crossed swords mark, incised and impressed marks.

11.5in (29cm) high

$600-1,000   FRE

A late 19th/early 20thC Meissen porcelain figure, modeled as a woman feeding birds, her apron filled with crumbs, underglaze blue crossed swords mark, incised 'L 73'.

10.5in (26.5cm) high

$1,000-1,200   FRE

An early 20thC Meissen porcelain group, modeled by Professor Paul Scheurich, depicting a lady and her attendant, seated cross-legged holding a gilded apple behind her back, whilst the eastern attendant pleads with her, clinging to the folds of her skirt, blue cross sword mark, incised signature 'SCHEURICH 19'.

11in (28cm) high

$3,600-4,400   L&T

A 20thC Meissen model of five putti, personifying the five Senses, painted in polychrome enamels on a rockwork base, crossed swords and other incised marks, some damages and restoration.

6in (15.5cm) high

$1,000-1,400   WW

A pair of early 20thC Meissen porcelain figures, depicting a gentleman suitor and his companion, blue underglaze crossed swords marks.

18.5in (47cm) high

$8,000-12,000   FRE

A 20thC Meissen model of Harlequin, posing before a tree stump on a flower encrusted base, crossed swords mark, minor chip to one of the flowers.

7.75in (20cm) high

$800-1,200   WW

A Meissen blanc de chine figure, of Diana the Huntress, impressed and blue cross sword marks 'Weifs', incised 'A 1046'.

11.75in (30cm) high

$1,400-1,800   L&T

A mid-19thC Meissen figure of a badger, after a model by J. J. Kandler, the snarling crouching figure naturalistically painted, raised on an oval base, blue crossed swords mark.

7.75in (20cm) high

$1,400-2,000   L&T

A 19thC Meissen porcelain figure of an elephant, standing on a naturalistic base, blue crossed swords mark.

12.25in (31cm) high

$3,000-4,000   L&T

A 19thC pair of Meissen model pugs with a puppy, painted in shades of brown, wearing blue collars with gilt bells, the female with crossed swords mark in blue and incised '1169'.

9.5in (24cm) high

$6,000-8,000   SOTA

A 19thC Meissen figure of a pug with a puppy, sitting with one paw raised, the puppy sitting beneath her stomach, naturalistically painted, blue crossed swords mark.

8.75in (22cm) high

$2,000-3,000   L&T

A pair of late 19thC Meissen magpies, each with long tail extending upwards, perched on a naturalistically modeled tree trunk, blue painted crossed swords mark.

20.75in (53cm) high

$5,000-6,000   L&T

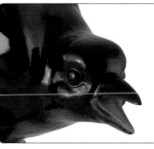

A late 19th/early 20thC Meissen porcelain figure, of a Danish hound, the seated dog naturalistically painted in brown and white, blue crossed swords mark.

6.75in (17cm) high

$1,000-1,600   L&T

A 19thC Meissen model of a magpie, perched on a rocky base, canceled crossed swords mark, good restoration to the beak.

20.75in (53cm) high

$1,000-1,400   WW

PORCELAIN

MINTON

The Minton factory was founded at Stoke-on-Trent, Staffordshire, England, in 1793, by Thomas Minton. The factory initially produced earthenware. From c1798 to c1810 Minton produced soft paste porcelain wares. They tended to be thinly potted with a slightly grayish glaze, sometimes with black flecks in it. The majority of wares were decorated with Neoclassical designs. After 1821 Minton made hard paste porcelain. It is rarely flawed and usually covered with a thin, glassy, smooth glaze. Wares tend to be copies of Sèvres or Meissen.

In 1849 Joseph-François Léon Arnoux became artistic director and decoration became richer, with vibrant ground colors – particularly turquoise – and excellent gilding. The factory became famous for its majolica wares. In 1873: 'Minton' mark became 'Mintons'. The factory remains active today.

A Minton bone china flatback model of a German peasant couple, standing on a green base inscribed 'Berne'.

c1825   5.75in (14.5cm) high

$400-600   **WW**

A Minton colored parian model of Red Riding Hood, impressed mark and date code, the basket's handle restored.

1864   6.25in (16cm) high

$160-240   **WW**

A late 19thC Minton parianware group of Ariadne and the panther, probably by John Bell, holding a draping cloth, on a rectangular plinth, impressed mark, date code, damages.

1864   12in (30cm) wide

$1,200-1,800   **L&T**

A Minton porcelain 'Wellington' vase, painted with brightly colored flowers, against a powder blue gilt enhanced ground, raised on a socle foot and pedestal base.

11.75in (30cm) high

$2,400-3,600   **L&T**

A Minton vase, painted with a woodpecker on a turquoise cloisonné glaze, printed and impressed marks with date code, the neck reduced and restored.

7in (18cm) high

$300-500   **WW**

A Minton bone china ormolu-mounted reticulated vase and cover, signed by Antonin Boullemier, on a dark blue ground, impressed marks and dated, cover restored.

1873   11.25in (28.5cm) high

$1,400-2,000   **WW**

A Minton pâte-sur-pâte vase, depicting two doves, flowers and arrows, applied gilt ring handles, impressed marks, date code.

1876   9.75in (24.5cm) high

$1,000-1,400   **WW**

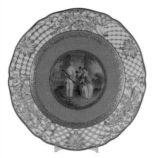

A Minton plate, with a reticulated border of flowers and lattice work, the well painted with a musician entertaining two young ladies before a waterfall scene, signed by Anton Boullemier, within a pink and gilt border, impressed and printed marks, date code.

1890   10.5in (26.5cm) diam

$1,800-2,400   **WW**

A pair of late 19th/early 20thC Minton plates, the borders decorated with three pâte-sur-pâte panels of young girls and cherubs, signed 'AB' and 'A Birks' for Albion Birks, restored.

10.5in (27cm)

$600-1,000   **WW**

A Rockingham figure of a beggar boy, wearing a green tunic edged in gilt, on a naturalistically encrusted circular base, incised 'N36'.

1826-42   *5in (12.5cm) high*

$1,600-2,000   **NEA**

A Rockingham spill vase, the panel painted by Thomas Searle, within matt and burnished rectangular gilt border, gilt rims, painted Griffen mark in orange.

c1830   *4.25in (11cm) high*

$700-900   **NEA**

A rare Rockingham hexagonal scent bottle, applied with naturalistically molded flowers and foliage, painted with gilt foliage within a gilt rim, flower finial.

c1830-42   *5in (13cm) high*

$1,000-1,200   **NEA**

A Rockingham pot pourri basket, painted with a river landscape, encrusted with flowers and foliage, on acanthus feet, printed griffen mark in puce and 'C3' in gilt.

c1830-42   *4.25in (11cm) diam*

$1,600-2,000   **NEA**

SAMSON

Opened in Paris in 1845, Edmé Samson's factory made copies of Chinese, German and English porcelain, French faience, Dutch Delft, and some Strasbourg wares.

It was known for its excellent copies of Meissen and Chinese porcelain. However, its fakes of English soft paste porcelain are easier to detect, as Continental hard paste was used.

All wares originally had 'S' within mark, but this has proved easy to remove. Production ended in 1969 and the factory's molds were sold in 1979.

A pair of late 19thC Samson models of lovers, after Derby, painted marks, minor damages.

12.5in (31.5cm) high

$500-700   **WW**

A large late 19thC Samson model, 'The Music Lesson', after Chelsea, gold anchor mark and gilt Samson mark, some restoration.

13in (33cm) high

$600-1,000   **WW**

A 19thC Samson model of a Kakiemon elephant, based on a 1680 Japanese model, raised trunk, red and cobalt blue saddle, well-modeled details.

11in (28cm) high

$1,400-2,000   **FRE**

A late 19thC Samson assembled garniture, in the Worcester manner, comprising three vases and covers, each of hexagonal form, the dark blue ground with gilt scroll framed panels painted with flowers and exotic birds, faux Worcester fret mark.

Largest: 16in (41cm) high

$2,400-3,600   **L&T**

A pair of late 19thC Samson Worcester-style jugs, painted with birds and gilded foliage, the spouts molded as bearded faces, unmarked, one handle restored.

8.25in (21cm) high

$400-600   **WW**

PORCELAIN

A large 19thC Samson gilt-bronze mounted porcelain brule-parfum, in the Chinese taste with an acorn knop and scrolling handles, above a foliate pierced rim, raised on a fluted wreath cast socle and shaped square base, decorated with carp on a mottled cobalt ground, gilt details.

30in (76cm) diam

$20,000-30,000   **FRE**

A late 19thC Samson hexagonal-section bottle vase, decorated in the Chantilly style with flowers, leaves and insects, hunting horn mark.

7.25in (18.5cm) high

$200-300   **WW**

A 19thC Samson tea urn and cover, in the Japanese style, raised on three gilt painted boys with pewter nozzle.

14in (35.5cm) high

$600-1,000   **FRE**

A set of twelve 19thC Samson porcelain plates, in the Chinese export style, each decorated with floral sprays centered by a pseudo armorial crest.

9.5in (24cm) high

$1,400-2,000   **FRE**

SÈVRES

With the decline in popularity of Meissen in the mid-18thC, the Vincennes/Sèvres factory in France (est. 1740) became arguably the most important porcelain factory in Europe.

- First director, Claude-Humbert Gérin, made a soft paste porcelain much whiter than that of other French factories.
- In 1745 Louis XV granted the factory a 20-year exclusive privilege to produce porcelain.
- Early wares heavy in form and painted with small flower sprays with gilt trellis and scrollwork borders.
- 1748: goldsmith Jean Claude Chambellan Duplessis hired to create new Rococo forms. Lighter, more elegant shapes.
- From 1753, other factories forbidden to use Vincennes subjects, colors, and gilding by the king.
- The factory moved to Sèvres, near Paris in 1756.
- Hard paste porcelain used from 1768. Colored and patterned grounds with little of the body left showing.
- Late 1770s: Sèvres produced strictly geometric shapes based on antique vases and urns. Subdued sepia/grays instead of bright Rococo colors and decorated with Classical motifs.
- Early 1780s: 'jeweled' (drops of enamel) decoration introduced.
- Following the French Revolution, porcelain sold to be decorated in Paris and London.
- Rich 'Empire' style developed early 19thC.
- Art Nouveau style adopted in late 1890s. Art Deco in 1920s.
- Currently, produces simplified versions of 18thC wares.

A large Sèvres bisque statue, entitled 'Après le Bain', with a metal band around the foot, engraved 'Sèvres 1845'.

1845   26.75in (68cm) high

$10,000-16,000   **L&T**

One of a pair of late 19thC Sèvres porcelain, bisque and gilt bronze mounted candelabra, blue marks.

14.75in (37.5cm) high

$3,000-4,000   **FRE**

A pair of 19thC Sèvres style porcelain figures of Cupid & Psyche, enriched with gilt, formed as Cupid seated on rockwork, and Psyche seated on a draped rock concealing Cupid's bow, on molded bases, pseudo Sèvres mark.

11in (28cm) high

$1,600-2,400   **FRE**

A pair of 18thC Sèvres ormolu vases, mounted in the 19thC, each body decorated with reserves of figures in 18thC costume within a gilt border, all on a bleu celeste ground, gilt details throughout.

27in (68.5cm) high

$20,000-30,000 **FRE**

CLOSER LOOK: SÈVRES COVERED VASE

The vase was made in the late 19thC – possibly to commemorate the 1892 quadricentennial of Columbus' discovery of the Americas.

The shape of the vase, and features such as the finial on the cover and the mask scroll supports on the base, recall the Neoclassical style of 150 years before. However, if this vase had been made in the 18thC the gilt mounts would have been more restrained and more of the porcelain left undecorated.

The faces of Columbus and the cherubs have been skillfully painted, with exceptional detailing. This is also evident in the details shown in the fabrics.

The vase is decorated with high quality raised gilding.

A late 19thC Sèvres commemorative porcelain and gilt bronze covered vase, the ovoid sides painted with Columbus discovering the New World, the reverse depicting a winged cherub holding aloft an American flag, raised by three mask scroll supports, ending on a tri-form base and claw feet.

22.5in (57cm) high

$4,000-6,000 **FRE**

A 19thC Sèvres vase, with domed lid and berry finial over a painted body with a scene depicting Napoleon on horseback, on a gilt enhanced ground, raised on a socle base.

37.5in (95cm) high

$6,000-8,000 **FRE**

A late 19thC large Sèvres-style porcelain Art Nouveau vase, with gilt bronze finial, sides painted with a bust-length portrait of a young beauty and a gilt-enriched ground, on a socle base.

26in (66cm) high

$4,000-6,000 **FRE**

A pair of late 19thC Sèvres-style vases and covers, the body with painted with rural scenes framed by shaped molding with twin masks, underglaze blue painted mark.

10.5in (27cm) high

$2,400-3,600 **L&T**

A pair of late 19thC Sèvres jeweled 'Hollandaise' vases and underdishes, with a 'jeweled' frame and depicting a Classical figure, the other flowers, trophies and a dove.

7.5in (19cm) high

$4,000-6,000 **L&T**

A pair of early 20thC Sèvres-style apple-green gilt metal mounted covered vases, with scroll handles, painted with scenes of lovers, raised on socle bases, and signed 'M. Gravey'.

30.5in (77.5cm) high

$3,000-4,000 **FRE**

A pair of Sèvres French silver-mounted porcelain vases, each of baluster form with a beaded rim and gilt snowflake decoration on a cobalt ground, raised on a circular foot, dated.

1922-23　　　*19in (38cm) high*

$5,000-6,000　　　**FRE**

A pair of late 19thC Sèvres-style porcelain and ormolu candelabra, the ovoid sides painted with romantic scenes of lovers and floral bouquets, against gilt-enhanced turquoise ground, flanked by twin goat-form handles and surmounted by ornate foliate scrolling branches, raised on triform sphinx cast feet.

21.75in (55cm) high

$4,000-6,000　　　**L&T**

A 19thC Sèvres biscuit porcelain model of Cupid, standing on one foot upon a lavender cylindrical plinth, mounted with a gilt metal candle-holder in the form of roses, incised 'L's' mark, damages.

14.75in (37.5cm) high

$300-500　　　**WW**

A Sèvres porcelain covered sugar bowl, with a berried finial, decorated with reserves of foliate sprays on a gilt enriched bleu celeste ground, decorators mark for Claude Antoine Tardy, gilders mark for Jean Chauvaux.

c1780　　　*4.25in (11cm) high*

$3,000-4,000　　　**FRE**

A Sèvres ecuelle, cover and stand, decorated with a band of alternating large and smaller panels enclosing flowers and chinoiserie garden scenes united by floral festoons enclosed by a double band of pearls within gilt bands, all against a lime green ground, crowned interlacing L's and date letters 'FF' in gold, painter's mark of a flower in gold.

c1783

$10,000-14,000　　　**SOTH**

A Sèvres écuelle, cover and stand, with gilt side handles, painted with colorful bands of scrolling foliage between apple-green bands, interlaced 'L's' marks in gilt enclosing 'LL' and blue enamel marks, some restoration and wear.

1789　　　*8in (20.5cm) diam*

$800-1,200　　　**WW**

An 18thC Sèvres porcelain ecuelle and cover, with later decoration, the domed cover and sides with naturalistic entwined scroll handles, painted with oval reserves depicting figural port scenes, against a blue ground enriched with gilt, painted interlaced green 'L' mark.

6.25in (16cm) high

$3,000-5,000　　　**L&T**

A Sèvres écuelle, cover and stand, painted with a garland of flowers below a gilt honeycomb border, minor wear to the gilding, restoration to the knop, various printed marks.

1847　　　*9in (23cm) diam*

$700-900　　　**WW**

A 19thC Sèvres-style wine cooler, painted on one side with Classical figures in a coach being drawn by lions, the other side with flowers, on a dark blue ground within gilt borders, canceled interlaced 'L's' mark, some wear and scratching to the enamels.

6.75in (17cm) high

$700-900　　　**WW**

A Sèvres cup (Gobelet Enfancé), painted each side with a harbour scene by Morin, against a blue ground with gilded dots (mouches d'or). Interlaced 'L's', date letter 'O' and painter's mark 'M' in blue.

c1767   3.5in (8.8cm) high

$1,600-2,400   SOTH

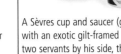

A Sèvres cup and saucer (goblet litron of the first size), the cup decorated with an exotic gilt-framed scene of a Turk seated smoking on a terrace, two servants by his side, the saucer painted with a panel of a group of travelers in an Egyptian landscape, both against a beau bleu ground, an elaborate diaper scrollwork cartouche running around the edge of the rims. Interlacing 'L's' and date letters 'bb' in blue, painter's mark 'LG' possibly for Etienne-Henry Le Guay.

c1779

$11,000-13,000   SOTH

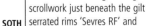

A Sèvres cup and saucer (goblet litron of the first size), decorated with a beau bleu ground, a gilt laurel wreath medallion enclosing a basket with flowers and fruit against a pale yellow ground, wide bands of elaborate gilt foliage scrollwork just beneath the gilt serrated rims 'Sevres RF' and painters mark 'LG' in blue enamel to the base, incised 'Louis'.

Louise-Antoine le Grand (1776-1817) was employed by the Sèvres factory as a gilder and painter.
c1793-94

$5,000-6,000   SOTH

CLOSER LOOK: SÈVRES CUP AND SAUCER

Charles Nicolas Dodin was considered to be one of the best miniature artists at Sèvres and was top of the artists' hierarchy.

His work made its way into the best French and other European collections, including those of Louis XV and his mistresses, Madame de Pompadour and Madame du Barry, as well as Louis XVI and Catherine the Great of Russia.

For much of his career Dodin painted mythological and allegorical figures and genre scenes based on works of the great masters of the 17thC and 18thC. He used engravings, and sometimes the original works, to guide him.

A Sèvres cup and saucer, the cup finely decorated by Charles-Nicolas Dodin with a scene of children playing instruments, dressed in revival costumes accompanying a girl playing the harpsichord. The saucer decorated with a similar terrace scene of a young painter behind his canvas looking at his young model, his pupil sitting on a pillow by his side, a large column just visible behind heavy green velvet drapery, the bleu nouveau ground decorated with finely tooled elaborate gift festoons and strapwork alternated by classical vases. Blue interlaced L's mark enclosing date letter 'ff', painter's mark 'k' for Dodin, gilder's mark for Le Guay, incised 36 to cup and 37 to saucer.

Charles-Nicolas Dodin worked 1754-1803. The scenes are taken from two of the overdoors painted by Carle Vanloo for Madame de Pompadour's Salon de Compagnie at the Château de Bellevue and engraved by Fessard.
c1783

$60,000-70,000   SOTH

A 19thC Sèvres-style porcelain covered cup and trembleuse stand, the domed lid with a berry finial, the tapered cylindrical sides with twin scroll handles, painted with an oval reserve depicting a bust length portrait of a lady, within a turquoise jeweled border and against a pink gilt enriched ground, the conforming stand painted with trophy motifs, interlaced S-mark, signed 'Moriot'.

$700-900   FRE

A small 19thC Sèvres-style teapot and cover, each side painted with figures on a blue ground, enriched with gilding and jeweling, interlaced 'L's' to the base, some restoration.

5in (13cm) high

$500-700   WW

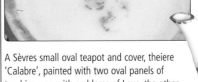

A Sèvres small oval teapot and cover, theiere 'Calabre', painted with two oval panels of trophies, one with emblems of Love, the other with maritime associations including a compass and an anchor, reserved on a pale-pink ground with blue and gilt oeil de perdrix ground, the cover with floriform finial, smudged and indistinct remnants of marks, minor wear.

c1775   4.25in (11cm) high

$3,000-4,000   DN

PORCELAIN

An 18thC Sèvres porcelain ewer and saucer, each molded in high relief with bullrushes and branches, painted with shaped reserves of exotic birds and shell motif, against gilt-enhanced cobalt blue 'L's' marks, saucer bears paper label 'Coleccion SANTARELLI, Buenos Ayres'.

Ewer 5.5in (14cm) high

$6,000-7,000   **L&T**

A late 19th/early 20thC Sèvres gilt-bronze mounted porcelain clock garniture, comprising a clock and pair of ewers, the clock with porcelain dial painted with Roman numerals above two figures in 18thC costume and surmounted by an urn finial with lion mask handles hung with garlands and centered by a portrait medallion, the ewers with griffin handles decorated with recumbent females, raised on a circular base, the case stamped '8 Pe Mourey 74'.

Clock 20in (51cm) high

$3,000-4,000   **FRE**

SPODE

An early 19thC Spode ice pail, cover and liner, with gilt scroll handles, decorated in the Imari palette with flowers and bold foliage, painted Spode mark and pattern number '1599' with an additional liner.

12.25in (31cm) high

$3,000-4,000   **L&T**

A pair of Spode bone china ovoid vases, each painted with a panel of a young lady on a gilded blue ground, each base inscribed in French with a semi-erotic verse, painted factory marks, each with some good restoration.

c1825   *6in (15.5cm) high*

$2,000-2,800   **WW**

A garniture of three early 19thC Spode flanged top beakers, decorated with pattern '3994' with purple convolvulus flowers and gilded leaves on a white ground, painted marks in iron red, minor damages.

$800-1,200   **WW**

A Spode bone china basket, the sides molded as scallop shells, painted in polychrome enamels, the interior highlighted with shades of pink, unmarked.

c1810   *6in (15cm) high*

$1,000-1,600   **WW**

An early 19thC Spode comport, painted with a scene of York Minster within a molded gilt border of foliage, stylized flowers and shells, painted 'Spode' mark, minor cracks.

13.5in (34cm) diam.

$600-800   **WW**

An early 19thC Spode box and cover, richly decorated in pattern no. 1166, with polychrome flowers on a blue and gilt scale ground, painted pattern mark, minor wear to the gilding.

2.75in (7cm) high

$900-1,100   **WW**

A pair of early 19thC Spode cups and saucers, richly painted with flowers, the cups with an elaborate gilded rim, painted mark.

5.75in (14.5cm) high

$700-900   **WW**

ESSENTIAL REFERENCE: TUCKER

The Tucker porcelain factory was established in 1825 by William Ellis Tucker in Philadelphia, Pennsylvania. First US porcelain factory of note.
- Early wares painted with scenes in sepia and dark brown.
- In 1823 the firm became 'Tucker & Hulme' and then 'Tucker Hemphill' in 1831.
- 1833-36: the factory run by Joseph Hemphill with Tucker's brother, Thomas, as manager.
- During Hemphill period, wares became much richer. Patterns derived from Sèvres. Heavy gilding with brightly painted flower decorations.
- Factory closed in 1838.

A rare Philadelphia Tucker porcelain vaseform pitcher with polychrome floral sprays.

9.25in (23cm) high

$3,600-4,400　　**NA**

A mid-19thC Tucker Philadelphia pitcher, with scalloped rim, hand-painted with sprays of flowers, unmarked, chip to spout, a few flakes to glaze.

8.5in (21.5cm) wide

$1,200-1,800　　**DRA**

VIENNA

Porcelain factory founded in 1719 in Vienna, Austria, by Claudius Innocentius Du Paquier, with the assistance of staff from Meissen.
- Body: distinctive smoky tone, sometimes greenish. Similar to Meissen wares in form but with denser decoration: chinoiseries, fleurs des inde, naturalistic flowers (from 1725, before they appeared at Meissen) and extensive use of trellis work or 'Gitterwerk'. Known for Baroque style.
- 1744: Du Paquier relinquished factory to the state. Factory adopted the Austrian shield as a mark.
- c1750: new patterns introduced on Rococo tablewares.
- Plain bases used from mid-1760s.
- 1784: ailing factory unsuccessfully offered for sale. But under the direction of Konrad von Sorgenthal, the factory was transformed into a prosperous concern.
- Simple geometric forms and wares decorated in strong colors and raised gilding. Joseph Leithner introduced a dark-blue glaze in the 1790's, known as 'Leithner blue'.
- Factory closed in 1864.
- Late 19thC: other factories in Vienna and the surrounding area producing similar wares with the style now known as 'Vienna'.

CLOSER LOOK: VIENNA VASE

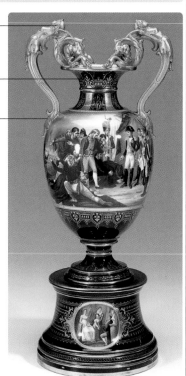

The flared neck is embellished with twin scroll handles in the sinuous, Rococo Revival style. 18thC Rococo handles would be less ornate than these 19thC examples.

Borders of solid color alternating with a gilded pattern are typical of Vienna.

The gilding on late 19thC Vienna wares copied the heavy, three-dimensional style that had been introduced in the late 18thC.

Sensitive painting of complex scenes – such as this interior featuring scenes from the life of Napoleon Bonaparte – were deftly handled by the factory's artists and appealed to the fascination with history that was popular at the time.

A late 19thC Vienna porcelain covered urn, the amphora-shaped body with pierced handles and a fluted neck, the body decorated with an oval reserve of a young beauty holding a floral bouquet, within a gilt border on an iridescent oxblood ground, gilt details throughout.

21in (53.5cm) high

$10,000-14,000　　**FRE**

A late 19thC Vienna porcelain vase, painted with Napoleonic interior scenes, against a gilt enriched cobalt blue ground, blue beehive mark.

29in (73.5cm) high

$16,000-20,000　　**FRE**

A late 19thC Vienna porcelain cabinet vase, 'Reflection', decorated with a portrait on an iridescent sang du boeuf ground with gilt highlights, painted and blue underglazed marks, signed 'Wagner'.

7in (18cm) high

$1,200-1,800   **FRE**

A large Royal Vienna covered vase, painted with three Classical beauties, with raised gilt floral decoration, the gilt metal mounted cover with a pinecone finial, blue beehive mark.

c1890   *33.5in (85cm) high*

$10,000-14,000   **FRE**

A set of twelve late 19thC Vienna porcelain plates, each painted with a young draped beauty within riverside and garden landscapes, entitled verso, blue beehive mark.

9in (23cm) diam

$14,000-18,000   **FRE**

A late 19thC framed oval Vienna porcelain plaque, finely painted with a biblical scene depicting Samson & Delilah, within a baroque gilt enhanced border.

16.25in (41cm) wide

$5,000-6,000   **FRE**

A late 19thC Vienna porcelain cabinet plate, depicting a Gypsy woman, within a gilt enriched celadon luster border, blue beehive mark, illegible inscription to the reverse.

9.5in (24cm) diam

$600-800   **FRE**

A late 19th/early 20thC Vienna porcelain cabinet plate, depicting the figure of Echo, within a cobalt and gilt enhanced border, underglaze blue beehive mark, framed.

9.5in (24cm) diam

$900-1,100   **FRE**

A late 19thC Vienna cabinet plate, depicting Napoleon's withdrawal from Russia, signed 'Wagner', within a red and gilt enhanced border, underglaze blue beehive mark, framed.

9.5in (24cm) diam

$3,000-4,000   **FRE**

A rare cased set of six mid-18thC Vienna custard cups and covers, each painted in polychrome with forget-me-not sprigs beneath leaf trails, shield marks.

3.25in (8.5cm) high

$1,600-2,400   **WW**

A Vienna coffee can and cover, painted with a battle scene between the Romans and the Sabines, painted shield mark, the knop broken and repaired.

c1804   *3.5in (9cm) high*

$1,400-1,800   **WW**

A 19thC Vienna-style coffee can and saucer, painted with a man sitting cross-legged beside a woman with an arrow through her heart, raised gilding to the colored panel ground.

$900-1,100   **WW**

ESSENTIAL REFERENCE: WORCESTER

Porcelain factory founded in 1751. Took over the stock and secrets of Lund's Bristol porcelain factory the following year.

- First porcelain of soft paste, including soaprock (steatite).
- 1751-56: useful wares, especially tea wares, and vases. Chinoiserie motifs in underglaze blue/enamel colors.
- c1751-53: blue and white and 'famille verte' polychrome wares produced.
- c1752-54: incised cross or line mark used.
- cl755-60: polychrome decoration crisp and clean. Almost all patterns based on Chinese prototypes.
- Transfer printed wares appear c1757. At first overglaze in black, by 1760 also underglaze in blue.
- 1760-76: most blue and white pieces marked with a crescent.
- 1760s: much rich enamel painting apparently executed outside the factory.
- Post 1760s saw a tendency to imitate Sèvres.
- The factory was bought by Thomas Flight in 1783 for sons, Joseph and John. Formula for paste modified.
- 1793-1807: named 'Flight & Barr'.
- 1807-14: named 'Barr, Flight & Barr'
- 1814-40: named 'Flight, Barr & Barr'.
- 1840: amalgamated with factory started by R. Chamberlain with production moving to their workshops.
- 1852: renamed 'Kerr & Binns'.
- 1862: renamed 'Royal Worcester'. Period of elaborate, richly gilded/painted and jeweled decoration.
- 1870s-80s: Japanese influence.
- 19th/early 20thC: many wares decorated with rich bunches of flowers or fruit on a cream or light ground.
- Factory still active.

A Worcester feather molded coffeepot and cover, painted in blue with two birds above leafy tendrils, 'C' mark, rim crack.

c1765   *9in (23cm) high*

$600-800   **WW**

A Worcester mustard pot and cover, printed in blue with flowers and butterflies, printed crescent mark, small chips to the knop.

c1770

$300-500   **WW**

A Worcester teapot and cover, printed in blue with flower sprays and butterflies, crescent mark, a small crack to the tip of the spout.

c1770   *7.5in (19cm) high*

$300-500   **WW**

A large Worcester blue and white teapot and cover, decorated with the 'Mansfield' pattern, blue crescent mark, knop riveted.

c1770   *8.25in (21cm) high*

$500-600   **WW**

An 18thC Worcester covered jug, with strap handle, blue painted with floral sprays and butterflies.

11.5in (29cm) high

$800-1,200   **DAH**

A Worcester tankard, printed with Liberty seated among trophies of war, a portrait of George II, and a warship, 'RH Worcester' mark and anchor rebus for Richard Holdship.

c1755-60   *6.25in (16cm) high*

$2,400-2,800   **WW**

A Worcester 'King of Prussia' mug, printed in black by Robert Hancock with a half-length portrait of Frederick the Great above the date '1757' gesturing towards trophies of war and battle honours, 'RH' monogram for Hancock and anchor for Richard Holdship.

1757 was a year into the Seven Years War (1756-63) which saw Prussia, Hanover and Great Britain allied against the might of Austria, France and much of the Holy Roman Empire. The names inscribed on the flags are Frederick's victories or those of his marshals against France and Austria. The outcome of this truly global war was to see two relatively small powers emerge with significant gains, Prussia supplanting the Holy Roman Empire in importance in the German region and Britain supplanting France as the major European colonial power (France would loose most of her North American possessions).

3.25in (8.5cm) high

$1,000-1,400   **DN**

A fine Worcester cylindrical mug, printed in black from a design by Robert Hancock with the arms of the Grand Lodge and the motto 'Amor Honor Et Justitia Sit Lux Et Lux Fuit' amidst Masonic emblems, with three figures to the left, paper labels for the Zorensky Collection and the Sir Jeremy Lever Collection, a 2cm haircrack to the rim.

c1760-62   *4.75in (12cm) high*

$2,000-3,000   **WW**

PORCELAIN

A Worcester blue and white sauceboat, painted with the 'Little Fisherman' pattern, open crescent mark.

c1765   6in (15.5cm) high

$700-900   WW

c1760

$500-700   WW

A Worcester two-handled sauceboat, painted in blue with a Chinese landscape to the interior, the exterior with four chinoiserie cartouches, workman's mark, minor wear and damages.

6.5in (16.5cm) high

A Worcester strap-fluted sauceboat, painted in blue with flowers and leaf sprigs, open crescent mark.

c1770-80   5.5in (14cm) high

$300-500   WW

A Worcester blue and white fluted jug, painted in blue with the Mansfield pattern, painted crescent mark.

c1760   3.75in (9.5cm) high

$1,000-1,400   WW

A Worcester shell molded pickle dish, painted in blue with the 'Two-Peony Rock Bird' pattern, workman's mark to the base, two rim chips.

c1754-58   3.5in (9cm) high

$400-600   WW

A Worcester shell molded pickle dish, painted in blue with the 'Two-Peony Rock Bird' pattern, workman's mark to the base.

c1754-58   4.25in (11cm) high

$800-1,000   WW

A Worcester leaf molded pickle dish, painted in blue with the 'Two-Peony Rock Bird' pattern, workman's mark, minor damages and restoration.

c1754-58   4.5in (11cm) high

$400-600   WW

A Worcester leaf molded pickle dish, painted in blue with the 'Two-Peony Rock Bird' pattern, workman's mark, a small chip to one point.

c1755-60   4in (10cm) high

$900-1,100   WW

A Worcester pickle dish, painted in blue with the 'Pickle Leaf Daisy' pattern, the exterior molded, workman's mark in blue.

c1760-65   5.5in (14cm) high

$1,200-1,600   WW

A Worcester pickle dish, painted in blue with the 'Pickle Leaf Vine' pattern, crescent mark, minor glaze chips to the rim.

c1760-70   3.25in (8.5cm) high

$200-400   WW

A Worcester 'Blind Earl' sweetmeat dish, painted in blue with leaves and insects, open crescent mark.

The design originated at the Chelsea porcelain factory and was also produced at Worcester from the 1750s. In the 19thC the pattern was named after the Earl of Coventry, who lost his sight in a riding accident. He ordered a service in this pattern so that he could feel the raised decoration.

c1765   6in (15cm) high

$1,800-2,400   WW

A small Worcester basket with reticulated sides, printed in blue with the 'Pine Cone' pattern, crescent mark.

c1770-80   4.5in (11.5cm) high
$800-1,000   WW

A Worcester chestnut basket and cover, with applied twig and flower handles, the lobed body printed with quatrefoil flower heads, crescent mark, damages and restoration.

c1770-75   8in (20.5cm) high
$600-800   WW

A Worcester basket with pierced rim, printed in blue with 'The Pine Cone' pattern, open crescent mark.

c1775-85   8.5in (21.5cm) high
$500-700   WW

A Worcester molded salad bowl, printed in blue with various flower sprays and a hatched border, open crescent mark.

c1775-85   9.75in (24.5cm) high
$800-1,200   WW

A Worcester blue and white bowl, painted in the 'Floral Queen' pattern.

c1770   6in (15.5cm) high
$500-700   WW

A Worcester molded leaf dish, printed in black with three butterflies within a painted pale green border, unmarked, the handle broken and repaired.

c1757   7in (17.5cm) high
$800-1,000   WW

A Worcester octagonal plate, painted in the Kakiemon palette with the 'Quail' pattern, unmarked, rim chip and crack.

c1760   9.25in (23.5cm) high
$200-400   WW

A pair of Worcester basket stands with pierced floral rims, painted with flower sprays, the handles formed as twigs with applied flower heads, unmarked, damages and restoration.

c1765   10in (25.5cm) high
$1,200-1,600   WW

A Worcester 'Blind Earl' sweetmeat dish, painted in the Japanese style with flowers within a border of iron red, black and gilt starbursts, paper label for the Zorensky Collection.

c1765-70   6in (15cm) high
$1,600-2,400   WW

A Worcester plate, painted with the 'Sir Joshua Reynolds' pattern within a gilt-decorated blue border, an upper case 'W' mark, paper label for the M. H. Stieglitz Collection.

c1770   7.5in (19cm) high
$700-800   WW

A Worcester double leaf molded dish, painted with chrysanthemum and prunus in the Imari palette, paper label for the Zorensky Collection, restored cracks.

c1770   10.25in (26cm) high

$300-500   **WW**

A late18thC Worcester 'Blind Earl' sweetmeat dish, painted in the 'Rich Queen's' pattern, square seal mark in blue, some restoration.

6.25in (16cm) high

$700-900   **WW**

A Worcester Imari palette dish, of kidney form in the 'Pavilion' pattern, the central reserve depicting a pavilion, prunus tree and clouds, the border with alternating foliate and dragon panels, with gilt highlights.

10in (25.5cm) long

$600-800   **FRE**

An early Worcester sauceboat, silver shape, molded with Rococo scrollwork, the scroll handle with pronounced thumb-rest, painted in colored enamel with Chinese figures and flowers, the interior with flowers and foliage, on footed base, cracked.

c1753   7.5in (19cm) wide

$600-700   **NEA**

A small Worcester jug, richly painted in the Imari palette with the 'Queen Charlotte' pattern, seal mark to the base.

c1770   3.25in (8cm) high

$1,000-1,400   **WW**

A Worcester teapot and cover, painted in polychrome enamels, with four Chinese figures and a cat, applied flower finial, unmarked.

c1770   7in (18cm) high

$1,000-1,600   **WW**

A Worcester feather-molded baluster cream jug, with scroll handle, painted in the famille rose palette, with flowering shrub, a crane, and an insect, workman's mark.

c1760   3.5in (9cm) high

$3,600-4,400   **DN**

A Worcester blue scale porcelain teapot, with floral reserves on a blue scale ground, gilt details, underglazed blue half moon mark.

c1770   5.5in (14cm) high

$800-1,200   **FRE**

A pair of 18thC Worcester pierced circular baskets, the blue scale ground painted with garlands, blue square seal mark, one repaired.

7.5in diam

$3,000-5,000   JN

A Worcester blue-ground guglet and fluted basin, the guglet of octagonal pear shape, painted with two large gilt-edged panels of exotic birds, the neck reserved with two smaller panels of birds in flight.

c1768-70   Basin 11in (28cm) wide

$16,000-20,000   SOTH

A Worcester two-tiered scallop shell sweetmeat dish, painted with flowers and encrusted with polychrome shells, unmarked, restored.

c1765-70   7.5in (19cm) high

$1,200-1,800   WW

A pair of Worcester blue-scale ground hexagonal vases and covers, painted with Kakiemon style panels of birds and flowers within elaborate gilt frames against a blue-scale ground, fretted square mark in underglaze-blue.

c1770   11.75in (30cm) high

$22,000-26,000   SOTH

A Worcester scale blue coffee cup and saucer, painted with panels of flowers, square seal marks.

c1770

$300-500   WW

A Worcester bowl, decorated with a bleu céleste ground within a gilt border, crossed swords mark with '9' between the blades, some wear to the enamel.

c1775-85   6.25in (16cm) high

$500-700   WW

Left: A Flight & Barr circular scalloped topographical fruit plate, with a gilt rim, the border decorated in sepia with strawberry plants, the well also decorated in sepia with a view of 'West Wycombe Park, the seat of Sir John Dashwood King, Bart', with fishermen by a river in the foreground, painted mark 'Flight & Barr, Wor.r Manufacturers to their Majesties' and place name.

c1795   9in (23cm) diam

$400-600   L&T

Center: A Flight & Barr scalloped oval single handled topographical fruit dish, with a gilt rim, the border decorated in sepia with strawberry plants, the well also decorated in sepia with a view of 'Cowes Castle, Isle of Wight', painted mark 'Flight & Barr, Wor.r Manufacturers to their Majesties' and place name.

c1795   8in (20cm) wide

$700-800   L&T

A Barr Worcester tea service, comprising a teapot, cover and stand, a sugar bowl, milk jug, cake plate, slop bowl, six tea cups, five coffee cans and six saucers, richly decorated in gilt leaves and floral swags on a dark blue ground, incised marks.

c1798

$2,400-3,600   WW

Right: A Flight & Barr circular scalloped topographical fruit plate, with a gilt rim, the border decorated in sepia with strawberry plants, the well also decorated in sepia with a view of 'Friar's Carse, Dumfries-shire, the seat of Robert Riddell, Esq', with fishermen by a river in the foreground, painted mark 'Flight & Barr, Wor.r Manufacturers to their Majesties' and place name.

c1795   9in (23cm) diam

$600-800   L&T

CLOSER LOOK: BARR, FLIGHT AND BARR VASE

Barr, Flight and Barr's Neoclassical decoration was increasingly exuberant and sophisticated.

The marbled ground painted around the neck of the vase is typical of Worcester at this time.

This vase is in the fashionable Neoclassical urn shape and features dolphin and shell handles. These are less restrained than many examples of the period and have been extravagantly gilded.

The flowers are almost lifelike. Worcester was renowned for its high quality painting during the early 19thC.

An early 19thC Flight Barr and Barr Worcester plaque, painted with flowers on a dark green ground, probably by Samuel Astles, in a gilt and velvet frame, impressed marks.

11in (28cm) high

$1,800-2,400 **WW**

A Barr, Flight & Barr two-handled vase, shield-shaped body painted with a panel of flowers against a blue ground within a gilt frame, reserved on a black and white marbled ground, the shoulders set within gilt dolphin and shell molded handles, raised on a gilt square base and four paw feet, puce script mark.

c1810 *14.25in (36cm) high*

$9,000-13,000 **SOTH**

An early 19thC Flight Barr and Barr muffin dish and cover, printed in black with farming figures and harvest scenes on a pale yellow ground, impressed crowned 'FBB' mark, some wear to the gilding.

8.25in (21cm) high

$700-800 **WW**

A Flight Barr and Barr Worcester soup tureen, cover and stand, painted with a band of leaves and flowers in purple and gilt, impressed mark to the stand, some wear to the gilding and a small restored chip.

c1825

$500-700 **WW**

A pair of 19thC Worcester porcelain 'Dr. Syntax' plates, titled 'Dr. Syntax reading his town (?)' and 'Dr. Syntax loses his wig', each scene within a gilt-enriched cobalt border decorated with floral sprays.

8.5in (21.5cm) diam

$1,400-1,800 **FRE**

A pair of Royal Worcester candlestick figures, modeled as a young man and woman carrying baskets on their shoulders, details highlighted in pink, green, blue and gilding, green printed marks, date code.

1864 *11in (28cm) high*

$700-900 **WW**

A pair of Royal Worcester figural casters, molded as a boy and a girl in Victorian dress, printed marks.

c1880 *7in (18cm) high*

$800-1,200 **WW**

A pair of Blush Worcester porcelain figural vases by James Hadley, depicting a girl and boy playing a whistle and drinking from a jug, each flanking an ovoid urn, on rockwork circular bases.

c1890 *7.25in (18.5cm) high*

$2,000-2,400 HT

A Royal Worcester miniature Toby jug, standing wearing a red coat and holding a goblet, printed mark and date code.

1931 *3.5in (9cm) high*

$140-200 WW

A pair of Royal Worcester figures, 'Joy' and 'Sorrow', by James Hadley, printed marks, date code, slight scratches and crazed.

1932 *9.5in (24cm) high*

$1,600-2,000 A&G

A Royal Worcester model of a sheep, standing on a green base with head turned to dexter, modeled by B Bargas, printed mark and model number '3155'.

c1936 *5in (13cm) high*

$1,200-1,800 WW

A Royal Worcester figure of Wellington, from the Famous Military Commanders series, modeled by Bernard Winskill, limited edition number 324 of 750, raised on wooden display stand, with certificate and original packing.

17in (43cm) high

$2,400-2,800 HALL

A Royal Worcester figure of Napoleon Bonaparte, after David, from the Famous Military Commanders series, modeled by Bernard Winskill, limited edition number 179 of 750, raised on wooden display stand, with original certificate and packing.

15.75in (40cm) high

$1,600-2,400 HALL

A Royal Worcester vase, decorated with chrysanthemums on a blush ground, printed mark with date code, some wear to the enamels and gilding.

1890 *11.25in (28.5cm) high*

$300-400 WW

An unusual pair of Royal Worcester vases, each supported on the backs of three black swans on trefoil bases, the purple glaze fading to white at the shoulders, restored rim chip to one vase, printed factory mark and date code.

1863 *8.5in (21.5cm) high*

$800-1,200 WW

A pair of Royal Worcester porcelain vases, of waisted form painted by Jas. Stinton with pheasants, signed, with gilded rim and foot.

1922 *7.5in (19in) high*

$2,000-3,000 HT

A late 19thC Royal Worcester part dinner service, comprising a meat plate, ten dinner plates and soup plate, decorated in blue, red and gilt with stylized flowers and foliage and decorative bands, printed and impressed marks.

Meat plate 17.25in (44cm) wide

$240-360   **ROS**

A Royal Worcester low comport, painted by J. Ruston, the gold-painted body with a jeweled border and edged vignettes, painted with satyrs and nymphs being attacked by a grotesque monster.

12in (30.5cm) diam

$800-1,000   **SWO**

A pair of Royal Worcester vases by Harry Davies, each pedestal ovoid vase enamelled with castles and ruins against a mountainous and woodland landscape with figures to the foreground, each within gilt reserve and against cobalt ground, the shoulders applied with gilt highlighted and scroll molded handles below a flared neck, all raised on canted square plinth base, green printed mark and model number '1969', date code.

1909   *20in (50.5cm) high*

$12,000-18,000   **HALL**

A Royal Worcester plate, decorated with a girl standing in the front door of a thatched cottage, signed 'C. Creese', titled 'Harrington' to the reverse, printed mark and date code.

1930   *8.75in (22.5cm) high*

$200-300   **WW**

A Chamberlain's Worcester shaped rectangular tray, painted with a titled view 'Osterley Park', within a surround of applied brightly colored shells and seaweed, molded gilt scroll and foliate rim, red-painted script mark and title.

c1840   *13.25in (33.5cm) wide*

$1,600-2,000   **SOTH**

A pair of Chamberlain's Worcester plates, the centers painted with flowers, the pink borders with gilt coral trails, printed marks.

c1845   *9.5in (24cm) diam*

$500-700   **WW**

An early 19thC Chamberlain's Worcester plate, the well decorated with chrysanthemums in overglaze blue enamel, the border with flowers in the Kakiemon palette, printed mark.

9in (23cm) diam

$140-200   **WW**

A Chamberlain's Worcester model of a milkmaid, wearing a plumed hat and with a milk churn hanging from one arm, painted mark, restored, one churn missing.

c1830   *7in (17.5cm) high*

$100-300   **WW**

A 19thC Chamberlain's Worcester cup and saucer, well painted with colorful flowers encircled by gold foliage on a blue ground, printed marks.

$700-900   **WW**

An early 19thC pair of Chamberlain's Worcester plates, a matching cup and saucer, and a waste bowl, all decorated in the Imari style with pattern number 276.

8.5in (21.5cm) diam

$500-700   **WW**

A Chamberlain's Worcester double-walled reticulated sugar bowl, the handles painted as bamboo, painted mark.

c1850   *5.5in (14cm) high*

$600-1,000   **WW**

BELLEEK

Founded in 1857 in the village of Belleek, Ireland, by John Caldwell Bloomfield, David McBirney and Robert Armstrong, Belleek Pottery initially produced earthenware fired with peat. These early wares included floor tiles and hospital ware.

- In 1863, a number of Stoke-on-Trent craftsmen joined the firm and it began to successfully produce Parian porcelain.
- By 1865, Belleek had established a growing market throughout Ireland and the UK and was exporting pieces to the US, Canada and Australia.
- The factory produced a wide variety of wares, including porcelain vases, flower-pots and centerpieces, often decorated with flowers, or marine motifs. The factory also produced a range of approximately 30 figures and busts. Belleek's most extensive range was tea ware. More than 36 patterns have been used, including 'Shamrock', 'Tridacna', and 'Neptune'. They are typically off-white, green or pink colored.
- The openwork baskets, with applied flowers, for which Belleek is famous, were designed and developed by William Henshall, one of craftsmen from Stoke-on-Trent. The earliest baskets to be introduced were the 'Henshell', 'Convolvulus', 'Twig', 'Sydenham' and 'Shamrock' designs. The finest is thought to be 'Rathmore'.
- Covered baskets were particularly difficult to produce as both pieces were made at the same time and were prone to failure.
- The history of the factory has been divided into nine periods, and the marks change accordingly.
- The factory is still in operation today.

A late 19thC Belleek oval lidded basket, the cover applied with thistles, shamrock and roses, impressed 'Belleek Co. Fermanagh' mark, the basket handles missing, other minor damages.

12.25in (31cm) high

$1,100-1,500   **WW**

A Belleek porcelain reticulated fruit basket, having a basket weave center bowl with an interlaced border applied with various flowers and branch-form handles, impressed 'BELLEEK' and 'IRELAND'.

9.5in (24cm) diam

$1,000-1,400   **FRE**

A Belleek porcelain reticulated covered basket, of oval form with a latticework body and interlaced loop border applied with roses, thistles and shamrocks and with twin branch-form handles, the cover similarly decorated, impressed 'BELLEEK' and 'IRELAND'.

12in (30.5cm) wide

$1,600-2,000   **FRE**

A pair of 19thC Bing & Grondhal bisque figures, depicting Jason and his golden fleece and Venus holding an apple, impressed marks.

13.75in (35cm) high

$2,400-3,600   **L&T**

A set of twelve late 19thC Bodley and Son porcelain plates, by J. Birkeek, and retailed by Bailey, Banks & Biddle, Philadelphia, each painted with different game bird, printed mark.

9in (23cm) diam

$2,000-3,000   **FRE**

A Champion's Bristol teapot, with an associated pottery cover, painted blue 'X' mark

c1770-1780   *8.25in (21cm) high*

$500-700   **WW**

A set of twelve 19thC Capodimonte porcelain plates, decorated with different armorial crests within a gilt border, the rims molded with continuous Classical landscapes depicting figures in various pursuits, blue underglazed mark.

10in (25.5cm) diam

$2,400-3,600   **FRE**

PORCELAIN

A late 18thC Chantilly plate, painted in blue with a floral design, the rim lobed and molded, unmarked.

9.5in (24cm) diam

$100-160   **WW**

A Copeland Parian bust of Princess Alexandra, raised on a socle, sculpted by F. M. Miller for the Crystal Palace Art Union, impressed marks including the date.

1863   *11in (30cm) high*

$360-440   **WW**

A Copeland Parian bust of Spring, sculpted by L. A. Malempré, impressed marks including publication date.

1870   *12.25in (31cm) high*

$400-600   **WW**

A late 19thC Copeland china trough and stand of elongated rectangular form, with scrolling rim, the sides painted with holly, printed Copeland mark and registration mark.

Trough 25in (63cm) wide

$1,400-2,000   **L&T**

A pair of 19thC Copenhagen bisque porcelain figures in the form of Classical figures, raised on square bases, blue wave mark.

13in (33cm) high

$3,000-4,000   **L&T**

A late 18thC Copenhagen tureen and cover, of oval form, the cover with pear-form finial, the borders with molded basket work, painted with flower sprays and further flower sprigs.

12.5in (31.5cm) high

$1,600-2,400   **L&T**

CLOSER LOOK: GIRL IN A SWING ÉTUI

'Girl in a Swing' is the name attributed to a London porcelain factory, established by Charles Gouyn, which operated from 1749-59 from his Bennet Street home.

Gouyn was a china retailer and jeweler who specialized in making novelties such as scent bottles, small figures, étuis and bonbonnières.

The name was derived from some figures attributed to his factory, which are now in London's Victoria & Albert Museum and the Boston Museum of Fine Arts.

An H & R Daniel botanical dessert service, comprising a tazza, two sauce tureens, stands and covers, four dishes, four small stands, twelve plates, each piece painted with a different flower, damages and restoration.

c1835

$800-1,200   **WW**

A Doccia plate, painted with scattered floral sprays in the manner of Chinese famille rose.

c1760   *10.5in (27cm) diam*

$300-400   **WW**

A late 18thC Doccia model of a young woman, wearing a purple shawl and a dark blue skirt, holding a spotted yellow bundle, restoration to her right arm.

5.5in (14cm) high

$1,800-2,400   **WW**

A rare Girl in a Swing étui, the cylindrical body delicately painted with flower sprays, the lid formed as the head of a young lady, wearing a mask and a white headscarf, her eyes set with single cut diamonds.

c1755   *5in (12.5cm) high*

$10,000-12,000   **WW**

A Höchst figure of a little barrel maker, large haircrack through his body, crowned wheel mark in underglaze blue, raised hand restored.

c1765   4in (10cm) high

$600-800   **SOTA**

A Höchst figure of a boy leaning forward with outstretched arm, holding a bird, standing on a naturalistic base, wheel mark in underglaze blue, incised 'N' and '18'.

25in (10.5cm) high

$1,200-1,600   **GORL**

A Höchst figure of a girl, holding a grapevine, on a rockwork base, wheel mark in iron red, minor damages.

c1760   6.25in (16cm) high

$800-1,200   **WW**

A late 19thC Hutschrenreuther porcelain plaque, 'Marguerite', the standing figure with daisies in her hair, numbered '311', signed 'Wagner'.

7.25in (18.5cm) high

$3,000-4,000   **FRE**

A blue and white coffee cup, probably Isleworth, painted with a mountainous Chinese landscape, minor chips and firing faults.

c1760-70   3in (8cm) high

$1,000-1,400   **WW**

A pair of English pâte-sur-pâte vases, probably by George Jones, of flattened ovoid form, the sides painted and hand-tooled in white slip with a nymph and a cherub fishing beside a pond, with gilt loop handles and marked in gilt '5639 13'.

c1880   6in (15cm) high

$4,000-6,000   **FRE**

A late 18thC Kloster-Veilsdorf figure of a bacchante, draped with an applied grapevine and with flowers garlanded in her hair, restored.

7.5in (19cm) high

$700-800   **WW**

An Isaac Broome parian bust of Ulysses S. Grant, signed 'BROOME Sculp'1876 LENOX Pottery 1914'.

9.75in (24.5cm) high

$2,000-4,000   **DRA**

A Limoges porcelain plaque, 'Gypsy', painted with a dark-haired beauty adorned in gold jewelry, wearing a head scarf.

$1,200-1,600   **FRE**

A Limoges chocolate set, comprising: a tray, a chocolate pot and cover, a sugar bowl and cover, a milk jug and three cups with covers, molded with foliate scrolls and painted with sprays of flowers within gilt borders, printed marks.

c1900

$400-600   **WW**

PORCELAIN

A Christian's Liverpool teapot and cover, painted with flowers in polychrome enamels, the shoulders with gilding over a blue ground, the knop formed as a flower, minor damages.

c1770-75   8.75in (22cm) high

$600-1,000   **WW**

A late 18thC Liverpool porcelain teapot and cover, painted with flower garlands in polychrome enamels.

                                        8.25in (21cm) high

$700-800   **WW**

A pair of Longton Hall figures of an abbess and her novice, seated reading from religious texts, unmarked, restoration to both.

c1755-60   5in (12.5cm) high

$2,400-2,800   **WW**

A Lowestoft blue and white teabowl, printed with the 'Good Cross Chapel' pattern, rim crack.

c1780-90   3in (7.5cm) high

$1,000-1,400   **WW**

ESSENTIAL REFERENCE: LUDWIGSBURG

Ludwigsburg was one of the many porcelain factories to emulate Meissen wares.

- The factory was founded in Württemberg, Germany, in 1758 by Duke Karl Eugen, starting in a barracks but later moving to a small castle.
- Its first director was Joseph Jakob Ringler, who remained there until 1802.
- Ringler had stolen the secret formula from his previous employer, the Vienna factory, and went on to sell it to Höchst, Strasbourg and Nymphenburg.
- Ringler brought with him Gottlieb Friedrich Riedel, who had been director of painting at Frankenthal.
- Riedel's influence led to the creation of some of Ludwigsburg's finest wares, the Rococo figures.
- Some of the best Rococo pieces were modeled by Johann Christian Wilhelm Beyer.
- Ludwigsburg has a smoky gray-brown tinge to the body of a piece.
- On areas of a figure that have been left white, this grayish glaze gives it the appearance of marble.
- The figures are crisply modeled but tend to lack the movement of Meissen, appearing rather stiff with bland faces.
- Wares were decorated in subtle pastel shades which complimented the smoky tone of the Ludwigsburg glaze.
- The key colors are grayish pinks, blues and greens with yellow, iron-red, black and gilding.
- Ludwigsburg bases vary widely from simple, mottled green-brown grass or rockwork mounds and slabs, to rich Rococo forms, with gilded highlights.
- Despite the input of Neoclassical sculptor Johann Heinrich von Dannecker in the 1790s, and a brief revival at the turn of the century, the factory went into decline and closed in 1824.

A late 18thC Ludwigsburg figure of a female folk dancer, holding a percussion instrument in each hand, raised on a small scrolled base, painted and incised marks, minor damages.

                                        6in (15.5cm) high

$1,000-1,400   **WW**

A Ludwigsburg group of a fortune teller, modeled by Johann Valentin Sonnenschein, interlacing 'C' in underglaze blue, restored.

c1775   8.25in (21cm) high

$800-1,200   **SOTA**

A pair of late 18thC Ludwigsburg figures of putti musicians, one playing a violin, the second a triangle, raised on plinths, crowned double 'C' monogram marks, minor damages.

5.5in (14cm) high

$500-700 **WW**

A Lynton bough pot and cover, of bombé form, the central panel painted and signed by Stefen Nowacki, with a scene of a Dutch man o' war and other ships, the reverse with shells, seaweed and coral, the turqouise ground with a raised gilt lattice, gilt rim, detachable pierced cover with circular gilt flower holders, printed marks in gilt.

10.5in (27cm) wide

$2,000-3,000 **NEA**

A 20thC Lynton bower pot and cover, painted by Stefan Nowacki with a scene of ships at sail in a stormy sea before a cliff-top fort in the distance, within a richly gilded panel on a blue-scale ground, the cover pierced with seven holes, printed factory mark.

7.25in (21.5cm) high

$800-1,200 **WW**

A pair of Mennecy cups and trembleuse saucers, painted with sprays of pink roses and other blooms, the cup handles formed as stalks issuing from leaves and berries, incised 'D.V' marks, minor wear.

c1760

$3,400-4,000 **WW**

An early 19thC New Hall part tea service, comprising teapot and cover, sugar bowl, cover and stand, milk jug, cake plate, slop bowl, five teacups, three coffee cups and six saucers, decorated with oak leaves and acorns in gilt and dark blue, pattern number 524, some damages.

$500-700 **WW**

A pair of 19thC Niderviller urns and covers, each cover surmounted by acorn finial with bisque fern leaf decoration, the body with applied bisque floral garlands and with female mask handles on a pink and gilt ground, with opposed armorials, one depicting Romulus and Remus suckling, with the initials 'SPQR', above reeded support and faux marble plinth, applied mark to foot.

14in (36cm) high

$2,000-3,000 **L&T**

A mid-18thC molded Nymphenberg plate, the center painted with a landscape scene in a Rococo vignette, bordered by leafy swags, impressed mark.

10in (25.5cm) diam

$1,200-1,800 **WW**

A late 19thC Paris porcelain and gilt-metal-mounted vase centerpiece.

17in (43cm) wide

$2,000-2,400 **DN**

An early 19thC Pinxton coffee can, painted with a scene of a double-arched bridge over a river, a very faint hairline crack near the base.

3.25in (8cm) high

$600-800 **WW**

A Rockingham tea service, comprising teapot and cover, sugar bowl and cover, milk jug, bowl, fourteen plates, twenty one cups and nine saucers, pattern number 1461, with a different botanical painting on each piece, printed marks, some damages.

c1840

$2,600-3,000 **WW**

PORCELAIN

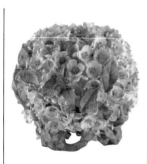

A mid-19thC Staffordshire porcelain vase, encrusted all over with apple blossom, some damages.

7in (18cm) high

$200-300 **WW**

A Swansea molded teacup and saucer, with a wishbone handle, painted with pink roses and gilt sprigs, unmarked.
c1820

$600-800 **WW**

A Tournai teapot (théière globulaires) and cover, from the Duc D'Orléans service, decorated with a blue band set with gilt floral festoons flanking two large geometric medallions enclosing ornithological and two small round medallions enclosing butterflies, the cover with an acorn finial and similar decoration, the base with the names of the birds in black script. '10(...)' in underglaze blue and incised 'B' to the pot, '12' in underglaze-blue to the cover.

In 1787 the Tournai factory received an order for a service for Philippe-Joseph, Duc d'Orléans (1747-93). It is not known whether the entire service was delivered to the Palais-Royale in Chantilly, France, but it is certain that not all pieces were delivered in 1791. This extensive service comprised a total of 1,593 pieces, of which 594 were sold to the Prince of Wales. In total there were three different shapes of teapots made for the service, the théière de forme calabre, théière litron and théière globulaire, all of which were produced in two sizes. This teapot of the largest size, another teapot of this size is kept in the Royal Collection in Windsor. Not even the Royal Manufactory at Sèvres ever produced a service of this extraordinary size. By way of comparison, the Sèvres service for Louis XV (1753-55) consisted of 493 pieces, and the service made for Catherine the Great of Russia (1776-79) comprised 706 pieces.
c1787

4.75in (12cm) high

$26,000-30,000 **SOTH**

ESSENTIAL REFERENCE: UNION PORCELAIN WORKS

The Union Porcelain Works was a large American factory that produced porcelain heavily influenced by German porcelain.
● The company was founded in Brooklyn, New York, in 1861, by Thomas Carll Smith (1815-1901).
● Much of the company's wares were produced from a hard paste porcelain.
● Produced inexpensive robust wares, such as door plates and knobs. It also produced commemorative vases, such as the 'Centenary' range, and tableware, including oyster plates.
● Karl Müller was art director from the early 1870s and introduced a characteristically bizarre style, his designs featuring mandarin-head finials, polar bear handles and rabbit-form feet.
● The factory closed in the 1920s.

A rare Union Porcelain Works Century vase, designed by Karl Mueller, with buffalo handles decorated in pâte-sur-pâte with busts of George Washington and several vignettes of historical moments, signed with UPW medallion, small chip to bison horn, light wear to gilt at rim.

The large, original example was made for The Philadelphia Centennial Exposition of 1876. This is one of the 14 smaller versions produced after it.
12.75in (32cm) high

$22,000-26,000 **DRA**

A molded and polychromed porcelain ice pitcher, designed by Karl L. H. Müller, the 'Uncle Sam' pitcher, molded with walrus spout and polar bear handle on ovoid body, molded with relief figures of King Gambrinus, the Norse God of beer, offering a drink to Brother Jonathan, a character from Royall Tyler's comedy, 'The Contrast', who came to symbolize America and Uncle Sam, the obverse with a fight scene between Bill Nye and Chinese Gambler AH Sin, popular characters of the time, signed 'Union Porcelain Works Greenpoint, N.Y.'.

9.75in (25cm) high

$8,000-12,000 **FRE**

A porcelain figure of two putti and a goat, possibly Vauxhall, the goat munching on grapes, raised on a scrollwork base with applied flowers, unmarked, damages and restoration.

c1758-60   6in (15cm) high

$2,600-3,000   WW

A 19thC painted ceramic tile, by Joseph Zasche (Austrian, 1821-1881), with a scene after Albert Jules Edouard's 'La Music sur la Terrasse', framed.

Tile 10in (25.4cm) high

$500-600   FRE

A 19thC English loving cup, with turquoise ground, decorated with gilt scrollwork reserved with a rectangular panel depicting a fanciful bird, the reverse with a river landscape.

c1875   9.5in (24cm) wide

$600-800   NEA

An English painted porcelain plaque, depicting a man wearing a fur coat and holding a spear climbing rocks, possibly John the Baptist, dated and signed 'Slocomb'.

1881   11.25in (28.5cm) high

$700-800   FRE

A 19thC bisque figure of Cupid, stringing his gilt-brass bow, seated on a draped pedestal with quiver below, on an elliptical serpentine marble base with Neoclassical gilt-metal braces, on turned feet.

14in (36cm) high

$3,600-4,400   L&T

A pair of 19thC bone china botanical plates, and a matching tazza, lavishly painted with colorful flowers, together with five dishes with similar decoration, the tazza cracked.

10.5in (27cm) diam max

$400-600   WW

An English porcelain cylindrical inkwell, the top painted with a band of flowers, the side with three figures in a landscape, unmarked.

c1825   4in (10cm) high

$600-800   WW

A bone china plaque painted with the Aintree legend 'Red Rum', standing beneath a tree before a winding river, signed 'Leighton Maybury', painted mark and dated, framed.

1977   14.5in (37cm) high

$1,000-1,600   WW

An English bone china commemorative cup and saucer, printed with a border of safari animals and titled 'Souvenir of the British Empire Exhibition, Wembley, 1925'.

$120-180   WW

A mid-19thC English bone china plaque, painted with a Swiss alpine view, verso with iron-red inscription 'Viege or Visp with Monte Rose painted by R. Abbot', mounted in giltwood and gesso frame.

Plaque 6.5in (16.5cm) wide

$1,400-1,800   DN

A 19thC bone china jug, painted with bands of flowers on a gilt ground, with the initials 'AB' to one side and 'CB' to the other within oval panels, unmarked, some wear to the gilding.

7in (18cm) high

$1,000-1,400   WW

A blanc de chine porcelain figure, modeled after the Barberini Faun, seated on a tree stump, applied with fruiting vines, raised on a Rococo scroll base.

13.75in (35cm) high

$2,800-3,200   **L&T**

Four plates, by Joseph Crawhall II, each hand-painted with exotic birds, with two examples bearing thumbnail head and shoulder self-portraits on reverse, all signed, three also dated 'Oct 1885', 'Oct 1885' and 'Nov 1885'.

1885

$3,000-4,000   **A&G**

A late 19thC French painted ceramic tile, by Laure Levy (French, 1866-1954), with scene depicting a coastal chateau and figures in a small rowing boat, signed 'Laure Levy', framed.

8.25in (21cm) high

$400-600   **FRE**

A Louis XV style blue porcelain and gilt-metal-mounted urn, the upper half with floral garlands and opposing ribbon tied oval portrait medallions, the leafy scroll side supports with female portrait heads and lower hairy paw feet, the fluted spreading foot on a shaped plinth base.

24in (61cm) high

$800-1,000   **L&T**

A pair of 20thC Continental porcelain yellow-ground vases and covers, in the Worcester style, painted with panels of parakeets and flowers, unmarked, minor wear to the gilding.

14.25in (36cm) high

$400-600   **WW**

A pair of 18th/19thC French Kakiemon style vases on brass mounts, of octagonal bottle form, scroll leaf-painted neck, the ovoid body painted with floral sprays and blue and red butterflies, brass mount to base.

8in (20.5cm) high

$1,800-2,400   **FRE**

A French polychromed and gilt porcelain deep dish, oblong shape decorated with crossed anchors and French and American flags above 'The Steamer Chateau Yquem' within a scrolled gilt reserve.

c1900   *15in (38cm) wide*

$800-1,200   **FRE**

A pair of early 20thC Chelsea style porcelain figures, modeled as a seated gentleman and a lady, he with a dog at his feet, she with a sheep, gold anchor mark.

7.5in (19cm) high

$800-1,200   **FRE**

An 18thC Continental porcelain molded cylindrical étui, painted in purple with scenes of young ladies and gentlemen before trees and Classical plinths, a restored chip.

4.5in (11.5cm) high

$1,400-2,000   **WW**

A 19th/20thC Continental porcelain tea service, comprising a tray, teapot and cover, sugar bowl, milk jug, four cups and four saucers, decorated with panels of birds and flowers on a yellow and gilt ground, printed overglaze marks.

$100-300　　　　　　　　　　　　　　　　WW

A pair of 19thC Continental sweetmeat figures, modeled as musicians, painted with birds, insects and flowers, elaborate 'F' mark to the base, some restoration.

7.25in (18.5cm) high

$400-600　　　　　　　　　　　　　　　　WW

A 19thC miniature porcelain basket of seashells, either side pierced with a hole, unmarked.

2in (5cm) high

$600-800　　　　　　　　　　　　　　　　WW

A pair of 19thC German porcelain figures, modeled as a shepherd and shepherdess, on naturalistic base, underglazed blue pseudo 'Augustus Rex' marks.

9in (3.5cm) high

$1,200-1,800　　　　　　　　　　　　　　FRE

A late 19thC German porcelain plaque, depicting an interior stable scene of two horses fighting while a stable hand intercedes, an officer standing by, framed.

Plaque 15in (38cm) wide

$6,000-10,000　　　　　　　　　　　　　FRE

A German porcelain plaque, 'The Prodigal Son in the Tavern', after Rembrandt Van Rijn, depicting a Dutch interior with a cavalier and his mistress, spurious impressed cross swords mark, framed.

Rembrandt's painting showed himself and his wife Saskia.

6.75in (17cm) high

$3,000-4,000　　　　　　　　　　　　　　FRE

A large Italian ceramic model of a cockerel.

26.5in (67cm) high

$2,400-3,000　　　　　　　　　　　　　　L&T

An Italian porcelain model of a dancing man, wearing a green jacket, standing on one leg and holding a posy of flowers, raised on a circular base, two fingers chipped.

c1780-90　　　　　*7in (17.5cm) high*

$4,000-5,000　　　　　　　　　　　　　　WW

THE POTTERY MARKET

The pottery market has seen a move away from a market where age alone would guarantee strong prices. Any piece that has come on the market that is early, an unusual shape, and particularly well painted has sold well. Dated pieces retain their popularity.

In delftware, patriotic and topographical scenes have grown in popularity, whereas simply painted chinoiserie pieces have been quite sluggish. Unusual subject matter and shape, such as the wig stand on page 69, have been at a premium.

Naïve pottery, with good provenance, has been a strong seller. The Shelley collection in the US saw strong prices for redware, particularly for a piece that ticks all the boxes, like the lidded jar on page 72.

Creamware is a perpetual favorite. The market is fuelled by interior decorators who like plain creamware in interesting shapes. Commemorative ware has to have a good subject to attract much interest. The same can be said for transfer-printed ware.

Interesting and unusual subject matter will add value and interest. Collectors are extremely discerning and search out the rare and exceptional pieces.

DELFT

A pair of Lambeth delft blue and white plates, painted with shepherd and shepherdess in romantic landscape with ruin.

9in (22cm)

$1,300-1,500 DN

An English delft sweetmeat or pickle tray, London or Liverpool, painted in blue with floral sprays within a diaper band border.

c1760

$2,000-2,400 DN

A small delftware plate, probably Lambeth, painted with stylized tulips on a pale blue ground, some crazing to the glaze.

c1720-30 *9in (23cm) diam*

$400-600 WW

A delftware dish, painted with a tulip design within a geometric border, possibly Bristol or Brislington, minor good restoration.

c1740 *13in (33cm) diam*

$3,000-4,000 WW

A large blue and white delftware dish, possibly Bristol, minor damages.

c1720 *14in (36cm) diam*

$500-700 WW

A delftware charger, painted in blue with a castle surrounded by boats, on a powdered manganese ground, possibly Wincanton or Bristol.

c1740-1750 *11.5in (29.5cm) high*

$800-1,200 WW

A mid-18thC delftware charger, painted with a stylized border of flowers and pineapples, some restoration to the rim.

13.5in (34cm) high

$600-800 WW

A delftware Adam and Eve charger, painted in polychrome with the doomed couple flanking a tree around which a serpent coils, a few small rim chips and glaze lacking from the rim.

From the 1630s to the 1730s, blue-dash chargers, made of tin-glazed earthenware with abstract, floral, religious, patriotic or topographical motifs, were produced by London and Bristol potters. They were decorated in a broad, rough style, in blue, green, tawny-yellow, and rich purplish-brown. The image of Adam and Eve was particularly popular. The fruit which Eve is handing to Adam is typically orange in color, so it is possible that these dishes are intended as a satire on the ascension of William and Mary of Orange.

c1740   13in (33.5cm) high

$7,000-9,000   WW

A late 17thC oval Delftware three-footed bowl, with rope-twist handles, the interior painted with a figure, the sides with rockwork, plantain and foliage, perhaps Brislington, a few small glaze chips.

8.25in (21cm) high

$2,000-4,000   WW

A large 18thC delft bowl, painted in blue with figures in a village setting, the interior with trees, some restoration to the foot rim.

10.5in (26.5cm) high

$1,000-1,400   WW

An 18thC polychrome delftware dish, painted with a pattern of stylized flowers and a banded hedge, minor chips to the glaze at the rim.

13.5in (34cm) diam

$600-800   WW

An 18thC delftware plate with a scalloped rim, painted in blue with a fence, peonies and fronds of foliage, the border with panels of lattice and flowers, minor rim flakes.

8.75in (22cm) diam

$300-500   WW

A mid-18thC delftware dish, painted in polychrome enamels with a pattern of star flowers and leaf fronds within a stylized floral border, minor wear to the enamels.

13.5in (34cm) diam

$2,000-3,000   WW

An English delft blue and white shallow bowl, possibly Bristol, painted with a bird in flight above sponge-decorated trees, blue dash border,

c1700.   9in (22cm) diam

$2,000-2,400   DN

An early 18thC London delft blue and white powder bowl, well painted with a stylized fish within a lappet border, some rim and footrim chips.

9in (23cm) diam

$1,600-2,400   DN

A mid-18thC delftware bowl, painted in polychrome enamels with a landscape scene, minor cracks and glaze chips.

6.75in (17cm) high

$800-1,200 WW

An 18thC delftware bowl, painted in polychrome enamels with flowers and insects above a palisade, the interior painted in blue with concentric bands and a floral spray, some damages.

10.5in (27cm) high

$500-700 WW

An 18thC English delft polychrome bowl, decorated with scrolling foliage to the rim, the well decorated with chinoocherrie scene with a fence, bold flowers and foliage and an exotic bird in flight.

13.75in (35cm) diam.

$1,200-1,600 L&T

A mid-18thC delftware small rectangular flower brick, painted in blue with peony and other flowers above a palisade, the top pierced with nineteen symmetrically arranged holes, '2' mark, damages.

5.5in (14cm) high

$500-700 WW

An English delft flower brick, probably London, painted in blue in panels of Oriental flowering shrubs with birds in flight, rim chips and wear to leading edges.

c1760 *5.75in (14.5cm) long*

$1,200-1,600 DN

A London delft blue and white urn, molded with two masks and painted with churches within a landscape of sponge decorated trees,

c1760. *6in (15cm) high*

$1,600-2,000 DN

CLOSER LOOK: DELFT WIG STAND

A wig stand was an important accessory at a time when wigs were fashionable.

Delftware was inspired by Chinese ceramics and so Oriental decoration is typical

The blue washed areas are 'trekked' or outlined in black, which characterizes a good deal of the delftware in the late 17th/18thC.

Typically, the ceramic is covered with a glaze with many 'pin holes' which were caused when air bubbles in the glaze exploded during firing.

A delft wig stand with top section supported on a double-knopped stem and stepped conical foot, painted in shades of manganese and ocher in the Transitional style.

c1700 *7in (17cm) high*

$10,000-12,000 DN

An 18thC Dutch Delft model of a blue and white seated dog, wearing a collar and holding an object in its mouth, damages.

6.5in (16.5cm) high

$1,200-1,600 WW

An early 18thC delftware gallipot or cylindrical drug jar, decorated with concentric manganese bands, probably London, broken and restored.

6.25in (16cm) high

$800-1,200 WW

A pair of 19thC Dutch Delft tea canisters, with metal mounts and covers, decorated with panels of figures in seascapes on a scrolling foliate ground, minor damages.

5in (12.5cm) high

$300-500 WW

A Dutch Delft octagonal-section baluster vase, De Metalen Pot, painted in shades of iron-red, green and blue with a lappet shoulder of panels of single flowers above a field of floral sprays, iron-red mark.

c1700

$500-750 DN

A late 17th/early 18thC German faïence charger, possibly Frankfurt, decorated after a Wan-Li original, some glaze flakes.

15.75in (40cm) diam.

$600-800   **SOTA**

An 18thC Frankfurt faïence dish, decorated after Wan-Li examples, some minor chips and flakes.

15in (38.5cm) diam.

$1,000-1,200   **SOTA**

An Eloury-Porquier Quimper platter, painted with a cornucopia pattern including a bird and butterflies, with rope twist handles, painted monogram mark, one handle restored.

c1850   *20.75in (53cm) high*

$300-500   **WW**

A faïence jug, probably Spanish, painted in blue with geometric and foliate bands, the neck bearing the inscription, 'Soy de Manuela Cerrian de Miguel' and the date, the neck and spout damaged.

1852   *9.75in (24.5cm) high*

$100-300   **WW**

A German faïence tankard, with a pewter cover, the lid with an inscription, and engraved with the initials 'F.G.M.W.' and the date, impressed marks to the lid, damages.

1754   *10.25in (26cm) high*

$500-700   **WW**

An Italian 18thC faïence plate, probably Savona, the octagonal well decorated in blue with rabbits and a bird, within a shaped foliate border, damages and restoration.

10in (25.5cm) diam

$6,000-8,000   **WW**

An 18thC French faïence waisted tambour decorated jardinière, with twin rope-twist handles and decorated with blue line and foliate bands, on a heavily carved ebonized stand.

19.75in (50cm) wide

$1,600-2,400   **L&T**

A late 18thC Continental faïence model of a cat, seated on a rectangular base, its right forepaw resting on a mouse, probably Brussels.

5.5in (14cm) high

$4,400-5,000   **WW**

An Italian maiolica tile, molded in relief with a sunburst panel inscribed 'IHS', painted in a ocher glaze and reserved on a blue ground.

9in (23cm)

$1,000-1,200 DN

A 19thC Cantigalli twin-handled vase, each side painted with a Roman profile portrait surrounded by musical and Classical motifs, the handles formed as snakes above a grotesque mask, cockerel mark to the base, one handle restored.

12.5in (32cm) high

$800-1,200 WW

A Naples maiolica albarello, painted in blue with a townscape and inscribed in manganese and dated.

1775   *10.5in (27cm) high*

$1,000-1,400 DN

A late 18thC Naples maiolica albarello, typically painted in blue with a panel of a townscape, footrim chip.

7.75in (20cm) high

$500-700 DN

REDWARE

Redware is the term used to describe the everyday porous red-brown pottery produced largely in the US from the 17thC.

- Early redware was fairly crude in shape and typically covered in lead glaze in browns, yellows, orange or copper green to make it watertight.
- Decoration is bold and lively. The finish is distinctly rustic. Simple slip-decoration was popular from the late 17thC.
- Some wares were made at small potteries, like that of Andrew Duché, and by part-time potters.
- Although redware became less common during the 19thC when mass-produced functional ware became readily available, it continues to be made today.

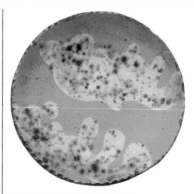

An early 19thC redware toddy plate, probably Hartford, Connecticut, with free-form mottled yellow slip with green splotches, from the Shelley Collection.

4.75in (12in) diam

$3,000-4,000 POOK

A 19thC North Carolina or Pennsylvania redware pie plate, with yellow, green, and brown slip dot and circle flower decoration on an orange-glazed ground.

8.25in (21cm) diam

$2,000-3,000 POOK

A 19thC Pennsylvania redware pie plate, probably Dryville, with green and brown four-line slip decoration, from the Shelley Collection.

7.75in (19.5cm) diam

$6,000-8,000 POOK

A 19thC Pennsylvania redware pie plate, impressed 'W. Smith Womelsdorf', from the Shelley Collection.

7.75in (20cm) diam

$6,000-8,000 POOK

An American redware plate, by Simon Singer (1822-94) Haycock Township, Bucks County, Pennsylvania, inscribed 'M. Singer Applebackville, Bucks Co. Penna', from the Shelley Collection.

12.5in (32cm) diam

$3,000-4,000 POOK

A Chester County, Pennsylvania vibrant redware flowerpot and undertray, possibly by Vickers Pottery, from the Shelley Collection.

c1820   *6.75in (17cm) high*

$5,000-6,000   **POOK**

An early 19thC Pennsylvania redware flower pot and undertray, with vibrant yellow and black slip decoration on an orange glaze, from the Shelley Collection.

$1,000-1,200   **POOK**

A Chester County, Pennsylvania earthenware jar, attributed to Vickers Pottery, with scraffito leaf decoration, inscribed 'H.g', and dated, from the Shelley Collection.

1808   *8in (20.5cm) high*

$10,000-12,000   **POOK**

A 19thC American redware flower pot, attributed to Absalom Bixler, Earl Township, Lancaster County, Pennsylvania, with relief bird figure, from the Shelley Collection.

6in (15cm) high

$30,000-40,000   **POOK**

A mid-19thC Pennsylvania molded redware jar, Mechanicsburg, Lancaster County, the front and back with recessed panels with relief figures of George Washington, inscribed 'Washington', the sides with relief figures of hunter and deer, inscribed 'Swope Pottery' for Henry Swope, with overall manganese splash decoration on an orange glaze ground, the base impressed 'GALL', from the Shelley Collection.

9.25in (23.5cm) high

$5,000-7,000   **POOK**

An American redware canister, North Carolina, of coiled form with bands of yellow and green slip on an orange-glazed ground, from the Shelley Collection.

c1800   *6.5in (16.5cm) high*

$12,000-14,000   **POOK**

An American glazed redware lidded jar, Montgomery County, Pennsylvania, all on an orange ground, from the Shelley Collection.

c1780-1840   *10.5in (26.5cm) high*

$20,000-30,000   **POOK**

A late 18th/early 19thC Bristol County, Massachusetts, green-glazed redware covered jar, ovoid form with green copper oxide glaze, the cover with reduced band, minor wear to cover edge.

10.5in (26.5cm) high

$30,000-40,000   **SK**

An English redware canister, with brown squiggle line decoration, initialled 'R.O.', dated.

1764   *4.75in (12.5) high*

$3,000-4,000   **POOK**

An Astbury-type redware mustard pot and cover, sprigged with pipe clay ornaments, restoration to the cover.

c1740   *3.5in (9cm) high*

$500-700   **WW**

A 19thC redware globular pot-pourri vase and cover, decorated with flowers, butterflies and insects, minor damages.

10.5in (26.5cm) high

$200-400   **WW**

POTTERY

A redware pitcher, probably Chester County, Pennsylvania, with overall black manganese glazing and relief initials 'JF', with relief birds and stars, from the Shelley Collection.

c1800-10   10.5in (26.5cm) high

$6,000-8,000   **POOK**

A molded redware pitcher, Virginia, attributed to Solomon Bell, with relief hunting scene, retaining orange glaze with green and brown slip decoration, from the Shelley Collection.

8in (20cm) high

$4,000-6,000   **POOK**

A 19thC redware puzzle jug, possibly Pennsylvania, with bird spout and overall dark brown manganese glaze and white dots.

From the Shelley Collection.

6in (15cm) high

$8,000-10,000   **POOK**

A Staffordshire redware teapot and cover, in octagonal shape and molded in relief with Oriental subjects.

c1755   4in (10cm) high

$1,200-1,600   **DN**

A Staffordshire redware teapot, of Elers type, cylindrical form with short spout, sprigged with stylized flowers, carved wood replacement cover.

c1700   4in (10cm) high

$3,000-3,600   **DN**

An redware standish, Montgomery County, Pennsylvania, with dog finial, inscribed 'William Hamalman Medinger 1855', from the Shelley Collection.

William was the father of Jacob Mendiger.

7.75in (19.5cm) high

$3,000-7,000   **POOK**

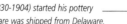

An redware ring vase, Montgomery or Bucks County, Pennsylvania, dated, from the Shelley Collection.

1815   8.75in (22cm) high

$6,000-8,000   **POOK**

An pierced redware footed covered dish, by David Haring (1801-71), Nockamixon Township, Bucks County, Pennsylvania, with rope-twist handles, retaining an overall green glaze, from the Shelley Collection.

6in (15cm) high

$24,000-30,000   **POOK**

A 19thC redware bird-on-stump whistle.

8in (20.5cm) high

$300-700   **POOK**

CLOSER LOOK: REDWARE WALL POCKET

Daniel Peter Shenfelder (1830-1904) started his pottery c1869. Clay for his stoneware was shipped from Delaware, while red clay was dug on his own property. The pottery also made bricks.

In redware Shenfelder made fancy pie plates, vases, sponge cake dishes and large plates with flower designs on them. The applied decoration was carried out by his daughter Mary.

This is a very rare piece by Shenfelder and probably his finest exisiting work .

Shenfelder used this stamped mark on his work.

A 19thC redware wall pocket, Reading, Pennsylvania, with mask decoration and yellow glaze with green and brown splash, impressed 'D.P. Shenfelder, Reading, PA', from the Shelley Collection.

10.75in (27.5cm) high

$44,000-56,000   **POOK**

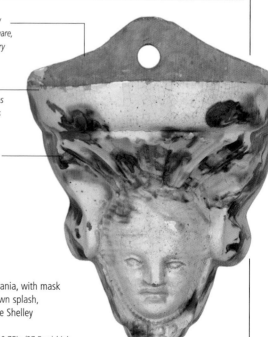

An 18th/19thC English large brown-glazed slipware charger, with honey-colored zigzag, scroll and waved line design, below a toothed rim.

17.75in (45cm) wide

$4,000-6,000 HALL

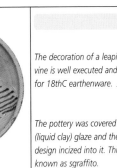

A slipware plate, Southwestern Pennsylvania, the center with three black, green and yellow tulips arising from a yellow heart surrounded by bands of wavy yellow and green slip decoration, all on an orange-glazed background, dated.

1816 12in (30.5cm) diam

$100,000-120,000 POOK

A Continental Moravian slip-decorated plate, with yellow and manganese petal decoration, dated, from the Shelley Collection.

1824 11.5in (29cm) diam

$4,000-6,000 POOK

CLOSER LOOK: SLIPWARE CHARGER

The decoration of a leaping stag with a tree and flowering vine is well executed and exceptionally sophisticated for 18thC earthenware.

The pottery was covered with a layer of slip (liquid clay) glaze and the outline of the design incised into it. This technique is known as sgraffito.

The design was then embellished with further colored slips to enhance the finished charger.

Dated ceramics such as this one tend to command a premium.

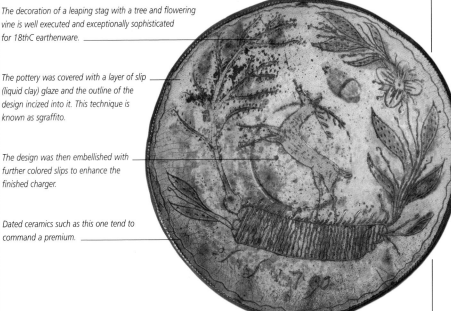

A late 18thC American earthenware charger, attributed to Isaac Stout, Bucks County, Pennsylvania, with sgraffito decoration, the center with a leaping stag, flanked by tree and flowering vine and fence in orange, green, yellow and brown slip, dated, from the Shelley Collection.

1790 14in (35.5cm) diam

$100,000-120,000 POOK

An earthenware barber's bowl, with profuse yellow, green, cream and brown slip flowers, vines and line decoration, dated, from the Shelley Collection.

1791 6.5in (16.5cm) diam

$1,000-2,000 POOK

A 19thC English earthenware bird whistle, in the form of a brown-glazed parrot with yellow slip decoration and round base.

5in (13cm) high

$400-600 POOK

A 19thC Devon slipware bottle vase, decorated with three stenciled fern fronds.

8.5in (21.5cm) high

$200-400 WW

An English 19thC slipware model of a cradle, decorated in a buff glaze with a pattern of swirls and geometric motifs in dark brown, the base unglazed, damages.

11.5in (29.5cm) high

$1,000-1,400 WW

POTTERY

ESSENTIAL REFERENCE: AGATEWARE

Agatewate is made from colored clays which are combined to suggest the veining of a hard stone like agate. It was made in ancient Roman times and was popular in 18thC England.

- Initially, the clays were mixed randomly, resulting in broad veining. Thomas Whieldon greatly improved agateware in the 1740s by using white clays stained with metallic oxides. The resulting clay was prone to blurring and so it was shaped in two-part moulds, polished after firing, and glazed.
- A typical golden-yellow glaze is on early ware, but after about 1750 it is transparent or blue gray.
- Josiah Wedgwood used the process to make onyx or pebbled vases closely imitating natural agate.

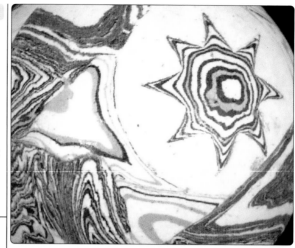

A mid-18thC agateware compressed circular teapot and cover, minor faults.

5.25in (13.5cm) high

$800-1,000   **WW**

A mid-18thC solid agateware sugar bowl and cover, with a cylindrical body and flattened knop, some good restoration to the cover.

4.5in (11.5cm) high

$300-500   **WW**

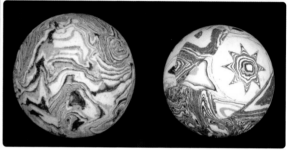

Two similar Staffordshire agateware balls. c1750

2in (5cm) diam

$1,200-1,600   **DN**

CREAMWARE

Creamware was developed c1740 by the potteries of Staffordshire, England. An improved type was made in 1765 by Josiah Wedgwood, who called it 'Queen's ware' in honour of Queen Charlotte.

- The clay was mixed with flint to produce a ware that was durable, relatively cheap, light weight and as thin as porcelain.
- Creamware was versatile and could be finely molded before being printed or painted, under and over the glaze.
- By the late 18thC, creamware had become the standard household pottery, driving many tin-glazed earthenware factories out of business.

A late 18thC Liverpool creamware commemorative mug, of cylindrical form, decorated with 'America Declared Independent July 4 1776',

5in (12.5cm) high

$5,000-7,000   **FRE**

A Liverpool creamware cylindrical mug, transfer-printed with 'An East View of Liverpool Light House & Signals on Bidston Hill'.

1796   *4.75in (12cm) high*

$2,000-3,000   **WW**

A Liverpool creamware commemorative mug, decorated with ribbon border inscribed with the names of sixteen states and the verse 'Oh Liberty thou Goddess Heavenly bright. Profuse of Bliss and pregnant with delight Eternal pleasures in they presence reign and smiling plenty leads thy wanton train',

6.25in (16cm) high

$2,000-3,000   **FRE**

A late 18th/early 19thC transfer-printed creamware commemorative mug, the cylindrical form decorated with the Ropemaker's arms and inscription 'Behold our support'.

6in (15cm) high

$1,000-1,600   **FRE**

An early 19thC pink luster and magenta transfer-printed creamware mug, decorated on each side with an eagle and shield, 'E Pluribus Unum' and 'May Success Attend Our Agriculture Trade'.

4in (10cm) high

$1,800-2,200   **FRE**

A Liverpool printed Pilchard Fishery creamware commemorative jug, decorated with a vignette of a brig under a press of sail and titled 'SUCCESS TO THE PILCHARD FISHERY', verso with an oval panel of a woman with cornucopia titled 'PEACE AND PLENTY', beneath the spout inscribed to 'MICHAEL & JANE TONKIN'.

c1790   *5.75in (14.5cm) high*

$2,400-3,600   **DN**

An early 19thC Liverpool pitcher, with Hope on one side, a ship flying the American flag on the other, and spread-winged eagle and shield with a Jefferson quotation.

9in (23cm) high

$800-1,200   **FRE**

CLOSER LOOK: CREAMWARE TEAPOT

A gilt hand-decorated creamware presentation pitcher, each side decorated with a three-masted ship flying the American flag, a figure of a man with a hammer burying a barrel, the inscription 'John Dockity' under spout enclosed by floral vine, band at top and trellis border at foot.

8.25in (21cm) high

$2,000-3,000   **FRE**

It is decorated on both sides with an iron red floral wreath, inscribed 'No Stamp Act' on one side and 'American Liberty Restored' on the other.

The teapot has a crabstock spout and handle.

The fact that the teapot was made in England for the American market to celebrate the repeal of the act illustrates how important trade with the American colonies was to British industry.

This piece documents a significant moment in American history. This is only the fourth known example. The other three are in the Smithsonian, Colonial Williamsburg, and the Peabody-Essex Museum in the US.

An early 19thC Liverpool creamware marriage pitcher, decorated on one side with 'The Arms of Deering', the reverse with 'The Arms of Carver' and below the spout, with the initials 'ED'.

11in (28cm) high

$1,600-2,400   **FRE**

A pre-Revolutionary War English creamware teapot and cover, of ovoid form, from the Shelley Collection

The 1765 Stamp Act was a tax imposed on the American colonies by the British Government. It required the colonists to pay a tax on every piece of printed paper they used. Once in effect, the tax met with great resistance as the colonists insisted that they could be taxed only with their consent and it was repealed in the following year.

1765-1766   *5in (12.5cm) high*

$160,000-200,000   **POOK**

POTTERY

A Staffordshire creamware teapot and cover modeled as a cauliflower, bullet-shaped with auricular handle,

c1765.   6in (15cm) high

$2,000-3,000   **DN**

A probably mid-18thC Astbury/Whieldon type creamware figure of a musician, some good restoration.

5in (12.5cm) high

$1,000-1,200   **WW**

A black transfer-printed and polychromed punch bowl, probably Herculaneum, the interior decorated with oak leaf border and rare ship-building scene heightened in polychrome above 'John Johnson', the exterior decorated with the Great Seal of the United States, Washington Map of the United States, King Neptune, and 'His Excellency General George Washington, Marshall of France...'.

11in (28cm) diam

$4,000-6,000   **FRE**

PEARLWARE

A late 18thC pearlware oval straining dish, with decorative piercing and a green underglaze border.

13in (33.5cm) diam

$400-600   **WW**

A large late 18thC pearlware meat dish, painted in blue with a Chinese figure holding a parasol before a pagoda, molded feathered rim, unmarked, minor damages.

20.5in (52cm) diam

$300-500   **WW**

A Staffordshire pearlware commemorative plaque, for Queen Caroline, molded in relief with bust profile of George IV's infamous wife, painted in shades of blue, green and ocher, reserved on pink luster ground.

Caroline of Brunswick married George IV whilst he was the Prince of Wales. George had already married a Catholic, Maria Fitzherbert, but he needed a wife who was Protestant and of royal blood if he wanted to ascend the throne. The marriage was unhappy. Caroline was forbidden to see their only daughter, Charlotte, and from 1814 she travelled in Europe, leading a bohemian and decadent life. After the death of George III in 1820, Caroline returned to England. Despite great popular support, George IV was determined that she would never be crowned Queen and had her barred from his coronation. Caroline fell seriously ill on the day of the coronation and died three weeks later, convinced she had been poisoned.

c1820   6in (15cm) diam

$800-1,200   **DN**

A mid-19thC Swansea pearlware plate, painted in red, blue and green with a vase of flowers in the well and a garlanded border, with luster details, impressed 'Dillwyn Swansea' mark.

8.5in (22cm) diam.

$600-1,000   **WW**

An 18thC unusual pearlware candle niche, painted in blue with a young man wearing a necklace.

c1750   *9.75in (25cm) high*

$1,200-1,600   **WW**

An early 19thC brown-glazed pearlware jug, printed in yellow with a portrait of Lord Nelson on a ground of flowers and scrolls, a small chip to the spout.

6in (15cm) high

$500-700   **WW**

A large early 19thC pearlware punch pot, printed in blue with figures in a Chinese riverscape, unmarked, the damaged spout with a metal replacement.

15.75in (40cm) high

$400-600   **WW**

A pearlware mug, printed in blue with panels of buildings on a floral ground, minor damages.

c1825   *5.5in (14cm) high*

$200-300   **WW**

A pearlware harvest jug, painted with a mock heraldic shield, between two figures above the motto 'Farmers Arms', an inscription under the spout, damages.

1808   *8.75in (22.5cm) high*

$300-400   **WW**

A matched pair of Staffordshire pearlware figural groups, the oblong molded base with sponged decoration.

6.5in (16cm) long

$5,000-7,000   **NA**

A 19thC Staffordshire pearlware spill vase, modeled as a tree stump with three recumbent sheep at the base amid applied flowers and grass, minor damages.

8.75in (22.5cm) high

$300-400   **WW**

PRATTWARE

A dated Staffordshire Prattware model of a tallcase clock, painted in shades of blue, green and ocher, restored.

1794   *9in (23cm) high*

$800-1,200   **DN**

A Staffordshire Prattware model of a tallcase clock, painted in shades of blue, green and ocher.

c1800   *8in (20cm) high*

$600-800   **DN**

A Prattware caster, painted with a repeated floral motif, the pierced top with radiating ocher stripes, damages.

c1800   *5in (12.5cm) high*

$100-300   **WW**

A small early 19thC Prattware flask, each side molded with figures and decorated in blue, green, yellow and ocher.

2.5in (6.5cm) high

$500-700   **WW**

POTTERY

MOCHAWARE

Mochaware is a type of slip-glazed earthenware made to resemble mocha stone (moss agate). It was popular in the UK, France and the US from the late 18thC to the late 19thC.

- Early pieces feature seaweed-like slip decoration which resembles mocha stone.
- The surface consists of layers of slip, usually a base coat topped with one of the more distinctive motifs arranged within glaze bands of contrasting color. There may be as many as twenty six of these decorative bands on a large piece such as a jug.
- Mochaware motifs include seaweed, earthworm, cat's eye, and marble or tortoiseshell.

A 19thC rare Mochaware covered bowl, with blue, black and green bands and seaweed decoration on a brown ground.

11in (28cm) diameter

$12,000-14,000   POOK

An early 19thC Mochaware basin, with looping earthworm decoration, base chips.

10.75in (27.5cm) diam.

$8,000-10,000   SK

An early 19thC Mochaware covered chamber pot, with looping earthworm decoration.

8.5in (21.5cm) high

$3,000-4,000   SK

A Mochaware cylindrical mug, decorated in brown, cream and caramel-colored combed slip between green bands.

c1800   6in (15cm) high

$5,000-6,000   WW

A large mid-19thC Mochaware jug, a replacement metal handle and other damages.

12.5in (32cm) high

$800-1,200   WW

STAFFORDSHIRE

The Staffordshire ceramics trade developed round five main English towns – Stoke-on-Trent, Burslem, Hanley, Tunstall, and Longton which were home to over 1,000 factories by the end of the 19thC, including Wedgwood, Spode and Ridgeway.

- The rich natural resources of clay and coal made Staffordshire an ideal location. White clay was also brought in from Dorset, Devon and Cornwall.
- Designers and potters moved between factories, so many similar shapes and patterns emerged.
- During the 19thC, the Staffordshire companies became increasingly well known for their pottery figures, which were copies of high-quality porcelain. These pieces were often inspired by Derby and Chelsea and depicted rustic, allegorical or biblical scenes.
- The ceramics industry has declined in recent times, but several companies still flourish in the Staffordshire area.

A 19thC pearlware Toby jug, wearing a long red coat and resting a foaming jug of ale on his knee, unmarked.

9.5in (24cm) high

$300-400   WW

An early 19thC Staffordshire pearlware Toby jug, restoration to the hat and feet.

9.75in (25cm) high

$1,000-1,200   WW

A Staffordshire Toby jug, with black tricorn hat and pink jacket, holding a foaming jug of ale, on canted square brown-line base .

c1825   9.5in (24cm) high

$240-360   DN

A Staffordshire Toby jug and cover, with black tricorn hat and jacket holding a foaming jug of ale and a pipe, on canted square red-line base.

c1840   10.25in (26cm) high

$240-360   DN

A Staffordshire Toby jug, black tricorn hat and brown jacket, seated with a foaming jug of ale, canted square base.

c1830   *9.5in (24cm) high*

$300-500   **DN**

A Staffordshire pearlware Toby jug, typically modeled seated holding a foaming mug of ale, flaking and old repairs.

c1820   *9.5in (24cm) high*

$400-600   **DN**

A pearlware Toby jug, possibly Yorkshire, typically modeled seated with foaming jug of ale, painted and sponged with colored enamels.

c1835   *10in (25cm) high*

$300-500   **DN**

A Victorian Staffordshire earthenware foot bath, with twin cast foliate handles and gray glaze with green diagonals.

$300-400   **BIG**

A Staffordshire Gaudy Welsh presentation pitcher, of baluster form, inscribed 'Mary Brayshaw Died Febry 3 1837 aged 62 years'.

8in (20.5cm) high

$800-1,200   **FRE**

Two 19thC Staffordshire figures of the Queen of Prussia and Queen Victoria.

Tallest 16.5in (42cm) high

$300-400   **POOK**

A pair of 19thC Staffordshire figures of the Duke and Duchess of Edinburgh.

17.25in (44cm) high

$400-600   **POOK**

A rare Staffordshire pottery two-handled leech jar and cover, bearing the gilt inscription 'Leeches' on a dark blue banner, with pierced lid.

11.75in (30cm) high

$4,000-6,000   **WW**

A pair of 19thC Staffordshire models of King Charles spaniels, damages.

7.5in (19cm) high

$100-300   **WW**

A mid-19thC Staffordshire part dessert service, comprising seven plates and three dishes. painted with views of 19thC American life, including views of Native American Indians at Lake Winnipesaukee, the White House and figures above the Hudson River, all within gilded pale blue borders and titled to the reverse.

$2,000-3,000   **WW**

POTTERY

An early 19thC Staffordshire silver resist luster ovoid jug, with angular handle, decorated with spots and ears of wheat beneath scaling.

c1810

4.25in (11cm) high

$200-300   **NEA**

A 19thC pottery lusterware model of a lion, resting on a marbled base, some restoration.

10.25in (26cm) high

$200-400   **WW**

A black transfer-printed and pink luster box, rectangular form, the lid decorated with a naval battle scene of the Constitution and the Java, interior with Sunderland splotches.

6in (15cm) wide

$400-600   **FRE**

TRANSFER-PRINTED WARE

Transfer printing was a cheaper and quicker alternative to hand painting. It was used from the late 18thC to mass produce ceramics.

- Blue and white chinoiserie designs, like the extremely popular 'Willow' pattern, were often applied to table wares.
- The decoration on early pieces can exhibit huge variances in shade. Some very rare examples were filled in by hand using colored enamels.
- Production had vastly increased by c1815, and by c1835 it was possible to print smoother designs in several colors.
- Transfer-printed ware may be distinguished from hand painting by the cross-hatching created by the engraving on the copper plate. Sometimes the edges of the printed design are not a perfect match.
- Transfer printing is still used to decorate ceramics today.

A historical blue transferware platter, Bennett Pottery, Baltimore, oblong form decorated with 'Pickett's Charge Gettysburg' enclosed by an oak leaf and acorn border with portrait medallions of General Robert E. Lee, General William. S. Hancock, General Jas Longstreet and General G.G. Mead.

13in (33cm) wide

$1,000-2,000   **FRE**

An historical blue and white transfer decorated A 1920s Staffordshire pottery platter, by James and Ralph Clews, Cobridge, England, depicting the 'Landing of Gen. LaFayette at Castle Garden New York 16 August 1824,' with printed title, and impressed maker's mark on the reverse.

19in (48cm)

$2,000-3,000   **SK**

A large Copeland and Garrett New Stone dish, printed in blue with the 'Grasshopper' pattern, printed and impressed marks, some wear and scratching.

c1840   *19.75in (50cm) diam.*

$400-600   **WW**

A Herculaneum Pottery blue and white charger, printed with 'View in the Fort, Madura' from the Indian series.

c1820   *13in (33cm) diam*

$500-700   **DN**

A pair of 19thC Hicks, Meigh and Johnson blue printed venison dishes, each with scalloped, gadrooned border, the well decorated with figures beside a tree on a riverine landscape with a pagoda behind.

c1822-35   *21.5in (55cm) wide*

$1,600-2,400   **L&T.**

A blue transferware well and tree platter, Jones & Son, 1826-1828, decorated with 'Death of General Wolfe' from the 'British History' series.

20in (51cm) wide

$2,000-4,000   **FRE**

A John & William Rigdway, Hanley historical blue transferware platter, decorated with 'Deaf & Dumb Asylum, Hartford Connecticut', from Ridgway's 'Beauties of America' series, within a rose and leaf medallion border.

1814-30   *14.75in (37.5cm) wide*
$1,000-2,000   **FRE**

A large Rogers pearlware dish, printed in blue with a figure tending an elephant, impressed marks.

c1820   *20.75in (53cm) high*
$400-600   **WW**

A 19thC blue and white meat dish, possibly Spode, depicting one Eastern scene with square buildings, overhanging trees and figures in the foreground.

19in (48cm) wide
$900-1,100   **JN**

A Ralph Stevenson, Cobridge, historical blue transferware platter, decorated with 'New York, Esplanade and Castle Garden', within a leaf and vine border, signed on ship's sail.

18.5in (47cm) wide
$3,000-5,000   **FRE**

A Canadian F. T. Thomas of Quebec transfer-printed plate, showing a scene of the 'St Louis Gate Porte St Louis' and with transfer-printed border of beavers amidst foliage.

9.75in (24.5cm) diam
$200-300   **TCF**

A Canadian F. T. Thomas, Quebec 'View Looking North From The Citadel' transfer-printed octagonal platter, from the 'Scottish Quebec Views' series.

c1874   *13.75in (35cm) wide*
$1,600-2,400   **TAC**

An Enoch Wood and Sons, Burslem, historical blue transferware platter, decorated with 'Christianburg Danish Settlement on the Gold Coast of Africa', within a shell border with irregular center.

1819-46   *20.5in (52cm) wide*
$2,400-3,600   **FRE**

An Enoch Wood & Sons, Burslem, historical blue transferware platter, decorated with 'Castle Battery New York', within a shell border with circular center.

1815-1846   *20.5in (52cm) wide*
$2,000-4,000   **FRE**

A mid 19thC Ridgeway 'Corey Hill' pattern tableware set, blue underglaze with chinoiserie decoration with flowers, buildings and scrolls embellished with red, green and pink enamel, some pieces highlighted with gilt, several backstamped with pattern name and/or make, including dinner plates, salad or luncheon plates, soup plates, dessert plates, cups, saucers, small shallow scallop-rimmed bowls, small shallow bowls, small plates, small serving bowls, butter pats, round serving bowls with handles, a round footed bowl, a covered butter dish with drainer, an oval footed serving bowl, an oval footed sauce dish with undertray, oval platters, a teapot, a covered sugar bowl, a cream jug, a chocolate pot, covered jar and a small jug, 162 pieces total, minor chips.

$2,000-4,000   **SK**

An early 19thC historical blue transferware platter, unknown maker, decorated with 'Sandusky', within a rose and scroll border, mismarked 'Detroit'.

16.25in (41cm) wide
$5,000-7,500   **FRE**

POTTERY

A James and Ralph Clews, Cobridge, historical blue transferware pitcher, decorated with 'Landing of Gen. Lafayette at Castle Garden New York, 16 August, 1824', within floral borders.

1829-36   *9in (23cm) high*
$3,000-4,000   **FRE**

A John & William Ridgway, dark-blue soup tureen and cover, with 'Cambridge College, Massachusetts', from the 'Beauties of America Series: Almshouse, Boston'.

15.5in (39cm) wide
$3,000-5,000   **NA**

A 19thC Ridgways 'India Temple' pattern hexagonal soup tureen, cover and two hexagonal stands, with printed mark.

c1814-30
$1,600-2,400   **L&T**

A graduated pair of 19thC blue printed ceramic footed twin-handled soup tureens and covers, decorated with figures in landscape settings, unmarked.

14.25in (36cm) and 13.5in (34cm) wide
$1,400-2,000   **L&T**

A Bathwell & Goodfellow medium-blue footbath, the interior depicting a pastoral view, printed overall with Italianate architectural and harbour views, unmarked.

19.75in (49cm) long
$2,000-4,000   **NA**

A James and Ralph Clews, Cobridge, historical blue transferware water pitcher, of ovoid form, decorated with 'Landing of Lafayette at Castle Gardens, New York, 16 August, 1824', within floral borders.

1829-36   *9.75in (25cm) high*
$600-1,000   **FRE**

A rare James and Ralph Clews, Cobridge historical purple transferware flask, decorated with 'Hudson, Hudson River' from 'Picturesque Views' series.

1829-36   *9.5in (24cm) high*
$3,000-5,000   **FRE**

A Canadian F.T. Thomas of Quebec transfer-printed teapot, with scene of Lorette Falls, Chutes de Lorette, cracked.

Note the desirable beaver motif, hidden in the branches near the rim.

8in (20cm) high
$1,000-2,000   **TCF**

A Ralph Stevenson & Williams, dark-blue Staffordshire pierced center bowl, printed title in underglaze-blue 'Vine Border: Battle of Bunker Hill'.

10in (25cm) long
$4,000-6,000   **NA**

A Turner's patent ironstone part dinner service, comprising three tureens and covers, four dishes, two sauce tureens and three stands, twelve ashets, fourteen bowls, eight side plates, a gravy boat, and two tureen covers.

Large tureen14in (35cm) wide

$4,000-6,000 L&T

A Turner's stone china plate, painted with pine and flowers in the Imari palette, painted mark 'Turner's Patent'

8.25in (21cm) diam.

$80-120 WW

A 19thC Mason's Ironstone part dinner service printed and painted with stylized chrysanthemum and foliage in the Imari palette, comprising a large twin-handled soup tureen and cover, a rectangular vegetable tureen and cover, a rectangular vegetable dish, two square vegetable tureens and covers, two twin-handled sauce tureens, covers and stands, five graduated ashets, a square-form dish, twenty-seven dinner plates, eighteen soup plates, fourteen dessert bowls, fifteen side plates and six cheese plates, impressed mark 'Mason's patent ironstone china'.

$8,000-12,000 L&T

A 19thC ironstone rectangular Imari pattern ashet, decorated in the typical palette.

21in (53cm) wide

$1,600-2,400 L&T

An early 19thC Mason's ironstone 'Japan' pattern vase and cover, impressed mark 'Mason's patent ironstone china'.

16in (40.5cm) high

$3,000-5,000 L&T

An early 19thC ironstone 'Japan' pattern fruit cooler and liner, with twin dragon's head handles.

8.75in (22cm) high

$2,000-3,000 L&T

A matched pair of early 19thC ironstone 'Japan' pattern sauce tureens and covers, each of ribbed form, with flower-head finial and twin shell-form handles, above a pierced gilt leaf decorated oval foot, one impressed with 'Mason's patent ironstone china'.

7.75in (20cm) high

$1,600-2,400 L&T

A set of early 19thC ironstone 'Japan' pattern cider jugs, each with a serpent handle, two Mason's Patent Ironstone with blue printed mark.

Largest: 5.5in (14cm) high

$3,000-5,000 L&T

A matched set of three 19thC Mason's ironstone red-printed tureens, covers and two stands of serpentine octagonal form, two covers, both stands and two bodies decorated with a chinoiserie landscape scene, the other cover and body decorated with an English figural landscape with building, together with one ladle.

14in (35cm) wide

$700-900 SET L&T

POTTERY

A Palissy style circular charger, by Mafra of Caldas De Rainha, with applied lizards, a tortoise, a snake and worms on a bed of extruded clay, impressed mark.

c1880   10.5in (26cm) diam

$800-1,000   **SWO**

A late 19thC Portuguese Palissy style dish, decorated with a pair of lizards fighting on a mossy base, with two stag beetles, impressed factory marks, some restoration.

7in (18cm) diam

$140-200   **WW**

A mid-19thC English phrenological head, as an inkwell, stamped 'By F. Bridges, Phrenologist'.

5.5in (14cm) high

$500-700   **WW**

A shouldered Decalcomania vase, of tapering cylindrical form, with narrow neck, decorated with opposed gothic panels and figures of angels and saints on a cream painted ground.

Decalcomania is a decorative technique by which engravings or prints are transferred onto pottery or other materials. It was invented in England by the Frenchman Simon Francois Ravenet in the 1750s. The term Decalcomania was coined in the 1870s.

12.25in (31cm) high

$700-1,100   **L&T**

STONEWARE

Stoneware is made by mixing clay with a stone flux and firing the mixture at high temperature to fuse the ingredients. The first European stoneware was made towards the end of the Middle Ages in Germany.

- It was more durable and watertight than earthenware. This made it particularly suitable for making stein: the lidded drinking vessels popular in Germany.
- Stoneware was often given a decorative salt glaze. Unglazed stoneware includes Wedgwood's Basalt and Jasper wares.
- White stoneware was very popular, as it emulated the properties of Oriental porcelain.
- Stoneware was eventually superseded in popularity by pale, opaque earthenwares like creamware.

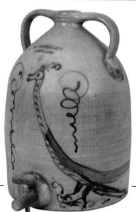

An American 19thC six-gallon stoneware water jug, impressed 'M. Woodruff Cortland', with vibrant goony bird decoration, from the Shelley Collection.

This humourous bird is an unusual and desirable form of decoration.

18in (45.5cm) high

$50,000-60,000   **POOK**

A dated stoneware English Bellarmine jug, typically molded with a mask to the neck and with three raised oval panels, one with Tudor rose surmounted with a crown, the central example with a coat of arms and the third with 'ER' cypher for Queen Elizabeth I surmounted with a crown.

1576   7in (18cm) high

$8,000-10,000   **DN**

A dated stoneware English Bellarmine jug, typically molded with a mask to the neck and with three raised oval panels, one with a Tudor rose surmounted with a crown, the central example with royal coat of arms and the third with a portcullis.

1576   8in (20cm) high

$8,000-10,000   **DN**

A 17thC Spanish salt-glazed wine jug, with applied bacchic mask motifs flanked by four rams, and further applied relief decoration.

24in (61cm) high

$6,000-8,000 **FRE**

CLOSER LOOK: STONEWARE JUG

The decoration featuring a woman with a parasol and exaggerated hoop skirt is very unusual. Birds and flowers are more usual subjects for stoneware jugs.

Bold decoration in a deep blue such as this is highly sought after by collectors.

Stoneware jugs and crocks were essential household items in the 18th and 19thC. They were used for storage.

The shape of stoneware vessels changed in the mid-19thC. Ovoid vessels tend to date from the first half of the century, while cylindrical containers date to the second half.

A 19thC stoneware jug, with cobalt decoration, inscribed indistinctly 'gal that wo_ the water', from the Shelley Collection.

8.25in (21cm) high

$50,000-60,000 **POOK**

A mid-19thC cobalt blue decorated stoneware crock, embellished with a stylized flower blossom, and Albany slip-glazed interior, marked 'ALBANY, N.Y.'.

11.75in (30cm) high

$400-600 **SK**

A mid- to late 19thC stoneware jug with parrot, with applied handle, marked 'WHITES UTICA,' impressed maker's mark, chips.

11in (28cm) high

$400-600 **SK**

A mid- to late 19thC blue stoneware jug, ornamented with a bird perched on a branch, marked 'HENRY LUTHER Amsterdam NY,' with lip chips.

13.75in (35cm) high

$400-600 **SK**

A New York City cobalt blue floral stamp-decorated stoneware jug, attributed to Clarkson Crolius, minor imperfections.

c1800 *14.5in (37cm) high*

$2,000-4,000 **SK**

A large late 19thC English stoneware jug, with twin handles, decorated with molded hunting scene.

19in (48cm) high

$1,400-2,000 **L&T**

A Raeren stoneware and pewter-mounted bauerntanzrug, the brown-glazed body molded with a frieze of dancing couples under arcs, the neck with ribbed decoration.

1598 *10.25in (26cm) high*

$5,000-7,000 **SOTA**

A late 16thC large Siegburg pewter-mounted schnelle, molded in relief with three identical panels depicting Christ, Mary Magdalene and Saint Anne, signed 'HH' for Hans Hilgers.

14.75in (37cm) high

$7,000-9,000 **SOTA**

A 17thC German salt-glazed stoneware Bellarmine jug, decorated all over with a mottled 'tiger ware' glaze, handle restored.

9in (23cm) high

$400-500 **DN**

ESSENTIAL REFERENCE: BELLARMINE

Bellarmine jugs (also known as graybeard jugs) were one of the most common forms of German stoneware. They were made from the mid-16thC to the late 18thC and exported throughout Europe. They were also made in England.

- They were originally made in Flanders to ridicule Cardinal Robert Bellarmine (1542-1621), who was a great opponent of the Reformed Church there. It is believed that it was common for Protestants wishing to insult the Cardinal to smash the jugs, after drinking.
- These corpulent, typically salt-glazed, jugs had a rude likeness of the cardinal and his large, square, ecclesiastical beard at the neck.
- They vary greatly in height and were mainly used in taverns as decanters between the cask and the table, with the smaller pieces used as drinking mugs.
- At one time the jugs were also frequently used as 'witch bottles'. This entailed filling the jug with certain articles, sealing it and burying it. This was done in order to deflect a witch's curse.

A 17thC German stoneware jug of Bellarmine type, with loop handle and typically molded with a mask to the neck above an oval cartouche of a lion rampant, manufacturing faults.

10.5in (27cm) high

$1,000-1,200   DN

A 17thC German brown salt-glazed stoneware Bellarmine jug, typically molded with a mask above an oval boss with a stylized flowerhead, decorated all over with a tiger glaze.

9in (23cm) high

$800-1,200   DN

A 17thC German salt-glazed stoneware Bellarmine jug, typically molded with a mask and decorated with a gray-green glaze, some footrim chips.

7.25in (18.5cm) high

$600-800   DN

A late 18th/early 19thC incized and cobalt blue-decorated stoneware flask, ovoid flattened form with cobalt-filled incized monogram 'HAH', flower blossom and scrolled foliate motifs, neck repair.

7in (18cm) high

$8,000-12,000   SK

A dated blue-decorated stoneware hip flask, possibly New York, the front inscribed with the initials 'P.F.K', within a stylized pot of flowers, flanked by trailing vines, the back with the same initials above a large sunflower.

1853   *5.5in (14cm) high*

$18,000-22,000   POOK

A late 19thC stoneware ring bottle, probably New York, with overall blue glazing, inscribed with suns and stars on one side and a stylized basket and trailing vine on the other.

7.75in (20cm) high

$7,000-9,000   POOK

A Bennington, Vermont stoneware three-gallon crock, with cobalt butterfly and rose amidst scrolls, by J. Norton & Co.

c1840   *12.75in (32cm) high*

$1,000-2,000   NA

A Galesville, New York stoneware six-gallon churn, with cobalt pea fowl and plant, of swelled cylindrical form, marked 'W.A. LEWIS'.

c1860   *18.75in (47cm) high*

$10,000-16,000   NA

An early 19thC incized cobalt blue-decorated stoneware jar, possibly by David Morgan, New York City, with applied lug handles, and minor chips.

9in (23cm) high

$2,000-3,000 SK

A late 18th/early 19thC incized floral-decorated stoneware jar, probably from New York City or northern New Jersey, repaired handles.

9.5in (24cm) high

$2,000-3,000 SK

A 'Quinces' cobalt blue stoneware jar, by Clarkson Crolius Sr., New York City, with impressed maker's mark and minor rim and base chips.

1797-1815 *10in (25.4cm) high*

$4,000-5,000 SK

A Harrisburg, Pennsylvania stoneware crock, stamped 'Wilson's & Young', with cobalt floral decoration.

c1855 *11in (28cm) high*

$5,000-7,000 POOK

A stoneware batter jug, with wire and wood handle, decorated with cobalt blue leafage, impressed 'Cowden & Wilcox / Harrisburg PA'.

7.5in (19cm) high

$5,000-6,000 ALD

An American stoneware crock, decorated with a Fulper bird in colbalt blue, with twin molded handles, cover with chipped edge.

12.75in (32.5cm) high

$300-500 ALD

A large 18thC salt-glazed stoneware mug, decorated with 'The Punch Party', metal mount to the rim, unmarked, damages.

7in (17.5cm) high

$600-1,000 WW

A London salt-glazed stoneware mug, possibly Vauxhall or Mortlake, inscribed 'Geo Pearce 1735', later silver mounts hallmarked for London 1921, faint crack in base.

9in (23cm) high

$6,000-8,000 DN

A Staffordshire salt-glazed stoneware teapot and cover, painted in colored enamels with sprays of flowers reserved on a dark red/brown ground, with naturalistically modeled twig spout and handle.

c1760 *4in (10cm) high*

$1,200-1,600 DN

A set of three mid-19thC Doulton stoneware barrels, decorated with bands of molded vine leaves and the Royal coat of arms, named 'brandy', 'rum' and 'gin', one with tap, impressed mark 'Doulton and Watts, London'.

13in (33cm) high

$1,800-2,400 L&T

A mid- to late 19thC cobalt-decorated stoneware three-part water cooler, Philadelphia or Baltimore, flattened lid on bulbous filter segment and straight-sided base decorated with crossed floral fronds and banding, some chips.

4in (10cm) high

$6,000-10,000 FRE

A pair of 19thC blue stoneware candlesticks, the columns and flared bases painted with flowers, unmarked.

8in (20.5cm) high

$400-600 PAIR WW

POTTERY

CLOSER LOOK: STONEWARE STAG

This stoneware folk art figure of a stag is highly unusual and virtually in mint condition, making it desirable to collectors.

The figure was hand molded and has a very expressive face with a carved, open mouth and full set of teeth.

The stag rests on a shallow platform with its legs stretched forwards. It has a paddle-form tail.

The tan glaze is decorated with cobalt spots.

An exceptional stoneware figure of a recumbent stag, probably western Pennsylvania, with blue dot highlights, expressive open mouth, resting on a free form platform.

c1875

$100,000-120,000   14.5in (37cm) long   **POOK**

A 17th/18thC stoneware globular money box, the buff body partly glazed, with a knopped finial, some restoration.

3in (7.5cm) high

$400-600   **WW**

A 19thC white stoneware pot-pourri basket and cover, painted with a border of flowers, impressed '3' and painted pattern number.

5.5in (14cm) high

$400-600   **WW**

WEDGWOOD

A 19thC Wedgwood black basalt plaque, molded with a maiden playing a lyre with Cupid holding a wreath, 'Wedgwood' impressed.

6.75in (17cm) high

$400-600   **WW**

A mid-19thC Wedgwood basalt hedgehog crocus pot and underplate, modeled with openwork body, raised on a quatreform base, impressed 'Wedgwood'.

These hedgehog-shaped pots were designed to hold crocus bulbs and were used indoors.

10in (25.5cm) wide

$1,000-2,000   **FRE**

A pair of Wedgwood black basalt inkwells modeled as sphinx couchant, on rectangular plinth bases with urns between their fore-paws, the urns with liners, impressed marks, one liner a replacement, some minor damage and repair.

c1800   6in (15cm) long

$2,000-3,000   **DN**

A 19thC Wedgwood bronzed basalt vase, of pedestal ovoid form, the plain body with two applied gilded handles and raised on circular pedestal base, impressed 'Wedgwood' and incized '943'.

12.25in (31cm) high

$1,000-1,400 **HALL**

A 19thC Wedgwood hedgehog crocus pot, the creamware body glazed throughout in green luster, with naturalistic finish, impressed mark, lacking stand.

8.25in (21cm) long

$400-600 **HALL**

A 19thC Wedgwood blue jasper ware cheese bell and stand, with a frieze of cherubs playing musical instruments, the stand with further oak leaf and acorn band, impressed mark.

11in (27.5cm) diam

$700-900 **L&T**

A 19thC Wedgwood blue jasper ware cheese bell and stand, with a continuous frieze of Classical female figures, above a band of acorns and oak leaves, the stand with similar band, impressed mark.

12.75in (32cm) diam

$1,000-1,400 **L&T**

A pair of late 19thC Wedgwood green jasper ware bottle vases and stoppers, each with four Classical figures, impressed mark and backstamp for Humphrey Taylor & Co., one stopper restored.

10.5in (26.5cm) high

$700-900 **WW**

A pair of 19thC Wedgwood black jasper ware covered urns, the ovoid sides decorated in applied white relief with a band of Classical maidens, raised on socle bases, impressed marks.

8.75in (22cm) high

$700-1,100 **L&T**

An Adams blue-jasper oval two-handled sugar box and cover, sprigged in white relief with Classical subjects, the cover surmounted with a swan finial, impressed mark, cracked.

c1800 *6.75in (17cm) wide*

$400-600 **DN**

A 19thC blue jasper ware cheese bell and stand, with rope-twist finial above bands of acorns and oak leaves and a continuous hunting scene.

11.5in (29cm) diam

$800-1,200 **L&T**

A late 19thC German black jasper ware inkwell, the globular well decorated in applied white relief with signs of the zodiac, the dished stand sprigged in white with a band of oak leaf and figural oval reserves.

5in (13cm) high

$600-1,000 **L&T**

TERRACOTTA

A large early 19thC terracotta chinoiserie vase, on circular foot and square painted softwood faux marble plinth.

102cm high

$7,000-9,000 **L&T**

A late 19thC terracotta model of a pug, the well-molded cast glazed brown, the face applied with two glass eyes.

11in (28cm) high

$400-600 **FRE**

CHINESE REIGN PERIODS AND MARKS

Imperial reign marks were adopted during the Ming dynasty, and some of the most common are illustrated here. Certain emperors forbade the use of their own reign mark, lest they should suffer the disrespect of a broken vessel bearing their name being thrown away. This is where the convention of using earlier reign marks comes from – a custom that was enthusiastically adopted by potters as a way of showing their respect for their predecessors.

It is worth remembering that a great deal of Imperial porcelain is marked misleadingly and pieces bearing the reign mark for the period in which they were made are therefore especially sought after.

Early periods and dates

Xia Dynasty	*c2000 - 1500BC*	Three Kingdoms	*221 - 280*	The Five Dynasties	*907 - 960*
Shang Dynasty	*1500 - 1028BC*	Jin Dynasty	*265 - 420*	Song Dynasty	*960 - 1279*
Zhou Dynasty	*1028 - 221BC*	Northern & Southern Dynasties	*420 - 581*	Jin Dynasty	*1115 - 1234*
Qin Dynasty	*221 - 206BC*	Sui Dynasty	*581 - 618*	Yuan Dynasty	*1260 - 1368*
Han Dynasty	*206BC - AD220*	Tang Dynasty	*618 - 906*		

Ming Dynasty Reigns

Hongwu	*1368 - 1398*	Jingtai	*1450 - 1457*
Jianwen	*1399 - 1402*	Tianshun	*1457 - 1464*
Yongle	*1403 - 1424*	Chenghua	*1465 - 1487*
Hongxi	*1425 - 1425*	Hongzhi	*1488 - 1505*
Xuande	*1426 - 1435*	Zhengde	*1506 - 1521*
Zhengtong	*1436 - 1449*		

Ming Dynasty Marks

大明嘉靖年製
Jiajing
1522 – 1566

大明隆慶年製
Longquing
1567 – 1572

大明萬曆年製
Wanli
1573 – 1619

大明天啟年製
Tianqi
1621 – 1627

崇楨年製
Chongzhen
1628 – 1644

Qing Dynasty Marks

大清順治年製
Shunzhi
1644 – 1661

大清康熙年製
Kangxi
1662 – 1722

大清雍正年製
Yongzheng
1723 – 1735

大清乾隆年製
Qianlong
1736 – 1795

嘉慶年製
Jiaqing
1796 – 1820

大清道光年製
Daoguang
1821 – 1850

大清咸豐年製
Xianfeng
1851 – 1861

大清同治年製
Tongzhi
1862 – 1874

大清光緒年製
Guangxu
1875 – 1908

大清宣統年製
Xuantong
1909 – 1911

Republic Period

崇楨年製
Hongxian (Yuan Shikai)
1915 – 1916

THE ORIENTAL MARKET

The rising interest in Buddhist and Imperial history and the recent creation of a consuming middle class in mainland China has pushed recent auction prices skyward. Consequently the areas that are doing particularly well are ceramics and works of art that were originally made for the home market. Chinese export wares such as armorial porcelains, which are traditionally popular with European and American buyers but are not to the Chinese taste, continue to lose ground unless they are exceptional.

Early ceramics have always been desirable, and they are even more so now. The market for transitional blue and white wares from c1640-50 as well as Kangxi porcelains (1662-1722) even those made for export if in Chinese shapes. However, the greatest demand is still for item of mark and period.

Late Qing and even republic period (mid 20th century) pieces with spurious earlier reign marks are selling well above estimate consistently and this area of collecting is available to many more people than those seeking ever scarcer mark and period porcelain. The trend can also be seen in contemporary Chinese art where a market exists that was not there ten years ago.

Qing dynasty Jade, scholar's objects, domestic Chinese furniture and Cloisonné have all been in strong demand. The glut of period and reproduction pottery burial figures has resulted in the only real area of Chinese art collection to experience a decline in demand and subsequent price.

A weaker domestic Japanese market and declining Western collecting base has contributed to a flat Japanese market. The very best examples of Satsuma, cloisonné, and Buddhist art has all done well at auction, mostly bought by Western collectors. Japanese porcelain has struggled recently to achieve prices comparable to ten or fifteen years ago.

Like the Japanese market South East Asian material has experienced less demand within the middle market ($3,000-10,000) than the Chinese market, the very best examples of Korean ceramics and Khmer stone figures have been in high demand but overall it is a hit and miss period for Japanese and South East Asian works of art.

Robert Waterhouse, Freeman's, Philadelphia

A Chinese Yangshou culture pottery Neolithic jar, decorated with geometric designs and four loop handles.

c2000 BC 10.25in (26cm) high

$800-1,000 WW

A Chinese pottery Han Dynasty vase, molded round the shoulder with animals and masks beneath a degraded green glaze, old wear and damage.

11in (28cm) high

$400-600 WW

A pair of Chinese Han Dynasty graypottery burial figures of female attendants, signs of red and black pigment, on a contemporary wood stand.

Tallest 11.75in (30cm) high

$3,000-5,000 FRE

A Chinese Han Dynasty pottery horse head, of typical Han form, potted with a curved neck, strong jaw and open strong mouth, two holes potted to the top of the head, signs of sediment.

2.25in (5.5cm) high

$300-500 FRE

A Chinese Tang Dynasty sancai pottery model of a horse, modeled as a long-legged pony, brown body, buff face and green saddle, all four legs attached to a rectangular pottery base.

$5,000-7,000 FRE

A Chinese late Song Dynasty yingqing model of a boat, of squat proportions and light celadon glaze, with openwork superstructure and hull decorated with molded lotus joined by scrolling leaves.

3in (7.5cm) long

$400-800 FRE

A Chinese Song Dynasty water dropper, in the form of a recumbent ox, with molded body, open mouth and horns, blue underglazed highlights to celadon-white ground, raised on four bracket feet.

3in (7.5cm) wide

$1,000-1,600 FRE

A Chinese Song Dynasty Jizhou bottle jar, of ovoid form, potted with a short fluted neck, the body splashed with brown-buff colorspots over a brown to black glaze, underside glazed black.

9in (23cm) high

$1,200-1,600   FRE

A large Indo-Chinese Song Dynasty celadon-glazed bowl, incised exterior border to deep sides showing elongated leaves, the interior incised lotus flower medallion to centre and foliate leaf border to sides, some crazing to underglaze, slight wear to interior and rim.

11in (28cm) diam

$1,400-2,000   FRE

A 12thC Chinese tortoiseshell-glazed bowl, of deep U-shape form, brown glaze with light yellow suffusion, raised on circular unglazed foot.

4.5in (11.5cm) diam

$500-900   FRE

A large Chinese Yuan Dynasty tea-dust type glazed stoneware wine jar, of compressed ovoid form, small rim mouth and short neck, all over a circular base.

20in (51cm) high

$2,000-3,000   FRE

A Chinese Yuan Dynasty tea-dust type glazed stoneware wine jar, of ovoid form, the short neck supports an everted rim, the glaze runs from light brown at the broad shoulder to dark green to a circular foot.

32in (81cm) high

$1,600-2,400   FRE

A Chinese late Song or Yuan period 'hare's fur' glaze bowl, rounded sides raising from a small straight potted unglazed foot, overall black glaze with brown russet rim and 'hare's fur' markings to the interior.

$800-1,200   FRE

A Chinese Ming period Cizhou painted slip pottery figure of Quanyin, modeled wearing a robe-like headdress and partially open robe, knees crossed, over a graduating base.

13in (33cm) high

$600-1,000   FRE

A large Chinese Ming period Cizhou urn, of baluster form, white slip over a stoneware body, exposed lugs to shoulder, painted sparely with iron-brown bands to the neck and shoulder and abstract work to the body.

30in (76cm) high

$1,400-2,000   FRE

A large Chinese late Ming Dynasty green-glazed vase, the globular vase surmounted by a long slender neck, with a fine crackled green glaze thinning at the neck.

14.5in (47cm) high

$1,500-2,000   FRE

A Chinese Wanli period blue and white ovoid vase, the body painted with the 'Three Friends of Winter': pine, prunus and bamboo formed as trees forming four shou characters, the base with a four-character Xuande mark, but Wanli.

7in (18cm) high

$7,000-9,000 **WW**

A Chinese Wanli period Kraak porcelain double gourd vase, decorated around the lower body with flower sprays and symbols in pomegranate-shaped panels, the upper bulb with panels of flowers and foliage.

10.75in (27cm) high

$4,000-5,000 **WW**

A Chinese Wanli period blue and white double gourd vase, painted with sparrows in flight, amidst the 'Three Friends of Winter', unmarked, the neck reduced.

c1600 *11.5in (29cm) high*

$1,600-2,400 **WW**

A large Chinese Wanli period blue and white ovoid vase, decorated with four panels containing lotus and chrysanthemum, and with smaller floral panels to the shoulder, cracked and repaired around the rim.

14.25in (36cm) high

$4,000-5,000 **WW**

A Chinese Wanli period Kraaksporselein pear-shaped bottle vase, decorated in underglaze blue with precious objects and fruiting branches.

12.5in (32cm) high

$800-1,200 **DN**

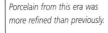

A Chinese blue and white Transitional vase, painted with bamboo, peony and four birds squabbling in mid air, beneath finely incised bands.

c1640 *7.75in (19.5cm) high*

$3,000-4,000 **WW**

A Chinese Transitional porcelain small jar, decorated in underglaze blue with birds in pomegranate branches, rui border.

4.75in (12cm) high

$1,000-1,600 **DN**

A Chinese blue-painted bottle vase, Kangxi period, with long neck above globular body, decorated with a continuous landscape scene depicting scholars, literati and sages enjoying the beauties of the surrounding lake, pavilions, bridges, boats and mountains.

17.5in (44.5cm) high

$26,000-36,000 **L&T**

CLOSER LOOK: KANGXI BLUE AND WHITE VASE

Porcelain from this era was more refined than previously.

The quality of the painting is exceptional, with plenty of well-executed details in the expressions on the faces and the clothing.

The glaze tended to be glassy and very thin.

Landscape scenes painted in the Kangxi era often suggest a craggy remoteness. They tend to wrap around the piece rather than be limited to panels.

A large Chinese Kangxi period blue and white baluster vase, the flared neck with a band of key fret above a continuous scene of nine figures, including a fisherman casting in a mountain lake, a jui fungus mark.

17in (43cm) high

$60,000-70,000 **WW**

ORIENTAL

A 17thC Chinese blue and white ovoid vase and cover, painted with alternate roundels of dragon and phoenix divided by lotus, the shoulder with prunus flowers on cracked ice, chips around the rim of the cover.

11.5in (29cm) high

$2,000-3,000   **WW**

A Chinese Kangxi period blue and white gourd vase, painted with scrolling foliage and lotus flowers, six-character Chenhua mark.

9.25in (23.5cm) high

$4,000-5,000   **WW**

A Chinese blue-painted 'Red Cliff' vase, with flared neck and square tapered body, the neck decorated with bamboo, two sides decorated with the two 'Odes to the Red Cliff' by the Song poet Su Dongpo (1037 - 1096), two sides with finely painted landscapes, unglazed foot rim with glazed recess bearing six-character Kangxi mark and period.

This is one of a number of 'Red Cliff' vases made in the 1690s and painted with identical scenes, possibly taken from woodblock prints, which appear to be from the same kiln in Jingdezhen. The Red Cliffs of the poem were purported to be the site of the Battle of the Red Cliffs in AD208.

c1690   *21.5in (55cm) high*

$50,000-60,000   **L&T**

A Chinese blue-painted square tapering vase, Kangxi mark and period, the flared neck decorated with bamboo, each side of the body with a panel of different plants: magnolias, chrysanthemums, prunus and lotus, all with birds in the branches, two opposed sides with poems, unglazed foot with glazed recessed square bearing six-character mark.

This is one of a group of similar vases made in the 1690s, which appear to be the productions of a small number of non-imperial kilns in Jingdezhen.

c1690   *21.5in (54.5cm) high*

$56,000-64,000   **L&T**

A Chinese Kangxi period blue and white bell-shaped candlestick, decorated with the wa wa playing on a fenced terrace, a flower spray round the narrow neck, beneath four auspicious symbols, small frits, six-character Chenghua mark but Kangxi.

5.5in (14cm) high

$1,600-2,400   **WW**

A Chinese Kangxi period blue and white vase, painted with six figures, plantain and rockwork, small chips around the foot rim, together with a wood cover.

8.5in (21.5cm) high

$2,000-3,000   **WW**

A Chinese Kangxi period blue and white brush stand, cylindrical form with an open mouth, painted to show a rocky village landscape.

5.75in (14.5cm) high

$2,000-2,400   **FRE**

A Chinese Kangxi period blue and white baluster vase, painted with two scaly four-clawed dragons, in pursuit of pearls of wisdom above breaking waves, the base with an artemesia leaf, together with a wood cover and stand.

11.25in (28.5cm) high

$6,000-7,000   **WW**

A small Chinese Kangxi period blue and white pear-shaped vase, decorated with three panels of peony and chrysanthemum.

6in (15.5cm) high

$600-800   **WW**

A Chinese Kangxi period blue and white double gourd vase, decorated with scrolling lotus, the base with an artemesia leaf, old restoration to the neck.

10.5in (26.5cm) high

$800-1,000   **WW**

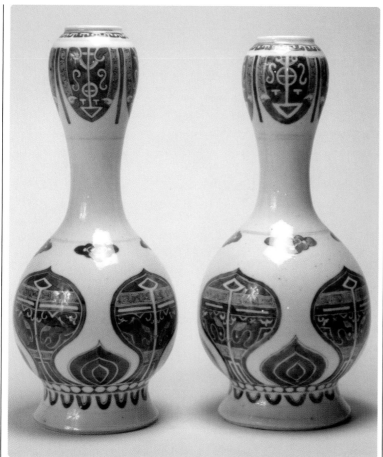

A pair of Chinese Kangxi period bottle vases, with onion necks and decorated in underglaze blue with archaistic lappets.

11.75in (30cm) high

$3,600-4,400 **DN**

A Chinese Kangxi period blue and white ewer and cover, decorated with two Europeans sitting naked on rockwork amidst flowers and foliage, one holding a scythe, frits and firing cracks.

7in (18cm) high

$2,000-4,000 **WW**

A Chinese Kangxi period blue and white triple gourd vase, of graduating triple-gourd form, painted with violet blue to show a leaf border to slender neck, cranes, Fu lions and Buddhistic symbols, neck may have been ground down.

9in (23cm) high

$700-900 **FRE**

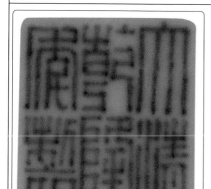

A Chinese Qianlong period blue and white Ming-style vase, painted with a frieze of archaic foliage between upright and pendant stiff leaves, the neck applied with a pair of cylindrical handles joined by a key fret band, Qianlong six-character seal mark.

7.75in (19.5cm) high

$16,000-20,000 **WW**

An 18thC Chinese blue and white guglet with a hua shih glaze, decorated with panels of figures, flowers and butterflies.

9.5in (24cm) high

$900-1,300 **WW**

An 18thC Chinese blue and white ovoid vase, decorated with four dragons amidst clouds above a band of breaking waves.

8.25in (21cm) high

$2,400-3,000   **WW**

A small Chinese blue and white vase, painted with two panels of figures, the base with a six-character Kangxi seal mark but later.

7in (18cm) high

$1,100-1,300   **WW**

A large pair of 19thC Chinese blue and white vases, with wood bases.

23.5in (60cm) high

$60,000-70,000   **SOTP**

A Chinese blue and white vase, painted with birds and lion dogs, amidst rocks and waves, the neck reduced.

10.75in (27.5cm) high

$600-800   **WW**

A 19thC Chinese Export baluster vase, decorated in underglaze blue with two pairs of Dutch fishermen, four-character Kangxi mark.

7.5in (19cm) high

$500-700   **DN**

A Chinese 19thC blue and white beaker vase, potted with a trumpet mouth and splayed foot, painted in rich violet blue tones to show a Lao Tzu with attendant amongst rock work and trees to the mouth and neck, four immortals to the bulbous body and two figures among a mountainous forest to the foot.

18in (45.5cm) high

$1,600-2,400   **FRE**

A pair of 19thC Chinese blue-painted flasks, each having shoulders decorated with stylized scrolling foliage, the sides with dragons amongst clouds, some damage.

11.5in (29.5cm) high

$3,600-4,400   L&T

A 19thC Chinese blue and white double gourd vase, decorated with prunus on a blue ground, four-character Kangxi mark.

12.25in (31cm) high

$300-500   WW

A 19thC Chinese Transitional-style blue and white sleeve vase, painted with two ducks and a woodcock amidst lotus, the shoulder and foot with incised bands, the rim with a firing fault and small chip.

10.75in (27cm) high

$240-360   WW

A 19thC Chinese blue and white small rouleau vase, decorated with warriors and panels of calligraphy, a four-character Kangxi mark.

10.5in (26.5cm) high

$800-1,200   WW

A 19thC Chinese blue and white Transitional-style sleeve vase, painted with aquatic birds amidst lotus, between anhua bands.

14.75in (27cm) high

$1,100-1,500   WW

A 19thC Chinese blue and white yen yen vase, painted with figures fishing from a boat and in discussion, in a rocky landscape, unmarked.

16.75in (42.5cm) high

$1,400-2,000   WW

(Center) A pair of 19thC Chinese Export Canton candlesticks, worked in the typical Canton palette, blossoming trees, rockworks and pagodas.

12in (30.5cm) high

$400-600   FRE

(Outside) A pair of 19thC Chinese Export Canton vases, the neck paneled by a leaf border, the body worked in Canton palette, the base with floral sprays.

12in (30.5cm) high

$1,800-2,200   FRE

A pair of large 19thC Chinese blue-painted vases and covers, decorated with dragons chasing birds of wisdom amongst the clouds, some damage.

24.5in (62cm) high

$3,600-4,400   **L&T**

A 19thC Chinese rouleau vase with painted decoration on a blue ground, depicting vases and boxes on stands and tables with flowers.

18in (46cm) high

$3,000-4,000   **L&T**

A 19thC Chinese blue and white tulip vase, decorated with scrolling chrysanthemum, damage to the neck.

9.75in (24.5cm) high

$600-800   **WW**

A 19thC Chinese blue and white vase, with a tall central neck with five apertures to the lobed body.

9.75in (24.5cm) high

$800-1,000   **WW**

A 19thC Chinese bottle vase, decorated in iron red and blue with a landscape scene and figures crossing a bridge beneath willow with mountains in the background.

14.5in (37cm) high

$2,000-3,000   **WW**

A pair of Chinese blue and white ovoid vases, decorated with birds perched on rockwork from which peonies grow.

c1900

6.75in (17cm) high

$800-1,000   **WW**

A pair of Chinese Export covered vases, the domed lids with f-lion finials, the baluster sides decorated with figures and pagoda within a continuous landscape.

12.5in (32cm) diam

$2,000-3,000   **L&T**

A 19thC Chinese blue and white moon flask, slender neck painted with a leaf border, the flat oval body applied with qilong to the shoulder in reverse, the body is painted with two oval panels depicting warring horsemen paneled by a foliate scrolling diaper.

10in (25.5cm) high

$1,400-2,000   **FRE**

A Chinese probably Tianqi period dish, with everted rim and decorated in underglaze blue with a figure of a sage beneath the moon.

8.75in (22cm) diam

$1,600-2,000 DN

A pair of 17thC Chinese blue and white dishes, painted with deer, bats and shrubs, contained in silk-lined case.

6.25in (16cm) high

$2,000-2,400 A&G

A Kangxi circular blue and white dish, decorated with fruit and leaves, bearing label of Jeffrey Waters, London, small chips to rim.

6.25in (16cm) diam

$2,400-2,800 A&G

A Kangxi period Chinese blue-painted charger, boldly decorated with a dragon and foliage to the well, blue-painted character mark.

13.25in (34cm) diam

$4,000-5,000 L&T

A 17th/18thC Chinese Swatow charger, of deep dished form with bronzed metal rim, blue-painted with a trellis work border interspersed with panels painted with stylized flowers, the well painted with an exotic bird amongst a profusion of flowers and foliage.

18in (45.5cm) diam

$1,400-1,800 L&T

A pair of Chinese blue and white dishes, with foliate rims and painted with flowering tree peonies issuing from rockwork, the backs with three flowering branches, with six-character Kangxi marks, one with a hair crack, both with rim chips.

14in (36cm) high

$3,600-4,400 WW

A pair of Chinese Kangxi period blue and white porcelain bowls, the lobed sides decorated with figure on a junk within a stylized foliate and geometric paneled border.

10.5in (26.5cm)

$3,000-4,000

L&T

A Chinese Kangxi period blue and white molded dish, painted with four birds, a butterfly and flowers.

9in (23cm) high

$300-500

WW

A Chinese Yongzheng period blue and white dish, the interior painted with a continuous scrolling lotus in a circular cartouche, the exterior with a similar lotus scroll, six-character mark of Yongzheng, one repaired crack.

8in (20.5cm) high

$2,400-3,000

WW

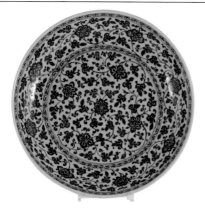

A large Chinese Qianlong period blue and white saucer dish, decorated with scrolling lotus flowers and leaves, unmarked.

c1780

14.5in (37cm) high

$8,000-12,000

WW

A Chinese Qianlong period Ming-style small saucer dish, decorated on the interior with a tied bouquet of lotus flowers and leaves, the rim and exterior with a continuous flower scroll, small rim crack and chips. Qianlong six-character mark.

4.5in (11.5cm) high

$1,600-2,000

WW

A Chinese Qianlong period blue and white rectangular dish, decorated with a pagoda landscape, light damage.

11.5in (29cm) high

$200-300   WW

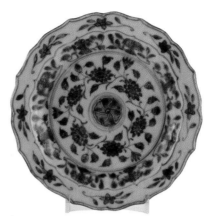

An unusual 18thC Chinese blue and white Ming-style dish, painted with a band of asters, other flowers and foliage, unmarked.

6.25in (16cm) high

$600-800   WW

A Qianlong period Chinese Export shaped rectangular meat dish, decorated in blue with a river landscape.

13.5in (34.5cm) wide

$500-700   DN

A Chinese Qianlong period export canted rectangular meat dish, decorated in underglaze blue with a river landscape.

18in (46cm) wide

$500-700   DN

A pair of 18thC Chinese Export blue and white vegetable dishes, each decorated in underglaze blue with riverside landscape views with figures and pagoda.

14.75in (37.5cm) wide

$1,600-2,400   L&T

A pair of 18thC Chinese blue and white porcelain chargers, each decorated in underglaze blue with courtiers by pagoda, within a geometric border with foliate reserves.

14.5in (37cm) diam

$8,000-10,000   L&T

A pair of 18thC Chinese Export chargers, for the Near Eastern market, decorated in underglaze blue with foliate wreath within a border of finger citron and peaches.

14in (35.5cm) diam

$1,000-1,600   DN

A Qianlong period Chinese Export shaped oval dish, decorated in underglaze blue with figures by a pavilion in a river landscape.

15.25in (39cm) wide

$500-700   DN

A large 18thC Chinese blue and white dish, the center painted with two squirrels on a grape vine beneath bamboo within a border carved with stylized scroll work, a faint rim crack.

15.5in (38.5cm) high

$500-700   WW

A Chinese Kangxi blue dragon circular dish.

1821-1850

10in (25.5cm) diam

$400-600   JN

A Chinese Wanli period Kraaksporselein barbed bowl, decorated in underglaze blue with a grasshopper and butterfly with a peony, paneled borders.

6in (15cm) high

$700-1,100 DN

A Chinese Kangxi period blue and white bowl, painted inside and out with a procession of four dragons, each with a lotus, six-character Chenghua mark, but Kangxi, a small rim chip.

8.25in (21cm) high

$1,200-1,600 WW

A Chinese Kangxi period blue and white bowl, blue double rings to base, of compressed globular form, gently flared rim, painted with a diaper to rim, lingzhi head band, enclosing a body of Indian lotus flowers and shou characters, blue ring to a short circular foot.

3in (7.5cm) wide

$1,200-2,000 FRE

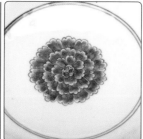

A large Chinese Kangxi period foliate-rimmed blue and white bowl, modeled around a deep U-shaped body, the interior is incised to show sixteen lotus petals, the interior rim is paneled with a blue border of floral sprays, the interior medallion shows a very finely painted peony enclosed by double blue rings, the exterior is equally well painted to show petal-shaped panels of peony and lotus flowers, over a short circular foot, Kangxi Lingzhi mark in blue double circles.

10in (25.5cm) diam

$5,000-7,000 FRE

CLOSER LOOK: KANGXI BLUE AND WHITE BOWL

The false gadroon border around the rim of the bowl is repeated around the foot.

Flowers and plants were a popular decorative theme for Kangxi potters. Here, bamboo and flowering prunus are entwined around the sides of the bowl.

The mark inside the bowl dates from 1426-35, although the bowl was made over 200 years later. Potters used earlier marks to pay tribute to their ancestors.

The base is decorated with a floral medallion.

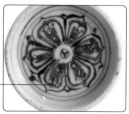

A rare Chinese Kangxi period blue and white bowl, decorated with bamboo and flowering prunus above a band of false gadroons, the rim with a key fret border, Xuande six-character mark to the interior.

5in (13cm) high

$20,000-30,000 WW

A Chinese Qianlong period bowl with a flared rim, painted in blue and underglaze copper red with three lion dogs chasing brocade balls, the base with a six-character Qianlong seal mark.

7.75in (19.5cm) high

$1,000-1,200 WW

A second half 18thC Chinese armorial large bowl, painted in blue with a crest of Larken within a Fitzhugh band and borders, small chips to the rim.

11.75in (30cm) high

$1,200-1,600 WW

A 19thC Chinese square-section bowl, the interior painted in blue with the eight Daoist Immortals encircling a dragon, the exterior with a raspberry glaze, six-character Xuande mark.

10.5in (26.5cm) high

$800-1,200 WW

A 19thC Chinese blue and white oval basket, the center painted with a scene of boats on a river, pierced sides and blue-banded decoration to the rim.

10.5in (27cm) wide

$200-300 ROS

A pair of 19thC Chinese square-section flaring bowls, the exteriors decorated with a continuous lotus scroll in underglaze blue with gilt outlines, the interior and foot glazed in turquoise, each with a six-character seal mark.

5in (12.5cm) high

$1,200-1,600
WW

A large modern Chinese bowl, painted in the Yuan style, with lotus, breaking waves and precious objects.

16.25in (41cm) high

$200-400
WW

A late 18thC Chinese Export tureen, cover and stand, of typical farming hamlet scene, good leaf-shaped finial to slightly domed cover, rectangular base applied with animal head handles, over a shaped rectangular stand.

Stand 14.25in (36cm) wide

$1,600-2,000
FRE

A late 18thC Chinese Export blue and white tureen, of rectangular form, the domed cover is surmounted by a gilded berry finial, the base is applied with two molded interlaced handles to the shoulder also partially gilded, painted in a blue canton palette.

12in (30.5cm) wide

$1,000-1,400
FRE

A late 18thC Chinese Export blue and white tureen and cover, of oval form, domed cover surmounted by a scrolled leaf, butterfly and ruyi clouds to cover, the base applied with two large shell-shaped handles, typical palette painted to body.

14in (35.5cm) wide

$1,600-2,400
FRE

A Chinese Kangxi period blue and white porcelain teapot, of fluted conical form with domed cover and rigid handle, spout replaced.

7.25in (18.5cm) high

$700-900
L&T

A Chinese Kangxi period wine pot in the form of a pomegranate, decorated in underglaze blue with pomegranates and flowering branches.

4.75in (12cm) high

$2,000-2,400
DN

A 19thC Chinese blue and white Cadogan teapot, formed as a peach, and painted with birds perched amidst flowers and foliage.

8.25in (21cm) high

$400-600
WW

A Chinese Kangxi period blue and white brushpot, painted with a fisherman on a riverbank watching a swooping bird catch his fish while his rod lies at his feet, all in a continuous mountain river landscape, a hair crack.

6.5in (16.5cm) high

$6,000-8,000
WW

A large 19thC Chinese Kangxi style blue and white brush pot, decorated with male figures in a landscape scene, the reverse painted with a feather.

10in (25.5cm) diam

$1,600-2,400
L&T

A Chinese blue and white cylindrical brushpot, decorated with scrolling leaves and lotus flowers, a four-character Xuande mark.

c1900   *5.5in (14cm) high*

$600-1,000
WW

ORIENTAL

A 17thC Chinese Export ware small wine cup decorated in underglaze blue with a dragon.

1.5in (4cm) high

$300-500   **DN**

A Chinese Kangxi period blue and white wine cup, with 19thC silver metal mounts.

4.25in (10.5cm) high

$500-700   **WW**

A Chinese blue and white Kangxi stem cup, with three young boys in a garden, bears label 'Glasgow art galleries and museums', slight crack.

3.75in (9.5cm) high

$2,000-3,000   **JN**

A Chinese chamber pot, from the Nanking Cargo, painted in blue with a trailing vine, 'Christie's Nanking Cargo' label.

c1750   6in (15.5cm) high

$500-700   **WW**

A Chinese blue and white barrel-shaped mug, painted with peony and prunus issuing from rockwork, small rim chip.

c1780   15.25in (13.5cm) high

$140-200   **WW**

An 18thC pair of Chinese blue and white silver shaped sauce boats, each painted with birds, rockwork, and flowers beneath pine trees, one handle damaged.

10in (25cm) high

$300-500   **WW**

A large 18thC Chinese blue underglazed porcelain tile, of tall rectangular form, well-painted scrolling cloud diaper over two court officials writing at a table.

17in (43cm) high

$1,000-1,400   **FRE**

A pair of probably 19thC Chinese garden seats decorated with flowers and precious objects in white slip on a pale blue ground.

19in (48cm) high

$6,000-7,000   **DN**

A pair of 19thC Chinese Export tea bowls and two saucers, the bowls with European white metal handles, one of the saucers has the seal stating 'Duveen, Liverpool'.

$200-400   **DN**

A 19thC Chinese blue and white beehive-shaped waterpot, Kangxi mark.

3.75in (9.5cm) high

$200-400   **WW**

CLOSER LOOK: IMPERIAL 'DRAGON' STEM CUP

When the bowl is exposed to the light a double dragon which has been superimposed into the porcelain is revealed.

The bowl has been incised with a dragon chasing a pearl which became a prominent decorative symbol in 15thC China. A dragon can symbolize success, wealth, power, bravery and nobility. If it loses the pearl it becomes helpless and incapable of action.

Monochrome wares were made for the four altars used for imperial ceremony and sacrifice. Brilliant yellow ceramics were used at the Altar of Earth. Because they were destined for the Imperial family they are of the highest quality.

The chenghua reign mark refers to the period from 1465-87.

A rare Chinese Imperial 'Dragon' stem cup, deep U-shaped form, incised to show a dragon chasing a pearl, with double dragon superimposed into the porcelain revealed when exposed to light, the bowl is supported above a circular base, Chenghua blue six-character mark.

Deaccessioned from the Shanghai Museum between 1993-96.

5.5in (14cm) high

FRE

$3,000-5,000

A 16thC Zhengde single yellow-glazed circular shallow dish, hairline crack.

1.75in (4cm) high

$6,000-7,000　**A&G**

A Chinese Kangxi period Imperial Lemon-yellow saucer dish, finely potted with shallow curved sides rising from a short circular foot, covered in a bright imperial lemon-yellow glaze, Kangxi blue six-character mark to base.

7in (18cm) diam

$3,000-5,000　**FRE**

A Yongzheng circular shallow dish, painted with green foliated medallions on yellow ground, two repaired small chips to rim.

5.75in (15cm) diam

$4,000-5,000　**A&G**

An 18thC Chinese Imperial Yellow dragon incised bowl, the exterior incised finely to show two elongated dragons chasing the flaming pearl of happiness among clouds, the interior and exterior are glazed in a rich lemon yellow, unglazed base, Chenghua blue six-character mark.

5.25in (13cm) diam

$4,000-6,000　**FRE**

A Chinese Guangxu period yellow-glazed bowl with everted rim, incised on the exterior with dragons chasing flaming pearls above rockwork and breaking waves, six-character mark of Guangxu.

6.75in (17cm) high

$1,200-1,800　**WW**

ORIENTAL

A Chinese Kangxi period blanc de Chine standing figure of Guanyin, with traces of original red pigment.

15.25in (39cm) high

$200-300   **WW**

An early 18thC Chinese blanc de Chine figure of Guanyin, seated on rockwork holding a child in her arms, some damage.

7in (17.5cm) high

$600-800   **WW**

A Qianlong blue blanc de Chine group, of a woman with a child on her shoulders and a young girl at her side carrying a mask, standing on a plain unglazed base.

c1750   *7in (18cm) high*

$600-800   **JN**

A 20thC Chinese blanc de Chine figure of Guanyin, standing holding a flask, and raised on a lotus throne, some good restoration.

19.75in (50cm) high

$160-240   **WW**

A first half 17thC Chinese blanc de Chine model of a Buddhistic lion dog, seated with his left paw on a brocade ball, some restoration.

20.75in (53cm) high

$2,000-3,000   WW

A rare Chinese Kangxi blanc de Chine model of a European figure, seated on the back of a standing kylin, its head turned to dexter, minor good restoration.

c1700   *5in (13cm) high*

$2,000-3,000   WW

A pair of 19thC Chinese Export porcelain blanc de chine figures of parrots, perched on tree stumps, with rock-form bases.

17.5in (44cm) high

$2,000-3,000   NA

A 17thC Chinese blanc de Chine tripod censer, decorated with the eight trigrams and raised on animal mask feet.

9.5in (24cm) high

$1,000-1,400   WW

A Chinese blanc de Chine rhinoceros horn libation cup, applied with molded kylin and prunus.

c1700   *5.75in (14.5cm) diam*

$1,000-1,400   WW

A 17th/18thC Chinese qingbai molded silver rimmed lotus-form bowl, of deep U-shape with a molded foliate rim mounted in a silver band, molded lotus petals worked to the body, raised on a small circular foot.

6in (15cm) diam

$500-700   FRE

An 18thC Chinese white-glazed incised dish, modeled after earlier examples, the porcelain dish of slightly rounded form with plain cavetto, the center incised to show a floral blossom issuing broad leaves, raised on an unglazed white porcelain foot.

11in (28cm) diam

$1,600-2,400   FRE

A Chinese Ming Dynasty white slip-glazed porcelain vase, of slender pear-shaped form, slightly flared mouth, waisted slender neck leading to a globular body, raised on a circular foot, glaze of light blue at rim to white with crackle underglaze.

16.5in (42cm) high

$3,000-5,000   FRE

A Chinese cylindrical brushpot, molded in high relief, with two geese beneath lotus upon which a kingfisher is perched, four-character molded Qianlong seal mark, a few small chips to the molding.

5in (12.5cm) high

$500-700   WW

A large probably 18thC Chinese flambé vase, heavily potted with a small rim mouth of mushroom glaze above a shouldered ovoid body finely glazed raspberry, blue and purple to the exterior and interior, raspberry glaze to base.

8in (20.5cm) high

$1,000-2,000   FRE

A small 18thC Chinese bottle vase, decorated with a copper red glaze with considerable green flecking.

8.25in (21cm) high

$200-400   WW

An early 19thC Chinese red flambé-glazed inverted pear-shaped vase, with elephant heads to the shoulders.

11in (28cm) high

$2,400-3,000   WW

A 19thC Chinese red flambé-glazed bottle vase, together with a hardwood stand.

15.25in (39cm) high including stand

$2,200-2,800   WW

A probably 19thC Chinese Oxblood vase, short potted neck glazed light celadon, ovoid raspberry body over a tapered unglazed foot, the underside glazed light celadon with a splash of raspberry.

3.5in (9cm) high

$500-700   FRE

A 19thC Chinese copper red bottle vase, the color thinning from the neck to a mushroom tone.

11.75in (30cm) high

$300-500   WW

A 19thC Chinese flared shallow bowl, decorated with an all-over flambé red glaze, draining from the rim.

10.5in (27cm) diam

$200-400   WW

An 18thC Chinese Langyao bottle vase, long slender neck leads to short globular body above a long cylindrical foot, the glaze runs from light whitish celadon from the mouth to rich raspberry to the body and exterior of the foot, the base is glazed white.

9.25in (23.5cm) high

$3,600-5,000 FRE

An early 18thC Chinese Langyao miniature vase, heavily potted with a short slender neck, open white glazed mouth, wide shoulder, raspberry red glaze thinning at the rim and shoulder, the base white with double blue ring, minor chipping to base.

An 18thC Chinese Langyao water pot, sloping ovoid sides, small-rimmed mouth, the glaze thins from light mushroom to raspberry to the base, the base is glazed.

3.5in (9cm) diam

$800-1,200 FRE

4.25in (11cm) high

$400-600 FRE

An 18th/19thC Chinese Langyao brush vase, circular cylindrical form, glaze runs from raspberry around the rim to light celadon to the body and interior, glazed base, chips to interior of mouth.

4.75in (12cm) diam

$500-700 FRE

A Chinese 19thC Langyao peach bloom vase, potted with a slender neck above a compressed globular body, light raspberry glaze running from the rim, mottled green spots to the body, recessed unglazed marked base, knife cut marks to base, Qianlong blue archaic mark.

7in (18cm) high

$500-700 FRE

A 19thC Chinese peachbloom-glazed brush washer, the base with a six-character Kangxi mark.

4.75in (12cm) high

$200-400

WW

A Chinese possibly Kangxi period peach bloom amphora, of typical form, open mouth with slender neck above a shouldered body and recessed base above a wood stand, Kangxi blue six-character mark, repair to neck.

5.5in (14cm) high

$700-1,000

FRE

A pair of early 19thC Chinese coral-red bowls.

5.5in (14cm) diam

$7,000-10,000

SOTP

A 20thC Chinese coral-glazed eggshell porcelain ovoid vase with a flared neck, a fine gold line rim, the base with a four-character gilt 'shen de tang zhi' mark: hall for the cultivation of virtue.

10.25in (26cm) high

$1,200-1,600

WW

A 17thC Chinese porcelain blue glazed vase, of globular shape with a tall neck, having 18thC ormolu scrolled mounts.

17in (44cm) high

$5,000-6,000   SWO

A 17thC Chinese bowl, with a slightly everted rim covered in a deep blue monochrome glaze, six-character Xuande mark.

7.5in (19cm) high

$1,600-2,400   DN

A Chinese Qianlong period blue ground teabowl and saucer, decorated in gilt with lotus and dragons, some wear, small chips and probably associated, each with a Qianlong seal mark.

4.5in (11.5cm) high

$400-600   WW

A Chinese Qianlong period blue monochrome dish, of slightly rounded form, brown fired rim, strong blue underglaze raised on a thin circular foot, Qianlong seal mark.

10.5in (26.5cm) diam

$2,000-3,000   FRE

An 18thC Chinese powder blue monochrome vase, of tapering shouldered form, good even powder-blue glaze over white porcelain circular base unglazed.

12in (30.5cm) high

$500-700   FRE

An 18thC Chinese flambé brush wash, rich raspberry ground glaze highlighted with blue and purple, good unglazed wide mouth, interior glazed raspberry, the base glazed a dark brown, minor scratching to the interior.

5in (12.5cm) diam

$600-1,000   FRE

An 18th/19thC Chinese blue ground saucer dish, molded and carved as a lotus flower, cracked and riveted.

12.75in (32.5cm) high

$100-300   WW

A Chinese lobed blue ground bowl, decorated in gilt with a stork, jui fungus, and mandarin ducks swimming amidst lotus, gilt seal mark for Xianfeng.

5.5in (14cm) high

$200-400   WW

A 19thC Chinese powder blue ovoid vase, decorated in gilt with panels of figures, on a scrolling ground, some wear to the gilding.

10in (25cm) high

$300-500   WW

ESSENTIAL REFERENCE: FAMILLE VERTE

Literally meaning 'green family', Famille Verte was adopted during the Kangxi period (1662-1722).

● It evolved from the five color Wucai style.

● The predominant colors are bright apple green and iron red, combined with blue, yellow and aubergine. With the exception of cobalt blue and copper red, these enamels were painted over the glaze.

● Flowers combined with black speckled diapers are common in small patterns. Larger designs include landscapes and gardens, figures, the Eight Precious Things, and the Eight Buddhist Emblems. Some designs may include the coats of arms of wealthy northern European families as many large dinner services were commissioned.

● Famille Verte was produced well into the 20thC, but the most desirable pieces are from the Kangxi period.

A Chinese Kangxi period porcelain famille verte baluster vase, converted to a lamp with good gilt-bronze mounts, well-painted with Buddhistic symbols to a green scrolling border to the shoulder, the body painted with a continuous figural scene.

Porcelain 10in (25.5cm) high

$1,400-2,000   FRE

A pair of Chinese Kangxi period famille verte bottle vases, decorated with phoenix amongst peony.

7.75in (19.5cm) high

$1,200-1,600   DN

A 19thC Chinese famille verte baluster vase, painted with six panels containing flowers, four-character mark.

14.5in (37cm) high

$600-800   WW

A pair of 19thC Chinese famille verte rouleau vases, painted with the eight horses of Mu Wang.

10.25in (26cm) high

$1,600-2,400   WW

A 19thC Chinese porcelain famille verte vase, of tapering rectangular form, leaf border to neck, scrolling leaf border to four panels depicting mountain landscapes, good cast bronze base mount stamped 'R860'.

Porcelain 19in (48cm) high

$800-1,200   FRE

A pair of late 19thC Chinese Canton famille verte vases, decorated with panels of figures and birds in branches, one with a small rim chip.

10in (25cm) high

$500-700   WW

A large late 19thC Chinese famille verte covered jar, of baluster form, the cover of domed form, surmounted with a gold finial, the green ground enameled with butterflies and floral sprays.

25in (63.5cm) high

$1,400-2,000   FRE

A pair of Chinese Kangxi period famille verte ewers and covers, decorated with bands of flowers and foliage around the bodies.

8.75in (22.5cm) high

$2,800-3,200   WW

A 19thC Chinese famille verte ewer, the cylindrical body divided by three horizontal shallow ribs, and decorated with fabulous animals, in yellow and aubergine on a green swirling ground, damage to the spout.

14.25in (36.5cm) high

$900-1,100   WW

A Chinese Kangxi period famille verte molded dish, decorated with a phoenix in flight above a lion dog, the border with panels of birds, beasts, flowers, trees and rockwork, lingzhi mark, a faint rim crack.

9.5in (24cm) high

$2,400-3,000   WW

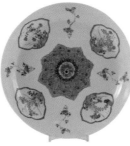

A Chinese Kangxi period famille verte saucer dish, painted with flowers inside cartouches, and a central stylized flower, the center with a drilled hole.

10.5in (26.5cm) high

$300-500   WW

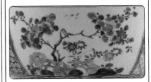

A pair of Guangxu famille verte enameled chargers, well-enameled Roman key border green ground rim enameled with lotus leaves and shou symbols, the yellow ground interior is enameled to show an iron red and black dragon among white blossoms.

c1900   *16in (40.5cm) diam*

$1,200-1,800   FRE

A Chinese Kangxi period famille verte bowl, decorated with panels of flowers and foliage, the interior decorated with lotus, leaves and flowers, rim chips.

11.5in (29.5cm) high

$1,600-2,000   WW

A matched pair of 19thC Chinese famille verte fish bowls, enameled with floral sprays and animals to a scrolling green lead ground, one enameled with fish and reeds to the interior.

15in (38cm) high

$1,200-2,000   FRE

A pair of 19thC Chinese famille verte Buddhistic lion dogs, on their backs playing with brocade balls, and raised on reticulated bases, both with some repairs.

5in (13cm) high

$700-900   WW

A Chinese Kangxi period famille verte libation cup, enameled on the biscuit with lion mask and Wang characters, applied dragon handles.

3.75in (9.5cm) high

$1,600-2,000   DN

FAMILLE ROSE

A small Chinese Yongzheng period famille rose vase, loosely painted with colorful flowers, the neck reduced.

6.5in (16.5cm) high

$360-440   WW

A Chinese Yongzheng period famille rose vase, painted with figures and foliage, and with a flying bat, cracked to the neck.

10in (25.5cm) high

$900-1,300   WW

An unusually large Chinese Qianlong period famille rose moonflask.

19.25in (49cm) high

$300,000-400,000   SOTP

A rare Chinese Qianlong period yellow famille rose wall vase, Qianlong mark.

8in (20cm) high

$80,000-100,000   **SOTP**

A small Chinese Qianlong period famille rose double vase, painted with flowering branches issuing from verdant rockwork, the reverse with further flowers and foliage.

5in (13cm) high

$5,000-7,000   **WW**

A pair of large late 18th/early19thC Chinese famille rose vases, each with well-balanced long flared slender neck, above shouldered globular body, painted in mirror image from mouth to base to show four blackbirds amongst peony, floral sprays, gnarled tree trunks and flying butterflies, over drilled wood bases, possibly Qianlong blue seal mark drilled through.

22.5in (57cm) high

$16,000-24,000   **FRE**

A small pair of 19thC Chinese famille rose vases, each painted with two black ducks beneath rockwork and peony, each with calligraphy to the reverse, each marked with 'Ju ren tang zhi' (Hall where Benevolence Resides).

5.5in (13.5cm) high

$2,000-2,400   **WW**

A 19thC Chinese famille rose ovoid vase with tall flaring neck, decorated with three maiden immortals riding in a log boat amidst breaking waves, the neck painted with Shoulao and an attendant, Qianlong six-character mark.

12.25in (31cm) high

$2,200-2,600   **WW**

A pair of 19thC Chinese famille rose gourd-shaped vases, painted with panels containing bats, flowers and lanterns, one with a rim crack.

15.75in (40cm) high

$5,000-6,000   **WW**

A 19thC Chinese famille rose moon flask, one side painted with figures hunting, the reverse with pheasants on rockwork, all on a coral ground scrolling foliage, flowers and shou characters, the base with a four-character mark, small rim fault.

14.25in (36cm) high

$2,000-2,400   **WW**

A 19thC Chinese famille rose landscape floor vase, of baluster form, applied with four Qilong to the shoulder, and four Fu lions and lug handles, well-painted to the interior of the flared scalloped mouth, neck and body showing a procession and landscape.

23.5in (59.5cm) high

$5,000-7,000   **FRE**

A pair of 19thC Rose Medallion baluster floor bases, well-painted and applied with gilded qilong to the shoulder and Fu dog handles, scalloped flared mouth, the body painted with a procession of approximately forty-five figures painted in four reverse panels on a ground of green scrolling leaves and butterflies.

35in (89cm) high

$16,000-20,000   **FRE**

A 19thC Chinese Canton famille rose baluster vase, decorated with panels of figures and flowers.

14in (35.5cm) high

$600-800   **WW**

A pair of 19thC Chinese famille rose moon flasks, painted with battle scenes and phoenix, on a pink and leaf scroll ground, one with damage to the neck.

10.25in (26cm) high

$500-700   WW

A 19thC Chinese famille rose pear-shaped vase, decorated with long life symbols and continuous lotus scroll on a pink ground, the foot encircled by a band of false gadroons, the neck with a jui scroll.

6.75in (17cm) high

$600-800   WW

A Chinese Republic period famille rose bottle vase, of globular form, a long slender neck leads to a body finely painted to show five boys playing in a garden, above a well-carved wood stand, Qianlong iron red four-character mark.

6.5in (16.5cm) high

$1,600-2,400   FRE

A Chinese Republic period famille rose brush pot, of cylindrical form, painted orange and black to the body to show lady attendants in discussion.

7in (18cm) high

$600-1,000   FRE

A large Chinese Republic period famille rose brush pot, of cylindrical form, painted with a detailed continuous landscape and a black inscription and red seal mark.

7.5in (19cm) high

$700-900   FRE

A pair of 19th/20thC Chinese famille rose covered jars, converted to lamps, painted green, blue and orange to show court attendants in a summer garden, drilled and wired over a timber stand.

20in (51cm) high

$1,000-1,400   FRE

A 20thC Chinese famille rose bottle vase, decorated with butterflies and flowers, the base with a six-character Xuantong mark but later.

16in (40.5cm) high

$2,000-2,800   WW

A pair of 20thC Chinese mille fleurs ovoid vases with cylindrical necks, each decorated overall with densely packed flower-heads and foliage, one neck damaged, six-character Qianlong marks.

13.5in (34cm) high

$1,800-2,400   WW

A pair of massive first half 20thC Chinese famille rose bottle vases, each painted with three panels containing vases and baskets with flower set against a mille fleurs ground, the bases with four-character Qianlong marks in iron red, together with stands, one with damage to the neck.

23in (58.5cm) high

$6,000-8,000   WW

A pair of Chinese Yongzheng period famille rose saucers, delicately painted with two small children playing with a lady seated on a daybed, one damaged.

4.5in (11.5cm) diam

$600-800   **WW**

A Chinese Export Yongzheng period famille rose plate, painted in bright and brilliant enamels to show an official in a riverscape followed by an attendant.

8.5in (21.5cm) diam

$1,000-1,400   **FRE**

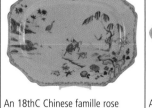

A Chinese Qianlong period famille rose plate, decorated with a pagoda landscape.

8.75in (22.5cm) diam

$200-300   **WW**

A pair of Chinese Qianlong period octagonal famille rose plates, decorated with flowers, storks and butterflies.

8.75in (22.5cm) diam

$300-500   **WW**

An 18thC Chinese famille rose chamfered rectangular dish, decorated with a boy riding a buffalo amidst landscape.

13in (33cm) high

$600-800   **WW**

A Chinese Qianlong period famille rose and bianco-sopra-bianco oval molded dish, decorated with a central panel depicting an elephant and rider, flanked by flowers and rockwork.

8.75in (22.5cm) high

$1,800-2,400   **WW**

An 18thC Chinese famille rose dish, painted with two colorful birds on a flowering branch.

12.5in (32cm) diam

$1,200-1,600   **WW**

A mid-19thC Chinese Canton famille rose tazza, decorated with six figures in a garden.

9.5in (24.5cm) high

$120-200   **WW**

A 19thC Chinese Canton famille rose dish, painted with twelve figures in a garden and on a veranda.

14.75in (37.5cm) diam

$1,400-1,800   **WW**

A 20thC Chinese famille rose peach dish, decorated with a peach tree bearing six ripe fruit, Yongzheng seal mark.

7.75in (19.5cm) diam

$500-700   **WW**

CLOSER LOOK: FAMILLE ROSE LOTUS BOWL

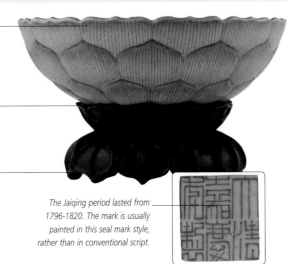

The porcelain has been molded and decorated to resemble a lotus flower. The delicate famille rose decoration is highlighted with gilding.

This shape is echoed in the carved wood base.

In China the lotus flower is a symbol of purity as it is a beautiful flower that rises from muddy waters. It is also one of the eight Bhuddist symbols of good fortune.

The Jaiqing period lasted from 1796-1820. The mark is usually painted in this seal mark style, rather than in conventional script.

A Chinese late Jiaqing period famille rose medallion bowl, decorated with four circular cartouches of figures and landscapes, on a sgraffito blue ground, the interior in underglazed blue with a central circular cartouche of two figures with an oxen in a landscape, Jiaqing six-character seal mark, some repair.

5.75in (14.5cm) high

$4,000-5,000   **WW**

A Chinese Jiaqing period famille rose lotus molded shallow bowl, the interior glazed in turquoise, the petal molded exterior painted in pink and white, the recessed foot with a six-character Jiaqing mark in iron red, together with a carved wood stand.

7in (18cm) high

$7,000-9,000   **WW**

A large Quianlong famille rose hunting bowl, the exterior with two shaped panels depicting a hunting scene with dogs and European riding horses. The interior with a European hunting man holding his gun and two dogs.

11.25in (28.5cm) diam

$4,000-5,000   **SOTA**

A Chinese famille rose Mandarin palette bowl, decorated with panels of figures at leisure before watery landscapes, on a coral ground, a rim crack.

c1780   *11.5in (29cm) high*

$700-900   **WW**

An important Chinese Export porcelain punchbowl, with an enameled exterior of the Hongs at Canton with western figures and ornate inner borders, the flags depicted are those of Denmark, France, Sweden, Britain and Holland.

c1780-85   *14.5in (37cm) diam*

$60,000-100,000   **NA**

A Chinese famille rose medallion bowl, well-painted with panels of birds, butterflies and flowers, on a complex yellow diaper ground, six-character Qianlong mark.

8.75in (22cm) high

$900-1,100   **WW**

A Chinese Qianlong period famille rose porcelain bowl, the sides decorated in polychrome with reserves depicting figures in scenic views.

10.25in (26cm) diam

$1,600-2,000   **L&T**

A rare pair of Chinese Daoguang period famille rose phoenix bowls, each finely decorated with four mythical birds amidst flowers and foliage, bordered by fine gilt bands, each with a four-character 'shen de tang zhi' mark: hall for the cultivation of virtue, one with minor damage.

5.75in (14.5cm) high

$5,000-7,000   **WW**

A Chinese famille rose bowl, decorated on the exterior with flower heads on a geometric ground, the interior with cockerels beneath a tree, Daoguang six-character mark but later, restored.

7.25in (18.5cm) high

$300-500   **WW**

A pair of Chinese Daoguang period famille rose bowls and covers, decorated with colorful medallions, each piece with a six-character Daoguang mark.

3.5in (9cm) high

$2,400-3,600 PAIR   **WW**

A Chinese Daoguang period famille rose landscape bowl, the deep bowl with a shaped and gilded rim, leading to a continuous landscape scene with a black inscription, Daoguang iron red seal mark to base.

6.75in (17cm) diam

$900-1,100   **FRE**

A 19thC Chinese rose medallion gilt-bronze-mounted porcelain punch bowl, with a beaded and pierced rim, the bowl decorated with alternating reserves of figures and floral studies, raised on a pierced stepped base, the handles cast with garlands.

15.5in (39.5cm) diam

$3,000-5,000   **FRE**

A large 19thC Chinese blue ground jardinière, decorated with four famille rose panels of figures in landscapes, lion mask handles beneath the rim.

16in (41cm) high

$3,000-4,000   **WW**

A Chinese famille rose bowl, painted with a mille fleurs design on a gilt ground, four-character Qianlong mark, but later.

5.5in (14cm) high

$500-700   **WW**

A 19thC Chinese famille rose phoenix bowl and cover, decorated with five mythological birds, amidst colorful foliage and flowers, the base and cover with an iron red jui fungus.

4.5in (11cm) high

$500-700   **WW**

A large famille rose bowl, decorated with panels of exotic birds, flowers, rockwork and bamboo on a pink ground, a star crack to the base.

c1900

15.75 (40cm) high

$140-200   **WW**

A 20thC Chinese famille rose mille fleurs U-shaped bowl, four-character Qianlong mark.

2.75in (7cm) high

$300-500   **WW**

An 18thC Chinese famille rose teapot and cover, painted with birds amidst rockwork and flowers.

7in (18cm) high

$1,600-2,000 WW

A Chinese Qianlong period famille rose teapot and cover, decorated in pseudo tobacco leaf style.

8.25in (21cm) high

$1,800-2,400 WW

A 20thC Chinese famille rose teapot and cover, finely painted with ten figures in a garden, the base with a six-character Guangxu mark.

6.75in (17cm) high

$800-1,200 WW

A Chinese Yongzheng period famille rose small teabowl and saucer, painted with colorful deer, and a monkey in a peach tree.

$500-700 WW

A Chinese Tongzhi period, Canton famille rose teabowl and saucer, each piece decorated with panels of figures and calligraphy.

5in (12.5cm) high

$500-700 WW

A pair of Chinese Guangxu period famille rose flared U-shaped cups, each finely painted with a dragon and phoenix amidst clouds and above bands of breaking waves, the rims with square scrolls, each with a six-character Guangxu mark.

2.75in (7cm) high

$600-1,000 WW

A 19th/20thC Chinese famille rose cup and saucer, glazed in a puce ground, the U-shaped cup is enameled to the interior to show a pink peony, the exterior of both is finely painted to show a village landscape.

$500-700 FRE

ORIENTAL

One of a pair of 18thC Chinese Export covered baluster vases, painted with a panel of green enameled frogs, grasshoppers and red lotus flowers, over wood stand.

11in (28cm) high

$1,200-1,600 PAIR   **FRE**

An 18thC Chinese famille rose group depicting the twin Genii of Harmony and Mirth, both seated on a rock, one with an open green robe, holding a scepter, the other in a yellow robe, holding a lotus flower, with a bat painted on the plinth.

8.5in (21.5cm) high

$1,600-2,400   **L&T**

A 19thC Chinese famille rose model of a standing phoenix, on a pierced rockwork base, some restoration.

12in (30.5cm) high

$200-400   **WW**

A large 20thC Chinese famille rose model of Buddhai Ho Shang, seated wearing floral robes and raised on a hardwood throne, the base with an impressed mark.

10.5in (27cm) high

$1,400-2,000   **WW**

A 20thC Chinese famille rose model of a scholar seated on a tiger, holding a scepter in his right hand and with a short sword to his back.

12.5in (32cm) high

$200-300   **WW**

An 18thC Chinese famille rose cylindrical box and cover, probably for silk, the exterior finely decorated with lotus, bats and peaches, and with formal flowers to the top, the interior turquoise-glazed with a central projection and a flange pierced with nine holes.

1.75in (4.5cm) high

$10,000-14,000   **WW**

A Chinese cylindrical Mandarin palette mug, decorated with a panel of figures, a minor fault to the rim.

c1780   *5in (13cm) high*

$400-600   **WW**

An 18thC Chinese famille rose circular tureen and cover, the knop painted with an iron-red chrysanthemum head, the handles in the form of shells, the cover and body painted with peacocks, peonies, rockwork and gilt bamboo.

10.25in (26cm) wide

$2,400-3,600   **L&T**

An 18thC Chinese Export desk set, well-painted in puce, famille rose and black enamel to the rear, the cover to the ink trough is painted with floral sprays and song birds, the inkwells painted to all four sides, black, puce and two famille rose scenes, one well-repaired.

8.5in (21.5cm) wide

$2,600-3,200 FRE

A 19thC Chinese famille rose tazza, decorated with scrolling lotus on a lime green ground.

4.75in (12cm) high

$1,000-1,400 WW

A set of four Chinese Republic period famille rose porcelain plaques, well-painted landscape, four columns of black script and red seal mark, rosewood frame.

48in (122cm) high

$1,000-1,400 FRE

A pair of early 20thC Canton garden seats, each profusely decorated with flowers on a green ground and with opposed rectangular panels painted with ladies in domestic settings, surrounded by bossed borders.

18.75in (47.5cm) high

$3,400-4,000 L&T

A pair of 20thC Canton garden seats, decorated with scrolling foliate borders, raised bosses and alternating panels of good luck symbols on a pink ground and exotic birds in a rocky landscape.

19.25in (49cm) high

$2,000-3,000 L&T

FAMILLE NOIRE

An unusual Chinese Kangxi period (1662-1722) famille noire octagonal vase, black ground decorated with green scroll work and petal medallions paneling twenty-eight allegorical scenes, Kangxi blue six-character mark to impressed base.

Literally meaning the 'black family', famille noire has black ground of brownish pigment from cobalt and manganese overlaid by a thin greenish enamel.

The decoration on 17th/18thC wares was of higher quality and more detailed than 19thC famille noire.

19.75in (50cm) high

$2,000-3,000 FRE

A Chinese early Kangxi period famille noire vase, heavy construction, wide rim over a short neck leading to a slightly shouldered cylindrical body, decorated with green lotus flowers issuing leaf scrolls.

10in (25.5cm) high

$1,600-2,000 FRE

A pair of mid-19thC Chinese Kangxi style famille noire vases, each of tapered square form decorated with cherry blossoms.

19.5in (39.5cm) high

$4,000-6,000 FRE

A 19thC Chinese famille noire cylindrical vase, decorated with flowering prunus.

11.5in (29cm) high

$400-600 WW

A pair of Chinese Yongzheng period armorial plates, well-painted with the arms of Lord Ross of Halkhead and the motto 'Think On'.

1732   *9in (22.5cm) high*

$3,000-4,000   **WW**

A pair of Chinese Armorial en grisaille decorated bowls, the rim decorated with flower sprigs to each side and crests to top and bottom, the well with gilt border and decorated with a copy of a European print 'The Rescue of Andromeda' showing Perseus driving his sword into the sea monster.

c1745   *9.25in (23.5cm) diam*

$3,000-4,000   **L&T**

A Chinese famille rose armorial plate, decorated in the center with the arms of Gale.

c1745   *9in (23cm) high*

$1,000-1,400   **WW**

A pair of Chinese famille rose armorial plates, painted with the arms of Willey, the rim with three flower sprays, some damage and restoration.

c1745   *9in (23cm) high*

$100-300   **WW**

A Chinese Qianlong period porcelain saucer dish, the white ground with grisaille decoration and centered by a coat of arms for the Saunders family, enriched with gilt.

9in (22.5cm) diam

$400-600   **L&T**

A pair of Chinese Qianlong period en grisaille small armorial pudding bowls, each painted with a shield-shaped coat of arms.

6.25in (16cm) high

$500-700   **WW**

A late 18thC Chinese armorial sauce tureen and cover, decorated with oval crests of a hand holding a cross and encircled by the motto 'Deo Juvante', some wear.

7.75in (19.5cm) high

$900-1,100   **WW**

A pair of early 19thC Chinese armorial oval trencher salts, decorated with gilt crests within a gilt and black lattice border, some wear to the gilding.

4in (10.5cm) high

$500-700   **WW**

An 18thC Chinese Imari part dinner service, with a geometric border interspersed with oval flower panels, the well with boldly painted chrysanthemums, comprising a serving plate and twenty dinner plates.

Serving plate 12.25in (31cm) diam

$4,000-6,000   L&T

An 18thC Chinese Imari charger, painted with gilt sprays of chrysanthemums, peony, and a butterfly in cobalt blue, orange and gilt.

16in (40.5cm) diam

$700-900   FRE

An 18thC Chinese Imari chamber pot.

6.5in (16.5in) diam

$800-1,200   SOTA

An 18thC Chinese Imari covered tankard, gilt metal rimmed cover and thumb piece, painted with orange and gilt pomegranate and cobalt blue foliate sprays to a molded tapering cylindrical body, missing partial fruit finial.

11in (28cm) high

$1,200-2,000   FRE

A rare late 18thC probably Chinese sectional armorial Imari ewer, of classic Georgian style, molded shell-form cup and base, leaf molded handle, the cup painted with a crest, iron-red, cobalt blue and gilt scrolls and floral garlands throughout.

11in (28cm) high

$800-1,200   FRE

A set of three 19thC Chinese Imari porcelain dishes, decorated in underglaze blue and iron red with scrolling foliage and trellis panels, centered by flowering urns.

8.25in (21.5cm) diam

$1,100-1,300   L&T

CHINESE POLYCHROME

A Chinese Transitional Wucai sleeve vase, painted with eight figures, pine and a vertical band of jagged rocks, the neck with two boys holding fly whisk, the neck damaged.

Wucai literally means 'five colors' and refers to porcelain painted with overglaze enamel colors: red, yellow, black and occasionally turquoise.

c1640-50   16in (40.5cm) high

$600-800   WW

A large Chinese early Kangxi period Wucai beaker vase, the flared mouth leads to a tapering neck painted to show blue rock work and red and blue chrysanthemums over a scale-like red ground, the bulbous center shows yellow and red pomegranates over square patterned ground, the outswept base is painted to show a broad leaf border on a cross hatched and flower red ground, repainted interior.

15.5in (39.5cm) high

$2,000-4,000   FRE

CLOSER LOOK: QIANLONG BOTTLE VASE

By the Qianlong period Chinese porcelain was very fine and white and so decoration was often used sparingly to display this.

Much decoration from the Qianlong period is in this painterly style and features rocky landscapes with pavilions similar to this one.

En grisaille decoration refers to painting in different tones of gray and black.

Potters at this time created neat, smooth ceramics with rounded footrims.

A Chinese Qianlong period pear-shaped bottle vase, with a long slender neck, well-decorated en grisaille with pavilions in a rocky landscape.

16.5in (42cm) high

$52,000-60,000   WW

ORIENTAL

A 17thC Chinese Wucai jar, decorated in underglaze blue and colored enamels with boys amongst scrolling foliage, the shoulders with peony and chrysanthemum, cracks.

9.5in (24cm) high

$900-1,100   **DN**

CLOSER LOOK: QILIN BOTTLE VASE

The bottle vase shape originated in China, possibly in the late Tang dynasty (618-907).

The vase is painted with three qilin. The qilin is a hybrid: it is usually portrayed with hooves like a horse, a tail like an ox, a deer's body with scales in five colors and backward antlers.

Despite its appearance it was a peaceful, benevolent creature.

As a hybrid the qilin had the potential to metamorphose and the three depictions on the vase may reflect this.

An 18thC Chinese copper-red and blue underglazed bottle vase, everted rim over a slightly waisted slender neck issuing from a compressed bulbous body, freely painted with three copper-red qilin with blue eyes.

10in (25.5cm) high

$7,000-9,000   **FRE**

A Chinese Kangxi period Gu shaped vase, decorated with molded panels of ladies and flowers.

11.5in (29cm) high

$1,800-2,200   **DN**

A small Chinese pear-shaped vase, decorated with a green spotted peachbloom glaze, the base with a six-character Kangxi mark and paper label for 'B and V Lake Collection'.

2.5in (6cm) high

$400-600   **WW**

One of a pair of 18thC Chinese Export covered baluster vases, the covers are surmounted by orange acorn finials painted with lotus leaves and a blue diaper to rim, the bases are painted with a scrolling blue and pink border to the neck and base, flanking a panel of green enameled frogs, grasshoppers and red lotus flowers, over wood stand.

11in (28cm) high

$1,200-1,600 PAIR   **FRE**

A pair of Chinese Export underglaze blue and clobbered rectangular section vases and covers with dog of fo finials.

c1800   11.5in (29cm high) high

$1,600-2,400   **DN**

A 19thC Chinese Canton enamel brush pot, of long cylindrical form, enameled to show a blue and red scrolling ground and a finely painted yellow dragon chasing a pearl in reverse, Qianlong six-character mark.

4.25cm (11cm) high

$1,000-1,400   **FRE**

A pair of 19thC Chinese vases, decorated in polychrome, with figures in a garden.

5.5in (14cm) high

$1,400-2,000   **WW**

A large 19thC Chinese baluster vase and cover, molded in relief with the po ku or a hundred antiques, all on a yellow ground, damage to the neck.

25.25in (64cm) high

$1,600-2,400   **WW**

A large 19thC Chinese pink sgraffito ground vase, decorated with figures and stylized butterflies, faint body crack.

24.5in (62cm) high

$1,400-1,800   **WW**

A large 19thC Chinese baluster vase, decorated in iron red, with lion dogs at play amidst brocade balls, the reverse with four columns of calligraphy.

24in (61cm) high

$300-500 **WW**

A probably late 19thC Chinese Yenyen vase, decorated in colored enamels with shou and phoenix medallions on a yellow ground, six-character Kangxi mark.

18.5in (47cm) high

$2,400-3,600 **DN**

A Chinese ovoid vase and cover, painted with lotus on a yellow ground.

c1900 *8.75in (22cm) high*

$100-300 **WW**

One of a pair of Chinese Guangxu period Dayazhai vases, of globular form, gilt rim leading to a typically painted scene of songbirds among flowing wisteria and blossoms, minor wear to body, three-character mark and Dayazhai seal to shoulder, Yong Qing Chang Chun iron red character mark.

9in (23cm) high

$1,400-2,000 **PAIR** **FRE**

A Chinese Republic period vase, the neck with dragon handles, the body painted with two panels containing a young man and woman in a landscape, and panels with Tang dynasty poems, all on an iron red and blue ground, with a Qianlong mark, but Republican period.

13in (33cm) high

$2,000-4,000 **WW**

A Chinese Republic period puce enamel vase, gilt-rimmed straight neck, with a blue lotus flower diaper neck above a finely painted body showing scholar and consort resting, black inscription to body, iron red four-character mark.

The Chinese Republic period (1911-49) saw much political turmoil and ended with the founding of The People's Republic of China.

9in (23cm) high

$300-500 **FRE**

An 18th/19thC Chinese molded twin-fish vase, each carp with well defined scales and open mouth, base drilled.

10.25in (26cm) high

$800-1,200 **WW**

A Chinese, Tianqi/Chongzhen period, hexagonal Wucai small dish, decorated with the 'Three Friends', pine, prunus and bamboo.

c1630 *5in (13cm) high*

$2,000-3,000 **WW**

A Chinese, Chongzhen period, porcelain Wucai hexagonal small dish, decorated with insects on pomegranate.

c1630 *5.5in (14cm) high*

$800-1,200 **WW**

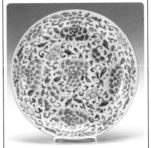

A Chinese late Ming period Wucai charger, deep-edged circular charger, orange line border enclosing yellow, green and orange enameled foliate scrolls, together with a timber stand.

10.5in (26.5cm) high

$300-500 **FRE**

A rare Chinese Kangxi period Kakiemon style plate, of slightly rounded form, brown rim, the interior enameled yellow, blue, green and iron-red to show songbirds and pine trees, blue leaf inside double blue rings.

8.5in (21.5cm) diam

$600-1,200 **FRE**

ORIENTAL

A small Chinese porcelain canted square stand, Yongzheng mark and period, decorated with dragons on a yellow ground, bears 'Sydney L Moss Ltd' label.

4.25in (10.5cm) wide

$1,600-2,400   L&T

A Chinese Qianlong period magic square calligraphic saucer dish, painted in iron red and black, with Arabic script.

6in (15cm) high

$1,400-2,000   WW

An 18thC Chinese Export charger, slightly raised rim painted with blue scrolling diaper interrupted by orange and gilt panels and foliate sprays, the interior is painted with a central medallion of vases, rock work and floral sprays.

15in (38cm) diam

$800-1,000   FRE

An unusual 19thC Chinese Kakiemon plate, of molded petal form, slightly U-shaped, painted to the interior to show three tigers, green enameled figure and a bamboo grove.

9.5in (24cm) diam

$800-1,000   FRE

An unusual 19thC Chinese Kakiemon plate, of molded petal form, slightly U-shaped, painted to the interior to show three tigers, green enameled figure and a bamboo grove.

9.5in (24cm) diam

$800-1,000   FRE

A pair of 19th/20thC Chinese Canton plates, decorated with figures in various pursuits in mountainous landscapes, one with a faint hairline.

8.5in (21.5cm) high

$1,400-1,800   WW

A pair of 20thC Chinese cultural revolution propaganda chargers, with Mao and Lin Biao, both of slightly rounded form, ivory crackle glaze, transfer painted with script.

11in (28cm) diam

$1,000-1,400   FRE

A Chinese Wanli period Wucai bowl, the exterior brightly painted with four figures divided by lanterns, the rim with stylized flowers, the interior with an underglaze blue five-clawed dragon, a six-character Wanli mark, cracked and riveted.

6.5in (16.5cm) high

$2,400-3,600   WW

A Chinese Wanli period Wucai lower section of a covered box, decorated on the exterior with four dragons contesting flaming pearls, Wanli six-character mark, some damage.

8.25in (21cm) high

$3,000-4,000   WW

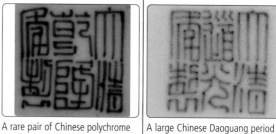

A rare pair of Chinese polychrome crane bowls, each decorated with a wide band, the birds standing and in flight amidst rockwork and jui beneath pine, each with a six-character Qianlong mark.

5.5in (14cm) high

$4,000-6,000   WW

A large Chinese Daoguang period yellow-glazed dragon bowl, Daoguang mark.

7.25in (18.5cm) diam

$16,000-20,000   SOTP

A Chinese Kangxi period brinjal bowl, decorated with splashes of yellow, green and aubergine, repairs.

7.5in (19 cm) high

$160-240　　WW

A large 19thC Chinese Canton bowl, painted with panels containing figures on a ground of flowers and foliage, some faults.

15.5in (39.5cm) high

$400-600　　WW

A Chinese Guangxu period bowl, decorated in iron red and enamels with dragons above waves, six-character Guangxu mark in blue.

6in (15cm) diam

$700-1,100　　DN

A Chinese Guangxu period enameled fish bowl, well-enameled roman key band to rim, enameled with a ruyi border above a body of blue and green lotus leaves and white egrets, enameled to the interior to show iron-red fish.

16in (40.5cm) high

$2,000-3,000　　FRE

A 20thC Chinese eggshell porcelain bowl, the exterior decorated with peacocks amidst rockwork and peony, the interior with a blue scaly dragon, six-character Qianlong mark, boxed.

9.75in (24.5cm) high

$1,300-1,700　　WW

A Chinese Kangxi period biscuit porcelain model of Li Po, the drunken poet, decorated in green, aubergine and yellow.

7.5in (19cm) high

$1,200-1,600　　WW

A Qianlong polychrome-colored figure of a man, in brightly colored robes.

c1770　　*7.5in (19cm) high*

$800-1,000　　JN

A late 19thC enameled porcelain model of Kannon seated over a beast, well-modeled figure seated open-legged, draped in a gold, green and red enamel robe, handles supported by a gold sword, the beast enameled green with a purple scrolling tail.

10in (25.5cm) high

$1,000-2,000　　FRE

A flambé glazed stoneware model of a warrior, wearing a long red cloak.

c1900　　*15in (38cm) high*

$1,200-1,600　　WW

A pair of Chinese Kangxi period, enamel on biscuit seated lion dogs, each decorated in aubergine, yellow and green.

11.5in (29cm) high

$6,000-8,000　　WW

A pair of Chinese Kangxi period biscuit figures of Buddhist lion dogs, seated on rectangular stands, each decorated in yellow, green and aubergine, extremities restored.

7.5in (19cm) high

$700-1,100　　WW

A pair of 18thC Chinese Export porcelain models of Indian elephants, each with its head lowered and standing four square, decorated with pale tangerine-colored skins and black beady eyes.

6.75in (17cm) high

$8,000-12,000　　WW

A rare early 19thC Chinese Export porcelain lantern cover of naïve cat form, body of incised white and black spotted glaze, pierced eyes, ears, mouth, underside and quatrefoil medallion to rear, boxed.

9in (23cm) long

$5,000-6,000　　FRE

An early 20thC Chinese Export model of a pug dog, modeled seated, decorated with an orange coat, wearing an iron-red collar with a gilt bell, black pupils and claws.

11in (28cm) high

$600-1,000　　FRE

A Chinese Export Qianlong period tobacco leaf mug, finely painted in the typical palette of gilt, orange, cobalt blue, pinkish yellow and green leaves, with small floral sprays over a white ground, bamboo molded handle.

5.5in (14cm) high

$3,400-4,000   FRE

One of a pair of large late 18thC Chinese Export mugs, hand painted figural scene to the blue paneled front, multi-color and blue floral sprays to the rear, applied with a handle also painted with a blue floral swag.

5.5in (14cm) high

$1,000-2,000   FRE

An unusual 18thC Chinese fan-shaped tea canister and cover, the lid inscribed 'Hexsan', the side painted with a small figure in a boat beneath a massive rock and pine trees, a small chip to the lid and some wear.

4in (10cm) high

$600-800   WW

An 18thC Chinese three-color model of a basket of peaches, the fruit graduated, leading from a circular scalloped basket from five, four, three, and lastly a single fruit, all applied with leaves.

5.75in (14.5cm) high

$500-1,000   FRE

A Chinese Export Qianlong period tureen and stand, of shaped rectangular form, slightly domed cover surmounted by orange flower model and animal heads to shoulder, painted to the cover, body and stand with floral swags.

10in (25.5cm) high

$3,000-4,000   FRE

A small 18thC Chinese Export sacred bird and butterfly tureen, of oval form, gilt finial surmounting a domed cover over a base applied to with two gilt handles, decorated with orange painted floral swags and birds, with gilt bands.

8in (20.5cm) wide

$1,000-1,600   FRE

A 19thC Chinese rectangular cricket cage, one face painted with figures and a spotted horse, four further faces reticulated, the stopper lacking,

8in (20.5cm) high

$700-900   WW

A pair of 20thC Chinese small oval jardinières, standing on four legs, decorated with shaped cartouches depicting maidens in interiors and landscapes.

10.25in (26cm) high

$1,000-1,200   WW

ESSENTIAL REFERENCE: KAKIEMON

Kakiemon is a style of decoration named after the potter Sakaida Kakiemon (1596-1666), who is credited with its introduction.

- The wares are very smooth, milk-white porcelain with a flawless glaze over which decorations are overpainted in orange-red, green and lilac-blue, sometimes with yellow, turquoise and gold.
- Kakiemon patterns are mainly flowers and figure motifs. The elements are asymmetrically and sparsely painted, enhancing the prominent white ground.
- The quality of this ware set a standard for European porcelain in the early 18thC.

A Japanese Kakiemon porcelain winepot or teapot, with arched handle, fixed with chrysanthemum flower pinions, above globular body, the cover decorated in polychrome enamels with a garden scene, the body with plant scrolls, with gilt highlights.

c1680   *5in (13cm) high*

$2,400-3,600   **L&T**

A late 17thC Japanese Kakiemon tokkuri, flared open mouth, short neck, square rectangular body, painted with a blue leaf band to neck, green scrolls amongst orange flowers to shoulder, the four panels of the body are painted differently, probably depicting the seasons, with yellow and orange flowers to purple tress branches and green, blue and yellow rock work, some repair.

11in (28cm) high

$6,000-10,000   **FRE**

A Japanese Kakiemon teabowl, delicately painted with a Bijin, with an attendant holding a fan between two birds, the reverse with bamboo and a peony spray.

c1700   *3in (7.5cm) high*

$1,400-2,000   **WW**

A large 18thC Japanese Kakiemon basin, molded deep U-shape, brown rim leading to a band of green scrolling leaves surrounding yellow and iron red fruit and flowers, the central medallion painted to show ho-o birds over rock work and blossoming trees, floral sprays to the exterior.

13.5in (34cm) diam

$2,400-3,600   **FRE**

A late 18th/19thC Japanese Kakiemon bottle vase, of square pear bottle form, painted iron-red scroll to long straight neck, iron-red scroll to long straight neck, four different floral sprays to body, square recessed base.

11.75in (30cm) high

$1,400-2,000   **FRE**

JAPANESE IMARI

Imari porcelain is the European name for the porcelain made for export at Arita on Kyushu, and shipped from the port of Imari from the late 17thC.

- Imari porcelain is richly decorated in dark underglaze blue and red enamels and gold or silver, combined with turquoise, green, aubergine and yellow enamel in the form of flowers, figures, ships, etc.
- Production of Imari porcelain was given a boost when instability in China disrupted the Dutch East India Company's supply of porcelain, forcing the Dutch to turn to Japanese producers.

A pair of 17thC Japanese Imari jars with covers.

c1680   *22in (56cm) high*

$16,000-20,000   **SOTP**

One of a pair of late 17thC and later Imari bottle vases, of pear shape, painted red scrolling neck, unusual green leaf panel neck, the body painted with four cobalt-blue paneled cherry blossom scenes.

9in (23cm) high

$2,400-3,600 PAIR   **FRE**

A large Japanese Imari baluster vase and cover, typically decorated with panels of landscapes and flowers, on a blue ground with gilt and iron red chrysanthemums, some extensive restoration.

c1700   *27in (69cm) high*

$900-1,100   **WW**

ORIENTAL

A large early 18thC Japanese Imari baluster vase and cover, typically decorated with panels containing shi shi and cranes amidst bamboo, together with a carved wood stand, minor damage.

24in (61cm) high

$1,200-2,000   WW

An early 19thC Imari covered tea caddy, of tall rectangular form, cylindrical cover painted to show gilt, cobalt blue and iron red chrysanthemum and peony.

7.5in (19cm) high

$500-900   FRE

A late 19thC Japanese Imari vase, the shoulder underglazed and enameled to depict bamboo leaves and ducks amongst peony, surrounded by a ground of small vignette of landscapes.

32in (81cm) high

$3,600-4,400   FRE

An unusual late 19thC Imari kendi, of garlic mouth form, trumpet neck, ovoid body with wide short spout, decorated in cobalt blue, orange, gilt and green to show ladies in the pursuit of leisure.

9.5in (24cm) high

$600-1,000   FRE

A 19thC Japanese Imari double gourd vase, of bulbous double form, well painted in cobalt blue, gilt and orange, showing ho-o, dragons and floral sprays.

13in (33cm) high

$1,000-2,000   FRE

A pair of large 19thC Japanese Imari vases and covers, each of baluster form, with shi-shi finials, finely decorated with bands of flowers and foliage with further pots of flowers, red painted signature.

24.75in (63cm) high

$5,000-7,000   L&T

A 19thC Japanese Imari ginger jar and cover, decorated in the typical palette with exotic birds and foliage, the domed lid surmounted by a fu-lion finial.

15in (38cm) high

$600-1,000   L&T

A large late 19thC Japanese 'turtle back' Imari bottle vase, of compressed ovoid form issuing from a long slender neck, the body is molded with graduating hexagonal panels, each painted cobalt blue, gilt and orange, showing songbirds, floral sprays and landscapes.

28in (71cm) high

$3,000-4,000   FRE

A late 19thC Japanese Imari bottle vase, well painted, of tall rectangular form, small domed neck, painted with floral panels in reverse, signed.

8in (20.5cm) high

$1,000-1,400   FRE

A large late 19thC Japanese Imari vase on stand, extremely well painted and gilded, typical palette of cobalt blue, gilt and orange depicting fans and medallions of ho-o birds and figures to a detailed blue and orange scrolling diaper and ground.

32in (81cm) high

$10,000-14,000   FRE

A large 19thC sectional Imari lantern, of cylindrical pillar form, hexagonal base, cylinder column painted to show coiling gilt dragons on a white porcelain ground, the pierced domed and hexagonal cover well painted in the typical Imari palette.

46in (117cm) high

$14,000-20,000   FRE

A pair of 19thC Japanese Imari censers, of compressed globular form, the cover surmounted by blue applied dragon, the pierced body painted orange, cobalt and light blue to show cloud scrolls, the body applied with two dragons in reverse to the shoulder, the base painted with a gilt fan motif.

17.5in (43cm) high

$7,000-10,000 **FRE**

A Japanese Fukugawa Imari ovoid vase, decorated with three panels, containing iris, peony and a pair of mandarin ducks, some glaze cracks, three-character mark, together with a wood stand.

c1900 *10in (25cm) high*

$200-400 **WW**

A Japanese Arita Imari dish, decorated with a central basket of flowers and with panels of prunus and chrysanthemum to the border.

c1700 *11.25in (28.5cm) high*

$1,000-1,400 **WW**

An unusual early 18thC Japanese Imari saucer, painted with figures leading a buffalo, and seated with a large flask inscribed 'FW'.

5in (13cm) high

$1,000-1,400 **WW**

A pair of late 19thC Japanese Imari chargers, of slightly rounded form, gilt scrolls over a black ground to the rim, four seasonal landscapes to the interior over a ground of grayand red.

16in (40.5cm) diam

$1,600-2,400 **FRE**

A pair of 19thC Japanese Imari chargers, decorated to the border with stylized flower heads and phoenix, and to the well with bold flowers and foliage with a central flower head.

14.5in (37cm) high

$1,400-1,800 **L&T**

A late 19thC Japanese Imari charger, of slightly rounded form, painted with two village scenes in reverse among of ground of scrolling blue and gilt leaves, blue foliate sprays to underside, seven spur marks to base.

16in (40.5cm) diam

$800-1,200 **FRE**

A late 19thC Japanese Imari charger, of slightly rounded form, depicting gray and green enameled horses on a white ground, red scroll and grassy hill to the foreground.

16in (40.5cm) diam

$800-1,200 **FRE**

A late 19thC Japanese Imari bowl, of deep U-shape form, orange geometric diaper to interior broken by four vignettes of green enameled floral sprigs and roundrels of ho-o birds, the central medallion painted to show a gold and orange peony.

8in (20.5cm) high

$1,000-1,400 **FRE**

A large 19thC Japanese Imari bowl, of deep U-shape form, shaped gilt rim, enameled green, iron-red and blue to the interior showing six panels painted in reverse to the sides and a central medallion of ho-o and flowers, blue underglazed floral sprays to underside, six blue character marks.

$1,000-1,600 **FRE**

A rare late 17th/18thC Japanese Imari model of bijin, brightly painted with black hair, iron red robe with green and blue leaved thistles and gilt chrysanthemum.

4in (10cm) high

$8,000-10,000 **FRE**

A late 18th/early 19thC Japanese Imari model of a boy, blue and orange robe, the urn painted with orange and iron red scrolls and winged ho-o bird-like figures.

8.25in (21cm) high

$4,000-6,000 **FRE**

ESSENTIAL REFERENCE: SATSUMA

Satuma wares are named after a feudal province at the southern tip of the Japanese island of Kyushu.

- Due to its close proximity to the Korean peninsula, the Satsuma province benefited from an influx of Korean master potters following the Japanese invasion of Korea in 1597.
- The first wares were simple tea ceremony vessels decorated with crackled yellow glaze on a cream ground.
- The Satsuma potters had began to learn enameling, gilding and other decorative techniques from Arita and Kyoto by the end of the 18thC.
- The best Satsuma pieces were produced from the mid-19thC. These are essentially paintings in miniature and took several months to make.
- Satsuma patterns include figures, flowers and Japanese fauna. Many Satsuma designs use perspective to create complex multi-layered scenes.
- Quality varies from the oldest, carefully decorated pieces and the later, gaudy items made for the export trade.

A late 19thC Japanese Satsuma vase, well-painted, figural and landscape scenes to gilt and blue gourd panels, signed 'Ryozan'.

5.5in (14cm) high

$1,600-2,000   **FRE**

CLOSER LOOK: SATSUMA VASE

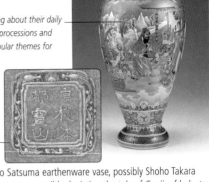

The high quality, complex gilding covers the neck of the vase and the bird-form handles. It was applied on top of the glaze and so stands proud of the surface.

The repeated motifs were usually painted freehand.

Scenes of people going about their daily business, or showing processions and ceremonies, were popular themes for decoration.

The mark states that the vase was made in Kyoto – one of the main areas of Satsuma production.

A 19thC Meiji Kyoto Satsuma earthenware vase, possibly Shoho Takara Honzan, with shogun crest, possibly depicting the tale of Genji, of baluster form, heavily gilded body, the slightly bulbous mouth leads to a pair of applied bird-form handles, the neck painted with a patchwork of gold, red, blue and brown leading to a body finely painted to show a phoenix in flight above a detailed landscape and figures to one side and a winter landscape and figures in reverse, roman key border to base, gold seal mark signed Kyoto.

38in (96.5cm) high

$20,000-24,000   **FRE**

A large Meiji Satsuma earthenware vase, by Hosai, finely enameled tapering shoulder-form vase, rim mouth above a short neck, the shoulder enameled with blue, orange and gold chrysanthemums, the body is enameled with floral sprays above a cobalt blue crosshatched border and scrolling base, blue enamel Shimazu family crest, enameled 'Dai Nippon Ijuin Satsuma Yaki'.

Meiji pieces date from 1868-1912.

19in (38cm) high

$5,000-7,000   **FRE**

A 19thC Satsuma oblong dish, decorated with warriors in a battle scene within a fan-painted panel, two corners slightly chipped and craze.

$3,000-4,000   **A&G**

A Japanese Meiji period Satsuma dish, painted with four ladies and a child in a pentagonal panel, four-character seal mark.

7in (18cm)

$1,400-1,800   **WW**

A rare late 19thC Japanese Satsuma earthenware Fu lion model, well potted to show open painted mouth and eyes, gilt and cobalt blue collar, and bow around his midsection, gilt signature to base.

11.75in (30cm) high

$4,000-6,000   **FRE**

A rare late 19thC Japanese Satsuma earthenware model of a buffalo and boy, modeled as a dark-haired boy ascending a recumbent buffalo, decorated with a gilt rope, saddle and tunic finely enameled with cobalt blue, red and gold, well potted.

6.5in (16.5cm) high

$6,000-8,000   **FRE**

A late 19thC Japanese Satsuma koro, cover and stand, with a pierced lid and carrying handles, the bodies painted with warriors.

6in (15cm) high

$600-1,000   **JN**

A pair of 19thC Satsuma square tapered vases, painted with panels of male and female figures, with ebonised wood stands.

4.75in (12cm) high

$400-600   A&G

A late 19thC Satsuma earthenware model of an official, the figure seated in a horseshoe-style chair, dressed in an open robe, fan in hand, the robe and fan very finely painted with scroll work and feathers, gold detail to the face, wood grain to the chair.

11in (28cm) high

$3,000-5,000   FRE

A large early 20thC Japanese Satsuma floor vase, of baluster form, enameled gold, green and white to show figures to a winter landscape, gold diaper and birds in low relief to neck.

43in (109cm) high

$2,400-3,600   FRE

An early 20thC Japanese Satsuma earthenware tea caddy, by Bizan in the style of Yabu Meizan, of tall rectangular form, associated silver cover, depicting four panels: 'Girl's Day Festival', 'Lake Biwa' and wisteria all surrounded by bordering flowers.

5in (12.5cm) high

$3,600-4,400   FRE

OTHER JAPANESE CERAMICS

One of a pair of late 19thC Japanese Seto vases, of baluster form, flared mouth issuing from a neck applied with two molded handles, the body is raised on a circular base, very finely painted blue on a white ground to show flowers and scrolls to the rim and base and fine songbirds and blossoms to the body.

18in (45.5cm) high

$1,000-1,400 PAIR   FRE

A massive pair of 19thC Japanese blue and white jardinières, the bodies painted with pheasants amidst flowers and foliage, the necks with cranes and cloud scrolls.

20.5in (52cm) wide

$1,000-1,600   WW

A Japanese blue and white quatre-lobed jardinière, painted with sparrows in flight above breaking waves.

c1900   7.5in (19cm) high

$160-240   WW

An early 20thC Japanese reticulated vase, with a central solid cylinder, painted in blue with irises, six-character mark, together with a wood stand.

c1900   10.5in (26.5cm) high

$5,000-7,000   WW

An Edo period Arita model of a Karashishi.

c1700   9in (23cm) high

$7,000-9,000   SOTP

A Japanese Edo period Arita-style dog model, probably Kutani, well-potted puppy with cheerful expression, gilt and red-painted eyes and mouth, painted with light orange and black markings.

4.5in (11.5cm) high

$1,000-1,200   FRE

A pair of early 18thC Arita models of puppies, both modeled as seated cheerful puppies, legs and head over their chests, painted with gilt and red collars, eyes and mouths, black spots to face, body and ears, repaired.

7.5in (19cm) high

$8,000-10,000   **FRE**

CLOSER LOOK: ARITA COCKEREL AND COPY

Potters working in and around the town of Arita made models such as the one on the right for export to Europe from the late 18thC.

The French factory Samson made copies of Oriental and European porcelains. They may have been commissioned to make a copy of the original Japanese model.

The red, green, gold and black glazes are typical of decoration on Arita porcelain.

The enameled bamboo sprigs echo the bamboo molding of the base.

An 18th/19thC Japanese Edo period Arita model of a cockerel and a matched Samson model, modeled seated open-mouthed over a bamboo molded oval base, well-painted iron-red face and tail feathers, gilt beak and tail feathers, feathers to the body painted black and red, green enameled bamboo sprigs to base.

14in (35.5cm) high

$6,000-8,000   **FRE**

A pair of 17thC and later Japanese dog models, one Arita and a matched model, the Arita dog modeled on all fours, tail coiled, head slightly down-turned, painted with green, iron-red and black spots, iron-red collar and mouth, together with an earthenware seated model decorated in a similar fashion.

Arita dog 8.5in (21.5cm) high

$28,000-32,000   **FRE**

A 19thC Japanese blue and white Arita lacquered vase, with a flared blue and white neck and circular base, and a central body lacquered black and red to show a deer amongst pine trees.

15in (38cm) high

$1,400-2,000   **FRE**

A large 19thC Japanese earthenware Seto ware vase, attributed to Seto, of tapering shouldered form, short neck painted light sky-blue leading to a cream ground, body incised and applied to show a white dragon emerging from a dark blue sea.

24in (61cm) high

$4,000-6,000   **FRE**

A late 19thC Japanese studio earthenware vase, by Kozan, of baluster form, gosu blue hydrangea, chrysanthemum and gilt butterflies on a cream ground, signed 'Kozan, Makuzu'.

$4,000-6,000   **FRE**

ESSENTIAL REFERENCE: NABESHIMA

Nabeshima porcelain was made from the late 17thC in Okawachi, north of Arita, on Kyushu, Japan.

- The porcelain was named after the ruling clan who patronised its production.
- The majority of the production was flatware.
- The body is virtually flawless and potted very thinly.
- The most common themes are seasonal flowers or wintry trees, sometimes combined with underlying or juxtaposed patterns derived from waves, trelliswork or basketry. The intricacy of this decoration suggests the use of a stencil or some kind of transfer-printing technique.
- Nabeshima designs are often outlined in underglaze blue with enamel infilling of iron red, turquoise, yellow, pale manganese, and black detailing. The glaze is of a soft, pale, grey-blue tone.

A 17th/18thC Japanese blue and white Nabeshima footed dish, of slightly rounded form, underglazed blue depicting chrysanthemums and leaves, 'comb tooth' pattern to foot.

7.75in (19.5cm) diam

$1,000-1,400   **FRE**

A 18th/19thC Japanese Nabeshima dish, of circular form depicting gifts underglazed in blue and a profusion of hydrangea in red, yellow and green enamels.

6.5in (16.5cm) diam

$2,000-3,000   FRE

A 19thC Japanese Nabeshima 'bamboo' dish, of slightly rounded form, slight peak to interior of dish, blue underglazed ground, enameled green, white and gold to depict snow-capped bamboo grove and gilt spring, spur marks to base.

7.25in (18.5cm) diam

$800-1,200   FRE

A rare late 19thC Japanese Nabeshima celadon and blue underglazed dish, center molded with the sixteen-petal kiku, blue underglazed dragons and scrolls.

12in (30.5cm) diam

$800-1,200   FRE

A Japanese porcelain vase, designed by Makuzu Kozan, painted with lilies on a shaded green ground, the base with a six-character mark.

8.25in (21cm) high

$3,000-4,000   WW

A late 19thC Japanese studio porcelain vase, by Kozan, of baluster form, depicting iris and white reeds on a celadon ground, signed 'Makuzu Kozan'.

8in (20.5cm) high

$1,200-1,600   FRE

A pair of late Meiji/early Taisho period Kutani vases by Watano, each of baluster form, decorated with a continuous mountainous landscape between bands of foliate decoration.

18.5in (47cm) high

$5,000-7,000   FRE

PERSIAN & MIDDLE EASTERN CERAMICS

A probably 12thC Persian conical bowl, decorated with geometric patterns in green and brown, damaged and restored.

6.5in (16.5cm) high

$500-700   WW

A probably 12thC Persian pottery bowl, decorated with a stylized floral pattern in green and brown.

9.25in (23.5cm) high

$500-600   WW

A probably 12thC Middle Eastern pottery bowl, decorated with four yellow panels, surrounded by black swirling motifs, sections broken and re-glued.

8.5in (21.5cm) high

$400-500   WW

An 18thC Persian blue-painted kendi, the neck and shoulders decorated with bands of stylized flowers and foliage, the sides with panels of birds and animals within landscapes, black painted mark.

8.5in (21.5cm) high

$18,000-24,000   L&T

An unusual 20thC sawatow Islamic influenced white enameled blue glazed charger, the large slightly rounded charger painted with a floral diaper edge, floral springs in reverse to the cavetto, and a central medallion of three radiating blossoms issuing broad leaves, raised on a circular foot with unglazed sand infused base.

17in (43cm) diam

$1,400-2,000   FRE

A 16th/17thC Chinese cloisonné gu beaker, decorated with scrolling lotus on a turquoise ground, six-character Jingtai mark, some surface wear.

12.25in (31cm) high

$5,000-7,000   **WW**

CLOSER LOOK: CLOISONNÉ CARP

Models of carp leaping were popular during the Qianlong period, (1736-1795) often in the form of porcelain tureens and jadeite vases.

The demand for quality gilt-bronze and cloisonné items has increased greatly in the last 5 years.

The pair were modeled to inspire the auspicious symbolism of a fish leaping at the dragons gate - a successful person standing out from others.

The quality of the pair is total, from well-carved 'sea scroll' wood base to heavy gilt-bronze mounts, thick multi-layer enamel, and well-reticulated fins.

They were likely produced from an Imperial workshop. They are in excellent condition - only minor stress has occurred to the fins, not a bad toll for 200 years

A pair of rare Chinese Qianlong/Jiaqing period cloisonné carp, mirror modeled, of free-flowing naturalistic form with mouth open, fins and tail shaped in the manner of jumping, decorated with red head, blue and black eyes, pink, white and red scales, positioned above a scrolling gilt metal sea, over a carved wood base.

12in (30.5cm) high

$60,000-80,000   **FRE**

A large Chinese Qianlong period cloisonné enamel tripod censer and cover, with a compressed globular body rising from three tall gilt lion-mask-headed legs, set at the shoulder with two large rectangular handles, profusely decorated around the exterior with leafy lotus strapwork between gilt lappets and keyfret bands, the domed cover surmounted by a pierced gilt dragon finial.

18.75in (47.5cm) high

$30,000-40,000   **WW**

A pair of late 18thC Chinese cloisonné ovoid vases, decorated with prunus, lotus and chrysanthemum.

9.5in (24cm) high

$4,000-6,000   **DN**

A19thC Chinese cloisonné gu shaped vase, decorated with taotie masks and stylized decoration on a blue ground.

11in (28cm) high

$700-1,100   **DN**

A pair of 19thC Chinese cloisonné bottle vases, each decorated with flowers, foliage and rockwork, on a geometric white ground, the necks with a continuous lotus scroll.

11in (28cm) high

$2,000-2,400   **WW**

A late 18th/early 19thC Chinese cloisonné and bronze tripod censer, possibly re-gilded, the cover pierced, domed and surmounted by a squirrel above a fruit vine, over a compressed globular base mounted with animal heads and vine to the shoulder, raised on three long gilded legs, medallion to underside of body, Ming four-character mark.

8in (20.5cm) high

$700-900   **FRE**

An 18th/19thC Chinese cloisonné tripod censer, finely enameled compressed globular form, raised on three short legs and with two arch-form handles, enameled to show twelve Indian lotuses joined by scrolling leaves, together with a later carved wood and jade-mounted cover, Ming four-character mark.

5in (12.5cm) high

$3,400-4,000   **FRE**

An 18th/19thC Chinese cloisonné bowl, decorated with two phoenix amidst a continuous flower and leaf scroll above a band of stiff leaves, Jingtai mark.

8.75in (22.5cm) high

$500-700 WW

A 19thC Chinese cloisonné censer, with gilt metal mounts to the rim and with lion dog handles, all raised on three elephant head feet, the base with a four-character Jingtai mark.

6.25in (16cm) high

$5,000-7,000 WW

A 19thC Chinese oval quatrefoil-section cloisonné bowl, decorated with a continuous lotus scroll in black on a yellow ground.

10in (25cm) high

$700-900 WW

A 19th/20thC Chinese cloisonné censer, with a gilt rim, each side decorated with a panel of Arabic script, raised on three feet.

5.5in (14cm) high

$1,000-1,200 WW

One of a pair of late 19thC Chinese cloisonné jardinières, of shaped rectangular form, Indian lotus joined by scrolling leaves, gilt Roman key edge above wood stands.

6in (15cm) high

$600-800 PAIR FRE

A pair of Chinese cloisonné shallow dishes each decorated with Pekinese, birds and trees.

c1800 *5.5in (14cm) diam*

$360-440 DN

CLOSER LOOK: CHINESE CLOISONNÉ PLAQUES

The cloisonné technique dates back to 1400BC. To create the design thin strips of metal were soldered onto the surface of the plaques to form individual cells. These were filled with powdered enamel and then fired in a kiln.

The plaques were made in the 18thC and have survived exceptionally well. Any damage to the enamel would be costly to repair and so their good condition adds to their value.

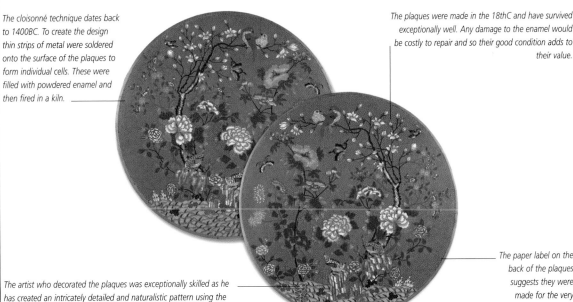

The artist who decorated the plaques was exceptionally skilled as he has created an intricately detailed and naturalistic pattern using the enamels.

The paper label on the back of the plaques suggests they were made for the very lucrative French market.

A pair of Chinese Qianlong period cloisonné circular plaques, each depicting exotic birds, blossom and bold flowerheads, against a blue ground.

Bears French paper label 'Fabrique d'Emaux Cloisonne de Teuo-Tcheng. La seule et veritable fabrique d'emaux cloisonnes de Teuo-Tcheng se trouve a Peking en dehors de la porte Tsien-men vers le milieu de la rue Yan-mei-tchou-sie-kiai (cote nord)'.

15.5in (39.5cm) diam

$24,000-30,000 L&T

A pair of late 19thC Chinese cloisonné altar sticks in the form of elephants, modeled standing over rectangular double lotus-form plinth bases with yellow and blue alternating enameled bands, the elephants mounted with candle holders.

24in (61cm) high

$3,000-4,000   **FRE**

A pair of Chinese, Qianlong/Jiaqing period, cloisonné candlesticks, each with butterflies on a blue ground, the base with endless knots on a blue ground.

3.75in (9.5cm) high

$1,000-1,400   **DN**

A 18thC Chinese cloisonné belt hook, decorated with stylized flowers on a turquoise ground, the terminal formed as dragon's head.

4in (10.5cm) high

$2,400-3,600   **WW**

A second half 19thC Chinese carved hardwood box and cover, set with cloisonné panels decorated with dragons.

7.5in (19cm) high

$440-560   **DN**

A 19th/20thC Chinese cloisonné peach-form covered box, cover featuring enameled yellow ground panel depicting five Fu bats surrounded by a blue lotus flower and scroll body, the interior enameled to show bats and cloud scrolls.

7in (18cm) high

$600-1,000   **FRE**

JAPANESE CLOISONNÉ

A 19thC Japanese cloisonné palace vase, attributed to Ando, of baluster form, depicting doves, songbirds, wisteria, peonies to a ground off brown pyrites.

The Ando company was established by Ando Jubei in 1880. The Ando trademark, referred to as the 'flower' or 'Maltese Cross' or 'sand dollar', is typically formed in wire in the center of the base.

54in (137cm) high

$10,000-14,000   **FRE**

A rare early 20thC Japanese cloisonné enamel nagari-gusuri vase, by Ando, of baluster form, depicting leaves and grapes in low relief over a transmutation mottle brown ground, Ando mark to base.

6in (15cm) high

$1,600-2,400   **FRE**

One of a pair of late 19thC Japanese cloisonné vases, attributed to Hattori, of baluster form, depicting a blue iris on a taupe ground with good diaper pattern to border, shakudo mounts.

15in (38cm) high

$2,400-2,800 PAIR   **FRE**

An unusual early 20thC Japanese cloisonné vase, by Ando, of baluster form, depicting flying doves, on a graduated blue to soft orange ground, silver mounts, mark of Ando Jubei.

14in (35.5cm) high

$2,600-3,000   **FRE**

A small early 20thC Japanese cloisonné vase, by Ando, of baluster form, depicting koi fish swimming on a light green ground, silver mounts, Ando mark to base.

2.75in (7cm) high

$3,000-5,000   **FRE**

An early 20thC Japanese cloisonné moriage vase, attributed to Hattori, depicting white flowers and reeds in low relief on a celadon ground.

6in (15cm) high

$1,200-1,600 | FRE

An early 20thC Japanese cloisonné enamel basse-taille vase, by Kawaguchi, of baluster form, depiction Kannon aside a green coiled dragon in low relief, the silver base incised with splashing waves, marked with S inside double triangle to base, minor damage.

7in (18cm) high

$1,200-1,600 | FRE

A late 19thC Japanese cloisonné basse-taille vase, by Kumeno, of pear-shaped form, elongated neck depicting a profusion of flowers on a purple to clear enameled ground incorporating a gin bari technique, the silver base incised with a profusion of waves, signed 'Kumeno Teitaro'.

15.5in (39.5cm) high

$1,600-2,400 | FRE

One of a pair of late 19thC Japanese cloisonné vases, in the style of Namikawa, attributed to Shibata, of baluster form, depicting gifts of the takaramono and various formed cartouches depicting Japanese birds and flowers all on a black ground, border work characteristic of the early Namikawa workshop.

7in (18cm) high

$2,000-3,000 PAIR | FRE

An extremely rare late 19thC Japanese cloisonné and enameled solid gold vase, by Namikawa Sosuke, the elongated baluster-form vase depicted alternating herringbone design incised into a solid gold body encased in a red to clear enamel solid gold mounts, impressed seal mark to solid gold base.

7.5in (19cm) high

$40,000-60,000 | FRE

A late 19thC Japanese cloisonné vase, by Hattori Tadasaburo, of baluster form, depicting furling lotus leaves and blossoming lotus on a light blue ground, signed with an impressed mark Hattori on leaf.

12.5in (32cm) high

$4,000-6,000 | FRE

A late 19thC Japanese Ota Tamashiro cloisonné vase, fashioned in the Namikawa style, ovoid form depicting prunus and songbirds over a midnight blue ground, the shoulder with geometric diapering, signed 'Ota'.

3.5in (9cm) high

$3,000-5,000 | FRE

A late 19thC Japanese cloisonné enameled basse-taille vase, by Kumeno Teitaro, of compressed ovoid form, on a rare indigo ground depicting daisies and spider mums, incised alternating decorations to silver body.

3in (7.5cm) high

$6,000-8,000 | FRE

An early 20thC Japanese cloisonné basse-taille vase, by Kumeno Teitaro, compressed ovoid form with a long slender neck, the shoulder depicting flying cranes and speckled gold stone, the body depicting splashing waves incised in silver, impressed mark to base.

4.5in (11.5cm) high

$2,000-3,000 | FRE

A Japanese cloisonné vase, by Namikawa Yasuyuki, of ovoid form with elongated neck depicting a sprig of blossoming flowers and butterflies all in gold wire with shakodo mounts on a blue ground, signed silver tablet, 'Kyoto Namikawa'.

3.75in (9.5cm) high

$4,000-6,000 | FRE

A Japanese Namikawa Yasuyuki cloisonné vase, of ovoid form with stout neck and geometric pattern, signed 'Kyoto Namikawa'.

3.25in (8cm) high

$16,000-24,000 | FRE

A late 19thC large Japanese cloisonné gin bari vase, of baluster form, depicting a multitude of flowers and birds on a blue ground, damage.

24.5in (62cm) high

$6,000-8,000   **FRE**

A pair of late 19thC Japanese cloisonné vases, of baluster form with flared mouth, well-enameled silver wired floral garden amongst a bamboo fence to dark blue ground, diaper neck and foot, gilt metal mounts and wood stands.

17in (43cm) high

$4,000-6,000   **FRE**

A late 19thC Japanese cloisonné censer, in the style of Namikawa, on a yellow speckle ground, with dragons, butterflies and phoenixes associated cover with banded butterflies.

3.5in (9cm) high

$1,200-1,600   **FRE**

A large late 19thC Japanese cloisonné covered urn, attributed to Namikawa Workshop, of compressed octagonal form applied with two handles, eight faceted panels, body and cover depicting various mythological creatures on speckled ground incorporating arabesque shield designs to outer body and well-detailed geometric diapering and pattern banding by a profusion of detailed flower heads.

17in (43cm) diam

$14,000-20,000   **FRE**

A pair of rare late 19thC Japanese cloisonné enameled censers, by Hattori Tadasaburo, depicting solid gold dragons amongst silver waves, silver covers.

Hattori Tadasaburo was one of the great artists in the golden era of Japanese enamels. He was active in the late 19th/early 20thC.

4in (10cm) diam

$6,000-8,000   **FRE**

CLOSER LOOK: JAPANESE CLOISONNÉ KORO

Namikawa Yasuyuki (1845-1927) was one of the greatest artists of his era. A former Samurai, he began his artistic career c1868 and founded his own studio.

He helped to develop a semi-transparent mirror black enamel that became the hallmark of most of his work.

His attention to detail enabled him to create intricate wirework designs. His early pieces are traditional in subject matter, featuring stylized botanical and formal geometric motifs. In general, his later work is more pictorial and shows nature scenes or views from around Kyoto, where he worked.

In 1896 he became Imperial Craftsman to the court of the Emperor Meiji, guaranteeing a domestic market for his work and increasing its value. He retired in 1915 and his company closed soon afterwards.

A late 19thC Japanese cloisonné koro, by Namikawa Yasuyuki, depicting white crane and pine on a soft green landscape over a light blue ground, silver pierced cover, signed 'Kyoto Namikawa' on a raised silver tablet.

3.5in (9cm) high

$20,000-30,000   **FRE**

A late 19thC Japanese cloisonné jar and cover, in the style of Honda Yasuburo, of ovoid form, depicting arabesque shields with alternating mythological creatures, cover banded with ju-i beads, gilt kiku finial and mounts.

5in (12.5cm) high

$4,000-6,000   **FRE**

A late 19thC Japanese cloisonné Namikawa style koro, with detailed design in fine gilt wire depicting various roundrels with a kiku finial and slightly domed cover, the shoulder with draped tapestry designs.

4in (10cm) high

$3,000-5,000   **FRE**

A late 19thC Japanese cloisonné koro, in the style of Namikawa, depicting various roundrels of alternating creatures amongst stylized waves on a black ground with gilt wire intricately detailed and gilt kiku finial.

4.5in (11.5cm) high

$2,400-3,600   **FRE**

A Japanese cloisonné sake pot, in the style of Namikawa Yasuyuki, of short ovoid form, with complex geometric borders and designs, the base with a profusion of waves and kiku.

7in (18cm) diam

$5,000-7,000 FRE

A late 19thC Japanese cloisonné creamer, in the style of Namikawa, depicting stylized waves and kiku with complex geometric roundrels.

6in (15cm) long

$3,000-4,000 FRE

A late 19thC Japanese cloisonné Kyoto school ewer, in the style of Namikawa, depicting fine gilt wire and roundrels with a stylized geometric pattern, possibly lacking cover.

7in (18cm) high

$1,000-1,200 FRE

A late 19thC Japanese cloisonné teapot, in the style of Namikawa Yasuyuki, depicting arabesque shield design with alternating kirin and ho-o, the shield banded by Mikado family crest.

Handle up 7in (18cm) high

$4,000-6,000 FRE

A Japanese Meiji period cloisonné rectangular box and domed cover, decorated with a flowering prunus on a silver foil ground, slight wear.

8.25in (21cm) high

$240-360 WW

A 20thC Japanese cloisonné small box and cover, finely decorated with quail and flowers reserved on a pale blue ground, gilt interior engraved with houses.

3.5in (9cm) high

$500-700 DN

A rare pair of late 19thC Japanese cloisonné kogos, male and female in the style of Honda Yasuburo, depicting various butterflies and moths, the borders with various family mons, the base with rare speckle ground.

3.5in (9cm) diam

$5,000-6,000 FRE

A Japanese Meiji period cloisonné square tray, decorated with a cockerel, a chick pecking at the grass at its feet, the rim decorated with dragonflies on a floral and foliate scroll, the reverse with a circular cartouche of fruit and nuts on a blue ground, two-character inscription, possibly Hosen, and red seal.

10.75in (27.5cm) high

$2,400-3,600 WW

A late 19thC Japanese cloisonné rectangular tray, decorated with a mallard drake in flight, signed 'Namikawa Sosuke', some surface cracks.

6in (15cm) wide

$6,000-8,000 DN

A rare late 19thC Japanese cloisonné two-fold table screen, in the style of Namikawa Kyoto school, depicting ho-o and dragons with bordering kiku design and well-designed coiled gilt wire, base depicting solid silver filigree stylized waves and kiku, verso with a solid gilt finish depicting cranes and Mount Fuji, mounted with alternative silver hinges and wood frame.

8.5in (21.5cm) high

$5,000-7,000 FRE

A rare 19thC Japanese plique-a-jour lantern cover, attributed to Ando Workshop, of oval form, depicting a landscape with temples, a waterfall and a profusion of foliage.

5in (12.5cm) high

$6,000-8,000 FRE

ORIENTAL

A pair of 19th/20thC Chinese hexagonal-section enamel vases, painted with birds, butterflies, deer and buffaloes.

15in (38cm) high

$1,200-2,000   **WW**

A pair of late 19thC Chinese bronze and champleve enamel ovoid vases with bands and pendant lappets of enamel.

12.5in (32cm) high

$400-600   **DN**

A Chinese bronze and champleve enamel koro and cover with kylin finial.

c1900   *15in (38cm) high*

$140-200   **DN**

A Canton enamel wine pot and cover, of Near Eastern form and decorated with two heart-shaped panels, Shoulao and other figures.

16in (41cm) high

$1,100-1,300   **DN**

A fine Canton enamel fishbowl of circular shape, the center decorated with flowers and fruit on a turquoise background, the deep, rounded sides and everted rim decorated with fruit and flowers against a vibrant blue background, the exterior with three writhing stylized dragons on a turquoise background, some restoration.

c1800   *16.5in (42cm) diam.*

$5,000-7,000   **SOTA**

A Chinese Canton enamel square-section vase, each face painted with a songbird amidst flowers and foliage, all on a blue scrolling lotus ground.

8.75in (22cm) high

$1,200-2,000   **WW**

A 20thC Chinese Canton enamel supper set, comprising eight fan-shaped dishes and a circular central dish, decorated with figures and a rocky landscape, cased.

17in (43cm) high

$600-800   **WW**

A Chinese Ming period bronze foliate-form vase, of ribbed foliate baluster form, layered foliate baluster form, layered foliate short neck, applied with two dragons in reverse, raised on a circular foot.

11in (28cm) high

$3,000-4,000   **FRE**

A 17thC Chinese bronze gu-shaped vase, of archaic form.

13.5in (34cm) high

$400-600   **WW**

A Chinese bronze vase, the body with shield-shaped panels, the waisted neck with fabulous animal handles, six-character Qianlong mark.

13.5in (34cm) high

$3,600-4,400   **WW**

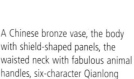

A 19thC Chinese bronze vase and cover, formed as a compressed pumpkin, cast with figures and shou characters, the base with a six-character Xuande mark.

5.75in (14.5cm) high

$2,000-3,000   **WW**

A 17thC Chinese Ming Dynasty bronze meiping, wide rim over a short waisted neck leading to broad shoulder rounding to tapering body over a hexagonal base raised on lingzhi scrolling feet joined by low shaped apron.

12in (30.5cm) high

$3,000-4,000　　FRE

A Chinese late Ming Dynasty bronze archaic Ku-form vase, square flared mouth over square pillar body incised with archaic style coiled dragons on Greek key ground.

6in (15cm) high

$400-600　　FRE

A late 17thC Chinese bronze yen yen vase, cast with a wide flared foliate mouth, tapering to a neck banded with a diaper and lingzhi heads leading to a shouldered body cast with ruyi head in high relief, raised on an openwork circular base, with ruyi and beaded scrolling apron.

17in (43cm) high

$1,200-1,600　　FRE

A 19thC Chinese bronze pear-form vase, the slightly flared mouth issues from a waisted slender neck leading to an ovoid body raised on a circular foot, signed 'Sen'.

7.5in (19cm) high

$500-700　　FRE

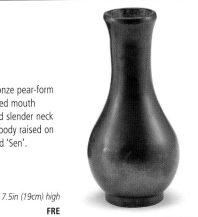

An 18th/19thC Chinese bronze archaic style vessel, heavily cast bronze vessel with two free-hanging handles to the shoulder over a circular base, signs of corrosive patination.

13in (33cm) high

$300-500　　FRE

A 17thC Chinese bronze censer, the body cast with taotie masks, the foot with geometric motifs, the handles formed as animal heads, six-character Xuande mark.

7.75in (19.5cm) high

$800-1,200　　WW

A 19th/20thC Chinese bronze incense burner and cover, with an animal knop and side handles, the body decorated with the eight trigrams.

10.75in (27cm) high

$240-360　　WW

A 17thC Chinese bronze incense burner, in the form of a kylin, standing four square, traces of gilding, slight damage.

8.25in (21cm) high

$400-600　　WW

A 17thC Chinese bronze censer, formed as a pumpkin, the handles as rats, all decorated with gold highlights and raised on three tall feet, some damage.

5.25in (13.5cm) high

$2,000-3,000　　WW

A 17thC Chinese bronze tripod censer, with curved handles and taotie masks cast to the body, the wood cover with a carved soapstone knop, raised on an elaborate lotus stand.

11.25in (28.5cm) high

$2,000-3,000　　WW

A 17thC Chinese bronze censer, the body cast with taotie masks, the rim with fabulous animals, the handles cast as animal heads.

2.25in (5.5cm) high

$600-1,000　　WW

A Chinese Ming dynasty bronze lozenge-shaped koro and cover, with kylin finial and scroll handles, the sides with archaistic decoration.

14.5in (37cm) high

$1,300-1,500   **DN**

A 17th/18thC Chinese well-cast gold-splash bronze tripod censer, of compressed globular form cast with hoop handles to rim, with irregular gold splashes, raised on three triangular feet, good patina, Xuande six-character mark.

4.5in (11.5cm) wide

$700-1,100   **FRE**

An 18th/19thC Chinese '100 character' bronze censer, of ovoid form, the pierced cover surmounted by a Fu dog, the body applied with qilong handles with the body decorated with bats to one side and four columns of twenty-five characters to the other, raised on three dragon feet mask feet, signs of water patination to interior and feet.

10.5in (26.5cm) high

$1,000-1,400   **FRE**

A Chinese bronze censer, cover and stand, finely modeled and pierced with dragons and clouds, the sides with ring handles and beasts leaping over waves, six-character Xuande mark, but possibly 18thC.

7.5in (19cm) high

$9,000-11,000   **DN**

A late Western Zhou period Chinese bronze ritual food vessel (gui), of circular convex form, the two large handles with animal head ornaments projecting from the sides, raised on a tall foot-rim and square base, all decorated with vertical ribbing and simplified border decoration of animal heads and rosettes, with a later inscription to the interior.

10.25in (26cm) high

$40,000-50,000   **L&T**

A Chinese Zhou period bronze ritual vessel (Pou), the body with three vertical flanges, each section with taotie masks on a leiwen ground.

7in (18cm) high

$1,600-2,400   **WW**

A Chinese, Western Han Dynasty, bronze Xian, or steamer, with taotie mask and ring handles, in three sections.

13.75in (35cm) high

$800-1,200   **DN**

A pair of Chinese Qianlong period bronze incense burners of compressed globular form, shallow beaded rim, applied with two lion masks supporting free-hanging ring handles, raised on a small fluted foot, Qianlong six-character mark.

7in (18cm) diam

$3,600-4,400   **FRE**

An 18th/19thC Chinese gold-splash bronze brush wash, of cylindrical form with everted rim, heavily gold-splashed wall, raised on a flared circular foot.

9in (23cm) wide

$800-1,000　　　　FRE

A 19thC Chinese bronze and mixed metal jardinière, of octagonal form, rim inlaid with silver Roman key diaper, applied with two lion mask handles in reverse, with six panels applied with copper five-claw dragon flanked by eight mixed metal Buddhist symbols over a conforming base.

10in (25.5cm) diam

$400-600　　　　FRE

A Chinese late Ming dynasty gilt-bronze figure of Guanyin, seated in lalitasana mudra, a figure of Buddha in his crown.

9in (23cm) high

$7,000-9,000　　　　WW

A Chinese Qianlong period gilt-bronze figure of Buddha, seated in lalitasana mudra, on a tall rectangular stand, nine-character Qianlong mark, nimbus missing.

7.7in (19.5cm) high

$2,000-3,000　　　　WW

A rare 16th/17thC Ming dynasty gilt-bronze figure of Wen Ch'ang, the god of literature, seated wearing elaborate robes with cloud scroll borders, a scholarly headdress and holding a sceptre, raised on a hardwood stand.

9.25in (23.5cm) high

$24,000-30,000　　　　WW

An 18thC or later Tibeto-Chinese gilt-bronze figure of Vajrabhairava in Yabyum, with his shakti, the bull-headed and multi-armed god trampling on prone figures on a lotus throne, some repair.

6in (15cm) high

$1,200-1,600　　　　WW

An 18thC Chinese bronze model of a billy goat, standing four square on an associated rectangular stand, traces of gilding.

4.75in (12cm) high

$400-600　　　　WW

A rare pair of 18thC Chinese Qianlong period gilt-bronze Buddhist lions, the mythical beasts standing four square, each with a tightly curled mane and bushy eyebrows, the prominent back bones with well-cast coats falling to either side and with extravagant flowing tails, their mouths agape baring their teeth and protruding tongues, both richly gilded with original pigment remaining.

9.25in (23.5cm) high

$40,000-50,000　　　　WW

An 18thC Tibeto-Chinese gilt-bronze figure of Tsong Ka Pa, seated in lalitasana mudra, his robe incised and with lotus blossoms at each shoulder.

9.6in (24cm) high

$5,000-7,000   **WW**

A Chinese early Qing period bronze rabbit-form incense burner, the long-eared rabbit cast on all fours, downcast face, hollowed open section to the center of the back, fine patina.

6.5in (16.5cm) high

$700-900   **FRE**

A Chinese early Qing period bronze rabbit-form incense burner, the long-eared rabbit cast on all fours, downcast face, hollowed open section to the center of the back.

6.5in (16.5cm) high

$700-900   **FRE**

A Chinese late Ming period bronze brush rest, modeled as a smiling boy reclining over an elbow.

3in (7.5cm)

$1,000-1,600   **FRE**

A rare Chinese Ming Dynasty gold lacquered bronze statue of the infant Buddha, standing on a single lotus base, typically modeled with left arm bent pointing upwards, right downwards, simple tunic modeled to show a four-claw dragon.

6.25in (16cm) high

$3,000-4,000   **FRE**

A Chinese late Ming/early Qing period bronze Fu lion, heavily cast model, open mouth, scrolling fur to head, body and tail, the head opens, hinged at the rear, paw supported above a pierced ball, over a carved wood stand.

Lion 11in (28cm) high

$2,000-3,000   **FRE**

A Chinese pair of bronze oil lanterns, each of pagoda form, with hexagonal body above turned and pierced column and foot.

20.5in (52cm) high

$1,600-2,400   **L&T**

A Chinese bronze belt hook, inset with turquoise, silver and gold, probably Warring States period, cracks.

6.25in (16.5cm) high

$400-600   **WW**

A Chinese Han-style bronze belt buckle, inlaid with silver geometric designs.

5in (13cm) high

$600-800   **WW**

A Chinese Ming Dynasty bronze mirror of circular form, fluted recessed rim around a central pierced knob, good patina to underside.

8.5in (21.5cm) diam

$160-240   **FRE**

A 19thC Japanese model of a hawk, with hawthorn blossom decoration, the hawk perched on a bronze rustic bow.

20in (51cm) high

$5,000-7,000 **A&G**

A late 19thC Japanese bronze female figure, wearing long robes and a headdress, on oblong base.

11.5in (29cm) high

$300-400 **A&G**

A large 19thC Japanese bronze censer, decorated with panels of water birds, amidst lotus, reeds and breaking waves, the handles as the rice god Daikoku beneath a giant bag of rice, the reticulated lid with sages beneath a pine tree, a six-character inscription to the base.

17in (43cm) high

$2,000-4,000 **WW**

A Japanese Meiji period bronze jardinière, decorated with two quail, heightened in gold and silver, beneath foliage and flowers, the base inset with a later signed panel.

10.25in (26cm) high

$1,200-1,600 **WW**

A Japanese Meiji period bronze figure of a hawk, raised on a later painted wooden base.

6in (15cm) high

$2,000-4,000 **FRE**

A Japanese Meiji period bronze and mixed metal plaque, depicting a hawk atop a branch looking to the night sky.

22.75in (58cm) wide

$16,000-20,000 **FRE**

A Japanese Meiji period bronze group, of two tigers attacking an elephant, rootwood base with presentation plaque inscribed, 'Presented to Dr W.C. Davey by the Senior Staff of the Dunlop Rubber Company, Kobe, Japan, April 8th, 1936'.

15.75in (40cm) wide

$3,000-4,000 **DN**

A Japanese bronze bowl, cast with a band of birds and flowers.

c1900 *12.25in (31cm) high*

$300-400 **DN**

A 19thC Japanese bronze vase, cast in relief with carp and crayfish amongst crashing waves.

12.25in (31cm) high

$200-300 **DN**

A Japanese Meiji period bronze vase, of naturalistic form, with leaf, twig and berry decoration, and a hardwood base.

8.5in (21.5cm) high

$240-300 **ROS**

A large 18th/19thC Japanese bronze temple bell, of dome form, cast to show four seasonal scenes to the body, dragon head hook bracket, beaded paneling to the top and pierced to the base, cast with chrysanthemum to prong.

32in (81cm) high

$5,000-7,000 **FRE**

A late 19thC Japanese bronze koro, by Suzuki Masayoshi, signed 'Dai Nippon Suzuki Masayoshi Zo', missing figure to base, possibly a bird.

51in (129.5cm) high

$1,400-2,000 **FRE**

A pair of early 20thC Japanese bronze and gilt figures, decorated with gilt headdress and robes, above an inlaid wood stand.

7in (17cm) high

$7,000-9,000   FRE

A late 19thC Japanese bronze vase, of pear shape, applied with a tiger over rock work, mark to base.

14.5in (37cm) high

$800-1,000   FRE

A late 19thC Japanese bronze vase, of ovoid form, rimmed mouth above a short neck worked to show a large bear over rock work raised on a circular base.

15in (38cm) high

$1,400-2,000   FRE

A late 19thC Japanese bronze, mixed metal and silver-covered tripod burner of Koro, the pierced silver cover worked with thirteen applied flowers, covering a bronze ovoid body worked to show three doves in a grass bed, mark to base.

5.5in (14cm) high

$4,000-6,000   FRE

A 19th/20thC Japanese bronze presentation vase, of elongated pear-shaped form, flared trumpet mouth, applied with a single gilt metal chrysanthemum.

11in (28cm) high

$1,000-1,200   FRE

An early 20thC Japanese bronze elephant, modeled with trunk down, large long tusks and ears, marked.

8in (20.5cm) high

$400-600   FRE

A Japanese bronze vase, finely cast with a band of irises and leaves, signed 'Shomei' or 'Masaaki'.

c1900   *10in (25cm) high*

$1,400-1,800   DN

A Chinese early Ming dynasty copper revolving bracelet, the main band with dragons and pearls, perspex stand.

2.75in (7cm) diam

$800-1,200   DN

An early 19thC Japanese copper lacuna lacquered vase, of meiping form, broad shoulder below a short neck and flared mouth, the body shows gold, silver and tin tone, recessed circular foot.

11in (28cm) high

$2,000-3,000   FRE

A rare Japanese Qing Dynasty copper traveling folding pricket, of compressed triangular form, expanding to reveal tri-bracket rotating openwork platform base, three arm vertical pricket stand, and circular support, impressed mark.

13in (33cm) high

$2,000-3,000   FRE

ORIENTAL

A Chinese Export silver box, the rectangular hinged top decorated with immortals atop cloud banks looking down on attendants astride fish and turtles and surrounded by a sea serpent, the front and sides decorated with a continuous village scene, marks rubbed.

c1860   *7.75in (20cm) wide*

$2,400-3,600   **FRE**

A Japanese Meiji period silver and mixed metal vase, of baluster form, decorated with a continuous river scene, 'Spink & Sons' label to the underside.

10in (25.5cm) high

$1,400-2,000   **FRE**

A late 19thC Japanese silver and enamel vase, well-enameled slender neck vase, over a triform base, enameled to show flowers and birds.

7in (18cm) high

$5,000-7,000   **FRE**

A 19th/20thC Japanese silver and enamel censer, of ovoid form, the surmounted domed cover worked to show berries and leaves, the body well-enameled in various colors to show highlighted flowers.

5.5in (14cm) high

$1,600-2,400   **FRE**

A 19th/20thC Japanese silver presentation covered censer, of typical form, pierced foliate cover, molded tripod base, applied with a single gilt metal chrysanthemum, pressed mark.

6in (15cm) high

$2,000-3,000   **FRE**

A late 19thC Japanese silver miniature chest, hoop handle surmounting a tall rectangular chest, pressed with blossom flowers, two latched doors revealing four wood drawers with silver handles.

6in (15cm) high

$1,400-2,000   **FRE**

A late 19thC Japanese silver miniature chest, with a hoop handle surmounting a tall rectangular chest, pressed to show songbirds and blossoms, with two latched doors revealing three black lacquered drawers.

5.5in (14cm) high

$1,400-2,000   **FRE**

A late 19thC Japanese silver cigar box, of rectangular form, worked to show in high relief carp, lotus flowers and reeds over a hammered ground, impressed mark to base.

9.5in (24cm) long

$2,400-4,800   **FRE**

An Edo period shakudo tsuba, signed 'Otsuki Korin', and two fushi Kasirae.

The tsuba 3in (8in) high

$7,000-9,000   **SOTP**

A Japanese Edo period iron shakudo tsuba, of oval form, carved in low relief to show a dragon to either side, signed.

3in (7.5cm) diam

$500-700   **FRE**

A Japanese Meiji period mixed metal Samurai warrior, wearing a uniform inlaid with gilt-metal stylized flower heads and circles, wearing a katana and carrying a spear, standing on a naturalistic base.

9.5in (24.5cm) high

$9,000-11,000   **L&T**

A Japanese Meiji period pair of mixed metal vases, each with flared neck and globular body decorated with birds in flight above a riverine reeded landscape, signed.

6.25in (16cm) high

$6,000-10,000   L&T

A pair of late 19thC Japanese mixed metal vases, of cylindrical form, lion masks to the shoulder in reverse, worked to show a songbird amongst a blossoming tree.

12in (30.5cm) high

$1,400-2,000   FRE

One of a pair of late 19thC Japanese mixed metal vases, of trumpet form, well inlaid with silver gilt-bronze to two archaic-form handles and the rim, the body applied with gilt-bronze, silver and copper to show floral sprays and well-cast song birds.

12in (30.5cm) high

$2,000-4,000 PAIR   FRE

A 20thC Himilayan mixed metal vajra, inlaid with lapis lazuli, coral and turquoise.

8.25in (21cm) high

$500-700   WW

One of a pair of 19th/20thC Japanese mixed metal vases, of sectional form, gilt metal ground, two white enamel panels applied with mixed metal to show floral sprigs and birds.

6in (15cm) high

$600-1,000 PAIR   FRE

A Japanese silver-colored metal novelty box and cover, formed as an artillery shell with a reeded copper base band, engraved with prunus blossom and with a gilt interior, stamped mark, 8.25oz (260g).

6.25in (16cm) high

$300-400   DN

A 17th or 18thC Indian white metal circular vase, with an everted rim chased with foliate decoration, the sides with scrolling foliate borders and a band of repoussé figures, on four bun feet.

4in (10.5cm) high

$900-1,100   L&T

A Japanese komai tea caddy, of hexagonal form, the cover and shoulders decorated with geometric designs, the sides with alternate panels of vines and landscape scenes, signed.

5in (13cm) high

$5,000-6,000   L&T

An unusual 19thC Japanese metal inro, inset with eight emblems, and signed on a pad.

2.25in (5.5cm) high

$600-800   WW

A Chinese hand mirror, with a white jade handle, the back set with a spinach jade bi, with semi-precious stones, with a Charlotte Horstmann invoice from the 1950s.

11.75in (30cm) high

$1,400-1,600   WW

A rare 19thC Thai rose gold and gilded sectional offering bowl, of overall ovoid form, comprising of four sections, a small domed cover revealing a second open-work handled flat domed cover enclosing an openwork rim and footed bowl fitting a Y-shaped bowl.

7in (18cm) high

$3,000-4,000   FRE

A 19thC Thai gilt metal figure of Sakyamuni, standing, hand raised in abhaya mudra, face in expression of joyful meditation, over a graduated plinth.

29.5in (75cm) high

$1,000-1,400   FRE

A Chinese silver-colored metal three-piece tea service by Luen Wo, of baluster form chased with dragons amidst clouds, with lobed rims and dragon handles, on five-tow feet, engraved with a monogram, stamped marks, 42.25oz (1412g) gross.

Luen Wo was a prolific maker located at 42 Nanking Road, Shanghai at the end of the 19thC and beginning of the 20thC.

The tea pot 9.25in (23.5cm) long

$5,000-7,000   DN

A 17thC Chinese jade carving of a recumbent horse, the stone with brown inclusions.

3.5in (9cm) high

$700-1,100 WW

A probably 19thC Chinese white jade carving of two love birds, on a lotus leaf and clasping a jui fungus.

3in (7.5cm) high

$10,000-12,000 WW

A pair of Chinese green jade carved models of horses, each in movement wearing reins and a long decorative saddlecloth, on fitted hardwood stands.

4in (10cm) wide

$1,600-1,800 L&T

A 19th/20thC Chinese jade carving of a recumbent kylin, the stone flecked with brown.

2.75in (7cm) high

$1,200-1,600 WW

A Chinese celadon-colored jade carving of a mythical beast, baring its teeth and raised on a wood stand.

5.5in (14cm) high

$400-600 WW

A Chinese jade carving of a fabulous animal.

3.25in (8cm) high

$120-200 WW

A Chinese probably Ming dynasty calcified jade carving of a recumbent horse, with a monkey clambering on its back.

3in (7.5cm) high

$6,000-10,000 WW

A Chinese jade carving of two fish, embracing a pearl.

4in (10cm) high

$300-500 WW

A Chinese late Qing Dynasty white jade bird grouping, of long rectangular form, carved to show six birds joined by a swag of grain, detail-carved feathers and base, over a wood stand.

9in (23cm) long

$1,400-2,000 FRE

A Chinese pale celadon jade carving of a drum, surrounded by three boys.

3in (8cm) high

$900-1,100 WW

A 19thC Chinese celadon and russet jade figure of Quanyin, well-carved, worked to show a flowing headdress, left hand holding a vase, draped in flowing robe, over a double lotus throne.

14in (35.5cm) high

$4,000-6,000 FRE

A Chinese pale green jade carving in the form of a flowerhead, the central spirally carved stamen formed as an incense holder, with subsidiary bowl-form flowerhead, surrounded by carved leaves.

3.5in (9cm) wide

$20,000-30,000 L&T

An 18thC Chinese jade vase, made for the Mughal market, the spherical body crisply carved with stylized flowers and foliage between bands of stiff leaves, the cylindrical neck carved with a lotus pattern, the interior set with a darker green reticulated jade panel, the two handles formed as buds.

4in (10cm) high

$14,000-20,000   WW

A Chinese late Qing Dynasty white and brown russet jade vase, of shouldered rectangular form, tapering flared mouth above four well-carved panels depicting scholars amongst mountainous forests, tall rectangular base.

14in (35.5cm) high

$2,000-3,000   FRE

An 18thC or later Chinese white jade pouring vessel, finely carved with a bifid dragon to the rim, and a lion mask beneath the spout, each side with a phoenix roundel, together with a hardwood stand.

4.75in (12cm) high

$5,000-6,000   WW

A small Chinese jade twin-handled koro and cover, the cover decorated with a lion dog, above three elephant head and ring handles, the body with twin dolphin head and ring handles, with carved lion head decoration above three paw feet.

3.75in (9.5cm) high

$2,000-2,400   L&T

A 17thC Chinese jade fish gong, the green stone with hardstone eyes, wood stand.

17.75in (45cm) long

$3,600-4,400   DN

A pair of Chinese circular jade screens, each applied with various hard stones depicting exotic birds amongst flowers and rockwork, with a pierced decorative hardwood stand.

12.25in (31cm) diam

$12,000-14,000   L&T

A 19thC Chinese pale green jade carved and pierced shaped contemplation screen, with central character mark and relief carved geometric decoration, on pierced stand.

9.5in (24cm) wide

$5,000-7,000   L&T

A 19thC Chinese jadeite pendant, carved with a peach, two Buddhist hand citron and a bat.

2.75in (7cm) high

$400-600   WW

A 19thC Chinese white jade pendant, carved on one side with boys riding a hobby horse the other with a lady at a loom.

2.25in (5.5cm) high

$3,000-4,000   WW

A pair of Chinese white jade bangles.

3in (8cm) diam

$1,100-1,300   **WW**

A pair of oblong green onyx bookends, with painted bronze double-budgerigar mounts on foliated boughs.

5.25in (13cm) high

$700-900   **A&G**

A 19thC Chinese 24k gold and jade dress ring, the delicately modeled ring set with a fine spinach green round cabochon stone to a hand-worked bezel showing coiled dragons, inscription to verso.

Stone 0.25in (0.5cm) diam

$900-1,100   **FRE**

A 19thC Chinese jade belt buckle, carved with two moths.

3.5in (9cm) high

$700-1,100   **WW**

A Chinese Qing Dynasty golden zitan and celadon jade-mounted scroll weight, of long rectangular form, fitted with a well-carved celadon jade handle in the form of joined scrolling mythical beasts.

8.75in (22cm) long

$2,400-3,600   **FRE**

A 19thC and later Chinese zitan seal box, the box of rectangular form, the cover waisted at the sides, the base fitted with three paneled bays over bracket feet, enclosing three celadon jade seals with the characters for happiness, prosperity and longevity in three different scripts.

4.5in (11.5cm) long

$800-1,200   **FRE**

HARDSTONE / SOAPSTONE

A Chinese late Ming Dynasty gilded black limestone Quanyin, the single carved section worked to show a seated Quanyin, down cast head covered in a long free-flowing robe, left knee raised supporting the left arm grasping a rolled scroll, hollowed base, signs of a red lacquer.

8.5in (21.5cm) high

$500-700   **FRE**

A 17th/18thC Chinese soapstone carving of Guanyin seated, wearing robes finely incised and decorated in gilt with roundels and borders, her hair, face and other details picked out in black and red.

7.5in (19cm) high

$6,000-8,000   **WW**

A 19thC Chinese yellow soapstone carving of a seated figure, wearing robes and holding a tablet, one foot restored.

5in (12.5cm) high

$700-900   **WW**

A 19thC Chinese white Shoushan stone figure of Quanyin, finely carved to show a downcast head, her left hand holding a sceptre with one knee bent, good detail to the face and robe.

9in (23cm) high

$1,400-1,800   **FRE**

A 19thC Chinese moss agate cup, the body carved with small studs.

1.5in (4cm) high

$300-500   **WW**

A 20thC Chinese hardstone censer and cover, with a lion dog knop and handles, a wood stand.

5in (13cm) high

$800-1,000   **WW**

A late 18thC Chinese huanghuali snuff box, of square 'face' form, the slightly domed oval cover reveals a hollowed interior, the base worked to show recessed branch-like inclusions, raised over four branch-like legs.

2.5in (6.5cm) wide

$400-600   **FRE**

An exceptional Chinese Qianlong period burl wood scroll pot, of slightly waisted cylindrical form, the fine textured protruding and knotted burl wood body ranges in color from gray to dark brown, over a huanghuali solid section base with eleven rows of inscribed script and two artist's seals with red pigment, calligraphic inscription to base.

10in (25.5cm) high

$30,000-40,000   **FRE**

A 18thC Chinese huangyangmu/boxwood libation cup, of oval form, incised rim over a body finely carved in high relief to show an openwork base issuing a peach branch and leaves forming a handle, the exterior finely carved to show a continuous scene of gentlemen in pursuit of leisure with attendants.

3in (7.5cm) high

$2,400-3,600   **FRE**

A Chinese Qing Dynasty huangyangmu/boxwood circular 'upside-down' dice box with four dice, of circular form, worked with a thin beaded cover, opening to reveal a base recessed with 12 hollows, enclosing four ivory dice.

2.5in (6.5cm) diam

$400-600   **FRE**

A 19thC Chinese huanghuali Qin-form box, the box of instrument form inlaid with mother-of-pearl and brass.

10in (25.5cm) long

$1,200-1,600   **FRE**

A 17thC Chinese Kangxi period huanghuali seal chest, of tall rectangular form, the top panel inlaid with ivory to show stylized dragons to the corners within a framed border, the two matched doors and side panels decorated with matching inlaid bands, revealing three long huanghuali drawers, raised one a beaded and finely scrolling shaped base, original brass hardware.

14in (35.5cm) wide

$8,000-10,000   **FRE**

A Chinese Qing Dynasty Imperial huanghuali artemisia leaf-form box, of two well-matched parts, the finely figured huanghuali ribbed cover carved in medium relief to show stem and veins, over a deep base.

7.5in (19cm) long

$5,000-7,000   **FRE**

A 17thC Chinese Yinxiang period huanghuali and brass-bound seal box, of tall square form, the flat domed lid opens to reveal a fitted brass-bound tray, terminating in a scrolling shaped apron and bracket footed base.

6in (15cm) wide

$1,200-1,600   **FRE**

A 19thC Chinese Muzhen period tanxiang or sandalwood pillow, with two incised characters within an intaglio medallion carved in imitation of a rubbing reading 'prolong the years' with inscription:

'Ye Xiangzhi, zi: Zidong said that, while plowing the land of Xianyang, [he came across] an ancient roof tile piece with the words 'prolong the years' written in reverse and that could barely be seen', the underside inscribed with two inscriptions, the first reads 'The Han Emperor Huangdi bestows this rhapsody, the great wing rises, the clouds fly and scatter. After distinguishing oneself across the country, I return to my home town, comforted by knowing that brave soldiers are protecting the four corners', the second inscription reads 'Bowing to the Stone Tower, someone copied the Han dynasty Stele of Dafeng Rhapsody'.

11in (28cm) long

$16,000-20,000   **FRE**

An unusual Chinese late Ming period huanghuali saddle, of typical U-shape form, rectangular Greek key incised sides, two iron-bound arches, one carved to show a Fu lion.

14in (35.5cm) long

$3,600-4,400   **FRE**

A Chinese early Qing Dynasty 'golden thread' zitan brush pot, of five-plank construction, rounded joined edge, raised on four bracket feet, recessed base, fine 'golden thread' throughout.

4.75in (12cm) high

$3,600-4,400   FRE

A possibly 18thC Chinese Zitan wood flower vase, of lotus petal section.

16in (41cm) high

$1,200-1,600   DN

A small 18thC Chinese zitan peach blossom or foliate-form brush pot, of hexafoil form, seven-plank construction, scalloped beaded rim, the underside incised to show a flower petal.

4.25in (10.5cm) high

$3,000-4,000   FRE

An 18thC Chinese zitan and embedded pebble brush pot, of single section form, well-hollowed interior revealing a gold thread grain, the exterior wall very finely embellished to resemble a tree trunk and abstractly a 'ghost face'; with delicately hollowed trunk recesses and weathered surfaces partially engulfing a mottled green pebble, raised on three small bracket feet.

6in (15cm) high

$20,000-30,000   FRE

A Chinese Qing Dynasty 'golden thread' zitan brush pot, of inverted waisted section form, constructed of five shaped panels.

4in (10cm) high

$3,600-4,400   FRE

A 19th/20thC Chinese Zitan brush pot, of thin cylindrical form, well-carved to show sages among a mountainous landscape, gnarled panel in reverse.

8in (20.5cm) high

$900-1,100   FRE

An 18thC Chinese zitan brush pot, of tree trunk form, one side naturally formed with gnarled irregular swirling veined surfaces, interrupted with apertures, verso inscribed with the phase 'Zuoren youem yidian shuzin' or 'A man requires a measure of a merciful heart', followed by a seal, the polished rim leading to a cliff-like naturally irregular interior.

6.25in (16cm) high

$10,000-14,000   FRE

A rare 18thC burl-zitan ink stone cover and hongmu base, four-character inscription to stone, the naturalistic-shaped porous stone inscribed with four-character seals to the base, covered by a single section of hollowed burl zitan with fine golden thread and black tight grain figuring, over a shaped hongmu base, raised on four bracket feet.

6.25in (16cm) wide

$3,000-4,000   FRE

A Chinese mid-Qing Dynasty zitan square corner box, of rectangular form with highly figured grain, the cover with rounded edge and beaded rim, over a match base.

4in (10cm) wide

$600-1,000   FRE

A rare Chinese Qing Dynasty zitan watch stand, section construction and banjo form, carved in medium relief in a European rococo style, circular beaded recess worked to the center.

5.5in (14cm) long

$700-1,100   FRE

A 14th/15thC Tibetan purple zitan lacquered Buddha figure, finely carved figured seated in dhyanasana with hands in abhaya and varada mudras, face with delicate features, open flowing robe, over a double lotus throne, with relic intact to base.

7in (18cm) high

$8,000-12,000   **FRE**

An 18thC Chinese huamu burl brush pot and nanmu stand and cover, the single section partially reticulated burl wood pot finely hollowed, the exterior reveals a cameo-like skinned body of yellow hues, terminating in matched nanmu shaped cover and openwork base.

7.5in (19cm) high

$9,000-11,000   **FRE**

A pair of Chinese late Qing Dynasty hongmu lanterns, of square form, with insert panels fitted to a humpback jointed frame.

20in (51cm) high

$1,000-1,600   **FRE**

A 19thC Chinese hongmu framed mirror, of tall rectangular form with a band of stylized lotus flowers issuing leaves joining Fu bats framing a recessed Greek Key band framing a period mirror, iron free-hanging hook.

16in (40.5cm) high

$1,000-1,600   **FRE**

A pair of 18th/19thC Chinese hongmu metamorphic or folding book stands, folding to reveal a rectangular book platform, supported by a hinged adjustable stand.

21in (53.5cm) wide

$1,000-1,400   **FRE**

A 19thC Chinese hongmu brush pot, hollowed from a single trunk, resembling the Chinese symbol of eternity of two raised square tiers and two recessed squares, issuing from a single large square, raised on four small bracket feet.

3in (7.5cm) high

$3,000-4,000   **FRE**

A Chinese Qing Dynasty hongmu tray, of simulated bamboo rectangular form, the gallery edge worked to show bamboo stems joined at the corners, single plank base.

20in (51cm) long

$1,100-1,500   **FRE**

An unusual 19thC hongmu bone or ivory inlaid picnic box, of four tier sectional form, each inlaid with three bands of bone or ivory oval panels, the twin hinged handles carved in low relief to show tight scrolls locked in place by two grasshopper-form pins surmounted to the cover, the shaped base carved with scroll work.

16in (40.6cm) wide

$1,000-1,600   **FRE**

A Chinese late Ming/early Qing period wood carved figure of Quanyin, carved with down-turned dressed head, flowing robe, holding a child in her arms, standing over a lotus throne, signs of color pigment.

14.5in (37cm) high

$1,200-1,600   **FRE**

A 17thC or later Chinese hardwood carving of Guanyin, seated with one knee raised, resting on pierced rockwork, paper label for 'Spink & Son', some old repairs.

10.25in (26cm) high

$2,400-3,600   **WW**

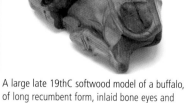

A large late 19thC softwood model of a buffalo, of long recumbent form, inlaid bone eyes and inset horns.

15in (38cm) long

$400-600   **FRE**

A late 18th/early 19thC Japanese burl wood basket, carved from a single section of burl wood, the hoop handle of three branch form, the rounded tray reveals an oval openwork hollow, the underside reveals a fine gnarled and knotted surface, overall finely enhanced.

13in (33cm) high

$3,600-4,400   **FRE**

A small 19thC Japanese burl wood lingzhi-form tray, finely figured stand enhanced to show an aged five head lingzhi, delicately worked continuation to underside, tomobako reads 'camphor wood free-form carved tea tray', signed Shiro or Haku Dou Saku.

6in (15cm) high

$400-600   **FRE**

An early 19thC Japanese okimono of a wasps' nest, hollowed and enhanced wood nest, enclosing three free-moving ivory grubs, and five sedentary ivory grubs, enclosed in a tomobako box.

3.5in (9cm) high

$2,400-3,800   **FRE**

A 19thC Japanese boxwood okimono of a boar, modeled seated with legs carved in fine detail verso, raised front legs, head held high looking forward, inlaid with ivory eyes and tusks, finely carved hair and detail throughout, enclosed in a 19thC black lacquer box.

2.5in (6.5cm) high

$3,000-5,000   **FRE**

A 19thC Japanese wood netsuke, carved as a warty toad crouched on a sandal.

2.25in (6cm) high

$700-900   **WW**

A 19thC Japanese root wood hibachi, extensively hollowed from a single waisted oval trunk section, thick incised edge, gnarled and polished tight grain exterior, two-plank pine base, missing copper insert.

25in (63.5cm) wide

$1,200-1,600   **FRE**

A 19thC Japanese wooden inro, decorated with lotus branches, flowers and leaves, a two-character mark to one end.

3.5in (8.5cm) high

$1,000-1,400   **WW**

A Japanese ivory and boxwood figure of a man with a broom, incomplete.

c1900   *9in (23cm) high*

$700-1,100   **DN**

A 19thC Japanese Komai kidney-shaped box and cover, decorated in gold and silver with pavilions in a landscape.

2.5in (6cm) high

$800-1,200   **WW**

A 19thC Japanese Noh mask, possibly Otobide, carved wood, gilt pigment on gesso, gilt metal eyes, storage box.

9in (23cm) high

$300-500   **FRE**

A 19thC Japanese Noh mask, possibly Shaka Buddha, carved wood polychrome over gesso, gilt metal eyes, inscribed to the interior.

11in (28cm) high

$240-360   **FRE**

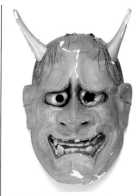

A 19thC Japanese Noh mask, Buaku, carved wood, polychrome over gesso, gilt horns, one gilt metal eye, one missing.

9in (23cm) high

$300-500   **FRE**

A 19th/20thC Japanese Noh mask, Choreibeshimi, carved wood polychrome over gesso, insert gilt metal eyes.

9in (23cm) high

$400-600   **FRE**

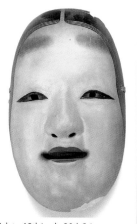

A late 19th/early 20thC Japanese Noh mask, Ko-omote, carved wood polychrome over gesso, storage case.

9in (23cm) high

$300-500   **FRE**

A 19th/20thC Japanese Noh mask, carved wood painted and gilt highlights, applied hair, with storage bag.

9in (23cm) high

$800-1,200   **FRE**

A 20thC Japanese Noh mask, Fukai, carved wood polychrome over gesso with storage bag.

9in (23cm) high

$400-600   **FRE**

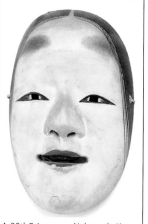

A 20thC Japanese Noh mask, Ko-omote, carved wood and polychrome, inscribed to the interior, minor losses, with storage bag.

9in (23cm) high

$400-600   **FRE**

A 19thC Burmese gilt and black lacquered wood Buddha figure, seated in padmasana with the right hand in bhumispara mudra.

5.5in (14cm) high

$240-360   **FRE**

A rare Burmese Qing Dynasty polychrome wood articulated tattoo model, of male adult form, articulated torso and limbs, white polychrome body painted red and black depicting significant tattooed areas.

9in (23cm) high

$700-1,100   **FRE**

A Thai carved wood and gilt reclining Buddhistic figure.

40.25in (102cm) long

$800-1,000   **DN**

A 17thC Chinese Bitong period bamboo brush pot, of slender cylindrical form, gently flared mouth carved in medium to high relief to show a continuous mountainous landscape with a figure over a mule or donkey ascending followed by an attendant, the verso carved to show plum blossoms in high relief.

4.25in (11cm) high

$1,600-2,400   **FRE**

A 19thC Chinese bamboo brushpot, decorated with figures on a veranda beneath foliage, the reverse with four columns of calligraphy.

5.25in (13.5cm) high

$300-500   **WW**

A late 19th/early 20thC bamboo brushpot, carved with two travelers in a landscape.

6in (15cm) high

$300-400   **DN**

An 18th/19thC Chinese bamboo model of a snake, of twisting coiled form, detail enhanced body and well-polished gold brown patina, Japanese torobako box reading 'natural bamboo root snake okimono'.

3in (7.5cm) high

$1,400-2,000   **FRE**

An 18thC Chinese shaped bamboo brushpot, carved in shallow relief in liu ching technique with figures crossing a bridge in a landscape.

5in (13cm) high

$500-700   **DN**

A late 19thC Chinese bamboo brushpot carved with figures and attendants in a landscape.

6.25in (16cm) high

$400-500   **DN**

An 18thC Chinese rhizome bamboo seal, the tapering cylindrical body with rhizome growths issuing from a cylindrical growth issuing from a cylindrical stem supported by three smaller stems, incised with two characters to base, red pigment to seal.

2in (5cm) high

$4,000-6,000   **FRE**

A pair of Chinese carved bamboo cylindrical incense boxes, pierced and carved with immortals in a bamboo grove.

12.5in (32cm) high

$600-800   **DN**

A 17th/18thC Chinese bamboo root brush pot, of gnarled bamboo root form, the interior lacquered black.

3.75in (9.5cm) high

$1,000-2,000   **FRE**

A small Chinese Qing Dynasty bamboo skin brush pot, of tall square form, of five-plank construction, raised on four low relief carved bracket feet.

3.75in (9.5cm) high

$300-400   **FRE**

An 18thC Chinese shaped bamboo brushpot, carved in shallow relief in liu ching technique with figures crossing a bridge in a landscape.

5in (13cm) high

$500-700   **DN**

A large 19thC Chinese bamboo brush pot, finely carved pot in medium relief, carved to show a continuous garden scene with scholars amongst pine trees and a scrolling sea.

7in (17.5cm) high

$400-800   **FRE**

A bamboo and shell seal, of square form, carved in high relief and openwork to show a scholar among a pine tree grove, signed for early Qing Dynasty to side, shell or horn incised seal plate, associated silver inlaid lacquer box.

$500-700   **FRE**

A Chinese Qing Dynasty double form gourd and stand, of fine golden brown patina, over a circular bracket footed wood stand.

9.5in (24cm) high

$200-400   FRE

A Chinese Qing Dynasty elongated gourd, long brown stem issues from an elongated double gourd form body, good golden brown patina, with modern wood stand.

18in (46cm) high

$600-800   FRE

A Chinese Qing Dynasty triple gourd and stand, the graduated triple gourd raised on an open work scroll form stand.

13in (33cm) high

$800-1,200   FRE

A Chinese Qing Dynasty partially lacquered knotted gourd and stand, the knotted neck issuing from a broad compressed double gourd body, over a fine circular base supporting four free-moving spheres.

16in (40.5cm) high

$800-1,200   FRE

A pair of Chinese Qing Dynasty natural double form gourds on sectional gourd stands, the bound stem coil in mirror image issuing from golden brown double gourds over pierced stands of gourd centres.

10in (25.5cm) high

$1,000-1,600   FRE

A 19thC bamboo bound form natural gourd bottle, enhanced by binding to resemble bamboo stem fitted with wood stopper and yellow jadeite ring, raised on a root wood stand.

11in (28cm) long

$500-700   FRE

A 19thC Japanese natural gourd, of waisted double form, fine white metal stopper, cloth bound enclosing an ivory ring or hyowa netsuke, fine golden brown to dark brown patina, encased in tomobako.

10in (25.5cm) high

$600-1,000   FRE

A 19thC Japanese double hyowa netsuke and spout natural gourd, fine slight double gourd form, fitted with wood stopper, brass fitted nozzle or spout, cloth supporting an ivory and tortoiseshell hyowa netsuke, silk case and tomobako.

8.5in (21.5cm) high

$800-1,200   FRE

HORN

A rhinoceros horn libation cup, carved in the form of a lotus flower with waves around the base, with two small snails to the interior, some damage.

4.25in (11cm) wide

$32,000-40,000   L&T

A Chinese rhinoceros horn libation cup, carved with a guei dragon and archaistic patterns.

3.25in (8.5cm) high

$400-600   DN

An early 19thC Chinese carved rhinoceros horn seal, finely carved with a phoenix on a ground of scrolling lotus.

3in (7.5cm) high

$300-500   DN

A late 16th/early 17thC Chinese carved red lacquer incense box and cover, decorated with lychees amidst foliage, on a diaper molded ground, cracks and chips.

3in (7.5cm) high

$8,000-10,000   **WW**

A Chinese export lacquer games box, with folding chess/backgammon board and a drawer containing an export ivory red and white chess set, complete but damaged.

$1,200-1,600   **DN**

A Chinese Qianlong period Imperial lacquer edict case, of rectangular form, carved in high relief, the front panel shows a two-character medallion 'Jade Temple'.

18in (45.5cm) wide

$5,000-6,000   **FRE**

A 17thC or later Chinese red lacquer cup, with a loop handle and three feet, decorated with fruiting lychee, beneath a key fret band, a metal lining, damages.

3in (8cm) high

$1,000-1,200   **WW**

A Chinese gilt metal-mounted red lacquer wall vase, carved with five bats around a shou character, fixed wood stand.

c1800   *7in (18cm) high*

$4,000-5,000   **WW**

CLOSER LOOK: LACQUER DISH

Lacquer has been used since c400BC. Layers of sap from the Rhus vernicifera tree create a hard surface that can be carved in relief.

It was a speciality of craftsmen in the Court workshops of Peking from the 16thC.

The dish is carved in deep relief with four figures and a pagoda, beneath a pine tree. The borders are decorated with flowers and foliage. The dish has survived in remarkable condition.

The six-character mark relates to the Jiajing period which lasted from 1522-66.

A Japanese Meiji period gold lacquer hexagonal box and cover, containing three lozenge-shaped boxes and covers, decorated with a mountainous landscape, and with stylized motifs.

5in (12.5cm) high

$1,000-1,600   **WW**

A 19thC Japanese lacquer square box and cover, decorated with a phoenix on a black ground, gilt leaf scroll borders.

11.25in (28.5cm) wide

$500-700   **DN**

A rare Chinese Jiajing period red lacquer octagonal dish, molded and carved, cracks and losses.

6.75in (17cm) high

$10,000-12,000   **WW**

ESSENTIAL REFERENCE: INRO

An inro is a small rectangular box made up of sections, used to hold herbs or tobacco.

- Inros are usually decorated with lacquer.
- In the absence of pockets in traditional Japanese costume, inros hang from the obi (sash) of the kimono using a netsuke (toggle).
- In use in Japan from the mid-16thC, inros are still made today.

A 19thC Japanese gold lacquer inro, decorated on each side with lakes and mountains.

3.5in (9cm) high

$1,400-1,800   **WW**

A pair of 19thC Japanese inro, including a five-case inro with orange-brown lacquer to a brown lacquer body showing a seated figure fitted with an agate omjime and frog form toggle, together with a well-lacquered butterfly six-case inro with stained ivory omjime and a very well carved nut kagamibuta, signed 'Masatama'.

$1,200-1,600   **FRE**

A pair of Chinese Jiaqing period blue Beijing glass shallow bowls, each incised on the base with a four-character Jiaqing mark.

6.5in (16.5cm) high

$5,000-7,000 WW

A large late 18th/early19thC Chinese Beijing sapphire-blue glass vase, the ovoid body with a tall flared neck and chamfered rim, unmarked.

14.5in (36.5cm) high

$8,000-10,000 WW

A 19thC or earlier Chinese Beijing glass compressed baluster vase, the white metal body with a claret red foot rim and mouth.

5in (12.5cm) high

$800-1,200 WW

A Chinese yellow Beijing glass compressed circular vase.

4.5in (11cm) high

$300-500 WW

A 19thC Chinese Beijing amethyst glass bowl, raised on a small foot, a rim bruise.

4.25in (11cm) diam

$140-200 WW

A Chinese Beijing glass bowl, the white metal overlaid in green with shibumpkin swimming amidst lotus flowers and leaves, wheelcut Qianlong four-character mark but later, with wood stand.

6.75in (17cm) high

$500-700 WW

A 20thC Chinese Beijing amber-colored glass bottle vase, the base with a four-character Qianlong mark.

14.5in (37.5cm) high

$400-800 WW

SNUFF BOTTLES

A 19thC Chinese lavender-colored jadeite bottle, with flecks of apple green.

2.25in (6cm) high

$1,700-1,900 WW

A Chinese jade snuff bottle, carved with a pavilion and figures in a watery landscape.

2.75in (7cm) high

$2,000-3,000 WW

A 19thC Chinese jade snuff bottle, carved with a horse beneath a willow tree.

3in (8cm) high

$1,200-1,600 WW

A rare Chinese celadon jade rectangular snuff bottle, carved with birds and bamboo.

2.5in (6.5cm) high

$6,000-8,000 WW

A Chinese Qianlong period pale celadon jade snuff bottle, formed as a fabulous fish amidst pomegranate leaves, other leaves and scrolls.

3.5in (9cm) high

$7,000-9,000　　WW

An early 19thC Chinese celadon jade pebble-form snuff bottle, of tall pebble form, well-hollowed, square jadeite stopper.

3in (7.5cm) high

$1,000-1,400　　FRE

A 19thC Chinese famille rose double-necked molded snuff bottle, decorated with a multitude of small figures.

2.75in (7cm) high

$700-900　　WW

A Chinese possibly Guangxu period porcelain snuff bottle, of flattened double gourd form, decorated with bats on a yellow ground and a lapis lazuli stopper, four-character mark of Guangxu.

2.5in (6.5cm) high

$1,000-1,400　　WW

A Chinese porcelain snuff bottle, decorated with the eight horses of Mu Wang.

3.5in (9cm) high

$600-1,000　　WW

A Chinese probably Yongzheng period turquoise-glazed porcelain snuff bottle, cylindrical form, orange glass and ivory stopper, Yongzheng seal mark to base.

3in (7.5cm) high

$600-1,000　　FRE

A 19thC Chinese ivory snuff bottle, carved as a quail, the eyes inlaid in horn.

1.75in (4.5cm) high

$1,600-2,000　　WW

A Chinese ivory snuff bottle, one side finely engraved with a recumbent figure beside a water buffalo, the reverse with sixteen lines of minute calligraphy.

2.25in (6cm) high

$1,300-1,500　　WW

A pair of 19thC ivory snuff bottles, of squat ribbed vegetable form, turned domed cover, raised on pierced wood stands.

3.5in (9cm) high

$1,400-2,000　　FRE

A 19thC Chinese 'laque burgauté' snuff bottle, decorated on one side with figures on a pavilion, the other with a bird perched on a branch, Qianlong four-character mark.

3.25in (8cm) high

$2,600-3,000　　WW

An early 19thC Chinese cinnabar lacquer on porcelain snuff bottle, of cylindrical form, lacquer on porcelain carved to show a continuous garden scene, matched red glass stopper.

3in (7.5cm) high

$500-700　　FRE

A 17thC Chinese jichimu yoke-back chair, the protruding top rail supported by a recessed paneled and scrolling openwork back rest, shaped applied apron below pad hand rests, all above a beaded apron continuing to the straight rounded legs, joined by a flat rectangular footrest and partially rounded stretchers.

44in (105.5cm) high

$2,000-3,000   FRE

A pair of large 17thC Chinese yumu and lacquer Official's Hat chairs, the shaped back rail supported by an S-shaped plain back rest, the heavily constructed rectangular framed and cane seat over a shaped apron continuing down the leg, rectangular foot rest and rounded stretchers joining slightly rounded and beaded legs.

48in (122cm) high

$5,000-7,000   FRE

A pair of Chinese early Qing Dynasty lacquered jumu and iron-mounted yoke-back chairs, the S-shaped arms supported by straight iron and shaped jumu posts, a single plank seat over a straight apron continuing to the legs, rounded foot rest and stretchers.

47in (119cm) high

$2,000-3,000   FRE

A 17th/18thC Chinese yumu partially lacquered low-back Southern Official's back chair, with a well-carved and beaded ruyi scroll shaped apron to three sides and below three rounded stretchers a slightly higher rounded back stretcher.

40in (101.5cm) high

$800-1,200   FRE

A late 18thC Chinese black-lacquered yumu horseshoe-back chair, the back is supported by a pierced Shou character, the panel worked to show Buddhistic symbols, shaped apron, all over a foot rest and straight low stretchers joining rounded legs.

41in (104cm) high

$1,600-2,000   FRE

A pair of 18thC Chinese yumu yoke-back chairs, the protruding top rail, supported by a solid S-shaped back rest, sinuously rounded scrolling arms and side posts, rectangular framed seat with woven cane rest, S-shaped apron leading to a foot rest and four low joined rounded legs.

46in (117cm) high

$1,600-2,400   FRE

An 18thC Chinese root wood armchair, the square-form back and shaped armrests comprised of an open lattice work of gnarled joined root-like protrusions finely enhanced to show a tight light brown figured grain, flat yumu insert seat all over an openwork apron and four strong straight gnarled legs.

35in (89cm) high

$8,000-10,000   FRE

A pair of 18thC Chinese bamboo horseshoe chairs, of split cane beaded horseshoe back, supported by an open lattice work back rest, the arms supported by three straight posts, lacquered square seat, all raised on stretcher straight legs.

36in (91.5cm) high

$600-800   FRE

A pair of 19thC Chinese yumu low back Southern Official's hat chairs, the slightly concave back rail supported by a plan S-shaped back rest, shaped arms supported by plain posts, rectangular insert seat, shaped apron continuing down the legs, straight plain footrest and double cross stretchers to the side, signs of lacquer.

38in (96.5cm) high

$1,000-1,400 PAIR   FRE

An unusual 19thC Chinese jichimu wingback armchair, of Western influence, the high straight caned back rest framed by two D-form wings and supported by seven palmate head back rails, the straight arm rest supported by a single low stretcher, the square-framed caned seat raised over two cabriole carved front legs and outswept rear legs.

44in (112cm) high

$6,000-8,000   FRE

A rare Chinese late Ming Dynasty tielimu and iron-mounted folding stool, jiaowu, of simple X-form design, woven cotton seat paneled by two square-form seat sections, the apron of both carved in high relief to show scrolling leaves within a beaded edge, the two rounded legs are joined by concealed iron pins and mounts, the joining foot rest fitted to the lower section of both legs, raised on flat rectangular feet.

15in (38cm) high

$4,000-6,000 FRE

A pair of large Chinese Ming Dynasty hongmu caned waisted square stools, caned square insert framed top, waisted fluted and straight apron, rounded high hump-back stretchers joining straight slightly rounded legs terminating in high hoof-shaped feet.

24.5in (62cm) wide

$6,000-10,000 FRE

A pair of Chinese Ming Dynasty yumu square waisted stools, of single plank and panel construction, swan-neck shaped plain apron issuing from cabriole legs joined by high hump-back and shaped stretchers, terminating in hoof foliate carved feet.

22.5in (57m) wide

$1,800-2,200 FRE

A 17th/18thC Chinese folding huanghuali stool, Jiaodeng, of eight piece construction, woven cotton seat set to two rounded legs, joined with brass foliate mounts concealing brass pins, the top and bottom horizontal section forming the seat frame and stretched feet, highly figured warm toned patina.

18in (45.5cm) high

$10,000-14,000 FRE

An unusual Chinese Qing Dynasty softwood horse-shoe back and storage stool, the single section horse-shoe back rest surmounted a softwood hollowed single section trunk, fitted with a hinged demi-lune seat opening to reveal a storage space, iron banding to cylindrical body, all over a circular base raised on bracket feet.

24in (61cm) high

$800-1,200 FRE

A Chinese early Qing Dynasty root wood stool, of naturalistic form, oval rounded body highlighted by a highly figured open grain, somewhat resembling a brain or coiled animal model.

14in (35.5cm) high

$6,000-8,000 FRE

An unusual Chinese early Qing Dynasty root wood and softwood stool, the base of interconnected root wood pierced to show three openwork medallions, softwood insert seat, applied with three iron free-hanging handles.

15in (39cm) high

$1,600-2,400 FRE

A 17th/18thC Chinese root wood stool, the seat incised to show a lotus leaf, gnarled naturalistic apron and four tree trunk-form legs.

14in (35.5cm) high

$2,000-3,000 FRE

A Chinese early Qing Dynasty root wood stool, of naturalistic form, light brown highly figured grain, trunk-form legs, friction polished seat.

14in (35.5cm) high

$1,600-2,400 FRE

A large 17th/18thC root wood stool, of tripod form, flat friction polished seat, over a tree trunk form body and tree tapering gnarled legs.

21in (53.5cm) high

$1,600-2,400   FRE

A rare pair of Chinese mid-Qing Dynasty root wood stools, of circular form, fitted with insert lacquered seat surface, partially enveloped by gnarled root wood descending to an openwork and protruding interlacing lattice apron above four gnarled and delicately enhanced naturalistically formed legs.

20in (50cm) high

$13,000-15,000   FRE

An 18thC Chinese root wood stool, fine gold patina, tight figured grain and of cylindrical form, recessed seat.

20in (51cm) high

$5,000-7,000   FRE

An 18thC Chinese root wood stool, fine golden brown patina, gnarled body under a flat seat surface.

20in (51cm) high

$1,400-2,000   FRE

A 17th/18thC Chinese yumu bench, of rectangular form, the heavy single plank top, fine beaded and molded edge, raised on rounded rectangular legs with beaded apron continuing to plain spandrels, resting on floor rails, well-figured grain.

57in (145cm) wide

$3,000-4,000   FRE

An 18th/19thC Chinese brown lacquered and caned day bed, the framed caned rectangular top over recessed side structured straight legs, molded brackets and shaped apron.

76in (193cm) wide

$600-1,000   FRE

A Chinese early Qing Dynasty jumu recessed leg bench, of plank top form with flared ends, recessed straight legs flanked by joined phoenix head carved spandrels and shaped apron band, continuing to leg interior, well-figured surface.

46in (117cm) wide

$700-900   FRE

A 20thC Senufo hardwood bed, worked from a single section, braced head rest, rail to edge, with four inset tapering legs.

78in (198cm) long

$800-1,200   FRE

A 17thC Chinese nanmu black lacquered triangular table, of unusual 'turtle black' parquetry framed top, over a thin waist bulging wide curvilinear apron carved in high relief to show a beaded edge interrupted by shell-like medallions, raised on board cabriole legs terminating in low hoof feet.

72in (183cm) wide

$1,000-1,400 **FRE**

CLOSER LOOK: MING SIDE TABLE

The table has a large well-figured single plank top. A lesser table would have two or three thin planks set to the framed edge.

The table has thick single section rounded high-hump back stretchers rather than joined split joinery.

There are signs of dry lacquer to underside, this was often used during the late Ming early Qing period to guard against rot and insect attack. Later 19/20thC examples have a painted black lacquer imitating the correct late Ming lacquer.

There is good wear to feet and edge indicating correct wear consistent with age and use.

A Chinese late Ming Dynasty huanghuali side table, of single plank ice plate framed top, double rounded edge, all over a straight rounded high hump-back stretcher supporting eight oval molded open medallions, raised on well-rounded cylindrical legs, well-figured grain throughout.

$60,000-80,000 **FRE**

A 17thC Chinese burl hualimu and tielimu square table, the partially lacquered thick single plank top shows age hollows and surface scarring, over a small waist, the apron carved in medium relief to show scrolling dragons framing a single character, the straight beaded legs joined by high humpback stretchers, terminating in hoof feet.

26in (66cm) wide

$14,000-20,000 **FRE**

A 17th/18thC Chinese huangulai flush-sided side table, the well-figured single rectangular-plank ice-plate framed top shows mortise and tenon joints to edge, over a plain beaded apron, above a high hump-back stretcher joining four straight square legs, terminating in high hoof feet.

33in (84cm) high

$40,000-50,000 **FRE**

A Chinese early Qing Dynasty jumu lacquered recessed-leg table, the thick single plank top terminating in shaped everted flanges, over a thin straight apron, the recessed legs paneled by scroll bracket-like spandrels, straight legs joined by two straight cross stretchers at both ends, minor traces of lacquer.

57in (145cm) wide

$1,000-1,400 **FRE**

A rare 17th/18thC tielimu folding wine table, the detached two-plank framed 'ice plate' edge top with hinged apron fits into two straight leg trestles, joined at the end by two rounded rectangular stretchers, good period wear to surface.

42in (106.5cm) wide

$800-1,200 **FRE**

A Chinese early Qing Dynasty softwood sectional square flush-sided table, comprising two triangular sectional tables, flush side legs joined by straight low stretchers, the longest edge carved in low relief to show coiled lotus leaves issuing from a lotus medallion, and Greek key frieze, terminating in hoof and square feet.

54in (137cm) wide

$1,000-1,200 **FRE**

CLOSER LOOK: ROOT WOOD TABLE

Root wood tables were designed to remove the scholar from his work and the straight lines of his study or office, and place him amid the undulating, swaying and uncontrolled flow of nature.

It is rare for tree roots to grow in this way to produce four practical legs.

It is rare to find an 18thC table – most date from the 19thC. It would have been costly when new.

The softwood table top is finely inserted and fitted with fine bamboo tenons.

A rare 18thC Qing Dynasty hetaomu and root wood side table, the rectangular highly figured Hetaomu insert single plank top joined by visible and raised bamboo mitered plugs, all above a fine and delicate bulging apron of open and gnarled root-work, raised on naturalistically enhanced cabriole legs and hoof feet.

52in (132cm) wide

$30,000-40,000 **FRE**

ORIENTAL

A large Chinese early Qing Dynasty yumu partially lacquered recessed leg altar table, of plank rectangular top applied with two shaped flanges, over beaded rounded straight legs and scrolling spandrels, joined at the ends by openwork panels depicting rock work.

100in (254cm) wide

$3,000-4,000   **FRE**

A large 18thC Chinese tielimu recessed legged painting table, the solid single plank top mounted with two everted flanges, all over a straight bracket apron, raised on straight round legs, joined at the end by two rounded short stretchers.

85in (216cm) wide

$1,600-2,400   **FRE**

An 18thC Chinese yumu and conglomerate liver stone insert side table, Tiaozhuo, the rectangular stone insert top resembling gold on red lacquer framed by highly figured yumu planks with ice-plate edge, short pierced key fretted waist, bead straight apron continuing down the slight cabriole leg, terminating in square scroll feel, sign of lacquer.

43in (109cm) wide

$3,600-4,400   **FRE**

An 18th/19thC Chinese hongmu and nanmu-burl wood waisted center table, the square insert burl-wood top framed by four well-figured hongmu planks of 'ice-plate' edge, waisted and beaded apron joined by a high straight stretcher with three vertical struts, joining four straight and beaded legs terminating in hoof feet.

37in (94cm) wide

$2,400-3,600   **FRE**

A Chinese mid to late Qing Dynasty huanghuali recessed leg side table, of rectangular insert single plank and frame top, surmounted by two fluted triangular flanges, over straight beaded and joined legs, matched apron, legs joined by high pierced apron and solid feet to the side.

37in (94cm) wide

$20,000-30,000   **FRE**

A Chinese Qing Dynasty black lacquered wine table, the rectangular lacquered top rest over a thin waist and beaded apron carved to show stylized Fu bats and scrolls terminating at openwork and carved scrolling corners mounts, straight legs, interrupted by a scrolling hoof, continuing as a recessed straight leg terminating in a second scrolling hoof, signs of gilt lacquer.

60in (152.5cm) wide

$2,400-3,000   **FRE**

A 19thC Chinese rosewood altar table, the narrow rectangular top of mitered design above a frieze of open lotus scrolls, baluster and roundels, centered by a scroll work medallion, the ends similarly decorated, on square section legs with underscrolled feet carved with lotus fronds and united by upswept stretchers.

77.25in (196cm) wide

$5,000-6,000   **L&T**

A Chinese late Qing Dynasty black lacquer and bamboo square table, the well-lacquered black top rest over an open lattice work apron, raised on four straight low stretcher legs.

34in (81cm) high

$600-1,000   **FRE**

A Chinese Qing Dynasty hetaomu and lacquered bamboo side table, the double plank hetaomu top rests over an open lattice work of woven split bamboo lacquered brown, raised on six straight legs, joined by a rectangular foot base.

44in (112cm) wide

$600-800   **FRE**

A late 19thC Chinese huang huali center table, formed of two D-shaped sections, with a relief carved and marquetry frieze and pierced corner brackets above shaped legs and scroll feet.

46in (116.5cm) diam

$1,300-1,500   **DN**

A mid-19thC Chinese hardwood side table, with a rectangular marble top above a carved frieze, on scroll carved cabriole supports raised on a platform.

62.25in (158cm) wide

$30,000-40,000   **SOTH**

A rare Chinese late Ming Dynasty huanghuali and partially lacquered stand, in a waisted kang table form, carved in low relief to show interlaced Indian lotus leaves and qilin to the center and lion or dragon masks to the knee of cabriole legs, terminating in claw feet.

15.5in (39.5cm) long

$3,000-4,000 **FRE**

A 17thC Chinese huanghuali kang table, the rectangular single plank 'ice-plate' framed top rests over a thin waist and beaded slightly bulging apron, raised on straight cabriole legs terminating in scrolling hoof feet.

75in (190.5cm) wide

$12,000-16,000 **FRE**

A 17thC Chinese huanghuali kang-form table stand, the fine double plank insert and 'ice-plate' framed fluted and beaded edge over a plain waist, finely carved and beaded curvilinear apron continuing to cabriole legs, terminating in low hoof feet.

18in (46cm) wide

$20,000-30,000 **FRE**

A 17thC Chinese huanghuali waisted kang table, of double insert plank framed top, fluted and beaded edge, the beaded scrolling apron carved in low relief to show interlacing scrolls issuing from the apron edge to show a delicate ruyi, straight knee cabriole legs, terminating in scrolling hoofs.

35in (89cm) wide

$10,000-20,000 **FRE**

An 18thC Chinese hongmu table stand, of kang form and two-plank insert and 'ice plate' edge construction with apron and high hump-back stretcher and scrolling legs carved to simulate bamboo shoots, good patina.

27ins (68.5cm)

$4,000-6,000 **FRE**

An 18th/19thC Chinese carved cinnabar lacquer table stand, of kang table form, the rectangular surface incised with cross-hatched motif over a Greek key edge and waisted diaper band, the wide shaped and beaded apron encloses a detailed ground carved in high relief showing Indian lotus flowers issuing scrolling leaves, continuing to cabriole legs terminating in hoof feet.

19.5in (49.5cm) wide

$4,400-5,600 **FRE**

A 19thC Chinese bamboo, coconut and hongmu 'turtleback' stand, in the form of a recess legged altar or side table, the hongmu framed rectangular top of parquetry coconut shell, the apron and straight legs of bamboo veneer.

20in (51cm) wide

$2,400-3,600 **FRE**

A 19thC Chinese tielimu waisted kang table, of single insert plank and panel top, fluted everted rim, the scroll-shaped apron beaded to the edge continuing to the cabriole legs, terminating in single scroll lingzhi feet.

36in (91.5cm) wide

$800-1,700 **FRE**

A Chinese Qing Dynasty tielimu and burl wood square waisted table, of single burl wood insert plank construction, framed by four tielimu planks, the scrolling shaped apron carved in low relief to show ruyi scroll and foliate scroll to the cabriole leg, beaded apron edge continuing to a straight leg terminating in a scrolling hoof.

30in (76cm) wide

$600-800 **FRE**

A pair of 19thC Chinese black lacquered softwood waisted tables.

20in (51cm) wide

$1,200-2,000 **FRE**

An early 20thC Chinese hongmu kang table, of Western influence, the single insert plank and panel top over a triple rounded molded edge, unusual twisted and joined 'rope twist' high stretcher joining simulated bamboo straight legs.

59in (150cm) wide

$3,000-4,000 **FRE**

ORIENTAL

A 17thC Chinese single section 'tiger fur' stand, of rectangular form with slight undulating surface over a scrolling 'thorn' openwork apron raised on four slightly outswept bracket feet, fine 'tiger fur' figured surface.

14in (35.5cm) long

$2,000-3,000   FRE

A 17th/18thC Chinese yumu Fu Guai or shrine, insert with a detailed etched bronze basin, worked to show scholar on mule with attendants to the central medallion and diaper band to edge, a bulging apron carved in Ming style to show ruyi scrolls issuing from the edge, cabriole legs, scroll pad feet, raised on a circular sectional base, joined by fine butterfly.

22in (56cm) high

$1,000-1,600   FRE

An 18thC Chinese hongmu stand, the single section of rectangular form, terminating in two well-rounded ribbon scroll ends, well-figured patina.

17in (43cm) long

$1,000-1,600   FRE

An 18thC huamu burl scrolling ribbon-form stand, worked from a single section of highly figured burl wood, the long rectangular surface with rounded edge and gradually rounded ends to well-scrolled feet, rich brown patina.

23in (58.5cm) long

$8,000-10,000   FRE

A Chinese Qing Dynasty hongmu stone-inset stand, the orange-veined white stone inset to rounded hongmu frame above flush-side corner legs recessing at the knee, raised on scrolling feet.

14in (35.5cm) long

$600-800   FRE

A 19thC Chinese hongmu stand, of recessed oval form, the base finely embellished to simulate a gnarled root wood of intertwined and protruding figure-like growths, together with a fitted box.

5.5in (14cm) long

$500-700   FRE

An 18thC Chinese huangyangmu/boxwood reticulated stand, highly figured rounded edged surface with minor period inclusions, the base of finely embellished gnarled and protruding stylized roots reticulated resembling a near floating surface, dark coffee brown patina.

13in (33cm) high

$8,000-10,000   FRE

An 18th/19thC Chinese huangyangmu/ boxwood tea ceremony stand, of short circular naturalistic form, enhanced to show a light brown hue figured surface punctuated with several hollows and recesses.

6.5in (16.5cm) wide

$1,400-2,000   FRE

An 18th/19thC Chinese hongmu reticulated stand, of tall cylindrical form, carved from a single section finely enhanced to show a flat surface to the top, over a base of interlaced joined root-like protrusions, enhanced to show small wood hollows, and branch-like growths, fine rich brown to black patina.

9in (23cm) high

$1,600-2,000   FRE

A 19thC Chinese boxwood scholar's stand, the flat polished burl figured surface shows minor natural inclusions and undulation, raised on an interlacing network of root-form base.

8in (20.5cm) wide

$1,600-2,000   **FRE**

An unusual 18thC Chinese huangyangmu/boxwood stand, carved from a single section of well-figured huangyangmu simulating a root wood stand, carved and worked to show six protruding legs and various scrolling gnarled and recessed surfaces.

18in (45.5cm) wide

$12,000-16,000   **FRE**

A 17thC Chinese tielimu coffer, Liansanchu, the single plank rectangular framed top flanked by two everted flanges, all over a bank of three drawers, above a frieze of double-plank boards divided by a single vertical strut, raised on straight rounded and beaded legs, joined by a simple shaped apron.

66in (167.5cm) wide

$8,000-10,000   **FRE**

A Chinese early Qing Dynasty yumu and lacquered coffer, the long single plank top terminates in two everted flanges, over a bank of three short drawers, flanked by two carved spandrels, all above a two-door cabinet framed by two plain panels, raised on straight legs.

74in (188cm) wide

$1,000-1,400   **FRE**

A small Chinese late Ming Dynasty square corner black lacquered cabinet, the two heavily lacquered rounded framed doors open to reveal two long drawers flanking a pair of short drawers, pebble texture to lacquer.

23in (58.5cm) wide

$600-1,000   **FRE**

A Chinese late Ming/early Qing Dynasty tapered jumu cabinet, Yuanjiaogui, of slender proportions, protruding top frame with rounded corners supported on splayed posts enclosing two matched doors, all above a plain panel bisected by a single vertical strut, plain apron, the interior fitted with a shelf and a pair of drawers, baitong fittings, highly figured grain.

37.5in (95.5cm) wide

$8,000-12,000   **FRE**

A large Chinese Qing Dynasty hongmu square corner cabinet, of tall rectangular form, well-matched framed and panel sides and doors, opening to reveal a shelf over a bank of two short drawers, the base shelf rest over a plain beaded apron, raised on straight legs.

48in (122cm) wide

$10,000-12,000   **FRE**

A pair of 19thC Chinese hardwood sectional cabinets, each with pierced rectangular frame surmounted by an iron handle above four removable sections.

27.25in (69cm) high

$1,200-1,600
DN

A late 19thC Japanese cabinet, with open shelves surmounted by an ornate tiered temple roof design pediment, with fretwork panels depicting scrolls, serpents and sun motifs, with pierced gallery below and open shelves under, flanked by carved serpent-entwined uprights, the side panels decorated with inlaid leaf and flower pattern motifs, raised on carved legs.

50in (127cm) wide

$4,000-6,000
A&G

A late 19thC Japanese carved giltwood and black lacquer shrine, the tall rectangular cabinet encloses three sliding door shrines, surrounded by well-carved giltwood dragons and scrolls above three well-lacquered drawers, raised on a base of three short and two long wood-veneered drawers.

36in (91.5cm) wide

$700-900
FRE

An early 20thC Japanese gold on red lacquer chest, well-lacquered gold and silver over a red ground showing fans and circles enclosing stalks and songbirds, two doors reveal eight pull and sliding drawers, over a four-legged stand decorated in gilt scrolls.

20.5in (52cm) high

$2,000-3,000
FRE

A late 18th/early 19thC Chinese black lacquer and gilt-decorated cabinet on stand, the shaped and molded pediment above two doors opening to an arrangement of drawers centered by a recessed pagoda section incorporating pierced fretwork panels, the stand with a pierced frieze, on hipped square section legs, claw-and-ball feet, damage, repair.

34.5in (88cm) wide

$5,000-6,000 **DN**

A 19thC Chinese Export lacquer secretary desk, in two parts, the upper section with shaped pediment and carved cartouche above two doors opening to fitted compartments, the lower section opens to reveal more compartments with drawer below on cabriole legs ending in paw feet.

65in (165cm) high

$3,000-4,000 **FRE**

A Chinese late Qing Dynasty agate chalcedony table screen and stand, the beveled rectangular insert screen mottled with brown inclusions to a translucent ground, resembling a mist-filled mountainous landscape, supported by a carved and openwork zitan stand.

5.5in (14cm) high

$1,600-2,400 **FRE**

An 18thC Chinese nanmu table screen, openwork tall rectangular panel showing a bamboo tree ascending from rock-work, fitting within a bracket stand.

32in (81cm) high

$2,000-3,000 **FRE**

A late 18thC Chinese fossil stone table screen, the rectangular paneled fish bone pattern fossil stone panel fitted into a finely carved and reticulated hardwood base, pierced rectangular central insert panel and shaped side spandrels, the apron carved with a central character medallion, fu bats and bird-like figures, the rectangular feet are carved in low relief to show Fu bats.

24in (61cm) high

$14,000-20,000 **FRE**

A Chinese Qianlong period root wood reticulated and huanghuali table screen, fitted over a huanghuali base with double lotus supporting arms issuing from a plain frieze framed by four dragon coiled spandrels, raised on scrolling bracket feet.

27in (68.5cm) high

$30,000-40,000 **FRE**

A pair of 20thC Chinese ivory table screens, of typical rectangular form, applied in high relief to show immortals amongst clouds, fine ink work to reverse with inscription.

19in (40cm) high

$3,000-4,000 PAIR **FRE**

CLOSER LOOK: CHINESE SCREEN

The screen features the Eight Immortals or Pa Hsein. They are one of the most popular subjects for decoration in China. The term 'Eight Immortals' is used to represent happiness and the number eight has become lucky thanks to its association with the immortals.

The carved sections of minerals and semi-precious stones used to decorate the screen stand proud of the lacquer ground to give a three-dimensional affect. It is evidence that the screen was a luxury item when it was made.

The screen is in good condition which adds to its desirability.

The combination of auspicious symbols and materials would have had a great resonanace for the screen's makers.

A 19thC Chinese spinach and celadon jade, rose quartz, lapis and coral four-panel screen, Hongmu framed red lacquer ground inlaid with brass, applied with various color jade, quartz, lapis, coral and other minerals to show immortals and female figures among rock work and floral sprays, glazed later, metal hanging hooks surmounting panels.

79in (200.5cm) high

$20,000-30,000   FRE

A 19thC Chinese eight-panel screen, set with forty two blue and white porcelain panels, depicting figures in various pursuits in rocky landscapes, some damages and repairs.

57in (145cm) wide

$9,000-11,000   WW

A Chinese wallpaper-on-wood paneled screen, comprising twelve panels, decorated with ducks and carp in a pond surrounded by blossoming trees and flying birds, the lower section undecorated.

128.75in (327cm) wide

$4,000-6,000   L&T

A 19thC eight-panel coromandel black lacquer screen, one side with figures in the pursuit of leisure, lotus flowers and egrets on the other.

84in (213.5cm) high

$4,000-6,000   FRE

THE FURNITURE MARKET

The market for antique furniture continues to improve thanks to a number of factors. Quality furniture is being seen as a suitable alternative to investing in shares, property or gold for many people who are tired of or disillusioned with these traditional investments. And, on the whole, furniture has seen a steady increase in value over the last ten years. High-end furniture has been an excellent investment. Television programmes about antiques, and books such as *Miller's Antiques Price Guide,* have educated buyers about the importance of looking for quality as well as original condition, provenance and fine patina. Consequently, today's buyers are far more discerning about what they buy than many of their predecessors were twenty years ago.

A major influence on the market for antique furniture is the effect of foreign buyers who are taking advantage of the weak dollar to buy in the US at prices the local market is unwilling to afford. This is particularly true of furniture that originally came to the US from continental Europe. This area could provide a good opportunity for investment.

Early American William and Mary and Queen Anne furniture has seen strong collecting interest. Pieces with provenance are particularly sought after. This is particularly true when provenance is combined with excellent quality and rarity as was seen when the Shelley Collection was sold in 2007.

Values for 18thC furniture, while not at the height they were eighteen years ago, are slowly picking up and these pieces can work well in today's more minimal interiors. Oak in particular has seen a resurgence. On the East Coast traditional Chippendale, Federal and Empire furniture is still in vogue and for the right piece the sky's the limit. Meanwhile, prices for provincial copies of these styles of furniture, are fairly static as supply is able to keep up with demand. On the West Coast and in areas such as Texas and Florida, high-end signed French furniture with Rococo gilt bronze mounts remains popular.

Mid to late 19thC middle-range furniture is struggling. But again any piece at the high end, with good provenance, signed, with good patination and in original condition will fetch a premium. Aesthetic taste or Eastlake-style furniture, for which there is a high level of demand, continually out-strips expectations.

This is an excellent time to buy, particularly good quality middle range furniture. When the market picks up, prices seem set to rise.

An early 19thC ash and fruitwood comb-back Windsor armchair, with two-piece horseshoe-shaped arms and D-shaped seat on turned legs.

$800-1,200 WW

A painted ash, oak and pine Windsor armchair, repair.

c1800

$2,000-2,400 DN

A set of six early 19thC ash and elm Windsor armchairs, the spindle-filled hoop backs with pierced splats above saddle seats, on ring-turned and splayed tapering legs.

$10,000-12,000 SET L&T

A harlequin set of four early 19thC Windsor low-back armchairs, in ash, fruitwood and elm, three with crinoline stretchers.

$2,400-3,000 WW

An early 19thC fruitwood wheel-back Windsor armchair, with an elm seat, old worm.

$800-1,200 WW

A pair of mid-19thC ash, beech and elm high wheel-back Windsor armchairs, each arched back with central pierced vase splat above the crescent arm rail, above the dished solid seat on baluster-turned tapering legs, and an H-shaped stretcher, damage, lacking part.

$1,000-1,400 DN

FURNITURE

A Victorian yew wood Windsor chair, raised on turned legs united by a crinoline stretcher.

$2,000-2,400   **L&T**

A Victorian yew wood Windsor chair, of typical form, united by a crinoline stretcher.

$2,200-2,600   **L&T**

A Victorian yew wood Windsor chair, raised on turned legs united by a crinoline stretcher.

$2,000-2,400   **L&T**

A late 17thC turned maple great chair, the ball-and-ring-turned finials over a three-slat back, and rattan seat supported by turned legs joined by double box stretcher.

$1,600-2,400   **POOK**

A mid-18thC oak child's high chair, damage, repair.

c1750

$1,600-2,000   **DN**

An early 19thC George III primitive ash armchair, the back with chamfered uprights and scalloped central rail, solid seat with splayed feet.

48in (122cm) high

$20,000-30,000   **SOTH**

A mid-19thC ash, oak and elm child's high chair, the square back with triple-spindle splat above a pair of turned arms with baluster terminals, centered by a woven seat on turned and square-section legs with peripheral stretchers.

14.5in (37cm) wide

$1,200-1,600   **DN**

A harlequin set of four ash and fruitwood spindle-back side chairs, with rush seats.

$500-600 SET   **WW**

A Boston William & Mary crook-back maple armchair, the arched crest over an upholstered back and seat flanked by molded and scrolled arms with voluted hand holds and baluster supports resting on turned and blocked front legs terminating in Spanish feet joined by ball- and ring-turned medial stretcher and square side stretchers, from the Shelley Collection.

$20,000-30,000   POOK

A late 17thC Massachusetts turned maple great chair, the back with three slats flanked by sausage- and ring-turned stretchers, retaining remnants of an old Spanish brown surface, from the Shelley Collection.

$8,000-10,000   POOK

A Southeastern Pennsylvania William & Mary walnut wainscot armchair, with a pierced and scalloped crest, raised panel back flanked by downward sloping arms and turned blocked legs joined by baluster- and ring-turned medial stretch and double side stretchers, from the Shelley Collection.
c1720

$40,000-60,000   POOK

A Pennsylvania walnut wainscot armchair, with recessed tombstone panel back, with ring-turned and block-front legs, joined by baluster- and ring-turned medial stretcher and square side stretchers, from the Shelley Collection.
c1720

$25,000-30,000   POOK

A Pennsylvania walnut wainscot armchair, with straight crest and three-slat back, flanked by scalloped arms, supported by square molded-edge legs joined by stretchers, from the Shelley Collection.

c1720

$21,000-25,000   POOK

A Philadelphia Queen Anne walnut armchair, with scalloped crest, the molded arms with scrolled handholds, the legs joined by a baluster and ring medial stretcher, ending in Spanish feet.

c1730

$18,000-22,000   POOK

A walnut wainscot armchair, the crest with diamond inlays, above a raised panel with line inlays, with turned and blocked legs joined by baluster- and ring-turned medial stretcher, retaining an old black surface, from the Shelley Collection.
c1720

$110,000-130,000   POOK

A Pennsylvania walnut wainscot armchair, with scalloped crest and raised panel back flanked by scrolled plank arms with baluster-turned supports above a plank seat resting of turned and block front legs, joined by a baluster- and ring-turned stretcher, from the Shelley Collection.
c1720

$28,000-32,000   POOK

A Pennsylvania walnut wainscot armchair, flanked by bold square arms with rolled handholds, with blocked and turned legs with bobbin- and ring-turned stretchers.

This chair, with its straight back and overall proportions, reflects the Philadelphia interpretation of the Cromwellian armchair.
c1725   43in (109cm) high

$90,000-110,000   POOK

A Southeastern Pennsylvania William & Mary wainscot armchair, with arched and scalloped crest, raised panel back and downward sloping arms supported by blocked and turned legs, joined by baluster- and ring-turned front stretcher and square side stretchers, retaining an old mellow patina, from the Shelley Collection.

c1725

$25,000-30,000   POOK

A Pennsylvania transitional William & Mary walnut armchair, the arched crest rail over a solid splat and scrolled arms above a plank seat supported by turned and blocked legs terminating in Spanish feet and joined by baluster- and ring-turned stretcher, from the Shelley Collection.

c1735

$10,000-15,000   POOK

A Queen Anne Bermudan cedar corner chair, with two pierced and fluted splats above a slip seat resting in a scalloped frame, supported by front cabriole leg with lambriquin knee terminating in trifid foot, from the Shelley Collection.

c1750

$4,500-6,500   POOK

A Pennsylvania, possibly Lancaster County, Queen Anne walnut armchair, with an upholstered back and seat, massive downward sloping arms with baluster supports, scalloped seat frame, and cabriole front legs terminating in crooked feet, retaining desirable old dark finish, the back and arms with evidence of tack holes of the original upholstery.

c1750

$45,000-50,000   POOK

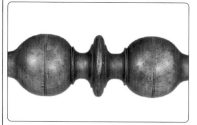

A maple armchair, attributed to the workshop of William Savery or Solomon Fussell, Philadelphia, the five-splat back flanked by scrolled arms with baluster supports over a rush seat with applied scalloped skirts, supported by cabriole front legs terminating in crooked feet and joined by boldly turned ball- and ring-turned stretcher, from the Shelley Collection.

c1750

$120,000-140,000   POOK

A late 18thC Massachusetts Chippendale grain-painted roundabout chair, old surface, minor imperfections.

31.25in (79.5cm) high

$17,000-20,000   SK

A walnut wainscot side chair, with pierced and scalloped crest, above a paneled back and plank seat supported by blocked and turned front legs joined, from the Shelley Collection.

c1720

$6,500-7,500   POOK

CLOSER LOOK: QUEEN ANNE ARMCHAIR

The cupid's bow crest, with projecting molded ears, and vasiform splat suggest the chair was made during the transition of the Queen Anne and Chippendale styles.

The breadth of this chair, as well as the outward serpentine scrolled arms, crooked feet and plain rear legs are typical of Philadelphia chairs of this period.

The chair has a desirable old mellow patina.

The rush seat has an applied scalloped skirt.

The cabriole front legs are joined by massive ball-turned stretcher.

A Philadelphia Queen Anne Savery-type tiger maple armchair.

c1750

$35,000-40,000   POOK

A Pennsylvania walnut wainscot side chair, with a pierced and scalloped crest above four molded slats, over a plank seat supported by turned and blocked front legs, joined by baluster- and ball-turned front stretcher and double square side stretchers, from the Shelley Collection.

c1730

$15,000-20,000   POOK

A set of six Queen Anne walnut chairs, probably from Virginia, with yoked back and shaped split solid seats, two inscribed 'T. Smith', many old repairs and reinforcements.

These chairs were on exhibition for many years at the Mitchie Tavern Museum, Charlottesville, Virginia.

c1740

$25,000-30,000   FRE

Left:
A Philadelphia Queen Anne figured maple side chair, attributed to William Savery, with cupid's bow crest and vasiform splat, over a period rush seat with scalloped skirt supported by chamfered cabriole front legs joined by boldly turned medial stretcher, terminating in crooked feet, retaining an excellent old dry surface.

c1745

$25,000-35,000   POOK

Right:
A Philadelphia Queen Anne maple side chair, attributed to William Savery, with cupid's bow crest and vasiform splat, over a period rush seat, with applied scalloped skirts supported by chamfered cabriole front legs joined by a bulbous medial stretcher, terminating in crooked feet.

c1745

$10,000-15,000   POOK

A Philadelphia Queen Anne walnut dining chair, the scrolled crest over a solid splat and compass slip seat supported by shell-carved cabriole legs with voluted returns, terminating in drake feet.

c1750

$7,500-9,500   POOK

FURNITURE

A Delaware Valley maple and pine banister-back side chair, the carved arch crest over a star punched back and rush seat, supported by double stretchers, from the Shelley Collection.

Another chair from the same set, purportedly belonging to John Gill I, founder of Haddonfield, New Jersey, is in the Newark Museum.
c1710

$65,000-85,000   **POOK**

A Pennsylvania William & Mary banister-back armchair, with an arched and curved crest rail with punched star decoration, bold outward scrolling arms, rush seat, with turned legs joined by baluster- and ring-turned medial stretcher, from the Shelley Collection.
c1720

$20,000-25,000   **POOK**

A pair of Delaware Valley banister-back side chairs.
c1720

$100,000-150,000   **POOK**

49.5in (125.5cm) high

POOK

CLOSER LOOK: LADDER-BACK ARMCHAIR

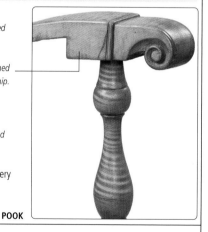

The six arched slats tend to be thinner on 18thC chairs than on earlier examples. The posts have extended to create the back legs and are topped by turned finials .

The scrolled arms terminate in volute-carved handholds with baluster-turned supports, suggesting a high standard of craftsmanship.

The rush seat has an applied scalloped skirt.

The chamfered cabriole front legs terminate in crooked feet and are joined by bold ball- and ring-turned front stretcher.

A tiger maple ladder-back armchair, attributed to the Fuller-Savery School, Pennsylvania.
c1750

$500,000+   **POOK**

A set of four Pennsylvania ladder-back side chairs, with four-slat back and turned medial stretcher, retaining old dry surface, from the Shelley Collection.
c1760

$10,000-15,000   **POOK**

An important Delaware Valley ladder-back armchair, the slat back over a rush seat supported by turned legs joined by a bold medial stretcher, retaining an excellent early blue painted surface.
c1760

$50,000-80,000   **POOK**

ESSENTIAL REFERENCE: SHAKER

The Shakers were a Christian group formed in mid-18thC Lancashire, England. Under the leadership of Ann Lee, known as Mother Ann, a small group immigrated to America in 1774.

- Shaker brothers and sisters were celibate and practised separation from the world, pacifism, the confession of sin, and communal ownership of property. Women were seen as equal to men. The Shakers' emphasis on simplicity, harmony and perfection within the community led to the development of a distinctive arts and crafts tradition.
- Shaker furniture tended to be devoid of decoration and had to fit its purpose. Designs were based on the simple forms of 18thC design, such as the ladder-back chair.
- The Shakers used traditional construction techniques, such as mortise-and-tenon joints that were pegged, nailed, or dovetailed. As making furniture was seen as another way of praising God, the level of craftsmanship was extremely high. Wood was smoothly finished and no tool marks were left on the finished pieces.
- Furniture was sometimes painted or stained red, red-brown, yellow, or dark blue.
- The Shakers also sold their surplus products to people outside their communities. They reached the height of their ministry in the mid-1800s.

A Shaker brown-stained birch armed rocking chair, from Enfield, New Hampshire, with graduated arched slats, and vase-turned supports on shaped rockers, original surface.

c1840   47in (119.5cm) high

$13,000-15,000   **SK**

Two late 19th/early 20thC Shaker number 7 ladder-back rush seat rocking chairs, with bar back, four arched slats, and one with mushroom finial on shaped arms.

$800-1,200   **FRE**

A Newport, Rhode Island maple and hickory high-back windsor armchair, with shaped concave crest, and D-shaped saddle seat, old refinish, imperfections and restoration.

c1760-70   44.75in (113.5cm) high

$4,000-5,000   **SK**

A Lancaster County, Pennsylvania sack-back windsor armchair, with rare tall bow back, knuckled arms, and baluster-turned legs, retains an old dark brown varnished surface, from the Shelley Collection.

c1770

$9,000-11,000   **POOK**

A fan-back windsor side chair, Lancaster County, Pennsylvania, with blunt arrow feet, the chair retaining a green surface with yellow pinstriping, from the Shelley Collection.

c1770

$6,000-8,000   **POOK**

A Philadelphia sack-back windsor armchair, the outward-flaring arms with knuckle handholds, with blunt arrow feet, retaining an exceptional early ochre surface, from the Shelley Collection.

c1770

$25,000-30,000   **POOK**

A pair of painted sack-back windsor chairs, attributed to Francis Trumble, Philadelphia, Pennsylvania, old red-painted surface over earlier yellow and original black, very minor repair.

c1775   37.75in (96cm) high

$20,000-25,000   **SK**

An 18thC windsor fan-back side chair, Rhode Island or Eastern Connecticut, the concave serpentine crest rail with scroll-carved terminals, original Spanish brown-painted surface.

35in (89cm) high

$8,000-10,000   **SK**

A pair of late 18thC brown-painted windsor side chairs, possibly Rhode Island, original surface, minor imperfections.

38in (96.5cm) high

$5,500-7,500   **SK**

A late 18thC New England paint-decorated sack-back windsor chair, on vase- and ring-turned supports, with turned up legs joined by swelled stretchers, 19thC century yellow-painted surface with red pinstriping and black bands.

36in (91.5cm) high

$10,000-15,000   **SK**

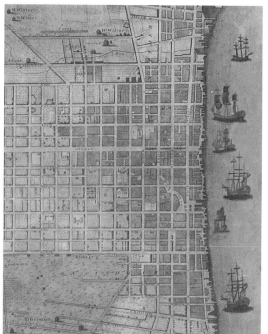

A New York continuous arm brace-back windsor chair, bearing the stamp of Matthias Bloom, retaining an old black surface.

c1790

$1,000-1,500   **POOK**

PROVENANCE: Typed note on seat underside 'Red Windsor Arm chair-Given to B.C. and E.M. Tilghman by Emily R. Cheston in 1916.' The chair may have originally been part of the furnishings of the Fisher family home, Wakefield, in Germantown.

c1800   *44in (112cm) high*

$35,000-40,000   **FRE**

A Pennsylvania red-painted bamboo turned windsor armchair, with four spindles to the crest nine spindles, turned posts, shaped seat, turned legs and H-stretchers old red-painted finish.

A late 18thC Lancaster County, Pennsylvania grain-painted and carved fan-back windsor side chair, old surface, 19thC paint over earlier colors, minor imperfections.

35in (89cm) high

$3,500-4,500   **SK**

One of two late 18thC Philadelphia sack-back windsor armchairs, each with carved hand-holds over seat, and baluster-turned and tapering legs.

$900-1,100 TWO   **FRE**

A Baltimore writing arm windsor chair, retaining an old gray/brown surface, stamped 'Jacob Daley'.

c1807-1820

$700-1,000   **POOK**

A set of four early 19thC Pennsylvania bow-back windsor side chairs, each with a seven-spindle back and splayed bamboo legs, retaining an old varnish surface.

$4,000-5,000   **POOK**

A pair of early 18thC William & Mary fruitwood mortised benches, each with baluster- and ring-turned splayed legs, from the Shelley Collection.

97.5in (247.5cm) long

$5,000-6,000   **POOK**

A Philadelphia William & Mary walnut settle bench, the back with straight crest rail and five raised panels, above downward sloping arms and paneled ends, supported by straight square front legs terminating in ball feet.

c1740

$100,000-150,000   **POOK**

A mid- to late 18thC Delaware Valley painted pine settle, the back with ten raised panels over a deep seat flanked by lollipop arms resting on a cut-out base, retaining its original blue surface, from the Shelley Collection.

75in (190.5cm) wide

$32,000-38,000   **POOK**

A bow-back windsor settee and three bow-back windsor chairs, by James Always and Joseph Hampton, New York City, with bowed crest rail, and branded 'J ALWA HMO'.

1795-96   *83in (211cm) wide*

$12,000-18,000 SET   **SK**

An early 19thC green painted and stenciled arrow-back windsor settee, with a flat crestrail with black and gold linear decoraton and matching seat, on turned legs with stretchers.

72in (183cm) long

$1,200-1,800   **FRE**

An early 19thC painted pine bench, the top with molded front edge over a dramatically scalloped skirt supported by boot jack legs, retaining an exceptional red and black grain decorated surface.

80.5in (204.5cm) long

$10,000-15,000   **POOK**

FURNITURE

A Queen Anne walnut chair, the cartouche-shaped back and seat covered with 18thC textile.

c1710

$3,000-4,000   DN

An early 18thC walnut chair, later banding.

c1720

$600-1,000   DN

A pair of George I walnut side chairs, the burr-veneered vase-shape splat backs with bell-shape needlework drop-in seats on shell-carved cabriole legs to pad feet, old restoration.

$5,000-7,000   WW

A pair of George II walnut and beech side chairs, each with vasiform-shaped and banded splat and leaf-carved top rail above a drop-in seat, raised on shell-carved cabriole legs ending in pad feet.

c1730   20in (51cm) wide

$3,000-4,000   FRE

A George II walnut chair, on shell-carved legs and carved claw-and-ball feet.

c1735

$600-800   DN

A George II walnut chair, repair, later elements.

c1740

$600-1,000   DN

An early 20thC George I style set of fifteen dining chairs, and a matched pair of armchairs.

$12,000-16,000 SET   DN

A pair of late 19th/early 20thC George II style mahogany hall chairs.

$1,000-1,400   DN

A pair of George III mahogany side chairs, the shaped top rail above a carved splat, the stuffed-over serpentine front seat above molded and chamfered front legs with pierced brackets, the legs united by a stretcher, old restorations and replacements.

$4,000-5,000   WW

A George III mahogany chair, the shaped top rail above a Gothic arch pierced splint and drop-in seat, raised on cabriole legs with trefoil feet.

$1,200-1,800   L&T

A Philadelphia Chippendale walnut side chair, with yoke crest rail with center shell and carved volutes, pierced urn-shaped splat, slip seat straight front rail with carved shell to center, on shell-carved cabriole legs and claw-and-ball feet.

c1750

$10,000-15,000   **FRE**

Three Philadelphia Queen Anne walnut side chairs, each with serpentine crestrail and center shell rolled volutes, pierced vase splat, shell-carved cabriole legs and pad feet.

PROVENANCE: A hand written note attached to one chair reads ' This chair and the two like it belonged to Andrew Forsythe, my Great-grandfather, and came to me through my father, Andrew F. Russel, are genuine Chippendale and came from England, and are to her knowledge 160 years old and how much older we do not know – Nov. 1904 Danville, Pa. Helen M. Russel.'

c1755

$20,000-25,000   **FRE**

A pair of North Carolina or Virginia carved mahogany side chairs, with vigorously shaped crests, pierced splats and frontal cabriole legs with C-scrolls in outline at the arch above the carved claw-and-ball feet, rear raking feet include platforms, old refinish.

c1760   40.5in (103cm) high

$13,000-15,000   **SK**

A Philadelphia Chippendale walnut dining chair, the shell-carved crest over a pierced splat and trapezoidal slip seat supported by shell-carved cabriole legs terminating in claw-and-ball feet.

c1765

$3,000-4,000   **POOK**

A pair of New York Chippendale mahogany side chairs, each with serpentine crestrail above a pierced splat, molded trapezoidal seat rail, and cabriole legs carved with elongated shells.

c1770   39in (99cm) high

$8,000-12,000   **FRE**

A late 18thC Chippendale birch carved side chair, possibly New Hampshire, the serpentine molded crest rail centering carved leafage against a punched background continuing to scrolled terminals, on raking molded styles and a pierced scroll carved gothic splat, on trapezoidal slip seat and molded Marlborough legs with pierced brackets and molded square stretchers, old surface.

37.5in (95.5cm) high

$4,500-5,500   **SK**

A Boston Chippendale carved mahogany side chair, with serpentine crest and a central carved ornament, over-upholstered seat and front square legs with rope-carved beading.

A similar example has been identified as follows: 'this Marlborough leg chair is one of five in institutional collections from an original set that probably numbered eight chairs and was owned by the wealthy Quincy family of Boston. Josiah Quincy, Jr., and his bride Abigail Phillips acquired the chairs in 1769 for their Short Street residence. In 1806, thirty years after Quincy's death, the chairs were moved to the family homestead at Braintree, where they furnished the east and west parlors in 1880'.

1760-75   38in (96.5cm) high

$2,500-3,500   **SK**

CLOSER LOOK: A SET OF GEORGE III DINING CHAIRS

The shield-shaped backs, with pierced splats decorated with a vase of flowers, were probably inspired by George Hepplewhite's The Cabinet-Maker and Upholsterer's Guide (1788).

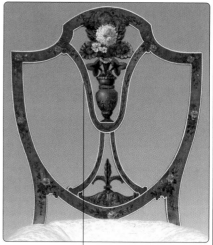

Sets of chairs became popular from the mid 18thC onwards.

Square tapered legs are typical of Hepplewhite's designs.

The shield-shaped backrests feature a splat painted with a flower-filled urn, surrounded by foliate trails.

A set of eight George III satinwood and painted dining chairs, comprising two armchairs and six sidechairs.

c1790

50in (19.75cm) wide

$40,000-60,000   **FRE**

A set of six George III mahogany and hide upholstered dining chairs, on shell-carved cabriole front legs and outswept rear legs, on pad feet.

$7,000-9,000 SET   **L&T**

A set of sixteen George III mahogany dining chairs, to include an armchair.
c1790

$14,000-20,000 SET   **DN**

A set of eight George III mahogany dining chairs, each with an X-shaped splat, stuffed-over leather seat and square tapering legs, including two elbow chairs, faults and repairs.
c1790

$3,000-4,000 SET   **DN**

A set of six George III mahogany dining chairs, the arched top rail on pierced and waisted splat with fluted base, drop-in seat in blue tapestry covering, raised on square tapering legs joined by stretchers.

$4,400-5,000   **HT**

A set of seven George III mahogany chairs, including an elbow chair, with arched top rail over pierced and waisted splat with heart to base, drop-in seats and floral needlework covering, on square tapering legs joined by stretchers.

$800-1,200 SET   **HT**

A set of seven late George III mahogany dining chairs, to include an armchair, each molded rectangular back with triple vertical bar splats, above a bow-fronted seat on molded square-section tapering legs, repair.
c1810

$2,400-3,600 SET   **DN**

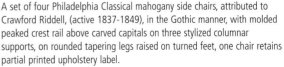

A set of three Rhode Island Federal carved mahogany side chairs, old surface, one with replaced crest.
c1795   *39in (99cm) high*
$50,000-60,000 SET   **SK**

A Boston Federal carved and inlaid mahogany shield-back side chair, old surface, minor imperfections.
c1800   *37.5in (95.5cm) high*
$15,000-20,000   **SK**

A set of four Philadelphia Classical mahogany side chairs, attributed to Crawford Riddell, (active 1837-1849), in the Gothic manner, with molded peaked crest rail above carved capitals on three stylized columnar supports, on rounded tapering legs raised on turned feet, one chair retains partial printed upholstery label.
33in (84cm) high
$10,000-15,000   **FRE**

A pair of paint-decorated side chairs, attributed to Samuel Gragg, Boston, Massachusetts, white-painted surface with polychrome and gilt seashell, rope-twist and foliate designs.

Label on underside of seat reads 'Beal.' Beal of Boston was a known retailer of Gragg chairs.
c1825   *35.5in (90cm) high*
$5,000-6,000   **SK**

A pair of early 19thC Baltimore Federal painted and decorated cane-seat side chairs, slightly curved flat crest rail centering a hand-painted landscape enclosed by shaped reserves above three vertical shaped spindles decorated with bellflowers and rose, serpentine seat on turned legs with turned frontal stretcher painted with rose, gilt and cream paint on green-blue.
$10,000-15,000   **FRE**

A set of six Pennsylvania grain-painted and stenciled side chairs, the yoked crest and shaped splat on plank seat, with turned legs, stenciled and hand-decorated with Classical devices.
c1830
$5,000-7,000 SET   **FRE**

Four Pennsylvania yellow-painted and stenciled side chairs, with scrolled crest rail and shaped splat decorated with fruit and flowers, on a plank seat and turned legs.
c1840
$1,500-2,000   **FRE**

A set of six stencil- and paint-decorated 'UNION' balloon-back side chairs, probably from Pennsylvania, with shaped crests and seats on splayed legs, some restoration.
c1840-60   *33.5in (85cm) high*
$1,500-2,500   **SK**

A set of six figured maple gothic chairs, with shaped crest, three gothic arches, tapering spindles and cane seat.
c1835
$2,000-3,000 SET   **FRE**

A set of seven George III mahogany dining chairs, to include one armchair.
c1810

$1,600-2,400 SET   **DN**

A set of eight early 20thC George II style mahogany dining chairs, the broad backs carved with rosettes and leaves, centered by pierced vase-shaped splats, on square-section legs and H-stretchers.

25.25in (64cm) wide

$3,400-4,000 SET   **DN**

A set of eight 19thC mahogany hoop-back dining chairs, the husk carved top rails above pierced splats centered by leaf-carved rosettes, above serpentine floral woolwork drop-in seats on molded square tapering legs, including two carvers with bold acanthus carved outscrolling arms.

$8,000-12,000 SET   **L&T**

A set of eight 19thC mahogany Gothic Chippendale dining chairs, the yolk-shaped top rails above relief-carved splats decorated with ogee tracery, on molded square-section legs, the two armchairs with outscrolling leaf-carved terminals.

$16,000-24,000 SET   **L&T**

A set of twelve late 19thC mahogany dining chairs, in the Sheraton manner, the rectangular backs with leaf-carved crestings and triple spar splats above close-nailed hide stuff-over seats, on molded tapering legs with spade feet, including two carvers.

$12,000-16,000 SET   **L&T**

A set of eight late 19thC Chippendale Revival dining chairs, the yolk-shaped top rails carved with leaf scrolls above Gothic pierced splats and drop-in bow-front seats, on square-section legs united by stretchers, including two carvers.

$3,000-4,000 SET   **L&T**

A set of twelve late 19thC mahogany hoop-back dining chairs, in the Hepplewhite taste, with pierced wheatsheaf splats above drop-in seats on square tapering legs united by stretchers, the pair of carvers of a later date.

$10,000-12,000 SET   **L&T**

A set of twelve Chippendale style mahogany dining chairs, the serpentine top rails above pierced splats decorated with quatrefoils and drop-in seats, on cabriole legs ending in claw-and-ball feet.

$4,000-6,000 SET   **L&T**

A set of ten George III style mahogany dining chairs, comprising two armchairs and eight side chairs, the carved and pierced backrest above a drop-in seat raised on straight legs.

38in (96.5cm) high

$4,000-6,000 SET   **FRE**

A set of six early 19thC Regency mahogany side chairs, each with inlaid and reeded tablet crest rail and reeded support enclosed by reeded stiles with rosette ears, trapezoidal green horse-hair-covered seats, reeded seat rail and legs ending in spade feet, rear legs canted.

$10,000-12,000   **FRE**

A set of eight William IV sabicu dining chairs, possibly Anglo-Indian, the volute-carved bar backs above scroll-and-rosette-carved middle rails and drop-in seats, on lappet-carved and reeded tapering legs, including two carvers.

Sabicu wood or sabicu has a rich mahogany color. It is fairly heavy, hard and durable, and was selected for the stairs of the Great Exhibition of London in 1851.

$11,000-13,000 SET   **L&T**

A set of ten late 19thC Regency-style mahogany dining chairs, with foliate carved splats, overupholstered seats and fluted legs

$5,000-7,000 SET   **POOK**

ESSENTIAL REFERENCE: THONET

Michael Thonet (1796-1871) is well known for his revolutionary bentwood chairs.

- Thonet perfected his steam-bending process in 1842. Once softened with steam or boiling water, the wood could be molded into almost any shape with the aid of a press. Beech was particularly suitable. This technique meant that furniture could be constructed from far fewer component parts and did away with dovetails or joints as the pieces could be held together with simple screws and nuts.
- In 1853, Thonet set up his own furniture company, Gebrüder Thonet, with his five sons. Within 20 years, it had offices in London and New York and, by the end of the 19thC, Gebrüder Thonet was operating more than 50 factories. The company had soon gained a reputation for innovation and contemporary design, which it maintained throughout the 20thC.
- From as early as the 1850s, Thonet produced furniture that could be packed flat for shipping and then assembled at its destination. The incredibly successful 'Number 14' chair was designed in 1859 and 50 million were sold by 1930. The No. 14 epitomised Thonet's brand of functional furniture for the masses rather than furniture as a signifier of wealth.
- The firm is still active today.

A set of six Austrian Thonet bentwood dining chairs, with scrolling backs, upholstered seats and conforming legs and under stretcher, each stamped 'Thonet'.

$800-1,200 SET   **DUK**

A set of eight mid-/late 19thC French mahogany dining chairs, with ormolu-mounted crest and seat rail on square tapering legs.

$4,000-5,000 SET   **POOK**

A set of nineteen Victorian oak dining chairs, in the 'Gothic' style, the baluster-turned padded backs and overstuffed seats, raised on turned tapered legs carved with flower-head motifs and ending in ceramic casters.

Some chairs are signed below the seat rails by an upholsterer for 'J. & T. Scott of Edinburgh'.

$18,000-24,000 SET   **L&T**

A set of four Victorian mahogany balloon-back dining chairs, with leaf-carved back above serpentine overstuffed seats upon turned front supports.

$100-140 SET   **ROS**

A set of six Victorian mahogany dining chairs.

c1870

$1,100-1,500 SET   **DN**

A set of eight 19thC Portuguese Rococo style dining chairs, comprising two armchairs and six sidechairs, each with shield-shaped backrest with a shell-carved toprail above a padded seat, raised on cabriole legs, carved at the knees with acanthus leaves and centered by a shell, ending in claw-and ball-feet.

Armchair 49.25in (117.5cm) high

$5,000-7,000 SET   **FRE**

A set of eight late 19thC Victorian oak and leather upholstered dining chairs, including two armchairs.

$2,400-3,000 SET   **DN**

FURNITURE

A pair of 19thC Louis XV style carved beech chairs.

$500-700   DN

A pair of Charles II walnut hall chairs, the arched and carved top over the caned backrest and seat, raised on scrolling legs united by a pierced and carved stretcher.

50in (127cm) high

$2,800-3,600   FRE

A pair of Moravian walnut chairs, each with heart cutout backs, plank seats and splayed legs, together with similar oak example.

c1750

$1,000-1,400   POOK

A George IV mahogany hall chair, in the manner of Gillows, the heavily carved shell back to a tapering seat on ribbed tapering legs.

$900-1,100   WW

A pair of William IV mahogany hall chairs.

c1835

$1,400-1,800   DN

HALL CHAIRS

Introduced in Britain from the 17thC, hall chairs were designed to be placed in the entrance hall where they would be used by tradesmen and tenants waiting to be called into one of the main rooms.

- Hall chairs are rarely upholstered and usually lack arms.
- They are of sturdy construction.
- Hall chairs were also symbols of social status and were therefore increasingly made of mahogany, with solid backs and dished or shaped seats. Designs were bold and simple and were frequently embellished with the painted crest or coat of arms of the family who commissioned them.
- Thomas Chippendale, George Hepplewhite and Thomas Sheraton all included designs for hall chairs in their design books.

CLOSER LOOK: PAIR OF HALL CHAIRS

Derived from the Graeco-Roman vocabulary of architecture and ornament, C-shaped scrolls were a popular Neoclassical motif, and thus often appeared in Regency designs. Here, a pair of out-facing C-scrolls 'support' a larger, reeded scroll that terminates in stylized flowerheads.

Characteristically, the back legs of these chairs are in plain saber form, while the front legs are turned and embellished with tapered reeding – a form of convex molding particularly fashionable in the early 19thC.

Originating in Europe during the 12thC, heraldic decoration provided a visual means of representing the position and status of an individual, a family, or an organisation in society. Polychrome-painted and set in recessed roundels, the crests of these chairs are no longer attributable but, in the form of a hand holding aloft a scroll, probably indicate the owner's involvement in politics or the law.

A pair of Regency or George IV carved mahogany hall chairs, in the manner of Gillows.

c1820

$4,400-5,200   DN

An oak stool or side table, the rectangular top above a fluted and castellated frieze, above baluster-turned legs with peripheral stretchers and turned feet, the top probably later associated, damage, repair.

c1680   30.75in (78cm) wide

$2,600-3,200   DN

A George II elm stool, possibly a milking stool.

c1750   7.75in (20cm) high

$300-500   DN

A late 17thC style oak joined stool, with a molded edge rectangular top to a shaped and molded frieze, the block and turned legs with peripheral stretchers.

15.25in (38.5cm) wide

$900-1,100   WW

A 19th/20thC oak longstool, in mid-17thC style, the rectangular seat above a shaped frieze on baluster-turned and carved legs, joined by peripheral stretchers, damage.

48.5in (123cm) wide

$1,100-1,500   DN

A 19th/20thC Charles II style joined oak stool.

$300-500   DN

A late 18thC George III white painted hall stool, pierced saddle-shaped seat with a fluted frieze, on conforming square tapering legs, surmounted by scroll carving, painted decoration refreshed.

This stool was almost certainly made by Robert Child (d.1782) for Osterley Park House, Middlesex, England. This painted stool with its fluted frieze and legs capped by scroll pilasters is designed in the 'Roman' manner introduced and popularized by the court architect of King George III, Sir William Chambers and Robert Adam in the 1760s.

21.25in (54cm) wide

$32,000-40,000   SOTH

A George III mahogany framed stool, the rectangular seat above four carved cabriole legs on pad feet, damage, repair.

c1760   22.5in (57cm) wide

$800-1,200   DN

A Louis XVI painted stool, the padded seat covered in ivory damask, over a bellflower-carved frieze raised on turned tapered leaf-carved legs.

$2,600-3,000   L&T

A black painted and parcel-gilt stool in George III style, the needlework seat depicting floral garlands.

49.25in (125cm) wide

$800-1,200   DN

An unusual late 18thC Chinese Export stool, the rectangular framed caned seat of slight concave form, above four delicate cabriole legs terminating in pad feet.

18.5in (47cm) wide

$1,000-1,400   FRE

FURNITURE

ESSENTIAL REFERENCE: GILLOWS

Gillows of Lancaster (est. c1730) designed and made a vast quantity of furniture for the nobility, the gentry, and the newly emerging middle classes.

- Most 18thC Gillows furniture was made in the Neoclassical style, without decoration. Such pieces followed the designs of George Hepplewhite and Thomas Sheraton.
- After c1770, the furniture had an austerity reflecting that of contemporary architecture.
- Writing, library and dressing furniture often had hidden compartments and ingenious arrangements of small drawers.
- Gillows has always produced high quality furniture for the domestic and export markets and the firm is still active today.

A pair of Regency cross-framed stools, attributed to Gillows of Lancaster, the button-upholstered silk seats above scrolling X-frame legs with roundel patera terminals and central bosses, on ball feet united by pole stretchers, one stool of very slightly larger dimensions.

Largest: 21.75in (55cm) wide

$8,000-10,000　　　**L&T**

A large George IV rosewood upholstered stool, the drop-in seat above a molded rounded frieze on reeded turned and tapered legs.

30.25in (77cm) wide

$3,000-4,000　　　**L&T**

An early Victorian rosewood footstool.

c1840

$300-500　　　**DN**

A Southern European painted and upholstered stool, the rectangular top covered in close-nailed embossed leather, on carved blue-and-gilt-painted cabriole legs and scrolled feet, joined by an X-stretcher.

23in (58cm) wide

$1,600-2,000　　　**L&T**

A Victorian period carved giltwood stool, the rectangular overstuffed seat covered in brightly colored geometric needlework, above a paneled frieze and raised on spiral turned tapered legs.

32.75in (83cm) wide

$1,200-1,600　　　**L&T**

A pair of Victorian period rosewood stools, with blue suede upholstered drop-in seats, raised on C-scroll X-form supports and joined by turned stretchers.

18in (46cm) wide

$6,000-8,000　　　**L&T**

A mid-19thC mahogany adjustable piano stool.

$400-500　　　**DN**

A pair of Victorian period rosewood and upholstered stools, with blue suede upholstery, the circular drop-in seats within parcel-gilt-molded surrounds on triple scroll supports and molded cabriole legs with pad feet, undersides bear makers labels, 'W Constantine & Co., Leeds'.

19.75in (50cm) diam

$7,000-9,000　　　**L&T**

A mid-Victorian rectangular stool, the floral needlework-covered seat with braiding above a cream and gilt gesso base decorated with shells, scrolls and foliage, having a serpentine frieze and cabriole legs.

37in (94cm) wide

$1,600-2,000　　　**WW**

A matching pair of Victorian giltwood rectangular stools, upholstered in a colored striped material to cabochon frieze and cabriole legs with leaf carving.

24in (61cm) wide

$3,000-4,000 WW

CLOSER LOOK: SHELL-SHAPED STOOL

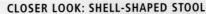

The 19thC saw a growing interest in fanciful furniture such as this stool, as well as the increasing use of mechanisms such as the one used here to raise and lower the seat.

The stool has been decorated with good, strong, deep carving.

The wood has an attractive color and shows excellent patination.

The carved paw feet have highly defined claws – proof that it is a quality piece.

A 19thC French carved walnut adjustable stool, in the form of an open shell, raised on a central lobed column containing a threaded mechanism, and three cabriole legs with carved paw feet.

c1860 *23.75in (60cm) high*

$5,000-7,000 RGA

A pair of 19thC Louis XV style giltwood banquettes, each with a tapestry-upholstered seat and foliate-carved, voluted armrests, leaf-carved rails, raised cabriole legs ending in scrolled toes.

78in (198cm) wide

$12,000-16,000 FRE

A rare 17thC oak child's box chair, of hexagonal design, the raised plank back with pierced strapwork cresting and pierced corner frets around a painted hexafoil medallion, the uprights slotted to receive a tray table, the interior formerly with a plank seat above a foot warming pan below, the front door on butterfly hinges with clasp and staple catch, clasp missing.

This intriguing and practical design allows a child little movement and affords safety. The tray has a simple self-securing action. This example shows Scots and Scandinavian influences.

34.5in (88cm) high

$10,000-12,000 L&T

A 20thC George III style carved mahogany framed window seat, the shaped seat flanked by scrollover arms, above a fluted and patera-carved frieze on square-section cabriole legs and tapering feet.

39.5in (100cm) wide

$1,000-1,400 DN

A Regency mahogany high chair, the shaped back with scrolling top rail, caned back and seat with restraining bar, on turned and octagonal legs on turned X-form stretcher, the legs with an adjustable foot rest, on a conforming base.

37in (94cm) high

$1,200-1,600 DUK

A Regency mahogany metamorphic library steps armchair, the bar back above a lion mask carved leaf-carved middle rail and downswept underscrolled arms with roundel bosses on ball supports, on front saber legs with molded tapering feet and splayed rear legs, a threaded screw releasing four internally hinged treads, the whole decorated with ebony lines.

$7,000-9,000 L&T

FURNITURE

A 17thC Dutch walnut Baroque armchair, with floral leather upholstery.

45in (114cm) high

$4,000-5,000   SOTA

A pair of 17thC style Northern European carved walnut high-back armchairs, with rectangular padded backrest and seat, the armrests with leaf-carved handholds, raised on turned and barley-twist supports, joined by stretchers, raised on bun feet.

25.25in (64cm) wide

$2,000-3,000   FRE

A pair of late 17th/early 18thC Italian walnut and parcel gilt armchairs, damage.

27.5in (70cm) wide Est

$4,000-5,000   DN

A walnut armchair, with later elements.

c1700   *24in (61cm) wide*

$1,000-1,200   DN

A matched pair of 19thC Moroccan walnut 'Savonarola' armchairs, each decorated with mosaic bone inlay in the Damascus taste, the shaped back rails with vignettes of ladies in the 17thC costume, composed of bone and cut metal, the slatted arms above solid seats, on downswept slatted cross-frame legs.

37.75in (96cm) high

$4,000-6,000   L&T

A George II probably Irish mahogany open armchair, the caddy-molded back with a serpentine top rail above a bold acanthus-carved ribband splat and padded outscrolling arms with rosette and trailing acanthus leaf-carved terminals, the close-nailed stuffover seat on leaf-carved cabriole legs with acorn pendants, ending in claw-and-ball feet.

$7,000-8,000   L&T

A pair of George III style simulated bamboo cock-pen armchairs of recent manufacture, each rectangular back above a pair of conforming arms, the upholstered square seats on turned tapering legs and stretchers.

$700-900   DN

A pair of 20thC George III style carved mahogany elbow chairs, each shaped square back with pierced ladder splats, above a pair of serpentine shaped arms and dished square seats, on molded square-section legs and H-shaped stretchers.

$1,200-1,600   DN

A mahogany elbow chair.

c1780 and later

$1,100-1,500   DN

A George III carved mahogany elbow chair, and a side chair of similar design after Sheraton, damage, repair.

c1790

$400-500 THE TWO   DN

A George III fruitwood corner armchair, the scroll arms above pierced vase-shaped splats with turned supports to a drop-in seat in square chamfered legs united by peripheral stretchers.

$800-1,200 WW

A George III mahogany library bergère armchair.

c1810

23.75in (60cm) wide

$2,400-3,000 DN

A George III oak and elm armchair.

c1810

$360-440 DN

CLOSER LOOK: QUEEN ANNE CHAIR

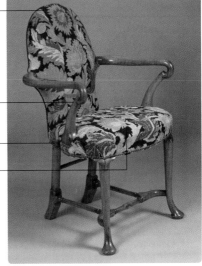

The shaped spade back has an arched top. This chair is upholstered with contemporary gros point polychrome needlework.

The walnut of the tightly furled shepherd's crook arms, the legs and the stretchers is all of a beautiful patinated mellow color.

The back legs have squared toes joined to the front legs by turned stretchers.

The rounded seat is raised upon turned legs with tobacco leaf-carved knees terminating in outswept pad feet to the front.

An English Queen Anne walnut open armchair with contemporary needlework.

c1710

24in (61cm) wide

$170,000+ PAR

An 18thC walnut Régence armchair, the padded armrest carved with leaves, the seat rail carved with a scallop, with embroidered upholstery, on cabriole legs.

42.25in (107.5cm) high

$4,000-6,000 SOTA

A walnut armchair, some damage, repair.

c1720

27.5in (70cm) wide

$6,000-7,000 DN

An early 18thC probably Spanish carved walnut armchair, with shaped padded back, down-scrolled arms, rectangular padded seat on turned and block legs joined by stretchers, with light brown velvet upholstery.

$2,000-3,000 SOTA

A pair of mid-18thC Continental mahogany open armchairs, the foliate carved arms are outward scrolling, on fully carved cabriole legs terminating in scroll feet.

$5,000-7,000 POOK

A fine George II period mahogany open-arm chair, with deep carving to the front cabriole legs and arm supports.

c1755

37in (94cm) high

$100,000-110,000 BLY

A pair of George III mahogany framed 'Gainsborough' armchairs, the rectangular backs with serpentine crestings above out-scrolling padded arms with acanthus scroll-carved in-swept terminals and stuff-over seats, on square tapering sunken field molded legs ending in block feet and united by chamfered H-stretchers, upholstered in close-nailed yellow damask.

31.5in (80cm) wide

$70,000-80,000   L&T

A pair of George III mahogany library armchairs, with an upholstered back and seat, raised on square legs united by straight stretchers one now raised on brass casters, the whole carved with blind fretwork.

c1775   27in (68.5cm) wide

$14,000-20,000   FRE

A 'French Chippendale' style carved mahogany framed fauteuil, the back of serpentine-arched cartouche-shaped outline above outscrolling padded arms with leaf and cabochon-carved terminals, the arm supports swept into the seat rails, the front apron with florets flanking rocaille, on cabriole rear and front legs embellished with foliage and ending in stiff acanthus scroll feet, the whole in close-nailed burgundy velvet upholstery.

$4,000-6,000   L&T

A George III giltwood and upholstered armchair, the oval back, padded open arms and seat covered in patterned cream silk, the leaf-carved downswept molded arms above a bowed front rail and tapered fluted leg, re-gilded.

$3,000-4,000   L&T

An 18thC walnut fauteuil, in the French Hepplewhite taste, the rounded rectangular back above padded outscrolling arms and molded serpentine seat rail, on molded cabriole legs ending in tapered feet.

$6,000-10,000   L&T

A set of four 18thC 'French Hepplewhite' painted walnut fauteuils, the cartouche-shaped backs with floret crestings, the serpentine seats with floral-carved front rails, on molded and shell-carved tapering cabriole legs on tapering feet, overpainted in ivory and green.

$8,000-12,000 SET   L&T

A pair of French Louis XVI-style beech fauteuils, the oval backs lead to cushioned elbow rests, scrolling reeded arms, paterae-capped leg shoulders, over reeded column front legs, not upholstered.

c1800   38in (96.5cm) high

$2,000-4,000   FRE

A mid-18thC Irish style library armchair, the arm supports carved as scaly beasts with a concave seat rail, carved scrolling foliage on acanthus-capped cabriole legs with dolphin feet.

$3,000-4,000   WW

An Empire style gilt-bronze-mounted mahogany fauteuil de bureau, the curved backrest with a lyre-form splat above a leather-upholstered seat, raised on square tapered legs headed by female busts and ending in paw feet.

24.25in (62.25cm) wide

$3,000-4,000   FRE

A pair of Regency period simulated rosewood open armchairs, the overscrolled bar backs decorated with anthemia above volute scroll middle rails and reeded underscrolled arms, the split cane upholstered seats with buff leather squabs and reeded rails, on reeded saber legs.

$3,200-4,000   L&T

A Regency mahogany Grecian style library chair, in the manner of Gillows of Lancaster, the arched wraparound back of 'cut-away' design, the cresting boldly carved with Neoclassical leaf scrolls above volute carved 'hips', with short turned and reeded legs.

$5,000-7,000   L&T

An Empire mahogany armchair, by Jacob Freres,with reeded volute scroll-carved top rail, the downswept spreading arms with reeded lotus-carved shoulders and terminals, the similarly carved legs tapering to carved paw feet headed by anthemia and rosettes, the front seat rail stamped verso 'JACOB FRERES. R. MESLEE'.

$10,000-14,000   L&T

A William IV rosewood armchair, button-upholstered in pale green damask covering, arched back, padded open arms with scroll ends on shaped supports, overstuffed seat, leaf-carved turned legs with brass toes and casters.

c1835

$600-800   HT

A William IV mahogany library bergère armchair, faults.

c1835

$1,600-2,000   DN

An Anglo-Indian carved ebony armchair, the rectangular back with stylized shell-carved pediment, above reeded downswept arms, with foliate-carved terminals, above a profusely carved frieze, turned tapering and lappet-carved legs, damaged, repair.

c1840

$2,000-2,400   DN

A mid-19thC Anglo-Indian carved ebony easy chair, from Galle District, Ceylon, the caned scroll back with a foliate-carved crest rail, over scroll open arms, raised on shell-carved saber legs ending in claw-and-ball feet.

$6,000-10,000   L&T

A rare Black Forest carved oak rocking chair, decorated to resemble tree root, covered in antique hide with brass studding.

c1860

$23,000-28,000   RGA

A 19thC mahogany 'Gainsborough' armchair, in the Chippendale taste, elaborately carved with leaf scrolls, on four cabriole legs bearing cabochon motifs, the front knees descending to tightly scrolled feet.

c1870

$13,000-17,000   RGA

A pair of unusual Renaissance style carved walnut armchairs, each with a padded back and seat, the leaf-carved armrests continuing to handholds modeled as heads of Native American chiefs, raised on leaf-carved, in-curved legs, joined by an H-stretcher and ending in paw feet.

26.75in (68cm) wide

$4,000-6,000   FRE

A 19thC polished steel R. W. Winfield & Co. patent rocking chair, Birmingham, England, the rectangular back above downswept arms forming the rocking base, with black hide slung seat and padded arms, the crossrails secured by bronze nuts.

25.75in (62cm) wide

$2,000-3,000   L&T

FURNITURE

A late 19thC oak framed Orkney chair, faults.

$1,600-2,400   **DN**

A pair of late 19th/early 20thC George III style black-painted and parcel gilt armchairs, damage, repair, some recent painting.

$1,400-1,800   **DN**

UPHOLSTERED ARMCHAIRS

A Charles II walnut or beech wing armchair, upholstered in red velvet with applied needlework fragments, raised on carved scrolling legs.

c1685   27in (68.5cm) wide

$8,000-12,000   **FRE**

A George II mahogany and upholstered wing armchair.

c1750

$6,000-8,000   **DN**

An American Queen Anne mahogany upholstered easy chair, signed 'N Bowen', Marblehead, Massachusetts, the serpentine crest above shaped sides and outward-scrolling arms with concave fronts tapering to the straight seat frame resting on frontal cabriole legs with conforming knee returns, joined to the raking chamfered rear legs by block, vase and ring-turned stretchers, very minor imperfections.

c1755   50in (127cm) high

$30,000-40,000   **SK**

A George III mahogany easy chair, the serpentine crest over scrolled arms supported by square molded legs,

c1770

$4,000-6,000   **POOK**

A George III mahogany wing armchair, damage, repair.

c1780   32.25in (82cm) wide

$1,600-2,000   **DN**

A 19thC Louis XV style giltwood and painted 'bergère a oreillies', upholstered in 18thC Aubusson tapestry, the arched foliate-carved top rail above a padded back and loose cushion seat, the front seat rail carve to match, raised on leaf-carved cabriole legs ending in scrolling toes.

30in (76cm) wide

$3,000-4,000   **FRE**

A pair of George III style mahogany and upholstered wing armchairs, covered in stylized blue heraldic pattern fabric, raised on square tapered legs terminating brass cappings and casters.

$3,200-4,000   **L&T**

A late 19th/early 20thC Louis XV style carved giltwood and composition highback wing armchair, the frame decorated throughout with carved acanthus and scroll motifs, the rectangular wing back above a pair of downswept arms with scroll terminals, the seat on cabriole legs and scroll feet.

31.75in (81cm) wide

$1,400-2,000 DN

A Louis XVI style mahogany and gilt-bronze mounted swivel desk chair by Francois Linke, the arched back, padded scroll arms and loose cushion seat covered in yellow fabric, raised on turned fluted legs, headed by paterae and terminating in toupie feet, underside stamped 'F. Linke' in two places.

c1900 *24.5in (62.25cm) wide*

$6,000-8,000 FRE

A late 19th/early 20thC green buttoned leather-upholstered tub shaped armchair.

$1,000-1,400 DN

A late 19th/early 20thC George II style studded leather-covered tub armchair.

36.75in (119cm) high

$3,000-4,000 DN

An early 20thC George III style mahogany and red leather-upholstered wing armchair.

$3,000-4,000 DN

A walnut and upholstered armchair, stamped 'Howard & Sons', on baluster-turned tapering legs at the front, on later casters of recent manufacture, on rear leg stamped 'Howard & Sons Limited, Berners St'.

c1800 and later *31.5in (80cm) wide*

$6,000-7,000 DN

A Regency mahogany library bergère, upholstered in buttoned red leather, the seat frame resupported.

c1820

$24,000-30,000 SOTH

A Regency mahogany and leather-upholstered tub armchair, the rectangular back, out-scrolled arms and seat covered in close nailed button upholstered green leather, chaneled arm ends and seat rail, with circular bosses on ring-turned tapering legs with brass caps and casters.

$7,000-9,000 L&T

A William IV mahogany framed and button-upholstered hide patent 'self-acting' library wing armchair, by George Minter of London, the back with adjustable 'rake' action, the seat with adjustable 'pitch' and an apron fitted with an integral sliding footrest, on a cantilever action, the legs stamped 'G. MINTER,55 GERRARD STREET SOHO VR PATENT 2007'.

George Minter is listed as a cabinet-maker, undertaker, bath chair and wheelchair maker working from various addresses in London, England, from the 1820s to the 1850s.

44in (111cm) high

$7,000-9,000 L&T

ESSENTIAL REFERENCE: BIEDERMEIER

- The main period of production was between c1805 and 1850.
- Biedermeier furniture was simple, Classical, and functional.
- Biedermeier was essentially a middle-class style, though it was also used in the private areas of noble houses. It placed emphasis on practicality and comfort. Furniture was, therefore, moderate in size, round in shape, comfortable and homely.
- It employed straight lines and lacked decorative carvings. Classical motifs were often used for decoration. However, the most important decorative feature was the grain of the wood, which was then emphasized with various pyramidal and fountain-like shapes. The most fashionable woods were mahogany and less costly local woods like walnut, cherry, pear, birch and ash.
- Upholstery was generally flat and square, made of silk or horsehair.
- By the mid-19thC, the style had begun to seem dowdy. It was at this time that it was given the name 'Biedermeier': a satirical term meaning 'the decent common man'. The style continued to decline in popularity until the beginning of the 20thC when it once again became much sought after and widely copied.

A pair of mid-19thC Biedermeier mahogany love seats, with straight crests, brass finials and animal paw feet on a plinth base.

38.5in (151.5cm) wide

$1,400-2,000　　　　**POOK**

A Biedermeier satin birch wing armchair, upholstered in green and cream-striped floral tapestry covering, button-upholstered back, padded arms with scroll ends on shaped supports, overstuffed seats and splayed legs.

$900-1,100　　　　**HT**

A late 19thC French mahogany-framed bergère, in the Empire taste, the arms with anthemion details on Egyptianesque caryatid supports tapering to saber legs on carved paw feet.

$900-1,100　　　　**L&T**

A pair of mid-20thC Victorian style Kelim upholstered armchairs, in the manner of Howard & Sons, raised on ebonized turned tapered legs ending in casters.

$3,000-4,000　　　　**L&T**

A matched pair of late 20thC George III style mahogany-framed wing armchairs, each arched rectangular back above overscrolling arms, on molded square-section legs and stretchers.

32.25in (82cm) wide

$1,100-1,300　　　　**DN**

SETTLES, SETTEES AND SOFAS

An 18thC and later oak box seat settle, the carved top rail over four portrait-carved fielded panels above a lunette-carved back rail, between leaf-carved tapering uprights and open arms above a plank seat with sliding central well, over a long lunette-carved landscape panel to the front, between stile-end supports.

4.5in (126cm) wide

$5,000-6,000　　　　**HALL**

A pair of 19thC William and Mary style stained walnut framed and upholstered settees, on ribbed inverted baluster legs with corrugated blocks united by pierced serpentine cross stretchers with leaf-carved boss finials, on bun feet.

55in (140cm) wide

$7,000-9,000　　　　**L&T**

CLOSER LOOK: CHIPPENDALE SOFA

The design of this sofa is derived from an example in the third edition of Chippendale's 'The Gentleman and Cabinet-Maker's Director'.

The design of Chippendale's 'French' chairs, such as these, was ingeniously adapted to suit his clients by the subtle use of carved ornament, adapted to suit the decor of the room in which they were to be placed.

The various elements of the design and carving of this sofa, with its serpentine mahogany frame carved with Rococo motifs, bear particular similarities to a suite (including a pair of sofas) supplied by Thomas Chippendale to the Earl of Dumfries for Dumfries House in 1759.

The eight cabriole legs have acanthus-carved terminals and scroll toes.

A George III carved mahogany sofa, in the manner of Thomas Chippendale, with serpentine back, seat and scroll arms, legs damaged and repaired, lacking scroll toes to outer back legs, elements of frame later.

It is possible that this sofa was part of a commission given to Chippendale by Sir Robert Burdett for Ramsbury Manor in Wiltshire.
c1770
83.5in (212cm) wide
$80,000-100,000 DN

A George III Chippendale mahogany sofa, with an arched back, outward flaring arms, serpentine front seat rail, and square molded legs joined by stretchers.
c1780 90in (228.5cm) wide
$10,000-12,000 POOK

A late 18thC Continental, possibly Italian, giltwood chaise longue, with a shell-carved curved back and footrest and loose cushion seat, raised on square tapered legs, carved with guilloche and carved at the knees with acanthus and shells.
86in (218.5cm) wide
$6,000-8,000 FRE

A George III carved giltwood sofa, with faults, wear and surface chipping.
c1780 73in (185cm) wide
$5,000-7,000 DN

A suite of Louis XVI giltwood seat furniture, comprising a pair of bergères and four 'fauteuils a la reine', raised on round tapered fluted, leaf-carved legs, the bergères stamped 'I. B. LELARGE'
c1780
$40,000-60,000 FRE

A Neoclassical Italian carved giltwood serpentine wallbench, raised on tapering, leaf-motif legs with scrolled acanthus heads and ball feet, the seat has a serpentine profile, with a frieze with florette-centered tablets within swags of husks,
c1785
$24,000-32,000 PAR

A George III mahogany camel-back settee, the padded back and out-scrolled padded arms raised on blind fretwork carved legs, ending in casters.
26in (66cm) wide
$4,000-6,000 FRE

A 19thC George III style mahogany camel-back settee.
36.5in (93cm) high
$6,000-8,000 L&T

A George III style upholstered and mahogany settee, the arched back, outscrolled arms and cushioned seat covered in rose check fabric, on shell and scroll-carved cabriole legs with pad feet.
77in (195cm) wide
$7,000-9,000 L&T

An 18thC Chippendale mahogany sofa, the serpentine back with outscrolled arms raised on six legs joined by straight stretchers.

72in (183cm) long

$4,000-5,000　　　　　　　　**FRE**

A Maryland Federal mahogany sofa, the sloping crest with central pediment, flanked by molded arms with knuckled hand holds, retaining period under-upholstery.

c1805,　　　　　　*81in (206cm) long*

$3,000-4,000　　　　　　　　**POOK**

A Classical maple carved, paint and gilt-decorated recamier, probably from New York, with open scrolled sides, rush slip seat, and original faux tiger maple surface.

1805-15　　　　　　*32in (81.5cm) high*

$5,000-6,000　　　　　　　　**SK**

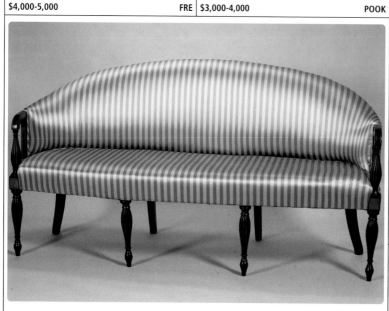

A Federal mahogany carved and inlaid settee, signed 'J Short,' Newburyport, Massachusetts, the arched back continuing to downward-sloping sides and scrolled handholds inlaid with interrupted-line stringing on vase and ring-turned reeded supports, above satinwood panels bordered by checkered banding, all resting on frontal vase and ring-turned reeded legs, and flaring, raking rear legs, refinished, minor restoration.

c1813　　　　　　*71in (180.5cm) wide*

$10,000-15,000　　　　　　　　**SK**

A Classical carved mahogany ormolu-mounted sofa, probably from Baltimore, retains fragments of printed paper label inscribed 'Baker / Baltimore..' and chalk inscription on right arm, 'EL.'

c1815　　　　　　*79in (200.5cm) wide*

$2,000-4,000　　　　　　　　**FRE**

A Classical carved mahogany recamier, with scrolled and carved back rail, on leaf-carved feet ending in brass caps on casters.

c1820　　　　　　*74in (188cm) long*

$2,500-3,500　　　　　　　　**FRE**

An early 19thC New York Classical carved mahogany sofa, with carved supports, reeded shaped seat rail and reeded tapering legs on casters, restoration, crest rail detached.

$5,000-6,000　　　　　　　　**FRE**

A Classical carved mahogany sofa, the arched crest rail above scrolled fruit and cornucopia carved arms, molded seat rail and feather and hairy paw feet.

c1825　　　　　　*75in (190.5cm) long*

$1,500-2,500　　　　　　　　**FRE**

A Philadelphia Classical carved mahogany sofa, rolled cresting with leaf-carved scrolled ends, the arm supports carved with cornucopia above feather-, scroll- and paw-carved feet.

c1825

$1,200-1,800　　　　　　　　**FRE**

CLOSER LOOK: GERMAN EMPIRE SOFA

A rare German Empire sofa, based on designs by Karl Friedrich Schinkel, Berlin, solidly constructed and carved from beechwood and decorated with Neoclassical motifs.

Karl Friedrich Schinkel (1781-1841) was a prominent Prussian architect who worked predominantly in the Neoclassical style.

He was influenced by Greek rather than Imperial Roman architecture - possibly as a reaction to its link to the recent French occupiers.

Later, Schinkel embraced the Neo-Gothic style. The Bauakademie (English Building Academy) he built in Berlin, is considered a forerunner of modern architecture due to its use of red brick and the relatively streamlined facade of the building. By ignoring historical conventions, the building - which has since been demolished - was a forerunner of the clean-lined 'modernist' architecture that would become prominent in Germany early in the 20th century.

Schinkel also designed the Iron Cross medal of Prussia, and later Germany.

c1825

$30,000-40,000

The corners are formed by columns rising from lancette-shaped leaves and topped by spheres.

The seat a deux corps and backrest are upholstered and covered in golden colored silk fabric worked in blue with a wreath of laurel incorporating an urn.

The sides are formed by winged and horned lions above circular medallions of laurel incorporating a lyre with eagle-headed finials.

The back is lightly curved and centered by a wreath of laurel incorporating musical instruments, the rectangular border formed by acanthus incorporating tambours.

53in (134cm) wide

SOTA

An early 19thC Regency brass-inlaid simulated rosewood window seat, with deeply reeded saber legs and S-scroll-armed seat frame.

c1815

$20,000-28,000 PAR

A Regency mahogany framed 'Grecian' couch, the serpentine volute-carved top rail with gadrooned cresting and outscrolling acanthus carved arms, the molded seat rail on turned and lappet-carved legs ending in brass socket casters.

88.5in (225cm) wide

$2,000-3,000 L&T

An early 19thC Empire mahogany and parcel gilt sofa.

92.5in (235cm) wide

$3,600-4,400 DN

One of a pair of Regency rosewood couches with a shaped show-wood back with scrolled and lobed crest, the outswept scrolling arms decorated with acanthus leaf carving, standing on molded saber legs ending in well-chased casters.

In the 18th and early 19thC the Classical designs borrowed from the ancient world were incorporated into all elements of buildings, furnishings and decoration. The obvious influences of ancient Rome and Greece can be seen in this sofa and the theme would undoubtedly have been carried through into the side chairs and open armchairs that would have been commissioned at the same time. Such seating furniture would have been placed in the formal drawing rooms of the period to show the owner's standing and their understanding of the Neoclassical taste. The size of such formal rooms would require suites of seating furniture to be positioned in symmetry to complete the ordered aesthetics of the Georgian period.

c1820.

34in (86cm) high

$70,000-80,000 PAIR RGA

A George IV mahogany-framed sofa, the shaped rectangular back flanked by scroll arms, above the rectangular seat on saber legs gilt-brass lion-paw caps and casters, damage.

c1825   80in (203cm) wide
$900-1,300   DN

A pair of late Regency mahogany framed chaise longues, in the manner of Gillows of Lancaster, each with an arched and padded lotus scroll-carved three-quarter arm above a seat with carved acroteriae and squab cushion, on short gadrooned and reeded tapering legs with brass socket casters, upholstered in ivory silk damask with bolster cushions.

73.25in (186cm) wide
$9,000-13,000 PAIR   L&T

A William IV carved mahogany and upholstered sofa, with foliate-carved armrests.

c1830   82.25in (209cm) wide
$1,200-1,600   DN

A William IV mahogany settee, leaf-carved wavy top rail, above a padded back and loose cushion seat, the armrest upon turned supports, raised on bulbous lobed legs, ending in casters.

c1835   60in (152.5cm) wide
$2,400-3,600   FRE

A William IV rosewood sofa.

c1835   89.25in (227cm) wide
$6,000-7,000   DN

A William IV carved mahogany sofa, in the manner of Williams and Gibton.

88.5in (225cm) wide
$1,200-1,600   DN

A William IV, probably Anglo-Indian, carved rosewood day bed.

c1835
$2,000-3,000

77.5in (197cm) wide
DN

A 19thC mahogany and gilt-metal-mounted salon suite, in the Empire taste, comprising a pair of canapes, with downswept arms with rosette terminals, on winged sphinx caryatid supports, on turned legs with anthemion-cast mounts and gilt-metal feet, with four armchairs.

Canapes 55in (140cm) wide
$16,000-20,000   L&T

CLOSER LOOK: PAINTED SETTEE

The three lyre splats are a typical Federal feature.

The scrolled seat features grapevine panels on an ivory ground.

The turned legs are joined by flat leaf-decorated stretchers.

The crest is decorated with a panoramic landscape, with the sun rising over rolling, wooded hills.

A mid-19thC painted settee, attributed to William F. Snyder, Mifflintown Chair Works, Juniata, Pennsylvania, inscribed 'A.B. Hart' on underside.

74.25in (188.5cm) wide

$130,000-150,000 **POOK**

A Philadelphia late Federal mahogany sofa, the gadrooned crest with hound head ears, above foliate-carved arms and reeded apron supported by animal paw feet.

c1830

$3,000-5,000 **POOK**

A Philadelphia Classical carved mahogany sofa, the bar-turned crest with leaf-carved ends, outscrolled arms with rosettes and acanthus and fruit-carved facings, cornucopia and leaf-carved legs with hairy paw feet.

c1825 *89in (226cm) long*

$1,500-2,500 **FRE**

A Philadelphia Classical mahogany sofa, with elaborate foliate and rosette carvings, and animal paw feet.

c1835 *78in (198cm) wide*

$1,200-1,800 **POOK**

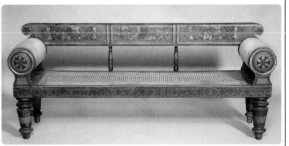

A Baltimore, Maryland painted and decorated classical settee, with gilt, green and orange leafage, and simulated ormolu mounts above the rolled, upholstered arms.

c1840 *31in (79cm) high*

$9,000-12,000 **SK**

A 17thC oak 'credence' or folding table, the semi-circular folding top over an overlapping lunette and foliate-carved frieze, with central short frieze drawer between canted sides on heavy front corner ring-turned supports, with matching slender supports to the back corners and conforming single gate to the back, over a single plank shelf stretcher, above a shaped apron on heavy block feet.

The term 'credence table' is thought to come from the Italian credenza as these tables may have been used as serving boards. The best early oak tables feature fine quality carving and deep color and should have been well preserved.

36.5in (92.5cm) wide

$16,000-24,000   **HALL**

A 17thC oak drop leaf refectory table in the Flemish taste, the flanked top with pull-out leaves at either end and above a chaneled frieze with central fluted table, with gadrooned and under bulb-turned legs headed by tablets and fluted capitals on bun feet.

111in (282cm) wide (extended)

$3,600-4,400   **L&T**

A late 17thC oak refectory dining table, the rectangular top composed of four well-figured planks with cleated ends, the frieze with shaped corner frets enclosing a pair of frieze drawers with turned handles, on square-section legs with chamfered corners united by stretchers.

64.5in (164cm) wide

$3,200-3,600   **L&T**

A fruitwood and oak rectory table, the top 16th/early 17thC, the base of 20thC construction, the triple plank top with cleated ends, the base with X-frame trestle legs, damage, repair.

124.5in (316cm) wide

$6,000-10,000   **DN**

An early 18thC Italian walnut refectory table, some damage.

89in (226cm) long

$6,000-8,000   **DN**

A 19thC French walnut refectory table, the rounded rectangular plank top on associate molded square legs and sloping bar feet joined by a bar stretcher.

89.5in (227cm) long

$3,400-4,000   **L&T**

An early 19thC American New England pine sawbuck table, with rectangular top over X-supports, retaining old red wash surface.

94in (239cm) long

$7,000-9,000   **POOK**

A late 19th/early 20thC oak draw-leaf refectory table, in 17thC style, the rectangular top above carved cup and cover legs headed by lion mask terminals, above an H-shaped stretcher and block feet.

83.5in (212cm) wide

$4,000-6,000   **DN**

A Boston William & Mary birch, maple and painted pine tavern table, the rectangular molded edge top over a frame with single drawer supported by blocked and turned legs joined by high and low baluster- and ring-turned stretchers, retaining an old painted black surface, from the Shelley Collection.

c1730

$32,000-38,000 POOK

A Pennsylvania walnut tavern table, the oval top above a frame with single drawer supported by baluster-turned and blocked legs joined by H-stretcher, retaining an old mellow surface, from the Shelley Collection.

c1740 36.25in (92cm) diam

$25,000-30,000 POOK

A Pennsylvania walnut tavern table, having a molded top with single molded lip drawer, over pronounced scrolled front apron, all resting on baluster-turned and blocked legs with molded stretchers, from the Shelley Collection.

c1745 31in (78.5cm) wide

$10,000-15,000 POOK

A Chester County, Pennsylvania, William & Mary walnut tavern table, the rectangular top overhanging a base with single drawer with line and berry inlay, above a scalloped apron with double inlaid turned legs joined by boldly turned outside stretchers, from the Shelley Collection.

c1750 33in (84cm) wide

$20,000-25,000 POOK

A Pennsylvania walnut tavern table, the oval top above a frame with single drawer supported by baluster legs joined by box stretchers, from the Shelley Collection.

c1750 31.75in (80.5cm) wide

$5,000-8,000 POOK

A mid-18thC New England Queen Anne maple and pine tavern table, the rectangular overhanging top with breadboard ends on a straight skirt with drawer, with block-, vase-, and ring-turned tapering legs ending in pad feet, old surface, imperfections.

46in (117cm) wide

$4,000-5,000 SK

A Queen Anne painted pine and oak tavern table, possibly Delaware, with an oblong top and baluster-turned legs joined by turned stretchers, retaining its original blue-gray painted surface.

c1750 22.75in (58cm) wide

$33,000-38,000 POOK

A Pennsylvania walnut tavern table, the molded-edge battened lift top overhanging a base with two drawers, the left inlaid '1770', an elaborate scalloped skirt supported by baluster-turned legs joined by square stretchers, from the Shelley Collection.

43.75in (111cm) wide

$22,000-28,000 POOK

FURNITURE

A late 17thC oak gateleg oval table, with bobbin-turned legs and stretchers.

$700-900   DN

A late 17thC Charles II oak gateleg table, the oval top with drop leaves, raised on turned legs united by stretchers.

39in (99cm) wide

$500-900   FRE

An early 18thC oak gateleg table, the oval top above end frieze drawers with shaped aprons, on turned baluster and block legs united by peripheral stretchers.

54in (137cm) wide

$2,400-3,600   WW

PEDESTAL TABLES

A Regency mahogany and satinwood crossbanded breakfast table, the top with snap-over action above a plain spreading column on outswept reeded legs ending in plain brass caps and casters.

64in (163cm) wide

$2,000-3,000   L&T

A Regency mahogany and satinwood crossbanded rectangular breakfast table.

c1820   *63.75in (162cm) wide*

$1,300-1,500   DN

A Regency rosewood and satinwood banded breakfast table, damage, repair.

c1820   *28.75in (73cm) high*

$4,000-5,000   DN

A Regency rosewood circular breakfast table, the circular top with marquetry border and bead-molded edge, above the turned stem and shaped plinth issuing four downswept legs, brass lappet cast caps and casters.

c1820

$12,000-16,000

50.5in (74cm) diam

DN

An American New York Federal mahogany breakfast table, with acanthus-carved standard, supported by carved legs, with animal paw feet.

c1825   *26.5in (67.5cm) wide*

$3,000-5,000   POOK

A Regency rosewood circular tip-up-top breakfast table, raised on an octagonal tapering column with triform base and paw feet.

54in (137cm) diam

$2,800-3,200   A&G

A Regency rosewood and brass-strung tilt-top breakfast table, the circular top with gadrooned edge and plain frieze on a stepped and beaded square-section pillar and concave platform base, raised on four saber legs ending in brass paw caps and casters.

53in (134cm) diam

$4,400-5,600   L&T

CLOSER LOOK: GILLOWS TABLE

The quality of Gillows construction is evident in the 'invisible' wavy join to the decorative veneers and the bold execution of the edge and feet moldings.

The burr-figured and quarter-veneered top has an egg and dart molded edge and burr-veneered frieze with molded lip.

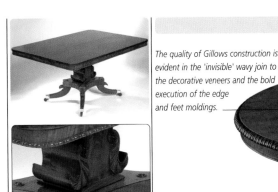

The molded detail on the central pillar is another typical Gillows detail, often encountered on the fold-over and sofa tables made by this firm.

The spreading hexagonal pillar features central gaitered banding with an ogee-molded collar below, and sits on a triform platform base with rounded terminals and gadrooned bun feet with recessed casters.

A late Regency mahogany breakfast table, the rectangular top with beaded edge above a square pilaster flanked by boldly carved and scrolled volutes on quadruped base with reeded scroll-cut saber legs headed by roundels and ending in brass casters.

59.5in (151cm) wide

$3,600-4,400   **L&T**

A late Regency amboyna and rosewood circular tilt-top breakfast table, by Gillows of Lancaster, the base stamped 'GILLOWS' on the upper tenon.

50.5in (128cm) diam

$30,000-40,000   **L&T**

A George IV rosewood circular breakfast table.

c1825   44in (112cm) diam

$1,600-2,400   **DN**

A George IV mahogany breakfast table, the top above a plain frieze and column stem issuing three outswept legs on carved lion paw feet and concealed casters, damage, repair.

c1825   47.25in (120cm) diam

$1,000-1,400   **DN**

A George IV mahogany breakfast table, the rounded rectangular top with a reeded edge, raised on a turned column support and four downswept legs terminating in brass capped casters.

c1820   56in (142cm) wide

$2,000-3,000   **FRE**

A fine George IV circular rosewood tilt-top dining table of excellent figuring, in the manner of Gillows, set on a tapered column with lower carved collar to triform base.

c1825   54in (137cm) wide

$14,000-18,000   **RGA**

A mid-19thC, probably Scottish, mahogany breakfast table.

51in (130cm) diam

$14,000-20,000   **DN**

A William IV circular 'goncalo alves' breakfast table, the circular top above a plain frieze on a turned and lappet-carved stem, issuing three outswept legs, and on scroll-carved gilt casters, damage.

c1835   54.75in (139cm) diam

$5,000-7,000   **DN**

A William IV mahogany circular breakfast table, with faults.

c1835   47.25in (120cm) diam

$1,000-1,400   **DN**

A large Pennsylvania Queen Anne walnut dining table, the shaped skirt supported by cabriole legs terminating in trifid feet.

c1760   *51.25in (130cm) wide*

$9,000-11,000   **POOK**

A Southeastern Pennsylvania William & Mary large walnut gateleg dining table, the oblong top supporting two demilune leaves, above a frame with two drawers and scalloped skirt, supported by baluster- and ring-turned and blocked legs joined by stretchers, retaining an old mellow finish, from the Shelley Collection.

c1730   *59in (150cm) widest*

$70,000-80,000   **POOK**

A Chippendale mahogany dropleaf dining table, the rectangular top over a cutout frame supported by acanthus-carved cabriole legs terminating in hairy paw feet.

c1760   *42in (106.5cm) wide*

$6,000-8,000   **POOK**

A late 18thC New Hampshire or Massachusetts, Queen Anne tiger maple and maple dining table, with dropleaf top, cabriole legs, and pad feet, old refinish.

47.75in (121cm) long

$12,000-14,000   **SK**

A Maryland Federal mahogany three-part dining table, probably Baltimore, each section with oval line inlaid frame supported by square tapering legs with bellflower chain and banded cuffs.

c1795   *46.75in (118.75cm) wide*

$4,000-6,000   **POOK**

A Baltimore, Maryland, Federal two-part mahogany dining table, with reeded edge on conforming skirt and ring-turned and tapering reeded legs.

c1815   *48in (122cm) wide*

$1,500-2,500   **FRE**

A Massachusetts Federal mahogany two-part dining table, each section with a rounded-corner top supported by acanthus-carved capitals.

c1820   *each section 45.25in (115cm) wide*

$1,500-2,500   **POOK**

An early 19thC Baltimore mahogany three-part banquet pedestal base dining table, with reeded edge and turned supports on carved tripod base.

47.75in (121.5cm) wide

$20,000-25,000   **FRE**

A Neoclassical carved mahogany dropleaf table, attributed to Thomas Seymour, Boston, with old surface, imperfections.

c1820   *43.75in (111cm) wide*

$25,000-30,000   **SK**

A Baltimore Sheraton two-part banquet table, with two D-shaped ends with single leaves resting on reeded, turned legs.

c1825   *91.5in (232.5cm) wide*

$2,500-3,500   **POOK**

FURNITURE

A mid-19thC Victorian rosewood oval breakfast table, with molded edge and hinged top, the lobed, baluster stem on four cabriole legs with scrolled feet and casters.

28.75in (73cm) high

$700-900   **DN**

A George III mahogany three-pedestal dining table, comprising a center section and two D-shaped ends, raised on turned standards and ending in saber legs, together with two leaf extensions.

c1800   *81in (206cm) wide open*

$7,000-9,000   **FRE**

A 19thC Regency mahogany twin pedestal dining table, the top with reeded edge and two additional leaves, on baluster supports and downswept reeded tripod bases ending in brass claw caps and casters, with alterations and restorations.

118in (300cm) long

$16,000-20,000   **L&T**

A George III mahogany triple pedestal dining table, with tapered cylindrical pedestals supported by cabriole legs terminating in brass casters, with two leaves.

c1770   *191in (485cm) long*

$50,000-60,000   **POOK**

A Regency period, probably Scottish, mahogany twin pedestal dining table, the rectangular top with molded edge and single leaf, on fly arm supports above a pair of beehive-turned pillars each on a lappet-hipped and reeded downswept quadruped base ending in finely cast brass caps and casters.

67.75in (172cm) wide

$3,200-3,600   **L&T**

A George IV mahogany twin pedestal dining table, with two additional leaf insertions, the rectangular top with rounded corners, each pedestal formed of a turned and reeded stem, the plinth on four hipped and downswept legs, scroll feet and casters.

c1825   *29in (74cm) high*

$4,000-6,000   **DN**

A William IV, possibly Scottish, mahogany three-pedestal dining table, the center pedestal with drop-down leaves and a single drawer at either end flanking D-shaped ends, each raised on acanthus-carved standards, in-curved rectangular platform and carved lion paw feet.

c1835   *97in (246cm) wide open*

$10,000-14,000   **FRE**

A mid-19thC William IV mahogany three-pedestal dining table, each pedestal with baluster-shaped stem, on three down-curved legs on brass casters, together with two additional leaves.

29.25in (74cm) long

$12,000-16,000   **SOTA**

An 18thC and later mahogany twin pedestal dining table, each 'D' end centered by a rectangular central section, with two leaf insertions, adapted, parts associated, repairs.

29in (74cm) high

$2,000-3,000   **DN**

A 20thC George III style mahogany triple pedestal dining table, with two additional leaf insertions.

30.75in (78cm) high

$8,000-12,000   **DN**

A 20thC mahogany triple pedestal dining table.

115.5in (293cm) long

$1,200-1,600   **DN**

DROPLEAF TABLES

A George II mahogany dropleaf dining table, the rounded rectangular top above a plain frieze, raised on turned tapered legs ending in pad feet.

Extended 109.5in (278cm) wide

$2,600-3,000   **L&T**

An early 18thC mahogany dropleaf dining table, formerly part of a larger table.

c1730   *56.75in (144cm) long*

$1,200-1,600   **DN**

A George II mahogany dropleaf dining table, rectangular top incorporating twin hinged flaps, on shell terminals, carved cabriole legs and claw feet.

c1750   *28.25in (72cm) high*

$1,500-$1,900   **DN**

An exceptionally large George III mahogany dropleaf dining table, the well-figured top of substantial gauge (1.25in/ 3cm), above a plain frieze on turned gate-action legs ending in pad feet.

78.75in (200cm) wide

$60,000-80,000   **L&T**

A late 18th/early 19thC mahogany dropleaf dining table, the oval top incorporating two hinged leaves, on square-section legs, damage, and repair.

71in (180cm) wide

$1,500-1,900   **DN**

An early 19thC George III mahogany hunt or 'wake' table, surface marks and wear.

27.5in (70cm) high

$1,000-1,400 DN

A drawleaf dining table, by William Birch, High Wycombe, the square top inlaid with a chequer band, raised above square chamfered legs, linked by crossed stretchers centered by an inlaid rosette.

29.5in (75cm) high

$2,000-2,400 L&T

A 20thC Irish mahogany wake table, the narrow oval dropleaf top with rounded edge above eight molded and chamfered square section legs with double gate action.

84.25in (214cm) wide

$5,000-7,000 L&T

EXTENDING TABLES

A George III mahogany D-end extending dining table, the later crossbanded top incorporating the rectangular central section with two hinged leaves, on square-section tapering leg, damage, repair.

c1800 *89in (226cm) wide*

$2,000-3,000 DN

A Regency mahogany triple section dining table in the manner of Gillows, crossbanded rectangular top with two additional leaves on slender turned and reeded tapering legs.

c1810 *161.5in*
(410cm) extended

$50,000-60,000 SOTH

CLOSER LOOK: EXTENDING DINING TABLE

The brass-mounted scissor frame is stamped 'WILKINSON PATENT LONDON'. This ingenious form of extension allows the table to be reduced as a small foldover side table when not in use. Other leading firms of the period also experimented with this form of action, most notably Gillows of Lancaster.

The top consists of three well-figured full leaves and a narrow half leaf, all with a reeded edge.

The ring-turned tapering baluster legs end in brass socket casters.

A Regency period mahogany patent 'scissor-action' extending dining table, by Wilkinson & Wilkinson of London.

106.75in (271cm) wide

$30,000-36,000 L&T

A Regency mahogany extending dining table, with one leaf insertion, the molded rounded rectangular top above a plain frieze, raised on reeded turned tapered legs terminating in brass cappings and casters.

88.5in (225cm) long

$5,000-6,000 L&T

A Regency extending mahogany dining table, in the manner of Gillows of Lancaster, the rounded rectangular top with reeded edge and two additional leaves on a sliding draw rail extension, the ebony-banded frieze above eight slender ring-turned tapering legs ending in brass socket casters.

99in (242cm) wide

$8,000-12,000 L&T

A late Regency mahogany extending dining table, the rounded rectangular top with three additional leaves above a plain frieze with lipped edge on lotus-turned tapering legs ending in brass socket casters.

117in (297cm) wide

$8,000-10,000　　　　　　　　**L&T**

A late Regency mahogany extending dining table, with repair.

c1820　　　　*107.75in (274cm) long*

$1,600-2,400　　　　　　　　**DN**

A George IV mahogany D-end dining table, the frieze to each end decorated with ebonized stringing, raised on turned tapering legs, complete with two spare leaves.

108in (274cm) long

$4,000-5,000　　　　　　　　**A&G**

A mahogany George IV extending dining table with two additional leaves.

104.25in (265cm) long

$8,000-12,000　　　　　　　　**SOTA**

A William IV mahogany extending dining table, molded edge top including four additional leaves on reeded turned tapering legs, with two detachable central legs.

c1830　　　　*149.5in (380cm) long extended*

$24,000-30,000　　　　　　　　**SOTH**

A Victorian plum pudding mahogany extending dining table, the rectangular top with molded edge above the molded frieze, on lappet-carved and octagonal baluster legs, brass caps and casters, with two additional leaf insertions.

c1840　　*53.5in (136cm) wide unextended*

$6,000-8,000　　　　　　　　**DN**

An early Victorian mahogany extending dining table, the oval top with one leaf.

c1840　　　　*84.75in (215cm) long*

$2,600-3,600　　　　　　　　**DN**

A Victorian mahogany extending dining table, with three additional leaves, faults, repair.

c1840　　*59.5in (151cm) wide unextended*

$4,000-6,000　　　　　　　　**DN**

A large Victorian oak extending dining table, with eight leaf insertions, the rounded rectangular top above a molded and chamfered frieze, raised on turned and faceted baluster legs headed by carved flowerheads and terminating in rope-twist carved 'ankles', with brass-mounted cappings and ceramic casters.

85.5in (551cm) long

$9,000-11,000　　　　　　　　**L&T**

FURNITURE

ESSENTIAL REFERENCE: ROCOCO

By the 1730s, the heavy, symmetrical Baroque style was discarded in favor of the lighter, more colorful Rococo style. This style respected and imitated nature, and favored asymmetry, which allowed a more realistic representation of the disorder of the natural world.

- Forms were embellished with delicate repeating rock and shell patterns (the term Rococo being derived from 'rocaille' meaning rockwork), light grotesques, chinoiseries and scrolls. The S-scroll, derived from the Classical volute, was extremely prominent, as were cartouches made up of multiple S- and C-scrolls. Furniture carved in this style was frequently smothered with gesso and gilding to create lavish works of art.

- The Rococo period was also strongly influenced by the Orient. The practise of japanning furniture (applying a shellac varnish to the surface in an imitation of Japanese lacquer) was widely used in Europe and America.

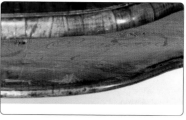

An unusual northern Italian Rococo walnut, olivewood and burlwood console table, probably Lombardy, the shaped quarter-veneered top with rounded fore corners inlaid with a cartouche above a single drawer, raised on cabriole legs with scrolling tops ending in stylized hoof feet, the dust board signed indistinctly 'Sagrind'.

c1750   47.25in (120cm) wide

$40,000-50,000   **FRE**

A pair of Irish George III style pine console tables, formerly with marble tops, the rectangular top over an egg and dart frieze carved with shells and scrolls, raised on cabriole legs ending in claw-and-ball feet.

50.5in (128.5cm) wide

$6,000-8,000   **FRE**

A late Regency mahogany console table, the rectangular top with boldly gadrooned edge and ogee ripple-molded frieze, on volute scroll legs ending in massive carved lion paw feet, united by a shaped shelf stretcher.

42.25in (107cm) wide

$4,000-6,000   **L&T**

A set of two early 19thC and later walnut and carved mahogany console tables, of recent construction, each shaped walnut top above an acanthus-carved scrolling leg.

$600-1,000   **DN**

An Anglo Indian rosewood console table.

c1825   55in (140cm) wide

$4,000-5,000   **DN**

A William IV rosewood, giltwood and marble-mounted console table, faults.

c1835   41in (104cm) wide

$4,000-5,000   **DN**

A pair of Neoclassical giltwood and gesso marble-top pier tables, of break-bowfront outline with concave sides, each with marble top inlaid with colored anthemion stems and arabesques around a halved fan patera, each frieze with ribbon-tied giltwood festoons and four Wedgwood style green jasperware medallions flanking a central jasperware tablet decorated with Classical muses, on square tapering legs decorated with trailing bell flowers on guttae style block feet, both with marbleized green-painted decoration.

42.25in (107cm) wide

$20,000-30,000　　　　**L&T**

A large Louis XVI style giltwood console, the legs joined by an undulating stretcher rail, carved with flower-filled urns, adapted.
c1900　　　　*119in (302cm) wide*
$30,000-40,000　　　　**FRE**

A Rococo style giltwood console table and mirror, the shaped marble top over an ornate pierced scroll carved and foliate-carved frieze, raised on cabriole legs united by acanthus and foliate-carved stretchers, the mirror with a central beveled rectangular plate within a gadrooned frame and floral etched margin plates, surmounted by a cartouche flanked by lions.

Console 56in (142cm) wide
$7,000-9,000　　　　**FRE**

A pair of George III style mahogany satinwood and marquetry demi-lune console tables, of recent manufacture.
35.75in (116cm) wide
$1,600-2,400　　　　**DN**

A pair of late 19th/early 20thC George III style mahogany and paint-decorated console tables, the shaped top painted to show a lute and ribbon swags to the frieze over straight tapering legs.

34.5in (87.5cm) wide
$3,000-5,000　　　　**FRE**

SIDE TABLES

A late 17thC Charles II walnut center/side table, molded top above a channeled frieze and scroll apron to all sides, with a single drawer, the square and bobbin-turned legs joined by conforming stretchers.
35in (89cm) wide
$30,000-40,000　　　　**SOTH**

A Charles II oak side table, the rectangular top above a mitre-paneled drawer, on baluster-turned legs and an H-stretcher.
41.75in (106cm) wide
$1,100-1,500　　　　**DN**

A William and Mary oak side table, with faults.
c1690　　　　*32in (81cm) wide*
$4,000-6,000　　　　**DN**

An early 18thC William and Mary walnut side table, the molded top above a drawer with boxwood stringing, front apron with pierced fret brackets, square and bobbin-turned legs joined by conforming peripheral stretchers.
33in (84cm) wide
$24,000-30,000　　　　**SOTH**

An 18thC and later George I walnut veneered side table, the rectangular top with quarter-matched veneers within feathered stringing and crossbanding, above a single frieze drawer above an arcaded frieze, on turned tapering legs with wavy X-form stretcher and ball feet.
30in (76cm) wide
$9,000-11,000　　　　**DUK**

A mid-18thC occasional dropleaf side table, of small proportions, the re-entrant cornered top with caddy-molded edge and rear dropleaf above plain frieze, on four scroll-carved slender cabriole legs ending in pad feet.
26in (66cm) wide
$10,000-14,000　　　　**L&T**

FURNITURE

A mid-18thC Dutch walnut and marquetry side table.

29in (74cm) wide

$4,000-6,000   **DN**

A George III mahogany side table, the rectangular top now with an additional rouge marble top above two frieze drawers, raised on canted square legs ending in block feet, the whole carved with blind fretwork and gothic tracery.

c1770   *31in (79cm) high*

$8,000-10,000   **FRE**

A George III satinwood, purpleheart and tulipwood-crossbanded demi-lune table, the top with a halved fan patera bounded by pole trophies united by ribbon-tied swags of ivy, on legs with inlaid simulated flutes, headed by tablet capitals with brass caps.

48in (122cm) wide

$8,000-12,000   **L&T**

A satinwood marquetry and kingwood-crossbanded side table, the top with central feather fan marquetry reserve, above a crossbanded frieze and on square-section tapering legs, damage, repair, adapted in part.

c1800 and later   *43in (109cm) wide*

$2,600-3,200   **DN**

A Regency walnut, rosewood-veneered satinwood-crossbanded and parcel-gilt side table, the narrow lobed top above an entablature frieze, centered by a sunken lozenge, on turned and reeded tapering legs united by an undulating shelf stretcher on toupie feet.

c1810   *78in (198cm) wide*

$200,000-300,000   **L&T**

A Regency mahogany side table, in manner of William Trotter of Edinburgh, the rectangular top above a frieze drawer and scroll-carved kneehole flanked by two short drawers with gadrooned handles, on volute scroll-carved cabriole front legs ending in scrolled feet and headed by sunken field capitals, the rear legs of turned tapering design.

46in (117cm) wide

$2,400-3,000   **L&T**

A mid-19thC American Rococo revival faux marble and rosewood side table, possibly Vermont, the shaped top above a conforming skirt with concealed drawer with flanking turned pendants on scroll-carved brackets and legs, the vase and ring-turned posts joined by a shaped central stretcher, original surface, minor imperfections.

37.5in (95.5cm) wide

$3,000-5,000   **SK**

A George III inverted bowfront serving table.

c1810   *48.5in (123cm) wide*

$3,600-4,400   **DN**

A William IV period mahogany serving table of impressive proportions, the top of break-bowfront outline with molded frieze on eight turned tapering legs with bold acanthus leaf-carved capitals, on ring-turned feet.

113.5in (278cm) wide

$14,000-16,000   **L&T**

A 19thC Swiss Beromünster style Baroque walnut and marquetry side table, the rectangular top topped with étagère, inlaid with mahogany banding enclosing hunting scenes and centered by coat of arms, above two drawers, flanked by square baluster-shaped carved supports joined by marquetry-inlaid tier, on plinth base.

43.5in (110cm) wide

$5,000-7,000   **SOTA**

A 19thC Irish mahogany serving table, the rectangular top with molded edge above plinth frieze on boldly carved volute-scroll front legs decorated with stiff leaf and foliate bosses, the rear legs of plain square section design.

82.75in (210cm) wide

$10,000-14,000   **L&T**

A late 18thC satinwood and rosewood-banded writing table, possibly Channel Islands, the quadrant-beaded frieze with a drawer, on faceted tapering column terminating in petal-shaped lobes, the shaped base with bold leaf-carved paw feet.

c1795   29.25in (74.5cm) wide

$6,000-8,000   **L&T**

An American Philadelphia Federal mahogany writing table or desk, the rectangular top above apron with drawer to each end, on ring-turned and reeded legs, inverted pear-form feet, stamped 'T. Elwyn' on frame.

Thomas Elwyn came to Philadelphia in 1797, but moved to New Hampshire after marrying that same year. He did however maintain a house on Sansom Street in Philadelphia.

c1815   54in (137cm) long

$12,000-16,000   **FRE**

A Regency mahogany writing table, attributed to William Trotter of Edinburgh, the top inset with a black and gilt Greek Key tooled skiver and a sunken corrugated edge of vertical reeds, the frieze with sunken quadrant beading, enclosing a pair of drawers with foliate-cast pull handles and opposing simulated drawers, on baluster-turned legs headed by chamfered tablet capitals and ending in brass socket casters.
William Trotter is the most famous of the Scottish Furniture Makers and worked from 9 Princess Street, Edinburgh, from 1810 until 1833. During his lifetime Trotter worked for all the important Houses in Scotland, including Parliament House, Edinburgh in 1822 in readiness for the visit of King George III

60.25in (153cm) wide

$9,000-11,000   **L&T**

A Regency mahogany writing table.

c1820   30in (76cm) wide

$1,200-1,600   **DN**

A pair of George IV mahogany writing tables, attributed to Gillows, each with an opposing false drawer,

c1825   26.5in (67cm) wide

$6,000-7,000   **DN**

A William IV or early Victorian mahogany writing table, with two frieze drawers.

c1835   45.25in (115cm) wide

$1,300-$1,500   **DN**

A Victorian Louis XV style burr walnut and kingwood-crossbanded writing desk, the serpentine-shaped top with an inset leather writing surface, over a shaped frieze with one drawer, raised on square cabriole legs decorated with gilt metal mounts.

32.5in (82.5cm) wide

$3,600-4,400   **L&T**

A 19thC Boulle marquetry writing table, in 'premiere partie' cut brass and scarlet tortoiseshell, the shaped aprons with Bacchus mask mounts, on cabriole legs headed by caryatids, the whole decorated with arabesques and foliate cast gilt-metal mounts.

55in (140cm) wide

$4,000-6,000   **L&T**

A mahogany, marquetry and gilt-metal-mounted writing table, stamped 'COLLINSON & LOCK', also stamped '....LONDON 3971' to the drawer.

Collinson & Lock was founded in 1870 by F. G. Collinson and C. J. Lock, former employees of the cabinet-makers and furnishers Jackson and Graham. With their experience of the revivalist styles the new firm became a leading 'Art Manufacturer', employing designers such as Edward Godwin, Henry Batley and Thomas Collcutt, many of whose designs were included in their first catalogue, 'Sketches for Artistic Furniture' (1871). Their furniture was exhibited in London (1871), Vienna (1873) and at the Philadelphia Exhibition (1876). The company was absorbed by Gillows in 1897, also exponents of revivalist furniture since the 1860s.

35.75in (91cm) wide

$6,000-8,000   **DN**

A late Victorian mahogany writing table, the rectangular top with molded edge and gilt-tooled red leather inset, above two long drawers on turned tapering and fluted legs headed by stylized Corinthian capitals.

c1880   72.5in (184cm) wide

$2,400-3,000   **DN**

FURNITURE

A Victorian walnut kingwood and floral marquetry writing table, in the French style, with gilt-metal mounts, the molded edged serpentine oblong top with inset oval green leather writing surface, and marquetry floral sprays to each corner, frieze drawer with gilt foliate handles, raised on cabriole legs with splayed feet.

32in (81.5cm) wide

$1,400-1,800 HT

A George III style figured table, the shaped rounded rectangular top with an inset tooled green leather writing surface, above a frieze fitted with twelve drawers, raised on reeded tapering legs.

c1900 *78.25in (199cm) wide*

$10,000-14,000 L&T

An oak writing table, by James Shoolbred & Company, one drawer stamped by maker.

c1900 *36.25in (92cm) wide*

$900-1,100 DN

An Edwardian satinwood and painted writing desk, painted throughout with trailing flowers, the crossbanded rectangular top centered by a musical trophy over a frieze drawer, raised on carved square tapered legs.

42in (106.5cm) wide

$3,000-4,000 FRE

A mid-18thC Louis XV kingwood and rosewood bureau plat, the rounded rectangular top with an inset leather writing surface, over three real and two opposing dummy frieze drawers, with lateral slides, raised on cabriole legs, ending in hairy paw feet.

65.25in (165.5cm) wide

$4,000-6,000 FRE

A Louis XVI style gilt-bronze-mounted mahogany and plum pudding mahogany bureau plat, by Gervais-Maximilien Eugene Durand, the rectangular leather inset writing surface above one long drawer flanked by two short deep drawers, raised on square tapered fluted legs, the whole outlined in gilt-bronze, the underside stamped 'G. Durand'.

Gervais-Maximilien-Eugene Durand was born in Paris 1874 and he was the first of three generations of highly successful cabinet makers, exhibiting widely at the series of International Exhibitions. In 1890 his son, Frederic-Louis joined the firm which became known as Durand & Fils.

c1800

$4,000-6,000 FRE

A French satinwood bureau plat, the inverted molded-edge breakfront top with an inset cloth to a raised galleried back with two pairs of leather-fronted drawers, the base with two frieze drawers, one with a brass label for 'P.A. Dunmas 24-26 Rue Notre Dame, Paris', on turned tapering fluted legs with gilt-brass sabots.

43.5in (110.5cm) wide

$2,000-3,000 WW

LIBRARY TABLES

A Regency mahogany kidney-shaped library table, in the manner of Gillows of Lancaster, the frieze with beaded edge on boldly beaded end standards filled with slender baluster uprights, on splay legs ending in finely cast brass foliate caps and casters.

37in (94cm) wide

$10,000-12,000 L&T

A Regency partridgewood and satinwood-banded library table, in the manner of Gillows, the rectangular top with rounded corners, above two drawers and a small pen drawer and two opposing false drawers, lyre-shaped trestle supports and two pole stretchers, each support issuing two downswept legs, lappet-cast gilt-metal caps and casters, damage, repair, legs possibly reduced in length.

c1820 *57.75in (147cm) wide*

$8,000-10,000 DN

A Regency mahogany partners' library table, the rounded rectangular top with matched flame veneers above a pair of frieze drawers to either side and a beaded edge, the large turned central pillar boldly carved with stiff lotus leaves and a gadrooned socle above a quadrapartite platform base, on gadrooned bun feet with recessed casters.

54.5in (138cm) wide

$4,000-6,000 **L&T**

A William IV rosewood library table, the rectangular top with molded edge above a beaded frieze enclosing a pair of drawers, on baluster-shaped end standards and scroll-carved trestle base with bun feet.

55in (140cm) wide

$4,000-5,000 **L&T**

An Irish William IV rosewood library table, the rounded rectangular top above a two real and two opposing dummy frieze drawers, raised on twin end supports united by a turned cross stretcher, terminating in molded scroll feet.

57.5in (146cm) wide

$5,000-6,000 **L&T**

A William IV Gothic style oak and leather-inset library table.

c1835 *65.75in (167cm) wide*

$5,000-7,000 **DN**

A George IV rosewood library table, the rectangular top with rounded corners above a pair of shallow frieze drawers, flanked by scroll brackets on ring-turned and ribbed baluster supports with leaf-and-dart-carved collars, the leaf scroll feet with sunken brass casters.

60in (152.5cm) wide

$3,000-4,000 **WW**

A 19thC partridgewood library table, the rounded rectangular top with gilt-tooled tan skiver and key fret-pierced gilt-metal three-quarter gallery above a pair of sunken field frieze drawers, on similarly molded end standards on dual splay saber legs ending in brass paw caps and casters.

40in (101cm) wide

$10,000-12,000 **L&T**

An early Victorian rosewood library table.

c1840, *50.25in (128cm) wide*

$2,400-3,000 **DN**

An early Victorian rectangular mahogany library table, with molded frieze, raised on scrolling end supports united by a single understretcher, on splay legs and carved bun feet.

54in (137cm) wide

$1,000-1,200 **A&G**

A 17thC and later Antwerp tortoiseshell and ebony table, the top adapted from a cabinet door inlaid in the center with a star-shaped motif inlaid in bone, the surrounding strapwork enriched with inlay of tortoiseshell, a flat single drawer fitted below, supported on spirally fluted legs joined by a stretcher veneered en suite to the top.

53in (134cm) wide

$20,000-24,000　　　　　　　　　　**SOTA**

An early 18thC Queen Anne walnut center table, the boarded top with cleated ends, ogee arch frieze above square and baluster-turned legs joined by peripheral stretchers.

25.25in. (64cm) high

$10,000-16,000　　　　　　　　　　**SOTH**

A 19thC Swiss Beromünster style Baroque mahogany, walnut, fruitwood and marquetry-inlaid table, the rectangular molded table top inlaid with banding and hunting scenes, in the middle with text and dated, on square baluster-shaped legs joined by stretcher, with four extending leaves.

1712　　　*67in (170cm) wide without leaves*

$7,000-9,000　　　　　　　　　　**SOTA**

An early 18thC American Queen Anne mahogany slab table, with oblong marble top with thumb-molded edge, overhanging a base with scalloped skirt supported by cabriole legs with volute-carved knee blocks, terminating in trifid feet.

45.5in (115.5cm) wide

$30,000-40,000　　　　　　　　　　**POOK**

A late 18thC Spanish walnut and bone-inlaid center table, with faults.

58.25in (148cm) wide

$1,800-2,200　　　　　　　　　　**DN**

A late 18thC George III mahogany rent table, the circular top over a frame with four drawers, above a turned standard supported by downward sloping molded legs terminating in brass casters.

43in (109cm) wide

$3,000-5,000　　　　　　　　　　**POOK**

A George III mahogany revolving oval drum table, the leather-inset oval top above a frieze with alternating drawers and hinged compartments, on a columnar standard supported on downswept tripod legs raised on casters.

c1800　　　*36in (91.5cm) wide*

$8,000-10,000　　　　　　　　　　**FRE**

A Regency rosewood center table, in the manner of Gillows of Lancaster, of small proportions, the rounded rectangular top with beaded edge above a beaded frieze with full width drawer, on reeded dual splay supports decorated with roundels and trestle base with four stiff leaf-carved saber legs united by a waisted platform stretcher.

36.75in (93cm) wide

$6,000-8,000　　　　　　　　　　**L&T**

A Regency mahogany drum library table, the molded circular top with an inset leather writing surface, above four real and four simulated frieze drawers, on a ring-turned column support ending in three reeded downswept legs terminating in brass caps and casters.

50in (127cm) wide

$11,000-13,000　　　　　　　　　　**L&T**

CLOSER LOOK: REGENCY CENTER TABLE

Multi-functional furniture was popular in the Regency period because it was useful in varied social settings in the fluid arrangements of rooms.

This table has the usual tilt-top, which enabled the table to moved from room to room or put against the wall when not in use.

The use of calamander veneers reflects the contemporary taste for highly exotic timbers. The evolving fashion for Neoclassical design is here allied to the taste for a playful Gothick, a romantic version of ecclesiastical gothic in domestic settings.

The inlays are a reflection of the revival of interest in early Boulle-inspired brass inlaid French furniture, the Prince Regent being an avid collector of such items during the auctions following the French Revolution.

A Regency calamander and parcel-gilt center table, with boulle inlays, the top veneered with figured veneers of calamander with a Boulle-inspired running brass border of S-scrolls, florettes and stylized anthemions within two inset brass lines. The frieze with a running brass Boulle-interlaced geometric pattern offset by tiny inlaid circles. The turned baluster base support with bands of gilt gesso and a boldly carved acanthus base above knulled carving, all inlaid with brass and supported by four giltwood leafy carved lion paw feet on casters.

c1815

51in (129.5cm) wide

$160,000-180,000   **PAR**

A late Regency mahogany drum library table, by James Winter & Son, London, with four cockbeaded frieze drawers with lion mask cast-brass pull handles, drawer stamped 'James Winter & Son 101 Wardour St. Soho. London'.

48in (122cm) wide

$8,000-12,000   **L&T**

A Regency mahogany drum library table.

c1820   45.75in (116cm) diam

$6,000-10,000   **DN**

A George IV pollard oak and parcel-gilt drum table, the circular top above a frieze of drawers and dummy drawers, raised on anthemion carved trefoil supports and a circular base with carved trefoil toes.

c1825   52.5in (133.5cm) diam

$6,000-8,000   **FRE**

A 19thC George I style giltwood center table, the ornate foliate scroll-carved rectangular molded top above a cavetto lattice and bellflower frieze, raised on acanthus-carved cabriole scroll legs.

46.75in (119cm) wide

$9,000-13,000   **L&T**

A William IV rosewood drum library table, the circular top with a gilt-tooled burgundy skiver above four frieze drawers with foliate cast-brass pull handles, on boldly turned and lappet-carved column and triform base with tapered bun feet and recessed casters.

53.75in (134cm) wide

$8,000-10,000   **L&T**

A 19thC Anglo-Ceylonese ebony and specimen wood center table, the octagonal top with radiating veneers and a gadrooned edge, raised on turned supports, united by a galleried under-tier and ending in four cabriole legs with carved claw feet.

10.25in (26cm) wide

$4,000-6,000   **L&T**

A late 19thC Roman 'Sites of the Grand Tour' micro-mosaic, sample marble and parcel giltwood occasional table, the top with a depiction of Saint Peter's Basilica and Piazza, with eight segments around with depictions of view of Rome, comprising the Pantheon, the Tomb of Caecilia Metella, the Senator's Palace, the Forum, The Flavian amphitheatre, the Temple of Vesta, the Castel Sant'Angelo and the Arch of Titus, surrounded by a border of various marbles and hardstones including lapis lazuli, Siena, portoro, brocatello and others, and interspersed with malachite and lapis lazuli borders, all in a marmo nero Belgio ground, the parcel giltwood and ebonized frieze below with three maiden's masks and three panther's masks, the fluted pedestal below with lobed and acanthus-carved capital and acanthus-carved and waisted socle, with three cavorting putti on the circular base with three projecting plinths, on acanthus-carved paw feet, restored.

26in (66.5cm) diam

$80,000-120,000   **DN**

A late 19thC mahogany drum table of George III style, the molded circular top inset with tooled-leather writing surface, above six frieze drawers, alternating with dummy drawers, on paneled square section column and plinth base.

54.5in (138cm) diam

$7,000-11,000   **L&T**

A late 19thC walnut, thuya, marquetry and gilt-metal-mounted center table, the frieze drawer centered by a painted porcelain plaque.

46.5in (118cm) wide

$6,000-8,000   **DN**

A 20thC George III style mahogany and fiddle back mahogany drum table, the top above four small drawers, above an octagonal tapering stem with downswept legs, brass caps and casters.

30.25in (77cm) diam

$2,000-2,400   **DN**

A Neoclassical style giltwood painted and marble center table, the circular marble-inlaid top sits above a plinth column applied with three giltwood swans raised on a triform base.

45in (114.5cm) diam

$2,400-3,600   **FRE**

A Neoclassical style giltwood painted and marble center table, the circular inlaid-marble top supported by a gilded and ebonized column applied with three winged birds, above a triform base.

45in (114.5cm) diam

$2,400-3,600   **FRE**

A late 19th/early 20thC style French giltwood and composition center table, with marble inset top, stylized shell and foliate-carved frieze above square section cabriole-shaped legs, damage.

39in (99cm) wide

$900-1,100   **DN**

A late 19th/early 20thC walnut and crossbanded hall table.

$1,200-1,600   **DN**

A late 19th/early 20thC Vienna style porcelain and giltwood center table, the dished circular top decorated with a reserve of a flower girl on the steps, gilt details within a bleu celeste border, raised on three porcelain and gilt supports.

23in (58.5cm) diam

$8,000-12,000   **FRE**

FURNITURE

A late 19thC Louis XV style kingwood and marquetry bijouterie cabinet, the shaped rectangular top with an inset glazed panel, opening to reveal a velvet-lined interior, raised on square cabriole legs terminating in sabots.

39.5in (100.25cm) wide

$2,400-3,600   **FRE**

A late 19thC rosewood and marquetry bijouterie table.

21.75in (55cm) wide

$2,400-3,000   **DN**

A late 19thC walnut and floral marquetry vitrine table, with shell-centered leaf-carved aprons and shell and fruiting vine-carved cabriole legs ending in talon-and-ball feet.

29.25in (74cm) wide

$3,000-4,000   **L&T**

An Edwardian mahogany and satinwood crossbanded bijouterie table, the frieze decorated with ribbon-tied penwork swags, on lyre-shaped end standards with brass wires and applied roundels.

19.75in (50cm) wide

$3,000-4,000   **L&T**

A Regency nest of three rosewood occasional tables.

c1820   *17in (43.5cm) wide*

$1,000-1,400   **DN**

An Edwardian nest of four painted satinwood 'Quartetto' tables, the largest painted with ribbon-tied and swagged urns around a pair of cherubs cavorting in the clouds, the remaining tops decorated with festoons of flowers.

26.75in (68cm) high

$5,000-7,000   **L&T**

A mid-18thC mahogany 'handkerchief' table, the triangular top with conforming dropleaf above a plain frieze on turned legs ending in pad feet.

28in (71cm) high

$2,000-3,000   **L&T**

A late 18thC American Pennsylvania painted poplar table, the oblong battened lip top over a frame with a single drawer and turned legs terminating in pad feet, retaining its original red and yellow swirl decoration and brass hardware.

30in (76cm) high

$30,000-40,000   **POOK**

A Louis XVI ormolu-mounted mahogany 'vide poche', attributed to Jean-Henri Riesener, the rectangular top with hinged flat raised on columnar stiles continuing to fluted legs, raised on round tapered capped feet joined by an entwined shaped stretcher, the whole outlined with ormolu.

'Vide Poche' is the French term for a small table or dish in which the contents of pockets may be emptied.

c1775   21.5in (54.5cm) wide

$14,000-20,000   **FRE**

An early 19thC Swedish marble-top occasional table, in the Empire taste, the gray fossil marble top above a mahogany-veneered frieze on three painted and parcel-gilt inswept tapering legs headed by Egyptianesque carved bird head terminals and brass-strung amaranth tablet capitals, each leg with stiff leaf carving at its center, united by a marble undertier.

29.5in (75cm) high

$4,000-6,000   **L&T**

A George IV mahogany side or center table, with shaped top.

c1830   43.75in (111cm) wide

$1,400-1,800   **DN**

A French transitional walnut and tulipwood-inlaid petit table, the top of serpentine outline with molded brass-bound edge, radially veneered and centered by a female sun mask, on cabriole legs, possibly reduced, united by a similarly veneered undershelf and ending in leaf-cast sabots with hoof feet.

17.75in (45cm) wide

$2,000-2,400   **L&T**

A 19thC scarlet japanned and gilt chinoiserie occasional table, the top with snap-over action, decorated with riverside pagodas and birds, on a slender spirally fluted baluster column and downswept tripod base painted with foliage, ending in giltwood ball feet.

30.25in (77cm) high

$1,200-1,600   **L&T**

A late 19thC French kingwood and tulipwood parquetry petit table, in the manner of Francois Linke, the top of serpentine outline with trellis bandings and raised brass-bound edge, the frieze with Rococo leaf-cast mounts, on cabriole legs with trailing leaf-cast putto mask figures ending in scroll-cast sabots.

29.5in (75cm) high

$4,000-6,000   **L&T**

A 19thC French rosewood, crossbanded and floral marquetry kidney-shaped occasional table, the top with heart motif pierced gallery and a festoon of wheat and flowers above a similarly inlaid frieze drawer and under-shelf, on cabriole legs, the whole with gilt-metal mounts ending in paw caster feet sabots.

27in (69cm) wide

$6,000-8,000   **L&T**

A 19thC Anglo-Indian Singhalese ebony and specimen wood occasional table, the octagonal top with radiating veneers and pewter line inlay, above a scroll-carved frieze, the acanthus-turned column support ending on a tripod base with claw-and-ball feet.

20.5in (52cm) wide

$3,000-4,000   **L&T**

A George IV style pollard oak coffee table, the rectangular cane top surmounted by a removable veneered center section above a reeded frieze and raised on turned and reeded legs terminating in brass cappings and casters.

59.5in (151cm) wide

$5,000-6,000   **L&T**

A Louis XV style gilt-bronze-mounted marquetry two-tier side table, marquetry-inlaid graduating tiers raised on tapering legs ending in sabots.

38in (96.5cm) high

$14,000-20,000   **FRE**

A late 19th/early 20thC Middle Eastern hardwood camel carved occasional table, the kidney-shaped top with wide fruiting scrolling foliate-carved border, supported on the back of a naturalistically carved camel, standing on elongated octagonal plinth base.

30in (76cm)

$7,000-8,000   **L&T**

An Edwardian mahogany and marquetry occasional table, by James Shoolbred & Company.

c1910   22in (56cm) wide

$500-600   **DN**

A late Georgian mahogany and satinwood-crossbanded sofa table, with two short drawers to the frieze, raised on splay legs terminating in brass capped feet and casters.

33.5in (85cm) wide

$2,400-3,000　A&G

An American Philadelphia Classical mahogany sofa table, rectangular top and conforming, round-cornered leaves with molded edge on a molded apron, raised on ring-turned and tapering reeded urn-form supports joined by scroll stretcher, arched leaf-carved and molded legs ending in brass caps.

c1815　29.75in (75.5cm) wide

$6,000-8,000　FRE

A Scottish Regency mahogany and rosewood-crossbanded sofa table, with flame-figured top with quadrant beaded edge on a beaded platform base raised on hipped and molded saber legs ending in boldly cast foliate caps and casters.

41.75in (106cm) wide

$14,000-18,000　L&T

An unusually small Regency period mahogany sofa table, the top with a reeded edge above a frieze containing a drawer on one side, a dummy on the reverse, flanked by molded tablets, raised on end supports and downswept legs decorated overall with reeded moldings, in the manner of Gillows of Lancaster.

The reeded decoration to the end support as well as the legs is a feature found in recorded examples of the work of the Gillows workshop in Lancaster illustrated in the 'Gillow Archive', Westminster City Library, London.

c1815　28in (71cm) high

$20,000-30,000　RGA

A Regency rosewood and cut brass-inlaid table, on a pillar and platform base raised on saber legs ending in paw caps and sabots, the whole decorated in brass arabesques and stringing.

28.5in (72cm) high

$4,000-5,000　L&T

A Regency rosewood and cut brass-inlaid sofa table, the end standards of waisted form, on dual splay saber legs headed by gilt-metal rosettes and ending in lion paw caps and casters.

43.5in (110cm) wide

$8,000-10,000　L&T

A Regency mahogany sofa table, the rectangular top incorporating a pair of hinged flaps above two frieze drawers and two opposing false drawers, on square-section trestle supports, each issuing a pair of reeded downswept legs, brass caps and casters, repair.

c1820　37.5in (95cm) wide

$4,000-6,000　DN

A late Regency burr ash and oak sofa table, with central support and pedestal base.

c1825　65.5in (166cm) wide

$3,200-4,000　DN

A Continental Biedermeier fruitwood sofa table, the molded canted rectangular hinged twin-flap top above two frieze drawers, dummy drawers to the reverse, on faceted baluster column and shaped quadrapartite base with square tapering down scrolled legs with spreading feet.

56in (142cm) wide

$5,000-7,000　L&T

A Regency mahogany sofa table, faults.

c1820　28.25in (72cm) high

$1,200-1,600　DN

A Federal cherry inlaid dropleaf table, probably southeastern New England, outlined in stringing, on conforming skirt centering a patera, refinished, minor imperfections.

c1790   20.25in (51.5cm) wide

$4,000-6,000   **SK**

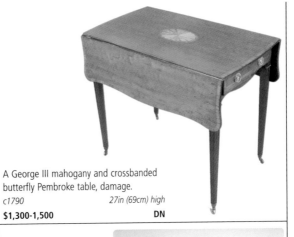

A George III mahogany and crossbanded butterfly Pembroke table, damage.

c1790   27in (69cm) high

$1,300-1,500   **DN**

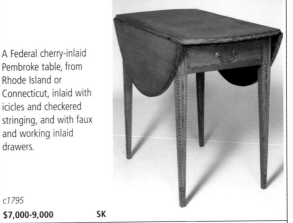

A Federal cherry-inlaid Pembroke table, from Rhode Island or Connecticut, inlaid with icicles and checkered stringing, and with faux and working inlaid drawers.

c1795

$7,000-9,000   **SK**

A late 18thC Chippendale walnut Pembroke table, rectangular top and shallow drop leaves, apron drawer with brass bail on square grooved and chamfered legs with X-stretcher.

Made from the 1750s, Pembroke tables were named after the first lady to order one. They had two side-flaps supported on hinged brackets which opened up to form the table top, and nearly all were fitted with casters. They were used for taking meals, playing cards, writing and needlework. They were largely replaced in the early 19thC by sofa tables.

47in (119.5cm) long

$3,000-4,000   **FRE**

A Federal mahogany-inlaid Pembroke table, probably from New York, edged and outlined in stringing, inlaid with ovals, and banded lower edge joining the square tapering legs, refinished, imperfections.

1795-1800

$4,000-6,000   **SK**

A Regency rosewood and satinwood-banded pedestal Pembroke table, damage.

c1820   28.75in (73cm) high

$3,000-4,000   **DN**

A George IV mahogany Pembroke worktable, with two drawers opposing false drawers.

c1825   16in (41cm) wide

$1,000-1,500   **DN**

A mahogany and marquetry Pembroke table, with frieze drawer at one end.

c1900   30in (76cm) wide

$800-1,200   **DN**

FURNITURE

A George III mahogany folding card table, with faults.

c1780   *35.75in (91cm) wide*

$400-600   **DN**

A George III mahogany folding card table, with faults.

c1780   *35.75in (91cm) wide*

$400-600   **DN**

A Dutch walnut and floral marquetry serpentine folding card table, damage, repair.

c1780   *28.25in (72cm) wide*

$4,600-5,000   **DN**

A George III mahogany and rosewood-crossbanded demi-lune foldover card table, the top decorated with an arched band of engraved marquetry leaf fronds above a boxwood-strung frieze, on square tapering legs with gaitered feet.

38.25in (97cm) wide

$10,000-12,000   **L&T**

A George III mahogany and marquetry demi-lune card table, bears Leeds City Art Gallery paper label.

c1810   *41.75in (106cm) wide*

$1,600-2,400   **DN**

A Regency mahogany and brass-inlaid card table, the rectangular top with canted corners and inlay of scrolling brass work against an ebonized ground, the frieze with conforming brass inlay and ebony stringing, on ring-turned tapering legs with ball feet.

35.5in (90cm) wide

$1,600-2,400   **DUK**

A satinwood and tulipwood-crossbanded folding card table, the D-shaped top opening to a baize inset, above a plain frieze centered by a tablet panel with oval reserve, on square-section tapering legs, on later spade feet.

c1810   *37in (94cm) wide*

$4,000-6,000   **DN**

A Regency rosewood and satinwood-banded folding card table.

c1820   *36in (91cm) wide*

$1,000-1,400   **DN**

A Regency rosewood and satinwood-banded card table, damage, with repair.

c1820   *35.75in (91cm) wide*

$1,800-2,400   **DN**

A Regency rosewood folding card table, damage, with repair.

c1820   *36.25in (92cm) wide*

$1,000-1,400   **DN**

A Regency mahogany and kingwood-crossbanded folding card table, the rectangular top with canted front corners above twin shaped trestle supports and a shaped stretcher, each trestle issuing a pair of down-swept legs, on gilt-brass lion paw caps and casters, damage.

c1820   *35.75in (91cm) wide*

$700-900   **DN**

A Regency pollard oak and ebony-strung card table, with faults.

c1820   *35in (89cm) wide*

$2,000-3,000   **DN**

FURNITURE

A Bermuda Queen Anne cedar tea table, the rectangular tray top over a case with shaped apron supported by cabriole legs terminating in Spanish feet, from the Shelley Collection.

c1730   31.25in (79.5cm) wide
$12,000-18,000   POOK

A mid-18thC New England Queen Anne maple tea table, the oval overhanging top on a valanced canted skirt joining four block-turned and splayed legs ending in pad feet, old finish, repairs.

35.25in (90cm) wide
$10,000-12,000   SK

A Queen Anne pine tea table, the removable tray top over a frame with scalloped skirt supported by cabriole legs terminating in slipper feet.

c1760   36.25in (92cm) wide
$9,000-11,000   POOK

A Queen Anne mahogany tea table, the scalloped tray top over a straight frame supported by cabriole legs terminating in pad feet.

c1765   27in (68.5cm) wide
$3,500-4,500   POOK

A Philadelphia Chippendale mahogany card table, with an oblong folding top and ovolo front corners, the base with cabriole legs terminating in claw-and-ball feet.

c1765   30in (76cm) wide
$5,500-6,500   POOK

A Baltimore Hepplewhite mahogany card table, the demilune top with molded edge, over a frame with oak leaf inlay and checkered skirt supported by square tapering legs with bellflower chain and banded cuffs,

c1790   36in (91.5cm) wide
$4,500-5,500   POOK

A Philadelphia Federal mahogany inlaid folding top card table, serpentine top above conforming skirt, with tapering legs.

c1800   35.75in (91cm) wide
$4,000-5,000   FRE

A New Hampshire Federal inlaid mahogany games table, the rectangular top with ellipitic front and canted corners with inlaid edge on conforming frieze inlaid with panels and ovals at corners and front, on pointed double tapering legs inlaid with bellflowers, refinished.

c1800   38in (96.5cm) wide
$10,000-15,000   FRE

A New Hampshire or Massachusetts Federal mahogany inlaid card table, with elliptic front, and inlaid edge on conforming skirt inlaid with satinwood, mahogany and contrasting geometric banding.

c1800   35in (89cm) wide
$18,000-20,000   SK

FURNITURE

A pair of New York Classical carved mahogany games tables, with a shaped top, radiating veneer opening to felted interior on conforming skirt.

c1815　　　　　　　　　　*36in (91.5cm) long*

$25,000-35,000　　　　　　　　　　**FRE**

CLOSER LOOK: CARD TABLE

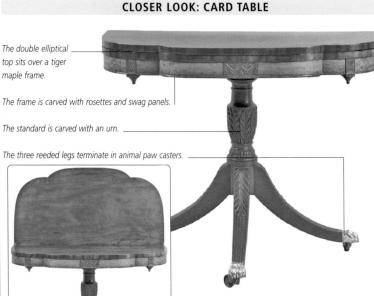

The double elliptical top sits over a tiger maple frame.

The frame is carved with rosettes and swag panels.

The standard is carved with an urn.

The three reeded legs terminate in animal paw casters.

A New York Federal mahogany card table.

c1815　　　　　　　　　　*35.75 in (91cm) wide*

$50,000-60,000　　　　　　　　　　**POOK**

A pair of early 19thC New England Federal mahogany and bird's eye maple card tables, with shaped front and skirt.

36.25in (92cm) wide

$10,000-15,000　　　　　　　　　　**FRE**

A Classical carved and stenciled mahogany card table, attributed to Anthony G. Quervelle (1789-1856), Philadelphia, the oblong top veneered and stenciled in gilt with Classical devices, above a molded and gadrooned skirt on scrolled four-part leaf-carved support on shaped platform, acanthus- and paw-carved feet, casters.

c1820　　　　　　　　　*39in (99cm) wide*

$24,000-28,000　　　　　　　　　　**FRE**

ESSENTIAL REFERENCE: DUNCAN PHYFE

Duncan Phyfe (1768-1854) designed fashionable and high quality furniture, which helped to transform American cabinet-making.

- Phyfe was born in Scotland and immigrated to the United States as a teenager. In 1792, he moved to New York City and within three years had opened his own store. By 1843, he was one of the richest men in the city.

- Phyfe's designs were based on a series of European styles, including Sheraton, Regency and Empire. He designed a wide range of furniture, especially large and ambitious pieces for dining rooms, using the best mahogany in elegant proportions and with fine details.

A New York Classical carved and brass-inlaid card table, attributed to Duncan Phyfe, the rectangular top with canted corners above swan, acanthus and lyre-form support, on a shield-shaped platform with inlaid tablet at front, raised on waterleaf and hairy paw carved feet, casters.

c1820　　　　　　　　　*36in (91.5cm) wide*

$24,000-28,000　　　　　　　　　　**FRE**

A 19thC painted games table, the checkerboard top with candle turret, above two drawers and turned legs, together with a hogscraper candlestick.

23.5in (59.5cm) high

$3,000-$5,000　　　　　　　　　　**POOK**

A late Regency rosewood card table, probably by Gillows of Lancaster, the beaded swivel top with baize inset above a faceted spreading column decorated with two bold graduated bands of beading on a quadrapartite platform base raised on scroll-cut feet with gilt-metal shell caps and casters.

The Gillows sketch book illustrates several foldover tables with this distinctive treatment of the column i.e. both spreading and faceted with graduated rows of beaded or gadrooned molding.

36.5in (93cm) wide

$6,000-8,000   L&T

A 19thC black boulle marquetry folding card table, of serpentine rectangular form, the top inlaid with brass, the frieze inlaid to all four sides, between cabriole legs on gilt sabots.

35in (89cm) wide

$6,000-8,000   DN

A George IV mahogany and satinwood-crossbanded folding card table, the D-shaped top above a plain frieze on turned and reeded tapering legs, repair.

c1825   36.25in (92cm) wide

$1,800-2,400   DN

A Victorian walnut folding card table, faults.

c1870   36.25in (92cm) wide

$1,000-1,400   DN

A Victorian burr walnut envelope card table, the molded edged swivel top opening to reveal green baize lining, frieze drawer with turned wood handles, on turned tapering and fluted legs with brass toes and casters.

23in (58.5cm) wide

$1,400-1,800   HT

TEA TABLES

A George II mahogany tea table of dished rounded oblong form, plain frieze on club legs with pad feet.

27in (68.5cm) wide

$4,000-5,000   HT

A George III mahogany folding tea table.

A George II carved mahogany serpentine front tea table, with frieze drawer below the hinged top.

c1740   36.25in (92cm) wide

$2,000-3,000   DN

c1790   34.25in (87cm) wide

$800-1,200   DN

FURNITURE

A George III mahogany demi-lune folding tea table.
c1790
35.75in (91cm) wide
$1,400-2,000   DN

A Regency mahogany tea table, the D-shaped folding top above the strung frieze, on turned tapering legs.
c1820
35.75in (91cm) wide
$900-1,100   DN

A Victorian ebony and yew wood folding tea table, of oblong form, with marquetry and gilt-metal mounts, the swivel top with central cartouche depicting a vase of flowers on a scrolling foliate ground, opening to reveal interior with shaped baize lining, the mildly breakfront fascia with projecting corners, raised on fluted turned tapering legs with brass toes.
34in (86.5cm) wide
$2,400-3,600   HT

A probably Continental mahogany folding tea table, the rectangular top with waved edge above a conforming frieze on a pierced shaped stem and plinth base, with four scroll feet and later casters, damage.
c1870
33.75in (86cm) wide
$800-1,200   DN

GAMES TABLE

A George II mahogany fold-over games table, the top with projecting re-entrant corners enclosing guinea wells and baize inset above a frieze drawer in a cockbeaded surround, on lappet-carved tapering legs, with gate action, on pad feet.
35in (89cm) wide
$3,000-4,000   L&T

A Regency period rosewood and line-inlaid foldover games table, the rectangular top with canted corners and swivel action above a frieze with four canted corners, on four inswept scrolling legs, fluted and gilded on the angles, headed by giltwood ball capitals, ending in brass paw cappings and casters.
36.75in (93cm) wide
$3,000-4,000   L&T

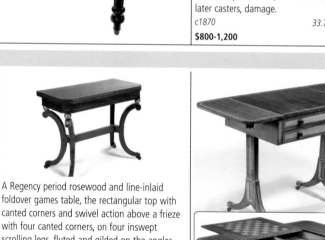

A 19thC and later Regency style rosewood and satinwood-inlaid combined games and sofa table, the rectangular top incorporating a pair of hinged flaps, and centered by an inlaid chess board, the sliding section revealing the backgammon board, above a false drawer and a drawer, and two opposing false drawers, on square section trestle supports, each issuing a pair of downswept legs with brass caps and casters.
29in (74cm) wide
$3,000-5,000   DN

A Regency period mahogany and zebrawood-crossbanded foldover games table, the rounded rectangular top with broad crossbanded edge and subsidiary inner banded lines above conforming inlaid frieze, on four ring-turned part-ebonized pillar supports and four reeded tapering saber legs ending in brass paw caps and casters.
34.75in (88cm) wide
$7,000-9,000   L&T

A 19thC walnut, purpleheart and bird's-eye maple-veneered fold-over games table, in the manner of Gillows of Lancaster, the top with arabesque inlaid corners enclosing a baize inset above an extending drawer with detachable side frieze mounts forming a center standing table, the sunken frieze with central lozenge above turned and fluted tapering legs, the whole with banded and line-inlaid decoration.

35.75in (91cm) wide

$6,000-8,000   **L&T**

A 19thC Victorian burl walnut games table, by A. Blain, Liverpool, the shaped hinged triangular top opening to a baize inset surface marked at the corners with dishes, raised on cabriole legs with acorn and leaf-carved toes ending in casters, the slide out back with runners stamped.

48in (122cm) wide

$1,400-2,000   **FRE**

A 19thC Anglo-Indian games table, the octagonal top inlaid with an ivory and carved hardwood games surface, above a sectioned frieze with carved figural panels and four sandalwood-lined fitted drawers, on an octagonal carved column support raised on a carved four-point star base.

26in (66cm) high

$2,400-3,200   **FRE**

A Victorian burr walnut serpentine folding games table.

c1870   *35.75in (91cm) wide*

$2,000-3,000   **DN**

A Victorian japanned papier mâché gilt-painted pedestal games table, the circular top with mother-of-pearl chequer board center on a slender baluster support and a circular platform on three short splay feet.

24.25in (61.5cm) diam

$700-900   **HALL**

A Louis XVI style gilt-bronze-mounted mahogany fold-over games table, by Gervais-Maximillien-Eugene Durand.

c1880   *33.25in (84cm) wide*

$7,000-9,000   **FRE**

A Napoleon III gilt-bronze-mounted burl walnut, marquetry and ebonized game table, the rectangular top with rounded fore corners inlaid with a flower-filled urn opening to a baize-lined playing surface, raised on round tapered stop-fluted legs.

c1890   *33in (84cm) wide*

$2,400-3,200   **FRE**

FURNITURE

A George II oak lowboy, the rectangular top with cavetto-molded edge above a full width caddy-molded frieze drawer and a scroll-carved apron flanked by two conforming short drawers with brass open back plated drop handles, on tapering legs ending in pointed pad feet.

30in (76cm) wide

$2,000-3,000   **L&T**

A Louis XV ormolu-mounted tulipwood and bois de bout poudreuse, the rectangular top with a hinged center section with a mirror on the reverse, flanked by hinged side panels opening on velvet-lined wells above a slide-out writing surface and single drawer flanked by an arrangement of drawers and raised on slightly hipped cabriole legs ending in scrolling leaf-cast sabots, the whole inlaid with foliate sprays, the underside bearing spurious 'BVRB jme' stamp.

c1760   35.75in (90cm) wide

$4,000-6,000   **FRE**

A Louis XVI mahogany rafraichissoir, attributed to Jean-Joseph Gegenbach Dit Canabas, the rectangular top inset with gray marble and a pair of copper liners flanked by wells, above a plain rounded frieze with one drawer raised on slightly hipped abriole legs joined by two platform stretchers, ending in casters.

c1770   24in (61cm) high

$10,000-14,000   **FRE**

A George III mahogany kneehole dressing table.

c1790

$600-1,000

38.25in (97cm) wide

DN

A Louis XVI walnut, tulipwood, harewood and marquetry poudreuse, the central hinged flap on a ratchet support between a pair of similar hinged covers revealing a partially fitted interior, on bell flower-inlaid square tapering legs ending in fluted brass sabots.

c1790   31in (79cm) wide

$8,000-10,000   **L&T**

A late George III bowfront mahogany dressing table, damage, repair.

35.5in (90cm) wide

$800-1,200   **DN**

An Irish Regency mahogany dressing table, possibly Cork, the rounded rectangular top with a solid three-quarter gallery, above a central frieze drawer and arched reeded apron, flanked by two further short drawers to either side, raised on spiral reeded legs terminating in brass cappings and casters.

48in (122cm) wide

$10,000-12,000   **L&T**

A Regency mahogany and ebony-strung gentleman's enclosed dressing table, the rectangular hinged top opening to a fitted interior, incorporating a raising mirror and later lidded compartments above an arrangement of four drawers and a commode drawer on turned tapering legs, gilt-brass caps and casters, damage, repair.

c1820   22.75in (58cm) wide

$1,200-1,600   **DN**

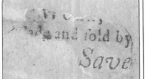

A Delaware Valley Queen Anne transitional walnut dressing table, bearing the label of William Savery (1721-87), the base with a single drawer (with label) above three small drawers flanked by fluted quarter columns, over a scalloped skirt supported by cabriole legs terminating in trifid feet, the highly figured drawers retain their original brasses.

31in (80cm) wide

$110,000-130,000 **POOK**

CLOSER LOOK: DRESSING TABLE

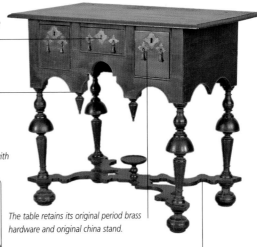

The molded edge top overhangs a case with three short drawers.

The arched skirt has an applied beaded edge and conical drops supported.

The bold oblong inverted trumpet turned legs are joined by an elaborate serpentine cross stretcher with turned dished china stand.

The table retains its original period brass hardware and original china stand.

This exceptional example represents the highest achievement in Philadelphia William & Mary furniture. A nearly identical example can be found at the Philadelphia Museum of Art.

A Philadelphia William & Mary mahogany dressing table.
c1720 *27.5in (70cm) wide*

$600,000+ **POOK**

A Delaware Valley Queen Anne walnut dressing table, the molded edge top overhanging a case with one long and two short drawers, supported by square cabriole legs terminating in Spanish feet, retaining its original brass hardware and old surface, from the Shelley Collection.
c1750 *29.75in (75.5cm) wide*

$22,000-28,000 **POOK**

A New England Queen Anne mahogany dressing table, with three drawers, beaded surrounds and a shaped skirt hung with turned pendants.
c1750 *33in (84cm) wide*

$8,000-12,000 **FRE**

A 19thC Chippendale style mahogany dressing table, with four thumb-molded drawers, shell carving, and cabriole legs ending in pad feet.
42.5in (108cm) wide

$800-1,200 **FRE**

An early 19thC Federal paint-decorated dressing table, a 'D'-shaped box with single drawer on ball feet above the projecting overhanging top, on straight apron joining square tapering legs, yellow-painted case with freehand fruit and seashells, the legs with bellflowers, all bordered by contrasting black and green banding, imperfections.
36in (91.5cm) high

$3,500-5,500 **SK**

A Neoclassical carved mahogany and mahogany veneer dressing chest with mirror, attributed to Thomas Seymour, Boston, original brass pulls, old surface, imperfections.
c1820 *76.5in (194.5cm) high*

$17,000-20,000 **SK**

A Massachusetts Classical carved mahogany, mahogany veneer and brass-inlaid dressing table, with leaf carving and floral rosettes, a mirror and seven drawers, refinished.
c1820-25 *39.5in (100.5cm) wide*

$4,000-5,000 **SK**

A 19thC Dutch mahogany and marquetry dressing table, lacks mirror supports, inlaid throughout with scrolling foliage, the oval mirror over a rectangular top and one frieze drawer, raised on twin scroll supports with carved paw feet.

39in (99cm) wide

$3,000-4,000   **FRE**

A Sheraton Revival satinwood and rosewood-crossbanded dressing table, the rounded rectangular swing mirror with re-entrant corners between slender uprights and two stage back drawers above a re-entrant cornered top enclosing a pair of frieze drawers on slender tapering legs inlaid with ebony lines on spade feet.

35.75in (91cm) wide

$4,000-6,000   **L&T**

A 20thC George III style satinwood gentleman's enclosed dressing table, the rectangular top incorporating two hinged flaps enclosing a fitted interior, with central ratchet-adjustable mirror flanked by lidded compartments, repair.

24.75in (63cm) wide

$1,000-1,400   **DN**

TRIPOD TABLES

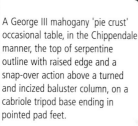

A George III mahogany 'pie crust' occasional table, in the Chippendale manner, the top of serpentine outline with raised edge and a snap-over action above a turned and incized baluster column, on a cabriole tripod base ending in pointed pad feet.

28in (71cm) high

$6,000-8,000   **L&T**

A George III mahogany tripod table, the circular top with pie crust edge above the baluster-turned stem, on three downswept legs with stylized pad feet.

c1760   *29.5in (75cm) diam*

$4,000-6,000   **DN**

A George III mahogany supper table, the circular top pierced and carved with dish wells, each enclosed by leaf carving, raised on a leaf-carved standard and a tripod base, ending in claw-and-ball feet.

c1760   *32in (81cm) diam*

$7,000-9,000   **FRE**

A George II style mahogany tea table, the pie crust top over a birdcage and foliate-carved baluster standard with carved cabriole legs terminating in pad feet.

c1760   *29in (73.75cm) diam*

$1,400-2,000   **POOK**

A Philadelphia Chippendale mahogany tilt-top tea table, the circular top with molded edge tilts on a birdcage support and a ring-turned post, with flattened ball on tripod base of cabriole legs tapering to pad feet on platforms, old surface, very minor imperfections.

c1755   28.5in (72.5cm) high

$45,000-50,000   **SK**

CLOSER LOOK: TRIPOD TABLE

The table top has an old, dry surface.

The dish top sits over a circular birdcage and baluster standard. The birdcage mechanism was more popular in the US than the UK.

The cabriole legs have unusual intaglio carved knees terminating in pad feet.

A Chester County, Pennsylvania Queen Anne walnut tea table.

c1765

$16,000-20,000

34.5in (87.5cm) wide

POOK

A Philadelphia Queen Anne mahogany candlestand, the circular, molded, dished tilting top on a slender turned support with suppressed ball standard, on cabriole legs with snakehead feet.

c1760   19.5in (49.5cm) diam

$4,000-6,000   **FRE**

A Chester County, Pennsylvania, Queen Anne tiger maple tea table, the dish top tilting on a birdcage and baluster-turned standard supported by cabriole legs terminating in snakehead feet, retaining an old dry surface, from the Shelley Collection.

c1770   30.75in (78cm) wide

$12,000-18,000   **POOK**

A Philadelphia Queen Anne mahogany tea table, the circular dish-molded tilting top on birdcage support, columnar shaft with suppressed ball standard on cabriole legs terminating in snakehead feet.

c1770

$5,000-7,000   **FRE**

A Philadelphia Chippendale mahogany tea table, the circular tilting dish top over a birdcage and suppressed ball standard, supported by cabriole legs terminating in claw-and-ball feet.

c1770   33in (84cm) diam

$8,000-10,000   **POOK**

FURNITURE

A New York Chippendale mahogany tea table, the top with gadrooned edge tilting on a birdcage and baluster-turned standard, supported by cabriole legs terminating in claw-and-ball feet.

c1770   *34.25in (87cm) wide*

$4,000-7,000   **POOK**

A Philadelphia Chippendale mahogany tea table, the circular top with molded rim, with birdcage on tapering support with suppressed ball and tripod base ending in slipper feet.

c1775

$3,000-4,000   **FRE**

A late 18thC Chester County, Pennsylvania Chippendale walnut tilt-top tea table, original surface, minor imperfections.

34.75in (88.5cm) diam.

$10,000-15,000   **SK**

An early 19thC Pennsylvania tiger maple and poplar game table, with a blue and black checkerboard tray top, above a turned standard and tripod base, from the Shelley Collection.

27in (68.5cm) high

$12,000-18,000   **POOK**

A New York Classical carved and inlaid mahogany candlestand, with band-inlaid top on acanthus-carved urn-form support ending in leaf-carved and paw feet.

c1820   *27in (68.5cm) wide*

$4,500-5,500   **FRE**

A Catawba County, North Carolina, walnut candlestand, the circular rotating top on a baluster-turned birdcage and vase- and ring-turned support on tripod cabriole leg base with paneled knees continuing to pad feet, mellow patina.

c1830   *26.75in (68cm) high*

$4,000-6,000   **SK**

A late George III satinwood and purpleheart-crossbanded oval work table, the hinged top above a cylindrical wool well, on slender tapering legs, requiring restoration.

21.75in (53cm) wide

$5,000-7,000   **L&T**

A George III style Edwardian satinwood and polychrome-painted work table, the octagonal hinged top above a foliate-painted frieze, on square-section tapering legs and an X-shaped stretcher.

c1910   *16in (41cm) wide*

$2,000-2,400   **DN**

A pair of Edwardian George III style mahogany and inlaid work tables.

c1910   *16.25in (41cm) wide*

$900-1,300 PAIR   **DN**

A Federal mahogany work table, school of John and Thomas Seymour, Boston, the top with ovolo corners above two cockbeaded drawers, the ends with flame mahogany panels bordered with cockbeading, with pull-out bag frame to the right, all on quarter-engaged fluted vase and ring-turned reeded and tapering legs on turned feet and brass cap casters, replaced brasses, old finish.

c1805   *30.5in (77.5cm) high*

$24,000-30,000   **SK**

A Federal inlaid mahogany sewing table, attributed to John and Thomas Seymour, Boston octagonal band inlaid top with single compartmented drawer, bag drawer below, on ring-turned and slender vasiform reeded posts, tall turned feet.

c1810   *27.25in (69cm) high*

$14,000-20,000   **FRE**

A New England Federal pine polychrome and gilt-decorated work table, the top painted with a landscape showing a group of buildings at a water's edge with an oval reserve, bordered by flowers and cornucopias, the sides and legs decorated with a variety of flowers, seashells and leafy wreaths, imperfections, paint wear.

c1810   *28.75in (73cm) high*

$10,000-12,000   **SK**

A Regency mahogany and ebony-strung work table, the hinged top on ratchet support and inlaid with a brass star to each corner, on lyre-shaped end standings applied with brass wires, on dual splay legs ending in Rococo cast caps and casters.

30in (76cm) high

$3,000-4,000   **L&T**

A Regency rosewood combined games and work table, the sliding and ratchet adjustable top opening to a backgammon board.

c1820   *24.5in (62.5cm) wide*

$3,000-4,000   **DN**

A Regency rosewood and boxwood-strung oval drum-shaped work table, the hinged lid enclosing a lined interior above two false drawers on a turned and parcel-gilt column and four saber legs on ball feet.

c1820   *32in (81cm) high*

$3,000-5,000   **DN**

A Regency mahogany and sycamore-strung workbox on stand, with knopped legs and casters.

c1820   *18.5in (47cm) wide*

$1,400-2,000   **DN**

An early 19thC, possibly Irish, yew wood and specimen wood pedestal table, the rectangular top inlaid with a central radiating veneer design with fan spandrels, cross and feather banding, the frieze with a reel-molded drawer, divided with a central pin cushion, on a ring-turned baluster stem to quatreform base on bun feet, one foot missing, minor veneer loss.

21in (53.5cm) wide

$3,000-4,000   **WW**

FURNITURE

A William IV rosewood work table, the rectangular top with rounded corners above a fitted frieze drawer and upholstered needlework basket, on square tapering uprights with platform feet, with applied turned decoration and lobed feet.

24in (61cm) wide

$2,600-3,000   **DUK**

A mid-19thC mahogany Pembroke work table, the rectangular top incorporating twin hinged flaps, above two short and one long drawer, and three opposing false drawers, on turned tapering legs, brass caps and casters, damage.

19in (48cm) wide

$800-1,200   **DN**

A mid-19thC Anglo-Indian rosewood work table, with a fitted interior of compartments above a leaf and roundel-carved frieze with scrolled angle frets and wool well, on a foliate-carved and pierced trestle base with inscrolling feet.

32.25in (82cm) wide

$4,000-6,000   **L&T**

A 19thC American New England Sheraton tiger maple work stand, with three drawers and turned legs, the middle drawer inscribed on underside 'Clark Van Gorden Feb. 12 1856'.

17.25in (43.75cm) wide

$4,000-5,000   **POOK**

A Napoleon III gilt-bronze mounted tortoiseshell and brass boule marquetry ebonized and rosewood sewing table, the shaped rectangular top monogrammed 'NP', opening to a mirror on the reverse and an interior fitted with a sliding shelf above a slide out basket raised on cabriole legs, cast at the knees with chutes continuing to shell-cast sabots.

c1860   *22.5in (57cm) high*

$2,400-3,600   **FRE**

A Victorian rosewood combined games and work table, the rectangular top with central chess board above a drawer and sliding workbag on twin spiral-turned supports, and trestle feet with a stretcher and on four carved lion paw feet with concealed casters.

c1860   *20.75in (53cm) wide*

$800-1,200   **DN**

A Victorian figured walnut combined games and work table, the rectangular hinged top with bird's eye maple and walnut chessboard, opening to reveal a divided interior and workbag, above scroll terminals and a baluster-turned stem above cabriole-shaped downswept and cabochon-carved legs with scroll-carved feet, and brass casters, damage, repair.

19.75in (50cm) wide

$800-1,200   **DN**

A late 19thC Victorian rosewood and sycamore-strung work table, the hinged cover with mirror within, losses.

22.5in (57cm) wide

$600-1,000   **DN**

A French gilt-metal-mounted oval work table, the marble top with pierced three-quarter gallery, above a drawer and a solid undertier, cabriole shaped square-section legs with gilt-metal terminals and sabots.

23.5in (60cm) wide

$1,400-1,800   **DN**

An Edwardian satinwood octagonal work table, the hinged top opening to a removable tray incorporating open and lidded compartments, above pleated fabric covered sides, on square-section tapering legs, damage.

c1910   *29.25in (74cm) high*

$1,200-1,600   **DN**

An Edwardian mahogany oval worktable, the hinged rectangular top above a workbag, on square-section tapering legs and an X-shaped stretcher, on spade feet.

19.25in (49cm) wide

$900-1,100   **DN**

A French walnut and iron-bound chest, in late Gothic style, the studded iron banding pierced with trefoils and terminating fleur-de-lys, on a plinth base, incorporating 15thC elements.

75.5in (192cm) wide

$10,000-12,000   SOTA

A Continental walnut and wrought iron-bound coffre fort, probably late 16th/early 17thC, of rectangular form with multiple iron straps attached by rivets secured by scrolled under-wires verso and an iron hasp and staple lock, the corners also reinforced with angle irons, the hinged top revealing a void, on short baluster-turned feet.

38in (97cm) wide

$5,000-7,000   L&T

A late 16th/early 17thC style paneled oak chest, hinged lid above twin-paneled front, centered by bog oak and holly parquetry lozenges, above shaped brackets and stile feet, repair.

30.25in (77cm) wide

$3,000-4,000   DN

A Charles II and later paneled oak chest, the hinged rectangular top above a triple-paneled front and frieze carved with lunette and foliate motifs, on later stile feet, repair, later elements.

44.5in (113cm) wide

$600-800   DN

A Charles II paneled oak chest, with damage, repair.

c1670   *48in (122cm) wide*

$500-700   DN

A Charles II oak mule chest.

c1680   *30.75in (129cm) wide*

$3,000-4,000   DN

A late 17th/early 18thC oak and elm boarded chest, the hinged rectangular top above later carved initials 'G M', on integral seat, damage, later elements to feet.

18in (46cm) wide

$700-900   DN

A mid-18thC Welsh oak coffer bach, the molded edge top with later hinges, with a twin fielded panel front above a girdle molding and two drawers, fitted later brass plate handles, on bracket feet.

26in (66cm) wide

$1,200-1,600   WW

An early 18thC and later North Italian carved cypress wood, coffer with foliate-paneled front, the cover interior with pen and ink decoration.

56.75in (144cm) wide

$3,000-4,000   DN

A late17th/early 18thC Connecticut River Valley oak and pine joined chest, old surface, lower front rail carved with intials 'R.B.', imperfections.

41.25in (105cm) wide

$18,000-22,000   **SK**

A William & Mary walnut blanket chest, probably Lancaster County, Pennsylvania, with a lift lid, double raised panel front and two drawers, all resting on bold bun feet.

c1725   *48.5in (123cm) wide*

$55,000-65,000   **POOK**

A Pennsylvania walnut blanket chest, the lift lid over a dovetailed case with two drawers supported by ogee bracket feet, retaining an old dry surface.

c1760   *49in (124.5cm) wide*

$4,000-5,000   **POOK**

A Pennsylvania painted and decorated blanket chest, molded rectangular top decorated with shaped reserves above case with similarly shaped reserves, inscribed 'Cadarina Weisen 1769' with two drawers below, bracket base.

51.5in (129.5cm) wide

$1,800-2,200   **FRE**

A Lancaster County, Pennsylvannia walnut blanket chest, the lift lid with inlaid panel with central star cartouche, over a case with initials 'IS', flanked by potted tulips, above two drawers supported by bracket feet, dated.

1777   *48in (122cm) wide*

$20,000-25,000   **POOK**

A Lehigh County, Pennsylvania dower chest, the case decorated with soldiers on horseback, roosters, pinwheels, etc., all on green ground, dated.

1779   *48in (122cm) wide*

$6,000-8,000   **POOK**

A Lebanon County dower chest, painted red and black, the molded rectangular lid opening to a well fitted with a till, the case decorated with a heart inscribed 'Susanna Dussing Anno 1782' on molded base with bracket feet.

A handwritten note on underside inscribed ' Lebanon, Dec. 26 1870 This chest was the property of grandfather John Bernhard Embick and his first wife Susanna Dussing and was purchased by me for the sum of $2.00 on the above date. John Jacob Embick, father Israel Embick was three years old when his mother Susannah Dussing died. Grand. John Bernhard Embick second wife's name was Susanna Ishler & to mother's knowledge they had... children. Grand. John Bernhard Embick third wife Elizabeth Smith & they had six children. '

51in (129.5cm) wide

$3,000-5,000   **FRE**

A Lebanon County, Pennsylvania dower chest, by Christian Selzer, Jonestown, the lid decorated with two floral panels, the case with two panels with potted tulips, the left pot is signed indistinctly, the sides with black and white pinwheels.

c1780   *43.75in (111cm) wide*

$15,000-20,000   **POOK**

A Lancaster County, Pennsylvania walnut architectural marriage chest, with the initials 'ALXL', flanked by tombstone panels with stars and pilasters with heart cutouts, appears to retain its original strap hinges and bail brasses, dated.

1785   *50in (127cm) wide*

$2,500-3,500   **POOK**

A Berks County, Pennsylvania painted pine dower chest, the front with central double arched panel with two rearing black unicorns with orange tulips and flower vines, within an elaborate sawtooth border flanked by two arched panels with tulip trees on a red ground, all resting on straight bracket feet with center drop, retaining original wrought iron strap hinges, grab lock and side carrying handles.

c1785   *48.5in (123cm) wide*

$18,000-22,000   POOK

A painted and stenciled blanket chest, probably from Berks County, Pennsylvania molded rectangular top opening to well with till, the base decorated with shaped reserves, one inscribed 'Maria Catrina Bushen 1788', and enclosed by tulip sprays, the sides decorated with pinwheels, drawers and molded base below.

48in (122cm) wide

$10,000-12,000   FRE

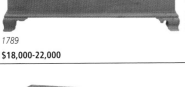

A Lancaster County, Pennsylvania walnut blanket chest, the case with sulfur-inlaid potted tulip vines, birds and pinwheels, supported by ogee bracket feet, dated.

1789   *48in (122cm) wide*

$18,000-22,000   POOK

A late 18thC walnut inlaid dower chest, probably from Chester County, Pennsylvania, containing a lidded till with two hidden drawers, and old eagle brass pulls, refinished, minor imperfections and restoration.

47.25in (120cm) wide

$12,000-15,000   SK

A late 18thC painted and decorated blanket chest, probably from Lancaster County, Pennsylvania, the case decorated with hearts at the corners, the front decorated with arches enclosing flowers, hinges removed.

48in (122cm) wide

$3,000-5,000   FRE

A late 18thC New England pine smoke- and paint-decorated six-board chest, the lift top with chamfered edge opens to an interior with till, above nail-constructed box with triple-arch cut-out ends, original surface.

50in (127cm) wide

$3,000-4,000   SK

A late 18thC Lehigh County, Pennsylvania dower chest, the front decorated with two stylized hearts with interior stars and stippling on a grained reserve, above two drawers and straight bracket feet.

48.5in (123.5cm) wide

$25,000-30,000   POOK

A late 18thC Pennsylvania painted dower chest, the lift lid over a case with the initials 'KW 1786' and 'Magdalena Waldin 1790', with a salmon cartouche on a blue ground, over two drawers, supported by bracket feet.

47.75 (121.5cm) wide

$3,000-4,000   POOK

A late 18thC Berks County, Pennsylvania painted pine dower chest, decorated on the front and sides with potted tulips, architectural columns, and heart corners, over three short drawers, supported by bracket feet.

48in (122cm) wide

$7,000-10,000   POOK

A late 18thC Lehigh County, Pennsylvania painted dower chest, inscribed 'Hanna Eister 1790 Gebert Diese Kist', above two stylized green sponge-decorated hearts centering on an orange and black pinwheel and tulip tree flanked by similar stars and tulips and heart corners on an ochre and red stippled ground, the ends with bold red and ivory stars, above three green sponge-decorated drawers retaining original hardware, supported by spurred straight bracket feet, retains original decorative wrought iron strap hinges.

46.25in (117.5cm) wide

$150,000-200,000   POOK

FURNITURE

CLOSER LOOK: DOWER CHEST

Decorated chests such as this example show the vibrant colors used by 18th and 19th century artists.

The top and front are profusely decorated with tulip vines, parrots, stars, and other motifs. Many of the itinerant painters had been trained in the Old World, so these traditional European designs suggest a nostalgia for the homeland among the settlers in the New World.

The painting style of the parrots on the front and sides is reminiscent of drawings by Pennsylvania fraktur artists such as Otto and Mertel.

A Berks County, Pennsylvania painted dower chest, supported on ogee bracket feet, dated.

1803   47.75in (121.5cm) wide

$500,000+   POOK

A late 18thC Lancaster County, Pennsylvania painted dower chest, by the Compass Artist, the lift lid over a case decorated with three panels of red and white flowers on a blue ground supported by bun feet.

There are only four dower chests known by this artist.

49.5in (125.5cm) wide

$40,000-50,000   POOK

A late 18thC Berks County, Pennsylvania painted dower chest, the front decorated with three tombstone panels depicting unicorns and rampant lions, the sides with potted tulips, all on a salmon ground, supported by short bracket feet.

48in (122cm) wide

$22,000-28,000   POOK

A Lebanon County painted pine dower chest, the top having two square panels, the front with three arched stippled panels on an orange ground, above three similar stippled drawers, resting on ogee stippled bracket feet.

c1800   51.75in (131.5cm) wide

$3,000-4,000   POOK

A Pennsylvania painted dower chest, the lid and case decorated with clover panels with potted tulips.

c1800   50in (127cm) wide

$3,000-4,000   POOK

A Northampton County, Pennsylvania painted dower chest, the lid with pinwheels and stars, over a case with three panels of potted tulips on a red ground, over three drawers supported by bracket feet, dated.

1801   48in (122cm) wide

$4,000-5,000   POOK

A Pennsylvania walnut blanket chest, probably Berks County, with sulfur-inlay 'Cadarina Moser', above potted tulips supported by ogee bracket feet, dated.

1801   48.25in (122.5cm) wide

$12,000-18,000   POOK

An early 19thC paint-decorated poplar dower chest, probably from Ohio, with a symmetrical arrangement of flowers and leaves and applied medial molding, with very minor imperfections.

48in (53cm) wide

$18,000-22,000   SK

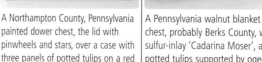

A 19thC painted pine miniature dower chest, from Lebanon County, rectangular lid with molded edge fitted with a molded glazed frame enclosing a watercolor and ink drawing of two birds perched on tulips over a heart, on a base similarly fitted with a glazed frame enclosing a watercolor and ink drawing of a heart and tulips, flanked by carved red-painted hearts, shaped bracket base.

16in (40.5cm) wide

$3,000-4,000 FRE

A paint-decorated poplar dower chest, probably decorated by a member of the Kriebel family, Pennsburg vicinity, Pennsylvania, containing secret compartment, and lettered 'Jacob Hubner 1815'.

49in (124.5cm) wide

$30,000-40,000 SK

An early 19thC painted and vinegar-grained blanket chest, molded rectangular top above conforming case fitted with a till, the case incised with three tombstone shaped reserves, molded bracket base.

51.5in (131cm) wide

$3,000-4,000 FRE

An early 19thC New Hampshire fancy paint-decorated dome-top trunk, dove-tail constructed rectangular box with wire-hinged lid, yellow and rust paint, black borders with ovolo corners, minor imperfections.

23in (58.5cm) wide

$2,500-3,500 SK

An early 19thC New Hampshire Federal grain-painted chest over drawers, the hinged rectangular top with ovolo corners opens to an interior above a case of two half-drawers, all flanked by ring-turned quarter-engaged columns continuing to vase- and ring-turned legs, original bail brasses, original painted surface simulating flame mahogany with stringing, minor imperfections.

48in (122cm) wide

$5,500-6,500 SK

An early 19thC Centre County, Pennsylvania painted dower chest, initialled 'DW', the top and case remaining in pristine condition, profusely decorated with trailing tulip vines, pinwheels, and hearts on a red ground, the base with lower sawtooth border supported by black-painted flaring French feet, retaining original wrought iron lock and strap hinges.

48in (122cm) wide

$250,00-350,000 POOK

An early 19thC New England painted pine blanket chest, the lift over case with two drawers and scalloped skirt supported by bracket feet, retaining its original red and black grained surface.

39.25in (99.5cm) wide

$4,500-5,500 POOK

A Mahantongo Valley, Pennsylvania painted pine dower chest, decorated with kneeling children flanking facing birds perched in a stylized tulip tree, within a potato stamp border on a blue ground, supported by turned feet.

This form is one of the rarest in Pennsylvania decorated furniture.

c1835-40 *47in (119cm) wide*

$55,000-65,000 POOK

A Pennsylvania painted poplar blanket chest, with dovetailed case, three drawers, and turned feet, retaining a pristine sponge-decorated surface, dated.

1844 *47.5in (121cm) wide*

$6,000-8,000 POOK

A mid 19thC Shaker pine grain bin, with a long lift lid and boot jack ends, retaining an old dry surface.

96in (244cm) wide

$4,500-5,500 POOK

A Soap Hollow, Pennsylvania painted blanket chest, with typical diamond escutcheon flanked by floral sprigs, the initials 'CW' and pillars above a potted tulip vine, all on a vibrant red background supported by floral-decorated ebonized feet, dated.

1874 *44in (112cm) wide*

$13,000-15,000 POOK

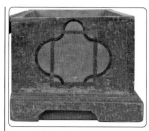

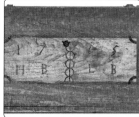

A Berks County, Pennsylvania miniature painted poplar marriage chest, of dovetailed construction, the lid with an ivory cartouche on a green stippled ground, inscribed '1765 HB LB' centering on interlacing tulip vines, the front with an outlined ivory cartouche with two birds flanking a tulip, the ends with conforming cartouches, all on a green stippled case with center scalloped drop and straight bracket feet, retaining its original wrought iron strap hinges.

1765   *19.5in (49.5cm) wide*

$300,000-400,000   **POOK**

A Berks County, Pennsylvania painted poplar dower chest, the front inscribed 'Maria Elisabed Webern', above two panels with birds and tulips centering two polka dot mermaids holding a stylized tulip, flanked by dogs chasing a stag and saddle horse with birds, the ends with stippled panels and heart corners, retaining its original hardware and boldly molded plinth base, dated.

1773   *49in (124.5cm) wide*

$50,000-60,000   **POOK**

A Lancaster County, Pennsylvania painted dower chest, by the Embroidery Artist, the lid with typical sawtooth border panel surrounded by florettes over a case with a large ivory panel decorated with tulip vines, pomegranates, etc., inscribed 'Catharine Mauren', supported by bun feet, dated.

1795   *50in (127cm) wide*

$45,000-55,000   **POOK**

A painted and decorated poplar black unicorn chest, with dovetailed case and hinged top over two thumb-molded drawers, original decorated surface of blue-green ground, and inscribed 'Bern, Berks County [Pennsylvania], Adam Minnich 1796'.

The 1810 census lists an Adam Menick (born between 1765 and 1784) living in Bern Township, Berks County, Pennsylvania. The early settlers of Pennsylvania produced such chests to contain household items gathered for a woman's impending marriage, and painted and decorated the chests with symbols from German folklore. They were often inscribed with a woman's or a man's name.

50in (127cm) wide

$500,000+   **SK**

CLOSER LOOK: CHARLES II CHEST

Following the Restoration of Charles II in 1660, walnut became the most popular wood for English furniture.

The building boom that followed the Great Fire of London in 1666 led to specialization within the furniture trade. Chests and other case furniture were made by cabinetmakers while chair making became a specialized task. While the nobility commissioned extravagant pieces of furniture, simpler well-crafted pieces were made for city merchants and the country gentry.

This chest has deep, crisp carving which is evidence that it was made by a skilled craftsman.

Decorative techniques such as marquetry also became common – probably as a reaction to the severity of design during Oliver Cromwell's rule.

A Charles II walnut, oak and bone marquetry chest-of-drawers.
c1680   36.25in (92cm) wide
$8,000-10,000   **DN**

A late 17thC Charles II yew wood chest-of-drawers, the molded rectangular top over two short drawers and three graduated long drawers, raised on stile feet.
38in (96.5cm) wide
$5,000-7,000   **FRE**

A late 17thC William and Mary oak chest-of-drawers, the rectangular top above three graduated drawers, each with carved and fielded panels, raised on bracket feet.
32.75in (83cm) wide
$2,000-3,000   **FRE**

A walnut-veneered and oak-crossbanded chest in the George I manner, the quarter-veneered top with herringbone-banded and crossbanded edge, the graduated and lipped drawers with brass drop handles between caddy molded uprights, on skirted base with bracket feet.
30in (76cm) wide
$2,000-4,000   **L&T**

A George II burr walnut and featherbanded chest-of-drawers, the quarter-veneered top with molded edge above a brushing slide.
c1735   228.5in (90cm) wide
$26,000-36,000   **DN**

A George II mahogany dressing chest, the caddy-molded top with a brushing side, cockbeaded drawers, with solid brass escutcheons and ring handles.
34in (86cm) wide
$5,000-7,000   **L&T**

An early 18thC and later oak and walnut chest-of-drawers, the rectangular top above two short and three long graduated drawers, on bracket feet, damage, repair.
39.75in (101cm) wide
$1,600-2,400   **DN**

A mid-18thC burr elm and checker-banded chest, with quarter-veneered top, the cockbeaded drawers with Rococo cast brass handles and escutcheons, on bracket feet.
31in (79cm) wide
$20,000-24,000   **L&T**

A mid-18thC George II mahogany chest of four graduated drawers, with slide.
30.75in (78cm) wide
$2,000-3,000   **DN**

FURNITURE

A Pennsylvania William & Mary walnut blanket chest.

c1730   47.5in (120.5cm) wide

$5,000-6,000   **POOK**

A Southeastern Pennsylvania William & Mary walnut chest-on-chest, the molded edge top over two short and one long drawer divided by a single arch molding, resting on a base with two drawers, flanked by sunken paneled sides, supported by bun feet.

c1730   39.75in (101cm) high

$80,000-100,000   **POOK**

A Philadelphia William & Mary chest-of-drawers, the oblong top with applied molded edge overhanging a case with four drawers separated by double arch moldings, cove-molded base resting on flattened ball-turned feet, possibly retaining period engraved plate brasses.

c1735   32.5in (82.5cm) high

$16,000-20,000   **POOK**

A Philadelphia William & Mary mahogany chest-of-drawers, with five short and three long drawers separated by double arch moldings supported by bracket feet.

c1740   41in (104cm) high

$2,000-3,000   **POOK**

A Pennsylvania Chippendale tiger maple chest-of-drawers, the molded edge top over a case with four drawers supported on ogee bracket feet, retaining period plate brasses.

c1770   33.5in (85cm) high

$7,000-8,000   **POOK**

A Pennsylvania Chippendale walnut child's chest, the molded cornice over a case with five short and four long drawers, flanked by chamfered columns, supported by ogee bracket feet, retaining its original brasses and an old surface.

c1780   25.5in (64.75cm) high

$30,000-40,000   **POOK**

A late 18thC Pennsylvania painted chest-of-drawers, the molded top over a case with three short over three long drawers, flanked by fluted quarter columns, supported by ogee bracket feet, retaining a 19thC vibrant red and yellow grained decoration.

40in (101.5cm) wide

$40,000-50,000   **POOK**

A late 18thC Chippendale mahogany reverse serpentine chest-of-drawers, probably from Massachusetts, with four graduated drawers on bracket feet, repairs.

36in (91.5cm) wide

$6,000-8,000   **SK**

A New Hampshire or Massachusetts Federal tiger maple and maple chest-of-drawers, with four thumb-molded drawers, old refinish, and minor imperfections.

c1800   40.5in (103cm) wide

$4,500-5,500   **SK**

A late 18thC Federal mahogany inlaid bow front chest-of-drawers, with four drawers with oval bird's eye inlaid borders, old oval brasses not original, refinished, some damage.

40.5in (103cm) wide

$3,000-4,000   **FRE**

A Federal figured maple and cherry chest-of-drawers, rectangular case above deep drawer with faux double drawer molding and three graduated drawers, all cock-beaded, on bracket feet.

c1800   43.5in (110.5cm) wide

$2,000-3,000   **FRE**

A Middle Atlantic States Federal mahogany-inlaid bow front chest, imperfections.

c1800   42.25in (107.5cm) wide

$3,000-4,000   **SK**

A Pennsylvania painted poplar chest-of-drawers, with two short over three long drawers, flanked by chamfered stiles, supported by turned feet, retaining its original salmon surface with black swirl decoration, and the original brass pulls and escutcheons.

c1810   48.5in (123cm) high

$40,000-50,000   **POOK**

A Massachusetts Federal mahogany four-drawer chest, with inlaid edge, wide cockbeaded drawers, on short vasiform turned legs, and tall turned feet, refinished.

c1810   38.25in (97cm) high

$2,000-3,000   **FRE**

An early 19thC Northwestern Vermont Federal bird's-eye maple and cherry veneer chest-of-drawers, the rectangular overhanging top above a cockbeaded case of four graduated drawers on cut-out feet, replaced brasses, refinished, minor imperfections.

38.5in (98cm) wide

$3,500-4,500   **SK**

An early 19thC Federal inlaid swell-front chest-of-drawers, the swelled top with contrasting dart-inlaid edge above four graduated drawers and shaped apron continuting to bracket feet, stamped eagle and star brasses.

41in (104cm) wide

$2,000-3,000   **FRE**

A cherrywood and tiger maple 'bonnet' chest, with cork-banded 'bonnet' drawers outset, above three graduated wide drawers on tall turned feet, refinished, new brass pulls.

c1825   42.75in (108.5cm) wide

$1,200-1,800   **FRE**

A Classical inlaid cherry and maple chest-of-drawers, from Pennsylvania or Ohio, rectangular top above three short cock-beaded drawers, band-inlaid deep desk drawer, over three cock-beaded long drawers, shaped skirt and feet.

c1830   43in (109cm) wide

$2,500-3,500   **FRE**

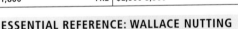

A mid 19thC Shaker maple and pine tailoring table, probably Mount Lebanon.

94in (239cm) wide

$5,000-6,000   **POOK**

ESSENTIAL REFERENCE: WALLACE NUTTING

Wallace Nutting (1861-1941) was a Congregational minister turned author, photographer, and entrepreneur. He became the principal authority on early American furniture for much of the early 20thC and played an important role in the development of a colonial revival aesthetic and ideology.

- When ill health forced him to give up his vocation in 1904, he turned to photography and sold prints including 'colonials' – images of women in period costume and in historical settings.
- In 1905, he moved to Southbury, CT and hired a team of women to hand-color his prints. He sold more than 5,000,000 of these, making over $1,000 per day.
- In 1912, he moved to Framingham, MA and began buying historic buildings.
- In 1916 he opened the five buildings to the public and began collecting American antiques for the homes.
- In 1917, he opened a furniture factory in Saugus, MA to make reproductions of his antiques . His workmen used modern techniques to make accurate copies of historical pieces.
- While his furniture copied designs from the past Nutting would not permit it to be artificially aged; it was either painted ebony or varnished so that it looked like new.
- Early pieces were marked with an "old tyme" paper label. From the early 1920s it was branded.

A Soap Hollow, Pennsylvania painted chest-of-drawers, dated, manufactured by John Sala, with typical scrolled backsplash and red and black grained case, with yellow cockbeaded drawers, the case adorned with stenciled floral decoration, the sides with recessed black panels each with bird, leaf, dog and stylized floral tree decoration, inscribed 'JE 1853', resting on tall turned feet.

1853   37in (94cm) wide

$30,000-40,000   **POOK**

A Wallace Nutting carved oak 'Sunflower chest', branded on both drawers.

45.25in (115cm) wide

$7,000-8,000   **POOK**

FURNITURE

A George III mahogany serpentine chest-of-drawers, with damage.

c1790   *41.75in (106cm) wide*

$10,000-12,000   **DN**

A George III mahogany serpentine chest, the top with molded edge and projecting corners above two short over three long graduated and cockbeaded drawers with brass drop handles, on bracket feet.

44in (112cm) wide

$12,000-16,000   **L&T**

A small 18thC and later walnut dressing chest, with feather and crossbanding, the burr-veneered top with a slide, the drawers with replaced handles and escutcheons, on bracket feet

$5,000-7,000   **WW**

A George III oak and mahogany crossbanded chest-of-drawers, the rectangular top above two short and three long graduated drawers, on bracket feet.

c1810   *44in (112cm) wide*

$1,000-1,600   **DN**

A late George III mahogany serpentine chest, the boxwood-strung top with crossbanded edge, above four cockbeaded drawers with bone escutcheons and brass pull handles, on shaped apron and high splayed bracket feet.

37.5in (95cm) wide

$7,000-9,000   **L&T**

A George III mahogany chest-of-drawers, attributed to Gillows, the molded top over a brushing slide and four long graduated drawers flanked by fluted quarter columns, raised on splayed bracket feet.

43in (109cm) wide

$4,000-6,000   **L&T**

A Regency mahogany and ebony-strung bowfront chest, the top with crossbanded frieze above four long graduated drawers and oval stamped brass handles emblematic of Nelson's battles, on splayed bracket feet.

36.25in (92cm) high

$4,000-6,000   **L&T**

An early 19thC mahogany and marble-topped chest, in the Empire taste, possibly Russian, the drawers with lion mask ring handles and anthemion cast escutcheons, with similar mounts to uprights, legs with front facing gilt-metal paw feet.

36.5in (92.5cm) wide

$6,000-8,000   **L&T**

A Regency mahogany bowfront chest-of-drawers, with repair.

c1820   *42in (107cm) wide*

$1,200-1,600   **DN**

A mid 18thC German Baroque walnut commode, possibly Dresden, the waved front accommodating four long drawers, on bun feet.

44in (112cm) wide

$8,000-10,000   **SOTH**

A Swedish Rococo gilt-brass-mounted walnut and sycamore commode, the liver-veined marble top of serpentine outline above three short feather-banded drawers and two long drawers, raised on slightly splayed bracket feet.

c1750   *51in (129.5cm) wide*

$7,000-9,000   **FRE**

CLOSER LOOK: GEORGE III COMMODE

Henry Hill was a cabinet maker, auctioneer and agent for the Sun Insurance Company from about 1740 to 1777. Although he gained commissions from elsewhere, his clientele was mostly based in his native county of Wiltshire, England.

The well-fashioned serpentine front is a sign of quality craftsmanship.

The keeled front angles and distinctively shaped apron, as well as thick cockbeaded moldings are characteristic of the work of Henry Hill of Marlborough.

The well-figured mahogany top has excellent patination

The brushing slide reveals an arrangement of fitted compartments, which again indicates a piece of fine quality.

A George III mahogany serpentine-fronted commode attributed to Henry Hill of Marlborough, the top drawer opening to a baize-inset slide, moving to reveal an arrangement of compartments, lacking former ratchet adjustable mirror.

c1770   *41.75in (106cm) wide*

$70,000-80,000   **DN**

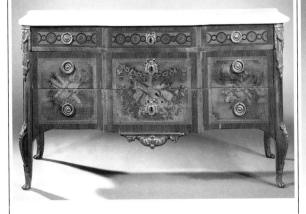

A kingwood, rosewood and amaranth marquetry commode, stamped 'F.RUBESTUCK', white marble top above breakfront housing three frieze drawers and a pair of long drawers inlaid with an arrangement of musical trophies flanked by panels depicting scientific trophies, the sides inlaid en suite, applied with mounts of gilt-bronze, raised on cabriole legs.

Francois Rübestuck (c1722-1785), in spite of a relatively short career, demonstrated great ability to interpret the styles of his day: the Louis XV period, the Transitional period, and the Louis XVI period. He is notable for a number of commodes and secrétaires veneered in Chinese or Japanese lacquer of the Louis XV period. His later work is notable for its marquetry panels, particularly those depicting musical trophies.

c1770   *58.25in (148cm) wide*

$70,000-80,000   **SOTA**

A Transitional tulipwood, stained fruitwood and amaranth marble top commode, the marble top of breakfront outline above two drawers with quarter-veneered reserves, the side panels veneered to match, raised on slightly hipped cabriole legs ending in sabots, stamped 'Stumpf, JME'.

c1770   *38in (96.5cm) wide*

$4,000-6,000   **FRE**

FURNITURE

A German small Neoclassical commode, veneered in fruitwood, tulipwood and ebonized wood forming a trellis at the top, cubicle parquetry to the sides.

c1780   30.25in (77cm) wide
$7,000-9,000   SOTA

A late 18thC Louis XVI rosewood and parquetry commode, possibly by Stumpf, the red-gray marble top above three short drawers and two long drawers, raised on square tapered legs, the whole inlaid with parquetry reserves, the sides veneered with diaper panels.

49.5in (126cm) high
$12,000-16,000   FRE

A George III mahogany commode, the shaped top of serpentine form over four long graduated drawers raised on splayed bracket feet.

c1780   42in (106.5cm) wide
$3,000-4,000   FRE

An 18thC Dutch burr walnut bombé commode, the serpentine-molded top over three long graduated drawers, flanked by outset corners, raised on scroll feet.

32.75in (83cm) wide
$2,400-3,600   L&T

ESSENTIAL REFERENCE: MARQUETRY

A late 18thC Transitional French provincial rosewood tulipwood and marquetry commode, with breche d'aleps marble top, each side panel decorated with a large urn, on cabriole legs ending in gilt-metal sabots.

37.5in (95cm) wide
$7,000-9,000   L&T

An 18thC Maltese walnut and boxwood-strung serpentine-front commode.

43.25in (110cm) wide
$12,000-16,000   DN

A late 18thC Italian walnut and marquetry commode, decorated throughout with marquetry, depicting Classical motifs and foliage, the rectangular top above three long drawers on square section tapering and fluted legs, damage, repair.

The decorative technique of marquetry was developed by Dutch cabinetmakers and introduced to Britain in the early 18thC.

It is a type of decorative veneer: small pieces of colored woods and/or materials such as ivory, bone and mother-of-pearl were laid out in a pattern and then applied to the carcass of a piece of furniture.

There were several forms: floral marquetry was fashionable from c1660-90 and seaweed or arabesque from c1690.

Marquetry fell out of fashion in the early 18th century in England, but was revived in the 1760s and 1770s.

c1780   47.5in (121cm) wide
$14,000-20,000   DN

A late 18thC German Neoclassical walnut and rosewood-banded commode, the rectangular top over three long drawers, raised on squat square tapered legs.

48in (122cm) wide
$7,000-9,000   FRE

A George III mahogany serpentine-front commode, the molded edge top above three long graduated drawers, with dummy fronts and satinwood edging and stringing, with gilt-brass swan neck handles, on bracket feet.

40in (101.5cm) wide
$7,000-9,000   WW

An Italian olivewood and boxwood-strung serpentine-front commode.

c1800   *35.5in (90cm) wide*

$12,000-16,000   **DN**

CLOSER LOOK: ITALIAN NEOCLASSICAL COMMODE

The marquetry decoration covers the top, front and sides of the commode and is bordered by bands of geometric motifs which are continued onto the legs and feet.

The commode is similar to the work of Giuseppe Maggiolini who was renowned for austere furniture decorated with pictorial marquetry.

Many different types and colors of timber were used to build up the pictures – here they are views of Classical buildings.

Most Maggiolini furniture is in the 18thC French style but decorated with marquetry rather than veneers.

An early 19thC Italian inlaid walnut commode, the later top with Carrera marble, the two drawers decorated with sunburst motifs, feather and geometric banding flanked by inlaid reeding, raised on square tapering legs.

52.5in (133cm) wide

$7,000-9,000   **A&G**

A late 18thC northern Italian Neoclassical walnut, burl walnut and marquetry commode, from Lombardy, in the manner of Giuseppe Maggiolini, the rectangular top with scroll banding, above three graduating long drawers inlaid with architectural parquetry, side veneered to match, raised on square tapering legs.

54in (137cm) wide

$36,000-44,000   **FRE**

A 19thC American mahogany commode, the cockbeaded drawers with brass drop-handles between spiral-twist turned Ionic style pilasters, on boldly carved lion paw feet.

46.5in (118cm) wide

$2,000-3,000   **L&T**

A pair of French marble-topped stained wood commodes, of Louis XVI style, each with molded veined red marble top above three drawers, carved with drapery swags, above stiff leaf frieze with central trophy tablet.

30in (76cm) wide

$7,000-9,000   **L&T**

A pair of 19thC continental mahogany convex commodes, line-inlaid overall, each with molded convex rectangular top above three long graduated drawers, on square tapering legs.

46.5in (101cm) wide

$11,000-13,000 PAIR   **L&T**

A pair of Italian Neoclassical style walnut commodes, the rectangular tops over two short drawers and two long drawers, flanked by half pilasters and raised on square tapered legs.

40in (101.5cm) wide

$3,000-4,000   **FRE**

A 19thC Victorian painted bombé commode, the shaped molded top centered by a floral reserve flanked by ho-ho birds, over two long drawers with conforming decoration, raised on splayed square tapered legs.

40in (101.5cm) wide

$4,000-6,000   **FRE**

A Continental carved walnut serpentine-fronted commode, in the early 18thC style, the two doors opening to the interior painted with heraldic devices to the reverse of the doors.

71.25in (181cm) wide

$3,000-4,000   **DN**

A second quarter 18thC George I walnut cabinet-on-chest, with ogee cornice above two break-arch panel inlaid quarter-veneered doors enclosing three reverse graduated long drawers, the base with three further drawers, on later bracket feet.

43.25in (110cm) wide

$6,000-8,000   DN

A William and Mary walnut oyster-veneered and marquetry cabinet-on-chest, the top and base associated, the molded cornice above one frieze drawer and a fall-front inlaid with foliate reserves, centered by a flowering urn opening to reveal a fitted interior with drawers, pigeon holes and a mirrored door, the lower section with two short and two long drawers, with further marquetry-inlaid panels, raised on later squat bun feet.

45.75in (116cm) wide

$9,000-11,000   L&T

An 18thC German walnut and fruitwood-inlaid 'Aufsatzschrank', restorations to cornice, altered.

73.25in (186cm) high

$5,000-7,000   SOTA

A George II walnut and featherbanded chest-on-chest.

c1740   67.75in (172cm) high

$7,000-9,000   DN

A George II walnut and feather-banded chest-on-chest, the cavetto molded cornice over three short and three long graduated drawers, flanked by reeded canted corners, the lower section with three further long graduated drawers, raised on bracket feet.

37.5in (95cm) wide

$16,000-20,000   L&T

A mid-18thC walnut and satinwood-banded chest-on-chest, the cavetto cornice above two short and six graduated drawers with brass drop handles headed by fluted angles and centered by a brushing slide, on high shaped bracket feet.

41.25in (105cm) wide

$16,000-20,000   L&T

A mid-18thC George II walnut and feather-banded chest-on-chest, raised on later bracket feet.

42.75in (108.5cm) wide

$12,000-16,000   FRE

A Philadelphia William and Mary walnut high chest, the molded cornice above two short and three long drawers, resting on a base with three drawers and scalloped skirt supported by trumpet-turned legs joined by serpentine stretchers.

c1730   62.5in (159cm) high

$10,000-12,000   POOK

A Maryland Queen Anne tiger maple high chest, the base with four drawers and scalloped skirt supported by cabriole legs terminating in unusual stocking trifid feet.

c1750   37.5in (95cm) wide

$8,000-10,000   POOK

A mid-18thC New England Queen Anne mahogany high chest, the upper section with fitted drawer, above eight further drawers, changed hardware.

41.75in (106cm) wide

$20,000-30,000   FRE

A mid-18thC Pennsylvania Queen Anne walnut high chest, the upper case with molded cornice above seven thumb-molded drawers, the lower case with five drawers on a shaped skirt and cabriole legs carved with shells and stockinged drake feet.

44in (112cm) wide

$17,000-20,000   FRE

A North Shore Massachusetts Queen Anne walnut carved scroll-top high chest-of-drawers, replaced brasses, refinished, minor imperfections.

c1750   82.5in (209.5cm) high

$30,000-35,000   SK

A Delaware Queen Anne walnut high chest in two parts, the upper section with a cove cornice, three small drawers, over three long drawers, over a base with four short drawers, scalloped skirt, and cabriole legs terminating in slipper feet, appears to retain its original brasses.

c1750   39.75in (101cm) wide

$8,000-12,000   POOK

A New England painted cherry two-part highboy, retaining a later orange and black surface.

c1770   37in (94cm) wide

$4,000-5,000   POOK

A Pennsylvania Chippendale walnut high chest, in two parts, the upper section with a dentil-molded cornice with elaborately scalloped skirt supported by cabriole legs terminating in claw-and-ball feet.

c1780   75in (190.5cm) high

$7,000-10,000   POOK

An 18thC Connecticut River Valley Queen Anne cherry scroll-top high chest-of-drawers, with central thumb-molded fan-carved drawer, flanking short drawers and graduated long drawers below.

38in (96.5cm) wide

$25,000-30,000   SK

A late 18thC Connecticut Queen Anne cherry carved high chest-of-drawers, old brasses, refinished, restoration.

84.75in (215.5cm) high

$24,000-28,000   SK

FURNITURE

A late 18thC Salem, Massachusetts Queen Anne tiger maple high chest-of-drawers, with five thumb-molded graduated drawers, above four further drawers.

37.5in (92cm) wide

$80,000-100,000   **SK**

A late 18thC Eastern Connecticut Queen Anne carved maple high chest-of-drawers, old brasses, refinished, minor imperfections.

73.25in (186cm) high

$26,000-30,000   **SK**

TALL CHESTS

A Pennsylvania Queen Anne walnut tall chest, the molded cornice above three short drawers and four long drawers, centered by a faux drawer with fall front, enclosing a fitted interior with raised tombstone panel prospect drawer, all flanked by smooth quarter columns.

c1760   *41.4in (105cm) wide*

$7,000-8,000   **POOK**

A New England Queen Anne tiger maple chest-on-chest, the upper section with four long drawers resting on a base with four drawers and tall straight bracket feet.

c1765   *38.5in (98cm) wide*

$4,000-5,000   **POOK**

A Pennsylvania Chippendale walnut tall chest, the molded cornice above a cast with five short and five long drawers, flanked by a chamfered corner case, each with a single carved flute, supported by ogee bracket feet.

c1780   *37in (94cm) wide*

$5,000-6,000   **POOK**

A late 18thC Pennsylvania Chippendale walnut tall chest, the drawers flanked by fluted quarter columns supported by ogee bracket feet.

37.5in (95cm) wide

$4,000-5,000   **POOK**

A late 18thC Chippendale tiger maple and maple tall chest-of-drawers, probably from Massachusetts, with six thumb-molded drawers, and replaced brasses, refinished, minor imperfections.

36in (91.5cm) wide

$6,500-8,500   **SK**

A late 18thC Chippendale tiger maple tall chest-of-drawers, probably from New Hampshire, with two thumb-molded half drawers and five graduated long drawers, retains some original brasses.

36in (91.5cm) wide

$6,000-8,000   **SK**

A late 18th/early 19thC Chippendale red-painted maple tall chest-of-drawers, from New Hampshire or Massachusetts, with old surface, old replaced brass pulls, and minor imperfections.

A late 18thC Pennsylvania Chippendale walnut tall chest, molded cornice above ten drawers, molded quarter columns, ogee bracket feet.

38.5in (98cm) wide

$8,000-10,000   **FRE**

36.25in (92cm) wide

$12,000-15,000   **SK**

ESSENTIAL REFERENCE: DEEP RUN SCHOOL

Furniture belonging to the Deep Run School, or attributed to the Deep Run Decorator, is decorated with a distinctive painted decoration.

- A salmon pink ground was painted to create a swirled, woodgrain effect.
- The affect was completed by painted 'cat's eyes' which resemble knots in the wood.
- Other decorative motifs included *'Sechsterns'* (a star within a circle) and stylized tulips.
- The furniture was often highlighted with yellow moldings and black paint detailing.

An early 19thC Bucks County, Pennsylvania painted semi-tall chest, probably Deep Run School, the molded cornice over a case with four drawers supported by ogee bracket feet, retaining its original black swirl decoration on a salmon ground, the sides with typical cat's eye design.

35.25in (90cm) wide

$30,000-40,000   **POOK**

CHEST-ON-CHEST

A William & Mary mahogany secretary desk, the double dome cornice above two raised arched panel doors enclosing an elaborately fitted interior with scalloped valances and serpentine drawers, over a lower section with fall front with ampitheatre interior and well, and four drawers supported by Spanish front feet and bun back feet.

c1720   *92in (233.5cm) high*

$60,000-80,000   **POOK**

A Queen Anne walnut secretary, probably Chester County, Pennsylvania, the molded cornice over two scalloped panel doors enclosing elaborately fitted interiors with multiple valuables drawers and scalloped pigeon holes and secret compartments, above a fall front desk and four drawers supported by bracket feet.

c1740   *85in (216cm) high*

$50,000-60,000   **POOK**

A Pennsylvania Queen Anne cherry secretary, the double dome cornice over two raised panel doors, enclosing a fully fitted interior, resting on a base with slant lid and pagoda interior, above a case with two candle drawers supported by straight bracket feet.

c1745

39.5in (100cm) wide

$35,000-45,000   POOK

A Chippendale cherry carved chest-on-chest, possibly from Concord, Massachusetts, with a carved fan on thumb-molded drawer, and ten further drawers, with replaced brasses, refinished.

The construction of this chest bears a strong resemblance to Concord-made furniture.

c1780   38.5in (98cm) wide

$20,000-30,000   SK

A late 18thC Connecticut Chippendale cherry chest-on-chest, the broken arch bonnet with inlaid rosettes flanking inlaid demilune pediment, retains original brasses.

84in (213cm) high

$9,000-11,000   POOK

A Baltimore, Maryland Federal inlaid mahogany secretary bookcase, the slant-front desk opening to a fitted interior, married top and base, veneer patches, some mends to case, hardware not original, repair to lock plate on top of desk, back left foot partially restored.

c1800   80.5in (204.5cm) high

$10,000-15,000   FRE

A Massachusetts Hepplewhite mahogany secretary desk, the upper section with two glazed doors, resting on a base with flip top writing surface and three drawers supported by flaring French feet with overall birdseye maple edges.

c1800   37.5in (95.25cm) wide

$1,500-2,500   POOK

A Federal inlaid mahogany secretary desk, in three parts, the scrolled cornice with central inlaid tablet above two glazed doors and inlaid cylinder desk top opening to fitted interior, with four graduated drawers below, all raised on French bracket feet.

$6,000-8,000   FRE

A Boston, Gothic revival mahogany veneer and carved desk and bookcase, two glazed doors open to a three-shelved interior above the pull-out writing surface and butler's drawer, that reveals a desk with a writing surface, over cupboards each with a single fixed shelf, brasses may be original, some surface imperfections.

c1820   117.25in (298cm) high

$18,000-22,000   SK

A George III mahogany secretary bookcase, the broken-arch bonnet over two mullioned doors, resting on a lower section with butler's desk and three drawers.

c1770

$12,000-16,000 POOK

A George III mahogany secretary desk, the lower section with a fall front enclosing a fitted interior with shell-carved prospect door, above four drawers supported by ogee bracket feet.

c1770 *81in (205.5cm) high*

$5,000-7,000 POOK

An early 19thC Regency rosewood veneer three-part secretary, with two brass mullion doors, flanked by gilded pilasters, above a lower section with butler's desk.

40in (101.5cm) wide

$5,000-6,000 POOK

A Regency mahogany secrétaire bookcase, the deep secrétaire drawer with fitted interior and a short deep drawer, adapted, the pair of paneled doors between lattice-inlaid uprights.

50.5in (128cm) wide

$3,000-4,000 L&T

A Regency mahogany secrétaire bookcase, with twin glazed doors above four drawers, losses.

c1815 *37in (94cm) wide*

$2,000-3,000 DN

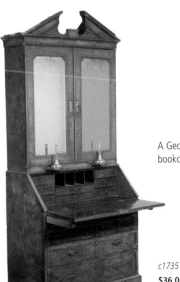

A George II walnut bureau bookcase.

c1735 *39.5in (100cm) wide*

$36,000-44,000 DN

A Victorian mahogany bureau bookcase in 18thC style, with fitted interior, the drawers between cluster column corners on leaf-carved ogee bracket feet.

48.25in (122cm) wide

$4,000-6,000 L&T

An 18thC Georgian walnut and elm bureau cabinet in two parts, the associated lower section with a fall front opening to a fitted interior, raised on bracket feet.

37.75in (96cm) wide

$8,000-12,000 FRE

FURNITURE

A late George III painted satinwood and tulipwood crossbanded low bookcase, the top with pierced brass gallery and border of trailing flowers, with reeded projecting corners and painted lozenge trellis sides.

c1790   64in (128cm) wide

$24,000-30,000   **L&T**

An early 19thC Regency simulated rosewood and parcel-gilt open bookcase, the gray marble top above a frieze with stellar motifs between a pair of stylized roses, on caryatid uprights flanking two reeded shelves.

40.5in (103cm) wide

$70,000-80,000   **SOTH**

A Regency rosewood low library bookcase, with a molded frieze applied with Neoclassical bronze mounts, the open shelves flanked by gilt-wire trellis doors with pleated red silk linings and rosettes to each corner.

81.25in (206cm) wide

$6,000-8,000   **L&T**

A Regency mahogany double-sided waterfall bookcase, the arched top above four graduated open tiers, raised on twin end supports, ending in reeded downswept legs terminating in brass hairy paw caps and casters.

60.25in (153cm) wide

$7,000-9,000   **L&T**

A pair of early 19thC Anglo-Indian rosewood and gilt-metal-mounted bookcases, the shelves flanked by brass-mounted split baluster columns on skirted brass-bound bases and gilt-brass talon and ball feet.

c1835   40.25in (102cm) wide

$12,000-16,000   **L&T**

A Regency mahogany waterfall bookcase, with two open shelves above an arrangement of six small drawers and a further shelf between molded uprights, on splay bracket feet.

36in (91.5cm) wide

$4,000-6,000   **DUK**

CLOSER LOOK: REGENCY SECRÉTAIRE

Heinrich Ludwig Goertz was born in Hanover but emigrated to England in 1800 where he was employed by the Royal Family for over quarter of a century.

The quality of this pair of cabinets and their high style design is reminiscent of furniture supplied to the Prince Regent (later George IV) at Carlton House in London and the Royal Pavilion in Brighton.

The three shelves are supported on finely-turned gilt-brass baluster uprights joined by cross-framed engine-turned braces centered by rosette bosses.

The fall fronts open to reveal a fitted interior with pigeon holes and drawers, a hide writing slope and pen trays, above cupboard doors fitted with gilt-brass trellis grilles backed by silk.

A rare pair of Regency rosewood and gilt-brass-mounted secrétaire bookstands, attributed to Heinrich Ludwig Goertz.

c1810   66.5in (169cm) high

$40,000-50,000   **L&T**

A 17thC and later Flemish tortoiseshell, ebonized and ivory-inlaid cabinet-on-stand, the galleried top over an arrangement of drawers inlaid with hunting scenes, centered by a cupboard door, opening to reveal a parquetry-veneered temple style interior, the rectangular stand with three conforming drawers, raised on spiral turned supports joined by stretchers.

41in (104cm) wide

$10,000-12,000   **FRE**

A 19thC Spanish tortoiseshell, ivory, rosewood and ebonized cabinet-on-stand, in Baroque style, the top with pierced railing and gilt-bronze mounts, the central door with coat of arms and Classical figure, flanked on each side by two columns, between four drawers containing sixteen Classical scenes, the stand with three short drawers, each with two Classical scenes, on spiral legs, all-over applied with small rosettes and ivory-inlaid putti and masks, all sides with inlaid light wood banding, incorporating earlier elements.

51.25in (130cm) wide

$30,000-40,000   **SOTA**

A Dutch tortoiseshell, ebony and ebonized cabinet-on-stand.

c1700 and later   *34.75in (88cm) wide*

$16,000-20,000   **DN**

A Walnut and cross-banded chest-on-stand, on later turned bun feet, faults, repair.

c1700   *41in (104cm) wide*

$6,000-8,000   **DN**

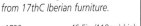

An Indo-Portuguese Goan padouk and marquetry 'contador'.

The bird carving on the feet derives from 17thC Iberian furniture.

c1730   *46.5in (118cm) high*

$60,000-70,000   **DN**

A late George III mahogany cabinet-on-stand, the rectangular top above two doors opening to an arrangement of satinwood-veneered drawers, the stand with a plain frieze on square section tapering legs headed by patera terminals, on spade feet.
c1810

$3,000-4,000   DN

A Regency mahogany secrétaire, in the manner of Gillows of Lancaster, the deep secrétaire with ebony stringing and fitted interior, the drawers with foliate cast gilt-brass bandings and ebonized pull handles, with reeded tapering legs.
39in (110cm) wide

$6,000-8,000   L&T

An 18thC japanned cabinet-on-stand, the cabinet with two cupboard doors painted with Classical figures on a black ground, elaborate brass hinges and lock plate, enclosing an interior with various drawers, painted with Chinoiserie scenes of birds and figures in landscapes, the stand with shaped apron, on cabriole legs with pad feet.

Japanning - a process where items were coated with layers of colored varnish to imitate genuine Chinese or Japanese lacquer - was first used in Europe in the mid-17th century. It was used on anything from small boxes to large pieces of furniture and was often combined with chinoiserie decoration.

38.75in (98cm) wide

$12,000-16,000   L&T

A 19thC German walnut, ivory and pewter-inlaid cabinet-on-stand, probably Braunschweig, with two doors depicting satyrs, a central maenad and Medusa head, above drawer, on stand with crossed stretchers.

48.75in (124cm) high

$5,000-7,000   SOTA

A 19thC Japanese black and gilt lacquer cabinet-on-stand, the two paneled cupboard doors decorated with figures and buildings in landscapes enclosing an architectural balconied interior, with galleried shelves, drawers and doors, on British stand with pierced fretwork frieze and triple cluster column legs, scrolled spandrels, on chamfered block feet.

36in (91cm) wide

$8,000-10,000   L&T

A Louis XV style gilt-bronze-mounted amaranth mahogany cartonnier, the upper section with six tooled leather-covered drawers above a writing slide, raised on cabriole legs terminating in gilt-bronze sabots, stamped twice to the underside 'L. Cueunieres, Ebeniste'.
c1880

31in (79cm) wide

$16,000-20,000   FRE

An 18thC North Italian fruitwood and kingwood-veneered display cabinet, the lower section with extractable surface above two-door front, inlaid with lozenge-shaped marquetry.

82.25in (209cm) high

$10,000-12,000   **SOTA**

A late 18thC and later Dutch walnut and floral marquetry display cabinet, damage, repair, the marquetry later.

84.75in (215cm) wide

$11,000-13,000   **DN**

A late 18th/early 19thC Dutch walnut and marquetry display cabinet-on-chest.

37in (94cm) wide

$7,000-9,000   **DN**

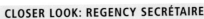

William (c1703-1763) and his son John (1729-1796) Linnell were important London carvers and cabinet-makers. Initially working in the Rococo style, John had adopted the Neoclassical style by c1765. He was among the craftsmen commissioned by Robert Adam to make furniture to his Neoclassical designs.

Both father and son were accomplished carvers and would have had similarly skilled workers among their 40 employees. This can be seen in the quality of the shell-carved cresting at the center of the arched top.

The lower section has two ogee-molded frieze drawers over two oval panel parquetry-banded doors, opening to reveal two further small drawers.

The cabinet is raised on shell and scroll bracket feet.

An important George III period mahogany, padouk and inlaid display cabinet, attributed to William and John Linnell, two glazed panel doors enclose adjustable shelves.

31.5in (80cm) wide

$140,000-200,000   **L&T**

A mid-19thC and later pine cabinet, with repair.

52in (132cm) wide

$2,400-3,600   **DN**

A French Empire mahogany side cabinet, the marble top above a full length door, below an arched frieze between turned columns headed by engine turned capitals decorated with anthemia, on bun feet.

64in (163cm) high

$3,000-4,000   **L&T**

A pair of mahogany side cabinets in the George III manner, with brass diamond trellis doors.

$6,000-8,000   **L&T**

A pair of French Paul Sormani mahogany and kingwood vitrines, applied with gilt-bronze mounts, the painted panel door flanked by curve and beveled edge glass doors, signed 'P SORMANI & FILS, 10 RUE CARLOS'
c1880   *59in (150cm) high*

$110,000-130,000   **SOTH**

A late 19th/early 20thC Venetian painted side cabinet, with an apron drawer raised on tapered Doric style supports, united by a wavy X-shaped stretcher.

34in (86.5cm) wide

$6,000-8,000   **FRE**

A late 19thC Louis XV style gilt-bronze-mounted rosewood Vernis Martin vitrine, with a single glazed door, the whole decorated with reserves.

30in (76cm) wide

$7,000-9,000   **FRE**

An Edwardian mahogany and inlaid display cabinet, of serpentine form, the projecting cornice with faux flutes and vine scrolls interspersed by roundels, the four panel doors decorated with ribbon-tied paterae, the whole highlighted with abalone shell inlay.

64.5in (164cm) wide

$16,000-20,000   **L&T**

A Georgian style mahogany bowfront standing corner cabinet, with astragal door enclosing shelves, a fielded paneled door below, raised on shell-carved dwarf cabriole legs with claw-and-ball feet.

29in (c73.5m) wide

$800-1,200   **A&G**

A late 19thC Louis XV-style kingwood and Vernis Martin vitrine.

Vernis Martin was a japanning technique developed in France in the reign of Louis XIV (1643-1715). It is named after the brothers Martin, but it is used to describe similar work by other craftsmen. It was not as durable as the oriental lacquerwork but it had a brilliancy that made it highly fashionable.

52.75in (134cm) wide

$9,000-11,000   **L&T**

A late 19th/early 20thC Louis XV style gilt-bronze-mounted mahogany Vernis Martin vitrine, with a single glazed door headed by caryatids and decorated with amorous reserves, raised on downswept legs.

41.5in (105.5cm) wide

$7,000-9,000   **FRE**

An Edwardian mahogany and marquetry-inlaid side cabinet, in the manner of Edwards & Roberts, the paneled cupboard doors inlaid with flowering cornucopia and angel mask motifs, raised on bellflower-carved square tapered legs.

72in (183cm) wide

$6,500-7,500   **L&T**

An Edwardian mahogany display cabinet, the rectangular top above a blind fret frieze, and two astragal glazed doors, above two drawers, on carved cabriole-shaped legs ad stylized claw-and-ball feet.

c1910   *48in (122cm) wide*

$1,200-1,600   **DN**

An Edwardian mahogany and marquetry standing corner cupboard, with dentil cornice and faux fluted frieze, the base with a pair of fielded panel satinwood-banded doors inlaid with musical trophies and foliage.

41in (104cm) wide

$9,000-11,000 WW

An Edwardian rosewood and marquetry display cabinet, retailed by Maple & Co, bearing ivorine retailer's plaque.

43in (109cm) wide

$7,000-9,000 DN

An early 20thC satinwood and polychrome-painted bowfront display cabinet, the door centered by a portrait of a female, damage.

28.25in (72cm) wide

$6,000-8,000 DN

SIDE CABINETS

One of a pair of early 18thC Italian walnut side cabinets, damage, repair.

76.5in (194cm) wide

$20,000-24,000 PAIR DN

A late 18thC German pair of Louis XVI mahogany demi-lune side cabinets, the marble tops above a central drawer and two drawers hinged on either side, a large compartment below with corrugated door, the legs inlaid in brass and fluted, tapering at the bottom.

47.5in (121cm) wide

$20,000-30,000 SOTA

A pair of 18thC style black lacquer and gilt chinoiserie bowfront corner cupboards, the doors painted with birds, pagodas and scenes from domestic life, enclosing shaped shelves, with brass cock's heads hinges, on skirted cavetto molded bases.

35.5in (90cm) high

$1,600-2,400 L&T

A second half 18thC and later Italian burr yew corner cupboard.

21.75in (55cm) wide

$1,000-1,600 DN

An early Regency satinwood and rosewood crossbanded side cabinet, the associated marble top above an inlaid frieze and a pair of silk-lined cabinet doors with roundel-applied corners, on short square tapering legs.

c1805 *40.5in (103cm) wide*

$56,000-64,000 L&T

A Regency rosewood mahogany-veneered and parcel-gilt breakfront side cabinet, with three sunken field frieze drawers above a cupboard door with circular frame molding and lozenge frame molding to the flanking doors, divided by reeded uprights headed by corrugated capitals, on short faceted legs with brass ball feet.

Many stylistic aspects of this cabinet suggest the hand of the London furniture maker John McLean. In particular, the use of reeded or corrugated decoration within a sunken 'tablet'.

48in (123cm) wide

$36,000-44,000 L&T

CLOSER LOOK: REGENCY SIDE CABINET

The corners of the front are decorated with gilt-bronze paterae-trailing husks.

Both the cupboard doors and the sides are inset with lacquer panels painted with figural landscapes.

The front of the cabinet is centered by a gilt-bronze satyr mask.

The serpentine apron is embellished with gilt-bronze ribbon-tied foliate mounts headed by chimera.

A Louis XVI style gilt-bronze-mounted kingwood and tulipwood lacquer meuble a hauteur d'appui, retailed by Ch. Deville & J. Maubert Sucrs, Paris, the rectangular verde antico marbled top over egg and dart molding, opening to a shelved interior, on waisted bracket feet, many of the mounts stamped 'MB', the backboard with a partially effaced retailers brand 'Ch DEVLLE K. MAUBERT SUCR 281 Avenue de l'Opera et Rue Gaillon PARIS'.

c1880

$24,000-30,000

62in (157.5cm) wide

FRE

A matched pair of late 19th/early 20thC carved oak cabinets, in the Gothic taste, of slightly varying proportions.

57.5in (146cm) wide

$8,000-12,000 PAIR　**DN**

A pair of early 20thC George II style satinwood and marquetry demi-lune side cabinets, each with marquetry reserves throughout depicting musical trophies, bell flowers and paterae, each with a central covered door, above square section tapering legs, damage, repair.

33.75in (86cm) wide

$12,000-16,000　**DN**

A late 19th/early 20thC Anglo-Indian carved rosewood and satinwood cabinet, the rectangular top with molded edge above a central door and flanking panels carved profusely with scrolling and meandering foliate motifs, on a plinth base.

47.25in (120cm) wide

$2,000-3,000　**DN**

A late 19th/early 20thC satinwood and marquetry cabinet.

43.25in (110cm) wide

$2,400-3,600　**DN**

A Regency brass-inlaid rosewood chiffonier, the shelved back with a three-quarter pierced brass gallery, the lower section with two frieze drawers over grille doors, raised on splayed feet.

c1815   36.75in (93.25cm) wide

$5,000-7,000   **FRE**

A Regency mahogany chiffonier bookcase, the arched back above two shelves on S-scroll and brass vine supports, the glazed base with a pair of cabinet doors decorated with a brass foliate trellis, on plinth base with bun feet.

35in (89cm) wide

$2,000-3,000   **L&T**

A Regency rosewood and brass-mounted chiffonier.

c1820   42in (107cm) wide

$2,000-3,000   **DN**

A mid-19thC mahogany chiffonier, with shelf above two doors.

42.5in (108cm) wide

$1,000-1,400   **DN**

A late Regency chiffonier, attributed to a design by Thomas King, the pair of paneled doors, enclosing an adjustable shelf, between broad pilaster uprights decorated with elongated lotus stems and dual carved rosettes.

A similar example with pleated doors and ledge back is illustrated in Thomas King's Sketch Book (1835), the carving on the uprights is identical.

50in (127cm) wide

$3,600-4,400   **L&T**

A Victorian mahogany chiffonier, frieze drawer with brass lion mask handles.

36in (91.5cm) wide

$1,000-1,600   **HT**

A Victorian burr walnut breakfront credenza, with a central paneled and arabesque door, the whole with gilt-metal mounts.

73in (185cm) wide

$5,000-7,000   **L&T**

A Napoleon III kingwood, tulipwood marquetry and bronze-mounted side board, on scrolled feet, all-over inlaid with floral marquetry.

57.5in (146cm) wide

$12,000-16,000   **SOTA**

A Victorian figured walnut and marquetry breakfront side cabinet, the rectangular crossbanded top above a central door, flanked on each side by a glass-paneled door, divided by ebonized columns, on a plinth base, damage.

c1870   73.25in (186cm) wide

$8,000-10,000   **DN**

FURNITURE

A Victorian burr-walnut and kingwood crossbanded side cabinet, faults.
c1870   *59.5in (151cm) wide*
$2,000-3,000   **DN**

A third quarter 19thC tortoiseshell, brass marquetry and ebonized side cabinet, with black marble top, faults.
$2,000-3,000   **DN**

A last quarter 19thC Victorian burr-walnut, inlaid and ebonized breakfront credenza.

64.5in (164cm) wide
$4,000-6,000   **DN**

A French kingwood credenza, by François Linke, applied with gilt-bronze mounts, of bowed breakfront form, the frieze drawer above a panel door inlaid with radiating veneers and flanked by open marble shelves with mirror backs, the inside backs of the locks stamped 'C LINKE SERRURERIE PARIS'.
c1890   *57.75in (147cm) wide*
$20,000-30,000   **SOTH**

BEDSIDE CABINETS

A George III mahogany night table or commode, with faults.
c1790   *19in (48cm) wide*
$1,200-1,600   **DN**

A George III mahogany washstand.
c1790   *13in (33cm) wide*
$500-700   **DN**

A George III mahogany tray-top commode, with damage.
c1790   *22.75in (58cm) wide*
$1,200-1,600   **DN**

A mahogany bedside cupboard, with damage.
c1790 and later   *19.25in (49cm) wide*
$500-700   **DN**

A George III mahogany bedside cupboard, the top with pierced carrying handles.

17.25in (44cm) wide
$5,000-7,000   **L&T**

A pair of George III style mahogany night commodes.

22in (56cm) wide
$4,000-5,000 PAIR   **L&T**

A pair of Regency mahogany bedside cupboards.

c1820
$11,000-13,000 PAIR   **DN**

A pair of early 19thC satinwood and ebony bedside tables, with bowfront checkered tambour doors, on slender square tapering legs.
32in (82cm) high
$4,000-6,000 PAIR   **L&T**

A matched pair of early 20thC beech and pine simulated bamboo bedside cabinets.
The largest 15.75in (40cm) wide
$1,600-2,400   **DN**

A late 19th/early 20thC mahogany and gilt-metal-mounted bedside cupboard.
17.75in (45cm) wide
$1,400-2,000   **DN**

A late 17thC oak buffet of narrow proportions, the pendant and strapwork-carved frieze inscribed with the initials 'MBM' and dated, above a Celtic style strapwork-carved cupboard door, a small guilloche-carved door and a larger strapwork-carved door with wrought iron loop handles, between channel-molded uprights and paneled sides, on stem feet.

1696   66.5in (169cm) high
$6,000-10,000   **L&T**

A late 17thC Flemish oak and lignum vitae buffet, the top with crossbanded decoration, with carved lion mask capitals on columns, the cupboard doors enclosing a shelved and inlaid interior, on a skirted apron with cabochon frieze and projecting corners carved with cartouches, on boldly turned spherical feet.

72in (183cm) wide
$4,000-5,000   **L&T**

An Elizabethan oak court cupboard, the rectangular top with molded edge and geometric inlaid frieze on gadrooned and carved melon-turned supports with ionic style capitals, the lower shelf enclosing a gadrooned full width drawer on similarly turned supports united by an inlaid undershelf, on stem feet, period and later parts.

47.25in (120cm) wide
$3,200-4,400   **L&T**

An early 17thC oak livery cupboard, the rectangular two-plank top over a dentil-molded and lunette-carved frieze and a rectangular single paneled cupboard door with nulled molded border, flanked to each side by matching canted panels, between two palmette-carved cup-and-cover supports over a lunette-carved long frieze drawer, above an open cupboard and two heavy front corner leaf-carved baluster supports, over a wavy scroll front rail on block front feet.

48.25in (122.5cm) wide
$6,000-10,000   **HALL**

A 17thC and later Charles II oak court cupboard, the rectangular molded top above a carved frieze and two tiers separated by a drawer, raised on foliate-carved cup-and-cover and scroll-capped supports, on a molded plinth base.

49.5in (125.5cm) wide
$1,400-2,000   **FRE**

A 19thC and later carved oak cupboard, in part constructed from old timbers, damage, repair.

51.25in (130cm) wide
$1,500-1,900   **DN**

An early 18thC 'cwpwrdd deuddarn', with a pair of fielded panel doors, the left with an interior locking bar, flanking a central panel above three frieze drawers and a pair of twin-panel doors, enclosing a shelf, brass work later, one panel door missing lock.

57in (145cm) wide
$1,600-2,400   **WW**

FURNITURE

An oak dresser base.

c1660 and later   75.5in (192cm) wide

$3,000-4,000   **DN**

An early 18thC oak dresser, the twin boarded top with a molded edge and canted corners above three frieze drawers, fitted later brass handles and escutcheons, with a girdle moulding on turned baluster block legs with turned feet.

89.75in (228cm) wide

$7,000-9,000   **WW**

A Welsh oak dresser base, with a molded edge top, an elaborate scalloped skirt and cabriole front legs terminating in slipper feet.

c1750   75in (190.5cm) wide

$6,000-10,000   **POOK**

A late 18thC George III oak dresser.   71in (180.5cm) wide

$4,800-5,200   **DN**

A Georgian mahogany dresser, fitted with six short drawers with later embossed brass handles and inlaid lozenge-shaped bone escutcheons, with a pair of paneled doors, raised on bracket feet.

62in (157cm) wide

$3,000-4,000   **A&G**

An 18thC rectangular oak dresser, three short drawers fitted to the frieze, with brass drop handles, a pair of paneled doors below with heavy iron hinges, raised on later bun feet.

84in (213cm) wide

$2,000-2,400   **A&G**

A small 18thC oak dresser, the boarded top above an applied molded frieze and two drawers, fitted replaced pierced brass plate handles and escutcheons above a shaped apron on square legs, old restoration.

20in (51cm) high

$1,600-2,400   **WW**

A late 18thC oak dresser, with a molded edge top above four frieze drawers, fitted replaced brass plate handles with shaped aprons on ring-turned baluster supports to a stretchered pot board, restoration and replacements.

80in (203cm) wide

$2,000-2,400   **WW**

A George III fruitwood low dresser, with molded edge top, two small central cockbeaded drawers with brass drop handles, flanked on either side by a large drawer, raised on club-front legs and pad feet.

68in (172.5cm) wide

$2,400-2,800   **HT**

CLOSER LOOK: PAINTED CORNER CUPBOARD

The construction of painted cupboards is usually much simpler than this – suggesting this was made for a wealthy family. Similarly, glass was relatively expensive at the time, adding to the probability that the original owners were people of means. The dentil-molded cornice and paneled pilasters are further evidence of quality.

A Lancaster County, Pennsylvania poplar hanging cupboard, the molded cornice over a single door with wrought iron ram's horn hinges, above a lower shelf with scalloped sides, retaining its original red-painted surface, from the Shelley Collection.

c1740   *36in (91.5cm) high*

$19,000-21,000   **POOK**

A Lancaster County, Pennsylvania two-part corner cupboard, the dentil-molded cornice over a single arched door, flanked by paneled pilasters, resting on a base with single drawer and raised panel cupboard door supported by ogee feet, retaining an old green and brown surface, from the Shelley Collection.

c1785   *80.5in (204.5cm) high*

$35,000-40,000   **POOK**

A mid-18thC Hudson Valley painted barrel-back two-part corner cupboard, the interior ceiling with shell and cherub polychrome decoration flanked by stop-fluted palisters supported by a blocked base with carved ogee bracket feet, retaining original old Spanish brown surface, from the Shelley Collection.

86.5in (219.5cm) high

$12,000-18,000   **POOK**

A probably mid-18thC ebonized and red 'combed' kitchen dresser.

American painted dressers of this type and size are scarce. The stylish features of this example possibly indicate a New England provenance and the use of crisply executed caddy and re-entrant moldings suggests an early date.

76.25in (194cm) high

$10,000-20,000   **L&T**

A Lancaster or Berks Couty, Pennsylvania painted pine schrank, the stepped cornice with ivory dentil molding, above a blue case with raised panel doors with stippled center and red surround, retaining their original rattail hinges, resting on a base with red ogee mid-molding and ivory stippled drawers, supported by tall bracket feet, from the Shelley Collection.

c1770   *79.5in (202cm) high*

$220,000-250,000   **POOK**

A late 18thC New England painted pine step-back cupboard, the molded cornice over three open shelves, and a base with raised panel doors supported by shoe feet, retaining a red and black surface.

54in (137.25cm) wide

$3,000-5,000   **POOK**

A late 18thC Lancaster or Berks County, Pennsylvania painted pine hanging corner cupboard, with molded cornice over raised panel door with rattail hinges, over a scalloped base, retaining an old red surface with stippled door panel, from the Shelley Collection.

34.5in (87.5cm) high

$20,000-25,000   **POOK**

A Lehigh Country, Pennsylvania decorated poplar cupboard, the upper section with a bold cover cornice, above two glazed doors, the base with three drawers, two doors, and French bracket feet, the case boldly decorated with ochre and red graining and smoke-decorated doors.

c1810   *65in (165.5cm) wide*
$33,000-36,000   **POOK**

A Pennsylvania painted two-part Dutch cupboard, the molded cornice over two glazed doors flanked by turned half columns, resting on a base with three drawers and two raised panel doors supported by bracket feet, retaining an old yellow surface.

c1820   *89.5in (227.5cm) high*
$6,000-10,000   **POOK**

A Pennsylvania poplar two-part Dutch cupboard.

c1830   *51.5in (130.75cm) wide*
$2,500-3,500   **POOK**

An early 19thC Pennsylvania painted poplar hanging corner cupboard, with molded cornice and raised panel door, retaining an old green-over-red surface, from the Shelley Collection.

24.5in (62cm) wide
$6,000-8,000   **POOK**

An early 19thC Virginia yellow pine hanging corner cabinet, the recessed panel door surrounded by picture frame molding, enclosing an interior with scalloped shelves, retaining old green surface, from the Shelley Collection.

41in (104cm) high
$7,000-9,000   **POOK**

An early 19thC South-Eastern United States, brown-painted yellow pine and punched tin pie safe, projecting molded top above two hinged doors each with three panels showing Antebellum mansions flanked by stars, opening to three shelves, the sides with the same punched tin panels, on square slightly tapering legs, original surface with minor imperfections.

42in (106.5cm) wide
$10,000-15,000   **SK**

An early 19thC Pennsylvania painted one piece corner cupboard, the molded cornice over a glazed door and two cupboard doors supported by bracket feet, retaining its original ochre grain decoration.

85in (216cm) high
$6,000-7,000   **POOK**

A Pennsylvania painted pine architectural corner cupboard, the molded cornice over two arched doors enclosing a salmon interior with scalloped shelves flanked by doric pilasters, above two cupboard doors, retaining a blue surface.

60.5in (153.5cm) wide
$4,000-6,000   **POOK**

A painted and decorated corner cupboard, by Peter Hunt, Provincetown, Massachusetts, molded cornice above recessed panel door opening to shelf, molded base, painted yellow with polychrome figure of St. Joan on horseback enclosed with broders of flourishes, hearts and flowers and the inscription 'Province A.D. 35.'

1935   *25in (63.5cm) wide*
$2,000-2,500   **FRE**

CLOSER LOOK: WALNUT SCHRANK

With its dramatic profiles, fully inlaid fascia, Baroque carved panel, and marquetry floral inlay, this piece embodies the height of Pennsylvania German cabinetry.

The design shows how the High Baroque style, popular in Germany at the time, was recreated in the New World by immigrant craftsmen. Similar, later pieces tend to show many influences, this piece has just one.

The Lancaster First Reformed Church has a record for the birth of a son to John and Anna Maria Spoor in 1749. They were most likely the original owners of the piece, probably made to signify the building of a new home or other special event.

A Lancaster County, Pennsylvania walnut schrank, the molded cornice over a frieze panel inlaid 'Iohanes Spohr A Maria Spohrin anno 1760', with floral sprigs, over a case with a floral-carved raised panel, over an astragal panel with tulip, scroll, and star inlay, flanked by linen-fold pilasters and double raised panel sides, resting on a lower section with five drawers and boldly molded base, from the Shelley Collection, dated.

1760   *85in (216cm) high*

$350,0000-400,000   POOK

A Pennsylvania Queen Anne walnut wall cupboard, the upper section with two paneled doors enclosing a fitted interior, over scalloped recess opening with single shelf, the base with two over three long drawers, resting on straight bracket feet with center drop, from the Shelley Collection.

c1750   *79in (200.5cm) high*

$60,000-70,000   POOK

A Lancaster County, Pennsylvania walnut two-part pewter cupboard, the dentil molded cornice over three shelves with spoon racks and plate rails flanked by pronounced scalloped and spurred sides, resting on a base with three lipped drawers and two raised panel doors with rattail hinges, flanked by sunken panel stiles supported by straight bracket feet, retaining an expectional fine old surface, from the Shelley Collection.

c1750   *82in (208cm) high*

$50,000-60,000   POOK

A Southern Pennsylvania figured walnut one-piece corner cupboard, flanked by canted sides with picture frame molding, on bracket feet, from the Shelley Collection.

c1760   *84in (213.5cm) high*

$5,000-7,000   POOK

A Lancaster County, Pennsylvania walnut hanging corner cupboard, the molded cornice over a raised panel door with scalloped relief and rattail hinges, above a single drawer, flanked by canted paneled sides above a molded base, retaining its original brass pull, from the Shelley Collection.

c1770   *33.75in (85.5cm) high*

$4,000-6,000   POOK

A Eastern Shore, Virginia yellow pine clothes press, with raised and arched panel doors flanked by raised panel sides, supported by straight bracket feet, from the Shelley Collection.

c1770   *66in (167.5cm) high*

$50,000-60,000   POOK

A Philadelphia Chippendale mahogany desk.

c1775

$15,000-25,000   FRE

FURNITURE

A Pennsylvania walnut two-part cupboard, the molded cornice over two glazed doors, flanked by fluted quarter columns, above a pie shelf with lollipop sides, three short drawers, and two cupboard doors supported by ogee bracket feet.

c1780　　　*99.5in (252.75cm) high*

$4,000-6,000　　**POOK**

A late 18th/early 19thC two-part Federal cherrywood linen press, probably from New Jersey, with two panel doors containing shelves, and beaded drawers on bracket feet.

48in (123cm) wide

$5,000-7,000　　**FRE**

A Pennsylvania step-back pine cupboard, in two parts, the upper section with molded cornice above two glazed doors flanked by fluted pilasters, the lower section with two lip-molded drawers and two raised panel doors on a flush molded base.

c1800

$5,500-7,500　　**FRE**

A Pennsylvania walnut two-part cupboard, the upper section with a molded cornice, over two glazed doors flanked by fluted pilasters, resting on a lower section with three line-inlaid drawers and two raised panel doors supported by bracket feet.

c1810　　　*51.5in (130cm) wide*

$8,000-10,000　　**POOK**

A Pennsylvania poplar two-part Dutch cupboard, the upper section with carved cornice, above two paneled doors flanked by spool-turned quarter columns, over a base with three drawers and two doors supported by turned feet.

c1820　　　*84.5in (214.5cm) high*

$5,500-6,500　　**POOK**

A Mid-Atlantic States cherry corner cabinet, with molded cornice above glazed door above three molded drawers and two recessed panel doors.

c1825

$3,000-4,000　　**FRE**

An early 19thC Pennsylvania cherry two-part corner cupboard, the molded cornice over an arched glazed door and lower section with single drawer and two recessed panel doors supported by flared bracket feet.

83.75in (212.5cm) high

$4,500-5,500　　**POOK**

An early 19thC Pennsylvania poplar one-piece corner cupboard, retaining an old red-stain surface.

32in (81.5cm) wide

$5,000-7,000　　**POOK**

A Pennsylvania Dutch walnut cupboard, with a molded cornice over two glazed doors and five candle drawers, flanked by turned half columns, resting on a lower section with three drawers and two doors supported by bracket feet.

c1830　　　*59in (150cm) wide*

$3,500-5,500　　**POOK**

A Pennsylvania Classical maple and cherrywood corner cupboard, with two glazed doors flanked by shaped pilasters, the lower section with two faux drawers flanking working drawer, on turned feet.

c1835

$3,000-4,000　　**FRE**

A mid- 9thC Pennsylvania poplar two-part Dutch cupboard, with glazed doors flanked by reeded and chamfered pilasters, above a pie shelf and lower section with three short drawers and two doors supported by turned feet.

93.5in (237.5cm) high

$2,500-3,500　　**POOK**

A late 18thC George III mahogany sideboard, with bowfront top over two highly inlaid bottle drawers flanking a central drawer supported on square tapering line-inlaid legs on spade feet.

66in (167.5cm) wide

$5,000-7,000   **POOK**

A George III mahogany serpentine sideboard, the brass gallery flanked on each side by a deep drawer, on square-section tapering legs and spade feet, damage.

c1790   67in (170cm) wide

$1,200-1,600   **DN**

A George III mahogany bowfront sideboard, some damage.

c1790   54.5in (138cm) wide

$8,000-10,000   **DN**

A late 18thC George III mahogany sideboard, the serpentine front with central long drawer, flanked by two bottle drawers and two cupboard doors, supported by square tapering legs with paterae and entwined serpent inlays, terminating in spade feet.

90in (228.5cm) wide

$9,000-11,000   **POOK**

A late George III mahogany and tulipwood-crossbanded sideboard, of break-bowfront outline, the staged tambour back with corner swing doors above a tablet-centered frieze drawer, the top veneers with 'plum pudding' figuring and end-facing pot cupboard.

46.75in (119cm) wide

$4,000-5,000   **L&T**

A late Georgian mahogany serpentine-front sideboard, decorated with boxwood edging, fitted with a single drawer to the frieze with a convex panel door, and a deep drawer, all fitted with lion mask ring handles, raised on square tapering legs with spade feet.

53.5in (136cm) wide

$1,000-1,400   **A&G**

A George III mahogany and banded bowfront sideboard, the rectangular shaped top above a central drawer with sliding writing surface and four further drawers, around the central arch on square section tapering legs, and spade feet, damage, possibly adapted.

c1810   42in (107cm) wide

$1,600-2,400   **DN**

An early 19thC late George III mahogany and sycamore-strung bowfront sideboard.

66in (168cm) wide

$3,600-4,400   **DN**

A Regency mahogany and boxwood-strung and inlaid twin pedestal sideboard, with inverted breakfront enclosing three frieze drawers and beaded doors enclosing shelves.

54.25in (138cm) wide

$5,000-6,000   **L&T**

A Regency mahogany sideboard, with a pair of concave-fronted drawers and deep cellaret drawer flanked by a deep drawer and an out-swinging cellaret drawer with lead lining, with lion mask handles.

83.5in (213cm) wide

$3,400-4,000   **L&T**

A Regency mahogany and boxwood-strung sideboard, of break bowfront form, the stage back with four tambour doors above a 'plum-pudding'-figured top with three inlaid frieze drawers flanked by a deep cellaret drawer, paneled as two, and a cupboard door, with brass oval-stamped handles, the arched recess with a pair of tambour doors, on partridgewood-veneered uprights and square tapering legs with leaf-carved capitals and gaitered feet.

79.5in (202cm) wide

$7,000-8,000   **L&T**

A Baltimore Hepplewhite mahogany sideboard, the serpentine top with line- and barber pole-inlaid edge, over a case with a single drawer and four doors, all with oval and line inlays supported by square tapering legs with interlacing line inlay and banded cuffs.

c1795   *75in (190cm) wide*

$15,000-20,000   **POOK**

A late 18thC Middle Atlantic States Federal inlaid mahogany sideboard, the bow-shaped top above drawer and two doors flanked by two curved cabinet doors, raised on eight square tapering legs, inlay throughout.

72.5in (184cm) wide

$7,000-9,000   **FRE**

A Federal mahogany inlaid sideboard, probably from New Hampshire, with elliptic front and inlaid edge above a case of flaming birch and mahogany crossbanded drawers, with old brasses, refinished.

c1800   *41.75in (106cm)*

$45,000-55,000   **SK**

A Connecticut or New York Hepplewhite mahogany sideboard, the rectangular top over a case with four short drawers, flanking a door supported by square tapering legs with bookend-inlaid capitals and two series of oval chain inlays.

c1800   *60in (152.5cm) wide*

$6,000-8,000   **POOK**

A Massachusetts Federal mahogany carved and mahogany veneer server, with bowed front, ovolo corners and double-beaded edge, old replaced brasses, minor imperfections.

c1810-15   *39in (99cm) wide*

$8,000-12,000   **SK**

An 18th/19thC Federal inlaid mahogany sideboard, possibly from Rhode Island, with bowed center section, and pencil line inlay, refinished, repaired and with some damage.

56in (142cm) wide

$9,000-11,000   **FRE**

A Massachusetts or Rhode Island Federal mahogany-inlaid sideboard, with inlaid edge, projecting elliptical front, on a conforming case with four drawers, with replaced brasses, refinished.

c1815 *66in (167.5cm) wide*

$5,500-7,500   **SK**

An early 19thC Southern Federal mahogany hunt board, with central cupboard door flanked by four drawers supported by square tapering legs.

47.5in (120.5cm) wide

$5,500-7,500   **POOK**

A Classical mahogany carved and mahogany veneer sideboard, probably from Salem, Massachusetts, with ring- and ball-turned decorative edge, replaced brass pulls, refinished, and restored.

c1825   *47.5in (120.5cm) wide*

$6,000-8,000   **SK**

A Baltimore, Maryland Federal mahogany server, with two outset and beaded drawers and recessed double doors, turned tapering legs, some damage, refinished.

c1825   *46.5in (118cm) wide*

$3,500-4,500   **FRE**

A Regency mahogany twin pedestal sideboard, satinwood crossbanded and boxwood line-inlaid overall, the D-shaped reeded center section with two molded frieze drawers, flanked on each side by a pedestal with reeded rectangular caddy top above two molded cupboard doors, the lower flanked by spirally reeded columns, on reeded short sabre legs.

100.5in (225cm) wide

$3,400-4,000   L&T

A small late Regency bowfront mahogany sideboard in the manner of Gillows, the shaped top above three frieze drawers around an arched apron, raised on reeded turned tapered legs.

41.5in (105cm) wide

$4,000-5,000   L&T

A Regency mahogany and marquetry serpentine-fronted sideboard, faults, repair.

c1820   *65in (165cm) wide*

$6,000-8,000   DN

A late Regency mahogany sideboard.

c1820   *65in (165cm) wide*

$2,000-3,000   DN

An early 19thC mahogany pedestal sideboard, decorated all over with satinwood crossbanding, boxwood stringing and inlaid urn motifs, the small raised back with carved scrolling decoration, the center section fitted with three small drawers to the frieze, flanked by the pedestals, each with a hinged cover and false drawer above an arched paneled door, recessed and flanked by turned pilasters enclosing a bottle drawer and shelves, raised on turned tapering feet.

94in (239cm) wide

$3,000-4,000   A&G

A George IV mahogany pedestal sideboard, faults.

c1825   *81in (206cm) wide*

$5,000-6,000   DN

A William IV mahogany twin pedestal sideboard, of inverted breakfront type, with four molded frieze drawers and a pair of paneled cupboard doors flanked by columnar uprights, the whole enhanced by flame-figured and plum pudding veneers.

90.25in (229cm) wide

$2,000-3,000   L&T

A George IV Scottish mahogany pedestal sideboard, the pedestals fitted with two drawers above a cupboard door, the left opens to slide-out shelves, the right opens to a cellaret, each carved with acanthus supports, raised on leaf-carved feet.

c1830   *80.75in (205cm) wide*

$4,000-5,000   FRE

A William IV mahogany pedestal sideboard.

c1835   *71.25in (181cm) wide*

$1,600-2,400   DN

A South West German or Alsace Renaissance oak, walnut and fruitwood-parquetry cabinet, built in three sections, the top frieze sculptured with winged putti, flowers and a central cartouche, the central part with two architectural doors decorated with acanthus leaves, winged putti and scallop shells, flanked and divided by turned columns, the lower corpus with one long drawer, flanked by two lion heads, each holding brass rings, sides paneled, on ball feet, dated.

1626   *82.75in (210cm) wide*

$20,000-30,000   **SOTA**

A late 17thC Dutch ebony, ebonized and rosewood Baroque cupboard or 'Kussenkast', the lower part with two larger doors above two drawers, all doors divided and flanked by pilasters, upper and lower part divided by lion-headed drawer, paneled sides, ball feet, damages.

97.75in (248cm) high

$13,000-15,000   **SOTA**

A 17thC Dutch oak and ebonized five-door Renaissance cupboard, the frieze with male and female masks, above three small paneled doors and two large geometrical paneled doors, paneled sides, overall with ebonized banding, altered.

78.75in (200cm) high

$6,000-8,000   **SOTA**

A 17thC Dutch oak and ebonized Renaissance cupboard, alterations.

73.25in (186cm) high

$7,000-9,000   **SOTA**

A 17thC South Netherlandish Renaissance carved oak cupboard, with doors depicting allegorical figures, all flanked and divided by fluted pillars, two drawers with lion-headed handles, on ball feet.

84.25in (214cm) high

$13,000-15,000   **SOTA**

A 17thC and later Dutch Renaissance oak and ebony cupboard, the interior with two pierced doors and one drawer, the lower frieze carved with acanthus leaves, alterations.

56.75in (114cm) wide

$6,000-8,000   **SOTA**

A 17thC Dutch Baroque oak, ebony and rosewood cupboard or 'Kussenkast', the protruding cornice above a pair of raised paneled doors, enclosing an interior with shelves and one drawer, flanked and divided by pilasters with Corinthian capital, a long drawer below, sides with panels and pilaster, on large ball feet, alterations.

80in (203cm) wide

$24,000-28,000   **SOTA**

A mid-18thC North German walnut, ivory and pewter parquetry and marquetry cabinet, Braunschweig Rococo, the corners with elegant floral inlay and rocaille carvings, on rocaille-carved curved feet.

84.25in (214cm)

$60,000-70,000 **SOTA**

A mid-18thC Dutch Rococo burr walnut display cupboard, pair of glazed doors, the lower section now also fitted with glazed doors, ball feet.

94.5in (240cm) high

$9,000-11,000 **SOTA**

A mid 18thC German walnut, fruitwood and mother-of-pearl marquetry Baroque cabinet, probably Frankfurt, the door with male figure of Justice, a griffin and a baldequin, on bun feet.

79in (201cm) high

$60,000-80,000 **SOTA**

A mid-18thC South-German Baroque walnut, fruitwood and marquetry cabinet, the lower part with hinged central sloping fall front, above central door, on six bun feet, alterations.

65in (162cm) wide

$10,000-14,000 **SOTA**

A late 18thC French pine standing cupboard, the upper section with two field paneled cupboard doors, the base with three drawers above two doors on stile legs, damage.

56in (142cm) wide

$1,200-2,400 **DN**

A late 18thC oak standing corner cupboard.

c1790 *39.75in (101cm) wide*

$2,400-3,000 **DN**

A 19thC South German walnut and burr walnut cupboard, possibly Freiburg, in Baroque style, the frieze with male masks alternating fruit above two sculptured doors, each with a male and female mask, opening to a later interior flanked by columns, sides paneled.

100in (254cm) wide

$9,000-11,000 **SOTA**

An early 19th century North Wales oak deuddarn, with panel doors, one revealing a fitted interior of two short drawers and two pigeonholes, over two short frieze drawers above two doors to the base, fitted with turned wooden handles with mother-of-pearl centers, raised on tall bracket feet.

44in (112cm) wide

$5,000-6,000 **HALL**

An early 19thC Welsh oak press, with a pair of arched fielded panel doors enclosing later shelves with a quadruple-panel front base above a pair of apron drawers on molded stile feet, handles later, one drawer missing its base.

54.5in (138.5cm) high

$6,000-8,000 **WW**

A massive 19thC French provincial walnut buffet a deux corps, with two molded paneled cupboard doors, flanked by concave doors, the projecting lower section with three cupboard doors, shaped apron, on scrolled feet.

93in (236cm) wide

$6,000-8,000 **L&T**

A pair of pitch pine press cupboards, each decorated all over with simulated bamboo mouldings, above two short drawers, on ring-turned feet.

53.75in (136cm) wide

$5,200-6,000 **L&T**

A Flemish oak cabinet, in late Gothic style, the front inserted with panels carved in relief with Gothic tracery, two doors in the center, the sides with broad linen fold panels, one above the other, upper lock detached.

46.5in (118cm) high

$6,000-8,000 **SOTA**

WILLIAM & MARY STYLE

Named after the English King and Queen who reigned from 1689-1694, the William and Mary style was introduced in America at the end of the 17thC.

- The William and Mary style was a New World version of the European Baroque style.
- The style was rich, elegant and highly embellished. As in the Baroque style, Classical motifs, like scrolls, spirals and columns, were used in exaggerated form. Wood was often veneered or painted, which led to walnut and maple replacing oak as the most popular woods.

An 18thC Pennsylvania William & Mary cherry secretaire, with double bonnet top, two doors over five drawer base and slant front enclosing fitted interior.

89in (226cm) high

$15,000-20,000   **POOK**

A Classical mahogany and mahogany veneer secretary desk, attributed to Elijah Sanderson (1751-1825) Salem, Massachusetts, with fitted interior.

A note glued to desk drawer inscribed 'The secretary was made by Elijah Sanderson of Salem Mass about 1800. His house was on Federal Street and his shop was across the street. Emery Abbot Mulliken 1897.' An additional note inscribed 'This secretary was once the property of Miss Eliza Sanderson and was made by her father Elijah Sanderson at his shop about the year 1800.' Elisa Sanderson, the child of Elijah and Mary Mulliken Sanderson, was born in Salem in 1791.

c1820   *45.5in (115.5cm) wide*

$6,000-8,000   **FRE**

A Montgomery County, Pennsylvania cherry corner cupboard, with a glazed upper section resting on a base with three drawers.

c1825   *50.5in (128cm) wide*

$2,500-3,500   **POOK**

A Federal mahogany and bird's-eye maple-inlaid desk bookcase, probably from New Hampshire, with a hinged slanted writing surface, four drawers, two cupboard doors and two bottle drawers, refinished.

41.5in (105.5cm) wide

$6,500-8,500   **SK**

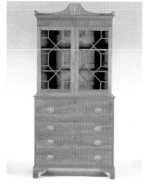

A Massachusetts Federal inlaid mahogany secretary bookcase, with double glazed doors opening to two shelves, fitted interior and three cock-beaded drawers.

c1800   *43in (109cm) wide*

$8,000-12,000   **FRE**

A Connecticut Queen Anne maple secretary desk, the bonnet top with two raised panel doors, over a base with blocked interior and four drawers, resting on straight bracket feet.

c1770   *36in (91.5cm) wide*

$20,000-30,000   **POOK**

A Philadelphia mahogany five-part secretary bookcase, with overall brass line inlays, the upper section with a molded cornice over two doors with carved mullions, flanked by turned columns, above three short drawers and one long drawer, resting on a lower section with two concave doors, supported by animal paw feet.

c1825   *94in (238cm) high*

$8,000-12,000   **POOK**

A late 18thC Dutch mahogany armoire, the cornice of swan neck outline centered by acanthus scroll and laurel swag above a pair of well-figured arched panel doors enclosing shelves and five shallow drawers, the lower part of bombé form with three long cockbeaded drawers, on a shaped apron and boldly carved claw-and-ball feet headed by stiff acanthus, the whole with Neoclassical gilt metal handles.

97.25in (247cm) high

$6,000-10,000 **L&T**

A late 18thC Normandy carved oak armoire, with profusely carved cornice, panel doors and drawer.

84.75in (215cm) high

$3,200-4,000 **DN**

An early 19thC French oak armoire, the arched bonnet with foliate and cherub decoration.

88in (223.5cm) wide

$8,000-10,000 **POOK**

A French walnut and cherrywood armoire, the arched cavetto cornice above a pair of asymmetric paneled doors with pierced brass escutcheons inscribed 'E.P. 1834', enclosing a shelved and hanging interior.

92.5in (235cm) high

$2,400-3,600 **L&T**

CLOTHES PRESS

A late 18thC black lacquer and gilt-japanned clothes press, some repair.

c1780 *41in (104cm) wide*

$6,000-8,000 **DN**

A George III oak press cupboard.

c1780 *60in (152cm) wide*

$1,400-1,800 **DN**

A George III oak press cupboard, damage, repair.

c1780 *78.75in (200cm) wide*

$1,600-2,400 **DN**

A late 18thC French carved oak press cupboard or 'deux corps', with a cornice and two doors above drawers and further doors.

88in (224cm) high

$3,200-4,000 **DN**

A George III mahogany linen press, with a dentil cornice above a pair of fielded and crossbanded paneled doors enclosing sliding shelves, two short and two long graduated drawers below fitted later molded brass handles, raised on bracket feet.

50in (127cm) wide

$2,400-2,800   **A&G**

A Regency Channel Islands mahogany linen press, inlaid stringing, the detachable cornice above a pair of rosewood-banded doors enclosing two slides, the four drawers fitted with embossed shell brass plate handles.

51.25in (130cm) wide

$3,000-4,000   **WW**

A Regency mahogany clothes press, the arched and molded cornice above two doors, enclosing five sliding trays, above two further doors enclosing sliding trays on outswept bracket feet.

37in (94cm) wide

$5,000-6,000   **DN**

A mid-19thC Victorian mahogany linen press.

43.25in (110cm) wide

$600-800   **DN**

A George IV mahogany linen press, with a pair of paneled cupboard doors opening to four sliding adjustable shelves, above two short drawers and two long drawers raised on bun feet, the top right drawers stamped 'Wilson 68 Great Great Queen St. London'.

c1820   *50.5in (128cm) wide*

$4,000-6,000   **FRE**

An early 19thC mahogany linen press, the molded and beaded cornice over two paneled and crossbanded doors with brass trim and leaf-carved cusped corners now enclosing a hanging space, two short over two long drawers with pierced brass ring handles, beaded base and turned bun feet.

78.75in (200cm) high

$2,000-3,000   **HT**

A late 19thC North European mahogany clothes press.

55in (140cm) wide

$1,800-2,200   **DN**

A Regency mahogany break-front wardrobe, the detachable molded cornice above a pair of rectangular panel doors, enclosing a later rail, previously with slides, the doors divided by a ribbed and turned girdle, on a plinth base.

94.75in (240.5cm) wide

$9,000-$11,000 **WW**

An early 19thC Scottish mahogany wardrobe, the molded cornice above veneered frieze, over two cupboard doors with graduated molded panels, enclosing hanging space, above three short drawers, shaped apron, on stile feet.

62.25in (158cm) wide

$2,400-2,800 **L&T**

A Regency mahogany breakfront wardrobe.

c1820   *91.25in (232cm) wide*

$6,000-8,000 **DN**

A Victorian mahogany compactum.

c1860   *82.75in (210cm) wide*

$1,400-1,800 **DN**

An early 20thC mahogany and satinwood wardrobe.

44in (112cm) wide

$500-700 **DN**

A Victorian mahogany break-front wardrobe, in the French Rococo taste, the arched cornice with leaf-scroll cresting above a mirrored door flanked by a pair of arched and asymmetric panel doors with ribbon-tied torch and quiver trophies, on a shaped apron and short acanthus-carved cabriole legs, enclosing fitted and hanging interiors, a serpentine-front dressing chest, of two short over three long graduated drawers with Rococo-carved decoration and scrolling gilt-metal handles, on short leaf-carved cabriole legs, and a swing mirror kneehole dressing table, of similar design, en suite, possibly made by Whytock and Reid.

94.5in (240cm) wide

$9,000-11,000 **L&T**

A Victorian satin walnut break-front wardrobe, with detachable cavetto molded cornice above a central beveled rectangular plate flanked by a pair of panel doors, enclosing slides and hanging rails, on a plinth base.

88in (223.5cm) wide

$800-1,000 **WW**

FURNITURE

An American Massachusetts mahogany block-front kneehole desk, the base resting on short claw-and-ball feet.

c1765   31.25in (79.5cm) wide

$3,000-5,000   **POOK**

A Sheraton Revival satinwood-crossbanded and floral-painted kneehole desk, by Edwards & Roberts, the top of inverted break-front form with gilt-tooled tan leather skiver above a frieze drawer flanked by hipped tapering pedestals each with four short graduated drawers, on splay legs, the sides decorated with ribbon-tied lyre trophies.

41.75in (106cm) wide

$9,000-11,000   **L&T**

A satinwood and mahogany-banded kneehole desk, the rectangular top with later leatherette inset, and with rear superstructure with pierced three-quarter gallery, above an arrangement of five drawers around the central kneehole, on square-section tapering legs, and later block feet, damage, the top later associated.

c1910 and later   49.5in (126cm) wide

$700-900   **DN**

A 20thC cream-painted and parcel-gilt kneehole desk, in 19thC Continental style, the rectangular top with green leather inset above an arrangement of seven drawers around the central kneehole, on squat cabriole legs and scroll feet, damage.

46in (117cm) wide

$1,100-1,300   **DN**

A George II feather-banded walnut kneehole desk, the quarter-veneered top above a compartmentalized long drawer.

30.25in (77cm) wide

$8,000-10,000   **FRE**

A George II yew wood kneehole secretaire desk, with boxwood and ebonized stringing, the walnut top crossbanded, all fitted replaced brass plate handles, on bracket feet.

32in (81cm) high

$5,000-7,000   **WW**

An early George III mahogany serpentine-fronted kneehole desk, with crossbanded and strung molded top, the front and sides outswept to fluted angles.

47.75in (121cm) wide

$5,000-7,000   **DN**

A large mahogany partners' desk, in the manner of Thomas Chippendale, the rectangular top with gilt-tooled burgundy skiver above a fluted and swag-carved frieze with a pair of arched central drawers above substantial wreath-carved pedestals, each with twin lion mask and husk-carved pilaster uprights, ending in hairy paw feet, the sides similarly carved and decorated.

78.75in (200cm) wide

$10,000-12,000   **L&T**

A George III mahogany partners' desk, the rectangular brown tooled leather insert top over three frieze drawers, flanked by two banks of three drawers.

54in (137cm) wide

$2,400-3,600   **FRE**

A late 19thC George III style octagonal mahogany partners' desk, by H. Samuel, London, the shaped top with outset corners and a tooled green inset leather writing surface over a paneled frieze with four drawers, shell and seaweed-carved pedestals, each with three further long graduated drawers, flanked by paneled cupboard doors, raised on a carved plinth base, the top of the pedestal stamped 'H. Samuel, London', in several places.

53in (135cm) wide

$80,000-100,000   **L&T**

An early 19thC mahogany partners' desk, the top above three sunken field frieze drawers to either side with foliate-cast brass ring handles, each pedestal with three drawers opposed by paneled cupboard doors, on plinth bases.

59in (150cm) wide

$5,000-7,000   **L&T**

A 19thC patridgewood partners' desk, with tooled skiver and leaf-carved edge above three frieze drawers to either side and floret and ribbon-carved lip, each pedestal with three frieze drawers opposed by fielded panel cupboard doors edged with leaf-carved mouldings, on similarly carved plinth bases.

60in (152cm) wide

$6,000-10,000   **L&T**

A Victorian mahogany pedestal partners' desk, the rectangular top with leather inset above an arrangement of drawers around the central kneehole, the opposing side with three drawers above two doors, on plinth bases.

c1860   *60.5in (154cm) wide*

$5,600-6,400   **DN**

An early 20thC George II style mahogany double sided library desk, pedestals with six graduated drawers in two tiers, the opposing sides with a cupboard enclosing a shelf, on carved ogee bracket feet.

64in (163cm) wide

$24,000-36,000   **SOTH**

A Victorian partners' pedestal desk, one drawer bearing stencilled makers name 'J.J. BRYNE G. HENRY ST. DUBLIN'.

54.25in (138cm) wide

$5,000-6,000   **DN**

An Edwardian mahogany partners' desk, the tooled black hide top with gadrooned edge, the desk on short leaf-carved cabriole legs with claw-and-ball feet.

60.25in (153cm) wide

$3,000-5,000   **L&T**

A George III style yew partners' pedestal desk, of recent manufacture.

72in (183cm) wide

$1,600-2,400   **DN**

A late 17thC century oak bureau, the rectangular fall opening to a fitted interior incorporating an arrangement of small drawers, above two short and two long miter-paneled drawers, on stile feet, damage, repair.

31.5in (105cm) wide

$7,000-9,000 DN

A George I walnut and feather-banded bureau, the fall front enclosing a stepped fitted interior with pigeon holes, drawers and a covered well, below are two short and two long-graduated drawers, raised on later bracket feet.

42in (107cm) wide

$3,000-5,000 L&T

A George I walnut bureau, the drop-front reveals an interior fitted with pigeonholes flanked by two small drawers above a tooled green leather writing surface, over three long drawers, raised on bracket feet.

c1730 *41in (104cm) wide*

$2,000-4,000 FRE

A George II walnut bureau, the herringbone-banded top above a sloping crossbanded fall enclosing a fitted interior above three long graduated drawers with pierced brass bat-wing handles on shaped bracket feet.

c1740 *41.25in (105cm) wide*

$3,000-5,000 DN

A George III mahogany bureau, the fall front enclosing a pagoda interior with blind fretwork, over a case with fretwork corners supported by an elaborately carved bracket base.

c1760 *42in (106.5cm) wide*

$5,000-7,000 POOK

A George III mahogany bureau, damage.

c1780 *36.5in (93cm) wide*

$800-1,200 DN

A late 18thC George III lacquered secrétaire bureau, with sloping hinged flap, enclosing a writing interior, above five drawers, on bracket feet, damages to lacquer work.

41.75in (106cm) high

$15,000-17,000 SOTA

A George III mahogany bureau, the fall front enclosing a fitted interior with star-inlaid prospect door, over a case with four drawers supported by flaring French feet.

c1790 *42.5in (108cm) wide*

$1,200-1,600 POOK

A late 18thC George III oak bureau, with fall front above four graduated drawers.

37.75in (96cm) wide

$700-900 DN

A late 18thC Italian Lombard walnut and crossbanded bureau, faults, repair.

44.5in (113cm) wide

$34,000-40,000 DN

A Pennsylvania William & Mary walnut slant-front desk, the fall front enclosing an amphitheatre interior with well above two short and two long drawers supported by bun feet, from the Shelley Collection.

c1730   42.5in (108cm) high

$7,500-9,500   POOK

CLOSER LOOK: HEPPLEWHITE SLANT-FRONT DESK

The desk is fitted with an elegant arrangement of drawers and pigeonholes which were hidden behind the fall front. This style of desk was often used in bedrooms as a combined desk and chest-of-drawers, in which case it was called a bureau secretary.

The eagle inlay is typical of furniture made in the early 19thC Hepplewhite style as it combined Neoclassical and patriotic American symbolism.

A Lancaster, Pennsylvania Hepplewhite mahogany slant-front desk, the fall front enclosing a fully fitted interior with satinwood valences, tambour prospect door and side drawer covers, above a case with four line-inlaid drawers flanked by chamfered stiles, above a scalloped skirt with eagle inlay supported by flaring French feet, with its original eagle brasses.

c1800   41.25in (104.75cm) wide

$16,000-20,000   POOK

A mid-18thC Queen Anne maple slant-lid desk, possibly Framingham, Massachusetts, the fall front opens to an interior of valanced compartments and five drawers above a case of two thumb-molded half-drawers and three graduated long drawers, all on bracket feet, most of the engraved brass escutcheons and drawer pulls are original, original surface.

40in (101.5cm) wide

$20,000-30,000   SK

A Massachusetts Chippendale mahogany block-front, slant-front desk, with lid opening to a blocked and shell-carved interior above four drawers, restoration.

c1775   39.5in (100.5cm) wide

$10,000-15,000   FRE

A Massachusetts Federal mahogany and mahogany veneer reverse serpentine slant-lid desk, with an interior of six drawers and eight valanced compartments, above four cockbeaded drawers, refinished, repaired.

c1790   41.75in (106cm) wide

$3,000-5,000   SK

A late 18thC Pennsylvania inlaid walnut slant-front desk, thumb-molded slant top opens to reveal a fitted interior above four beaded drawers flanked by chevron-shaped inlay on a shaped inlaid skirt, bracket feet.

41in (104cm) wide

$7,000-10,000   FRE

A Federal mahogany-inlaid tambour desk, from Massachusetts or New Hampshire, the central door with an inlaid eagle, and fold-out writing surface, old brasses, refinished, restored.

c1800   39.5in (100.5cm) wide

$9,000-11,000   SK

An Amesbury, Massachusetts Federal mahogany-inlaid desk bookcase, the top section with three cockbeaded short drawers above two hinged doors opening to two drawers and four valanced compartments, flanking a central inlaid door with wavy birch oval panel and border of maple banding and stringing, opening to three compartments, all on projecting lower section of fold-out lid and case of four cockbeaded graduated drawers on slightly flaring French feet and valanced skirt, turned wooden pulls, original finish, imperfections.

c1805   61.75in (157cm) high

$4,000-6,000   SK

An Indiana 'extra grade' Wooton desk, with Renaissance Revival gilt and burl-veneered exterior and ebonized and birdseye maple interior.

74in (188cm) high

$20,000-30,000   POOK

FURNITURE

An 18thC Italian walnut, satinwood and marquetry bureau, with sloping fall inlaid with a basket of flowers within a parquetry border and enclosing a fitted interior of four drawers around a shaped arched open recess, two frieze drawers above two long drawers inlaid sans traverse with similar decoration, on square tapering legs.

48in. (122.5cm) wide

$16,000-20,000   **SOTH**

A late 18thC probably Dutch Continental mahogany bombé bureau, with fully fitted interior.

38in (99cm) wide

$1,200-1,600   **DN**

An early 19thC Dutch mahogany and marquetry cylinder bureau.

54in (137cm) high

$3,000-4,000   **DN**

An early 19thC and later walnut bureau, the rectangular fall opening to a fitted interior with a central door surrounded by an arrangement of five drawers and a well section, above a drawer, the stand with two short drawers on baluster-turned tapering legs, and an X-stretcher, on turned bun feet, damage, repair.

26.5in (67cm) wide

$1,800-2,200   **DN**

A late 19thC mahogany and ebony-mounted bureau cabinet, by Lamb of Manchester, the top of one drawer stamped 'LAMB MANCHESTER'.

29.25in (74.5cm) wide

$7,000-9,000   **DN**

A late 18thC German mahogany and brass-mounted cylinder bureau, bronze-galleried top above cylinder opening to reveal a writing interior and sliding surface.

48.75in (124cm) wide

$9,000-11,000   **SOTA**

A 19thC French Empire gilt-brass mahogany bureau à cylindre, with a fitted interior, with central clock with countwheel bell striking anchor escapement, signed 'Bechot'.

63.75in (162cm) high

$13,000-15,000   **SOTA**

A Regency mahogany and gilt-metal-mounted cylinder bureau, stamped 'W Priest 1-2 Tudor Street, Blackfriars', with pierced gallery and red marble-inset top, the fall enclosing a fitted interior, the sliding leather inset writing surface with central rachet-adjustable section, on turned tapering legs, brass caps and casters.

c1820   32.75in (83cm) wide

$3,000-4,000   **DN**

A George IV pedestal cylinder desk, the reeded top above a roll front with fitted interior and writing slide, on bracket feet, the whole inlaid with ebony lines, the top drawer stamped 'T. Willson 68 Great Queen Street, London'.

53in (135cm) wide

$7,000-9,000   **L&T**

A late 19thC Louis XVI style mahogany and gilt-bronze-mounted bureau à cylindre, the fall with fitted interior and a brushing slide with inset baize writing surface, raised on turned fluted legs terminating in toupie feet.

30in (76cm) wide

$2,400-3,600   **FRE**

An Edwardian satinwood cylinder bureau, crossbanded with ebony stringing and foliate marquetry, with fitted interior and writing slide, the drawers with brass ring handles, raised on square tapering legs with spade feet and casters.

36in (91.5cm) wide

$4,000-6,000   **HT**

A mahogany, partridge-wood and harewood-crossbanded Carlton House desk, by Gillows of Lancaster, the center of the frieze drawers stamped 'GILLOWS', on turned and fluted tapering legs headed by stiff lotus leaf capitals.

54.75in (139cm) wide

$16,000-18,000   **L&T**

A late Victorian satinwood and marquetry Carlton House desk.

First named in a cost book of Gillows in 1796, Carlton House desks are named after the residence of the then Prince of Wales.

48.25in (122.5cm) wide

$9,000-12,000   **WW**

An Edwardian mahogany Carlton House desk, crossbanded with stringing, the frieze drawer over kneehole flanked on either side by two small drawers, brass drop handles, raised on square tapering legs and spade feet.

53.25in (135.5cm) wide

$1,600-2,400   **HT**

A 19thC burr walnut and arabesque inlaid bureau de dame, the fall enclosing a fitted interior of drawers and pigeon holes above a well, on cabriole legs, decorated with Rococo cast giltmetal mounts and sabots.

33.5in (85cm) wide

$3,000-4,000   **L&T**

A Louis XV style kingwood and amaranth bureau de dame, the slant front opening to an arrangement of drawers, the frieze drawer raised on cabriole legs cast with chutes, the gallery stamped 'ML BB'.

28.75in (73cm) wide

$3,000-5,000   **FRE**

A 19thC English kingwood, crossbanded and porcelain-mounted bonheur du jour, the serpentine top with a frieze drawer applied with porcelain panels, on cabriole legs united by cross stretchers with a porcelain medallion boss.

A bonheur du jour is a delicate lady's writing desk with a flat writing surface with tiered drawers and compartments at the back. It was introduced in the 18thC and became increasingly popular in the 19thC. This design, which is common in 19thC French furniture, is rare from an English workshop. The usual Sèvres porcelain panels have been substituted by delicately painted English examples.

54.75in (139cm) wide

$8,000-10,000   **L&T**

A late 19thC mahogany, satinwood-banded and chequer-strung English bonheur du jour, in the Louis XVI taste, the wide skiver draws forward to reveal a pen try and inkwell recess, on inlaid and reeded tapering legs headed by simulated flutes and ending in brass casters.

41.75in (106cm) wide

$9,000-11,000   **L&T**

An Edwardian satinwood, crossbanded and painted bonheur du jour, the raised top fitted with two short drawers and one long drawer, the lower section with a further frieze drawer, raised on slightly splayed slender square tapered legs.

21in (53.5cm) wide

$2,400-3,600   **FRE**

A late 1600s William & Mary painted mirror, the sarcophagus top retaining its original marblized surface.

28.25in (72cm) high

$4,000-6,000   POOK

A William & Mary mirror, with walnut veneer frame enclosing an elaborate silk-on-silk needlework bezel with scalloped edge.

c1690   *29.75in(75.5cm) high*

$5,000-7,000   POOK

A Queen Anne burl walnut veneer looking glass, with arched crest and bolection-molded frame enclosing two beveled glass plates, the upper with cut floral decoration.

c1710   *39in (99cm) high*

$3,000-5,000   POOK

An American Queen Anne mahogany looking glass, with scalloped and pierced crest over a bolection-molded frame with beveled edge plate.

c1710   *30.75in (78cm) high*

$3,000-5,000   POOK

A pair of German giltwood console mirrors, possibly Dresden.

In the early 18th century King Friedrich August 'der Starke' I (1670-1733) of Saxony, chose Dresden to be his glamorous cultural metropolis. As part of this program, in 1709 the 'Zwinger', an ensemble of beautiful buildings and gardens was started. The main artist was the sculptor Balthasar Permoser (1651-1732), whose style was to remain dominant in Saxony and Brandenburg for the coming decades. In 1945 it was completely destroyed and took 20 years to rebuild. These mirrors were undoubtedly made after Permoser's death. Apart from South German Rococo influences they also reflect features from the works of Johann August Nahl and of other leading designers.

78.75in (200cm) high

$45,000-55,000 PAIR   SOTA

A George II mahogany looking glass, with scrolled crest and stepped mirror plates with gilt liner, retaining an old dry surface and original glass.

c1730

$8,000-12,000   POOK

A mid-18thC George II walnut and parcel-gilt-framed wall mirror, scrolled broken pediment with eagle surmount, rectangular plate flanked by leaf and berry festoons, some regilding and with a later beveled plate.

66in (167cm) high Est.

$12,000-16,000   SOTH

An unusual and small George II yew wood mirror, with a shaped cresting and apron with wrong iron candle arm, the mirror plate within an arched molded frame.

8.25in (21cm) wide

$6,000-8,000   L&T

An American Queen Anne walnut veneer looking glass, the scalloped crest with parcel-gilt shell over a base with candlearm.

c1760   *26in (66cm) high*

$2,500-3,000   POOK

An early George III mahogany-framed wall mirror, the rectangular plate within a cartouche-shaped frame surmounted by a pierced central anthemion, damage.

c1760   38.5in (98cm) high

$700-900   DN

A Georgian burl veneer looking glass, with pierced and scalloped crest and gilt liner.

c1770   42in (106.75cm) high

$1,500-2,000   POOK

A Chippendale mahogany looking glass, with scalloped crest and base.

c1770

$800-1,200   POOK

A mid-18thC mahogany and parcel-gilt wall mirror, with broken-arch pediment, decorated with central gilt cartouche and dentil molding, the original mirrored plate below flanked by applied carved foliate side supports.

26in (66cm) wide

$2,500-3,000   A&G

A Chippendale mahogany looking glass, the scrolled crest with parcel-gilt phoenix above a rectangular plate with gilt liner and scrolled base.

c1780   26.75in (68cm) high

$500-700   POOK

A late 18thC Chippendale mahogany and giltwood mirror, with swan's neck cresting centering a phoenix, surmounting a shaped frame, and giltwood liner enclosing mirror plate, regilded.

66in (167.5cm) long

$7,000-9,000   FRE

An 18thC Flemish carved giltwood wall mirror, the beveled rectangular plate with eight further margin plates, the molded frame surmounted by a scrolling foliate carved cresting.

45.75in (116cm) high

$7,000-9,000   L&T

A George III mahogany-framed wall mirror, the cornice decorated with scallop shell motif, flanked by bellflowers, with acanthus leaf brackets to each side and foliate carved scrolls below.

30in (76cm) wide

$800-1,200   A&G

A small pair of 18thC carved giltwood looking glasses, the rectangular plates within ornate openwork foliate and scroll-carved frames.

19.75in (50cm) high

$17,000-19,000   L&T

A George III period mahogany wall mirror, the later rectangular plate within an ornate openwork Rococo scroll-carved frame.

41.25in (105cm) high

$8,000-10,000   L&T

A pair of 19thC George III style carved giltwood mirrors, in the manner of Thomas Chippendale.

36in (91.5cm) wide

$50,000-60,000   **FRE**

CLOSER LOOK: GIRANDOLE MIRROR

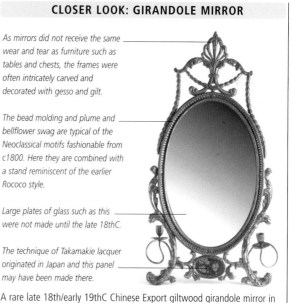

As mirrors did not receive the same wear and tear as furniture such as tables and chests, the frames were often intricately carved and decorated with gesso and gilt.

The bead molding and plume and bellflower swag are typical of the Neoclassical motifs fashionable from c1800. Here they are combined with a stand reminiscent of the earlier Rococo style.

Large plates of glass such as this were not made until the late 18thC.

The technique of Takamakie lacquer originated in Japan and this panel may have been made there.

A rare late 18th/early 19thC Chinese Export giltwood girandole mirror in the George III style, the oval plate within a fluted and bead-molded frame, surmounted by a stylised plume and bellflower swag cresting, the openwork apron centered by a Takamakie lacquer panel and issuing two outscrolling candle branches.

18.75in (47cm) wide

$7,000-9,000   **L&T**

A pair of late George III giltwood and gesso pier mirrors, the corrugated ovolu frames with a leaf paterae to each corner surmounted by scrolled and festooned crestings.

35.75in (91cm) high

$8,000-10,000   **L&T**

A pair of George III style carved giltwood wall mirrors, the shaped rectangular beveled plates within ornate open Rococo scroll frames, surmounted by ho-ho birds.

30.75in (78cm) wide

$1,500-2,500   **FRE**

An American giltwood convex mirror, with spread-winged eagle pediment and foliate drop, retaining an unidentified partial maker's label.

c1800   40in (101.5cm) high

$2,000-3,000   **POOK**

An early 19thC American massive giltwood convex mirror, the foliate crest with opposing eagle heads flanking a plinth with spread-winged eagle.

60in (152.5cm) high

$12,000-16,000   **POOK**

A giltwood convex mirror, with eagle crest and carved foliate drop.

c1800   50in (127cm) high

$12,000-14,000   **POOK**

A Regency giltwood convex wall mirror, the circular plate within a reeded ebonised slip and molded frame with applied ball spacers, surmounted by an eagle cresting, over acanthus-carved apron from which issue two outscrolling branches.

40in (102cm) high

$6,000-10,000   **L&T**

A Regency giltwood and gesso convex wall mirror, the circular plate within a reeded ebonized slip and ball-molded frame, surmounted by a flaming urn finial, the foliate-carved apron centered by a lion mask medallion.

53in (135cm) high

$7,000-9,000 **L&T**

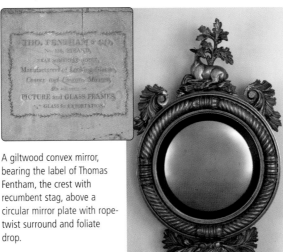

A giltwood convex mirror, bearing the label of Thomas Fentham, the crest with recumbent stag, above a circular mirror plate with rope-twist surround and foliate drop.

c1800 *41.5in (105.5cm) high*

$7,000-9,000 **POOK**

A giltwood overmantel mirror, in Regency style, of recent manufacture, the sphere-mounted frieze above acanthus and lyre-mounted panels and three beveled plates flanked by reeded split columns.

57in (145cm) wide

$1,400-1,800 **DN**

A Regency giltwood overmantel mirror, the rectangular plate surmounted by an eagle cresting and flanked by fluted columns headed by flaming torches.

46in (117cm) high

$6,000-8,000 **L&T**

A Regency carved giltwood and gesso overmantel mirror, the rectangular plate surmounted by a cavetto-molded cornice, over a Greek key- and drapery-carved frieze, flanked by Doric pilasters headed by lion mask motifs.

53in (135cm) wide

$8,000-10,000 **L&T**

A Regency giltwood pier glass, the oblong plate below a frieze of classical charioteers flanked by foliate cluster columns headed by Egyptian caryatids, molded cornice with applied orbs over stiff leaf banding flanked by lion masks, molded base and ebonized plinth.

47.5in (120.5cm) high

$1,000-1,500 **HT**

An American Federal large giltwood mirror, molded cornice with acorn drops, above a foliate-decorated frieze, with églomise panel.

c1825 *59in (150cm) high*

$2,500-3,500 **POOK**

An American late Federal stencil-decorated mirror, with églomise panel of a church.

c1825 *27in (68.5cm) high*

$3,000-5,000 **POOK**

An American Classical New England stencil-decorated mirror, the rectangular frame with gilt-stenciled floral designs and square corner blocks with rosettes, minor imperfections.

c1825 *27in (68.5cm) long*

$2,500-3,000 **SK**

A 19thC 'mid-18thC' style giltwood and gesso overmantel mirror, the cartouche-shape frame with ten subsidiary plates divided by acanthus-carved scrolls surmounted by an outstretched eagle above an icicle-carved frieze and scallop shell pendant.

59in (150cm) wide

$4,500-5,500 **L&T**

A Victorian gilt composition wall mirror, the profusely decorated and pierced pediment above a central plate flanked by two further plates, above a scroll and cabochon-decorated pendant frieze, damage.

c1870   *39.5in (100cm) wide*

$1,500-2,000   **DN**

A Victorian giltwood and gesso picture frame wall mirror, the rectangular beveled plate within an ornate shaped openwork foliate, shell and S-scroll frame.

                              41.75in (106cm) wide

$6,000-10,000   **L&T**

A 19thC Flemish carved and stained pine mirror, in the Baroque taste, the frame with scrolling foliage and leafage around a medieval mask, flanked by male masks at the corners and spire finials.

                               57in (145cm) high

$5,000-7,000   **L&T**

A 19thC French giltwood cushion wall mirror, the beveled octagonal mirror plate in molded frame with further sloping mirror panels, with acanthus-carved angles and pierced cartouche cresting.

36.25in (92cm) wide

$5,000-7,000   **L&T**

One of a pair of 19thC French wall mirrors, each with rectangular mirror plate in molded frame with harebell chain to the top, surmounted by stepped pediment with three urns.

18.25in (46cm) wide

$12,000-18,000 PAIR   **L&T**

A 19thC French giltwood wall mirror, the rectangular mirror plate in rope-twist frame, with Greek key tablet top and triple cartouche surmount, suspending floral swags.

34.75in (88cm) wide

$3,000-4,000   **L&T**

One of a pair of 19thC Rococo style carved and parcel-gilt walnut-framed wall mirrors, losses, repairs.

36.5in (93cm) high

$2,000-2,500 PAIR   **DN**

A 19thC gilt gesso Rococo design overmantel mirror, with three panels surmounted by a ho-ho bird, fruiting vines and scrolls.

61in (155cm) wide

$2,500-3,000   **A&G**

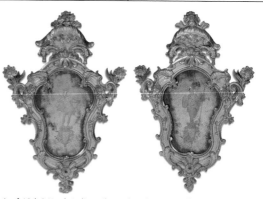

A pair of 19thC North Italian giltwood and gesso wall mirrors, each of cartouche-shaped form, boldly carved with flower heads and acanthus scrolls, the festooned crestings with pendant trefoil decorated friezes, the plates with oxidised silvering centered by engraved representations of medieval-style knights on Rococo plinths, holding a short sword and spear respectively.

23.25in (59cm) wide

$7,000-9,000   **L&T**

A 19thC French giltwood pier mirror, the rectangular plate with bas relief carved inner slip bordered by four subsidiary plates, the Baroque-style cresting with a festooned surmount, the scroll-carved frame entwined with carved flower-heads.

38.5in (98cm) wide

$5,000-7,000   L&T

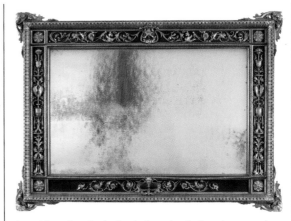

A late 19thC Italian ebonized and giltwood wall mirror, the rectangular plate within margin plates decorated with marlins, scrolling masks, flowering urns and paterae to the corners, the stop-fluted outer frame with foliate scroll corners.

50in (127cm) wide

$3,000-3,500   L&T

A late 19thC Victorian carved oak-framed arch-topped wall mirror, probably adapted from a cheval mirror, later elements.

73.25in (186cm) high

$1,000-1,500   DN

A late 19thC French giltwood wall mirror, the rectangular mirror plate in mirrored, molded and foliate-carved frame, with mirrored cartouche surmount centered by a carved basket of flowers.

21.75in (55cm) wide

$4,000-5,000   L&T

A Victorian mahogany-framed cheval mirror, with arched plate, inverted tapered supports with extending candle holders, scrolled feet joined by a stretcher.

$500-700   GIL

An Empire gilt-bronze-mounted mahogany cheval mirror, by Johannes Klinckerfus, the arched mirror plate within a mahogany frame set with gilt-bronze stars, supported by columns, joined by circular baluster-shaped supports, on down-scrolled feet, allover fitted with gilt-bronze mounts.

c1815-1820   41.75in (106cm)

$30,000-40,000   SOTA

A Regency mahogany and ebonised cheval mirror, the rectangular plate flanked by baluster-turned supports surmounted by urn finials, on plinth bases and four gilt-metal scroll feet, with casters, damage.

c1820   36.25in (92cm) wide

$2,500-3,500   DN

An Edwardian mahogany cheval mirror.

c1910

$2,500-3,000   DN

FURNITURE

A walnut dressing mirror, later gilt repair.

c1740   20in (51cm) wide
$800-1,200   DN

A George II walnut dressing mirror, faults.

c1750   23.75in (60cm) high
$700-900   DN

A mid-18thC George III mahogany and parcel-gilt dressing table mirror, with serpentine-fronted base.

                    26.75in (68cm) high
$700-900   DN

A George III mahogany dressing table mirror, with bow-fronted base.
c1800   24in (61cm) wide
$500-700   DN

A George III mahogany bowfront dressing table mirror, faults.
c1810   21.75in (55.5cm) wide
$400-600   DN

An early 19thC George III mahogany and sycamore-strung dressing table mirror, the shield-shaped plate held in twin serpentine uprights, on a serpentine-fronted base with three drawers, on waisted bracket feet.
                    25.25in (61.5cm) high
$1,500-2,000   DN

A George IV mahogany dressing table mirror, the adjustable oval plate held in twin serpentine uprights, the bowfront base with three drawers, on waisted bracket feet.
c1825   22.5in (57cm) high
$1,000-1,500   DN

A 19thC French brass toilet mirror, the circular looking glass supported by a demi-lune bracket, leading to two free-swing candle holders, the column decorated with a leaf and berry motif.
                    15.5in (39.5cm) high
$800-1,200   FRE

An American Pennsylvania late Federal mahogany and tiger maple shaving mirror.
c1835   29.25in (75.25cm) wide
$4,000-5,000   POOK

SHELVES

An early George III set of oak hanging shelves.

c1760   38.5in (98cm) wide
$400-600   DN

A late 18thC American Pennsylvania mahogany hanging corner shelf, with elaborately scalloped sides and seven tiers.

                    42.5in (108cm) high
$6,000-10,000   POOK

A George III mahogany wall-shelf, with three graduating tiers above two drawers, the whole carved and pierced with fretwork.
c1775
$2,500-3,000   FRE

A pair of Regency chinoiserie-painted open wall shelves, of serpentine-sided outline, each with an arched cresting above three open shelves flanked by corner shelves, the whole bordered with giltwood foliage and pendant husks and decorated with scenes from Chinese courtly life, each on a pierced acanthus leaf apron centered by a carved cabochon.

31in (79cm) wide

$6,000-8,000 L&T

An early 19thC American yellow pine hanging corner shelf, with beaded edge shelves and scalloped base, retaining a blue surface.

39.5in (100.5cm) high

$4,000-6,000 POOK

An early 19thC American painted pine hanging shelf, with scalloped sides and plate racks above a lower section with pegs, retaining an old ocher surface.

41.75in (106cm) wide

$5,000-7,000 POOK

A mid-19thC American pine hanging shelf, with cut-out scrolled ends joining four shelves, and painted dark brown.

30in (76cm) wide

$2,000-2,500 SK

A pair of Victorian mahogany whatnots, the acanthus-carved arched backs above five serpentine graduated tiers, raised on baluster spiral-turned upright supports.

32.5in (82cm) wide

$5,000-7,000 L&T

A set of 19thC mahogany hanging wall shelves.

41.25in (105cm) high

$700-1,000 DN

A set of 19thC French walnut hanging shelves.

42.5in (108cm) wide

$700-1,000 DN

ÉTAGÈRE

A pair of Regency style black japanned and painted bronze étagères, the three rectangular tiers with chinoiserie decoration, raised on turned supports.

25in (63.5cm) wide

$3,000-4,000 FRE

A Continental rectangular mahogany étagère, with four tiers and a stepped top.

c1830 *31in (79cm) wide*

$1,000-1,500 DN

A William IV rosewood three-tier whatnot, the scroll supports with scroll terminals.

c1835 *44.5in (113cm) wide*

$2,000-2,500 DN

ESSENTIAL REFERENCE: BLACK FOREST WARES

Though named after Germany's Black Forest region, Black Forest carvings were first created in Switzerland in the early 19thC. By the 1850s their work was receiving acclaim at international exhibitions from London to Chicago to Paris.

- In Europe, Black Forest wares became a symbol of wealth with many of the finest pieces becoming part of Royal collections or those of elite Victorian travelers. There was great demand in the US for pieces featuring native animals such as eagles.
- Examples featuring dogs are rarer than those featuring bears and required greater skill, so these tend to be more desirable. Signed pieces and those by certain families, like the Huggler family, command a premium.

A German Black Forest carved walnut hat/umbrella stand, with a spread-winged eagle above a shield-form mirror and mountain goat.

c1895   *88in (223.5cm) high*

$12,000-16,000   **POOK**

A 19thC century finely carved Black Forest dog hall stand, modeled as a long haired terrier seated on its hind legs begging, raised on a naturalistic shaped base with inset drip tray.

43in (103cm) high

$15,000-20,000   **L&T**

A George IV period mahogany hat and coat stand, the ring-turned twin section stem with lotus leaf-cast brass hooks and central stick supports, the whole ending in a cast iron square dished base.

70.75in (180cm) high

$6,000-8,000   **L&T**

A late Victorian bamboo hall stand, raised on four open step legs with two chrysanthemum and bat-carved trays, the stem with root and bar supports.

79.5in (202cm) high

$700-1,000   **WW**

A cold painted cast iron hall stand, the rectangular canted corner base on leaf-scroll feet with a central reeded stem with paw-scroll supports and an eight-ring stick division, above three tiers of open scroll hooks.

72in (183cm) high

$1,500-2,000   **WW**

A Victorian cast iron stick stand, painted black, the top with six circular apertures to a lift-out tray.

25in (63.5cm) high

$500-700   **WW**

A late 19th/early 20thC turned brass and iron corner stickstand, the base with lift-out tray, faint stamped registration number.

24.5in (62cm) high

$500-700   **WW**

A late 19th/early 20thC turned brass and cast iron semi-circular stick stand, with five divisions.

25.5in (65cm) high

$700-900   **WW**

An early 20thC turned brass and cast iron four-division stick stand, with lift-out tray.

24.5in (62cm) high

$400-600   **WW**

A carved mahogany and caned tapering cylindrical stick stand, with a lift-out zinc liner.

25.25in (65cm) high

$1,500-2,000   **WW**

A late 19thC painted sheet iron dummy board stick stand, decorated with a terrier.

24in (61cm) high

$4,000-5,000   **DN**

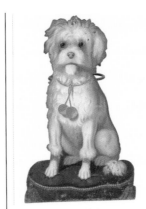

A pair of George I carved giltwood torchères, the bead-molded dished tops with an undulating frieze with acanthus-carved baluster-turned column supports, ending on three conforming cabriole scroll legs.

43.75in (111cm) high

$7,000-9,000   **L&T**

A George II mahogany kettle stand, with pie crust top, damage to top edge.

c1730   *18.5in (47cm) high*

$4,000-6,000   **DN**

A mid-18thC George II mahogany candle or kettle stand.

27.25in (69.5cm) high

$4,000-5,000   **DN**

CLOSER LOOK: GEORGE III CANDLESTANDS

The dished top with piecrust border is typical of candlestands made in the Chippendale style and highly desirable to collectors, especially when found on a period piece.

A pair of stands will be worth up to three times as much as a single example.

The stands were designed to hold little more than a candlestick. Any excess pressure may cause the pole to break – usually where it meets the top or the legs.

The deep carving and turning on the pole are signs of a quality piece.

The colour and patination of the wood also add to the desirability of the stands.

A pair of George III mahogany candlestands, some damage.

In a report on these stands, author R.W. Symonds notes that half of one of the lengths has been restored and states that this 'damage was caused through something falling on the top through the explosion of a German bomb at Ovenden House, Sundridge, Kent, the country residence of Lord Plender on the night of April 19th, 1941'.

c1760   *42.25in (107cm) high*

$40,000-50,000   **DN**

A Louis XVI painted torchère stand, with Sienna marble top, raised on three leaf-carved supports, ending in a triform base.

46in (117cm) high

$2,500-3,500   **L&T**

A pair of mahogany torchères.

c1780 and later   *71in (180cm) high*

$2,000-3,000   **DN**

FURNITURE

A late 18thC New England apple-green-painted candlestand, the square tray top with applied beaded edge on a vase and ring-turned support and tripod cabriole leg base, old surface.

26in (66cm) high

$1,500-2,500   **SK**

A Federal New Hampshire cherry candlestand, the oval top above a ring-turned swelled post and tripod base of shaped tapering legs ending in spade feet, old surface.

c1800   27.75in (70.5cm) high

$2,000-3,000   **SK**

A Pennsylvania walnut and poplar painted stand, the square top over a straight frame supported by molded splay legs, retaining an old blue surface.

c1800   26.75in (68cm) high

$2,500-3,500   **POOK**

A Pennsylvania windsor stand, with a dish top and a bamboo-turned, tripod base joined by stretchers, retaining an old brown surface, from the Shelley Collection.

c1810   26in (66cm) high

$11,000-13,000   **POOK**

An early 19thC Federal paint-decorated game board candlestand, probably from New England, the black squares painted with stars, and tripod cabriole leg base, minor imperfections.

28in (71cm) high

$16,000-20,000   **SK**

A New Hampshire Federal birch red-washed tilt-top candlestand, the octagonal top on a vase- and-ring turned support, and tripod base of shaped tapering legs ending in spade feet, original surface.

c1810   30in (76cm) high

$20,000-25,000   **SK**

A New England Federal red-painted cherry stand, the rectangular top above a single deep drawer and straight skirt joining square tapering legs, original brass, original surface, imperfections.

c1810   31.75in (80.5cm) high

$2,500-3,500   **SK**

A Maine Federal painted one-drawer stand, the square overhanging top above a drawer with shaped facade and straight skirt joining square tapering legs, original surface painted yellow bordered by simulated black stringing and tan banding, original brass pulls, minor imperfections.

c1810   29.5in (75cm) high

$15,000-20,000   **SK**

A Maine Federal cherry-inlaid candlestand, the square top bordered by banded inlay of contrasting woods, on a vase and ring-turned support and a tripod base of arched legs, original surface.

26.25in (66.5cm) high

$3,500-4,500   **SK**

A Pennsylvania Sheraton pine one-drawer stand, with black marbleized top and drawer front, resting on turned legs with tall tulip feet, retaining its original ochre grain paint, from the Shelley Collection.

c1820   20in (51cm) wide

$5,000-7,000   **POOK**

A Pennsylvania painted poplar and pine one-drawer stand, the top with stippled orange border centering on a pinwheel on a yellow ground, the splayed legs with tigered decoration, from the Shelley Collection.

c1820   18.5in (47cm) wide

$10,000-15,000   **POOK**

An unusual Regency cast iron gueridon, in the manner of Thomas Hope, the top inset with a central bronze medallion depicting Virgil reading to figures inscribed: 'VIRGILIVS APVD MECENATEM TVA MECANAS HAVD MOLLIA JVSSA', the fluted Ionic style column surmounted by a winged sphinx with a lizard with prey in its jaws above an anthemion-cast base of three inscrolling monopaediae with claw feet.

30in (76cm) high

$4,500-5,500   **L&T**

A pair of 19thC walnut and satinwood sculpture pedestals, with rouge marble tops.

43.75in (111cm) high

$4,000-6,000   **L&T**

A 19thC French giltwood torchère, the molded circular top on hexagonal and acanthus-carved baluster column, on three S-scrolled legs.

12.75in (32cm) diam

$1,000-1,500   **L&T**

A pair of Neoclassical satinwood and painted pedestals, the crossbanded molded square tops on a paneled square tapered column, painted with urns and trailing bellflowers, raised on molded plinth bases.

47.5in (120.5cm) high

$3,000-5,000   **FRE**

A 19thC oak and walnut candlestand.

34.75in (88cm) high

$800-1,200   **DN**

A pair of 19thC French Empire style marble-topped mahogany demi-lune pedestals, each with black marble D-shaped top above bowfront column with gilt-metal winged Classical maiden mount, on molded plinth with further mounts.

21.75in (55cm) wide

$4,500-5,500 PAIR   **L&T**

A pair of Empire style stained fruitwood pedestals, of square tapered form, applied with a gilt-metal mount.

66in (167.5cm) high

$3,000-5,000 PAIR   **FRE**

A 19thC Venetian giltwood and polychrome lacquer blackamoor torchère, the figure standing upon a gondola holding a fan and supporting an elaborately draped plinth 'revealed' at one corner to show a carved and molded edge, on a faceted column applied with a swag and an octagonal plinth base raised on four large paw feet.

42.5 in (108cm) high

$5,000-7,000   **L&T**

A North Italian walnut, ebonised and painted wood blackamoor pedestal, the molded circular top supported on the head of a carved kneeling figure, on molded circular plinth base.

15.74in (40cm) diam

$2,500-3,000   **L&T**

An elaborately carved Italian walnut torchère stand, the circular molded top resting on the head of a winged sphinx, standing on cartouche-shaped base with paw feet.

18.25in (46cm) diam

$2,000-3,000   **L&T**

FURNITURE

A pair of Neoclassical style carved mahogany figural torchère stands, each with a marble top supported by Classical maidens, raised on claw feet.

40in (101.5cm) high

$3,000-5,000　　　　　　**FRE**

A pair of late 19thC cast iron torchères by Antoine Durenne, both stamped 'A. Durenne' on base.

61.5in (156cm) high

$7,000-10,000　　　　　**POOK**

A pair of Empire style stained fruitwood pedestals, of square tapered form, applied with a gilt-metal mount.

66in (167.5cm) high

$3,000-5,000　　　　　　**FRE**

A George III mahogany adjustable writing table, the ratchet-adjustable top above a false drawer, and two flanking drawers with divided interiors, the revolving height-adjustable stem on four downswept legs, pad feet and brass casters.

c1780　　　　26.25in (67cm) wide

$3,000-5,000　　　　　　**DN**

A pair of Regency mahogany reading stands, the tops with molded book-rests on brass quadrant ratchet supports and brass thumbscrews to adjustable columns, on baluster columns with gadrooned triform bases with underscrolled feet decorated with roundels.

29.25in (74cm) high

$7,000-9,000　　　　　　**L&T**

A Regency mahogany duet stand, shaped supports with two brass candle arms on tripod base.

44in (112cm) high

$2,000-2,500　　　　　**GORL**

A William IV mahogany folio stand, with trellis-framed wings on adjustable ratchet supports, on dual outsplaying legs ending in brass paw caps and casters.

24in (61cm) wide

$4,000-6,000　　　　　　**L&T**

A William IV rosewood adjustable duet stand.

c1835

$6,000-8,000　　　　　　**DN**

A mid-19thC walnut quintet music stand, with turned central finial, with five brass candle sconces, on a turned column, supported on a tripod base.

49.5in (126cm) high

$2,500-3,500　　　　　　**DN**

A 19thC mahogany, simulated rosewood and brass-strung Campaign duet stand, the lattice-framed rests with hinged folding mechanism flanked by a pair of engine-turned gilt-brass sconces, on an adjustable turned and ringed column with acanthus-carved base, on downswept tripod base ending in brass box casters.

19.75in (50cm) wide

$8,000-12,000　　　　　**L&T**

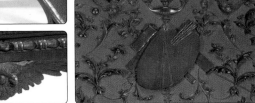

A late 19th/early20thC carved mahogany artist's folio stand, the hinged panel carved with a central palette and brushes within a surround depicting flowering foliage and two birds within a paterae and scroll-carved border, above a frieze carved with an owl in flight, on anthemion-carved trestle supports, with a lion mask below, above a pair of downswept legs with scroll feet, the panel above signed 'L Fruillini, Firenze'.

$6,000-10,000 DN

A George III mahogany and boxwood-strung oval urn table, the top with galleried edge and cup slide above an undulating frieze on slender splayed square tapering legs ending in spade feet.

14in (36cm) wide

$2,500-3,500 L&T

A George III mahogany kettle stand, the galleried top above a slide.

c1780 *13in (33cm) wide*

$3,000-5,000 DN

A military washbasin, the silver-plated basin sits fitted into a brass inlay mahogany rectangular box.

c1820 *16in (40.5cm) wide*

$1,000-1,500 FRE

A 19thC Continental rosewood bird's eye maple and tulipwood billet doux, the rectangular fall front inset with a beaded needlework panel, opening to reveal an interior fitted for writing, raised on upright supports and downswept part-ebonized legs.

21in (53.5cm) wide

$800-1,200 FRE

A William IV rosewood teapoy, the hinged top opening to a fitted interior with two bowl apertures and a lidded canister, on a baluster-shaped stem and lobed plinth with four scroll feet and concealed casters.

c1835 *30in (76cm)*

$800-1,200 DN

A Victorian figured walnut teapoy, the hinged oval top above the molded and gadrooned frieze on the baluster-turned and reeded stem issuing three leaf-carved downswept legs and scroll-carved feet, damage.

c1860 *28.75in (73cm) high*

$700-900 DN

FURNITURE

A George III brass-bound mahogany cellaret on stand, the hinged lid opening to a plain interior well, with flanking loop handles, on later square tapered legs ending in brass cappings and casters.

c1780   17.5in (44.5cm) wide
$3,000-5,000   **FRE**

An American Norfolk, Virginia Federal mahogany cellaret, rectangular lift lid fitted with a brass plate inscribed 'Capt. E. Kennedy United States Navy', and opening to fitted well of fifteen compartments and back counter board, above three graduated cockbeaded drawers flanked by reeded panels, on ring-turned tapering legs with inset brass bails to sides, repairs to rear corners of top.

PROVENANCE: Captain Edmund P. Kennedy of Norfolk, Va., had command of the famous ship, The Hornet, in 1825, and sailed to the West Indies and Gulf of Mexico.
c1800   40.5in (103cm) high
$12,000-16,000   **FRE**

CLOSER LOOK: GEORGE III CELLARET

This oval cellaret with its fluted lid relates to a number of well-known examples from collections that are attributed to Gillows.

This coopered shape is typical for cellarets. However, the fluted lid with finial and carved legs lift it above the norm.

The cellaret was made from well-figured mahogany and has an excellent patina – adding to its desirability.

Gillows is also known to have made a number of cellarets with reeded baluster legs.

A George III mahogany cellaret, in the manner of Gillows, some loss to top finial.

The term 'wine cooler' is commonly interchangeable with the term 'cellaret'. However, not all wine coolers are cellarets – a cellaret has a lockable lid, making it a 'little cellar', a wine cooler does not.
c1800   26.75in (68cm) wide
$30,000-35,000   **DN**

A George III mahogany and crossbanded octagonal cellaret, with later baize-lined interior on tapering square-section legs with brass casters, the whole decorated with boxwood lines.
18.5in (47cm) wide
$1,500-2,000   **L&T**

A George III mahogany and brass-bound wine cooler, of oval section, with twin carry handles and later ogee bracket feet.

31.25in (79cm) wide
$1,400-1,800   **L&T**

A George III mahogany cellaret.

c1810   20.5in (52cm) wide
$800-1,200   **DN**

A Regency mahogany sarcophagus cellaret, in the manner of Gillows, later carved overall with foliate decoration, the rounded rectangular shallow domed hinged lid above heavily gadrooned feet with wood casters.
32.75in (83cm) wide
$4,000-6,000   **L&T**

A Regency mahogany table cellaret, with domed top and square-section tapering body, damage, later elements.
c1820   17.25in (44cm) high
$800-1,200   **DN**

A William IV mahogany cellaret, the interior stamped 'JAMES WINTER & SONS 101 WARDOUR ST. SOHO, LONDON'.
c1835   30in (76cm) wide
$3,000-4,000   **DN**

A Pennsylvania William & Mary maple daybed, the adjustable back with an arched crest and three splats supported by baluster-turned stiles, the rush seat supported by boldly turned legs joined by ball- and ring-turned stretchers, from the Shelley Collection.

c1730   68in (172.5cm) wide

$22,000-28,000   **POOK**

A Pennsylvania American poplar rope bed, with diamond headboard and footboard and scalloped pillow guards, retaining its original vibrant blue painted surface, from the Shelley Collection.

c1790   76.5in (194.5cm) long

$2,000-4,000   **POOK**

A Pennsylvania poplar rope bed, with a pronounced scalloped headboard and turned posts, with a flatterned finial and turned spade feet, from the Shelley Collection.

c1800   77in (195.5cm) long

$2,000-4,000   **POOK**

A Pennsylvania painted rope bed, retaining its original exuberant black wavy swirls on salmon ground decoration, from the Shelley Collection.

c1800   76in (193cm) long

$10,000-15,000   **POOK**

A Pennsylvania painted child's rope bed, , retaining its original salmon grained decorated surface, from the Shelley Collection.

c1800   76.75in (195cm) long

$1,200-1,800   **POOK**

A New England windsor painted bamboo-turned hooded cradle, with original red-brown surface and yellow striping.

c1810   13in (33cm) wide

$4,000-6,000   **SK**

An early 19thC Philadelphia Federal cherry tall post bed, with carved acanthus leaves, and lamb's tongue treatment over the turned tapering legs.

     50.5in (128.5cm) wide

$5,000-7,000   **SK**

A Federal carved mahogany and mahogany veneer canopy bed, possibly Salem, Massachusetts, old surface.

c1823   89.5in (227.5cm) high

$7,000-9,000   **SK**

A late 18th/19thC oak child's cradle, the canopy with shaped frieze above paneled back and sides.

21.25in (54cm) wide

$700-900   DN

An early 19thC late Empire mahogany cradle, the supporting columns carved with acanthus leaves and resting on lion paws, the interior lined with mustard-coloured silk, retaining pillow and duvet.

53.25in (135cm) wide

$3,000-5,000   SOTA

A William IV mahogany and canework cradle.

c1825,   *39.5in (100cm) wide*

$400-600   DN

An Empire mahogany and gilt-bronze-mounted bed, the columns at the front supporting Medusa mask roundels, with engine milled socle collars.

c1810   *78.75in (200cm) long*

$2,000-2,500   DN

A 19thC Anglo-Indian 'European Classical Revival' style ebonised rosewood four-poster bed.

$10,000-20,000   GUIN

A late 19thC Anglo Indian carved and stained hardwood four-poster bed, the openwork headboard with lion and unicorn cresting.

88.5in (225cm) long

$8,000-12,000   DN

A 19thC George III style mahogany four-poster bed.

79.5in (202cm) long

$10,000-12,000   DN

A late 19thC Louis XV style rosewood and marquetry bedstead, with gilt-brass mounts, the headboard with applied brass trade label for 'DRUCE & CO Upholsters & Cabinet Makers, Baker Street, London. W. From Second Hand Department'.

81in (205cm) long

$4,000-6,000   WW

A 17thC and later South German marquetry miniature table cabinet, of various woods, the front doors inlaid with floral motif, opening to an arrangement of drawers around a central door, all with marquetry depicting townscapes, on a modern plinth base.

9.75in (24.5cm) high

$2,000-3,000   FRE

A rare American Queen Anne miniature painted pine and maple tall chest, in two parts, the top with a cove cornice above two small drawers over three long drawers, resting on a base with two small drawers, pronounced scalloped skirt, and cabriole legs terminating in crooked feet.

c1750   *48in (122cm) high*

$20,000-30,000   POOK

A late 18thC American miniature blanket chest, Lancaster County, Pennsylvania, the front with typical incised shell carving with trailing vines, above two shell-carved drawers, flanked by delicately chamfered and fluted corners supported by short ogee carved bracket feet, from the Shelley Collection.

15.5in (39.5cm) wide

$20,000-30,000   POOK

A late 18thC Louis XIV style amaranth and walnut miniature bureau mazarin, the rectangular parquetry-inlaid top above one small drawer and one deep drawer flanked by banks of three drawers, raised on square tapered legs joined by shaped stretchers ending in bun feet, stamped 'I Viez'.

12.5in (32cm) high

$1,200-1,800   FRE

A Regency rosewood and sycamore-strung miniature chest of drawers.

c1815   *14.5in (37cm) wide*

$1,500-2,000   DN

An American Clay Township, Lancaster County, Pennsylvania painted pine miniature blanket chest, by Joseph Long Lehn (1798-1892), with iron red ground, green, red, and yellow pinstriping and découpage floral sprays.

8.25in (21cm) wide

$1,200-1,600   POOK

A Victorian walnut miniature chest of drawers, the rectangular top above two short and three long drawers, on a plinth base.

c1880   *20.5in (52cm)*

$400-600   DN

An 19thC Louis XV/XVI style kingwood and parquetry miniature commode, the later ebonized wood top above three drawers on slightly hipped cabriole legs, fitted with gilt-bronze leafy mounts throughout.

10.75in (27.5cm) wide

$1,200-1,600   FRE

FOLK ART

THE FOLK ART MARKET

Last year's sale of part of Dr Donald A. Shelley and his wife Esther's pioneering collection helped to confirm Folk Art's place at the heart of American collecting. Dr Shelley, who was probably the first to research the purpose and creators of fraktur, amassed a diverse collection of unusual pieces including dower chests, William and Mary pieces and a painted box by Jacob Weber. While he began collecting when the interest in Folk Art was beginning, the buyers for his collection will have seen the market grow and mature.

Folk Art collectors are not alone in valuing quality and condition but above all rarity. And so, prices achieved for pieces from the Shelley collection show what can happen when something is right in every respect or so rare to be considered one of a kind. Similar items showing less originality in the design, in poorer condition or that are relatively common are unlikely to perform as well.

At the top end of the market collectors continue to prize exceptional and rare pieces. Ceramics, and especially redware (see pages 66-9), still attract a great deal of attention. Jugs and bowls with exquisite decoration are very collectible and are probably a good investment. Early pieces and those with strong, graphic decoration remain popular, particularly stoneware crocks (see pages 82-3).

The top end of the horn and scrimshaw field is also doing well and the market for quilts – particularly the better 19th century examples – continues to improve.

Fraktur remains a popular area, with rare and colorful pieces reaching five-figure prices. Condition is extremely important, as is proven provenance. The top end of the market is doing extremely well, whereas the lower end continues to stagnate.

As more and more is known about these early American art forms it is possible for buyers to research their chosen field more easily. However, fakes are known and so it is important to buy from a reputable source such as an established dealer or auction house.

Ron Pook, Pook & Pook, Downingtown, Pensylvannia

ESSENTIAL REFERENCE: HEINRICH BUCHER

Heinrich Bucher was originally thought to have been the maker of the small decorated boxes, or Schmuckkasten, found with his name on them. However, there is now a theory that he was the owner and the boxes had a common maker.

- Schmuckkasten were a traditional gift in Germanic Europe and the tradition continued within the Pennsylvania German community. They were used to hold sewing accessories, trinkets and personal keepsakes.
- The boxes marked Heinrich Bucher are usually of thinly milled pine, cedar or poplar, constructed with fine dovetails, pinned bottom and top boards, punch-decorated sheet tin hinges and lock hasps.
- The boxes have a red, blue or blue-green ground decorated with stylized flowers, vines and pinwheels laid out with a compass.
- Forms vary from dome- and flat-top to sliding-lid as well as coopered round or oval band boxes and bride's boxes.
- Some are lined with Lancaster County newspapers from 1812-38 or a pencil or ink inscription of owner.

A Chester County, Pennsylvania cherry dresser box, with a lift lid, front line and berry inlays resting on short straight bracket feet, from the Shelley Collection.
c1760   *10in (25.5cm) wide*
$10,000-15,000   **POOK**

A late 18thC Pennsylvania small painted pine slide-lid ditty box, probably Lancaster County, the body with zigzag and dot decoration, the lid with trailing vine decoration, from the Shelley Collection.
7.5ins (19cm) long
$11,000-15,000   **POOK**

A late 18th/early 19thC rectangular painted and decorated pine storage box, by Heinrich Bucher, Berks County, Pennsylvania, with hinged lid and tin hasp, the lid with house and tulip decoration, inscribed 'H.L', the sides with tulips, all on a black ground, from the Shelley Collection.
10.5in (26.5cm) wide
$4,000-6,000   **POOK**

A late 18th/early 19thC painted and decorated oval bentwood ribbon box, marked Heinrich Bucher, Berks County, Pennsylvania, the fitted lid with elaborate potted flowers and dot and sawtooth border, the sides with profuse floral decoration on a blue/black ground, from the Shelley Collection.
16.5ins (42cm) wide
$75,000-100,000   **POOK**

An early 19thC Centre County, Pennsylvania decorated oval band box, with delicate vine, tulip and drape decoration with floret-decorated border on a red surface, inscribed on the underside of the lid 'Jacob Burl 1811', from the Shelley Collection.

14.25in (36cm) wide
$70,000-100,000   **POOK**

CLOSER LOOK: PENNSYLVANIA COMPASS BOX

The blue ground is profusely decorated all over with red and white stylized flower, fan, and leaf motifs.

The latch and escutcheon are made from punched sheet iron.

The design – which is almost symmetrical – was laid out with the aid of a compass before being hand-painted.

The box has a single drawer.

The sale price represents an auction record for this type of box.

A Lancaster County, Pennsylvania poplar and pine polychrome-decorated compass box, from the Shelley Collection.

c1800-1840
$375,000-400,000
16in (40.5cm) wide
POOK

A Pennsylvania painted Conestoga wagon box.

The Conestoga wagon was developed in the Conestoga Creek region of Lancaster County, Pennsylvania, c1725. Designed to carry heavy loads over bad roads, the floor curved up at each end to prevent the contents shifting. Initially used by farmers, they were later used to carry goods to frontier stores and settlements and return with frontier produce. Before the railroads crossed the Allegheny Mountain Range c1850 goods were transported by wagon train. The wagons were also used by families moving West. Their household goods were kept on board while they walked or rode alongside. At night, they slept sheltered beneath the wagon.

1819
$30,000-50,000
16in (40.5cm) high
POOK

An early 19thC fancy blue paint-decorated dome-top box, attributed to Moses Eaton (1753-1833), Massachusetts and New Hampshire, (or M.E. Jr. 1796-1886 New Hampshire), dovetail-constructed rectangular box with wire-hinged lid, iron latch, with all over shaded blue putty painted decoration with brown borders, minor imperfections.

18in (45.5cm) wide
$6,500-8,500
SK

An Academy painted pine box, signed 'Emily Emerson Northfield Vermont', paint wear, dated.

1826
$4,000-6,000
10in (25.4cm) wide
SK

A early 19thC paint-decorated poplar dome-top box, from New York, with hinged lid and iron lock, with imperfections.

25.75in (65.5cm) long
$10,000-12,000
SK

An early 19thC New England painted dome-top 'Joshua's Box', dovetail-constructed rectangular pine box with hinged lid, painted gray with black lettering and striping, minor imperfections.

27.5in (70cm) wide
$2,500-3,500
SK

A possibly Virginia painted pine salt box, with a lift-lid and single drawer, retaining its original yellow flowers and green leaf decoration on a red ground.

c1835
$1,000-$1,500
10.5in (26.5cm) wide
POOK

A 19thC Central Pennsylvania, Mahantongo Valley, canted-side storage box, with typical red and yellow stamped rosettes on a green ground, from the Shelley Collection.

11.5ins (29cm) wide
$23,000-28,000
POOK

FOLK ART

An early 19thC Connecticut or possibly East Douglas, Massachusetts, paint-decorated tinware trunk, dome-topped with hinged lid and wire handle, white band on front with floral and foliate decoration on a black ground, minor paint wear.

10in (25.4cm) wide

$4,500-6,500   SK

CLOSER LOOK: JACOB WEBER BOX

The front of all known boxes decorated by Weber (1772-1865), feature a two- or three-story Georgian-style house with many windows. The house is shown symmetrically and in three dimensions and is flanked by trees, with low hills in the foreground.

Like most Weber boxes this one has shaped bracket feet and edge-molded bottom bands.

In common with other examples of his work, it is secured with an oversized sheet tin hasp which hinges downwards to meet a wire loop in the front board to which a lock was attached.

The side and top panels of Weber's boxes were painted freehand with tulips. Sometimes fans and arches define the corners.

The painted decoration is typically blue-green, blue, light green or yellow ground with the decoration built up with two or three layers of color.

A painted pine storage box, by Jacob Weber, of Fivepointville, Lancaster County, Pennsylvania, inscribed 'Maria Weber 1850', from the Shelley Collection.

10in (25.5cm) wide

$140,000-180,000   POOK

A 19thC dome-top box, dovetail constructed, the top painted with a couple and four children in a rural landscape, the front with a red house beside a river with sailing vessels and a sidewheeler, minor imperfections.

20in (51cm) wide

$8,000-10,000   SK

A 19thC Pennsylvania painted and decorated rectangular slide-lid candlebox, of pegged construction with an ochre ground, the lid decorated with grapes and leaves, the sides with roses, from the Shelley Collection.

10in (25.5cm) long

$4,000-5,000   POOK

Left: A large mid- to late 19thC Shaker red-painted oval covered box, probably New England, original red paint.

13.5in (34.5cm) wide

$6,500-8,500   SK

Right/Top: A large late 19thC Shaker covered oval box with label, attributed to David Meacham Jr., New Lebanon, New York.

12in (30.5cm) wide

$10,000-15,000   SK

Right/Bottom: A mid to late 19thC Shaker yellow-painted oval covered box, probably New England, original yellow paint.

13.5in (35.5cm) wide

$6,500-8,500   SK

A set of four late 19thC, probaby New England graduating green-painted Shaker oval covered boxes, the boxes with pine top and bottom with bent maple sides, the two smaller boxes joined with three fingers and secured with copper tacks, the two larger with four fingers, paint wear, stains.

10.5in (26.5cm) wide (largest)

$10,000-15,000   SK

A graduating set of five late 19th/early 20thC red-painted Shaker oval boxes, the covered boxes with pine tops and bottoms and bent maple sides with lapped finger construction, the smallest and largest with fingers facing left, the other three facing right, imperfections.

11.5in (29cm) wide (largest)

$7,000-9,000   SK

A 19thC Vermont putty-painted dome-top box, square dovetailed with wire hinges, the exterior with brown putty decoration on a mustard and green ground, the front centered with a compass flower decoration, minor paint loss.

17.25in (44cm) wide c1900

$1,500-2,000   SK

A Lancaster County, Pennsylvania painted slide-lid candlebox, decorated with tulip trees, facing birds and initials 'EH', all on a yellow ground with green corners and red edges

8.5ins (21.5cm) wide

$5,000-6,000   POOK

A late 19th/early 20thC American painted 'Snakes and Ladders' game board, late rectangular panel with applied breadboard ends, the playing surface painted red, blue, and black on a white ground with blue and red borders, age crack.

23.75in (60.5cm) high

$65,000-75,000   SK

A 19thC American polychrome-painted wooden checkerboard with red diamond border, square panel with molded edges, the center painted with black and creamy white checks outlined in red, the salmon-painted border with red diamonds with intersecting yellow lines and outlined in blue, the molding painted yellow, panel bowed, scattered paint losses.

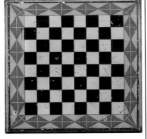

16in (40.7cm) high

$3,000-4,000   SK

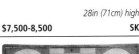

A late 19thC painted Parcheesi board, retaining its original red, green, yellow, black, and olive surface.

19.25in (49cm) high

$2,000-3,000   POOK

An early 20thC American polychrome-painted Parcheesi game board, rectangular panel with breadboard ends, the playing surface painted red, black, green and mustard on a creamy white ground.

28in (71cm) high

$7,500-8,500   SK

A late 19th/early 20thC painted American pine carom game board, with recessed corner pockets and applied molding, the playing field painted in dark red and mustard.

31in (78.5cm) high

$6,000-8,000   SK

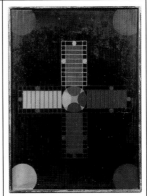

A 19thC Canadian polychrome-painted double-sided game board, with a red and gold painted checkerboard, black-painted game piece sections, the reverse painted with a Parcheesi game in red, yellow, sepia, and green on a black background, age crack, minor wear.

28in (71cm) wide

$5,000-6,000   SK

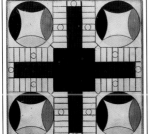

A late 19th/early 20thC polychrome-painted Parcheesi game board, square panel, the playing field painted red, black, green and yellow on a creamy white ground, applied mitered frame.

17.25in (44cm) wide

$4,500-5,500   SK

A 19thC American polychrome-painted double-sided game board, one side painted with Parcheesi board with black-painted molding, the other side painted with a yellow and grey checkerboard with gray border, molding losses.

18.75in (47.5cm) wide

$4,000-5,000   SK

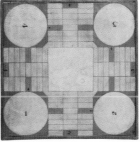

A small, late 19th/early 20thC American painted Parcheesi board, square panel with applied molding, the playing surface painted in muted tones of red, green and creamy white, black painted numerals.

12.5in (32cm) wide

$6,500-7,500   SK

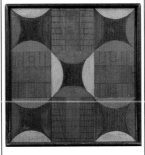

An early 20thC American polychrome-painted wooden Parcheesi game board, square panel with applied molded frame, the playing surface painted in shades of red, green, blue, gold and creamy white.

19in (48.5cm) wide

$3,000-4,000   SK

CLOSER LOOK: SCHIMMEL EAGLES

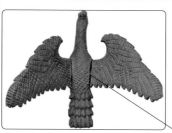

Wilhelm Schimmel (1817-90) was a German immigrant carver who arrived in Cumberland County, PA c1860. Remembered for his unpredictable and drunken behaviour, he was nevertheless supported by the local community who no doubt saw it as their duty to shelter and care for others.

The eagles have a central body, head, leg and base section. The separate wings, decorated with deep angular cuts, were joined to the body using a shallow mortise and glue.

The original red, yellow and brown decoration has been varnished over.

Schimmel used the German word 'Vogel' to describe his eagles.

This example has been brightly painted – probably using left over household paints.

Both these eagles are from the Shelley Collection.

Above: A carved and polychrome-decorated pine standing eagle.

14.5in (37cm) high

$250,000-300,000   **POOK**

Right: A carved and painted pine standing eaglet.

6.75in (17cm) high

$60,000-80,000   **POOK**

A figure of a smiling woman, attributed to Manly L. Lundberg, the woman wears a white hat, coat, and muff, unsigned, carved and painted walnut figure, mounted on a square wooden base with chamfered edges, craquelure to varnished surface.

It is believed that Manly L. Lundberg was born c1908 in Reads Landing, Minnesota. He started carving figures and writing poetry after being hospitalized for a spinal injury he received during his service in the Marine Corps. He lived a simple life in a small cabin in Southern Minnesota and occasionally sold his sculptures. He tried, without great success, to sell them from a van he designed and built which he took on a cross country trip to California. He died in 1973.

12.5in (32cm) high

$1,200-1,800   **SK**

A late 19th/early 20thC pair of mink furrier's counter figures, possibly New York State, the carved wood and composition figures with tack eyes, leather ears, wire claws, and brown wool flocking, imperfections.

15.75in (40cm) long

$800-1,200   **SK**

A late 19th/early 20thC polychrome-painted papier-mâché Georgia Bottle Man, molded papier-mâché covered bottle in the form of a man seated on a handled pot, the man with lift-off head with inset glass eyes, wearing a black jacket with red collar, and green trousers, loss on foot.

11.75in (30cm) high

$500-800   **SK**

A 19thC Pennsylvania carved and gessoed figure of a dog.

14in (35.5cm) high

$3,500-4,500   **POOK**

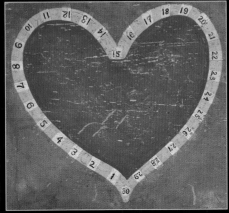
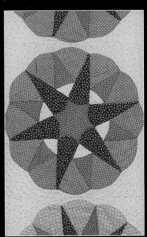

A small late 19thC Lehnware painted covered canister, Joseph Lehn, Elizabeth Township, Lancaster County, Pennsylvania, lathe-turned vessel decorated on the cover with strawberries, the sides with stylized flowers, in shades of red, green, white and brown on a pink ground.

5.5in (14cm) high

$2,000-3,000 SK

CLOSER LOOK: JOSEPH LEHN SUGAR BUCKET

The turned lids and plank bottoms were made from turned poplar. The knobs on the lids were mass produced and bought rather than made by Lehn.

Joseph Lehn made open and covered sugar buckets. They are a slightly tapering cylinder in shape with the sides made from eleven tapering oak staves.

The buckets were painted with a salmon pink ground, then combed or figured with a darker red wash in vertical diagonal bands.

Trailing vines and floral buds were a common decoration.

An American sugar bucket, by Joseph Lehn, Lancaster County, Pennsylvania, of stave construction with iron straps, retaining original salmon surface with floral and vine bands, from the Shelley Collection.

Joseph Lehn (1798-1892) of Elizabeth Township, Lancaster County, Pennsylvania, was a farmer who supplemented his income by making finely turned and paint-decorated wooden table items, coopered buckets and small cabinet pieces.

A prolific maker, he is best known for his egg cups, covered saffron boxes and small footed bowls painted with floral motifs on blue, pink and yellow ground colors.

$1,200-1,800 POOK

A late 19thC Lehnware covered saffron cup, Joseph Lehn, Elizabeth Township, Lancaster County, Pennsylvania, lathe-turned footed vessel decorated on the cover and sides with strawberries, in shades of red, green, and white on a pink ground.

These spice cups follow the style of earlier Continental prototypes and have a stylistic tie to early 19thC Neoclassicism with their urn-shape form and undulating swag-pattern borders.

4.25in (11cm) high

$2,000-3,000 SK

An American turned poplar lidded treen canister, with green and yellow leaf and dot decoration on a burnt orange ground, from the Shelley Collection.

c1800 *6.25in (16cm) high*

$10,000-12,000 POOK

A Pennsylvania cherry watch hutch, with slide-lip top, with a bold ogee cornice and chamfered stiles over a molded base, retaining an old dry surface, from the Shelley Collection.

c1800 *8.5in (21.5cm) high*

$14,000-18,000 POOK

A 19thC Pennsylvania elaborately turned poplar covered canister, with red and black polychrome decoration, from the Shelley Collection.

9.25in (23.5cm) high

$1,800-2,200 POOK

An early 19thC Virginia tooled leather key basket, with heart and star decoration.

8.5in (21.5cm) high

$6,500-8,500 POOK

A collection of thirty seven New England and Pennsylvania baskets, to include splint oak, sewing, creel, swing handle, etc.

$12,000-15,000 POOK

A Lancaster County, Pennsylvania walnut straight edge, with sulfur-inlaid initials 'IS', with bird, star, and potted tulip inlays, dated, from the Shelley Collection.

1800 *22.5in (57cm) long*

$30,000-50,000 POOK

ESSENTIAL REFERENCE: FRAKTUR

The tradition of creating illuminated texts arrived in America with settlers from Germanic Europe. The term, which originally meant a form of broken lettering, now means a variety of illustrated texts from the 18th and 19th centuries.

Types include:

- Vorschrift: writing samplers such as penmanship example booklets, tunebooks and bookplates.
- Zierschrift: decorative writing.
- Liebesbriefe: love letters or house blessings, presentation fraktur and rewards of merit. These are almost exclusively an American form.
- Daafschein: birth record, these are one of the most common types of fraktur.
- Geburts- und Taufscheine: birth and baptismal certificates. A vast number of printed ones exist, the majority contain date and details of the child's birth but not his or her baptism. Taufscheine were handmade or printed; they were mass-produced from the early 1780s and by the late 1800s had gone from a Pennsylvania German custom to a national trend.
- Taufwunsch: godparent's greeting. Usually record the first name of the child. They were often given to the child wrapped around a coin. Many were stored rolled up.

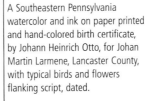

A Southeastern Pennsylvania watercolor and ink on paper printed and hand-colored birth certificate, by Johann Heinrich Otto, for Johan Martin Larmene, Lancaster County, with typical birds and flowers flanking script, dated.

1766   *16.5in (42cm) wide*

$1,800-2,200   **POOK**

A Lancaster and Northumberland Counties, Pennsylvana ink and watercolor fraktur, by Johann Heinrich Otto, for Anna Cathariena Ullrich, with central printed script surrounded by hand-colored birds and floral vines, with a period faux tiger frame, dated.

Johann Heinrich Otto (active c1762-c1797) was a talented fraktur artist whose work shows an attractive balance of color and form. He used repeated motifs which were often identical in shape but decorated with different patterns. A master of the parrot motif, his exuberant floral designs and crowns of righteousness provided inspiration for many other artists.

1770   *15.5in (39cm) wide*

$3,500-4,500   **POOK**

A Southeastern Pennsylvania watercolor and ink on paper fraktur, possibly by Johann Heinrich Otto, with central cartouche with sawtooth border flanked by parrots, mermaids and scrolling vines with stylized flowers, dated.

1783   *16in (41cm) wide*

$3,000-4,000   **POOK**

A birth record attributed to Moses Connor, Jr. (active 1800-1832), titled 'Birth Record: Jerusha Webber Born Aug't 23, 1802', unsigned, the back of the record inscribed in ink 'A gift from a friend, and you remember the giver. Joan F. Jackman', watercolor and ink on paper, depicting the birth inscription flanked by two fanciful birds perched on leafy branches, in original light blue painted wooden frame, toning.

Moses Connor, Jr., was born in Hopkinton, New Hampshire, on October 25, 1774. In 1808 he moved to Wolfeboro, New Hampshire. Good at penmanship, Connor began writing family records, which he continued for the next 20 years. By 1813, he had developed a style that included hearts, flowers, vines, diamonds and birds, most of which have large beaks. Connor died sometime after 1832.

9in (23cm) high

$7,000-9,000   **SK**

An early 19thC family record picture, probably Maine, watercolor and ink on paper, depicting a rectangular reserve with a spreadwing eagle and an American shield inscribed 'WE ARE ONE,' grasping a banner in its beak which is inscribed 'BIRTHS AND MARRIAGE OF CORNELIUS AND REBECCA ADAMS,' above a panel with the inscribed vital statistics of the couple 'Cornelius Adams Born December 1st 1782,' 'Rebecca Davis Born March 22nd 1787,' in oval reserves and 'THEY WERE MARRIED June 7th 1804,' in a heart-shaped reserve flanked by flowering branches, enclosed in a leafy border, toning, edge and corner losses, in a period molded wood frame.

12in (30.5cm) high

$20,000-25,000   **SK**

ESSENTIAL REFERENCE: JOHANN KREBS

Johann Friedrich Krebs (1749-1815, active 1784-1812) was a Prussian soldier who, like many others, decided to stay in the US after the Revolutionary War.

- He settled near Harrisburg, Pennsylvania, where he taught at a number of Lutheran schools.
- He is credited with helping to make Taufscheine (birth or baptismal certificates) popular. As well as making hand-drawn fraktur he filled in hundreds of printed examples.
- Krebs' work was often hastily produced and while a great quantity of it survives there are relatively few quality pieces. Some of these offer a remarkable window on Pennsylvania German life with subjects such as a squabbling man and woman.
- A popular subject for his work were Biblical texts or pictures, particularly the tale of the Prodigal Son – a popular story for fathers to tell their sons – which he told many times using just two or four pictures.

A Southeastern Pennsylvania ink and watercolor birth certificate, by Johann Friederich Krebs, for Benjamin Gruber, the central heart with printed and hand-drawn script surrounded by tulips, flowers, decoupage, dated.

1809   *15.25ins (39cm) wide*

$1,000-1,500   **POOK**

A Bucks County Pennsylvania ink and watercolor birth certificate, by Johann Friederich Krebs (active 1784-1812), the central heart with printed and hand-drawn script surrounded by parrots, tulip vines, flowers, dated.

1806   *15.5ins (39cm) wide*

$2,500-3,500   **POOK**

A Berks County, Southeastern Pennsylvania, ink and watercolor fraktur, by Martin Brechall (active 1783-1830), with central script flanked by shields, tulips and floral pinwheels, dated.

1807   *16.25in (41cm) wide*

$3,500-4,500   **POOK**

A Dauphin County, Pennsylvania, watercolor and ink on paper birth and baptismal certificate, for Sarah Stauffer, with central script flanked by parrot, birds, tulip vines and stylized flowers in shades of blue, red, yellow and green, dated.

1813   *15.5in (39cm) wide*

$2,000-3,000   **POOK**

A Manor Township, Pennsylvania watercolor and ink on paper Haussegen (house blessing), with central cartouche enclosing script flanked by tulip vines arising from pots and perched birds in shades of blue, yellow, red, orange and green, dated.

1822   *15.5in (39cm) wide*

$3,500-4,500   **POOK**

A family record for the Mallery family, signed and dated 'Drawn by William Murray May 11th 1824', watercolor and ink on paper, depicting the vital statistics of Samuel Mallery, his wife Nabby Hurd and their eight children, ornamented with hearts, a pineapple and a floral border, in a period molded giltwood frame, toning, crease, repaired tears, stains.

1824   *15in (38cm) high*

$2,000-3,000   **SK**

A Warwick Township, Lancaster County, Pennsylvania cut paper and watercolor birth certificate, minor toning, creases.

Scherenschnitte – or paper cutting – was a popular pastime in Pennsylvania German communities.

c1824   *12.5in (32cm) wide*

$6,000-8,000   **SK**

An ink and watercolor on paper fraktur, for Sara Kessler, by Martin Brechall (Southeastern Pennsylvania, active 1783-1830), the central script bordered by hearts and religious verses, later script added announcing her death in 1826.

15.5in (39cm) wide

$1,500-2,500 POOK

A Southeastern Pennsylvania ink and watercolor lover's knot, an early label verso reads 'Jonathan Helffenstein February 1833', dated.

1833 *6.5in (16.5cm) square*

$2,500-3,500 POOK

A watercolor and ink on paper birth record, by Henry Young, for Christopher Marsh, with typical central hearts with script and sawtooth borders, flanked by birds, tulips, stars and flowers, dated.

Henry Young (active 1817-61) lived in Centre County, Pennsylvania, and used several distinct conventionalized formats in his certificates. These include women with their hair arranged high on their head and wearing an Empire-style gown and men wearing colorful waistcoats and tailcoats. The figures usually stand on a patch of green grass. Other identifying motifs include large roses with leaves, stylized birds, a tripod table and an eight-sided star.

1831 *9.5in (24cm) high*

$4,000-5,000 POOK

A Schuylkill County, Pennsylvania watercolor and ink on paper fraktur birth certificate, marked 'Elizabeth Williams, 1833', with vibrant pots of flowers and tulips flanking a central circle with script written sideways.

14.25in (36.5cm) wide

$4,000-5,000 POOK

A mid- 19thC Pennsylvania set of six watercolor and ink on paper birth certificates, for the Hartman family, by J. S. Ellsworth, Four-Corners Flowers Artist'.

9.5in (24cm) wide

$2,000-3,000 SET POOK

A Monson, Maine framed illustration, given on the occasion of marriage, 'For Miss Harmony B. Merritt...Monson March 13th 1841. A present from Torrey aged 76', watercolor and ink on paper depicting a couple holding hands, an angel blowing a trumpet accompanied by the inscription: 'A Female Angel with her trump is here presented, to guard the name of Harmony B. Merritt.,' with the words 'Respect' and 'Love' embellished with scrolled foliage, billing doves, and flower blossoms, in a period molded giltwood frame, minor toning, foxing, minor stains, light creases.

21.75in (55cm) high

$1,500-2,000 SK

A Daniel Peterman (York County, Pennsylvania, active 1819-1864), ink and watercolor fraktur, for Henry Baily, the central script surrounded by female figures, parrots, and tulip vines, signed lower middle 'Daniel Peterman'.

1861 11.5in (29.5cm) wide

$3,500-4,500 POOK

CLOSER LOOK: MAHOGANY TEA CHEST

This unusual chest was made with high quality fittings and has survived in near mint condition.

Each panel is decorated with inlaid quatrefoils. The rectangular body has canted corners and a hinged lid with a kingwood sloping edge.

The scroll handle is hallmarked with lion passant and makers initials 'J.S.'.

Inside is a pair of rectangular canisters, lead-lined with sliding faceted cover and turned ebonized lid with inset disc engraved with a crest, flanking a further canister with sliding domed cover.

An early George III mahogany tea chest, with silver-lined inlay and ebonized moulding, the front inset with pierced Gothic escutcheon.

10.25in (26cm) wide

$24,000-30,000   WW

A George II burr walnut bombé tea caddy, the hinged lid with a scroll handle, opening to reveal a compartmented interior with brass fittings, raised on squat bracket feet.

8in (20.5cm) wide

$5,000-6,000   L&T

A George III fruitwood 'apple' tea caddy, the hinged lid opening to reveal a lined interior.

4in (10cm) high

$3,400-4,000   L&T

A George III fruitwood 'apple' tea caddy with hinged lid.

4.5in (11cm) high

$2,200-2,600   L&T

An 18thC fruitwood 'pear' tea caddy, of typical form, the hinged lid with a curved stalk.

6.75in (17cm) high

$3,000-4,000   L&T

An 18thC fruitwood 'pear' tea caddy, of typical form, the hinged lid with a curved stalk finial.

7.5in (19cm) high

$8,000-10,000   L&T

A late 18thC George III mahogany tea caddy of oval section, with bone-inset diamond escutcheon, the interior with subsidiary cover.

6in (15cm) wide

$800-1,200   DN

A late 18thC George III mahogany and marquetry tea caddy, the hinged cover with fan patera in an oval reserve and cavetto edging, the interior previously with twin divisions, lacking interior divisions.

12in (30.5cm) wide

$240-360   **DN**

A late 18thC George III tortoiseshell-veneered tea caddy, of rectangular section, with ivory banding.

5in (12.5cm) wide

$4,000-6,000   **DN**

A George III tortoiseshell and ivory-strung decagonal tea caddy, the front inset with a vacant shield within a gold and mother-of-pearl dot border, with drape above a bright cut escutcheon, the hinged top with a gold loop handle and dot star, the inner lid with a turned ivory handle, with key.

5in (12.5cm) high

$11,000-13,000   **WW**

A late 18thC Georgian rolled paper tea caddy, of navette form with brass finial, inlaid with foliage on a scroll ground, opening to reveal a satinwood inner lid.

7.5in (19cm) wide

$1,400-2,000   **HT**

A late 18thC George III satinwood and crossbanded tea caddy, of oval section, the cover with brass swing handle, the interior with metal lining.

6.25in (16cm) wide

$1,300-1,700   **DN**

A George III harewood and marquetry-inlaid tea caddy, the square sides and domed lid inlaid with stylized trailing bell flowers and burr wood oval panels, opening to reveal a conforming covered interior.

5.75in (14.5cm) wide

$3,000-4,000   **L&T**

A late George III rosewood and brass bound tea caddy, the hinged lid enclosing a compartmented interior with brass fittings, raised on bracket feet.

8.75in (22cm) wide

$2,000-3,000   **L&T**

A George III walnut and parquetry tea caddy, the ogee molded hinged lid, opening to reveal a compartmented interior with brass fittings, raised on later claw-and-ball feet.

8.5in (21.5cm) wide

$1,800-2,200   **L&T**

A George III mahogany and kingwood crossbanded tea caddy, of cubic form, the hinged lid opening to reveal a parquetry-inlaid interior with covered compartments.

5in (12.5cm) wide

$800-1,200   **L&T**

A George III ivory tea caddy, of canted rectangular form, with tortoiseshell inlay and silver mounts, the hinged lid enclosing a covered compartment.

4in (10cm) wide

$2,400-3,600   **L&T**

A late George III mahogany tea caddy, elaborately inlaid throughout with boxwood stringing, ivory flowerheads, roundels and mother-of-pearl, the hinged lid revealing a central cut glass bowl flanked by lidded compartments, the underside of lid radial-veneered, the whole raised on ball feet.

12.5in (31.5cm) wide

$3,000-$5,000   **L&T**

A Regency rosewood and sycamore-strung tea caddy, of sarcophagus form, with repoussé brass and ring handles, the fitted interior with twin subsidiary caddies with hinged covers and a central cut glass bowl.

c1815　　*13in (33cm) wide*

$200-300　　　　**DN**

A late George III or Regency burr yew wood and gilt-brass-mounted tea caddy, with twin subsidiary covers within.

c1810　　*8.25in (21cm) wide*

$500-700　　　　**DN**

A Regency rosewood tea caddy, of sarcophagus form, the interior with twin subsidiary caddies and a glass bowl.

c1815　　*15in (38cm) wide*

$560-640　　**DN**

A Regency pen work tea caddy, of canted rectangular form, decorated with griffins, foliage chequer banding and geometric designs, the hinged lid enclosing a covered compartmented interior.

7in (18cm) wide

$1,800-2,400　　**L&T**

A Regency mahogany and brass molded tea caddy, of rectangular form with ebonized and brass moulding, sand winged brass escutcheon, the lid with an ivory ball finial, opening to a compartmented interior comprising three removable lidded mahogany tea containers.

c1815　　*10.5in (26.5cm) wide*

$1,400-2,000　　**FRE**

A Regency rosewood tea caddy, of sarcophagus form.

c1815　　*13.5in (34cm) wide*

$600-800　　**DN**

An early 19thC Regency tortoiseshell tea caddy, with retail label for 'F. L. Hausburg, Goldsmith & Jeweller, Old Post Office Building, Liverpool'.

7in (18cm) wide

$5,200-6,000　　**FRE**

A Regency tortoiseshell and ivory tea caddy, of canted rectangular form, the hinged lid enclosing two conforming covered compartments.

7in (18cm) wide

$4,000-6,000　　**L&T**

A Regency bowfront tortoiseshell tea caddy, the radiating fluted front with a domed hinged lid, opening to reveal two covered compartments, raised on four ball feet.

7in (17.5cm) wide

$3,600-4,400　　**L&T**

A Regency tortoiseshell tea caddy, of serpentine form, the molded hinged top opening to reveal two lidded wells raised on bun feet.

c1820　　*8in (20.5cm) wide*

$2,400-3,600　　**FRE**

A Regency blonde tortoiseshell tea caddy, of sarcophagus shape with ivory stringing, the hinged cover with a plated ball finial, to a twin-lidded interior with turned ivory handles, on ball feet.

8.25in (21cm) wide

$3,000-4,000　　**WW**

An early 19thC Regency tortoiseshell tea caddy, the pagoda-form top of serpentine outline with brass name plate, over a conforming body with a brass escutcheon, opening to a compartmented interior, on ball feet.

7.5in (19cm) wide

$1,400-2,000　　**FRE**

A late Regency tortoiseshell bowfront tea caddy, with silver stringing and a floral mother-of-pearl-inlaid front, the hinged pagoda lid with a plaque inscribed 'J & E Lister to F H & M Firth', the interior with a pair of lidded compartments with vegetable ivory handles, on turned feet.

7.5in (19cm) wide

$3,600-4,400   **WW**

An unusually large Regency gonzalo alves and crossbanded tea caddy, of sarcophagus form and with twin lion-mask-and-loop handles, the molded top enclosing a typical fitted interior with an associated Bristol blue glass mixing bowl, raised on claw-and-ball feet.

17in (43cm) wide

$3,600-4,400   **L&T**

An early 19thC oak fruitwood and boxwood parquetry-decorated tea caddy, the hinged lid revealing star-inlaid liner, together with parquetry-decorated caddy spoon.

$600-800   **LOC**

A Regency chinoiserie-decorated tea caddy, the hinged lid opening to reveal a foliate penwork-decorated interior with two lidded wells, the swelled side with cornucopia loop handles, raised on brass feet.

8.75in (22cm) wide

$600-1,000   **FRE**

A large George IV tortoiseshell tea caddy, of bombé form, the carnet molded hinged lid enclosing a twin-lidded interior with central cut glass bowl, with ivory paterae bun side handles and conforming feet.

13in (33cm) wide

$5,00-7,000   **L&T**

A George IV or William IV rosewood and mother-of-pearl-inlaid tea caddy, of sarcophagus form, twin subsidiary caddies within, damage.

c1830   *12.75in (32.5cm) wide*

$400-600   **DN**

An early 19thC yew wood tea caddy, with banding and stringing, the hinged lid to a pair of hinged lidded canisters flanking a later glass bowl.

12.25in (31cm) wide

$440-560   **WW**

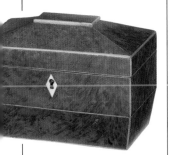

An early 19thC burr yew wood tea caddy, with boxwood stringing, the interior previously divided.

7.5in (19cm) wide

$300-500   **WW**

A George IV tortoiseshell tea caddy, the hinged pagoda top with a vacant plaque, the interior with a single lidded compartment, the front with a pressed fan motif and with beaded mounts, on ball feet.

4.5in (11.5cm) wide

$3,000-5,000   **WW**

A George IV tortoiseshell tea caddy, with white metal stringing, the sides with pressed Gothic windows, the hinged pagoda lid with an ivory finial, the inner lid with ivory banding and finial, revealing a divided interior, on brass ball feet, with key.

7in (8cm) high

$12,000-16,000   **WW**

A Victorian dome-top burl walnut tea caddy, with parquetry banding, opening to reveal a twin compartment interior, the covers lacking.

c1840   *8in (20.5cm) wide*

$240-360   **FRE**

BOXES

A mid-19thC cut brass and tortoiseshell tea caddy, the hinged cover to a pair of yew wood-lidded canisters.

9.5in (24cm) high

$800-1,200   **WW**

A Victorian papier mâché tea caddy, with simulated malachite borders and floral-decorated, the hinged lid to a pair of lidded compartments with mother-of-pearl floret handles.

9.25in (23.5cm) wide

$400-800   **WW**

A Victorian papier mâché tea caddy, by Jennens and Bettridge, of bombé form, with canted corners, polychrome-decorated and inlaid mother-of-pearl, the hinged lid with a pair of lidded compartments and mother-of-pearl handles, the underside stamped 'Jennens & Bettridge Makers to the Queen', '9' over '19' and painted '52'.

9.75in (25cm) wide

$1,000-1,600   **WW**

A 19thC Sorrento ware tea caddy, the walnut ground with multi-strung borders, the hinged lid centered with a marquetry panel of figures dancing, the inside with a floral panel and a pair of hinged lidded canisters with marquetry figure panels.

10.75in (27.5cm) wide

$700-900   **WW**

A late 19thC French lacquered brass inlay tea caddy, of rectangular form, the blue lacquer ground finely inlaid with brass foliate scroll work, the hinged lid encloses two covered caddies and weights.

8in (20.5cm) wide

$600-1,000   **FRE**

A 19thC French rosewood, cut pewter, brass and ivory tea caddy, of slight bombé form, the hinged lid to a pair of lidded compartments.

8.75in (22cm) wide

$600-1,000   **WW**

A Victorian satinwood and polychrome-decorated tea caddy, with crossbanding and stringing, the hinged lid to a pair of hinged canisters decorated with portrait miniatures of a lady and gentleman, flanking a bowl aperture.

11.5in (29cm) wide

$1,200-1,600   **WW**

A late 19thC Chinese lacquer tea caddy, of concave-sided octagonal form, decorated with figures and foliage, the hinged lid to a pair of lidded pewter canisters, on carved giltwood claw feet.

9in (23cm) wide

$700-900   **WW**

A 19thC continental papier mâché tea caddy, decorated with oriental scenes, the hinged lid to a divided interior.

8.75in (22cm) wide

$300-500   **WW**

An early 20thC Chinese hexagonal painted wood tea caddy, decorated figures in garden landscapes, the hinged lid with a lift-out pewter canister, on carved giltwood winged claw feet.

6in (15cm) high

$500-700   **WW**

A George V tortoiseshell and silver-mounted tea caddy, of octagonal form, the hinged cover velvet-lined with remains of foil to the interior, hallmarked Birmingham.

1910   *4.75in (12cm) wide*

$1,000-1,400   **WW**

An 18thC Indo-Portugese tortoiseshell and ivory work box, the paneled sides with foliate and scale decoration, opening to reveal a foliate scroll-inlaid compartmented interior with central well and inset mirror plate.

4in (10cm) high

$6,000-8,000   **L&T**

A mid-17thC Charles II elaborate needlework casket, with raised work flowers, insects, birds, fruit, trees and man and woman on an ivory satin ground.

12.5in (32cm) wide

$7,000-8,000   **POOK**

A late George III oyster laburnum box, the hinged lid with mirror inset to the underside, with fitted interior above two drawers, later adapted with divisions in the drawers as a collector's cabinet, one drawer containing shells.

19.25in (49cm) wide

$1,000-1,200   **DN**

An early 19thC Vizagapatam ivory workbox, decorated throughout with trailing foliage and anthemion and with oval side carrying handles, the hinged lid enclosing a lidded and compartmented interior above a drawer.

11.25in (28.5cm) wide

$2,000-3,000   **L&T**

A late Regency blonde tortoiseshell work box, with white metal stringing, the hinged lid with an inset plaque to a paper-lined vacant interior, on brass ball feet.

12in (30.5cm) wide

$3,000-4,000   **WW**

An early 19thC Indian Vizagapatam ivory box, of domed waisted form, with etched bands of interlaced leaves and flowerheads, ribbed lid, on outsplayed bracket feet.

11.5in (29cm) wide

$2,000-3,000   **L&T**

A fine early 19thC Indian Vizagapatam ivory work box, of sarcophagus form, the reeded lid and sides decorated with bands of fruiting vines, opening to reveal a fitted interior, raised on lobed bun feet.

13in (33cm) wide

$5,000-7,000   **L&T**

A William IV or early Victorian rosewood and mother-of-pearl-inset workbox, of sarcophagus form with bun feet with foliate panels to cover and front, the fitted interior with lift out tray.

c1835   *12in (30.5cm) wide*

$360-440   **DN**

A mid-19thC Victorian mahogany and parquetry work box, of sarcophagus form, the top with geometric inlay, above ogee sides, on bun feet, with a brass swing handle at each end, the velvet-lined fitted interior with lift out tray.

12.5in (20cm) wide

$900-1,100   **DN**

A mid-19thC rosewood combined musical and sewing box, in the form of a piano, the fitted interior with various implements, some associated.

11.5in (29cm) long

$1,000-1,400   DN

A 19thC Anglo-Indian workbox, possibly Vizagapatam, with inlaid rosewood exterior, the hinged lid opening to reveal a sandalwood interior over a long drawer to the base, with losses.

14in (35.5cm) wide

$1,000-1,200   HALL

A 19thC Anglo-Ceylonese bone-inlaid calamander and specimen wood box, Galle District, of shaped rectangular form, the hinged top opening to a bone-inlaid specimen wheel to the reverse and two tiers of compartmentalized trays fitted with specimen wood lids.

15in (38cm) wide

$1,400-2,000   FRE

A 19thC Anglo-Indian Vizagapatam ivory-inlaid hardwood dressing box, with chevron banding and inlaid throughout with scrolling foliage and stylized motifs, centered by a shaped reserve depicting two peacocks standing beneath a tree, the hinged lid opening to reveal a compartmented interior with covered wells, a removable tray and mirrored plate.

18in (46cm) wide

$4,000-6,000   L&T

A late 19thC Victorian walnut, marquetry and crossbanded workbox, with ogee molded sides.

14in (35cm) wide

$500-700   DN

A late 19thC Ceylonese calamander and ivory-inlaid workbox, with scalloped sides, the interior inlaid with ivory engraved in red and black ink and silver wire-inlaid chevron-decorated borders. Rear elevating section with five drawers incorporating three-quarter-length portraits of a king and dignitaries and the front section with two compartmentalized removable trays, each compartment lid of the lower tray inlaid with a different specimen wood.

The scalloped interior is a design derived from 18thC bible boxes produced under Dutch colonial patronage in Matara, a town in the Galle district. Parallels can also be drawn with the ripple and scalloped mouldings featured on some 17th and 18thC furniture produced in the Netherlands. The central figure in this box seems to be wearing a stylized British naval uniform and one wonders if it could be a representation of William IV. The figures in profile could well represent Ceylonese noblemen.

17.75in (45cm) wide

An Anglo-Indian horn and ivory sewing box, Vizagapatam, with pierced and lac decoration, the sandalwood interior with divided and lidded compartments.

8.5in (21.5cm) wide

$400-600   WW

$8,000-10,000   SOTH

A Newport, Rhode Island, Federal maple and mahogany-inlaid lap desk, the top centring a rosewood star and oval within a rectangle of stringing, corner quarter fans and rosewood edging, on conformingly inlaid case, the facade centring a shield, the sides with small drawers fitted with brass bail pulls, on a later mahogany base, refinished.

c1810   20.75in (52.5cm) wide

$4,000-5,000   **SK**

A Regency mahogany and brass-bound miniature writing slope.

c1815   7in (18cm) wide

$500-600   **DN**

A George IV mahogany boxed writing slope, by T. Handford, with brass corners and sunken handles, the interior with two trade labels 'T. Handford Improved Writing Desk Manufactory No. 7 Strand, London', the other promoting a traveling trunk.

22in (55.5cm) wide

$600-1,000   **WW**

A 19thC leather writing slope, gilt and silver-gilt mounts to all corners and rope-twist gilt-metal handles.

Made by F West, No 1 St James's Street, London, and manufacturer to Queen Victoria. Original interior of green leather and velvet with gold tooling, lined with green silk and fitted with a removable green-tooled leather blotter pad. The first removable tray contains gilt and silver-gilt tools and objects including a pen tray with spaces for ink bottle, vesta box and candle holder, scissors, ruler, rubber and dividers, as well as gold pen, pencil, seal, knife and spatula. On either side of the tray is a book: a journal to record notes and addresses, and a cash book, started by the owner in 1856, to record income and expenditure. Under the first tray is a second, to hold stationery. Below is a secret floor for secret correspondence. All the gilt-metal mounts, including the screws, are engraved. The original owner was Lady Jane Lissey Harriet Levett, who was given the box as a wedding present in 1856. She used the cashbook from 1856 until just before the birth of her third child in November 1863.

c1855   15in (38cm) wide

$14,000-18,000   **RGA**

A late19thC Victorian walnut and parquetry-banded combination workbox and writing slope, with fitted interior.

11.75in (30cm) wide

$300-500   **DN**

A 19thC Indian Khatamkari stationery box, ivory-veneered within borders of geometric patterns, the hinged lid revealing a sandalwood interior of five graduated divisions, some losses.

8.25in (21cm) wide

$300-500   **HALL**

A Victorian burr walnut stationery cabinet, having a pierced fret fitted interior, damages.

14in (35.5cm) high

$300-500   **WW**

BOXES

A late 17th/early 18thC probably Spanish ebonized and tortoiseshell table cabinet, the hinged lid above a concave compartment and a pair of paneled doors, enclosing a cupboard door and seven drawers.

20.5in (52cm) wide

$3,000-5,000   **L&T**

An early 18thC Italian bone-inlaid ebony table cabinet, Naples, the drawers inlaid with circular motifs, the sides with bale handles and shaped inlaid designs, the back with similar inlay raised on bun feet.

30.5in (77.5cm) wide

$7,000-9,000   **FRE**

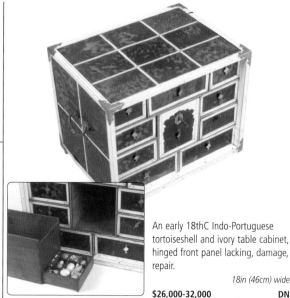

An early 18thC Indo-Portuguese tortoiseshell and ivory table cabinet, hinged front panel lacking, damage, repair.

18in (46cm) wide

$26,000-32,000   **DN**

A Chester County, Pennsylvania Chippendale walnut spice box, the molded cornice over a single door with elaborate line and berry inlay with central eight-point star within a crosshatched circle surrounded by a whimsical scrolling vine and crosshatched border, enclosing an interior with nine drawers, supported by spurred bracket feet.

c1765   *16.5in (42cm)*

$60,000-80,000   **POOK**

A mid-late 18thC Indo-Portuguese tortoiseshell and ivory table cabinet, the paneled sides with applied bronze flower-head motifs the fall-front opening to reveal a fitted interior with an arrangement of 11 drawers.

20in (50.4cm) wide

$24,000-30,000   **L&T**

A late 18thC Colonial rosewood and padouk table cabinet.

15in (38.5cm) wide

$4,000-5,000   **DN**

A Victorian walnut table cabinet, the doors opening to three drawers within.

13in (33cm) high

$300-500   **DN**

An unusual French mahogany and rosewood traveling pharmacist's case, the rectangular case with a pair of doors, opening to an interior fitted to accommodate small apothecary jars, mixing elements etc., the drawers fitted with a mortar and pestle, some drawers marked for various substances, many original elements remaining.

c1850   *12in (30cm) wide*

$2,600-3,000   **FRE**

A late 18thC pine red-painted apothecary chest, possibly Middle Atlantic States, the dovetail-constructed beaded case of thirty graduated drawers, retains old labels on drawerfronts, old brass ring pulls, repairs.

30in (76cm) high

$2,600-3,000   **SK**

A late 18th/early 19thC American painted pine apothecary chest, possibly New England, rectangular case of nine drawers, replaced brass pulls, old black-painted surface, the drawer fronts with yellow lettering, imperfections.

34.5in (87.5cm) wide

$3,000-4,000   **SK**

A mid-19thC mahogany apothecary's cabinet, with ten glass medicine bottles, some with contents and original labels, and interior section with a set of scales with brass pans and weights, this section lifting out to reveal a further removable compartmented section with glass mortar, measure, two small pill jars and two further small medicine bottles, with booklet 'Cox's Companion to the Family Medicine Chest, one shilling'.

10.5in (27cm) wide

$700-900   **DN**

A 19thC mahogany apothecary's box, the fitted double doors enclosing a fall-down drawer base, revealing a single drawer and bottle compartments, all containing various sized bottles and containers.

11.5in (29.5cm) wide

$1,100-1,500   **WW**

A matched pair of George III mahogany cutlery boxes, of serpentine-fronted form with sloping covers and fitted interiors, each crossbanded in tulipwood, one with additional chequer banding.

14.25in (36cm) high

$1,400-2,000   **L&T**

A pair of late 18thC George III mahogany and sycamore-strung serpentine-fronted knife boxes, with fitted interiors.

14.5in (37cm) high

$5,000-6,000   **DN**

A pair of George III style mahogany cutlery urns, each with lobed rising upper section revealing a stepped fitted interior, the stiff leaf acanthus-carved body on spreading circular molded foot, with a separate circular mahogany base.

31.25in (79cm) high

$4,000-5,000   L&T

A pair of 20thC George III style mahogany and boxwood-strung urn lamp bases, each on a spreading foot and octagonal plinth, repair, damage, possibly converted from cutlery urns.

22.75in (58cm) high

$3,000-4,000   DN

A Continental ebonized, mother-of-pearl-inset and amboyna liqueur cabinet, with hinged top, front and sides, the fitted interior with fifteen engraved glasses and four engraved decanters, one decanter broken, lacking one glass.

c1880   *13in (33cm) wide*

$600-1,000   DN

An Edwardian oak tantalus, with mirrored back and drawer below, containing three associated cut glass spirit decanters, and three drinking glasses.

13.5in (34.5cm) wide

$240-360   ROS

A late 19thC Victorian oak and silver plated metal-mounted tantalus, with three cut glass decanters and stoppers.

15.5in (39.5cm) wide

$400-500   DN

A late 19thC burr oak and brass-mounted tantalus, with three associated glass decanters and stoppers.

16.25in (41.5cm) wide

$700-900   DN

A 19thC and later brass bound oak games compendium, the cover and front doors opening to a fitted interior containing wood chess and draughts pieces, bone dice, dominoes, playing cards and other items, reconditioned.

14in (35.5cm) wide

$1,400-1,800   DN

An early 19thC and later oak and oyster walnut-cased cards compendium, the interior later refitted, with playing cards, Bezique markers, die, leather shakers, etc.

12.25in (31cm) wide

$400-600   DN

A silver-plated metal and pietra dure gaming box, of recent manufacture, bearing spurious inscription 'Dunhill'.

13in (33cm) wide

$800-1,000   DN

A Victorian gilt-tooled leather cased games compendium, inscribed 'W.&J. MILNE, Makers. 126 Princes St. EDINBURGH', with ivory Staunton pattern chess set, draughts counters and other items.

c1880   *12.5in (31.5cm) wide*

$1,600-2,000   DN

A George IV rosewood and brass-mounted traveling jewelry case, with fitted interior and drawer below.

c1830   12.25in (31cm) wide
$500-700   DN

A Regency satinwood bijouterie box, the hinged lid centered by a reserve depicting Mercury in his chariot being drawn by swans, opening to reveal a compartmented interior, the sides with loop handles, raised on bun feet.

c1820   9in (23cm) wide
$500-700   FRE

A late 19thC Boulle-work brass and faux tortoiseshell jewelry casket, with two concealed drawers beneath the fitted interior.

10in (25cm) wide
$2,400-3,000   DN

An 18thC and later Anglo-Indian ivory, tortoiseshell, and penwork casket, the tortoiseshell panels banded by ivory and centered by cartouches, the cover with figures flanking a mother-of-pearl heart, flattened ivory bun feet.

c1745   7in (18cm) wide
$1,800-2,200   FRE

A Georgian tooled leather trunk, bearing the label 'Edward Smith', with elaborate brass tack decoration of crowns, tulips, and the initials 'G.R.' (George Rex).

c1760   40.5in (103cm) wide
$2,000-4,000   POOK

A late 18thC George III carved and stained wood box, in the form of a Doric columnar pedestal, probably for a bottle, the upper section and capital hinged as the cover, hinge bereft.

13in (33cm) high
$400-600   DN

A George III mahogany table top book press, the base with drawer.

c1800   21.25in (54cm) high
$900-1,300   DN

A George III kingwood, marquetry and crossbanded jewelry and dressing casket, with fully fitted interior.

c1800   12in (30cm) wide
$1,800-2,200   DN

A late 18thC George III mahogany cutlery tray, of rectangular form, with brass handle above two serpentine divisions.

16.25in (41cm) wide
$500-700   DN

An early 19thC and later polychrome-painted domed casket, probably Scandinavian.

19.75in (50cm) wide
$600-800   DN

A late 19thC Swiss carved wooden tobacco box, in the form of the head of Shylock, the cover carved as a hat, with scrolling hair and beard, flanked by two receivers.

16.75in (42cm) high
$1,400-1,800   L&T

A 19thC Swiss carved softwood box, modeled as chickens perched on a wheat sheaf, opening to reveal a plush-lined interior.

11.75in (30cm) wide

$1,400-1,800 **L&T**

A Victorian coromandel and brass bound toilet box, by Toulmin & Gale, the hinged cover with an inset plaque initialed 'A', with a compartmented interior and drawer to the side and front.

12.25in (31cm) wide

$500-700 **WW**

An Austrian or German oak domestic posting box, the cover carved in relief with a maiden with a hand mirror within a foliate reserve above the slot, with cavetto edges, the front with pierced and relief-carved foliage around a roundel with a bird, with glass backing.

c1880 *14.25in (36cm) wide*

$240-360 **DN**

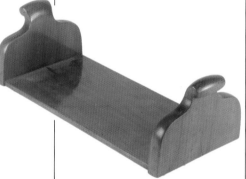

A late 19thC Victorian mahogany bookrest.

18.5in (47cm) long

$300-500 **DN**

An unusual Victorian period ebonized paneled casket, the cavetto hinged top, front, sides and back comprising small glazed watercolors of landscapes, with a lined interior and bracket feet, underside bears makers label, 'J.P. White, Cabinet Manufactory, College Hill, Shrewsbury'.

11.5in (29cm) wide

$900-1,300 **L&T**

A 19thC Chinese painted tea chest, the top decorated with flowers and a butterfly, the front with figures.

12.25in (31cm) wide

$240-360 **WW**

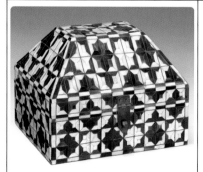

An Ottoman mother-of-pearl and horn casket, having a high canted lid, the exterior covered with mother-of-pearl and horn parquetry.

12in (30.5cm) wide

$700-1,100 **FRE**

A late 19thC continental thuyawood, crossbanded and brass bound serpentine-fronted cigar cabinet.

11in (28cm) wide

$600-800 **DN**

A Louis XV lacquer and gilt-bronze-mounted inkstand, the shaped base decorated with a wild boar and foliage, with two inkwells and a seated Buddha, raised on four scroll feet.

c1760   19in (48cm) wide

$4,000-6,000   **FRE**

A French gilt-metal-mounted fruitwood desk stand, with central foliate cast handle flanked by cut glass ink and pounce pots with foliate cast covers, the rectangular section base with twin concave pen recesses and a drawer below, on four winged paw feet.

c1830   10.25in (26cm) wide

$240-360   **DN**

A George IV or William IV ebony, ebonized and Boulle style brass marquetry deskstand.

c1830   14in (35.5cm) wide

$800-1,200   **DN**

A Victorian silver-gilt and malachite inkstand, by John Eldershaw Brunt, London, shaped rectangular stand cast and chased with naturalistic flowers, foliage and bees, fitted with two silver-gilt-mounted and lined inkwells, hinged domed covers, foliate scroll handles leading to floral swags, acorn finials, dated.

1837   11in (28cm) wide

$40,000-50,000   **SOTH**

A mid-19thC Continental gilt-bronze-mounted marmo nero Belgio inkstand, with raised handle above a cylindrical decorated porcelain inkwell, with foliate cast cover, flanked by two cut glass wells with foliate cast covers, the rectangular base with concave pen recess, on four foliate cast feet, elements associated.

12.25in (31cm) wide

$300-400   **DN**

A Napoleon III gilt-metal-mounted inkwell, of cubic form, the cover applied with a laurel and oak leaf wreath, the sides with winged figures and hippocamps against a black enamel ground.

c1860   4in (10cm) high

$700-900   **FRE**

A late 19thC Régence style gilt-brass-mounted, rosewood, ebony and brass boulle marquetry encrier, fitted with two pen rests centered by a handle and inkpots above a single drawer, the whole veneered with boulle marquetry, raised on paw feet.

14in (35.5cm) high

$1,600-2,400   **FRE**

A late 19thC Louis XV style ormolu and tiger's eye desk ornament, modeled as a kneeling cherub holding aloft a globe, raised on a canted stepped pedestal base.

9.5in (24cm) high

$6,000-8,000   **L&T**

A 19thC gilt-bronze figure of Cupid with a bow and a dead bird, on a rosewood-veneered plinth with gilt-metal mounts.

7in (18cm) high

$300-400   **GIL**

A late 19th/early 20thC Japanese bronze and ivory-mounted desk stand, cast with two bull elephants, the animals portrayed in combat, on a naturalistically cast base, with recess for pens at the front and lidded compartment for ink to the right, lacking inkwell from within.

17.25in (44cm) wide

$1,600-2,000   **DN**

A late 19thC French bronze model of a seated mariner, probably a desk stand, portrayed reclining on a barrel, smoking a pipe, a capstan behind him.

6.5in (16.5cm) high

$300-400   **DN**

A late 19thC Swiss carved softwood novelty inkstand, modeled as a collared Labrador, the head hinged to reveal an ink bottle aperture, the paws holding the trunk-form pen tray.

10.5in (27cm) wide

$1,600-2,400   **L&T**

An 18thC French fruitwood finely carved heraldic snuff box

c1790 3in (8cm) wide

$800-1,000 RDER

An 18thC snuff box bellows, with inlaid brass studs 'Forget Me Not'.

c1790 5.25in (13cm) wide

$800-1,000 RDER

An 18thC Dutch boxwood snuff shoe.

c1790 3.5in (8.5cm) long

$1,200-1.400 RDER

ESSENTIAL REFERENCE: SNUFF TAKING

The widespread taking of snuff in the Western world dates from the beginning of the 18thC, though it is likely that the habit was practiced before this.

- Early snuff boxes were similar to tobacco boxes in form, except for the lids which were hinged (rather than lift-off) which prevented much accidental spillage. John Sandy's 'hidden hinge' snuff box, which completely prevented spillage, was not invented until late in the 18thC. This snuffbox prevented snuff from leaking into the owner's pocket.

- Due to the popularity of snuff-taking, vast quantities of gold and silver snuff boxes were produced in the late 18thC and the early 19thC. New mechanical techniques ensured a plentiful supply of relatively inexpensive sheet silver from which these boxes were made. Decoration varied from simple engine-turning to more extravagant boxes depicting hunting scenes etc in enamel. Wooden and coquilla nut snuff boxes were also extremely popular, and are now very collectable. Some were carved with erotic designs.

- 'Table snuff boxes', or snuff mulls, measuring 3.5-4.75in (9-12cm) were probably used after dinner, when a host would offer guests snuff from a communal box.

- By the mid-19thC, the snuff taking habit had begun to decline.

An 18thC French coquilla nut man with cap snuff box.

c1790 Profile 2.75in (7cm) wide

$1,600-2,000 RDER

An 18thC Dutch brass tobacco box, with rare rasp in lid.

c1790 5in (12.75cm) long

$500-700 RDER

A French erotic snuff box, with straw interior.

c1800 2.5in (6cm) diam

$600-1,000 RDER

A 19thC 'Robinson delivers Friday from the Cannibals' transfer print papier mâché snuff box.

The print is reversed – has to be read in a mirror

c1820   3.5in (9cm) diam

$600-800   **RDER**

An early Tunbridge Ware snuff box, with print of Brighton Pavilion.

c1820   1.75in (4.5cm) diam

$160-240   **RDER**

A matched pair of early 19thC timber snuff boxes, of boot form, the timber boot reveals a hollowed interior from a sliding cover, the cover and boot inlaid with brass.

6in (15cm) long

$800-1,000   **FRE**

A Stobwasser papier mâché painted portrait snuff box, inscribed 'Mlle Ludens, la favourite de P.P. Rubens', of Susanna Lunden after Debucourt's engraving of Rubens painting, signed, numbered 6868 lid and base.

It is most important that lid and base have the same number.

Johann Heinrich Stobwasser (1740-1829) was a German japanner who specialized in small objects, notably boxes very finely painted with portraits, landscapes, mythological scenes etc.

c1825   3.75in (9.5cm) diam

$2,800-3,200   **RDER**

An early 19thC papier mâché theatrical snuff box of Kean, possibly playing Iago.

Edmund Kean (1789-1833), was an unrivaled tragic actor. His successes included Shylock, Richard III, Hamlet, Othello, Iago and Lear.

4.25in (10.5cm) diam

$1,400-1,800   **RDER**

A 19thC French pressed boxwood box, 'Mme Angot et Nicolas'.

These snuff boxes date back to the Directoire period, and the successful opera-comique 'Madame Angot ou la poissarde parvenue'. The play was performed in 1797 at the 'Theatre 'd'Emulation'. The author, Antoine Eve, known as Maillot, was paid five hundred francs. The takings of the play were five hundred thousand francs, a considerable sum at the time. Madame Angot is the kind of common, vulgar, ill-mannered woman who suddenly becomes rich.

c1830-40   3.25in (8cm) diam

$800-1,000   **RDER**

A Scottish treen stippled toad sycamore snuff box, with glass eyes.

c1840   2.5in (6cm) long

$800-1,000   **RDER**

A Tunbridge snuff box.

c1840   1.25in (3cm) diam

$120-160   **RDER**

A rare Tartan Ware curved snuff box, the cover painted with a dog and two puppies, with wooden hinge, in red, green and yellow striped tartan, one end restored.

3.75in (9.5cm) wide

$300-500   **DN**

BOXES

A 17thC English hardwood wassail bowl, probably Lignum Vitae, ribbed and waisted.

8in (20.5cm) high

$1,800-2,200   **DN**

A large 18thC boat-shaped burr bowl, with fine old patina.

17.75in (45cm) wide

$5,000-7,000   **POOK**

A 18thC North American delicate burlwood boat-shaped bowl, from the Shelley Collection.

11in (28cm) long

$24,000-30,000

POOK

A treen single handled scoop, with incized stylized tree decoration.

4.75in (12cm) high

$400-600   **WW**

A large 18thC burr oak bowl.

21in (53.5cm) diam.

$4,000-5,000   **WW**

An 18thC treen bowl, of oval form.

18in (46cm) wide

$600-1,000   **WW**

A late 18th/19thC carved round burl bowl, with flat bottom.

12in (76cm) diam

$800-1,200   **POOK**

A late 18th/early 19thC burl bowl, with fine old patina.

13in (33cm) diam

$4,000-6,000   **POOK**

A 19thC burl timber bowl, of circular form, with a simply turned rim, restored bottom.

16in (40.5cm) diam

$900-1,100   **FRE**

A Scandinavian stained birch treen bowl, the adzed body with tramline decoration and broad flange handle, opposed by a small shaped lug.

10.25in (26cm) wide

$700-900   **L&T**

A dated Victorian carved coconut shell vessel, carved to one side with a ship under sail and inscribed 'FANTEE', the other side carved with a Jack Tar holding a Union Jack, a spout at one end with a caricature, a paper label within inscribed 'carved by an old sailor on the Barque Fantee on a voyage from West Africa about 1852'.

1852   *4.75in (12cm) long*

$240-360   **DN**

A mid-Victorian staved wooden cream pail, of laburnum and sycamore, inscribed 'From the Athole Plantations, Dunkeld. Cam' ye by Athole, lad wi' the Philabeg, Down by the Tummel, or banks o' the Garry, Saw ye the lads, wi' their bonnets an' white cockades, Leaving their mountains to Follow Prince Charlie. Anderson. Bookseller. Dunkeld.'

24in (10.5cm) wide

$360-440   **L&T**

A late 18thC George III mahogany adjustable candle stand, adapted.

A George III mahogany cheese coaster.

An early 19thC Norwegian birch-wood tankard, the dome lid centered by a relief-carved lion motif, the cylindrical sides with a scroll handle with a lion-form thumb piece, raised on conforming lions, carved bracket feet.

10in (25cm)

7.75in (20cm) high un-extended | *c1800*   *16.5in (42cm) wide*

$200-300   **DN** | **$900-1,100**   **DN** | **$1,200-1,600**   **L&T**

A mid-19thC oak hanging spoon rack, damage, repair.

13in (33cm) wide

$200-300   **DN**

A mid-19thC Scandinavian carved and stained softwood lidded jug, of tapering form and coopered construction, later elements.

11.5in (29cm) high

$300-500   **DN**

A mid-19thC turned mahogany revolving bobbin stand, for eight reels.

11in (28cm) high

$300-500   **WW**

BOXES

A French architectural model of a staircase, the two story structure has a parquetry floor, baluster column stair case, two hinged doors to the side walls.

c1860

$18,000-22,000 FRE

A pair of matching 19thC carved and turned coquilla nut and treen ornaments, the basket bases with screw-off covers having a screw-off acorn-shaped finial.

7in (17.5cm) high

$1,400-1,800 WW

A set of two Victorian skimming ladles, with turned mahogany handles and pierced bowls, one stamped 'JONES, DOWN ST. W. BRIS'.

Longest 25.5in (65cm) long

$800-1,200 L&T

LEFT: A late 19thC small treen pug dog inkwell, with green glass eyes and bared teeth, with leather collar, lacking interior fittings.

4in (10cm) high

$500-700 L&T

CENTER: A late 19thC treen pug dog inkwell, with glass eyes and leather collar.

5in (13cm) high

$600-800 L&T

RIGHT: A late 19thC treen pug dog tobacco box, the naturalistic carved head with glass eyes and blackened patination, enclosing a copper-sleeved interior, his neck bound with a leather collar.

7.75in (20cm) high

$1,600-2,400 L&T

An unusual late 19thC Colonial carved coconut cup and cover, finely carved with cherubs, pierced love hearts, a firing cannon, a tribal warrior and other scenes, mounted on an associated silver stand, hallmarked.

1919 *8.75in (22cm) high*

$1,600-2,400 L&T

A 19thC timber articulated model, good period patina, sectional model, finely detailed face and torso, over a later stand.

69in (175cm) high

$50,000-60,000 FRE

A carved and painted softwood humidor of Victorian style, in the form of a pug dog's head, the hinged head revealing a void interior, with inset eyes and carved collar.

14in (35cm) high

$2,000-2,600 L&T

A mid-19thC Victorian ebonized wood and ivory-mounted spinning wheel.

36.25in (92cm) high

$600-1,000 DN

A Tunbridge Ware walnut folding writing box, the lid with mosaic view of Eridge Castle, the interior fitted with two sovereign drawers.

15in (38cm) wide

$800-1,200 **DN**

A Tunbridge Ware rosewood box, with tessera panel of a seated dog.

2.25in (5.5cm) wide

$300-500 **DN**

A Tunbridge Ware rosewood glove box, the domed cover with tessera rose spray, the sides with a deep mosaic band, on black ground.

10.5in (27cm) wide

$500-700 **DN**

A Japanned Tunbridge Ware box, in the manner of Wise, the lid decorated with a chinoiserie scene, the interior lined with turquoise paper.

8in (20cm) wide

$300-400 **DN**

A Tunbridge Ware ebony jewelry box, possibly by Hollamby, the lid with photographic ware image of a 19th century coastal bay on the Isle of Wight, substantial losses to tessera mosaic bands.

11.5in (29cm) wide

$200-400 **DN**

A Tunbridge Ware rosewood jewelry box, with tessera panel of Edward, Prince of Wales, the interior with removable tray.

8in (20.5cm) wide

$300-400 **DN**

A Tunbridge Ware rosewood stamp box, depicting the head of the young Queen Victoria.

1.5in (4cm) wide

$160-240 **DN**

A small Tunbridge Ware holly sewing box, the pin-hinged lid with foliate mosaic panel and van dyke borders.

4.25in (11cm) wide

$160-240 **DN**

A small Tunbridge Ware rosewood jewelry box, the canted cornered lid with tessera mosaic flower spray on a black ground.

5in (12.5cm) wide

$300-500 **DN**

A late 19thC Victorian yew wood and Tunbridge Ware box, the cover with a depiction of a Gothic ruin.

8.25in (21cm) wide

$240-360 **DN**

A Victorian rosewood Tunbridge Ware tea caddy, the tapering body with a band of roses and a hinged dome lid with a castle view, the twin-lidded interior with ebonized handles.

10in (25.5cm) wide

$1,100-1,500 **WW**

BOXES

A Tunbridge Ware walnut folding writing box, the lid with mosaic view of Eridge Castle, the interior with two fitted sovereign drawers.

15in (38cm) wide

$500-700 DN

A 19thC Tunbridge Ware rosewood box, with tessera panel of a seated dog

2.25in (5.5cm) wide

$200-400 DN

A late 19thC Italian Sorrento Ware olivewood and marquetry box, decorated with scenes in the Classical taste, the interior stamped 'L.GARIGIULO'.

7.25in (18.5cm) wide

$240-360 DN

A large Tunbridge Ware rosewood desk stand, with Boyce, Brown and Kemp label, fitted lidded box between a pair of ink bottles

11.75in (30cm) wide

$1,000-1,400 DN

A Tunbridge Ware view of The Pantiles, attributed to Henry Hollamby, in tessera frame, some losses to corners.

8.75in (22cm) wide

$500-700 DN

A Tunbridge Ware whitewood cylindrical 'Twenty Guineas' counter box, with line decoration, containing three bone dice.

1.5in (3.5cm) high

$160-240 DN

A Tunbridge Ware walnut 'Cleopatra's needle' thermometer, with ivory vernier scale, floral mosaic and perspective cube marquetry panels.

7.75in (20cm) high

$300-500 DN

Two Tunbridge Ware rulers, an unusual 12in (30cm) rule with parquetry roundels, losses to one end, and a 9in (23cm) rule, with tesera mosaic panel.

$160-240 DN

A Tunbridge Ware rosewood sovereign ball, inlaid eight-point stars within reeded roundels.

$360-440 DN

A Tunbridge Ware tessera panel of Shakespeare's Birthplace, Stratford-Upon-Avon, reputedly by Henry Hollamby.

7.5in (19cm) wide

$360-440 DN

A Tunbridge Ware visiting card case, by Edmund Nye, one side with Berlin Work cartouche and the other side a spray of flowers.

4.25in (10.5cm) high

$800-1,000 DN

Two Mauchline Ware novelty pin cushions, one in the form of a stool with a view of Stirling Castle from back walk and inscribed 'bought in the Douglas Room of the Royal Palace of Stirling', the other in the form of a pail, with a view of Folkestone Church.

Larger 3in (7.5cm) high

$160-240 DN

A Mauchline Ware stained and natural sycamore quaich, with views of 'cottage in which Burns was born' and 'Alloway Kirk', and inscribed 'the dark portions of this wood are warranted to have grown on the banks of the Ayr and the light, on the banks of the Doon'.

4.25in (10.5cm) wide

$200-300 DN

A Mauchline Ware photograph frame, of shaped rectangular form, with an oval aperture and easel back, with views of Killiecrankie, Pitlochrie and Ben Vracky.

5.5in (14cm) high

$200-300 DN

A Mauchline Ware disc-shaped snuff box, painted with a view 'Dumbarton Castle', with remnants of zinc lining, hair crack to cover.

3.75in (9.5cm) diam.

$160-240 DN

A Mauchline Ware staved wood quaich, the body bound with wicker, inscribed to the base and dated.

1852 *4in (10cm) wide*

$160-240 DN

An early Mauchline Ware visiting card case with slip top, with lithographic views of landscapes and animals.

4in (10cm) high

$160-240 DN

A novelty Tartan Ware parasol-shaped pin cushion, in McBeth tartan.

5.25in (13.5cm) high

$500-700 DN

Two Tartan Ware visiting card cases, one with Prince Charlie pattern and photographic image of a lady and child, the other in MacDonald pattern with a wooden hinge.

Larger 4.25in (11cm) high

$800-1,200 DN

Two Tartan Ware cylindrical rolled tape boxes, in McDuff pattern with a photographic image of Widow Wadham and Uncle Toby, the other in Stuart pattern.

Both 2.5in (6.5cm) high

$300-500 DN

A Tartan Ware thermometer, in Caledonia tartan, with an ivory centigrade scale and mercury filled tube.

9.75in (25cm) high to suspension loop

$300-500 DN

A Tartan Ware brass-handled brush, in Clan Stuart tartan, possibly for brushing dust from wine bottles.

9.75in (25cm) long

$300-500 DN

A Tartan Ware 'PORTRAIT ALBUM', in Stuart tartan enclosing photographic portraits of Victorian ladies and gentlemen, the morocco leather spine with gilt-tooled decoration and title.

6in (15cm) high

$600-1,000 DN

A late 15thC Northern French carved walnut figure, dressed in a cloak over armour, his right foot placed on a representation of the devil, with traces of polychrome.

29in (74cm) high

$8,000-12,000   SOTH

A 17thC Italian carved reliquary, in the form of a life-size bust.

23.5in (59.5cm) high

$1,200-2,000   POOK

A 17thC Spanish polychrome wood figure of a female saint, probably St. Eulalia, her robes richly decorated to stimulate floral embroidery and partly gilt, the eyes inserted and of glass.

65in (165cm) high

$16,000-20,000   SOTA

A late 16th/17thC Continental carved and painted wood model of a female saint, portrayed crowned and holding a Bible, flaking overall.

20.5in (52cm) high

$4,400-5,000   DN

A late 17thC carved oak caryatid figure.

20in (51cm) high

$700-900   WW

A pair of 17thC Italian carved walnut models, probably saints, comprising a semi-robed male figure and a blind-folded female figure, both on later carved walnut triform socles with ebonized and gilt-metal-mounted bases, losses.

Taller 12.25in (31cm) high

$440-560   DN

A set of four English carved and polychromed female figures, representing the Four Seasons.

c1750

11.5in (29.cm) high

$3,400-4,000   POOK

A 19thC American carved walnut figure of George Washington, Pennsylvania, with a waistcoat, vest and ruffed cuffs.

19.5in (49.5cm) high

$12,000-16,000   POOK

A pair of carved oak finials, in the manner of Sir Robert Lorimer, depicting opposed praying female figures.

18.25in (46.5cm) high

$700-900   L&T

A 19thC carved oak wall-mounted figure, of a jester in cap and bells, with both hands outstretched and eyes raised, formerly holding an item, now lacking.

17.5in (44cm) high

$1,300-1,700   L&T

A pair of Victorian carved oak busts, depicting Mozart and Beethoven, each raised on a socle base.

11.5in (29cm) high

$2,400-3,000   L&T

An early 19thC fully carved American spread-winged eagle, with an open beak and red tongue, detailed carved feathers, and talons grasping a circular plinth, retaining its original ebonized surface.

45in (115.5cm) wide

$50,000-70,000 **POOK**

A 19thC American carved and painted wooden eagle wall plaque, the relief-carved spread-winged figure with an American shield, portrayed grasping an olive branch in its talons, flanked by carved and gilt-tasseled American flags.

50.25in (127.5cm) wide

$90,000-100,000 **SK**

A 19thC carved and painted eagle lectern, the eagle with outstretched wings perched on orb and mounted on a triangular-paneled and shell-carved support and molded and scrolled base, the back of eagle fitted with wrought iron shelf and support.

74in (188cm) high

$2,400-3,600 **FRE**

A pair of 16thC carved oak lions, the standing, fully maned lions raised on naturalistically carved scroll bases, with later molded oak pedestals, probably originally sections of a chimney piece or architectural fitting.

Both 24.5in (62cm) wide

$2,400-3,600 **L&T**

A 19thC carved wood lion mask, with ring handle to mouth.

$700-900 **L&T**

One of a pair of early 19thC carved giltwood lion masks.

10.25in (26cm) high

$4,400-5,000 PAIR **L&T**

A 19thC carved pear-wood figure of a lion, the seated lion raised on an oval base inscribed 'O G 1864'.

3.5in (9cm) high

$5,000-7,000 **L&T**

A 19thC American carved and polychrome-decorated alligator, Pennsylvania, from the Shelley Collection.

13.25in (33.5cm) long

$10,000-14,000 **POOK**

A late 19th/early 20thC American carved and painted stag figure, by John Reber, Pennsylvania, from the Shelley Collection.

15.5in (39.5cm) high

$4,000-8,000 **POOK**

A 19thC Swiss 'Black Forest' carved walnut group, depicting fighting stags, one stag attacking another, which has fallen to the ground, within a naturalist forest landscape, in a glazed display case.

19in (48cm) high

$12,000-16,000 **L&T**

1: A late 19th/early 20thC Swiss carved wood tobacco box in the form of an owl, perched on naturalistic base, with inset eyes.

10.25in (26cm) high

$3,000-4,000 **L&T**

2: A late 19th/early 20thC Swiss carved wood tobacco box in the form of an owl, standing on naturalistic base with tree trunk veneers.

These figures are often referred to as Black Forest carvings.

12.75in (32cm) high

$2,000-3,000 **L&T**

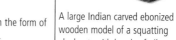

A large Indian carved ebonized wooden model of a squatting elephant, with bands of gilt-heightened decoration.

27.75in (70cm) long

$3,000-5,000 **L&T**

A dated Italian carved and painted family crest, inscribed verso 'Ants. Julianus Imolensis SCVL'.

1681   *38in (95.5cm) high*
$11,000-13,000   **POOK**

An 18thC carved and painted coat of arms, depicting a lion and unicorn with central quartered shield reading 'Honi Soit Qui Mal Y Pense'.

27.5in (70cm) wide
$16,000-20,000   **L&T**

A late 18thC armorial panel, within original frame, the painted coat of arms above an inscription: 'The above Arms, Peter Davies of Broughton…'.

23.5in (59.5cm) wide
$5,000-6,000   **L&T**

A George III carved giltwood coat of arms of the Earl of Darnley, the painted central shield below a crown and flanked by a pair of griffins, verso bears letter from the College of Arms.

12.25in (31cm) wide
$10,000-14,000   **L&T**

An early 19thC painted square coach panel, within a later molded giltwood frame, depicting two lions holding a central quartered shield, bears motto 'QUONDAM HIS VICIMUS ARMIS'.

11in (28cm) square
$2,600-3,200   **L&T**

A 19thC coach panel within a later ornate giltwood frame, depicting the lion and unicorn flanking the quarter shield of Great Britain inscribed 'QUIS SEPERABIT MDCCXXXIII', some restoration and re-painting.

19in (48cm) wide
$2,600-3,200   **L&T**

A Victorian painted coach panel, now within a fluted giltwood frame, depicting twin lions holding oval coats of arms below a crown, one bears motto 'TRA JUNCIA IN UNO', lower scrolls read 'VIRTUS MILLE SCUTA', some restoration and re-painting.

17in (43cm) wide
$2,600-3,200   **L&T**

A pair of 19thC Persian polychrome-painted and parcel giltwood panels of rectangular form, each decorated with flowers and birds within decorative borders.

30in (77cm) and 32.75in (83cm) wide
$2,000-2,400 PAIR   **DN**

A George III carved pine Ionic pilaster capital, later adapted as a wall bracket.
c1770 and later   *14.25in (36cm) wide*
$600-800   **DN**

A carved giltwood and gesso wall bracket of Louis XV style, the serpentine simulated marble top on central carved cherub within a double foliate scroll surround.

23.75in (60cm) wide
$2,000-2,400   **L&T**

An early 19thC carved giltwood crown wall mount, formerly part of a larger item.

14.25in (52cm) wide
$1,100-1,500   **L&T**

An early 20thC Indian carved hardwood presentation scroll case, the cylindrical hinged case carved in relief with animals and scrolling foliage, opening to reveal a velvet-lined interior, raised on carved lion supports, the rectangular base with ornate fret-pierced apron and angel-form bracket feet.

21.5in (55cm) wide
$1,500-1,900   **L&T**

A pair of carved giltwood wall brackets, the shell-carved tops with ornate openwork Rococo-carved supports, one 18thC.
15in (38cm) high
$8,000-10,000   **L&T**

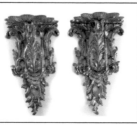

THE CLOCKS MARKET

The romance of the tallcase clock continues to pull American buyers, so long as the clock is in perfect condition; any damage and you can take a zero off the price of a perfect example. Generally, the market for American clocks remains strong, especially for clocks that are new to the market. The exception to this is shelf clocks which are struggle to find buyers.

The most desirable English tallcase and bracket clocks continue to be those made in the late 17thc and early 18thC by names such as Thomas Tompion, Joseph Knibb, Henry Jones, Daniel Quare and Joseph Windmills. However, collectors are also becoming increasingly interested in their apprentices and successors, so prices for clocks by Samuel Aldworth, Brounker Watts, Daniel Delander and William Webster are staying very strong. The same can be said about later 18thC makers such as Ellicott, Vulliamy, Mudge & Dutton, McCabe and Frodsham. Collectors will pay extra for clocks by these and similar makers.

Another important factor is the aesthetics of the clock where the cases have the very best proportions and originality with all components starting life together. Most clocks of this age will have had some restoration and as long as this has been carried out honestly and sympathetically it will not affect the value.

Until relatively recently many collectors confined themselves to Philadelphia or London makers, believing their work represented the best quality available. However, buyers are beginning to realise that many makers outside the main centers, particularly those working in the major 18th and 19thC ports and towns, had a clientele who demanded the best clocks and the skills to provide them. As a result, prices are rising for good-quality tallcase clocks no matter where they were made. Consequently, ordinary Philadelphia and London clocks are not doing as well as they were, and good mahogany tallcase clocks are now representing very good value for money.

Carriage clocks made by the renowned makers such as Garnier, Jacot, Drocourt, Le Roy, Margaine and Soldano still remain highly desirable. No matter who the maker, collectors are looking for examples which retain their original escapement and, if possible, the original leather-covered traveling case and key. Case style also influences desirability, with gorge (grooved) cases traditionally more desirable than other case styles such as the corniche. A further selling point is complicated movements such as those with day, date and alarm or moon phase or other unusual features, but that said, the market is still buoyant for clocks with plain dials and simple cases.

The market for the substantial English carriage clocks with chain fusee movements also remains strong, especially the traveling four-glass examples in mahogany or rosewood cases.

Demand for early lantern clocks has been strong. Here we are seeing the clocks that have been conserved and not over polished achieving the best prices.

TALLCASE CLOCKS

A late 17thC and later arabesque marquetry eight-day tallcase clock, the five-finned pillar outside countwheel bell-striking movement, signed 'Jos: Jackman Londini Fecit', case with 19thC restoration.

Joseph Jackson is recorded as working from 1690-1716.

81in (206cm) high

$8,000-10,000   **DN**

A Queen Anne walnut and arabesque marquetry quarter chiming eight-day tallcase clock, the substantial six-finned pillar movement with anchor escapement, chiming the quarters on a graduated nest of six bells and with inside countwheel hour strike on a further bell, the dial with calendar aperture, ringed winding holes and subsidiary seconds dial, signed 'Tho: Carter, London'.

Thomas Carter is listed as being admitted to the Clockmakers Company in 1690.

c1700   95.25in (242cm) high

$40,000-60,000   **DN**

A walnut marquetry month-going chiming tallcase clock, dial signed 'Char Cabrier, London', the three-train movement with six ring-turned knopped pillars, bell-striking and chiming the quarters on six bells, five wheel trains, movement and case associated.

c1705   98in (38.5cm) high

$40,000-60,000   **SOTH**

A Queen Anne oak thirty-hour tallcase clock, the posted countwheel bell-striking single handed movement with rectangular section-steel uprights, and signed 'Luke Wise, Reading'.

Luke Wise is recorded as working in Reading c1686-1710.

c1710   80.75in (205cm) high

$3,000-4,000   **DN**

CLOCKS

An early 18thC ebonized thirty-hour tallcase clock, the four-finned pillar outside countwheel bell-striking single-handed movement, with brass dial with calendar aperture, the chapter ring with sliced sword hilt half hour markers and signed 'Geo: Booth Manchesft'r'.

George Booth is recorded working c1758-88, however various details within the construction and decoration of the movement, dial and case of this clock suggest a date of manufacture within the first 20 years of the 18thC.

80in (204cm) high

$3,000-4,000   **DN**

CLOSER LOOK: GEORGE II TALLCASE CLOCK

The French script for the days of the week within the arch suggests that this clock was originally made for a French client.

The case features an ogee caddy above break-arch cornice with foliate scroll blind fretwork infill to frieze and integral pilasters to hood door.

The trunk has a herringbone banded burr figured door and panel inlaid sides on conforming base with double skirt.

James Hubert is recorded as working in London 1712-30.

A George Graham walnut tallcase clock, dial signed along the lower edge 'Geo: Graham, London', with seconds dial and calendar aperture with pin hole adjustment, the movement with five latched knopped pillars, dead beat escapement with bolt and shutter maintaining power, rack striking on a bell, punch numbered '724', restored case.

c1735   91in (231cm) high

$110,000-130,000   **SOTH**

A George II walnut eight-day tallcase clock, with trip repeat, the five finned pillar rack and bell-striking movement, the seconds dial, signed 'Tho. Baker Portsmouth', the case with break-arch molded cornice and frieze and integral pilasters to the hood door above herringbone banded break-arch trunk door.

c1740   85.5in (217cm) high

$16,000-20,000   **DN**

A George II burr-walnut quarter chiming eight-day tallcase clock, with day of the week to arch, the substantial five-finned pillar movement with anchor escapement, chiming the quarters on a graduated nest of six bells and rack striking the hours on a further bell, the brass break-arch dial with calendar aperture and subsidiary seconds dial, the arch with days of the week titled in French, signed 'James Hubert, LONDON'.

c1725   93in (236cm) high

$22,000-30,000   **DN**

A Philadephia Queen Anne curly maple tallcase clock, the flat top bonnet enclosing an eight-day works with brass face inscribed 'Edward Duffield Philadelphia', retaining an old mellow surface.

c1740 91.25in (232cm) high
$80,000-100,000   POOK

An early/mid-18thC Pennsylvania walnut tallcase clock, with a flat top bonnet enclosing a square brass dial, inscribed 'John Wills Philada', above a waist with a double raised panel door, flanked by chamfered corners, above a paneled base supported by a molded plinth, from the Shelley Collection.

85.5in (217cm) high
$12,000-14,000   POOK

A mid-18thC Philadelphia Queen Anne yellow pine tall case clock, the flat top bonnet enclosing a thirty hour works with brass face, inscribed 'Joseph Wills'.

87in (221cm) high
$5,000-6,000   POOK

A Pennsylvania William & Mary walnut tallcase clock, with a sarcophagus-form bonnet enclosing a brass-face works, inscribed 'Jacob Gotshalk Philadelphia', from the Shelley Collection

c1760 87in (221cm) high
$7,500-8,500   POOK

A Willis Town, Chester County Pennsylvania Queen Anne walnut tallcase clock, by Isaac Thomas (1721-1802), with 12-inch brass dial, with chapter ring and maker's boss engraved 'Isaac Thomas, Willis Town' and an eight-day brass, five-pillar movement with rack and snail strike and recoil escapement powered by two brass-cased weights and regulated by a strap brass pendulum rod and bob, old surface, imperfections.

c1765 99in (251.5cm) high
$65,000-85,000   SK

An 18thC Chester County, Pennsylvania Chippendale walnut tallcase clock, the broken arch bonnet bearing the mother-of-pearl inlaid date '1771', enclosing a thirty-hour works with a brass face, inscribed 'Bentley Darlington', above an eight-pointed star, above two hunters, one with an falcon, the other with a bow, over a stylized street scene with tavern, from the Shelley Collection.

98.25in (249.5cm) high
$20,000-30,000   POOK

A Delaware Valley Chippendale mahogany tallcase clock, the broken arch bonnet with blind fretwork enclosing an eight-day works with brass face.

c1775 91.5in (232.5cm) high
$5,000-9,000   POOK

An early 18thC and later inlaid mahogany month-going tallcase clock, the dial with calendar aperture and recessed subsidiary seconds dial with subsidiary ring calibrated for the lunar month and penny moon, composite.

91.25in (232cm) high

$4,000-5,000 DN

A mid 18thC red and gilt-japanned eight-day tallcase clock, by Robyat, London, the twin train movement striking on a bell, the brass dial with subsidiary seconds dial, the trunk door decorated with chinoiserie scenes.

95.5in (242cm) high

$8,000-10,000 L&T

A George II oak eight-day tallcase clock, with four-pillar rack and bell-striking movement, the brass dial with calendar aperture and subsidiary seconds dial, signed 'Thomas Russell, BEDFORD'.

c1750 79in (201cm) high

$2,200-2,800 DN

A mid-18thC George II walnut eight-day tallcase clock, with four-finned pillar outside countwheel bell-striking movement, the brass dial with calendar aperture, subsidiary seconds dial, signed 'Jno. Ingram, Spalding'.

81in (206cm) high

$4,000-5,000 DN

A George III oak thirty-hour tallcase clock, with four-finned pillar outside countwheel bell-striking movement, the dial signed 'Wooley Codnor'.

James Woolley (c1695-1786) was a renowned UK provincial clockmaker.

c1750 81in (206cm) high

$5,000-6,000 DN

A George II oak thirty-hour tallcase clock, the posted countwheel bell-striking movement with columnar uprights, dial with calendar aperture and signed 'Edward Bilbie CHEWSTOKE'.

c1750 77.5in (197cm) high

$2,400-3,000 DN

A George III mahogany tallcase clock, the arch top dial signed 'John Smithyes, Great Saffron Hill, London' above a strike/silent dial, the chapter ring central date and seconds dial, with two-train five pillar movement with alarm mechanism.

92in (233.5cm) high

$13,000-15,000 DUK

A George III scarlet-japanned eight-day tallcase clock, with five-pillar rack and bell-striking movement, the dial signed 'John Mason, LONDON', with silvered rocking Chronos figure, case re-decorated.

c1770 86.5in (220cm) high

$3,600-4,400 DN

A George III oak eight-day tallcase clock, with four-pillar rack and bell-striking movement, the dial signed 'Rich'd Tyler, WALLINGFORD' on reduced plinth base.

Richard Tyler is recorded as working in Wallingford 1740-82.

c1770 81in (206cm) high

$1,400-2,000 DN

A George III oak eight-day tallcase clock, with four-pillar inside countwheel bell-striking movement, the dial signed 'John Brice DEAL'.

John Brice is recorded as working in Sandwich, Kent c1795.

c1780 79in (201cm) high

$1,800-2,400 DN

A George III oak thirty-hour tallcase clock, the countwheel bell-striking movement signed 'Anthony Lynch, NEWBURY'.

Anthony Lynch is recorded as working in Newbury c1781.

c1785   77in (196cm) high

$1,600-2,000   DN

An 18thC Dutch marquetry and burl veneer tallcase clock, the sarcophagus top with blind fretwork frieze enclosing an eight-day brass face, signed 'Johs Uswald Amsteldam', with dioramic rocking ship harbor scene and two-bell mechanism.

94.5in (240cm) high

$24,000-30,000   POOK

An 18thC Dutch burl veneer tallcase clock, the molded cornice over a frieze with blind fretwork enclosing a brass face, two-bell, eight-day works with silver dial, with line-inlaid door and chamfered stiles.

99in (251.5cm) high

$7,000-10,000   POOK

A late 18thC Dutch burr walnut tallcase clock, the brass dial signed 'Johannes Van Wyk en Zoon Amsterdam', with date, day, month, moonphase and the ships automaton in the arch rocking to and fro' connected to the going train of the anchor movement, rack Dutch quarter striking on two alternating bells, alarm removed, associated to the burr walnut-veneered case, with bell top surmounted by a giltwood Atlas and two angels.

106.75in (271cm) high including Atlas

$20,000-24,000   SOTA

A George III oak eight-day tallcase clock, the four-pillar rack and bell-striking movement with brass dial with subsidiary calendar and seconds dials and signed 'Rich'd Boxall Godalming', the arch with 'STRIKE/SILENT' dial.

c1790   80.75in (205cm) high

$2,200-2,600   DN

A late 18thC mahogany eight-day tallcase clock, by Charles Graham, Edinburgh, the twin train movement with anchor escapement, with moon phase to arch, the shaped trunk door flanked by inset brass pilaster columns.

110 in (279cm) high

$3,200-4,000   L&T

A late 18thC George III mahogany eight-day tallcase clock, with center seconds and moonphase to arch, the five-pillar rack and bell-striking movement with deadbeat escapement, the brass break-arch dial with arched calendar aperture and silvered nameplate 'BENJ'N ROSE, SWATHLING', the arch with rolling moonphase behind scroll-engraved lunettes.

82in (208cm) high

$5,000-6,000   DN

A late 18thC Reading, Pennsylvania Chippendale mahogany tallcase clock, the broken arch bonnet with dentil molded cornice and frieze with applied carving, enclosing an eight-day works, signed 'Daniel Rose Reading'.

98in (249cm) high

$25,000-35,000   **POOK**

A Lancaster, Pennsylvania Federal mahogany tallcase clock, by George Hoff (1733-1816), with painted rocking ship movement works, with day and date chapter ring.

90in (228.5cm) high

$20,000-25,000   **FRE**

An Easton, Pennsylvania Chippendale cherry and tiger maple tallcase clock, the broken arch bonnet with pineapple finial enclosing a thirty-hour works, inscribed 'Christian Bixler Easton No 224', retaining an old crackled surface.

c1800   90in (228.5cm) high

$9,000-11,000   **POOK**

A late 18thC Reading, Pennsylvania walnut tallcase clock, with a broken arch bonnet enclosing a brass face works, inscribed 'No 122, John Keim', from the Shelley Collection.

$18,000-20,000   **POOK**

A Hackensack, New Jersey Federal inlaid mahogany tall-case clock, by William Dawes, the double scroll cresting with inlaid fan rosettes and two urn and spire brass finials, painted face having an oval landscape painting with figure above, chapter ring and seconds chapter ring, day display, with oval inlaid barber pole stripe panel, the base with square barber pole inlay panel, on French bracket feet.

c1800   94in (239cm) high

$26,000-30,000   **FRE**

A Federal mahogany inlaid tallcase clock, with an eight-day, brass time and strike movement with tin-cased weights, wooden pendulum rod and unsigned painted iron dial, dial relined and colors enhanced, imperfections.

92in (233.5cm) high

$5,000-8,000   **SK**

A Philadelphia Federal mahogany tallcase clock, the broken arch bonnet enclosing an eight-day works with painted face, signed 'Benjn Clark Philadelphia', retaining an old cracked varnish surface.

c1800   89in (226.5cm) high

$7,000-9,000   **POOK**

A Pennsylvania painted tallcase clock, the broken arch bonnet enclosing a thirty-hour works, signed 'Samuel Breneisen Reading', retaining its original salmon and black surface.

c1800   88in (223.5cm) high

$8,000-10,000   **POOK**

A Massachusetts Federal mahogany dwarf clock, the arched bonnet enclosing an eight-day works, signed 'John Bailey Jr. Hanover'.

c1805   *50in (127in) high*

$45,000-55,000   **POOK**

A New Jersey Chippendale mahogany tallcase clock, the broken arch bonnet enclosing an eight-day painted dial works.

c1810   *94in (238cm) high*

$4,500-5,500   **POOK**

A Berks County, Pennsylvania painted poplar tallcase clock, the associated works inscribed 'Peter Gifft', the broken arch bonnet, with yellow and red trim with salmon tulips on a blue background, from the Shelley Collection.

c1810   *88in (223.5cm) high*

$20,000-25,000   **POOK**

An early 19thC Lebanon walnut and ebonized tallcase clock, by Emanuel Meyli, double scroll cresting with inlaid rosettes and urn and spire finials, with painted moon-phased face, sweep second hand and date indicator.

95in (241.5cm) high

$7,000-9,000   **FRE**

A Massachusetts Federal mahogany tallcase clock, the arched bonnet with pierced fretwork enclosing an eight-day works with painted face, signed 'Aaron Willard Boston', over a case with brass top fluted quarter columns.

c1810   *90.5in (230cm) high*

$25,000-35,000   **POOK**

A Federal Newburyport, Massachusetts mahogany-inlaid tall clock, by David Wood, with stylized sunburst in the arch, and an eight-day brass time and strike movement, signed 'David Wood, Newburyport', imperfections.

c1815   *82in (208cm) high*

$25,000-28,000   **SK**

A Gilmanton, New Hampshire pine-cased dwarf clock, by Noah Ranlet, with an eight-day time and strike, weight-powered brass movement engraved 'Ranlet', and signed 'Noah Ranlet, Gilmanton', restoration.

c1820   *6.5in (118cm) high*

$9,000-11,000   **SK**

A Hingham, Massachusetts Federal mahogany dwarf clock, by Joshua Wilder, with eight-day weight-driven timepiece with fall-off strike and alarm, signed 'Warranted by J. Wilder, Hingham', restoration.

c1825   *50.5in (128.5cm) high*

$60,000-80,000   **SK**

CLOCKS

An 18thC and later George III green-japanned tallcase clock, the four-pillar anchor escapement movement signed 'Rich Mason, St. Albans', with strike silence above a seconds dial.

82in (208cm) high
$9,000-11,000   **FRE**

A George III mahogany tallcase clock, by Harvey of Weymouth, the arch top dial with a rotating ball moon phase dial, with subsidiary seconds dial and date aperture, the eight-day movement striking on a bell.

90in (228.5cm) high
$9,000-11,000   **DUK**

A Grandmother clock, the eight-day movement with anchor escapement, the dial chased with foliage, the arched roundel inscribed 'Tempus Fugit', in Georgian style mahogany case.

60.5in (153.5cm) high
$5,000-7,000   **HT**

An early 19thC mahogany eight-day tallcase clock, by Andrew Smith, Tranent, the twin train movement with anchor escapement, the painted dial with subsidiary seconds and date dial.

81in (206cm) high
$3,000-4,000   **L&T**

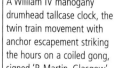

An early 19thC mahogany and crossbanded tallcase clock, the twin movement with anchor escapement striking the hours on a bell, the dial signed 'J. & G. Leithhead, Galashiels'.

85.75in (218cm) high
$2,000-3,000   **L&T**

A William IV mahogany drumhead tallcase clock, the twin train movement with anchor escapement striking the hours on a coiled gong, signed 'P. Martin, Glasgow'.

81.5in (207cm) high
$2,200-2,600   **L&T**

A Regency mahogany eight-day tallcase clock, with five-pillar rack and bell-striking movement, with dial with subsidiary second dials and signed 'William Samuel Archer, Hackney', the break-arch pedimented case with fretwork crest and canted angles to hood above break-arch door, on flush-shaped panel-fronted plinth base with double skirt.

c1820   *87.5in (222cm) high*
$6,000-8,000   **DN**

A Scottish William IV mahogany tallcase regulator, by John Clark, Forfar, the movement with dead-beat anchor escapement, maintaining power and striking on a gong.

80.75in (205cm) high

$3,000-5,000   **L&T**

An oak tallcase regulator clock, with subsidiary seconds dial, the eight-day movement striking on two bells and a gong, brass cased weights and ebonized pendulum, the dial inscribed 'Willliam Tritschler, Carlisle'.

20.5in (52cm) wide

$4,000-5,000   **A&G**

A 19thC mahogany tallcase clock, the four-pillar anchor escapement movement with a strike silent above a chapter ring with Roman and Arabic numerals, signed 'Edward Clarke London'.

87.5in (222cm) high

$3,000-4,000   **FRE**

A 19thC carved and stained oak tallcase clock, the twin train movement with anchor escapement, the leaf scroll pediment centered by a cockerel, the silvered dial with subsidiary seconds and calender dial, the lion mask carved trunk door between fruiting vine pilasters and leaf scroll-carved sides.

90 in (229cm) high

$2,000-2,600   **L&T**

An early 20thC green-japanned quarter chiming eight-day grandmother clock, the triple train movement with platform lever escapement and chiming the hours and quarters on five gongs, with 'CHIME/SILENT' dial to arch.

67.75in (172cm) high

$3,000-4,000   **DN**

A William III ebonized bracket clock, the five-finned pillar twin fusee rack and bell-striking movement with verge escapement, pull quarter repeat work removed, signature erased.

c1695   *14.5in (37cm) high excluding handle*

$10,000-14,000   **DN**

A French boulle marquetry bracket clock, by Francois Rabby, Paris, the caddy top with flame finials above larger foliate finials and a balustrated frieze, the anchor escapement striking on a bell, the backplate engraved 'Rabby Paris'.

c1700   *23.5 in (60cm) high*

$10,000-14,000   **L&T**

A George III ebonized bracket clock, the five-pillar twin fusee movement now with half deadbeat escapement, the dial with blanked off false bob aperture, calendar aperture and signature plaque 'Chater & Sons, LONDON', the arch with 'Strike/Silent' ring.

c1760   *15.5in (40cm) high*

$4,600-5,200   **DN**

An early 18thC Régence ormolu-mounted tortoiseshell and brass boulle marquetry bracket clock, the dial with enameled Roman numerals decorated with winged infants, set in arched case surmounted by Father Time.

14in (35.5cm) high

$2,000-2,600   **FRE**

A George III mahogany bracket clock, the five-pillar twin fusee rack and bell-striking movement with trip repeat, with verge escapement, the brass dial with calendar aperture and silvered nameplate 'Will'm Wall, Richmond' beneath 'Strike/Silent' dial.

c1775   *19.5in (50cm) high*

$12,000-14,000   **DN**

A George III ebonized bracket clock, by John Carter, London, the dial with silvered chapter ring and subsidiary silent/strike dial, the striking eight-day twin chain fusee movement with anchor escapement.

19.25in (49cm) high

$5,000-6,000   L&T

A late 18thC American Charlestown, South Carolina mahogany bracket clock, the works with white painted face and engraved back plate, signed 'Josh'a Lockwood Charles Town'.

17in (43cm) high

$9,000-11,000   POOK

A rare 18thC Chinese Export padouk bracket clock, the arched face painted with a port scene, with a single train fusee movement with a foliate engraved backplate.

27in (69cm) high

$5,000-6,000   L&T

A Regency rosewood bracket clock, by James McCabe, the twin train eight-day movement striking the hours and half hours on a bell, the dial serial no.1337.

17in (44cm) high

$14,000-18,000   L&T

A late 18thC Austro-Hungarian ebonized quarter striking bracket clock, the four-pillar triple train movement with verge escapement, trip repeat and visible stopwork to the backplate, the dial with false bob aperture, with silvered boss bearing signature 'Chater, London' flanked by subsidiary dials 'Nicht Repl:/Repedit', 'Schlagt/Sch: Nicht'.

15.75in (40cm) high

$1,800-2,400   DN

A Regency bracket clock, by John Caney, the eight-day twin train fusee movement on a bell, the arched case a stepped top surmounted by a pineapple finial and side sound frets, the white painted dial signed 'John Caney, 33 Cheapside, London'.

19.75in (50cm) high

$4,000-5,000   L&T

A Regency rosewood bracket clock, by Payne, the eight-day twin fusee movement with anchor escapement and striking on two bells, the white painted dial signed 'Payne, New Bond Street, London'.

24in (61cm) high

$7,000-9,000   L&T

An early 19thC Swedish giltwood bracket clock, by Emil Lagerstrom, Enkoping, the twin train movement striking on a bell, on bracket suspending fruiting terminals and with acanthus-carved center.

29.25in (74cm) wide

$8,000-10,000 L&T

A George III mahogany bracket clock, with trip repeat, the five-pillar twin fusee rack and bell-striking movement with anchor escapement, the dial signed 'Younge & Son, London'.

c1820 *15.75in (40cm) high*

$4,000-5,000 DN

A William IV brass-inlaid mahogany small bracket clock, the five-pillar twin fusee gong-striking movement with anchor escapement signed 'VINER NEW BOND STREET LONDN', some damage.

c1835 *13.75in (35cm) high*

$5,600-6,400 DN

A Victorian Gothic Revival bracket clock, by J. W. Benson, with an eight-day fusee movement, the silvered dial signed 'J. W. Benson, Ludgate, London'.

23.5in (60cm) high

$2,200-2,800 L&T

A large late 19thC mahogany and gilt-metal-mounted bracket clock, unsigned, with triple fusee movement, quarter chiming Westminster and eight Bells, with a mahogany wall bracket.

Clock 26.25in (67cm) high

$6,000-7,000 DN

A 19thC Victorian gilt-metal-mounted quarter chiming bracket clock, the substantial four-pillar triple fusee movement chiming the quarters on nine bells and striking the hours on a gong with rise/fall regulation, the brass dial with 'FAST/SLOW', 'CHIME/SILENT' and 'CHIME ON EIGHT BELL/WESTMINSTER CHIME' subsidiary dials, unsigned.

28.75in (73cm) high

$4,400-5,000 DN

A late 19thC bracket clock, by Payne & Co., no. 4560, fitted eight-day movement striking on a gong, made in New Bond Street, London.

20in (51cm) high

$900-1,300 A&G

A late 19thC bracket clock, the two train movement by Winterhalter & Hoffmeyer, with 'SLOW/FAST' and 'CHIME/SILENT' dials.

22in (56cm) high

$2,400-3,000 DN

An American mahogany pillar and scroll shelf clock, by Erastus Hodges (1781-1847), with thirty-hour 'east-west' wooden movement, iron weights and pendulum, damage.

30.5in (77.5cm) high

$16,000-20,000 **SK**

An early 19thC French Empire mantel clock, with eight-day outside countwheel bell-striking movement, dial signed 'Cleret a Orleans'.

19.25in (49cm) high

$1,200-1,600 **DN**

An American Massachusetts pine and maple cased transitional shelf clock, by William Sherwin, thirty-hour time and strike, weight powered movement.

c1830 *30.5in (77.5cm) high*

$7,000-8,000 **SK**

A William IV rosewood small five-glass mantel clock, with trip repeat, with five-pillar twin fusee bell-striking movement, unsigned.

c1830 *10.5in (27cm) high*

$4,000-4,600 **DN**

A mid 19thC Victorian brass skeleton timepiece, unsigned, the four-pillar single fusee movement with half-deadbeat escapement, with later ebonized wood base.

9.5in (24cm) high

$700-900 **DN**

A mid 19thC French Louis XV style ormolu mantel clock, the outside countwheel bell-striking movement stamped 'HY. MARC, PARIS' to backplate.

14.5in (37cm) high

$800-1,200 **DN**

ESSENTIAL REFERENCE: THOMAS COLE

A Victorian patinated and gilt brass tripod timepiece, the single train movement with six-wheel train and deadbeat escapement set between stepped plates, the dial with subsidiary seconds dial and signed 'THO'S COLE, LONDON', supported on triform frame with turned and carved ivory finial and supporting the pendulum with heavy silvered ball bob from the center, on base applied with adjustable silvered calendar.

A late 19thC Louis XV style gilt and patinated bronze mantel clock, modeled as a cherub supporting the movement atop a fluted classical pedestal, the white enameled dial signed 'Frd. Berthoud, A Paris'.

21.75in (55cm) high

$8,000-10,000 **L&T**

Thomas Cole was born in Nether Stowey, Somerset, UK in 1800, the second son of the renowned and learned local clockmaker James 'Philosopher' Cole. His brother James Ferguson Cole, who was two years older, learned the trade from his father before moving to London in 1821 to become one of the country's most eminent horologists. Thomas Cole joined his brother in London from 1823 until 1829 when they went their separate ways and by 1845 he was advertizing himself as a 'designer and maker of ornamental clocks'. He exhibited at the Great Exhibition in 1851 as well as in Paris in 1855 and again in London in the 1862 British International Exhibition. He died from typhoid fever in 1862. The current example displays the originality and quality of design coupled with the finest workmanship for which Thomas Cole became famous.

c1860 *19.25in (49cm) high*

$20,000-24,000 **DN**

A 19thC French gilt-bronze and metal mantel clock, modeled as Napoleon firing a cannon, map to his feet inscribed, 'Montezan'.

15.75in (40cm) wide
$2,400-3,000   L&T

A Louis XV style ormolu mantel clock, the eight-day bell-striking movement signed 'HY. MARC A PARIS'.

c1870   *14.5in (37cm) high*
$1,600-2,000   DN

A late 19thC German cuckoo clock, fitted eight-day twin fusee movement, striking on a single gong.

19.5in (50cm) high
$2,000-2,400   A&G

A late 19thC French gilt-bronze and enamel clock, in the Persian taste.

11.5in (29cm) high
$2,000-2,400   L&T

A late 19thC Louis XV style gilt bronze mantel clock.

20.5in (52cm) high
$1,400-2,000   L&T

A late 19thC French boulle and ormolu mounted shelf clock, the works signed 'H&F Paris'.

29in (74cm) high
$1,600-2,000   POOK

A late 19thC Black Forest carved shelf clock, with carved wolves, birds, etc.

28.25in (72cm) high
$2,600-3,200   POOK

A 19thC French gilt bronze-and-slate shelf clock, the works stamped 'Marti'.

26.5in (67.5cm) high
$1,400-2,000   POOK

A late 19thC French black slate and brass mantel clock, marked 'Lloyd Payne & Amiel Paris Make', the bronze panel sides with Arcadian scenes.

17.75in (45cm) wide
$1,700-1,900   L&T

A late 19thC Anglo-French brass timepiece, the eight-day movement with platform lever escapement, with a globe which rotates giving the time.

11.75in (30cm) high
$3,000-3,600   DN

A 19thC French mantel clock, the silk suspension movement striking on a bell and signed 'Ch. Duillet'.

14.25in (36cm) high
$800-1,200   HT

A late 19thC French brass and patinated bronze small novelty lighthouse timepiece, unsigned, the eight-day movement with a form of a double-wheel duplex escapement.

9.75in (24.5cm) high
$2,600-3,000   DN

A late 19thC French brass novelty windmill timepiece, with aneroid barometer and thermometers, the eight-day movement with platform escapement.

17in (43cm) high

$3,000-4,000 DN

A French 'Japonisme' gilt-bronze and champlevé enamel clock, the sides decorated with berried branches, insects and birds, surmounted by a lion dog.

9.75in (25cm) high

$1,200-1,600 L&T

A French bronzed spelter elephant novelty swinging mystery timepiece, the movement with tic-tac escapement, internal short bob pendulum.

c1900   11in (28cm) high

$900-1,300 DN

A late Victorian oak four-glass mantel clock, the four-pillar single fusee movement with anchor escapement, the dial signed by retailers 'R. H. HALFORD & SONS'.

c1900   11.45in (29cm) high

$1,600-2,000 DN

An Edwardian mounted tortoiseshell timepiece, by William Comyns, with piqué-inlaid decoration, and in fitted leather case, with marks for London, stamped 'CARRINGTON & CO.', initialed.

1906   5in (13cm) high

$2,000-3,000 L&T

A Tiffany & Co. enameled miniature timepiece, and key, signed indistinctly, stamped 'ARGENT DORE 0,925 STERLING SILVER 84' and numbered 4236.

2.75in (7cm) high

$1,400-2,000 L&T

A tortoiseshell and piqué-decorated table clock, with silver frame, white enamel dial and French movement, with marks for London.

1913   4.25in (11cm) high

$2,400-3,600 L&T

An early 20thC Bulle electric mantel timepiece, the movement with locking crown wheel and contacts for the electromagnetic coil pendulum, the chapter ring inscribed 'Georges Bernard, DINARD'.

13in (33cm) high

$1,000-1,600 DN

A Swiss gilt-brass inclined plane gravity timepiece, Imhof for the Musée International d'Horlogerie, La Chaux-de-Fonds, Switzerland, with fifteen-jewel movement and white dial set onto an inclined mahogany plane annotated with days of the week, in original box with instruction manual and spare inclined plane stand.

24in (61cm) wide

$1,300-$1,700 DN

An early 20thC French red-japanned 'floating turtle' novelty mystery timepiece, attributed to Grubelin for Dreyfous, Paris, the eight-day movement with platform lever escapement operating horizontal ring magnet to move the floating turtle within the pewter dish annotated with Roman numeral chapters and Arabic quarters to rim.

11.5in (29cm) wide

$4,600-5,600 DN

A 19thC French gilt-bronze and marble clock garniture set, the clock with works signed 'Paillard Paris', the candelabra each with six candle-arms and three putti-supports.

Clock 29in (74cm) wide

$12,000-16,000   POOK

A late 19thC French white marble and gilt-metal mounted clock garniture, in the Empire taste, with eight-day twin train movement striking the hours and half hours on a bell, indistinctly signed, the backplate stamped 'S.C. Paris'.

Clock 21in (53.5cm) high

$2,000-3,000   L&T

A 19thC French ormolu and white marble clock garniture, the twin train eight-day movement striking the hours and half hours on a bell, the backplate stamped 3887, with a pair of candelabra.

Clock 13in (33cm) high

$3,600-4,400   L&T

A 19thC French porcelain and gilt-bronze clock garniture, the inset 'jeweled' porcelain panels painted with scenic views and rural scenes, with a pair of Classical style ewers.

Clock 15in (38cm) high

$2,400-3,000   L&T

A French gilt-bronze and porcelain clock garniture, the porcelain dial surmounted by an orb finial with a berried knop and a portrait of a beauty below, with flanking griffin mask handles, the urns decorated with reserves of figures in 18thC costume, all on a bleu celeste ground.

c1890   *Clock 17.5in (44.5cm) high*

$3,000-4,000   FRE

A late 19thC gilt-bronze and marble three-piece clock garniture, with Bacchus and two cupids centered by a globular blue-enameled clock, on a veined green marble oval base, with a pair of gilt-bronze figural candelabra, one a bacchic child, the other a satyr.

Clock 15.5in (39.5cm) high

$6,000-8,000   FRE

A Louis XVI style gilt-bronze and Carrara marble clock garniture, the enameled dial with Roman numerals surmounted by a recumbent baccante and supported by winged infants atop goats hung with a lambrequin and bacchic vines, the matching urns with berried knops and mask handles cast.

c1900   *Clock 19in (48cm) high*

$8,000-12,000   FRE

A French gilt-bronze, porcelain and champlevé three-piece clock garniture, the porcelain dial surmounted by an urn finial, with flanking painted plaques depicting flower girls, the urns decorated with Classical figures.

c1900   *Clock 18in (45.5cm) high*

$10,000-14,000   FRE

A Regency rosewood clock, the gilt foliate-engraved face with a silvered engine-turned dial, the case surmounted by carrying handle.

9in (23cm) high

$8,000-10,000 L&T

A repeating carriage clock, signed 'Charles Frodsham', two-train fusee movement, underslung ratchet tooth lever escapement with compensation balance and maintaining power.

c1860 *8.5in (21.5 cm) high*

$28,000-32,000 SOTH

A French champlevé-enameled carriage clock, the eight-day gong-striking movement with silvered platform lever escapement.

4.75in (12cm) high

$3,600-4,400 DN

A late 19thC French gilt-brass and enamel carriage clock, retailed by Cooke & Kelvey, Calcutta, the repeating lever escapement movement striking on a wire, with a leather traveling case.

8in (20cm) high

$3,000-4,000 L&T

A late 19thC French brass carriage clock, with push-button repeat, unsigned, the eight-day gong-striking movement with silvered platform lever escapement.

5.25in (13.5cm) high

$800-1,200 DN

A late 19thC French brass carriage clock, unsigned, the eight-day two-train gong-striking movement with silvered platform lever escapement, with original leather case.

6.5in (16.5cm) high

$700-1,100 DN

A late 19thC French carriage clock, by Drocourt for J. W. Benson, London, the two-train gong-striking movement with silvered platform lever escapement.

5.75in (14.5cm) high

$1,800-2,400 DN

A late 19thC French carriage timepiece, possibly attributable to Brunelot, Paris, the eight-day movement with silvered platform lever escapement.

6in (15cm) high

$1,500-!,900 DN

A late 19thC French brass carriage clock, by C. A. Richard & Cie, the eight-day two-train gong-striking movement with replaced platform lever escapement and push button repeat, excluding handle

5.75in (14.5cm) high

$900-1,100 DN

A late 19thC French lacquered brass carriage clock, with two-train gong-striking movement, the dial signed and retailed by 'GOLDSMITHS & SILVERSMITHS Co. Ltd', in a corniche type case.

5.5in (14cm) high

$900-1,300 DN

A late 19thC French brass carriage timepiece, by Henry Jacot, the eight-day movement with replaced platform lever escapement, in a corniche type case.

5.75in (14.5cm) high

$340-400 DN

An early 20thC brass-cased four-glass carriage clock, with French repeat movement striking on two gongs, retailed by Howell & James Ltd., London.

6in (15cm) high

$400-600 ROS

CLOCKS

ESSENTIAL REFERENCE: LANTERN CLOCK

Lantern clocks were made almost entirely of brass and comprized a square case on ball or urn feet, a large circular dial with a chapter ring extending beyond the width of the case on early examples, a single hour hand, and a large bell and finial. They usually had ornate pierced fretwork on top of the frame.

Because of their relatively simple construction, lantern clocks were frequently copied in the 19thC and have been faked in modern times.

Patina and oxidation, symmetrical engraving on the center dial and the clear resonance of the bell help identify a genuine piece.

The characteristic pierced fretwork crown on a lantern clock should fit well into the original feet holes. If not, it has been replaced; sometimes because of damage to the original, but occasionally with a crown bearing the signature of a maker to enhance value.

A Charles II brass lantern clock, the posted countwheel bell-striking movement formerly with verge escapement and pendulum swinging between the trains, now with anchor escapement, the dial with vestigial alarm disc, signed 'Thomas Wheeler Londini Fecit'.

Lantern clocks are weight-driven wall clocks, shaped like a lantern, which were first seen in the UK c1620.

c1680   15in (38cm) high

$6,000-8,000   **DN**

A 20thC Continental painted white metal peddler clock, with pendulum and key.

15.5in (39.5in) high

$440-560   **ROS**

A 19thC picture clock, depicting a coastal view with figures beside a church, the church set with a clock movement, oil on canvas, in original gilt wood and gesso frame.

39in (99cm) high

$800-1,200   **L&T**

An early 20thC American folk art carved wooden automaton clock, the electric powered clock animating fourteen carved figures.

27.75in (70.5cm) high

$22,000-30,000   **SK**

CLOSER LOOK: MUSICAL DIORAMA

The diorama is modeled as a coastal town with a crenellated tower and watermill flanking a bridge with other gabled buildings behind.

The music is played via a pinned cylinder and steel comb mounted within the base.

The scene is set under a glass dome which has a landscape painted to the rear.

The molded ebonized wood base incorporates operating plungers and pull-wind cord to left-hand side.

There is an automata of a procession of cavalry over the bridge, turning water wheel to the mill and paddle steamer which rocks back and forth to the foreground.

A late 19thC musical automaton diorama, unsigned.

20.75in (53cm) high

$3,000-4,000   **DN**

A Jaeger-Le Coultre Atmos timepiece, in a fitted case.

Jean Leon Reutter, a French engineer, was working on utilizing the change in temperature and atmospheric pressure to wind a clock early in the 1920s. Patents were taken out in 1928 and 1930. The early models were not particularly successful commercially. They had a glass tube which held mercury, a liquified gas and a saturated vapour. The differences in pressure caused a rocking movement in the tube. The movement was transferred to the winding mechanism by a ratchet wheel. Later, ethyl chloride was substituted as a reagent. The Atmos clocks were manufactured by the Swiss firm of Jaeger-Le Coultre. They were marketed in the UK from 1934 by De Trevars Ltd. of Regent St. London W.1.

8.75in (22cm) high

$1,000-1,400   **SWO**

A Jaeger-Le Coultre traveling clock, with satin finished dial, hinged cover which doubles as an easel-back stand, with pouch, box and documents.

1.75in (4.5cm) long

$300-400   **L&T**

WALL CLOCKS

A George II thirty-hour posted wall clock, the movement with rectangular section posts, the anchor escapement and countwheel strike on a bell mounted above the top plate, with hook and spike wall mounting to rear.

c1730   *11in (28cm) high*

$3,000-3,600   **DN**

A French Louis XVI Ormolu Cartel wall timepiece, the enamel dial signed 'Le Nepveu Paris', movement with tapered plates and tic-tac escapement, silk suspended sunburst pendulum, repeating work removed.

17.25in (44cm) high

$5,000-6,000   **SOTA**

A George III mahogany tavern timepiece, the five-pillar weight-driven movement with five-wheel train, anchor escapement and tapered plates, with salt-box type case, lacking brass bezel and minute hand.

c1790   *38.5in (98cm) high*

$4,000-5,000   **DN**

A late 18thC George III black japanned tavern timepiece, the four-pillar weight-driven movement with anchor escapement and tapered plates, the salt-box type case with fretwork ears, the recessed panel door painted with a Lakeland view with pavilion, with pendulum adjustment flap to right-hand side.

46in (117cm) high

$5,000-6,000   **DN**

An American Federal mahogany banjo clock, possibly Simon Willard & Son, Massachusetts.

c1815   *33in (84cm) high*

$5,000-7,000   **POOK**

An American 'banjo' clock, attributed to Aaron Willard, Jr., Boston, the reverse-paintings on glass with 1812 battle scene and four captains' names, eight-day brass weight-powered movement with 'T-bridge' suspension.

c1815   42in (106.5cm) long

$10,000-14,000   **SK**

A Regency Edinburgh mahogany wall clock, the enameled roman dial with single train movement, signed 'A. Philipp Edinburgh'.

59in (150cm) high

$4,000-6,000   **L&T**

A large American Federal mahogany and eglomise wall clock, with mirror plate and panel showing buildings on a village green, without works.

c1820   62in (157.5cm) long

$1,500-2,000   **FRE**

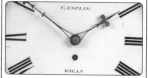

A Victorian mother-of-pearl-inlaid rosewood dial timepiece, the four-pillar single fusee movement with anchor escapement, signed 'G. ESPLIN, WIGAN'.

c1840   17.5in (44cm) diam

$900-1,100   **DN**

A Victorian rosewood and mother-of-pearl marquetry drop dial wall clock.

c1860   22.5in (57cm) high

$900-1,100   **DN**

An unusual mid-19thC Austrian large oak wall regulator, the single train movement with deadbeat escapement, A-shaped plates and Huygens endless rope system winding via a large wheel and click mounted on the backboard, the dial with subsidiary seconds and calendar dials and signed 'Josef Kotek'.

56in (142cm) high

$1,800-2,400   **DN**

A late 19thC American Ithaca calendar clock.

60.5in (153.5cm) high

$6,000-10,000   **POOK**

A late 19thC American Boston, Massachusetts No. 60 wall regulator clock, by Edward Howard.

92in (233cm) high overall

$40,000-50,000   **POOK**

A large Vienna style wall clock, with a single train movement with long pendulum with brass-faced bob.

72in (183cm) high

$3,000-4,000   **DUK**

A 19thC Black Forest wall clock, the case inlaid with mother of pearl roundels.

$300-360   **ROS**

A late 19thC Black Forest carved wall clock.

47in (119.5cm) high

$6,000-7,000   **POOK**

THE BAROMETER MARKET

The market for barometers has consolidated. While buyers remain relatively selective, prices are strong for the right pieces. There has always been a market for classic examples and those by the best makers, and this continues. A barometer which shows quality in its design, construction and mechanism will always find a buyer, and this has not changed. For example, a good, early, fine mercury stick barometer by a famous maker such as John Patrick or Daniel Quare is relatively rare and likely to be of a high quality, so prices for such pieces are strong due to their historical importance.

The same can be said for later pieces which present themselves as the best of their period, hence 19thC examples by makers such as Adie and Dollond are commanding good prices. However the same cannot be said for mid to late 19thC barometers of average quality by lesser makers. Examples which are more

standard in their design and function are not doing as well as they were. On the other hand, wheel barometers with an unusual layout – upside down examples or those with the dial in the center – are doing well with buyers prepared to pay for innovation or novelty. Prices for polytechnic and Fitzroy barometers in original condition are gaining strength.

Particularly hard hit are the more ordinary mercury barometers which people are nervous of buying because of ill-founded fears that new laws may prohibit the sale and even the repair of instruments containing mercury. Exports to the US have suffered considerably as a result. Consequently, the market for aneroid barometers has grown stronger. Finally, condition and originality have always had a bearing on value, in today's selective market such factors are becoming increasingly important.

STICK AND CISTERN BAROMETERS

A late 17thC walnut cistern tube stick barometer, with cross-grain molded ogee outline arched pediment above caddy-molded panel-veneered case, the scale annotated for 'Sumer' and 'Winter', with signature 'Henry Wynne' London.

40.5in (103cm) high

$7,000-9,000   DN

A William and Mary walnut cistern tube stick barometer, in the manner of John Patrick.

c1695   *47.25in (120cm) high*

$5,000-7,000   DN

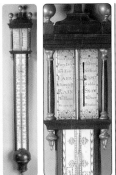

A Queen Anne walnut cistern tube stick barometer, with thermometer, attributed to Stephen Davenport or John Patrick, London, with restored paper scale calibrated from 0 at the top down to 90.

c1715   *39in (99cm) high*

$7,000-9,000   DN

A George II mahogany cistern tube stick barometer, by Edward Scarlett, London, with silvered vernier scale and bayonet-shaped tube, the mercury thermometer signed.

c1740   *35.75in (91cm) high*

$6,000-8,000   DN

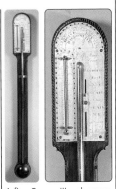

A fine George III mahogany cistern tube stick barometer, with hygrometer or Triple Weather Glass, the vernier scale with arched hygrometer scale above Fahrenheit and Reaumur mercury thermometer and signed 'B. Martin, London'.

c1760   *37in (94cm) high*

$7,000-9,000   DN

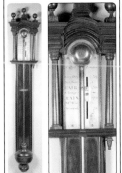

A George III mahogany cistern tube stick barometer, vernier scale signed 'J. Bird, London'.

c1760   *44in (112cm) high*

$5,000-6,000   DN

A George III mahogany cistern tube stick barometer.

c1765   *37in (94cm) high*

$3,000-4,000   DN

A George III mahogany cistern tube stick barometer with hygrometer, by Henry Pyefinch, London.

c1770   *39.75in (101cm) high*

$3,000-4,000   DN

A George III mahogany cistern tube stick barometer, silvered vernier register signed 'Dollond, London'.

c1770   *39.5in (100cm) high*

$5,000-6,000   DN

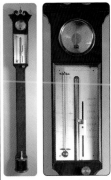

A fine George III mahogany cistern tube stick barometer, with whalebone hygrometer and ivory cistern float.

c1770   *43.75in (111cm) high*

$8,000-10,000   DN

BAROMETERS

A late 18thC inlaid mahogany mercury wheel barometer, signed 'Ja's Gatty No 130 High Holborn, LONDON'.

37in (94cm) high

$4,000-5,000   DN

A rare inlaid and crossbanded mahogany mercury wheel barometer, attributed to Christopher Bettally, London.

c1790   37.5in (95cm) high

$7,000-8,000   DN

CLOSER LOOK: WHEEL BAROMETER

The stepped caddy pediment is an unusual feature. Other examples of this style of barometer made by John Hallifax have a simple, domed pediment.

The restrained design of the trunk is enhanced by book-matched walnut veneers.

The form and design, with its centrally placed dial, is very rare.

The reading ring is well engraved, with a central brass panel engraved with a foliate panel and the name of the maker.

A rare George II walnut siphon tube wheel barometer, with a 7.5in (19cm) register calibrated in inches and also divided 0-30 corresponding to the decimal divisions of the barometric inches, the brass center signed 'John Hallifax Barnsley Inv:f fecit'.

c1730   45in (114cm) high

$40,000-50,000   DN

A George III satinwood mercury wheel barometer, the 10in (25.5cm) silvered register calibrated in inches and signed 'Anone No. 26 High Holb'n, London' beneath hygrometer and arched Fahrenheit scale alcohol thermometer.

c1805   41.5in (105cm) high

$1,800-2,400   DN

A George III inlaid mahogany mercury wheel barometer, the 8in (20.5cm) silvered register calibrated in inches and signed 'P. Gally, London' the Fahrenheit scale alcohol thermometer flanked by foliate inlaid oval paterae.

c1810   39in (99cm) high

$2,200-2,600   DN

A rare George III mahogany upside-down mercury wheel barometer, the silvered register calibrated in inches above ivory setting pointer adjustment disc with spirit level signed 'JAMES LIONE No 81 high Holbn'n, LONDON'.

c1810   37.5in (95cm) high

$10,000-12,000   DN

A George III mahogany mercury wheel barometer, the 8in (20.5cm) silvered register calibrated in inches and signed 'P. Manticha, LONDON', with brass setting pointer to glass beneath arched Fahrenheit scale alcohol thermometer.

c1815   36in (92cm) high

$1,100-1,300   DN

A Regency inlaid mahogany mercury wheel barometer, the 8in (20.5cm) silvered register calibrated in inches, signed 'G. Testi & Co, Chester' with Fahrenheit scale alcohol thermometer.

c1820   38.5in (98cm) high

$1,400-1,800   DN

A Regency mahogany mercury wheel barometer, the 8in (20.5cm) silvered register calibrated in inches and signed 'A. Alberti, Sheffield'.

c1825   39in (99cm) high
$1,300-1,500   DN

A William IV large rosewood wheel barometer with timepiece, the clock dial signed 'French Royal Exchange, London' with pillar single fusee movement with platform lever escapement to front-plate, with Fahrenheit scale mercury thermometer and hygrometer similarly signed.

c1830   49.25in (125cm) high
$4,400-5,600   DN

A William IV mahogany mercury wheel barometer, by Francis Amadio & Son for John Mangiacavalli, London.

c1835   37.75in (96cm) high
$3,000-4,000   DN

A satinwood crossbanded mercury wheel barometer signed 'C. Maspolli, Manchester, Warranted'.

c1840   49.5in (126cm) high
$2,800-3,600   DN

An early Victorian brass-mounted mahogany mercury wheel barometer, with bowfront mercury Fahrenheit scale thermometer flanked by brass pilaster and hygrometer, with spirit level signed 'Gardner & Dowling, Belfast'.

c1840   43.75in (111cm) high
$1,800-2,200   DN

An early Victorian rosewood combination drop-dial wall clock and mercury wheel barometer, the register inscribed 'P. BREGAZZI Patentee Nottingham No. 44', with registration kite mark for 25 September 1843 to the Royal Coat of Arms, with a drop-dial wall clock with four-pillar single fusee movement.

c1843   41.25in (105cm) high
$6,000-8,000   DN

An early Victorian mahogany mercury wheel barometer, the 10in (25.5cm) register calibrated in inches and signed 'DOLLOND, LONDON', with bowfronted Fahrenheit scale, alcohol thermometer, the base with hygrometer.

c1845   40.5in (103cm) high
$4,600-5,200   DN

A Victorian mahogany mercury wheel barometer, register signed 'Watkins & Hill 5 Charing Cross London' and inscribed 'REGISTERED 1586 SEPT'R 14TH 1848 No. 201', lacking setting pointer adjustment disc.

c1848   39in (99cm) high
$1,600-2,400   DN

A Victorian oak combined stick and wheel barometer, the register signed 'N. Whitehouse 2 Cranbourn Str. Leicester Square', with brass setting pointer adjustment disc and Fahrenheit scale mercury thermometer to the shaped base section beneath.

c1850   36.5in (93cm) high
$4,000-6,000   DN

A late 19thC oak-cased barograph, with six-part vacuum chamber within lacquered brass armature operating inked pointer for the rotating paper scale lined drum.

15in (37.5cm) wide

$1,200-1,800   DN

An early 20thC thermobarograph, with seven-part vacuum chamber, operating inked pointer for the paper scale lined drum and secondary pointer to record the temperature.

14.75in (37cm) wide

$1,500-1,700   DN

An oak-cased barograph, with four-part vacuum chamber, with inked pointer for the rotating paper scale lined drum, the base plate signed 'GRIFFIN & TATLOCK, LONDON No F.6135".

c1915   *13.5in (34cm) wide*

$700-800   DN

A chrome plated barograph, with two-part vacuum chamber within electroplated armature operating an inked pointer for the paper scale, with a curved mercury tube thermometer.

c1925   *14in (35cm) wide*

$2,600-3,600   DN

An ebonized cased micro-barograph, with thirteen-part vacuum chamber with inked pointer for the paper scale lined drum and inscribed 'SHORT AND MASON, LONDON... No. 957/45.

c1925   *14.25in (36cm) wide*

$1,000-1,200   DN

A mid 20thC mahogany cased barograph, with eight-part vacuum chamber within lacquered brass armature operating inked pointer for the rotating paper scale lined drum.

14in (36cm) wide

$900-1,100   DN

A late 18thC Ramsden brass telescope, inscribed 'RAMSDEN, LONDON', thumbwheel rack and pinion fine focusing, single drawtube focusing, 2in (5cm) subject lens, dust cap, dent to body, two lenses replaced.

22in (56cm) long

$3,000-5,000   FRE

A 19thC brass portable telescope, by W. Harris & Co, with a 3.5in (9cm) objective lens, thumb-operated fine turning, brass dust cover, tripod, timber adjusting handle, original box.

42in (106.5cm) long

$3,000-4,000   FRE

A Dollond floor telescope, with thumb-operated fine focus, 2in (5cm) objective lens, timber tripod stand, signed 'Dollond, London' to tube.

c1840   *37.5in (95cm) long*

$2,400-3,600   FRE

A 19thC brass floor telescope, 2in (5cm) objective lens, dust cover, timber tripod stand.

58in (147.5cm) long

$5,000-6,000   FRE

A composite 19thC brass telescope, signed on the backplate 'T & R. Willats, 98, Cheapside, London'.

17.75in (45cm) high

$800-1,000   ROS

A late 19thC hand-held 1.5in (4cm) refracting telescope, with four draws, the first signed 'DOLLOND, LONDON' with lens covers.

8.25in (21cm) long closed

$700-800   DN

A set of two similar early 20thC leather-covered brass three draw telescopes, by Broadhurst, Clarkson & Co., Ltd.

33.25in (84.5cm) long extended

$200-300   ROS

A set of two similar early 20thC wood and brass three-draw telescopes.

33.25in (84.5cm) long extended

$160-240   ROS

An early 19thC brass spyglass, by Cox, London, with a removable dust cover, an eight-draw tube, coarse focus, tortoiseshell grip, and a 1.5in (4cm) lens.

31in (79cm) long

$1,200-1,600 FRE

A brass spyglass, coarse focus from an eight-draw tube, 1.5in (4cm) subject lens, new blue shagreen skin hand grip.

c1850 *24in (61cm) long*

$1,600-2,000 FRE

A 19thC brass spyglass, by Cox, Devenport, removable dust cap, tortoiseshell hand rest, seven pull draw tube, 1.5in (4cm) subject lens, and a slide cover eye piece.

22in (56cm) long

$1,000-1,400 FRE

A brass spyglass, by Rojs & Co. Regency Street Piccadilly, three-pull draw tube, swinging cover over eye lens, 1.5in (4cm) subject lens, pop dust cover, tortoiseshell hand grip.

c1850 *24in (61cm) long*

$1,200-1,800 FRE

A late 18thC style lacquered brass Culpeper type microscope, in original fitted pyramid case, with a quantity of accessories including three other objective lenses and three bone slides.

$1,300-1,500 GORL

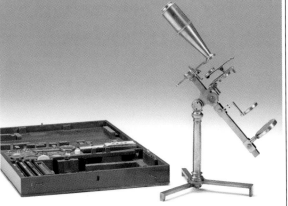

An early 19thC Bate 'Jones Most Improved' type brass compound microscope, signed, substage condenser and plano/concave mirror, six objectives, three lieberkuhns, live box, and cone.

16in (40.5cm) high

$7,000-9,000 FRE

A late 19thC brass compound monocular microscope, with rack-and-pinion focusing, micrometre screw adjustment, signed 'J. Swift & Son, London.' in a case with extras.

12.25in (31cm) high

$400-500 DN

A 19thC lacquered brass binocular microscope, by' C. Collins, Optician, 157, Gt Portland St, London'.

19.75in (50cm) high

$700-800 ROS

An exceptional early 18thC brass circumferentor, inscribed 'Willz Collier Fecit', the silver-plated compass dial finely inscribed with direction and decoration of foliate scrolls, enclosed by a dome glass cover and brass dust cover, the outer arch pierced and supported by six arms, with original mahogany, ebony and parquetry box.

13.5in (34cm) diam

$22,000-28,000 FRE

A mid 18thC French cube dial, by D. Beringer, small magnetic compass on paper gore-covered dial applied with four adjustable tin dials, for various latitudes.

8in (20.5cm) high

$1,200-1,600 FRE

SCIENTIFIC INSTRUMENTS

A Chinese metal and enamel traveling sundial, with an integral compass.

4.5in (11.5cm) high

$400-500   WW

A brass table dip needle, by Philip Harris, the circular face encloses the dip needle and measured dial.

c1900   8in (20.5cm) high

$1,000-1,600   FRE

An early 19thC mahogany-cased two-day marine chronometer, with a gimbal-mounted silvered dial, subsidiary seconds and up/down dial, with retaining screw, signed on the dial 'McLachlan, London'.

6.75in (17cm) wide

$4,000-6,000   L&T

An early 20thC ivorine pocket weather forecasting calculator, signed 'NEGRETTI & ZAMBRA, LONDON', the middle for 'BAROMETER AT SEA LEVEL' and the center pierced with three sectors annotated 'FALLING', 'STEADY' and 'RISING' and inscribed 'PAT. NO. 6276/15', in original box with instructions titled 'WEATHER FORECASTER'.

14in (5.5cm) diam

$170-200   DN

An early 20thC brass table weather forecasting calculator, formed as three discs, the outer calibrated in inches for the barometer reading to the top edge and for wind direction to the lower edge, the middle ring is annotated for 'STEADY', 'RISING' and 'FALLING', the center with instructions for use, inscribed 'NEGRETTI & ZAMBRA, LONDON, PATENT 6276, 1915'.

4.75in (12cm) diam

$1,600-2,000   DN

A japanned metal hair hygrometer, with four-inch ceramic register calibrated for 'RELATIVE PERCENTAGE HUMIDITY' and signed 'NEGRETTI & ZAMBRA, LONDON'.

The instrument uses the relative expansion and contraction of hair with changes in moisture in the air to measure relative humidity.

c1935   4.25in (11cm) diam

$60-100   DN

A carved wood weather house, with polychrome-printed silhouettes of male and female figures each in the 16thC style dress, the instrument is a form of hygrometer, as the twisted gut suspension absorbs moisture it expands causing the beam onto which the figures are mounted to pivot.

c1900   8in (20cm) wide

$80-160   DN

A mid-19thC mahogany-cased brass portable dipleidoscope, the brass bed with three leveling screws mounted with angled prism, bubble level and magnetic compass needle.

4in (10cm) wide

$2,000-2,800   DN

A boxed set of rare mechanical slides, including twelve glass colour slides of England, the timber viewer is operated by a swing handle.

c1860

$1,400-1,800   FRE

A 19thC French medical shock machine, supported on a mahogany rectangular base are four gilt-metal conductors attached to two supporting brass bars, and a velvet-covered head rest.

10in (25.5cm) long

$500-600   FRE

A 19thC magnifying glass, the sliding magnifying glass cased in carved shell with silver mounts.

3.5in (9cm) diam

$200-300   **FRE**

A 19thC John Brown amputation set, comprizing a timber-handled saw, two spare blades, steel grips, cases.

18in (45.5cm) long

$400-600   **FRE**

A set of twelve eye surgery instruments, Weiss, the steel blades are set to ivory handles, in a fitted leather box.

c1850   Longest 5in (12.5cm) long

$120-160   **FRE**

A set of thirteen 19thC Philharmonic tuning forks, J. Walker, encased in a fitted box.

Longest 6in (15cm) long

$200-300   **FRE**

A 19thC draftsman's set, complete ivory and steel set comprizing approximately 25 pieces, including watercolors enclosed under the instrument tray, in a brass-inlaid rosewood box with key.

13in (33cm) wide

$2,000-3,000   **FRE**

A George III table celestial globe, by J & W Cary, London, on a molded and turned mahogany tripod base.

1802   19in (48cm) high overall

$5,000-6,000   **WW**

A pair of terrestrial and celestial table globes, by G. & J. Cary, London, the maps colored, the terrestrial globe with losses to southern Italy and Greece, minor losses and abrasions elsewhere, the celestial globe with restored section to South and section rebuild to North, the supporting rings of brass, on original stands of mahogany and ebonized wood, the rings also with small losses and abrasions.

1828   12in (30.5cm) diam.

$8,000-10,000   **SOTA**

A William IV Newton's terrestrial globe, with printed segments and a label 'Newton's New and Improved Terrestrial Globe Accurately Delineated From the Observations of The Most Esteemed Navigators and Travellers To The Present Time, London, Published 1st January 1832'.

43.5in (110.5cm) high

$30,000-40,000   **WW**

A Victorian armillary sphere, the central terrestrial globe bounded by an arrangement of calibrated brass horizons and outer celestial ring marking the constellations, on a short turned cabochon-carved column and pierced scrolling tripod base.

44in (112cm) high

$8,000-10,000   **L&T**

An American 19thC terrestrial globe, by Gilman Joslin, Boston, of typical sphere form, constructed of twelve colour paper gores, with a brass meridian, over a timber stand.

18in (46cm) high

$2,000-3,000   **FRE**

A late 20thC decorative 8in (20.5cm) terrestrial globe on a patinated bronze figural stand, unsigned, the twelve gores printed with a facsimile of Woodward's map, supported by a figure of Atlas on a circular grained wood base.

20.75in (53cm) high

$400-600   **DN**

Edward Everard Arnold (New Orleans, 1824-1866), 'Sch'r H.B. Metcalf, Capt'n Charles L. Murden', signed and dated 'Arnold 1859 pinxt', oil on canvas, two patch repairs, scattered retouch, minor paint losses.

40in (101.5cm) wide

$26,000-32,000   SK

Ralph Eugene Cahoon, Jr. (Cotuit, Massachusetts, 1910-1982), signed, oil on masonite depicting sailors netting fish and mermaids.

27.75in (70.5cm) wide

$24,000-30,000   SK

Raffael Corsini (Turkish, active 1830-1880), 'Barque Juniata, Capt. Joseph Cheever Entering Smyrna April 22th 1852', signed, gouache on paper, in original walnut veneer frame.

23.5in (59.5cm) wide

$28,000-32,000   SK

Antonio Nicolo Gasparo Jacobsen (American/Danish, 1850-1921), portrait of the British steamer 'Circassia', signed and dated 'A Jacobsen 1881', oil on canvas, vessel identified on bow and pennant.

60in (152.5cm) wide

$32,000-40,000   SK

19thC American School, portrait of a four-masted ship, unsigned, oil on canvas, framed.

30in (76cm) wide

$3,000-4,000   FRE

A 19thC Chinese School, oil on canvas, ''CENTENNIAL' HONG KONG. SEPT. 1878', unsigned, titled below, in a Chinese carved wooden frame, minor craquelure.

32.25in (82cm) wide

$24,000-30,000   SK

TEXTILES

A sailor's embroidered woolwork picture, of the 'Prince Consort', the battleship in full regalia, draped with flags, above a crowned banner.

33.75in (86cm) wide

$8,000-12,000   L&T

A Victorian sailor's woolwork picture of ship, flying the red ensign, entitled 'HMS QUEEN 1850' within a simulated rosewood frame.

28in (71cm) wide

$6,000-8,000   L&T

A mid-19thC sailor's woolwork picture of a naval gunboat, steam and sail, with raised padded embroidered sails and black cotton rigging, silver thread anchors.

Framed 15in (39cm) wide

$1,000-1,200   KT

A mid-19thC embroidered woolwork picture of HMS 'Marlborough', the 131 gun steam and sail ship flying blue and red ensigns.

Framed 14in (36cm) wide

$1,200-1,600   KT

A late 19thC sailor's woolwork, worked with a three masted merchantman on an emerald green scudding sea, the hull worked in black and red with grey and white guns holes and port holes.

Framed 22in (56cm) wide

$1,400-1,800   KT

A mid-19thC embroidered sailor's woolwork, worked with four ships of the line, with black cotton rigging, black beaded gun-ports, on a scudding sea and calm sky in shades of green.

Framed 18.5in (47cm) wide

$2,200-2,800   KT

A 19thC engraved whale's tooth, depicting an eagle, American shield and flags, and Christ upon the cross, inscribed 'M.T.' and 'M.D.S.', some areas with red sealing wax, on a rosewood base.

7in (18cm) high

$12,000-16,000   SK

A powder horn, with engraving and inscription 'MARCH ye A 1762 CROWN POINT STEPHEN DYAR,' surrounded by vessels flying British flags, and carved wooden butt plug.

A genealogical search indicates that Stephen Dyar (Dyer, Dier) was born in Weymouth, Massachusetts, October 20, 1741, to Joseph and Jane (Stephens [Stevens]) Dyar. He married Leah Bate(s) October 25, 1764. In the Massachusetts Soldiers and Sailors in the Revolution, Dyar was enlisted as a Minute-man in various lengths of service between April 19 1775 and April 26, 1778.

c1762   *11.5in (29cm) long*

$6,000-8,000   SK

A 19thC carved and engraved whale's tooth, depicting a three-masted bark with carved hull, and the initials 'P.M.' engraved in script.

6in (15cm) long

$4,000-5,000   SK

A scrimshaw horn, of Masonic Interest, decorated with sailing ships and the City arms of Edinburgh and Glasgow above views of notable buildings: St. Giles Cathedral, Holyrood Palace, Edinburgh University, Tron Church, St. Andrew's Church, St. George's Church, Nelson Monument, Melville's Monument, George Herriot's Hospital, Royal Institution, Register Office, with a lower banding of Masonic emblems and symbols, signed: 'carved by D. Gourlay, Plumber aged 68'.

15in (38cm) long

$2,400-3,200   L&T.

A French and Native American war powder or blowing horn, inscribed 'George Losch Anno 1762', carved with the Royal Coat of Arms, New York, a hunter with dogs and a deer, and 'Map of America' showing the river and military forts from Albany to Lake Champlain and Lake Ontario, heightened with black and red.

Provenance: This horn may have been made for George Losch, a gunpowder maker of Philadelphia County, who, along with Oswold Eve, signed an agreement to furnish 'good strong and well seasoned' gunpowder in one year's time to the Committee of the Secrecy of the Continental Congress, January 11, 1776. The committee members included Benjamin Franklin, Robert Morris and Silas Dean.

12in (30.5cm) long

$16,000-20,000   FRE

A scrimshaw-decorated walrus tusk, incised to one side with a clipper.

18.5in (47cm) long

$1,200-1,600   L&T

NAUTICAL ANTIQUES

An early 19thC midshipman's training model, of a fully rigged tea clipper, the absence of sails clearly delineating the positions of masts, rigging and supporting chain mounts, made in dark stained pine and beech.

96.75in (246cm) wide

$5,000-7,000   **L&T**

A painted pine ship model, of a Mediterranean trading vessel, the painted deck with naturalistically modeled cranking wheels, ships wheel and bell, with full rigging, on a trestle stand.

83in (211cm) wide

$5,000-7,000   **L&T**

An early 20thC gaff-rigged pond yacht, with a painted hull and planked deck, with a later two-wheeled carriage.

66.5in (169cm) high

$2,400-3,000   **L&T**

A silver model, of a four-masted English Royal galleon the 'Mary Rose' by Alfred James, Francis William & Arthur Walter Pairpoint, London, in full sail with men on deck, cannons and flying pennants, on a four-wheel base, on a mahogany plinth with title plaque and an oak carrying case 58.75oz (1828g).

The 'Mary Rose' was launched in 1511 and served as flagship in King Henry VIII's fleet. She was one of a new type of purpose-built warship equipped with gunports to enable artillery broadsides to be fired. She was sunk on 19th July 1545 off Portsmouth during a battle with the French fleet which had attacked the English coast. After many years of excavation, the ship was finally raised from the sea bed in 1982.

1920   19in (48.5cm) long

$5,000-6,000   **DN**

A working pond model of a yacht, Birkenhead, gaff-rigged, timber body, cotton/silk sail, with timber stand.

c1920   24in (61cm) high

$1,000-1,600   **FRE**

An American 'from scratch' pond model of a yacht, timber body and keel, with two linen sails, on a timber stand.

c1940   20in (51cm) high

$700-1,000   **FRE**

An American 20thC cased painted near-scale ship model, made by Peter Ness, 'The Flying Cloud, New York'.

41.5in (105.5cm) wide

$1,600-2,000   **FRE**

An early 20thC painted wood half model, of a ship mounted on a molded mahogany backboard, labeled 'Maria a Hinde. Built by Workman Clarke & Co. Limited Belfast 208 29 13 11 hold'.

64in (162cm) long

$4,400-5,200   **L&T**

A large early 20thC painted wood half model, of a ship on a molded maple backboard.

92.25in (234cm) long

$4,000-5,000   **L&T**

An early 20thC painted wood half model, of a ship mounted on a mahogany backboard, labeled 'S. S. William Hinde 160x22 6x11 9 hold. Built by Workman Clark & Co. Limited Belfast'.

51.25in (130cm) long

$6,000-7,000   **L&T**

'There is No Second', Schooner Yacht America, Isle of Wight 1851', diorama, by William E Hitchcock (1928-2006, Massachusetts), in a molded giltwood frame.

The yacht 'America' was designed by George Steers for The New York Yacht Club in 1851, in an effort to challenge the British, who had a reputation for yachting supremacy. The 'America' raced in England against fifteen yachts in the annual 53-mile race around the Isle of Wight, conducted by the Royal Yacht Squadron, and won by two minutes. She won the next race, against England's fastest the 'Titania', by nearly an hour. When Queen Victoria was told of the triumph, she asked who was second; the famous reply was: 'There is no second, your Majesty.' A cup was presented to the New York Yacht Club, who offered it to any yacht capable of defeating them, a challenge which has become known as the 'America's Cup'.

33in (84cm) long

$1,000-2,000   **SK**

A late 19thC ship diorama, half black model of a five-masted ship, in a glazed case, corrosion of small metal parts.

37in (94cm) wide

$3,600-4,400   **SK**

A diorama by Erik A. R. Ronnberg Sr., 'Arctic Steam Whalers off Herschel Island c1890', signed.

1986   56.5in (143.5cm) wide

$2,000-2,600   **SK**

Robert F. Kurtz, diorama of the schooner 'William M. Yerkes', the model taken from an oil painting by S. F. M. Badger, in a glazed molded mahogany frame with gilt liner.

1983   22.25in (56.5cm) wide

$1,600-2,400   **SK**

A brass-hooded and gimbaled binnacle, by Calvin & Winfrid O. White Co., Boston and New York, fitted onto a full-sized mahogany circular pedestal, on rectangular plinth, cast iron compensating arms, pedestal with copper plate.

$1,500-2,000   FRE

A ship's brass pedestal-mounted telegraph, by J.W. Ray & Co., Liverpool and London, from a large steamship.

46in (117cm) high

$900-1,300   FRE

A mid-to late 19thC German Universal Skaphe sundial, by A. Meisser, Berlin, patented by H. Schmeisser, with copper hemisphere on a cobalt-glazed ceramic stand.

6in (15cm) high

$1,500-2,000   FRE

A 19th/20thC portable brass foghorn, by H.R. Holland, with leather strap and adjustable horn.

20.25in (51.5cm) long

$400-600   FRE

A pair of 19th-early 20thC port and starboard copper lamps, by Stuurboord and Bakboord, with clear glass lenses.

13.75in (35cm) high

$300-400   FRE

Left: An early to mid-20thC Japanese copper and brass diving helmet.

18.5in (47cm) high

$1,500-2,000   FRE

Right: A late 19th/early 20thC brass and copper diving helmet, by A.J. Morris & Co., Boston.

18in (45.5cm) high

$4,400-5,600   FRE

A late 19thC shellwork shadowbox, from Barbados, with exotic shells.

The poem on reverse reads 'All the royal gems of the world's kingdoms, Don't compare with Poseidon's humblest creatures, Whose perfection and color are without equal, And are there to be found on our coastal beaches.', comes with printed label 'New Curiosity Shop McGregor St, Barbados W.I. ...Fancy Work ....'

16in (40.6cm) wide

$5,000-6,000   FRE

A Victorian sailor's shell double valentine, in an octagonal hinged glazed case, one side with 'SOUVENIR FROM BARBADOS', the other with a galleon.

28.5in (72cm) wide open

$10,000-12,000   L&T

THE MUSIC BOX MARKET

The inspiration for the design of the familiar cylinder musical box may be found in some of the more complex musical clocks of the 18th century. These clocks could play simple tunes provided by a series of tuned bells that were struck by small hammers which were, in turn, activated by a rotating, pinned cylinder.

At the end of the 18th and during the early 19th century, technology allowed the bells to be replaced with a steel comb consisting of tuned teeth. As this was a much more compact arrangement, more notes could be provided in a given space allowing the musical arrangers greater opportunities to produce elaborate music.

Technical developments, mostly made by Swiss engineers, throughout the 19th century reduced the cost of these machines to such an extent that many households could afford this form of entertainment.

By the mid 1880s, German engineers had developed a more robust system where the musical information was provided via an easily interchangeable disc rather than the more vulnerable, and mostly fixed, cylinder. This system had many advantages, including the opportunity to allow the manufacture of a large selection of titles.

The early 20th century saw the introduction of many marvelous technical advances. Recordings of live music and the introduction of the wireless eventually made the musical box redundant.

Condition is of the utmost importance when considering values. Interest in antique musical boxes has increased over the past 40 years and restoration techniques have been developed to enable a musical box to provide a performance today that is equal to that when it was first produced.

MUSIC BOXES

A Swiss '2 per turn' cylinder musical box, Nicole Frères, serial no. '43038', playing 12 airs, movement overhauled, case repolished, cylinder 12in (30.5cm) long.
c1860   22in (56cm) wide
$8,000-10,000   PGO

A Swiss cylinder musical box, movement overhauled, original tune sheet, cylinder 9in (23cm) long.
c1870-1890   20in (51cm) wide
$4,000-5,000   PGO

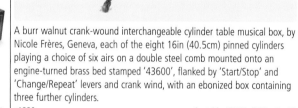

An eight-air cylinder musical box, by Ami Rivenc, original tune sheet, original finish to case, movement restored.
c1880   14in (35.5cm) wide
$3,600-4,400   PGO

A French cylinder musical box, by L'Epee, No. '54846', playing six airs, case refinished, movement over-hauled. cylinder 8in (20.5in) long.
c1885   16.75in (42.5cm) wide
$3,600-4,400   PGO

A burr walnut crank-wound interchangeable cylinder table musical box, by Nicole Frères, Geneva, each of the eight 16in (40.5cm) pinned cylinders playing a choice of six airs on a double steel comb mounted onto an engine-turned brass bed stamped '43600', flanked by 'Start/Stop' and 'Change/Repeat' levers and crank wind, with an ebonized box containing three further cylinders.
c1880   the table 46.75in (119cm) wide
$10,000-14,000   DN

A late 19thC Swiss burr thuya wood musical box, with a row of six graduated bells and a 16in (40.5cm) comb playing ten airs, winding handle and two levers, on later inlaid stand, playing card numbered '5079'.
31.5in (80cm) wide
$8,000-12,000   L&T

A late 19thC Swiss eight-air musical box, with 11in (4.25cm) cylinder playing on hooked teeth, no. 3522 in inlaid rosewood case.

20in (50cm) wide
$1,000-1,400   GORL

An 18ct gold half hunter pocket watch, cuvette inscribed 'PARKINSON & FRODSHAM... LONDON', the reverse with blue enameled floral border around a monogrammed shield-shaped cartouche.

1.25in (3.5cm) diam

$800-1,000   L&T

An open face pocket watch, 18ct gold, the white dial and movement signed 'W Batty & Son, Manchester 53248'.

$1,200-1,600   CHT

A metal-cased Jaeger-LeCoultre pocket watch, open faced with date and alarm, circular champagne dial with black Roman numerals, the center section as an alarm dial, with further date aperture, the base fitted with a folding strut, movement number 1967826, movement stamped 'K911' to the reverse, the case numbered 11003 and 1186679, with original black leather slip.

$1,000-1,600   ROS

A Belle Époque diamond set fob watch, the front millegrain collet set to the center with an old European cut diamond, set with single cut diamonds and borders of channel set caliber cut onyx.

Fob 2in (5cm) long

$1,200-1,600   L&T

An Art Deco platinum and diamond cocktail watch, with single cut diamond set bezel, fitted to a mesh link strap, clasp stamped '9ct'.

6.5in (16.5cm) long

$2,000-3,000   L&T

An Art Deco cocktail watch, caliber cut emeralds and single cut diamonds.

$2,000-2,600   L&T

An Art Deco lady's platinum cocktail watch, the case inset with old cut diamonds and shaped baguette cut onyx, fitted with 9ct gold mesh strap.

$500-600   ROS

An Art Deco cocktail watch, set with single cut diamonds, to a ribbon strap, mounts stamped 18ct.

$1,600-2,400   L&T

An Art Deco style diamond and sapphire-set 14ct white gold cocktail watch, inscribed.

$900-1,100   CHT

A Baume & Mercier gentleman's gold wrist watch, stamped '750', '18K' and numbered '205688 35041'.

Dial 1.5in (3.5cm) diam

$2,000-3,000   L&T

A Baume & Mercier lady's 18ct gold wrist watch, numbered '404523 38244T2'.

Dial 1in (2.5cm) wide

$1,200-1,600   L&T

A 1970s Swiss Bulova lady's wristwatch, white gold, with 16 diamonds, silver clockface, blackened hands, quartz clockwork, matted original bracelet.

1in (2.5cm) wide

$400-600   KAU

A 'Must de Cartier' lady's wristwatch, the winder fitted with sapphire cabochon.

$400-600   ROS

A 'Must de Cartier' lady's tank watch, silver gilt case, fitted with original black leather strap, case number cc21050.

$1,000-1,600   ROS

A 18ct gold Cartier tank wristwatch, the dial having two faces for different time zones, the tonneau-shaped case with two sapphire cabochon crowns, the dial, movement and case signed, boxed.

$5,000-7.000   CHT

A 1960s Dunhill gentleman's silver wristwatch, marked on back 'Swiss Chronometer', with original black leather strap.

$1,700-2,200   BLO

A lady's diamond Jaeger-LeCoultre cocktail watch, the bracelet box set with round brilliant cut diamonds.

$7,000-10,000   L&T

A gold Jaeger-LeCoultre gentleman's 18ct gold wristwatch, 18ct gold, automatic movement, the dial, movement and case signed 'Jaeger-le-Coultre'.

$1,000-1,600   CHT

A Longines gentleman's wristwatch, 9ct gold, the silvered dial with subsidiary seconds dial and Roman numerals.

$300-400   CHT

A Longines gentleman's gold wristwatch, 14ct gold, automatic movement, with subsidiary seconds, the dial, movement and case signed 'Longines'.

$1,000-1,200   CHT

A Longines gentleman's wristwatch, 9ct gold case, the champagne dial with Arabic numerals, baton indices and subsidiary seconds dial, with original guarantee.

$500-700   CHT

An Omega 18ct white gold lady's bracelet watch, diamond set lugs, the square silvered dial with baton markers, cal. 484 seventeen jewel movement, triple signed.

.75in (1.5cm) diam

$1,000-1,400   GHOU

An 1960s Omega gentleman's 18ct gold wristwatch, cal. no. 600, 17 jewels, center seconds with date, brown leather strap, working condition, dial needs clean or replacement.

$700-900   BLO

A 1980s Swiss Omega Seamaster-Cosmic gentlemen's wristwatch, stainless steel, silver clockface.

1.25in (3cm) diam

$500-700   KAU

A Patek Philippe gentleman's 18ct gold wristwatch, signed face, Buren Grand Prix movement, in 18ct gold hallmarked case by Dennison of England, with black strap with 14ct gold buckle, good clean working order.

$1,100-1,300   BLO

A Piaget lady's 18ct gold wristwatch.

$800-1,000   ROS

A gentleman's 14ct yellow gold case wristwatch, by Audemars Piguet, case no. 8765, including an 18ct yellow gold wide mesh flexible bracelet.

$6,000-8,000   FRE

A Rolex 'Oyster Perpetual Explorer' gentleman's stainless steel bracelet watch, reference number '5500', serial number '891137'.

1.25in (3.5cm) diam

$2,800-3,200   GHOU

A Rolex Oyster gentleman's wristwatch, perpetual day-date movement, 18ct yellow gold flexible bracelet.

$10,000-12,000   FRE

A Rolex 'Oyster Perpetual Datejust' stainless steel gentleman's bracelet watch, the silvered dial with baton markers, sweep center seconds and date aperture at 3 o'clock, twenty-seven jewels, reference number '16030', serial number '891137', plain bezel, screw back and conforming bracelet.

1.25in (3.5cm) diam

$1,400-1,800   GHOU

A Tudor Rolex Oyster gentleman's wristwatch, on stainless steel Rolex jubilee bracelet, the dial, movement and case signed.

$300-400   CHT

A Tissot gentleman's wristwatch, in a stainless steel case, the square silvered dial with baton indices, the movement, case and dial signed 'Tissot'.

$160-240   CHT

A Vacheron & Constantin gentleman's 18ct gold wristwatch, the movement, case and dial signed 'Vacheron & Constantin'.

$2,400-3,000   CHT

THE SILVER MARKET

Whether they are buying a mid-19thC tea service or a provincial silver spoon, collectors are becoming far more interested in the history of the silver they are buying. They want to know about the inscriptions, crests and monograms on salvers, mugs, and trophies as well as the social history behind spoons and other wares. This means that pieces with provenance are becoming increasingly desirable.

Of course, quality remains important to buyers, as does condition. It is also noticeable that people are looking for good, clear, tidy hallmarks. As ever, any enamel work must be pristine as restoration to even the slightest damage is virtually impossible.

The market for collectibles such as small boxes, card cases and vinaigrettes continues to grow, with condition becoming more important. The demand for 19thC silver is still quite strong and the recent dearth of good Georgian silver on the market means that when pieces do come up for sale there is a lot of interest.

20thC tea services, trays and salvers are rarely worth more than the bullion price unless they are stylish, Art Deco examples, or of great artisitic merit, in which case they are increasing in value. Pieces by the big names of 20thC design such as Archibald Knox are also doing better than those by less well known names unless, of course, they are particularly stylish.

Its rarity makes a big difference to the value of provincial Scottish silver. Buyers look for the less common hallmarks but are also willing to pay for pieces in good condition. Again, the political and social history behind any piece of Scottish silver will make a difference to its value.

A Dutch silver beaker, by David Reyniers, Dordrecht, engraved below the flared rim with strapwork, fruit clusters and scrolls partly terminating in masks and possibly later engraved with ships below, the base inscribed with the initials 'NMIP', fully marked at the base, 11.25oz (350g).

1614   *7in (17.5cm) high*

$8,000-12,000   **SOTA**

A Dutch silver beaker, by Herman Maetyssen, Deventer, date letter 'L', the body engraved with strapwork and scrolling foliage and a fruit cluster below a phoenix, with the initials 'BA' and 'GK' and two housemarks within a shield, fully marked at the base, 15.8oz (493g).

c1634   *7.5in (19cm) high*

$44,000-52,000   **SOTA**

A Dutch silver beaker, Jan Lubbers Langeweerd, Groningen, engraved with the personifications of Hope, Faith and Charity inscribed on one side with 'LUE', housemark 'AILIENS', the base applied with a corded girdle above cast bands, fully marked below, 5.9oz (183g).

1636-37   *5.25in (13.5cm) high*

$16,000-24,000   **SOTA**

A set of six Victorian silver straight tapering beakers, by William Ker Reid, London, with a molded spreading foot and engraved with armorials, the interiors gilt, 27.5oz (855g).

1848   *4in (10cm) high*

$8,000-10,000   **DN**

A French silver gilt engraved 'Freesia' beaker, by Puiforcat, molded and engraved with bands, on a reeded circular foot, first standard mark, engraved '1928-1978', 7.5oz (237g).

3.5in (9cm) high

$400-600   **DN**

A William IV silver goblet, by Robert Garrard II, London, with a reeded rim, 8oz (254g).

1833   *6.5in (16cm) high*

$1,600-2,000   **DN**

A Victorian silver campana shaped goblet, by William Horton, London, 8.5oz (266g).

$800-1,000   **DN**

A Savage, Lyman & Co. of Montreal embossed and engraved sterling silver presentation goblet, with band of maple leaves, engraved circular monogram and motto, the interior with gold wash, the foot with beaded ring and with stamped maker's marks.

The motto 'Tria Juncta In Uno' and the armorial under the encircled monogram are those of the Order of the Bath. Meaning 'Three Joined In One', the motto refers to the union of England, Scotland and Wales. Created by George I in 1725, it is the fourth highest order of chivalry. This goblet was most probably produced for a Canadian recipient of the honour, or an existing member who moved to Canada.

6.25in (16cm) high

$2,000-3,000   **TCF**

A George II sterling silver tankard, possibly Jason Kingman or John Kentish, London, the domed lid above a bulbous body with scrolling loop handle, the repoussé decoration possibly of a later date, 26oz (737g).

1772   *8.25in (21cm) high*

$3,000-4,000   **FRE**

A late George III sterling silver tankard, of traditional form with a curved spout and bands of ribbed decoration, marks rubbed, possibly stamped 'JE', 25oz (708.5g).

1808   *7in (17.75cm) high*

$800-1,000   **FRE**

A late George III sterling silver tankard, Nicholas Hearnden, London, with a hinged, domed lid, decorated throughout with a ribbed design, 14oz (397g).

1814   *6.75in (17cm) high*

$2,400-3,600   **FRE**

A Victorian silver embossed baluster beer jug, by Martin, Hall & Co., Sheffield, with flowers, foliage and scrolls, a mask spout, a double-scroll handle and a domed cover with a chair-back thumb piece, with a presentation inscription, 24.25oz (755g).

1861   *8in (20.5cm) high*

$1,200-1,600   **DN**

A Victorian sterling silver flagon, Robert Roskell, Allan Roskell & John Mortimer Hunt, London, the lid and rim chased with a band of oak leaves, the spout molded as a satyr mask, the scrolling handle molded with berries, the spreading body decorated with a continuous band of strapwork and rinceaux, the interior silver gilt, 82oz (2324.5g).

1883   *12in (30.5cm) high*

$9,000-11,000   **FRE**

A George II Exeter provincial silver pint mug, maker's mark 'JC' (untraced) and engraved beneath 'DD' over 'JY', the front later engraved with a crest, 12.5oz (389g).

1747   *5in (13cm) high*

$1,400-2,000   **DN**

A George III silver mug, by Thomas Wallis I, London, and later embossed with flowers, leaves, scrolls, rocaille and a cartouche, the foot rim repaired, 10.5oz (330g).

1776   *4.75in (12cm) high*

$600-800   **DN**

A George III mug, by Robert Pinkney and Robert Scott II, Newcastle, with baluster-shaped body and engraved initials, with scrollwork handle, on spreading foot, 12.25oz (347g).

5.25in (13.5cm) high

$900-1,100   **A&G**

A George III provincial silver two-handled pedestal cup, by John Langlands I & John Robertson I, Newcastle, later embossed with flowers, foliate scrolls and rocaille cartouches, 14.75oz (463g).

6.5in (16.5cm) high

$600-800   **DN**

A Victorian silver baluster mug, by George Unite, Birmingham, embossed with an oval reserve and floral swags under a husk band, with a leaf-capped S-scroll handle, on a circular pedestal foot, 10.25oz (319g).

1870   *6.25in (16cm) high*

$400-600   **DN**

METALWARE

A Gorham martelé silver child's cup, 'Morning Glory' pattern, 7 oz (198.5g).

c1899   *3in (7.5cm) high*

$2,400-3,600   **FRE**

A Britannia silver and silver-gilt repoussé cup and cover, George Lambert, London, the knop in the form of a standing nude.

1900   *12in (30.5cm) high*

$2,000-3,000   **FRE**

An English silver miniature trophy, of double-handled cup form with foot, engraved 'The Earl Grey Challenge Cup for Hunt and Military Teams Presented By His Excellency The Governor General 1909', with double curved detail to base of handles, the base stamped with SSH & Co maker's mark and Sheffield hallmarks.

1911   *4in (10cm) high*

$240-360   **TCF**

A silver punch bowl by The Goldsmiths and Silvermiths Co. Ltd, London, the ebonized stand with a silver panel inscribed 'Presented to Lieutenant Colonel W. Anthony, C.M.G. by His Highness The Khan of Kalat in recognition of his valuable services in the promotion of Horse Breeding, 1923-1925', 68.5oz (2136g).

16.5in (42cm) wide

$1,300-1,500   **DN**

A silver vase-shaped trophy cup and cover by Mappin & Webb, Birmingham, in George III Neo-classical style with reeded borders and twin handles, with a cast urn of flowers and husk swag band, the cover with an urn finial, 43.75oz (1366g).

1926   *15in (38cm) high*

$1,200-1,600   **DN**

ESSENTIAL REFERENCE: JEAN BATTEN

Jean Gardner Batten (1909-1982) was one of the most illustrious and glamourous aviatrix heroines of the 1930s, and a national hero in her native New Zealand.

- Born in Rotorua, New Zealand, she was inspired by the pioneering flights of Charles Lindberg and Charles Kingsford Smith.
- Determined to become a pilot, Batten moved to London in 1930 to take flying lessons, qualifying for both her private 'A' license and commercial pilot's license in 1931. That year, Amy Johnson set the record for flying from England to Australia in 20 days, and Batten embarked on a course to beat that record.
- In 1933 Batten made two failed attempts at Johnson's record. She succeeded on her third attempt, flying the 10,500 miles from London to Darwin in 14 days and 22 hours, smashing Johnson's record by 6 days. Her return flight to England made her the first ever pilot to fly the round trip of England-Australia-England.

A silver flying trophy cup and cover by Asprey & Co., Ltd, London, the cover with an orb and eagle finial, on a tapering stem and a round base, on an ebonized socle with an inscribed silver plaque 'Blind Flying Challenge Cup, Presented by Lady Hay Drummond-Hay, President of the Women's International Association of Aeronautics, 1936' and 'Jean Batten, 1937-8', 19oz (593g).

15.5in (39cm) high

$7,000-9,000   **DN**

TEA AND COFFEE WARE

A Queen Anne octagonal teapot and stand, teapot designed by Anthony Nelme, London, the burner and stand designed by John Fawdery, London, armorial-engraved baluster, covered spout with scroll thumb piece, associated crested stand with scroll supports, 27oz (869g).

Teapot 1709, burner and stand 1710
8.75in (22cm) high altogether

$36,000-44,000   **SOTH**

A George III sterling silver teapot on stand, by George Hindmarsh, London, the lid with a floral garland, the oval body with repoussé floral trails surrounding cartouches, above a hinged stand, raised on shell feet, 31oz (879g).

1781   *10.25in (26cm) high*

$3,000-4,000   **FRE**

A Victorian silver baluster teapot, by William Moulson, London, engraved with a variant of the Cellini pattern, the domed cover with a lobed finial, with a loop handle, 21.25oz (660g).

1858   *9in (23cm) long*
$500-700   **DN**

A Victorian silver shaped oval straight-sided teapot, by Robert Harper, London, engraved with foliate scrolls, ovolo borders and a helm crest, the cover with a lobed oval finial, with an ivory loop handle, 11.25oz (352g).

8.75in (22cm) long
$700-900   **DN**

A Victorian sterling silver teapot, probably William Chawner, London, retailed by Munday, 6 Gt. Portland St., with a roundel knop and leaf-cast handle with bone spacers, the body decorated with floral bouquets and foliage, raised on scrolled toes, 27oz (765.5g).

1884   *5.5in (14cm) high*
$800-1,000   **FRE**

A George II silver straight tapering coffee pot, by Peter Archambo I, London, engraved with a crest and armorial, 28.5oz (891g).

1729   *9in (23cm) high*
$8,000-10,000   **DN**

A George II sterling silver coffee pot, by Thomas Heming, London, with acorn knop and treen handle, spout chased with shells, body decorated with floral cartouches, raised on a circular foot, 31oz (879g).

1752   *11.25in (28.5cm) high*
$2,400-3,600   **FRE**

A George II sterling silver coffee pot, by William Cripps, London, of plain baluster form with a pineapple finial, the body centered with an armorial crest, having a woven split reed handle, raised on a circular foot, 16oz (453.5g).

1753   *10in (25.5cm) high*
$2,000-3,000   **FRE**

A George III sterling silver coffee pot, probably Charles Wright, London, the body entwined with foliate trails and acanthus leaves, wooden handle, 30oz (850.5g).

1759   *11in (28cm) high*
$2,000-4,000   **FRE**

A George III sterling silver coffee pot, London, of baluster form centered by an armorial crest and having a leaf cast spout, the lid with an acorn finial, shaped wood handle, raised on a circular foot, marks rubbed, 26oz (737g).

1762   *10in (25.5cm) high*
$2,000-3,000   **FRE**

A George III silver baluster coffee pot, by William Grundy, London, with a double scroll ebonized handle, on a circular foot, engraved with an armorial, 30.5oz (955g).

1770   *10.5in (24.5cm) high*
$2,400-3,600   **DN**

A George II silver straight tapering small coffee pot, the maker's mark indistinct, London, with a shallow domed cover with a bell finial, and an ebonized double scroll handle, 12.5oz (395g).

1773   *6.75in (17cm) high*
$700-900   **DN**

A George III sterling silver coffee pot, by John Denzilow, London, with an urn-form finial and bone handle, beaded spout and circular foot, 29oz (822g).

1784   *12.5in (32cm) high*
$2,400-3,600   **FRE**

A French silver coffee pot, by Francois-Thomas Bernard, Paris, with an acorn knop, the leaf-cast spout with a ram's mask tip, the rosewood handle ending in a female mask, raised on a circular foot cast with leaf-tips, 34oz (964g).

c1838   13in (33cm) high
$3,000-4,000   FRE

A Victorian silver oval and straight tapering coffee pot, by Samuel Smily, London, with an ivory double scroll handle and pineapple finial, inscribed 'B 1902-1927', and stamped beneath 'Goldsmiths Alliance Limited, Cornhill, London', 27.5oz (856g).

9.25in (23.5cm) high
$800-1,000   DN

A late 19thC American silver coffee pot, decorated throughout with Rococo motifs, the rim and foot with a Greek-key border, monogrammed, 35oz (992g).

12cm (30.5cm) high
$2,000-3,000   FRE

An Edwardian, Queen Anne-style sterling silver coffee pot, Goldsmiths & Silversmiths Co., London, of paneled form with a domed lid and finial, the curved spout opposed by an ebony loop handle, 24oz (680g).

1909   11.75in (30cm) high
$600-800   FRE

A George III silver vase-shaped cream jug, by John Bull, London, engraved with leaves, bands and a cartouche, 3.25oz (107g).

1790   5.5in (14.5cm) high
$500-700   DN

A George III Irish silver oval milk jug, by Gustavus Bryne, Dublin, with a shaped and molded rim, a reeded loop handle and fluted sides engraved with floral bands and wreath cartouches, 4.5oz (147g).

1802   4.75in (12cm) high
$360-440   DN

A Victorian silver baluster-shaped hot-water jug, by Edward & John Barnard, London, with a scroll handle and a domed cover with an ivory finial, stamped beneath 'Widdowson & Veale, Strand', 25.5oz (797g).

1866   9.5in (24cm) high
$800-1,000   DN

A Tiffany & Co. sterling silver water jug, the hinged lid with a leafy knop above spout with strainer, the entire body with repoussé foliate and leafy decoration, raised on a circular foot, the underside with an elaborate monogram, 26oz (737g).

c1886   8.25in (21cm) high
$3,000-5,000   FRE

A Victorian silver vase-shaped hot-water jug, by Edward Hutton, London, 18.75oz (584g).

1887   11.75in (30cm) high
$1,000-1,200   DN

ESSENTIAL REFERENCE: JAPONISME

Japonisme – or Japonaiserie – was a decorative style inspired by Japanese designs. The exhibitions of Japanese art and design which followed the recommencement of trade with the West in the 1850s influenced many designers.

- Popular motifs included chrysanthemums, birds and flowers, and stylized branches.
- Metalworkers often produced silverware featuring Japanese motifs or with mixed metal decoration.

An American silver Japanese style pitcher, by Tiffany & Co., with a globular body and a cylindrical neck, hexagonal spot-hammered and applied and engraved with bamboo, a fly caught in a spider's web and a dragonfly, with an angular loop handle, stamped marks and nos. '5066', '1254', 34.75oz (1080g).

8.5in (21.5cm) high
$18,000-22,000   DN

A Dutch cow creamer, with a fly finial, the curling tail forming the handle, .833 standard, 5.5oz (178g).

5.25in (13.5cm) long
$800-1,000   DN

A George IV silver compressed round teapot, by John Houle, London, part-fluted flush-hinged cover on four leaf-chased feet, the body engraved with a crest, with a silver milk jug, the marks worn, with a gadrooned rim and leaf-chased scroll handle and an old Sheffield plate sugar basin, 9.25oz (288g).

1821   *Teapot 6.5in (16.5cm) diam*
$700-900   DN

An American six-piece silver tea service, by Edward Lownes, Philadelphia, including two teapots, a hot water pot, waste bowl, creamer and covered sugar bowl, lid of sugar slightly different, the waste bowl, covered sugar base, one teapot and hot water pot bear maker's mark, some very small dents, no noticeable repairs or re-solders, 178oz (5046g).

c1825
$5,000-7,000   FRE

A William IV silver compressed round and melon fluted three-piece tea service, probably by William Barett II, London, chased with floral panels, the conforming domed cover with a flower finial, with a leaf-capped loop handle, on four flower and shell feet, 47.5oz (1478g).

1831   *Teapot 12.25in (31cm) long*
$1,000-1,200   DN

A Victorian silver four-piece baluster-shaped tea and coffee service, by Joseph & Albert Savory, London, engraved with C-scrolls, foliage and diaper panels, engraved with intials 'F.O.S.', 75.5oz (2358g).

1845-6   *Teapot 10.5in (26.5cm) long*
$2,400-3,600   DN

A four-piece American sterling silver tea/coffee service, comprising a coffee pot, teapot, milk jug and covered sugar bowl, 85oz (2410g).

c1850   *Coffee pot 11.5in (29cm) high*
$2,000-3,000   FRE

An American sterling silver three-piece tea and coffee service, P. B. Sadtler & Son, Baltimore, comprising a coffee pot, a teapot and a sugar bowl, chased and embossed with flowers, foliage and vignettes of castles and bridges, centered by monogrammed cartouches and raised on socle bases, the coffee pot unmarked, 95oz (2693g).

c1850   *Coffee pot 11.75in (30cm) high*
$3,000-4,000   FRE

A French silver cream jug, sugar bowl and a twin-handled bowl and cover, by A. Aucoc, each of baluster form with a central molded girdle, post 1838 1st standards departments mark, 26.75oz (838g) (the jug loaded).

Cream jug 5.25in (13.5cm) high
$500-700   DN

A Victorian sterling silver four-piece tea and coffee service, by James Dixon & Sons, Sheffield, comprising a coffee pot, teapot, sugar bowl and cream jug, each with a gadrooned rim and raised on ball feet, the pots with treen handles and knops, 63oz (1786g).

1866   *Coffee pot 9in (23cm) high*
$2,000-3,000   FRE

A Victorian silver baluster-shaped four-piece tea and coffee service, by Samuel Smily, London, with beaded leaf scroll handles, leaf and scroll-chased borders and feet, scroll cartouches engraved with etoille crests, each marked beneath 'Goldsmiths Alliance Limited, Cornhill, London', 94oz (2922g).

1870   *Coffee pot 11in (28cm) high*
$5,000-7,000   DN

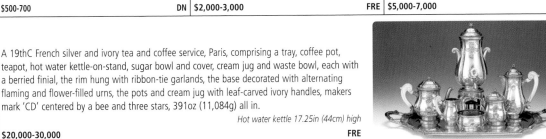

A 19thC French silver and ivory tea and coffee service, Paris, comprising a tray, coffee pot, teapot, hot water kettle-on-stand, sugar bowl and cover, cream jug and waste bowl, each with a berried finial, the rim hung with ribbon-tie garlands, the base decorated with alternating flaming and flower-filled urns, the pots and cream jug with leaf-carved ivory handles, makers mark 'CD' centered by a bee and three stars, 391oz (11,084g) all in.

Hot water kettle 17.25in (44cm) high
$20,000-30,000   FRE

A Victorian four-piece sterling silver tea and coffee service, London, comprising a pyriform coffee pot, a globular teapot, both with bird finials to the covers, an open sugar bowl and a creamer, all with scroll handles and beaded edges, maker's mark 'GB', 71oz (2013g).
1871

$2,000-3,000   **FRE**

A Victorian four-piece tea set, of tapering oval form with straight spouts, chased with foliage around blind oval cartouche and foliate bands, Sheffield and London, 73oz (2270g).

1879, 1880.

$2,400-3,600   **HT**

A late 19thC American Gorham sterling silver five-piece tea and coffee service, comprising a teapot, coffee pot, creamer, covered sugar and waste bowl, with lobed foliate decoration, monogrammed 'M', 95oz (2693g).

Coffee pot 10in (25.5cm) high

$2,400-3,600   **FRE**

A late 19thC Chinese silver eight-piece tea and coffee service, comprising a teapot, coffee pot, tea kettle on stand, lacking handle, covered sugar bowl, creamer, slop bowl, hot water pitcher, sugar tongs and a tray, each of simulated bamboo form with applied bamboo decoration, signed, 182oz (5160g).

Tray 27.5in (70cm) wide

$7,000-9,000   **FRE**

An American Gorham martelé sterling silver after-dinner coffee service, comprising a coffee pot, sugar bowl and cream jug, each of baluster form chased throughout with foliage enclosing cartouches, the coffee pot with bone spacers to handle, marks for 'Wendell G. Arnold, Silversmith', 37oz (1049g).
1898   Coffee pot 12in (30.5cm) high

$9,000-11,000   **FRE**

A late Victorian silver three-piece oblong 'bachelors' tea service, by Charles Stuart Harris, London, each profusely embossed with flowers, leaves, scrolls, diaper and cartouches, on ball feet, the teapot with a composition handle and finial, 25.25oz (786g).
1898   Teapot 8.5in (22cm) long

$500-700   **DN**

An Edwardian silver four-piece tea set, with gadrooned shell-mounted rims and raised on ball feet, 68oz (2114g).
1906, 1907, 1911

$1,400-2,000   **HT**

A silver four-piece circular pedestal tea service, in the Regency style by D. & J. Wellby Ltd, London, each with shell and gadroon shoulders, egg and dart rim and double snake handle, on a reeded circular foot, 87oz (2708g).

1910-11   Teapot 11.25in (28.5cm) long

$2,000-3,000   **DN**

An early 20thC American seven-piece Reed and Barton silver tea and coffee service, comprising a teapot, coffee pot, kettle-on-stand, creamer, covered sugar bowl and a tray, 291oz (8250g).
Tray 27in (68.5cm) wide

$5,000-7,000   **FRE**

A Tiffany & Co. sterling silver tea and coffee service, comprising a teapot, coffee pot, cream jug, covered sugar bowl, waste bowl and two-handled tray, of rectangular form, with canted edges, the teapot and coffee pot with bone rings to handles, 220oz (6237g).
1913   Coffee pot 8.5in (21.5cm) high

$10,000-12,000   **FRE**

A silver four-piece oval tea service, by Mappin & Webb, Birmingham, with pierced borders and scroll handles, each on four leaf and paw feet, engraved with a monogram, the service 54.25oz (1688g).
1915   Teapot 12in (30.5cm) long

$1,200-1,600   **DN**

A 20thC sterling silver tea and coffee service, Elkington & Co., Birmingham, comprising a teapot, coffee pot, hot water kettle-on-stand, covered sugar bowl, waste bowl and cream jug, each of lobed form, the pots all with wooden handles, 170oz (4819.5g).

1920 *Kettle 9.5in (24cm) high*

$3,000-4,000 **FRE**

A 20thC Continental silver tea and coffee service, comprising a coffee pot and teapot with pheasant head spouts, a covered sugar bowl and a creamer, of lobed melon form, the covers with acorn finials, stamped '800'.

Coffee pot 9in (23cm) high

$1,000-1,600 **FRE**

A 20thC Cartier silver-gilt coffee service, comprising a coffee pot with ebony handle, cream jug and covered sugar bowl monogrammed 'S', together with an associated Reed & Barton sterling silver-gilt circular salver, 86oz (2438g).

Coffee pot 12in (30.5cm) high

$3,000-4,000 **FRE**

A silver four-piece canted oblong tea service, by James Deakin & Sons, Sheffield, with shaped handles and foliate scroll feet, 58.5oz (1825g).

1923-24 Teapot 11in (28cm) high

$800-1,200 **DN**

FLATWARE

A George III silver rectangular snuffer stand, the maker's mark worn, London, with a gadrooned border, scroll handle and four hoof feet and engraved with a crest, and with a scratch weight '8=12' beneath, 8oz (252g).

1764 7in (18cm) wide

$700-900 **DN**

A set of four George III sterling silver shell-form dishes, London, each with an armorial crest, raised on shell feet, marks rubbed, 15oz (425g).

1768 4.5in (11.5cm) wide

$1,000-1,400 **FRE**

A late 19thC American set of four Kirk & Sons sterling silver compotes, with chased and embossed decoration, 96oz (2721g).

9.5in (24cm) wide

$7,000-9,000 **FRE**

A pair of sterling silver bonbon dishes, London, each reticulated shell-form dish with a figural handle, raised on dolphin supports, makers mark 'EJG', 22oz (624g).

1908 5.5in (14cm) wide

$2,000-3,000 **FRE**

A set of four silver shaped round compotes, by The Goldsmiths & Silversmiths Co. Ltd, London, each embossed with floral swags on a matt ground, with shell and scroll borders and engraved with a monogram, 73.25oz (2283g).

1908-1913 Largest 11in (28cm) diam.

$3,000-4,000 **DN**

A pair of Tiffany & Co. sterling silver tazzas, each with strawberry-cast border, raised on a circular foot, monogrammed, 29oz (822g).

c1916 8in (20.5cm) diam

$2,000-3,000 **FRE**

A set of four 20thC Continental silver shell-form condiment dishes, J. Piault, in the Rococo style, monogrammed, 47oz (1332g).

7in (18cm) long

$800-1,000 **FRE**

An American sterling silver oval dish, with embossed scrolling and floral pattern and pierced rim, the bowl with engraved 'AB' monogram and the back stamped 'STERLING 925 1988', with '1355' in a diamond.

7in (18cm) wide

$200-300 **TCF**

METALWARE

BASKETS & BOWLS

A George II silver basket, by Paul Lamerie, London, the center armorial engraved, on cast and chased supports, flower garlands between, the oval bat pierced and engraved with scrolls and foliage, the rim interrupted by shells and mounted at each end with putti heads against shells, the swing caryatid handle cast and chased with flowers, engraved with scratchweight '61 = 1/4', 59oz (1856g).

1739   *14in (37.5cm) wide*

$360,000-440,000   **SOTH**

A George III sterling silver pierced basket, by William Plummer, London, the ornate openwork paneled sides with a swing handle and shell-cast rim, raised on a pierced Rococo scroll foot, 38oz (1077g).

1760   *14.5in (37cm) wide*

$4,000-6,000   **FRE**

A Dutch silver sweetmeat basket, by Johannes Schiotling, Amsterdam, the oval body pierced and engraved with geometrical patterns, applied with garlands and ribbon-tied medallions with double portraits, the interior divided into four pieces, fully marked, including 1795 control mark for Rotterdam, 11oz (345g).

1777   *7in (17.5cm) wide*

$16,000-20,000   **SOTA**

A Dutch silver sweetmeat basket, by Johannes Schiotling, Amsterdam, of shaped oval form on four claw-and-ball feet, the sides pierced and engraved with geometrical patterns, with beaded rims, central flowers and foliage beneath, fully marked below, including a 1795 control mark for Gouda, 10.7oz (334g).

1783   *6in (15.5cm) high*

$16,000-20,000   **SOTA**

A Dutch silver basket, by Antonie van Luthervelt, Utrecht, with twig handles at the side, together with a detachable wirework bottle frame, both also struck with a 1795 control mark for Utrecht, fully marked and engraved 'L:A:V:V:', 34.4oz (1070g).

1798   *11.5in (29cm) wide*

$13,000-17,000   **SOTA**

A Regency sterling silver basket, by William Bateman, London, of oblong form with a gadrooned edge and reeded swing handle, the sides with foliate-embossed and chased decoration, 33oz (935g).

1815   *13in (33cm) wide*

$3,000-4,000   **FRE**

A French silver jardinière, the shaped oval body on four supports, the rim openworked and applied with medallions and garlands, with two handles, with original metal liner, 93.8.oz (2660g).

c1880   *19.25in (49cm) wide*

$24,000-30,000   **SOTA**

A silver lobed oval cake basket, by Walker and Hall, Chester, with a beaded and gadrooned inter-woven swing handle and shaped rim, a lobed oval bowl with foliate pierced round panels and engraved with foliate scrolls on a beaded oval foot, 28.5oz (888).

1907   *14in (35.5cm) long*

$1,000-1,200   **DN**

A 20thC sterling silver centerpiece on stand, by Charles & Richard Comyns, London, of oval form with a pierced Vitruvian scroll rim above ribbon-tied medallions, with flanking ram's mask handles raised on foliate-cast feet, the stand with conforming decoration throughout, each monogrammed with a coat of arms, 73oz (2069g).

1925   *15in (38cm) wide*

$4,000-6,000   **FRE**

A Belgian silver brandy bowl, makers mark 'GL', Maaseik, the openworked handles decorated with flowers, marked below, 8.2oz (256g).

c1690   *10.25in (26cm) wide*

$16,000-20,000   **SOTA**

A William III Britannia standard silver monteith, by Anthony Nelme, London, lion mask pendant handles, the body embossed and chased on either side with a cartouche, on armorial engraved on a scalework background, the other engraved with initials 'WH', the collar with shaped mask and scroll border, 57oz (1796g).

1699   *11.5in (29cm) diam*

$54,000-60,000   **SOTH**

A George IV Irish silver round bowl on foot, maker's marks for William Law and possibly William Nelson, Dublin, half reeded, the everted rim with reeded scroll and shells, engraved with a belted crest and motto, 18.5oz (578g).

1820   *8.25in (21cm) diam*

$1,600-4,400   **DN**

A George IV Irish silver wine cooler, probably Edward Twycross, Dublin, with repoussé cartouches surmounted by eagles, the handles chased with shells and foliage, with a later silver-plated liner, 71oz (2013g).

1825   *11in (28cm) high*

$5,000-6,000   **FRE**

A Victorian sterling silver rose bowl, possibly Adams & Foster, London, with a silver-gilt bowl and hung with rose garlands, raised on a circular foot, 49oz (1389g).

1860   *12.5in (32cm) diam*

$4,000-6,000   **FRE**

An American silver footed bowl, with applied cast scallop shell and foliate feet, the bowl with engraved acanthus leaf border, rope-twist rim and applied stylized floral and foliate border to base.

The base is marked with a capital 'S' in a circle, perhaps indicating The Shepard Manufacturing Co. of Massachussetts.

c1860   *5.5in (14cm) high*

$1,600-2,400   **TCF**

A Victorian silver gilt oval bowl London, retailed by Dobson, 32 Piccadilly, the ornate part-fluted and foliate-pierced sides with ram's mask and loop handles and ruby glass liner, raised on a spreading oval foot, 26oz (737g).

1873   *11in (28cm) wide*

$1,600-2,400   **L&T**

A Tiffany & Co. sterling silver porringer, with a pierced foliate handle, decorated throughout with repoussé flora and fauna, 9.1oz (258g).

c1880   *9in (23cm) wide*

$700-900   **FRE**

A 19thC American silver repoussé punch bowl, The Loring Andrews Co., Cincinnati, chased and embossed with foliage, fruit, exotic birds, shells and vignettes of castles, raised on a conforming domed foot, 40oz (1134g).

11.75in (30cm) wide

$6,000-8,000   **FRE**

A Victorian silver Monteith, London, of typical form, the fluted sides with twin scroll handles, chased and embossed with dolphins and foliage, raised on a circular foot, 41oz (1162g).

1885   *12.25in (28.5in) diam*

$5,000-7,000   **L&T**

A pair of late 19thC American Dominick & Haff sterling silver bowls, retailed by J. E. Caldwell & Co., Philadelphia, the lobed bowls with openwork foliate-chased borders, 46oz (1304g).

12in (30.5cm) diam

$1,200-1,600   **FRE**

An American sterling silver foot centerpiece bowl, retailed by Bailey, Banks and Biddle, with an elaborate foliate-pierced rim and lobed basin, raised on a circular foot similarly chased, 92oz (2608g).

7in (18cm) high

$5,000-7,000   **FRE**

A large Victorian sterling silver punch bowl, by Charles Stuart Harris, London, 72oz (2041g).

1893   *5in (38cm) diam*

$3,600-4,400   **FRE**

A late Victorian small silver punch bowl, by Job Frank Hall, London, embossed with acanthus and engraved 'Roseberry from Louisa & Lucy Cohen, May 7 1897', with a glass liner, 10.75oz (335g).

1896   *7.25in (18.5cm) diam*

$400-600   **DN**

A Victorian sterling silver reticulated bowl, London, the shaped openwork sides decorated with exotic birds amongst scrolling foliage, centered by a vacant cartouche, raised on four openwork shell feet, 35oz (992g).
1897   *11.75in (30cm) diam*
$2,000-4,000   **FRE**

A Victorian sterling silver monteith bowl, Birmingham, the pierced undulating rim above a repoussé band of masks, raised on a circular foot, marks rubbed, 53oz (1502g).
1898   *10.5in (26.5cm) diam*
$3,600-4,400   **FRE**

An American Whiting sterling silver bread bowl, in the martelé style, the rim with poppy repoussé decoration, 14oz (397g).

14.5in (37cm) wide
$500-700   **FRE**

An Edwardian sterling silver pierced urn, Chester, of flattened campana form, the gadrooned, rim over a reticulated scrolling band and lobed body , 45oz (1275g).
1907
$3,000-4,000   **FRE**

An early 20thC American sterling silver and silver gilt-plated 'Vitruvian' pattern flower-arranging bowl, retailed by W. W. Wattles & Sons, 61oz (1729g).
15.5in (39.5cm) wide
$1,600-2,400   **FRE**

An American Gorham sterling silver centerpiece bowl, the wide everted rim decorated with C-scrolls and floral garlands, 56oz (1587g).
c1914   *16in (30.5cm) diam*
$1,600-2,400   **FRE**

A pair of Irish George III sterling silver covered vegetable dishes, by William Hamy & J. Scott, Dublin, each of rectangular form with a berried leafy knop, the handles molded as palm fronds, raised on fluted tapered legs ending in claw-and-ball feet, 44oz (1247g).
1810   *9.5in (24cm) wide*
$10,000-14,000   **FRE**

A Regency sterling silver soup tureen and cover, by John Houle, London, of oval form with a gadrooned rim and leaf-cast handles, the cover with a detachable foliate handle, the lobed body raised on four leaf-cast feet with scrolled toes, 144oz (4082g).
1811   *16in (40.5cm) wide*
$12,000-16,000   **FRE**

A George IV silver hot water urn, by Smith, Tate, Hoult & Tate, London, with shell-cast gadrooned rim and collar, the lobed body engraved with a family crest above a spigot, upon a square, gadrooned base and raised on anthemion-cast paw feet, 178oz (5046g).
1820   *16.25in (41cm) high*
$9,000-11,000   **FRE**

An early 19thC French silver-gilt soup tureen, the cover with a leaf-cast acorn finial and etched and chased with anthemion hung with drapery and with a leaf-cast rim, the handles cast with swans, all raised on a circular foot, 88oz (2495g).
16.75in (42.5cm) wide
$10,000-12,000   **FRE**

A pair of Victorian sterling silver covered entrée dishes, by Robert Garrard, London, each of lobed domed form surmounted by a griffin finial and engraved with a coat of arm bearing the motto 'mea Gloria fides', the underplate of conforming shapes with a ribbon tied rim, 103oz (2920g).
1854   *11in (28cm) diam*
$10,000-12,000   **FRE**

A pair of American Samuel Kirk & Sons silver repoussé covered entrée dishes, chased and embossed with scrolling foliage and vignettes of castles, houses, bridges, birds and rowboats, raised on four scroll feet, 94oz (2665g).
c1860 · 13.5in (34cm) wide
$14,000-18,000 · **FRE**

An American sterling silver covered vegetable dish, with removable handle and engraved with a family crest, 46oz (1304g).
13in (33cm) wide
$800-1,000 · **FRE**

A Peruvian silver covered tureen, with a leafy knop and loop handles, raised on claw-and-ball feet, 74oz (2098g).
12.5in (32cm) wide
$800-1,000 · **FRE**

A pair of George III silver sauceboats, probably William Skeen, London, on three shell-and-hoof feet, gadrooned rim, leaf-capped flying scroll handle, 25oz (804g).
1766 · 7.5in (19cm) long
$8,000-10,000 · **SOTH**

A late George II silver sauce boat, by David Mowden, London, with a shaped rim, a flying scroll handle, pad feet and later embossed with flowers and scrolls, 3oz (94g).
1755 · 5.25in (13.5cm) high
$180-240 · **DN**

A pair of George III silver sauceboats, probably by John Arnell, London, each with a leaf-capped flying scroll handle, a repair near one handle, 18.5oz (582g).
1775 · 6.75in (17cm) long
$2,000-3,000 · **DN**

A pair of George III oval pedestal sauceboats, maker's mark rubbed, possibly Charles Fuller, London, with reeded rims, loop handles and on oval bases, engraved with a double crest and a monogram, 16oz (504g).
1814 · 7.25in (18.5cm) long
$1,600-2,400 · **DN**

A pair of Victorian silver oval sauceboats, by Martin, Hall & Co., Sheffield, with shaped rims, leaf-capped flying scroll handles, anthemion and trefid feet and engraved with a crest, 17.75oz (559g).
1898 · 7.5in (19cm) long
$1,200-1,600 · **DN**

SALVERS

A pair of George III silver waiters, by Richard Rugg London, each centered by a coat of arms, within an ornate trellis-pierced and foliate-chased border, raised on three scroll feet, 30oz (850g).
1762 · 7.75in (20cm) diam
$2,400-3,600 · **L&T**

A George III sterling silver salver, by John Parker & Edward Wakelin, London, having a shaped gadrooned border bearing an armorial crest, the reverse inscribed 'No. 83, 18-12', 17oz (482g).
1768 · 9.5in (24cm) diam
$600-800 · **FRE**

A George III silver salver, of plain circular form with beaded border, raised on claw and ball feet, marks for Hester Bateman, London, 31oz (964g).
1782 · 12in (30.5cm) wide
$2,000-3,000 · **HT**

A pair of George III silver waiters, by Robert & Thomas Makepiece, London, of oval form with a molded edge, engraved armorial raised on four scroll feet, engraved crest to underside, 42oz (1191g).
1793 · 10.75in (27.5cm) wide
$4,000-6,000 · **L&T**

A pair of George III oval silver waiters, London, with gadrooned rims and central armorial and crest to edge, raised on conforming scroll feet, makers mark 'WB', 40 oz (1134g).

1799   *11in (28cm) wide*
$3,000-4,000   **L&T**

A George III silver waiter, the center chased with an initial within a scroll and floral festoon border, on bracket feet, marks for Peter and William Bateman, London, 17.5oz (544g).

1805   *10in (25.5cm) wide*
$700-900   **HT**

A pair of George III oval silver waiters, London, with gadrooned rims and conforming scroll feet, makers mark 'J.C.', 44oz (1247g).

1807   *12in (30.5cm) wide*
$5,000-6,000   **L&T**

A George III sterling silver salver, London, bearing armorial crest, makers mark 'BS.IS', 37oz (1049g).

1810   *12.5in (32cm) diam*
$1,200-1,600   **FRE**

An American Gorham sterling silver fish platter, of oval form with a leaf-cast border, the raised ends mounted with figures of jockeys astride hippocamps, 70oz (1984g).

1913   *28in (71cm) long*
$11,000-13,000   **FRE**

A pair of George IV silver waiters, London, of oblong form, with gadrooned rims, raised on four acanthus-cast paw feet, makers mark 'W.B.', 40oz (1134g).

1820   *10.5in (27cm) wide*
$2,000-3,000   **L&T**

A pair of Continental silver gilt circular plaques, profusely embossed with swag, ribbon and bellflower decoration intersected by bust profiles, with ribbon and pole border.

11in (28cm) diam
$500-700   **A&G**

A set of four sterling silver-gilt dishes, Garrard & Co., London, each of scalloped form centered by a coat of arms.

1921   *7.5in (19cm) diam*
$3,000-4,000   **FRE**

A pair of George III silver card trays, London, Storey & Elliot, of shaped circular form with shell and gadrooned cast rim, centered by an engraved armorial crest, raised on three scroll feet, 22oz (624g).

1810   *6.75in (17cm) diam*
$2,000-3,000   **L&T**

A Victorian sterling silver tea tray, by Richard Martin & Ebenezer Hall, Sheffield, with pierced galleried sides and engraved decoration, 174oz (4933g).

1893   *22.75in (58cm) wide*
$12,000-16,000   **FRE**

A silver tea tray, by Hawksworth, Eyre & Co. Sheffield, of oblong form, the shell and scroll-cast rim with twin double scroll handles, 110oz (3118g).

1915   *26.25in (67cm) wide*
$4,000-6,000   **L&T**

A large American Gorham sterling silver tray, of shaped oval form with a reeded border, monogrammed, marked, 84oz (2381g).

1917   *23in (58.5cm) wide*
$2,000-3,000   **FRE**

A 20thC American Gorham sterling silver tea tray, of rectangular form with a scrolling floral cast border and open carrying handles, monogrammed, 108oz (3062g).

28in (71cm) wide

$3,000-4,000 FRE

A silver tray, by Thomas Bradbury & Sons, Sheffield, with a molded border, re-entrant corners and engraved with a presentation inscription, 115oz (3758g).

1935 *26.5in (67cm) long*

$2,000-3,000 DN

A Sheffield silver tray, of oval form, the loop handles molded with stiff leaves, chased with a band of scrolling foliage, 84oz (2612g).

1939. *24.5in (62cm) wide*

$2,400-3,600 HT

A Scottish silver-mounted oak sugar caster, by Ferguson & MacBean of Inverness, marked 'F&M', camel, 'INV's, Edinburgh 1891-92.

Ferguson & MacBean's work often specialized in items of historical revivalism as with the Celtic knotwork here. The silver studs to the knotwork borders, the use of stained hardwood is reminiscent of their high quality dirk handles. From the quality it must be assumed that the wooden body was specially commissioned from a wood carver and mounted in-house.

6.5in (16.5cm) high

$4,000-5,000 L&T

A pair of continental silver pepperettes, each modeled as a partridge, 9oz (255g).

c1910. *4in (10cm) high*

$3,600-4,400 L&T

A set of four late Victorian novelty salts, by Saunders & Shepherd Ltd, modeled as miniature cradles, with marks for Birmingham, and matched spoons, (London), 3.5oz (99g) total.

1896 *2.25in (6cm) long*

$800-1,000 L&T

A pair of Victorian novelty cartridge-form peppers, by Horace Woodward & Co. Ltd, with marks for London 2oz (57g).

1887 *2.5in (6cm) high*

$4,000-5,000 L&T

ESSENTIAL REFERENCE: TRAPRAIN LAW

In 1914 a hoard of more than 150 pieces of native and Roman silver was found at Traprain Law near Edinburgh. It included spoons, bowls and other tableware, some with Christian symbols.

- Four coins were discovered which help to date the find to some point in the 5thC AD. The quality of some of the items suggests that they may have come from as far afield as Rome, Ravenna, or possibly Antioch or Constantinople.
- It may be that the silver represented a payment from the Romans to secure the support of the local Votandini tribe.
- Most of the pieces had been cut up, and one of the few whole objects was a triangular bowl now displayed at the National Museum of Scotland.
- Much of the haul was restored and copies were made under licence and sold to the public.

A pair of silver Traprain salts, with marks for Edinburgh, with incuse marks for 'Brook and Sons, of George Street' and mark of an 'S' in a diamond punch, 3.5oz (99g).

1930, 1934 *3in (7.5cm) wide*

$500-700 L&T

A rare strawberry-form nutmeg grater, Birmingham, by Hilliard and Thomason, the semi-matt-finished naturalistically formed body with hinged opening and pierced hinged steel grille.

1860 *1.5in (4cm) long*

$15,000-17,000 L&T

A Canadian sterling silver stilton scoop, with gilt washed interior and barley-twist handle, stamped 'STERLING 3' and with a flower motif, together with original fitted box marked 'G. Seifert QUEBEC'.

8.75in (22cm) long CAD

$400-600 TCF

A set of Birks sterling silver bright cut flatware.

This hand-engraved pattern was introduced in 1894. Standard knives would have had mother-of-pearl or ivory handles, so a fish knife has been added.

Large spoon 8.75in (22cm) high

$80-120 TCF

METALWARE

A Charles II trefid spoon, by William Law of Edinburgh, makers mark of 'WL' conjoined with crown above and pellet below, the trefid end with engraved initials 'AG / SB' to reverse of terminal, the slightly tapering stem with shaped stylized foliage terminal to bowl with long rat tail to center, 1.7oz (52.9g).

William Law first appears within the Edinburgh Goldsmiths records on 14th March 1662 where he is commanded to make as his assay 'ane silver coupe with ane cover graven and ane voupe in Robert Lawis shop', his overseers were Edward Cleghorne, Alexander Scott and Alexander Reid. He is then admitted as a master and freeman of the trade on 14th June 1662. Law's mark is also encountered as a Deacons mark as he was elected Deacon from 1667.

7.75in (20cm) long

$6,000-8,000 L&T

A rare Scottish provincial apple corer, by Joseph Pearson of Dumfries, with long hemispherical scoop with simple reeded socket mount to a turned stained wood handle, makers mark 'IP' only.

This is the only recorded example of a Scottish provincial apple corer, while it is a standard form for an English example. The placement of the marks and original provenance strongly suggest a local manufacture to Dumfries and therefore Joseph Pearson.

c1800   6in (15.5cm) long

$1,000-1,200 L&T

OTHER SILVERWARE

A sterling silver tea caddy, London, retailed by Goldsmiths & Silversmiths Co., of canted square form with a cylindrical cover and ball knop, 8oz (227g).

1937   5in (12.5cm) high

$500-700 FRE

A sterling silver caddy, London, retailed by Munsey & Co., Ltd, Cambridge, of paneled octagonal form with a wooden knop and beaded decoration to the rim and base, makers mark 'CE', 19oz (539g).

1913   5.25in (13.5cm) high

$1,000-1,200 FRE

A Scottish gilt table snuff box, by Peter Ross of Aberdeen, marked 'PR', struck twice, 5.2oz (147g).

This box imitates but falls short of the high quality examples being produced in Birmingham by makers such as Nathaniel Mills.

c1820   3.25in (8.5cm) wide

$1,600-2,400 L&T

ESSENTIAL REFERENCE: CASTLE TOPS

Embossed or engraved silver card cases, snuff boxes or vinaigrettes decorated with views of famous landmarks such as castles and historic houses are known as 'castle tops'.

- They were made from the 1830s, many as souvenirs for wealthy tourists. Early examples feature a scene on both sides of the box, later ones usually have a scene on one side only.
- One of the most renowned makers was Nathaniel Mills, who was based in Birmingham.
- The quality of Mills' work is such that the relief decoration can stand up to 0.25in (1cm) away from the surface of the box.
- Landmarks featured include Windsor Castle and Westminster Abbey. The more unusual or famous the subject, the greater the value of the box is likely to be.
- Other decoration may include chasing with flowers, leaves and C-scrolls.

An early Victorian 18ct gold snuff box, by Nathaniel Mills, Birmingham, the lid chased with Warwick Castle, with an inscription, dated 1839, to the Right Honourable George Guy, Lord Brooke.

2.75in (7cm) wide

$9,000-11,000 L&T

A Victorian silver table snuff box, by William Elliott, London, of rectangular form, the hinged lid chased and embossed with a hunting scene depicting hounds attacking a wild boar within an oak leaf and acorn border, the sides and base with engine-turned decoration, 11oz (312g).

1849   4.25in (11cm) wide

$1,600-2,400 L&T

A 19thC probably Swedish silver snuff box, gilt to the interior.

3in (7.5cm) wide

$100-160 FRE

A late 19thC Continental, probably Dutch, silver marriage box, decorated throughout with reserves of floral garlands and marked at the corners with figures within porticos, 16oz (454g).

5.5in (14cm) wide

$1,600-2,400 FRE

A 19thC Northern European silver snuff box, marked '0.800', the rectangular box enameled to the lid to show a white horse.

3in (7.5cm) wide

$300-400   FRE

A late 19thC Continental silver oval patch box, apparently unmarked, the hinged cover engraved with dancing figures amidst Renaissance motifs.

3.25in (8.5cm) wide

$700-900   L&T

A Continental silver oval box, import marked for Chester 1911, embossed with Arcadian lovers, the sides with martial trophies and foliage, 3oz (94g).

4in (10cm) wide

$200-300   DN

A sterling silver jewel box, London, the hinged top with wavy etched decoration opening to a velvet line interior raised on bun feet, makers mark 'CD'.

1922   *6in (15cm) wide*

$600-800   FRE

A George III silver inkstand, London, of boat shape form, with a bead-molded rim, surmounted by three cut glass bottles and raised on pierced, bladed bracket feet, makers mark 'W.P.', 28oz (794g).

1784   *11in (28cm) wide*

$1,600-2,400   L&T

A Victorian silver desk stand, by Joseph & John Angell, London, with two pen recesses, on four acanthus feet, and with a central round sand box with a shaped-round taperstick cover flanked by two silver mounted cut glass ink wells, 17.25oz (538g).

1840   *9.75in (25cm) wide*

$1,000-1,600   DN

A Edwardian sterling silver and cut glass standish, by George Jackson and Edward Fullerton, London, with an elaborately pierced three-quarter gallery incorporating a letter stand, the whole edged with shell-work and centered by two cut glass ink pots with silver lids and collars and a pen tray, raised on claw-and-ball feet, 21oz (595g).

1909   *10in (25.5cm) wide*

$2,400-3,600   FRE

A Georgian style silver desk inkstand, by Millar and Wilkinson London, of rectangular form with shaped rounded ends, beaded edge, bright cut and pierced fern leaf pattern sides, two Bristol blue glass inkwells and central frame for a chamberstick, lacking, and replaced by a continental box and cover, the whole on claw-and-ball feet, 20oz (567g).

1911   *10in (25cm) wide*

$1,400-2,000   L&T

A sterling silver standish, by D. & J. Welby, London, of rectangular form with bail handles to the sides, the compartmentalized hinged top opening to reveal an ebonized wood pen rest, glass inkwells and sandpot, raised on bracket feet.

1925   *9.75in (25cm) wide*

$3,000-4,000   FRE

A pair of Britannia standard silver picture frames, London, with shell and foliate scroll-chased and embossed decoration.

7.75in (20cm) wide

$2,000-3,000   L&T

A pair of Britannia standard silver photograph frame, London, of upright form. oval to center, the ground with raised rose detail and splay feet, maker's mark 'M&LS'.

6.5in (16.5cm) wide

$1,200-1,800   L&T

METALWARE

A Victorian silver-mounted dressing table mirror, by William Comyns & Sons Ltd, London, the openwork border centered with a grotesque mask with urns, fruit, mermaids and putti amidst scrolling foliage and a vacant reserve below, with a beveled plate, the easel back covered with fabric.

16in (41cm) high

$2,400-3,600   DN

A George III silver table bell, London, possibly John Reily, well-turned baluster handle, the bell with threaded detail and gadrooned edge.

1817   4.5in (11.5cm) high

$2,400-3,600   L&T

A silver table bell, London, of traditional form, ivory baluster handle.

1933

$800-1,200   L&T

A French silver and cut glass jam pot, Ambroise Mignerot, Paris, the cover with a plumed knop above a cut glass insert, the body with griffin-form handles, decorated with a band of flower maidens alternating with vines, 20oz (623g).

11in (28cm) high

$2,000-3,000   FRE

A silver round tapered vase, maker's mark worn, Sheffield, with twin lion mask hinged handles and a shaped rim, 24.75oz (769g).

1911   11.75in (29.5cm) high

$800-1,000   DN

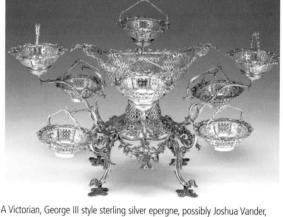

A Victorian, George III style sterling silver epergne, possibly Joshua Vander, London, after a design by Thomas Pitts, on four openwork cartouche feet, the foliate-chased swag aprons surmounted by a pierced shaped oval basket with a scroll and leaf-cast rim, from which emanate eight outscrolling branches, four supporting pierced baskets, the remaining four hanging, 165oz (4678g).

1890   26in (61cm) high

$36,000-44,000   FRE

A mid-18thC and later assembled English silver and cut glass cruet set, comprising a stand, marks for 'Sam Wood, London, 1751', one larger and two smaller casters, marks for 'Davis Thompson, London 1751', two stoppered bottles with silver collars, marks for 'Birmingham, 1881', 35oz (992g).

8in (20.5cm) high

$1,600-2,400   FRE

A six-piece silver condiment set, Sheffield, Walker and Hall, with leaf-clasped legs and paw feet, comprising four circular salts and a pair of lidded mustard posts, with liners and associated spoons, 58oz (1644g).

$2,400-3,600   L&T

A set of six late George III silver parcel-gilt egg cups, by William Eaton, London, each with molded girdle and a round foot with an egg and dart border, each engraved with a crest, 14.75oz (463g).

2.75in (7cm) high

$1,200-1,600   DN

A pair of Elizabeth II silver gilt wine coasters, by Roberts & Belk, Sheffield, profusely embossed with vine, shells and flowers.

1972   6in (15cm) diam

$800-1,000   A&G

A George III silver wine funnel, by Peter & Anne Bateman, London, 2.5oz (81g).

1796   4.25in (11cm) high

$600-800   DN

A pair of mid-20thC French silver wine caddies, each of woven basket form with twist handles, the first example marked 'Christofle', the other marked 'Boulenger', 22oz (624g).

Longer 11in (28cm) long

$300-400   **FRE**

A silver shaving mug and brush, by Levi & Salaman, Birmingham, the mug with a hinged cover, broad scroll handle and gilt interior, the brush of inverted baluster form.

1902   *The mug*
4.75in (12cm) high

$800-1,000   **DN**

A set of three George III 'Ships Decanters' labels, by George Fenwick, Edinburgh, with integral suspension loops, suspended by belcher link chains, inscribed for 'PORT', 'SHERRY' and 'CLARET', 0.75oz (23.7g).

1806-7   *3.75in (9.5cm) wide*

$2,400-3,000   **L&T**

A Scottish provincial spirit label, by William Constable, Dundee, with reeded border, incised 'BRITISH WINE', suspended from a belcher link chain, marked Edinburgh 1817-1818, 'WC', duty head, 0.3oz (10g).

1817-18   *1.5in (4cm) wide*

$600-800   **L&T**

A pair of Scottish provincial spirit labels, by Alexander Cameron of Dundee, inside 'SHERRY', suspended from integral suspension loops by a belcher link chain, marked 'C', thistle, pot of lilies, 'AC', thistle, 0.3oz (9g).

c1825   *1.75in (4.5cm) wide*

$1,200-1,600 PAIR   **L&T**

A Scottish provincial spirit label, by John Blair of Dundee, incised for 'MADEIRA', suspended from a belcher link chain, marked thistle, pot of lilies, 'JB', thistle, pot of lilies, 0.3oz (10g).

c1830   *1.75in (4.5cm) wide*

$1,200-1,600   **L&T**

A Scottish provincial caddy spoon, by 'WL', possibly William Leighton, Dundee, pot of lilies struck twice, of Fiddle pattern with large fluted shell bowl, marked 'WL', 0.4oz (12g).

3.75in (9.5cm) long

$1,200-1,600   **L&T**

A Scottish provincial caddy spoon, Dundee, pot of lilies struck thrice, of Old English pattern with deep scoop shell bowl, marked 'D', 0.4oz (12g).

3.25in (8.5cm) long

$800-1,000   **L&T**

A Scottish provincial caddy spoon, by Alexander Cameron, Dundee, of Fiddle pattern, with scoop shell bowl, marked 'AC', 'C', thistle, pot of lilies, 0.4oz (11g).

3.75in (9.5cm) long

$1,000-1,200   **L&T**

METALWARE

A George III Scottish provincial shoe buckle, by James Wildgoose, Aberdeen, with simple reeded design, the clasp and tongue of shaped semi-circular design with arrow head terminals, marked 'IW', 0.2oz (6g).

c1770   1.75in (4.5cm) wide
$400-600   **L&T**

A pair of Scottish provincial shoe buckles, by William Scott, Dundee, the borders with diamond spacers, the inner and outer borders both with beaded details, with shaped steel tongues, marked 'WS', pot of lilies, total weight 3.9oz (121g).

c1780   3.25in (8cm) wide
$1,200-1,600   **L&T**

A pair of George III shoe buckles, by Robert Gray, Glasgow, Edinburgh, with flower-head-, scroll- and leaf-chased details, with shaped steel tongues, date letter lacking to both.

c1790   2.75in (7cm) wide
$1,600-2,400   **L&T**

A Scottish belt buckle, attributed to Alexander Ritchie, Iona, formed as vine leaf and branch form, marked 'CS*FS', Chester, Rg. No. 391329, 3.7 oz (105g).

1905-1906,   5.5in (14cm) wide
$600-800   **L&T**

A cased set of six Victorian menu holders, probably by William Hutton, each in the form of a woodcock or a grouse upon a turned silver gilt base.

1906   1.5in (4cm) high
$2,400-3,600   **LAW**

A set of six Edwardian place card holders, with polychrome enamel decoration to the front, depicting game birds and a fox, with marks for Chester, 9.5oz (269g).

1903   1.5in (3.5cm) high
$7,000-9,000   **L&T**

A pair of Victorian menu stands, by L. Emmanuel, each of easel back form, modeled as a fox running past a gate, with marks for Birmingham, 1.5oz (42g).

1895   2in (5.5cm) high
$2,000-3,000   **L&T**

A late Victorian novelty vesta case, London, maker's mark 'J.B.A.B.', of plain form, designed as a shoe, with hinged cover and suspension ring.

1878   2.75in (7cm) long
$2,400-3,600   **L&T**

An Edwardian vesta case, maker Samson Morden & Co., Chester, the flat hinged cover inscribed 'HIS MASTER'S VOICE', above the associated cast motif, additionally inscribed to the under of cover 'WITH THE COMPLIMENTS OF THE GRAMOPHONE CO LTD'.

1907   1.75in (4.5cm) wide
$2,000-3,000   **L&T**

A late Victorian novelty vesta case, maker probably G. Loveridge & Co., Birmingham, designed as a footballer's leg and a ball, initialed in script, also inscribed 'C. & M. PATENT'.

1884   2.25in (5.5cm) long
$3,000-4,000   **L&T**

A Victorian tobacco pipe case, by M. C. &Co., Edinburgh, the case in the form of the pipe, with pull-off stem held in place by steel pricker, the hinged 'bowl' section with pinned clasp, engraved with conjoined gothic initials 'CBF', with pipe, 1.5oz (46.7g).
This maker's mark unrecorded in the records of the Edinburgh Assay Office.

                      5in (13cm) long
$1,400-1,800   **L&T**

A Victorian patent silver cigar tool, by Jane Brownett and Alexander Jones, London, with a fold-out steel blade and piercer and a hinged flap to enable it to be used as a rest, engraved with an Earl's coronet and cypher, and stamped with a registration lozenge.

1880   2in (5cm) long
$500-700   **WW**

A souvenir thimble, 'GREAT YARMOUTH', by Henry Griffith and Son, Birmingham.

1930
$100-140   **WW**

A German silver-colored metal circular sugar bowl, pierced with buds and foliage, with an undulating floral C-scroll rim, on three scroll feet, with a shaped clear glass liner, 12.5oz (390g).

6in (15cm) diam

$300-400   DN

A Chinese silver-colored metal bowl, embossed with dragons and characters on a matted ground between stiff leaf borders, unmarked, 14oz (441g).

6.5in (16.5cm) diam

$360-440   DN

A set of six Far Eastern silver-colored metal dishes, with flower-embossed paneled borders, stamped '800' and 'K.S.', 22.25oz (696g).

4.5in (11.5cm) diam

$300-400   DN

A late 19thC Continental Renaissance Revival silver-colored pilgrim flask wine flagon, embossed to one side with a central princely figure in late 17thC costume with warriors and arms at the cardinal points on a scrolled ground, and a pseudo crest to the other side, the lid embossed with a grotesque mask, 45oz (1285g).

15.25in (38.5cm) high

$3,000-4,000   DN

An Anglo-Indian silver-colored metal wine bottle cover, pierced with birds and animals amidst foliage and with similarly engraved cartouches, with a bottle-top hung from chains and a removable base, 17.25oz (541g).

12in (30.5cm) high

$500-700   DN

An early 20thC Chinese silver-colored metal cocktail shaker by Hing Ching, straight-tapered and chased with flower sprays on a hammered ground, 15.75oz (493g).

9in (23cm) high

$900-1,100   DN

A Spanish, silver-colored metal desk stand, Madrid, with a bell topped box, two with swan finials to the covers and another with a parrot, the rectangular base with bowed ends and a pierced gallery, assayer's or maker's mark 'N CHANEROI', the bell lacking the clapper, 27.75oz (865g).

1822-23   *9in (23cm) long*

$3,600-4,400   DN

A set of twelve late 19thC Chinese small silver-colored metal wine cups, each applied with a dragon, makers mark 'WA' not traced, 9.25oz (288g).

c1900

$500-700   DN

An Irish silver-colored metal hour glass, maker's marks of Edward Twycross and Edward Power of Dublin (maker's marks only), with three shaped supports, the cover with initials 'EC' and the base with a crest, 1.25oz (43g).

3in (7.5cm) high

$1,100-1,300   DN

A white metal mounted novelty scent bottle, modeled as a fish with shagreen body and hinged head with stone set eyes, containing a glass scent bottle.

14in (35.5cm) long

$4,000-5,000   L&T

An Edwardian silver napkin ring, with a polychrome-enameled dolphin boss, by an unascribed maker, 'DG', Birmingham.

1905

$200-300   WW

An early 20thC Continental silver scent bottle case, modeled as a fish, with naturalistic imbrication, the hinged head inset with red glass eyes, import marks for London.

c.1900   *3in (8cm) wide*

$300-360   ROW

A novelty Victorian smoker's companion in the form of a pig, her curly tail a removable smoker's tool, standing by a 'trough' for matches, upon a painted wood base, by JB, possibly John Brumfit.

1885   *3in (8cm) wide*

$400-600   LAW

A silver bulldog, by Berthold Muller, standing solidly and with a removable head.

1910   *5.5in (13.5cm) long*

$2,000-3,000   L&T

METALWARE

SILVER PLATE

A silver-plated circular-pedestal large punch bowl, embossed with fruiting vine on a matted ground, with a conforming pierced band and a cable rim.

16.5in (42cm) diam.

$1,200-1,600   **DN**

A French plated round tureen on foot and cover, by Christofle, with twin bifurcated leafy handles, the domed cover with a bead outlined finial.

13.75in (35cm) wide

$300-400   **DN**

A pair of 19thC plated two-handled pedestal wine coolers, of lobed form with C-scroll handles and scroll outlined rims, each engraved with an armorial.

14.5in (36.5cm) high

$1,600-2,400   **DN**

A Sheffield plate hot water-heated covered roast server, of typical form with floral cast handles and egg and dart border, on outscrolling feet.

12in (30.5cm) high

$1,200-1,600   FRE

An early 20thC silver-plated revolving supper set, with four Bakelite turned handles, with covered tureen, four entrée dishes, four blue-glass-lined salts and four Georgian-style casters.

21.5in (54.5cm) high

$1,600-2,400   FRE

An American silver plate centerpiece, possibly by The Meriden Britannia Co., the center column surmounted by a lobed dish and four arms with lobed dishes, supported on four columnar supports, further raised on a base mounted with the figures of Neptune, Galatea and sea creatures, bears a presentation plaque from the government of Bolivia.

40in (101.5cm) high

$16,000-24,000   **FRE**

A late 19th/early 20thC silver-plated metal and ebonized wood mounted mechanical wine pourer, with Archimedes screw mechanism.

11.5in (29cm) high

$500-700   **DN**

A mid-20thC French silver plate mint julep serving set, comprising six cups and an undertray, each with applied hunting motif.

Tray 13in (33cm) wide

$600-800   **FRE**

A set of twelve small pattens by Christofle, of threaded serpentine form engraved initials 'A T' to center.

6in (15cm) diam

$500-700   **L&T**

A pair of Regency 'tôle-peinte' chestnut urns, the black grounds decorated in gilt with scrolling foliage and insects, with peaked lid and lion's mask and loop handles, raised on a socle foot.

11.75in (30cm) high

$3,600-5,000 **L&T**

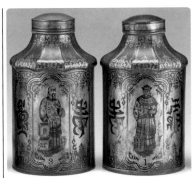

A pair of painted metal cover urns, of Classical urn form, the domed covers surmounted by an acorn finial, finely painted with gilt leaf wreathes to the cover, a village scene to the urn, with free-hanging ring handles to the shoulder supported by a lion mask, over circular bases.

c1830 *12in (30.5cm) high*

$3,600-4,400 **FRE**

A pair of early 19thC Regency tôle tea canisters, of cylindrical form with sectioned tapered covers, the central panel decorated with Chinese figures and characters on a gold field against a red painted ground.

18.75in (48cm) high

$2,400-3,600 **FRE**

A pair of 19thC tôle painted canisters, numbered '1' and '4', on a green ground, converted to lamps.

12.5in (32cm) high excluding fittings

$500-700 PAIR **FRE**

A late 19thC Victorian japanned, parcel gilt and mother-of-pearl-inset tin tea canister, of cylindrical form, decorated with figures in a boat before a church.

c1890 *18in (45.5cm) high*

$900-1,100 **DN**

A pair of Regency tôle painted bird cages, of pagoda form, the ornate stepped fluted tops with pineapple finials, over open wirework cylindrical sides.

51in (130cm) high

$16,000-24,000 **L&T**

A 19thC American Pennsylvania red tôle coffee pot, with yellow and ivory floral decoration and goose neck spout, from the Shelley Collection.

10in (25.5cm) high

$24,000-30,000 **POOK**

A 19thC American New York black tôle document box, possibly by Butler, with bird and floral decoration, from the Shelley Collection.

9.25in (23.5cm) wide

$16,000-24,000 **POOK**

METALWARE

A rare American pewter lidded pitcher, attributed to Johann Phillip Alberti, Philiadelphia, (1754-80), with heart shaped spout, the body with double C-scroll handle, inscribed 'MM Georg Leonart Muller 1763', from the Shelley Collection.

Muller appears to have lived in Lebanon and was a member of Hill Evangelical Lutheran Church.

7.75in (19.5cm) high
$36,000-44,000 **POOK**

A rare American pewter flagon, attributed to Johann Phillip Alberti, Philadelphia, (1754-80), with a ball-shaped thumb piece, a lid with heart-shaped spout and body with double C-scroll handle and inscription 'Georg-Kichen 1763', from the Shelley Collection.

15in (38cm) high
$50,000-60,000 **POOK**

An American pewter pint mug, attributed to Robert Bonnynge, Boston, with solid molded S-scroll handle and moon-face terminal, likely owner's initials 'AF' impressed on handle top.
1731-63
4.5in (11.5cm) high
$14,000-20,000 **SK**

An American Queen Anne pewter teapot, attributed to Johann Phillip Alberti, Philadelphia, (1754-80), with bright-cut chased vines and floral and bird decoration, from the Shelley Collection.
6.25in (16cm) high
$36,000-44,000 **POOK**

A mid-to late 18thC American pewter chalice, attributed to Johann Christoph Heyne, Lancaster, Pennsylvania (1752-81), from the Shelley Collection.
8.75in (22cm) high
$30,000-40,000 **POOK**

A set of five American graduated pewter measures, New York City (1770-1800), together with a gallon-size measure, New York City (1760-80), impressed with an 'A' on the rim, from the Shelley Collection.
Tallest 13in (33cm) high
$14,000-20,000 **POOK**

A late 18th/early 19thC American pewter chalice, attributed to William Will, Philadelphia, (1764-98), from the Shelley Collection.
7.75in (19.5cm) high
$7,000-9,000 **POOK**

BRASS

A German brass covered flagon in Gothic style, the gourd-shaped body supported by a trumpet-base inscribed 'Gewidmet von Lehrer kolleg. Misburg. 1904', tall incurved neck, applied with dragon spout and dragon handle, golden patina.
16in (41cm) high
$3,000-4,000 **SOTA**

A Victorian brass fish tank, the castellated top above glazed panel sides, flanked and divided by cluster columns, on a plinth base.
21.75in (55cm) wide
$1,600-2,400 **L&T**

A pair of rare 18thC brass Indian palace guards, modeled as a pair of archaic tigers standing on hind legs, set with red glass eyes, inscribed stripes to body.
7.5in (19cm) high
$1,000-1,600 **FRE**

An early 19thC European brass traveling lamp, the hinged door with a beaded top edge to a central holder and two apertures, an embossed star back and oval chimney, the back with a folding stand.

5.5in (14cm) high

$240-360 WW

A brass alms dish, with embossed decoration, the center with Samson and the lion and a text border 'Vis Vitae Transeat In Exemplum', the reverse with a later hook.

14.25in (36cm) diam.

$400-600 WW

A late 19thC brass fireman's helmet, from the Merral's Mill Fire Brigade, Haworth, the high comb embossed with acorns and oak leaves, pierced and molded badge, leather and brass chain chin strap.

The Merral's Mill Fire Brigade was disbanded in 1898.

10in (25.5cm) high

$1,200-1,600 HT

COPPER

A Victorian copper triple-tier mold, stamped 'PC' for Powys Castle.

8.25in (21cm) high

$400-600 HALL

A 19thC copper boiler of oval form having twin loop ring handles on a molded base.

24in (61cm) diam.

$1,200-1,600 LOC

A Victorian copper wall-mounting jardinière, with balloon back decorated with crown and twin-headed spread bird above cylindrical pan.

$240-360 LOC

A Dutch copper log bin, embossed 'A.M. 1684'.

20.75in (53cm) high

$800-1,200 DN

A Victorian copper and brass tea urn of typical form.

21.75in (55cm) high

$200-300 ROS

OTHER METALWARES

A late 18thC American tin wrigglework coffee pot, by Willoughby Shade, Tulpehocken, Pennsylvania, the body elaborately decorated with birds, flowers, etc., inscribed 'Hannah Reinert' and stamped on the handle 'W. Shade', from the Shelley Collection.

10.5in (26.5cm) high

$12,000-16,000 POOK

A set of rare 18thC lock picks, twelve adjustable iron key arms lead from a single iron rod, leather case.

$500-700 FRE

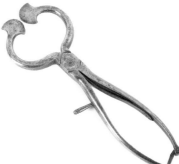

A pair of late George III polished steel sugar cutters.

9.5in (23.5cm) long

$300-400 WW

THE GLASS MARKET

Anyone who has broken a wine glass will appreciate the rarity of an early drinking glass and wonder how something so fragile can survive so long. It is perhaps not surprising then that glasses from the 18th century, especially heavy balustroids and wine glasses with intricate air twist stems, continue to find buyers willing to pay for their longevity and beauty.

Collectors continue to look for pieces which required a high level of craftsmanship in their manufacture. Introducing and manipulating air, color and mercury twists within fragile stems, crafting knops and balusters, and drawing out bowls and feet all required a level of skill which meant these pieces were made in relatively small numbers and sold as luxury items in their day and they remain desirable and valuable pieces today.

On all glass, any damage should be avoided as it will almost always lower value considerably. Repairs are costly. It is always better to buy from a reputable source who can give you a detailed receipt detailing what you have bought.

Also in demand are rummers (a type of goblet) and early 19th century decanters. Decanters should have their original stopper; check that the design and decoration fit with that of the decanter itself and that the stopper fits the neck properly. Many decanters and stoppers are numbered. The value of a decanter lacking its original stopper will be around half one that retains its original stopper.

Early 19th century colored glass represents particularly good value for money at the moment, especially Bristol green and blue examples.

While the past year has not seen any landmark sales of pre-20th century glass, high prices continue be paid for mid 19th century paperweights by Baccarat, St Louis and others, and original enamelled 'Mary Gregory' glasses. By comparison, 18th century Continental glass is underrated and good value.

Mid to late 19th century Bohemain glass is another area that continues to do well. Again, buyers are looking for pieces in excellent condition and which show exceptional craftsmanship in every area of design and creation: from the blowing and casing of the glass (encasing a layer of clear glass with a layer of colored) to the level of detail in the cutting and finishing of the decoration. Running a thumb over the surface of the glass will show how deep the cutting is; the deeper and finer the better the quality of the piece is likely to be. Any engraving should add fine detail to the subject matter and create a sense of realism.

The fact that much early glass was handmade means no two pieces will be exactly the same. This adds a charm to a pair or set of similar pieces which will not be seen in more recent mass produced items.

As well as age, value for money has a part to play in the desirability of antique glass – many examples are more affordable than a modern copy despite their age.

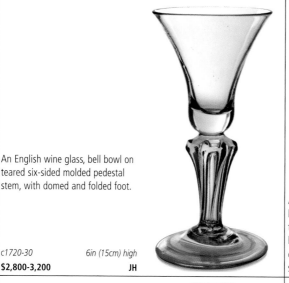

An English wine glass, bell bowl on teared six-sided molded pedestal stem, with domed and folded foot.

c1720-30   6in (15cm) high
$2,800-3,200   **JH**

An English baluster wine glass, bell bowl, triple annulated knop over teared inverted baluster and base knops, folded foot.

c1720-30   6in (15cm) high
$1,500-1,700   **JH**

An English light baluster wine glass, round funnel bowl over angular ball and inverted baluster knops, domed foot.

c1730-40   6.75in (17cm) high
$2,000-2,500   **JH**

An unusual English bucket bowl balustroid wine glass, teared triple-knop stem, folded foot.

c1730-40   5.75in (14.5cm) high
$800-1,000   **JH**

An English wine glass, drawn trumpet bowl, plain stem, on high conical folded foot.

c1730   6in (15cm) high
$280-320   **JH**

An English wine glass, round funnel bowl engraved with a flower and bird in flight, plain stem, folded foot.

c1730-40   *6in (15cm) high*

$280-320   **JH**

An English composite stem wine glass, drawn trumpet bowl with plain stem section over knopped multi-spiral air twist stem.

c1740-50   *7in (17.5cm) high*

$1,300-1,500   **JH**

An English wine glass, waisted bucket bowl on double series air twist stem with mercury corkscrew tape surrounded by four-ply band.

c1745-50   *6.25in (15.5cm) high*

$1,300-1,500   **JH**

An English wine glass, round funnel bowl engraved with a fruiting vine, on air twist stem with two mercury spirals.

c1745-50   *6in (15cm) high*

$800-1,000   **JH**

An opaque twist wine glass, the flute-molded ogee bowl supported on a double series stem and conical foot.

c1770   *5.25in (13cm) high*

$700-900   **DN**

A mixed twist stem wine glass, round funnel bowl, central air twist stem, the gauze surrounded by two opposing white tapes.

c1760   *6in (15cm) high*

$1,100-1,300   **JH**

An English wine glass, lipped ogee bowl, on multi-spiral opaque twist stem with central swelling knop.

c1760   *5.75in (14.5cm) high*

$900-1,100   **JH**

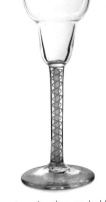

A pan-top wine glass, on double series opaque twist stem, with central gauze surrounded by two tapes.

c1765   *6in (15cm) high*

$900-1,100   **JH**

An opaque twist wine glass, the ogee bowl supported on a double series stem and conical foot.

c1770   *5.25in (13cm) high*

$500-700   **DN**

An ovoid bowl wine glass, engraved with a hunting scene and a castle, on hexagonal facet-cut stem.

c1765   *5in (12.5cm) high*

$1,200-1,400   **JH**

A pair of late 18thC facet-stemmed short wine glasses, bowls engraved and polished, stems cut with diamond facets, on conical feet.

c1790

$800-1,000   **DN**

A wine glass, on hexagonal facet-cut stem.

c1775   *5.75in (14.5cm) high*

$220-260   **JH**

GLASS

An English ale glass, drawn trumpet bowl engraved with hops and barley, plain stem, folded foot.

c1730-40   *7in (17.5cm) high*
$380-440   **JH**

A large English champagne and ale glass, the bowl engraved with fruiting vine stock and ears of barley, on a multi-spiral air twist stem.

c1745-50   *8in (20cm) high*
$1,700-2,000   **JH**

One of a pair of champagne or ale glasses, elongated ogee bowl, with hexagonal facet-cut stem with central swelling knop.

c1765   *7in (17.5cm) high*
$1,000-1,200 PAIR   **JH**

A late 18thC English dwarf wrythen ale glass, on a rudimentary stem.

5.5in (12.5cm) high
$100-120   **JH**

A late 17thC pale-green tint roemer, the ovoid bowl on a hollow stem applied with prunts beneath a milled band and high spun foot, cracked.

$500-600   **DN**

An English square-based rummer, the bowl with engraved and polished band and slice cutting.

c1800   *5.25in (13.5cm) high*
$240-280   **JH**

One of a pair of English square-pedestal-based rummers, the bowls engraved with swags and birds on a perch.

c1800   *5.25in (13.5cm) high*
$500-600 PAIR   **JH**

An English press-molded rummer, made in imitation of a cut glass example, with imitation polished printies.

c1860-70   *5.5in (14cm) high*
$50-70   **JH**

An early 19thC English rummer, ovoid bowl, capstan stem.

5.5in (12.5cm) high
$120-140   **JH**

An early 19thC English barrel rummer, on bladed knop stem.

4.75in (12cm) high
$100-150   **JH**

An English cordial glass, fluted round funnel bowl with solid base, double series opaque twist stem with central gauze surrounded by two flat tapes.

c1765   *6.25in (15.5cm) high*
$1,400-1,600   **JH**

An English drawn trumpet double series cordial glass, with bowl with engraved border, the stem with central air core surrounded by multi-spiral tapes.

c1745-50   *6.25in (15.5cm) high*
$2,000-2,500   **JH**

A rattafia glass, small elongated bowl over double series opaque twist stem, with central gauze surrounded by four tapes.

c1765   *7.25in (18.5cm) high*
$2,000-2,500   **JH**

One of a pair of rare, miniature facet stem liqueur glasses, the bowl cut with twelve slice-cut panels, on diamond-cut stem and panel-cut foot.

c1770   *3.5in (9cm) high*

$840-920 PAIR   **JH**

A late 18thC English firing glass, teared trumpet bowl, flared foot.

3.5in (9cm) high

$160-240   **JH**

An English jelly glass, petal molded.

c1830-40   *4.5in (11.5cm) high*

$40-50   **JH**

An English jelly glass, honeycomb-molded, domed foot.

c1760   *3.75in (9.5cm) high*

$280-360   **JH**

An English syllabub glass, with pan top, panel-molded bowl, on panel-molded domed and folded foot.

c1760   *4in (10cm) high*

$280-320   **JH**

An early 18thC sweetmeat glass, with an ogee-molded bowl, raised on an octagonal hollow stem and domed molded foot.

6.25in (16cm) high

$480-560   **WW**

An early 18thC sweetmeat glass with a flat-cut bowl and shaped rim, above an octagonal stem and domed foot.

5.75in (14.5cm) high

$600-800   **WW**

A whisky tumbler, flute cutting with mirror cutting on base.

c1810   *3.5in (9cm) high*

$100-150   **JH**

A whisky tumbler, with blaze cutting over flutes.

c1810   *3.5in (9cm) high*

$100-150   **JH**

A mid-18thC plain glass tumbler, of gently tapered form.

c1750   *6in (15.5cm) high*

$300-400   **JH**

An early 19thC English glass custard or punch cup, barrel bowl with flute cutting and a stick-down handle.

2in (5cm) high

$50-70   **JH**

A late 19thC English glass custard cup, stick-up handle.

2.75in (7cm) high

$30-40   **JH**

GLASS

One of a pair of Bristol blue decanters, with lozenge stoppers.

c1780-90   11.25in (28.5cm) high

$1,000-1,500 PAIR   JH

A pair of late 18thC cut-glass decanters, with bullseye stoppers, the necks with three faceted concentric rings.

11.5in (29.6cm) high

$700-900   WW

A rare, full-sized Bristol blue decanter, with three bladed neck rings and lozenge stopper.

Full-sized Bristol blue decanters are rare.

c1790-1800   11in (28cm) high

$650-750   JH

A pair of early 19thC cut glass decanters, with mushroom stoppers, the bodies faceted and diamond cut, minor chips.

10.75in (27.5cm) high

$400-600   WW

A mallet-shaped decanter and stopper, engraved with diamonds and cut with a band of flutes around the foot.

10.75in (27.5cm) high

$350-450   WW

An early 19thC green glass decanter and disc stopper, of club form.

9.5in (24cm) high

$600-800   DN

A William IV green cut glass decanter and stopper, cut with prismatic steps to its neck above vertical pillars and star-cut base, the original spire stopper cut to match.

c1835   14in (35.5cm) high

$1,100-1,300   RGA

One of a pair of shaft and globe decanters, scale-cut neck, lens-, flute-, and diamond-cut body, with hollow blown stopper.

c1860-70   13in (33cm) high

$350-400 PAIR   JH

A Stevens & Williams green-cased decanter and stopper, intaglio cut and engraved with grapes and vine leaves.

c1910   7.5in (19cm) high

$620-680   JH

A mid 19thC Stourbridge yellow- and white-overlaid glass jug, with two matching goblets, decorated with large leaf motifs and with lobed flared feet, a few small chips.

Jug 12.25in (31cm) high

$350-450   WW

A claret jug, engraved all over with ears of barley and rye.

The decoration signifies this was made for beer not claret. A beer jug of this sophistication is unusual.

c1870   10.75in (27cm) high

$550-650   JH

A shaft and globe claret jug, with slice-cut neck and lens-cut body, with cut strap handle and hollow blown stopper.

c1880   10.75in (27cm) high

$250-300   JH

GLASS

A pair of English sealed and dated mallet-shaped wine bottles, of olive tint, with string rims, seals stamped MN 1733, some surface scratching.

8in (21cm) 9in (23cm) high

$9,000-11,000 DN

An 18thC Dutch green glass bottle, painted with a portrait of Maarten Harpertszoon Tromp, within a foliate border, the decoration probably later.

8.25in (21cm) high

$900-1,100 WW

A Regency oak, burr and rosewood decanter stand, the quadraform stand fitted with four amber glass bottles, with turned wood stoppers, the reeded stem with a pineapple finial.

19in (48cm) high

$6,000-10,000 L&T

An 18thC blue glass finger bowl, the body flat-cut with diamonds, applied scallop and gadroon edge silver mount.

5.25in (13.5cm) diam

$1,000-1,200 FLD

A 19thC ormolu and glass centerpiece, gilt-bronze base with three satyr caryatids joined by a band of vine and grape leaves, supporting a clear cut glass bowl.

11.75in (30cm) high

$1,200-1,600 DRA

A 19thC New England Glass Co. bride's bowl, with pink overlay Mount Washington cameo on Pairpoint quadruple silver-plated stand, marked on the base 'Pairpoint Mfg. Co'.

7.5in (19cm) diam

$1,500-2,000 DRA

A shallow-cut glass salt, on air-beaded knop stem and shallow-cut foot.

c1760   *2.5in (6.5cm) high*

$150-200 JH

An early 19thC heavy diamond-cut glass salt and stand.

There are many salts in this style without a stand. Some had silver stands which have been melted down. Without a stand it is usually worth $60-80.

2.5in (6.5cm) diam

$200-250 JH

A late 18thC boat-shaped glass salt, Van Dyke-cut rim, fluted bowl with notch cutting, on circular foot with square lemon-squeezer pedestal base.

3.25in (8.25cm) high

$120-160 JH

GLASS

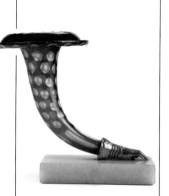

A Victorian glass cornucopia vase, the cut glass vessel overlaid in blue with cast gilt-metal hand terminal and raised on a marble plinth.

7.75in (20cm) high

$1,000-1,200 **L&T**

A late 19thC French Empire style gilt-bronze-mounted cut crystal urn, with twin ram's mask angular handles, raised on a socle base.

12.25in (31cm) high

$2,000-3,000 **L&T**

One of a pair of Continental blue overlay glass shield-shaped vases and covers, each with two clear glass scroll handles cut and engraved with oval panels of sports men and trophies above laurel swags and stepped clear glass base.

c1900 *10.5in (27cm) high*

$15,000-20,000 PAIR **PART**

A large 19thC Bohemian glass goblet and cover, ten-sided bowl finely engraved with a stag, deer and woodland against the ruby-overlaid ground, on knopped stem and ten-sided foot, cover with spiral rim and acorn finial.

20.25in (51.5cm) high

$6,000-8,000 **GORL**

A pair of Bohemian enameled glass vases, of cylindrical form with a spreading base, ruby to clear glass decorated in enamels depicting pansies, with gilt highlights.

c1900 *14in (35.5cm) high*

$1,000-1,200 **FRE**

A mid-19thC Baccarat glass paperweight, set with a variety of colorful canes, including silhouette canes of a deer, a goat, an elephant, a cockerel, a horse, a dog, and flowers, on a bed of upset latticinio, with date cane.

1847 *3.25in (8.5cm) diam*

$3,000-4,000 **L&T**

A 19thC Baccarat paperweight, scattered millefiori and Gridel silhouette canes on ruffled upset muslin, with signature date cane.

1848 *3in (7.5cm) high*

$2,000-3,000 **DRA**

A Baccarat dated paperweight, set with millefiori canes.

1848 *2.25in (6cm) diam.*

$2,000-3,000 **WW**

A Baccarat dated scattered millefiori paperweight, the clear glass set with assorted colored millefiori canes, including silhouettes of a horse, a butterfly, a stag, a goat, a cockerel, and a monkey, amongst short lengths of latticinio tubing, dated on a single cane.

1848   *2.25in (6cm) diam*

$2,000-3,000   **DN**

A 19thC dated Baccarat paperweight, scattered millefiori and Gridel silhouette canes on ruffled upset muslin, with signature date cane.

1848   *3in (7.5cm) high*

$2,000-3,000   **DRA**

A Saint Louis paperweight, the clear glass set with tightly packed, brightly colored short lengths of assorted ribbons and tubing.

3.25in (8cm) diam

$600-800   **DN**

A 19thC cranberry glass table luster, painted with alternate panels of portraits and flowers between gilt scrolls, hung with ten clear glass lusters, minor wear and chips.

12.5in (31.5cm) high

$1,200-1,800   **WW**

A pair of 19thC glass luster candlesticks, each worked with an etched fan neck, with ten descending lusters, surrounding a tapering column, over a circular base.

9in (23cm) high

$1,600-2,400   **FRE**

A pair of pale green glass lusters, with enamel decoration and gilded crenulated top, with two tiers of cut prisms.

c1900   *14in (35.5cm) high*

$800-1,200   **DRA**

A 19thC glass scent bottle and stopper, overlaid in white and painted with a floral garland, some wear to the enamel.

7in (18cm)

$500-700   **WW**

A 19thC French faceted glass casket, with gilt-metal banding, feet and handles, containing two glass scent bottles with stoppers, decorated with gilt stars.

5.5in (14cm) high

$1,000-1,200   **WW**

THE JEWELRY MARKET

Diamonds continue to be more than just 'a girl's best friend' – buyers are willing to pay for large, good quality stones, especially if they are in an attractive period setting. As ever, quality pieces in good condition and which are typical of the era in which they were made, sell for good prices.

Early 20thC jewelry tends to be more popular than mid- to late-19thC pieces, possibly because the settings are more delicate. There is still a market for 19thC pieces, but those that sell well are usually exceptionally good examples of their type and in excellent condition. The value of Belle Époque jewelry, dating from c1910-15, looks set to rise as buyers become increasingly enamoured with its light style.

Art Deco jewelry continues to appeal to many buyers, both those looking for period pieces and others who appreciate the modernity of the settings and feel they have a contemporary look despite their age. Many Art Deco jewels are set with diamonds, adding to their desirability in the marketplace.

Buyers are also willing to pay a premium for signed pieces by makers such as Cartier and Boucheron – even plain gold bracelets signed by names such as these will fetch far more than unsigned pieces.

Post-war jewelry, especially Scandinavian pieces from the 1950s, 60s and 70s, is an up and coming collecting area. The majority of the pieces, particularly those made in Sweden, are signed often pass unnoticed at auctions, fairs and in shops. A little research on the Internet can enable buyers to uncover hidden gems while prices remain reasonable.

The market for vintage costume jewelry remains strong but has moved on. While the big names such as Chanel, Dior, Trifari and Schiaparelli continue to attract buyers and high prices, collectors are willing to pay more than previosuly for a piece which is a great design even if it is not signed.

EARLY JEWELRY

An early 19thC moonstone and diamond pin, the moonstone panel carved in relief with a running fox, within a rose cut diamond-set border.

1.25in (3cm) wide

$6,000-8,000   L&T

A 19thC French gold-mounted Antique style multi-gem-set intaglio pin, incized with zodiac symbols, probably by Jules Wiése, stamped 'JW' with French control marks.

2.5in (6.5cm) wide

$2,400-3,000   L&T

An early 19thC diamond pin/pendant, claw-set with graduated old mine cut diamonds, the border set with rose cut diamonds.

1.5in (4cm) wide

$1,400-2,000   L&T

An early 19thC diamond bird pin, with old mine and single cut diamonds, with ruby cabochon-set eye, with three old mine cut diamonds.

1.5in (3.5cm) wide

$4,000-6,000   L&T

A mid-18thC niello decorated plaid pin, with engraved bosses with knot work, crosshatched and star designs, engraved 'MS 1781', unmarked, 2.7oz (84g).

3in (7.5cm) diam

$1,800-2,400   L&T

A mid-18thC dated ring pin, engraved and stamped with semi-circular and prick dot border, with later engraved script initials 'CF' unmarked, 4oz (124.5g).

1795   3in (7.5cm) diam

$1,000-1,600   L&T

A Scottish plaid pin, by Charles Jamieson of Inverness, marked 'CJ','INS', dromedary and 'CJ' on its side, engraved with original owner's initials 'DM*KF', 2.5oz (77.75g).

1797   4in (10cm) diam

$2,000-2,600   L&T

ESSENTIAL REFERENCE: JACOBITE JEWELRY

An 18thC memoriam pin of Jacobite interest, the canted square rock crystal enclosing a lock of hair, in collet-set gold mount with two scroll mounts to reverse and hinged pin, the back of the closed setting engraved with a crown with 'L Lovat / M:G / SF' below.

$5,000-6,000   L&T

An 18thC Jacobite secret service ring, the oval cabochon emerald in a simple collet mount with open work to shoulders and simple shank, the reverse of the closed back setting engraved 'CR / III / 1766'.

The significance of this unassuming item of 18thC jewelry is far greater than it appears. Once defeated by the English troops in 1746 at the Battle of Culloden, Prince Charles Edward Stuart (Bonnie Prince Charlie) fled to the safe haven of France to reunite with his father. He and a large proportion of the Scottish population still considered him the rightful heir to the Scottish throne. Even after this final defeat at Culloden, Charles and his father James for many years still held hopes to overthrow the English rule of Scotland and planned for another attack on the throne to claim back their rightful place in Scotland. These plans were not helped by the outlawing of Scottish traditions by the victorious English monarch and the fact that the reprisals for supporting the Jacobite cause included death. The population which backed Prince Charles had to find other ways to show their support in secret and this is where the wealth of poetry and songwriting blooms, the common factor in all writings is the fact that neither James' nor Charles' names were ever uttered but the significance was not lost to their supporters. This theme carried on to the applied arts in crafts such as silver, carvings, glass and jewelry. This ring was used as a 'signature' when traveling with correspondence from Charles. No document could carry a signature or seal, as if the bearer was found in possession of such marked papers by government troops, he would almost certainly have been sentenced to death. Therefore this ring would accompany the messenger to show that documents had originated from Charles and were considered official. This Jacobite secret service provided an invaluable service to Charles who had to keep all his loyal supporters abreast of his plans and movements. The cipher of CR III 1766 is also important as this is the year that Charles' father James died in France. Charles now considered himself the rightful King of Scotland and gave himself the title King Charles III, rather than Prince of Wales, which even in exile he still used.

$30,000-40,000   L&T

A 16thC French gilded bronze and engraved portrait medallion, with burnished mirror verso revealing an open compartment, the portrait depicting Henry III, the border inscribed in capital letters: 'HENRICVS III D G FRANCORVM ET POLANIAE REX 1584'.

4.25in (11.1cm) high

$12,000-16,000   L&T

A Scottish George III memoriam ring, with double enameled borders inscribed 'Mrs Bailie of Polkemmet. OB '10' apr 1799: AE'48' 'Lord Polkemmet. OB.' 14 MAR. 1816: AE'79', marked 'IG', along with two domed glass-covered lockets of hair.

$1,000-1,400   L&T

19ᵀᴴC JEWELRY

A Victorian gold-mounted oval shell cameo pin, with a glazed locket containing a scroll of hair, inscribed 'JAMES ANTHONY, STEEL MARCH 1864' and signed 'NERI'.

2in (5cm) long

$700-900   L&T

A late 19thC Holbeinesque pin, with central ruby and seed pearl cluster, and decorated with enamel and seed pearls.

1.5in (4cm) wide

$4,000-5,000   L&T

A gold and Pertabghar enamel pin, decorated with mythical beasts within foliate scrolls and an outer scroll border.

1.25in (3cm) wide

$400-800   L&T

A Victorian shamrock pin, collet-set to the center with a rose cut diamond, three petals set with a circular cut sapphire within rose cut diamonds.

0.5in (1.5cm) long

$1,500-1,700   L&T

A late Victorian heart-shaped pin, set with an old European cut diamond, a circular cut ruby and sapphire, within a border of half-pearls.

1in (2.5cm) long

$2,000-3,000   L&T

A 19thC pin, with an Earl's crown surmounted by an egret feather, set with old European cut diamonds, with oval cut sapphire, in a case.

2.25in (5.5cm) long

$1,500-1,900   L&T

A Victorian multi-gem-set pin, set with three oval and pear cut rubies, and old European cut diamonds, surmounted by a bouton pearl and suspending a large pearl drop.

1.5in (4cm) wide

$4,000-6,000   L&T

A Victorian closed crescent pin, set with graduated circular cut sapphires and an inner border of smaller old European cut diamonds.

1.5in (3.5cm) diam

$1,600-2,400   L&T

A Montrose agate-set pin, of cross form with applied foliate-engraved crown set with three orange cabochons, unmarked.

c1870   1.75in (4.5cm) wide

$500-600   L&T

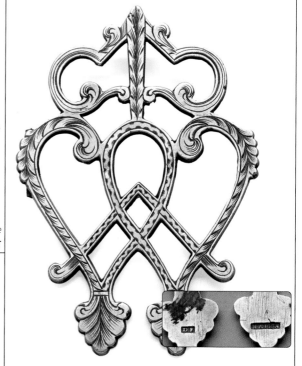

A Victorian gold-mounted Scottish pebble pin, reverse stamped with a registration number, with box stamped 'TESSIERS LTD… LONDON'.

1.5in (4cm) diam

$1,200-1,600   L&T

A gold pebble-set garter pin, unmarked.

2.5in (6.5cm) wide

$1,200-1,600   L&T

A rare Scottish provincial luckenbooth pin, by Daniel Ferguson of Nairn, of typical conjoined double heart form with stylized 'Inverness' spectacles surmounting, with all-over finely engraved detail, 0.7oz (24g).

Little is known about the early career and training of Daniel Ferguson, it appears that originally he trained and traded purely as a watchmaker, and established this business in 1837 aged 23. The main output of named works are clocks and watches with signed dials and movements. For this reason and the total lack of known marked pieces, one must assume that whilst capable of making items, Ferguson either retailed or did not mark his items. It should also be noted that only a small amount of work is known with his Inverness mark (DF INVSS) and an assumption that he only marked a small proportion of his work seems fair. So far only three examples of items marked by Ferguson in Nairn have been recorded, no matter the number unrecorded to date these must still be considered amongst the rarest provincial marks in Scotland.

c1840   3in (7.5cm) high

$4,000-6,000   L&T

A gold-mounted pebble pin, with panels of agate and hardstones, set with six raised circular cut foil backed crystals, the center with circular cut citrine, unmarked.

1.25in (3.5cm) diam.

$500-700   L&T

A Celtic Revival Tara pin, by Waterhouse of Dublin, intricately cast with Celtic motifs.

4in (10cm) wide

$1,000-1,600 — **L&T**

A gold-mounted pebble pin, with detailed engraved border of Celtic and interlaced designs, between panels with agates and hardstone, the center applied with engraved saltire with applied crown, unmarked.

1.75in (4.5cm) diam.

$1,500-1,700 — **L&T**

A Scottish Royal plaid pin, by William Robb of Ballater, inscribed '19 ERI 04', Edinburgh, 3oz (93.5g).

Presented by King Edward VII to his ghillie on the Balmoral estate on his retirement. The pattern is worn by the Balmoral Highlanders.

1898-99   *3.25in (8.5cm) diam*

$6,000-8,000 — **L&T**

A Scottish provincial grouse claw pin, in tablet punch, the claw with mounts, the terminal set with an oval cut citrine in top-twisted collet setting, marked 'JAS. RAMSEY / DUNDEE'.

c1900   *3.25in (8.5cm) long*

$500-700 — **L&T**

A Scottish silver plaid pin, by R. W. Forsyth Ltd., with cairngorm within Celtic knots and scrolls, with marks for Edinburgh.

1910   *3.75in (9.5cm) diam*

$1,200-1,600 — **L&T**

A Highland plaid pin, by Henry Tatton, Edinburgh, with engraved Celtic knotwork panels divided by engraved bosses, the center claw-set with a circular cut citrine.

1919-20   *3.25in (8cm) diam.*

$800-1,200 — **L&T**

A Highland plaid pin, by R. W. Forsyth, Edinburgh, with alternate panels of Celtic knotwork and intertwined Celtic beasts, claw set with a circular cut citrine.

1925   *3.25in (8.5cm) diam.*

$800-1,000 — **L&T**

A Celtic plaid pin, by Thomas K. Ebutt, Edinburgh, with engraved Celtic bosses and knotwork panels around a raised claw-set circular cut citrine.

1926-27   *3.25in (8.5cm) diam.*

$560-680 — **L&T**

A Victorian gold Scottish pebble bracelet, with padlock clasp, with glazed hair panel to reverse, inscribed 'SIR WALTER SCOTT'.

8in (20cm) long

$4,400-5,000 — **L&T**

A gilt hardstone bracelet, the links composed of granite-backed agate panels with central pyramid agates.

$1,000-1,400 — **L&T**

A 19thC gold bracelet, composed of faceted belcher links with pierced oval links, with a heart-shaped fob, set with a cushion cut garnet, with a George III quarter guinea dated '1804', in a fitted case.

7.5in (19cm) long

$600-1,000 — **L&T**

A Renaissance Revival demi-parure, comprizing hinged bangle and matching pendant earrings, applied with putti and rose cut diamonds around the central oval mother-of-pearl plaque, hand painted with an enameled portrait, in a fitted case.

Bangle 2.5in (6.5cm) wide

$8,000-12,000 — **L&T**

A Victorian gold ruby and rose cut diamond bangle, of hinged design.

2.5in (6.5cm)

$1,000-1,400 — **L&T**

A Victorian rock crystal pendant, carved as a heart and surmounted by a crown set with four rose cut diamonds and fringed by pearls.

2.25in (6cm) long

$1,600-2,000 — **L&T**

A Victorian gold memorial pendant, with panel containing woven hair, inscribed 'WALTERUS. DECR. XI MARGERETA. DECR. 3. 1858' and 'CARLAOTTA. H.J. HOPE SCOTT OCTR. 26 1858 RIP'.

2in (5.5cm) long

$2,000-3,000   L&T

A possibly Indian aquamarine and gold necklace, comprizing ten light blue pillow cut stones, the largest 50 carats, for a total of approx. 249 carats, set in 24K gold die-struck setting.

c1900   16in (40.5cm) long

$12,000-20,000   POOK

A late 19thC American large sterling silver heart-shaped locket, enameled with a shield containing three books and the word 'VERITAS'.

2.5in (6cm) high

$250-300   BB

A late 19thC amethyst heart pendant, the large faceted heart-shaped amethyst, approximately 1.5in (4cm) x 1in (3cm) suspended from a rose cut diamond suspension loop, attached to a black silk cord necklace.

$3,600-4,400   DN

An early 19thC multi-gem-set pendant, set with cushion cut gems, including citrine, amethyst, chrysoberyl, rock crystal, aquamarine, garnet and pink topaz.

2.75in (7cm) long

$3,000-4,000   L&T

A Victorian gold-mounted verse crystal intaglio pendant, the high-domed crystal depicting a bird resting on a fruiting branch, within bead borders.

1.5in (4cm) diam

$2,000-3,000   L&T

A Victorian amethyst riviére necklace, composed of oval cut amethysts, suspending matched detachable pear cut amethyst drop, swallow surmount.

15.75in (40cm) long

$2,000-2,600   L&T

A matched Belle Époque suite, the necklace with a single cut diamond-set bow-tied ribbon, with a pearl, surmounting knife bars, collet-set with diamonds, suspending a pearl drop, within diamond-set borders, the earrings similar.

Necklace 20.5in (52cm) long

$6,000-8,000   L&T

A Victorian gold and banded agate Prince Albert memorial stick pin, dated 1861 and a possible gift from Queen Victoria, engraved to the reverse 'in remembrance of the beloved Prince Dec 14th 1861 from VR'.

$1,700-2,000   DN

A Victorian 18ct gold-mounted gentleman's mourning ring, box-set with an old European cut diamond, with black enameled panels to the shank.

$5,000-6,000   L&T

A Victorian diamond ring, set with three graduated old European cut diamonds, with rose cut diamonds between and scroll-pierced gallery.

$8,000-12,000   L&T

A pair of Belle Époque pearl and diamond earrings, each composed of a bow-tied ribbon, set with graduated old European cut diamonds, with a pearl drop, within a shaped surround, millegrain collet-set with graduated old European cut diamonds.

1.25in (3cm) long

$6,600-8,000   L&T

EARLY 20THC JEWELRY

A Guild of Handicraft silver pendant, by C. R. Ashbee, depicting the tree of life with a turquoise enameled medallion and two hanging natural pearls, monogrammed 'L.C.' on verso.

Pendant 1.5in (4cm) high

$6,000-8,000

An Art Nouveau Charles Horner silver necklace, set to the front with a greenish-blue enameled panel, suspending a drop collet set with a circular cut orange gem, made in Chester.

1908   9.75in (25cm) long

$500-700   L&T

An Art Nouveau Liberty & Co. enameled silver pendant, by Charles Fleetwood Varley, the hand-painted enamel plaque depicting silhouetted trees against a sunset, applied with turquoise enameled foliate motifs, possibly by Jessie M. King, suspending a baroque freshwater pearl drop.

A Victorian landscape and seascape painter, Varley's enameled scenes were more often set into lids for silver or pewter boxes. Jewelry by Varley is rare and, although unmarked, this piece exemplifies his use of softly enameled, deep colors within a foliate border, also enameled in complimentary tones.

2in (5cm) long

$1,600-2,400   **L&T**

A Theodor Fahrner Jugendstil silver pendant, with simulated ivory pierced panel set with chrysoprase, marcasite and white enamel, signed with monogram 'TF' and stamped '935'.

$1,000-1,600   **L&T**

An Art Nouveau 9ct gold necklace, possibly by Sydney & Co., collet-set with graduated circular cut moonstone cabochons, with rope-twist borders, within a wirework surround, suspending a moonstone cabochon drop, suspended from a fancy link chain.

24.75in (63cm) long

$3,600-4,400   **L&T**

An Edwardian 15ct gold pendant, alternately composed of collet-set circular cut amethysts and plain oval links, suspending a seed-pearl-set scroll-form drop, also collet-set with two circular cut amethysts.

20.5in (52cm) long

$1,400-2,000   **L&T**

An Edwardian necklace, collet-set with graduated circular cut garnets, interspersed by floret-set seed pearls, the front fringed by graduated pear cut garnet drops, to a fine belcher link chain, in a fitted case.

17.75in (45cm) long

$1,200-1,600   **L&T**

An Edwardian 9ct gold necklace, with belcher links, set with small spherical opal beads, interspersed by faceted cushion cut rock crystal beads, flanked by opal cabochons.

19.75in (50cm) long

$2,400-2,800   **L&T**

An Edwardian multi-gem-set necklace, the front of scroll design, claw-set with three circular cut pink tourmalines and two cushion cut peridots, set with graduated seed pearls, with a belcher link chain.

15.75in (40cm) long

$2,400-2,800   **L&T**

A Harry Dixon hammered sterling pin, set with a citrine, hand incized 'HARRY DIXON SF 1933 Sterling 925 9'.

2in (5cm) wide

$500-700   **DRA**

An Edwardian floral pin/ pendant, the central old European cut diamond within border of circular cut demantoid garnets and heart cut opal cabochons.

0.75in (2cm) diam

$3,600-4,400   **L&T**

A Murrle Bennett & Co. 15ct gold pin, set with a central amethyst cabouchon and collar-set with three seed pearls.

$1,400-2,000   **FLD**

A Heinrich Levinger Art Nouveau pin, modeled as a stylized dragonfly with green plique-a-jour wings and cabochon cut, collar-set moonstone body and garnet eyes.

4.25in (10.5cm) long

$4,000-5,000   **FLD**

A Murrle Bennet & Co. 15ct gold pin, with central set emerald within pierced borders with three seed pearls, with a freshwater pearl drop, stamped to reverse.

$900-1,100   **FLD**

A Scottish Arts and Crafts hammered silver bar pin, set with amethyst and corded wirework, stamped maker's mark 'King'.

$200-400   **L&T**

A pair of Edwardian style multi-gem-set earrings, each designed as an insect, with circular cut ruby-set thorax, oval cut opal cabochon-set abdomen and seed-pearl-set wings, suspending a collet-set round brilliant cut diamond drop.

1in (2.5cm) long

$2,000-3,000   **L&T**

An early 20thC platinum-mounted ring, claw-set with an old mine cut diamond.

$9,000-11,000   **L&T**

JEWELRY

A 1930s Art Deco silver and paste ring.

$220-250   TDG

A Belle Époque fob watch, the front millegrain collet-set with an old European cut diamond, set with single cut diamonds and borders of channel-set calibre cut onyx, suspended from a long black cord.

Fob 2in (5cm) long

$1,100-1,500   L&T

An Art Deco necklace, the front claw-set to the center with nine graduated round brilliant cut diamonds, flanked by graduated clusters of three vertically set diamonds and five baguette cut diamonds, the detachable front may be worn as a bracelet and the remaining section as a bandeau.

16.25in (41.5cm) long overall

$40,000-60,000   L&T

A pair of cufflinks, with a bar millegrain-set with single cut diamonds, and set to each end with a collet-set high-domed ruby cabochon.

Terminals 1in (2.5cm) long

$3,000-4,000   L&T

A pair of ruby- and diamond-set cufflinks with baton-shaped terminals.

Terminals 0.75in (2cm) long

$1,600-2,000   L&T

A pair of French gold-mounted sapphire cufflinks, with channel-set border of calibre cut sapphires, with terminals set with a circular cut sapphire cabochon.

Terminals 0.75in (2cm) long

$3,000-3,600   L&T

A pair of Boucheron cufflinks, collet-set with an oval cut sapphire cabochon, each sapphire of an intense blue hue, signed and stamped 'OR 750'.

Terminals 0.75in (2cm) long

$8,000-12,000   L&T

A pair of sapphire and cowrie shell cufflinks, possibly Trianon.

Terminals 0.75in (2cm) long

$2,000-2,800   L&T

A pair of French white gold and platinum sapphire cufflinks.

Terminals 0.5in (1.5cm) long

$4,000-6,000   L&T

A pair of Boucheron 18ct gold-mounted onyx and ruby cufflinks, numbered 'A3403216'.

Terminals 0.75in (2cm) long

$3,000-4,000   L&T

A pair of platinum-mounted sapphire- and diamond-set cufflinks.

Terminals 0.5in (1.5cm) long

$2,800-3,600   L&T

A pair of French Van Cleef et Arpels platinum-mounted diamond cufflinks, signed and numbered '42885 BTESGOG'.

Terminals 0.75in (2cm) long

$4,400-5,600   L&T

A pair of Bulgari cufflinks, each set with four round brilliant cut diamonds, signed.

Terminals 0.75in (2cm) diam

$5,200-6,000   L&T

A pair of novelty cufflinks, attributed to David Webb, each designed as a hexagonal bolt with screw-turned post, unmarked, tests as gold.

Fronts 0.5in (1cm) diam

$2,400-3,600   L&T

A pair of Bulgari novelty cufflinks, with two-color graduated circular button-form terminals, conjoined by belcher links, signed.

Terminals 0.5in (1.5cm) diam

$1,700-2,000   L&T

A pair of early gold-mounted cufflinks, the terminals each set with a rose cut rock crystal above initials in gold scrolling script, within a red border, with closed back setting.

Terminals 0.5in (1cm) diam

$3,000-4,000   L&T

A pair of cornelian intaglio-set cufflinks, within a broad bezel conjoined by belcher links, unmarked, tests as gold.

$2,400-3,000   L&T

A pair of cufflinks, each claw-set with a sugar-loaf cabochon cut emerald, stamped '750' and 'PSN'.

Terminals 0.5in (1.5cm) long

$4,600-5,600   L&T

A pair of 14ct white gold cufflinks, each terminal millegrain collet-set with a square cut coral cabochon, within a surround of rose cut diamonds, conjoined by belcher links.

Terminals 0.5in (1cm) long

$2,400-3,000   L&T

An 18ct gold-mounted gentleman's dress set, each circular terminal millegrain collet-set with a circular cut sapphire cabochon, within a surround of rose cut diamonds, with blue guilloche enameled border and outer white enameled edge.

Terminals 0.5in (1.5cm) diam

$7,000-9,000   L&T

A Chanel Maltese Cross pin, with green, red and pink poured glass cabochons in gilt-metal settings.

1990s.   *2.5in (6.5cm) wide.*

$180-240   **PC**

A pair of Chanel earrings, gold tone metal set with faux pearls surrounded faux rubies and faux seed pearls, marked 'Chanel'.

late 1960s   *1in (2.5cm) diam*

$300-500   **PC**

A Coro Duette, 'Quivering Camelias', gilt-metal set with clear and emerald rhinestones and green enamel, the trembling flowers mounted on springs, signed with patent numbers.

1940s   *3in (7.5cm) long*

$400-500   **PC**

A Coro chateleine pin, of a girl walking a dog, gold tone metal set with turquoise, pink and red crystals, signed 'Coro'.

1950s   *Girl 2in (5cm) high*

$340-320   **PC**

An 'en tremblant' flower pin, by Kramer for Dior, rhodium-plated setting with pavé-set rhinestones and a large clear rhinestone in the center, unmarked.

1960s   *2.5in (6.5cm) long*

$120-200   **PC**

A Christian Dior heart-shaped pin, with co-ordinating star and drop earrings, silver tone setting with oval, round and navette aquamarine, chalcedony, pale green and fuchsia pink prong-set pastes.

1960s   *Pin 3.5in (7cm) wide*

$440-520   **PC**

A Christian Dior wreath pin and co-ordinating earrings, silver tone metal with gold metal decoration, prong-set with clear rhinestones, marked 'ChrDior 1959'.

1959   *Pin 2.5in (6.5cm) high*

$500-700   **PC**

A Christian Dior swordfish pin, silver tone metal prong-set with clear rhinestones, a red rhinestone eye and dangling faux baroque pearls.

1960s   *4.25in (11cm) long*

$360-560   **PC**

A pair of earrings, Mitchell Maer for Christian Dior, silver tone metal set with black and clear crystal rhinestones with faux baroque pearl drops, signed 'Christian Dior by Mitchell Maer'.

1950s   *2in (5cm) long*

$200-300   **PC**

A rare Christian Dior faceted paste pin, signed.

1962   *3in (7.5cm) long*

$280-320   **TDG**

A pair of Christian Dior earrings, silver tone metal with prong-set citrine and clear rhinestones, marked 'Christian Dior 1958'.

1958   *1.5in (3.5cm) long*

$160-240   **PC**

A Stanley Hagler floral pin and earrings set, with petals and leaves of faux pearls and seed pearls, and clear crystal rhinestones, hand-wired to filigree gold-plated backings.

Early 1990s.   *Pin: 3in (7.5cm) long*

$320-400   **PC**

A Stanley Hagler flower pin, with brown plastic leaves, citrine glass beads and a brown onyx cabochon, signed 'Stanley Hagler N.Y.C'.
This unusual design was probably made to order.

1980s   *3.5in (9cm) diam*

$160-240   **PC**

A Miriam Haskell floral and fruit motif pin and earrings, with silvered faux 'black' baroque and seed pearls on a filigree gilt-metal casting.

1950s.   *2in (5cm) long.*

$240-320   **PC**

A Joseff of Hollywood bar pin and earrings, 'Russian gold' setting with faux rubies, signed 'Joseff Hollywood'.

1940s   *Pin 3.5in (9cm) long*

$200-280   **PC**

A Joseff 'Sun God' pin, in 'Russian gold' with clear rhinestone eye tremblers.

1940s.   *3in (7.5cm) diam.*

$500-600   **PC**

A rare Joseff 'Moon God' with ruff pin, 'Russian gold' with clear rhinestone eye tremblers.
Moon God pins without the ruff are almost 1/3rd the price.

1940s.   *2.5in (6.25cm) diam.*

$600-800   **PC**

A Joseff 'Russian gold' chatelaine camel pin, with faux ruby, emerald, citrine, jade and aquamarine crystal cabochons.

1940s.   *1.25in (3cm) wide.*

$500-600   **PC**

A collection of bee pins, by Joseff of Hollywood.
1940s

LARGE BEE $140, MEDIUM BEE $120, SMALL BEE $60 EACH   **PC**

A Rebajes stylized 'African head' copper pin, with copper wire necklace and earrings.

Late 1940s.   *3in (8cm) high*

$440-520   **PC**

A Regency flower pin and earrings, gold-plated setting with topaz and aurora borealis crystals, marked 'Regency'.

1950s   *Pin 3in (7.5cm) diam,*

$120-200   **PC**

An Elsa Schiaparelli pin and earrings, with prong-set leaves of pale green and pink Lucite on a gold-plated backing.

1950s.   *Pin: 3.5in (9cm) long*
$600-800   **PC**

An Ian St. Gielar flower pin, with iridescent shell petals, an amber-red glass center encircled by topaz crystal rhinestones.

Late 1990s.   *3.5in (9cm) diam.*
$320-400   **PC**

A 1980s Hervé van der Straeten 'Primitive' necklace, the gilt-metal mask applied with gilt-studded ceramic discs forming the hair, pendant cabochon amethyst stones forming earrings, the chain formed from beaten metal medallions, maker's plaque to reverse.

17in (43cm) long
$1,200-1,600   **KT**

A Trifari poinsettia pin, designed by Alfred Philippe, with faux rubies and diamonds configured in imitation of the 'invisible setting' technique developed by Van Cleef and Arpels.

1950s.   *2.75in (7cm) diam.*
$1,300-1,700   **PC**

A pair of Trifari carnation earrings, red, green and clear diamante in 'invisible setting'.

1950's   *3cm (1.25in) long*
$200-260   **PC**

A Weiss Christmas tree pin, japanned metal set with green, red, yellow, pink and clear crystal rhinestones, marked 'Weiss'.

1950s   *2.75in (7cm) high*
$200-300   **PC**

A pair of Weiss earrings, prong-set with aurora borealis rhinestones, marked 'Weiss'.

1.5in (3.5cm) long
$90-130   **PC**

A pair of Weiss earrings, gold tone metal prong-set with green, citrine and clear aurora borealis rhinestones, marked 'Weiss'.

1.5in (3.5cm) long
$80-120   **PC**

A pair of Weiss earrings, the central pink rough-cut stone surrounded by lilac green and pink baguettes.

3cm (1.25in) long
$100-140   **PC**

An 18thC Jacobite interest enamel patch box, the lid with portrait of Prince Charles Edward Stuart.

With an accompanying note stating 'This box was presented by Prince Charles Edward to Captain John Burnett of the R H Arty'.

2.5in (6.5cm) diam

$3,000-4,000   **L&T**

An early George III double partition silver spice box, with crest of a hand with motto 'MANENT OPTIMA CAELO' and script initials 'GM', the interior with engraved galleon with legend 'James Miller Grocer in Canongate 1773', unmarked.

c1775   3.25in (8.5cm) high

$2,000-3,000   **L&T**

An 18thC Gujarat mother-of-pearl round box, with florette on cover picked out in red.

4in (11cm) diam

$4,000-6,000   **DN**

A George III engraved silver counter box, the pull-off cover with a miniature portrait of a young girl behind glass, unmarked.

c1800   75in (2cm) diam

$400-500   **WW**

A 19thC Continental tortoiseshell pique-gold and mother-of-pearl-inlaid box, the hinged lid inlaid with a mythological scene, opening to reveal an interior with removable tray, the sides decorated with Classical maidens and castles.

5.5in (14cm) wide

$30,000-40,000   **L&T**

A Victorian gold-mounted agate presentation table snuff box, the lid engraved with the presentation border 'PRESENTED BY COLONEL DUGALD CAMPBELL R.A. TO ARTHUR CAMPBELL WRITER TO THE SIGNET 1848'.

1848   2.75in (7cm) wide

$10,000-14,000   **L&T**

A rare Scottish silver, Castle Douglas provincial snuff mull, by Adam Burgess of Castle Douglas or Dumfries, the cow horn body with carved seal head terminal, the hinged cover with applied thistle design with circular cut amethyst, marked 'AB', ruined castle, 'D', fouled anchor.

It has often been the case that this combination of the makers mark for Adam Burgess and the ruined castle mark signify his time working in Castle Douglas rather than Dumfries. It does seem a little hopeful that the surviving body of work featuring these marks comes from this short period, of eleven months. There can be no firm differentiation, between these periods unless the items are fully hallmarked in Edinburgh, as is often the case, and the time line examined. This maker is generally known for his flatware.

c1835   4.25in (11cm) long

$5,000-7,000   **L&T**

A French rose gold-mounted and lined tortoiseshell box, the cover with central glazed shell cameo carved with a Classical figural scene, with an outer blue-enameled border, with French control marks.

3.25in (8cm) long

$2,400-4,000   **L&T**

A Scandinavian silver-mounted cowrie shell snuff box, indistinctly marked.

c1850   3.25in (8cm) wide

$240-320   **ROS**

A gold-mounted agate snuff box, with flat hinged cover and scroll-form thumb piece.

2.5in (6.5cm) wide

$500-700   **L&T**

A 19thC banded agate-mounted gilt-metal casket, on four ball feet.

6.5in (16.5cm) wide

$1,200-1,600 DN

A Scottish market agate scent bottle, by J Cook & Sons, Birmingham, the screw-off cap set with a circular cut amethyst.

c1890 *4.25in (11cm) long*

$700-900 L&T

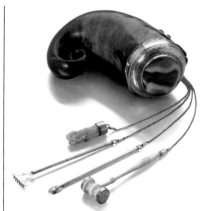

A gold-mounted curly horn table snuff mull, the cover engraved and set with a cabochon-banded agate, the body applied with a thistle mount with tools, paw, snuff spoon, rake and ivory mallet, suspended from a belcher link chain, the mounts unmarked.

5in (13cm) long

$8,000-10,000 L&T

A gilded multi-gem-set box, the hinged cover decorated with rope-twist scrolls, enamel, seed pearls and other gems, around a cut garnet cabochon, with Swedish import marks.

1.5in (4cm) long

$360-480 L&T

A deep blue enamel decorated gold box, apparently unmarked, with hinged cover, and decorated with a diaper pattern.

3.5in (9cm) long

$2,000-3,000 L&T

A 19thC French gilt-bronze and agate jewelry casket, scroll-engraved with applied relief pendant mounts and inset with fourteen different agate panels.

5.75in (14.5cm) long

$800-1,200 DN

A French yellow metal and red-enameled compact, with carved oval jade and rose cut diamond-set thumb-piece, with mirror, two lidded compartments and a lipstick holder inside.

3in (7.5cm) long

$1,200-1,800 L&T

A white metal-mounted ivory patch box, inlaid and painted to the underside with a miniature portrait of an Elizabethan lady, unmarked.

3.5in (9cm) long

$700-900 L&T

A silver-mounted tortoiseshell mechanical nécessaire, retailed by Goldsmiths & Silversmiths Co., London, with fitted interior, the front with a spring mechanism opening to reveal further compartments, marks rubbed.

Nécessaire is a French term for a small box of silver, leather-covered wood, porcelain or enamel, which carries everything 'necessary' for a lady's daily requirements.

1912 *7.5in (19cm) wide*

$4,000-6,000 FRE

A French red-enameled compact, with jade and rose cut diamond thumb-piece, with mirror, lidded compartments, lipstick holder inside.

3in (7.5cm) long

$1,200-1,800   L&T

A rose gold multi-gem vesta case, decorated to the front with a question marks set with rose cut diamonds, a sapphire and ruby.

1.5in (4cm) long

$800-1,000   L&T

A gilt-metal-mounted lapis lazulis box, with scroll-form thumb-piece.

3.5in (8.5cm) long

$400-600   L&T

A French gold-mounted jadeite box, with diamond-set thumb-piece, and French control marks, stamped '750'.

3.5in (9.5cm) long

$1,400-1,800   L&T

An engraved gilt-bronze singing bird box, numbered 51 and in its original box, with inscription by Chevob & Co (previously Baker-Troll & Co), Geneva, Switzerland.

c1890   *1.5in (4cm) high*

$11,000-13,000   RGA

A 19thC German sterling silver, enamel and ivory automaton singing bird box, the bird with red, blue and green plumage beneath a carved ivory lid, raised on four ivory bun feet.

4.25in (11cm) wide

$5,000-7,000   FRE

ESSENTIAL REFERENCE: BIRD TABATIÈRES

- The mechanical singing bird tabatières were made as early as the 1780s as a rich man's toy, made from precious metal or tortoiseshell.
- Tabatière is a French word meaning 'snuffbox', but has come to be used to describe all small, high quality boxes, including the 'singing bird' tabatières, which originated in Geneva, Switzerland, developed by Pierre Jaquet-Droz towards the end of the 18thC.

A red enamel and gilt-metal singing bird box, on small lion paw feet, the cover in ivory carved with a bird. When the operating lever is activated the lid opens and the bird pops up through the grille and begins to sing. At the same time the bird rotates 180 degrees backwards and forwards, opens and shuts its beak and flaps its wings. It then returns to the box and the lid closes.

c1890   *5cm (2in) high*

$16,000-22,000   RGA

CLOSER LOOK: SINGING BIRD CAGE

The mechanism is very intricate, comprising a clockwork movement which works a series of rods that move the birds' heads from side to side, open and close the beaks and flap the tails and wings, whilst working a bellows, which gives the birds their song.

The birds take it in turns to move their heads from side to side and sing.

The vast majority of singing bird cages were made for the home, where they were played on special occasions to amuse the family, but some were made for shop premises and had a penny-in-the-slot mechanism. These examples are much more difficult to find today.

A very rare late 19thC singing bird cage with three birds, operated by a penny-in-the-slot mechanism.

c1890   *58.5cm (23in) high*

$16,000-18,000   RGA

OBJETS DE VERTU

A pair of Elkington & Co. cloisonné vases, depicting birds and grasses, signed to vase and impressed mark under foot.

11in (28cm) high

$34,000-40,000   HT

A 19thC Austrian ebonized and enamel-inset table cabinet, with figure-decorated pediment, two doors concealing three small drawers and long frieze drawer.

9in (23cm) high

$4,000-5,000   L&T

A 19thC French 'Japonisme' champlevé enamel and gilt-bronze jardinière, probably by Barbedienne.

13.25in (34cm) high

$4,000-5,000   L&T

A 19thC Limoges enamel plaque, depicting an Elizabethan court scene, surrounded by enameled plaques decorated with rinceau and masks, framed.

11in (28cm) high

$5,000-6,000   FRE

ESSENTIAL REFERENCE: CHESS

Chess became very popular in the 18thC and 19thC when many sets were made. These were most often made from carved or turned wood, though ivory, bone and tusks were also used. Ivory and exotic woods, such as rosewood, are the most valuable now, as are examples earlier than the 18thC. The export markets of China and India were particularly strong. Britain, Germany and France were also good producers.

- The official set of the World Chess Federation is known as the Staunton Set. It was designed by Nathaniel Cook for Jacques & Sons in 1849, and was endorsed by and named after Howard Staunton, a famous English Grand Master.
- Sets should be complete and undamaged. Period boxes can add value. The inclusion of a chess board is not necessary.

An American Gorham sterling silver and champlevé chamberstick, with a dolphin-form handle, monogrammed 'VHS'.

c1893   *4in (10cm) diam*

$5,000-7,000   FRE

A large early 20thC Limoges enamel plaque, with a profile bust of Minerva with a plumed helmet, against a scrolling copper-colored ground.

20in (51cm) wide

$7,000-9,000   FRE

IVORY

A late 19th/early 20thC Viennese enameled silver and jewel-mounted chess set.

21.75in (55cm) square

$26,000-32,000   FRE

An ivory snuff box, the cover painted to show a view from a country house.

c1830   *3.5in (9cm) diam*

$400-500   FRE

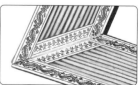

A 19thC Vizagapatam quill and ivory frame, backboard lacking.

8.5in (21cm) wide

$1,100-1,300   L&T

A set of six 19thC French ivory figures, each standing on a walnut and ebonized barrel, comprising: a conductor, a flautist, an accordian player, a lute player, a double bassist, and a bagpipe player.

6in (15cm) high

$10,000-12,000 L&T

A pair of 19thC ivory plaques, with carved angels with cupids, representing the Arts, in carved wood frames.

7.25in (18cm) wide

$3,000-4,000 A&G

A 19thC ivory plaque, depicting classical figures, cherubs and dolphins in the sea, in a red leather fitted case.

4.25in (11cm) high

$1,800-2,400 L&T

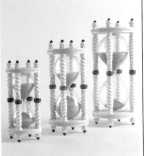

A set of three 19thC Indo-Portuguese graduated ivory and tortoiseshell sand glasses.

Largest 10.25in (26cm) high

$8,000-10,000 L&T

A late 19thC Indo-Portuguese turned ivory, tortoiseshell and rosewood chalice.

12in (31cm) high

$8,000-12,000 L&T

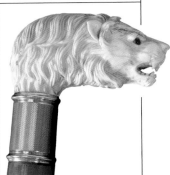

A late 19thC carved ivory and yellow metal-mounted Malacca walking stick, the metal mount stamped '18CT'.

35.5in (90cm) high

$1,600-2,000 DN

MINIATURES & SILHOUETTES

A small oval oil-on-poplar panel profile portrait of a gentleman, Jacob Eichholtz (American 1776-1842), attributed.

9in (22.5cm) high

$8,000-10,000 POOK

A pair of 19thC Indian portraits on ivory, of Shah Jehan and wife Mumtaz Mahal.

4in (10cm) high

$800-1,200 DN

A miniature watercolor-on-ivory portrait of Jeremiah Kahler, Boston, MA, unsigned, attributed to Henry Pelham (1749-1806), in gold frame.

2in (5cm) high

$4,000-6,000 FRE

A pair of miniature watercolor-on-paper portraits of Charles Sherwin and his wife Hanna, unsigned, attributed to Rufus Porter (American, 1792-1884), the sitters identified in an inscription on the reverse also 'came from Warwick Mass to Windham, Vt.' in original eglomise mats and molded giltwood frames, foxing and minor toning.

c1830 *3.25in (8.5cm) wide*

$6,000-8,000 SK

OBJETS DE VERTU

An early 19thC English School watercolor-on-ivory portrait miniature of a gentleman, unsigned, in a gilt metal frame, the reverse enclosing a lock of hair set with three seed pearls.

3in (7.5cm) high

$600-800 FRE

A pair of English School portrait miniatures, depicting a man and woman dressed in black and seated by red drapery, framed.

c1830 *3.25in (8.5cm) high*

$500-700 FRE

An early 18thC oil on copper English School portrait miniature of a gentleman, unsigned.

2.75in (7cm) high

$2,600-3,200 FRE

An 18thC English School portrait miniature, 'Sir Francis Drake', unsigned, watercolor and gouache on vellum, with 'Sir F. Drake 1587'.

4.75in (12cm) high

$600-800 FRE

An American School portrait silhouette of William Merritt Chase, signed and dated 'M. P. Parker Fed. 28, 1906,' and inscribed by the sitter.

11.75in (30cm) high

$3,000-4,000 FRE

An American School portrait silhouette of Thomas Eakins, inscribed and signed 'My Dear Mrs. Parker many thanks for your skillful silhouette, Thomas Eakins,' framed.

c1905 *9in (23cm) high*

$6,000-8,000 FRE

A 19thC English School silhouette group, inscribed James Sword and Fancy, reverse-painted on glass, framed, verso with inscription, 'Harriet B. Buttrick' and printed framer's label, 'Samuel Jennings, Carver, Gilder and Printer Seller, London'.

c1840 *13in (33cm) wide*

$400-800 FRE

A pair of Continental wax portrait reliefs, probably depicting the King and Queen of Naples, dated and inscribed to the reverse 'Franciscus Pieri fecit', mounted and framed.

1756 *18.75in (47.5cm) wide overall*

$4,000-5,000 DN

SEALS

A Georgian multi-gem-set fob seal, with rose cut amethyst-set base, with entwined borders of oval cut rubies and rose cut diamonds.

1.5in (3.5cm) wide

$1,400-2,000 L&T

A late 18thC gold-mounted fob seal/locket, with cornelian inset base, inscribed 'SEMPRE' with miniature by A. Delatour.

Portrait 1in (2.5cm) long

$1,600-3,000 L&T

A 19thC blackamoor fob seal, the head carved from banded agate with an old cut diamond collar and surmount, on a gold base set with a cornelian intaglio carved with an armorial.

1.5in (4cm) high

$7,000-8,000 **DN**

A large 19thC glass wax seal, with simulated tooled surface, the base marked 'P.R.'

4in (10cm) high

$500-700 **FRE**

A 19thC French ivory and silver wax seal, the seal inscribed with 'nec spe nec metu', seal base marked 'P.J.'.

4in (10cm) high

$600-800 **FRE**

A 19thC silver owl model wax seal, with green glass eyes, ebony and 'O.N/N.O' mark, marked '26, 5, 33'.

2.5in (6.5cm) high

$360-480 **FRE**

OTHER OBJETS DE VERTU

A late Victorian silver gilt chatelaine, by William Comyns, the clip suspending a pair of scissors with cast sheath (Chester 1896), an aide memoir (Birmingham 1896), a gilt-metal thimble case/pin cushion, and a needle case (Chester 1898).

10.5in (26.5cm) long

$900-1,300 **L&TA**

A white metal-mounted agate-handled knife, with an impressed leather case.

5.5in (14cm) long

$800-1,200 **L&T**

A gentleman's travelling companion, the silver and fishskin case has several inscriptions and dates, including '1727', '1777' and '1875', the case encloses a pencil, toothpick, fruit knife, ear sprout, tweezers, and other items.

4in (10cm) high

$1,500-2,000 **FRE**

A Scottish provincial page turner, by Ferguson and Macbean, Inverness, marked 'F&M, camel, INVS', with 'Edinburgh 1896' marks, the handle formed from a roe deer antler, initialed 'R.C.R'.

18.75in (47.5cm) long

$1,000-1,400 **L&T**

A 19thC agate goblet, of campana form and with lobed decoration.

5.5in (14cm) high

$1,600-2,000 **L&T**

A 19thC Italian 'marmo giallo' marble tazza, in the Neoclassical style, the reeded bowl with twin scroll handles and lion mask motifs.

8in (20.5cm) wide

$3,600-4,800 **L&T**

A late 19thC Italian Grand Tour specimen marble pen tray, modeled as a Roman trough, underside bears hand written label dated '1823'.

6.75in (17cm) wide

$1,200-1,800 **L&T**

A 19thC near pair of Neoclassical style gilt-bronze and Sienna marble inkwells, one stamped 'Tiffany & Co.'.

Tallest 5in (12.5cm) high

$1,000-1,600 **FRE**

A novelty miniature gem-set moss agate dish, decorated with enamel, seed pearls and red stone.

4in (10cm) wide

$1,400-2,000   **L&T**

A pair of 18thC North Italian gilt-brass-framed scenic micro mosaic panels, depicting verdant cappriccio landscapes with temple follies and passing figures, within cavetto molded frames with beaded inner slips.

6.75in (17cm) wide overall

$80,000-100,000 PAIR   **L&T**

A 19thC Italian micromosaic plaque, depicting St Peter's Square, Rome.

11in (28cm) wide

$16,000-20,000   **FRE**

A late 19thC Italian silver and micromosaic crucifix, the cross inset with views of Rome and a silver figure of Christ, the reverse inscribed 'Roma' and dated.

1899   *7in (18cm) high*

$1,100-1,500   **FRE**

A 19thC King's bronze and ivory brush corkscrew, the ivory brush surmounts a bronze column base with patent label to front.

$700-900   **FRE**

A bronze, brass and timber corkscrew, barrel-shaped handle, brass screw, bronze barrel column base.

c1840   *6.5in (16.5cm) high*

$260-400   **FRE**

A 19thC Italian olivewood corkscrew, timber and iron, with a rectangular double handle grip.

8in (20.5cm) high

$500-700   **FRE**

A 19thC American horn and silver corkscrew, the shaped antler handle is applied with two silver mounts decorated to show vine leaves.

6.5in (16.5cm) high

$800-1,200   **FRE**

An American sand picture in a bottle, with ship Wm. H. Cook and patriotic eagle, by Andrew Clemens, McGregor, Iowa, dated.

Andrew Clemens was born in Dubuque, Iowa, in 1857. At the age of five he became deaf after a bout of encephalitis. He earned his livelihood by painstakingly arranging colored sand with a few hand-made tools to make pictures in glass bottles.

1888   *6.75in (17cm) high*

$12,000-16,000   **SK**

A sand glass, with hand-blown glass, supported by three mahogany barley-twist columns, over three bun feet.

c1840   *15in (38cm) high*

$2,000-3,000   **FRE**

A pair of 19thC sand glasses, with hand-blown glass, one is tartanware, the other is of turned mahogany.

7in (18cm) high

$1,100-1,500   **FRE**

A goat's hair sporran, the cantle with motto 'MANU FORTI', with marks 'FERGUSON BROs/INVss', and marks for Inverness.

c1870.   *6.25in (16cm) wide*

$1,000-1,200   **L&T**

A Highland dress sporran, by Wilson and Sharp, Edinburgh, with long link sporran chain.

1928   *75in (20cm) long*

$2,200-3,000   **L&T**

A Victorian novelty purse, formed as a miniature sporran, chased as a horse hair sporran set with orange cabochons, the mounts unmarked.

3.75in (9.5cm) high

$1,000-1,200   **L&T**

An early 19thC loggerhead 'blond' turtle shell.

36.5in (93cm) long

$6,000-8,000   **L&T**

A lion (*Panthera leo*) taxidermy specimen, head mount.

c1900

$400-600   **GIL**

A Nyala Antelope (*Tragelaphus angasii*) taxidermy specimen, shoulder mount facing right.

$400-600   **GIL**

A Zebra (*Equus quagga*) skin game rug.

$2,000-2,400   **GIL**

An early 20thC American gilt-painted metal money box, modeled after Independence Hall.

9in (23cm) high

$320-400   **FRE**

An early 20thC American rustic tree root frame, composed of gnarled and entwined tree roots applied to a rectangular wooden frame.

39x47in (99x119.5cm)

$5,000-6,000   **SK**

An early 20thC American tramp art double lamp, bank, and storage box.

28.25in (72cm) wide

$8,000-10,000   **SK**

An early 20thC American chip-carved tramp art footed box.

17.75in (45cm) high

$1,000-1,500   **SK**

A Regency papier-mâché and gilt-brass table coaster, the pierced wheels previously leathered, one with remains.

12.25in (31cm) wide

$3,000-4,000   **WW**

ESSENTIAL REFERENCE: FABERGÉ MARKS

A guilloché enameled silver cigarette case, by Fabergé, hallmarked St. Petersburg, 88 standard, workmaster initials of August Hollming, Fabergé in Cyrillic and scratched inventory number '19334'.

c1912   *4.5in (11.5cm) long*

$70,000-90,000   **JACK**

A silver and guilloché enamel desk clock, by Fabergé, workmaster Henrik Wigstrom, scratched inventory number '25483', stamped with the workmaster's initials 'H.W.' and Fabergé in Cyrillic, hallmarked St Petersburg

1908-17   *4in (10cm) diam*

$120,000-160,000   **JACK**

Peter Carl Fabergé (1846-1920) was a Russian goldsmith and jeweler. He took over the family concern in 1870, which soon became the leading jewelers in St Petersberg, receiving the Imperial appointment in 1881.

Branches were later opened in Moscow (1887), Kiev (1907) and London (1906). At the height of its activity, Fabergé employed more than five hundred members of staff.

Motifs were usually inspired by the 18thC French style, though some later products are Art Nouveau in style.

A Faberge enamel cigarette case, engine-turned ground, diamond-set thumb piece, and marked 'Faberge', work master Henrik Wigstrom, with workmaster's initials, 88 standard, with London import marks.

c1910   *3.25in (8cm) wide*

$28,000-36,000   **FRE**

A 20thC blue enamel and silver gilt pill box, with enamel over an engine-turned ground, two diamonds, the cover with a lapis lazuli panel and a further diamond, pseudo Fabergé marks.

1.25in (3cm) high

$1,600-2,400   **FRE**

A Russian silver and enamel frame, with an engine-turned ground, surmounted ribbon-tied drapery set with a cabochon ruby, 88 standard, pseudo Fabergé marks, with leather case.

4.5in (11.5cm) high

$1,400-1,800   **FRE**

A small 20thC Russian silver enamel box, with pseudo Fabergé marks.

$2,600-3,200   *4in (10cm) wide*

A late 19thC Russian silver and enamel cigarette case, from St Petersburg, with foliate champlevé enamel, the lid centred by a view of St Petersburg, the reverse with birds.

4in (10cm) wide

$5,000-6,000   **FRE**

A Russian enamel silver brooch, maker's mark 'XN', designed as a ribbon garter, with applied dates '1877' and '1878', with imperial Queen's crown, with original box.

1.75in (4.5cm) long

$800-1,000   **L&T**

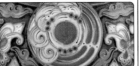

A Russian silver gilt and enamel kovsh, possibly by luka Khaimovich Lozinskii, modeled with a horse head handle, bearing assay mark for 'A. Romanov' Moscow.

1894   5in (12.5cm) long

$2,000-3,000   **FRE**

A matched set of six late 19thC Russian silver salts, with marks on five for St Petersburg, assay master A. Riktera, with stylized polychrome enamel decoration, each with a blue glass liner.

c1899-1903   1.5in (3.5cm) wide

$1,000-1,200 SET   **L&T**

A late 19thC Russian spoon and maple spoon, work master MC, the bowl with champlevé enamel decoration, the maple spoon also with champlevé enamel, import marks for '1908'.

c1896-1908   Longest 8in (20.5cm) long

$1,200-1,600   **L&T**

CLOSER LOOK: CLOISSONÉ ENAMEL BOX

An early 20thC Russian silver scent bottle, decorated with purple guilloché enamel and gold, rubies and rose cut diamonds, the stopper with colorless stone.

3.5in (8.5cm) high

$6,000-8,000   **L&T**

The box is decorated with pan-Slavic motifs. The pan-Slavic revival was a mid-19thC movement based on the study of Russian history and a number of celebrated 17thC works of art.

Fedor Rückert was a Fabergé workmaster and his chief supplier of enamelwares. He was born in Moscow, of German origin, and made articles in Moscow in cloisonné enamel. Fabergé's Moscow signature often obliterates Ruckert's initials. Ruckert also sold his cloisonné objects independently, which explains why a number of his pieces bear no Fabergé signature.

A Russian silver gilt and cloisonné enamel box, with marks for Fedor Rückert, marked to the underside.

c1908-17   2.75in (7cm) wide

$150,000-200,000   **L&T**

Four Russian silver napkin rings, each with polychrome enamel-decorated floral designs, three with workmaster's mark of 'MC' and one 'H', import marks.

c1910   2in (5cm) wide

$3,600-4,400   **L&T**

A Russian silver enameled miniature kovsch, with 'plique a jour' border and trefid handle, the plain exterior with traces of gilding, with control marks.

1908-1917   3.75in (9.5cm) long

$800-1,000   **L&T**

A Russian silver and cloisonné enamel-decorated salt, designed as a miniature throne with hinged lid to the seat.

5.75in (14.5cm) high

$5,000-6,000   **L&T**

A 20thC Russian silver gilt and enamel icon, depicting Christ with saints and apostles, beneath a silver gilt repoussé oklad.

12.25in (31cm) high

$900-1,300   **FRE**

A Russian silver gilt and enamel cased tête-à-tète, comprising two cups and saucers, a waste bowl with swing handle, two dishes, two spoons and a strainer, maker's mark in Cyrillic 'LFO', in a fitted case with a Soviet retailer's stamp to interior.

c1925   Waste bowl 4.25in (11cm) diam

$9,000-11,000   FRE

A cased set of twelve late 19thC Russian silver and enamel teaspoons, retailed by Samuel Kirk & Sons, Baltimore, 84 standard.

$3,000-4,000   FRE

A Russian silver gilt enamel cigarette case, by Khlebnikov, St Petersburg, with hinged lid and medallion portrait of Czar Alexander II, vesta case and strike.

1876   4in (10cm) wide

$17,000-21,000   FRE

SILVER

A late 18thC/early 19thC Russian multi-panel icon, the central image of the Madonna and Child enthroned and encircled by twelve panels depicting scene from the life of Christ.

10in (25.5cm) wide

$1,800-2,400   FRE

An early 20thC Russian silver-colored tea glass holder, maker's mark 'EC' 84 Kokoshnik mark Moscow 1908-1917, with later .875 standard marks for Moscow.

1927-58

$300-500   DN

A 19thC Russian silver-colored napkin ring, by Stephan Wakeva, possibly for Fabergé, 84 Zolotnik mark St Petersburg, maker's mark 'S.W.'

1896-99   1.5in (4cm) high

$500-600   DN

A late 19thC Russian silver-colored tea glass holder, by Alexander Joseph Fuld, Cyrillic maker's mark 'A.F', later engraved in Cyrillic and dated 1925, 84 Zolotnik mark Moscow 1885.

$220-300   DN

A Russian silver-colored cigarette and vesta case, with a concealed vesta case, maker's mark 'A.B.' (possibly Aron Berg), 84 Zolotnik mark.

post-1896   4in (10cm) long

$1,100-1,500   DN

A Russian silver cigarette case, marked '84, B.C. 1869', the gilt interior covered by a hinged lid, of rectangular form.

1869   5in (12.5cm) wide

$500-700   FRE

An early 20thC Russian niello silver cigarette case, the cover depicting a harness racer and horse.

3.75in (9.5cm) wide

$600-900   FRE

A Kasimir Malevich/State Porcelain Factory Russian porcelain plate, in abstract geometric 'suprematist' pattern, signed and dated on back.

1923   *9.5in (24cm) diam*

$7,000-11,000   **SDR**

A late 19thC Russian Kornilov St. Petersburg porcelain five-piece tea service, comprising a teapot, covered sugar bowl, creamer, cup and saucer, red factory mark to underside, blue factory mark to cup.

Teapot 4.5in (11.5cm) high

$1,000-1,400   **FRE**

A Russian Kuznetsov ceramic and silver-mounted bowl, the mounts by the Fabergé workshop, work master KV, St Petersburg pre-1899.

3.25in (8cm) diam

$4,400-5,000   **L&T**

A 19thC Russian lacquer box and cover, the cover painted with figures in a troika pulled by three horses.

5.25in (13.5cm) wide

$600-700   **L&T**

A 19thC Russian lacquer box and cover, the cover painted with figures in a troika pulled by three horses.

4.5in (11.5cm) diam

$400-600   **L&T**

A 19thC Russian lacquer box and cover, the cover painted with figures in a troika pulled by three horses.

3.5in (9cm) diam

$400-600   **L&T**

A Russian lacquer box, underside of the lid bears triple gilt imperial double eagle and Cyrillic inscription.

9.5in (24cm) wide

$1,400-2,000   **L&T**

A Russian bronze equestrian figure group, 'Charging Cossacks', medium brown patina, inscribed 'Cyrillic' and 'Fabr. C. F. Woerffel', on a black marble base.

17in (43cm) high

$6,000-7,000   **FRE**

An early 20thC Russian bronze figure group, light brown patina, modeled as a Cossack on horseback kissing a young lady farewell, signed indistinctly 'A.M. Bo**g**'.

10.5in (26.5cm) high

$6,000-7,000   **FRE**

A late 19thC bronze 'Pointer', after Nicolai-Ivanovitch Lieberich (Russian, 1828-1883), inscribed 'Lieberich' and with Fabr. CF. Woerffel foundry mark.

13.75in (35cm) long

$1,700-2,000   **FRE**

LIGHTING

A Victorian octagonal bronze hall lantern, the pagoda-form top with a faceted bell-shaped corona, with a gadrooned apron with a pine cone finial.

31.5in (80cm) high

$7,000-9,000   **L&T**

A late 19thC Victorian wrought iron, stained and leaded glass lantern, one foot replaced.

25.25in (64cm) high

$400-600   **DN**

A bronze and gilt-bronze three-light hall lantern, in the manner of Osler, with trailing acanthus and berried finial uprights.

42.5in (108cm) high

$4,000-6,000   **L&T**

An early 20thC George III style gilt-brass and glazed hexagonal hall lantern.

23.25in (59cm) high

$2,000-2,500   **DN**

A set of six early 20thC brass and opaque glass hexagonal-section lanterns, in the Gothic style.

43.25in (110cm) high

$3,000-4,000 SET   **DN**

A pair of early 20thC George III style brass hexagonal-section hall lanterns, later replaced Perspex panes.

32in (81cm) high

$6,000-7,000 PAIR   **DN**

A set of three 20thC glass hanging lanterns.

18in (46cm) high

$1,200-1,800 SET   **DN**

WALL LIGHTS

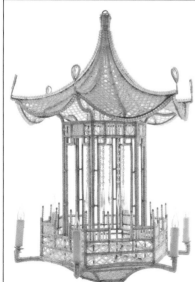

A pair of French pagoda-shaped 'bird-cage' lanterns, with strands of faceted glass beads.

The overall design closely resembles decorative ceiling lights made by the Parisian firm of Bagues in the 1930s and thereafter.

c1950

$60,000-80,000 PAIR   **PAR**

33.5in (85cm.) high

A pair of George III giltwood girandoles, in the Chippendale style, the shaped divided plates within ornate Rococo scroll-carved frames, surmounted by stylized ho-ho birds.

57in (144.5cm) high

$70,000-100,000   **L&T**

A pair of 19thC brass wall candelabra, cast in Rococo style.

14in (35.5cm) high

$1,200-1,600   FRE

A pair of Victorian gilt-brass three-branch wall lights, in Gothic taste.

10.25in (26cm) high

$600-1,000 PAIR   WW

A pair of 19thC Continental Louis XV style gilt-bronze three-light wall appliqués.

20in (51cm) high

$800-1,200 PAIR   DN

A pair of late 19thC American gilt-bronze three-light wall sconces.

20in (51cm) high

$600-800   FRE

A pair of 20thC Continental gilt-metal twin-light wall appliqués, each with urn-cast sockets above drip pans.

10in (25.5cm) wide

$1,200-1,600   DN

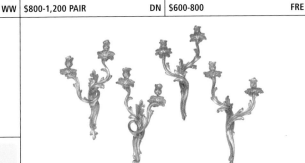

A set of two pairs of early 20thC Louis XV style gilt-metal twin-light wall appliqués.

The larger pair 17.25in (44cm) high

$800-1,200   DN

SILVER CANDLESTICKS

One of a suite of twelve early 20thC gilt-metal wall appliques, each cast with twin scrolling branches supported by a mythical winged and crowned figure on a scrolled fish-tail support, with molded flame-glass shades.

$10,000-12,000 SET   L&T

A pair of early 20thC French bronze four-light figural wall appliqués, cast as a male and female Bacchante.

17.75in (45cm) wide

$10,000-12,000   DN

A pair of late George II cast silver hexafoil candlesticks, by James Gould, London, engraved with armorials, the nozzles unmarked, 42oz (1309g).

1750   *9.25in (23.5cm) high*

$4,000-5,000   DN

A set of four late George II cast silver Rococo candlesticks, by John Pollock, London, the bases each with a cartouche engraved with an armorial, 90oz (2797g).

1753   *10.75in (27.5cm) high*

$10,000-15,000   DN

A pair of second quarter 20thC Italian wirework and carved giltwood twin-light wall appliqués, modeled with rising ears of wheat.

18.5in (47cm) high

$700-1,000   DN

A pair of 20thC Louis XVI style gilt-metal wall appliqués.

11.5in (29cm) high

$200-300   DN

A pair of mid-18thC Augsburg silver candlesticks, with scalloped bases.

6.75in (17cm) high

$3,500-4,500   POOK

A pair of George III silver candlesticks, by John Carter II, London, engraved with a castle crest, loaded.

1768　　　*10.25in (26cm) high*
$2,000-3,000 PAIR　　　**DN**

A pair of George III cast silver table candlesticks, London, William Cafe.

1774　　　*7.75in (20cm) high*
$6,000-8,000　　　**L&T**

A pair of William IV silver shaped circular candlesticks, by Hy. Wilkinson & Co., Sheffield, with scroll and leaf outline acanthus knops and capitals, loaded.

1836　　　*8in (20cm) high*
$700-1,000 PAIR　　　**DN**

A pair of Polish silver repoussé Sabbath candlesticks, stamped '84 standard', makers mark 'ZM', assay mark 'AT'.

1887　　　*15.25cm (39cm) high*
$2,000-3,000　　　**FRE**

A pair of Louis XV style gilt-bronze five-light candelabra.

c1890　　　*23.5in (59.5cm) high*
$3,500-4,500　　　**FRE**

A set of four Victorian sterling silver candlesticks, Hawksworth, Eyre & Co., Ltd, Sheffield, each with columnar standard and Corinthian capital.

1891　　　*7in (18cm) high*
$2,800-3,200 SET　　　**FRE**

A pair of Victorian candlesticks, by Gold & Silversmiths Co., Ltd, of Classical form with urn-shaped nozzles, swag and paterae square-tapered stems, filled, engraved with inscription 'St. M.T.C. Grand National – 1st Prize, 1900', London.

1899　　　*9.25in (23.5cm) high*
$1,000-1,500　　　**A&G**

A pair of silver square candlesticks, by Hawksworth, Eyre & Co. Ltd. Sheffield, embossed in the Adam style with urns, stiff leaves, oval pendants and rams' masks, loaded.

1905　　　*8.5in (21.5cm) high*
$1,500-2,000　　　**DN**

A pair of silver candlesticks, in George II style, by Fordham & Faulkner, Sheffield, loaded.

1914　　　*9.25in (23.5cm) high*
$700-900　　　**DN**

A pair of 20thC Continental silver lion-form Sabbath candlesticks, the bases with reserves of Old Testament scenes and applied with frogs and beetles.

*　　　7.5in (19cm) high*
$2,000-2,500　　　**FRE**

A pair of German silver five-light four-branch candelabra in late 17thC style, import marked for London. 93.25oz (2905g).

1945　　　*12.25in (31cm) high*
$6,000-8,000　　　**DN**

A pair of silver hexagonal two-branch candelabra, by Richard Comyns, London, 55.5oz (731oz).

1972　　　*10.75in (27cm) high*
$3,000-4,000　　　**DN**

A Gothic three-knop brass candlestick, retaining old desirable verdigris patination.

c1450

$8,000-10,000   **POOK**

A mid-drip brass candlestick, with 'great bell' base.

c1540   *11in (28cm) high*

$14,000-18,000   **POOK**

A mid-17thC Dutch brass 'Heemskirk' candlestick.

9in (23cm) high

$1,000-1,500   **DN**

A first half 18thC Scandinavian copper alloy hexagonal candlestick, later elements.

9.5in (24cm) high

$600-800   **DN**

A pair of Louis XV brass candlesticks.

c1750   *10.25in (26cm) high*

$400-500   **DN**

A pair of German brass pricket candlesticks, inscribed 'Thomas Henning ver Ehret dise Leuchter, Ao:1762 no Aprilis',

1762   *19in (48.5cm) high*

$3,000-4,000   **DN**

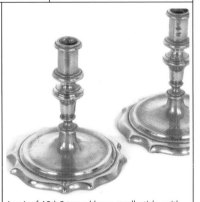

A pair of 18thC turned brass candlesticks, with serpentine edged bases.

5.5in (14cm) high

$450-550   **WW**

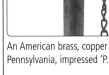

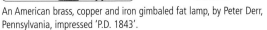

An American brass, copper and iron gimbaled fat lamp, by Peter Derr, Pennsylvania, impressed 'P.D. 1843'.

10.75in (27.5cm) high

$8,000-12,000   **POOK**

A pair of late 19thC Elkington & Co gilt-brass luster candlesticks, in Grecian taste, fitted for electricity.

9in (23cm) high

$800-1,000   **DN**

A pair of Victorian brass altar candlesticks, the knopped stems with colored glass prunts.

24.25in (61.5cm) high

$1,000-1,500   **WW**

A pair of late 18thC painted and parcel giltwood and composition candle holders, modeled with standing amorini, chips and losses.

12.5in (32cm) high

$200-300 DN

A pair of Regency bronze luster candlesticks, with urns issuing anthemion pierced fronds hung with faceted glass drops, each on three monopaedic eagle mask supports.

34cm high

$2,000-3,000 L&T

A pair of Regency patinated and gilt bronze candlesticks, cast as urns on dolphin stems.

c1815 *5.75in (14.5cm) high*

$600-800 DN

A pair of early 19thC Chinese pewter prickets, impressed mark.

11in (28cm) high

$600-800 FRE

A pair of second quarter 19thC Restoration gilt and patinated bronze luster candlesticks, hung with glass pendants.

$600-800 DN

A pair of 19thC French bronze candlesticks in the Empire taste, the drip pans hung with faceted drops and upheld by Egyptian male figures, with circular rouge marble bases.

9.5in (24cm) high

$1,200-1,600 L&T

A pair of 19thC Louis XV style gilt-bronze and Chinese porcelain candelabra, with turquoise glaze figures, on Rococo bases.

10in (25.5cm) high

$4,000-6,000 FRE

A pair of French Empire bronze and gilt-bronze twin-handled metamorphic candlesticks, each with reversible cover, mounted with griffin finial and to the reverse with flowerhead nozzle, raised above an urn with elephant handles.

15in (38cm) high

$10,000-15,000 L&T

A pair of late 19thC bronze cassolettes, in the form of urns on stands, the domed lids with fir cone finials above ram's head-decorated bodies on triform chain-hung stands with hoof feet.

12.25in (31cm) high

$2,000-2,500 L&T

A pair of last quarter 19thC French gilt-bronze and 'marmo rouge' griotte mounted twin-light candelabra.

9.5in (24cm) high

$700-900 DN

A pair of 19thC French three-branched candelabra, each modeled as a cherub holding a cornucopia of flowers.

17.25in (44cm) high

$1,500-2,000   L&T

Two Empire style bronze and brass candlesticks, modeled as Grecian male and female figures holding torchères.

22.25in (56cm) high

$2,000-2,500   L&T

A late 19thC pair of French Empire bronze candelabra, with stems formed as Classical maidens, each on marble bases.

17in (43cm) high

$2,000-3,000   FRE

A pair of late 19thC Continental gilt and patinated bronze candlesticks, on green serpentine marble bases.

9.75in (24.5cm) high

$350-450   DN

A pair of late 19thC Louis XV style gilt-bronze twin-light candelabra, cast as scrolling foliage.

13in (33cm) wide

$700-1,000   DN

An early 20thC French parcel silvered and gilt-bronze three-light candelabrum, the triform base with three addorsed swans.

18in (46cm) high

$400-600   DN

An 18thC Italian carved walnut altar candlestick, with later electrical fitment.

27.5 in (70cm) high

$400-600   DN

A pair of late 17th/early 18thC Italian carved wood, silver and gilt gesso floor standing candlesticks.

68.25in (173.5cm) high

$4,000-6,000   HALL

A pair of French gilt and patinated bronze six-light candelabra, now mounted as lamps.

c1825   *29.5in (75cm) high*

$4,200-4,800   FRE

A pair of 19thC turned oak pricket candlesticks.

27.5in (70cm) high

$800-1,200   DN

CLOSER LOOK: REGENCY CANDELABRA

Colza lamps were hugely in demand before the dawn of electricity and were subsequently redundant, unless reutilized for electric light.

The upper section is based upon a large two-handled vase and cover acting as the reservoir for the Colza oil used to feed the lamps and utilizing the fluted ormolu arms as conduits to the glass-shaded burners.

The arms are embellished with lotus leaves and the vases have acanthus mounts. These reflect the knulling of the bases and the lotus flower finials of the tops, typifying the Neoclassical inspiration of the lights.

The tops of the tripod bases have a circular concave frieze with a running border of florettes and acanthus leaves above a reversed finial with knulled decoration centred by an ormolu knop. The bases reflect this device.

The distinctive design is one often used in Neoclassical schemes, but the detailing reflects the more robust revival of interest in the antique seen in the works of Thomas Hope and George Smith and popularized by Ackermann's widely circulated designs.

In the ancient world cranes represented fidelity and were messengers of the gods. Here, they may be taken from a family crest.

James Smethurst existed for some time as a purveyor of fine furnishings, adding '& Co' to the name of his business after 1814.

Each tripod base has three tapering molded supports with circular stepped bases and with rams' heads to the top and lion paw feet.

A rare pair of Regency bronze and ormolu three-light candelabra, label of James Smethurst, 138 New Bond Street, consisting of detachable upper lights, which sit upon bronze circular tops with tripod bases.
c1810

72in (183 cm)

$300,000-400,000   **PAR**

A 19thC bronze Egyptianesque Colza oil lamp, with flaming finial and coiled serpent-mask handle, the bowl cast with a Pharaoh mask, adapted for electricity.	A pair of Egyptianesque bronze and ormolu Colza oil lamps, probably by William Bullock, with fluted socles and triform platforms with winged monopaedic chimera corner ornaments.	A pair of French Empire bronze and ormolu candelabra, the green-veined marble bases with ormolu mounts, each now with two electric lights.	A French Empire period gilt and patinated bronze lamp, the reeded and leaf-cast column raised on a square base with applied mounts, fitted for electricity.
15.25in (35cm) wide	*19.75in (50cm) high*	*c1815*	*37.75in (96cm) high*
$2,000-3,000 **L&T**	**$6,000-8,000** **L&T**	**$90,000-100,000** **PAR**	**$5,000-6,000** **L&T**

A pair of Charles X gilt and patinated bronze lamps, the reeded columns raised on triform bases with applied swan mounts, fitted for electricity.	A mid 19thC Continental painted and parcel-gilt porcelain twin-handled vase, later adapted as a table lamp.	A pair of 19thC gilt and patinated bronze lamps, formed as Roman oil lamps, with seated figures depicting 'L'Etude' & 'Philosophie', on square green marble bases.	A pair of 19thC Louis XVI style gilt-bronze mounted 'sang du boeuf' urns, the upright leaf-cast handles ending in female masks, now mounted as lamps.
21.5in (54.5cm) high	*17in (43cm) high*	*13.75in (35cm) high*	*Urn 17in (43cm) high*
$10,000-12,000 **L&T**	**$1,100-1,300** **DN**	**$8,000-10,000** **FRE**	**$13,000-17,000** **FRE**

A pair of Chinese famille rose vases, decorated with warriors and nobles in mountainous landscapes, converted to lamps.

32.25in (82cm) high

$6,000-8,000   **L&T**

A late 19thC Louis XVI style gilt and patinated bronze lamp, with urn-form spiral fluted body supported by three female caryatids.

19in (48cm) high

$3,000-5,000   **FRE**

A pair of late Victorian gilt-brass table lamps, in the Gothic taste, the knopped and leaf-cast stems on cinquefoil pierced triple leaf-form bases, adapted and wired for electricity.

36.5in (93cm) high

$8,000-10,000   **L&T**

A pair of French Empire style gilt and patinated metal storm lamps, the glass shades raised by three cabriole supports surmounted by swan finials.

18in (46cm) high

$4,500-5,500   **L&T**

A late 19thC Elkington silvered metal centerpiece adapted as a table lamp, with three addorsed sphinxes.

12.25in (31cm) high

$420-480   **DN**

A late 19thC brass table oil lamp, with four adorned columns above a plinth with seated hounds, with later electrical fitments.

22in (56cm) high

$1,800-2,200   **DN**

A brass and decorated glass table oil lamp.

c1900   *31in (79cm) high including shade*

$300-400   **DN**

A pair of Louis XVI style marble and gilt-bronze-mounted lamps, the stems surmounted by palmette-form fittings and applied with lion mask motifs.

37.5in (95cm) high

$6,000-8,000   **L&T**

A pair of bronze and gilt-bronze lamps, modeled as figures of the Duke of Wellington and Napoleon, wired for electricity.

26.5in (67cm) high

$3,500-4,500   **L&T**

A pair of early 20thC carved and painted wood figures of Nubian women, now adapted as lamp bases.

38.25in (97cm) high

$2,200-2,800   **L&T**

A pair of 20thC gilt and patinated metal table lamps in the Restoration style, each with faux oil burner above a faceted glass reservoir.

26.5in (67cm) high overall

$2,000-2,500   **DN**

An early 18thC oak fire surround, the molded overhanging cornice on ring-turned straight baluster supports above a back composed of fielded panels, above a rectangular mantel shelf, on paneled jambs, adapted.

72in (183cm) wide

$2,400-3,400　　　　　**L&T**

A late 18th/early 19thC carved pine and gesso chimneypiece, in the Adam style.

73.25in (186cm) wide overall

$3,400-4,000　　　　　**DN**

A Regency or George IV cast iron hobgrate, with foliate-cast cresting and uprights.

c1820

$1,000-1,500　　　　　**DN**

A rare California Clay Products (CALCO) fireplace surround, composed of thirty-nine tiles embossed with Mayan warriors and glyphs.

1920s　　　　*44in (112cm) high*

$3,000-4,000　　　　　**DRA**

A George III engraved brass and iron firegrate.

c1780 and later　　*32.25in (82cm) wide*

$7,000-9,000　　　　　**DN**

A Regency cast iron fire basket, of urn form with loop handles, hung with drapery above an ash drawer.

32in (53.5cm) wide

$3,000-4,000　　　　　**FRE**

A William IV iron fire basket, with cast brass mounts, over a rope-twist border of four leaf-molded ball feet.

26in (66cm) wide

$5,000-6,000　　　　　**HALL**

A late Victorian cast iron and brass fire grate, with a fan cresting and serpentine front with urn finials.

32.75in (83cm) wide

$1,200-2,000　　　　　**WW**

A 20thC cast iron and brass-mounted fire grate, the basket with arched backplate and twin urn finials at the front.

22.75in (58cm) wide

$900-1,300　　　　　**DN**

A George III polished steel bowfront fender.

50in (127cm) wide

$1,400-1,800　　　　　**WW**

A Victorian pierced brass fender.

46in (117cm) wide

$240-300　　　　　**WW**

A late 19thC Louis XVI style French gilt-bronze adjustable fender, with swagged spirally fluted urns and flambeau finials.

13.75in (35cm) wide

$900-$1,100　　　　　**DN**

A rare pair of New York Federal brass andirons, from the workshop of Richard Wittingham, with ball and finial terminals, with classically engraved plinths.

c1810   *21.75in (55cm) high*

$8,000-10,000   **POOK**

A pair of brass andirons, of a Neoclassical form.

c1820-1840   *12in (30.5cm) high*

$600-1,200   **FRE**

A pair of wrought iron andirons, the fronts with flattened disc finials.

14.75in (37.5cm) high

$220-280   **WW**

A late 19thC pair of Continental gilt-metal and cast iron mounted chenets, each with a cloaked putto beside a brazier.

8.75in (22cm) high

$600-800   **DN**

A pair of late 19thC gilt-metal chenets, in the Neoclassical style, each with swagged urn above a frieze.

$600-800   **DN**

A late 19thC Louis XV style gilt-bronze fire screen and chenets, of ornate Rococo form.

Fire screen 31in (78.5cm) high

$3,400-4,000   **FRE**

A late 19thC Louis XV style pair of French patinated and gilt-bronze chenets.

13.5in (34cm) wide

$2,400-3,200   **DN**

A pair of late 19thC Victorian cast iron andirons, the uprights cast as the Duke of Wellington.

16.25in (41cm) high

$700-900   **DN**

A pair of firedogs, in the manner of Ernest Gimson, each with cut-out circular rosettes, chased with flowering foliage above a pierced panel below on wrought iron stand.

25.25in (64cm) high

$2,000-3,000   **L&T**

A pair of Roycroft style andirons, made of black-enameled curled elements, complete with cross-bar, unmarked.

Provenance: From the living room at Vancroft, the Wellsburg, W.Va., home designed by the Pittsburgh architects Alden and Harlow and built at a cost of more than $1,000,000 as a hunting lodge for Joseph B. Vandergrift in 1901.

c1901   *36.5in (92.5cm) high*

$2,800-3,600   **CRA**

A rare pair of Roycroft andirons, made of black-enameled curled elements with twisted rings, large orb-and-cross incorporated in design.

c1901   *31in (78.5cm) high*

$7,000-9,000   **DRA**

A pair of painted fire irons, the iron terminating in a painted iron model of a duck's head, some losses.

c1920   *12in (30.5cm) high*

$1,500-2,000   **FRE**

An 18thC northern European wrought iron trammell, or 'chimney crane', with a line of ratchet teeth to one side supporting an adjustable arm with mounting ring above an overscrolled pot hook at the lower end, the lever handle with embossed brass collar, with inscription 'WAM/ACNK/ELVET/ANNO 1790'.

94cm high

$1,200-1,600   **L&T**

A late 19thC New York State North Wind face-carved wood, iron, and leather bellows, impressed 'W.R. PRIES 433 CANAL OF N.Y.'.

32.5in (82.5cm) high on stand

$7,000-9,000   **SK**

A Victorian cast iron doorstop, modeled as a standing elephant.

10in (25cm) long

$1,000-1,600   **L&T**

A pair of late 19thC Victorian painted iron door porters, cast as Punch and Judy.

11.75in (30cm) high

$300-400   **DN**

A Central Pennsylvania painted pine fireboard, decorated with angels, tulips and birds.

The source of the decoration comes from the same printed fraktur which inspired the furniture of the Mahantongo Valley.

c1900

61in (155cm) wide

$10,000-12,000   **POOK**

A cast iron 'Wedding Dance' stove plate, dated.

1746   *26in (66cm) high*

$2,600-3,200   **POOK**

A Portsmouth, New Hampshire painted leather fire bucket, inscribed 'No2', with the name 'G.K. Haswell F.F.S' (Federal Fire Society) enclosing the date.

1789   *11.75in (30cm) high*

$5,000-7,000   **POOK**

A George III mahogany and brass-banded peat bucket, of navette form, with brass swing handle and liner.

14.5in (37cm) wide

$6,000-8,000   **L&T**

A pair of late 19th/early 20thC copper and brass log buckets.

15in (38cm) diam

$800-1,000 PAIR   **DN**

A late 20thC pair of limestone peat bucket planters, of spirally reeded tapering form, each with a bronze-bound frieze and base.

26in (66cm) high

$6,000-8,000   L&T

CLOSER LOOK: CAST IRON URNS

Each urn would originally have stood upon a cast iron stove with a door to the front to allow coals to be inserted and lit and a vented tray at the bottom to allow a controled input of oxygen and to collect the spent ash. The urn, while adding a classically decorative element to an otherwise utilitarian article, also assisted in the radiation of heat and incorporated a vent pipe at the rear which would have led out through the wall of the room to a chimney or directly to the outside of the building. The size, elaborate detail and obvious cost of such stoves would only allow their installation in the grandest of houses of the period and as such they are extremely rare.

The body is decorated with a pair of mythical bearded masks united by trailing swags of flowers and a fluted border.

The lower section has conforming cast leaf decoration.

These urns correspond very closely to a pen and gray wash manuscript design in a volume of drawings amongst the Carron papers at the Scottish Record Office with exactly the same dimensions, allowing a confident attribution to the Carron Iron Co, Falkirk, Scotland.

One of a pair of cast irons urns of Classical inspiration, the lids with cast leaf decoration topped by a flame finial, on a flared socle and squared plinth.
c1780.

39in (99cm) high

$40,000-50,000 PAIR   RGA

A pair of modern cast iron Versailles style garden planters, with 'fish scale' side panels on four lotus-cast uprights with pineapple finials, green painted.

24.75in (63cm) wide

$5,000-7,000   L&T

A Regency cast iron garden bench, the back with reeded lozenge trellis splats with bifurcated outscrolling terminals.

60in (153cm) wide

$3,600-4,800   L&T

A French suite of faux bois furniture.
c1930

Table 42in (106.5cm) diam

$1,800-2,400   POOK

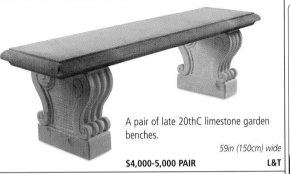

A pair of late 20thC limestone garden benches.

59in (150cm) wide

$4,000-5,000 PAIR   L&T

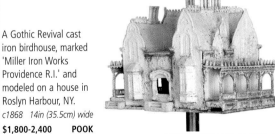

A Gothic Revival cast iron birdhouse, marked 'Miller Iron Works Providence R.I.' and modeled on a house in Roslyn Harbour, NY.
c1868   14in (35.5cm) wide

$1,800-2,400   POOK

A large 19thC cast iron figural fountain, in the form of a female water carrier, formerly painted.

64.25in (163cm) high

$9,000-11,000   L&T

A Victorian cast iron and painted model of a greyhound by Coalbrookdale, indistinctly marked to cartouche base, 'B. DALE…', rear with patent lozenge, formerly part of a large item.

19in (48cm) high

$4,000-5,000   **L&T**

A late 19thC patinated bronze garden fountain, cast as a nubian youth holding aloft a water lily flower stem, the base cast with water lily leaves.

21.25in (54cm) high

$1,000-1,600   **L&T**

A late 19thC cast iron garden ornament, of a Newfoundland dog, in the full round, painted dark gray.

54.5in (138.5cm) long

$60,000-70,000   **SK**

A 19thC architectural model of an eagle, standing over a black-painted plinth base.

33in (84cm) high

$1,600-2,000   **FRE**

A late 19thC Victorian foliate cast iron finial, cast in two halves.

37.5in (95cm) high

$400-600   **DN**

A pair of early 20thC lead models of putti, emblematic of Spring and Summer.

25.5in (65cm) high

$1,800-2,400   **DN**

MARBLE

A pair of 19thC Cornish marble sphinx, attributed to the London Serpentine Company.

28in (71cm) wide

$2,400-3,600   **L&T**

A pair of carved Travertine marble sphinxes.

35.25in (89.5cm) wide

$1,800-2,400   **FRE**

A pair of 19thC Louis XV style gilt-bronze-mounted marble urns on pedestals, each of campana form with an oak leaf carved rim with an egg and dart collar, the handles cast with grotesque masks.

57in (145cm) high

$60,000-70,000   **FRE**

A pair of Louis XVI style gilt-bronze and molded glass pedestals, each with a circular green marble top upon a faceted standard and leaf-cast shaped square base.

39.5in (100cm) high

$4,400-5,600   **FRE**

A pair of Empire style gilt-bronze-mounted porphyry pedestals and urns, each urn with a rim cast with bacchic vines above two handles cast as swans, the base cast with rinceaux and medallions.

66in (167.5cm) high

$26,000-32,000   **FRE**

A 19thC specimen marble pedestal, the square top with a cylindrical column support and molded square base.

44in (111.5cm) high

$2,200-3,000   **L&T**

A molded copper horse jumping through hoop weather vane, attributed to A. L. Jewell & Co. Waltham, Massachusetts, 1852-1867,

The first full-time commercial weathervane manufacturer was Alvin L. Jewell of Waltham, Massachusetts, near Boston, starting in 1852. Jewell, a gifted designer and craftsman, created a line of weathervane forms imitated by later businesses. He was also the first to publish a catalogue of his designs. His vanes were made of copper molded in iron forms, which had been cast from carved wood models. Each part of the vane was molded in two symmetrical halves joined with solder. This new method allowed Jewell and his followers to massproduce identical vanes. Jewell's hollow copper vanes were clear, simple forms, easily recognized from any viewpoint. They were an immediate success. After Jewell's death (in a rooftop fall) in 1867, his business and patterns were sold at auction.

75 in (190cm) high

$160,000-200,000 SK

A Hackney horse weather vane, 'Lady Seaton', by Eugene Morahan (American, 1869-1949), signed.

This weather vane sat atop an 8,000 square foot Massachusetts carriage house owned by industrialist William Henry Moore. The weather vane was fashioned after Moore's favorite prize-winning mare, Lady Seaton.

c1912   94.75in (240.5cm) high

$33,000-40,000 SK

A large 19thC full-bodied copper Dexter horse weathervane, with cast head, retaining a verdigris finish.

21in (53cm) high

$8,500-10,000 POOK

A copper jumping horse and rider weathervane, from the Isaac Clothier Stables and Carriage House in Villanova, Pennsylvania, attributed to Kenneth Lynch & Sons.

c1920   90in (228.5cm) high

$6,000-10,000 POOK

A late 19thC weather vane depicting St. Julien with sulky, attributed to J. W. Fiske, New York, full-bodied molded sheet copper with cast iron horse's head and driver's hands, with black metal stand, with imperfections.

40in (101.5cm) long

$24,000-28,000 SK

A late 19thC American large sheet copper rooster weather vane, with imperfections.

39in (99cm) high

$9,000-12,000 SK

A late 19th/early 20thC American gilded molded sheet copper rooster weather vane, loss to lower shaft.

24in (61cm) wide

$5,000-7,000 SK

A late 19th/early 20thC American molded sheet copper gamecock weather vane, bronze painted surface over earlier gilt surface, dents.

18.75in (47.5cm) high

$3,500-4,500 SK

A 19thC full-bodied copper bull weathervane, with a cast iron head, retaining its original gilt surface.

13in (33cm) high

$10,000-14,000 POOK

A late 19thC American molded copper and zinc cow weather vane, probably Cushing & White, Waltham, Massachusetts, mounted on a copper rod, seam separation, bullet holes.

28.5in (72.25cm) wide

$26,000-30,000 SK

A late 19th/early 20thC American copper and zinc bull weather vane, full body sheet copper figure with zinc head and horns, mounted on a copper rod, surface restoration.

27in (68.5cm) wide

$13,000-16,000 SK

A 19thC full-bodied copper leaping stag weathervane, retaining an old gilt and verdigris surface.

22in (56cm) high

$30,000-35,000 **POOK**

A late 19th/early 20thC molded copper leaping stag weather vane, possibly by E. G. Washburne & Co., New York City and Danvers, Massachusetts.

32in (81cm) long

$12,000-15,000 **SK**

A late 19thC sheet iron dolphin fish weathervane, with diamond-form spire.

29.5in (75cm)

$2,000-3,000 **POOK**

A late 19thC American wooden trumpeteer weather vane, mounted on an iron rod supported on a wooden base, losses, old repair.

47.25in (120cm) total height

$3,500-4,500 **SK**

A late 19th/early 20thC American gilded molded sheet copper codfish weathervane, later gilded surface, dents.

32.25in (82cm) wide

$2,500-3,500 **SK**

A rare late 19thC American molded sheet copper sphinx weather vane, weathered verdigris surface with traces of gilt, no stand, bullet holes.

This weathervane was manufactured by J. L. Mott Iron Works of New York and Chicago, who made it in three sizes: 4ft, 5ft and 6ft. This example was the shortest, selling when new for $75, and it was once installed atop a textile manufactory in Wilbraham, Massachusetts.

49.5in (125.5cm) long

$70,000-100,000 **SK**

A large wrought iron and copper bannerette weathervane, the wind indicator with whimsical scrollwork and the banner dated.

1908 *122in (310cm) high*

$3,500-4,500 **POOK**

A 20thC molded sheet copper dog weather vane, attributed to Joseph Davis, Skowhegan, Maine.

27.75in (70.5cm) long

$5,000-6,000 **SK**

ESSENTIAL REFERENCE: WHIRLIGIGS

Whirligigs are a form of weathervane. There are two types: single-figures with rotating paddle-like arms and multi-figures that are moved by a propeller and a series of gears and rods.
- The more complicated or unusual the subject, the higher the value. Because they were kept outside few examples from the 19thC have survived and so they can be very valuable.

A Folk Art peacock weather vane, with enameled feathers, unmarked, some losses to enamel.

25.5in (64.5cm) high

$4,000-5,000 **DRA**

An early 19thC New England carved and polychrome-painted wood and zinc soldier whirligig, the figure with black hair and moustache, wearing a black-painted sheet zinc bicorn hat, a blue jacket with a red sash, white trousers and black boots, and black-painted saddles, including metal wall mount.

20.5in (52cm) high

$30,000-35,000 **SK**

An Afshar rug, the zigzag field with eleven polychrome lozenge medallions, within cream cartouche border between multiple bands.

74.75in (190cm) long

$700-900 **L&T**

A late 19thC Bakshaish carpet, north Persia.

206in (523cm) long

$20,000-24,000 **FRE**

A large Bakshaish carpet, the camel field with all-over rosette, lozenge and serrated leaf pattern, within blue turtle palmette border, worn.

244in (620cm) long

$6,000-8,000 **L&T**

A late 19thC Aimaq Belouch rug, northwest Afghanistan.

89in (226cm) long

$1,000-1,200 **FRE**

A Bidjar carpet, the crimson field with all-over palmette, rosette and foliate lattice, within indigo turtle palmette and angular vine border between camel and blue bands.

145in (368cm) long

$5,000-6,000 **L&T**

A large Fereghan carpet, the indigo field with all-over herati pattern, brick-red turtle palmette and vine border between blue bands.

244in (620cm) long

$11,000-13,000 **L&T**

A Hamadan carpet, west Persia.

c1920-30 *120in (305cm) long*

$2,400-3,000 **FRE**

A Hamadan carpet, west Persia.

c1920 *208in (528.5cm) long*

$7,000-9,000 **FRE**

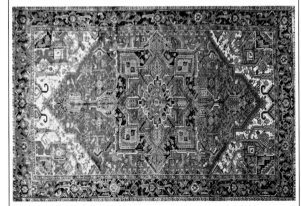

A Persian Heriz room-size rug, with medallion, in tones of red.

c1970 *146in (371.5cm) long*

$900-1,300 **DRA**

A Heriz carpet, the red field with central indigo and ivory medallion suspending pendants, ivory and red spandrels, within indigo rosette and leafy vine border between blue, red and yellow bands.

148.5in (377cm) long

$1,800-2,400 **L&T**

A Heriz carpet, the red field with central indigo and red medallion suspending pendants, ivory and red spandrels, within indigo turtle palmette and vine border between red and cream bands.

129in (328cm) long

$1,100-1,500 **L&T**

A Heriz rug, with a blue medallion on a red field with navy border.
c1920   *68in (173cm) long*
$3,000-4,000   **POOK**

A Heriz room-size rug, with central medallion on a red field with navy border.

The town of Heriz to the north-east of Tabriz, produces distinctive carpets with patterns based on formal town designs.

Both all-over and medallion designs are woven.

Heriz carpets are characterized by their angular rendering of the design elements. The medallions are often star-like in form.

c1930   *134in (340.5cm) long*
$2,800-3,600   **POOK**

An Isfahan carpet, the ivory field with central red and blue medallion suspending pendants, within red palmette and leafy vine border between indigo and ivory bands.
    216in (550cm) long
$6,000-8,000   **L&T**

A Persian Kashan rug, with floral pattern in rose tones, some areas of wear.
c1910   *82in (208cm) long*
$1,000-1,200   **DRA**

A Kashan carpet, central Persia.
c1920   *165in (419cm) long*
$4,400-5,600   **FRE**

A Kashan carpet, central Persia.
c1920   *157in (399cm) long*
$6,000-8,000   **FRE**

A late 19thC Kashan silk prayer rug, central Persia.
    81in (205.5cm) long
$6,000-8,000   **FRE**

A silk Kashan prayer rug, the ivory field with claret vase issuing tree-of-life pattern, claret spandrels, within claret palmette and floral border between peach and light blue bands.
    79.5in (202cm) long
$3,000-4,000   **L&T**

A Kashan silk rug, the ocher field centered by an urn issuing a spray of flowers, within navy spandrels, conforming border and guard stripes.
    82in (208cm) wide
$4,000-5,000   **DN**

A Kashan prayer rug, the indigo field with floral tree-of-life-pattern, red spandrels, within indigo floral cartouche border between cream bands.
    77in (196cm) long
$2,000-2,800   **L&T**

A Kashan part-silk prayer rug.
    92.5in (235cm) long
$600-800   **DN**

A Kashan silk rug.

78in (198cm) long

$5,200-6,000   DN

A Lavar Kerman room-size rug, with central medallion and floral pattern.

c1910   108in (274.5cm) long

$8,000-10,000   POOK

A Kerman carpet, southeast Persia, with 'JERREHIAN BROTHERS' printed cloth label on back of carpet at each end.

c1930-40   240in (609.5cm) long

$8,000-9,000   FRE

A Persian Kerman palace-sized carpet, hand-woven wool with all-over stylized florals on a burgundy ground.

1940s   266in (675.5cm) long

$18,000-24,000   JACK

A late 19thC Kurdish long rug, northwest Persia.

109in (277cm) long

$1,000-1,500   FRE

A mid-19thC Kurdish rug, northwest Persia.

69in (175.5cm) long

$2,000-3,000   FRE

A Persian Mahal carpet, the red field with all-over palmette and vine lattice.

149.5in (380cm) long

$2,000-2,600   L&T

A Mahal rug, northwest Persia.

1930s   84in (213cm) long

$400-600   WW

A Qashqai carpet, the indigo field with three ivory and red hooked lozenge medallions, red spandrels, within ivory palmette and scrolling vine border between red and blue bands.

107.5in (273cm) long

$1,800-2,200   L&T

A Qashqai rug, the plain brown field with central ivory medallion, plain indigo spandrels with inscription to each end.

These rugs are produced in Fars province, Southwestern Persia.

86.5 in (220cm) long

$1,000-1,500   L&T

A Sarouk rug, west Persia, Mahajeran type design.

c1920   91in (231cm) long

$3,200-4,000   FRE

A Sarouk carpet, west Persia.

c1930-40   248in (630cm) long

$3,000-4,000   FRE

TEXTILES

A late 19thC Sarouk Fereghan carpet, west Persia.

155in (393.5cm) long

$8,000-10,000   **FRE**

A Sarouk Fereghan rug, the rose field with central ivory stepped lozenge medallion suspending pendants, within shaped indigo palmette and floral vine border with outer rose band.

85.75in (218cm) long

$4,800-5,600   **L&T**

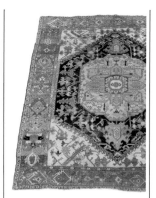

A late 19thC Serapi carpet, northwest Persia.

138in (350.5cm) long

$5,000-6,000   **FRE**

A Serapi runner, the red field with five indigo linked elongated lozenge medallions, within blue, cream and red stylized vine borders.

154.25in (392cm) long

$1,400-1,800   **L&T**

A Serapi rug, with central medallion on an ivory field with blue corners and red border.

c1910   *78in (198cm) long*

$10,000-12,000   **POOK**

A Shahsevan kelim, the indigo field with all-over pattern of polychrome serrated hexagons.

135.75in (345cm) long

$2,000-3,000   **L&T**

A Shiraz carpet, southwest Persia.

1940s   *111in (282cm) long*

$500-600   **WW**

A Tabriz carpet, northwest Persia.

An early 20thC Tabriz rug, northwest Persia, outer end of rug with a linen border with woven inscription: 'JERREHIAN BROTHERS/RUGS OF QUALITY'.

83in (211cm) long

$3,000-4,000   **FRE**

A late 19thC Tabriz silk prayer rug, northwest Persia.

64in (162.5cm) long

$6,000-8,000   **FRE**

A late 19thC Tabriz silk prayer rug, northwest Persia.

68in (172.5cm) long

$8,000-10,000   **FRE**

c1900   *171in (434.5cm) long*

$7,000-8,000   **FRE**

A large Tabriz style garden carpet, the cruciform field with central foliate roundel and fifteen rectangular tree and vase panels to each quarter, within indigo scrolling floral vine border between palmette bands.

240in (610cm) long

$5,000-7,000 **L&T**

A large Tabriz carpet, the rose field with all-over pattern of palmettes, flowers, vine and strapwork, within café-au-lait cartouche and floral vine border between green bands.

236.25in (600cm) long

$24,000-30,000 **L&T**

ESSENTIAL REFERENCE: TABRIZ

Following the Safavid conquest of Persia (now Iran), four royal workshops for weaving carpets and textiles were established in Kashan, Kerman, Isfahan (now Esfahan) and Tabriz. These grew into the four great centers of production.

- The earliest Persian carpets, produced in the 15th/16thC, are associated with Tabriz.
- Tabriz rugs generally use the symmetric (Turkish) knot.
- Tabriz designs are the most diverse in Persia, including a wide variety of curvilinear and geometric patterns. These include several variations of the medallion-and-corner design, paneled garden, vase, hunting, pictorial, etc.
- The palette of Tabriz rugs is also extremely varied, including very vivid and pastel colors.

A Persian Tabriz room-size rug with central medallion, in tones of red.

c1970

150in (381cm) long

$1,400-2,000 **DRA**

An unusual Persian Tehran Masonic rug, the plain cream field woven with central masonic devices and inscribed 'Lodge of Teheran 1541' in Persian above and English below.

41.75in (106cm) long

$1,100-1,500 **L&T**

A pair of Tehran prayer rugs, each with an ivory field centered by flowering trees below a red mihrab, within a blue border and multiple guard stripes.

82in (208cm) wide

$1,200-1,600 **DN**

A Zeigler Mahal carpet, the abrash camel field with all-over herati pattern, within rust-red rosette and floral vine border between blue and camel bands.

166in (422cm) x 148.5in (377cm)

$10,000-12,000 **L&T**

A large Zeigler carpet, the rust-red field with small blue and ivory medallion and large palmette and scrolling leafy vine pattern, within indigo palmette and floral vine border between olive and cream bands.

206.75in (525cm) x 148.5in (377cm)

$14,000-18,000 **L&T**

A woven wool carpet, in Zeigler style, retailed by Liberty, the deep orange field decorated with foliage in camel and cream tones, within conforming borders and cream guard stripes.

169.25in (430cm) wide

$8,000-12,000 **DN**

A Zeigler style carpet, the cream field with all-over large palmette and vine pattern, within brown palmette and angular vine border between brown bands.

171.25in (435cm) long

$8,000-10,000 **L&T**

A Northwest Persian runner, with seven medallions on a brown field with red border.

c1910

137in (348cm) long

$3,400-4,000 **POOK**

A North Persian pictorial rug.

c1920

79in (200.5cm) long

$4,000-6,000 **FRE**

A Chelaberd rug, the red field with central cream lozenge and indigo cruciform motif.

67.75in (172cm) long

$1,500-2,000 **L&T**

A Chi Chi rug, northeast Caucasus.

c1900 *74in (188cm) long*

$4,000-6,000 **FRE**

A Gendje rug, the brown field with all-over lattice and star pattern.

87in (221cm) long

$1,600-2,400 **L&T**

A late 19thC Karabagh rug, south Caucasus.

95in (241.5cm) long

$2,000-2,600 **FRE**

A Chelaberd rug, the red field with central ivory lozenge and green cruciform medallion flanked by ivory eagle's wings.

80.25 in (204cm) long

$3,000-3,600 **L&T**

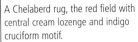

A late 19thC Kasim Ushag rug, south Caucasus.

97in (246.5cm) long

$3,000-4,000 **FRE**

A Caucasian Kazak rug, in indigo and madder red.

c1930 *103in (260cm) long*

$1,800-2,200 **DRA**

A Kazak long rug, with repeating medallions on a blue field with running dog border.

c1910 *78in (198cm) long*

$3,000-4,000 **POOK**

A Kazak throw rug, with three medallions on a red field with ivory border.

c1900 *86in (218.5cm) long*

$3,000-4,000 **POOK**

A Kazak throw rug, with three medallions on a blue field with red and blue borders.

c1910 *104in (264cm) long*

$3,000-4,000 **POOK**

A Kazak long rug, the indigo field with two elongated red and ivory medallions.

108.5in (276cm) long

$3,000-4,000 **L&T**

A Moghan Kazak rug, the field with four blue rectangles containing polychrome stepped, hooked lozenge medallions.

71.75in (182cm) long

$3,000-4,000 **L&T**

ESSENTIAL REFERENCE: KAZAK

Rugs from the Kazak district in western Caucasus, Eurasia, are epitomized by bold and open designs,

- Wool pile is long and usually much more loosely woven than rugs of the North and East of Caucasus. This results in striking, less detailed designs. These designs are often based on early classic Persian and Anatolian forms.
- With a primarily village-orientated nature of production, Kazak mainly produces small rug-sized pieces and runners, which also display the bold designs to best effect.
- The best Kazak rugs are woven with bright vibrant colors that are not conflicting. Pieces made after 1800 may include harsh chemical dyes, like oranges and purples, which stand out from the traditional, natural colors.

A Kazak throw rug, with four medallions, and red and white striped border.
c1900   *98in (249cm) long*
$5,000-6,000   **POOK**

A Kuba rug, east Caucasus, dated '1323'.
1905   *109in (277cm) long*
$3,000-4,000   **FRE**

A Kuba rug, the abrash brown field with three ivory and red medallions.
49.25in (125cm) long
$900-1,300   **L&T**

A late 19thC Lenkoran rug, southeast Caucasus.
119in (302.5cm) long
$3,600-4,400   **FRE**

A Lenkoran long rug, southeast Caucasus.
c1900   *119.5in (304cm) long*
$2,000-2,600   **WW**

A late 19th/early 20thC Lenkoran area runner, southeast Caucasus.

150in (375cm) long
$1,000-1,500   **WW**

A late 19thC Perepedil rug, east Caucasus.

57in (145cm) long
$3,000-4,000   **FRE**

A Peshawar Serapi room-size rug with geometric floral pattern in rust-colored pattern.
120in (305cm) long
$1,500-2,000   **DRA**

A late 19thC Shirvan rug, east Caucasus.

59in (150cm) long
$2,400-3,300   **FRE**

TEXTILES

A Shrivan rug, the navy field centered by red and ivory abstract medallions, within a chevron and flowerhead-decorated border within multiple guard stripes.

86.5in (220cm) long

$1,500-1,900 DN

A Shirvan rug, the ivory field with all-over red and blue stylized pattern.

70.5in (179cm) long

$3,000-4,000 L&T

A late 19th/early 20thC Shirvan rug, southeast Caucasus.

86in (219cm) long

$3,600-4,400 WW

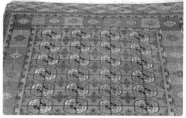

A Caucasian Soumac carpet, the red field with three columns of seven polychrome hooked lozenge medallions.

105in (267cm) long

$2,400-3,300 L&T

A Caucasian runner, with repeating medallions and human figures on a red ground with multiple borders.

c1910 *66in (167.5cm) long*

$1,000-1,500 POOK

A Caucasian carpet.

132.25in (336cm) long

$3,000-4,000 DN

TURKISH RUGS & CARPETS

An early 19thC Beshir prayer rug, south Turkestan.

82in (208.5cm) long

$4,000-6,000 FRE

An early 20thC Kazak khilim, Turkestan.

152in (386cm) long

$900-1,300 FRE

A late 19thC Oushak carpet, west Anatolia.

138in (350.5cm) long

$8,000-10,000 FRE

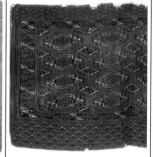

A 19thC Saryk Turkoman chuval, east Turkestan, cotton highlights.

61in (155cm) wide

$2,000-3,000 FRE

A Tekke kapunuk, the U-shaped band with red and indigo serrated scrolls on an ivory ground, within inner ivory hatched and outer X-bands, with original tassels.

46.5in (119cm) long

$6,000-7,000 L&T

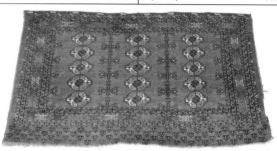

A Tekke Ensi rug.

67.75in (172cm) long

$600-800 DN

An Ushak carpet, the red field with all-over large blue palmette and cruciform motif pattern, reduced and border re-sewn to one side.

183.5in (466cm) long

$6,000-7,000   **L&T**

A large Ushak carpet, the red field with all-over pattern of large light blue palmettes and cruciform motifs.

275.5in (700cm) long

$9,000-10,000   **L&T**

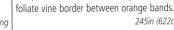

A large Ushak carpet, the red field with all-over serrated blue medallion, palmette and serrated leaf pattern, within blue lozenge, tulip and foliate vine border between orange bands.

245in (622cm) long

$16,000-20,000   **L&T**

A late 19th/early 20thC Turkestan Chyrpy, probably Uzbek.

43in (109cm) long

$400-600   **FRE**

A late 19th/early 20thC Turkestan Chyrpy, probably Uzbek.

41in (104cm) long

$400-600   **FRE**

A late 19thC Yomud asmalyk, west Turkestan.

45in (114.5cm) wide

$1,000-1,400   **FRE**

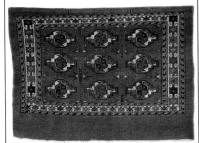

A mid-to late 19thC Yomud Group chuval, west Turkestan.

43in (109cm) wide

$1,200-1,600   **FRE**

A late 19thC Yomud Group khordjin, west Turkestan.

37in (94cm) wide

$1,000-2,000   **FRE**

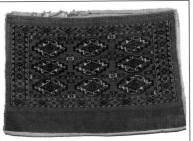

A Yomut juval, the red field with three columns of three guls, original back.

45.75in (116cm) x 29.5in (75cm) high

$300-400   **L&T**

A 19thC Western Turkoman tentband (Ak Yup), west Turkestan.

The present tentband is knotted on adjacent warps, like a piled rug, rather than on alternating warps as is typical of mixed technique tentbands. As such, the knots are viewable from the back of the tentband.

438in (1,112.5cm) long

$7,000-9,000 FRE

A Turkish silk rug, the rose field with all-over palmette and leafy vine pattern.

62.5in (159cm) long

$1,500-1,900 L&T

OTHER RUGS & CARPETS

A Chinese saddle cover, comprising two sewn shaped ivory panels, each with central deer and two leather bosses.

52.25in (133cm) long

$600-1,000 L&T

An 18thC Chinese wool carpet, dark blue edge, ivory ground with light blue lotus flowers issuing leaves.

96in (30.5cm) long

$3,000-4,000 FRE

A Chinese, late Qing Dynasty rug, central medallion of eight floral sprigs to a blue ground within two diaper borders.

102in (259cm) long

$1,500-2,000 FRE

A 19thC Chinese voided velvet carpet, the mid-brown velvet woven with purple and coral-pink peonies and scrolling foliage.

82.5in (210cm) wide

$1,200-1,800 KT

A 19thC Tibetan tiger rug, of rectangular form, woven wool pink and brown striped tiger on a blue ground.

55in (139.5cm) long

$9,000-13,000 FRE

A late 19thC Tibetan rug, depicting two multi-color dragons chasing a flaming pearl and ruyi clouds.

72in (183cm) long

$800-1,400 FRE

A Laristan carpet, north India.

c1920 *165in (419cm) long*
$4,000-5,000 FRE

An Indian carpet.

c1940 *142in (360.5cm) long*
$2,400-3,300 FRE

An Afghan rug.

126in (320cm) long
$900-1,300 DN

A late 18th/early 19thC Ladik prayer rug, central Anatolia, inscribed in Armenian 'GLR' and includes a 'cross of Jerusalem' in the stepped mihrab.

62in (157.5cm) long
$3,000-3,600 FRE

A Konya long rug, central Anatolia.

c1875 *124in (315cm) long*
$3,600-4,400 FRE

A woven carpet in Aubusson style, of recent manufacture.

165in (419cm) wide
$2,000-3,000 DN

A 20thC woven carpet, the brown field with an acanthus scroll-decorated border, bearing label to underside 'TUBERVILLE SMITH & SON LTD'.

220in (560cm) wide
$700-1,100 DN

TAPESTRIES

A 17thC Flemish tapestry, woven in wool and silk with exotic birds, animals and foliage surrounding an architectural arch, the wide fruit-woven border with oval reserves depicting landscape views, bears Royal coat of arms.

12.25 (285cm) long
$10,000-12,000 L&T

A 17thC continental verdure tapestry depicting the Trojan Horse and robed figures, reduced, faded and with general wear and tears overall.

124in (315cm) wide
$11,000-13,000 DN

A 17thC Continental verdure tapestry, depicting hunting dogs attacking a bear in a wooded landscape, with later brass hanging rod, some wears, tears and fading.

118in (300cm) wide
$2,400-3,300 DN

A mid-18thC French Beauvais tapestry panel, designed by Jean Baptiste Oudry, with an owl being tormented by other birds, originally a sofa back, condition poor to the center.

49.25in (125cm) long
$7,000-8,000 L&T

TEXTILES

An American large wool and cotton hooked rug, with central basket of flowers flanked by the numerals '18' and '63', scattered losses, repairs, dated.

1863   *52in (116.5cm) wide*

$6,000-8,000   **SK**

A late 19th/early 20thC wool and cotton penny rug, composed of concentric discs of multicolored wool fabric edged with blanket stitching, arranged and sewn in an oblong hexagonal design on an off-white cotton backing.

90in (228.5cm) long

$3,000-4,000   **SK**

An early 20thC American wool pictorial hooked rug, with houses and Christmas trees, with multicolored striped border, mounted on a wooden frame, scattered wear, fading.

40.25in (102cm) wide

$1,500-2,000   **SK**

ESSENTIAL REFERENCE: GRENFELL RUGS

British doctor, Wilfred Grenfell was sent to Newfoundland in 1892 to establish a medical mission.

- The women of Newfoundland made hooked rugs from narrow strips of wool or cotton hooked closely together through linen or burlap backing. Grenfell hit upon the idea of supplementing impoverished women's incomes making similar rugs, many of which he designed himself, and selling them in the cities.
- Grenfell encouraged the women to form cooperatives and helped to transform the economy of this impoverished area.
- The rug makers were given kits created by Grenfell's wife that included everything they needed for the work.
- The earliest Grenfell rugs were made of wool and cotton, whilst later examples are often made from donated dyed silk stockings.
- Grenfell rugs are decorated with scenes that reflect the environment of Newfoundland, including fishing scenes and dog teams.
- Grenfell rugs were sold in several shops in Canada, New York and Philadelphia from 1910 to the late 1940s.

An early 20thC Grenfell pictorial hooked mat with dog sled scene, Grenfell Labrador Industries, Newfoundland and Labrador, woven maker's label affixed to the reverse, mounted on wood stretchers.

40in (101.5cm) wide

$2,500-3,500   **SK**

An early 20thC American wool and cotton pictorial hooked rug, depicting a house flanked by a well sweep and pine tree with a dog, cat, and flowers in the foreground, mounted on a wood frame.

38 in (96.5cm) wide

$1,500-2,000   **SK**

An early 20thC American wool and cotton pictorial hooked rug, depicting a house, five chickens, and two geese, mounted on a wood frame, minor fading, toning, and losses.

41in (104cm) wide

$5,000-7,000   **SK**

A 20thC American 'Wool Starbust' hooked rug, square shaped with central radiating star motif in shades of red and blue, mounted on a wood frame.

38in (97cm) square

$200-300   **SK**

A large hooked rug, from Madison, Wisconsin, original design by Edna Bullard, with 117 squares, each with a different floral sprig or object, comprised of polychrome yarns.

1946   108x144in (274.5x366cm)

$5,500-6,500   **FRE**

A mid-20thC Massachusetts hooked rug, with Pearl K. McGown pattern, a 'Dutch' design with tulips and hearts within a border of flowers in urns and flowerheads at corners, worked in polychrome yarns on a burlap ground.

$250-350   **FRE**

An American woven wool and Linsey-Woolsey zigzag quilt, with rows of brown and red unglazed worsted wool triangles stitched together.

c1820   72in (183cm) wide

$5,000-6,000   **SK**

A mid-19thC Baltimore appliqué album quilt, with an assortment of floral arrangements in chintz, cotton, and calico fabrics, all within a bow and swag border.

$16,000-20,000   **POOK**

CLOSER LOOK: ALBUM QUILT

Album quilts are made up of individually decorated blocks which are pieced together. This one is composed of sixteen printed and plain fabric blocks. Green and red motifs on a white ground are common.

They were made to commemorate significant events such as a marriage or as a gift to friends who were moving West and so feature symbols or events which would have been significant in the makers' and the recipients' lives.

Motifs include Baltimore's monument honoring George Washington, a fire pumper truck flanked by American flags, in support of volunteer fire departments, a building, likely the nation's capitol, floral urns, a heart-shaped floral wreath commemorating Baltimore's fallen Mexican-American War heroes, birds, wreaths, and hearts linked by brotherhood, each square separated by a grid of red fabric.

The border is decorated with swags, flower blossoms and rosettes flanked by red and green sawtooth borders.

A pieced and appliquéd cotton Baltimore album quilt, some motifs padded or embroidered with wool yarns, edged in red, two squares signed, one with a pen and ink image of a bird with a banner inscribed 'Sarah Shafer Baltimore 1850,' another square signed ' John Hadly', unbacked.

107in (272cm) wide

$30,000-40,000   **SK**

A rare and important Captain Hosea C. Wyman Civil War Baltimore album quilt, dated.

Made by the captain's wife, Judith Dicks Wyman. According to family history Captain Wyman was lost at sea in 1879 along with his son, Clifford Wyman.

1863   81in (206cm) high

$14,000-18,000   **JDJ**

A 19thC appliqué crib quilt, with swag border,

34in (86.5cm) wide

$6,000-7,000   **POOK**

A Lebanon or Lancaster County, Pennsylvania pieced cotton 'Carpenter's Wheel' quilt.

c1885   85.5in (217cm) wide

$7,000-9,000   **SK**

A late 19thC American Pennsylvania vibrant pieced crib quilt, with a central checkboard diamond panel within a sawtooth border with diamond corners and scalloped edge.

41in (104cm) wide

$25,000-30,000   **POOK**

A late 19thC American pieced and appliquéd 'Four Pots of Flowers' quilt.

76in (193cm) wide

$8,500-9,500   **SK**

A late 19thC 'Burgoyne Surrounded' quilt, commemorating the American Revolutionary War Battle of Saratoga where British General Burgoyne surrendered on October 17, 1777.

69.5in (176.5cm) wide

$1,800-2,500   **SK**

A Trapunto appliqué quilt.

Trapunto is quilting in which the design is outlined with two or more rows of running stitches and then padded from the underside to achieve a raised effect.

80in (203.5cm) wide

$3,500-4,000   **POOK**

A rare Amish wool crib quilt with pieced stars, blocks, and bars in various colors.

44.5in (113cm) high

$13,000-15,000   **POOK**

TEXTILES

An early 18thC needlework panel, worked with a lady shepherdess and gentleman in an idealized landscape with buildings to the distance.

20in (51cm) wide

$2,000-2,600   DUK

An American Philadelphia wool-on-linen needlework, depicting a bird perched on a floral tree atop a grassy landscape.

c1750   *11.75in (30cm) high*

$22,000-28,000   POOK

An American canvaswork picture, probably Boston, depicting a shepherdess, sheep, spotted dog, cow and exotic bird in tree, and brick house beyond, worked in polychrome wool yarns, in original frame.

c1750   *16in (40.5cm) high*

$50,000-60,000   FRE

A mid-18thC English pictorial needlework, with two figures in a pastoral setting with animals and birds.

18in (45.5cm) high

$5,600-6,800   POOK

A mid-18thC needlework picture, the central oval depicting a pastoral scene of a shepherd and shepherdess with gambolling lambs, the shepherd playing a flute, enclosed by flowerhead and foliate motifs, within a molded maple frame.

35.25in (80cm) high

$3,000-4,000   L&T

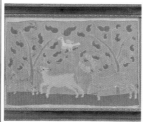

A mid-18thC American wool needlework and felt picture, possible Pennsylvania, depicting a landscape with stag, doe and fawn below a tree with a dove.

12.5in (32cm) wide

$3,400-4,000   POOK

A framed mid-18thC embroidered picture worked in tent stitch with colored wools, depicting Tobias leaving home for Medea (slightly worn and reworked in parts).

22.75in (58cm) high

$1,400-1,800   L&T

A mid-18thC French tent stitch needlework, depicting figures in a landscape within a floral border.

32.5in (82.5cm) high

$4,000-6,000   POOK

An early 19thC English wool and silk-on-linen needlework picture, depicting a woman seated in front of her house with dog, fisherman, butterfly, cherry tree and perched peacock, with a gilt-lined ogee frame.

22in (56cm) wide

$18,000-22,000   POOK

A 19thC American wool-on-cloth trapunto needlework picture, with birds perched in a cherry tree, retaining paper label verso, inscribed 'Miss Elizabeth L. Baker, Bernardsville, New Jersey'.

30.5in (77.5cm) high

$5,000-6,000   POOK

A 19thC wool- and chenille-on-silk needlework picture.

22.5in high

$300-400   POOK

A 19thC woolwork picture of two hounds amongst foliage, signed 'Linwood', with gilt frame.

17.25in (44cm) wide overall

$1,200-1,600   DN

An 18thC silk needlework, depicting a central urn with flowers.

7.5in (19cm) square

$2,600-3,200   POOK

A silk-on-linen needlework, with trumpeting angels and seated figures flanking the ten commandments, dated.

1744   15.5in (39.5cm) wide

$900-1,300   POOK

An early 19thC English silk, chenille and paint-on-silk pictorial needlework, depicting a young husband and wife with their two children, dog and nanny in a landscape, signed in stitch under mat 'Viclor'.

13.5in (34.5cm) wide

$5,000-7,000   POOK

A silk-on-linen needlework wrought by Miss Margaret Smith, the central brick house flanked by trees with animals and figures on a green lawn within a floral vine border.

16.5in (42cm) high

$6,000-8,000   POOK

SAMPLERS

One of a pair of needlework samplers in silk on linen inscribed, 'Nancy Martindale 1761' on one, the other '1759' with alphabets, numbers, flowers, scenes, figures, trees and animals.

16in (41cm) high

$3,000-4,000 PAIR   POOK

CLOSER LOOK: NAPOLEONIC WAR SAMPLER

The brown linen ground is worked with a soldier and a sailor with Britannia medallion to the center and a lion and unicorn beneath. This eye-catching central image adds to the sampler's appeal.

The overall design is well balanced and finely stitched.

The borders and the panels either side of the main verse are formed of entwined flowering vines.

Text that comments on current affairs is highly desirable. Here the mottoes read: 'Britain Rule Nia' (Britannia Rule), 'God Save the King', 'O the Roast Beef of Old England', the upper verse 'if the French should invade us they shall be taught, How dearly one inch of our isle must be bought, Hand and Heart one and all for the land that is free, And we'll soon drive those Plunderers into the sea, Britons strike home hearts of oak'.

A rare Napoleonic war sampler, 'Briton's Protection', by Mary Millward.

1804   Framed 20in (51cm) high

$8,000-10,000   KT

A needlework sampler, worked in silk threads on a loosely woven wool ground, signed and dated 'Mary Vowles, November 21 1794 FINIS', in a later molded wood frame, small losses to backing fabric.

17in (43cm) wide

$2,400-2,800   SK

An embroidered sampler, by Ann Spencer and also bearing the name of her teacher 'Mrs C Hall', worked in couched and looped silks and in Algerian eye and cross stitch, with large trees and pots of harebells, the ground scattered with little birds and beasts with 'Lord of All Power' verse to the center.

c1800   Framed 14.25in (36cm) wide

$1,200-1,800   KT

An embroidered sampler, by Amy Langdon, 'Life how short, Eternity how long', the cream wool ground completely smothered with tiny figures, animals, a central red house, parrots, butterflies, roosters, angels, carnation and daisy border.

1802   18.5in (47cm) wide

$6,000-8,000   KT

TEXTILES

A Chester County, Pennsylvania wool and silk-on-linen needlework picture, of two peacocks, inscribed 'CM' and '1745'.

10in (25.5cm) high

$25,000-30,000   **POOK**

A Philadelphia silk-on-linen needlework, wrought by Mary Laskey, attributed to Mary Zeller's school, the building surrounded by a hairy goat, stag, birds, insects and lawn with figures and animals, dated.

1795   21.5in (54.5cm) high

$20,000-25,000   **POOK**

A Folwell School, Philadelphia silkwork picture, the Nativity worked in silk and chenille threads and watercolor on a silk ground, retains section of original eglomise with needleworker's initials 'E.C', original giltwood frame, dated.

PROVENANCE: Of extraordinary size, only four works of this subject are known to exist. All have been attributed to the instruction of Godfrey Folwell, 1799-1855.

1812   35in (89cm) wide

$50,000-60,000   **FRE**

An early 19thC American silk needlework picture, worked with silk threads and watercolor-painted faces, depicting a mother seated on a chair reading to her child, with a young lady playing a harp in a landscape, tears, creases, in a period molded giltwood frame.

20in (51cm) wide

$7,500-9,500   **SK**

A needlework family register, worked in silk and chenille threads on a linen ground, signed and dated 'Wrought by Charlotte Baker, Franklin (Massachusetts)', with applied brass corner rosettes, toning, fading, dated.

1822   19.25in (49cm) high

$2,000-3,000   **SK**

A Pennsylvania silk, chenille, spangles and paint-on-silk needlework picture, from the Lititz Moravian Girls' School, inscribed on the tablet 'Hannah Mary M'Conaughy Lititz May 1825', with original gilt frame.

1825   20.5in (52cm) wide

$35,000-40,000   **POOK**

A rare Lititz, Pennsylvania silk, chenille and paint-on-silk memorial, inscribed 'In Memory of my sister Mary Jane Annan'.

c1825   21in (53.25cm) wide

$5,000-7,000   **POOK**

A Montgomery County, Pennsylvania silk-on-linen needlework picture, depicting four types of birds perched on a tree, inscribed 'An Aerial Scene. Mary Rees 1828'.

This is only one of four known works from this school.

10in (25cm) high

$5,500-6,500   **POOK**

An American 19thC silk and paint-on-silk needlework memorial, depicting a young woman seated beside an urn, below a willow tree with a town in the background.

13.25in (33.5cm) wide

$2,500-3,000   **POOK**

A folk art needlework woolen picture, depicting a spotted dog with a red collar and a three-flap side pocket with cross stitch border.

c1890   28in (71cm) wide

$4,500-5,500   **POOK**

An early 20thC Asian export patriotic silk embroidered picture, with an eagle and American shields and banner inscribed 'E. Pluribus Unum', under a canopy of stars worked with silk metallic threads, framed.

31in (78.5cm) wide

$900-1,200   **FRE**

A needlework sampler, worked with silk threads on a linen ground, signed and dated 'Elizabeth Auteracher worked in the 12 year of her age and finished this work March 28 1806 Hereford', in a contemporary mitred oak frame.

21.25in (54cm) high

$300-360   SK

A needlework sampler, silk threads on a linen ground, signed and dated 'Hannah Hildreth Aged 9/1808', in a molded giltwood frame, minor toning and foxing.

18.25in (46.5cm) high

$4,000-6,000   SK

A needlework sampler, worked in silk threads on a linen ground, signed and dated 'Mary Francis aged 9 years in the year 1811', in a contemporary wood frame.

22in (55.5cm) high

$1,800-2,200   SK

A needlework sampler, 'Mary H. Bateman Born Aug. 6 1818 Aged 10 yrs.,' stitched with silk on linen with the verse 'May truth and virtue guide thy heart, Nor hope nor peace nor joy depart.'

16.5in (42cm) wide

$4,000-5,000   SK

A needlework sampler, framed.

c1820   *15.25in (39cm) wide*

$440-560   DN

A needlework sampler worked in wool threads on a linen ground, signed and dated 'Sarah Greens Sampler Aged 12 1824', in a later molded wood frame, toning, stitch losses.

16.5in (42cm) high

$1,000-1,500   SK

A needlework sampler, 'Jane Halsey March 10 1825,' in silk on wool, depicting a large building, likely an academy, surrounded by a fence, plants and birds.

13in (33cm) wide

$1,600-2,000   SK

A large pictorial needlework sampler, in silk on linen, with several monograms, likely members of Louisa's family, and geometric floral and strawberry borders, signed 'Louisa Lamberts 1831,'.

24.5in (62cm) high

$5,000-6,000   SK

An unusual early 19thC needlework sampler, showing a kneeling figure of a black slave in chains above a field of sheep and inscribed 'Pity the negro slave, emancipated in 1832, Hannah Shiels', in mahogany frame.

10.25in (26cm) high

$8,000-10,000   L&T

TEXTILES

A New England silk-on-needlework sampler, inscribed 'Mary Thomas August', the script flanked by columns holding flower pots, tree, birds, alphabet and tulip border worked in satin cross, dated.

1793   *20.5ins (52cm) wide*

$9,000-11,000   **POOK**

A Lancaster County, Pennsylvania silk-on-linen sampler, wrought by Dolly Sheller, attributed to Miss Galligher School, the central script surrounded by hearts, geometric devices and a church with trees, dated.

1800   *17.5ins wide*

$6,000-7,000   **POOK**

A pair of Londonderry, New Hampshire silk-on-linen samplers, wrought by sisters Hannah and Mary McMurphy, each with central alphabet within a stylized border, dated.

1818   *Largest 14in (35.5cm) high*

$3,500-4,000 PAIR   **POOK**

A needlework memorial/Adams family register sampler, Lunenburg, Worcester County, Massachusetts, 'Wrought by Lucy Adams Aed 12', 'Wrought in 1819', stitched in silk on linen with the names and current ages of Lucy and her twelve siblings.

A genealogical record indicates that Lucy and her siblings were the children of Jonathan (b. March 5 1759, Groton, MA) and Elizabeth (Gary) Adams (b. Feb. 26, 1764, Lunenburg, MA). They were married Dec. 13, 1781, and their thirteen children were all born in Lunenburg, Massachusetts.

1819   *16.25in (41.5cm) square*

$3,000-4,000   **SK**

A needlework family record, 'Wrought by Adeline Patch Sept. 1823 Aged 11 yrs.,' from Middlesex County, Massachusetts, in silk on linen, with details of John Patch (b. July 23 1780), Abigail Trowbridge (b. May 29 1791) and their six children.

1823   *17in (43cm) wide*

$2,000-3,000   **SK**

A needlework sampler, 'Mary M. Case's Sampler wrought in the year 1828 in the 11 year of her age, Chelsea, Orange County, Vermont', worked in silk threads on a linen ground, fading, minor stains, in a period molded giltwood frame.

1828   *7.75in (45cm) wide*

$3,000-4,000   **SK**

An American silk-on-linen sampler, wrought by Sarah Livingston, Hollidaysburg, Huntingdon County, Pennsylvania, with alphabet and verse over potted flowers within a floral vine border, dated.

1834   *6.5in (42cm) wide*

$3,000-3,500   **POOK**

A Lancaster County, Pennsylvania silk-on-linen needlework sampler, wrought by 'Mary Ann Gardner', with lawn, house, trees, animals, figures, and strawberry border, dated.

1836   *19in (48.5cm) wide*

$3,000-4,000   **POOK**

A Virginia silk-on-linen sampler, wrought by Isabella Kirk with alphabet and verse over potted flowers, dated.

1836   *17.25in (44cm) wide*

$3,500-4,000   **POOK**

A York, Pennsylvania silk-on-linen needlework, wrought by Anna Mary Ebert, with alphabet over brick house within a floral border, dated.

1837   *18in (45.5cm) high*

$3,500-4,000   **POOK**

A Berks or Montgomery County, Pennsylvania silk-on-linen sampler, probably inscribed 'Sarah Krieble', with alphabet, floral bands, birds, deer, and potted plants, dated.

1841   *18in (45.5cm) wide*

$3,000-4,000   **POOK**

An embroidered pictorial sampler, by Ann Chapman, with short verse on the theme of mortality, large central Georgian house with climbing plants, within a parkland with rose arbours, lawns with a seated girl and her dog, an elegant young lady with a basket and presumably their parents to either side – a stout black garbed gentleman with his stick, and a bonneted lady with her kerchief, worked in silks on a cream wool ground.

1839   *Framed 17.25in (44cm) wide*
$6,000-8,000   **KT**

An English silk-on-linen needlework, wrought by Ann Bayley Pettipher, religious verse, Native American figures, trees and pastoral scenes, dated.

1858   *13in (33.5cm) wide*
$1,500-2,000   **POOK**

OTHER TEXTILES

A set of late 17thC English crewelworked bedhanging, heavily re-worked in the 1920s, comprising two large square curtains, two narrow curtains, a long fringed pelmet, three valance panels, two of which are 1920s.

89.75in (228cm) long
$16,000-20,000 SET   **KT**

A late 17thC 'bearing' or christening cloth, of pale blue/silver satin, with deep border of gold and silver bobbin lace, backed in pale blue silk, with hand-written note attached to one corner 'Christening cloth, Newton'.

75in (190cm) long
$1,800-2,400   **KT**

A late 17th/early 18thC English stumpwork, with spread-winged eagle, snakes and stylized floral and fruit trees.

11.75in (30cm) wide
$2,200-2,800   **POOK**

A Queen Anne pictorial beadwork, the center with vibrant blue, green, yellow, brown and tan pot with numerous intricate flowers flanked by recumbent stag, unicorn, lion and tiger

c1710   *15.5in (39.5cm) wide*
$4,000-5,000   **POOK**

A pair of embroidered and false-quilted cushions, the linen ground delicately worked in fine chain stitch with meandering foliage and exotic blooms, the reverse of linen covered with a lattice of yellow false-quilting stitch.

c1700-10   *Larger 19in (48cm) wide*
$11,000-13,000   **KT**

A pair of chinoiserie embroidered cushions, the linen ground embroidered with central phoenix motifs, the corners with oriental ladies below large parasols, the reverse with a lattice of fine chain stitch within foliate borders.

c1700-10   *18in (46cm) wide*
$3,000-4,000   **KT**

An early 18thC Italian embroidered mirror surround, with raised work central rocaille and acanthus scrolls worked mainly in couched silver threads, mounted onto crimson velvet, inset with an antique mirror plate, later braid border.

36in (90cm) square
$2,000-2,600   **KT**

A Continental stitching sample, inscribed 'Anno 1734', with various blocks of flame stitch, herringbone, tent stitch, eye stitch, etc., alphabet, flowers, potted fruit trees, birds, and flower-filled urn.

$5,000-6,000   **POOK**

TEXTILES

An unusual mid-18thC American needlework and felt picture, depicting a colorful bird perched on a cherry tree with lawn and flowers, the felt outlined in stitches.

$6,000-10,000   POOK

An 18thC linen panel with crewelwork embroidery, worked in colored wools upon a joined cream linen panel, the central cartouche with initials 'IAWR' below a coronet, surrounded by stylized flowers and pomegranates.

65in (165cm) long

$1,600-2,000   DN

An early 19thC American folk art needlework embroidery, with rows of human figures.

20in (51cm) wide

$4,000-6,000   POOK

A French copper-plate printed bedcurtain, with the 'Apotheosis of Franklin and Washington' printed in red on a cotton ground, comprised of three panels.

c1785   87in (221cm) wide

$8,000-10,000   FRE

A pair of silk portières woven with Glasgow rose pattern in jade green and black, some discoloration.

88 in (224cm) long

$700-1,100   DRA

An early 19thC printed cotton handkerchief, printed in green with 'Dr. B. Franklin's Maxims or Moral Pictures for Youth'.

17.5in (44.5cm) wide

$2,000-3,000   FRE

A Carlisle, Pennsylvania appliqué tablecloth, with colorful baskets of tulips and tulip trees.

c1900

$700-900   POOK

COSTUMES AND COUTURE

An 18thC infant bodice of 1720s silk lampas, the ground of light brown satin woven with yellow and blue leaf shapes, berries and lace patterns, lined in raspberry pink silk, adorned with gold bobbin lace, back laced.

13in (33cm) long

$1,800-2,200   KT

A pair of stays, of pale brown linen with green top-stitched detailing, green and white Chinese damask satin center panel, back laced.

c1760

$3,000-4,000   KT

A figured black silk gentleman's suit, the black silk ground woven with fine green stripes and small pink and blue lozenges, lined in ivory silk, matching breeches with small-fall front, the ivory satin waistcoat embroidered with wild flowers and oak leaves.

c1790

$10,000-12,000   KT

A late 1870s/early 1880s Worth labeled blue dolman jacket, with velvet collar, with engine-turned mother-of-pearl buttons to fasten, lined in navy self-striped satin, with vestigial blue satin hood with ribbon trim.

This has the printed gold-on-black Worth label which was used during the c1870-1885 period.

Chest 36in (92cm)

$1,100-1,500   KT

A Worth ball gown, with signature label to waistband, of pink damask satin woven with large bearded irises and swags of interlaced ribbons.

c1900

$4,600-5,600   KT

An Edwardian cream lace and embroidered tea dress, with elaborate naturalistic stumpwork embroidery with a centralized exotic bird motif, surrounded by stylized flora and fauna, glass buttons at shoulders and one side.

$600-800   FRE

A Liberty & Co. black and gold damask evening mantle, woven with leaf clusters against a checkered ground, large knotted tassels to the sleeve openings, large gilt thread buttons and fringed hem, un-lined, labeled 'Liberty & Co, Paris & London'.

c1915

$1,300-1,700   KT

A blue satin jacket for a Captain of the Guard, from Diaghilev's Ballet Russes 'La Boutique Fantasque', first performed 1919, designed by André Derain.

$700-900   KT

ESSENTIAL REFERENCE: BALLET RUSSES

The Ballet Russes (French for the 'Russian Ballet') was established in 1909 by Russian impresario Serge Diaghilev (1872-1929). The vitality, color and movement in Russian ballet created a sensation in Western Europe, and its influence can be seen in almost every area of the arts in the Art Deco period.

- The dancers were associated and trained with the Tsar's Imperial Ballet of St Petersburg. It used many of the works of the great choreographer Marius Petipa.
- The sets designed by Léon Bakst were brilliantly colored and featured a medley of Persian, Oriental and Russian influences. These inspired interior designers to move away from the restrained palette of the previous era. Textile designers embraced the colorful geometric patterns seen in the ballet.
- Two of the Ballet Russes's dancers, Ida Rubenstein and Vaslav Nijinsky, became the models for the 'Russian Dancers' by Demêtre Chiparus, the master of bronze and ivory sculpture.
- Art Deco furniture designers inspired by the ballet used colorful and exotic materials like Macassar ebony and palisander enriched with ivory, shagreen and lacquer in bold patterns such as sun-rays and checks.

A Lezghin outfit, for Diaghilev's Ballet Russes 'Thamar', first performed 1912, designed by Leon Bakst, comprising fuchsia pink satin frock-coat edged with silver braid stenciled with diamonds, hanging sleeves with inner blue satin sleeves striped with yellow silk, calico lining inked 'Frank George Heops', with a pair of yellow satinized cotton Turkish trousers adorned with silver braid and green ribbons, with inked label written in Russian, green satin belt with inked names 'Andreef, Bor, Alg'.

$27,000-31,000   KT

A 1920s Art Deco beaded dress, silk straight caftan sheath with shoulder-grazing sleeves, beaded with short cut bugle beads.

$500-700   **FRE**

A 1920s black silk floral medallion-jacquard Art Deco gown, unlabeled.

$500-1,000   **FRE**

A late 1930s/1940s Jeanne Lanvin black silk jersey 'Goddess' gown, with large woven silk label, numbered '2590.5'.

Bust approx 36in (91cm)

$2,600-3,200   **KT**

A rayon cream twill beaded skirt suit, pencil skirt with nipped-waist fitted jacket, 'key hole' neckline, with a trailing bellflower beaded motif in red, blue and gunmetal-gray on the back of the collar and left shoulder, unlined and unlabeled.

1940s

$300-400   **FRE**

A Jeanne Lanvin emerald green tulle ball gown, the boned strapless bodice with ruched and shirred panels, the separate petticoat with bouffant section to left hip to raise the skirt higher at that point to give an asymmetric hemline, labeled and numbered '6653'.

Summer 1949   *Bust 34in (86cm)*

$5,200-6,000   **KT**

An early 1950s Paquin black velvet and organza halter-necked gown, the slim fitted bodice with cross-over pleats of organza to the décolleté, with large organza bow to the back, bearing the Paquin 'Les Couturiers Associès' label.

Bust 36in (91cm)

$4,000-5,000   **KT**

An early 1950s Madame Grès black and white taffeta ball gown, with a play of black against white, labeled 'Grès, 1 Rue de la Paix, Paris'.

Bust 34in (86cm)

$3,000-4,000   **KT**

A Christian Dior goffered silk organza and velvet evening gown, the bodice with boning but not corseted, of cream organza with flounce of black organza emerging from the black velvet band below, stiffened inner petticoat, labeled and numbered '10893', and also labeled behind the main label '188337'.

1951   *Bust 32in (82cm)*

$16,000-20,000   **KT**

HUBERT de GIVENCHY
PARIS

An early Hubert de Givenchy orientalist dinner gown, comprising button-fronted bodice, cut wide at the shoulders, the over-skirt with nipped-in waist of beetle-wing black and green changeable silk, together with a black silk petticoat, labeled and numbered '3328'.

1952   *Bust 34in (86cm)*

$4,400-5,600   **KT**

A 1950s Jean Patou black wool crêpe cocktail gown, with corseted inner bodice.

Bust 34in (86cm)

$1,500-1,900   **KT**

A mid-1950s Madame Grès ball gown, the elaborately boned strapless bodice edged in garlands of silk blossom and roses, the dress formed from four layers of white and yellow chiffon, organza and taffeta and a final translucent overlay of glistening white horsehair which gives glimpses of the primrose yellow layers below and also ensures a perfect silhouette, labeled 'Grès, 1 Rue de la Paix, Paris'.

Bust 34in (86cm)

$7,000-8,000   **KT**

A Christian Dior shocking pink party dress, silk taffeta with silk gauze lining in the skirt, with large applied bow detail at front and an attached stand-up shawl, labeled 'Christian Dior New York.'

Fall 1958

$500-800 FRE

A late 1950s Simonetta stenciled satin and cut velvet evening coat, label removed.

$6,000-8,000 KT

A Pierre Balmain ball gown and matching evening coat, labeled and indistinctly numbered, the boned strapless bodice with ruched folds of ivory satin emphasising the curves of the breast in contrast to the tiny, fitted waist and enormous satin skirt with five internal layers of silk, tulle and horsehair petticoats, embroidered and appliquéd overall, faintly numbered '24, 418'.

1955 *Gown bust 34in (82cm)*

$40,000-50,000 KT

A late 1950s Pierre Balmain oyster satin evening gown, labeled and numbered '84-466'.

34in (86cm)

$7,000-9,000 KT

A Jean Dessès chine rose-print taffeta cocktail dress, detached label, with corseted inner bodice, with inner and outer taffeta skirts and layers of tulle petticoats, the overskirt draped and caught in place with a massive bow to one side, matching belt.

c1959 *Bust 38in (96cm)*

$3,600-4,800 KT

A late 1950s/early1960s Balenciaga oyster taffeta evening coat, no fastenings, the sleeve and front panels cut in one piece, the back and rear sleeves also cut in one piece, labeled 'Eisa'.

Chest 52in (132cm)

$8,000-10,000 KT

A Balenciaga petrol blue silk ball gown, hem encrusted in a 2in (5cm) wide band of tiered beading with molded white lily of the valley and globular beads, crystal discs and cream silk buds, labeled and numbered '93027'.

c1958-60 *Bust 34in (86cm)*

$3,400-4,000 KT

A Victor Saks leopard coat, with mink cuffs and collar.

1960s *Bust 40in (101cm)*

$1,600-2,000 FRE

A 1960s Bob Bugnand party dress, with rhinestone-, branch-coral- and mother-of-pearl-encrusted bodice, tussah silk tulip-shaped skirt with matching beadwork at hem, labeled 'Bob Bugnand, Paris'

Size 0-2

$800-1,200 FRE

TEXTILES

A 1960s black feathered column gown, with silk ribbon straps decorated with bows, back zip closure.

Size 6-8

$1,000-1,500   **FRE**

Monroe's status as one of the most iconic images of the 20th century, her links with JFK, along with the inclusion of two photographs apparently showing her wearing these trousers add to their desirability.

The label reads: 'Designed by Jax'. Jax was one of Marilyn Monroe's favourite designers and she also owned dresses by him.

The narrow, fitted look was typical of Jax's designs.

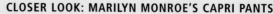

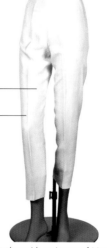

Marilyn Monroe's cream slubbed silk Capri pants, together with an image of Marilyn Monroe, seemingly wearing these pants, taken by Willy Rizzo in 1961, and another by George Barris taken in one of her last photo sessions in June 1962, two months before her death.

c1961-62   *Waist 25in (64cm)*

$10,000-12,000   **KT**

A 1960s Guy Laroche violet silk fox-trimmed opera coat, bright violet-red silk with large decorative buttons and black fox collar and cuffs, labeled 'Guy Laroche Paris'.

$400-600   **FRE**

A 1960s Rudi Gernreich tapestry mini dress, labeled 'Rudi Gernreich'.

$400-600   **FRE**

A 1960s leopard fur stroller coat, labeled 'Patchin Furs'.

Size medium

$3,000-4,000   **FRE**

A Cristobal Balenciaga primrose yellow silk ball gown, labeled, number is indistinct.

c1960   *Bust 36in (91cm)*

$6,000-8,000   **KT**

A Balenciaga hot pink and fuchsia matelassé cocktail ensemble, the sleeveless gown with jewel-neckline, the matching coat with three-quarter sleeves and fold-over lapels, labeled and numbered '33030'.

c1960   *Bust 36in (92cm)*

$6,000-7,000   **KT**

A Madame Grès navy pleated jersey evening gown, the fitted bodice with split to center front and with vertical splits, labeled.

c1960   *Bust 34-36in (86-91cm)*

$8,000-10,000   **KT**

An early 1960s Princess Galitzene feather-sequinned mini dress, the black silk ground entirely smothered in spiky pierced elliptical black sequins, labeled 'Irene Galitzene, Roma'.

Bust 34-36in (86-91cm)

$5,000-6,000   **KT**

A Pierre Cardin jewelled evening gown, entirely covered in gold and silver sequins in a giant hounds-tooth check repeat and further embellished with large rose-cut and elliptical pastes, labeled 'Pierre Cardin Paris'.

c1965   *Bust 34in (87cm)*

$11,000-13,000   **KT**

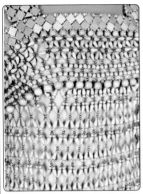

A rare Yves Saint Laurent 'African' Collection mini-dress, the beige silk/linen under-dress covered with a tunic of latticed wooden beads, lined in beige silk, labeled and numbered '14635'.

1967   *Bust 32in (82cm)*

$26,000-30,000   **KT**

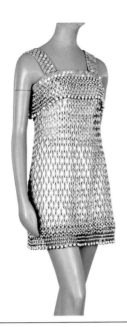

A 'Souper Dress', printed paper, probably Mars of Asheville, printed with the Andy Warhol design, original label with care instructions to neck.

c1968

Bust 34in (86cm)

$4,000-5,000   **KT**

A 1960s-70s Jean Lanvin haute couture evening gown, grass-green silk twill full-circle skirt, wide beaded 'grapevine' motif hunter green corset waist, unlined, labeled 'Jeanne Lanvin – Paris' and '49 01(?)' handwritten verso.

$1,400-2,000   **FRE**

An Emilio Pucci strapless beaded and jewel-encrusted evening gown, printed fine silk chiffon, heavily beaded with iridescent sequins, faceted crystal beads, and rhinestones, marked on a large black label 'EMILIO PUCCI / Firenze.'

$1,200-1,800   **FRE**

A Norman Norell beaded evening gown, sleeveless fitted full-length sheath decorated with ivory bugle beads and turquoise and magenta paisley designs, labeled 'Norman Norell' and 'Marsal'.

c1970   *Size 2-4*

$1,000-1,500   **FRE**

A Christian Dior brocade and beaded hostess gown, in Persian paisley brocade, labeled 'Boutique Christian Dior Paris / Made in France', and stamped '1754205'.

c1970   *Size 6-8*

$500-700   **FRE**

A 1970s Emilio Pucci silk jersey dress, labeled 'Emilio Pucci/Florence Italy' and 'Exclusively for Saks Fifth Avenue'.

Size 8

$500-700   **FRE**

A Hubert de Givenchy evening gown, of emerald green chiffon smothered in tiny pink and green floral sequins and adorned with paste tassels with shocking pink, green and mauve feathers, labeled and numbered '41763'.

c1970   *Bust 34in (86cm)*

$3,000-4,000   **KT**

A Christian Dior silk satin evening coat, labeled 'Christian Dior Paris/Automne 1971'.

Size 4

$400-500   **FRE**

A 1970s Yves Saint Laurent silk organza harlequin print shirtwaist dress.

Bust 34in (86cm)

$700-1,100   **FRE**

A 1980s Issey Miyake cotton kasuri dress, labeled 'Issey Miyake'.

Size small

$500-600   **FRE**

TEXTILES

A late 17thC French tapestry purse, woven in polychrome silk and metal thread, with central motif of a small brown dog below two birds bearing bunches of colored grapes, simple silver knots and pink floss silk tassels to the corners, lined in blue silk.

4.75in (12cm) wide

$2,000-2,800   **KT**

An early 20thC Orientalist micro-beaded purse, enamel Etruscan Revival frame with cut glass and cabochon jewels, the body of the purse beaded in the style of Persian prayer rug with tiny faceted metal beads.

$400-500   **FRE**

CLOSER LOOK: MIDAS OF MIAMI PURSE

The gold-painted wicker is in excellent condition with no wear or flaking.

The green velvet has faded a little but the red velvet cherries, which embellish it retain their vibrant color.

The green rhinestones add sparkling highlights.

The lining appears to be as-new with no marks or tears.

A Midas of Miami gold-painted wicker and green velvet purse.

1950s   *12in (30.5cm) wide*

$300-500   **PC**

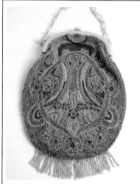

A 1920s-30s Art Deco purse, fine-beaded with a celluloid frame.

$600-800   **TDG**

A 1920s French Egyptian Revival microbeaded purse, blackened silver frame with a chain handle, depicting a Pharaoah and servant, with various hieroglyphics and symbols surrounding, beaded fringe.

$500-700   **FRE**

A 1920s-30s micro-beaded 'landscape' framed purse, with detailed romantic landscape depicting a house on a hill in a picturesque garden with a stream and two figures fishing, with a silver etched frame.

$500-700   **FRE**

A 1930s-40s Lederer of Paris natural alligator box purse, modified picnic basket shape with a lift-lid, opening to reveal an apple-green kid-lined interior, fitted with a matching mirror and case, and coin purse containing original 'Lederer' tag and also reading 'Porte Bonheur de Paris' with an attached drilled ten centime coin dated 1939.

$500-600   **FRE**

A 1940s python purse, hinged vanity wing with mirror and pouch.

$400-550   **TDG**

A 1950s black Coblentz alligator purse, small 'doctor's bag' shape with two loop handles and gold latch, lined in black and embossed 'Coblentz Original' in gold.

$600-800   **FRE**

An early 1960s Hermès forest-green leather purse, lined in soft green leather and with separate coin purse and mirror, with angular gilt-brass lifter-clasp stamped 'Hermès Paris'.

10in (26cm) long

$1,200-1,600   **KT**

A rare Pierre Cardin black and white purse.

c1960s

$360-440   **TDG**

A Cartier black alligator purse in fitted case, trapezoid shaped with calfskin lining, envelope flap with large gold bracelet handle, embossed on the interior 'Cartier / New York, Paris, London, Caracas / Made in France', with red satin-lined Cartier storage case.

$4,000-6,000   **FRE**

A large 1960s French black alligator purse or lady's briefcase, with an open pocket at the back with a separate document purse that pulls up, attached, kid-lined interior, by Reine Astrid.

$2,400-3,300 FRE

An Emilio Pucci velvet purse, shaped like an oversized coin purse, with a clamshell snap closure and loop top handle, with coral leather piping and trim.

1960s-70s

$500-600 FRE

CLOSER LOOK: HERMÈS KELLY BAG

Hermès made its first Kelly bag in 1935 as a more refined version of a saddlebag it had created three years earlier. It was known as the 'small tall bag with straps' until 1955 when it was renamed the 'Kelly bag' to commemorate Grace Kelly's marriage to Prince Rainier of Monaco. Its fame was boosted a year later when Princess Grace was photographed on the front cover of Life magazine, holding the bag, it was rumoured, to hide her pregnancy. Today it is celebrities such as Victoria Beckham who are seen carrying this classic bag.

The sections are saddlestitched together by hand at the Hermès workshop in Paris. A bag takes 20 hours to make.

Kelly bags fasten at the front with a padlock and rotating clasp; the lock is stamped 'Hermès-Paris'.

Kelly bags are so desirable there is always a waiting list for them. Add to this the fact that they improve with age, it is no wonder that the market for Kelly bags is consistently strong.

A Hermès sable crocodile Kelly bag, lined in soft kid leather, with matching padlock, two keys and fob stamped in gold and also to a gilt edged closure strap.

c1966   11.5in (29cm) long

$8,000-12,000 KT

A Hermès crocodile purse, 'Crocodylus porosus', soft black kid leather lining with side pockets, mirror and coin purse.

c1970   11in (28cm) wide

$1,700-2,100 KT

A 1970s Louis Vuitton train case, signature canvas traveling cosmetic and toiletry case, fitted with a slide-in bottle holder and a small suitcase-shaped box, with brass signed hardware and leather trim and luggage tag.

14in (35.5cm) wide

$1,400-2,000 FRE

A Pucci silk abstract printed purse, with heavy gold chain handle, opening to reveal two equally-sized accordion-sided sections lined in leather.

1970s   8.5in (21.5cm) long

$500-700 FRE

A Chanel black alligator purse, exterior pockets on both sides and interior zip pockets, embossed 'Chanel' and 'Made in Italy' in gold on interior, and with hanging Chanel logo charm.

$2,400-3,600 FRE

A Chanel quilted purse, soft black kidskin with front-flap and logo-latch, lined in burgundy leather and embossed 'Chanel' and 'Made in France' in gold on the interior.

$1,500-1,900 FRE

A Judith Leiber snakeskin purse, undyed python pouch-style evening bag with hinged frame closure, long shoulder strap which can tuck into the bag to form a clutch, with 'Judith Leiber' etched gold plate label.

$600-800 FRE

A Lana Marks 'Princess Diana' alligator purse, rich cognac front-flap top-handled bag with magnetic closure, alternate long shoulder strap, two main interior compartments.

$4,000-5,000 FRE

A 1980s Judith Leiber crystal minaudière, kidney bean-shaped with pave crystal surface, gold and semi-precious cabochon latch, fitted with coin purse, mirror comb and attached chain.

$700-900 FRE

A Chanel pebble-textured leather purse, rich wine leather front-flap design with decorative 'quilt' topstitching, brass logo turn-lock closure and hardware, chain shoulder strap, lined in logo jacquard and labeled 'Chanel/Made in Italy'.

$800-1,000 FRE

Audubon, John James, 'Mississippi Kite', London, R Havell, hand-colored engraving with aquatint and etching, plate CXVII from 'The Birds of America', with J. Whatman Turkey Hill watermark.
1831
$3,000-4,000　　　**FRE**

Barbault, Jean, 'Les plus beaux monuments de Rome ancienne', Rome, de l'imprimerie de Komarek, 69 [of 73] plates, near-contemporary pasted paper boards, contemporary calf backstrip, worn.
1761
$2,000-2,500　　　**L&T**

Burns, Robert, 'Poems, Chiefly in the Scottish Dialect', second edition, first Edinburgh edition, minor spotting, original boards, uncut, rebacked, chipped and soiled, joints and spine cracked.
1787
$3,000-4,000　　　**BLO**

Cambridge, Richard Owen, 'The Works', first collected edition, fifteen engraved plates and one facsimile, later half calf over marbled boards, a little rubbed.

1803
$500-600　　　**BLO**

Churchill, Sir Winston, 'The Story of the Malakand Field Force', first edition, six maps, foxed at beginning, original cloth, gilt, rubbed.

1898
$4,000-5,000　　　**BLO**

Coward, Nöel, 'Hernia Whittlebot Poems...with an appreciation by Nöel Coward', one of only 24 copies, signed inscription from Coward on verso of title, occasional light finger-marking.
1923
$1,000-1,500　　　**BLO**

Curtis, Edward S. 'The North American Indian', Volume II, 'Pima, Pagago, Quhatika, Mohave, Yuma, Maricopa, Walapai, Havasupai, Apache, Mohave', limited to 500 sets.
1908
$10,000-12,000　　　**SK**

Dickens, Charles, 'A Christmas Carol', first edition, trial issue, hand-colored etched frontispiece and three plates by John Leech, illustrations, some foxing, rebacked preserving original spine, a little rubbed and faded, preserved in modern cloth drop-back box.
1843
$7,000-9,000　　　**BLO**

Doyle, Arthur Conan, 'A Study in Scarlet', London, Ward, Lock and Co., first edition, first impression, six plates, late 19thC green pebbledash cloth, faint library stamp on endpapers, adhesion to page 8-9, lacking the two pp. advertisements at the beginning.
1888
$17,000-20,000　　　**L&T**

Hardy, Thomas, 'The Woodlanders', first edition, three volumes, half-titles, original dark green bead-grain cloth, volume one neatly repaired at head of lower joint, with minor rubbing to extremities, preserved in cloth drop-back box, a little rubbed and soiled.
1887
$4,800-5,200　　　**BLO**

Kane, Paul, 'Wanderings of an Artist among the Indians of North America, from Canada to Vancouver's Island and Oregon through the Hudson's Bay Company's Territory', London, Longman, Brown, Green et al, folding map, eight color plates, original brown cloth gilt, inner hinges weak, some leaves loose, contemporary owner's ink inscription on title page.
1859
$2,000-2,500　　　**L&T**

Kipling, Rudyard, 'The Jungle Book' and 'The Second Jungle Book', first edition, original gilt-pictorial, letters and decorated blue cloth, full-page and text illustration, together in custom 1/2 scarlet morocco and cloth slipcase.
1894 and 1895
$2,500-3,000　　　**FRE**

Luther, Martin, 'A Commentarie ...upon the Epistle of S. Paule to the Galathians', first English edition, Thomas Vautroullier, device on title, lacks *2 (? blank), some small tear, contemporary calf, gilt ornament on covers, rubbed, ends of hinges cracked, original ties.
1575

$4,500-5,500 BLO

Manson, James A, 'Sir Edwin Landseer', London and New York, the Walter Scott Publishing Co., Ltd. and Charles Scribner's Sons, photogravure frontispiece, 21 engraved plates, dark green morocco bound to a Cosway style for Sotheran & Co., gilt ruled and tooled turn-ins, marbled endpapers, slipcase.
1902

$12,000-16,000 BLNY

Orme, Edward, 'Orme's Graphic history of the life, exploits and death of Horatio Nelson', London: printed for, published and sold by Edward Orme… and by Longman, Hurst, Rees, and Orme, very rare earliest undated issue, engraved portrait, nine hand-colored aquatint plates, one full-page facsimile of Nelson's handwriting, contemporary half maroon morocco, with original printed label on upper cover.
1806

$5,000-6,000 L&T

Planché, James Robinson, 'Costume of Shakespeare's Tragedy of Hamlet [...Othello and Comedy of the Merchant of Venice]', title vignette hand-colored and heightened with gold, 36 hand-colored plates by G. Scharf, contemporary half calf, covers almost detached.
1825

$1,500-2,000 BLO

Rackham, Arthur and Barrie, J. M., 'The Peter Pan portfolio', London, Hodder & Stoughton, number 471 of 500 copies, signed by the publishers and the engravers, twelve color plates, original box.
1912

$6,000-7,000 L&T

Shakespeare, William, 'Macbeth', edited by William Davenant, eight edition, browned and spotted, margins trimmed with partial loss, modern half calf over marbled boards, new endpapers.
1710

$1,500-2,000 BLO

Verne, Jules, 'The Will of an Eccentric', first edition, Sampson Low & Co., plates, fold-out 'Noble Game of the United States of America'.
1900

$2,000-3,000 BLO

Verne, Jules, 'From the Earth to the Moon...and a Trip Round It', first English edition, Sampson Low & Co., original blue pictorial cloth decorated in gilt and black.
1873

$9,000-10,000 BLO

MODERN FIRST EDITIONS

Amis, Kingsley, 'Lucky Jim,' first edition, minor spotting to extreme edge of some ff., original boards, dust-jacket slightly darkened at spine, small closed tear near head of spine.
1953

$4,000-5,000 BLO

Burgess, Anthony, 'A Clockwork Orange', first edition, first issue, original boards, slight damage to spine, original dust-jacket, worn at corners, torn at foot of spine.
1962

$1,500-2,000 BLO

Christie, Agatha, 'Ten Little Niggers', London, for the Crime Club, by Collins, first edition, original orange cloth, dust jacket priced '7s 6d.', some short closed tears.
1939

$5,000-6,000 L&T

Christie, Agatha, 'The Mysterious Affair at Styles', first edition, light creasing to last f., contemporary inscription on front free endpaper, original decorated brown cloth, slight splitting to lower joint.
1921

$4,000-5,000 BLO

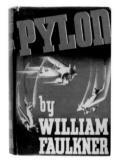

Eliot, T. S., 'The Waste Land', number 203 of 300 copies signed by the author, printed by the Officina Bodoni in Verona for Faber & Faber, original vellum-backed marbled boards, top edge gilt, others uncut, board slip-case a little rubbed with splits to joints, 4to.
1961
$3,500-4,000 BLO

Faulkner, William, 'Pylon', first trade edition, New York, original blue and black cloth, dust-jacket, chipped at head of spine, slight rubbing to fore-edges and upper joint, minor browning on lower panel.
1935
$400-500 BLO

Fleming, Ian, 'Casino Royale', first edition, first impression, full-page inscription from the author on front free endpaper, original boards, slightly cocked, first state dust-jacket without Times review, slightly chipped at head of spine.

The inscription reads 'To / the power behind / the publishers' throne! / from / the author / May 1953', presumably referring to somebody related to the publishers Jonathan Cape. 'Casino Royale' is always a desirable first edition and this example is in excellent condition which makes it even more collectible.
1953
$50,000-60,000 BLO

MILLER'S COMPARES

Fleming, Ian, 'Live and Let Die', first edition, original boards, first issue dust jacket without credit to Kenneth Lewis, a few light small marks/scratches but otherwise a very good example, 8vo.
1954
$16,000-18,000 BLO

Fleming, Ian, 'Live and Let Die', first edition, first state dust-jacket, slightly rubbed at joints, rubbed at corners with minor fraying to spine ends, two small closed tears, otherwise a very good example, 8vo.
1954
$23,000-25,000 BLO

First editions of Ian Fleming's James Bond novels are highly desirable. While condition is important to collectors, a signed copy – especially one dedicated to a close friend or colleague – will be hotly contested at auction.

These two copies of 'Live and Let Die' are in similar, good condition. The edition on the right has the first state dust jacket and a full-page inscription from Fleming on the front free endpaper. It reads: 'To Donald Crowther, Who helped with the coin!, from the author 1954'.

Donald Crowther seemingly worked at Spink, the London dealer and auctioneer of coins, medals, stamps, banknotes at this time, and must have advised Fleming on the 17thC gold coins being sold by 'Mr Big' in the plot of 'Live and Let Die'. The inscription adds to the connection between the author and the recipient and so the value increases.

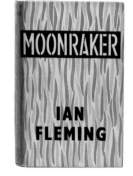

Fleming, Ian, 'Moonraker', first edition, issue with 'shoot, signed presentation inscription from the author on front free endpaper, original boards, dust-jacket, slightly rubbed at corners, spine slightly dulled.

The inscription reads: 'To E.B. Strauss, This 'Tagebuch eines, halbwüchsigen Spiones'!, Ian Fleming, 1955'.
1955
$20,000-24,000 BLO

Fleming, Ian, 'For Your Eyes Only', first edition, signed inscription from the author on front free endpaper, original boards, dust-jacket.

The inscription reads 'To Maureen, 'Just across the corridor'!, from Ian Fleming'. A penciled note at the front indicates that Maureen worked across the hall from his office, possibly at Kemsley Newspapers.
1960
$15,000-16,000 BLO

Forester, C.S., 'The African Queen', first American edition, Boston, ink name on front free endpaper, original textured cloth, dust jacket, skilful restoration to spine ends, corners and upper joint.
1935
$1,500-1,700 BLO

Golding, William, 'Lord of the Flies,' London, Faber and Faber, first edition, original red cloth, dustwrapper discolored, small tear on upper hinge.

1954

$3,000-4,000   **L&T**

Greene, Graham, 'Babbling April', Oxford, Basil Blackwell, original purple-grey boards, minor wear.

1925

$5,000-6,000   **FRE**

Haggard, Sir Henry Rider, 'King Solomon's Mines', neatly repaired without loss, original red cloth, rubbed, a few small stains to upper cover, spine faded and chipped, lower joint repaired.

1885

$2,200-2,600   **BLO**

Hemingway, Ernest, 'The Old Man and the Sea', first edition, first issue with 'A' and publisher's seal on copyright page, New York, original cloth, dust jacket, small closed tear near head of spine.

1952

$1,800-2,400   **BLO**

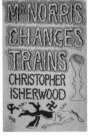

Isherwood, Christopher, 'Mr. Norris Changes Trains', first edition, Hogarth Press, light spotting to endpapers, original cloth, faded at spine and fore-edges, dust-jacket, neat restoration to edges and corners.

Scarce in dust jacket
1935

$2,500-3,000   **BLO**

Joyce, James, 'A Portrait of the Artist as a Young Man', first edition, New York, contemporary inscription on front free endpaper, original cloth, gilt lettering on spine slightly dulled.

1916

$2,400-3,000   **BLO**

Joyce, James, 'Ulysse', first edition in French, Paris, La Maison des Amis des Livres, from an edition of 100 copies on vélin d'Arches, original printed card wrappers, a fine copy, glassine dust jacket, torn and creased at fore-edges, in modern half calf drop-back box.

1929

$3,000-4,000   **BLO**

Lawrence, D. H., 'Sons and Lovers', first edition, with twenty pages of publisher's catalogue, ink name on front free endpaper, original blue cloth lettered in gilt, very slightly cocked.

1913

$1,500-2,000   **BLO**

Lessing, Doris, 'The Grass is Singing', first edition, original cloth, dust-jacket.

Lessing won the Nobel Prize for literature in 2007. This is her first novel.

1950

$800-1,200   **BLO**

Miller, Walter M., Jr., 'A Canticle for Leibowitz', Philadelphia & New York, J. B. Lippincott, first edition, original pink cloth, black cloth shelf back, light wear, with orange wrap-around label.

1960

$1,000-1,500   **FRE**

Mitchell, Margaret, 'Gone with the Wind', first edition, The MacMillan Company, New York.

This is the first edition, first issue of this Pulitzer prize winner for Literature in 1937.

1936

$3,000-4,000   **BLNY**

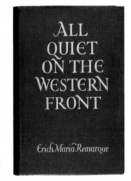

Remarque, Erich Maria, 'All Quiet on the Western Front', first English edition, original cloth, dust jacket, subtle restoration to fore-edges, spine ends and part of top edge of upper panel, spine lettering darkened.

1929

$1,200-1,600   **BLO**

Sassoon, Siegfried, 'Memoirs of a Fox-Hunting Man', first edition, light spotting to endpapers, original cloth, dust jacket.

1928

$1,800-2,200 BLO

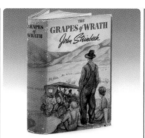

Steinbeck, John, 'Grapes of Wrath', New York: Viking, first edition, original pictorial grey cloth, light edge wear, several deep chips to dust jacket.

1939

$600-800 FRE

Waugh, Evelyn, 'Decline and Fall', first edition, plates by the author, original patterned cloth, dust jacket faded, spine faded and lower panel detached.

1928

$6,000-8,000 BLO

Wells, H.G., 'The Island of Doctor Moreau', first edition, first issue, 33 pages of advertisements, frontispiece, original pictorial cloth, slight darkening to spine and corners, slightly cocked.

1896

$1,000-1,500 BLO

Wells, H.G., 'The Invisible Man', first edition, first issue, two pages of advertisements, minor browning to endpapers and edges, original pictorial cloth lettered in gilt, spine and part of lower cover faded.

1897

$1,500-2,000 BLO

Wilde, Oscar, 'The Importance of Being Earnest', first edition, one of 1,000 copies, original salmon cloth with gilt designs by Shannon, slightly bumped and rubbed at corners.

1899

$2,200-2,800 BLO

Wodehouse, P.G., 'My Man Jeeves', first edition, first issue, Butler and Tanner printers, original brown cloth, frayed at spine ends with slight loss, undated.

1919

$500-700 BLO

Yeats, William Butler, 'The Countess Kathleen and Various Legends and Lyrics', first edition, Arthur Symons' copy with his ink inscription on front free endpaper.

1892

$4,000-6,000 BLO

CHILDREN'S BOOKS

Baum, L. Frank, 'The Life and Adventures of Santa Claus', colored title and 11 plates, original red pictorial cloth, inscribed L. Frank Baum / Hollywood / April 1907'.

1902

$6,000-7,000 BLNY

Bewick, Thomas, 'A New Lottery Book of Birds and Beasts for Children to Learn their Letters by as soon as they can Speak', first edition.

1771

$9,000-11,000 BLNY

Dahl, Roald, 'Charlie and the Chocolate Factory', first edition, first issue, New York, illustrations by Joseph Schindelman.

1964

$4,000-5,000 BLO

Disney Studios, 'The Pop-Up Mickey Mouse', New York, Blue Ribbon Books, original edition, original color pictorial boards, three color pop-up illustrations.

1933

$200-300 FRE

Greenaway, Kate, 'Mother Goose or the Old Nursery Rhymes', first edition, London and New York, George Routledge & Sons, printed in color from woodblocks by Edmund Evans.

First edition, first state in the rare pictorial cloth binding with no table of contents and no Evans seal added to the recto of the rear endpaper, plus all three textual errors. One of Kate Greenaway's loveliest publications for children.

1881

$2,000-3,000 BLNY

Milne, A. A., 'Winnie-the-Pooh', London, Metheun & Co., illustrated by Ernest H. Shepard, folding map at rear, original dark blue boards, number 182 of 350 copies signed by Milne and Shepard in 1926, jacket lightly rubbed, spine faded.

1926

$7,000-9,000 BLNY

Nicholson, William, 'An alphabet', London, Heinemann, 26 plates, original decorative boards, some rubbing to edges, owner's ink inscription on front endpaper.

1898 [1897]

$1,400-1,800   **L&T**

Potter, Beatrix, 'The Tale of Peter Rabbit', London, first edition, first printing, privately printed by Strangeways, colored frontispiece, 41 full-page line illustrations, all after Potter, inscription by C.E. Cobb dated June 1902.

1901

$50,000-70,000   **BLNY**

Rowling, J. K., 'Harry Potter and the Order of the Phoenix', London, Bloomsbury, first edition, presentation copy, inscribed on title-page 'To Chantelle, lots of love, J. K. Rowling X', original cloth, dust jacket, unread in mint condition.

2003

$2,500-3,000   **L&T**

Rowling, J. K., 'Harry Potter and the Philosopher's Stone', first edition, very slight darkening to ff, original pictorial boards, tiny nicks to the tips of the fore-corners and foot of spine corners, slightly cocked. *One of only 500 first edition copies released.*

1997

$30,000-40,000   **BLO**

Sendak, Maurice, 'Where the Wild Things Are', first edition, New York, Harper & Row, colored illustrations after Sendak.

First edition with the very rare first issue dust-jackett

1963

$4,800-5,200   **BLNY**

Tolkien, J.R.R., 'The Hobbit', first edition, full-page illustrations and map endpapers by the author, gilt figure of 'Smaug' to foot of upper cover.

1937

$6,000-7,000   **BLO**

DOCUMENTS

Byng, John, Admiral, executed by firing squad on the quarter-deck of HMS Monarque for neglect of duty (1704-57), 'Journal of Byng's Command of the Mediterranean Fleet in 1748', autograph manuscript, 121pp., numerous ink corrections, paper watermarked with Arms of Great Britain over 'GR', c1740s, wrappers with inscription.

c1740s

$35,000-40,000   **BLO**

Dickens, Charles, a cheque drawn on Messrs. Coutts and Co. for £500, paid to 'Self', signed by 'Charles Dickens', 'Twenty Ninth October 1864'.

$2,500-3,000   **L&T**

Staffordshire, Robert de Wicliff and Antony St. Quintin, quitclaim to John Depden all rights in the manor of Hanlay [Hanley], manuscript in Latin, on vellum, folds, a little browned, two red wax seals, one fine impression and the other cracked and with slight loss, Helagh (Yorkshire), 2nd October 1393.

Hanley, a suburb of Stoke-on-Trent.

6.5in (16.5cm)

$1,700-2,000   **BLO**

A grant by Sir William Phelipp, John Barney and others of the manor of 'Cokefeldhalle', Yoxford, Suffolk to John Manning, manuscript on vellum, in Latin, folds, four wax seals with remarkably fine and clear impressions, witnessed by Simon Felbrigg, John Hevening ham, John Fastolf and others, 21st July 1428.

10.75in (27.5cm) wide

$1,500-2,000   **BLO**

Robinson, W. Heath, five advertisements for the Duroid Co., printed from the original blocks.

$500-700   **L&T**

Morley, Alan, a collection of four Nosey Parker strip cartoons, numbers 393, 400, 440 and 503, pen, ink and blue pencil, each approximately twelve cells.

Each 9in (23cm) wide

$800-1,200   **L&T**

A set of twelve original ink 'Beau Peep' strip cartoons, as published in The Daily Star, numbered Sat. 132, Wed. 63 – Sat. 66, Mon. 31 – Sat 36.

$400-600   **L&T**

A set of ten signed original ink cartoons of cats, by Paul Wood, Jack Blyth, Wright, Dicky Howett, Richie and Pep, on paper or card, one numbered in ink in margin.

$400-600   **L&T**

A set of ten signed original golf cartoons, by Chris Wright, Jack Blyth, Sax, and Wing, ink on paper or card, three with number in ink in margin.

$400-600   **L&T**

Watkins, Dudley, 'Oor Wullie' and 'Ma & Pa Broon', both pen and ink over pencil, signed by Watkins.

Dudley Dexter Watkins (1907-69) was a comic artist, employed by publisher DC Thomson, who made his name drawing two comic strips for the Scottish Sunday Post newspaper: 'Oor Wullie' and 'The Broons'. Both were launched in a comic supplement published by the newspaper on March 8 1936. 'Oor Wullie' follows the adventures of an eight- or nine-year-old boy who gets into trouble, eats too many sweets and does his best to avoid girls. Most strips begin and end with him sitting on his trademark upturned metal bucket. 'The Broons' is a domestic comedy about a large family and presents a warm-hearted picture of urban Scottish life. The Broons all 'spoke' in broad Scottish dialect and rapidly became popular – by 1971 the Sunday Post had an estimated readership of just under three million, or 79 per cent of the adult population of Scotland.

1938

$10,000-12,000   **L&T**

Collins, Dennis and Dodd, Maurice, ten original ink strip cartoons on card of 'The Perishers', numbers L89-L98, each numbered and dated in the margin, stamped on verso 'Slade London'.

1977

$800-1,200   **L&T**

Fisher, Harry Conway 'Bud', 'Mutt and Jeff', original pen and ink cartoon drawing in five panels on card, depicts Jeff and a doctor attending an ailing Mutt, light fading, corners chipped, some minor scattered rubbing.

Created in 1907, Mutt and Jeff was the first successful daily comic strip in the United States and thus the beginning of a particularly American popular art form that reached millions through the massive circulations of the Pulitzer and Hearst newspaper empires. Lanky Mutt and short Jeff soon passed quickly into the American vernacular, becoming the basis for early films as well as comic books. The strip ran for nearly 75 years, though Fisher himself had stopped drawing the strips by 1932, when he had become wealthy enough to let another artist work under his license.

28in (72cm) wide

$500-700   **BLNY**

A W. & J. Gourlay feather golf ball, stamped with the maker's name and numbered 28 in ink, in mint condition.

$11,000-13,000   L&T

An Alex Patrick of Leven hand-hammered gutty ball, stamped 'A. Patrick' retaining most of the original paint.

$13,000-17,000   L&T

A 'Henley Union Jack' pattern gutty ball, in mint condition.

$8,000-10,000   L&T

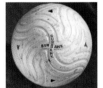

A Stowe Woodward 'Burbank' rubber-core ball, patterned with swirling-pattern grooves.

$2,500-3,500   L&T

A US Rubber Co. 'Tiger 1' yellow rubber-core ball, with circlet pattern.

$300-400   L&T

A Hutchison & Main, Springvale 'Hawk' bramble-pattern gutty ball, in original wrappers.

$750-850   L&T

A Tom Morris beech-headed longnose spoon, the scared head stamped 'T. Morris', horn insert to sole, lead counterweight, hickory shaft.

$3,000-3,500   L&T

A James J. Hutchison longnose playclub, the scared beech head stamped 'Hutchison', with horn insert, lead counterweight, hickory shaft, head cracked.

$900-1,100   L&T

A Robert Forgan longnose putter, the scared beech head stamped 'R. Forgan' and with Prince of Wales feathers, horn insert to sole, lead counterweight, the hickory shaft stamped 'R. Forgan & Son, St. Andrews'.

$1,700-1,900   L&T

A Cochranes Ltd Mammoth niblick, Edinburgh, with dot-pattern face, hickory shaft.

$12,000-14,000   L&T

An American Harry C. Lee & Co. backward putter, New York, aluminum head, hickory shaft.

$4,000-5,000   L&T

A Baltimore Putter Co. 'Triangular' putter, multi-faceted adjustable putter, hickory shaft.

$3,000-4,000   L&T

'Glasgow from the Green with Golfers in the Distance', by A. R. Grieve, signed, inscribed and dated on the reverse, watercolor.

1879   14.5in (36.5cm) wide

$2,500-3,500   L&T

SPORTING ANTIQUES

Charles Crombie, 'The Rules of Golf Illustrated', London, Derby & Sons, with 24 color lithographs, lettered cloth-backed boards, minimal soiling, boards slightly rubbed and soiled.

This elaborate album was issued by 'Golf Illustrated' to advertise Perrier. A limited edition of plate-marked proofs was also issued.
1905

$1,700-2,000 BLNY

A George Pietzcker sepia photograph, depicting the 1931 America Ryder Cup Team, including Sam Ryder and Walter Hagen.

16in (40.5cm) high

$16,000-18,000 L&T

A Ryder Cup Official Souvenir program, Southport, The Fourth International Golf Match, Monday & Tuesday, June 26-27, 1933, internally signed by Arthur J. Lacey, John Henry Taylor and Syd Easterbrook.

$2,000-3,000 FRE

A copy of Time Magazine, Vol. XVI no. 12, September 22, 1930, with a portrait of Robert Tyre 'Bobby' Jones Jnr to the cover.

$600-800 L&T

A late Victorian silver and enamel golfing vesta case, London, the obverse with an arched rectangular enameled panel of a golfer at the top of his back swing, the reverse with cursive initials.
1891   *2.25in (5.5cm) high*

$4,000-4,500 L&T

An Augusta National Golf Club 1939 Master's Tournament Series Ticket, March 26th-April 2nd, no. 298, signed by the winner Ralph Guldahl to the obverse and Sam Snead to the reverse.

$6,500-7,500 L&T

A Dunaverty Golf Club white metal medal, the obverse relief decorated with ribbon-tied crossed clubs and balls, the reverse inscribed 'Dunaverty Golf Club, 1889... Won by Mr William Reid', with cast surmount and right suspension, cased.

1.5in (4cm) diam

$1,100-1,400 L&T

A Gorham sterling silver and enamel vesta case, decorated to the obverse with a golfer lining up a putt.

2.25in (5.5cm) high

$8,000-10,000 L&T

A Copeland Late Spode pottery jug, relief-decorated in white with a scene of golfers in the round, on an olive-green and beige ground.

4.25in (11cm) high

$900-1,100 L&T

A Royal Doulton 'Colonel Bogey Whisky' water jug, the salt-glazed baluster body relief-decorated with a crest inscription and ornamental band and transfer-printed with two golfing scenes.

7.5in (19cm) high

$3,000-4,000 L&T

A Royal Doulton, Burslem blue and white transfer-printed plate, decorated with a golfing scene.

c1888   *12in (30.5cm) diam*

$10,000-14,000 L&T

Garrincha's 1962 World Cup final shirt, a match-worn Brazil No. 7 international jersey, some damage.

Manoel Francisco dos Santos (1933-83), known by his nickname Garrincha (Little Bird), was an outstanding Brazilian right winger and influential member of the 1958 and 1962 World Cup winning teams.

$30,000-40,000 GBA

A pair of black leather football boots, worn by Stanley Matthews in 1953.

These are a pair of Co-Op boots that were supplied to Matthews in exchange for his appearances in their stores to sign autographs.

$3,000-4,000 GBA

A leather soccer ball, with removable lid and internal ceramic pot. *c1920*

$1,000-1,200 RGA

A signed Manchester United 1968 European Cup final LP record, produced by Instant Records, with commentary from the match against Benfica at Wembley Stadium, the sleeve designed in the shape of a soccer ball and signed in blue biro by the 11 Manchester United finalists Alex Stepney, Pat Crerand, Bill Foulkes, John Aston, David Sadler, Shay Brennan, Nobby Stiles, Tony Dunne, Brian Kidd, George Best and Bobby Charlton.

$4,000-4,500 GBA

An F. A. Cup Final program for Tottenham Hotspur v Wolverhampton Wanderers, played at Stamford Bridge, Chelsea 23rd April 1921.

$4,500-5,500 GBA

'Pelé: Edson Arantes do Nascimento', a deluxe large-format limited edition book, published by Gloria Books with each copy personally signed by Pelé.

$1,100-1,300 GBA

A large sgraffito-technique Chelsea Football Club crest roundel, suitable for use as a table top.

This unique piece was owned by Raphael Djanogly OBE and was made at the time of the club's historic 1954-55 Championship winning season. The club crest was introduced under Ted Drake's management in 1953 as part of his modernization plans for the club.

42in (107cm) diam

$4,000-6,000 GBA

A important bronze plaque presented to Jules Rimet by the French Football Federation in 1931, designed by Abel La Fleur, the plaque signed 'Abel La Fleur - Sculp't.

21.75in (55cm) high

$8,000-12,000 GBA

A large spelter group of two footballers, signed Ulysse, the players modeled chasing the ball side-by-side, one with the ball 'mid-air' on his right foot.

16.5in (42cm) high

$600-800 GBA

A large spelter figure of a footballer, signed S. Kinsburger, modeled running with the ball at his right foot.

19in (49cm) high

$500-700 GBA

A chromium-plated figure of a footballer, modeled taking a powerful right foot shot, the ball sculpted separately on the marble base.

11.5in (29cm) high

$300-400 GBA

A red silk jockey's jacket, worn by Jem Mason, mounted in a display case with caption reading 'Jacket Worn by J. Mason, who rode Mr J. Elmore's 'Lottry', winner of the First National on this course'.

These silks were displayed in the County Stand at Aintree racecourse.
34in (86.5cm) high

$5,000-6,000   **GBA**

A 1950s jockey's jacket, in the famous Crazy Quilt colors, by Boyce & Rogers of Newmarket.

These colors were first registered in 1950 to Chesney Allen, a member of the Crazy Gang.

$1,000-1,500   **GBA**

Shergar's no. 18 number cloth from the 1981 Derby Stakes, signed by his jockey Walter Swinburn.

Shergar is one of the most famous horses of the 20thC. Having been retired to a stud in County Kildare, he was stolen and held to ransom. He was never seen again and is presumed to have been killed.

$9,000-11,000   **GBA**

A racing plate worn by Brown Jack when winning his historic sixth consecutive Queen Alexandra Stakes in 1934, mounted with a silver plaque.

1934   *8in (20cm) high*

$1,500-2,000   **GBA**

A Trigo 1929 Derby silk commemorative scarf, mounted, framed and glazed.
37.5in (95cm)

$160-240   **GBA**

A Blenheim 1930 Derby silk commemorative scarf.

$170-200   **GBA**

A 1912 Grand National souvenir display, created and signed by Arthur F. Meyrick, comprising hand-colored photographs of the 1912 Grand National winner 'Jerry M', Sir Charles Assheton-Smith (owner), Robert Gore (trainer) and Ernie Piggott (jockey), mounted with two locks of the horse's hair, in a modern frame.

22in (56cm) wide

$800-1,200   **GBA**

Jason Lowes, 'Desert Orchid', signed, watercolor and gouache, additionally signed to the mount by the trainer David Elsworth.

This original work has been reproduced as a limited edition print of 55, all signed by David Elsworth.

20.25in (52cm) wide

$3,000-4,000   **GBA**

The historic Aintree Racecourse mounting bell, inscribed 'Aintree Racecourse, 1831'.

This bell signaled to the jockeys to mount their horses.
13.75in (35cm) high

$20,000-25,000   **GBA**

The silver trophy, for the 1881 Chesterfield Cup at Goodwood, in the form of a sculptural group by Hunt & Roskell titled 'Sir Roger de Coverley and the Gypsies, Spectator,' hallmarked London, on a naturalistic base with a title plaque, inscribed 'Goodwood 1881', with the original oak fitted carrying case, with key.

A bronze, 'Gladiateur', by Pierre Lenordez (1815-1892), signed, mid-brown patina, the plinth cast with a panel inscribed with details of the 19thC French racehorse.

Trophies such as this were often the prize for races at this time, rather than cash. This is typical of the style of trophies offered, where a horse usually formed part of the design but rarely in a sporting context.

13.75in (35cm) wide
$10,000-15,000   **GBA**

1881   *Group 18.5in (47cm) long*
$45,000-55,000   **GBA**

A stuffed pike, mounted in a naturalistic setting with painted backboard, ebonized and gilt-lined, glazed, bowfront case, the back with attached advert for 'Geo. Bazeley, Taxidermist, Northampton'.

49in (124.5cm) wide

$1,200-1,600   L&T

A stuffed bream, by J. Copper & Sons, London, in a naturalistic setting with painted backdrop, a label to the interior inscribed 'Bream, 3lbs. 10ozs., Caught by H. Taylor, River Severn, at Upton on Severn, Sept. 25th 1927', ebonized and gilt-lined, glazed, bowfront case.

26.5in (67cm) wide

$1,600-2,400   L&T

A stuffed chub, by W. F. Home, London, in a naturalistic setting with painted backdrop, the ebonized and gilt-lined, glazed, bowfront case inscribed, 'Chub, 3lbs., Caught at Broxbourne by W. Perry, 15th Oct. 1924'.

22.5in (57.5cm) wide

$900-1,100   L&T

A stuffed chub, by W. R. Pape, Newcastle-upon-Tyne, mounted against grasses on a painted backdrop, inscribed, 'Cheshunt, 'Old Lea', July, 1933, Wgt 3lb. 12ozs., re-cased 1956', in an ebonized glazed case.

24.5in (62cm) wide

$300-400   L&T

A Hardy 'Perfect' all-brass salmon fly reel, pierced brass foot, turk's head locking nut above tension adjuster to rim, dished backplate, the faceplate stamped horizontal, oval, horizontal and rod-in-hand logs, Hardy replacement ebonite handle.

4in (10cm) diam

$2,000-3,000   L&T

A very rare 1896 Pattern Hardy brass and alloy 'Perfect' 4.5in (11.5cm) Salmon Fly Reel, seldom seen variant with backplate, frame and foot cast integrally in alloy and with dished alloy drum with large and small perforations, all left in 'bright' finish.

1895-97

$2,000-3,000   MM

A brass race check winch, made by J. Bernard & Son, London, with folding horn handle.

3.75in (7cm) diam

$1,200-1,600   TEN

A Hardy's 2.75in 1982 Special Edition 'Perfect' brass fishing reel, from the centenary boxed rod and reel set, in leather case with sterling silver presentation plate.

$3,000-4,000   MUR

A Hardy brass and alloy Perfect 3' reel.

$800-1,000   BRI

A pair of original New York Yankee Baseball Stadium chairs, painted blue, with plaque on back reading 'Yankee Stadium 50th Anniversary 1923-1973.'

32.5in (82.5cm) high

$1,700-2,000   DRA

A New York Yankees 1939 World Series signed baseball, with 22 signatures including 19 players who include Joe DiMaggio.

$1,200-1,800   DRA

A silver cigar case presented to pugilist Tom Sayers in 1860, manufactured by Hilliard & Thomason, the body engraved 'Presented by L. Abrahams to Tom Sayers, The Champion of the World', hallmarks for Birmingham, 1860, hinged lid.

Thomas Sayers was born in the deprived slum district of Pimlico, Brighton, England, on 25th May 1826. He is considered one of the most brilliant pugilists known and was involved in contests lasting up to 85 rounds. He became the bare knuckle Champion of England when he beat 'The Tipton Slasher' in 1857. He was elected into the Boxing Hall of Fame in 1954. Abrahams was named in contemporary newspapers as Sayer's promoter.

5.25in (13.5cm) high

$5,000-6,000   GBA

A large Bähr & Pröschild bisque shoulder head doll, with brown sleeping eyes, the open mouth with teeth, a dimple to the chin, earrings, replaced dark brown real hair wig, leather body with bisque forearms, wearing an old white dress, one brown leather shoe, marked '410'.

c1900   *24in (60cm) high*

$750-850   **WDL**

A large German B. S. W 'Wendy' bisque character doll, with deeply molded mouth, brown glass sleeping eyes and molded eyebrows, on a pink jointed composition body, wearing a blonde antique mohair wig and old, if not original, clothing, shoes and socks, marked on rear of head '2033', and in a heart 'B S W 537', small professional restoration of one finger on each hand.

                    23in (58.50cm) high

$35,000-45,000   **JDJ**

A Heubach 9573 Googley doll, with blue glass sleeping eyes, on typical composition body with molded shoes and socks, retains original brown mohair wig, straw bonnet and red and white print dress.

                    7in (18cm) high

$900-1,100   **JDJ**

A German Heubach Koppelsdorf 300.3 doll, with open/close eyes and mouth showing two teeth and a tongue, in knitted jacket.

c1920-25   *18in (45.5cm) high*

$300-500   **HB**

A Heubach doll, in all-original clothing, with shoulder plate attached to a cloth body, dressed in a white suit and straw hat.

c1900   *20in (51cm) high*

$500-700   **HB**

A Jumeau first series portrait doll, with glass eyes, original wig with curls, marked shoes and original green dress, with original spring in head, on eight-ball-jointed Jumeau body, marked with '3/0' in neck socket, body shows minor wear.

                    13in (33cm) high

$14,000-16,000   **JDJ**

A rare large French Têtê Jumeau, the unmarked size 16 pale bisque doll, with curly wig with long tails, original cork pate marked '16', brown paperweight eyes, open mouth, large composition/wood body, in glass case.

                    36in (91.50cm) high

$4,400-5,600   **JDJ**

A Kämmer & Reinhardt bisque head doll, with sleeping eyes, modeled and painted eyebrows, open mouth with teeth, pierced ears with earrings, dimples in the chin, with a blonde real hair wig with plaits, marked '191' and 'Ehlert'.

                    20in (50cm) high

$1,000-1,200   **WDL**

A Kestner 'Bru' doll, with sleeping eyes, open-closed mouth with molded teeth, multi-balled composition body with jointed ankle, with antique clothing and original wig with plaster pate, minor wear and paint touch-up to body.

                    18.50in (47cm) high

$3,500-4,500   **JDJ**

A Kestner character baby doll 152, with open/close eyes and mouth with molded tongue and teeth, dressed in a long white dress.

c1915-20   *13.75in (35cm) high*

$900-1,000   **HB**

A rare Simon & Halbig bisque head doll, with open mouth, replaced brown eyes, painted lashes, brown real hair wig, body in fifteen parts, wearing a short velvet suit, an old white shirt, an old embroidered straw hat and old red leather boots.

                    32in (80cm) high

$800-1,000   **WDL**

A pre-Greiner papier-mâché head doll, with glass eyes, stitched leather arms and hands, in original clothing.

c1860   29in (73.5cm) high
$500-600   DRA

An extremely rare Kaulitz doll, with papier-mâché head and painted brown eyes, red cheeks and a ginger wig, wearing an old blue dress, brown leather shoes, an old straw hat, stamped in red 'Germany'.

18in (45cm) high
$3,500-4,000   WDL

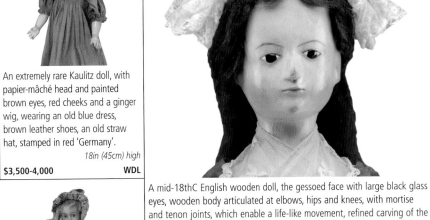

A wax head doll, with blue sleeping eyes, the open mouth with four teeth, a blonde original mohair wig, thirteen-part body, the left thumb missing, wearing old shoes and socks.

c1900   11.25in (28cm) high
$550-650   WDL

A mid-18thC English wooden doll, the gessoed face with large black glass eyes, wooden body articulated at elbows, hips and knees, with mortise and tenon joints, which enable a life-like movement, refined carving of the ankle bones, feet and hands, retains dark brown human hair wig which is topped by a lace mantua over a red silk brocade dress, beneath her dress are a plain chemise and an off-white quilted petticoat, stockings and red leather shoes with ties.

28in (71cm) high
$35,000-45,000   JDJ

DOLLS HOUSES

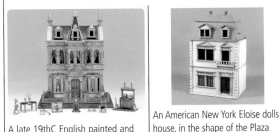

A late 19thC English painted and paper-covered Victorian dolls house, the three-storey house opens at the front to reveal four papered rooms, on a platform base, with assorted furniture.

32.5in (82.5cm) high
$20,000-30,000   FRE

An American New York Eloise dolls house, in the shape of the Plaza Hotel, with a hand-cranked elevator, with a group of dolls house furniture to include two Chinese Chippendale chairs, a washstand, a marble-top table, painted bed etc.

c1910   26.75in (68cm) wide
$9,000-11,000   POOK

A 'Mystery House' dolls house, distributed by F. A. O. Schwartz, with eight rooms, two hallways, stairway, windows, porch, moldings, period interior restored with antique fabrics, originally owned by Annie Pinkway Watt of New York City.

c1900   54in (137cm) wide
$12,000-14,000   BER

An early 20thC German M. Gottschalk dolls house, front section opens in two pieces to expose six rooms plus a closet, retains original wallpaper and flooring, second floor has spectacular crested arches.

37in (94cm) high
$8,000-10,000   JDJ

A late 19th/early 20thC painted card and paper model of Stowe House, depicted with trees either side of a lake in the foreground, in a rectangular-section glass display case, with ebonized wood base.

19in (48cm) wide
$300-400   DN

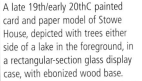

A late 19thC Viennese enameled and gilt-metal suite of dolls house salon furniture, comprising settee, three chairs and a table, all decorated with scenes of courting couples.

The settee 3in (7.5cm) wide
$900-1,100   DN

A pair of patinated lead maquettes, cast from models by George J. Frampton, made for Queen Mary's Dolls House, raised on L-shaped faux marble pedestal bases, one bearing monogram 'CF' and dated.

1922   10.25in (26cm) high
$1,500-2,500   L&T

A German painted Noah's Ark, with forty-two animals,

c1900   40in (101.5cm) wide

$5,000-6,000   **POOK**

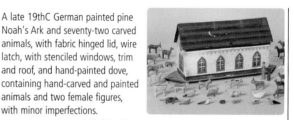

A late 19thC German painted pine Noah's Ark and seventy-two carved animals, with fabric hinged lid, wire latch, with stenciled windows, trim and roof, and hand-painted dove, containing hand-carved and painted animals and two female figures, with minor imperfections.

24in (61cm) long

$2,500-3,500   **SK**

A painted and carved miniature circus bandwagon and bandstand, by Frank Goldquist, Savannah, Illinois, dated March 9, 1948, the horse-drawn wagon with two drivers and eleven musicians together with a bandstand with carved musicians.

20in (51cm) long

$2,500-3,500   **FRE**

Two carved and painted miniature calliope wagons, by Frank Goldquist, Savannah, Illinois, dated Sept 20, 1951, and Oct 10, 1964, the first with a carved driver, the second a plastic driver.

Largest 19in (48.5cm) long

$2,000-3,000   **FRE**

An English carved and painted wood rocking horse, with real hair mane and tail, sheepskin saddlecloth, leather saddle, stirrups and bridle, raised on square-section pillar stand.

$1,100-1,300   **A&G**

An early 20thC large carved rocking horse, by F.H. Ayres, restored by Brian & Jean Tildesley.

48in (122cm) high

$9,500-10,500   **RGA**

A small rocking horse, restored, in very good condition.

PROVENANCE: This horse was acquired from Marguerite Fawdry, owner of Pollocks Toy Museum in Scala Street, London and the author of 'The English Rocking Horse'.

c1910   29in (73.5cm) high

$4,000-5,000   **RGA**

An early Lines Bros. painted wood and fabricated metal pedal car, with buff-colored bodywork and green-painted wheel arches and upholstery.

1942   55in (140cm) long

$3,000-4,000   **A&G**

An Austin A40 fabricated metal pedal car, in sky blue.

58in (147cm) long

$2,000-3,000   **A&G**

A Viktor Schreckengost enameled steel pedal car, of aeroplane form.

47in (119cm) wide

$3,500-4,500   **SDR**

A 1930s Industrial Modernism child's bicycle, painted metal, bears mark to both sides 'Kiddy Bike/Safe and Sound'.

40in (102cm) wide

$450-550   **L&T**

A late 20thC Japanese Chevrolet Corvette, white-lacquered and lithographed tinplate, battery-driven, with illuminated rear window, signed 'Corvette', 'Chevrolet' and 'Made in Japan', maker's mark Taiyo.

10.25in (25.5cm) long

$35-45   KAU

A Japanese Irco musical Cadillac, boxed example, battery-operated, plays music when moving forward, colorful graphics on box lid.

9in (23cm) long

$200-400   BER

A Japanese SSS sight-seeing tin bus, white with nickel side trim, features interior red seating, rubber tires and friction driver, boxed.

7.75in (19.5cm) long

$200-400   BER

A pair of Hauser military vehicles, tin and lithographed in olive, one in blue camouflage, includes six-wheel Krupp truck and anti-aircraft truck, with replacement wheels and breaks to windshields, missing some smaller accessories.

11in (28cm) long

$400-600   BER

A Tipp and Co. Hindenburg dirigible, boxed example, lithographed tin, painted in silver overall with celluloid propellers, swastika markings to fin and box.

The Hindenburg ran the first scheduled transatlantic flights, and remains the largest aircraft ever to take to the skies. It burst into flames in 1937, marking the end of commercial dirigibles.

11in (28cm) long

$2,800-3,200   BER

A small river boat, by Uebelacker of Germany, hand-painted tin, red and white hull, simple details to deck features canopy top on rear deck area, single stack, figurehead and brass plate on stern, repainted.

9in (23cm) long

$500-700   BER

A Martin orange vendor, lithographed and hand-painted tin, open cart contains embossed orange display, figure wears cloth shirt, spoke wheels painted red.

7.5in (19cm) long

$1,000-1,500   BER

A Spanish lithographed tin toy, with two bear cubs riding with larger bear driving motorcycle.

9in (23cm) long

$2,000-3,000   BER

A German lithographed tin toy, by Tipp & Co. depicting boy with blackboard, clockwork movement.

8in (20cm) high

$1,800-2,400   BER

CLOCKWORK

A Renault lithographed tin biplane, by Carl Rossignol of France, very colorful graphics, features seated pilot, three propellers, disc wheels, clockwork mechanism, repaint to propellers, minor break to fin bracket.

13.5in (34.5cm) wide

$600-800   BER

A lithographed tin biplane, by Distler of Germany, in red overall, single propeller, wing reads 'JD 2755', fuselage contains windows on sides, disc wheels, clockwork-driven, resoldered propeller, one wing replaced.

16.5in (42cm) wide

$600-700   BER

A hand-painted tin German Märklin zeppelin, in white with silver gondolas, striking scale and design, complete with celluloid propellers and clockwork mechanism, some overpaint to body.

c1910   *12in (30.5cm) long*

$4,000-5,000   BER

A rare German Bing limousine, dark blue, with green lining, black roof, orange hubs, includes chauffeur, clockwork motor, steerable front wheels and, unusually, cable for remote-control steering, which requires reattachment, both rear doors open, some surface corrosion.

c1920　　　　10.5in (27cm) long

$900-1,100　　　　**VEC**

A lithographed tin limousine, by Karl Bub of Germany, in maroon with light red striping and black roof, features full running boards, nickel head lamps, seated chauffeur, opening side doors, spoke wheels, clockwork driven, figure repainted, replaced lamps and bracket, wear to roof.

14in (35.5cm)

$1,500-2,000　　　　**BER**

A convertible B2 Torpedo open tourer, by Citroën of France, with nickel plate grill, full running boards, simulated soft top lays across back seat, celluloid windshield, clockwork driven.

c1920s　　　14.25in (36cm) long

$1,600-2,400　　　　**BER**

A hand-painted luxury limousine, by Carette of Germany, in white with blue striping and roof, red-trimmed window frames, embossed seating painted brown, beveled glass windows, nickel plated headlamps, rubber tires, spoke wheels, roof rail rack and clockwork driven, roof rail repainted, lamps replaced, dent to hood and roof.

This model is the largest in the series.

16in (40.5cm) long

$5,000-6,000　　　　**BER**

A rare Converse touring car, with fold-down canvas roof, heavy-gauge tin blue body with yellow running boards and red embossed seating, wooden dummy lights, spoke wheels, celluloid windshield and clockwork mechanism with centre body crank position, break at windshield, front wheels loose.

15in (38cm) long

$3,000-4,000　　　　**BER**

A Converse pressed-steel covered auto wagon, early example with three bench seats, original fringe surrounding roof with clockwork key at center, rubber tires, spoke wheels, paint worn but with traces of red and bright green flooring, black fenders, scarce example, wear to paint.

10.5in (26.5cm) long

$1,500-2,000　　　　**BER**

A Distler lithographed tin fire ladder truck, bright red, with seated fireman, extension ladder and clockwork mechanism.

11in (28cm) overall

$700-1,000　　　　**BER**

A lithographed tin limousine, by Distler of Germany, with electric headlights and rear licence, grill reads '603', in yellow with orange trim, blue sides, black rood and running boards, with seated driver, clockwork driven.

10in (25.5cm) long

$1,500-2,000　　　　**BER**

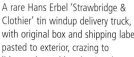

A rare Hans Erbel 'Strawbridge & Clothier' tin windup delivery truck, with original box and shipping label pasted to exterior, crazing to lithography and hand-painted frame.

$6,000-8,000　　　　**JDJ**

A limousine, by Hans Eberl of Germany, well-modeled lithographed tin example, colorful blues and gray with extensive gold trim highlights, features opening doors, seated driver, roof top luggage rack, side brake, spoke wheels, glass windshield, clockwork driven, restoration to bottom of one door, roof and fenders.

13.5in (34.5cm)

$2,000-2,500　　　　**BER**

A German Greppert and Kelch lithographed tin open tourer, in rich green and beige with red embossed seating, driver at wheel, clockwork mechanism.

1920s　　　7.75in (19.5cm) long

$700-900　　　　**BER**

A Gunthermann tinplate four-door sedan, large scale clockwork model in blue, plated parts, steerable front wheels, lacks bonnet motif, otherwise in good condition, with a fair condition illustrated box.

11in (28cm) long

$500-600　　　　**VEC**

A large hand-painted limousine, by Märklin of Germany, in deep blue with light blue pinstripes, features opening doors, glass windows, rear luggage rack and roof top rack, nickel steering wheel, side lamps, headlamps, rubber tires, ornate spoke wheels and clockwork mechanism.

A very desirable find, for its scale and design this example is arguably the finest made by Märklin.

18in (45.5cm) long

$25,000-30,000   BER

A Lehmann hand-painted and lithographed tin 'Tut Tut' toy, depicts suited gentleman with horn in mouth riding open auto, clockwork mechanism.

6.75in (17cm) high

$1,500-2,000   BER

A Märklin red clockwork racer, racing no. 7, cycle type wings to front wheels, lacks wheels to rear and with no clockwork motor, otherwise in good condition.

1934   15in (38cm) long

$600-800   VEC

An English Meccano tinplate racer, black open auto with red interior and fenders, clockwork mechanism, tool and extra screws.

9in (23cm) long

$350-450   BER

A saloon by Richter and Co. of Germany, depicts seated driver, luggage rack on striped roof, gold running boards, clockwork driven.

This is one of the more colorful and graphic of lithographed early toy autos.

5.75in (14.5cm) long

$2,000-3,000   BER

A lithographed tin ladder truck, by Tipp and Co. of Germany, open bench body with complete railing and three seated firemen, contains driver and ladder on supports, clockwork driven, spoke wheels.

8.5in (21.5cm) long

$1,000-2,000   BER

A lithographed tin luxury model limousine, by Tipp and Co. of Germany, with beige body and blue bonnet, roof and running boards, electric headlights, opening rear doors and clockwork mechanism, some scratches and denting to roof.

15in (38cm) long

$1,500-2,000   BER

A hand-painted tin Union ferry boat, by Gebrüder Bing of Germany, with open end deck, large covered cargo and passenger cabin, long stack, clockwork mechanism, restored.

16in (40.5cm) long

$1,000-1,500   BER

A hand-painted tin ocean liner, by Bing of Germany, four-stack model with red and white hull, upper deck cabin, railed sides, ten lifeboats, pilot's cabin, funnels, mast and clockwork mechanism, repainted.

27in (68.5cm) long

$5,000-6,000   BER

A hand-painted freighter, by Fleischmann of Germany, exact-scale depiction of ocean freighter, with red and black hull, white deck rail and cabin, grey stack with 'Eggo' decal on funnel, green catwalk, clockwork driven, great deck cap detail, some repaint, replaced flags.

21in (53.5cm) long

$1,000-1,500   BER

A hand-painted tin ocean liner, by Fleischmann of Germany, with red and black hull, it features upper deck, full cabin, two stacks, four lifeboats, two masts with ladders, clockwork mechanism, some corrosion, restored.

Modeled after the 'Albert Ballin' transatlantic liner.

19in (48.5cm) long

$1,500-2,000   BER

A hand-painted tin river boat, by Bing of Germany, with full canopy over entire deck, clockwork driven, side windows and railed sides.

19.5in (49.5cm) long

$2,000-3,000   BER

A 1920s American Ferdinand Strauss 'Tip-Top Porter', clockwork mechanism, some wear and chips, in good condition.

6in (15cm) high

$300-400 VEC

A lithographed tin 'Jacko the Organ Grinder' toy, by Distler of Germany, clockwork driven, depicts full figure with organ and dancing monkey on top, spoke wheels.

6.5in (16.5cm) long

$3,000-4,000 BER

A hand-painted tin Ferdinand Martin 'Le Petit Livreur' toy delivery boy, depicted pushing cart, wearing a cloth jacket, clockwork action, exceptional condition, boxed.

8in (20.5cm) high

$2,000-2,500 BER

A hand-painted and lithographed tin Lehmann 'Paddy the Pig' toy, the rider wearing a cloth jacket.

5.5in (14cm) high

$1,500-2,000 BER

A Lehmann lithographed tin 'Alabama Coon Jigger', with original box, figure holds Lehmann flag in hand, clockwork mechanism, unusual box.

10in (25.5cm) high

$800-1,000 BER

A Martin 'Piano Player', features cloth-dressed musician seated at tin piano with candles and music sheet, clockwork mechanism, repainted.

5in (12.5cm) high

$1,200-1,600 BER

A German 'Black Minstrel' clockwork toy, features a black woman playing a banjo accompanied by her gentleman caller, clockwork mechanism with music contained within the lady's hoop dress, when activated she appears to strum the banjo with her right hand as his upper body and head sway to and fro, while being propelled forward.

7.5in (19cm) high

$8,000-10,000 JDJ

A lithographed tin clockwork balloon salesman, features die-cut tin balloon seller with hand organ and toys, clockwork activates his eyes to roll, his hand to move up and down, and the toys to swing.

6.5in (16.5cm) high

$800-1,200 BER

A hand-painted tin figure of a minstrel, holding banjo in hand, good detail to large collar, clockwork mechanism.

7.75in (19.5cm) high

$1,200-1,600 BER

A Ferdinand Martin 'The Drunkard' toy, hand-painted tin head and hat, lead hands and feet, cloth body, holds wooden bottle and lead cup in hands, clockwork mechanism, rub to face paint.

8.25in (21cm) high

$800-1,000 BER

A Lehmann tinplate clockwork 'Climbing Monkey' toy.

8.75in (22cm) high

$50-70 ROS

A US Zone German clockwork Chuco 7403 Rolly Bear, brown and black glass eyes, black horizontally stitched nose, yellow felt scarf, felt pads, holding wooden staff, mounted onto two skates, each with four wheels, in near mint condition.

8.25in (20.5cm) long

$800-1,000 VEC

An Arcade cast iron 1927 Buick sedan, luxury styling, gold trim, black roof and full running boards, spoke wheels, white rubber tires, spare stencilled, missing driver, otherwise good condition.

8in (21cm) long

$1,200-1,800   BER

An Arcade cast iron yellow cab, in classic orange and black with seated nickel driver, painted disc wheels, stencilling on doors.

9in (23cm) long

$2,000-2,500   BER

An Arcade cast iron Chevrolet coupé, painted with grey body, black roof and runnings boards, silver trimmed grille, features nickel disc wheels with spare on trunk.

8in (20cm) long

$1,000-1,200   BER

A Hubley cast iron Hillclimber motorcycle, painted blue, classic depiction of seated racer on cycle, black trunk and motor, well detailed.

7in (18cm) long

$800-1,200   BER

A Kenton cast iron sedan, for Sears, made for familiar store, in large scale, painted red and black, silver spoke wheels, red centres, includes original driver, embossed spare.

12in (30cm) long

$2,000-3,000   BER

A Kenton cast iron cement mixer, with nickel rotary cement mixer on body, embossed open frame, white rubber tires.

9in (23cm) long

$1,500-2,000   BER

A Kilgore 'Tat' aeroplane, with yellow and green paint, cast rib wing, embossed 'TAT' on fuselage.

14in (36cm) long

$3,500-4,500   BER

A rare pressed steel American National Mack coal truck, with enclosed green cab with orange hopper body, rubber tires, painted wheels, orange trim, decals on grille and sides.

25in (64cm) long

$8,000-10,000   BER

A pressed steel Toledo 'Bulldog' coal truck with red doorless cab with black open body, chute slide, interior bed, side gate, rubber tyres, disc wheels, original celluloid windshield, decal on grille.

c1925   *25in (64cm) long*

$6,000-8,000   BER

A very rare Toledo Bulldog Mack circus truck, with orange open cab, green three panel van body, containing lithographed images of caged animals,

26in (66cm) long

$13,000-15,000   BER

A 19thC 'Always Did 'Spise a Mule' cast iron mechanical bank, original paint, good condition, patent information on base.

10in (25.5cm) wide

$3,000-4,000   DRA

A pre-WWII Dinky no. 22D Delivery Van, 'W.E. Boyce' type 1 with 'Hornby Series' embossed to underside of cab.

A very rare promotional van and the only one known. W. E. Boyce was a cycle shop on Archway Road in London in the 1930s and was apparently still trading under that name into the early 1960s.

$40,000-50,000   VEC

A very rare pre-WWII Dinky no. 28/1 trade box for six type 1 Delivery Vans, containing six vans, including no. 28a 'Hornby Trains', no. 28c 'Pickfords', no. 28c 'Manchester Guardian', no. 28d 'Oxo', no. 28e 'Ensign Cameras' and no. 28f 'Palethorpes', all with 'Dinky Toys' cast to underside of cab roof, all contained within yellow Trade Box with original internal dividers.

$70,000-80,000   VEC

A pre-war French-made Dinky 'Super Streamline' Saloon, 24E type but with no side window framing, thirteen bonnet louvres, red chassis and white Dunlop tires, with type 1 criss-cross chassis and type 1 radiator grill with diamond, possible repaint, unboxed.

$300-400   DN

A rare pre-war Dinky no. 28A 'Hornby' Delivery Van, type 2, yellow body, smooth blue hubs with white tires 'Hornby Trains British & Guaranteed' to both sides, slight fatigue with clear glue to underside, in excellent condition, paint and printing to both sides.

$2,000-3,000   VEC

A rare pre-war Dinky no. 28B 'Pickfords' Delivery Van, type 1, dark blue, blue metal wheels, slight distortion to shape, rear brace between wheelarches detached one side, some fading to one side, slight corrosion to same rear corner, in good condition.

$700-800   VEC

A rare Dinky no. 234 Ferrari, blue body, yellow triangle to front, blue plastic hubs, racing no. 5, overall in excellent condition.

$600-800   VEC

A Dinky no. 449 Chevrolet El Camino Pick-up, 'Mickey Thompson Enterprises' decals, promotional give-aways, in near mint condition, with near mint condition box.

$350-450   VEC

A South African Dinky no. 555 Dinky Ford Thunderbird, metallic blue, red interior, driver, white tyres, slight corrosion to hubs and damage to windscreen, good condition, including box, slight marks to end flap.

$600-800   VEC

A French Dinky no. 809 GMC US Army 6x6 Truck, military green with tilt, driver, white star to bonnet and sides, spun hubs, in near mint condition, with excellent condition, inner card and excellent condition detailed picture box.

$300-400   VEC

A French Dinky no. 810 Dodge DC56 Military Command Car, military green, plastic tilt, driver, aerial, decals, camouflage net missing, in mint condition, with good condition camouflage effect yellow card box.

$300-400   VEC

A French Dinky no. 824 Berliet Gazelle 6x6 Truck, military green with tilt and spun hubs, in good condition, with good condition detailed picture box.

$180-220   VEC

A Dinky no. 903 Foden Flat Truck with tailboard, violet blue cab, chassis, orange flatbed, mid-blue Supertoy hubs, black treaded tires, in near mint condition, with near mint striped lift off lid box.

$1,200-1,500   VEC

A Corgi no. 241 Ghia L.6.4, lime green, deep yellow interior, cast hubs, in mint condition, with near mint condition blue and yellow carded box, complete with Collectors Club folded leaflet.

$300-400   VEC

A Corgi no. 258 'The Saint' Volvo P1800, white, red interior, spun hubs, mint including blue and yellow carded box, superb example.

$700-900   VEC

A Corgi no. 270 'James Bond' Aston Martin DB5, silver, tire slashers, secret instruction pack containing unapplied decal sheet, lapel badge, spare bandit figure and folded leaflet, overall condition is mint, apart from very slight discoloration to door, with first issue wing-flap box.

$1,000-1,200   VEC

A Corgi no. 321 BMC Mini Cooper S, 'Rallye Monte Carlo', red with red interior, white roof with autograph signatures, spun hubs, racing number 2, in excellent condition, with good condition blue and yellow carded picture box with flash.

$550-650   VEC

A Corgi no. 328 Hillman Imp, 'Rallye Monte Carlo', blue body, white side stripe, off white interior, spun hubs, racing number 107, in mint condition, with mint condition display card and correct folded instruction sheet, outer blue and yellow carded box.

$600-800   VEC

A Corgi no. 340 Sunbeam Imp, 'Rallye Monte Carlo', blue body, cream interior, spun hubs, racing number 77, in excellent condition, with excellent condition display card and correct folded instruction sheet and good condition outer blue and yellow carded picture box.

$350-450   VEC

A Corgi 'Evening Standard' no. 421 Bedford Van, silver, black lower body, flat spun hubs, in near mint condition, with excellent condition blue and yellow carded box complete with Collectors Club folded leaflet.

$350-450   VEC

A Corgi no. 474 Ford Thames 'Walls Ice-cream' ice-cream van, with musical chimes, pale blue, cream, spun hubs, in near mint condition, with excellent condition inner pictorial stand, in good condition outer blue and yellow carded box.

$500-600   VEC

A Corgi no. 653 'Air Canada' Concorde, white, red, blue, near mint condition, in excellent condition correct issue blue and yellow carded box.

$500-600   VEC

A Corgi no. 1101 Bedford S-type Carrimore Car Transporter, rare issue finished with metallic mauve cab, blue trailer, flat spun hubs, in excellent condition, with near mint condition blue and yellow carded lift off lid box, complete with inner packing.

$800-1,000   VEC

A Corgi no. GS14 'Daktari' Gift Set, comprising Bedford giraffe transporter, Land Rover and cattle truck, plus various figures including Clarence the cross-eyed lion, overall conditions are near mint to mint, inner polystyrene packing is mint, outer blue and yellow picture box is good, although slightly creased, complete with picture header card which is excellent plus.

$800-1,000   VEC

A Corgi no. GS36 'Tarzan' Gift Set, comprising various vehicles and figures, mint condition, in excellent condition window box, although grubby around corners.

$400-500   VEC

An unusual Italian Alpia large clockwork trolley bus, wooden bodied, with six plastic wheels, includes opening doors to side and trolley poles, lacks driver mirror and clockwork spring requires attention, otherwise in excellent condition.

20.5in (52cm) long

$4,500-5,500   **VEC**

A rare AR Toys clockwork military ambulance, clockwork operation to rear wheels, red hubs with white tires, with soldier figure driver, opening rear door with rotary catch, some wear to edges, otherwise in good condition, with a fair condition plain card box.

$600-800   **VEC**

An unusual and rare German Blomer & Schuler flying car, with wings and propeller, futuristic shape with brick-red aluminum body, clockwork operation, with retractable wings and propeller to front, steerable front wheels, scratch above one rear wheel, otherwise in excellent condition.

7.75in (20cm) long

$700-900   **VEC**

A rare Britains no. 9526 Fordson Super Major Spud, black steering wheel, orange metal front wheel and 'Spud' rear wheel, complete with rear attachment, on excellent condition inner sliding plinth, with good condition card outer box, one side flap detached, tuck-in part of end flap missing.

$2,000-3,000   **VEC**

A Budgie Toys no. 298 Alvis Salamander Fire Crash Tender, black base, gray ladders and hose, in excellent condition, with excellent condition carded picture box with color folded leaflet.

$700-900   **VEC**

A Distler Electro Matic 7500 Porsche, battery-operated large scale tinplate model, removable hood reveals battery compartment, with selector lever to interior, rubber tires, steerable front wheels, some light wear and corrosion to interior of battery compartment, otherwise in excellent condition, with a good condition colorfully illustrated box and contemporary color leaflet.

10.25in (26cm) long

$900-1,100   **VEC**

A very rare G.I.S.E.A. Live Steam Tractor, front-loading fuel tray, brass radiator top, steel chimney, in excellent condition, with yellow plastic funnel and card 'Funziona Con Motore A Bapore', with instructions in Italian marked 'Gisea (Giocattoli Italiani Scintifici E Artistici) Milan', within plain brown card box, paper label to one end.

11in (28cm) long

$1,100-1,300   **VEC**

A German JNF tinplate American station wagon, metallic blue, with grey plastic roof-rack, detailed tin-printed interior, plated parts, friction drive with steerable front wheels, supplied with four card suit-cases to roof, in excellent condition.

10.25in (26cm) long

$600-800   **VEC**

A rare Kellerman no. 353 clockwork touring rider and male passenger, red bike, brown rider, blue and brown passenger, tin wheels, passenger rotates from hips as rider turns, in near mint condition, with good condition full color illustrated card box, and original key.

$1,500-1,700   **VEC**

An Italian Lima no. 3001 Auto Pompieri Fire Engine, red plastic body, with tinplate baseplate, battery operated, with yellow ladder, four firemen figures sealed in a plastic bag, some interaction between wheel hubs and tires, otherwise in near mint condition, with good condition colorfully illustrated box.

8.75in (22cm) long

$600-800   **VEC**

A Japanese Marusan 'Baby Scooter' pat no.4940, with rider and woman passenger, red and gray with 'Silver Pigeon' to rear, friction drive, scooter with clear windshield, tin blue wheels to front, slight mark on one side, otherwise in near mint condition, with excellent condition box with detail, full color picture to lid.

$1,000-1,500   VEC

A Matchbox Regular Wheels no. 72a Fordson Major Tractor, yellow plastic front and rear hubs with black tires, in mint condition, with type D color picture box.

$1,000-1,200   VEC

A Matchbox Regular Wheels no. 39b Pontiac Bonneville Convertible, cream interior with red steering wheel, crimson base with grey plastic wheels, in mint condition, with near mint condition type D color picture box.

$2,500-3,500   VEC

A Matchbox Regular Wheels no. 22c Pontiac GP Coupé, red, gray interior, black base and plastic wheels, in near mint condition, with good condition later issue F style box.

$1,000-1,500   VEC

A US Zone German Schuco 'Curvo 1000' motor cycle, blue with gray and cream engine detail, rider with red jacket and tan trousers, gauntlets, helmet, flat spot to front tire, otherwise in near mint condition, with good condition box, complete with instructions.

5in (13cm) long

$2,500-3,500   VEC

A Western German Schuco 5710 Elektro radio car, cream upper open body, red lower body, gold and cream plastic 'fins' to rear, lithographed interior, dashboard, plated lights, radiator, front and rear bumpers, windscreen frame, 'Schuco' to front of bonnet, one wheel hub corroded, otherwise in excellent condition.

11in (28cm) long

$1,100-1,300   VEC

A Limited Edition Solido 'James Bond - Goldfinger' Rolls Royce, from an edition of 100, complete with Goldfinger and Oddjob figures, mint condition including gold tube.

$800-1,000   VEC

A French VeBe large tinplate fire engine, with clockwork motor, elevation and extending controls to ladder, which is mounted on a revolving turntable, opening door to cab, wired for electric headlights, with tires and steerable front wheels, some surface corrosion to silver painted ladder, otherwise in good condition with rubber.

15.75in (40cm) long

$700-900   VEC

A Japanese Yonezawa 'Diamond' hood truck, friction drive, red with yellow plastic tilt, detailed tin-printed interior, plated parts, very light wear due to storage, otherwise in excellent condition with some inner packaging, with fair card box with illustrated lift off lid.

15.5in (39cm) long

$900-1,100   VEC

A pressed steel open-top car, of unconfirmed manufacture, grayish green, with cream interior, clockwork operation to rear wheels, poseable front wheels, rubber tires, some wear to upper edges but includes tinplate windshield surround and rear wheel cover.

11in (28cm) long

$700-900   VEC

TOYS

A rare Schuco miniature orange teddy bear, with black stitched face and metal eyes.

2.75in (7cm) high

$200-300   A&G

A rare Schuco miniature pink teddy bear, with black stitched face and metal eyes, faded and worn.

2.75in (7cm) high

$250-350   A&G

A pale gold Steiff center-seam mohair teddy bear, with boot button eyes, hump back and elongated feet, light brown vertical stitching to nose, Steiff button in ear, original pads.

This bear belonged to Pamela Winstanley (b.1910) and was sold together with photographs and a history of its owner. Center-seam Steiff are rare as one piece of mohair was sufficient to produced six and a half bear heads, so the head of the seventh bear was made from two pieces sewn together creating a seam down the middle of the head.

21in (54.5cm) high

$10,000-12,000   BWL

A Steiff beige bear with glass eyes, no buttons or tags.

17in (43cm) high

$200-400   BER

A Steiff blonde mohair 'Petsy' teddy bear, blue and black glass eyes, red vertically stitched nose, center seam, wired ears, fully jointed, felt pads, red clear stitching, hump, inoperative squeaker, mohair thinning and balding in places, pads holed, stuffing shifted at neck and tops of limbs, button with remains of red tag behind.

1928   *11in (28cm) high*

$3,500-4,500   VEC

A Steiff blonde mohair teddy bear, with brown woven nose and boot button eyes, together with a gift certificate, dated.

1908   *14in (35.5cm) high*

$3,000-4,000   HGS

A Steiff small brown mohair bear, lacks button in his ear.

c1907   *10in (25.5cm) high*

$1,000-1,200   TCT

An early American blonde mohair teddy bear, by an unknown maker, with original paw pads, glass eyes and stitched nose.

c1908   *11.5in (29cm) high*

$550-650   TCT

An early American blonde mohair teddy bear, by an unknown maker, with original paw pads, black stitched nose and mouth and boot button eyes.

c1908   *10in (25.5cm) high*

$700-900   HGS

A black drummer boy automaton, with papier-mâché head, leather eyes, in working order with drum sticks acting as speed regulator.

30in (76cm) high

$22,000-26,000 BER

A Lambert nargileh smoker automaton, by Leopold Lambert, with music playing the figure raises and lowers head, arm, pipe and teacup.

c1885 *21in (53cm) high*

$5,000-7,000 BER

A limited edition Steiff 'Musician Brown', from an edition of 1,200, with button, the wood-wool-stuffed felt figure with mohair hair and beard, cornet missing.

This is a replica of the 1911 'Musician Brown' figure.

1996 *15.25in (38cm) high*

$200-300 WDL

A Goblin Paints advertising figure, entitled 'Paint More Save More', the two goblins holding a paintbrush or a bag of cash, some damage.

19in (48cm) high

$900-1,100 LA

A set of four 19thC timber puppets, of sectional timber composition, joined cloth costume, naively painted, with stands.

18in (45.5cm) high

$2,000-3,000 FRE

A French clockwork-driven carousel, with figures and horses, tattered silk canopy, label on base.

12in (30cm) high

$3,000-4,000 BER

An English wooden baby carriage.

$1,800-2,400 GORL

A late 19th/early 20thC painted canvas circus banner, mounted on a wooden frame.

102in (259cm) high

$4,500-5,500 SK

A mid-20thC American painted canvas circus banner. 'Millard & Bulsterbaum 2894 W 8th St. Coney Island, N.Y.' stencilled lower right.

96in (244cm) high

$3,000-4,000 SK

A Fromann & Bunte transformation pack, third edition.

c1870

$200-300 BLO

A late Italian 19thC olive wood playing card box, in the form of a book with inlaid playing cards with sliding interior for four packs of playing cards.

6.75in (17cm) wide

$600-800 BLO

A stone figure, 'Owl', by Latcholassie Akesuk (1919-2000), E7-1055, Cape Dorset.

c1960   *10in (25.5cm) high*

$17,000-21,000   **WAD**

A stone figure 'Ecstasy', by Abraham Apakark Anghik, Salt Spring Island, signed in Roman, dated.

2001   *26in (66cm) high*

$6,000-10,000   **WAD**

A stone figure, 'Raven Man', by Abraham Apakark Anghik, Salt Spring Island, signed in Roman, dated.

2000   *37in (94cm) high*

$5,000-7,000   **WAD**

A stone figure, 'Musk Ox', by Barnabus Arnasungaaq, (b1924), E2-213, Baker Lake, signed in syllabics.

12in (30.5cm) wide

$12,000-16,000   **WAD**

A stone figure, 'Hawk', by Kenojuak Ashevak (b1927), E7-1035, Cape Dorset, signed in syllabics.

14in (35.5cm) high

$7,000-9,000   **WAD**

A stone figure, 'Archer', by Abraham Etungat, (1911-99), E7-809, Cape Dorset.

c1960   *17in (43cm) high*

$12,000-16,000   **WAD**

An antler carving, 'Running Bird', by Luke Iksiktaaryuk, (1909-77), E2-45, Baker Lake.

13in (33cm) high

$15,000-19,000   **WAD**

A stone figure, 'Owl Landing', by Osuitok Ipeelee (1923-2005), E7-1154, Cape Dorset.

1983   *15.25in (38.5cm) wide*

$5,000-7,000   **WAD**

A stone statue, 'Shaman's Head', by John Kavik (1897-1993), E2-290, Rankin Inlet.

c1970   *8.5in (21.5cm) wide*

$40,000-50,000   **WAD**

A stone figure, 'Standing Woman', by Sheokjuk Oqutaq, (1920-82), E7-919, Cape Dorset.

c1949   *5.5in (14cm) high*

$22,000-26,000   **WAD**

A stone figure, by John Pangnark (1920-80), E1-104, Arviat.

9in (23cm) long

$10,000-12,000   **WAD**

A stone statue, 'Many Faces', by John Tiktak, (1916-81), E1-266, Rankin Inlet, signed in syllabics.

12in (30.5cm) high

$50,000-60,000 WAD

A stone figure, 'Polar Figure', by Pauta Saila, (b1916), E7-990, Cape Dorset.

16in (40.5cm) high

$9,000-11,000 WAD

A stone and ivory figure, 'Dancing Walrus', by Pauta Saila, E7-990, Cape Dorset, signed in Roman.

c1975 *17in (43cm) high*

$9,000-11,000 WAD

A stone figure, 'Mother and Child', by George Tataniq, (1910-91), E2-179, Baker Lake, signed in syllabics and disc number.

11in (28cm) high

$10,000-12,000 WAD

A bone figure, 'Drummer', by Charlie Ugyuk, (1931-98), E4-341, Spence Bay.

18in (45.5cm) high

$10,000-12,000 WAD

A stone figure, 'Mother and Child', unidentified artist, Arviat.

11in (28cm) high

$17,000-21,000 WAD

A stone figure, 'Sedna Mother and Child', unidentified artist, Salluit.

c1950 *9in (23cm) high*

$22,000-30,000 WAD

A stonecut, 'Enchanted Owl', by Kerouac Ashevak (b1927), E7-1035, Cape Dorset, a/p, unframed.

1960 *26in (66cm) wide*

$50,000-60,000 WAD

A skin stencil, 'Polar Bear and Cub in Ice', by Niviaxie, (1908-59), E7-1077, Cape Dorset, 18/30, framed.

1959 *22in (56cm) wide*

$32,000-40,000 WAD

An appliqué wall hanging, by Jessie Oonark (1906-85), E2-384, Baker Lake, stroud, embroidery floss, thread, dated to tag.

1974 *73in (185.5cm) wide*

$32,000-40,000 WAD

An early 20thC Inuit carved ivory cribbage board, with animal heads projecting from the ends and two relief-carved heads on the playing surface.

16in (40.5cm) long

$1,100-1,300 SK

An Inuit incised ivory tusk, split section, one side with a whaling scene, two traditionally dressed men sitting on a European chair and stool, various animal and plant devices, and a winged fantasy creature, red pigment details.

c1900 *17.25in (44cm) long*

$5,000-7,000 SK

A 20thC Inuit ivory seal, age cracks.

6in (15cm) long

$360-440 SK

A 20thC Inuit stone carving, bust of a man wearing an animal headdress, appears phallic when viewed from behind, applied metal eyes.

6.75in (17cm) high

$2,600-3,600 SK

An Inuit carved wood mask, King Island, with exaggerated facial features and pierced at the eyes, nose and mouth.

c1900 *6in (15cm) wide*

$2,000-3,000 SK

A late 19thC Inuit painted carved wood bowl, the ovoid form with red and black rim and five stacked stylized animals on the inside.

11in (28cm) long

$3,000-4,000 SK

An early 20thC Inuit coiled basket, the round flat-bottom form with minimal geometric decoration, the lid with walrus ivory knob carved in the form of walrus heads, minor stitch loss.

10in (25.5cm) diam

$600-800 SK

NORTH EASTERN TRIBES

A pair of third quarter 19thC Northeast Iroquois beaded cloth and hide child's moccasins, the soft sole forms beaded on the vamps with multicolored floral and geometric devices using small seed beads, the silk-covered cuffs with larger bead edgings, minor bead loss.

4.75in (12cm) long

$1,200-1,600 SK

A mid-19thC Northeast beaded cloth bag, red trade cloth, decorated on both sides with multicolored variations of the C-scroll pattern, remnant silk edging.

5.5in (14cm) high

$800-1,200 SK

A mid-19thC Northeast Micmac quilled birch bark box, the rectangular lidded form with multi-colored chevron pattern sides and geometric lid, minor quill loss.

5in (12.5cm) long

$800-1,000 SK

A third quarter 19thC Northeast Micmac quilled Rococo Revival chair, the rosewood and walnut slipper chair with traditional polychrome-quilled birch bark panels on the seat and back, wear to quill work.

37in (94cm) high

$2,000-3,000 SK

A third quarter 19thC Northeast Huron moose-hair-embroidered birch bark cigar case, with male and female figures smoking pipes and perched birds on foliage, hair loss.

5in (12.5cm) high

$600-1,000 SK

A mid-19thC Northeast Iroquois beaded cloth corn husk doll and cradle, the female wearing traditional clothing of the period, with silver brooch/pin, minor loss.

Doll 11.5in (29cm) high

$12,000-16,000 SK

A first quarter 20thC Northwest coast carved and painted wood totem pole, carved with stylized human and animal forms, avian finial, and painted with early commercial colors.

34in (86.5cm) high

$4,000-6,000   **SK**

A last quarter 19thC Northwest coast carved wood bear, crouching on a round base, with front paws up and curled at the chest, traces of red and black pigment, cracks.

23.5in (59.5cm) high

$11,000-13,000   **SK**

A late 19thC Northwest coast Nootka carved wood mask, the hollow oval form with wide pierced down-turned mouth, round pierced eyes, and flattened nose, red, black and white pigment details, patina of use, written on the inside 'Old Native Dance Mask – Alaska – OR'.

11.75in (30cm) high

$2,400-3,600   **SK**

A mid-19thC Northwest coast Haida carved argillite, elaborate form with abstract European ship theme and two European-dress figures, damage, in two pieces.

15.25in (38.5cm) long

$8,000-10,000   **SK**

A pair of Algonquin moccasins, one moccasin has loose upper beaded portion.

c1850   *9in (23cm) long*

$300-400   **ALD**

A Northwest Coast Tlingit polychrome twined basket, with multicolored bands, the outside with multicolored fret and cross devices, small split.

c1900   *11.5in (29cm) diam*

$7,000-9,000   **SK**

PLAINS TRIBES

A Native American embroidered fringed hide shirt, possibly Northern Plains, the front placard, pocket, cuffs and shoulders decorated with dyed embroidered leaves and flowers.

c1900   *30in (76cm) high*

$3,000-4,000   **POOK**

A late 19thC Central Plains Lakota beaded hide man's vest, beaded on the front and back with multicolored geometric designs on a white background, minor bead loss.

20in (51cm) long

$2,000-3,000   **SK**

A pair of last quarter 19thC Central Plains Arapaho beaded hide woman's high-top moccasins, the hard sole forms with soft uppers stained yellow and red, with multicolored geometric detailing including a cross on one vamp and a circle on the other, brass beaded fringe along the side panels.

18in (45.5cm) high

$8,000-12,000   **SK**

A pair of last quarter 19thC Central Plains Lakota beaded hide possible bags, the rectangular forms beaded on the front and sides with multicolored geometric devices, tin cone and red horsehair drops from the sides.

21in (53.5cm) long

$11,000-13,000   **SK**

A last quarter 19thC Northern Plains Crow tomahawk and beaded hide drop, with ash handle pierced for smoking, a variant spontoon-style brass head, the handle wrapped with otter skin at the top.

Tomahawk 18.5in (47cm) long

$2,000-3,000   **SK**

A last quarter 19thC Plains pictograph drawing, titled 'Kills 3 Crows', colored pencil drawing depicting a warrior on foot counting coup on a wounded warrior, and a man and woman shot with arrows, unframed.

8.25in (21cm) wide

$2,400-3,600   **SK**

A Southwest Hopi polychrome carved wood Kokopelli katcina, the cottonwood hump-backed flute player carrying a rattle in one hand and a stick in the other, the body slightly twisted and with male genitalia, the black case mask with long tapered bill, old tag on the back, one arm re-glued.

$3,600-4,400   SK

A Southwest Hopi polychrome carved wood mudhead katcina, with arms to the sides and painted with black, white, red and dull pink pigments.

4.5in (11.5cm) high

$1,400-2,000   SK

A Southwest Sipikne, Hopi, polychrome carved wood Zuni Sun God katcina, the case mask with black stripes, large red ears, and snout.

2.75in (7cm) high

$1,600-2,400   SK

A Southwest Cochiti, Pueblo, polychrome pottery story teller figure, Sarafina Ortez, the seated female form with fourteen listeners.

8.25in (21cm) high

$1,300-1,700   SK

A Southwest polychrome pottery vessel, Margaret and Luther, Santa Clare Pueblo, the rounded form with stylized bird and rabbit devices on a buff slip.

3in (7.5cm) high

$400-600   SK

A late 19thC Southwest Acoma polychrome pottery pitcher, with handle between two stylized bird heads, one a spout, painted with black and red-brown abstract foliate designs on a cream-colored ground.

4.5in (11.5cm) high

$1,000-1,600   SK

A first half 20thC Southwest Paiute beaded coiled basketry bowl, the outside overlaid in a multicolored geometric pattern.

5in (12.5cm) diam

$500-700   SK

A Southwest Apache coiled basketry bowl, with concentric five-point star pattern, stains.

c1900   *15in (38cm) diam*

$1,000-1,600   SK

A Southwest Apache coiled basketry olla, with high shoulder and flared rim, decorated with zigzag and triangular devices, stitch loss.

c1900   *8.5in (21.5cm) diam*

$500-700   SK

A Southwest Navajo, Two Gray Hills, regional weaving, tightly woven with natural and synthetic dyed homespun wood, a storm pattern variant on a variegated gray background, black border.

c1940   *75.5in (192cm) long*

$2,000-3,000   SK

A last quarter 19thC Southwest Navajo, Germantown weaving, tightly woven with a multicolored serrated diamond pattern, a two-color stepped border, and fringe at one end, fading.

52in (132cm) long

$1,000-1,600   SK

A Southwest Navajo transitional weaving, natural and synthetic dyed homespun yarn, with serrated diamond, crosses, and arrow devices on a red background, wool loss.

c1900   *88in (223.5cm) long*

$1,000-1,600   SK

A Pre-Columbian Jalisco painted pottery couple, the female with hands on her drum-playing husband's shoulders, both with necklaces and ear ornaments, elaborate headdress, and painted detail.

100BC-AD250   *9.5in (24cm) high*

$1,200-1,600   **SK**

A Pre-Columbian Jalisco painted pottery female figure, seated with legs to the side, out-thrust arms, wearing a skirt, headdress, and nose ornament, red pigment detail, nose tip restored.

c100BC-AD250   *10.25in (26cm) high*

$600-800   **SK**

A Pre-Columbian Jalisco seated male pottery figure, the hollow hunch-backed form with hands to the ground, wearing ear discs and a headdress.

c100BC-AD300   *7.5in (19cm) high*

$1,000-1,600   **SK**

A Pre-Columbian Jalisco painted pottery figure, the seated female form with a bowl on her shoulder and one resting on her thigh, nose and ear ornaments with black and red body decoration, some restoration.

c100BC-AD250   *15in (38cm) high*

$1,000-1,600   **SK**

A Pre-Columbian Nayarit painted pottery figure, the standing female form with upturned arms, ears ornaments, and black and red body paint, restoration.

c100BC-AD250   *16in (40.5cm) high*

$1,200-1,600   **SK**

A Pre-Columbian Zacatecas painted pottery female figure, seated with hands to the side and black and red geometric decoration on the upper body.

c200BC-AD200   *11.5in (29cm) high*

$2,200-3,000   **SK**

A Pre-Columbian Colima painted pottery turtle-dog figure, with open spout tail, red shell and dog-like head.

c200BC-AD200   *6.5in (16.5cm) high*

$2,400-3,600   **SK**

A Pre-Columbian Colima painted pottery dog, the plump seated form with flared spout on the top of the head, upturned tail, and incised toothy grin, remnant black and red pigment.

c100BC-AD300   *9.25in (23.5cm) high*

$2,000-3,000   **SK**

A Pre-Columbian Chancay, Peru, painted pottery animal, the bulbous redware form with brown and white paint.

7.5in (19cm) high

$300-400   **SK**

A Pre-Columbian Inca, Peru, blackware stirrup-spout pottery vessel, in the form of a boat with a seated human figure at the helm, incised and relief-carved detail.

c1200-1400   *7.5in (17cm) high*

$400-600   **SK**

A Pre-Columbian painted pottery vessel, a whistling form with strap and spout double body, the front in the form of a seal, with dark brown and white pigment on red body.

6in (15cm) high

$700-900   **SK**

A Pre-Columbian Maya, El Salvador, polychrome cylinder, three elaborately dressed standing male figures on a buff-colored background with red and black framing lines, surface loss.

cAD650-900   *7in (18cm) high*

$1,600-2,400   **SK**

A Nok anthropomorphic terracotta figure, from Nigeria, some damage.
300BC-AD200   *8.25in (21cm) high*
$1,000-1,600   **BLA**

A Mambila figure, from Cameroon or Nigeria.
16in (41cm) high
$11,000-13,000   **BLA**

A late 19thC Yoruba reliquary guardian figure, from Nigeria.
18.75in (47.5cm) high
$9,000-11,000   **BLA**

A pair of early 20thC Yoruba Ibeji figures, from Nigeria.
10.5in (27cm) high
$700-900   **BLA**

A 19thC Dogon or Proto Dogon anthropomorphic figure, depicting a hermaphrodite protector.
11.25in (28.5cm) high
$7,000-9,000   **BLA**

An African Baule carved wood male figure, from Ivory Coast, seated on a stool with hands on knees, one palm out, the body and large head with finely carved detail, including a headdress with cowry shell edging and animal hair attachment, red, white, and black pigments, wood loss.
17in (43cm) high
$5,000-7,000   **SK**

An Ibo dance mask crest, from Nigeria.
c1900   *11in (28cm) high*
$1,600-2,000   **BLA**

A carved wood Idoma fetish mask, from Nigeria.
c1900   *16.5in (42cm) high*
$3,000-4,000   **BLA**

An early 20thC Ejagham helmet mask crest, from Nigeria
15in (38.5cm) high
$3,000-4,000   **BLA**

A 20thC Epa mask, from Nigeria, carved wood with traces of pigment.
44in (112cm) high
$1,200-1,600   **FRE**

A Karumba antelope form helmet mask, from Burkina Faso, surmounted with tall horns, forward-curved ears, twine issuing from holes to the edge, polychrome painting.
54in (137cm) high
$400-600   **FRE**

An African Guro carved wood mask, from Ivory Coast, the hollow form with long narrow nose, pierced narrow eyes, scarification marks, and tripartite coiffure, dark patina, cracked.
12.5in (32cm) high
$2,400-3,600   **SK**

An African Benin carved wood kola nut bowl, from Nigeria, the lidded form carved to represent a stylized antelope head, with incised detail, wood loss.

15.25in (38.75cm) long

$1,000-1,600 SK

An African Kuba carved wood box, from D. R. Congo, the crescent-shaped lidded form with relief-carved geometric decoration on the sides, top, and handle, traces of red pigment.

13.25in (33.5cm) wide

$1,200-1,600 SK

An African Kuba carved lidded box, from D. R. Congo, with incised geometric patterns, traces of red pigment, dark patina, minor wood loss.

6.5in (16.5cm) high

$900-1,300 SK

An early 20thC Bambara carved wood cane-top, from Mali.

21.5in (55cm) high

$1,600-2,400 BLA

An African Yoruba carved wood shango staff, from Nigeria, with cylindrical handle surmounted by a platform with a kneeling female figure holding a bird in one hand and a gourd shaped item in the other, the axe-shaped projection from head stained black on one side and with kaolin-filled incised lozenges, black surface.

17in (43cm) high

$2,000-3,000 SK

A South African Zulu carved wood ball-headed club, part of the shaft covered in fine two-color braided wire, dark patina.

22in (56cm) high

$1,000-1,600 SK

An early 20thC Dogon wooden door lock, from Mali.

19in (48cm) high

$1,200-1,600 BLA

An African Songye wood and metal ceremonial axe, Congo River Basin, the forged steel blade with elaborate open work and single-head projection on both sides, the wood handle covered with a copper sheath, patina of use.

Handle 15in (38cm) long

$1,600-2,400 SK

An Ashanti carved child's stool, from Ghana, the dished seat on an elephant support.

12.5in (31.5cm) wide

$200-300 WW

An African Kuba carved horn cup, from D. R. Congo, the gracefully curved form with relief-carved geometric and concentric circle devices, patina of use.

16in (40.5cm) long

$3,000-4,000 SK

An African ivory and horn sceptre, the handle with animal hair whisk and brass-braided wire wrap, the finial in the form of a dog head with inlaid eyes and teeth.

Handle 10.5in (26.5cm) long

$1,000-1,600 SK

A Benin bronze cat head, good cast, handle to back of head.

c1900 *5.5in (14cm) high*

$600-1,000 FRE

A large Yuat Rivershield, from New Guinea, carved wood with pigment and raffia ornamentation through the nose of five faces, one side with raffia tassels attached.

78in (198cm) high

$400-600   **FRE**

A Mendi village shield, from New Guinea, painted wood, with cloth handles to the rear.

65in (165cm) high

$900-1,100   **FRE**

A Mendi shield, from New Guinea, painted wood, rope handle leading to a triangle shape to the front.

60in (152.5cm) high

$600-800   **FRE**

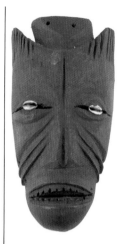

A carved and painted Sepik River mask, from New Guinea .

9.75in (24.5cm) long

$200-300   **WW**

A carved wood and painted Sepik River mask, from New Guinea, decorated with feathers and cowrie shells, some losses to the shell decoration.

29in (74cm) long

$400-600   **WW**

A carved wood and painted Sepik River standing figure, from New Guinea, with cowrie shell eyes.

34.75in (88.5cm) high

$600-800   **WW**

A Garamut slit drum, from New Guinea, carved sides with carved figural handles.

88in (223.5cm) long

$900-1,100   **FRE**

A shell pectoral bride price, with case, from New Guinea, Kina shell with woven red neck band, ornamented with cowrie shells and cuscus fur, covered in red pigment with detailed carrying case.

14in (35.5cm) high

$120-200   **FRE**

A 19thC Maori inscribed club, with bands of geometric carved decoration, the tip carved with a lion mask, inscribed 'A MIGHTY CHIEF FIRST CUT ME FROM THE TREE AND REDUCED ME TO THE STATE YOU SEE, A WARRIORS ARM SUSTAINED ME IN THE FIELD AND WITH MY HELP HE MADE MANY TO YIELD, COMMITED BY FATE TO CROSS THE BRINY WAVE FOR I WAS BOUGHT BY A SAILOR STOUT AND BRAVE TO OTAHEITE'S ISLE OF FAME, ST SINGAPATAM WAS THE FRIGATES NAME, WALDEGRAVE CAPTN APRIL 29 WE LEFT THE BAY IN THE YEAR 1830 WE SAILED AWAY'.

43.75in (111cm) long

$6,000-10,000   **WW**

A Baining mask, from New Britain, painted tapa cloth over a cane frame, large abstract head forming circular eyes and a complexly painted pattern to the front, elongated mouth shape, over a wood stand.

42in (106.5cm) high

$1,000-1,600   **FRE**

An early 18thC steel-mounted Italian flintlock holster pistol, the rounded banana-shaped lock with finely chiseled acanthus leaf at the tail and on the frizzen back, elegant shaped cock with floral chiseled cock retaining screw head, trigger cut and scrolled with foliate chiselling, replacement trigger guard, bulbous spurred pommel with chiseled acanthus leaves on both sides and floral butt cap en suite with cock retaining screw, pierced and cut steel blank escutcheon, finely cut foliate side plate, the two-stage barrel octagonal at the breech tapering to a slender muzzle with rubbed classical portrait head at the breech, plain tang, dark walnut full stock carved with foliate scrolls at the barrel tang, trigger guard finial and rear chiseled steel ramrod pipes, rubbed 'Anton Boniscolo' signature and replacement ramrod.

20.75in (53cm) long

$6,000-10,000   L&T

A mid-18thC silver-mounted flintlock three-stage cannon-barreled turn-off pistol, the dark walnut butt carved with a shell below the engraved barrel tang and with carved tear drops behind the cast silver trophy of arms side plate, engraved silver spurred pommel with grotesque mask butt cap in the form of leaves, rococo escutcheon engraved with a viscount's crest and coronet, signed 'Barbar, London 2' at the breech with 'IB' stamp for James Barbar and engraved acanthus leaves with London proof mark, with Keith Neal collection tag 'P 228' attached to the floral engraved trigger guard.

The crest and coronet is that of Lionel Tollemache (1734-1799), 5th Earl of Dysart. The 5th Earl was responsible for reshaping the gardens at Ham House, Richmond Park, Middlesex, UK. Ham House is now in the care of The National Trust given by the Tolleche family in 1948. Jacobus Barbero was apprenticed on October 7th, 1714 for seven years to his father Ludovicus in June 1737. In May 1741 he became Gentleman Armorer to King George II. In 1742 he was appointed Master of Gunmakers Company. The spelling of the name varies between Barber and Barbar. He died in April 1773.

11.75in (30cm) long

$9,000-11,000   L&T

A rare George II flintlock blunderbuss pistol, by Grice, with steel barrel and action, walnut butt and cappings.

c1755   14.25in (36cm) long

$4,400-5,200   RGA

An 18thC paktong flintlock, boxlock, turn-off cannon barrel pocket pistol, with 'PERRY-LONDON' within scrolls on each side of the lock, with full Birmingham hallmarks for '1777' and maker's mark 'CF' for Charles Freeth.

5.75in (14.5cm) long

$7,000-11,000   L&T

A 55 bore flintlock boxlock pocket pistol, London proved, the frame engraved with swags and 'Broomhead, London' in ovals, top safety, hidden trigger, plain walnut slab butt, with some original blued finish.

c1800   7.25in (18.5cm) long

$500-700   W&W

A George III double-barreled flintlock highwayman's pistol, by Brasher, with steel barrels and actions, walnut butts, in good condition.

c1810   15in (38cm) long

$9,000-11,000   RGA

A 42 bore flintlock boxlock pocket pistol, by Parker of Holborn, London, hidden trigger, partly chequered walnut slab butt with escutcheon.

c1820   5in (12.5cm) long

$1,000-1,400   W&W

A mid-19thC flintlock service pistol, by Dobson and Baker, with steel barrel and action, and walnut butt with brass cappings.

c1840   15in (38cm) long

$4,400-5,600   RGA

A flintlock pocket pistol, with octagonal steel barrel and brass lock, signed Noyes, Warminster, together with various flints and a bullet mold.

$800-1,200   SWO

An Irish 32 bore flintlock pocket pistol, by Dempsey, Dublin, with 4.25in (11cm) steel barrel, sliding safety and roller frizen, complete with ramrod, steel trigger-guard and butt cap, the chequered grip inlaid with a silver-colored metal escutcheon.

8in (20.5cm) long

$900-1,100   A&G

A Continental 36 bore brass cannon-barreled and brass-framed flintlock boxlock pocket pistol, top saftey which also locks the frizzen, flattened chequered walnut butt inset with silver studs, octagonal flared finial with flat brass cap.

7.5in (19cm) long

$700-900   W&W

A 19thC flintlock holster pistol, the lock struck with an eastern seal mark, with brass trigger guard and butt cap.

$500-700   SWO

An Eastern flintlock pistol, with wirework decoration.

$360-440   SWO

An early 19th Century Belgian Seaservice flintlock holster pistol.

$500-700   SWO

A Belgian Sea Service flintlock holster pistol.

$600-800   SWO

A flintwood Sea Service belt pistol, the lock stamped Woolley, Sargeant & Fairfax, with swivel ramrod and brass butt cap.

$800-1,200   SWO

A 120 bore Continental flintlock steel pocket pistol, signed Seglas, London, with tapering barrel, box-lock action signed on the right and inscribed 'London' on the left, engraved bag-shaped butt swelling towards the base and engraved sliding trigger-guard operating a safety-catch also locking the steel, engraving worn throughout.

5.5in (14cm) long

$1,000-1,400   TDM

A matched pair of Jacob or Peter Kunz (Kuntz) Kentucky pistols, SN and NSN, octagonal to round smooth barrels of approximately 45 calibre, the brass and side plates are engraved, each butt cap has a pierced finial extending up the grip, the flintlocks are each marked 'C. BIRD & Co PHILADa'.

The curly maple stocks with chequered wrists show the original red violin finish used by Kunz and other gunsmiths who learned their trade in the Lehigh Valley, PA, area. Peter and Jacob Kunz were born in the late 18thC in Whitehall Township, Lehigh City, PA. They later also worked in Philadelphia. The Kunz brothers were awarded a number of Franklin Institute awards for being the most accomplished gunsmiths in Philadelphia and for their fine craftsmanship. Like most gunsmiths, not all of their work was signed. However, pistols are quite easily identified by their characteristics, and this pair is signed 'P Kunz'. Kentucky pistols in matched pairs are extremely rare and desirable.

8.5in (21.5cm) long

$80,000-120,000   JDJ

A late 18thC pair of flintlock pistols, probably German, full length walnut stocks carved around the tang and the underside with Rococo scrolls, the gilt brass cast mounts chased with satyr's heads and trophies of war, the trigger guard with an Ottoman crescent length barrel.

13.5in (34.5cm) barrel length

$14,000-20,000   SOTA

A pair of 18thC duelling pistols, saw butt, silver mounted, hallmarked 'MB' for Matthew Boulton, flat pommel engraved with initials 'JG' for Joseph Gosling, his silver coat of arms inlaid into the left side of both pistols, silver ramrod pipes, and original ramrods, the replacement percussion locks signed 'William Powell', converted from flint, in original fitted oak case with various accessories.

1799

$14,000-20,000   L&T

A flintlock blunderbuss, by Aston, Manchester, 14in (35.5cm) long brass barrels, complete with ramrod, brass trigger-guard and butt cap.

29.25in (11.5cm) long

$1,600-2,400   A&G

A George III flintlock blunderbuss, scrolled brass trigger-guard and Damascus steel barrel, with walnut stock with brass capping, fitted with a spring-loaded steel bayonet, in good condition.

c1810   *32in (81.5cm) long*

$5,000-7,000   RGA

An early 19thC Dutch colonial flintlock blunderbuss, with swamped steel barrel strongly swelling and fluted towards the muzzle, inlaid with fine brass linear patterns and a central foliate panel, English regulation lock stamped with 'GR' crowned, hardwood full stock boldly carved with flowers on the right of the butt, brass regulation mounts and a pair of steel sling swivels, ramrod and fore-end cap missing, crack and repairs to stock.

44in (112cm) long

$1,000-1,400   TDM

An early 19thC percussion cap pistol, cross-hatched walnut stock, some engraving on side panels, sound condition, one screw needing replacement.

7.75in (19.5cm) long

$300-500 **BLO**

An early 19th Century French percussion belt pistol, with indistinct engraved marks to the lock.

$600-800 **SWO**

An American .54 US Marshall's percussion holster pistol, the lock stamped 'MIDDTN CONN.'
c1850

$1,000-1,400 **SWO**

A mid 19th Century percussion pistol, by Nock of London.

$700-900 **SWO**

An Irish 12 bore percussion travelling pistol, by Trulock of Dublin, with registration number 'DC-4692', walnut fullstock with plain brass mounts, swivel ramrod.

9in (23cm) long

$360-440 **W&W**

A 22 bore percussion belt pistol, with 4.75in (12cm) long octagonal steel barrel and swivel ramrod underneath, with steel butt cap and fitted with a small magazine.

9.5in (24cm) long

$640-760 **A&G**

A percussion Tower pistol, the lock stamped 'Tower'.

$400-600 **SWO**

An unusual French 34 bore all steel percussion boxlock pocket pistol, with turn-off rifled barrel with St Etienne proof, the frame stamped 'Vincent, Brevete SDGD', hidden trigger.

5.75in (14.5cm) long

$400-600 **W&W**

A pair of 19thC cased percussion pocket pistols, with foliate-engraved hammers, false breeches with silver line inlays, barrel tangs and fire-blued trigger guards, plain silver escutcheons, full walnut stocks with chequered butts, captive swivel ramrods, contained in original mahogany case lined with green baize with small powder flask and associated turn screw, with plain brass shaped escutcheon on case lid, the engraved flat-sided locks with safety slides and signed 'WESTLEY RICHARDS and WESTLEY RICHARDS LONDON', the Westley Richards trade card on the inside of the lid states 'Gun Manufacturer to His Royal Highness Prince Albert, 170 New Bond Street'.

The family of Westley Richards were Birmingham gunmakers of the highest renown during the latter part of the 18thC and throughout the 19thC. William started at 82 High Street, Birmingham, England in 1812, and opened a London shop at 170 New Bond Street in 1815.

$19,000-23,000 **L&T**

A 19thC double barrel percussion sporting gun, the top rib engraved 'Gasquoine and Dyson, Market Place, Manchester', finely engraved trigger-guard and butt plate tang, in a fitted mahogany case , numbered '1381'.

$2,400-3,600 **L&T**

A pair of percussion pistols, by Falisse and Trapmann à Liege, with round ribbed 4.75in (12cm) Damascus barrels and concealed triggers.

9.25in (23.5cm) long

$3,600-4,400 **GVI**

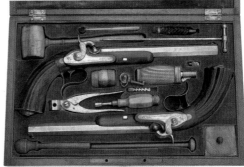

A fine pair of 19thC French percussion target and duelling pistols, by Jalaber Lamotte of St Etienne (1810-1855), with octagonal 9.75in (25cm) barrels with 0.5in (12mm) polygrove bores, the Damascus steel barrels stamped with French proof marks and stamped with the French barrel maker's name 'Massardite Peiegon', the French walnut stocks stamped with the stocker's name 'A Gonon', the trigger guard and locks engraved with foliage, maker's name inlaid in gold, cased with original accessories.

7in (18cm) long

$8,400-9,600 **GVI**

A fine cased pair of 80 bore silver-mounted percussion travelling pistols, by Westley Richards, London, with Birmingham proof marks and silver hallmarks for 1850, maker's mark 'hs', dated.

1851

$6,000-10,000 TDM

A pair of early 19thC mahogany cased percussion pistols, by Conway of Manchester, England with steel barrels and actions, walnut butts with silver cappings, including numerous accessories, the case bearing a retailer's label for 'Williams & Powell, Liverpool'.

c1830

9in (23cm) long

$11,000-13,000 RGA

A 19thC English pepperbox percussion pistol, six-barreled, the rounded German silver action engraved 'Charles Jones, 26 St James Street, London', in a mahogany case, with accessories.

Pistol 7.75in (20cm) long

$3,000-5,000 L&T

A rare 19thC long barrel pepperbox percussion revolver, by Foster of Wisbeach, with a walnut butt with engraved brass cappings.

c1840

11.5in (29cm) long

$9,000-13,000 RGA

A four-barreled 42 bore Mariette self-cocking ring trigger underhammer percussion pepperbox revolver, with turn-off twist barrels numbered 1 to 4, Liege proved, rounded scroll engraved frame, the butt strap stamped 'Mariette Brevete' and numbered '1346', with plain ebony grips.

8.75in (22cm) long

$700-900 W&W

An American six-shot percussion pepperbox pistol, with 3in (8cm) long steel barrel stamped 'Allen & Thurber, Worcester, patented 1837', with scroll-engraved action, the hammer stamped 'Allens Patent', with wood slabs to the grip.

7in (18cm) long

$900-1,100 BE

A six-shot 120 bore self-cocking bar hammer percussion pepperbox revolver, engraved 'Akrill Beverley'.

7.75in (19.5cm) long

$700-900 W&W

A South American 'Amazons' double barrel percussion pistol.

$360-440 SWO

A single-barreled 14 bore percussion sporting gun, with a 32in (81cm) long twist barrel, the lock and rounded hammer engraved with scrolls, light walnut halfstock with chequered fore-end and wrist, vacant oval escutcheon on underside of butt, engraved steel mounts, brass-tipped ebony ramrod with concealed worm, surface rust to barrel, otherwise in good working order and condition.

48in (122cm) long overall

$500-700 W&W

A single-barreled 16 bore percussion sporting gun, by W. Weston, Brighton, with a slender flat topped round 32in (81cm) long barrel from a Wogdon flintlock gun, with oval 'Wogdon' poincon at breech, the breech plug with two platinum lines, the lock and hammer engraved with dog tooth borders and scrolls, the plate with game birds and 'W Weston, Brighton', slender walnut halfstock with chequered wrist, the fore-end with silver cap and barrel wedge plates, steel mounts, the trigger guard with pineapple finial, the bow engraved with game dog and 'Stevens' in panel, the butt plate tang with game birds, small silver escutcheon engraved with crest and finials, in good working order, barrel slightly pitted overall, ramrod rib slightly damaged, minor defects to stock, no ramrod.

48in (122cm) long overall

$700-900 W&W

A Russian Crimean War period .704 calibre Belgian Brunswick military percussion rifle, with a 30.5in (77.5cm) long barrel, bayonet bar at muzzle and hinged rearsight, back action lock stamped 'P J Malberbe à Liege', walnut fullstock with regulation pattern heavy brass mounts including large patch box in butt, the oval escutcheon engraved with crowned cipher of Nicholas I, the butt plate tang engraved with Imperial eagle and 'No. 688', sling swivels, lock and barrel moderately pitted overall, otherwise in good working order, steel ramrod a good replacement.

46in (116cm) long overall

$3,600-4,400 W&W

A .577 calibre three-band Enfield percussion rifle, with a 39in (99cm) barrel with Birmingham proofs, the lock stamped with crown and 'Tower 1866', medium brown walnut fullstock with regulation pattern brass mounts, sling swivels, original steel ramrod.

55in (140cm) long overall

$800-1,200 W&W

ARMS & ARMOR

A Belgian six-shot 7mm DA PF pepperbox revolver, fluted cylinder with rifled barrels, Liege proved, loading gate on the right, folding trigger, chequered walnut grips, ejector rod screwed into the butt.

4.75in (12cm) long

$700-900   W&W

A Belgian six shot 7mm closed frame double action pinfire revolver, the 4in (10cm) long barrel tips up to allow removal of the cylinder, with folding trigger, plain walnut grips, Liege proved, the breech stamped 'Jongen Freres Brevette' and '1382', the frame and cylinder engraved with panels of scrolls, the frame numbered '9632', in good working order, dark patina overall, light pitting to cylinder, one grip chipped.

8in (20.25cm) long overall

$500-600   W&W

An English six-shot 7mm DA solid closed frame PF revolver, engraved 'Coles patent', Birmigham, England proved, scroll-engraved frame and breech, conventional loading gate but unusual ejector rod attached to the frame and cylinder pin, folding trigger, chequered walnut grips, in an original fitted oak revolver case with brass escutcheon in the lid and blue baize lining.

7.5in (19cm) long

$600-1,000   W&W

A Bentleys' calibre shot self-cocking percussion revolver, the hammer fitted with patent safety catch, with octagonal rifled 7.25in (18cm) barrel, with chequer grip, engraved 'J. Bentley & Son, Liverpool', patent no. '2955.425'.

12.5in (32cm) long

$1,200-1,600   A&G

A rare .177 calibre Accles & Shelvoke 'Warrior' side lever air pistol, second model, the frame stamped 'The Warrior Made by Accles & Shelvoke Ltd Birmingham' and 'F Clarke's Patent Nos Brit 351268 USA 568057', pressed horn grips, in general working order, small welded repairs to air chamber and front grip strap, the latter partly obliterating the serial number, otherwise in good condition.

$500-700   W&W

A .22 calibre pre WWII slant grip Webley Senior air pistol, serial number S11781, the barrel lug stamped '22/S', the rear plug secured by grub screw, no patent dates on barrel link or breech block, in good working order.

$800-1,200   W&W

A Westley and Richards 12 bore double barrel hammer shot gun, side locks engraved, chequered walnut stock, wooden ramrod, serial no. GT 5521, with 30in (76.2cm) barrels, and fitted within a brass-bound gun case with trade label and a leather case carrier.

33in (84cm) long

$1,100-1,300   WW

A 12 bore Holland & Holland Royal side-by-side sidelock ejector, with 27in (68.5cm) replacement barrels, 2.75in (7cm) chambers, gold-lined cocking-indicators, engraved with the initials 'GMKY', chequered ebonite butt plate, serial number A5451.

c1906

$14,000-18,000   L&T

A Wurfflein side-by-side cased rifle/shotgun combination, SN NSN, combination gun has 31in (79cm) round barrels marked 'JOHN WURFFLEIN PHILADA', 38 Cal rifle barrel and approx 20 ga. shot barrel, engraved right-hand lock is marked 'JOHN WURFFLEIN' and the left-hand lock is marked 'PHILADELPHIA', all iron hardware is finely engraved and the inside of the capbox door is marked 'TK No 6'.

$20,000-30,000   JDJ

A double-barreled 16 bore underlever pinfire sporting gun, by Reilly, 502 New Oxford Street, London, with 30in (76cm) long twist barrels, with London 15 bore proofs, number 10456.

45.5in (115.5cm) long overall

$1,000-1,200   W&W

A German VG5C semi-automatic rifle, SN 7538. Cal. 7.92 X 32 cartridge, spot-welded receiver with no finish and assembled basic block pieces of wood, with the serial number stamped into the buttstock. 4-33961 BK25, complete with canvas sling and magazine, and in working order.

These are very rare as most of the GI's brought home German guns that were more finely made instead of these.

$30,000-40,000   JDJ

A rare WWII Sedgeley Experimental Glove Gun, Cal. 38 S&W, no serial number, metal, with a 4.75x2.5in sheet metal backing with six holes for attaching to back of a heavy glove, small box on top with a sliding safety and an articulated, smoothbore 3in (7.5cm) bbl with a plunger adjacent to the bbl.

This experimental item was probably generated by the Office for Strategic Services for clandestine operations.

$7,000-9,000   JDJ

A very rare Colt Paterson No. 3 Belt Model Percussion Revolver, serial number 152, Cal. 34, with 5.5in (14cm) oct bbl with eleven grooves.

According to 'Flayderman's Guide to Antique American Firearms', only about 850 of the No. 2 & No. 3 Paterson revolvers combined were made between 1837-1840.

c1838

$160,000-200,000   JDJ

A rare Samuel Colt presentation cased colt model 1860 army percussion revolver, serial no. 4740, Cal. 44, 8in (20.5cm) round barrel.

This gun was presented to Edwin Oscar Perrin (1822-88) who served in the Civil War under Colonel Kit Carson. He was the Secretary of five Democratic National Conventions and, in 1868, was elected Clerk of the Court of Appeals in New York and reappointed to the same position by the court in 1870.

$70,000-90,000   JDJ

A rare pair of silver-plated Colt single action army revolvers, serial numbers 208657 and 208673, Cal. 45 Colt, with 4.75in (12cm) barrels.

These are the only known matched pair of engraved, silver-plated Colt single action revolvers with backstrap inscriptions.

Barrels 4.75in (12cm) long

$200,000-400,000   JDJ

A .36 calibre rim-fire U.S. Colt model 1871/72 cartridge converted pocket revolver, No. 4038 with 3.5in (1.5cm) blued round barrel stamped 'Colt's Pt. F.A. MFG. Co. Hartford. CT USA', engraved cylinder, case-hardened frame stamped with patent details on the left, case-hardened trigger, polished walnut butt, with matching numbers and retaining much original finish throughout.

8.5in (21.5cm) long

$1,600-2,400   TDM

A scarce Henry Nettleton-inspected Colt Cavalry single action army revolver, Cal. 45 Colt. serial number 48269, blue and case colored with 7.5in (19cm) bbl, marked with the date '1878'.

Henry Nettleton was the sub-inspector for only about 3,000 Colt Single Actions under inspector Capt. John E. Greer in 1878.

$30,000-40,000   JDJ

A rare Confederate Augusta Machine Works 12 stop revolver, SN 'L', 7.75in octagonal bbl, brass triggerguard and backstrap, distinctive bulged Augusta stocks.

Probably no more than ten examples of this gun are known.

$70,000-90,000   JDJ

A five-shot RF Smith & Wesson Model 1.5in tip-up SA revolver, with name, address and patent dates and engraved in Gothis script 'Fd Claudin Brevete a Paris, Boulevard des Italiens 38', number '34277', blued finish overall, rosewood grips.

7.75in (19.5cm) long

$1,000-1,200   W&W

A rare presentation Glahn engraved gold-plated single action army revolver, serial number 354396, Cal. 38-40, single action with 4.75in (12cm) barrel, fitted with rampant Colt medallion pearl grips, the barrel has an engraved presentation which reads 'To Arthur / from a Grateful County'.

There are only twelve gold engraved Colt single action guns from the total 357,859 single action guns manufactured in the first generation.

$160,000-240,000   JDJ

A 17thC Spanish rapier, cup-hilted, the grip of shaded and reeded ivory, long round-section quillons with two turned knops at the ends, the knuckle guard with central knop and cup-shaped handguard, the slender double-edged blade with central fuller stamped Solingen, with plain oval pommel.

Blade 42in (106.5cm) long

$1,000-1,600   L&T

A 17thC Spanish rapier, cup-hilted, the grip covered in black horse hair, with wide brass ferules, long round-section quillons with two flared knops at the ends, the knuckleguard with turned knop midway, with cup-shaped handguard, the slender double-edged blade with short central fuller stamped 'SOLINGEN', with plain but shaped pommel.

Blade 40in (101.5cm) long

$1,000-1,600   L&T

A 17thC Spanish rapier, cup-hilted, the grip tightly bound with a double twist of silver wire, long quillons and knuckle guard with turned terminals at each end, the cup handguard pierced and with scalloped top edge, the double-edged blade of triangular section, with a writhen-turned pommel.

Blade 34in (86.5cm) long

$1,600-2,400   L&T

A rare early 18thC English officers sword, with copper alloy heart-shaped shell guards, the knuckle guard with two swept-forward guards that join the shell guard midway, and short wrist guard, some small patches of gilding, with single edge lightweight blade with narrow fuller at back edge, damaged edge, wooden grip binding missing.

Blade 30in (76cm) long

$800-1,200   L&T

An early 18thC Scottish basket-hilted cavalry back sword, single edged, the hilt of conventional form with pierced cross guards joined at the pommel by a ring, large bun-shaped pommel, damaged blade edge and tip, deep corrosion on hilt and blade, grip missing.

Blade 31in (79cm) long

$800-1,200   L&T

An 18th Century Scottish basket-hilted sword, with a pierced-bowl hilt, the blade struck twice 'Andria Farara' within three X's, blade bent and cracked.

Blade 31in (79cm) long

$1,000-1,400   SWO

$9,000-13,000

An early 18thC Scottish basket-hilted broad sword, the wooden grip covered in black dogfish skin, the basket of traditional form with the guard of flat-section bar terminating at the shallow bun-shaped pommel cut with a groove to take the guard, missing wrist-guard with the remains of the leather liner, the broad double-edged blade with four narrow fullers for three quarters of the blade length, stamped with 'ss' blade-smith's mark and with the running wolf motif.

36.25in (92cm) long

L&T

An early 19thC Gibson, Thompson & Craig scarce stirrup-hilted Flank Company officer's sabre, in associated scabbard, with gilt-metal hilt, chequered ivory grip, the deeply curved blued blade engraved and inlaid in gold with martial trophies, royal arms, and makers' mark.

35 in (89cm) long

$600-1,000   L&T

A 19thC Prussian officer's dress sword, the fish skin grip to a gilt-brass hilt with Prussian eagle, the fullered blade with a steel scabbard.

Blade 30.5in (77.5cm)

$440-560   WW

A Prussian cavalry trooper's sword, broad shallow-curved 32.5in (82.5cm) long blade, stamps on backstrap including date '? 5.87', regulation heavy quality steel stirrup hilt with knucklebow and langets, plain pommel and eared backstrap, ribbed leather grip, in its steel scabbard marked en suite '86.R.1.1', some surface rust.

$900-1,100   W&W

A German State M1889 cavalry trooper's sword, straight pipe black 32in (81.5cm) long blade, double edged at point, with crowned crossed swords mark of 'C K Co', ribbed composition shaped grips, in steel scabbard with opposing hanging rings.

$1,100-1,500   W&W

A French curassier trooper's M An XI sword, straight 37.5in (95.5cm) double fullered blade, marked on backstrap '…Klingenthal mars (unclear) 1811', regulation brass hilt with flat guard into knucklebow, three sidebars, cap-shaped pommel, brass wirebound leather grip, stamps at forte and on hilt, with steel scabbard with two hanging rings.

$1,200-1,400   W&W

An early brass-handled dirk, the solid one-piece brass handle with ribbed grip and simple incised linear decoration to pommel, the blade reduced from a sword blade and marked 'ME FECIT', with a triple 'S' mark below.

17.75in (45cm) long

$12,000-16,000   **L&T**

A late 18thC Scottish dirk, with broad blade cut-down from a broadsword, incised with a series of marks on each side including a running wolf, a cross and orb, rootwood grip carved with a naive flowerhead on each face, formed with a pair of tall shoulders, each reinforced with a brass panel and brass disc pommel, in a contemporary leather scabbard with later brass mounts.

20in (50.5cm) long

$3,000-4,000   **TDM**

A highland dirk by Robert Mole & Sons, Birmingham, with etched blade, nickel-mounted hilt with hardwood grip carved with basket-weave designs enriched with nickel nails, associated steel pommel cap cast with a crown, in an associated scabbard with steel mounts cast with thistle foliage, and the hilt and scabbard inscribed '14LD.1' and '14LD.3' respectively.

1900   17.5in (44.5cm) long

$1,400-1,800   **TDM**

A Scottish provincial highland dirk, by J. Hodge of Inverness, with basket weave-carved handle with studded grip, claw set with circular cut citrine, the leather covered scabbard with applied mounts with pierced decoration and foliate engraved designs, the top mount with applied crest and motto for clan Fraser, the ensuite knife and two-prong fork set and carved similarly, marked 'J. Hodge'.

c1890   18in (46cm) long

$4,000-6,000   **L&T**

A Victorian gilt-metal-mounted dress dirk, of the 79th Regiment (The Queen's Own Cameron Highlanders), the basket weave-carved wood hilt with circular-cut cairngorm-set pommel, and thistle-, acorn- and foliate-cast mounts, contained in a similarly mounted leather scabbard, fitted with a companion knife and fork with matching pommels.

Dirk 16.5in (42cm) long

$5,000-7,000   **BE**

A late Victorian boy's Highland dirk and sgian dubh suite, the dirk with antler handles set with foil-backed stones to pommels, with spear point blades and two-prong bi knife, together with matching sgian dubh, the mounts unmarked.

A 'sgian dubh' is a Scottish ceremonial dagger.

Dirk 11.75in (30cm) long

$2,000-3,000   **L&T**

A Scottish provincial sgian dubh, by William B. Taylor of Inverness, marked 'W.B.T, INVss', Edinburgh 1919-20, the carved wooden handles with intertwined Celtic knotwork and leaf detail, with pin cap with simple knotwork border, the leather-covered scabbard with Celtic knotwork mounts.

1919-20   7in (17.5cm) long

$900-1,300   **L&T**

A 19thC American bowie knife, with faceted ivory hilt, the blade etched with various slogans, including 'I can dig gold from quartz, California Bowie Knife,' stamped 'Tiffany, Broadway, New York, U.S.A.'

12.75in (32.5cm) long

$800-1,200   **SK**

A rare Civil War Bowie knife, made by the C. Roby & Co. of West Chelmsford, MA., the Bowie blade with diamond-shaped flat grind with about 3in of back grind, oval steel handguard with turned, ribbed walnut handle with swelled middle, a brass ferrule and a cast brass eagle head pommel, marked on left ricasso 'C. ROBY & CO. / W. CHELMSFORD / MASS.', left side of blade is etched with crossed cannons and an American shield in a wreath, right side is etched 'US' in a wreath and another panel has crossed swords in a wreath.

1861-65   Blade 9.25in (23.5cm) long

$20,000-30,000   **JDJ**

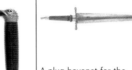

A plug bayonet for the Royal Guard of James II, with tapering double-edged blade etched with the inscription 'God save King James the 2', stamped with a King's Head mark and with the mark of the London Cutler's company, matching pommel and turned hardwood grip.

c1687   16.5in (42cm) long

$8,000-12,000   **TDM**

A 19thC Persian Jambiya, with curved blade chiseled with foliage over the lower half, carved bone grip decorated with a pair of courtly figures on each side, in its leather-covered wooden scabbard.

17.25in (44cm) long

$600-800   **TDM**

An Argentinian gaucho's dagger, steel blade with stamp, head of Liberty, libertad below, in .900 silver hilt, with 'LSB' monogram in gold, in silver scabbard by J.S. Ferra, superb condition, some minor blade oxidation.

c1900   Blade 6.25in (16cm)

$400-600   **BLO**

An Eastern dagger, with brass-mounted wooden holt, the brass and chased white metal scabbard with two brass suspension rings.

15.5in (39.5cm) long

$240-360   LFA

A Meiji period Japanese tanto, with carved ivory handle and sheath, decorated with numerous figures undertaking various activities, including fishing from a boat, with subsidiary side blade.

12in (30.5cm) long

$3,000-5,000   L&T

A 17thC East European war hammer, with steel head formed of eight pierced shaped flanges, molded slightly down-curved tapering rear spike, fluted neck, tapering tubular shaft retaining an early leather covering over cord, and modern leather thong.

26.75in (68cm)

$11,600-13,600   TDM

A late 18thC stonebow, by T. Barker, Warrington, with steel bow fitted with an early string with bone spacers, folding fore-sight, figured walnut tiller with turned steel knop-shaped finial, built-in gaffle, signed on the back-sight and engraved with a flower above and beneath.

28in (71.5cm) long tiller

$2,800-3,600   TDM

A Northern Italian close-helmet, the headpiece with a roped comb and pointed visor with a horizontal sight and pierced breathing holes, the neckplates to front and rear.

c1570   *9in (23cm) wide*

$7,000-11,000   FRE

A combed Morion helmet, retaining traces of original colored finish to the metal.

Helmets of this type were worn by foot soldiers and comparatively few survive outside major collections.

1560

$3,600-4,400   GVI

A 17thC English Civil War cavalry trooper's helmet, with a two-piece skull and rising peak with a three bar face guard, unusual form to the lobster tail, in very good condition.

$4,000-5,000   GVI

An officer cadet's helmet, from the Royal Military College.

c1881-1901   *11in (28cm) high*

$1,500-1,700   RGA

An Argentinean officer's 'Pickelhaube', of typical German form with patent leather skull, gilt spike and chinscales and gilt badge in the form of the Argentinean arms, pale blue and gilt rosettes, leather headband and cream silk lining, top of skull slightly depressed, some crazing to patent leather, silk lining split, otherwise in good condition.

c1910

$760-840   W&W

An English Civil War pikeman's suit of armor and helmet, comprising breast plate, back plate, tassets and helmet, the shoulder straps and tassets secured by hooks, in good condition.

c1640

$11,600-13,600   GVI

An early 17thC pair of German etched blue and blued gauntlets, each formed of a strongly flared and pointed cuff made in one piece with a riveted join at the inside of the wrist.

$6,000-10,000   TDM

A post-1902 officer's gilt and silver-plated shako badge, of the Highland Light Infantry.

$300-500   **W&W**

A WWI Tribute Cross, the gold paty cross with '22 Loyalty 1914' and 'Presented to W.J. Marshall by F.L.C.'.

This medal was awarded by Sir Frederick Lucas Cooke of London to his workers who enlisted in 1914. It is known to have been awarded in gold, silver and bronze.
1914

$300-400   **DNW**

An other rank's or bandsman's white metal shako plate, of the 74th Highlanders, in very good condition.

$400-600   **W&W**

A Victorian officer's die-struck silver-plated small shako plate, of the 16th (Harrogate) West York Rifles Volunteers, in good condition.

$640-760   **W&W**

An 1874 pattern other rank's brass Glengarry badge, of the 26th (Cameronians) regiment, brass lugs, cleaned and lacquered, in good condition.

$360-440   **W&W**

An 1874 pattern non-commissioned officer's gilt Glengarry badge, of the 71st (Highland Light Infantry) regiment, lacquered, in very good condition.

$500-700   **W&W**

An officer's silver-plated helmet plate, of the Sixth West York Militia, rose on original black patent leather, in very good condition.

$360-440   **W&W**

An officer's silver-plated forage cap badge, of the Fifth West York Militia, in very good condition.

$400-600   **W&W**

A Patiala Family Order Officer's breast badge, in silver-gilt and red and green enamel, no ribbon, extremely fine.

$1,100-1,300   **BLO**

An officer's cast silver-plated star headdress badge of the Second West York Militia, rose in the title scroll on rayed star, two lugs, in very good condition.

c1830   2.25in (5.5cm) wide

$700-900   **W&W**

A rare pair of WWII printed cloth badges, of the 202nd (Assam) line of communication area, in good condition.

$160-240   **W&W**

A scarce Vatican Order of Christ Knights gold and enamel breast badge, with crown in silver-gilt, slight enamel damage at suspension, extremely fine.

The Vatican Order of Christ is awarded in one class only and reserved for Roman Catholic Heads of State.

$800-1,200   **BLO**

A military general service medal, with three clasps 'Fuentes D'onor', 'Vittoria' and 'Pyrenees', clasps slightly buckled, edge knock, otherwise in good condition.
1793-1814

$2,000-3,000   W&W

A Peninsular War military general service medal, naming J. Rippen, Eighteenth Dragoons, with one clasp 'Sahagun & Benevente', minor edge bruises, in excellent condition.
1793-1814

$2,400-3,600   DNW

A Peninsular War military general service medal, naming George Small, Serjeant, 57th Foot Regiment, with one clasp 'Albuhera', with riband buckle, edge nicks, in very good condition.
1793-1814

$7,000-8,000   DNW

A Peninsular War military general service medal, naming W. Gunner, Serjeant, 88th Foot, with five clasps 'Talavera', 'Busaco', 'Fuentes D'Onor', 'Ciudad Rodrigo' and 'Badajoz', suspension claw refixed, few edge bruises, in very good condition.
1793-1814

$7,000-8,000   DNW

A rare Army of India medal, naming G. Hunter, 29th Light Dragoons, with three clasps, 'Allighur', 'Laswarree' and 'Capture of Deig', short hyphen reverse, officially impressed naming, edge bruising and contact marks, in very good condition.
1799-1826

$14,000-16,000   DNW

A very rare Army of India medal, naming T. Davis, 76th Foot, with four clasps 'Allighur', 'Battle of Delhi', 'Laswarree' and 'Battle of Deig', short hyphen reverse, officially impressed naming, edge bruising, in good condition.

Only twenty-three of these medals were issued with four clasps, including fourteen to British regiments, and five with this combination of clasps, all of which were awarded to the 76th Foot, known as Lord Lake's 'Handfull of heroes'.
1799-1826

$24,000-36,000   DNW

A rare German second class Iron Cross, the suspension loop marked 'KO', silver with magnetic steel center, possibly intended for display or exhibition, very fine or better, ribbon worn.

1813

$600-1,000   BLO

A Waterloo campaign medal, naming Thomas Morris, Second Battalion, 73rd Regiment Foot, naming re-engraved in contemporary large capitals, with replacement silver ball mount and straight bar suspension, some edge bruising and contact marks, in good condition.
1815

$2,000-3,000   DNW

A China campaign medal, naming P. A. Helpman, Lieutenant of H.M.S. Columbine, with replacement silver mount and contemporary gold swivel straight bar suspension, with gold buckle and brooch bar, edge bruising, in very good condition.
1842

$4,000-6,000   DNW

A Sutlej campaign medal, for Modkee 1845, naming Corporal William Sherman, 31st Regiment, with three clasps 'Ferozeshuhur', 'Aliwal' and 'Sobraon', slight contact to Queen's cheek, otherwise in very good condition.
1845-46

$2,000-3,000   DNW

An extremely rare first issue Victorian Royal Marine Meritorious Service Medal, awarded to Sergeant W. Maxwell, Royal Marine, with '1848' on the obverse and with dated edge.

$5,000-7,000   DNW

A very rare Canada general service campaign medal, naming 1673 Private J. Greenhil, First 60th Royal Rifles, with one clasp 'Red River 1870', officially impressed naming, in excellent condition.
1866-70

$3,000-4,000   DNW

An Empress of India silver medal, complete with neck ribbon, toned.

1877

$1,200-1,400   **BLO**

A pair of Sudan Campaign medals, naming Lieutenant Richard Wolfe, Second Dragoons (Scots Greys), Egypt and Sudan, 1882-89, with two clasps, 'The Nile 1884-85' and 'Abu Klea', undated reverse, and Khedive's Star, 1884-6, both in very good condition.

1882-89

$26,000-30,000   **DNW**

A British North Borneo Company campaign medal, naming 380 Private Momin, with one clasp 'Tambunan', bronze issue.

Initially seven silver and 116 bronze medals were made. In 1905/06 36 bronze were exchanged for silver.

1898-1900

$1,600-2,400   **DNW**

A Tibet medal, naming Cooly Gopal Sing Lama, Science & Technology Corps, with one clasp 'Gyantse', bronze issue, in excellent condition.

1903-4

$560-640   **DNW**

A rare George V second issue Commonwealth of Australia Meritorious Service Medal, awarded to J. F. Chapple, Gunner, Royal Australian Garrison Artillery, fixed suspension, in excellent condition.

$900-1,100   **DNW**

A rare German first class Iron Cross, two-piece screw back and flat plate fixing, pilot's issue, extremely fine.

1939

$300-400   **BLO**

A group of eight medals awarded to Nurse Estelle Smith, Army Nursing Service (India), comprising Award of Royal Red Cross, GVIR second class dated 1946, with 1939-45, Africa, Pacific, Italy stars, War, Defence and QEII Coronation medals, also British Red Cross Society Merit Award named E. Smith (née Stoddard), mounted as worn, extremely fine.

1939-46

$600-800   **BLO**

An Albanian Order of Scanderburg Grand Cross set, by Cravanzola of Rome, consisting of a sash badge in silver-gilt, and breast star in silver and enamel, complete with full dress sash, extremely fine and scarce.

This order was issued by the Italian Government occupying Albania during the WWII.

$3,000-4,000   **BLO**

A Bikaner Commendable Conduct silver medal, in extremely fine condition.

$800-1,200   **BLO**

A Kaiser-I-Hind medal, George VI issue, 2nd Class, with silver bar, complete with brooch buckle, in Garrard case of issue, dated, extremely fine.

1946

$1,000-1,400   **BLO**

A very rare Naval general service campaign medal, naming D/JX.146158 W. H. L. Flower, Leading Seaman, Royal Navy, with one clasp 'Bomb & Mine Clearance 1945-53', official correction to 'R.N.', in excellent condition.

1915-1962

$2,400-3,600   **DNW**

A scarce Bulgarian Order of George Dimitrov 14ct gold medal, decorated in red and white enamel, extremely fine.

Only 4,000 of this order were produced.

$500-600   **BLO**

A Roman redware flagon, North Africa, with erotic scene of a couple.

This piece may well have been used as a prize for a victorious gladiator.

5.5in (14cm) high

$1,400-1,800   ANA

A 4thC BCE late Etruscan amphora, creamy stoneware with red wash decoration.

8.25in (21cm) high

$560-640   ANA

A rare 6th-7thC Byzantine glass flask, green translucent glass of variegated iridescence, with mold-blown Christian symbols in relief.

5in (13cm) high

$3,000-4,000   ANA

A 2nd-3rdC Roman glass unguentarium, with variegated iridescence.

This was used to store perfume.

4.75in (12cm) high

$150-170   ANA

A large 3rdC Roman bronze statuette of Venus.

6in (15cm) high

$2,000-2,600   ANA

A 1st/2ndC Roman bronze draped goddess statuette.

2.25in (6cm) high

$1,200-1,600   ANA

A 1stC Roman bronze bust of Mars, of Romano-British style.

3.75in (9.5cm) high

$1,600-2,400   ANA

A 2nd/3rdC Roman terracotta toy horse, with harness

.

4.25in (11cm) long

$300-400   ANA

A 16thC-11thC BCE New Kingdom wooden boatman, wears white kilt, extensive deep red pigment of the torso and face and black pigment of the features and wig remaining.

10in (25.5cm) high

$600-800   ANA

A late Dynastic brilliant blue ushabti, wearing tripartite wig of darker blue glaze and royal beard.

715-332BCE   3.75in (9.5cm) high

$360-480   ANA

A late Dynastic beaded mask, multi-coloured beaded mask composition, with eyebrow and eye outlined in black with yellow infill and black pupil, yellow nose and red mouth in outline with yellow infill, surmounted by border of green cylindrical-shaped beads laid out in triangular fashion, constitutes face of mummy's shroud.

715-332BCE   5.25in (13.5cm) high

$400-600   ANA

An English violin, by William H. Luff, the two-piece back of faint medium curl with similar wood to the sides and head, the table of a medium grain and the varnish of a reddish color on a golden ground, labeled 'William H. Luff, Maker, London, 1986', with case and two silver-mounted violin bows.

14in (35.5cm) high

$6,000-8,000 GHOU

A French violin by Charles Adolphe Gand, the one-piece back with almost horizontal narrow curl, the ribs and head of similar curl, the table of fine grain, the varnish of orange/brown color, with original label 'Gand, Luthier de la Musique du Roi et du Conservatoire de Musique, Rue Croix de Petits Champs, No.24, Paris 1835'.

The back 14.25in (36cm) long

$4,400-3,600 HT

An English violin, by Joseph Hill, the two-piece back of medium curl with narrow curl to the sides and head, the table of medium grain and the varnish of a golden-brown color, with case.

c1700 *14in (35.5cm) high*

$10,000-12,000 GHOU

A violin, the two-piece back of faint broad curl with similar wood to the sides and head, the table of a medium grain and the varnish of a light reddish-brown color on a golden ground, labeled 'Antonius Hieronymus Fr. Amati Cremonen. Andrea fil. F. 1625'.

14in (35.5cm) high

$24,000-30,000 GHOU

A rare Italian violin, by Filippo Gragnani, the two-piece back of fine irregular curl with similar wood to the sides and head, the table of a fine grain widening to the flanks and the varnish of a light brown color, bearing a manuscript label signed 'Filippo Gragnani, Liburni, 18?...', with an Edward Withers' case, with two certificates of authenticity from William E. Hill & Sons stating the instrument has some characteristics of Gragnani.

14in (35.5cm) high

$88,000-100,000 GHOU

An English violoncello, by Lockey Hill, London, the two-piece back of plainish wood with faint medium curl to the sides, the later neck and head of plain wood, the table of a fine grain and the varnish of a golden-brown color, with soft case.

c1790 *29in (73.5cm) high*

$7,000-9,000 GHOU

An Italian violoncello, attributed to Antonio Mariani, the two-piece back of plain wood with similar wood to the sides and head, the tale of a medium grain narrowing to the flanks and the varnish of a rich red color on a golden ground, labeled 'Antonio Mariani fece in Pessaro 1761'.

29.75in (75.5cm) high

$16,000-24,000 GHOU

An early 20thC German violoncello, the two-piece back of faint medium curl with similar wood to the sides and head, the varnish of a reddish-brown color on a golden ground, labeled 'John Werro, importer and maker of musical instruments...', with case and two bows.

29.75in (75.5cm) high

$6,000-8,000 GHOU

A Neapolitan mandolin, by Luigi Emberger, the body of 18 plain sycamore ribs, the table and oval soundhole edged with multiple purfling, the scratch plate of tortoiseshell inlaid in ivory with a floral motif, twenty-five brass frets and brass machine heads with ebony pegs, labeled 'Anno 1932, Luigi Emberger, Via Belsiana no. 7, Roma' and stamped 'L. Emberger, Roman' on the face of the head.

23in (58.5cm) high

$2,400-3,600 GHOU

A classical Spanish guitar, by Marcelino Lopez Neito, labeled 'Marcelino Lopez, Luthier, Guitarra no. 73, 1955... Madrid', also signed on the label and bearing the maker's stamp to the inner back, with case.

$1,100-1,400 GHOU

A late 19thC small-bodied lady's guitar, with rosewood back and sides, ebony and boxwood-purled spruce table and open peg box, with home-made case.

$700-900 GHOU

A Hofner President model guitar, no. 4622, with original label, with hard case.

$1,000-1,200 GHOU

THE ARTS & CRAFTS MARKET

From Arts & Crafts ceramics to Tiffany lamps, Stickley chairs to Dirk Van Erp lamps, the market for American decorative arts continues to grow with new buyers and record prices every year. It is perhaps not surprising that smaller items such as pottery, tiles and lighting, which are easier to find a place in the average size home, continue to perform well, as does one-of-a-kind metalware. Prices for furniture remain strong, with good prices for key pieces with an original, pristine finish and which appeal to established collectors. These pieces are far from common and so they can command top dollar. The work of Gustav Stickley (particularly when associated with Harvey Ellis), Charles Rohlfs and the Roycrofters continue to be sought after, especially for hard-to-find rarities which have not been on the market before.

Those relatively new to the collecting field continue to maintain the value of well-designed furniture, without needing repair or renovation, and which will look good in a 21st century home. These pieces — which generally sell for under $6,000 — are often hotly contested.

Values for the mainstays of the Arts & Crafts pottery movement remain strong, especially pieces by Grueby, Rookwood, Roseville, Teco and Newcomb College. Outstanding pieces by George Ohr continue to sell for five-figure sums, especially the unique pieces he used to test glazes and other techniques. In the past year new record prices have been set for the work of Frederick Rhead, Artus Van Briggle and Pewabic. It is likely the resulting publicity will see increased demand — and higher prices — for their work. On the whole, collectors are willing to pay a premium for quality and unusual piece rather than for the name of a potter or pottery.

Lighting is in demand with prices for Tiffany and other American makers continuing to rise, especially if the decoration on the shade or base is unusual. The same is true of Art Glass.

David Rago, Rago Arts & Auction Center, Lambertville, New Jersey

CHELSEA / DEDHAM

A rare and early Chelsea Pottery Crackleware plate, incised in the Lotus pattern outlined in blue with rare green leaves, stamped 'CPUS/EEX'.

The crackle finish was inspired by the Oriental pottery seen by Hugh Robertson at the Centennial Exposition. His subsequent experiments bankrupted the firm, and it was reorganized in 1891 by a group of patrons, many of them members of Society of Arts and Crafts, Boston. The group of Boston investors encouraged Robertson to produce a commercially successful ware, while continuing to make artware. Working with his son William, Hugh perfected the crackle finish and applied it to tableware. In 1892, the pottery offered prizes to students at the Museum of Fine Arts School in Boston for 'the best design for a dinner-plate for reproduction by the Chelsea Pottery,' stipulating that the designs be blue, simple in treatment, on a gray crackled ground. Several designs, and those of other artists, were put into production. The Crackleware produced in Dedham (where the pottery moved in 1895, and remained until 1968), was a great commercial success.

10in (25.5cm) diam

$3,000-4,000   DRA

A Dedham Crackleware crab plate no. 2, with three small crabs and indigo and impressed stamps.

8.75in (22cm) diam

$1,800-2,200   DRA

A Dedham Crackleware breakfast plate no. 2, in the 'Dolphin' design, with indigo and impressed stamps.

8.75in (22cm) diam

$2,000-2,500   DRA

An early Dedham Crackleware plate, embossed with upside down dolphins, with die stamp 'CPUS', and with restoration to rim chip.

8.5in (21.5cm) diam

$800-1,200   DRA

A Dedham Crackleware plate, in the 'Elephant' pattern, with cobalt stamp and rabbit die-stamp.

6.5in (16.5cm) diam

$800-1,200   DRA

A rare Dedham Crackleware plate, in the 'Lion Tapestry' pattern, with cobalt stamp and rabbit die-stamp.

8.5in (21.5cm) diam

$1,000-1,500   DRA

A Dedham Crackleware deep plate, in the 'Mushroom' design, with indigo and impressed stamps.

8.5in (21.5cm) diam

$700-1,000   DRA

A Dedham Crackleware plate no. 1, in the 'Polar Bear' design, by Maude Davenport, with indigo and impressed stamps.

10in (25.5cm) diam

$2,000-2,500   DRA

A Dedham Crackleware shallow soup plate, in the 'Clockwise Rabbit' pattern, with 'KF' monogram, a Dedham postcard, and indigo and impressed stamps.

8.25in (21cm) diam

$1,500-2,000   DRA

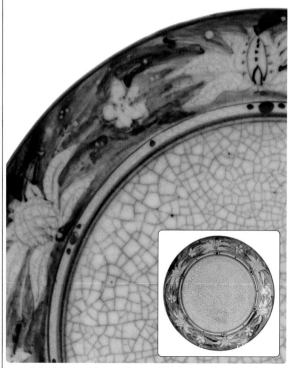

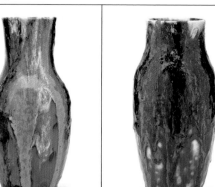

A Dedham experimental vase, by Hugh Robertson, with a thick, mottled green, amber, and white dripping volcanic glaze, marked 'Dedham Pottery/HCR/13/DP17F'.

c1895-1908   *11in (28cm) high*

$4,500-5,000   CRA

A Dedham experimental vase, by Hugh Robertson, covered in mottled brown, green, and amber volcanic glaze, marked 'Dedham Pottery/HCR'.

c1895-190   *7.5in (19cm) high*

$1,500-2,000   CRA

An early Dedham Crackleware plate no. 1, in the 'Raised Pineapple' design, with impressed cloverleaf with 'C.P.U.S., EEX'.

10in (25.5cm) diam

$1,200-1,800   DRA

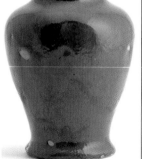

A Dedham experimental vase by Hugh Robertson covered in a thick blue-gray and oxblood glaze, incised Dedham Pottery HCR, in ink 'DE 23C'.

5in (12.5cm) high

$1,500-2,000   DRA

A Dedham Crackleware coffee pot, in the 'Clockwise Rabbit' pattern, with cobalt stamp.

9in (23cm) wide

$1,000-1,500   DRA

A Fulper Effigy bowl, the interior covered in Cat's Eye flambé glaze, and exterior in matte mustard, over a Cafe-au-Lait glaze, with vertical mark.

11in (28cm) wide

$800-1,200   DRA

A Fulper Faceted vase, covered in Khaki green, cobalt, and Cat's Eye flambé glaze, with vertical mark and glaze flake to base.

9.75in (25cm) high

$600-900   DRA

A two-handled Fulper vase, covered in a fine Chinese Blue crystalline flambé glaze, with vertical mark.

9.5in (24cm) high

$600-800   DRA

A large Fulper vase, covered in Chinese Blue flambé glaze, vertical mark.

10.5in (26.5cm) high

$1,200-1,800   DRA

CLOSER LOOK: FULPER LAMP

The shade is unusual because it combines glass and ceramic. These lamps are among the most innovative of Fulper's output.

The mushroom-shaped shade and base are typical of the organic shapes popular with Arts and Crafts potters.

Like many potteries involved in the Arts & Crafts movement, Fulper experimented with combinations of glazes. Here Cat's Eye has been allowed to run over the Flemington Green flambé glaze.

Fulper advertised these lamps as 'art pottery put to practical uses'.

A Fulper table lamp, mushroom-shaped shade with slag glass inserts over a two-socket baluster base, both covered in a mix of Cat's Eye and Flemington Green flambé glaze, vertical stamp and circular Vasekraft stamp, marked 'PATENT PENDING US AND CANADA', 1in (2.5cm) hairline from rim to glass.

21in (53cm) high

$18,000-20,000   DRA

GRUEBY

The Grueby Faïence Company was founded by William Henry Grueby (1867-1925) in Boston, Massachusetts in 1894. Initially the pottery made architectural bricks and tiles, but in 1897 it began to make art wares.

Grueby pioneered the use of thick, opaque matte glazes in rich shades of brown, ochre and especially moss green, which created a surface texture that resembled the skin of a watermelon.

The shape of each piece of earthenware was cleverly integrated with its decoration, the hand-thrown ceramic pieces were embellished with stylized hand-carved or relief patterns of motifs inspired by nature and including flowers, grasses, leaves and lotus blossoms.

Potters also used the Spanish cuenca technique where patterns are impressed into the clay to make ridges that kept the different colored glazes apart. The decoration was often used in contrasting colors, such as yellow petals on a green background.

The firm successfully combined mass production with hand craftsmanship, the simple, handmade clay bodies were decorated with standard patterns. The company was rewarded with a gold medal at the Paris Exposition of 1900, and a host of imitators.

Wares are usually marked with the name 'Grueby' alongside a vegetal motif.

A Grueby frieze of six tiles, decorated in cuenca with ivory and yellow water lilies and light green lily pads.

6in (15cm) square each

$5,000-8,000   DRA

A Grueby tile, decorated in cuerda seca, with houses on a hill by the seashore, stamped 'GRUEBY TILE BOSTON'.

4in (10cm) square

$3,000-4,000   DRA

A Grueby tile, with stag and tree, signed 'JS', minor fleck to corner.

4in (10cm) square

$3,500-4,500   DRA

DECORATIVE ARTS

A gourd-shaped Grueby vase, with full-height leaves under feathered matte green glaze, with circular pottery stamp/'ER'.

8in (20.5cm) high

$8,000-10,000   **DRA**

A tall Grueby vase, by Ruth Erickson, with full-height leaves alternating with yellow buds, and pottery circular stamp/'RE'.

11.5in (29cm) high

$12,000-15,000   **DRA**

A Grueby squat vase, with three rows of curled leaves under a superior matte green glaze, spherical pottery stamp '41 N', invisible restoration to two rim chips.

6in (15cm) wide

$6,000-8,000   **DRA**

A Grueby squat vessel, with tooled and applied rounded leaves, alternating with white buds, covered in a rich matte brown glaze, circular pottery stamp 'E.R.' and number sequence, several small glaze chips.

3.5in (9cm) high

$4,500-5,500   **DRA**

A Grueby fine and large vase, with ivory buds alternating with leaves under a rich matte mustard glaze, circular Pottery stamp/C.H., professional restoration to chips at base.

11in (28cm) high

$12,000-15,000   **DRA**

A Grueby vase, with yellow buds alternating with leaves under a fine matte green glaze, circular Pottery stamp/'ER/3/30', professional restoration to small rim chip.

12in (30.5cm) high

$10,000-12,000   **DRA**

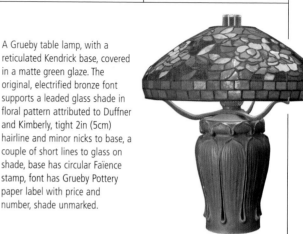

A Grueby table lamp, with a reticulated Kendrick base, covered in a matte green glaze. The original, electrified bronze font supports a leaded glass shade in floral pattern attributed to Duffner and Kimberly, tight 2in (5cm) hairline and minor nicks to base, a couple of short lines to glass on shade, base has circular Faïence stamp, font has Grueby Pottery paper label with price and number, shade unmarked.

Shade 19in (47.5cm) diam

$25,000-30,000   **DRA**

MARBLEHEAD

The Marblehead Pottery began as a craft therapy program to give 'quiet manual work' to convalescing 'nervously worn out patients' in the small fishing village of Marblehead, Massachusetts in 1905. Ten years later Dr Hall's Handcraft Shops had been bought by Arthur Eugene Baggs (1886-1947), who ran them as a commercial operation and remained as director until the company closed in 1936.

The pottery specialized in hand-thrown matte-glazed ceramics in simple, elegant shapes. Under the direction of chief decorator Hanna Tutt, tiles, vases, jars, garden ornaments and bowls were decorated by a team of artists with incised and painted geometric patterns, stylized flowers, animals, birds, insects and fish and sometimes Native American motifs.

Colored glazes were soft and muted and included blue, gray, wisteria, rose, yellow, green and tobacco brown. Occasionally several colors were combined on a single piece.

After the pottery closed, Baggs worked as Professor of Ceramic Arts at Ohio State University until his death.

Marblehead pottery is usually marked with the impressed outline of a ship accompanied by the initials MP, all enclosed within a circle, and sometimes including the initials AEB and/or HT (for Arthur E Baggs and Hanna Tutt).

A tear-shaped Marblehead vase, by Hannah Tutt, with stylized carnation in black on a dark green ground, and with ship mark/HT.

4.5in (11.5cm) high

$4,500-5,500   **DRA**

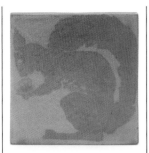

A rare Marblehead tile, matte-painted with a brown squirrel holding a brown and green acorn, against a matte mustard ground, stamped ship mark.

6in (15cm) square

$5,000-6,000 DRA

A large Marblehead vase, matte-painted by Hannah Tutt with wisteria branches in brown on a lighter brown ground, and with stamped ship mark 'HT'.

7in (18cm) high

$3,000-4,000 DRA

An early Marblehead tapering vase, incised with stylized leaf forms in black on a dark green ground, with ship mark 'MT'.

4.25in (11cm) high

$3,500-4,500 DRA

A Marblehead covered jar, in a dark matte green speckled glaze, with stilt-pulls to lid and ship mark.

6in (15cm) high

$2,000-3,000 DRA

A tall Marblehead cylindrical vase, covered in matte mustard speckled glaze, with ship mark.

9.25in (23.5cm) high

$2,000-3,000 DRA

A Marblehead vessel, ship stamp with glaze, and firing codes.

One of Arthur Baggs' early glaze experiments.

3.75in (9.5cm) high

$1,200-1,800 CRA

A Marblehead barrel-shaped vase, by Arthur Baggs, with flowers in charcoal on a dark green speckled ground, ship mark, artist's cipher.

9.5in (24cm) high

$3,500-4,500 DRA

A rare Marblehead flaring vase, with yellow blossoms and blue-gray leaves on a gray speckled ground, ship mark.

4.25in (10.5cm) high

$3,000-4,000 DRA

NEWCOMB

An early Newcomb College charger, painted by S. E. Bres in the Delft style with the old Newcomb Chapel, and the Newcomb College Pottery logo/97, 'NC/M/S.E.B./APR97/JM/26'.

8.75in (22cm) high

$6,000-8,000 DRA

An early Newcomb College bulbous vase, painted by M. O. Delavigne with stylized foliage in green on a light and dark blue ground.

1902   6.25in (16cm) high

$3,500-4,500 DRA

A tall and early Newcomb College vase, carved by Harriett Joor, with clusters of white flowers on green stems, and with a short, tight line from rim.

13.5in (34.5cm) high

$40,000-50,000 DRA

An early Newcomb College vase, painted by Bemis Sharp, with a band of yellow blossoms, marked 'NC/BS/JM/Q/AM75', glaze drip at rim, interior spiderlines barely show through.

1905   5.25in (13cm) high

$2,500-3,500 DRA

A Newcomb College transitional creamer, carved by Henrietta Bailey, with white nasturtium, 'NC/HB/FZ51/23/80/B'.

1913   4.5in (11.5cm) wide

$800-1,200 DRA

A Newcomb College squat transitional vase, carved by C.M. Luria with blue and yellow daffodils on a blue ground, 'NC/JM/CL/GU62/260/C'.

1914 5.75in (14.5cm) wide

$1,500-2,000 DRA

A Newcomb College Transitional squat vessel, sharply carved by Anna Frances Simpson, with irises on a blue and pink ground.

1917 8in (20.5cm) wide

$3,000-4,000 DRA

A Newcomb College transitional bulbous vase, crisply carved by A. F. Simpson, with tall pines, marked 'NC/AFS/JM/B/FV77/17'.

Anna Frances (Fanny) Simpson (d.1930) joined Newcomb as a student in 1902.

After graduation she worked as an Arts Craftsman from 1908 until 1923 and from 1924 until 1929 when she was one of the mainstays of the pottery.

Her work in pottery, embroidery and printmaking, showed a skill and individuality that won her several awards.

She was a prolific artist who produced beautifully carved and modeled pieces which were enhanced by subtle decoration.

1913 9in (23cm) high

$9,000-11,000 DRA

A large and fine Newcomb College transitional vase, carved by Sadie Irvine, with oak trees and Spanish moss in a sunlit landscape.

Sadie (Sarah Agnes Estelle) Irvine (1887-1970) was the decorator who introduced the oak, moss, and moon motifs to Newcomb Pottery. The scenic vases, which were immensely popular with the buying public throughout the 1910s and 20s, showed a trend away from the stylized Arts & Crafts designs of the past in favor of more naturalistic and conventional decoration.

She was the longest serving craftsman at the Newcomb Pottery. She joined the college as a freshman in 1902 and, after graduation, worked there until her retirement in 1952.

As a student at the Graduate School (from 1906-08) she was noted for her pottery decoration and embroidery. While pottery became the mainstay of her employment at Newcomb she also exhibited as a print maker and designed books.

Sadie Irvine filled many roles at the college. She was an Arts Craftsman from 1908-29 and went on to work as Pottery Decorator, Assistant, Assistant Instructor, and Instructor, a post she held for her final ten years at Newcomb.

1913 10.75in (27.5cm) wide

$15,000-18,000 DRA

A Newcomb College cabinet vase, carved by Sadie Irvine with a bayou scene against a pink sky.

1919 4in (10cm) wide

$3,000-4,000 DRA

A Newcomb College cylindrical vase, carved by Henrietta Bailey, with pink pine cones, marked 'NC/HB/JM/PV70/320', tight 1in (2.54cm) line.

1926 9.5in (24cm) high

$2,500-3,000 DRA

A Newcomb College bulbous vase, carved by Sadie Irvine, with trefoils, marked 'NC/JM/SI/KW82/179'.

1920 8.75in (22cm) high

$5,000-6,000 DRA

A Newcomb College vase, carved by Sadie Irvine, with tall oak trees along a river, an unusual and very crisp example, marked 'NC/SI/JM/150/IZ60'.

1917 9.75in (24.5cm) high

$11,000-15,000 DRA

MILLER'S COMPARES: NEWCOMB

An early Newcomb College biscuit jar and cover, carved by Lucia Jordan, with a motto on the cover, marked 'NC/BN92/Lucia Jordan/ JM/W'.

1907   *7in (17.5cm) high*

$10,000-12,000   **DRA**

A Newcomb College vase, carved by A. F. Simpson, marked 'NC/JM/35 /AFS/MR40'.

1922   *5in (12.5cm) high*

$3,000-4,000   **DRA**

DATING NEWCOMB POTTERY

From 1894 the majority of Newcomb Pottery was signed and dated using a system of marks.

Pieces usually have the name of the college or its mark (an N within a C), as well as potter's monogram, a letter for the clay body, and the cipher or the name of the decorator.

Pieces made between 1894 and 1899 usually have the month and year of production impressed on them as well as a registration number.

From 1901 to 1942 Newcomb combined the two marks so that each piece had a unique number. The new registration system consisted of sequential letters and numbers (1 through 100). These marks begin with a sequence of single letters e.g. A1-100, B1-100 etc, which encompasses late 1901 to early 1903, then moves into double letters e.g. AA1-100, BB1-100 etc; followed by AB1-100, AC1-100 etc; through to ZR1-100 in 1941.

Thus, for example, a piece with the number HC20 was made in 1915.

The early biscuit jar shown on the left features the clear, deep carving typical of early Newcomb wares. Carving has been used to define the landscape and suggest the texture of the leaves and grass.

Blocks of color have been used to fill the carved areas. The clear, bright colors are typical of early Newcomb wares.

The carved motto on the cover: 'Somewhere Above Us Live the Fulfillment of Our Dreams' adds to its desirability.

The later scenic vase on the right shows the atmospheric landscapes Newcomb decorators were renowned for in the 1920s, as a full moon lights a dreamy bayou scene with oak trees dripping with Spanish moss. However, these scenes were standard on Newcomb vases by the 1920s and are relatively common today.

The carving has been used to create a three-dimensional effect which is enhanced by the way the blue and green glazes have been shaded to give a feeling of depth to the scene. Additional colors would add to the value.

The artistry shown in the decoration of the vase was highly prized at the time but is not as sought after by collectors today.

A Newcomb College vase, by Marie DeHoa LeBlanc, with white blossoms, marked 'NC/MHLeB/JM/CN12/W'.

1908   *12.25in (31cm) high*

$6,000-8,000   **DRA**

A Newcomb College candlestick lamp, by Maude Robinson, with copper-faceted clip-on shade, signed 'NC/MROBINSON/AV73/JM'.

1906   *10.5in (26.6cm) high*

$7,000-9,000   **DRA**

A Newcomb College vase, carved by A. F. Simpson, with tall palm trees in front of a full moon.

6.5in (16.5cm) high

$10,000-12,000   **DRA**

A Newcomb College cylindrical vase, carved by A. F. Simpson with panels of white morning glories.

1928   *8in (20.5cm) high*

$3,000-4,000   **DRA**

A Newcomb College vase, carved by A. F. Simpson, marked 'NC/SN43/ 131/JH/AFS'.

1930   *11in (28cm) high*

$10,000-12,000   **DRA**

A Newcomb College Art Deco vase, in a light semi-matte green glaze.

9.5in (24cm) high

$3,000-4,000   **DRA**

A North Dakota School of Mines Bentonite clay vessel, by Allen, with yellow birds on a terra cotta ground, an indigo stamp and 'Allen'.

5.5in (14cm) high

$800-1,200   DRA

A North Dakota School of Mines low vessel, carved by Margaret Cable, with a band of teepees on a river front, with circular stamp/'M. Cable'.

7.25in (18.5cm) wide

$8,000-10,000   DRA

A North Dakota School of Mines vase, by Margaret Cable, with prairie rose under matte green glaze, indigo stamp 'M. Cable 44'.

8.5in (21.5cm) high

$1,500-2,000   DRA

A North Dakota School of Mines bulbous vase, carved by Margaret Cable and Flora Huckfield, 'Indian Travois,' with Native Americans on horseback, with indigo circular stamp, and carved 'CABLE-HUCK-INDIAN TRAVOIS 184'.

6.75in (17cm) high

$6,000-8,000   DRA

A North Dakota School of Mines squat vessel, decorated by Julia Mattson, with viking ships in blues and greens, and circular stamp/'JM'/'236'.

4.25in (11cm) wide

$2,000-3,000   DRA

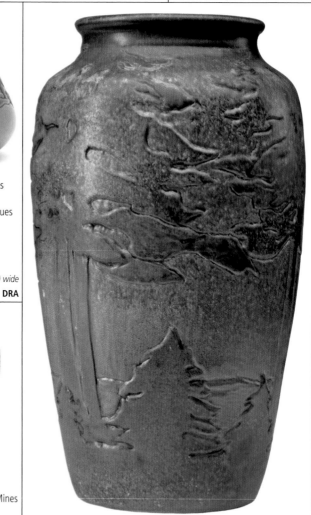

A North Dakota School Of Mines vase, carved by D. Nasset, with a chain of figures holding hands, covered in matte brown glaze, circular cobalt stamp and artist's signature.

4.5in (11.5cm) high

$1,500-2,000   DRA

A tall North Dakota School of Mines vase, excised by S. Sorlie with sheaves of wheat on a blue-gray ground, with indigo stamp and 'ELH-750, S Sorlie'.

8.5in (21.5cm) high

$7,000-10,000   DRA

A large North Dakota School Of Mines vase, carved with a forest landscape by Thorne and Flora Huckfield, and covered in a rare green, brown, and amber microcrystalline glaze, cobalt stamp 'Thorne-Huck-1445', restoration to 1in (2.5cm) rim chip.

10.5in (26.5cm) high

$9,000-12,000   DRA

ESSENTIAL REFERENCE: GEORGE OHR

Often called the father of the studio pottery movement, George Ohr (1857-1918) used a wheel and a homemade wood-burning kiln to produce skillfully hand-thrown wares in startling designs. Working almost exclusively in red earthenware, his pots are usually thinly potted with a lightweight, brittle body, which he manipulated by pinching, folding, crushing, twisting and pressing into highly unusual shapes.

He is often referred to as the 'mad potter of Biloxi' – his home town in Mississippi –where he built his studio and made more than 10,000 pots (or 'mud babies') between 1883 and 1907.

He mixed his own glazes, which are lustrous, mottled, and made up of the rich green and brown tones that are easily achieved in a wood-burning kiln. Other favorite colors include red, blue, bronze, purple, black, and orange. Ohr often combined mottled or speckled glazes, as well as metallic and crystalline effects.

After 1900 Ohr focused mainly on the simplicity and honesty of his work. A large proportion of his later work – known as bisque ware – was manipulated into pinched, asymmetrical sculptural shapes and left unglazed. He occasionally made wares with applied decoration, such as tendril-like handles, spouts, spikes and snakes. Other variations included the use of colored muds or clays marbled together, and some vessels were brushed with a mineral pigment.

Although Ohr's remarkable output throughout his unusual career included both practical and ornamental wares – vases jugs, inkwells, flowerpots and bowls – he sold hardly a single piece during his lifetime. He closed his studio in 1906.

A rare New Orleans Art Pottery vase, of orange clay covered in green speckled mirror glaze, probably by Ohr, impressed 'NEW ORLEANS ART POTTERY COMPANY BARONNE STREET', with minor fleck to rim.

5in (12.5cm) high

$7,000-10,000   DRA

A George Ohr 'Burnt Baby', with pinched rim over dimpled body, and remnants of original olive green glaze, no visible mark.

Damaged in pottery fire in October 1893, Ohr referred to these fire victims as his 'burnt babies'.

3in (7.5cm) high

$1,500-2,000   DRA

A George Ohr bulbous vase, with floriform pinched front and back, covered with bands of indigo and amber sponging on an amber ground, and die-stamped mark.

6in (15cm) high

$8,000-10,000   DRA

A George Ohr bulbous footed vase, with folded rim covered in bottle-green and raspberry mottled glaze, with restoration to small chip on rim and stamped 'G.E. OHR, Biloxi, Miss.'.

5in (12.5cm) high

$12,000-15,000   DRA

A George Ohr vase, deep in-body twist, covered in several glazes, pad inside stamped 'G.E. Ohr, Biloxi, Miss.', short, tight line to rim.

3.5in (9cm) wide

$16,000-20,000   CRA

A George Ohr tear-shaped vase, covered in gunmetal brown glaze, and hand-incised 'OHR BILOXI'.

5.25in (13.5cm) high

$2,000-3,000   DRA

A George Ohr cabinet vase, of squat spherical form, covered in green speckled glaze, and with die-stamped mark.

3.75in (9.5cm) wide

$2,000-3,000   DRA

A George Ohr cabinet vase, folded rim, covered in gunmetal brown and bright green matte glaze, with signed stilt pad, vase stamped, stilt pad incised 'G. E. OHR', minor nicks to paper-thin rim.

Stilt pads would normally have been snipped off, leaving little bumps to show where they had been. Either Ohr neglected to do this, or feared that removing it might destroy the delicate piece. Ohr's ego was such that he marked even his home-made kiln furniture. Evidently, these were made by pressing clay into small plaster molds into which he had scratched his name, thus the lettering is raised.

3.25in (8cm) wide

$3,500-4,500   CRA

A George Ohr vase, with deep in-body twist and floriform folds around rim, covered in semi-matte blue-gray glaze, stamped 'G. E. OHR Biloxi, Miss.', small nick to rim, touch-up to stilt-pull.

3in (7.5cm) high

$8,000-10,000   DRA

A George Ohr bud vase, with folded floriform rim, covered in mottled gunmetal glaze dripping over emerald green ground, script signature, 0.5in (1cm) surface scratch to body.

5in (12.5cm) high

$7,000-10,000   DRA

A George Ohr tapering vase of marbleized clay with loose indigo sponged pattern, stamped GEO. E. OHR BILOXI, MISS.

4.5in (11.5cm) high

$3,000-4,000   DRA

A George Ohr vessel, with two asymmetrical handles, covered in bands of matte pink, blue-green, and green, and with script signature.

4in (10cm) high

$10,000-12,000   DRA

A George Ohr small squat vessel, of white clay covered in emerald green mirrored glaze, and stamped 'BILOXI'.

4.25in (11cm) wide

$3,000-4,000   DRA

A George Ohr squat vessel, with floriform pinched front and back, covered in a dark green glaze, and with die-stamped mark.

4in (10cm) wide

$3,000-4,000   DRA

A George Ohr low vessel, covered in raspberry volcanic glaze, with bright green interior, stamped 'G. E. OHR Biloxi, Miss.', very slight loss to bubble at base.

Red glazes are notoriously fugitive and rare in pottery. Hugh Robertson at Dedham spent years trying to achieve them, working on a thick stoneware body, whereas Ohr managed this difficult glaze on an amazingly thin-walled vessel.

4in (10cm) wide

$6,000-8,000   CRA

A George Ohr vessel, white clay with closed-in rim, sponged cobalt and brown pattern, script signature.

White is the ultimate challenge to potters. This is white on the outside and inside, with blue sponge decoration. There is speculation that this may have been Ohr's answer to the blue-sponged kitchen ware being produced in Ohio and Illinois in the 1880s and 90s.

2.5in (6cm) high

$3,000-4,000   DRA

A George Ohr bisque-fired vessel, of brown clay with folded rim and dimpled front, stamped 'G.E.OHR Biloxi Miss.'.

5.75in (14.5cm) wide

$4,500-5,500   DRA

A rare George Ohr/Susan Frackelton bisque-fired bulbous pitcher, with a squeezed heart-shaped ribbon handle, and signed 'SF 99', with small chips to rim.

A rare and exceptional collaboration of the two potters, with an interesting iron oxide blush.

1899   *9in (23cm) high*

$6,000-8,000   DRA

A George Ohr bisque-fired pitcher, of marbleized clay, with script signature.

4.5in (11.5cm) wide

$5,000-6,000   DRA

A George Ohr bisque-fired cabinet vessel, of red scroddled clay with pinched rim, and script signature/'06'.

1906   *3in (7.6cm) wide*

$2,500-3,500   DRA

PEWABIC

A Pewabic plate, embossed with black rooks against gold lustered glaze, stamped 'PEWABIC'.

The luster has been carefully brushed from the edges of the crows, making them stand out in stark relief. There is something Classical about it, perhaps it's the triple bars dividing the panels which recall the triglyphs separating the reliefs of the frieze on the Parthenon.

10in (25.5cm) diam

$5,000-6,000   CRA

A tall Pewabic baluster vase, covered in Persian blue mottled glaze, and stamped Pewabic Detroit.

10.75in (27.5cm) high

$1,200-1,500   DRA

A Pewabic bulbous vase, covered in an unusual fire orange matte glaze, with circular stamp.

8in (20.5cm) high

$1,500-2,000   DRA

A fine, large, and early Pewabic vase, covered in thick lustered glaze dripping on ultramarine base, stamped 'PEWABIC' with maple leaves, grinding chip.

8in (20cm) high

$5,500-7,500   DRA

A Pewabic vase, covered in thick dripping matte amber glaze, circular stamp 'PEWABIC DETROIT'.

10.5in (26.5cm) high

$2,000-3,000   DRA

A Pewabic early vase, covered in matte flambé glaze, stamped 'PEWABIC' with maple leaves.

14.5in (37cm) high

$5,000-6,000   DRA

A rare Frederick Rhead/Santa Barbara footed bowl, decorated in wax-resist with a band of carp, stamped 'RHEAD STA. BARBARA'.

9.5in (24cm) wide

$18,000-20,000   DRA

A Frederick Rhead/Santa Barbara squat vessel, squeezebag-decorated with waves around the rim, and covered in sheer matte green glaze, the brown clay showing through, and with circular stamp.

4.25in (11cm) wide

$3,500-4,500   DRA

CLOSER LOOK: RHEAD SANTA BARBARA VASE

The vase is etched with a stylized landscape which reflects Rhead's interpretation of the California landscape, the lean, tall trees with a canopy of foliage are set against a midnight blue sky with the ocean and clouds beyond.

The vase and decoration are technically perfect in execution and were made by an artist at the pinnacle of his career. It came from a small studio that did not produce many Rhead pieces and is therefore highly desirable. This piece made a world record price at auction.

The etched design is unusual, squeezebag decoration is more common.

Rhead Santa Barbara pieces are stamped or have a paper label on the base with a potter sitting at a wheel and 'RHEAD POTTERY/SANTA BARBARA'.

A Rhead Santa Barbara vase, etched with a stylized landscape, stamped medallion of potter at kiln, a few hairlines.

Frederick Hurten Rhead (1880-1942) was born in England and trained there as a potter, working for companies such as Foley. In 1902 he immigrated to the US where he worked as an artist and art director for the Avon Faïence Company, Weller Pottery, Roseville Pottery, Jervis Pottery, University City, and Arequipa Pottery. By the time Rhead reached California and the Arequipa Pottery he had refined his art to the point where he was creating the best work of his career. His innovative decoration at this time was second to none. In 1913 he and his wife Lois left Arequipa and started their own pottery in Santa Barbara. They made garden ornaments, vases and bowls with an Oriental influence and covered with the innovative glazes Rhead developed. Despite his talents as a potter, Rhead's business was not a success and it closed in 1917. Rhead continued to work in research and education.

c1915   *11.25in (28.5cm) high*

$516,000 +   DRA

ROOKWOOD

Rookwood Pottery of Cincinnati, Ohio, is acknowledged to be the most important producer of American art pottery, in terms of quality, innovation, longevity, and volume. It was founded by Maria Longworth Nichols in 1880. With the financial backing of the Longworth family she employed the most competent local ceramic workers and the pottery flourished. However, it was not until William Watts Taylor took charge as manager, that it began to succeed financially as a business.

In 1889, Rookwood was awarded a Gold Medal at the Universal Exposition at Paris. The following year Mrs. Nichols retired from active participation and the Rookwood Pottery Company was incorporated in Ohio with Taylor as president. Employing over 50 staff artists, Rookwood created lines that would be imitated by companies all over the country, including their Standard, Sea Green and Vellum glazes.

Taylor died in 1913 and the pottery changed hands several times. It survived two World Wars and the Depression, but the wares were markedly inferior. In 1967 it closed for good.

A Rookwood Standard glaze vase, painted by Matt Daly with palm fronds, restored drill hole to bottom and chip to rim, flame mark/'S1406A/MAD'.

1898   *20ins (51cm) high*

$3,500-4,500   DRA

A Rookwood Standard glaze pitcher, painted by Kataro Shirayamadani, with silver overlay with pomegranates, hairlines to base, flame mark/'437A/S'/artist's cipher.

1890   *8.25in (21cm) high*

$5,000-6,000   DRA

A Rookwood Vellum vase, painted by Lenore Asbury with Canadian geese in flight over an indigo ground, and with flame mark/'XVI/913D/V/L.A.'

1916   8in (20.5cm) high

$2,000-3,000   DRA

CLOSER LOOK: ROOKWOOD STANDARD GLAZE VASE

Towards the end of the 19thC there was a growing respect for, and appreciation of, Native Americans. Many were photographed by the leading photographers of their day and the images seen by thousands.

This interest was reflected in a range of Rookwood Standard glaze vases and plaques which are as popular with collectors now as they were when new.

The portrait of Wanstall Arapahoe has been painted with exceptional quality and detail by Grace Young, who was one of Rookwood's best decorators.

The rich glazes have been used to create an image of almost photographic detail and show Wanstall in native dress and with characteristic dignity.

A Rookwood Standard glaze vase, by Grace Young, *Wanstall Arapahoe*, painted after the 1899 Rose & Hopkins photograph of Wanstall, flame mark/'581C'/artist's cipher and title, several scratches.

1900   13.5in (34cm) high

$12,000-15,000   DRA

A Rookwood Scenic Vellum plaque, by Lenore Asbury, *Along the River*, mounted in original frame, flame mark/'XVII/V/L.A.'/type-written title.

1917   Plaque: 9in (23cm) wide

$6,000-8,000   DRA

A Rookwood Scenic Vellum vase, finely painted by Sallie Coyne, flame mark/'XXIII/356F/SEC', uncrazed.

1923   5.25in (13cm) high

$3,000-4,000   DRA

A Rookwood Scenic Vellum plaque, *Winter*, painted by Sallie Coyne, with tall pines in a snowy landscape, mounted in original frame, Flame mark/'XVIII/SEC'.

1918   Plaque 12.25in (31cm) wide

$11,000-13,000   DRA

A Rookwood Vellum vase, painted by Ed Diers with light pink and yellow nasturtium blossoms on a blue ground, uncrazed, and with flame mark/'XXVII/915D/ED'.

1928   7in (18cm) high

$800-1,200   DRA

A Rookwood Scenic Vellum plaque, *Gathering Clouds*, painted by Ed Diers with overcast sky above a landscape, in original gilded frame, signed 'ED', flame mark.

8in (20.5cm) square

$8,000-10,000   DRA

A Rookwood Scenic Vellum vase, painted by Ed Diers, flame mark/'XXIV/295 C/V/ED', uncrazed.

1924   11in (28cm) high

$4,500-5,500   DRA

A Rookwood Vellum vase, painted by Ed Diers, flame mark/'XXVII/1369 D/V/ED', uncrazed.

1927   9.25in (23cm) high

$6,000-8,000   DRA

ESSENTIAL REFERENCE: ROOKWOOD GLAZES

The first glaze to establish Rookwood's professionalism as an art pottery was the Standard glaze, developed in 1884. The glaze was a translucent high gloss that gave all colors a yellow-brown hue. Pieces with Standard glaze are typically decorated with flowers.

Iris glaze, also developed in 1884, was an attempt to create a colorless glaze retaining the richness and depth of the Standard. Like Standard, the motifs displayed under the Iris Glaze are primarily floral, although there are examples of birds and animals and rare landscapes and seascapes.

Sea Green glaze, developed at approximately the same time, was used almost exclusively for seascapes and fish, because of its blue-green color, though it was also used for flowers.

Matte glaze was developed, with the help of Artus Van Briggle, around 1900 in response to Grueby's matte glaze. It was flat and opaque with a coarse texture and was applied in a wide variety of tones.

Vellum glaze, introduced in 1900, is considered the link between Rookwood's gloss and matte glazes. It diffuses the painted decoration (usually plants or landscapes) it covers, giving it an Impressionist appearance. Though usually clear, Vellum was also available with green and yellow tints.

The Jewel Porcelain glaze was first used in 1916. It employs air bubbles in clear gloss glaze, and therefore produces a similar effect to that of Vellum, but without the same waxiness.

A Rookwood Scenic Vellum plaque, painted by Lorinda Epply with windblown pines, in original frame, with flame mark/'XVI/LE'.

1916   *9.25in (23.5cm) high*
$10,000-12,000   DRA

A Rookwood Vellum vase, painted by Kate Van Horne with blue flowers in the Asian taste, flame mark/'XV/30E/V'/artist's cipher.

1915   *9in (23cm) high*
$3,000-4,000   DRA

A Rookwood Scenic Vellum vase, painted by E. T. Hurley, with a silhouetted landscape, flame mark/'IX/1664G/V/ETH', light peppering around shoulder.

1909   *12.5in (31.5cm) high*
$4,500-5,500   DRA

A Rookwood Scenic Vellum ovoid vase, by E. T. Hurley, flame mark/'XLVIII/S/ETH', uncrazed.

1948   *8.5in (21.5cm) high*
$3,500-4,500   DRA

A Rookwood Scenic Vellum flaring vase, painted by Elizabeth McDermott, flame mark/'1357E/V/EHM', uncrazed.

Unusual and good colors.
1916   *7.5in (19cm) high*
$3,000-4,000   DRA

A Rookwood bulbous vellum vase, painted by Fred Rothenbusch with violets on a shaded ground, and with flame mark/'V/989D/FR'.

1905   *8.25in (21cm) high*
$1,500-2,000   DRA

CLOSER LOOK: SCENIC VELLUM VASE

The Vellum glaze, introduced in 1900, created a diffused surface reminiscent of an Impressionist painting.

Pastel shades are usual, especially cream and blue.

Landscapes featuring trees and river views were popular decoration, particularly on large vases and wall plaques.

The decoration usually covers the entire surface of the ceramic.

A Rookwood Scenic Vellum plaque, painted by Fred Rothenbusch with a winter landscape, in original Arts & Crafts frame, with flame mark/'XII/FR'.

1912   *8in (20.5cm) wide*
$6,000-8,000   DRA

A Rookwood Scenic Vellum tapered vase, painted by Sara Sax, flame mark/ '1654D/V/V.'/artist's cipher.

1909   *9.5in (24cm) high*
$9,000-11,000   DRA

A Rookwood Scenic Vellum ovoid vase, by E. T. Hurley, flame mark/ 'XLVIII/S/ETH', uncrazed.

1948   *8.5in (21.5cm) high*
$3,500-4,500   DRA

A Rookwood Iris glaze bulbous vase, painted by Fred Rothenbusch with milkweed pods, with flame mark/'III/902C/FR'.

1903   *8.75in (22cm) high*

$4,000-5,000   **DRA**

A Rookwood Black Iris glaze tankard, with silver overlay, painted by Kataro Shirayamadani, with flame mark/'564D'/Japanese cipher.

1900   *9in (23cm) high*

$16,000-18,000   **DRA**

A Rookwood Iris glaze vase, painted by A. R. Valentien with pink roses, flame mark/ 'II/905B/' A.R.VALENTIEN, minor glaze miss.

1902   *15in (38cm) high*

$9,000-11,000   **DRA**

A Rookwood Carved Iris vase, by John D. Wareham, drilled hole on bottom, and flame mark/ '614C'/partial artist's signature/'W'.

1900   *12.5in (32cm) high*

$20,000-25,000   **DRA**

A Rookwood Wax Mat vase, painted by Jens Jensen, with red roses, flame mark/'XXIX/2932'/artist's cipher.

1929   *14in (35.5cm) high*

$2,000-3,000   **DRA**

A Rookwood Decorated Mat vase, by Kataro Shirayamadani, flame mark/'XXIX/6006'/Japanese cipher, some grinding chips.

1929   *11.5in (29cm) high*

$3,000-4,000   **DRA**

A Rookwood Wax Mat vase, painted by an unidentified artist with wild yellow and red roses, flame mark/'XXV/614C'.

1925   *13in (33cm) high*

$4,000-5,000   **DRA**

A later Rookwood Mat/Mat Moderne vase, by William Hentschell, with sprigs of leaves, flame mark/'XXIX/2790/WEH'.

1929   *11.5in (29cm) high*

$2,500-3,500   **DRA**

A later Rookwood Mat/Mat Moderne vase, by Wilhemina Rhem, with horses and rider, flame mark/'XXXIV/WR'.

1934   *5in (12.5cm) high*

$1,200-1,800   **DRA**

A rare Rookwood Z-Line inkwell, by A. M. Valentien, with swirling maiden under matte green glaze, flame mark/'III/407Z/X1023X/A.M.V.'

1903   *4in (10cm) high*

$4,000-5,000   **DRA**

A Rookwood Z-Line squat vessel, by A. M. Valentien, flame mark/'?51Z/ A.M.V', touch-up to shoulder.

1901   *3.5in (9cm) high*

$2,500-3,500   **DRA**

A rare Rookwood Z-Line vessel, flame mark/'Z/661'/partial paper museum label, firing lines and scaling to figure.

1901   *4.25in (10.5cm) high*

$3,000-4,000   **DRA**

A Rookwood Jewel Porcelain vase, by Arthur Conant, with sparrows in silhouette on a blooming branch, and with flame mark/'XX/932D/C'.

1920   *9.5in (24cm) high*

$3,000-4,000   **DRA**

A Rookwood Jewel Porcelain vase, by William Hentschell, with purple sprigs, flame mark/'XX/2499C/WEH'.

1920   *14in (35.5cm) high*

$8,000-10,000   **DRA**

A pair of tall Rookwood Jewel Porcelain urns, with dolphin handles painted by E. T. Hurley in the Oriental style, and flame marks/ 'XLVI/2634/5236/E.T.HURLEY'.

1946   *9.75in (25cm) high*
$2,000-3,000   **DRA**

A Rookwood Jewel Porcelain vase, by Jens Jensen, with large white and pink blossoms, and flame mark/ 'XXIV/S'/artist's cipher.

1934   *6.5in (16.5cm) high*
$1,500-2,000   **DRA**

A Rookwood Limoges-style pitcher, by Matt Daly, with swallows in flight, and horizontal stamp with mark '101A'.

1886   *12in (30.5cm) high*
$1,000-1,500   **DRA**

A Rookwood Limoges-style basket on lion's-head feet, painted by A. R. Valentien with butterflies, stamped 'A Rookwood 1882 45 A.R.V.', opposing hairlines.

1882   *20in (51cm) wide*
$600-800   **DRA**

A Rookwood high glaze Scenic plaque, painted by Sturgis Laurence, *Four-Master Bound In,* with large flame mark/ 'III/XII68X' /title and signature, and paper label.

1903   *14in (35.5cm) wide*
$40,000-50,000   **DRA**

A large rare Rookwood tile panel, consisting of 45 tiles depicting a landscape in matte glazes, and surrounded by 14 molding tiles and one row of border tiles in matte brown glaze, stamped 'RP'.

76in (193cm) wide
$25,000-30,000   **DRA**

A Rookwood tile, with oak tree, framed, back and edges covered by frame.

6in (15cm) square
$2,000-3,000   **DRA**

A rare Rookwood advertising tile, decorated in cuenca with a blue rook and the word 'Rookwood', mounted in period frame, does not appear to have been removed, minor nicks to two corners

An extremely rare example, these advertising tiles were not meant for commercial sale.

Tile 9in (23cm) wide
$30,000-35,000   **DRA**

A large Rookwood faïence ship medallion, stamped 'RP 375 E8131924'.

12in (30.5cm) diam
$2,500-3,500   **DRA**

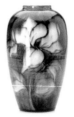

A Rookwood porcelain vase, painted by Jens Jensen, with flame mark/'XLIV/6869'/artist's cipher.

1944   *9in (23cm) high*
$2,000-3,000   **DRA**

An exceptional and rare Rookwood 'Cameo' cylindrical vase, painted by A. R. Valentien, with a wisteria branch in white pâte-sur-pâte, and with flame mark/'C/644/A.R.V.'/.

1893   *14.5in (37cm) high*
$14,000-18,000   **DRA**

A large Rookwood faïence wall pocket, heavily modeled with a bird perched on a grapevine, with flame mark/'XVI/2279', and a couple of glaze flakes.

1916   *13.75in (35cm) high*

$2,500-3,000   **DRA**

A Rookwood trial porcelain plate, depicting the twelve apostles under sheer ivory glaze, flame mark/'K8'.

12.5in (31.5cm) diam

$400-600   **CRA**

A Rookwood Production vase, embossed with swirling blossoms under cobalt glaze, flame mark/'XIV/516', small glaze nick to edge of leaf.

1914   *11in (28cm) high*

$2,500-3,000   **DRA**

A Rookwood silverplate-mounted earthenware tankard, the body molded with three frogs fishing, the rim further set with cast lily pads, impressed marks no. '775', cracked.

8.25in (21cm) high

$1,200-1,800   **L&T**

ROSEVILLE

Roseville Pottery was first established in 1890 in the town of Roseville, Ohio. Under the direction of its first general manager, George F. Young, it began by producing basic, but well designed, utilitarian stoneware. Roseville Pottery flourished and acquired a second pottery in Roseville and another in the nearby town of Zanesville, both former stoneware facilities.

In 1900, hoping to capitalize on the fame of Rookwood Pottery, Roseville launched its own range of art ware. This art ware was named 'Rozane': a contraction of the company name and the new Zaneville location, where all Rozane Ware was produced.

Initially, Rozane did little more than reproduce passable copies of Rookwood designs. However, in 1905 the firm introduced a series of original lines, including Della Robbia: designed by new art director, Frederick H. Rhead.

Frederick Rhead left Roseville in 1908, and was succeeded by his brother, Harry Rhead. The company began to fail and, by 1910 only the Zanesville pottery remained open.

With the onset of WWI, the production of art ware ceased in favour of returning to commercially viable mass production. Following World War II, sales declined steadily. Roseville closed in 1954.

A Roseville rare 'Azurean' baluster vase, painted by JL with bluebells, impressed mark 'RPCo/892/6/M'.

8.25in (21cm) high

$1,500-2,000   **CRA**

A Roseville green 'Baneda' wall pocket, gift store foil label.

8.25in (21cm) high

$3,000-4,000   **CRA**

A Roseville green 'Baneda' bulbous vase, unmarked.

10.25in (26cm) high

$1,500-2,500   **DRA**

A Roseville 'Blackberry' jardiniere and pedestal set, two nicks near top of pedestal, unmarked.

Total 28in (71cm) high.

$2,500-3,500   **CRA**

A pair of Roseville 'Blackberry' vases, unmarked.

6.5in (16.5cm) high

$800-1,200   **DRA**

A Roseville rare 'Cameo' jardinière and pedestal set, slight damage, unmarked.

33.75in (86cm) high in total

$1,800-2,200   **CRA**

DECORATIVE ARTS

A Roseville pink 'Cherry Blossom' bulbous two-handled vase, unmarked, two flecks and small burst to body.

10.5in (26.5cm) high

$1,000-1,500   **DRA**

A Roseville rare 'Cremo' vase, decorated with squeezebag floral design, unmarked.

9.75in (24.75cm) high

$9,000-11,000   **CRA**

A Roseville 'Della Robbia' baluster vase, incised with stylized jonquils in yellow and ochre, and green leaves on a celadon ground, restored rim, base chips, signed 'ES' and with medallion mark.

11in (28cm) high

$10,000-15,000   **CRA**

CLOSER LOOK: ROSEVILLE CARNELIAN VASE

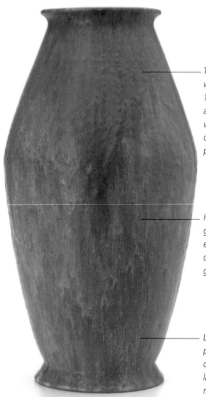

The Carnelian glaze was introduced in 1926. The mottled red and blue/green glaze is very popular with collectors – particularly in red.

Here, the pink-red glaze has been embellished with deep purple and green drips.

Like this one, many pieces were unmarked, others have a paper label or stamped ink mark.

A Roseville 'Carnelian III' large and rare ovoid vase, covered in a fine frothy pink and ochre glaze with deep purple and green drips, unmarked.

20in (51cm) high

$12,000-15,000   **CRA**

A Roseville 'Della Robbia' vase, excised with daisies and spade-shaped leaves on a forest green ground, Rozane seal, restoration to hairline through body and chips at base.

10.5in (26.5cm) high

$14,000-18,000   **DRA**

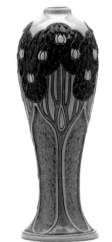

A Roseville 'Della Robbia' vase, incised and excised with stylized trees, artist signed MF, restoration to drilled hole on bottom, and chip at base.

8.75in (22cm) high

$12,000-15,000   **DRA**

A Roseville 'Della Robbia' five-color large bulbous vase, with daffodils in ochre, ivory, and green against a gray-blue ground, with reticulated geometric band around rim, artist's initials 'K.D.', chip to bottom, fleck and firing line to one flower.

12.5in (31.5cm) high

$20,000-25,000   **DRA**

A Roseville 'Blue Falline' bulbous vase, strong molded design, foil label.

8.25in (21cm) wide

$1,800-2,200   **CRA**

A Roseville red 'Ferella' vase, no. 511-10, unmarked.

10in (25.5cm) high

$1,000-1,500 DRA

A Roseville blue 'Fuchsia' floor vase, no. 905-18, impressed mark.

18in (46cm) high

$1,000-1,500 DRA

A Roseville green 'Panel' ovoid vase, with flaring rim, RV ink mark.

10.25in (26cm) high

$1,500-2,000 CRA

A Roseville 'Imperial II' flaring vase, covered in mottled orange and green curdled glaze, the body with threaded design, minute invisible touch-up to very top of rim, unmarked.

5.5in (14cm) high

$2,000-3,000 CRA

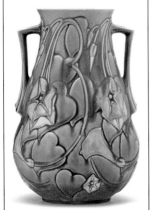

A Roseville green 'Morning Glory' vase, no. 730-10, unmarked.

10in (25.5cm) high

$1,000-1,500 DRA

A Roseville rare 'Olympic' footed two-handled vase, *Euryclea discovers Ulysses,* painted with Greek motif and key design around rim, with floral decoration on the rear side, restored handles and lines through lower portion of body, marked 'Euryclea discovers Ulysses'/Rozane 'Olympic' Pottery.

11in (28cm) high

$3,000-4,000 CRA

A Roseville 'Pauleo' vase, covered in mottled olive, red, ochre, and brown glaze, unmarked.

24in (61cm) high

$8,000-10,000 CRA

A Roseville tall blue 'Pine Cone' ewer, impressed mark, foil label to body.

15in (38cm) high

$2,000-3,000 CRA

A Roseville brown 'Pine Cone' wall pocket, no. 1283, impressed mark, minute fleck to tip of branch.

1,000-1,500 DRA

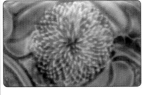

A Roseville 'Sunflower' bulbous vase, no. 488-6, unmarked, very crisp mold.

6in (15.25cm) high

$1,000-1,500 DRA

A Roseville blue 'Water Lily' vase, no. 83-15, impressed mark.

15in (38cm) high

$500-800 DRA

A Roseville 'Woodland/Fujiyama' vase, Rozane Ware seal, artist's initials 'ET', minor glaze loss.

9in (22.5cm) high

$600-800 DRA

SATURDAY EVENING GIRLS

The Saturday Evening Girls was originally a club, comprised chiefly of Italian and Jewish immigrant girls, who met at the North Branch of Boston Library in 1899.

In 1906, the club acquired a small kiln, and, by 1907, it had opened a pottery, headed by Edith Brown. The operation moved to larger premises and took the name of a local Revolutionary War hero and became the Paul Revere Pottery. There members produced hand-decorated ceramics, including bowls, vases, tea wares and dinner sets, and a popular line of children's breakfast sets.

Edith Brown died in 1932, signalling the end of the pottery. Though Mrs Storrow continued to fund the enterprise, it became clear that its expenses could not be met, and it closed in 1942.

CLOSER LOOK: SATURDAY EVENING GIRLS CHARGER

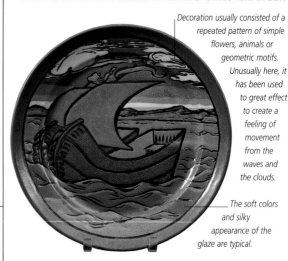

Decoration usually consisted of a repeated pattern of simple flowers, animals or geometric motifs. Unusually here, it has been used to great effect to create a feeling of movement from the waves and the clouds.

The soft colors and silky appearance of the glaze are typical.

A Saturday Evening Girls Pottery ship charger, incised and decorated by Albina Mangini, with white clouds and yellow horizon against a green and brown landscape, the blue sea with two single-mast ships with green sails and bodies in two shades of brown, all on blue ground, signed 'S.E.G. AM 4-14'.

1914   *12.5in (31.75cm) diam*

$17,000-22,000   **SK**

A Saturday Evening Girls low flaring bowl, painted with yellow stylized blossoms, and with Paul Revere stamp/'6-26/LS'.

1926   *10.25in (26cm) wide*

$1,000-1,500   **DRA**

A four-sided Saturday Evening Girls vase, decorated in cuerda seca, 'S.E.G./12-20/JMD', 'A.P.' on surface.

1920   *3.75in (9.5cm) high*

$1,500-2,000   **DRA**

A Saturday Evening Girls divided bowl, decorated in cuerda seca with a band of white irises on bright yellow ground, missing lid, restoration to chip, signed 'S.E.G./4.16'.

8.5in (21.5cm) wide

$400-600   **DRA**

A Saturday Evening Girls bowl, painted in wax-resist with white camellia, signed 'S.E.G./AM/10-16', two short, tight hairlines.

1916   *8.5in (21.5cm) wide*

$1,500-2,000   **CRA**

A Saturday Evening Girls Pottery 'Monumental' vase, decorated by Rose Bacchini, marked on base 'S.E.G. RB 10-17'.

1917   *20.5in (53cm) high*

$3,500-5,500   **SK**

TECO

A Teco vase, reticulated with narrow folded leaves in matte green glaze, stamped 'Teco'.

11.5in (29cm) high

$10,000-15,000   **DRA**

A Teco lobed vase, covered in blue matte glaze, and stamped 'TECO'.

5.25in (13.5cm) high

$1,000-1,500   **DRA**

A Teco two-handled organically-shaped vase, covered in smooth matte green glaze, and stamped 'Teco'.

8.5in (21.5cm) wide

$3,000-4,000   **DRA**

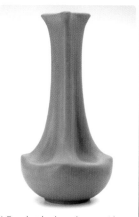

A Teco bottle-shaped vase, with dimpled four-sided neck, covered in smooth matte green glaze, and stamped 'Teco'.

16in (40.5cm) high

$3,500-4,500   DRA

A Teco gourd-shaped vase, covered in matte green glaze, stamped 'Teco 661', invisible, professional restoration to chip at rim and base.

10in (25.5cm) high

$4,000-5,000   DRA

VAN BRIGGLE

A former senior decorator at Rookwood Pottery, Artus Van Briggle relocated to Colorado Springs, Colorado in 1899 in the hopes of easing his tuberculosis. There, with his wife, Anna, he founded Van Briggle Pottery, favouring organic-shaped ceramic vessels decorated with sumptuous matt glazes.

Under Artus' direction, the company won medals in the 1903 Paris Salon and the 1904 Lousiana Purchase Exposition. Most of the finest Van Briggle ware was produced before the death of Artus in 1904. After this date, Anna controlled the company and it continued to produce high quality art wares in a variety of distinctive hues. She sold the factory in 1912.

Van Briggle Pottery remains in operation today, making it unique amongst other big potteries of the original art pottery period.

An early Van Briggle vase, embossed with stylized morning glories and covered in raspberry glaze with green accents, marked 'AA VAN BRIGGLE 1905 287'.

1905   *7in (18cm) high*

$1,500-2,000   DRA

An early Van Briggle vase, with two handles, embossed with red morning glories, small firing glaze scale inside one handle.

1904   *11in (28cm) high*

$7,000-9,000   DRA

CLOSER LOOK: VAN BRIGGLE VASE

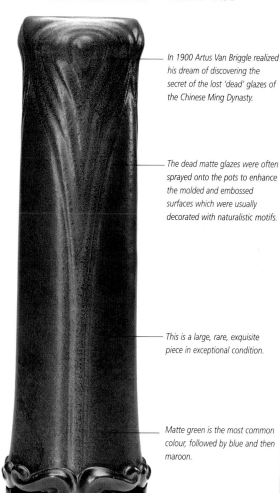

In 1900 Artus Van Briggle realized his dream of discovering the secret of the lost 'dead' glazes of the Chinese Ming Dynasty.

The dead matte glazes were often sprayed onto the pots to enhance the molded and embossed surfaces which were usually decorated with naturalistic motifs.

This is a large, rare, exquisite piece in exceptional condition.

Matte green is the most common colour, followed by blue and then maroon.

An early Van Briggle bulbous vase, embossed with mistletoe in red, blue and gray flambé.

1902   *6in (15cm) high*

$3,500-4,500   DRA

An early Van Briggle vase, embossed with geese and covered in matte green to chartreuse glaze, marked 'AA VAN BRIGGLE/5/1903/III'.

1903   *6.25in (16cm) high*

$8,000-10,000   DRA

An early and exceptional Van Briggle vase on stand, embossed with green peacock feathers on a rich purple ground, set on a bronze footed base, marked 'AA/VANBRIGGLE/1904'.

It is possible that this piece was made for the St. Louis World's Fair, 1904.

1904   *13in (33cm) high*

$45,000-50,000   DRA

DECORATIVE ARTS

An early Van Briggle two-handled vase, with trefoils covered in indigo and bright green glaze, marked 'AA/VAN BRIGGLE/1903/III/172', drilled hole to bottom.

1903   *12.25in (31cm) high*

$2,000-3,000   **DRA**

A Van Briggle bulbous vase, embossed with poppy pods under a dark green to medium green matte glaze, marked 'AA 1916'.

1916   *7.75in (19.5cm) high*

$1,500-2,000   **DRA**

A Van Briggle bowl, with heavily embossed leaves, under medium and dark green glaze.

1916   *10in (25.5cm) wide*

$1,500-2,000   **DRA**

A Van Briggle Mermaid center bowl in blue and turquoise, marked 'AA VAN BRIGGLE COLO. SPGS'.

9in (23cm) high

$500-800   **CRA**

A fine and rare Van Briggle tile, decorated in cuenca with trees, mounted in an Arts & Crafts frame, unmarked.

6.25in (16cm) square

$3,000-4,000   **DRA**

WELLER

Samuel A. Weller founded Weller Pottery in Fultonham, Ohio, in 1872. In 1888 the pottery moved to Zanesville and by 1893 was producing art ware. The next year Weller merged with Lonhuda Pottery but within two years the partnership had been dissolved. Weller produced a similar ware named Louwelsa.

Like Roseville, Weller only truly distinguished itself when it stopped copying Rookwood and created its own original lines. Weller lured Frederick Rhead from Roseville to create 'Jap Birdimal'. When this failed to prove as popular as 'Della Robbia', which Rhead created for Roseville, he hired Jacques Sicard, who designed the iridescent Sicardo Ware. By 1915, Weller Pottery claimed to be the largest art pottery in existence. By the end of WWI, production ware had replaced most of the better lines. It closed in 1945.

A Weller 'Coppertone' bulbous vase with two frogs perched on both sides of the rim, tight line parallel to rim, stamped mark.

7.5in (19cm) high

$1,000-1,500   **CRA**

A Weller 'Aurelian' lamp base, painted with gold carnations, metal collar fitted inside rim, incised mark, with four factory holes through base, excellent condition.

17.5in (44.5cm) high

$600-800   **DRA**

A rare Weller 'Camelot' cylindrical vase, embossed with masks and medallions, unmarked, some discoloration to glaze, typical of this line.

9.5in (24cm) high

$500-800   **DRA**

A Weller 'Eocean' bulbous vase painted by Elizabeth Blake with portrait of a kitten, few minor scratches to body and rim, incised mark/artist's name.

8in (20.5cm) high

$2,000-2,500   **CRA**

A Weller 'Dickensware' ewer beautifully carved with a golfer and caddy along a deeply incised line of trees, impressed mark, possible artist's signature in grass.

The finest example of 'golfer', with the decoration spanning the entire body.

11in (28cm) high

$4,000-5,000   **CRA**

A Weller 'Fru Russett' vase, with a dragon wrapped around its body, covered in a purple and blue-gray glaze, stamped 'WELLER'.

9.75in (24.5cm) high

$7,000-9,000 **DRA**

A Weller 'Hudson' vase, painted by Claude Leffler with irises on both sides, impressed mark and artist's mark.

15in (38cm) high

$4,000-5,000 **CRA**

A Weller 'Jap Birdimal' mug, decorated in squeezebag with a geisha and a cat, incised 'Weller Faïence/Rhead/X/G462'.

5.25in (13.5cm) high

$700-900 **DRA**

A rare matte green Weller vase, unmarked, the body with faint impressed decoration, and very minor grinding chip.

11.5in (29cm) high

$1,000-1,500 **DRA**

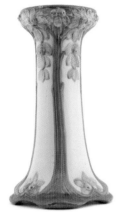

A rare Weller 'Voile' pedestal, decorated with tall fruit trees, marked '24' in ink, underglaze, and very minor chip to underside of base.

21in (53.5cm) high

$500-800 **DRA**

A Weller 'Woodcraft' tree-shaped vase decorated with a squirrel running down one side, and an owl perched in its hole, tight bruise and dark crazing line to rim, unmarked.

18.5in (47cm) high

$1,000-1,500 **CRA**

CLOSER LOOK: WELLER SICARD VASE

Jacques Sicard worked at Weller from 1902-1907. He used metallic lusters on an iridescent ground to decorate a range of simply shaped ceramics. The glaze was similar to one used by Tiffany & Co.

His designs often used floral or foliage motifs repeated all over the surface.

The majority of pieces were handpainted. Sicard is renowned as much for his painting as for his glaze technique.

This is a particularly large example.

A Weller 'Sicard' floor vase, extensively decorated with flowers and leaves in gold, against a nacreous purple, blue, and red ground, restoration to rim, a few minor abrasions or marks to body, signed and dated.

1902 *24.75in (63cm) high*

$4,000-5,000 **CRA**

OTHER FACTORIES

An Arequipa ribbed vase, covered in semi-sheer blue-gray glaze, the red clay showing through, stamped 'AREQUIPA CALIFORNIA'.

6in (15cm) high

$2,000-2,500 **DRA**

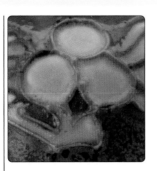

A Frederick Rhead period Arequipa vase, decorated in squeezebag and enamel, with oranges and leaves, with minor nicks to rim, and blue on white hand-painted Arequipa mark.

8.5in (21.5cm) high

$20,000-25,000 **DRA**

An Omar Khayyam/O. L. Bachelder tall cylindrical vase, covered in brown and black speckled mirrored glaze, and signed 'OLB'.

10.75in (27cm) high

$1,000-1,500 **DRA**

A pear-shaped Arthur Baggs vase, covered in a matte speckled blue glaze, and signed 'OHIO STATE/EB'.

4.5in (11.5cm) high

$500-800 **DRA**

An Arthur Baggs ovoid vase, with stylized blue and green leaves, probably from Ohio State, and incised 'AEB'.

5.25in (13.5cm) high

$1,000-1,500 **DRA**

A pair of Barol ovoid vases, decorated in cloisonné with a satyr and a wading bird, in polychrome lustered glazes, and signed 'Barol'.

9in (23cm) high

$5,000-6,000 **DRA**

A John Bennett bottle-shaped bud vase, painted with red quatrefoils on a turquoise ground, and in ink 'John Bennett East 24 NY/CR' in circle.

11in (28cm) high

$5,500-6,500 **DRA**

A John Bennett bottle-shaped vase, painted with chrysanthemums, in the style of Rozenburg and Japanese Kokutani wares, signed 'J Bennett New York 188?, Made by JB on his birthday.'

Among the few made of red clay, with exceptional color and clarity, an excellent example of Bennett's work.

11in (28cm) high

$4,000-5,000 **DRA**

An Edwin Bennett Albion pillow vase, in mottled tortoiseshell glaze, marked 'E. BENNETT POTTERY 1896'.

From his arrival in the United States in 1841, when he worked with his brothers in East Liverpool, Ohio, to his death in Baltimore in 1908, Bennett was one of the most commercially successful potters in American history. His output ranged from relief-molded yellow- and Rockingham-ware to art pottery. This pillow vase is of Albion ware, a short-lived pottery line.

1896

8.5in (21.5cm) high

$500-800 **CRA**

A Brouwer flaring vase, with flat shoulder, flame-painted in lustered gold and amber glaze, with small nicks to rim, and incised 'M' under whalebone/Brouwer.

6.5in (16.5cm) high

$2,500-3,000 **DRA**

A Brouwer flame-painted bottle-shaped vase, incised Brouwer mark with bone.

7.5in (19cm) high

$2,500-3,000 **DRA**

ESSENTIAL REFERENCE: JOHN BENNETT

John Bennett (1840-1907) trained as a ceramics decorator at Coalport, a British porcelain factory. In 1876, he immigrated to America and settled in New York City.

● As he was not a potter he imported English porcelain. However, he soon built his own kilns and employed potters who made a cream-colored body known as 'Bennett ware'.

● In 1878, he was engaged to teach pottery decoration at New York's newly formed Society of Decorative Art. He was replaced the following year with Charles Volkmar.

● He relocated in 1883 to West Orange, where he built a kiln, but did little further ceramic work. He died there in 1907.

A Brushguild biscuit jar and cover, carved by Lucy Perkins with an oxen frieze, and covered in a burnished bronzed glaze, incised 'LP' in a ribbon.

6.5in (16.5cm) wide

$7,000-10,000 **DRA**

A pair of California Faïence/Tully bookends, made of California Faïence cuenca tiles, mounted in wrought copper frames, and metal stamped 'TULLY'.

5.5in (14cm) wide

$4,000-5,000   DRA

A Chelsea Keramic Art Works experimental glaze plate, stamped 'CHELSEA KERAMIC ART WORKS, ROBERTSON & SONS'.

c1877-80   5.5in (14cm) diam

$3,000-4,000   CRA

A Chelsea Keramic Art bottle-shaped vase covered in a fine oxblood glaze, stamped 'CKAW'.

7.5in (19cm) high

$5,000-6,000   DRA

A Chicago Crucible bud vase, in frothy green glaze, unmarked.

8in (20cm) high

$500-800   DRA

A Claycraft vertical tile, with a California coastline scene, stamped 'CLAYCRAFT', in new Arts & Crafts frame.

Tile 3.75in (9.5cm) wide

$2,000-3,000   DRA

A Clewell copper-clad bottle-shaped vase, with a good verdigris patina, and incised 'Clewell/361'.

10in (25.5cm) high

$1,200-1,800   DRA

A Clewell copper-clad lidded jar, over a Claywood blank, with panels of flowers, unmarked, touch-up to interior lines.

6in (15cm) high

$1,200-1,800   DRA

A Clifton Crystal Patina bottle-shaped vase, signed 'Clifton 1906/148/CAP'.

1906   9in (23cm) high

$400-600   CRA

A Clifton Crystal Patina two-handled vase, signed and dated.

1906   7in (17.5cm) wide

$600-900   DRA

A Cook Nipur Ware vase, signed 'NIPUR' and 'Cook' mark.

9.5in (24cm) high

$4,000-5,000   DRA

A rare Paul Cox vase, carved with stylized cinquefoils in celadon and blue glossy glaze, incised 'CAP' cipher.

6.5in (16.5cm) high

$4,000-5,000   DRA

A Russell Crook salt-glazed stoneware vase, painted with lions on a dead-matte black and cobalt ground, unmarked.

9.5in (24cm) high

$6,000-8,000   DRA

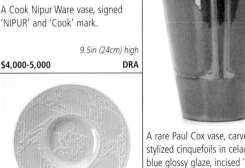

A Cowan charger, embossed with leaping maidens and foliage, covered in a leathery beige semi-matte glaze, and stamped 'Cowan' with flower.

12.75in (32.5cm) diam

$1,200-1,800   DRA

DECORATIVE ARTS

A salt-glazed stoneware vase, by Susan Frackelton, painted with oak leaves and acorns in indigo, and signed 'SF/I/II/927'.

8in (20.5cm) high

$11,000-14,000   **DRA**

CLOSER LOOK: DENVER DENAURA VASE

William Long, the founder of the Lonhuda Pottery, began the Denver China and Pottery Company in 1901.

The Denaura range featured low-relief-modeled Art Nouveau designs of native Colorado flowers and was similar to early Van Briggle wares.

Matte green was the most common glaze, however unlike the popular Grueby matte green glaze, Denver's had a satin finish.

A Denver Denaura squat vase, modeled and carved by William Long, covered in a dark green vellum glaze, stamped 'DENAURA DENVER', and incised 'DENAURA DENVER COL. U.S.A. 1903 #171/W.A.L.', two chips inside rim.

The best known example of Denaura, and the only one hand-signed by Long.

11in (28cm) high

$10,000-12,000   **DRA**

ESSENTIAL REFERENCE: SUSAN FRACKELTON

Susan Stuart Goodrich Frackelton (1848-1932) was the daughter of a brickmaker. She studied landscape painting and this influenced her ceramic decoration.

- In 1883, she established the Frackelton China Decorating Works in Milwaukee, employing many professionally trained decorators. With the sole exception of Graham Pottery, it was the only art pottery to use common salt-glazed stoneware.
- Whilst the Decorating Works was open, Susan Frackelton published a book on china painting, organised the National League of Mineral Painters, helped to develop a national school of ceramic art, and, in 1901, invented the gas kiln.
- Frackelton China Decorating Works closed in 1903. Though Susan Frackelton returned to ceramic work occasionally she no longer had her own kiln. Before the Saint Louis World's Fair in 1904, she abandoned pottery for good and relocated to Chicago where she lectured on a variety of subjects.

A rare Susan Frackelton stoneware covered jar, with applied decoration on a carved base, and incised 'SF 1898', small chip to interior of lid.

Shown in period photo from the Paul Evans book 'Tried by Fire'.

5in (12.5cm) high

$8,000-10,000   **DRA**

A Grand Feu baluster vase, covered in an exceptional and rare three-color flambé glaze and incised 'BR 1730/Grand Feu Art Pottery/L.A. Cal.'.

7.5in (19cm) high

$10,000-12,000   **DRA**

A Hampshire low bowl, embossed with water lily buds and lily pads under a smooth matte green glaze, with some wear to bottom, and stamped mark.

10in (25.5cm) wide

$500-800   **DRA**

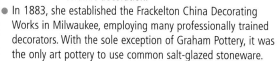

A Lenox/Gustav Stickley pair of porcelain soup bowls from Gustav Stickley's restaurant in the 34th Street Building, New York, with 'Als ik kan' mark, green Lenox stamp.

8.5in (21.5cm) diam

$2,000-3,000   **DRA**

An Inwood bottle-shaped bud vase, covered in purple and celadon mottled matte glaze, and incised 'Inwood Pottery NYC'.

5.75in (14.5cm) high

$500-800   **DRA**

A Jugtown vase, covered in a good Chinese blue glaze, with circular stamp.

7in (18cm) wide

$400-600   **DRA**

A Marie and Julian spherical vase, of burnished black clay with geometric pattern, signed 'Marie + Julian'.

4.5in (11.5cm) high

$2,000-2,500   **DRA**

A Lonhuda vase, slip-decorated with cowboys and Native Americans, stamped 'DENVER LONHUDA' with shield.

9in (23cm) high

$6,000-8,000   **DRA**

A Losanti porcelain vase, carved with acanthus leaves and covered in sheer celadon glaze, signed 'Losanti'.

4in (10cm) wide

$5,000-6,000 DRA

An Ella McKinnon / Quaker Road 'April' Studio tile, hand-pressed and carved with a young maiden holding flowers, hand-incised 'April, tree medallion, E.C.M., Quaker Road 1915', a couple of minor flakes to back edge.

Ella McKinnon is listed as a key figure in the Guild of Allied Crafts, Buffalo, 1910, itself a member of the National League of Handicraft Societies, Boston.

1915 6.75in (17cm) high

$2,000-3,000 DRA

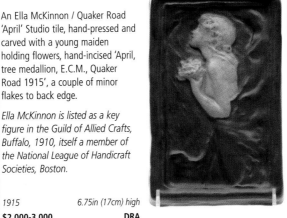

A tall Merrimac vase, with an exceptional gunmetal and green mottled glaze, several minor nicks, and probable mark covered by glaze.

15in (38cm) high

$20,000-25,000 DRA

A Merrimac small two-handled vase covered in frothy semi-matte green glaze, illegible stamp.

4in (10cm) high

$1,000-1,500 DRA

A rare Mueller vertical tile, decorated in cuerda seca with a farmer sowing seeds, signed on front 'MUELLER', a few minor edge nicks.

12.25in (31cm) high

$1,000-1,500 DRA

A large Norse baluster vase, incised with a Native American landscape of tepees and water on a bronze glaze base, stamped 'Norse', with small glaze nicks to body.

9.5in (24cm) high

$800-1,200 DRA

An Ouachita ovoid vase, embossed with berries and covered in matte green glaze, stamped 'OUACHITA HOT SPRINGS ARK' and incised 'S.E.S.'.

4.75in (12cm) high

$1,200-1,800 DRA

An Overbeck bulbous vase, deeply cut back with birds in flight and flora, in matte ivory on rose, and incised 'EH/OBK'.

5in (12.5cm) high

$6,000-8,000 DRA

An Owens Mission vase, with original oak stand, some flakes to paint, stamped 'OWENSART'.

11.5in (29.25cm) high

$1,800-2,200 CRA

A Pennsylvania Museum School of Industrial Arts squat vase, with carved neck, covered in mottled matte green glaze, and stamped 'PMSIA'.

6.5in (16.5cm) wide

$1,200-1,800 DRA

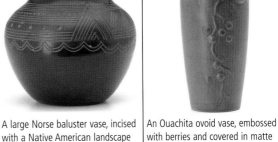

A rare embossed Redlands vessel, with a superior burnished glaze, and minor glaze flake to base, embossed 'Redlands Pottery' with tadpole.

3.5in (9cm) wide

$14,000-18,000 DRA

A Robertson (Los Angeles) small tapering vase, covered in blue and yellow crystalline glaze, stamped 'Los Angeles F. H. R'.

4.5in (11.5cm) high

$1,000-1,500 DRA

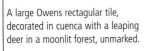

A large Owens rectagular tile, decorated in cuenca with a leaping deer in a moonlit forest, unmarked.

17.75in (45cm) wide

$3,500-4,500 DRA

A Henry Varnum Poor plate, incised and painted with a portrait of the artist's wife, Marion Dorn Poor, stamped floral Crow House mark, a few small nicks to rim.

Henry Varnum Poor (1888-1970) always considered himself primarily a painter, although his early commercial success was as a ceramic artist. He studied art at Stanford University, then in 1917 established a studio in San Francisco with his former student, Marion Dorn. He separated from his first wife, Lena Wiltz, and married Marion in 1919. They moved to Rockland County, New York that year, where he built a studio and home called Crow House. An image of the house became his pottery mark. In 1920 he began potting, for philosophical and practical reasons.

Marion Dorn (1896-1964) and Poor divorced in 1923. While married to Poor, she showed in the 'Exhibition of Industrial Art' at the Metropolitan Museum of Art. After divorcing Poor, she moved to London and continued a thriving career. She is best known for her carpet designs, which included carpets for Claridge's Hotel in London, the decorator Syrie Maugham, and the Diplomatic Reception Room of the White House. The British art connoisseur Harold Acton wrote of her work in Memoirs of an Aesthete (1948), 'Marion designed modernistic rugs which kept one's eyes riveted to the floor.'

8in (20cm) diam

$5,000-6,000   **CRA**

An Adelaide Robineau bud vase, covered in a fine amber crystalline glaze, minor grinding chips, signed 'AR' and circular stamp, restoration to 0.25in (0.5cm) chip under rim.

7in (17.5cm) high

$11,000-13,000   **DRA**

A tall, two-handled Rose Valley vase, covered in three-color matte flambé glaze, and 'Rose Valley' stamp/'RV' cipher, with flecks to rim, restoration around base.

14in (35.5cm) high

$4,000-5,000   **DRA**

A Frederick George Richard Roth squat stoneware lidded vessel, its base covered in gunmetal, indigo, and green flambé glaze, the sculptural lid modeled as a brown bear, each component signed 'FGRR', some chips and touch-ups.

The internationally renowned American sculptor, Frederick Roth, was born in Brooklyn in 1872. He was educated in Europe when his father's cotton business took the family to Germany. He learned sculpture in Vienna and in Berlin. He also learned pottery techniques at the Staffordshire potteries in England, and in Stuttgart, Germany, and for a time, modeled animal figures for the Doulton Potteries. He maintained a studio in New York from 1890, and participated in the St.Louis, 1904 and the Panama Pacific, 1915 Expositions. He taught at the National Academy, was President of the National Sculpture Society, and in 1925, won a major prize for a Central Park favorite, his statue of Siberian husky hero, Balto (the subject of a Disney movie). As chief sculptor for the New York City Parks Department from 1934 to 1936, he produced fountain statues and tile reliefs at the Central Park Zoo, Mother Goose near 72nd Street, and Alice in Wonderland, near 76th Street. His work is in the collections of the Metropolitan Museum of Art, the Detroit Institute of Arts, and Brookgreen Gardens. Morristown has his equestrian George Washington. He died in Englewood, NJ in 1944. His ceramics are extremely rare.

1920s   *11in (28cm) high*

$7,000-10,000   **CRA**

An extremely rare San Jose fifteen-tile panel, decorated in cuerda seca with a young man serenading a lady, in bright matte and semi-matte glazes, in near-mint condition, never mounted, unmarked, small glaze nick to one corner.

17.75in (45cm) wide

$20,000-25,000   **DRA**

ESSENTIAL REFERENCE: SHEARWATER

In 1928, Shearwater Pottery was founded in Ocean Springs, Mississippi, by Peter Anderson with the help of his parents, George Walter Anderson and Annette McConnell Anderson. The latter had studied at Newcomb and turned to her friend and professor, Mary Sheerer, for advice on glazing and firing.

● Though often similar to Newcomb in shape, Shearwater glazes were developed differently. Peter believed these would set it apart from other small potteries.

● The pottery later expanded to accommodate Peter's younger brothers, Walter Inglis and James McConnell, who became two of Shearwater's most important designers.

● Shearwater was severely damaged by Hurricane Katrina in 2005, but the workshop was rebuilt and the Anderson family continue to throw and decorate pottery to this day.

A Shearwater vase, embossed with pelicans under mottled blue and turquoise glaze, two tight lines to base, possibly from firing.

7in (17.5cm) high

$7,000-10,000   **DRA**

A Roblin Squat cabinet vase, with brown drips on a celadon flambé ground, and stamped 'ROBLIN/AWR'.

3.25in (8cm) wide

$2,000-2,500   **DRA**

A bulbous Annette and Paul St. Gaudens vase, with gun-metal glaze, incised signature and description, area of glaze scaling to rim.

1925   *10.5in (26.5cm) high*

$2,000-2,500   **DRA**

A Stangl Fish Hawk / Osprey large figure, no. 3459, impressed mark, excellent color, invisible restoration to line across one wing.

8.25in (21cm) high

$2,500-3,000   **DRA**

A rare small Steiger vase, carved with panels of Viking ships, covered in matte celadon glaze, and with circular stamp 'S.T.C./P.W.K'S'.

4in (10cm) wide

$2,000-2,500   **DRA**

A Strobl bell-shaped vase, covered in gun-metal glaze, and stamped 'SP 834'.

7in (18cm) high

$1,200-1,800   **DRA**

An L.C. Tiffany large ceramic vase covered in a rich matte green, amber and brown mottled glaze, several small chips around rim, incised 'LCT', etched 'P1233 L.C.Tiffany Favrile Pottery'.

16in (40.5cm) high

$4,000-5,000   **DRA**

An L.C. Tiffany small vase of white clay embossed with leaves covered in sheer amber glaze, restoration to base and rim, incised 'LCT'.

4.5in (11.5cm) high

$1,000-1,500   **DRA**

A University City spherical vessel, covered in celadon crystalline glaze, in orange ink 'C.U.1913'.

The University City Pottery (1910-15) was part of the American Woman's League. Talented members of the League were invited to University City to be taught by a notable group of ceramic artists and experts including Taxile Doat, Frederick H. Rhead, and Samuel and Adelaide Robineau. Their experiments determined that native clays were superior to the finest of Europe and were available in greater abundance. They also produced many noteworthy glazes. They won many prizes, including the Grand Prize at the International Exposition in 1911 at Turin, Italy.

5.25in (13.5cm) high

$18,000-22,000   **DRA**

A University City vase, attributed to Frederick Rhead, excised with stylized trees and covered in matte green glaze, incised 'UC 1911 5045'.

1911   *9in (23cm) high*

$5,000-8,000   **DRA**

An Albert Valentien baluster vase, embossed with stylized blossoms under an exceptional matte green alligatored glaze, with impressed cartouche and '321'.

Albert Valentien (1862-1925) became the first full-time decorator at Rookwood Pottery in 1881 and went on to control the decorating department. In 1887, he married Anna Marie Bookprinter, who was also a member of the department. The Valentiens left Rookwood in 1905, but remained in Cincinnati until 1908 when they moved to San Diego, California. There they set up the Valentien Pottery in c1911. Anna had tried unsuccessfully to interest Rookwood in sculptured designs inspired by Rodin, under whom she had studied. It was these designs, decorated with the then-popular matt finish, which were produced at the Valentien Pottery. In 1915 Albert was awarded a Silver Medal for his painting at the San Diego exposition. He did not exhibit any art pottery, and so it is assumed that all such work had ceased by this time.

8in (20cm) high

$4,000-5,000   **DRA**

A Frank X. Chamberlin / Salmagundi Club China-painted Volkmar mug, with Pierrot clowns, a snake handle, 'Eat, Drink, and be Merry,' to be read while drinking, and caricatures of twelve of its members on the bottom, artist's signature.

Founded in 1871 in New York as a sketching class, the Salmagundi became an artists' club which included artists like Frederick Church, George Inness, and Thomas Moran. Twenty-four mugs, provided by the Volkmar Pottery, were decorated every year, and sold at the library dinners to raise funds. The artist, Frank X. Chamberlin, was a New York-based magazine illustrator who did covers for Pearson's Magazine.

c1899-1910   6in (15cm) high

$1,500-2,000   **CRA**

A Volkmar bulbous vase, covered in matte green glaze, and incised 'Volkmar 1911'.

10.5in (26.5cm) high

$1,500-2,000   **DRA**

A Zark vase, covered in matte speckled turquoise and blue glaze, incised 'ZARK/J.A.C.'.

6in (15cm) high

$2,000-3,000   **DRA**

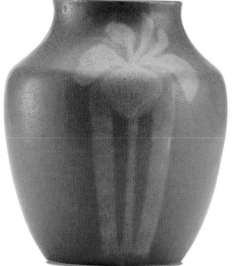

An exceptional Walrath bulbous vase, matte-painted with purple irises on long green stems against a deep green ground, incised 'Walrath Pottery'.

6.5in (16.5cm) high

$10,000-15,000   **DRA**

A rare Zark vase, matte-painted with stylized flora in black on dark green.

Zark Pottery was the name given to the art pottery produced by Robert Porter Bringhurst and the Ozark Pottery Company in St. Louis. The company, which was incorporated in 1906, was organised by Bringhurst, Clarence H. Howard and Arthur T. Morey, with the intention of dealing with all areas of pottery manufacture and distribution. Production started in 1907 and ended in 1910.

10in (25.5cm) high

$3,000-4,000   **DRA**

THE DECORATIVE ARTS MARKET

In the European Decorative Arts field, Arts & Crafts is the movement to watch, perhaps because it is a style that suits modern, more minimal interiors. Arts & Crafts pottery is selling well, in particular the big names such as the Martin Brothers and William de Morgan, and although prices for Pilkington's are levelling off they are still selling fairly well. The same can be said for the other stalwarts of the Arts & Crafts movement – the Tudric (pewter) and Cymric (silver) wares designed by Archibald Knox for Liberty & Co.

As far as Art Deco pottery is concerned, the work of Clarice Cliff continues to sell well. Its perennial popularity is perhaps due to the supply of fresh pieces which come onto the market every year and fetch good prices. At the same time there is a thriving collector's club and new books help to maintain interest levels.

Carlton Ware and Shelley have not had the same good fortune. This may be partly due to the perception that they need to be housed en mass in a display cabinet which is not fashionable at the moment. In comparison, pieces by Clarice Cliff, whose designs are more avant garde, can be shown singly to great effect. Prices for Art Deco figures by Lenci and Goldscheider continue to rise steadily and look set to go higher as more and more buyers are won over by their charms. Top prices continue to be paid for Wemyss ware, particularly pieces which are well painted, in bright colors and in perfect condition.

For any of these designers, any damage, especially to a relatively common piece, will lower values considerably.

The market for Continental Art Nouveau ceramics continues to be led by Zsolnay, particularly pieces which show fine moulding and exceptionally vibrant lustered glazing.

Furniture from the Arts & Crafts, Art Nouveau and Art Deco movements continues to sell well – especially if it is by a big name such as Émile Gallé or Émile-Jacques Ruhlmann. Pieces in the same style but without the 'hand of the master' are not doing as well, probably because buyers want a name and the cachet that goes with it. This has benefitted prices for pieces by lesser-known names, such as the Scottish Arts & Crafts designer Sir Robert Lorimer, which are performing above expectations.

In glass, the market for Whitefriars has levelled off over the past three or four years. However, rare pieces of Whitefriars – especially the designs of Geoffrey Baxter – continue to achieve high prices at auction.

Glass by the Art Deco master – René Lalique – is particularly strong at the moment. The same can be said for the cameo glass of Émile Gallé and Daum Freres as buyers continue to appreciate – and pay good prices for – the skilled craftsmanship of both factories' cameo glass. Perhaps, again, this is because displayed individually and in a good light, this glass can be the centerpiece of any room.

A Boch Frères large ovoid vase, enamel-decorated with floral bands in crackled glazes, stamped 'MADE IN BELGIUM/BOCH Fes./FABRICATION BELGE'.

20in (51cm) high

$5,000-6,000 SDR

A large Boch Frères vase, by Charles Catteau, with stylized blossoms, stamped 'Ch. Catteau/Made in Belgium/951 WD962'.

14in (35.5cm) high

$3,600-4,400 SDR

ESSENTIAL REFERENCE: BURMANTOFTS

Burmantofts Pottery was established by William Wilcock and John Lassey in the Burmantofts district of Leeds, Yorkshire in 1845. It was originally a brick and pipe factory.

- In 1879, the pottery passed to James Holroyd who started the production of 'architectural faïence'. The company began producing vases, jardinières, etc in the 1880s.
- In 1888, the company opened its own showroom in London and changed its name to The Burmantofts Company. The following year Burmantofts merged with five other Yorkshire companies to form the Leeds Fireclay Company.
- Early Burmantofts pottery was plain, including bulbous vases, with long slender necks. Later designs are more ornate. More ambitious glazes were used, with sgraffito decoration. The use of applied insects and serpents was popular.
- In 1904, the factory reverted mainly to production of architectural pieces. Production finally ceased in 1957.

A Bough three-handled luster tyg, decorated by Elizabeth Amour, the cylindrical body painted with garlands of fruit and bearing inscription 'Peep Through Their Stars Tonight I'll Make The Wine', painted marks, dated.

1920 *8in (20cm) high*

$2,000-2,400 L&T

A Brannam Pottery twin-handled vase, modeled with reptile handles, the body incised with scaly fish, incised 'WB C H Brannam, Barum 1907', minor glaze nicks.

8.5in (21.5cm) high

$600-700 WW

A Burmantofts faïence Persian vase, designed by Leonard King, painted with carnations, in shades of blue, aubergine and green on a white ground, impressed and painted marks, 'LK' monogram.

9.5in (24cm) high

$5,000-6,000 WW

A Burmantofts faïence Persian vase, designed by Leonard King, design 85, impressed marks, painted monogram, minor glaze loss.

9.75in (25cm) high

$1,400-1,600   WW

A rare Burmantofts faïence vase, designed by Leonard King, painted with birds amongst scrolling foliage, in ruby luster on a white ground, impressed marks, painted 'LK' monogram.

14.5in (36.5cm) high

$1,600-3,200   WW

A Burmantofts faïence Persian vase, designed by Leonard King, design 91, painted with mythical beasts, impressed and painted marks, 'LK' monogram, minor damages.

9in (23cm) high

$1,400-1,800   WW

A Burmantofts faïence vase, of waisted form and decorated with a continuous scene of entwined scaly dragons within a woodland setting, impressed 'Burmantofts Faïence England 2197' and black painted 'Col. 118/10'.

8.75in (22cm) high

$600-800   HALL

A Carlton Ware 'Chinaland' ginger jar and cover, printed and painted in gilt and colored enamels, printed and painted marks, 2948.

5.5in (14cm) high

$720-800   L&T

A Carlton Ware 'Fan' vase, shouldered ovoid form with applied lugs, printed and painted in gilt and colored enamels, printed and painted marks.

9.75in (25cm) high

$500-600   L&T

A Carlton Ware 'Parkland' vase, printed and painted in gilt and colored enamels, printed and painted marks, 3523.

6in (15cm) high

$1,100-1,500   L&T

A limited edition Clarice Cliff exhibition poster, from an edition of 250, illegibly signed.

$300-400   SK

A Carlton Ware 'Anemone' Handcraft bowl, printed and painted in gilt and colored enamels, printed and painted marks, 3694.

9in (23cm) across

$600-800   L&T

A Clarice Cliff 'Green Erin' pattern Bizarre Lynton coffee service, comprising a coffee pot, sugar basin, cream jug and four cups and saucers.

$3,000-4,400   GHOU

A Clarice Cliff Bizarre pottery teapot, of conical form, painted in the 'Gayday' design, the domed lid with oblong finial, triangular loop handle, black mark including 'Registration applied for' mark.

9.75in (25cm) wide

$800-1,200 HT

A Clarice Cliff Bizarre 'Yellow Cowslip' pattern 'Bon Jour' preserve and cover, painted in colors, printed mark, chips.

4.5in (11.5cm) high

$800-1,000 WW

A Clarice Cliff 'Rhodanthe' wall charger, painted in colors, printed mark.

16.5in (42cm) diam.

$700-900 WW

A Clarice Cliff Fantasque Bizarre 'Summerhouse' cylindrical preserve pot, painted in colors, printed mark, chip to inside rim.

3in (7.5cm) high

$200-300 WW

A Clarice Cliff Bizarre 'Crocus' pattern 'Athens' jug, painted with orange crocuses above green band, printed mark, minor restoration to foot rim.

6in (15cm) high

$240-300 WW

A Clarice Cliff Bizarre 'Newport' pattern shape '200' vase, painted in colors, printed mark.

7.5in (19cm) high

$1,300-1,500 WW

A Clarice Cliff Bizarre 'Forest Glen' pattern 'Daffodil' shape flower vase, shape no. 450, painted in colors, and a flower brick, printed marks.

13in (33cm) wide

$1,000-1,200 WW

A Clarice Cliff Fantasque Bizarre 'Windbells' part tea set, painted in colors, comprising teapot and cover, one cup, saucer and side plate, printed mark, old restoration to spout.

4.75in (12cm) high

$1,100-1,300 WW

A Clarice Cliff Bizarre 'Autumn' pattern 'Stamford' shape tea for two, comprising teapot and cover, milk jug and sugar basin, two cups, saucers and a side plate, printed marks, small chip to spout of teapot and a nick to the rim of one cup.

5in (13cm) high

$2,800-3,600 WW

ESSENTIAL REFERENCE: WILLIAM DE MORGAN

William de Morgan (1839-1917) was a stained glass designer before he became interested in ceramics.

- His work often includes stylized and grotesque flora and fauna inspired by medieval Persian, Moorish and Greek designs. These motifs are usually perfectly related to the shapes on which they are painted. These include decorative plates, vases, and, De Morgan's speciality, tiles.
- De Morgan's forms are painted either in luster, predominantly ruby and copper, or in 'Persian' colors, predominantly green, black, and turquoise.
- De Morgan initially painted blanks for other companies. In 1882, he began producing his own ceramics after relocating to William Morris's Merton Abbey Workshops.
- From 1892, he spent the winters in Florence where he worked for Cantagalli.
- He retired in 1907.

A Crown Devon large 'Fairy Castle' vase, painted and printed in gilt and colored enamels on a jade green ground, printed and painted marks '2406'.

15in (38cm) high

$1,600-2,400 L&T

A William De Morgan bowl, painted with a frieze of peacocks and serpents amongst apple trees, in ruby and sand luster, unmarked, hairline to top rim.

13in (33cm) diam.

$4,800-5,600 WW

A William De Morgan charger, painted to the well with a dragon and serpent roundel, the rim with Classical trumpeters in ruby luster, unmarked, restored.

17.25in (44cm) diam.

$2,600-3,200   **WW**

CLOSER LOOK: WILLIAM DE MORGAN VASE AND COVER

The cover is modeled with stiff leaf foliage and a bud finial

The two handles are modeled as winged grotesques, each with twin scrolled fish tails.

The vase and cover are decorated with a ruby and copper luster glaze.

The vase is molded in relief with bands of stylized scaly fish.

The design is similar to the two Livadia vases de Morgan made for the Tsar of Russia – either for his summer palace or his yacht.

A large William De Morgan 'Livadia' vase and cover, by Fred Passenger, 'FP' monogram, final off, chips.

15in (38cm) high

$22,000-30,000   **WW**

A William De Morgan vase, painted with panels of flowers and scrolling foliate in ruby luster, unmarked, repaired neck.

11.25in (28.5cm) high

$1,100-1,600   **WW**

A William De Morgan ruby and copper luster vase, painted with birds before stylized foliage, on a white ground, impressed Fulham tulip mark, glazed nick to top rim.

8.25in (21cm) high

$6,000-8,000   **WW**

A William De Morgan solifleur vase, painted with sprays of flowers and foliate, in ruby and copper luster on a white ground, unsigned.

8.25in (21cm) high

$1,800-2,200   **WW**

A William De Morgan Persian pedestal bowl, by Charles Passenger, painted with carnations, in shades of blue, aubergine, green and white, painted 'W. DE. MORGAN', 'CP' monogram, light hairline to rim.

4in (10.5cm) diam.

$1,000-1,200   **WW**

A William De Morgan twin-handled vase, by Joe Luster, painted with three birds above a crown and two crossed birds, impressed Sand's End roundel, painted 'JJ' mark, professionally restored neck and handles.

10in (25.5cm) high

$4,000-5,000   **WW**

A late Fulham period William de Morgan six tile panel, Mongolian pattern, each painted in the Persian palette with flowerheads and leaves, impressed marks.

Each tile 6in (15.5cm) across

$1,400-1,800   **L&T**

A William De Morgan 'Single Rose (Wild Rose)' tile, painted in shades of blue and green on a white ground, impressed 'Merton Abbey' mark, minor frits.

6in (15.5cm) square

$600-700   **WW**

A William De Morgan 'Chicago' tile, painted with two flowerheads in shades of blue, purple, green and brown on a blue ground, impressed tulip mark, minor rim chips.

8in (20.5cm) square

$1,900-2,200   **WW**

A William De Morgan 'Bedford Park Daisy' tile, painted with alternating panels of daisy and foliage sprays in shades of green, blue and yellow, impressed 'WD Morgan', restored chip to corner.

8.25in (21cm) square

$1,100-1,600 **WW**

A William De Morgan pottery tile, painted with two Chameleons, in shades of blue and green, impressed 'Sand's End' mark.

6in (15cm) wide

$8,000-9,000 **WW**

A William De Morgan six-tile panel, painted with an owl above a crescent moon amidst carnation flowers, in colors, on a blue ground, impressed Merton Abbey mark, framed.

18in (46cm) wide

$26,000-30,000 **WW**

A large De Porceleyne Fles tile panel, by Den Hoed, depicting a bird on 25 tiles, mounted on masonite, signed 'CD' with De Porceleyne Fles mark, and 'DELFT'.

28in (71cm) square

$2,000-3,000 **SDR**

An Auguste Delaherche bulbous four-handled vase, covered in mottled blue-green and brown glossy glaze, with circular stamp and '6860'.

7.25in (18.5cm) high

$1,300-1,500 **DRA**

An Auguste Delaherche large bulbous vase incised with bands of fruiting branches alternating with oxblood and indigo glaze, circular stamp 'AUGUSTE DELAHERCHE 1138'.

13.5in (34cm) high

$7,000-8,000 **DRA**

A Della Robbia pottery vase and cover, by 'LW', incised and painted with mice running and resting and holding up lanterns with their tails, in shades of green, cream and blue, incised and painted marks, incised 'Shirley', minor professional restoration.

6in (15cm) high

$1,700-2,000 **WW**

A Doulton Lambeth pottery vase, by Florence Barlow and Eliza Simmance, depicting a roundel of grouse with a beaded surround within foliate scroll borders in pale green, navy, blue and brown.

12.5in (32cm) high

$1,000-1,200 **HT**

A Doulton Lambeth stoneware Scotch whisky dispenser, decorated in shades of blue, green and ochre.

17in (43cm) high

$1,500-1,700 **GORL**

A Doulton Lambeth stoneware vase, by Hannah Barlow, sgraffito with ponies and cattle within beaded and stiff leaf banding, marks also for Emily Stomer.

11in (28cm) high

$1,500-1,700 **HT**

A pair of Royal Doulton stoneware vases, by Hannah Barlow, incised with a band of resting deer, between foliate borders, in shades of green, brown and white on a buff ground, impressed marks, incised monogram.

13.75in (35cm) high

$6,000-7,000 **WW**

A large early Doulton Lambeth stoneware vase, by Hannah Barlow, incised with a scene of running deer, the reverse deer at rest, between bands of incised and applied scrolling foliage, incised 'HB' to the body, impressed mark, dated, restored top rim.

1874   *17.25in (44cm) high*

$6,000-7,000   **WW**

A pair of Doulton Lambeth stoneware vases, by Hannah Barlow, incised with resting, grazing and galloping horses, between foliate bands, impressed mark, incised monogram and datemark, minor glaze nicks to base rim.

9.75in (25cm) high

$2,800-3,600   **WW**

A large Doulton Lambeth vase, by Hannah Barlow, with a high flared-collar neck decorated to the body with a deep scrafitto band of sheep in a landscape setting between interlaced scrolled borders, incised and impressed marks.

17in (43cm) high

$2,600-3,200   **FLD**

A large pair of Doulton Lambeth vases, by Edith Lupton, with a flared-collar neck decorated with hand-carved scrolled convolvulus between repeat pattern borders, incised and impressed marks.

12in (30.5cm) high

$2,000-2,600   **FLD**

A pair of tall Doulton Lambeth vases, by Florence Barlow, with high flared-collar necks decorated with pâte-sur-pâte birds in flight over an incised scrolled ground between foliate scrolled borders, incised and impressed marks.

11.5in (29.5cm) high

$2,800-3,600   **FLD**

A large Doulton Lambeth jardinière, of shouldered ovoid form, by Hannah Barlow, with a shallow collar neck decorated with a deep central band of sgrafitto decorated cattle in a landscape setting, between banded borders, incised and impressed marks.

13in (34cm) high

$2,200-3,000   **FLD**

A Royal Doulton Chinese jade figure of two cockatoos, designed by Charles Noke, painted in shades of green and white, printed and painted marks.

4.5in (11.5cm) high

$2,000-2,600   **WW**

A pair of late 19th/early 20thC Fulham Pottery stoneware bowls, probably designed by J. P. Seddon, each with brown glaze molded scroll, stylized floral and foliate decoration, impressed marks.

9in (22.5cm) high

$700-900   **L&T**

A Ludwig Gies 'Moon Sheep' glazed porcelain figure, model number 28809.

1926   *13.25in (33.5cm) high*

$6,000-7,000   **VZ**

A Goldscheider hanging double mask of a woman holding a black mask, with restoration to tight line around hanging hole, and stamped 'Goldscheider/Wien/Made in Austria'.

13.75in (35cm) high

$800-1,200   **SDR**

A Goldscheider figure of Diana, designed by Louis Marie Latour, model no. 4310, painted in colors, impressed marks, artist signature, repaired dog's tail, missing bow.

32.25in (59cm) high

$600-1,000   **WW**

A Goldscheider porcelain figure, 'Austrian Country Girl' by Josef Lorenzl, painted in colors, bears paper label, impressed marks with stamped signature, no. '7228/ 62/ 31'.

8.25in (21cm) high

$400-500   **L&T**

A Goldscheider pottery figural lamp, modeled as a night watchman, wearing a helmet and holding aloft a lantern, on shaped base, signed 'Latour', impressed 'No 3144.152.14'.

34in (86.5cm) high

$1,900-2,200   HT

A large 1930's Goldscheider figure of a female in Spanish style dress, with long flowing lace-effect dress and open fan raised to an oval base, small restoration to hair comb.

17.5in (45cm) high

$2,000-2,400   FLD

A large 1930's Dakon-Goldscheider figure of a Dolly Sister, with arms outstretched behind, dressed in a short bat-winged costume with cloche hat, in green and black-painted finish all set to a shaped base, molded signature with printed marks.

16in (41cm) high

$1,400-2,000   FLD

A Hammersmith stoneware figure, 'The Bull', designed by Harold and Phoebe Stabler, painted in colors, impressed Hammersmith Bridge mark, incised 'Potted by Harold Stabler', reverse signed 'Harold and Phoebe Stabler'.

1914   13in (33cm) high

$4,000-5,000   WW

A Hammersmith Bridge 'Buster Girl' figure, designed by Phoebe Stabler, painted in colors with bright pink bonnet and ribbon, impressed bridge mark, signature and pencil signature 'Grace Nelson'.

The figure also bears the unusual inscription: 'The Workshop, First Kiln Hammersmith Terr. London 1910'.

1910   7.25in (18.5cm) high

$1,100-1,300   WW

A Hancock & Son Morrisware vase, designed by George Cartlidge, tubeline decorated with red bell flowers, model C18-5, printed mark, painted facsimile signature, cracked.

9.75in (24.5cm) high

$700-800   WW

A rare Hancock & Sons Morrisware pot pourri, 'Essence of Past Summers', model C56-1, designed by Georges Cartlidge, tubelined with red roses on a green ground, printed mark, painted green facsimile signature, cover repaired.

8.75in (22cm) high

$1,400-1,600   WW

A George Jones pâte-sur-pâte plaque, designed by Frederick Schenk, decorated with two young girls by a lily pond, fringed with aquatic plants, on a charcoal ground, impressed factory mark.

c1880   12in (30.5cm) diam.

$900-1,000   WW

A Keramos figure of crouching lady, decorated in skin tone enamel, with printed marks to foot.

17.75in (45cm) high

$500-600   L&T

A Lenci ceramic figure, of a girl with skis, standing with hands on hips, wearing a headscarf and with original wooden ski poles, the whole raised on lozenge base, painted marks.

17.25in (43.5cm) high

$6,000-7,000   L&T

A Lenci, 'Ski Figure', painted in colored enamels and raised on a lozenge-shaped base (crack to base), painted marks 'Lenci/ Made in Italy/ FV/ 697', bears paper label.

17in (43cm) high

$7,000-8,000   L&T

A Linthorpe pottery vase, model no.415, designed by Dr Christopher Dresser, with geometric pane under a running olive-green and white glaze, impressed mark, facsimile signature.

8.75in (22cm) high

$1,100-1,300   **WW**

A Linthorpe pottery ewer, model no.957, designed by Dr Christopher Dresser, dome form, with angular handle, covered in a running olive, brown and white glaze, impressed marks, facsimile signature 'HT' monogram, professional restoration to rims.

6.25in (16cm) high

$1,900-2,200   **WW**

CLOSER LOOK: DRESSER VASE

Christopher Dresser (1834-1904) was the first industrial designer. He used design elements from other cultures and from nature to create his designs.

He created hundreds of distinctive designs for the Linthorpe Pottery, many covered in streaky glazes.

This vase is a tube form with central pierced foliate roundel.

Pieces are impressed with his facsimile signature and the initials 'HT' for Henry Tooth, the pottery manager.

A rare Linthorpe pottery vase, designed by Dr Christopher Dresser, impressed marks, facsimile signature.

8.75in (22cm) high

$3,400-4,000   **WW**

A late 19thC Copeland majolica jardinière stand, with a continuous frieze of molded Classical figures, between bands of molded floral swags, impressed mark.

24.75in (63cm) high

$2,000-2,400   **L&T**

A late 19thC Goldscheider majolica terracotta figure of a Nubian boy, holding out a wickerwork tray, wearing a straw hat and striped open neck shirt, on an integral canted plinth base.

27.75in (71cm) high

$14,000-16,000   **L&T**

An English majolica oval jardinière, hung with swags upon which putti sit, impressed mark for Joseph Holdcroft, some damages, together with a large majolica stand.

c1880   *32in (81cm) high on stand*

$1,100-1,300   **WW**

A George Jones majolica jardinière stand, in the form of a rustic garden seat, with circular top above three branch-form concave legs decorated with molded leaves, with central rope-form support on shaped triform base.

17.75in (45cm) high

$1,400-2,000   **L&T.**

A large 19thC George Jones ovoid majolica jardiniére, with yellow scalloped rim above dark blue body decorated with molded birds and flowers, the three feet formed from molded leaf forms, the interior turquoise glazed, impressed monogram.

18.25in (46cm) diam

$9,000-11,000   **L&T**

A George Jones majolica sardine dish and cover, with a blue-glazed basketweave molded base, the cover molded with leaves, sardine finial, yellow rims.

c1875   *8.25in (21cm) wide*

$800-1,200   **DN**

A Minton majolica chestnut dish, with a metal fitting to the center, some restoration, impressed marks and date code.

1871   *11.5in (29cm) wide*

$600-1,000   **WW**

A Minton majolica sardine dish and cover, the turquoise ground body molded with seaweed, the cover molded with three fishes, fish finial, brown rims, impressed marks, shape 1383.

8.75in (22cm) diam

$700-900   **DN**

A large Minton majolica stick stand, modeled as a heron standing on one leg and holding a wriggling fish in its beak, before a clump of bullrushes, raised on a circular base, signed by Paul Comolera, impressed marks and date code, damages and old restoration.

Paul Comolera (1818-97) was born in Paris, France. He was a fine sculptor known mainly for his birds in bronze.

1877   *40.5in (103cm) high*

$10,000-12,000   **WW**

A 19thC Sarreguemines majolica jardinière and stand, supported by three high-relief griffons and decorated with leaves and foliage, the circular stand with scalloped edge decorated with lion heads and foliage, impressed marks 'B majolica Sarreguemines 426'

15.75in (40cm) diam

$2,000-2,600   **L&T**

A Wedgwood majolica pie dish, the sides molded and painted with hanging birds amidst a grape vine, the lid with various game animals and a rabbit finial, some good restoration.

c1870   *10.5in (26.5cm) diam.*

$600-1,000   **WW**

A Wedgwood majolica game pie dish, molded with birds, flowers and foliage, some restoration, impressed marks including date code.

1872   *9.5in (24.5cm) high*

$600-800   **WW**

A pair of Royal Worcester majolica wall pockets, each modeled as a nest beneath a branch, with a bird perched on the side, impressed marks, one heavily restored.

c1875   *8.25in (21cm) high*

$600-1,000   **WW**

A late 19thC majolica model of an elephant, standing four-square with a castle upon its back, unmarked, the base broken across the front foot and reglued.

7.5in (19.5cm) high

$600-800   **WW**

A 19thC majolica teapot in the shape of an apple, a twig forming the handle and spout, the knop molded as a wren watching a fly, minor damages.

This exceptional price for a majolica teapot is due to the unusual shape and detailing – particularly the knop with the small wren watching a fly. Rarity and a whimsical subject are very appealing to collectors.

6.25in (16cm) high

$10,000-14,000   **WW**

A majolica tazza, molded with a horse chestnut leaf.

c1870   *9in (23cm) high*

$180-240   **WW**

A majolica sardine dish and cover, decorated with mottled brown and green glazes, unmarked, minor damages.

c1870,

8.5in (22cm) high

$400-600   **WW**

A 20thC majolica bear jug, with a pale brown glaze, the nose, ears and eyes painted black, painted registration and US patent mark.

7.75in (20cm) high

$70-110   **WW**

A 19thC majolica cachepot, the sides decorated with stags and hounds, the edges molded as bamboo, unmarked, damages.

8.5in (22cm) high

$400-600   **WW**

A Martin Brothers stoneware grotesque jar and cover, restoration to head, lid signed 'RW Martin & Brothers, London & Southall, 6-1888', base signed 'RW Martin Southall S. L.'.

1888   With stand: 8in (20.5cm) high

$16,000-20,000   **DRA**

A Martin Brothers stoneware vase, incised and painted with thistle on an amber ground, signed '11-1905 Martin Bros London & Southall'.

1905   10.25in (26cm) high

$3,000-4,000   **DRA**

A Martin Brothers stoneware vase, decorated with a floral pattern in the Renaissance style, restoration to neck and rim, marked '7-1888 RW Martin Bros London & Southall'.

1888   7.75in (20cm) high

$3,600-4,400   **DRA**

A Martin Brothers stoneware vase decorated with dragons, marked '7-1901 Martin Bros London & Southall'.

1901   11.5in (29cm) high

$1,200-1,800   **DRA**

A Martin Brothers stoneware grotesque spoon warmer, covered in cobalt and teal matte glaze, signed 'Martin London & Southall'.

9in high

$6,600-8,000   **DRA**

A Martin Brothers jardinière, painted with scrolling foliage and seed heads, incised marks to base, 'Martin Bros./ London & Southall/ 1-1896'.

1896   9.75in (25cm) high

$1,000-1,500   **L&T**

CLOSER LOOK: MARTIN BROTHERS BIRD JAR

The pottery is covered with a tonal blue to salt-glazed decoration. They are often called 'barrister birds'.

The bird is modeled with a sideways glance, a smiling expression, and a quizzical look.

The Martin Brothers produced a series of these birds – each one with its own personality.

Both the jar and cover bear the signature 'R.W. Martin & Bros London and Southall 11-1911'.

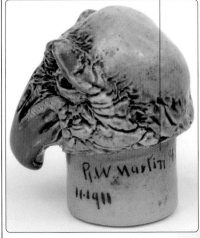

A Martin Brothers stoneware bird jar and cover, by Robert Wallace Martin, raised to a turned ebonized base.

1911   8in (21.5cm) high

$20,000-28,000   **FLD**

A Martin Brothers stoneware vase, incised and painted with magnolia flowers, in shades of white and ochre, incised marks and '1-1888 Martin Brothers London & Southall', repaired base.

1888   8in (20cm) high

$1,200-1,600   **WW**

A Martin Brothers stoneware vase, incised and painted with ferocious fighting dragons in shades of brown on a buff ground, incised '8-1894 Martin Bros, London & Southall'.

1894   8in (20cm) high

$7,000-9,000   **WW**

A large Martin Brothers sun mask jug, with a narrow-collar neck and lipped spout, decorated with a high relief sun mask below the spout over a patterned ground with tonal blue and ochre glazed finish, incised marks to the base.

1896   11.5in (29.5cm) high

$5,000-6,000   **FLD**

DECORATIVE ARTS

A Clement Massier twisted bud vase, with applied silver peapod vine on a lustered ceramic ground, a few very small nicks to top and bottom, signed 'C. M. Golfe Juan'.

6in (15cm) high

$1,000-1,500   **DRA**

A Mettlach Art Nouveau charger, by R. Thevenin, with a maiden picking irises in the forest, marked 'METTLACH VB GEGH... NACHBILDUNG GESCHUTZT 2547, R. Thevenin'.

15.75 in (40cm) diam.

$3,400-4,000   **DRA**

A rare Minton Art Pottery moonflask, designed by Dr Christopher Dresser, decorated with a stylized bird with an olive branch in its beak, enameled in colors on a terracotta ground, impressed marks, date code, with minor rim chips.

1867   *6in (15.5cm) high*

$12,000-14,000   **WW**

A 19thC Mintons stoneware bread plate, designed by AWN Pugin, the border decorated in blue with 'Waste not want not', impressed marks.

14in (35cm) diam

$1,200-1,600   **L&T**

A Minton charger, decorated with a kingfisher perched upon water lily leaves with butterflies and insects, within a Persian style border of scrolling flowers and foliage, picked out in tones of blue, turquoise, puce, green and yellow, impressed codes for 'November 1873' and marked 'D/15'.

1873   *15.75in (40cm) diam.*

$500-700   **HALL**

A large Minton Aesthetic Movement moonflask and cover, decorated in gilt with a dragon and pomegranate mon to both sides, on a purple ground, impressed marks, restored collar rim.

13in (33cm) high

$300-400   **WW**

A Minton Pottery charger, printed and painted with Classical figures riding a dolphin, impressed and printed marks.

87.75in (34.5cm) diam.

$240-300   **WW**

A Minton Aesthetic Movement moonflask, painted with panels by William Wise (c.1831-1889), impressed Minton marks, datemark, signed to the panels 'W Wise', hairlines to neck, minor repair to neck at shoulder.

1877   *10.25in (26cm) high*

$1,000-1,200   **WW**

A pair of Minton cloisonné jugs, ovoid form with loop handles, painted in colors and gilt on a pale blue ground with stylized flowers and foliage, unmarked, light wear to gilt.

5.75in (14.5cm) high

$700-900   **WW**

A pair of Minton cloisonné vases, designed by Dr Christopher Dresser, on integral stands, enameled in colors and gilt on a pink ground, impressed marks.

8.5in (21.5cm) high

$2,400-3,000   WW

A Minton cloisonné tea caddy and cover, painted with flowers and Chinese characters in colors and gilt on a salmon pink ground, unmarked.

In 1859, the Japanese ports reopened for trade, which caused a craze for all things Japanese in the Western world. Minton & Co. made porcelain copies of cloisonné wares with rich turquoise/pink enamel backgrounds with designs outlined in gold. Many were designed by Christopher Dresser (1834-1904). His designs were angular and modern, inspired by the 19thC Aesthetic Movement.

4.25in (10.5cm) high

$600-800   WW

ESSENTIAL REFERENCE: MOORCROFT

William Moorcroft (1872-1945)

● In 1897, James Macintyre & Co. established a design studio within its works headed by William Moorcroft. 'Aurelian' vases were printed patterns, whilst 'Florianware' was decorated in the emerging Art Nouveau style.

● In 1904, Moorcroft won a gold medal at the St. Louis International Exhibition. Afterwards, he insisted on adding his own initials or signature to the pottery that he designed, and overseeing the production of his work.

● Moorcroft resigned to establish his own company in 1912, with financial assistance from Liberty & Co. By this time, Moorcroft's patterns were simpler and bolder, usually with dark grounds and a clear glossy glaze. These included 'Pomegranate', 'Wisteria' and Hazeldine'.

● Queen Mary, a keen collector of Moorcroft's works, granted him a royal appointment in 1929. Shortly before William's death, his eldest son, Walter, took control of the pottery business, which was awarded another Royal Appointment in 1946.

● The pottery is still operating today.

A Moorcroft Florianware bowl with scalloped rim, decorated with anemones and poppies, printed mark, signed in green and with retailer's mark 'Made for J.W. Bridge Ltd, Accrington'.

c1902   *9in (23cm) diam.*

$1,300-1,700   L&T

A Moorcroft Florianware vase, of waisted form with two loop handles, tube lined with harebells on a white ground, signed to base over printed Florian mark.

c1902-04   *9.75in (25cm) high*

$3,600-4,400   HT

A Moorcroft Florianware miniature vase, the flattened ovoid body with tall neck and frilled rim, decorated with anemones and poppies on a white ground, printed factory mark, signed in green, retailers mark.

c1902   *6in (15cm) high*

$1,800-2,400   L&T

A James Macintyre & Co. Florianware vase, by William Moorcroft, with narrow-collar neck decorated in a version of the 'Peacock' pattern in blue, green and yellow over a two-tone blue ground between scale borders, printed marks and full green painted flash signature.

c1900-02   *10.5in (27cm) high*

$4,000-5,000   FLD

A James Macintyre 'Alhambra' vase, designed by William Moorcroft, painted in shades of salmon pink, red and blue, highlighted in gilt, printed mark.

c1903   *11.25in (28.5cm) high*

$2,200-3,000   WW

DECORATIVE ARTS

A large James Macintyre & Co. twin-handled footed bowl, designed by William Moorcroft, radially decorated in the 'Ochre Tulip and Forget-Me-Not' pattern, full green-painted signature.

This pattern was registered in 1898.

12in (31cm) wide

$3,600-4,400 FLD

A pair of Moorcroft Macintyre gourd-shaped vases, decorated with 'Revived Cornflower' or 'Brown Chrysanthemum' design within foliated cartouches, on mottled green and brown ground, green signature.

This is a good pair in a rare shape in excellent condition.

c1912 *4.75in (12cm) high*

$9,000-10,000 A&G

A pair of Moorcroft vases, by William Moorcroft, in the 'Late Florian' pattern, impressed marks and green painted flash signature.

The 'Late Florian' designs were made from c1918 and were popular through the 1920s and 30s. The exquisitely drawn poppies and tulips, with intricate surface patterns, were augmented by the use of strong, rich colors.

15in (38cm) high

$4,800-5,600 FLD

CLOSER LOOK: MOORCROFT TEA KETTLE

Unusual, rare shape, particularly collectable in an early pattern.

The kettle has an integral spout and high arched handle.

It is decorated in the 'Claremont' pattern over a tonal green and ochre ground. All Moorcroft's wares were handmade and the naturalistic designs were painted in raised slip.

It bears green painted flash signature, with marks for Shreve & Co, San Francisco.

A James Macintyre & Co. tea kettle, by William Moorcroft, small chip to tip of the spout.

c1905 *6.5in (17cm) high*

$9,000-10,000 FLD

A large James Macintyre & Co vase, designed by William Moorcroft, decorated in the 'Revived Cornflower' or 'Brown Chrysanthemum' pattern.

In August 1913 Moorcroft moved to Cobridge, he was still producing many of the MacIntyre patterns. The Moorcroft signature became larger and increasingly significant.

1910-13 *10in (26cm) high*

$8,000-9,000 FLD

A large James Macintyre & Co. jardinière, designed by William Moorcroft, decorated in the 'Celadon Pomegranate' pattern over a pale jade green ground, green painted flash signature.

The 'Pomegranate' design was introduced in 1910.

8in (20cm) high

$4,800-5,600 FLD

A William Moorcroft biscuit box and cover, decorated in the 'Claremont' pattern, impressed marks.

This pattern was registered in October 1903. It proved extremely popular and continued in production when Moorcroft opened his factory in Cobridge in 1913. This piece is a rare shape.

c1913-16 *6.5in (17cm) high*

$7,000-8,000 FLD

A William Moorcroft pedestal bowl, with high arched handles, decorated to the whole in the 'Pomegranate' pattern over ochre ground, painted signature, marked 'November 1913'.

5in (13cm) high

$4,400-5,200 FLD

A William Moorcroft biscuit box and cover, of rounded cube form, with applied twin loop handles and arched cover handle, decorated in the 'Pomegranate' pattern, over green to ochre color ground.

6.5in (17cm) high

$2,600-3,200 FLD

A William Moorcroft bowl, the exterior bears a band of Latin verse 'Vincit Omnia Veritas' (Truth conquers all) in tonal blue with light flambé glaze, impressed marks and blue painted flash signature.

5in (12.5cm)

$4,000-5,000 FLD

A William Moorcroft tea kettle, in the 'Spanish' pattern, full green painted flash signature, high small hairline to the base.

The Spanish design was introduced in 1910 and remained in production until the 1930's.

8in (20.5cm) high

$3,600-4,400 **FLD**

A pair of large Moorcroft baluster vases, each decorated in the 'Pomegranate' pattern, impressed marks, signed in green.

12.5in (32cm) high

$3,600-4,400 **L&T**

A 1930's Moorcroft ovoid vase, decorated in the 'Pansies' pattern, impressed marks, signed in green.

7 in (18cm) high

$1,200-1,600 **L&T**

A Moorcroft bowl and cover, to commemorate the coronation of Queen Elizabeth and King George VI, on blue and gray ground, impressed marks.

1937 5.25in (13cm) high

$600-700 **A&G**

An American Matt Morgan Art Pottery urn vase, decorated with a painted duck perched on a rock in front of a lake.

The Matt Morgan Art Pottery of Cincinnati, Ohio operated from 1882-1884. Before founding his own company, English-born artist Morgan had worked for a number of years as head of the lithographic department at Strobridge & Co., and worked briefly at the Dayton Porcelain Pottery.

12in (30.5cm) high

$6,000-7,000 **ANT**

A Bernard Moore vase, with roll collar neck decorated with a Viking long boat to rough seas in tonal luster glazes, with applied enamel and gilded highlights, painted signature.

7in (18cm) high

$2,000-2,600 **FLD**

A Bernard Moore cylindrical vase, decorated in flambé with panels of flowers printed marks.

9.5in (24.5cm) high

$600-700 **WW**

A Bernard Moore bowl, inscribed 'Fond Memory Brings The Light of Other Days', with scrolling carnation flowers, printed mark.

10in (25cm) diam

$1,200-1,600 **WW**

A Nippon urn, painted with farm and lake landscapes on both sides, the body pink and ivory with gilded details and handles, minor wear to gilt, green Nippon stamp.

16.5in (42cm) high

$1,500-1,700 **CRA**

A Pilkington's Lancastrian vase, designed by Richard Joyce, painted with a deer amongst cypress trees, in ruby and copper luster, impressed mark, painted artist cipher, datemark.

1914 6.25in (16cm) high

$2,000-3,000 **WW**

A Pilkington's Lancastrian solifleur vase, designed by William S. Mycock, painted with Persian motif in shades of blue, ruby and copper luster, impressed marks, painted artist cipher.

8.75in (22.5cm) high

$2,000-2,400 **WW**

A Pilkington's Lancastrian solifleur vase, designed by William S. Mycock, painted with a frieze of lions in shades of ruby and copper luster, impressed marks, painted cipher datemark.

1913 6.25in (16cm) high

$1,700-2,000 **WW**

A Pilkington's Lancastrian vase, molded in relief with simple, heart-shaped leaves, covered in an aventurine glaze, impressed marks.

7in (17.5cm) high

$360-480 **WW**

A Pilkington's Royal Lancastrian charger, by William S. Mycock, painted with a galleon at full sail, in blue on a mottled orange ground, impressed mark, painted artist cipher.

14in (35.5cm) diam.

$600-800 **WW**

A Pilkington's Lancastrian ginger jar and cover, by Richard Joyce, painted with hares boxing between stylized flowers in shades of ruby and sand luster, impressed marks, painted artists cipher, datemark.

1919 *5.25in (13.5cm) high*

$2,400-3,000 **WW**

A Carter Stabler & Adams Poole Pottery 'Persian Deer' pattern vase, shape no. 966, the pattern designed and painted by Ruth Pavely, the base with impressed and painted marks, with hairline crack.

From the collection of Roy Holland, Managing Director of Poole Pottery.

10in (25cm) high

$500-600 **WW**

A Carter, Stabler & Adams Poole Pottery architectural sculpture, 'The Galleon', designed by Harold Stabler, painted in colors, impressed mark, minor chips.

21.25in (54cm) high

$3,000-4,000 **WW**

A Poole Pottery Art Deco vase, signed by Truda Carter, painted by Ruth Pavely, shape no.846, painted with geometric flowers and foliage in shades of green, brown and black on a mushroom ground, impressed, incised and painted marks, minor hairline to top rim.

13in (33cm) high

$2,800-3,600 **WW**

A set of seven original Poole Pottery designs on paper, 'Sugar for the Birds' and 'Female Portraits', painted in colors and annotated, the original design by Olive Bourne.

$900-1,300 SET **WW**

A Quimper hand-painted ceramic figure, 'Bigoudene en Priere' by Alexander Goudie for La Musée de la Faïence, limited edition 28/250, painted maker's marks.

17in (43cm) high

$600-1,000 **L&T**

A Quimper hand-painted ceramic 'Paysan dans un Champ de Ble' figure, by Alexander Goudie for La Musée de la Faïence, limited edition 27/100.

20in (51cm) high

$1,400-1,800 **L&T**

A Quimper hand-painted ceramic 'Le Marin' figure, by Alexander Goudie for La Musée de la Faïence, limited edition 9/100, painted maker's marks and inscription by the artist 'Head and re-touching by my hand/ Goudie'.

20in (51cm) high

$2,400-2,800 **L&T**

An Adelaide Robineau porcelain vase, covered with blue crystals on a celadon ground, with artist's 'AR' medallion carved on its side, and marked '526', small bruise on rim.

4.5in (11.5cm) high

$13,000-17,000   DRA

A Rorstrand porcelain vase, carved with white and purple lilies, with green stamp with 'KL/15893/EG', and small nick to foot ring.

7.25in (18.5cm) high

$800-1,200   DRA

A Rosenthal porcelain figure of a snake charmer, painted in colors, printed mark.

8.25in (21cm) high

$360-440   WW

A Royal Copenhagen figure group, of intertwined male and female figures restrained to a rock, decorated in blue, gray and skin tone enamels, with printed marks to base.

18in (46cm) high

$1,000-1,400   L&T

A Royal Dux model of a dog, seated on a cushion, gray painted with highlights, pink seal to base.

10.25in (26cm) high

$700-900   L&T

A Royal Dux porcelain comport, the circular top molded with foliate swags and tassels, the tapering rocky stem flanked by a shepherdess, her sheep and a boy playing a whistle, raised on a circular base, in pale green and ivory with gilt highlights.

18in (45.5cm) high

$1,200-1,600   HT

A Rozenburg twelve-tile panel, painted after David Adolf Constant Artz (Dutch, 1837-1890), with a genre scene of a mother and two children at a kitchen table, framed, signed 'N. ARTZ Rozenburg Den Haag L5', original painting dates from 1884.

Panel: 24in (61cm) high

$2,000-2,600   DRA

A Rozenburg twelve-tile panel, painted after Johannes Christiaan Karel Klinkenberg (Dutch, 19thC), depicting a Dutch cityscape with canal, framed, signed 'N. Klinkenberg' and 'B. Rozenburg', small chip to one tile, 3in (7.5cm) corner line to other.

Panel 24in (61cm) wide

$2,400-3,000   DRA

A Rozenburg twelve-tile panel, painted after Cornelis Springer (Dutch, 1817-1891), depicting a Dutch cityscape with canal, framed, signed 'N. C. Springer B. Rozenburg'.

Panel 24in (61cm) wide

$3,200-3,800   DRA

A Rozenburg eggshell-faceted demitasse and saucer with flowers and a bird, signed Rozenburg Den Haag CH.

Saucer 4in (10cm) diam

$1,800-2,400   DRA

A Ruskin Pottery Kingfisher luster stoneware vase, tall cylindrical form, covered in a petrol luster glaze, impressed 'Ruskin, 1912'.

1912   *11.75in (30cm) high*

$2,000-3,000   WW

A large early high-fired Ruskin Pottery vase, having a footed compressed spherical base rising to a flared trumpet neck, with a deep purple flambé glaze with green-flecked decoration, impressed oval West Smethwick mark.

8.4in (21.5cm) high

$4,000-5,000   **FLD**

A high-fired Ruskin Pottery vase, decorated with a flambé tonal purple and red glaze with green flecks, impressed signature and date.

1925   *8.5in (22cm) high*

$1,600-2,400   **FLD**

A Johann Von Schwarz Art Nouveau vase, decorated in cuenca with a maiden in profile over multi-colored poppies, stamped '631 6 71' and illegibly initialed, a couple of minor grinding chips.

9in (23cm) high

$700-900   **DRA**

A German Art Nouveau plaque, by Johann Von Schwarz, with maiden and grapevine, stamped 'CH Q 99 VI'.

11in (28cm) wide

$2,800-3,600   **DRA**

A Teplitz corseted three-handled vase painted with golden sun, red ink stamp, 'TURN TEPLITZ-BOHEMIA R StK MADE IN AUSTRIA AMPHORA MK 5362'.

16.5in (42cm) high

$1,800-2,200   **DRA**

A Hans Thoma 'Mermaid' faïence relief plate, model no. 106, painted by August Gebhard, signed.

c1903   *18.75in (47.5cm) wide*

$4,000-5,000   **VZ**

A Troika Pottery vase, modeled in low relief, in shades of green and brown, painted mark, hairline crack.

10in (25.5cm) high

$1,300-1,500   **WW**

A Troika Pottery wheel lamp base, by Alison Brigden, modeled in low relief, in shades of blue and brown, painted marks.

10.5in (27cm) high

$800-900   **WW**

A Watcombe, Torquay, terracotta jug with brass neck and cover, the design attributed to Dr Christopher Dresser, with grotesque dragon handle, impressed birds feet mark, painted '3381'.

10in (25.5cm) high

$1,000-1,500   **WW**

A pair of Watcombe, Torquay terracotta wall brackets, modeled with a mythical dragon-like beast, glazed turquoise, printed 'Watcombe Torquay'.

6.75in (17cm) high

$600-800   **WW**

A Wedgwood fairyland luster 'Woodland Bridge' and 'Poplar Trees' pattern footed punch bowl, designed by Daisy Makeig Jones, painted and printed in gilt and colored enamels, printed and painted marks to base 'Z4968'.

11.5in (29cm) diam

$6,000-8,000 **L&T**

A Wedgwood vase and cover, painted with bands of flowers and geometric patterns and a central band of script, in shades of green, blue and yellow on a white ground, impressed and painted marks, painted date, cover cracked and finial re-stuck.

1880 *8.75in (22cm) high*

$200-280 **WW**

A Wedgwood matt green earthenware vase, designed by Keith Murray, shape no.4197, impressed and printed marks, facsimile signature.

6.25in (16cm) high

$300-500 **WW**

A Wedgwood earthenware vase, designed by Keith Murray, incised cream body covered in champagne, impressed and printed marks, facsimile signature.

6in (15.5cm) high

$400-500 **WW**

A Wedgwood earthenware vase, designed by Keith Murray, covered in a matt blue glaze, impressed marks, printed factory mark.

12.25in (31cm) high

$400-600 **WW**

A rare Wedgwood black basalt beaker vase, designed by Keith Murray, shape no.3884, with three carved chevron bands, printed mark, facsimile signature.

4in (10cm) high

$1,200-1,800 **WW**

A Weiner Werkstatte ceramic figure, modeled as a market seller, holding two baskets, his jacket with bold geometric design, painted in pale gray with orange details, impressed marks.

8.75in (22cm) high

$1,600-2,000 **L&T**

CLOSER LOOK: WEMYSS SLEEPING PIGLET

The sleeping pig is probably the rarest and most desirable of all Wemyss ware. The pigs were designed for children's nurseries and some had a slot in the back so they could be used as a money box. Others were personalized with a child's name and birthdate. Smaller versions were designed to be used as paperweights – these are rarer still.

Collectors are attracted by Wemyss' naive charm. The naturalistic decoration stands out on the clear white background and the more colorful, rare and well-painted the design, the more desirable the piece is likely to be. A sleeping pig decorated with shamrocks sold for over $38,000

Condition is very important: to create the vibrant colors the pottery was fired at a low temperature which means it is susceptible to chips and cracks, and restoration is expensive. As a result, pieces in perfect condition command a premium.

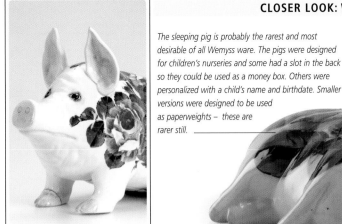

The piglet lies on its side with a contented smile on its face.

An early 20thC Wemyss Pottery pig, painted with roses, painted 'Wemyss' mark, old repair to front right foot.

16in (40.5cm) long

$1,600-2,400 **DRA**

An early 20thC Wemyss 'Sleeping Piglet' figure, decorated with cabbage roses, impressed mark 'Wemyss', minor restorations.

6.25in (16cm) long

$24,000-30,000 **L&T**

A Wemyss Pottery 'Cabbage Rose' pig, painted in shades of pink and green on a white ground, impressed and painted 'Wemyss'.

6.25in (16cm) wide

$1,600-2,400   **WW**

ESSENTIAL REFERENCE: WEMYSS

Wemyss ware was first produced in 1882 at the Fife Pottery. It was the brainchild of Robert Methven Heron, who was assisted by his sister, Jessie, the firm's manager Robert McLaughlan, and master painter, Karel Nekola.

- Wemyss was aimed at owners of country houses, especially those with a large retinue of servants. It exhibited a back-to-nature style, glorying in the fruit, flowers, birds and animals of the British countryside. Every piece is a unique work of art. It was sold exclusively by the London firm, Thomas Goode & Co.
- The range is diverse but it is best known for its pigs, cats and cabbage rose decoration.
- The pottery moved to Bovey Tracey, Devon in 1930, where it was made until 1957.
- Griselda Hill pottery began to make its modern Wemyss ware in 1985, and continues to do so to this day.

A post 1930 large Wemyss pig figure, decorated with cabbage roses, painted marks 'Nekola Pinxt', 'Plichta London' and 'Made in England'.

17.75in (45cm) long

$5,000-6,000   **L&T**

A post 1930 Wemyss cat figure, decorated with cabbage roses, painted mark 'Wemyss Ware/Made in England'.

13in (33cm) high

$4,000-5,000   **L&T**

An early 20thC Wemyss cat figure, decorated with cabbage roses, painted mark 'Wemyss Ware', restorations.

13in (33cm) high

$8,000-12,000   **L&T**

A post-1930 Wemyss cat figure, decorated with cabbage roses, painted mark 'Nekola Pinxt', 'Plichta/London England'.

13in (33cm) high

$5,000-6,000   **L&T**

An early 20thC Wemyss biscuit barrel, decorated with cabbage roses, lid inscribed 'Biscuits', painted mark 'Wemyss', crack to side, restored.

4.75in (12cm) high

$600-1,000   **L&T**

An early 20thC Wemyss pot-pourri jar and cover, decorated with cabbage roses and inscribed 'Gather Ye Rosebuds While Ye May', impressed mark 'Wemyss', minor restorations.

5in (13cm) high

$1,600-2,400   **L&T**

An early 20thC Wemyss 'Earlshall' small beaker vase, decorated with a rookery and windmill design, painted mark 'Wemyss'.

4.25in (11cm) high

$600-800   **L&T**

A Wemyss 'Drummond' flower pot, decorated by Karel Nekola, with cabbage roses, impressed mark 'Wemyss Ware/ R. H. & S.'

c1900   8.5cm (21.5cm) high

$2,000-3,000   **L&T**

A pair of Wemyss egg cups, one painted with dog roses, the other with sweet peas, each with painted and impressed marks.

2in (5.5cm) high

$3,000-4,000   **L&T**

A Wemyss luggie, decorated with cabbage roses, impressed and painted marks.

4.75in (12cm) high

$1,000-1,600　　　　　　　L&T

A small early 20thC Wemyss ewer and basin, decorated with cabbage roses, ewer with impressed mark 'Wemyss', basin with impressed mark 'Wemyss Ware/R. H. & S.'

Ewer 6.25in (16cm) high

$1,200-1,800　　　　　　　L&T

Left: A Wemyss loving cup, decorated with tulips, impressed mark 'WEMYSS WARE R. H. & S.'

7.5in (19cm) high

$1,600-2,400　　　　　　　L&T

Right: A Wemyss three-handled tyg, decorated with apples, impressed marks.

9.25in (23.5cm) high

$2,000-3,000　　　　　　　L&T

A Wemyss heart-shaped tray, decorated with dog roses, impressed mark 'Wemyss Ware/R. H. & S.', minor hairline crack.

c1900　　　　*11.5in (29cm) wide*

$1,000-1,600　　　　　　　L&T

A Wemyss twin-handled tray, decorated with cabbage roses, impressed mark.

17.75in (45cm) wide

$2,400-3,000　　　　　　　L&T

An early 20thC Wemyss 'Fife' flower bowl, decorated by James Sharp with tulips, impressed and painted marks 'Wemyss', restored mold crack.

11.25in (28.5cm) wide

$1,200-1,800　　　　　　　L&T

An early 20thC Wemyss covered honey box, cover and tray, decorated with beehive and bees, tray and box with painted marks 'Wemyss'.

Box 5.5in (14cm) long

$2,000-3,000　　　　　　　L&T

An early 20thC Wemyss covered honey box, cover and drip tray, decorated by Edwin Sandland with beehive and bees, drip tray with painted mark 'Wemyss', losing color from knop.

Box 5in (13cm) long

$1,600-2,400　　　　　　　L&T

A Wemyss low quaich dessert dish, decorated with beehive and bees, impressed mark 'Wemyss Ware/R. H. & S.', restoration to handles, firing crack.

c1900   7.75in (19.5cm) wide

$1,400-2,000   L&T

A large Wemyss preserve jar and cover, decorated with bees and beehive, red scalloped rim to pot and cover, impressed mark 'Wemyss Ware/ R. H. & S.', painted 'T. Goode & Co.' retailers mark, restoration to cover.

c1900   6in (15.5cm) high

$2,400-3,600   L&T

A post-1930 small Wemyss pig figure, decorated with thistles, painted mark 'Nekola Pinxt', 'Plichta/London/England/Made in England'.

4.25in (10.5cm) high

$1,400-2,000   L&T

A post-1930 small Wemyss pig figure, decorated with cornflowers, painted marks 'Nekola Pinxt', and 'Plichta London England', restored ears.

4in (10cm) high

$2,000-3,000   L&T

A post 1930 large Wemyss pig figure, decorated by Joe Nekola with thistles, painted marks 'Wemyss/Made in England'.

17.25in (44cm) long

$7,000-8,000   L&T

A post 1930 large Wemyss pig figure, decorated with red clover, painted 'Nekola Pinxt', 'J Plichta London' and 'Made in England'.

17.75in (45cm) long

$4,000-6,000   L&T

A small Wemyss plate, decorated with a carnation, impressed mark 'Wemyss Ware/R. H. & S.'

c1900   5.75in (14.5cm) diam

$500-700   L&T

A Wemyss 'Gordon' dessert plate, decorated with yellow irises, with impressed mark 'Wemyss/R.H. & S', and printed 'T. Goode & Co.' retailers mark.

c1900   8in (20.5cm) diam

$900-1,100   L&T

A Wemyss 'Gordon' dessert plate, decorated with violet poppies, with impressed mark 'Wemyss/R. H. & S.' and printed 'T. Goode & Co.' retailers mark, restored.

c1900   8in (20.5cm) diam

$1,000-1,600   L&T

An early 20thC Wemyss frilled vase, decorated with carnations, impressed mark 'Wemyss'.

5.25in (13.5cm) high

$1,000-1,600   L&T

A Wemyss low quaich dessert dish, decorated with raspberries, impressed and painted marks.

7.5in (19cm) diam

$2,000-3,000   **L&T**

A Wemyss low quaich dessert dish, decorated with strawberries, impressed mark 'WEMYSS WARE R. H. & S'.

7.25in (18.5cm) diam

$1,000-1,600   **L&T**

An early 20thC Wemyss sponge dish and liner, decorated by Karel Nekola with purple grapes and vine leaves on a black ground, impressed mark 'Wemyss', painted 'T. Goode & Co.' retailer's mark.

7.75in (20cm) diam

$1,800-2,400   **L&T**

A large Wemyss preserve jar and cover, decorated with purple grapes and vine leaves, impressed mark 'Wemyss Ware/R. H. & S.'

c1900   *6in (15.5cm) high*

$1,800-2,400   **L&T**

A large early 20thC Wemyss preserve jar and cover, decorated with greengages, impressed mark 'Wemyss', painted 'T. Goode & Co.' retailer's mark.

6.5in (16.5cm) high

$2,000-3,000   **L&T**

An early 20thC Wemyss biscuit barrel and cover, decorated with oranges, the cover inscribed 'Biscuits', impressed mark 'Wemyss' and painted 'T. Goode & Co' retailer's mark, restored lid and rim.

4.5in (11.5cm) high

$600-1,000   **L&T**

An early 20thC Wemyss 'Japan' vase, decorated with apples, impressed mark 'Wemyss'.

8.5in (21.5cm) high

$1,200-1,800   **L&T**

An early 20thC Wemyss miniature sample jug, decorated by Edwin Sandland with black cockerels, impressed and painted marks 'Wemyss', painted initials 'ES', restored handle.

2.25in (5.5cm) high

$2,000-3,000   **L&T**

A Wemyss 'BonJour' cream jug, decorated with two black cockerels and inscribed 'BonJour', impressed mark 'Wemyss Ware/R. H. & S.'

c1900   *2.75in (7cm) high*

$800-1,200   **L&T**

A large Wemyss tyg, decorated with black cock and hens, impressed marks 'Wemyss Ware/R. H. & S', minor hairline cracks.

c1900   *9.75in (24.5cm) high*

$3,000-4,000   **L&T**

A post-1930 small Wemyss pig figure, decorated with shamrocks, painted marks 'Nekola Pinxt', 'Plichta/London England/Made in England'.

4in (10cm) high

$800-1,200   **L&T**

A large Wemyss pig figure, decorated in a brown glaze, impressed mark 'Wemyss Ware/R H & S', minor restorations.

c1900   *17.75in (45cm) long*

$7,000-8,000   **L&T**

A large Wemyss pig figure, decorated by Joseph Nekola with black on white, painted marks 'Wemyss/ Made in England', restoration to tail.

19in (48cm) long

$5,000-6,000   **L&T**

A post-1930 large Wemyss pig figure, decorated by Joseph Nekola in black on a white ground, painted marks 'Wemyss/Made in England'.

17.75in (45cm) long

$5,000-6,000   **L&T**

A small Wemyss pig figure, decorated black on white, impressed mark 'Wemyss Ware/R. H. & S.', small chip to tail and one ear, other ear cracked at base.

c1900 — *4in (10cm) high*

$2,000-3,000 — **L&T**

A Wemyss 'Earlshall' jug, with a rookery design and inscription, and 'Earlshall Faire A.D. 1914', impressed mark 'Wemyss', hairline crack.

5in (12.5cm) high

$1,000-1,600 — **L&T**

An early 20thC Wemyss jug, decorated by Karel Nekola with stag and deer, impressed mark 'Wemyss' painted 'T. Goode & Co.' retailers mark, minor restoration to rim.

5in (13cm) high

$3,000-4,000 — **L&T**

A near pair of Wemyss thistle-shaped vases, painted in colors, both unmarked.

c1900 — *Taller 5in (12.5cm) high*

$800-1,200 — **L&T**

An early 20thC Wemyss hat pin holder, decorated with heather and inscribed 'Hat-Pins', impressed mark 'Wemyss', glaze frits to rim.

5.75in (14.5cm) high

$1,200-1,800 — **L&T**

A small Wemyss plate, decorated with two geese and inscribed 'BonJour', impressed mark 'Wemyss Ware/R. H. & S.', painted mark 'T. Goode & Co.'

c1900 — *4.75in (12cm) diam*

$800-1,200 — **L&T**

A late 19thC Wemyss 'Waverley' tray, decorated with forget-me-nots, impressed mark 'Wemyss', minor hairline crack.

17.25in (44cm) long

$2,000-3,000 — **L&T**

An early 20thC Wemyss pin tray, decorated by Karel Nekola with a garden bench bearing the inscription 'Soi satisfait des fruits des fleurs, même des feuilles/ Si c'est dans ton jardin à toi que tu les cueilles', impressed and painted mark 'Wemyss', hairline crack to underside, glaze chip.

5.75in (14.5cm) wide

$1,600-2,400 — **L&T**

A Zsolnay tile, with classical scene of satyrs and nude, under lustered glaze, stamped '7893 ZSOLNAY 36'.

11in (28cm) high

$2,000-2,600 — **DRA**

A Zsolnay figure, of a maiden with pitcher, covered in lustered glaze, pink five churches medallion, '86?2 36'.

11in (28cm) high

$1,200-1,400 — **DRA**

A Zsolnay owl figurine, 'Ketupa Ceylonensis,' covered in red glaze, small chips, five churches medallion '8771'.

13.5in (34.5cm) high

$1,100-1,500 — **DRA**

A Zsolnay jardinière, embossed with weeds and cattails, covered in a lustered glaze, touch-ups to several high points, Y-shaped line on body, five churches red medallion, '4055, 6127B, Korona'.

12in (30.5cm) high

$12,000-14,000 — **DRA**

A Zsolnay tapering Art Deco vase, with panels of birds of paradise in relief under lustered glazes, five churches medallion, illegible number.

8.25in (21cm) wide

$6,000-8,000   DRA

A Zsolnay boat-shaped center bowl, topped by two crimson red parrots, covered in marbleized, lustered gold glaze, five churches gold stamp 'MADE IN HUNGARY, 8805E'.

15in (38cm) long

$3,000-4,000   DRA

A Zsolnay vase, embossed with geraniums, covered in lustered glazes, hairline and restoration, five churches gold stamp, 'MADE IN HUNGARY, ZSOLNAY PECS, 6166'.

8.75in (22cm) high

$5,000-6,000   DRA

ESSENTIAL REFERENCE: ZSOLNAY

Zsolnay was founded by Miklós Zsolnay in 1853 in Pécs, Hungary. It began to expand after his son, Vilmôs, took control in 1865.

- Prior to the 1890s, Zsolnay produced ornate pieces inspired by Islamic pierced wares and traditional Hungarian wares.
- Vilmôs was influenced by the latest design movements across Europe, particularly the Art Nouveau movement. Zsolnay began to specialize in ceramics with crystalline metallic glazes.
- Forms are simple and naturalistic, with low-relief molded detail. Decorative motifs include tree silhouettes and red skies with lustrous surface.
- The factory still survives as a Hungarian State concern.

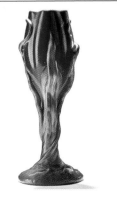

A Zsolnay tulip-shaped vase in lustered glazes, restoration to two rim chips, two small glaze bursts on base, green five churches stamp 'ZSOLNAY PECS 5495'

14in (35.5cm) high

$14,000-16,000   DRA

An Austrian Art Nouveau tall vase with white and blue blossoms, restoration to one petal and stem, stamped 'R. D. Z. HH 20882'.

19.5in (49.5cm) high

$2,400-3,000   DRA

An Arts & Crafts four-tile panel, painted with a figure of Pan below a flowering tree, with exotic birds and animals, painted monogram, framed.

30in (76cm) high

$2,400-3,000   L&T

A porcelain plaque, painted with a semi-clad female figure lying by a river reading a book with an urn by her side, in foliated gilt frame, bearing blue crossed swords mark and impressed no. '115'.

10.25in (26cm) high

$4,000-5,000   A&G

An Art Nouveau French studio pottery silver-mounted vase, the leaf-molded tapered oval body in dark green and chartreuse glaze, with sinuous silver mounts to the mouth and foot rims, inscribed signature to base.

c1900   *7in (18cm) high*

$1,600-2,000   FRE

A shouldered vase after Jessie M. King, painted on a porcelain blank with a frieze of girls gathering flowers in a woodland setting, painted initials to base.

8.25in (21cm) high

$700-800   L&T

MISS CRANSTON'S TEAROOMS

The temperance movement was becoming increasingly popular in Glasgow in the late 19th/early 20thC. In response, Miss Catherine Cranston, the daughter of a local tea merchant, opened a series of tearooms, the interiors of which were all partially designed by Charles Rennie Mackintosh.

- In 1903, Mackintosh was commissioned to completely re-design the building (including interior design, furniture and exteriors) that later became known as The Willow Tearooms.

A Miss Cranston's part tea set, blue printed in the Willow pattern, comprising a tea cup and saucer, a sugar bowl and a milk jug, printed marks 'Miss Cranston's, Willow, Adderleys Ltd'.

$600-800   L&T

An American Arts & Crafts Grandfather clock, with copper numbers, unmarked.

78in (198cm) high

$3,000-4,000 DRA

An American Arts & Crafts oak standing clock, the twin train movement with circular dial enclosed by inset blue glass spandrels.

71.75in (182cm) high

$1,100-1,300 L&T

An Arts & Crafts tallcase clock, with brass face, hardware and floriform inlay decoration.

78.5in (199cm) high

$8,000-10,000 SDR

A Secessionist style tallcase clock, in exotic hardwood veneers with mother-of-pearl inlay, brass banding and German movement.

83in (210.5cm) high

$800-1,200 SDR

An Aesthetic Movement ebonized mantel clock, for Thomas Russell & Son., 33 Piccadilly and Liverpool, with twin train movement, the case decorated in gilt and colored enamels with floral panels.

119in (47cm) high

$900-1,200 L&T

An Arts & Crafts design copper-cased timepiece.

9in (23cm) high

$400-500 A&G

An Aesthetic Movement clock, by Lewis F. Day, Edward & Sons, London and Glasgow, with twin train movement with ebonized case with molded cornice and flower-carved spandrels and set with two ceramic plaques.

15in (38cm) high

$900-1,200 L&T

A Liberty & Co. English pewter mantel clock, designed by Archibald Knox, model no. 0761, with blue/green enameled dial, stamped marks.

8.75in (22cm) high

$6,000-7,000 WW

An early 20thC Tiffany & Co. sterling silver travel clock, the case decorated with foliate sprays enclosing an oval medallion.

2.5in (6.5cm) wide

$2,000-2,600 FRE

A brass-cased wall clock, by Hector Guimard, the case decorated with cast whiplash foliage, hanging chain.

18in (46cm) high

$3,600-4,400 L&T

A Continental silver and enamel desk clock, in the style of Josef Hoffman, indistinctly marked.

3.5in (9cm) high

$1,800-2,400   FLD

An Art Deco gilt-bronze strut clock, with classic Art Deco hands, with an eight-day French movement with integral key, signed on dial and case 'Finnigans London & Paris', in original case.

c1920   *3.5in (9cm) wide*

$1,200-1,400   RGA

An Austrian Art Deco sub-miniature carriage clock, decorated with silver, sky blue guilloché enamel and black enamel, the back door decorated with silver in a basket weave pattern, eight-day movement with lever escapement, in its original leather case with its original key.

c1920   *2.25in (5.5cm) high*

$5,000-6,000   RGA

ESSENTIAL REFERENCE: CARTIER

In 1847, Louis-François Cartier took over the workshop of his former-master, Adolphe Picard, in Paris. Management passed to his son, Alfred in 1874, but it was Alfred's sons, Louis, Pierre and Jacques, who were responsible for establishing the worldwide brand name.

- The London branch was established in 1902, after Jacques and Pierre were sent to London to meet the requests prompted by Edward VII's coronation. Whilst still Prince of Wales, Edward had declared Cartier the 'Jeweler of Kings.' Cartier became the official supplier of the English Court from 1904. Pierre opened Cartier New York in 1909. Jacques remained in charge of the London branch

- Cartier is credited with producing the first wristwatch. It was designed in 1904 by Louis Cartier with the help of master watchmaker Edmond Jaeger, for aviator Alberto Santos-Dumont. Louis was also responsible for the 'Mysterious Clocks' and the 'Tutti Frutti' jewelry.

- After the death of Pierre in 1964, the businesses were sold and closed. In 1972, a group of investors led by Joseph Kanoui bought Cartier Paris. They bought Cartier London and Cartier New York back in 1974 and 1976 respectively, combining the Cartier interests in 1979 as 'Cartier Monde'.

A Cartier silver miniature boudoir clock, gilt and guilloché enamel, the white enamel dial signed 'Cartier', the back door in silver with engine turning, with fixed silver gilt handle, fine three-quarter plate eight-day lever movement with integral winding key.

c1920   *3.5in (9cm) high*

$8,000-9,000   RGA

A rare Cartier miniature strut clock, in the form of a camera, case constructed of gold, silver and leather, decorated with coral winding.

c1920   *2.75in (7cm) high*

$6,000-7,000   RGA

A German Art Deco sub-miniature carriage clock, decorated with light blue guilloché enamel and silver, eight-day three-quarter plate movement with lever escapement, fully marked on the case and numbered.

c1925   *1.5in (4cm) high*

$6,000-7,000   RGA

An early 20thC Art Deco gilt-bronze and enamel strut clock, dial marked 'Doxa' and 'Swiss made', with original box.

4in (10cm) wide

$2,600-3,200   RGA

A French Boucheron gold square travel or strut watch, the silvered dial with blue cabochon indicators, a red cabochon 2 and signed 'Boucheron', French eagle head poincons, International Watch Co. movement, cal.132, adjusted 5 positions and 2 temperatures.

c1930

$4,000-5,000   DN

An Art Deco walnut wall clock, with carved stylized floral motifs, Westminster chime, quarter strike pendulum movement.

c1930

$1,600-2,000   TDG

A Morgan Colt, New Hope, PA wrought iron armchair, with tan leather sling seat and backrest.

24in (61cm) wide

$4,500-5,500   **SDR**

A Morgan Colt, New Hope, Pennsylvania library table, with ebonized oak top and pierced metal-lined apron, on wrought iron base.

39.5in (100cm) wide

$15,000-18,000   **SDR**

A Grand Rapids Bookcase & Chair Co. settee and cube chair, with cloth-upholstered foam seats, paper label on settee.

settee 48in (123cm) wide

$1,600-2,000   **DRA**

A Harden square lamp table, with a lower shelf and legs mortised through the top, original finish with light overcoat, and paper label under shelf.

18.5in (47cm) wide

$2,500-3,000   **DRA**

A rare Frederick Harer, New Hope, Pennsylvania gateleg table, of mixed hardwoods with walnut top and through-tenon construction.

48 in (122cm) wide

$5,500-7,500   **SDR**

A Lakeside Crafts Shop magazine stand, with inverted V crest rail, square cut-outs, original finish, seam separations to shelves, and unmarked.

46.25in (117.5cm) high

$1,300-1,600   **DRA**

A Limbert double oval library table, with plank legs and square cut-out stretchers supporting a lower shelf, and branded under top.

47.5in (120.5cm) wide

$16,000-18,000   **DRA**

A Lifetime Puritan line console table, skinned original finish, decal in drawer, and paper label under drawer.

67in (170cm) wide

£5,000-5,500   **DRA**

A Limbert drop-arm settle, with loose seat and back cushions covered in cordovan leather, refinished, branded under arm.

76in (193cm) wide

$7,000-9,000   **DRA**

A Limbert china cabinet.

43.5in (123cm) wide

$6,000-8,000 **DRA**

A Limbert ebon-oak curved arm rocker, with geometric inlay, a corbel under each arm, and overcoated original finish.

30in (76cm) wide

$2,500-3,000 **DRA**

A rare early Limbert two-door bookcase, with leaded glass doors, on casters, stamped '334', marked in ink '334 1/2'.

c1905 *42in (106.5cm) wide*

$12,000-14,000 **DRA**

A pair of Michigan Chair Co. spindled cube chairs, with plank seats, one has loose cushion, partial paper label to dark one.

36in (91.5cm) high

$2,000-3,000 **DRA**

A Thomas Molesworth burlwood armchair, with tacked-on leather seat, hammered brass hardware and fabric-upholstered cushions.

A Paine Furniture Company bookcase, with square copper knob pulls, refinished, small holes in back.

48in (122cm) wide

$2,500-3,000 **DRA**

In 1931 Thomas Canada Molesworth (1890-1977) started the Shoshone Furniture Company in Cody, Wyoming. The western 'Dude Ranch' was a popular vacation destination. In a few short years Molesworth had made a name for himself furnishing the Moses Annenberg lodge and big hotels in Wyoming and Montana. In 1940 he received a commission to furnish the TE Ranch which had formerly belonged to Buffalo Bill. Edward Grigware, an old classmate from Chicago, collaborated with Molesworth on the TE Ranch project and several other commissions. Molesworth made furniture for some of the most prominent Americans of the 20thC. He furnished Eisenhower's den, the Rockefeller Ranch and the homes and retreats of several celebrities and captains of industry and commerce.

33in (84cm) wide

$30,000-35,000 **SDR**

ESSENTIAL REFERENCE: CHARLES ROHLFS

Charles Rohlfs (1853-1936) was an American furniture designer, who combined the solidity of the Arts & Crafts movement with Art Nouveau ornament and Norwegian craft influences.

- He opened the Charles Rohlfs Workshop in Buffalo, New York in 1898, where he employed eight craftsmen to execute his designs.
- His furniture was predominantly made from relatively pale oak with fretwork and sinuous carved decoration.
- Rohlfs mainly designed desks, chairs, small tables, and storage pieces.
- His furniture was well known in Europe, as well as America, and he made several pieces for Buckingham Palace.
- The workshop closed in 1928.

A Charles Rohlfs carved cedar-lined oak box, with hammered copper escutcheon, with original finish, small split to interior cedar, signed and dated.

1901 *14.5in (37cm) wide*

$15,000-17,000 **DRA**

A Charles Rohlfs tall-back hall chair, with shaped back slats, cut with stylised cloverleaf reticulation, impressed mark on back.

16.5in (42cm) wide

$9,000-12,000   **DRA**

A Charles Rohlfs floriform table, with carved top, reticulated legs, original finish with light overcoat, crack to one mortise.

26in (66cm) wide

$6,000-8,000   **DRA**

A Rose Valley folding stool, carved with rosettes, branded mark.

25in (63.5cm) wide

$6,000-8,000   **DRA**

An important Roycroft sideboard, with leaded-glass cabinet doors, mirrored back, copper hardware, and orb and cross mark on center stile.

65.5in (166.5cm) wide

$45,000-50,000   **DRA**

A Roycroft rare triple-door bookcase with three adjustable shelves per door, carved orb and cross mark.

69in (175 cm) wide

$10,000-13,000   **DRA**

A Roycrofters important rare oak cellaret, with wrought iron hardware, model no. 019, with the firm's carved orb and cross cipher.

40in (101.5cm) wide

$90,000-100,000   **SOT**

A Gustav Stickley flat-arm Morris chair, no. 332, with drop-in spring seat and loose back cushion newly recovered in dark brown leather, original finish, and color added to arms.

32in (81.5cm) wide

$10,000-12,000   **DRA**

A Gustav Stickley knock-down even-arm settle, with a twelve-inch horizontal back slat, and a loose seat cushion newly recovered, with black stamp on back stretcher.

84in (213.5cm) wide

$15,000-17,000   **DRA**

ESSENTIAL REFERENCE: GUSTAV STICKLEY

Gustav Stickley (1858-1942) trained as a stonemason before apprenticing himself to his uncle's chair factory. He was fascinated by the construction of furniture, and this is reflected in the emphasized functional details like dovetailing and exposed dowel-ends of his designs.

- He believed that furniture must 'fill its mission of usefulness'.
- In 1898, he traveled to England where he became interested in the Arts & Crafts movement, and the ideas of John Ruskin and William Morris. On his return, he set up the Gustav Stickley Company (est. 1898), making furniture inspired by Morris.
- In 1901, he renamed his business 'United Crafts'. He also began to publish a monthly magazine, 'The Craftsman'. The magazine was originally intended as a marketing tool for his furniture, but was later expanded to cover philosophy and architecture.
- Stickley's furniture was made from natural materials, like oak, leather and rush. The grain of the wood was emphasized with his hallmark fumed-ammonia finish.
- The company was taken over by Gustav's brothers, Leopold and John George in 1916, and renamed 'L & JG Stickley'. The company is still in business today.

A Gustav Stickley tall-back armchair, with a spindled back and a drop-in spring cushion recovered in light brown suede, stress cracks to lower side stretchers.

27.5in (70cm) wide

$3,500-4,500   **DRA**

A Gustav Stickley sidechair, with vertical slats and corbels, braided rush seat, unmarked.

The rare braided rush treatment is original.

c1901   *34in (86cm) high*

$3,000-4,000   **DRA**

An early Gustav Stickley chestnut window seat, unmarked.

c1901   *25in (63.5cm) wide*

$4,000-5,000   **DRA**

A Gustav Stickley Harvey Ellis-designed maple side chair, with rush seat, inlaid with pewter, copper, and fruitwoods, unmarked.

39.25in (99.5cm) high

$6,500-7,500   **DRA**

A Gustav Stickley oversized rocker, (no. 323) with drop-in spring seat covered in brown leather, red decal.

37in (94cm) high

$3,000-4,000   **DRA**

A pair of Gustav Stickley V-back billiards chairs, with five vertical back slats, tacked-on leather seats, and replaced burgundy leather.

26in (66cm) wide

$20,000-25,000   **DRA**

A Gustav Stickley oak poppy table, with floriform lower shelf and cut-out legs, original finish, color added to top, and partial paper label under top.

19.5in (49.5cm) wide

$16,000-18,000   **DRA**

A rare Gustav Stickley lamp table, with trumpeted cross-stretchers and legs mortised through the top.

25.5in (64.5cm) wide

$30,000-35,000   **DRA**

A Gustav Stickley leather top library table, unmarked.

Provenance: From the living room at Vancroft, the Wellsburg, W. Va., home designed by the Pittsburgh architects Alden and Harlow and built at a cost of more than $1,000,000 as a hunting lodge for Joseph B. Vandergrift in 1901.

c1901   *40in (101.5cm) wide*

$20,000-25,000   **CRA**

A rare Gustav Stickley tabouret, (no. 46) inset with hexagonal Grueby tile covered in indigo glaze.

This is exceedingly rare, especially with its original tile.

c1901   *21in (53cm) high*
$22,000-25,000   **DRA**

A tall Gustav Stickley chest of drawers, refinished, separation to top, with branded mark.

A Gustav Stickley Harvey Ellis-designed library table, delicate inlay of pewter, brass and copper, and medallions inlaid with galleons in various fruitwoods.

29.75in (75.5cm) wide
$80,000-90,000   **DRA**

36in (91.5cm) wide
$14,000-16,000   **DRA**

A fine Gustav Stickley paneled magazine stand, (no. 548) red decal in box.

A Gustav Stickley Harvey Ellis-designed drop-front desk, inlaid with pewter, copper, and fruitwoods, complete with original glass inkwells, early red decal.

A Gustav Stickley early double-door bookcase, (no. 525) with mitered mullions and three fixed shelves, early red decal.

1902   *43.75in (111cm) high*
$6,000-8,000   **DRA**

43.75in (111cm) high
$22,000-25,000   **DRA**

c1901   *45in (114cm) wide*
$18,000-20,000   **DRA**

An early Gustav Stickley server, (no. 955).

c1902.   *59.25in (150cm) wide*
$18,000-22,000   **DRA**

A Gustav Stickley eight-leg sideboard, (no. 817) with chamfered plate rack, branded mark.

70in (178cm) wide
$15,000-17,000   **DRA**

An L. & J. G. Stickley trestle table, the lower shelf mortised through the sides with keyed through-tenons, refinished, unmarked.

72in (183cm) wide
$4,500-5,500   **DRA**

An L. & J. G. Stickley rocker, with a drop-in spring seat and loose back cushion recovered in leather, shadow of 'The Work of...' decal, back stretcher.

36.5in (92.5cm) high

$3,500-4,000   DRA

An L. & J. G. Stickley even-arm settle, (no. 281) with drop-in spring seat, 'The Work of...' decal.

76in (193cm) wide

$5,500-6,500   DRA

An L. & J. G. Stickley magazine stand, with four shelves, original finish, stains to shelves, and branded 'The work of...' outside lower stretcher.

21in (53.5cm) wide

$2,500-3,000   DRA

A rare Stickley Brothers double oval lamp table, metal tag.

36in (91.5cm) wide

$2,500-3,000   DRA

A Stickley Brothers full-size paneled bed, with pewter and ebonized wood inlay, unmarked.

56.75in (144cm) wide

$16,000-18,000   DRA

A Stickley Brothers server, with two small drawers over a linen drawer, iron hardware, original finish to base, and color added to top.

48in (122cm) wide

$3,500-4,000   DRA

A Stickley Brothers sideboard, with three drawers and two doors, branded mark and decal.

50in (127cm) wide

$6,000-8,000   DRA

A large armchair, attributed to Charles Stickley, with broad drop-arms, a drop-in spring cushion covered in leather, original finish, color and finish added to arms.

34.75in (88.5cm) wide

$4,000-4,500   DRA

A J. M. Young drop-arm settee, with a drop-in spring cushion covered in leather, and a partial paper label.

79in (200.5cm) wide

$3,500-4,000   DRA

A pair of Edward Welby Pugin pitch pine 'Granville' chairs, each with carved molded tablet toprail with six central ebony roundels, on chamfered A-frame.

$5,200-6,000 **L&T**

A pair of 1860s Gothic Revival oak stools, each with a pierced Gothic apron on chamfered legs.

19in (48.5cm) wide

$4,000-6,000 **L&T**

A Gothic Revival oak window seat, the seat with chamfered arms raised on curved cross supports, linked by a stretcher.

54in (137cm) wide

$1,200-1,600 **L&T**

A Celtic Revival oak hall settle, attributed to Alexander Ritchie, the rectangular back carved with three panels of elaborately carved Celtic knotwork and mythical beasts, dated.

1899 *50.5in (128cm) wide*

$1,300-1,500 **L&T**

A Gothic Revival oak planter, fitted with a frieze of Minton tiles.

45.75in (116cm) wide

$1,200-1,600 **L&T**

An early 19thC Gothic Revival carved jardinière, possibly a design by A. W. N. Pugin, the top with reversible solid panel above a 'hob nail' carved frieze centered by lancet arches and trefoil spandrels, the plinth base with a broad frieze of pierced tracery enclosing a metal-lined void.

28.75in (73cm) wide

$2,400-3,000 **L&T**

A mid-19thC French Gothic Revival karelian birch desk and chair, the desk with spire finials over two cupboard doors joined by gothic tracery above a single drawer, raised on carved tapered supports, the chair with a caned high back, raised on round, tapered, beaded legs.

Desk 44in (112cm) wide

$3,000-4,000 **FRE**

A 19thC Gothic Revival oak court cupboard, the cornice with eight allegorical carved panels, above a single cupboard door above a single drawer raised on straight legs.

34in (86.5cm) wide

$1,000-1,200 **FRE**

A Gothic Revival painted casket, the pitched architectural cover with scalloped moldings, foliate diaper and a frieze of carved rosettes above sides decorated with foliate-painted sunken roundels.

34.75in (88cm) wide

$1,600-2,000 **L&T**

A late 19thC Gothic Revival giltwood archway, attributed to Peter Paul Pugin, the pointed lancet-arched dentil pediment enclosing a quatrefoil and tracery, with lozenges highlighted with punched work.

55in (140cm) wide

$2,400-5,000 **L&T**

A Scottish Arts & Crafts oak four poster bed, the canopy carved with Gothic tracery and with rosette and flowerhead motifs above a plain headboard with material covering, the front supports spirally molded and imbricated with flowerheads, shields and acorn motifs, joined by a shaped triple panel foot board corresponding to the canopy.

95in (242cm) high

$8,000-10,000 **L&T**

ESSENTIAL REFERENCE: CARLO BUGATTI

Carlo Bugatti (1856-1940) was an Italian designer who worked c1880-1910. He designed metalware, textiles, and ceramics, but he is best known for his furniture.

- Bugatti drew inspiration from nature, and Moorish, Egyptian and Japanese art. He was also inspired by the writings of Eugène Viollet-le-Duc, in particular his ideas on the use of decorative elements to draw attention to the structure of a piece, rather than disguise it.
- The particularly strong Moroccan influence can be seen in Bugatti's use of dark woods offset by bold colors and strong, geometric designs, ropework and tassels of silk and wool.
- Some pieces are inlaid with ebony, copper, and pewter. Copper may also be wrapped around uprights.
- Carlo was the father of Rembrandt Bugatti, the sculptor, and Ettore Bugatti, the car designer.

An Aesthetic Movement Carlo Bugatti piano stool, of ebonized wood inlaid with white metal kanji, with copper and bone accents, upholstered in camel skin.

20in (51cm) high

$10,000-12,000 SDR

An Aesthetic Movement Carlo Bugatti étagère, of ebonized wood inlaid in metal, bone and mahogany, with a patinated parchment panel, and copper-wrapped details.

c1905 23.25in (59cm) wide

$12,000-14,000 SDR

An oak bench, designed by Carlo Bugatti, with parchment, stenciled parchment, brass and brass nails.

c1902 46.75in (118.5cm) wide

$40,000-50,000 SOT

A partially ebonized oak bench, designed by Carlo Bugatti, with parchment, stenciled parchment, pewter, and copper.

c1902 46in (167cm) wide

$18,000-22,000 SOT

An oak corner chair, designed by Carlo Bugatti, with parchment, stenciled parchment, bone, metal cord, pewter, brass and brass nails.

c1902 28in (71cm) high

$14,000-16,000 SOT

A pair of walnut chairs, designed by Carlo Bugatti, with partially ebonized pewter and brass.

c1900 39.5in (100.5cm) high

$19,000-22,000 SOT

An oak pedestal designed by Carlo Bugatti, with parchment copper, pewter, silk cord and brass nails.

c1900 16.5in (42cm) wide

$20,000-24,000 SOT

An important and rare pine and partially ebonized oak Cartonnier, designed by Carlo Bugatti, with parchment, stenciled parchment, pewter, brass and bronze.

c1900 28in (71cm) wide

$90,000-100,000 SOT

A partially ebonized pine table, designed by Carlo Bugatti, with pewter and brass.

c1900 46in (117cm) wide

$16,000-20,000 SOT

A Scottish Arts & Crafts stained and ebonized beech armchair, inlaid with mother-of-pearl lozenges, the tall paneled back painted with a rook perched on prunus blossom, above curved open arms and solid seat raised on curved legs linked by stretchers.

$5,000-6,000   L&T

A George Walton walnut 'Philippines' side chair, the arched top rail with carved and gilded ribbon edging, centered by a pierced oval aperture above tall caned splat.

$5,000-6,000   L&T

An oak chair with leather upholstery, designed by Frank Lloyd Wright, from the Hillside Home School, Spring Green, Wisconsin.

c1904   40in (102cm) high
$34,000-40,000   SOT

A mahogany ladder-back chair, designed by Charles Rennie Mackintosh for W. J. Basset-Lowke for the guest bedroom of 78 Derngate, Northampton.

c1917   34.25in (87cm) high
$30,000-40,000   SOTH

A Scottish Arts & Crafts ebonized tub chair, the solid back and arms painted and inlaid with mother-of-pearl with the image of a maiden seated by a window, with two roundels to the arms depicting a windmill and a sailing ship.

$7,000-8,000   L&T

An Arthur W. Simpson, Kendal oak and leather-upholstered armchair and stool.

$2,000-3,000   L&T

An American Odd Fellows oak rocking chair, turned stiles with wide crest rail carved with 'all seeing eye', clasped hands and initials 'I.O.O.F', carved with three linked chains enclosing 'L.F.T.' and the lower 'The Brotherhood'.
c1900
$1,200-1,400   FRE

An armchair and two matching side chairs in the manner of Ernest Archibald, green-stained oak, each with pierced top rails above tapering splats.

$2,000-2,600   L&T

An ebonized wood armchair by George Walton, the back with upholstered panel and spindle panels above curved arms and outswept turned legs.

$2,400-3,000   L&T

A pair of Exhibition mahogany side chairs, by George Logan for Wylie & Lochhead, with tapering backs inlaid with stylized foliate motifs, highlighted with abalone shell.

These chairs were originally designed for the Royal Reception Room at the Wylie & Lochhead Pavilion at the Glasgow International Exhibition, 1901.
1901
$3,200-4,000   L&T

A set of eight Arts & Crafts oak dining chairs, including two carvers, each with slatted backs formed as plant totems with applied embossed metal facings.

$2,000-3,000 SET — L&T

An ebonized oak armchair, attributed to Philip Webb, for Morris & Co., with later loose upholstered cushions, with padded arms, the ladder back on an adjustable ratchet, with bobbin-turned supports.

$8,000-10,000 — L&T

A suite of stained oak boardroom furniture, in the manner of James Salmon Jnr., comprising a center table and eight matching chairs, the table with stylized company initials 'B.L. & Co.', the chairs, including two carver chairs, with broad top rails carved with sinuous plant forms.

Table 40.25in (102cm) wide

$4,600-5,200 SUITE — L&T

A pair of Russian Arts & Crafts birch armchairs, each with incised decorative motifs, each bears metal makers label 'КОНСYАСТВО/NO. 25'.

$1,600-2,000 — L&T

An Arts & Crafts oak settle, Edgar Wood, the high paneled back with shaped finials above a plank seat on stem feet.

71.25in (181cm) wide

$4,000-5,000 — L&T

ESSENTIAL REFERENCE: MOUSEMAN

Robert Thompson (1876-1955) was an English furniture-maker who signed every piece of furniture with his trademark carved mouse, giving him the name 'Mouseman.'

● Thompson was part of the 1920s crafts revival. He was interested in traditional tools and methods and consequently produced handcrafted oak furniture, inspired by 17thC designs. This furniture is characterized by an uneven, rippled surface created with an adze, a cutting tool with an arched blade.

● His workshop, now known as Robert Thompson's Craftsmen Ltd – The Mouseman of Kilburn, is still open.

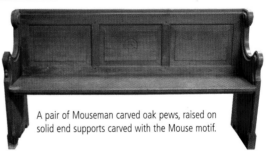

A pair of Mouseman carved oak pews, raised on solid end supports carved with the Mouse motif.

71in (180cm) wide

$4,000-5,000 PAIR — A&G

An oak and elm joint stool, Robert 'Mouseman' Thompson, the dished burr elm seat above four faceted baluster legs.

15.75in (40cm) wide

$1,600-2,000 — L&T

A Robert 'Mouseman' Thompson oak magazine rack.

17in (43.25in) wide

$800-1,000 — GORL

A Morris & Co. mahogany-framed sofa, upholstered in 'Squirrel' pattern wool fabric, raised on spirally fluted turned legs with brass caps and pot casters.

72.75in (185cm) wide

$2,000-2,800 — L&T

A Heal & Sons oak 'Letchworth' refectory dining table, bears inset maker's label.

71.25in (181cm) wide

$3,600-4,400   L&T

An inlaid mahogany side table, attributed to George Walton, the top with chevron banding above a frieze with chequer panels.

29in (73.5cm) wide

$1,200-1,600   L&T

An oak table, designed by George Walton, the top raised on hexagonal legs united by stretchers, on trestle feet.

28.75in (73cm) high

$4,000-5,000   L&T

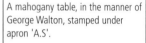

A mahogany table, in the manner of George Walton, stamped under apron 'A.S'.

33in (84cm) wide

$1,000-1,400   L&T

An Arts & Crafts oak gateleg table, the canted top above turned and blocked faceted supports linked by stretchers.

29.25in (74cm) high

$300-500   L&T

An Arts & Crafts oak dressing table, by Harris Lebus.

c1905

$2,400-3,000   TDG

An 1870s Holland & Son mahogany table, the top above three turned legs with ebonized collars raised on cross stretchers with chamfered curved feet, stamped marks.

41.75in (106cm) diam

$1,000-1,200   L&T

An oak occasional table, by Sir Robert Lorimer, the hexagonal paneled top with chamfered edging and exposed pegs above carved spirally molded supports linked by curved stretchers on shaped block feet.

12.25in (31cm) high

$5,400-6,000   L&T

An Arts and Crafts linen press, with four shelves and three drawers.

43in (109cm) wide

$2,000-2,600   DRA

An oak press, by Sir Robert Lorimer, the cornice carved with flower and berry sprigs, the doors carved with linen-fold panels and enclosing an interior fitted with drawers and hanging spaces.

69.75in (177cm) wide

$18,000-22,000   L&T

A 20thC Arts & Crafts walnut standing corner cupboard, in the manner of Stanley Davies, cushion-molded cornice and faceted frieze, doors with four raised panels and wooden loop handles, interior with hanging space.

40.75in (103.5cm) wide

$2,000-2,600   HT

An oak and marquetry-inlaid hall cupboard, by Shapland and Petter, Barnstaple, the single door paneled with elaborate foliate strapwork inlay, flanked by further panels, similarly decorated.

54in (137cm) wide

$1,600-2,400   L&T

An oak hall cupboard, designed by Earnest Archibald Taylor, for Wylie & Lochhead, with door inset with stained and leaded glass panel, above two further doors on stile supports, bears retailers label, stamped serial no '116663'.

c1900   79in (201cm) high

$3,200-4,000   **L&T**

An Arts & Crafts oak hall stand, by Shapland and Petter, Barnstaple , with embossed copper frieze, centered with an aneroid barometer dial, over central mirror and coat pegs, above marble-top glove drawer, with stick stand below, bearing inscription 'Fair Weather After You'.

52in (132cm) wide

$2,400-3,000   **L&T**

An Arts & Crafts mahogany with marquetry inlay display cabinet, in the style of Wylie & Lochhead, Glasgow, the three-quarter ledge back with spindle-filled three-quarter gallery central by a panel decorated with angular stemmed foliage, highlighted in harewood, requiring some restoration.

37.25in (120cm) wide

$1,700-2,200   **L&T**

An Arts & Crafts oak bureau, with Irish Celtic detail, with carved and stained decoration to fall front, top gallery and sides with mythical creatures and Celtic knots, copper stylized metalware, green-stained interior.

c1900

$1,600-2,000   **TDG**

An Arts & Crafts boarded and paneled oak chest, the triple-panel front centered with three dancing maidens in relief, the cut-out ends with carved female musicians.

52.5in (133cm) wide

$260-320   **WW**

A George Walton mahogany workbox, the shaped and paneled hinged lid with lined interior above two drawers on square tapering legs.

The form of this small workbox conforms to furniture designed by Walton for Elm Bank, York, characterized by its stripped down 18thC references and demonstrating a re-orientation in line from the vertical to the horizontal.

23.5in (59.5cm) wide

$4,000-6,000   **L&T**

An Arthur W. Simpson, Kendal oak wall cupboard, with open bookshelf with hinged dust protectors carved with rosettes above twin paneled doors similarly carved, bears paper label.

35.75in (91cm) wide

$2,400-3,000   **L&T**

An oak-framed three-fold draught screen, after C. F. A. Voysey, inset with three stained and leaded glass panels.

74.5in (189cm) high

$5,000-6,000   **L&T**

A Secessionist three-panel screen, leaded glass, brass, and velvet, unmarked.

Center panel: 63.5in (161cm) high

$5,000-6,000   **DRA**

A green-stained sycamore draught screen, George Logan for Wylie & Lochhead, each fold with stained and leaded glass panel depicting a stylized plant form, above linen panels painted with hearts.

72in (183cm) high

$4,000-6,000   **L&T**

An Arts & Crafts oak fire screen, design characteristic of Charles Voysey, metal tag 'House Furnishers, 36 Donegal St. Belfast, Bell & Mayrs Ltd.'

1907

$500-600   **SK**

A Scottish Arts & Crafts oak-framed fire surround, with a crewelwork wool panel worked with flowering foliage on a cream ground and surrounding aperture for fireplace.

47in (119cm) wide

$4,000-5,000   L&T

An oak overmantel mirror, by Arthur W. Simpson, Kendal, carved with panels of flowering foliage.

45in (114cm) wide

$2,000-3,000   L&T

An oak dressing mirror, by Liberty & Co., the mirrored plate with turned uprights having acorn finials and heart-pierced brackets.

32.5in (82.5cm) high

$700-900   L&T

An Italian Art Nouveau wood side chair, carved with two ladies' heads, a frog, and flowers, upholstered with pale silk, unmarked.

39in (99cm) high

$4,000-5,000   DRA

An Art Nouveau oak and marquetry-inlaid side chair.

$800-900   L&T

An early 20thC cast iron and oak seat, by Hector Guimard.

French architect and designer Hector Guimard (1867-1942) is best known for designing the entrances to the Paris Métro.

36in (91.5cm) high

$6,000-10,000   SOTH

An Art Nouveau mahogany armchair, in the manner of J. S. Henry, with upholstered panel back above curved arms and slatted gallery pierced with hearts, the upholstered panel seat on square supports linked by a stretcher.

$1,800-2,400   L&T

ESSENTIAL REFERENCE: LOUIS MAJORELLE

French cabinet-maker, Louis Majorelle (1859-1926) trained as a painter before taking over and industrialising his father's cabinet-making business in Nancy in 1879. He later established several workshops to increase his output.

- Majorelle was inspired by nature, the Art Nouveau movement and Emile Gallé.
- His furniture was usually made of dark hardwoods such as mahogany and rosewood, with fluid outlines and large, sculptural gilt-bronze mounts shaped as orchids or water lilies, alongside delicately carved, inlaid or marquetry decoration in fruitwoods, pewter, or mother-of-pearl.
- Majorelle also designed metalware, and he collaborated with the Daum brothers to produce a variety of lamps with glass shades and elegant bronze and iron mounts.
- Majorelle was one of the founding members of the École de Nancy.

A Louis Majorelle mahogany, tamarind wood and gilt-bronze 'Table Aux Nénuphars'.

c1902

$700,000+

36.5in (92cm) diam

SOT

A Louis Majorelle mahogany two-tiered tea table, with exotic wood marquetry design and gilded bronze handles, signed 'L. Majorelle'.

35in (90cm) wide

$6,000-8,000 **SOTP**

A set of four Emile Gallé Art Nouveau mahogany nesting tables, each with a different inlay, chestnut branch, gladiola stalk, irises, and poppies, unmarked.

Largest: 21.75in (55cm) wide

$6,000-8,000 **DRA**

An Art Nouveau mahogany and inlaid center table, attributed to Mackay Hugh Baillie Scott.

35.75in (91cm) diam

$7,000-8,000 **L&T**

ESSENTIAL REFERENCE: EMILE GALLÉ

Emile Gallé (1846-1904) was a furniture and glass designer, who founded the École de Nancy in 1901, based on the principles of medieval guilds.

- Gallé was influenced by the history of art, Symbolist poetry and literature, and particularly the natural world, which provided him with inspiration for shapes and well as decoration.
- Gallé's furniture was made from richly colored or exotic woods, such as rosewood, maple, walnut or fruitwoods.
- His tables and cabinets often stand on carved supports in the shape of dragonfly wings, or featured cornices carved with snails, moths or bats, etc. Other common decorative features include bronze mounts in the form of insects, fruitwood inlays in the shape of natural motifs, engraved verses by Victor Hugo, Paul Verlaine, and Charles Baudelaire.
- Many of Gallé's pieces were unique and were signed.

An Emile Gallé mahogany display cabinet, carved and inlaid with clematis, with a glass door over two fixed shelves, flanked by side shelves, unmarked.

31.5in (80cm) wide

$10,000-11,000 **DRA**

A 19thC Emile Gallé walnut folio stand, with exotic wood flower marquetry design, signed 'Gallé'.

30.25in (77cm) wide

$13,000-15,000 **SOTP**

An Art Nouveau satinwood standing desk, with small glazed door above shelf fronted by baluster-turned supports, inlaid fall front beneath, on square supports with shaped under tier, labeled Howard & Sons, Stamped 11429/5933 .

66in (167.75cm) high

$6,000-7,000 **BWL**

A Scottish Art Nouveau oak sideboard, inlaid with iridescent enamel heart motifs with cupboard doors inset with stained and leaded glass panels.

64.25in (163cm) wide

$5,000-6,000 **L&T**

An oak stickstand, by Shapland and Petter of Barnstaple.

c1905

$2,400-2,800 **TDG**

A mahogany coal purdonium, the hinged base inset with an oxidized plaque with stylized foliage, the sides with copper plate carrying handles the reverse with ivorene label 'Short & Hayes 25 London Road Southampton'.

38.5in (98cm) high

$1,200-1,600 **WW**

An Art Nouveau inlaid mahogany display cabinet, fitted with stained and leaded glass panel and flanked by marquetry inlaid doors.

73.75in (187cm) high

$4,000-6,000 **L&T**

An Art Nouveau mahogany-inlaid display cabinet, pierced and inlaid with Art Nouveau whiplash foliage and enclosing an astragal glazed door flanked by corresponding panels.

60.25in (153cm) wide

$5,400-6,000   **L&T**

An Art Nouveau mahogany music cabinet, with twin marquetry inlaid panel doors.

39in (99cm) high

$700-900   **L&T**

An Art Nouveau satinwood and inlaid display cabinet, with open shelf supported by turned columns, enclosing cabinet with single glazed door with inlaid panel.

60in (152cm) wide

$4,000-6,000   **L&T**

An Art Nouveau mahogany bureau bookcase, the lower section with sloping fall embellished with decorative copper hinges and two drawers.

76in (193cm) high

$1,000-1,200   **L&T**

An Art Nouveau inlaid mahogany display cabinet, the arched-ledge back with mirror plates on turreted supports, the whole decorated with stylized flowerheads on scrolling tendril stems, highlighted in abalone shell.

55in (140cm) wide

$7,200-8,000   **L&T**

A bentwood desk, designed by Josef Hoffmann, for Jacob et Josef Kohn, the curved ledge paneled back extended to the lower stretcher, with central beveled mirror plate, above inset writing surface, on curved and bracketed square open supports.

Josef Hoffman (1870-1956) was an Austrian architect and designer who created metalwork, jewelry and furniture. He was a leading member of the Vienna Secession, and one of the founding members of Wiener Werkstätte (est. 1903), for which he designed many tables and chairs in beechwood, mahogany, limed oak, and other ebonized woods. Inspired by the work of Charles Rennie Mackintosh, he favoured linear and geometric designs, though his bentwood designs have gently bent corners. Decoration on his furniture typically consists of open-centered rectangles with a ball motif at intersections,

c1900   *44.5in (113.5cm) wide*

$18,000-20,000   **L&T**

An Art Nouveau mahogany and inlaid bedroom suite, comprising a wardrobe, a dressing table, a pot cupboard and a pair of double bed ends.

82.75in (210cm) wide

$5,600-6,400 SUITE   **L&T**

A rosewood wardrobe, by Louis Majorelle, with wrought metal foliate panels above drawers with conforming handles, the central section with mirrored backplate above wrought iron jardinière base, branded signature mark.

98.5in (250cm) wide

$4,600-5,200   **L&T**

A rosewood display cabinet, Louis Majorelle, each inlaid to the hinges with foliate motifs in brass and mother-of-pearl.

71.25in (181cm) wide

$3,000-4,000   **L&T**

A pair of ebonized and parcel-gilt wood chairs, designed by Armand-Albert Rateau, each stamped 'AA RATEAU 1874'.

c1925   *37.25in (94.5cm) high*

$20,000-30,000 PAIR   **SOT**

A 1930s birch armchair, Gerald Summers, Makers of Simple furniture, single sheet of cut and bent birch plywood.

23.75in (60.5cm) wide

$34,000-40,000   **L&T**

A pair of Art Deco beech and palisander wood armchairs.

$1,500-1,700   **L&T**

A pair of Art Deco leather club chairs.

$3,000-4,000   **L&T**

A set of four Machine Age enamel and chrome metal chairs, unmarked.

29in (73.5cm) high

$1,000-1,200   **SK**

An Art Deco day-bed, in walnut veneers.

c1930

$2,800-3,200   **TDG**

An Art Deco Belgian thula wood dining table, the top with draw leaves supported by two square end columns in the center.

c1930   *Closed 42.25in (107cm) wide*

$3,200-4,000   **SK**

An Art Deco birch dining room suite, comprising a sideboard, a side cabinet, and extending dining table, the black laminated top above twin pillars with black plinths, and six matching chairs.

Table 62.25in (158cm) long

$1,500-2,000 SUITE   **L&T**

An Art Deco two-tier steel console table, with brass details and marble top.

72in (182.5cm) wide

$5,000-6,000   **SDR**

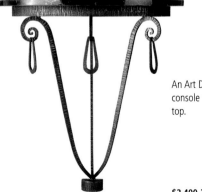

An Art Deco forged steel console table, with marble top.

32in (81cm) wide

$2,400-3,000   **SDR**

ESSENTIAL REFERENCE: GILBERT ROHDE

Gilbert Rohde (1894-1944) founded his New York design studio in 1927, and soon became known for his avant-garde ideas.

● Rohde's furniture was typically made from natural materials like American maple. The sparse hardware was typically metal. Exotic hardwood was used for veneers.

● Rohde had traveled in Germany and many of his pieces were inspired by the Bauhaus. Walter Gropius's influence, in particular, can be seen in Rohde's modular and sectional furniture.

● Much of Rohde's work was designed for corporate manufacturers, such as Herman Miller, Heywood-Wakefield and John Widdicomb. He designed innovative children's furniture for Krohler and a range of tubular steel seating furniture for Troy Sunshade Co. in 1933.

● Rohde's furniture is typically marked. Some custom furniture bears a paper label.

A Herman Miller four-drawer chest, by Gilbert Rohde, in walnut and ash with brass and ebonized wood pulls, Herman Miller label.

48in (122cm) wide

$2,400-3,000   **SDR**

An Art Deco maple chest of drawers, with ebony trim, the drawers with turned rosewood handles, turned tapering legs and brass feet.

39in (99cm) wide

$3,000-4,000   **HT**

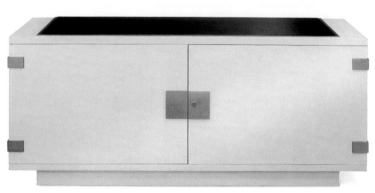

A two-door ivory lacquered chest, with black opaline top encircled with gilded bronze, by Jacques Adnet, opens to reveal two compartments with maple shelves.

69.25in (176cm) wide

$40,000-48,000   **SOTP**

An Art Deco burr walnut 'Gentleman's Fitment', two end wardrobes with a central section with cupboards, shelves and drawers including a white vitrolite-lined 'cool' cabinet.

118in (299.5cm) wide

$1,200-1,600   **HT**

A 1940s Fontana Arte Italian wall mirror, with shelf, clear and blue-tinted mirrored glass, gilt metal.

89.75in (228cm) high

$20,000-30,000   **L&T**

A white painted jardinière stand, in the manner of Koloman Moser, the oval spindle-filled gallery with black sphere spacers enclosing a liner.

36in (91.5cm) wide

$1,500-1,700   **L&T**

A Gabriel Argy-Rousseau pâte-de-verre vase, decorated with four naturalistic thistles on purplish ground, molded with 'G. ARGY-ROUSSEAU' mark.

c1920   6in (15cm) high

$6,000-7,000   DRA

A Gabriel Argy-Rousseau pâte-de-verre box and cover, decorated with formalized honesty leaves, base molded with 'G-ARGY-ROUSSEAU' mark.

c1920   3.75in (9.5cm) high

$4,000-5,000   DRA

A Gabriel Argy-Rousseau pâte-de-cristal paperweight, patterned with two moths in relief, molded 'G Argy-Rousseau' signature.

2.75in (7cm) high

$2,500-3,000   DRA

A Gabriel Argy-Rousseau pâte-de-verre veilleuse lamp shade, incized G.ARGY ROUSSEAU, painted FRANCE.

6in (15cm) high

$6,000-7,000   DRA

A Gabriel Argy-Rousseau pâte-de-verre cabinet vase, 'Masques', with two male masks surrounded by ivy leaves, incized G.ARGY ROUSSEAU.

4in (10cm) high

$3,000-4,000   DRA

ESSENTIAL REFERENCE: DAUM FRÈRES

In 1885, Jean-Louis Auguste and Jean-Antonin Daum took over their father's glass factory in Nancy, France, which became known as 'Daum Frères'. Inspired by the Gallé pieces shown at the 1889 Paris Exhibition, they started making art glass in the early 1890s.

- Early Daum pieces were inspired by nature and the countryside, and images from the East. Many of their trademark innovative techniques were designed to enhance this naturalistic decoration, such as the cloudy, mottled rich background, colored enamel detail, the martelé background, patterns at various depths (intercalaire pieces), and applied foil-backed decoration.
- Many new forms were created by the factory, including the 'Berluze' vase, distinguished by its long thin neck.
- Paul and Henri Daum, the sons of Auguste, and Michel Daum, son of Antonin, introduced the Art Deco style during 1920s. The shapes were simpler, and decorated with stylized geometric acid-etched patterns. At this time, electric lamps became an increasingly important area of production, some of which featured bronze or iron mounts designed by Louis Majorelle or Edgar Brandt.
- In 1962, the factory became a public company, and was renamed 'Cristallerie Daum'.

A Daum etched, engraved, applied, and internally decorated glass vase, patterned with sunflowers with applied centers and gilt leaves on streaked red ground, painted and engraved signature 'DAUM NANCY' with Cross of Lorraine mark.

c1900   15.75in (40cm) high

$3,500-4,500   DRA

A Daum Frères glass vase, the mottled brown and blue ground overlaid in tones of green and ocher, applied with a large spider at the center of its web, flanked by a beetle and a bee against a ground carved with briony leaves and applied with red berries, carved mark 'Daum, Nancy' and cross of Lorraine, underside engraved '54', enameled collection number '1990,472'.

The spider was a popular motif on Daum cameo glass but the very large and prominent spider on this vase is unusual. Unlike Gallé, Daum did not tend to use poetic quotations but with regard to another vase decorated with spiders and nettles a verse provided inspiration, 'I like the spider and I like the nettle, because they are unloved and because no-one looks on them with sympathy, rather everyone with reproval, at their doleful wishes' (See Noël Daum, Daum, Mastery of Glass, Lausanne 1985, p.56.)

c1905   16.5cm (42in) high

$80,000-90,000   SOTH

DECORATIVE ARTS

A Daum etched and enameled glass thistle vase, in autumnal palette on frosted opalescent ground, engraved signature 'Daum Nancy'.

16.75in (42.5cm) high
$7,000-9,000 DRA

A rare Daum Nancy freeform cameo and enamel vase, decorated with wild orchids and bumble bee, signed 'Daum Nancy' in gilt on underside.

10in (25.5cm) high
$18,000-22,000 JDJ

A Daum Nancy cameo and applied glass vase, pink and white acid-etched marguerites, each with a foil-backed applied cabochon center, pale yellow mottled background, acid-etched and gilded signature on underside 'Daum Nancy'.

15in (38cm) high
$25,000-30,000 JDJ

A Daum Nancy wheel-cut vase, autumnal leaf decoration, etched signature to underside of base.

15.5in (39.5cm) high
$2,000-3,000 FRE

A Daum Nancy cameo glass landscape vase, signed in cameo with 'Cross of Lorraine'.

c1910   *21in (53.5cm) high*
$5,000-8,000 FRE

A Daum internally decorated Art Deco vase, with gilt speckled inclusions, engraved 'DAUM NANCY' with Cross of Lorraine mark.

17in (43cm) high
$2,000-3,000 DRA

A Daum cabinet box and cover, etched, enameled and gilt with hydrangea and a border of dragonflies on opalescent ground, with applied glass cabochons, gilt signature 'Daum Nancy' with Cross of Lorraine mark.

c1900   *3.25in (8cm) diam*
$5,000-7,000 DRA

A Daum etched and enameled scenic vase, with continuous frieze of pond scene with egrets in flight, polychrome and gilt on pale green and mauve ground, gilt signature 'Daum Nancy' with Cross of Lorraine mark.

c1890   *8.5in (21.5cm) diam*
$7,000-9,000 DRA

A Victor Durand Art Nouveau threaded vase, in gold iridescence with green lappets, some minor losses to threading, polished pontil.

12in (30.5cm) high
$1,000-1,500 DRA

A Durand gold-lustered glass vase, with ivory swirls, signed 'Durand 1968-6'.

6in (15cm) high
$1,000-1,500 DRA

A Durand Glass ginger jar, with heavy ribbing, in deep amber graded to white, yellow interior, unpolished pontil with some roughness, and thumbnail hairline crack, no lid.

9.75in (25cm) high
$1,000-1,500 DRA

ESSENTIAL REFERENCE: GALLÉ

Emile Gallé (1846-1904) was a pioneer of the Art Nouveau style in France. He set up his first decorating workshop in Nancy in 1873.

- Gallé used the techniques of historical cameo glass-making, but took the process further by using up to five layers of different colored glass, which were cut away by hand to create subtle color gradations. He combined cameo techniques with enameling, mold casting, marquetry and inlay.
- Gallé's glass is highly naturalistic in form and decoration, incorporating flowers, particularly thistles, insects, plants, trees and fossils in the designs.
- Gallé began commercial production of Art Nouveau cameo in c1899. By 1900, the firm was the largest manufacturer of luxury glassware in Europe. Acid-etching was increasingly used on the 'standard' or middle range pieces, though the 'pièces uniques' were still handcrafted by Gallé and his master craftsmen.
- In 1901, Gallé established the École de Nancy, based on the the principles of medieval guilds.
- He died in 1904, leaving his widow to run the factory with Victor Prouvé as art director. A star by Gallé's signature indicates production after his death. The factory closed in 1936.

An Emile Gallé 'Jeanne D'Arc' cameo glass commemorative vase, with panel depicting Joan of Arc on a ground of arabesques, the verso with similar panel featuring a Cross of Lorraine, cameo signature 'Gallé'.

c1895   11in (28cm) high

$15,000-20,000   **DRA**

A glass marqueterie-de-verre vase by Emile Gallé, the delicately striped ground inlaid with four 'Colchium Autumnale', their petals finely carved, the foot applied and carved with leaf forms over foil highlights, engraved mark 'Gallé', enameled collection number '1990,473'.

Emile Gallé wrote to Victor Champier that he had created 'chalice-form blossoms that seek air and daylight' (see Sigrid Barten and Bernd Hakenjos, Keramik, Glas und Möbel des Art Nouveau, Museum Belerive, Zurich, 1980, p.48.) The designs for this series of vases, now in the Musée D'Orsay, are dated 1897 and the pieces were put into production in 1898. It was in this year that Gallé patented the term, 'marqueterie de verre'.

17.25in (44cm) high

$100,000-120,000   **SOTH**

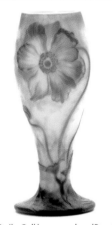

An Emile Gallé cameo glass 'Pavote' vase, with mauve poppies on martelé frosted ground, signed with cameo snail shell.

7.5in (19cm) high

$10,000-15,000   **DRA**

An Emile Gallé cameo glass vase, with mountainous landscape in mauve, blue, and green, on shaded yellow ground, with 'Gallé' cameo signature .

c1900   12.5in (31.5cm) high

$9,000-11,000   **DRA**

An Emile Gallé cameo glass vase, with wooded lakeland landscape in amber on frosted lemon-yellow ground, with 'Gallé' cameo signature .

c1900   7.75in (19.5cm) high

$2,500-3,000   **DRA**

An Emile Gallé cameo glass vase, patterned with red peony blossoms, vertical Japanese cameo signature.

c1900   18in (45.5cm) high

$3,500-4,500   **DRA**

An Emile Gallé cameo glass vase, in shades of purple, partly fire-polished, cameo signature 'GALLE'.

c1900   12.5in (31.5cm) high

$3,500-4,500   **DRA**

A large Emile Gallé marqueterie-de-verre vase, inlaid and carved glass, the boldly striated ground with two butterflies, the reverse with a third, engraved mark 'Gallé'.

c1900   23.5in (60cm) high

$100,000-120,000   **SOTH**

A Gallé cameo vase, the gray glass body covered in blue and amber glass and acid-etched with flowering convolvulus vines in a landscape, cameo signature to body.

13.75in (35cm) high

$4,000-5,000   **L&T**

An Emile Gallé cameo glass vase, the gray glass body overlaid in yellow and amethyst and acid-etched with the depiction of a lily pond with flowering plants, cameo mark 'Gallé'.

10.5in (26.5cm) high

$1,800-2,200   **L&T**

CLOSER LOOK: GALLÉ CAMEO GLASS LAMP

Up to five layers of glass were fused together before the outer layers were cut back using wheel carving and hand-work to create the design which stands out in relief.

Gallé studied botany and used this knowledge to great effect in his glass designs which feature highly naturalistic decoration.

Lamp design was revolutionized by the advent of electricity which allowed cameo glass shades and bases to be illuminated to make the most of both the light and the glass design.

The carver has cleverly graduated the color to give a feeling of added perspective.

An Emile Gallé large cameo glass vase, the graduated peach body cased in deep magenta and cut with a fern pattern, with scroll signature to the lower side.

19in (48cm) high

$3,000-4,000   **FLD**

A table lamp designed by Emile Gallé, 'Rhododendron', with mold-blown and wheel-carved cameo glass shade, base signed in cameo 'Gallé'.

c1925

18in (45.5cm) high

$200,000-250,000   **SOT**

An Emile Gallé cameo vase, decorated with honeysuckle in mauve against a shaded lemon-yellow ground, cameo signature.

9.5in (24cm) high

$1,800-2,200   **DRA**

An Emile Gallé electrified exhibition panel of marks and signatures, with a glass negative medallion against an etched brass mat, in gilded frame surrounded with various Gallé signatures.

1904   *16in (40.5cm) high*

$5,000-6,000   **DRA**

A 'Corolla' lamp by Emile Gallé, cameo glass and bronze, the lamp modeled as a lotus flower, the base cast as three leaves and a bud, cameo mark to glass 'Gallé'.

18in (46cm) high

$120,000-140,000   **SOTH**

ESSENTIAL REFERENCE: RENÉ LALIQUE

Previously a master jeweler, René Lalique (1860-1945) began experimenting with glass in his jewelry designs in the 1880s. He developed his interest in glass in the 1890s and opened a shop in Paris in 1902, making scent bottles and decorative wares for the commercial trade.

- Lalique first produced scent bottles for François Coty c1907, and then most other leading Parisian perfumeries. Many were made in the Art Deco style.
- Lalique is predominantly associated with pressed glass, but many of his thinner vases were molded. His pieces were primarily clear, opalescent or frosted, though many were produced in colored glass, which is now sought after.
- Between 1920 and 1930, Lalique produced designs for over 200 vases and 150 bowls, two of the most popular forms. The crisply molded details, quality of molding and virtuosity of the designs gave mass-produced pieces a 'one-off' feel.
- Virtually all pieces produced before Lalique's death in 1945 are marked 'R. Lalique'. Pieces made afterwards are marked 'Lalique'. The company is still operating, now under the name 'Cristallerie Lalique et Cie'.

A Lalique 'Acanthes' vase, cased butterscotch yellow glass with original bronze stand, molded 'R. LALIQUE' mark, introduced 1921.

Vase 11in (28cm) high

$30,000-35,000   **DRA**

A Lalique 'Acanthes' vase, cased red glass with original bronze stand, molded 'R.LALIQUE' and engraved 'Lalique' marks, introduced 1921.

Vase 11in (28cm) high

$20,000-24,000 **DRA**

A Lalique 'Antilopes' vase, clear glass with black enamel decoration, stenciled 'R. LALIQUE FRANCE' mark, introduced 1925.

10.75in (27.5cm) high

$30,000-36,000 **DRA**

A Lalique 'Aras' opalescent glass vase, molded with birds amongst thorny branches, etched mark 'R.Lalique, France', introduced 1924.

9in (23cm) high

$4,000-5,000 **L&T**

A Lalique 'Avallon' vase, deep yellow amber glass with original wood stand, wheel-cut 'R. LALIQUE FRANCE' mark and engraved 'No. 986', introduced 1927.

Vase 5.75in (14.5cm) high

$6,000-8,000 **DRA**

A Lalique 'Bandes De Roses' vase, clear and frosted glass with sepia patina, molded 'LALIQUE' with extended 'L' mark, introduced 1919.

9.25in (23.5cm) high

$4,000-5,000 **DRA**

A Lalique 'Bresse' vase, amber glass with whitish patina, stenciled 'R. LALIQUE FRANCE' mark, introduced 1931.

4in (10cm) high

$3,000-4,000 **DRA**

A Lalique 'Cariatides' vase and cover, clear and frosted glass with green patina, stenciled 'R. LALIQUE' twice, engraved 'Lalique', introduced 1920.

8in (20cm) high

$8,000-10,000 **DRA**

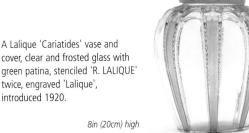

A Lalique 'Champagne' vase, bright green glass, engraved 'R. Lalique France, No. 1004', introduced 1927.

6.5in (16.5cm) high

$4,000-5,000 **DRA**

A Lalique 'Chamois' pattern vase, with Sienna patina, the base with acid-etched 'R. LALIQUE FRANCE' mark, introduced 1931.

4.5in (11.5cm) high

$1,500-2,000 **TGM**

A Lalique 'Courges' vase, cased opalescent glass with blue patina, molded 'R. LALIQUE' mark, introduced 1914.

7.25in (18.5cm) high

$3,000-4,000 **DRA**

MILLER'S COMPARES

A Lalique 'Courlis' vase, deep green glass with whitish patina, stenciled 'R. LALIQUE FRANCE' mark, introduced 1931.

6.5in (16.5cm) high

$7,000-8,000 DRA

A Lalique 'Courlis' vase, red amber glass with whitish patina, stenciled 'R. LALIQUE FRANCE' mark, introduced 1931.

6.5in (16.5cm) high

$11,000-13,000 DRA

Lalique created many variations of the same design even to the point of different pieces having cased interiors (pearly white), or patinated colors added to the exterior. However, mostly, the same forms were available only in a limited and specific grouping of colors. Relatively few forms were available in red.

And so the green and red vases above are typical of Lalique, whose red vases tend to be more valuable than other colors in the same design.

Red is rarer than green because it is harder to work with, being prone to 'burning' in the heat and becoming dull in tone.

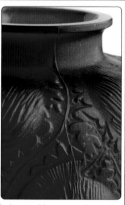

A Lalique 'Domremy' vase, emerald green glass with whitish patina, engraved 'R. Lalique France No. 979', introduced 1926.

8.25in (21cm) high

$5,000-6,000 DRA

A Lalique red amber glass vase, 'Domremy', designed by René Lalique, No. 979, etched 'R Lalique France No.979', introduced 1926.

8.5in (21.5cm) high

$3,500-4,500 WW

A Lalique 'Escargot' vase, deep red glass, molded 'R.LALIQUE' mark, introduced 1920.

8.25in (21cm) high

$25,000-30,000 DRA

A Lalique 'Espalion' vase, cased jade green glass, engraved 'R. Lalique France' mark, introduced 1927.

7in (18cm) high

$6,000-7,000 DRA

A Lalique 'Espalion' vase, blue glass, engraved 'R. Lalique France' mark, introduced 1927.

7in (18cm) high

$3,500-4,500 DRA

A Lalique 'Florence' vase, with brown enamel decoration and sepia patina, stenciled 'R. LALIQUE FRANCE', introduced 1937.

7.5in (19cm) high

$6,000-7,000 DRA

A Lalique 'Formose' vase, clear and frosted glass, molded 'R. LALIQUE' mark, introduced 1924.

6.75in (17cm) high

$2,000-2,800 DRA

A Lalique 'Gobelet Six Figurines' vase, clear and frosted glass with blue patina, engraved 'R. Lalique' mark, introduced 1912.

8in (20.5cm) high

$4,000-5,000 DRA

A Lalique 'Grenade' vase, engraved 'R. Lalique France' mark, introduced 1930.

4.75in (12cm) high

$2,600-3,200 **DRA**

A Lalique 'Gui' vase, pale pea green glass, molded 'R. LALIQUE' mark.

c1920 *6.5in (16.5cm) high*

$2,500-3,000 **DRA**

CLOSER LOOK: LALIQUE VASE

The cire perdue – or lost wax – technique involves making a plaster cast of the object to be made. This is coated with a layer of wax the desired thickness of the finished object and the central cavity of the mold is filled with clay. The mold is then heated until the wax melts and can be drained off. The space left is filled with molten glass.

This piece is remarkable in the depth of the relief decoration which would have been very difficult to achieve using this technique.

The details of the snakes' bodies have been highlighted with a sepia patina.

A René Lalique 'Huit Serpents' 'cire perdue' cast glass vase, the shoulders modeled with eight entangled serpents, engraved 'R.LALIQUE'.

Reptiles were a source of inspiration to Lalique throughout his life and they appear in some of his most spectacular creations such as the gold and enamel pectoral in the Gulbenkian Museum. The motif also appears in bronze and even on an evening handbag embroidered in silver thread on silk and with silver mounts cast as opposing snakes. In cire perdue, other pieces from this period include several vases, 'Quatre Serpents', 'Quatre Serpents et Grenouilles' and a plafonnier 'Quatre Grouped de Deux Serpents'.

8.25in (21cm) high

$120,000-160,000 **SOTH**

A Lalique 'Hirondelles' vase, clear and frosted with glass, grayish patina, molded 'LALIQUE' mark with extended 'L', introduced 1919.

9in (23cm) high

$14,000-16,000 **DRA**

A Lalique 'Lagamar' vase, clear and frosted glass with black enamel decoration, wheel-cut 'R. LALIQUE' mark, introduced 1926.

7.25in (18.5cm) high

$10,000-14,000 **DRA**

A Lalique 'Malesherbes' vase, clear and frosted glass with sepia patina, engraved 'R. Lalique France No. 1014', introduced 1927.

9in (23cm) high

$3,000-4,000 **DRA**

A Lalique 'Moissac' vase, topaz glass, wheel-cut 'R. LALIQUE FRANCE' mark, introduced 1927.

5in (12.5cm) high

$2,000-3,000 **DRA**

A Lalique 'Monnaie du Pape' vase, stenciled 'R. LALIQUE FRANCE' mark, introduced 1914.

9in (23cm) high

$3,000-4,000 **DRA**

A Lalique 'Nivernais' vase, bright green glass, engraved 'R. Lalique France, No. 1005', introduced 1927.

6.5in (16.5cm) high

$3,400-4,000 **DRA**

A Lalique 'Ormeaux' vase, red amber glass, engraved 'R. Lalique France' mark, introduced 1926.

6.5in (16.5cm) high

$3,000-3,600 **DRA**

A Lalique 'Ormeaux' vase, cased jade green glass, engraved 'R. Lalique France, No. 984'.

c1926 *6.5in (16.5cm) high*

$12,000-14,000 **DRA**

A Lalique 'Palissy' frosted glass vase, of ovoid form molded with shells, molded mark 'R. Lalique', introduced 1926.

6.75in (17cm) high

$1,700-2,000   **L&T**

A Lalique 'Pearls' pattern Agate glass vase, the base molded 'R. LALIQUE', introduced 1925.

Vases in the pearl pattern are scarce, as the pattern was usually used for scent bottles or dressing table sets. Furthermore, this example is in Agate glass, which is again scarce.

4.75in (12cm) high

$5,000-6,000   **TGM**

A Lalique 'Perruches' vase, pea green glass, engraved 'R. Lalique France', introduced 1919.

9.75in (24.5cm) high

$12,000-14,000   **DRA**

A Lalique 'Poissons' vase, deep red glass, engraved 'R. Lalique' and molded 'R. LALIQUE' marks.

c1921   *9.25in (23.5cm) high*

$20,000-25,000   **DRA**

A Lalique 'Rampillon' vase, yellow amber glass, wheel-cut 'R. LALIQUE FRANCE' mark, introduced 1927.

5in (12.5cm) high

$2,400-2,800   **DRA**

A Lalique 'Ronces' vase, red amber glass, molded 'R. LALIQUE' mark, introduced 1921.

9in (23cm) high

$5,000-6,000   **DRA**

A Lalique 'Sauge' vase, red amber glass with whitish patina, molded 'R.LALIQUE' mark, introduced 1923.

9.75in (25cm) high

$5,000-6,000   **DRA**

A Lalique 'Sirenes et Cabochons' vase, clear and frosted glass with sepia patina, molded 'R. LALIQUE' mark, introduced 1914.

7.75in (19.5cm) high

$11,000-13,000   **DRA**

A Lalique 'Sirenes Avec Bouchon Figurine' vase, with stopper, of clear and frosted glass, engraved 'R. Lalique France', flat chip to base of stopper, fleck to inner rim of vase, introduced 1920.

14in (35.5cm) high

$13,000-17,000   **DRA**

A Lalique 'Sylvia' vase, clear and frosted glass with blue patina, wheel-cut 'R. LALIQUE FRANCE' mark, introduced 1929.

8.5in (21.5cm) high

$9,000-11,000   **DRA**

A Rene Lalique vase, 'Tortues', molded clear glass with sepia patina, of globular form with a flared mouth, the surface covered with tortoises, molded 'R. Lalique' to underside, introduced 1926.

10.25in (26cm) high

$12,000-16,000   **FRE**

A large limited edition Rene Lalique 'Tourbillons' re-issue vase, with a deep wall relief-molded with spiral spiked motifs picked out in black enamel over the clear crystal ground, engraved signature and numbered '462 of 999' produced, complete with presentation certificate and box.

8in (21cm) high

$5,000-6,000   **FLD**

A Lalique 'Tournesol' opalescent vase, with remains of light staining, the base inscribed 'R. Lalique France No.1007', introduced 1927.

4.25in (11cm) high

$2,000-2,500   **TGM**

A Lalique 'Fleurons' pattern opalescent glass dish, with molded 'R.LALIQUE' signature, introduced 1935.

Values depend on the opalescence amongst other factors. This example has an excellent level of opalescence, making it desirable.

10.25in (26cm) diam

$800-1,000 **TGM**

A Lalique 'Gazelles' opalescent glass with blue patina dish, molded 'R. LALIQUE' and wheel-cut 'FRANCE' marks, introduced 1925.

11.5in (29cm) diam

$1,800-2,400 **DRA**

A Lalique 'Martigues' opalescent amber glass bowl, molded 'LALIQUE' mark.

14in (35.5cm) diam

$5,500-6,000 **DRA**

A 1980's Lalique 'Deux Moineaux' center bowl, clear and frosted glass, design no. 11000, engraved 'Lalique France'.

15.75in (40cm) long

$700-900 **DRA**

A Lalique 'Roscoff' opalescent glass bowl, engraved 'R. Lalique France' mark, introduced 1932.

13.75in (35cm) diam

$2,800-3,200 **DRA**

A Lalique 'Fauvettes' ashtray, amber glass, molded 'R. LALIQUE' and engraved 'R. Lalique France' marks. c1924. 6.75in (17cm) diam

$1,000-1,500 **DRA**

A Lalique 'Serpent' ashtray, electric blue glass, engraved 'R. Lalique' mark, introduced 1920.

4.5in (11.5cm) diam

$3,000-4,000 **DRA**

A Lalique glass ashtray, 'Statuette De La Fontaine' No.288, clear and frosted, engraved 'R Lalique', introduced 1925.

4.75in (12cm) high

$1,700-2,000 **WW**

A Lalique 'Nenuphar' inkwell, clear and frosted glass with gray patina, engraved 'Lalique' mark, introduced 1910.

2.75in (7cm) diam

$1,500-2,000 **DRA**

A Lalique 'Serpents' inkwell, in opalescent dark amber, engraved 'R. Lalique', introduced 1920.

6.25in (16cm) diam

$4,000-6,000 **DRA**

A Lalique 'Trois Sirenes' opalescent glass inkwell, with original cover, molded 'R. LALIQUE' mark, introduced 1921.

9in (23cm) diam

$15,000-17,000 **DRA**

A Lalique 'Cleones' opalescent glass box, molded 'R. LALIQUE' mark, introduced 1921.

10in (25.5cm) diam

$3,000-4,000 **DRA**

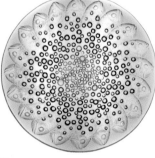

A Lalique 'Panier De Roses' oval box, clear and frosted glass with blue patina, molded 'R. LALIQUE' mark, introduced 1919.

3.5in (8.5cm) long

$2,500-3,000   **DRA**

A Lalique 'Quatre Papillons' box, opalescent glass with sepia patina, engraved 'R. Lalique France' mark, introduced 1911.

3in (7.5cm) diam

$3,000-4,000   **DRA**

A Lalique 'Quatre Scarabees' box, electric blue glass with whitish patina, molded 'R. LALIQUE' mark, introduced 1911.

3.5in (9cm) diam

$3,000-4,000   **DRA**

A Lalique 'Tokio' blue glass box, molded 'LALIQUE' and engraved 'France' marks, introduced 1921.

6.75in (17cm) diam

$9,000-11,000   **DRA**

A Lalique 'D'Aigle' automobile hood ornament, clear and frosted glass with original chrome collar on black glass bookend base, molded 'R. LALIQUE' mark, introduced 1928.

7in (17.5cm) high

$4,000-6,000   **DRA**

A Lalique 'De Coq' automobile hood ornament, clear and frosted glass, molded 'LALIQUE FRANCE' mark, with Lucite stand, introduced 1928.

7in (17.5cm) high

$2,500-3,000   **DRA**

A Lalique 'Grenouille' automobile hood ornament, clear and frosted glass, molded 'LALIQUE', engraved 'R. Lalique France' marks, introduced 1928.

2.5in (6cm) high

$13,000-15,000   **DRA**

A Lalique 'Hirondelle' car mascot, molded as a swallow, clear and frosted glass with chromium-plated part mount, molded mark 'R. Lalique/ France'. No. '1143'.

5.75in (14.5cm) high

$3,500-4,500   **L&T**

A Lalique 'Libellule' car mascot, clear and frosted glass with amethyst inclusion, mounted on removable turned brass plinth, molded mark 'R. Lalique', etched script mark 'R. Lalique/ France', no. '1145', chip to foot rim.

8in (20.5cm) high

$5,000-6,000   **L&T**

A Lalique 'Perche' automobile hood ornament, clear and frosted glass with gray patina, molded and stenciled 'R. LALIQUE FRANCE' mark.

6.25in (16cm) high

$1,500-2,000   **DRA**

A Lalique 'Pintade' automobile hood ornament, clear and frosted glass, wheel-cut 'R. LALIQUE FRANCE' mark, introduced 1929.

6in (15cm) high

$7,000-9,000   **DRA**

A Lalique 'Coq Nain' automobile hood ornament, clear and frosted glass, molded 'R. LALIQUE FRANCE' mark, introduced 1928.

8in (20.5cm) high

$1,500-2,000   **DRA**

DECORATIVE ARTS

A Lalique 'Daim' paperweight, clear and frosted glass, molded 'R. LALIQUE' mark, introduced 1929.

3in (7.5cm) long

$1,000-1,500 DRA

A Lalique 'Rhinoceros' paperweight, clear and frosted glass, stenciled 'R. LALIQUE FRANCE' mark, introduced 1931.

4.5in (11.5cm) long

$4,000-6,000 DRA

A Lalique 'Toby' paperweight, clear and frosted glass, stenciled 'R. LALIQUE FRANCE' mark, introduced 1931.

3.5in (9cm) wide

$1,500-2,000 DRA

A Lalique clear crystal 'Bellecour Sparrow' paperweight, frosted finish and light gray hue, relief-molded above blackberries, bears diamond point-engraved signature to the base, introduced 1927.

4.25in (11cm) high

$700-900 FLD

A Lalique 'Deux Figurines' clock, clear and frosted glass, with original decorated metal illuminating base, lower edge of clock polished, mostly inside base, and with internal fracture to one corner, unsigned, introduced 1926.

15.25in (39cm) high

$3,500-4,500 DRA

A Lalique 'Inseparables' frosted and opalescent timepiece, the single train movement with painted circular dial within glass case, molded with budgerigars, within fitted leather case, molded mark 'R. Lalique', etched script mark 'France No. 258'.

4.25in (11cm) high

$7,000-9,000 L&T

A Lalique 'Roitelets' clock, clear and frosted glass with black enamel numerals, original movement and hands, small internal bruise behind numeral 3, stenciled 'R. LALIQUE FRANCE' mark, introduced 1931.

7.5in (19cm) high

$3,000-5,000 DRA

A Lalique 'Cerises' rocker blotter, clear and frosted glass with sepia patina, original metal rocker, molded 'R. LALIQUE' mark, introduced 1920.

6.5in (16.5cm) long

$2,000-2,500 DRA

A Lalique 'Grupe de Six Moineaux' decorative motif, clear and frosted glass, stenciled 'R. LALIQUE FRANCE' mark, introduced 1933.

11.75in (30cm) long

$3,500-4,500 DRA

A Lalique 'Figurine' clear glass seal, etched in bas relief with a nude, blank seal, etched script mark 'R. Lalique, France'.

3.25in (8.5cm) high

$4,000-5,000 L&T

A Lalique 'Papillon ailes ferme' frosted glass seal, with original blue staining, blank seal, etched script mark 'R. Lalique'

2.25in (6cm) high

$2,000-2,500 L&T

A Lalique 'Sorbier' pendant, electric blue glass with blue silk cord, probably original, molded 'LALIQUE' mark, introduced 1920.

2in (5cm) long

$1,500-2,000 DRA

A Lalique 'Vase de Fleur' seal, clear and frosted glass molded as a vase of flowers, with applied gilt seal with monogram, etched mark 'Lalique'.

2.5in (6.5cm) high

$1,700-2,000 L&T

A Lalique 'William' glass, clear and frosted with blue enamel decoration, engraved 'R. Lalique France', introduced 1925.

5.75in (14.5cm) high

$600-800 DRA

A Rene Lalique design for a horn hair comb, ink and watercolor on BFK Rives parchment paper, with annotations in Lalique's hand, upper right.

Provenance: Lalique Family collection.

1900 *8.5in (21.5cm)wide*

$5,000-6,000 DRA

A Loetz iridescent green vase, with internal trailing tendril decoration and trefoil lip, engraved 'Loetz Austria'.

9.5in (24cm) diam

$2,000-3,000 DRA

A Loetz Witwe coupe vase, by Maria Licarz, in oilspot pattern, unmarked.

11.5in (29cm) high

$1,700-2,200 DRA

An early 20thC Loetz iridescent glass vase, of amphora form with twisted handles on a favrile ground, signed 'Loetz, Austria'.

7in (18cm) high

$800-1,000 FRE

An early 20thC Loetz iridescent art glass vase, decorated with a pulled feather design on green favrile ground, unsigned.

5in (12.5cm) high

$2,800-3,200 FRE

A Loetz glass vase, designed by Michael Powolny, ribbed amber body with black rim, on three applied black glass ball feet, unmarked.

6.25in (16cm) high

$350-450 WW

An early 20thC Loetz Art Nouveau silver overlay vase, the triform dimple body decorated with silver whiplash stemmed flowers over the green Papillion ground.

10.75in (27cm) high

$3,000-4,000 FLD

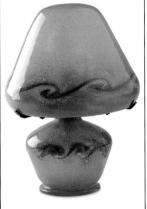

A Monart glass lamp and shade, the turquoise glass with green swirling bands and bubble inclusions, the shade of mushroom form above a squat shouldered base, bears original paper label 'VII.P/29.410'.

12.5in (31.5cm) high

$4,800-5,200 L&T

A Monart SA V glass vase, mottled blue and green.

9in (23cm) high

$700-900 L&T

A Monart A VII glass vase, mottled pink and purple.

6.75in (17cm) high

$500-700 L&T

A Monart JB VII glass goblet, surface decorated with blue, green, yellow and white.

7in (18cm) high

$2,000-2,500 L&T

A Monart RF IV glass vase, mottled red and orange with aventurine inclusions.

12in (30.5cm) high

$900-1,100 L&T

A Monart FI V glass vase, mottled pale green with aventurine inclusions.

15.25in (39cm) high

$1,100-1,300 L&T

A Monart D glass vase, mottled pale green and pink with aventurine inclusions, bears partial label.

14in (36cm) high

$700-900 L&T

A Monart KC glass vase, mottled green and orange.

7in (18cm) high

$1,000-1,200 L&T

A Monart HC VI glass vase, pale blue with bubble inclusions.

7in (18cm) high

$900-1,100 L&T

A Monart tapering glass vase, with yellow, blue and turquoise craquelure inclusions.

9in (23cm) high

$1,200-1,400 L&T

A Monart C VII glass vase, mottled green and blue with surface decoration.

7in (17.5cm) high

$900-1,100 L&T

A Le Verre Francais Art Deco vase, with stylized Japanese flora in red on mottled orange ground, engraved 'Le Verre Francais'.

19in (48cm) high

$3,500-4,000 DRA

A Charles Schneider mottled glass globular vase, in shades of pink and orange, engraved 'Schneider' mark.

c1925 *10in (25.5cm) high*

$800-1,000 DRA

A Schneider footed bowl, with bubble inclusions, raised on a turned amethyst glass column and spreading base, stencil-etched mark 'Schneider France'.

14.25in (36.5cm) high

$750-850 L&T

A large Schneider cameo glass vase, in a graduated orange to blue over mottled tan ground and cut in the 'Fig Tree' pattern with a repeat stylized foliate motif, murrine cane to base.

19.4in (49.5cm) high

$4,000-6,000 FLD

A Barovier 'Crepuscolo' vase, designed by Ercole Barovier, the clear-cased cream and amber glass with aventurine inclusions, the base with remains of factory paper label.

1933-35   12.75in (32cm) high

$1,500-2,000   QU

A 1930s Barovier flared glass vase, red cased with clear bubbles and side decoration.

11in (17.9cm) high

$3,500-4,500   PC

A Barovier & Toso 'Oriente' vase, designed by Ercole Barovier, honey-colored glass with silver-foil inlays and wavy bands of blue, purple, red, turquoise, yellow and green.

1940   7.25in (18cm) high

$8,000-12,000   PC

A Ferro-Toso-Barovier inverted bell-shaped 'Vetro Mosaico' vase, designed by Ercole Barovier, with murrines in opaque yellow and brown.

c1930   8.5in (21.4cm) high

$12,000-14,000   VZ

A Ferro-Toso-Barovier 'Autunno Gemmato' vase, designed by Ercole Barovier, the 'tortoiseshell' ground with silver inclusions and six large clear glass applications.

Ercole Barovier designed a group of thick-walled pieces in 1935-36 using decorative techniques, including Crepuscolo, Autonno Gemmato, Marina Gemmata and Laguna Gemmata. This piece is typical of the soft shapes used during this period which differ greatly from the lighter, more brightly colored pieces produced in the years following the Second World War.

1935-36   11in (28cm) high

$3,000-5,000   SOTH

A Seguso-Ferro 'Pulegoso' pale blue vase, designed by Ercole Barovier.

'Pulegoso' is translucent glass that is identified by a countless number of bubbles ('puleghe' in the dialect of Murano) contained in the glass, obtained by chemical reactions during the heating process.

1935-40   11in (28cm) high

$8,000-10,000   SOTH

An MVM Cappellin footed bowl or tazza, with amber-gold tinted glass, the base with 'MVM Cappellin Murano' acid stamp, designed by Vittorio Zecchin.

1922-25   4.25in (11cm) high

$800-1,200   QU

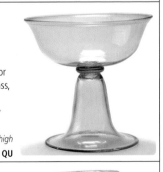

A Seguso Vetri D'Arte beaker vase, designed by Flavio Poli, cased in blue and red, the surface with shallow pulled lobes.

1937   8in (20cm) high

$2,500-3,000   QU

A Seguso Vetri D'Arte 'Pulegoso' footed vase, the green body with 'foamy' irregular internal air bubbles, diagonal ribbing, the side trails with fine gold foil inclusions terminating in handles.

c1940   12in (30.5cm) high

$2,000-2,500   QU

A Seguso Vetri D'Arte 'Sommerso A Bollicine' vase, in red glass with gold inclusions.

c1940   8in (20.5cm) high

$5,000-6,000   **SOTH**

A Fratelli Toso urn vase, the opaque black baluster body with gold foil inclusions and applied opaque red spiraling trail to neck and double handles.

c1915-20   14.5in (36cm) high

$3,000-4,000   **QU**

A Venini 'Laguna' bell vase, designed by Tomaso Buzzi, the milky pink body with melted fine gold foil inclusions.

1932   6.25in (15.5cm) high

$5,000-6,000   **QU**

A Venini 'Sommerso A Bollicine' vase, designed by Carlo Scarpa, the green body with randomly sized internal bubbles and gold foil inclusions arranged in columns, the base with 'Venini Murano' acid stamp.

1934-36   10.5 in (26.5cm) high

$5,000-6,000   **QU**

A Venini 'A Bolle' vase, of amorphous form, designed by Carlo Scarpa, decorated with a network of controlled internal bubbles, the base with 'Venini Murano ITALIA' acid stamp.

1936   6in (15cm) high

$2,000-2,500   **QU**

A Venini 'Battuto' vase, designed by Carlo Scarpa, the violet-black double gourd shaped body with hammered effect cut surface, the base with 'Venini Murano' acid stamp.

1940   9.5in (24cm) high

$18,000-22,000   **QU**

A Venini 'A Bugne' vase, designed by Carlo Scarpa in green glass, later factory signed 'venini italia'.

1940   12in (31cm) high

$45,000-50,000   **SOTH**

A Venini 'Opalino' vase, designed by Tomaso Buzzi, the blue glass with white lattimo border, circular label 'Venini Murano'.

1932   8.5in (21.5cm) high

$4,000-5,000   **SOTH**

A 'Cavallino' horse sculpture, the design attributed to Napoleone Martinuzzi for Zecchin-Martinuzzi, the red glass body with molded ribs and fine gold foil inclusions, with applied legs, tail and mane.

1933.   6.25in (16cm) high

$3,000-3,500   **QU**

An early 20thC Steuben 'Aurene' glass vase of flattened bottle form, applied with raised handles, signed 'Steuben Aurene' 1914'

13in (33cm) high

$8,000-9,000   **FRE**

A pair of Steuben amber and blue glass candlesticks, waffle mark.

c1920.   *12in (30.5cm) high*

$2,000-3,000   **DRA**

A tall Steuben gold Aurene vase, etched 'Aurene 2418', with a few short scratches.

16.75in (42.5cm) high

$1,100-1,500   **DRA**

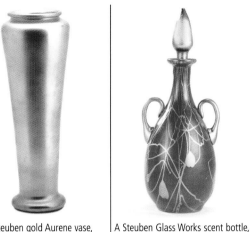

A Steuben Glass Works scent bottle, model no. 3048, decorated aurene glass, engraved 'Aurene' twice.

c1910-1915   *6.5in (16.5cm) high*

$24,000-28,000   **SOT**

A Steuben millefiori flower-form vase, iridescent gold coloring with heart, vine and millefiori decoration with applied gold Aurene foot, marked 'Aurene 578'.

11in (28cm) high

$18,000-22,000   **JDJ**

A Tiffany Studios favrile glass compote, with iridescent green rim on an opalescent base, engraved 'L.C.T. Favrile 1702C'.

6in (15cm) high

$2,000-2,500   **DRA**

A Tiffany Studios carved and internally decorated Favrile glass vase, with leafage in green on gold, engraved 'L.C.Tiffany Favrile 4252J'.

6.25in (16cm) high

$6,000-8,000   **DRA**

A Tiffany Studios leaded-glass window, with trophy center of crest, ribbons, acorns, oak leaves, and red 'jewels,' surrounded by swirling leaves, unmarked.

28in (71cm) wide

$9,000-10,000   **DRA**

An important Tiffany Studios aquamarine paperweight glass ornament, depicting a single fish swimming against a background of aquatic foliage in an aquamarine sea, engraved 'L.C.Tiffany Inc. Favrile 6508N'.

6.25in (16cm) high

$20,000-25,000   **DRA**

A Tiffany Studios gold Favrile floriform compote, with green tendrils, etched 'L.C.T. Favrille'.

8.5in (21.5cm) diam

$2,000-3,000   **DRA**

A Tiffany Studios gold Favrile pitcher, with green leaf and vine pattern, etched 1257, blacked-out number, 'L C TIFFANY-Favrile'.

8.75in (22cm) high

$3,500-4,500   **DRA**

An early 20thC Tiffany Furnaces Favrile glass and enamel vase, the slender stem and flared faceted rim raised on a blue/turquoise enameled base, stamped 'Louis C. Tiffany Furnaces, Inc. 151' with monogram.

13in (33cm) high

$1,000-1,500   **FRE**

ESSENTIAL REFERENCE: WEBB

In 1855, Thomas Webb (1804-1869) moved his company to Stourbridge, West Midlands, England, where, by 1859, it became known as Thomas Webb & Sons.

- In the late 19th/early 20thC, Webb produced cameo glass ranges combining clear glass and at least one other color (red, yellow, blue and white).
- The in-house cameo team was led by two brothers, George and Thomas Woodall. Their specialties were Classical, historical and mythological scenes.
- The factory also produced commercial cameo, generally decorated with floral motifs in white on yellow or white on red ground. Many of the best pieces were the work of Daniel Pearce and his son Lionel, who joined the company in 1884.
- After 1900, the new managing director, Congreve William Jackson, steered the family away from elaborate glass like cameo, as the market was declining rapidly.

A Webb blue cameo glass decorated bowl, the bright cobalt blue sphere layered in shades of blue and white, deeply cut and stippled overall in stylized floral repeating tapestry motif with six medallion elements, carved base stamped with circular 'Webb Gem Cameo' mark.

5in (12.5cm) diam

$11,000-15,000 **SK**

A Webb Gem cameo glass gilt-enameled vase, the gilt decoration by Jules Barbe, master decorator, decorated in the Japanese style, the body with red flowers in cameo, gilt branches and leaves on an intricate scroll decorate ground, chevron-decorated base rim, signed 'Thomas Webb & Sons/Gem Cameo'.

1888

$40,000-45,000 **SK**

A Thomas Webb & Sons cameo-carved glass solifleur vase, milky glass overlaid with peach and white, decorated with a butterfly amongst hibiscus flowers, unmarked.

7.5in (19cm) high

$2,000-3,000 **WW**

A Webb Gem cameo glass four-layer decorated vase, colorless crystal case in bright red and layered yellow over white cameo-cut and meticulously carved overall in repeating Asian influenced pattern, stamped 'Thomas Webb & Sons Gem Cameo'.

7in (18cm) high

$40,000-45,000 **SK**

A Webb Gem cameo glass Japonesque decorated bottle vase, in Webb raisin brown overlaid with white, cameo-cut and carved intricately with basketweave motif, above assorted blossoms, with bamboo, grasses and fern, intricate border motifs, stamped 'Thomas Webb & Sons Gem Cameo'.

8.5in (21.5cm) high

$20,000-25,000 **SK**

A Webb Gem cameo glass decorated vase, citron yellow overlaid in white cameo-cut and carved with a profusion of open-petaled roses. buds, leaves and stems with a moth, butterfly and ivy on the opposite side, marked 'Thomas Webb & Sons Gem Cameo'.

13.75in (35cm) high

$20,000-25,000 **SK**

A 'Clutha' green glass vase, by James Couper & Sons, Glasgow, with aventurine and milky inclusions.

6.25in (16cm) high

$1,800-2,200 **L&T**

An early 20thC pâte-de-verre pedestal bowl, by François Emile Décorchemont, with theatrical face mask handles, bears lozenge mark to the lower side.

c1920 *5in (13cm) wide*

$3,500-4,500 **FLD**

A D'Argenthal cameo glass cabinet vase, patterned with stylized amber fronds on pale green ground, with cameo signature 'D'Argenthal'.

c1905 *4.5in (11.5cm) high*

$800-1,000 **DRA**

A De Vez cameo glass vase, of tapering form, the lemon yellow body overlaid in amethyst and acid-etched with irises, etched cameo mark.

8in (20.5cm) high

$600-800 **L&T**

A pair of 1930's Art Deco Haida region enameled vases, decorated in the manner of the Wiener Werkstätte with fluted black line cartouches with enameled birds over a stylized black line leaf-and-flower ground.

5.5in (14cm) high

$600-800 **FLD**

A Haida school glass vase, decorated with a yellow and black grid enclosing carved concave roundels.

13.5in (34cm) high

$1,200-1,600 **L&T**

A Bohemian glass Wilhelm Kralik Sohn vase, the blue iridescent body with flashes of gold, green and purple, decorated with a random design of platinum iridescence with flashes of blue and green, housed within an Art Nouveau metal surround.

23in (58.5cm) high

$16,000-20,000 **JDJ**

A Legras enameled glass vase, decorated with a floral roundel on a mottled orange, yellow and opalescent round, signed 'Legras'.

18in (46cm) high

$4,000-5,000 **FRE**

A Muller Frères etched and enameled scenic vase, with wooded winter landscape in naturalistic colors on shaded mauve and amber ground, cameo signature.

4.25in (10.5cm) high

$1,200-1,600 **DRA**

A Muller Frères large cameo vase, of shouldered ovoid form and cased in deep magenta over cranberry over clear, acid-cut with large peony flowers in bud and full bloom with acid-cut signature to the side.

17.75in (45cm) high

$4,000-5,000 **FLD**

A Muller Frères cameo glass vase, the baluster glass body of clear glass overlaid in blue and acid-etched with a landscape scene, cameo mark.

10.5in (26.5cm) high

$1,500-2,000 **L&T**

A Quezal eight-light lily lamp, with gold iridescent assembled lily shades on a patinated metal base, shades engraved 'Quezal', base unmarked.

c1920 *18in (45.5cm) high*

$3,000-4,000 **DRA**

An early 20thC Stevens & Williams cased decanter, with frill-collar neck and hollow blown plume stopper, the body cased in green over clear and flash-cut with Classical inspired foliate scrolls and swags.

10.5in (27cm) high

$1,200-1,600 FLD

A Wiener Werkstätte gilded and enameled glass vase, decorated by Reni Schaschl, the body painted in white enamel with figures dancing through trees, with exotic flowering plants below, painted marks.

6.5in (16.5cm) high

$1,000-1,500 L&T

A Wiener Werkstätte enameled glass decanter and stopper, clear glass body painted in colored enamels with lattice design and further decorated in gilt with flower sprigs.

7.25in (18.5cm) high

$1,100-1,300 L&T

A 1920s German painted glass tazza, by Adolf Beckert, painted in gilt and black enamel with a procession of fauns, the tapered faceted stem on circular spreading base.

13in (33cm) high

$900-1,100 L&T

An Amalric Walter pâte-de-verre crab paperweight, in deep green and blue, incized 'A WALTER NANCY'.

2.5in (6.5cm) wide

$1,100-1,500 DRA

A Scottish Arts & Crafts stained, leaded and glass panel, depicting Saint Maurice (or Saint Victor) with a donor.

This panel is copied from the original late 15thC painting by Jean Hey, the Master of Moulins. The painting currently hangs in Kelvingrove Art Gallery and Museum, Glasgow. It was bequeathed to the city by Archibald McMillan in 1854 and is thought to be a fragment. A religious scene would originally have appeared to the left of the picture.

19.75in (50cm) high

$3,500-4,500 L&T

A pair of Aesthetic Movement stained, painted and leaded glass panels, each of rectangular outline, and painted with female figures within a border of panels painted with flowers, inscribed 'Painting' and 'Music'.

27in (69cm) high

$4,000-5,000 PAIR L&T

A pair of Aesthetic Movement large leaded-glass and painted windows, framed.

c1885.

33in (84cm) wide

$10,000-15,000 DRA

A pair of Scottish Arts & Crafts stained, leaded and painted glass panels, depicting 'Robert Bruce' and 'Queen Margaret'.

c1890 *38.5in (98cm) high*

$2,000-2,500 PAIR L&T

An American Philadelphia stained glass window.

PROVENANCE: From the mansion of financier Alexander Van Rensselaer, built in 1898, the corner of 18th and Walnut Street, now the flagship Anthropologie store.

1898 *42.5in (108cm) high*

$14,000-18,000 FRE

A Tiffany 'Hearts and Vines' four-panel table screen, each arched patinated bronze and favrile glass panel comprised of three sections, the upper section with twining leafy vines against a yellow ground, above mottled green glass lower sections, unmarked.

c1900 *16.5in (42cm) wide*

$2,000-3,000 FRE

An early 20thC leaded glass window, with a mosaic of colored glass depicting two pillars centering a robed figure holding a child, unsigned.

75in (191cm) high

$6,000-8,000   SK

A pair of stained, leaded and painted glass panels, by Guthrie & Wells Ltd., Glasgow, depicting 'Sir Percival and the Holy Grail', the other depicting the Grail with female attendants, signed and dated 'Guthrie & Wells Ltd.'.

c1930   *31.5in (80cm) high*

$10,000-12,000 PAIR   L&T

SCENT BOTTLES

A Lalique 'Dans La Nuit' scent display bottle, for Worth, sealed, and with original string labels (no contents), molded 'R. LALIQUE' mark, introduced 1924.

9.75in (24.5cm) high

$2,500-3,000   DRA

A Lalique 'Elegance' scent bottle, for D'Orsay, frosted glass with brown patina, with frolicking figures, partial label, molded 'R. LALIQUE' mark, introduced 1914.

3.75in (9.5cm) high

$4,000-5,000   DRA

A Lalique 'Imprudence' factice scent bottle, for Worth, clear glass with silvered edge detail, molded 'R. LALIQUE' mark, introduced 1938.

A factice is a large shop-window dummy.

9.5in (24cm) high

$1,500-2,000   DRA

A Lalique 'Jaytho' scent bottle, for Jay Thorpe, clear and frosted glass with sepia patina, molded 'MADE IN FRANCE' mark, introduced 1928.

6in (15cm) high

$800-1,000   DRA

A Lalique 'Je Reviens' scent bottle, for Worth, blue and opaque aqua glass in silver-metal case, introduced 1931.

This is the earliest version of this skyscraper design.

5.5in (14cm) high

$2,000-2,500   DRA

A Lalique 'La Perle Noire' scent bottle, for Forvil, clear and topaz glass, molded 'R. LALIQUE PARIS FRANCE' mark, stopper frozen, introduced 1922.

4.5in (11.5cm) high

$3,000-4,000   DRA

A Lalique 'La Phalene' scent bottle, for D'Heraud, clear and frosted Amberina glass, designed as a nymph with butterfly wings, molded 'R. LALIQUE' mark, introduced 1925.

3.5in (9cm) high

$7,000-8,000   DRA

A Lalique 'Le Jade' molded glass scent bottle and stopper, for Roget et Gallet, Paris, indistinct molded mark 'R.L. France'.

3.25in (8cm) high

$3,000-4,000   L&T

CLOSER LOOK: TRÉSOR DE LA MER SCENT BOTTLE

This presentation was made for Saks Fifth Avenue, and a corded label in the form of a booklet identifies this example as No. 72 from a limited edition of 100.

The opalescent glass shell-form box contains a clear and frosted glass pearl-form bottle.

The box and bottle are in the original red velvet presentation box lined in gold silk and blue velvet.

The presentation box retains its original Saks price tag affixed underneath, indicating a price of $50. Glass box retains partial label on inside lid and both the glass box and bottle are signed by Lalique.

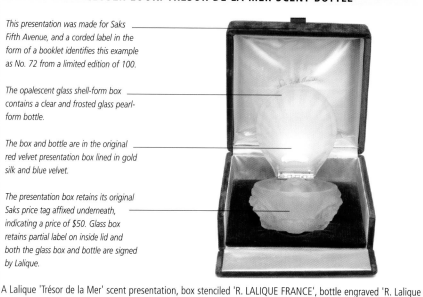

A Lalique 'Trésor de la Mer' scent presentation, box stenciled 'R. LALIQUE FRANCE', bottle engraved 'R. Lalique France'.

c1936   *Glass box 5.75in (14.5cm) long*

$200,000+   DRA

A Lalique 'Misti' scent bottle, for Piver, clear and frosted glass with blue patina, butterfly motif, molded 'R. LALIQUE' mark, introduced 1913.

2in (5cm) high

$3,000-4,000   DRA

A Lalique 'Narkiss' scent bottle, for Roger et Gallet, with company label and Shanghai perfumier's label in Mandarin Chinese, molded 'R.L.' mark, introduced 1912.

4in (10cm) high

$2,000-3,000   DRA

A Lalique 'Orchis' scent bottle', for Colgate, clear and frosted glass with rose patina, with label, molded 'R. LALIQUE' mark, introduced 1927.

3.5in (9cm) high

$2,500-3,000   DRA

A Lalique 'Rosace Figurines' scent bottle, clear and frosted glass with sepia patina, figural stopper version, engraved 'Lalique France' mark, introduced 1912.

5in (13cm) high

$3,500-4,500   DRA

A Lalique/Viard 'Roses' Baccarat scent bottle for D'Orsay, crystal bottle with stopper and cover, mounted with R. Lalique figural metalwork designed by Julian Viard, in lavender suede box with gold moiré interior, stamped 'RL' on metal, introduced 1912.

5.5in (14cm) high

$4,000-5,000   DRA

A Lalique 'Sans Adieu' scent bottle, for Worth, green glass with label, in wooden box, molded 'R. LALIQUE' mark, introduced 1929.

4.25in (10.5cm) high

$1,000-1,500   DRA

A Lalique scent atomiser, for D'Heraud, clear glass with black patina, original hardware, hose and ball (hardened), molded 'R. LALIQUE' mark, introduced 1924.

6.5in (16.5cm) high

$1,200-1,600   DRA

A 1920s Hoffman shoe-shaped scent bottle, black crystal with jade 'knot' stopper and enameled and jeweled metalwork, stenciled 'MADE IN CZECHOSLOVAKIA' mark.

4.5in (11.5cm) high

$18,000-22,000   DRA

A 1920s Hoffman scent bottle, pink crystal with enameled and jeweled metalwork on four sides, cupid and Psyche stopper with dauber stub, intaglio 'HOFFMAN' mark.

6.5in (16.5cm) high

$2,000-3,000   DRA

A 1930s Hoffman scent bottle, blue crystal with stylized jeweled metalwork, highly detailed stopper with dauber, intaglio 'HOFFMAN' mark.

6.6in (16.5cm) high

$3,000-4,000   DRA

A Piver 'Astris' Baccarat scent bottle, pink crystal with silver star-shaped label, stenciled 'BACCARAT' mark, boxed, introduced 1927.

2.75in (7cm) high

$8,000-9,000   DRA

A Gravier 'Cascade' Baccarat scent bottle, clear and frosted crystal with pale green patina, stenciled 'BACCARAT' mark, introduced 1926.

4.5in (11.5cm) high

$3,500-4,000   DRA

An Ybry 'Desir du Coeur' Baccarat scent bottle, pink crystal with stopper and enameled metal cover, in box with R. Lalique glass pendant and tassel, introduced 1926.

4in (10cm) high

$4,000-5,000   DRA

A Corday 'L'Heure Romantique' Baccarat scent bottle, crystal with gilded detail, stenciled 'BACCARAT' mark, introduced 1928.

3in (7.5cm) high

$400-600   DRA

A 1920s Ahmed Soliman set of three scent bottles, Czech crystal with enameled Egyptian goddesses, with jeweled screw caps, in green leather box.

7.5in (19cm) long

$2,000-3,000   DRA

A 1920s Aristo scent bottle, purple crystal with enameled and jeweled filigree metalwork, with dauber, stenciled line 'CZECHOSLOVAKIA', metal tag 'CZECHOSLOVAKIA', 'ARISTO' label.

3.25in (9cm) high

$800-1,000   DRA

A 1920s Czech scent bottle, blue and clear crystal with enameled and jeweled filigree metalwork, on 'lapis' ball feet, dancer stopper with dauber, stenciled oval 'MADE IN CZECHOSLOVAKIA' mark.

6in (15cm) high

$4,000-5,000   DRA

A 1920s Czech scent bottle, pink crystal with jeweled metalwork, stenciled oval 'MADE IN CZECHOSLOVAKIA' mark.

5in (12.5cm) high

$900-1,100   DRA

A Langlois 'Shari' scent bottle, Czech crystal with raised enameled detail, sealed, with label, stenciled 'BOTTLE MADE IN CZECHOSLOVAKIA' mark.

c1925   *4in (10cm) high*

$900-1,100   **DRA**

A 1920s Devilbiss scent bottle, enameled and gilded glass with gilded metal and cloisonné enamel stopper, metal and glass ornaments, with dauber, marked 'DEVILBISS'.

4.75in (12cm) high

$4,000-6,000   **DRA**

A Devilbiss scent atomiser, glass with black and orange decoration, with small acorn top, marked 'DEVILBISS', introduced 1926.

10in (25.5cm) high

$2,500-3,000   **DRA**

A Devilbiss scent atomiser, amber glass with wheel engraving, on detailed metal stem and foot, introduced 1926.

5in (12.5cm) high

$1,000-1,200   **DRA**

A 1920s Devilbiss scent atomiser, amber glass with gilded finish, with removable atomiser, paper label.

6.25in (cm) high

$500-700   **DRA**

An Arys 'Promenade Matinale' J. Viard scent bottle, made by Depinoix in clear and frosted glass with sepia patina, with label, boxed.

c1920   *4.5in (11.5cm) high*

$2,500-3,000   **DRA**

CLOSER LOOK: JULIEN VIARD SCENT BOTTLE

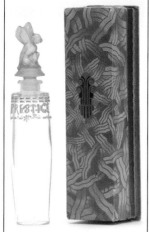

The 1920s saw a craze for Egyptian-inspired goods following the discovery of King Tutankhamun's tomb. Many scent bottles were made in shapes such as Pharoah's heads, sphinxes and pyramids, or decorated with heiroglyphics.

The fitted box was designed to complement the bottle. Having the original box will increase value significantly – particularly if it is in good condition.

The French sculptor Julian Viard was commissioned to design dozens of scent bottles by a number of manufacturers. Models were sent to glass houses to be made and then finished by Viard's workshop.

There is a wide variation in quality of Viard bottles, as there was a range of producers, but the quality of the surface decoration was usually of the highest standard.

A Gueldy 'Le Prestige' J. Viard scent bottle, clear glass with sepia patina, figural stopper, molded 'J. VIARD' mark, boxed, hinge tear to box, introduced 1922.

6in (15cm) high

$5,000-6,000   **DRA**

A Lubin 'Enigma' J. Viard scent bottle, formed as a crystal pyramid with golden sphinx, resting on a bed of lotus in original box with Egyptian scarab graphics, introduced 1921.

3.5in (9cm) high

$28,000-36,000   **DRA**

A Brecher 'Sous la Charmille' J. Viard scent bottle, made by Depinoix in glass with enamel detail, introduced 1924.

2.75in (7cm) high

$2,800-3,200   **DRA**

A Dubarry 'Blue Lagoon' J. Viard scent bottle, made by Depinoix in clear and frosted glass with multicolored patina, figural stopper, introduced 1919.

4in (10cm) high

$4,600-5,200   **DRA**

A 1930s Coty 'Muguet' scent bottle, crystal, sealed, with label, boxed, unwrapped for auction.

5in (12.5cm) high

$900-1,000   **DRA**

A deluxe issue Coty Crystal scent bottle, with enameled detail, attributed to Marcel Goupy, molded 'COTY France' mark.

c1925   *4.5in (11.5cm) high*

$1,000-1,200   **DRA**

A 1920s Coryse 'Rose d'Ispahan' scent bottle, clear and frosted glass with rose patina, sealed, with label.

6.75in (17cm) high

$1,000-1,200   **DRA**

A Salvador Dali 'Salvador Dali' factice scent bottle, in black (dark blue) glass, after his 1981 painting, 'Apparition du Visage de l'Aphrodite de Cnide dans un Paysage', introduced 1983.

12.5in (31.5cm) high

$1,200-1,600   **DRA**

A 1920s Dralle 'Ora e Sempre' scent bottle, crystal with cut stopper, in footed silvered metal holder.

3in (7.5cm) high

$1,500-2,000   **DRA**

A Guerlain 'Sillage' scent bottle, clear glass with raised enamel drapery and gilded detail, sealed, with label.

c1910   *5.5in (14cm) high*

$900-1,100   **DRA**

A Hermès 'Doblis' scent bottle, clear and green glass, with label, in paper box replica of Hermès building, Paris.

c1955   *3.5in (9cm) high*

$3,000-4,000   **DRA**

DECORATIVE ARTS

A 1950s Kesma 'Larmes de Nuit' scent bottle, clear and frosted glass, with label, in satin box, label to base reads 'Formule Legrain-Made in Egypt'.

5in (12.5cm) high

$2,000-3,000   DRA

A Lucien Lelong 'Jabot' scent bottle, clear and frosted glass, sealed, with label, boxed, introduced 1939.

3in (7.5cm) high

$800-1,000   DRA

A 1920s Marquis 'Niradjah' Depinoix scent bottle, black crystal with red cased crystal stopper, with label, in deluxe silver and yellow silk presentation box.

3.75in (9.5cm) high

$7,000-8,000   DRA

A 1920s Rochambeau figural scent bottle, blown glass in shape of a grape cluster with fabric leaves, with labels, in box.

4.5in (11.5cm) long

$600-800   DRA

A 1940s Schiaparelli 'Shocking', 'Sleeping', and 'Zut' mini scent bottle set, with glass bottles and metal and plastic screw caps, in satin-lined box.

3.5in (9cm) high

$1,800-2,400   DRA

A 1920s Vantines scent bottle and face powder gift set, frosted glass bottle with cork tip stopper, resting on a silk powder box trimmed with metallic fabric and Peking glass, with contents, boxed.

Bottle 1.75in (4.5cm) high

$1,400-1,600   DRA

A 1900s Yardley & Co 'White Roses' scent bottle gift set, clear crystal, with labels, in Art Nouveau box.

4in (10cm) high

$900-1,100   DRA

An Ybry 'Les Fleurs' scent bottle, crystal with pierced stopper hung with silk cord and enameled metal tag, boxed, introduced 1928.

3.5in (8.5cm) high

$1,800-2,400   DRA

A Tiffany Studios tulip lamp, the tulips are vibrant warm orange and yellow and the foliage is medium apple green to deep turquoise, the background is confetti glass, the base is an urn shape supported by five Art Nouveau columns, shade is signed 'Tiffany Studios New York 1905', signed on the burners 'P. Duplex A', base is marked 'Tiffany Studios New York'.

This glass is heavily textured so it sparkles to give the effect of sunset, thus this lamp is commonly referred to as the 'Sunset Tulip'. The base has a single socket and appears to be an original Tiffany conversion which makes this an extremely early Tiffany lamp. This lamp is a rare size.

Shade 14in (35.5cm) diam

$40,000-50,000   JDJ

An early 20thC Tiffany Studios bronze 'Windswept Tulip' lamp, with flowers on a blue confetti glass and string glass ground, the shade and base marked 'Tiffany Studios New York'.

21.5in (65cm) high

$80,000-90,000   FRE

A rare Tiffany mosaic peacock chandelier, peacock feather mosaic pattern in iridescent favrile pink, blue, purple and green glass, and finished with a green swirled peak eye, set against a solid bronze flat conical shade, lit by a very early six-socket cluster with Tiffany chain hooks, unsigned, socket cluster marked 'Benjamin Patents Mar 3 1903'.

38in (96.5cm) high

$70,000-80,000   JDJ

An early 20thC Tiffany Studios bronze 'Tyler Scroll' lamp, the scrolling decoration in dichroic glass on a graduated green ground, raised on a library base with oil font and arms, base and shade marked 'Tiffany Studios New York'.

25in (63.5cm) high

$30,000-40,000   FRE

A Tiffany Studios linenfold table lamp, shade signed on bottom of the apron 'Tiffany Studios New York 1827 Pat. Appl'd For', base is marked 'Tiffany Studios New York 584'.

Shade 19.25in (49cm) diam

$36,000-40,000   JDJ

A Tiffany Studios lamp, the shade is supported by a six-light candelabra base, lamp is finished with rare Linenfold glass top cap, shade is signed 'Tiffany Studios New York 1927 Patent Appl'd For', base is signed 'Tiffany Studios New York.

Shade 19in (cm) diam

$36,000-40,000   JDJ

A Tiffany Studios table lamp, with Woodbine shade on a bronze lamp base with adapted oil-font, a couple of minor breaks, stamped 'TIFFANY STUDIOS NEW YORK'.

17in (43cm) high

$24,000-28,000   DRA

A Tiffany Studios table lamp, with a Four Virtues gilt base with four sockets, a couple of short breaks, stamped 'TIFFANY STUDIOS NEW YORK', shade '1482', base '557'.

25.5in (64.5cm) high

$30,000-40,000   DRA

A Tiffany Studios pomegranate mosaic glass and bronze table lamp, upheld by a three-prong spider, over a three-socket cluster, signed on base 'Tiffany Studios, New York 370' and 'S182'.

16in (41cm) diam

$16,000-20,000   SK

A Tiffany Studios gilded bronze and brown glass lamp, the lampshade imitating pleated silk, signed 'Tiffany Studios New York 590' on the base and 'Tiffany Studios New York 1938, Pat.Appl'd for' on the lampshade.

19.75in (50cm) high

$16,000-20,000   SOTP

A Tiffany Favrile table lamp, the bell-form shade with twelve ribs in gold Favrile, the shade signed 'L.C. Tiffany L167L', the base signed 'L.C. Tiffany-Favrile', enlarged aperture on shade.

16.25in (41cm) high

$3,000-4,000   SK

A Tiffany Studios twelve-light Lily lamp, one shade broken, stamped 'TIFFANY STUDIOS NEW YORK. 382'.

21in (53cm) high

$13,000-15,000　　　　　**DRA**

A Tiffany Studios floor lamp, with a linenfold shade on a bronze harp base covered in verdigris patina, stamped 'TIFFANY STUDIOS NEW YORK', shade '1938 PAT APPL'D FOR', base '423'.

54.75in (139cm) high

$4,000-6,000　　　　　**DRA**

A Handel table lamp, acid-etched shade reverse-painted with pink roses and yellow butterflies, over a classical bronzed base, shade signed 'Handel 6688', and stamped 'HANDEL Lamps' with patent number.

23.25in (59cm) high

$12,000-16,000　　　　　**DRA**

A rare Handel floor lamp, its paneled cattail shade lined with caramel slag glass over a three-socket fluted bronzed base with sphinx, base marked 'HANDEL'.

63in (160cm) high

$36,000-44,000　　　　　**DRA**

A Handel table lamp, acid-etched shade reverse-painted with a Venetian scene, over bronzed base with two-tone patina, shade signed 'HANDEL 5935', and stamped 'HANDEL Lamps' with patent number, base unmarked, 0.5in (1cm) clamshell chip to interior.

25in (63.5cm) high

$10,000-14,000　　　　　**DRA**

A Handel table lamp, acid-etched glass shade obverse-painted with stylized leaves, over a three-socket bronzed base, shade signed 'A. 5940' and Handel patent no., base stamped 'HANDEL', crack around shade.

24.25in (61.5cm) high

$1,800-2,200　　　　　**DRA**

A Handel glass and bronze table lamp, reverse-painted with textured shade composed of six paneled sides, each panel hand-painted with stylized flowers on interior of shade, rests over three sockets, on ribbed standard raised on circular foot, signed 'Handel 6805' on rim, cloth Handel label on base.

c1920　　　　　*22in (56cm) high*

$3,000-4,000　　　　　**SK**

An Oscar Bach table lamp, with original Steuben gold Aurene globe shade, the lamp with pierced and sculpted brass-washed metal base with nude male figures, theatrical masks, and a satyr finial.

25.75in (65.5cm) high

$3,600-4,400　　　　　**SDR**

A pair of brass candlesticks, in the manner of W. A. S. Benson, with counterbalance ball, unmarked.

12.25in (31cm) wide

$500-700　　　　　**WW**

A Bergmann & Loetz cast bronze table lamp, the cast bronze base with figure of a water carrier before a Classical column with ring gallery mounted with a Loetz cameo glass shade, bears cameo signature.

13.5in (34cm) high

$5,000-7,000　　　　　**FLD**

An early 20thC Edgar Brandt marble and patinated metal hanging lamp, with domed marble shade in a metalwork frame suspended by wrought metal linked chain, signed.

14in (36cm) diam

$5,000-6,000 SK

A large gilt bronze and alabaster lamp by Edgar Brandt (1880-1960), the four conformingly pierced lancet supports above a circular fluted collar, on an octagonal Portor marble plinth, bronze base stamped 'E.Brandt'.

37.25in (95cm) high

$80,000-120,000 SOTH

An Edgar Brandt 'Cobra' lamp, gilt-bronze and internally decorated glass shade engraved 'Daum Nancy' with the Croix de Lorraine, base stamped 'E.BRANDT'.

c1925 *19in (48cm) high*

$24,000-30,000 SOT

A Daum 'rain scene' lamp, cameo and enamel glass decorated with rain scene on shade and base, cameo-carved rain drops extend diagonally around the shade and base to give the effect of being blown by the wind, signed 'Daum Nancy'.

13in (33cm) high

$32,000-36,000 JDJ

A pair of Art Nouveau bronze lamps with Loetz glass shades, cast from a model by Gustave Gurschner, cast marks, artist's signature and made in Austria, small chip to the rim of one shade.

19in (48.5cm) high

$14,000-16,000 WW

A wrought iron and glass table lamp by Muller Freres, the domed shade supported by a stylized scrolling stem, shade with etched mark 'Muller Frès/Luneville', base case with 'Th Béramy.

c1930 *25.25in (64cm) high*

$16,000-24,000 SOTH

A Pairpoint puffy lamp, with hummingbird and chrysanthemum shade.

21.25in (54in) high

$3,000-4,000 POOK

A Pairpoint Puffy pansy lamp, with four large panels reverse-painted in sienna, the exterior with gold enamel highlighting, shade rests on a four-arm base, shade signed 'The Pairpoint Corp'n'.,the base signed 'Pairpoint Mfg.', 'P' within a diamond and 'B3'.

Shade 12in (30.5cm) diam

$20,000-24,000 JDJ

A pair of Prairie School architectural wall lanterns, in bronze and glass, possibly designed by Frank Lloyd Wright, originally fitted for gas.

20in (51cm) high

$18,000-22,000 SK

A pair of Quezel wall lights, with iridescent glass and patinated metal, marked 'Quezel'.

19.5in (50cm) high

$9,000-11,000 SK

A Roycroft hammered copper and mica helmet-shade table lamp, Orb & Cross mark.

14.5in (36cm) high

$4,000-5,000 **DRA**

A Steuben Millefiori lamp, bright green leaf-and-vine decoration interspersed with millefiori flowers, set against a gold iridescent background with flashes of pink and green, base signed with white enamel mark 'Aurene Haviland & Co.'

8.5in (32.5cm) diam

$17,000-21,000 **JDJ**

A monumental Steuben moss agate chandelier, inverted bell-shaped shade mounted in metal frame, frame attached to two swirling stylized leaf designs leading to wrought iron arms supporting the shade.

14in (35.5cm) diam

$30,000-36,000 **JDJ**

A wrought iron and molded glass table lamp by Raymond Subes (1891-1970), the domed mottled orange shade above a tapering stem and circular base, mounted with stylized foliage.

27.5in (70cm) high

$30,000-40,000 **SOTH**

A Dirk Van Erp hammered copper and mica table lamp, windmill mark with box, original mica.

c1911 *16in (40.5cm) high*

$10,000-14,000 **DRA**

A Dirk Van Erp hammered copper and mica table lamp, its shade with spade-shaped riveted straps on a single-socket, pear-shaped base, windmill stamp with 'DIRKVANERP' and remnant of 'D'Arcy Gaw'.

16.5in (42cm) high

$8,400-10,000 **DRA**

A Gustav Stickley chandelier, with five hammered copper drops pierced with hearts and lined in original yellow glass cylinders, no visible mark.

37in (94cm) long

$20,000-28,000 **DRA**

An Art Nouveau Austrian table lamp, with glass, silk and patinated and textured metal, resting on an oak leaf-formed metal support backed by a caramel-colored silk shade.

25.75in (65cm) high

$2,400-3,000 **SK**

An Arts & Crafts hammered metal chandelier with Monk's heads, unmarked, brass-wash patina.

$2,000-2,800 **DRA**

A pair of forged iron tall candelabra, each with three bobeches and twisted shafts.

$2,400-3,000 **DRA**

A C. R. Ashbee silver hinged condiment jar, with jade cabochons and poppy-patterned spoon, CRA, lion, crest, and 'E' hallmarks.

3in (7.5cm) high

$3,000-4,000   DRA

A Canadian Birks Arts & Crafts sterling silver heavy gauge tea and coffee set, comprising a teapot, coffee pot, creamer and covered sugar, the bases stamped 'BIRKS STERLING 41/5'.

Coffeepot 10.8in (27.5cm) high

$3,000-4,000   TCF

A German Bruckmann und Söhne tall silver chalice, with hardstone cabochons and gilt interior, stamped 'B'.

11.25in (27.6cm)

$2,600-3,200   DRA

A Cartier enameled silver pin dish, by Jacques Cartier, initialed 'MMcK' in script, also inscribed 'THE FOUNTAIN OF WISDOM FLOWS THROUGH BOOKS', London.

1929   3.5in (9cm) high

$500-600   L&T

A pair of James Dixon & Sons silver candlesticks, marks for Sheffield.

1909   8.75in (22cm) high

$4,000-5,000   L&T

A Christopher Dresser silver toast rack, stamped 'H&H 2556', with registration mark, resoldering at base of one divider.

5in (12.5cm) wide

$400-600   DRA

A Jugendstil silver photograph frame, designed by Theodor Fahrner, set with chrysoprase cabochons, stamped marks.

2.25in (5.5cm) high

$1,600-2,400   L&T

A Gorham sterling silver Art Nouveau footed bowl, the rim decorated with floral baskets.

c1905

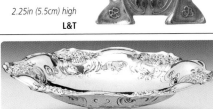

$1,300-1,700   FRE

A Guild of Handicrafts hammered sterling silver shaker, with jade cabochons, GH, lion, lion's head, and 'e' hallmarks.

The Guild of the Handicrafts was founded by C. R. Ashbee in the Cotswolds, UK, in 1888.

2.75in (7cm) high

$1,400-1,800   DRA

A William Hutton & Sons sterling silver milk pitcher, embossed and enameled with tulips, small flake to one enameled drop, anchor, lion, shield, 'H' hallmarks.

5.25in (13.3cm) high

$1,800-2,200   DRA

A five-piece 'Blossom' tea service, designed by Georg Jensen (1866-1935), comprising teapot, hot water pot, sugar bowl and milk jug, stamped 'Denmark', 'Georg Jensen/ Silversmiths Ltd', 'Sterling' and '2D', sides stamped with maker's hallmark.

22.25in (56.5cm) wide tray

$45,000-50,000   SOTH

An A. E. Jones hammered silver jar and cover, with applied cruciform decoration with turquoise ceramic cabochons, scratch to body, some minor dents, stamped 'A.E.J', anchor, rampant lion.

4.5in (11.4cm) high

$700-800   DRA

A Liberty & Co. Cymric hammered sterling silver spoon, marked L&Co, anchor, lion, 'D', CYMRIC, 394.

8in (20.3cm) long

$1,200-1,600   DRA

A Liberty & Co. sterling silver shaker, some losses to enamel and a few dents, L&CO, anchor, lion, 'I' hallmarks.

3.5in (8.6cm) high

$700-800   DRA

A Liberty & Co. 'Cymric' silver and enamel tea caddy and matching spoon, designed by Archibald Knox, Birmingham.

1903   *6in (15cm) high*

$12,000-14,000   L&T

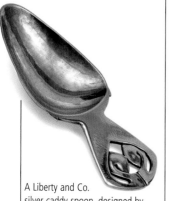

A Liberty and Co. silver caddy spoon, designed by Archibald Knox, with shovel-planished bowl below Celtic style intertwined handle.

3.5in (9cm) high

$700-900   FLD

A Liberty & Co. 'Cymric' silver vase, designed by Archibald Knox, stamped marks.

8.75in (22cm) high

$4,000-5,000   L&T

A Canadian Petersen sterling silver small tazza, with stamped maker's marks to base.

3in (7.5cm) high

$800-1,200   TCF

A Canadian Petersen sterling silver footed bowl, the interior with light gold wash, with stamped maker's marks to base.

3.5in (9cm) high

$1,000-1,500   TCF

A pair of Canadian Petersen sterling silver candlesticks, with applied curling leaf supports, with stamped maker's marks to base.

3.25in (8cm) high

$800-1,200   TCF

A Canadian Petersen sterling silver goblet, the bowl with gold-washed interior, the exterior engraved 'R', with stamped maker's marks to base.

4.5in (11.5cm) high

$1,500-2,000   TCF

A Canadian Proctor and Ellis Art Nouveau style sterling silver trophy, embossed with horses and carts in a band of panels around the rim, the base stamped 'PROCTOR STERLING 925/1000 FINE' and with the Ellis Brothers mark.

Ellis was the second of a small number of Canadian silver and jewelry companies taken over by Birks. Ryrie Brothers merged in 1917, Ellis Brothers in 1933.

6.25in (16cm) high

$1,500-2,000   TCF

A silver traveling shaving brush and cover, by Ramsden & Carr, with Tudor rose to the pull-off cover and inner mounted brush, with screw-turned base, London.

1904   *3.25in (8.5cm) long*

$700-900   L&T

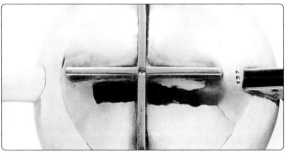

An important and rare silver-plated brass and ebony tea infuser, designed by Marianne Brandt, model no. MT 49, stamped '137' to the underside and to the rim of the lid.

c1927   *6in (15cm) wide*

$300,000-400,000   **SOT**

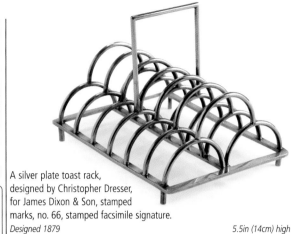

A silver plate toast rack, designed by Christopher Dresser, for James Dixon & Son, stamped marks, no. 66, stamped facsimile signature.

Designed 1879   *5.5in (14cm) high*

$8,000-10,000   **L&T**

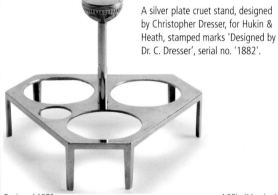

A silver plate cruet stand, designed by Christopher Dresser, for Hukin & Heath, stamped marks 'Designed by Dr. C. Dresser', serial no. '1882'.

Designed 1878   *4.25in (11cm) wide*

$1,000-1,500   **L&T**

A silver plate sugar bowl, designed by Christopher Dresser, for Hukin & Heath, in the form of a tureen, stamped marks.

5in (13cm) diam

$1,800-2,400   **L&T**

PEWTER

A pewter decanter, designed by Joseph Maria Olbrich, manufactured by Eduard Hueck, Lüdenscheid, with raised artist's monogram and 'EDELZINN/1865/E. HUECK'.

31.5in (34cm) high

$10,000-12,000   **SOT**

A pewter punch bowl, with green glass insert, designed by Albin Müller, manufactured by Eduard Hueck, Lüdenscheid, with artist's monogram to both sides.

17in (431cm) wide

$18,000-22,000   **SOT**

A pair of pewter candelabra, designed by Hugo Levan, model no. 4531, manufactured by J. P. Kayser Sohn, Krefeld, with raised mark 'KAYSERZINN/4531'.

10in (24.5cm) high

$10,000-12,000   **SOT**

A Continental pewter grotesque bird inkwell, attributed to Kayserzinn, with ceramic green liner, unmarked.

4in (10cm) high

$700-800   **WW**

A Liberty Tudric pewter biscuit barrel, designed by Archibald Knox, model 0194, stamped marks.

5.5in (14cm) high

$800-1,200   **GHOU**

A Liberty & Co. 'Tudric' pewter twin-branch table candelabrum, designed by Archibald Knox, stamped marks '0530'.

11.25in (28.5cm) high

$1,800-2,200   **L&T**

A pair of Art Nouveau Tudric vases, the underside stamped '8/Tudric/029'.

10in (25.5cm) high

$800-1,000   **HALL**

A polished pewter wall mirror, attributed to Alexander Ritchie, Iona.

16.25in (41cm) wide

$1,200-1,600   **L&T**

An Art Nouveau WMF pewter-mounted green glass decanter, the mounts with a maiden and whiplash foliage, with detachable stopper, stamped marks.

15in (38cm) high

$1,600-2,200   **L&T**

An Art Nouveau WMF pewter and glass épergne, the cut glass central vase and bowl supported by a spreading base cast with whiplash foliage, stamped marks.

19.75in (50cm) high

$1,200-1,600   **L&T**

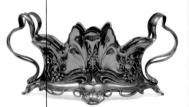

A WMF Art Nouveau polished pewter table centre, with embossed butterflies and curling organic forms and whiplash handles, with replaced green glass liner.

16.5in (42cm) long

$1,600-2,200   **FLD**

A WMF Art Nouveau polished pewter card tray, embossed with head and shoulder portraits of two ladies within lily-leaf-pierced borders, with stamped maker's mark to back.

9.5in (24cm) high

$600-800   **FLD**

An early 20thC WMF polished pewter basket, with the chestnut pattern and a clear glass liner, with stamped marks to base.

13in (33cm) high

$500-600   **FLD**

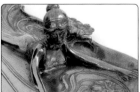

An Italian early 20thC Art Nouveau polished pewter tray, with high and low relief sculptural form of a maiden lying on a pond with outstretched arms, marked 'Achille Gambo' on the base.

14.25in (36cm) long

$250-350   **FLD**

A pair of American Boston School hammered copper bookends, each with a riveted enameled insert of a sailboat in polychrome, medium patina, unmarked.

6.25in (16cm) high

$2,000-3,000   **DRA**

An Elizabeth Burton copper jewelry box, with abalone shell inserts to top and to hinged clasp, stamped 'Burton' with hammer, cleaned patina.

6.75in (17cm) wide

$3,000-4,000   **DRA**

A Christofle 'Ecailles' dinanderie copper with silver vase, designed by Luc Lanel, factory stamped and 'B1G'.

c1920   *10in (25.5cm) high*

$2,800-3,200   **FRE**

A copper jardinière, attributed to Margaret Gilmour, with broad rim, repoussé decorated with Celtic knotwork on a hammered ground.

12.75in (32.5cm) wide

$1,000-1,500   **L&T**

A Gorham & Co. mixed metal copper and sterling silver small tray, the shaped rectangular tray with applied crabs on a 'cracked ice' surface.

1881   *10in (25.5cm) wide*

$3,500-4,000   **FRE**

A patinated copper and brass 'Teemaschine', designed by Albin Müller, manufactured by Eduard Hueck, Lüdenscheid, stamped with artist's monogram and 'EDUARD HUECK/2029' to underside of kettle.

11.75in (30cm) high

$3,000-4,000   **SOT**

A Newlyn School copper mirror, the frame repoussé-decorated with trailing foliage.

15.5in (39.5cm) high

$500-600   **L&T**

A large Newlyn School copper charger, with embossed central Viking style ship within poppy floral border.

22in (57cm) diam

$1,400-1,600   **FLD**

An Onondaga Metal Shops hammered copper coal bucket, with embossed floral design, new dark patina, stamped OMS.

16.5in (42cm) high

$3,000-4,000   **DRA**

An Onondaga Metal Shops hammered copper charger, cleaned patina, OMS stamp.

19in (48cm) diam

$1,000-1,500   DRA

An exceptional, rare Charles Rohlfs jewellery box, with riveted hammered copper hinges, and wooden key on chain, carved 'R, 1901', interior of lid has green tinted shellac, and lined in original red velvet, original finish, a few minor nicks.

1901   *8.5in (21.5cm) wide*

$24,000-28,000   DRA

A Roycroft brass-washed hammered copper vase, with silver overlay, light wear to patina, Orb & Cross mark.

6in (15cm) high

$1,000-1,500   DRA

A Roycroft brass-washed hammered copper bud vase, with full-height buttresses, Orb and Cross mark.

7in (17.5cm) high

$3,000-4,000   DRA

A rare pair of Roycroft hammered copper candlesticks, cleaned patina, Orb & Cross mark.

15in (38cm) high

$5,000-6,000   DRA

A Gertrude Twichell hammered copper and enamel hinged box, decorated in the Pre-Raphaelite style, signed.

Twichell (1899-1937) a graduate of the Rhode Island School of Design, was master craftsman in The Society of Arts & Crafts, Boston. This is an unusual example of her work in that it is enameled all around, and has figural decoration.

4.75in (12cm) wide

$10,000-12,000   DRA

A Secessionist metal-hammered copper jardiniere, with brass handles, possibly German or Austrian, embossed with owls and birds of paradise.

12in (30.5cm) high

$1,200-1,600   DRA

An Arts & Crafts hammered copper fire screen, embossed with a peacock on a branch, unmarked.

28in (71cm) high

$1,500-2,000   DRA

An Arts & Crafts hammered copper vase, with sea life design, artist's cipher 'C?J.', some dents, fine dark patina.

10.5in (26.5cm) high

$700-1,000   DRA

A Marie Zimmerman Arts & Crafts copper bowl, stamped 'M. ZIMMERMAN MAKER'.

c1920   *14.75in (37.5cm) diam*

$1,500-2,000   FRE

A Marie Zimmerman Arts & Crafts hand-hammered gilt-copper vase, in the form of an upright flower blossom, stamped 'MAKER-MARIE ZIMMERMAN' and '76'.

c1910   *5.75in (14.5cm) high*

$1,000-1,500   FRE

A brass trivet, by Margaret Gilmour, repoussé decorated with stylised butterfly and plant motifs, bears monogram mark.

10.5in (26.5cm) diam

$1,000-1,500   **L&T**

A pair of Gothic Revival brass candelabra, in the manner of Christopher Dresser, probably by Benham & Froud.

19.75in (50cm) high

$800-1,200   **L&T**

A brass charger, attributed to Margaret Gilmour, with central turquoise enamel roundel enclosed by repoussé decoration of Celtic knotwork.

23.5in (59.5cm) diam

$1,800-2,400   **L&T**

A brass wall sconce, after Margaret Gilmour, the backplate repoussé decorated with a peacock, and a pair of candle sconces below.

30.75in (78cm) high

$1,000-1,500   **L&T**

A Keswick School of Industrial Art brass charger, repoussé decorated with a stylised floral design and Celtic knotwork, stamped mark.

23.25in (59cm) diam

$1,000-1,500   **L&T**

A Keswick School of Industrial Arts brass wall mirror, repoussé decorated with stylised flora and wave pattern with entwined knotwork.

39.5in (100cm) wide

$6,000-7,000   **L&T**

A cast and wrought brass chamberstick, designed by Richard Riemerschmid, model no. 1459, manufactured by Vereinigte Werkstätten für Kunst im Handwerk, Munich.

7.5in (18.5cm) high

$20,000-25,000   **SOT**

A Wiener Werkstätte Aufsatz centerpiece coupé, designed by Josef Hoffman, with hammered and chased brass and ribbon handles, stamped 'WIENER WERKSTÄTTE JH MADE IN AUSTRIA'.

1925-131   *7.75in (20cm) high*

$26,000-32,000   **SDR**

A Scottish Arts & Crafts brass-framed mirror, repoussé decorated with Celtic beasts.

27.5in (70cm) wide

$1,000-1,500   **L&T**

A Scottish Arts & Crafts brass jardinière, the sides repoussé decorated with panels of flowering waterlilies.

12.5in (32cm) wide

$1,000-1,500   **L&T**

An Eric Gill 'St Martin of Tours' patinated bronze relief panel, with cast inscription 'St. Martin/ Pray/ For Us'.

This was originally commissioned in stone for Campion Hall, Brewer Street, Oxford, England.

1935   17.75in (45cm) high

$4,800-5,200   **L&T**

A pair of Heintz sterling-on-bronze tall candlesticks, in a pine needle pattern on a dark brown ground, stamped 'PAT.APD FOR 3078'.

14.25in (36cm) high

$1,500-2,000   **DRA**

A Jarvie bronze candlestick, embossed with spade-shaped leaves, unmarked, original patina.

13.75in (35cm) high

$5,000-6,000   **DRA**

A Lalique gilt-bronze medallion, an unrecorded design depicting a nurse tending a wounded soldier, engraved 'R. LALIQUE'.

Provenance: Part of the Lalique Family Collection.

c1915   2in (5cm) wide

$800-1,000   **DRA**

A Tiffany Studios gilded bronze 'Abalone pattern' desk set, comprising a double letter-holder, four blotter corners, an ink blotter, a pen-wipe holder, a perpetual calendar, paper clip, stamp box, cigarette box, and a pen tray, each piece stamped 'TIFFANY STUDIOS NEW YORK'.

$5,000-6,000   **DRA**

An Art Deco bronze plaque, decorated with allegorical figures in relief, mounted on fabric-covered wood board.

30.5in (77.5cm) wide

$1,500-2,000   **SDR**

A wrought iron and copper coal scuttle, designed by Dr Christopher Dresser, the body detailed with a band of riveted copper below conforming cover and ball finial.

18in (45cm) high

$280-320   **FLD**

A Norman Bel Geddes Ferris wheel-shaped bright chrome cocktail stand, with wire glass accessories and two 'Manhattan' chrome cocktail shakers, missing one rectangular glass insert, two replaced glasses, and one broken glass, unmarked.

24in (60cm) high

$6,000-7,000   **SDR**

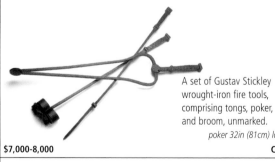

A set of Gustav Stickley wrought-iron fire tools, comprising tongs, poker, and broom, unmarked.

poker 32in (81cm) long

$7,000-8,000   **CRA**

A spelter table lighter, after Lorenzl, modeled as a young girl wearing a floral detailed trouser suit leaning against the lighter, bears signature.

7.5in (20cm) high

$600-700   **FLD**

A gilt and patinated bronze, 'Joan of Arc', by Louis Ernest Barrias (French, 1841-1905), signed 'E Barrias' and inscribed 'Vous avez pu m'enchainer/ Vous n'enchainerez jamais la Fortune de la France'.

28.5in (72.5cm) high

$5,000-7,000   **FRE**

A bronze figure, 'GRENADIER, 1st GUARDS 1815', by Sir Joseph Edgar Boehm (1834-1890), signed by the sculptor and with 'Elkington & Co.' foundry stamp.

22.75in (58cm) high

$4,000-6,000   **L&T**

A poured bronze figure, 'Two relay runners' by Friedrich Büschelberger rectangle base of black-gray marble, base signed 'Büschelberger'.

12in (30.5cm) high

$2,000-3,000   **VZ**

A gilt-bronze group, 'Mother & Daughter at a Well' by Emile-Joseph-Nestor Carlier, raised on a circular base, signed 'Carlier'.

27.5in (70cm) high

$5,000-7,000   **FRE**

A bronze figure, 'Nymph', by Albert Ernst Carrier-Belleuse, brown patina, signed 'A. Carrier'.

28.5in (72.5cm) high

$7,000-9,000   **FRE**

A late 19thC French bronze bust, of Rembrandt, after Albert-Ernest-Carrier-Belleuse, signed on waisted socle and square base.

19.75in (50cm) high

$2,000-3,000   **L&T**

A bronze bust, of Napoleon Bonaparte, by Renzo Colombo (Italian, d. 1885), inscribed 'R. Colombo' and dated.

1885   *22in (56cm) high*

$2,600-3,200   **POOK**

A bronze group of 'Charity', by Paul Dubois (1829-1905), with brown patina, signed 'P. DUBOIS' and with foundry seal 'REDUCTION MECANIQUE / A COLLAS'.

24.75in (63cm) high

$8,000-10,000   **L&T**

A bronze figure of a girl, 'Peace', by Edward Onslow Ford, (1852-1901), with green patination, raised on a rectangular green marble base, signed and inscribed 'London' and dated.

The date is significant as it is earlier than the Collie casts.

1889   *21.25in (54cm) high*

$8,000-10,000   **L&T**

A bronze sculpture 'L'age D'or', by Henri Fugere (French, 1872-1944), medium bronze and gold patinas, modeled as a nude female, her right arm raised and holding a floral spray, signed 'H. Fugere', and inscribed 'Salon des Beaux arts'.

35in (89cm) high

$4,000-6,000   **FRE**

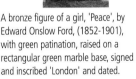

A bronze figure, 'La Vitesse', by Fréderic C. Focht, of a man on a rocket hurling an arrow, green-patinated and silvered, on a black marble base, signed 'Fred C. Focht'.

c1925   *34.75in (88cm) high*

$15,000-17,000   **SOTP**

A polychromed and patinated bronze, 'Femme de Mequinez', by Honore Henri Ple, raised on a waisted socle base, inscribed 'Henri Ple' and dated.

1883   *29.5in (75cm) high*

$30,000-40,000   **FRE**

A pair of gilt-bronze 'Mercury & Venus' figures, after Giambologna, raised on pedestal bases with applied silvered bronze relief panels.

33in (84cm) high

$3,000-4,000   **FRE**

A 19thC bronze figure of a naked male fencer, after Rudolf Kuchler (Austrian), the base incized with guilloché and signature, on a red-and-brown-veined marble plinth, sloping to the front.

16.5in (42cm) high overall

$2,400-3,600   **L&T**

A bronze plaque, by Albert Laliberté, of the profile of Marc Aurèle de Foy Suzor-Coté, molded 'Paris 1906'.

Marc Aurèle de Foy Suzor-Coté (1869-1937) was a French Canadian painter known for his Impressionist style paintings of Quebec.

8.75in (22cm) high

$4,000-6,000   **TSG**

A bronze group, 'Wrestlers', by Joseph-Maria-Thomas Lambeaux, dark brown patina, signed 'Jef. Lambeaux' and dated.

1895   *29in (73.5cm) high*

$4,000-6,000   **FRE**

A patinated bronze, 'Dancing Figure' by Josef Lorenzl, with silvered patination raised on a stepped green onyx base, signed in the bronze.

13in (33.5cm) high

$2,000-3,000   **L&T**

A silvered bronze figure, 'The Hoop Dancer', by Josef Lorenzl, mounted to a facet-cut onyx base, signed to the lower plinth edge.

11.5in (29.5cm) high

$5,000-6,000   **FLD**

A bronze statue of the devil, 'Le diablo demeure dans le patrimoine' ('The devil resides in the patrimony') by Albert Laliberte.

17.75in (45.5cm) high

$6,000-8,000   **TSG**

A gilded bronze figure, 'Dancer', by Josef Lorenzl, of a young naked woman in dance position, holding bouquets in both hands, hexagonal agate base, hexagonal condition plate singed 'Lorenzl, UC'.

c1928   *10.5in (26.5 cm) high*

$2,000-3,000   **VZ**

A bronze figure, 'Gladiator', by Ferdinand Lugerth (Austrian 1885-1915), brown/gold patinas, signed and monogrammed, raised on a verde antico marble base.

19.75in (50cm) high

$1,600-2,400   **L&T**

A gilt-bronze figure, 'Inspiration', by Eugene Marioton, Paris foundry, on a rouge marble base with applied mounts ending in toupie feet, signed 'Eug. Marioton, E. Colin & Cie'.

27in (68.5cm) high

$3,000-4,000   **FRE**

Two late 19th/early 20thC bronze figures of gentlemen, both holding swords, signed 'C. Masse'.

$10,000-12,000   **L&T**

A bronze, with dark brown patina, 'Cupid', after Auguste Moreau, modeled as a standing Cupid, with a marble column, and marble and bronze mounted base.

24in (61cm) high

$3,000-4,000   FRE

A bronze figure, after Charles Raphael Peyre, depicting Cleopatra with the asp, signed in the bronze.

40in (102cm) high

$2,400-3,600   L&T

A 19thC bronze figure of Psyche, after Pieffer, the figure holding an oil lamp in her right hand, and gilt bronze base inscribed 'Pieffer' and stamped 'TIFFANY & Co'.

20in (51cm) high

$3,600-4,400   FRE

A gilt bronze maquette, by Jean-Jacques Pradier, (called James Pradier, Swiss, 1790-1852), modeled as a seated draped beauty, at her feet sit five cherubs engaged in various pursuits, raised on a rectangular base inscribed 'Genius & Thought Enrich Industry & Industry Enriches the Nation', signed 'J. PRADIER' and with foundry mark.

10.75in (27.5cm) high

$1,600-2,400   L&T

A bronze female nude, by August Puttemans (1866-1927), signed in the bronze.

19in (48cm) high

$1,400-2,000   L&T

A bronze group, attributed to Charles de Sousy Ricketts, depicting a central naked man flanked by two female companions with another man lying indolently nearby, with dark patination.

5.75in (14.5cm) high

$2,000-4,000   JN

A bronze group, 'Io supported by Nymphs', designed by Charles de Sousy Ricketts, depicting the naked Io flanked and supported by a pair of nymphs, with rich dark patination, signed 'CR'.

Io was the daughter of Inachus, first king of Argos and was seduced by Jupiter who took on the guise of a cloud.

10.5in (26.5cm) high

$12,000-16,000   JN

A French 19thC pair of Etienne Alexandre Stella Classical females, allegorical to the seasons, dark brown patina, signed 'Stella'.

Tallest 38in (96.5cm) high

$20,000-30,000   FRE

A bronze bust, entitled 'La Sibylle', by Emmanuelle Villanis (active 1880-1920), signed 'E. Villanis', and inset with foundry seal for 'Société des Bronzes de Paris', stamped 'J. P. 5235'.

20.5in (52cm) high

$4,000-6,000   L&T

A bronze figure of a dancer, 'La Danseuse Nattova', by Prince Serge Yourievitch (1876-1969), on green marble base, numbered '120'.

8.75in (22cm) high

$2,400-3,600   L&T

An Art Nouveau gilt-bronze bust of a young girl, wearing a headscarf and shoulder length hair, her dress bound with a broad belt and buckle, on a square integral plinth base with canted corners, golden patination, indistinct incised signature to base, [?] 'Aut Nelson'.

17.25in (44cm) high

$3,600-4,400   **L&T**

A late 19thC Italian bronze of the Dancing Faun, after the antique, dark brown patina, raised in an ogee-molded circular marble base.

23.25in (59cm) high

$4,000-6,000   **L&T**

A 19thC bronze figure of the 'The Dying Gladiator', after the antique, with brown patina.

$4,000-6,000   **L&T**

A pair of late 19thC gilt-bronze figures, depicting Minerva and Mars, standing on stepped pedestals with masks and entwined marlin and foliate-decorated bands, on bun feet.

12.5in (32cm) high

$4,000-6,000   **L&T**

A bronze figure, 'The Borghese Warrior', after the antique, dark brown patina, with 'GLADENBECK BERLIN' foundry mark.

19in (48cm) high

$2,400-3,600   **FRE**

An early 20thC French School standing male nude, bronze dark green and verdigris patina, signed indistinctly with 'Cire A. Valsuani Perdue' foundry seal.

11.5in (29cm) high

$2,000-3,000   **FRE**

A 19thC bronze group,'ANIER DU CAIRE', by Antoine Bofill, (French/Spanish, 1875-1921), modeled as an Arab standing beside a mule, raised on a naturalistic oval base, signed 'A. Bofill' and with impressed monogram.

18in (46cm) high

$8,000-12,000   **L&T**

A late 19thC French bronze group, 'Jockey Up' by Isidore-Jules Bonheur, dark brown patina, signed 'I. Bonheur'.

25in (63.5cm) wide

$11,000-13,000   **L&T**

A bronze figure, 'Bull', by Isadore Jules Bonheur, (French, 1827-1901), dark brown patina, raised on a green marble base.

Bronze 21in (53.5cm) long

$4,000-6,000   **FRE**

A bronze figure, 'Tigress Feeding Her Cubs', by Auguste-Nicholas Cain (French, 1822-1894), modeled as a tigress standing with a boar in her jaws, her three cubs at her feet, signed 'A. Cain', with Susse Freres Edition, Paris, foundry marks and seal.

42in (106.5cm) wide

$10,000-12,000   **FRE**

A bronze figure, 'Figure of a Bulldog', by Charles Curry, signed in the bronze 'C Curry Sc'.

8.75in (22cm) wide

$1,600-2,400   L&T

A bronze figure, 'Cow and Calf', by Paul Eduoard DeLaBriere, (French, 1825-1912), yellow-brown patina, the base inscribed 'Cercle d'agricole de l'arr**met vouziers concours de machault'.

10in (25.5cm) high

$2,000-3,000   FRE

A bronze figure, 'Two Hounds', by Alfred Dubucand (French, 1828-1894), medium brown patina, signed 'A. Dubucand'.

6in (15cm) long

$600-1,000   FRE

A bronze figure, 'Lion and Boar', by Christophe Fratin (French, 1800-1864), yellow-brown patina, modeled as a lion holding a boar in its mouth, signed 'Fratin', with Theibaut Freres, Paris, foundry seal.

21.5in (54.5cm) long

$3,000-4,000   FRE

A bronze figure, 'Mountain Lion', by Evangelos Frudakis (American, b.1921), bronze, signed, on a black stained wood base.

10.25in (26cm) high

$400-600   FRE

A bronze lion group, by Georges Gardet, signed with foundry stamp.

c1900   *23.5in (60cm) long*

$15,000-17,000   G&H

A late 19thC German bronze group of a boy on a donkey, the boy seated on the donkey's back and raising a crop, with twin basket panniers either side, the foliate cast base inscribed 'HOCHMUTH'.

6.25in (16cm) wide

$400-600   DN

A bronze group, 'Jument Normande et son Poulain' (Normandy Mare and Foal), by Pierre Jules Mene (French, 1810-1879) inscribed on base 'P. J. Mene'.

24in (61cm) wide

$7,000-9,000   POOK

A rare bronze group, by Pierre-Jules Mene (French 1810-1879), cast by Coalbrookedale, modeled as a goat and kid, raised on a naturalistic cast oval base, signed 'P. J. MENE'.

9.5in (24cm) high

$2,000-3,000   L&T

A silvered bronze figure, 'The Falconer', Pierre Jules Mene (1810-1897), signed 'P. J. Mene'.

31in (79cm) high

$10,000-14,000   FRE

A French bronze model of an owl after Jules Moigniez, with outstretched wings, perched on a branch, signed 'J Moigniez', mounted on oval green marble plinth.

32.5in (82cm) high

$4,000-6,000   L&T

A French silvered bronze group, by Charles Paillet (1871-1937), modeled as a standing pheasant and two grouse, raised on a naturalistically cast rectangular base and green marble plinth, signed 'ch Paillet, Medaille d'or'.

21.5in (54cm) high

$5,000-7,000   L&T

A bronze fish group, 'Carpio Carpio', by Emile Rouff, signed.
c1910   *18.5in (47cm) long*
$6,000-7,000   **G&H**

A bronze figure, 'Leaping Deer', by Gerhard Schliepstein, with dark brown patina, probably executed by H. Noack, Berlin, the rear base edge signed 'G. Schliepstein'.

1924   10in (25cm) high
$4,000-6,000   **VZ**

A pair of early 18thC Continental, possibly Italian, ormolu figures of horses, each finely cast and chased horse rearing atop an associated black marble base.

31.5in (80cm) wide
$20,000-30,000   **FRE**

A pair of 18th century bronze female mask sphinxes each with decorative headdresses and tasseled drapes, on underscrolled plinth bases, dark green patination.
15.25in (39cm)
$6,000-8,000   **L&T**

A bronze sculpture, 'Furietti Centaur', after the antique, dark brown patina, raised on a stepped veined marble rectangular base.
6in (15cm) wide
$1,200-1,600   **L&T**

A pair of late 19th/early 20thC French marble and gilt-bronze urns, each with pineapple finial and lotus leaf cover, the swan neck handles with husk and foliate ribbons, the circular fluted and laurel socle on square inset corner base.
$9,000-11,000   **L&T**

A pair of mid-19thC bronze urns on marble columns of campana form, each with lobed lower section, reeded handles and spreading foot, on stepped cylindrical variegated green marble pedestal with bronze collar.
15.75in (40cm) wide
$3,000-4,000   **L&T**

A pair of 19thC Neoclassical French patinated bronze and gilt ewers, each with acanthus-cast scrolling handles, with griffin terminals raised on a black slate plinth.

15in (38.5cm) high
$6,000-8,000   **L&T**

A 19thC bronze ewer with foliate and leaf scroll decoration, the top with a triton and a sea nymph holding a conch shell above Classical scenes and foliate garlands, on a fluted spreading foot with plinth base.
22.25in (56cm) high
$600-800   **L&T**

A 19thC French bronze vase, cast with frolicking putti and trailing leaves, stamped 'Clodion' below one handle.
15.75in (40cm) high
$6,000-8,000   **L&T**

A French silvered bronze inkwell, 'Serpent Attacking Two Birds', after Pierre Jules Mene, raised on a green marble base, signed 'Mene'.
9in (23cm) wide
$1,000-1,600   **FRE**

A bronze and ivory, 'Sculpture Group', by Dambros, cast as two workers seated on a bench, signed in the bronze.

6.25in (16cm) high

$800-1,200   L&T

A bronze and ivory figure, 'Little Pierrot', by Georges Omerth, signed in the bronze, stamped number '5195', raised on a circular onyx base.

7.25in (18.5cm) high

$1,000-1,500   L&T

A bronze figure, 'Danseuse au Bandeau', by Paul Philippe, cold-painted and parcel-gilt bronze, carved ivory and onyx on wood plinth, cast by Rosenthal und Maedar, signed 'P.Phillipe' and 'RuM'.

c1925   29.25in (74in) high

$50,000-60,000   SOT

A carved ivory and bronze figure, 'The Source', by Ferdinand Priess, young woman in long, gold-painted garb, which exposes her right breast, leaning on a three-sided parapet wall with applied mythological face, surrounding an arc-shaped protruding base plate with round basin hollow.

c1925   11.5in (29cm) high

$20,000-30,000   VZ

A cold-painted and patinated bronze figure, 'Charleston Dancer', by Johann Philipp Ferdinand Preiss, carved and painted ivory and marble, base engraved 'F. Preiss'.

c1925   15in (38cm) high

$24,000-36,000   SOT

A pair of bronze and ivory bookends, Roland, Paris, depicting two seated jesters with eccentric headgear, each with birds perched on their knees, raised on marble plinths, signed on the plinths 'Roland Paris'.

6.25in (16cm) high

$3,600-4,400   L&T

A gilt bronze and ivory group, 'Skating Figures', by Louis Sosson, raised on an onyx plinth, signed to the base.

7.5in (19cm) high

$3,000-4,000   L&T

A 20thC French bronze and ivory erotic cigarette box, the hinged lid surmounted by a reclining female figure in full-length robe, opening to reveal her 'déshabillé'.

5.5in (14cm) wide

$1,200-1,600   L&T

An early 20thC Austrian cold-painted bronze figure, 'Running Moor', by Franz Bergman, holding a spear or staff, on a naturalistic base, impressed Bergman amphora, 'GESCHUTZT'.

9.5in (24cm) high

$1,600-2,400   FRE

An Austrian cold-painted bronze group, 'Concubine and Shahib', by Franz Bergman, in bronze, signed 'Nam Greb' with Bergman Amphora mark.

7.5in high (19cm)

$2,400-3,600   FRE

A Bergmann cold-painted bronze figure of a carpet seller, the standing figure holding a carpet, bearing Bergmann Amphora stamp.

8in (20.5cm) high

$3,000-4,000   FRE

A late 19th/early 20thC Austrian cold-painted bronze figure by Carl Kauba, in the form of a recumbent Native American smoking a pipe, signed 'C. Kauba'.

10in (25.5cm) high

$4,000-6,000   L&T

An early 20thC Austrian erotic bronze figure, modeled as a draped young lady, her gown opening to reveal her nude, on a raised marble base.

5.75in (14cm) high

$800-1,200   FRE

A large Austrian cold-painted bronze figure, cast as an Arabic water carrier, the turbanned male figure carrying an animal skin bladder on his back, naturalistic marble plinth.

19in (48cm) high

$3,000-4,000   L&T

An Austrian painted bronze group, depicting an Arabian teacher reading from a book to four children seated on a carpet.

5in (13cm) high

$700-900   A&G

A large Austrian cold-painted bronze figure, depicting an Native American realistically cast and painted holding a peace pipe in his right hand, stamped 'GESCHUTZT'.

20in (51cm) high

$12,000-16,000   L&T

A late 19th/early 20thC Austrian cold-painted bronze figure, in the form of an Arab riding a camel and holding a long rifle.

12in (30cm) high

$3,000-4,000   L&T

A late 19th/early 20thC Austrian cold-painted bronze boudoir lamp in the form of an Arab seated beneath a tent.

10in (25cm) high

$2,000-3,000   L&T

An early 20thC Austrian cold-painted bronze figure of the slave seller, standing on a tasseled carpet, chain around slave girl's arm is lacking.

8in (20.5cm) high

$2,400-3,600   FRE

A late 19th/early 20thC cold-painted bronze falcon, by Bergmann, perched on a rock, bears Bergmann Amphora, stamped 'GESCH'.

6in (15cm) high

$6,000-8,000   L&T

A Bergmann cold-painted bronze figure of a bison, stamped '4867' with Bergman Amphora and 'GESCHUTZT'.

11.5in (29cm) wide

$9,000-11,000   FRE

A Bergmann cold-painted bronze figure of a cockerel, realistically modeled and painted with inset glass eyes, bearing Bergmann Amphora stamp and 'GESCHUTZT'.

12in (30.5cm) high

$7,000-9,000   FRE

A Bergmann cold-painted bronze figure of a hen, with applied glass eyes, bearing Bergmann Amphora stamp.

8.25in (21cm) high

$1,000-1,600   FRE

An amusing late 19th/early 20thC Austrian cold-painted bronze figure in the form of a fox carrying a sandwich board.

8.75in (22cm) high

$3,000-4,000   L&T

A late 19th/early 20thC Austrian cold-painted bronze picture frame in the form of a cat peering around the frame.

6.5in (16cm) wide

$4,000-6,000   L&T

A large late 19th/early 20thC Austrian cold-painted bronze turkey, realistically cast and painted.

10in (25.5cm) high

$2,000-3,000   L&T

A late 19th/early 20thC Austrian cold-painted bronze mountain goat, raised on a naturalistic marble base.

14.25in (36cm) high

$7,000-9,000   L&T

An early 20thC Austrian cold-painted bronze figure of a bulldog, naturalistically cast and painted.

4in (10cm) high

$500-700   L&T

A late 19th/early 20thC cast and painted white metal blackamoor, modeled standing holding a lobed oval tray, on rug-draped, stepped plinth, indistinctly signed, damaged.

43.5in (110cm) high

$5,000-7,000   L&T

A Victorian painted cast iron model of a fox terrier.

9.25in (23cm) high

$600-1,000   L&T

A bronzed white metal figure of a racehorse and jockey taking a jump, by W. Zwick, with shaped wooden base.

22.75in (58cm) long

$800-1,200   ROS

A late 19th/early 20thC cold-painted bronze group of a jockey and gig, on foliate-decorated rectangular base.

12.25in (31cm) long

$8,000-10,000   L&T

A 19thC Italian marble figure of Lorenzo de Medici, after Michelangelo, with seated figure looking down in contemplation.

32in (81.5cm) high

$6,000-8,000   FRE

A gilt-bronze and ivory fashionable Victorian lady, by Armand Quernard (French, 1865-1925), on a canted white marble base, signed 'Quernard'.

13.5in (34cm) high

$5,000-7,000   L&T

A late 19thC Italian green marble and alabaster figure, modeled as a young woman leaning against a wall, her head turned to the left.

28in (71cm) high

$3,000-4,000   FRE

A late 19thC Italian marble figure of a flower girl, the standing figure with a flower basket in her arms, signed 'H Moreau'.

27.5cm (70cm) high

$3,000-4,000   FRE

A large plaster study, 'Love Triumphant', after N. F. Gillet (1712-1791), depicting Cupid resting against a festooned tree stump, on a plinth base, stamped Musée Du Louvre and inscribed around the top edge: 'Qui que tu sois, voici ton maitre.. il l'est le fut, ou le doit etre' (whoever you are, here is your master.. he is or he should be - i.e. love).

$5,000-7,000   L&T

A white marble bust of W.H. Cassells, by Hiram Powers, inscribed.

Walter Richard Cassells was a poet and critic of theology. He commissioned the bust in 1868.

24in (61cm) high

$11,000-13,000   L&T

A 19thC marble bust of a gentleman, by Peter Francis Connelly (American 1841-1902), raised on a socle base, signed 'P. F. CONNILLY, FECIT'.

21.25in (54cm) high

$1,600-2,400   L&T

A white marble bust of a lady, by Alfred Courtens (Belgian, 1889-1967), signed and dated, with a mahogany pedestal.

1921   31.5in (80cm) high

$4,000-6,000   L&T

A marble bust of a young girl, by Edouard-Charles-Marie-Houssin (French, 1847-1917), signed 'E. Houssin', on a gray marble socle.

11in (28cm) high

$6,000-10,000   L&T

A pair of early 20thC Italian specimen marble busts of blackamoors, composed of lapis lazuli, sienna, variegated rouge, white carrera and black marbles, on ogee-molded marble bases.

14.5in (37cm) high

$3,000-4,000   FRE

A pair of late 19thC specimen marble busts, 'Dante' and 'Beatrice', by F. Vichi, raised on canted rectangular marble bases, signed 'F.Vichi, Firenze'.

26.75in (68cm) high

$5,000-7,000   L&T

A 19thC marble stand, the conch shell dish top carved with a central satyr's head flanked by twin serpents and upheld on twin marlin supports on an oval mottled red and black marble pedestal base.

9.5in (24cm) high

$2,000-3,000   L&T

A pair of Blue John and black marble obelisks, the plinths with inset panels on square bases.

17.5in (44cm) high

$10,000-12,000   **L&T**

A 19thC Blue John and marble obelisk with white marble collars and a square plinth base.

14.25in (38cm) high

$9,000-11,000   **L&T**

A 19thC Blue John and marble urn on plinth, the urn with spreading foot on a square black base, the square plinth with white marble collars and outset base.

10in (25cm) high

$6,000-8,000   **L&T**

A 19thC Blue John urn with lobed lower section and separate socle, chips.

7.25in (18cm) high

$5,000-7,000   **L&T**

A Victorian Blue John goblet, the deep-dished bowl on a turned tapered stem, raised on a molded circular foot.

6in (15cm) high

$5,000-7,000   **L&T**

TERRACOTTA

A late 19th/early 20thC Austrian painted terracotta bust of a Nubian boy, by Goldscheider, model 1365, on plinth base, stamped 'Reproduction R**' and '1365/53'.

21.75in (55cm) high

$5,000-7,000   **L&T**

Left: An early 20thC Goldscheider painted terracotta bust, of a Nubian girl, Model 1102, wearing a turban and a low cut blouse, signed 'J du Perrant and Frederick Goldscheider', stamped 'Reproduction Réservée'.

26in (66cm) high

$5,000-6,000   **L&T**

Right: An early 20thC Goldscheider painted terracotta bust of a Nubian boy, model 1645, wearing a loosely draped robe, with plaque 'F. Goldscheider Vienna', stamped 'Reproduction Réservée'.

23.75in (60cm) high

$8,000-10,000   **L&T**

A late 19th/early 20thC Austrian painted terracotta figure, of a Nubian man, by Goldscheider, Model 895, with a necklace and robed garment, the base with plaque 'F Goldscheider Wien' and stamped 'Reproduction'.

23in (58cm) high

$5,000-6,000   **L&T**

A late 19th/early 20thC Austrian painted terracotta figure, of a seated Nubian youth, by Goldscheider, model 1048, playing a flute, with necklace and loosely draped loin cloth, with plaque stamped 'Goldscheider 1048, Reproduction Réservée'.

41.75in (106cm) high

$9,000-11,000   **L&T**

An early 19thC terracotta figure, depicting 'Diana with a greyhound', by Joseph Gott (1791-1850), signed and dated.

1824   *2.75in (7cm) high*

$7,000-9,000   **L&T**

A late 19th/early 20thC Austrian painted terracotta model of a cat, seated with a ribbon tied around its neck, with inset glass eyes; and another model of standing cat.

8in (20cm) wide and 10 in (25cm) wide

$2,000-3,000   **L&T**

A large Austrian painted terracotta group of two seated cats cradling a young kitten, with inset eyes and on a naturalistic grassy oval base.

18.25in (46cm) wide

$1,100-1,300   **L&T**

A 19thC pair of terracotta hounds seated on their haunches, gazing forward attentively, each wearing a collar, on plinth bases, some damages.

28.75in (73cm) high

$4,000-6,000   **L&T**

An area rug, with large leafy pattern, in the style of William Morris, in tones of dark red.

96in (244cm) long

$1,400-2,000 **DRA**

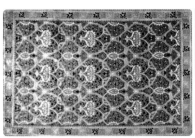

A room-size rug in an Iznik pattern, in the style of William Morris, on an emerald field.

144in (366cm) long

$1,400-2,000 **DRA**

An Arts and Crafts 'Hunting' carpet, designed by George Bain, machine woven with huntsmen with dogs, deer, boar and horses, made by Quayle & Tranter Ltd, Kidderminster, label to the reverse.

144in (366cm) long

$5,000-6,000 **L&T**

A 'Donegal' carpet, designed by Gavin Morton and G. K. Robertson, made by Alexander Morton & Co.

187.75in (477cm) wide

$28,000-32,000 **L&T**

A 1930s Nichols Chinese Art Deco room-size wool carpet, depicting an interior vignette surrounded by floral border, on jade ground.

175.5in (445cm) long

$3,000-4,000 **SDR**

A Scottish Art Nouveau silkwork-embroidered panel, a pair of birds perched on a stylized flowering tree reserved on a blue woven cotton ground.

28in (71cm) long

$2,200-2,800 **L&T**

Six panels of Morris & Co. floral-printed cotton fabric, some sewn as curtains, signed on selvage, some fading to one panel.

1880-1900 *56in (142cm) long*

$900-1,300 SIX **DRA**

A lacquered and gilded 'La Conquète du Cheval' panel by Jean Dunand (1877-1942), featuring two native riders in pursuit of five wild horses, signed 'Jean Dunand' lower left

24.5in (62cm) high

$60,000-70,000 **SOTP**

An André David lacquered 'Diane Chasseresse' panel, representing Diana hunting with two greyhounds in a cubist landscape, signed lower right 'A. David'.

63in (160cm) wide

$50,000-60,000 **SOTP**

THE MODERN MARKET

The appetite for the work of modern designers continues unabated with the work of George Nakashima, Paul Evans, Lucie Rie and Wendell Castle staying at the top of every collector's wanted list. There is increasing interest in the work of contemporary designers such as Ron Arad, and ceramics by European and American potters continue to lure buyers.

As the market grows established collectors are looking for pieces which show individuality while also being typical of a designer's work. So, handmade ceramics such as those by Rie and her contemporaries, and furniture by Nakashima with its natural, free edges, fit this bill.

We may also be seeing buyers starting to move away from production pieces in favor of one-off designs and prototypes which show the hand of the master. Similarly there is increasing demand for examples with provenance.

And where record prices are concerned there have been some new names on the block in the past twelve months including Gertrude and Otto Natzler, Wharton Esherick and Phillip Lloyd Powell. The Natzlers' hand-thrown ceramics covered with vibrant, volcanic glazes suit current trends. Similarly Esherick and Powell, who were friends with both George Nakashima and Paul Evans (Powell once shared a studio with Evans), made handcrafted organic furniture which is increasingly in demand by collectors. It is interesting to note that Powell is believed to have produced barely a thousand pieces, compared with the 10,000 that are reputed to have been made by Nakashima. This may have a bearing on prices for his work in the future.

Glass from the 20th century's major centers of excellence: the glasshouses of Scandinavia and Murano in Italy continues to find willing buyers, especially for examples which combine vibrant colors with modern forms and for big names such as Barovier, Venini and Seguso or design classics such as the Pezzato range by Fulvio Bianconi for Venini.

John Sollo, Sollo Rago Modern Auctions, Lambertville, New Jersey

An Alvar Aalto laminated birch chair, no. 31.

23in (58cm) wide

$6,000-7,000   **SDR**

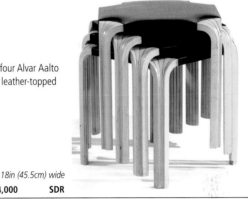

A set of four Alvar Aalto stacking leather-topped stools.

18in (45.5cm) wide

$3,000-4,000   **SDR**

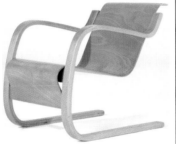

An Alvar Aalto tank chair, with birch frame and red wool upholstery.

30.5in (77.5cm) wide

$2,000-4,000   **SDR**

A Finnish molded fiberglass 'Pastille' chair, designed by Eero Aarnio, for Asko Lahti.

1967-1968

$1,500-1,900   **L&T**

A burr ash and fiddled sycamore cabinet-on-stand, designed by Fred Baier.

c1984   *63in (160cm) wide*

$12,000-14,000   **L&T**

A pink and green stained sycamore ply writing desk, designed by Fred Baier, the superstructure with pigeonholes and lidded stationary compartments, raised above a V-shaped support.

42in (106.5cm) wide

$15,000-17,000   **L&T**

A Baumann fils tambour draught screen, with undulating crest and slatted construction, bears makers label.

71.5in (181cm) high

$1,400-2,000   **L&T**

An early 1990s polished granite and wrought steel center table, designed by Paul Belvoir, the circular top supported by six scroll legs.

55in (140cm) diam.

$11,000-13,000   **SOTH**

MODERN DESIGN

A Fontana Arte coffee table, designed by Dulio Bernabe, with painted and gilded chiseled edge glass top on walnut base, signed 'Dube Fontana Arte'.

1955   *50in (127cm) wide*
$10,000-12,000   **SDR**

A lacquered wood desk, storage unit and console, designed by Osvaldo Borsani, for Techno, the desk with an inset writing surface, the storage unit on casters with supply drawer, file drawer and wastepaper compartment, the tripartite console with hinged side sections.

1982   *Desk 86.5in (220cm) wide*
$8,000-12,000   **SOTH**

A 1950s oak-veneered cabinet, designed by Osvaldo Borsani, the six cupboard doors each with a carved wood panel depicting an animal within an angled frame.

89.75in (228cm) wide
$12,000-14,000   **SOTH**

A limited edition 'San Demas' suite, designed by Mark Brazier-Jones, patinated bronze and printed hide upholstery, with winged terminals and claw feet.

The San Dema sofa was produced in a limited edition of 50 in bronze polished/patina and 50 in aluminum. The limited edition chairs were produced in 100 of each metal.

30in (76cm) high
$32,000-36,000   **SOTH**

A black lacquered wood and black painted steel table 'T102', designed by Osvaldo Borsani and Eugenio Gerli, for Tecno, one leg labelled 'Tecno/Milano'.

c1964   *46.5in (118.5cm) wide*
$10,000-12,000   **SOTH**

A Marcel Breuer bentwood chaise-longue, manufactured by Isokon Furniture Co., London, with manufacturer's label.

52in (132cm) long
$14,000-16,000   **SOT**

A Wendell Castle three-legged corner vanity, in exotic hardwoods and bird's-eye maple veneer, with stool upholstered in tufted leather, both signed 'Castle 92'.

1992   *Vanity 54in (137cm) high*
$8,000-10,000   **SDR**

A Wendell Castle miniature bronze 'Angel' chair, with verdigris patina, signed 'Castle 91'.

1991   *6.75in (17cm) wide*
$1,500-1,900   **SDR**

A 1980s armchair and ottoman, designed by Achille Castiglione, in green suede, the chair with L-shaped armrests, the ottoman formed of two curved sections on a black metal foot.

28.75in (73cm) high
$6,000-10,000   **SOTH**

A pair of Wendell Castle yellow molded plastic 'Molar' chairs, molded 'WC'.

32in (81cm) wide
$3,000-4,000   **SDR**

A 1970s circular resin and cornelian dining table, designed by Ado Chale, the table top fitted with an internal light, the side of the table top signed 'Chale'.

65.5in (166cm) diam.

$170,000-200,000   **SOTH**

A Kusch & Co 'TV-Relax' chaise-longue, designed by Luigi Colani, formed from shaped polyurethane foam covered in purple stretch fabric.

1969   *28.5in (72cm) high*

$7,000-8,000   **QU**

An Italian 'Tube' chair, designed by Joe Colombo, for Flexform, with vinyl-covered polyurethane foam, plastic cylinders, metal and rubber grips.

1969-1970

$10,000-14,000   **L&T**

An Italian games and dining table, designed by Joe Columbo, for Zanotta, twin top laminated in plastic with height adjusted legs in chrome-plated steel, each corner fitted with pull-out drink/ash trays.

1967   *38.5in (98cm) wide*

$3,600-4,400   **L&T**

A 1960s large four fold painted screen, designed and painted by Robert Crowder.

Crowder, an American, first visited Japan in 1934. The trip began a lifelong love affair with the country and its art. His training with the great painters Shunko Mochizuki and Shimamoto-sensei served him well after his repatriation to the United States in 1943. After a brief stay in Chicago, Crowder moved west, opening a gallery in Los Angeles in the neighbourhood of Greta Garbo and other Hollywood legends. He quickly became famous for his screens and fabulous textiles, which as recently as 2005 were ordered for an international redecoration of the Chanel boutiques.

Each panel 83.5in (212cm) high

$28,000-36,000   **SOTH**

A 1950s rosewood sideboard, designed by Robin Day, for Hille, with veined black marble top and four doors below, satinwood lined.

77in (186cm) wide

$1,400-1,800   **A&G**

A Donald Deskey six-drawer D-shaped kneehole desk, of painted and lacquered mahogany.

50in (127cm) wide

$5,000-6,000   **SDR**

A 'Trône' wrought iron chair, designed by André Dubreuil, bent and welded, the shield back rising to an exaggerated scroll, slubbed fabric seat.

c1985   *56.75in (144cm) high*

$34,000-40,000   **SOTH**

A Dunbar walnut cross-legged coffee table, with Murano glass mosaic tile top, green tag and paper label.

54in (137cm) wide

$5,400-6,000   **SDR**

A Dunbar walnut three-legged side table, its top inlaid with sixteen blue and green Natzler tiles, Dunbar metal tag.

15in (38cm) wide

$17,000-19,000 SDR

A Dunbar lacquered mahogany credenza, on brass legs with woven-front doors and interior shelves, brass tag.

62in (157.5cm) wide

$4,000-6,000 SDR

A Herman Miller 'ESU 400' storage unit, designed by Charles and Ray Eames, with colored masonite panels on polished chrome frame.

47in (119cm) wide

$6,000-8,000 SDR

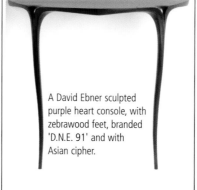

A Zenith Edition 'DAW' chair, designed by Charles and Ray Eames, with fiberglass seat and steel wire and walnut stand, with maker's label to base.

1950 *30in (76cm) high*

$4,000-5,000 QU

A Charles and Ray Eames armchair and ottoman, for Herman Miller, model nos 670 and 671, rosewood ply framed, upholstered in black leather.

$4,000-5,000 L&T

A David Ebner sculpted purple heart console, with zebrawood feet, branded 'D.N.E. 91' and with Asian cipher.

37in (94cm) wide

$7,000-8,000 SDR

A Wharton Esherick walnut armchair, with sculpted back and arms and leather strap seat, signed '1951 W.E.'.

1951 *23.5in (60cm) wide*

$19,000-23,000 SDR

A Wharton Esherick padouk single-arm prismatic bench, the base with small storage compartment and four banks of shallow pivoting drawers illuminated from under the seat.

Provenance: From the estate of Helene Fischer, one of Esherick's most prominent patrons. This piece was featured in the Brooklyn Museum exhibition, 'Masters of Contemporary American Crafts'.

1961 *94in (239cm) wide*

$130,000-170,000 SDR

A Paul Evans welded and etched steel 'Argente' sculpture/room divider, suspended from a patinated metal frame.

This rare piece was part of Evans' 1968 'Sculptures in the Fields' series. He created only three 'Argente' masterpieces and photographed them in a Bucks County field. The Field series is considered to be among the rarest and most important of all Evans' work.

1968 *85in (216cm) wide*

$140,000-160,000 SDR

A Paul Evans copper patchwork swivel cube chair, on castors.

30in (76cm) wide

$28,000-32,000 SDR

A Paul Evans sculpture-front wall-hanging cabinet, with slate top, and interior shelves, signed 'Paul Evans 67 D.C.'

1967   *81in (205.5cm) wide*

$100,000-120,000   **SDR**

A Paul Evans sculpted and painted steel cocktail table, with plate glass top.

1973   *36in (91.5cm) wide*

$24,000-28,000   **SDR**

A Paul Evans copper, bronze and pewter console, with smoked glass top, and matching upholstered stool.

54in (137cm) wide

$7,000-9,000   **SDR**

A 1970s chromium plate and brass patchwork four-poster bed, designed by Paul Evans, entirely covered in paneling, the upper rails fitted for curtains.

120.5in (306cm) long

$16,000-20,000   **SOTH**

A pair of Danish scimitar chairs, designed by Preben Fabricus and Jorgen Kastholm, upholstered in brown leather on steel frames, branded 'Denmark'.

32in (81cm) wide

$20,000-24,000   **SDR**

A 1950s white-painted wrought iron bed, designed by Giovanni Ferrabini, the headboard formed as a stylized coronet.

78.75in (200cm) long

$26,000-30,000   **SOTH**

A 1950s pair of Fontana Arte deep blue glass side tables, each with three curved stands supporting a circular top.

27.5in (70cm) high

$140,000-160,000 PAIR   **SOTH**

A 1950s pair of Fontana Arte glass and bronze consoles, each with a rectangular top above waisted supports joined by twin cylindrical stretchers.

63in (160cm) long

$26,000-32,000   **SOTH**

A Piero Fornasetti three-drawer 'Palladian' demi-lune chest, printed in black on white ground, with brass pulls, signed 'Fornasetti/Made in Italy' and with Fornasetti Milano label.

40in (101.5cm) wide

$9,000-11,000   **SDR**

A Piero Fornasetti metal 'Doberman' umbrella stand.

34.25in (87cm) wide

$1,000-1,500 SDR

A Gio Ponti black lacquered four-drawer desk, by Piero Fornasetti, printed with pistol and key motif in silver and gold, on brass feet, signed 'Fornasetti/Milano/made in Italy'.

35.25in (89.5cm) wide

$12,000-14,000 SDR

A Pedro Friedeberg red-enameled 'Hand and Foot' chair, with left hand seat on right foot base, signed twice 'PEDRO FRIEDEBERG'.

18.25in (46cm) wide

$10,000-12,000 SDR

A pair of bronze stools, designed by Elisabeth Garouste and Mattia Bonetti, each with an embroidered removeable cover depicting a star, both chairs marked 'BG' to one or two legs.

17in (43cm) high

$18,000-22,000 SOTH

Two Frank Gehry wiggle chairs, multiple layers of bonded corrugated cardboard finished at edges with brown hardboard.

c1972 *33.5in (85cm) high*

$1,500-1,900 SK

A German fiberglass 'Garden Egg' chair, designed by Peter Ghyczy, for Reuter Products, upholstered interior and articulated top.

1968

$1,500-1,900 L&T

A Herman Miller sofa, designed by Alexander Girard, upholstered in its original taupe and blue fabric, on aluminum frame.

72in (183cm) wide

$7,000-9,000 SDR

A pair of Allen Gould string chairs, on tubular black metal frames.

20in (50.5cm) wide

$3,400-4,000 SDR

A mid-20thC concrete and iron bench, designed by Willy Guhl.

76in (193cm) long

$19,000-23,000 SOTH

A Guillerme and Chambon oak sideboard, with two sliding doors inset with tiles and two end cabinets.

90.25in (229cm) wide

$9,000-11,000 SDR

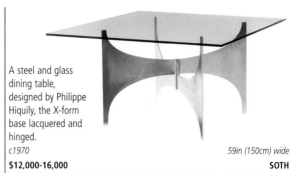

A steel and glass dining table, designed by Philippe Hiquily, the X-form base lacquered and hinged.
c1970
59in (150cm) wide
$12,000-16,000 SOTH

A 1970s pair of aluminum and injection-molded occasional chairs, designed by Knut Hesterberg.
28.5in (72cm) high
$10,000-14,000 PAIR SOTH

A Higgins 'Rondelay' screen, of multi-colored glass discs within original walnut frame.
94.5in (240cm) wide
$10,000-12,000 SDR

An Arne Jacobsen Swan chair, manufactured by Fritz Hansen, Denmark, seat in later purple upholstery, four-prong aluminum swivel base with manufacturer's label and control mark.
30in (76cm) high
$1,300-$1,700 SK

An 'Egg' leather and aluminum chair and ottoman, designed by Arne Jacobsen, model nos 3316 and 3127, manufactured by Fritz Hansen, Denmark, with manufaccturer's label.
c1958 *Chair 41in (104cm) high*
$30,000-36,000 SOT

A 1960s green lacquered bureau, designed by Maison Jansen, the fall front enclosing two shelves above an illuminated interior with tooled and gilt-leather surface.
45.5in (116cm) high
$16,000-20,000 SOTH

A pair of teak and simulated leatherette armchairs, designed by Pierre Jeanneret.
c1955 *35.5in (90cm) high*
$13,000-$15,000 SOTH

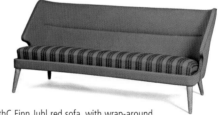

A mid-20thC Finn Juhl red sofa, with wrap-around back, single striped seat cushion in wool upholstery.
75in (191cm) wide
$4,000-5,000 SK

A set of four faux alligator vinyl-upholstered side chairs, designed by Finn Juhl, for Baker.
22in (56cm) wide
$2,000-3,000 SDR

A Vladimir Kagan cantilevered end table, with brass-trimmed top.
31in (78.5cm) wide
$9,000-11,000 SDR

A Dreyfuss walnut contour chair, designed by Vladimir Kagan, upholstered in white leather, 'Kagan-Dreyfuss' branded mark.
28.75in (73cm) wide
$16,000-18,000 SDR

A Vladimir Kagan curved floating sofa, on walnut frame, upholstered in indigo chenille.

82.5in (209.5cm) wide

$12,000-16,000   **SDR**

A steel two-seat leather settee, with tubular wall-mounted headrest, designed by Jorgen Kastholm and Preben Fabricius, for Bo-Ex.
1964

$8,000-12,000   **L&T**

An E. Kold Christensen 'PK-80' stainless steel daybed, designed by Poul Kjaerholm, with black leather tufted cushion.

74in (188cm) wide

$13,000-15,000   **SDR**

A pair of Poul Kjaerholm 'PK22' chairs, covered in brown leather.

25in (63.5cm) wide

$3,600-4,400   **SDR**

An early Knoll maple credenza, designed by Florence Knoll, on black metal legs.

72in (182.5cm) wide
$2,000-3,000   SDR

A Knoll walnut veneer vitrine cabinet, on iron base, Knoll Associates label, and IBM inventory tag.

48in (122cm) wide

$2,000-3,000   **SDR**

A Shiro Kuramata 'How High the Moon' chair, of nickel-plated wire mesh.

27.5in (70cm) wide

$12,000-14,000   **SDR**

A parchment and leather occasional 'drum' table, designed by Paul Dupré-Lafon, stamped to upper and lower leather rings 'HERMES-PARIS'.

24.5in (62cm) high

$20,000-24,000   **SOTH**

A 1960's pair of Swedish oiled teak and leather chairs, designed by I. Kofod Larsen, for Olof Persons Fatolindustri, marked 'Salen 799'.

30.25in (77cm) wide

$4,000-6,000 PAIR   **L&T**

A pair of Janette Lavèrrière iron rocking chairs, with leather seats.

47in (119cm) high

$5,000-6,000   **SDR**

A Philip and Kelvin Laverne bronze coffee table, the top depicting an Asian courtyard scene with light polychrome painted details, on bronze 'bundled' legs, signed 'Philip + Kelvin LaVerne'.

60.5in (154cm) wide

$10,000-12,000   **SDR**

A Philip and Kelvin Laverne bronze coffee table, etched with Creation detail from Michelangelo's 'Capella Sistina', signed 'Philip Kelvin Laverne/After Michaelangelo'.

65in (165cm) wide

$5,000-6,000   **SDR**

A pair of Christian Liagre corseted carved fir pedestals.

11.5in (29cm) wide

$3,200-4,400   **SDR**

An early walnut veneer center table, by David Linley, inlaid with macassar ebony, sycamore and burrwood.

c1985   *40in (102cm) wide*

$5,000-7,000   **SOTH**

A pair of Michele de Lucchi prototype 'First' stools, signed 'Michele de Lucchi'.

1992   *24.5in (62cm) wide*

$700-900   **SDR**

A white 'Eros' side table, designed by Angelo Mangiarotti, the conical base supporting a detachable kidney-shaped top.

1971   *25.5in (65cm) wide*

$15,000-17,000   **SOTH**

A pair of Bruno Mathsson 'Eva' armchairs, with original hemp webbing on bentwood frames.

23in (58.5cm) wide

$5,000-7,000   **SDR**

A Bruno Mathsson 'Pernilla' lounge chair and ottoman, with original hemp webbing on bentwood frames, branded marks.

25.5in (64.5cm) wide

$3,400-4,600   **SDR**

A Paul McCobb birch and black laminate men's wardrobe, with shirt drawers and doors, Paul McCobb metal label.

40in (101.5cm) wide

$2,400-3,000   **SDR**

A pair of 'Barcelona' chairs, designed by Ludwig Mies van der Rohe, model MR-90, bent chromed flat steel joined with chromed screws, original leather strapping.

29in (74cm) wide

$30,000-36,000   **SOTP**

A set of four 'Brno' chairs, designed by Mies van der Rohe, for Knoll International, these of a later production, manufacturer's marks to the base.
Designed 1930

$2,400-3,000　　　　　　　　**L&T**

A 1970s German Horn molded Baydur 'Kangaroo' armchair, finished in blue, designed by Ernst Moeckl.

Due to the angled legs, this chair is often known as the 'Kangaroo' chair. Available without arms, it is molded from a resilient form of structural composite polyurethane produced by Bayer and known as 'Baydur'.

30.5in (76.5cm) high

$200-280　　　　　　　　**QU**

A Borge Mogensen design leather-upholstered three seat settee, with wooden legs, unmarked.

76in (193cm) wide

$2,400-3,200　　　　　　　　**L&T**

A pair of James Mont lounge chairs, upholstered in original orange fabric, embroidered with Asian courtyard scene.

36in (94.5cm) wide

$10,000-12,000　　　　　　　　**SDR**

A James Mont glass top table, with plant stand base.

27.5in (70cm) high

$1,600-2,000　　　　　　　　**SDR**

A French bent tubular steel 'Djinn' chaise longue, designed by Olivier Mourgue, for Airborne, with foam and stretch wool fabric.
1965　　*22.5in (57cm) wide*

$2,400-3,000　　　　　　　　**L&T**

A Forrest Myers style bent steel console, with pair of matching two-seat benches.

Console 54in (137cm) wide

$2,400-3,000　　　　　　　　**SDR**

ESSENTIAL REFERENCE: GEORGE NAKASHIMA

George Nakashima (1905-1990) was an American of Japanese parentage. He trained as an architect, before turning to furniture design and manufacture.

- His first furniture was made in Seattle 1940-2, before he was interned following Pearl Harbour. In the camps, he met Gentauro Hikogawa, a man trained in traditional Japanese carpentry, who taught him the use of traditional Japanese hand tools and joinery techniques.
- In 1943, American architect, Antonin Raymond, sponsored Nakashima's release from the camp and invited him to his farm in New Hope, Pennyslvania. In 1946, Nakashima set up his 'craft furniture studio' there.
- His furniture is sturdy and made from solid wood, without veneers. Nakashima worked with the texture and organic structure of the wood, choosing pieces with knots and whorls.
- Σ He was influenced by Japanese woodwork, in particular the tea ceremony aesthetic.
- Despite the hand-worked appearance of his work, Nakeshima favored machine production, which set him apart from the crafts revival movement.

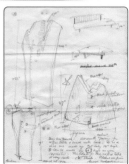

A walnut Conoid bench, designed by George Nakashima, with walnut butterfly joint, free edge seat, with hickory spindles on cylindrical tapering legs.

Accompanied by original paperwork and drawing signed and dated 1972. Inscribed on the underside, 'to the Donches George Nakashima May 1972.'

81in (206cm) long

$34,000-40,000　　　　　　　　**FRE**

A pair of walnut Conoid dining chairs, designed by George Nakashima.

With copy of original bill of sale dated 1968. Irving name to underside of chairs.

35.5in (90cm) high

$16,000-18,000   **FRE**

A pair of George Nakashima walnut slat-back open armchairs.

30in (76cm) wide

$10,000-12,000   **FRE**

A George Nakashima walnut lounge chair, with free-edge writing arm.

33in (84cm) wide

$10,000-12,000   **SDR**

A Conoid walnut coffee table, designed by George Nakashima, the freeform shape top with terminal support and single tapering leg.

With original order receipt and drawing signed and dated 1971.

37in (94cm) wide

$18,000-22,000   **FRE**

A walnut circular top dining table, designed by George Nakashima, with rectangular tapering legs.

57in (145cm) diam

$6,000-8,000   **FRE**

A George Nakashima English walnut freeform Conoid coffee table, with single board, the top with one butterfly joint.

1960   14in (36cm) high

$24,000-30,000   **SK**

A George Nakashima 'Minguren I' coffee table, with free-edge buckeye burl top, with natural occlusions and walnut base, with a copy of the original drawing.

1981   64in (162cm) wide

$300,000+   **SDR**

A George Nakashima walnut wall-hanging cabinet, marked with client's name.

72in (183cm) wide

$20,000-28,000   **SDR**

A credenza, designed by George Nakashima, with free-edge top with dovetails over three vertical sliding grilled doors backed with pandanus cloth, signed and dated 'George Nakashima'.

Accompanied by original drawing signed and dated 1979 and copy of bill of sale dated 1980.

1980   84in (213.5cm) wide

$40,000-50,000   **FRE**

MODERN DESIGN

A Herman Miller 'Thin Edge' rosewood chest, designed by George Nelson, with porcelain pulls, Herman Miller foil label.

33.75in (85.5cm) wide

$2,000-3,000   **SDR**

A Herman Miller three-seat sofa and club chair, designed by George Nelson, upholstered in dark olive-green wool.

sofa: 96in (244cm) wide

$4,000-6,000   **SDR**

An 'Embryo' chair, designed by Marc Newson, for Ideé, Japan, in green neoprene, tubular steel and aluminum.

c1988

$6,000-8,000

30.5in (77.5cm) high

SOT

A Mobilier 'Rio' sculptural lounge chair, designed by Oscar Niemeyer, with bent ash frame and black leather-upholstered cushion.

67in (170cm) wide

$16,000-18,000   **SDR**

A Knoll coffee table, designed by Isamu Noguchi, with plate glass top resting on a birch base.

50.25in (127.5cm) wide

$2,400-3,000   **SDR**

A pair of steel and leather chairs, designed by Arne Norell, each with detachable headrest, the exposed leather webbing elaborately buckled.

c1970

$18,000-22,000 PAIR

39in (99cm) deep

SOTH

A Kurt Ostervig rosewood partner's desk, with twelve drawers and four pull-out shelves.

67in (170cm) wide

$4,000-5,000   **SDR**

A Vernor Panton four-piece curved modular sofa, its wire framework upholstered in burgundy fabric.

96in (243.5cm) wide

$1,700-2,200   **SDR**

A pair of Verner Panton wire cone chairs, with upholstered seat pads.

25in (63.5cm) wide

$1,700-2,200   **SDR**

An 'Oryx' desk, designed by V. Pargigi and N. Prina, for Molteni and Co., with molded plastic top, glass, chrome plated steel.

1970   *40.5in (103cm) wide*

$1,400-1,800   **L&T**

An Italian teak consol table, designed by Ico and Luisa Parisi, for Singer Furniture Company, New York, with brass fittings, bears makers label.

1952   *70.75in (180cm) wide*

$17,000-20,000   **L&T**

ESSENTIAL REFERENCE: TOMMI PARZINGER

Tommi Parzinger (1903-1981) was born in Germany and settled in New York City in 1935, where he opened his first showroom, Parzinger Inc. in 1939. The company was renamed Parzinger Originals in 1946.

- Parzinger was trained as a painter and in metalwork, ceramics, glass and furniture design. He melded these talents into refined modern furniture with elegant detailing. His pieces were often covered in shimmering lacquer, leather, or precious wood veneer, with handmade pulls, metal studs and brass outlines. This gave his furniture a sense of luxury, which appealed to clients who found Bauhaus-style design too severe.
- Parzinger was at the height of his popularity in the 1950's, with clients including the Rockefeller, Mellon and Dupont families, as well as Marilyn Monroe.
- He also designed for other furniture manufacturers, including Charak Modern.

A Tommi Parzinger mahogany armoire, with ivory-lacquered doors in a subtle grid pattern, brass hardware and details, covering drawers and shelves, branded 'Parzinger Originals'.

One of only five known, this was the showroom model made exactly to Parzinger's specifications.

51.25in (130cm) wide

$20,000-24,000   **SDR**

A Tommi Parzinger four-poster queen-size bed, in solid mahogany stained deep brown with high polish finish, no. '185'.

64.5in (164cm) wide

$20,000-24,000   **SDR**

A Tommi Parzinger unique writing table, with 'Negro Marquina' marble top resting on a gold-stippled wrought iron base, with hand-forged details.

59.75in (151cm) wide

$14,000-18,000   **SDR**

A Tommi Parzinger six-drawer dresser, in mahogany stained deep brown with high polish, no. '217', and polished brass etched details.

72in (183cm) wide

$20,000-24,000   **SDR**

A pair of Tommi Parzinger armchairs,
upholstered in pumpkin velvet, on bleached maple bases.

27in (68.5cm) wide

$7,000-8,000   **SDR**

A Maria Pergay stainless steel bench.

47.5in (120.5cm) wide

$15,000-17,000   **SDR**

A pair of Charlotte Perriand gray fiberglass doors, with chrome hardware.

76.75in (195cm) high

$2,800-3,200   **SDR**

An Italian 'I Feltri' chair, designed by Geatano
Pesce, for Cassina, Milan, wool impregnated
with thermosetting resin, stitched edges, early
production.

1987

$5,600-6,400   **L&T**

A Cassina 'I Feltri' armchair, designed by
Gaetano Pesce, of thick resin-infused wool felt
and tied string laces, with padded, quilted fabric
seat.

1987   *48in (122cm) wide*

$3,600-4,400   **SDR**

An M. Singer & Sons four-drawer walnut dresser,
designed by Gio Ponti, with Singer labels.

47in (119cm) wide

$14,000-16,000   **SDR**

An M. Singer & Sons
Italian walnut three-
door sideboard,
designed by Gio
Ponti, enclosing
interior shelves and
drawers.

71in (180cm) wide

$17,000-19,000   **SDR**

A Gio Ponti oak
coffee table, with
glass top.

41.25in (105cm) wide

$8,000-10,000   **SDR**

MODERN DESIGN

A David Powell leather-covered fall-front writing desk, its interior with a patterned leather writing surface, satinwood drawers and file compartments, resting on a sculpted maple base.

At first the fall-front desk is a mystery – an ovoid capsule that steps far outside the traditional form to become sculpture. Yet, its interior, once revealed, is a feat of useful details, sinuous dovetailed satinwood drawers and chambers, a flawless desktop created from multi-colored leather strips, a functional balance to the exterior's sculptural finesse. Its creator was the under-recognized yet influential master furniture maker, David Powell (1926 - 2001). Born and trained in England, he was an apprentice to the foremost British furniture maker Edward Barnsley, then studied at the Royal College of Art. Powell started several design ventures in London, including making furniture for Queen Elizabeth II, before moving to the United States in 1969. He settled in Easthampton, Massachusetts where he practiced his craft and started the Leeds Design Workshop with business partner John Tierney, taking on students for almost fifteen years. His influence can still be felt among woodworkers in the area. Powell made relatively few pieces throughout his career, but treated each work as a masterpiece, combining his technical wizardry with a rigorous design sensibility.

1982   *54in (137cm) wide*

$16,000-20,000   **SDR**

A 1950s satin birch and vellum desk, attributed to Gio Ponti, the rectangular top with three drawers and rounded sides.

50.75in (129cm) wide

$90,000-100,000   **SOTH**

A Philip Lloyd Powell walnut New Hope armchair and ottoman, with fabric-upholstered cushions (not shown).

Chair 29.5in (75cm) wide

$6,000-8,000   **SDR**

A Harvey Probber extension mahogany and teak dining table, with two 18in (45.5cm) leaves, and six dining chairs, including two arm and four side. table:

78in (198cm) wide

$4,000-6,000   **SDR**

A Jean Prouvé oak dining table, with iron mounts and angular legs.

78.5in (199cm) wide

$40,000-50,000   **SDR**

A Jean Prouvé wall-hanging oak cabinet, with single sliding door and black metal shelf.

117.5in (298.5cm) wide

$16,000-18,000   **SDR**

A pair of Quigley single-door cabinets, designed by Samuel Marx, with silvered metal pulls and stylized 'Greek key' pattern, each with single interior shelf, both marked 'Quigley'.

30.5in (77.5cm) wide

$12,000-16,000   **SDR**

A pair of sycamore nightstands, attributed to Jacques Quinet, with bronze sabots and supports.

27in (68.5cm) high

$5,000-6,000 SDR

A unique 'Ring Couch', by Karim Rashid, manufactured by Galerkin, Gardena, California, with wood and steel frame with foam and vinyl upholstery.

2005 *178.5in (453.5cm) diam*

$19,000-23,000 SOT

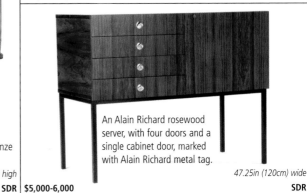

An Alain Richard rosewood server, with four doors and a single cabinet door, marked with Alain Richard metal tag.

47.25in (120cm) wide

$5,000-6,000 SDR

A Gerrit Rietfeld pine 'Zig-Zag' chair,

c1934 *30.5in (77.5cm) high*

$40,000-50,000 SOT

A red and cream-painted child's high chair, designed by Gerrit Thomas Rietveld, and executed by G. A. van de Groenekan, green leather seat and back, the underside stamped 'H.G.M. G.A v.d.Groenekan bilt Nederland'.

c1938 *35.5in (89.5cm) high*

$28,000-36,000 SOTH

A Willy Rizzo stainless steel coffee table, with integrated ice bucket on swivel base.

49in (124.5cm) diam

$3,400-4,000 SDR

An ISA 'Sheriff' sofa, designed by Sergio Rodrigues, in tropical hardwood with black leather cushions, with 'ISA' label.

81in (205cm) wide

$4,000-6,000 SDR

An OCA rosewood coffee table, designed by Sergio Rodrigues, with tray-style top, marked 'OCA'.

59in (150cm) wide

$3,000-4,000 SDR

A fruitwood-veneered and wrought iron cabinet, designed by Jean Royère, the cupboard doors with decorative hinges, enclosing an adjustable shelf.

c1953 *43.25in (110cm) high*

$10,000-12,000 SOTH

A 1950s pair of Knoll International '7 Up' chairs, designed by Eero Saarinen, with gray fabric upholstery and tubular chrome metal legs.

1948 *33.5in (85cm) high*

$400-500 QU

An M. Singer & Sons two-piece Italian walnut cabinet, designed by Bertha Schaefer, with angled doors covering speakers and shelves, 'Singer' labels.

1952 *40in (101.5cm) wide*

$2,400-3,200 SDR

An M. Singer & Sons Italian walnut cabinet with angled doors, by Bertha Schaefer, fitted with interior doors, 'Singer' label.

1952 *40in (101.5cm) wide*

$2,400-3,600 SDR

A ribbon coffee table, designed by Silas Seandel, its fiberglass base covered in gold leaf over a Chinese red finish, signed 'SILAS SEANDEL.

This coffee table was one of 15 commissioned by Bloomingdale's, New York.

1978 *56.5in (143cm) wide*

$6,000-7,000 SDR

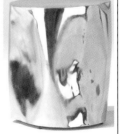

A stainless steel tub, designed by Silas Seandel, signed 'Silas Seandel'.

2003 *15.75in (40cm) wide*

$5,000-7,000 SDR

A 1960s chromium-plated metal and brushed aluminum-veneered console table, designed by Batistin Spade, with smoked glass top, the drawers with hinged circular concave handles.

48in (122cm) wide

$20,000-24,000 SOTH

A 1970s low marble and brushed metal coffee table, designed by Karl Springer, the stone top supported by brass-capped cylinders, one leg with artist's signature.

59in (150cm) long

$8,000-12,000 SOTH

A stainless steel rectangular dining table, designed by Karl Springer, with faux shagreen top, top marked with 'Karl Springer' tag.

72in (183cm) wide

$4,000-5,000 SDR

A corseted parchment-covered table, designed by Karl Springer.

16in (40.5cm) wide

$3,000-4,000   **SDR**

A four-door laminated tortoise-pattern parchment cabinet, designed by Karl Springer, flanked by a pair of suede-covered wall units with smoked glass shelves.

128in (325cm) wide

$5,000-6,000   **SDR**

A polished brass and black leather occasional table, designed by Karl Springer, the oval top on an angled cylindrical support, the underside signed 'Karl Springer 1990' in the leather, provenance Sir Paul Smith.

24in (61cm) wide

$10,000-12,000   **SOTH**

An XO 'Joe Ship', by Philippe Starck, with four black metal table legs and plate glass top.

Glass not part of the original design, but included here.

1982   50in (127cm) wide

$1,000-1,200   **SDR**

A Disform 'Miss Dorn' black metal chair, designed by Philippe Starck, upholstered in black leather.

1982   *21.5in (54.5cm) wide*

$800-1,200   **SDR**

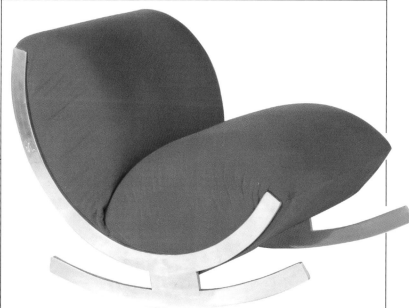

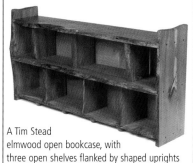

A Tim Stead elmwood open bookcase, with three open shelves flanked by shaped uprights with exposed joints.

68.5in (174cm) wide

$9,000-11,000   **L&T**

A Directional rocking chair, designed by Kipp Stewart, upholstered in tomato-red brushed fabric on polished steel base.

25in (63.5cm) wide

$2,400-3,000   **SDR**

A rare Paul Tuttle lounge chair, upholstered in stitched leather, on polished steel frame.

26in (66cm) wide

$4,400-5,200 SDR

A carved wood and vellum-covered travertine top console table, designed by Guglielmo Ulrich, with a textured surface, the four frieze drawers flanked by tapering supports.

67.75in (172cm) wide

$20,000-30,000 SOTH

A glass fiber reinforced polyester 'chairpiece' prototype, designed by Floris Van Den Broecke, upholstered in polyether foam and stretch Jersey wool.

1969

$8,000-10,000 L&T

A molded plywood 'Queen Anne' chair, designed by Robert Venturi .

24in (61cm) wide

$5,000-6,000 SDR

Two mid-20thC tall mahogany-veneered side cabinets, designed by Ole Wanscher, each with different brass handles and four tambour shutters, both with fitted interiors.

51in (130cm) wide

$12,000-16,000 SOTH

A Hans Wegner teak daybed, with slatted back and original upholstered drop-in cushion.

78in (198cm) wide

$6,000-7,000   **SDR**

A Hans Wegner teak wall unit, with two sliding doors enclosing shelves, over a six-drawer chest.

71in (180cm) wide

$4,000-5,000   **SDR**

A Hans Wegner 'Model 25' teak armchair, with woven rush seat and back.

28in (71cm) wide

$1,600-2,000   **SDR**

A banqueting table, designed by Rupert Williamson, of rectangular form with colored block supports.

1996   *236.25in (600cm) long*

$10,000-12,000   **L&T**

A Dunbar walnut long coffee table, designed by Edward Wormley, the top inset with six Tiffany tiles, green Dunbar metal tag.

77in (195.5cm) wide

$11,000-13,000 SDR

A 1940s sap walnut free-standing cabinet, designed by Edward Wormley, for Dunbar Furniture, on X-stretcher base with folding hinged doors enclosing a fitted interior, polished brass sabots to the feet.

51.5in (131cm) wide

$5,000-6,000 L&T

MODERN CERAMICS

A Bernard Leach earthenware bowl, decorated in trailing slip and colored glazes with fruiting vines, impressed St. Ives and monogram marks.

9.75in (24.5cm) diam

$1,100-1,300 L&T

A Bernard Leach, St Ives stoneware vase, covered with a deep gray-green speckled glaze, seal marks.

8in (20.5cm) high

$2,000-3,000 JN

A Bernard Leach 'Medieval' stoneware jug, modeled with a simple repeat pattern under an olive glaze, impressed 'BL' and 'St Ives' seals.

11.5in (29cm) high

$2,000-2,800 WW

A Shoji Hamada stoneware dish, off-white with dark brown foliate spray

19.5cm diam

$2,400-3,000 WW

A 1960s Shoji Hamada faceted bottle, with ladle-pour design.

7.5in (19cm) high

$5,000-6,000 SDR

A Rudy Autio porcelain slab sculpture of a torso, incized and painted with figural decoration, signed 'AUTIO/HKI/81'.

Made at the Arabia Factory in Helsinki, Finland, this piece is accompanied by an original letter from the artist discussing this piece and his great satisfaction with it.

1981   13.25in (33.5cm) wide

$7,000-8,000 SDR

A large Claude Conover earthenware vase, entitled 'Kabak', signed and titled.

20in (51cm) high

$7,000-8,000 SDR

A Richard Devore ovoid vase, with asymmetrical rim and 'torn' edges, under crackled light brown glaze.

13.75in (35cm) wide

$9,000-10,000   **SDR**

A Ken Ferguson hand-built oversized stoneware teapot, with rabbit-form handle covered in verdigris glaze.

23in (58.5cm) high

$7,000-8,000   **SDR**

A David Gilhooly marbleized ceramic two-piece sculpture, entitled 'Trip to California Stelae', featuring anthropomorphized frogs, signed 'Gilhooly 75'.

1975   *29in (74cm) high*

$4,000-5,000   **SDR**

A David Gilhooly two-piece earthenware sculpture, entitled 'Chief Fat Lazy Bullfrog', signed 'Gilhooly/76'.

1976   *21.5in (55cm) high*

$4,000-6,000   **SDR**

A Natzler tall chalice, covered in mottled sky blue and amber glaze, signed 'NATZLER', paper label 'L712'.

10in (25.5cm) high

$24,000-28,000   **SDR**

A Natzler small flaring bowl, covered in uranium volcanic glaze, signed 'Natzler'.

5.75in (15cm) diam

$7,000-8,000   **SDR**

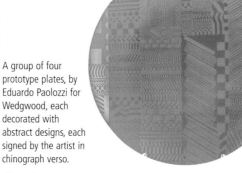

A group of four prototype plates, by Eduardo Paolozzi for Wedgwood, each decorated with abstract designs, each signed by the artist in chinograph verso.

These plates were prototypes to a series produced by Wedgwood in the late 1960s. The designs are derived from one of Paolozzi's screen prints and six production pieces were selected. These plates are one-off prototypes and they are unique as not all of them were in the final series.

10.25in (26cm) diam

$4,000-6,000 GROUP   **L&T**

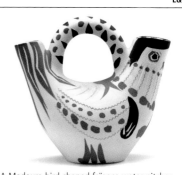

A Madoura white clay figural vessel of a peasant woman, designed by Pablo Picasso, with a face painted and incized on her apron, small chips to bottom rim, stamped 'Madoura/plein feu/D'apres Picasso'.

13.75in (35cm)

$5,600-6,400   **SDR**

A Madoura faïence plate, designed by Pablo Picasso, decorated with leaves, signed 'No. 17/Edition Picasso/67/150/Madoura'.

10in (25.5cm) diam

$3,000-4,000   **SDR**

A Madoura bird-shaped faïence water pitcher, designed by Pablo Picasso, signed '247/300. EDITION PICASSO 247/300/EDITION PICASSOMADOURA/PLEIN FEU'.

9in (22.5cm) high

$5,000-6,000   **SDR**

A Madoura ceramic wall plaque, designed by Pablo Picasso, depicting three figures in white on black matte ground, stamped 'EMPREINTE/ORIGINALE DE/PICASSO/MADOURA/PLEIN FEU'.

7.5in (19cm) wide
$6,000-7,000   **SDR**

A Polia Pillin square center bowl, decorated with birds in polychrome glaze.

11.5in (29cm) diam
$2,000-3,000   **SDR**

CLOSER LOOK: POLIA PILLIN VASE

Polia Pillin (1909-92) is known for her paintings and her painted pots and vases.

They are typically decorated with a young woman's face or dream-like images which were inspired by her experience during the holocaust.

This piece is an unusually large size.

It is fully signed to the base with Pillin's name.

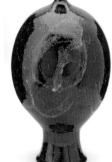

A Polia Pillin tall vase, painted with young ladies and fish, with a dreamlike quality.

22in (56cm) high
$3,600-4,400   **SDR**

A Polia Pillin studio vase, decorated with a strong red glaze, the base 'W + P Pillin'.
Pieces with plain glazes, particularly such vibrant ones, are scarce. Those covered with textured, 'volcanic' glazes like those produced by the Natzlers are even rarer.

9.5in (24cm) high
$2,000-2,600   **ANT**

A large Vincenzo Pinto faïence vase, embossed with tribal masks and covered in polychrome volcanic glaze, signed 'PINTO. V./VIETRI/ITALIA.'

24.5in (62cm) high
$2,000-4,000   **SDR**

A Richard Ginori earthenware dish, 'L'Amazone con Il Corno', designed by Gio Ponti, the red ground painted with a huntress astride a horse, a dog at her feet, black painted mark, 'Richard Ginori, M.229?368E, Gio Ponti'.

14in (35.5cm) diam
$11,000-13,000   **SOTH**

A Ken Price geometric ceramic vessel.

14.5in (37cm) wide
$7,000-8,000   **SDR**

A Ken Price tall sculptural vessel, with multiple spouts, covered in mottled brown glaze.

This piece is accompanied by a signed photograph of the piece from the artist along with a letter from Michael Frimkiss, from whom this piece was purchased.

1956   30.5in (77.5cm) wide
$15,0000-17,000   **SDR**

An Antonio Prieto footed bulbous stoneware vase, covered in mahogany and amber mottled glaze, signed 'Prieto'.

15.75in (40cm) wide
$3,400-4,000   **SDR**

A Daniel Rhodes stoneware sculptural torso, marked 'Rhodes'.

50in (127cm) wide

$7,000-8,000 SDR

A large stoneware bowl, by Dame Lucie Rie, the mottled pale turqoise ground within a broad bronze-colored band with 'dribbled' brown decoration, impressed 'LR' seal.

c1975 *64.75in (25.5cm) diam*

$14,000-16,000 SOTH

A porcelain bowl, by Dame Lucie Rie, the white ground decorated at the rim with a bronze band and brown 'dribbling', impressed 'LR' seal.

5.75in (14.5cm) diam.

$15,000-17,000 SOTH

A Lucie Rie stoneware bottle vase, ovoid with slender neck and flaring rim, glazed with a spiral blue, lavender and brown pitted glaze, impressed 'LR' mark.

Purchased from Lucie Rie at her Albion Mews studio 1982-3.

11.75in (30cm) high

$10,000-12,000 WW

A Royal Copenhagen cylindrical vase, designed by Axel Salto, with prunts covered in matte tortoiseshell glaze, incized 'Salto' and with green Royal Copenhagen stamp '/20685'.

6in (15cm) high

$3,000-4,000 SDR

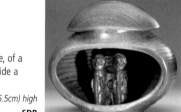

A Scheier ceramic sculpture, of a man, woman and child inside a mushroom-shaped pod.

10.5in (26.5cm) high

$2,000-2,800 SDR

A Scheier charger, depicting Adam and Eve, outlined in manganese on a celadon ground, signed 'Scheier-45'.

1945 *15in (38cm) diam*

$5,000-6,000 SDR

A Toshiko Takaezu ridged stoneware vessel, in mahogany, brown and amber matte glaze, signed '1965/Toshiko TAKAEZU/$65.00'.

1965 *11in (28cm) high*

$7,000-8,000 SDR

A Robert Turner ceramic kiln-shape vessel, entitled 'Circle Square #13', with slashes, covered in russet-colored glaze, signed 'Turner' in black marker, incized mark and title on label.

10in (25.5cm) high

$8,000-10,000 SDR

A Peter Voulkos anagama-fired stoneware bowl, in indigo, gray and rust brushed-on volcanic glaze, incized 'Voulkos 96'.

1996 *10.5in (26.5cm) diam*

$3,000-4,000 SDR

A Peter Voulkos stoneware charger, with gouged and incized surface under buff glaze, signed 'VOULKOS'.

78.5in (199cm) diam

$16,000-20,000   SDR

A Beatrice Wood faïence hen-shaped center bowl, with applied floral decoration, in pastel glazes, signed 'BEATO'.

16.5in (42cm) wide

$3,200-4,000   SDR

A Beatrice Wood large fish center bowl, in blue and white volcanic crackled glaze, signed 'BEATO'.

24in (61cm) wide

$6,000-7,000   SDR

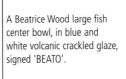

A Betty Woodman slab-built vessel, in sponged folk art amber and green luster glaze, stamped 'WOODMAN'.

1985   *5in (12.5cm) high*

$5,600-6,400   SDR

A Betty Woodman slab-built 'French Garden' jardinière, stamped 'WOODMAN'.

6.5in (16.5cm) high

$1,800-2,400   SDR

A Russell Wright long boat-shaped vessel, covered in turquoise and deep plum glaze, stamped script signature.

25in (63.5cm) long

$3,000-4,000   SDR

MODERN GLASS

An AVEM 'Anse Volante' handled vase, designed by Giorgio Ferro, of blue- and clear-cased green glass with an iridescent finish.

1952   *12.5in (31.5cm) high*

$3,600-4,400   QU

An AVEM vase, designed by Anzolo Fuga, of biomorphic near teardrop form with two applied tubular red flowers and a heart.

c1955   *17.5in (44.5cm) high*

$3,400-4,000   QU

A large Barbini 'Scavo' glass vase, with grape and amber pattern, incized 'Barbini Murano' on base.

16.75in (42.5cm) high   SDR

$2,400-3,000

A Barovier & Toso 'Corniola' vase, designed by Ercole Barovier, with seahorse-shaped handle, of marblized opaque red and black glass, with factory paper label numbered '22706'.

1959   *6.25in (16cm) high*

$3,200-3,600   QU

A Barovier & Toso 'Ambrati' mottled red bird sculpture, designed by Ercole Barovier, with opaque white swirl and lightly iridescent surface, the base signed 'Ercole Barovier 1954' and with factory paper label.

1954

$5,000-6,000   QU

A Barovier & Toso 'Crepuscolo' vase, designed by Ercole Barovier, the white opaque inner layer cased in colorless glass with aventurine inclusions, with remains of paper label to base bearing indistinct numbers.

This is a variant of the 1935/36 design by Barovier. For more information see 'Art of the Barovier', by Marina Barovier.

c1950   *13in (33cm) high*

$3,600-4,400   QU

A Barovier & Toso 'Eugeneo' double-handled vase, designed by Ercole Barovier, with fine gold foil inclusions and applied turquoise rim and foot.

1951   5.75in (14.5cm) high

$1,500-1,700   QU

A Barovier & Toso 'Pezzato' vase, designed by Ercole Barovier, overlaid with alternating striated amber and opaque white and striated turquoise panels.

1956   9in (23cm) high

$7,000-8,000   QU

A Barovier & Toso 'A Spina' vase, designed by Ercole Barovier, overlaid with opalescent white and turquoise panels giving a woven effect, the base engraved 'barovier & toso murano' and bearing the factory paper label.

1958   11.5in (29cm) high

$7,000-8,000   QU

A Dan Dailey cast and blown glass vase, entitled 'Surf Spray Rocks', from the 'Ocean Vase' series, sandblasted and acid-polished, signed on foot, marked 'O-4-79'.

1979   12.75in (32.5cm) high

$4,000-5,000   SDR

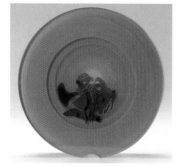

A Bohumil Elias laminated glass circular sculpture, with abstract design, signed 'Elias'.

7.5in (19cm) high

$1,200-1,600   SDR

A Tomas Hlavicka glass egg, laminated, cut and polished, on stand, engraved 'Tomas Hlavicka 2006'.

2006   7in (17.5cm) high

$1,200-1,600   SDR

A Tomas Hlavicka laminated, cut, and polished glass cube, signed and dated.

2005   4.25in (10.75cm) wide

$1,000-1,500   SDR

An Orrefors 'Graal' chalice, by Gunnar Cyren, decorated with nudes and animals, engraved 'ORREFORS EXPO Graal V 1149-78 Gunnar Cyren'

9in (22.5cm) high

$1,800-2,200   SDR

A Gaetano Pesce bowl, entitled 'Sans Titre No. 6', in blue glass with textured interior, signed 'G. Pesce'.

1989-1990   11.5in (29cm) diam

$5,000-6,000   SDR

A 1970's Salviati large freeform periwinkle glass vase, by Claire Falkenstein, with three opalescent supports, etched '10/24 Design Claire Falkenstein Salviati', with remnant of Salviati label.

16.25in (41cm) high

$3,000-4,000   SDR

A Steve Tobin figural sculpture, in black glass.

1985   *17in (43cm) wide*

$1,500-1,900   SDR

An Aureliano Toso 'Oriente' vase, designed by Dino Martens, overlaid with a dark violet and white star murrine, and multi-colored panels of opaque enamels, the neck with fine gold foil inclusions.

Murano glass historian Marc Heiremans shows that photographic archives identify this as model no.5139, one of the earliest model numbers given to the Oriente series. The Oriente range was introduced at the Venice Biennale in 1952, making this one of the earliest designs produced.

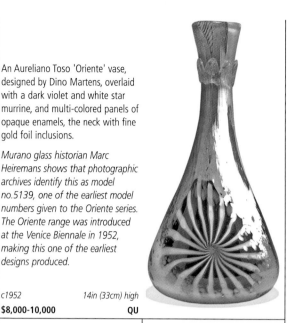

c1952   *14in (33cm) high*

$8,000-10,000   QU

An Aureliano Toso 'Oriente' fish sculpture, designed by Dino Martens, the body overlaid with sections of zanfirico rods, irregular multicolored panels of opaque enamels and with applied mouth and fins in colorless glass with gold foil inclusions.

1952   *12.5in (31.5cm) high*

$9,000-10,000   QU

A Fratelli Toso 'Stellato' vase, designed by Pollio Perelda, the colorless cylindrical body overlaid with large stylized star-shaped rectangular murrines comprized of green, blue, orange, red or brown rays, with two factory paper labels to the body.

c1953   *13.5in (34cm) high*

$12,000-16,000   QU

A Venini 'A Doppio Incalmo' ovoid vase with two adjacent openings, designed by Thomas Stearns, comprized of three sections in red on opaque white, transparent green and black, the surface lightly iridized, the base with 'venini murano ITALIA' acid stamp.

Thomas Stearns (1936-2006) was the first American to design for Venini and worked there from 1959-61 on a Fulbright Travel grant. He had studied at the Cranbrook Academy in the US. He won the Gold Medal at the 1962 Venice Bienalle but the judges rescinded the award when they realized he was American.

Incalmo is a very simple yet difficult technique — each section is separately blown and then joined together when hot. Most pieces are made of two parts, which tend to cool at different rates, so it has to be judged carefully. This one combines three parts, hence doppio incalmo. These pieces could not be mass-produced and only about 30 are known to exist. They are therefore rare and valuable.

1962   *4.5in (11cm) high*

$24,000-30,000   QU

A Venini glass sculpture with green, clear and amber layers, designed by Thomas Stearns, 'Cappello del Doge', the base etched 'Venini Murano Italia', with circular paster 'Venini S.A. Murano' with vase.

1962   *5.25in (13.5cm) wide*

$18,000-24,000   SDR

A Venini 'Sirena' figural vase, designed by Fulvio Bianconi, the green body with pulled limbs and neck opening, with 'venini murano ITALIA' acid stamp.

c1950   *14.5in (36.5cm) long*

$20,000-30,000   QU

A Venini 'A Canne' bottle, designed by Fulvio Bianconi, the colorless body overlaid with vertical alternating green and red stripes, the body marked with the 'venini murano ITALIA' acid stamp,

c1952   *16.25in (41cm) high*

$2,400-3,000   QU

A Venini 'A Canne' vase, designed by Gio Ponti, the colorless glass body overlaid with alternating blue, red, green violet and yellow canes, the base with 'venini murano ITALIA' acid stamp.

1955   *9in (22cm) high*
$7,000-8,000   **QU**

A Venini 'Tronco' cylinder vase, designed by Toni Zuccheri, the clear glass body overlaid with opaque butterscotch colored veins, giving an almost wood-like effect, the base engraved 'venini italia' and with factory paper label numbered '214/2',

1966   *13.5in (34cm) high*
$3,200-3,600   **QU**

A Venini 'La Fiamma' cylindrical vase, designed by Barbara del Vicario, the colorless glass body overlaid with sections of opaque white, turquise, blue and pink canes in a chevron pattern, the base engraved 'venini 86 Del Vicario', and with factory label,

1986   *15.75in (40cm) high*
$4,600-5,200   **QU**

A Venini large 'Pezzato' glass globe, designed by Fulvio Bianconi, in cobalt, red and green.

c1950   *16in (40.5cm) diam*
$1,000-2,000   **SDR**

A Venini 'Fazzoletto' glass vase, in turquoise and white incamiciato, etched 'Venini Murano ITALIA'.

                    10in (25.5cm) high
$800-1,400   **SDR**

A Venini 'sommerso' vase, by Laura Diaz de Santillana, with gold leaf on red ground, engraved 'Venini Laura 1987', circular label.

1987   *9.5in (24cm) high*
$1,000-1,400   **SDR**

A Venini 'Inciso' bottle and stopper, designed by Paoli Venini, in brown glass, acid stamped 'Venini Murano ITALIA'.

1950   *11in (28cm) high*
$5,000-6,000   **SOTH**

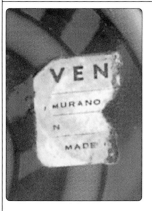

A 1950's Venini 'A Spirale' vase, designed by Fulvio Bianconi, with bulb formation at top, in transparent blue and red striped glass, with partial Venini label.

                    12.75in (32.5cm) high
$8,000-12,000   **SOTH**

A Venini screen, designed by Makio Hasuike (b.1938) glass and painted metal, five of the glass panels demonstrate glass techniques, engraved mark 'Venini, Italia, '85'. *Makio Hasuike worked for Seiko and designed 20 clocks for the 1964 Tokyo Olympics. In 1963, he moved permanently to Italy and has collaborated with many international companies.*

                    Each panel 19.5in (50cm) wide
$14,000-18,000   **SOTH**

A Vistosi 'Pulcino' bird, designed by Alessandro Pianon, the gray-blue blown body decorated with bands of alternating green and blue circular murrines and impressed murrine eyes, mounted on colorless thighs with applied bent metal legs.

This is a more unusual shape than the more commonly seen spherical orange bird.

1962   *12.5in (31.5cm) high*
$4,000-2,800   **QU**

An Arredoluce 'Triennale' brass floor lamp, with enameled metal shades and handles in primary colors.

69in (175cm) high

$3,400-4,000 SDR

An Arredoluce floor lamp, in enameled metal and chrome-plated steel on marble base.

79.5in (202cm) high

$1,600-2,000 SDR

A pair of Arredoluce chrome cylindrical lamps, with red enameled balls, one marked 'Arredoluce/Made in Italy'.

9.5in (24cm) high

$1,000-1.400 SDR

A pair of rare Arredoluce 'Cobra' table lamps, designed by Angelo Lelii, model number 12919, adjustable magnetic shades with transformers to the base, applied manufacturer's labels.

1962 *24.75in (63cm) high*

$4,000-5,000 L&T

A pair of Azucena 'LTE 8' standard lamps, designed by Ignazio Gardella, glass, marble, each spherical frosted glass shade with three lights and gilt-bronze supports, on a patinated metal cylindrical stem and triform white marble base.

1956 *68.5in (174cm) high*

$28,000-32,000 SOTH

A Mario Bellini 'Chiara' stainless steel floor lamp.

57in (144.5cm) high

$1,400-1,800 SDR

A pair of silver-mounted rose quartz candlesticks, by Paul Belvoir, stone column within silver surrounds, fully hallmarked for London.

2007 *12.75in (32.5cm) high*

$20,000-28,000 SOTH

An Italian Achille and Piergiacomo Castiglioni standard lamp, 'Flos', metal with sprayed resin.

1962 *52in (132cm) high*

$1,400-2,000 L&T

A Maison Desny desk lamp, designed by Jean Desny, with glass plates on chrome base.

4.75in (12cm) high

$4,000-6,000 SDR

A pair of Fontana Arte brass and plate glass double socket table lamps.

base 24in (61cm) high

$12,000-14,000 SDR

A 1950s Fontana Arte brass table lamp, with frosted glass shade, designed by Max Ingrand, waisted base and angular finial with handle, fitted for three lights.

25.5in (65cm) high

$28,000-32,000 SOTH

A Pierre Guariche wall-mounted lamp, with green perforated enameled metal shade.

46in (117cm) high

$4,000-6,000　　　　SDR

An 'Equilibrium' adjustable standard lamp by Pierre Guariche, gilt-bronze and black-painted metal, the pierced and painted shades on two joint stems balanced on stand, terminating in a ring foot.

1951　　　　76in (193cm) high

$28,000-32,000　　　SOTH

A Missaglia steel and marble gyroscope table lamp, the globular shade composed of polished steel strips, fitted for four bulbs, on a circular marble base with manufacturer's paper label.

26in (66cm) high

$4,400-4,800　　　SOTH

A pair of James Mont painted wood table lamps, with original parchment shades.

35in (89cm) high

$3,000-4,000 PAIR　　SDR

A Tommi Parzinger ceiling light, with frosted plate glass and radiating polished brass arms and finial.

20in (51cm) diam

$5,000-6,000　　　　SDR

A Tommi Parzinger eight-arm floor lamp, in gold-stippled wrought iron with silk shade.

79in (200.5cm) high

$12,000-16,000　　　SDR

A Seguso Vetri D'Arte glass and brass chandelier, designed by Flavio Poli, with green and yellow pendants hung in two circles, five bulb fittings.

51in (130cm) high

$14,000-18,000　　　SOTH

An Italian Sirrah chromed steel 'AM-AS' series table lamp, designed by Franco Albini, Franca Helg and Antonio Pira.

33in (84cm) high

$1,200-1,600　　　　L&T

A Stilnovo 'Dorane' table lamp, designed by Ettore Sottsass, with light blue Murano glass shade on powder blue coated metal base, clear Murano label.

8in (20cm) high

$1,000-1,500　　　SDR

A 1960s American chromed metal satellite table lamp, the six arms terminating in a spherical shade with a single socket, arms rotate on the baluster-form base.

26.75in (68cm) high

$1,300-1,700　　　　SK

A beryllium copper and bronze sculpture, 'Sound Sculpture' by Harry Bertoia (American 1915-1978).
71.75in (182.5cm) wide

$300,000-400,000   **FRE**

A steel sculpture 'Willow Tree' by Harry Bertoia.
12in (30.5cm) wide

$90,000-110,000   **FRE**

A silicon bronze double gong, in three parts, by Harry Bertoia.

108.75in (276cm) high

$300,000-400,000   **SDR**

A bronze and copper sculpture, 'Fan Tree', by Klaus Ihlenfeld (German/American) signed.
1962   *117.5in (298.5cm) wide*

$16,000-20,000   **SDR**

A Philip K. Laverne acid-etched and patinated bronze panel, with still-life of flower vase, in original bronze frame, signed 'Philip K. Laverne'
22.75in (58cm) wide

$3,000-5,000   **SDR**

A rare Philip and Kelvin Laverne sculpted bronze male figural bust, signed 'PHILIP KELVIN LAVERNE'.
22.25in (56.5cm) high

$10,000-12,000   **SDR**

A polished bronze abstract sculpture, 'Sawanna', by Dennis Mitchell, mounted on a slate base and monogramed 'DAM', inscirbed 'No.4' and dated.
1974   *25in high*

$5,000-7,000   **JN**

A Christian Peschke 'Cubist Head' bronze figure, hollow poured, with light brown patina, irregular structured surface.
2002   *38.5in (98cm) high*

$7,000-8,000   **VZ**

A Melvin Lindquist sugar maple flaring vase, signed 'L4 76/Sugar Maple'.

1976   8.75in (22cm) high

$1,600-2,400   **SDR**

A Rude Osolnik zebrawood bowl, with uneven rim, signed 'Osolniks Originals/Zebrawood.

6in (15cm) diam

$1,300-1,700   **SDR**

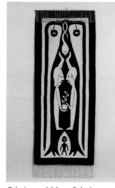

A John A. Sage yellow birch burl-wood bowl, with natural occlusions and free-edge rim, signed 'John A. Sage/1987 Yellow Birch/Burl'.

1987   14in (35.5cm) diam

$1,800-2,400   **SDR**

A Marian Kruczek bas relief figural triptych, with rectangular cast concrete inset with an assortment of metal, glass, stone, and plastic found objects, with incized details, inscribed maker's marks and dates, paper, label.

Marian Kruczek is from Krakow, Poland.

1962-63   Center panel 15in (38cm) high

$1,000-1,500   **SK**

A Hui Ka Kwong faïence sculpture, with black and yellow curls.

20.5in (52cm) high

$3,400-4,000   **SDR**

An Alexander Calder jute rug, with abstract design in red, blue, orange and black on natural ground.

79in (200.5cm) high

$7,000-8,000   **SK**

An Edwin and Mary Scheier woven wool tapestry, depicting 'Adam and Eve and the Tree of Knowledge of Good and Evil and the Serpent', entitled 'Adam and Eve', excluding fringe.

85in (216cm) long

$5,000-6,000   **SK**

A Jack Youngerman tapestry, from an edition of twelve.

103in (261.5cm) long

$3,000-4,000   **SDR**

An Olivetti 'Synthesis' coatrack/umbrella stand, designed by Ettore Sottsass, in metal and lacquered ABS plastic.

1973   59.5in (151cm) wide

$800-1,600   **SDR**

A Tecno model AT16 adjustable coat rack, designed by Osvaldi Borsani, leather, walnut, rosewood and aluminum, the leather-covered revolving stem with eight adjustable coat hooks terminating in spheres, suspended by extendable rods, with Tecno label to pole.

1961   132.5in (337cm) high

$12,000-14,000   **SOTH**

A Herman Miller 'Watermelon' clock, designed by George Nelson, with gold Howard Miller Chronopak label.

5in (12.5cm) high

$1,500-2,000   **SDR**

A National Animated Sign Co. lighted bellhop sign, marked 'National Animated Sign Co./Hot Springs, Arkansas/Phone 6420/America's Sign of Hospitality/SN-4073-A'.

$2,000-3,000   **SDR**

'Tout Paris A La Revue Des Folies Bergère', designed by Adrien Barrère (1877-1931), printed by Wall & Cie., Paris, restored and repaired.

This ten-sheet poster is the largest and most spectacular poster ever produced for Folies-Bergere. Depicting 'La Belle Otero' at the arm of Arthur Meyer, Louisa Balthy, Henri Rochefort, Brasseur and the Prince of Wales (far right).

1902   152.25in (386.5cm) wide

$22,000-26,000   SWA

'Liquore Strega', designed by Marcello Dudovich (1878-1962), printed by G. Ricordi, Milan, restoration, two sheets.

1906   80.25in (204cm) high

$22,000-26,000   SWA

'Sogno D'Un Valzer', designed by Leopoldo Metlicovitz (1868-1944), printed by G. Ricordi & C., Milan, restoration and restored loss, repaired tears, two sheets.

1910   78.5in (200cm) high

$28,000-32,000   SWA

'Gismonda', by Alphonse Mucha, (1860-1939) Maitre de l'affiche, pl. 27, printed by Chaix, lithograph in colors, in near mint condition, not linen-backed.

'Waverley Cycles', designed by Alphonse Mucha (1860-1939), printed by F. Champenois, Paris, folds, minor discoloration, wrinkles, creases and bubbling in image, matted and framed.

'La Maison Moderne', designed by Manuel Orazi, (1860-1934), printed by J. Minot, Paris.

1896   15.75in (40cm) high

$2,400-3,000   BLNY

1898   43in (109cm) wide

$22,000-26,000   SWA

1900   46in (117cm) wide

$18,000-24,000   SWA

'Clinique Cheron', designed by Théophile-Alexandre Steinlen (1859-1923), printed by Wall & Cie., Paris, depicting an animal lover and protector, restoration, folds.

1905   77.75in (138.5cm) high

$40,000-50,000   SWA

'Motocycles Comiot', designed by Théophile-Alexandre Steinlen (1859-1923), printed by Charle Verneau, Paris.

1899   77in (195.5cm) high

$40,000-48,000   SWA

'Ambassadeurs', designed by Henri de Toulouse-Lautrec (1864-1901), printed by Edward Ancourt, Paris.

1892   56in (142cm) high

$120,000-140,000   SWA

'California/America's Vacation Land', designed by Jon O. Brubaker, (1875-?) printed by Latham Litho. & Printing Co., creases, repaired.

The New York Central Lines began using posters as advertisements in 1925. This poster was the second one they ever issued.

1925   39.75in (101cm) high

$20,000-28,000   **SWA**

'Adirondack Mountains', designed by Walter L. Greene (1870-1956), printed by Latham Litho and Printing Co., New York, repaired tears and creases.

1930   40.25in (102cm) high

$7,000-9,000   **SWA**

'Over Old Indian Trails, The North Shore Line', designed by Oscar Rabe Hanson (1901-1926), printed by Gugler Litho, Milwaukee.

Hanson designed 29 posters from 1923-26. His graphic style and compositional ability made him one of the best US designers of his time.

c1926   42in (106.5cm) high

$8,000-10,000   **SWA**

'California - The Year 'Round', designed by Horney (dates Unknown), with a woman on horseback overlooking farmland, a mission and the Pacific Ocean, repaired tears and creases.

1934   41in (104.5cm) high

$10,000-14,000   **SWA**

'San Francisco-Hawaii Overnight!/Via Pan American - To The Orient', designed by Frank Mackintosh (dates unknown), with the Honolulu Clipper disgorging passengers, repaired.

This image celebrates the arrival in Honolulu from San Francisco of Pan American's most advanced, largest and last flying boat, the Boeing 314.

c1938   38.25in (97cm) wide

$10,000-14,000   **SWA**

'Pennsylvania Railroad/Atlantic City', designed by Sascha Maurer (1897-1961), depicting a woman with her back to the ocean facing Atlantic City's boardwalk, reflections of which are visible in the lenses of her sunglasses, restored, creases.

c1940   40.5in (103cm) high

$5,000-7,000   **SWA**

'Rockafeller Center, New York', designed by Leslie Ragan (1897-1972), printed by Latham Litho & PTG. Co. Long Island City, New York, restoration and overpainting.

c1933   41in (104cm) high

$7,000-9,000   **SWA**

'Grand Canyon', by an anonymous designer, silk screen on thick stock, framed.

The Grand Canyon National Park was established through an Act of Congress, signed by President Woodrow Wilson in 1919. Considered one of the Seven Natural Wonders of the World, the canyon stretches over 275 miles and was formed over the millennia by the Colorado River coursing over the rocks of the Plateau.

c1938   19in (48.5cm) high

$9,000-11,000   **SWA**

'Yellowstone National Park', by an anonymous designer, framed.

Yellowstone is America's first National Park. President Ulysses S. Grant signed it into being in 1872. The Park covers areas in three states, primarily Wyoming, but also Montana and Idaho.

c1938   19in (48.5cm) high

$6,000-8,000   **SWA**

'Golf in Northern Ireland', designed by Norman Wilkison (1882-1971), printed by S. C. Allen, London, restoration and repairs.

Wilkinson was a prolific poster artist for the British railway companies in the 1920's and '30's, and a renowned marine painter.

c1925   49in (124.5cm) wide

$20,000-24,000   **SWA**

'The Forth Bridge', designed by Henry George Gawthorn (1879-1941), printed by David Allen & Sons, London, restoration.

1928   49.75in (126.5cm) wide

$17,000-19,000   **SWA**

'London Underground, Nightly Carnival', Frederick C. Herrick (1887-1970), printed by The Baynard Press, London, folds and repairs, framed.

Herrick was the only British artist to participate in the1925 Parisian Exposition Internationales des Arts Decoratifs et Industriels Modernes. In a "cosmic fresco", he depicts cherubs flitting about constellations which represent Underground stops.

1924   49.25in (125cm) wide

$16,000-18,000   **SWA**

'A Pigsticking Meet, Visit India', designed by Henry George Gawthorn (1879-1941), printed by Shardlow Ltd., London, restoration and repairs.

In many of his finest posters, Gawthorn employed his signature, stylized graphic ability, to depict the privileged classes engaged in their exclusive and elegant pastimes.

                                    48.75in (124cm) wide

$10,000-12,000   **SWA**

'Madura', designed by M. V. Dhurandhar (dates unknown), printed by Cooper Litho., Bombay, with a festival parading through the streets before a temple.

c1925   40in (101.5cm) high

$6,000-8,000   **SWA**

'Australia/Great Barrier Coral Reef', designed by James Northfield (1888-1973), printed by J. E. Hackett, Melbourne.

c1935   40in (102cm) high

$10,000-12,000   **SWA**

'Bermuda - West Indies, Canadian National Steamships', unknown designer, restored loss and repaired tear.

c1935   37.5in (95cm) high

$4,800-6,000   **SWA**

'Zermatt', designed by Emile Cardinaux (1877-1936), printed by J. E. Wolfsberger, Zurich.

1908   40.75in (103.5cm) high

$9,000-11,000   **SWA**

'Visit Johannesburg/The Wonder City', by an anonymous designer, printed by William Brown & Davis, Durban, creases and repaired tears, folds.

                                    40in (101.5cm) high

$1,400-2,000   **SWA**

682

POSTERS

'I Want You', by James Montgomery Flagg (1877-1960), printed for the Leslie-Judge Co., NY, on paper, framed, repaired tears, wrinkles, creases and overpainting.

A prolific illustrator, Flagg was also an extremely patriotic citizen who designed 42 posters during WWI.

1917　　　　*39.75in (101cm) high*

$3,600-4,400　　　　**SWA**

'This Is The Enemy!' by Karl Koehler & Victoria Ancona, printed by Grinnell, New York, tears and creases.

This chilling image of a hanging reflected in the monocle of this high ranking member of Germany's military was the winner of the National War Poster Competition of 1942 held under the auspices of the Museum of Modern Art.

1942

$5,000-6,000　　　　**SWA**

34.25in (87cm) high

'We The People', designed by Howard Chandler Christy (1873-1952), with a Christy girl hovering over a scene of America's founding fathers signing the Constitution, repaired tears and crease.

1937　　　　*42.5in (108cm) high*

$3,600-4,400　　　　**SWA**

'Sun Valley', by an anonymous designer, with Gretchen Fraser against a backdrop of mountains, with the village of Sun Valley behind her, restored and repaired.

38in (96.5cm) high

$3,000-4,000　　　　**SWA**

'Pontresina/KLM', designed by Martin Peikert (1901-75), printed by Klausfelder, Vevey, with a woman lying on a red pillow lifting her legs to reach the sun overlooking a ski resort.

39.5in (100.5cm)

$1,500-2,000　　　　**SWA**

'Nunc Est Bibendum/ Le Pneu Michelin Boit L'Obstacle', designed by O'Galop (Marius Rossillon)(1867-1946), printed by Chaix, Paris, restored, repaired tears.

In 1894, at the international exhibition in Lyon, Michelin's staff had arranged a display of a large pile of tires. Rumour has it that when brothers André and Edouard Michelin saw the arrangement, one of them uttered 'If it had arms it would be like a man'. Shortly after this observation, O'Galop came to the brothers with an idea for a poster, based on a picture he had found of a portly German holding aloft a stein of beer and giving the Latin toast, 'nunc est bibendum' ('now is the time to drink', a line from an ode by Horace). In 1898, with this poster, O'Galop gave birth to Bibendum (the Michelin Man). Depicted at a banquet table, Bibendum is standing with a raised glass filled with everything that could puncture a tire. On either side of him are two deflated tires, the one on the left is John Dunlop, the one on the right the director of Continental Tires. The proud, inflated and healthy-looking Bibendum is not worried about the sharp objects in his glass, because, as the text reads 'the Michelin tire drinks obstacles'. The rare and historic poster was the first of hundreds of images using Bibendum all over the world, and as a tribute to the beloved icon's effectiveness, he is still appearing in ads over 100 years later.

'New Haven R. R.', designed by F. C. Veit, with black and white vignettes of skiers and a speeding train and a color image of a woman with curly hair below a yellow sky.

40.5in (102.5cm)

$3,000-4,000　　　　**SWA**

'Olympique Cycles', by Jean A. Mercier (1899-1995), printed by Publicite Vox, Paris, lithograph in colors, linen-backed.

1925　　　　*62in (159cm) wide*

$3,000-4,000　　　　**BLNY**

c1898　　　　*61in (155cm) high*

$16,000-18,000　　　　**SWA**

Dates	British Monarch	British Period	French Period	German Period	US Period	Style	Woods
1558–1603	Elizabeth I	Elizabethan	Renaissance	Renaissance	Early Colonial	Gothic	Oak Period (to c1670)
1603–1625	James I	Jacobean					
1625–1649	Charles I	Carolean	Louis XIII (1610–1643)			Baroque (c1620–1700)	
1649–1660	Commonwealth	Cromwellian	Louis XIV (1643–1715)	Renaissance/ Baroque (c1650–1700)			Walnut period (c1670–1735)
1660–1685	Charles II	Restoration			William & Mary		
1685–1689	James II	Restoration			Dutch Colonial	Rococo (c1695–1760)	
1689–1694	William & Mary	William & Mary		Baroque (c1700–1730)	Queen Anne		
1694–1702	William III	William III					
1702–1714	Anne	Queen Anne					
1714–1727	George I	Early Georgian	Régence (1715–1723)	Rococo (c1730–1760)	Chippendale (from 1750)		
1727–1760	George II	Early Georgian	Louis XV (1723–1774)	Neoclassical (c1760–1800)	Early Federal (1790–1810)	Neoclassical (c1755–1805)	Early mahogany period (c1735–1770)
1760–1812	George III	Late Georgian	Louis XVI (1774–1793) Directoire (1793–1799) Empire (1799–1815)	Empire (c1800–1815)	American Directoire (1798–1804) American Empire (1804–1815)	Empire (c1799–1815)	Late mahogany period (c1770–1810)
1812–1820	George III	Regency	Restauration Charles X (1815–1830)	Biedermeier (c1815–1848)	Late Federal (1810–1830)	Regency (c1812–1830)	
1820–1830	George IV	Regency					
1830–1837	William IV	William IV	Louis Philippe (1830–1848)	Revivale (c1830–1880)		Eclectic (c1830–1880)	
1837–1901	Victoria	Victorian	2nd Empire Napoleon III (1848–1870) 3rd Republic (1871–1940)	Jugendstil (c1880–1920)	Victorian	Arts & Crafts (c1880–1900)	
1901–1910	Edward VII	Edwardian			Art Nouveau (c1900–1920)	Art Nouveau (c1900–1920)	

Every antique illustrated in Miller's Antiques Price Guide 2009 has a letter code which identifies the dealer or auction house that sold it. The list below is a key to these codes. In the list, auction houses are shown by the letter A and dealers by the letter D. Some items may have come from a private collection, in which case the code in the list is accompanied by the letter P. Inclusion in this book in no way constitutes or implies a contract or a binding offer on the part of any of our contributors to supply or sell the goods illustrated, or similar items, at the prices stated.

A&G (A)
ANDERSON & GARLAND
Anderson House, Crispin Court,
Newbiggin Lane, Westerhope,
Newcastle upon Tyne, NE5 1BF
Tel: 0191 430 3000
www.andersonandgarland.com

ALD (A)
ALDERFERS
Alderfer's Auction Gallery
501 Fairgrounds Road
Hatfield, Pennsylvania 19440 USA
Tel: 001 215 393 3000
www.alderferauction.com

ANA (D)
ANCIENT ART
85 The Vale, London N14 6AT
Tel: 020 8882 1509
www.antiquities.co.uk

ANT (D)
Antique Gallery,
8523 Germantown Avenue,
Philadelphia, PA 19118
Tel: 001 215 248 1700
www.antiquegal.com

BE (A)
BEARNES
St Edmund's Court, Okehampton
Street, Exeter, Devon, EX4 1DU
Tel: 01392 207000
www.bearnes.co.uk

BER (A)
BERTOIA AUCTIONS
2141 Demarco Drive, Vineland NJ
08360 USA
Tel: 001 856 692 1881
www.bertoiaauctions.com

BLA (A)
BLANCHET ET ASSOCIÉS
3 rue Geoffroy Marie, 75009 Paris,
France
Tel: 00 33 1 53 34 14 44
blanchet.auction@wanadoo.fr

BLNY (A)
BLOOMSBURY AUCTIONS
6 West 48th Street, New York, NY
10036-190
Tel: 001 212-719-1000
http://ny.bloomsburyauctions.com

BLO (A)
BLOOMSBURY AUCTIONS
Bloomsbury House, 24 Maddox
Street, London W1 S1PP
Tel: 020 7495 9494
www.bloomsburyauctions.com

BLY (D)
JOHN BLY
Byappointment
Tel: 01442 823030
www.johnbly.com

BRI (A)
BRIGHTWELLS FINE ART
Fine Art Saleroom, Easters Court,
Leominster, Herefordshire HR6 0DE
Tel: 01568 611122
www.brightwells.co.uk

BRK (D)
BROOKSIDE ANTIQUES
44 North Water Street, New
Bedford, MA 02740 USA
Tel: 001 508 993 4944
www.brooksideartglass.com

BWH (P)
BIG WHITE HOUSE
Private collection

CHT (A)
CHARTERHOUSE
The Long Street Salerooms,
Sherborne, Dorset, DT93BS
Tel: 01935 812277
www.charterhouse-auctions.co.uk

CLV (A)
CLEVEDON SALEROOMS
The Auction Centre, Kenn Road,
Kenn, Clevedon, Bristol, BS21 6TT
Tel: 01934 830 111
www.clevedon-salerooms.com

CRA (A)
CRAFTSMAN AUCTIONS
333 North Main Street,
Lambertville, NJ 08530 USA
Tel: 001 609 397 9374
www.ragoarts.com

DA (D)
DAVIES ANTIQUES
c/o Cadogan Tate, Unit 6, 6-12
Ponton Road, London SW8 5BA
Tel: 020 8947 1902
www.antique-meissen.com

DAH (A)
DEE, ATKINSON & HARRISON
The Exchange Saleroom, Driffield,
East Yorkshire
Tel : 01377 253151
www.dee-atkinson-harrison.co.uk

DN (A)
DREWEATTS
Donnington Priory Salerooms,
Donnington, Newbury, Berkshire
RG14 2JE
Tel: 01635 553553
www.dnfa.com/donnington

DNW (A)
DIX NOONAN WEB
16 Bolton Street, London, W1J 8BQ
Tel: 020 7016 1700
www.dnw.co.uk

DRA (A)
DAVID RAGO AUCTIONS
333 North Main Street,
Lambertville, NJ 08530, USA
Tel: 001 609 397 9374
www.ragoarts.com

DUK (A)
HY DUKE AND SON
The Dorchester Fine Art Salerooms,
Weymouth Avenue, Dorchester,
Dorset DT1 1QS
Tel: 01305 265 080
www.dukes-auctions.com

FLD (A)
FIELDINGS AUCTIONEERS
Mill Race Lane, Stourbridge,
DY8 1JN
Tel: 01384 444140
www.fieldingsauctioneers.co.uk

FRE (A)
FREEMAN'S
1808 Chestnut Street,
Philadelphia, PA 19103, USA
Tel: 001 215 563 9275
www.freemansauction.com

GBA (A)
GRAHAM BUDD AUCTIONS
PO Box 47519, London N14 6XD
Tel: 020 8366 2525
www.grahambuddauctions.co.uk

GHOU (A)
GARDINER HOULGATE
Bath Auction Rooms, 9 Leafield
Way, Corsham, SN13 9SW
Tel: 01225 812 912
auctions@gardiner-houlgate.co.uk

GIL (A)
GILDING'S AUCTIONEERS
64 Roman Way, Market
Harborough, LE16 7PQ
Tel: 01858 410414
www.gildings.co.uk

GORL (A)
GORRINGES
15 North Street,
Lewes, East Sussex BN7 2PD
Tel: 01273 472503
www.gorringes.co.uk

GUIN (D)
GUINEVERE
578 Kings Road, London SW6 2DY
Tel: 020 7736 2917
www.guinevere.co.uk

GVI (D)
GARTH VINCENT
The Old Manor House,
Allington, Nr Grantham,
Lincolnshire, NG32 2DH
Tel: 01400 281358
www.guns.uk.com

HALL (A)
HALLS FINE ART
Welsh Bridge, Shrewsbury, SY3 8LA
Tel: 01743 231 212
www.hallsgb.com

HB (D)
VICTORIANA DOLLS
101 Portobello Rd, London, W11 2BQ
Tel: 01737 249 525

heather.bond@totalserve.co.uk

HGS (D)
HARPERS GENERAL STORE
301 Maple Avenue, Mt. Gretna, PA
17064 USA
Tel: 001 717 865 3456
www.harpergeneralstore.com

HT or HTV (D)
HARTLEY'S
Victoria Hall, Little Lane, Ilkley, LS29
8EA
Tel: 01943 816363
www.hartleyauctions.co.uk

JACK (A)
JACKSON'S
2229 Lincoln Street, Cedar Falls,
Iowa 5063 USA
Tel: 001 319 277 2256
www.jacksonsauction.com

JDJ (A)
JAMES D JULIA INC
PO Box 830, Fairfield, ME 04937,
USA
Tel: 001 207 453 7125
www.juliaauctions.com

JH (D)
JEANETTE HAYHURST FINE GLASS
32A Kensington Church St., London
W8 4HA
Tel: 020 7938 1539

JN (A)
JOHN NICHOLSONS
The Auction Rooms, 'Longfield',
Midhurst Road, Fernhurst,
Haslemere, Surrey GU27 3HA
Tel: 01428 653727
www.johnnicholsons.com

KAU (A)
AUKTIONHAUS KAUP
Schloss Sulzburg, Hauptstrasse 62,
79295 Sulzburg, Germany
Tel: 0049 7634 5038 0
www.kaupp.de

KT (A)
KERRY TAYLOR AUCTIONS
Unit C25 Parkhall Road Trading
Estate, 40 Martell Road,
Dulwich, London SE21 8EN
Tel: 020 8676 4600
www.kerrytaylorauctions.com

LA (A)
LAYS AUCTIONS
The Penzance Auction House,
Alverton, Penzance, TR18 4RE
Tel: 01736 361414
www.davidlay.co.uk

L&T (A)
LYON AND TURNBULL LTD.
33 Broughton Place,
Edinburgh, Midlothian EH1 3RR
Tel: 0131 557 8844
www.lyonandturnbull.com

LAW Ⓐ
LAWRENCES' AUCTIONEERS
The Linen Yard, South Street,
Crewkerne, Somerset TA18 8AB
Tel: 01460 73041
www.lawrences.co.uk

LFA Ⓐ
LAW FINE ART LTD.
Ash Cottage, Ashmore Green,
Newbury, Berkshire, RG18 9ER
Tel: 01635 860033
www.lawfineart.co.uk

LOC Ⓐ
LOCKE & ENGLAND
18 Guy Street, Leamington Spa,
CV32 4RT
Tel: 01926 889100
www.leauction.co.uk

MUR Ⓐ
TONY MURLAND AUCTIONS
78 High Street, Needham Market,
Suffolk, IP6 8AW
Tel: 01449 722 992
www.antiquetools.co.uk

NA Ⓐ
Northeast Auctions
93 Pleasant Street, Portsmouth, NH
03801 USA
Tel: 001 603 433 8400
www.northeastauctions.com

NEA Ⓓ
DREWEATTS
The Nottingham Salerooms,
192 Mansfield Road, Nottingham,
NG1 3HU
Tel: 0115 962 4141
www.dnfa.com/neales

PAR or PART Ⓓ
PARTRIDGE FINE ARTS PLC
144-146 New Bond Street, London
W1S 2PF
Tel: 020 7629 0834
www.partridgeplc.com

PC ⓅⒸ
PRIVATE COLLECTION

PGO Ⓓ
PAMELA GOODWIN
11 The Pantiles, Royal Turnbridge
Wells, Kent, TN2 5TD
Tel: 01435 882200
www.goodwinantiques.co.uk

POOK Ⓐ
POOK & POOK
463 East Lancaster Avenue,
Downington, PA 19335, USA
Tel: 001 610 269 4040/0695
www.pookandpook.com

QU Ⓐ
QUITTENBAUM
Hohenstaufenstraße 1, D-80801,
München, Germany
Tel: 0049 859 33 00 75 6
www.quittenbaum.de

RDER Ⓓ
ROGERS DE RIN
76 Royal Hospital Road, Paradise
Walk, Chelsea, London SW3 4HN
Tel: 020 7352 9007
www.rogersderin.co.uk

RGA Ⓐ
RICHARD GARDNER ANTIQUES
Swan House, Market Square,
Petworth, West Sussex GU28 0AH
Tel: 01798 343 411
www.richardgardenerantiques.co.uk

ROS Ⓐ
ROSEBERY'S
74-76 Knight's Hill, West Norwood,
London SE27 0JD
Tel: 020 8761 2522
www.roseberys.co.uk

ROW Ⓐ
ROWLEY FINE ARTS
8 Downham Road, Ely, Cambridge,
Cambridgeshire CB6 1AH
Tel: 01353 653020
www.rowleyfineart.com

SDR Ⓐ
SOLLO:RAGO MODERN AUCTIONS
333 North Main Street,
Lambertville, NJ 08530 USA
Tel: 001 609 397 9374
www.ragoarts.com

SK Ⓐ
SKINNER INC.
The Heritage on the Garden,
63 Park Plaza Boston MA 02116,
USA
Tel: 001 617 350 5400
www.skinnerinc.com
SOT Ⓐ
SOTHEBY'S (US)
1334 York Avenue, New York, NY
10021, USA
Tel: 001 212 606-7000
www.sothebys.com

SOTA Ⓐ
SOTHEBY'S (AMSTERDAM)
De Boelelaan 30, 1083 HJ
Amsterdam, Netherlands
Tel: 0031 20 550 22 00
www.sothebys.com

SOTH Ⓐ
SOTHEBY'S (LONDON)
34-35 New Bond Street, London,
W1A 2AA
Tel: 020 7293 5000
www.sothebys.com

SOTP Ⓐ
SOTHEBY'S (PARIS)
Galerie Charpentier,
76 rue du Faubourg, Saint Honoré,
75008 Paris, France
Tel: 00 33 1 53 05 53 05
www.sothebys.com

SWA Ⓐ
**SWANN GALLERIES IMAGE
LIBRARY**
104 East 25th Street, New York,
New York 10010
Tel: 001 212 254 4710
www.swanngalleries.com

SWO Ⓐ
SWORDERS
14 Cambridge Road, Stansted
Mountfitchet, Essex CM24 8BZ
Tel: 01279 817 778
www.sworder.co.uk

TAC Ⓓ
TORONTO ANTIQUES CENTER
276 King Street West, Toronto,
Ontario M5V 1J2, Canada

TCF Ⓓ
CYNTHIA FINDLAY
Toronto Antiques Centre,
276 King Street West, Toronto,
Ontario M5V 1J2, Canada
Tel: 001 416 260 9057
www.cynthiafindlay.com

TCT Ⓓ
THE CALICO TEDDY
www.calicoteddy.com

TDG Ⓓ
THE DESIGN GALLERY
5 The Green, Westerham, Kent,
TN16 1AS
Tel: 01959 561 234
www.designgallery.co.uk

TDM Ⓐ
THOMAS DEL MAR LTD
25 Blythe Road, London W14 0PD
Tel: 0207 602 4805
www.thomasdelmar.com

TEN Ⓐ
TENNANTS
The Auction Centre, Leyburn, North
Yorkshire, DL8 5SG
Tel: 01969 623 780
www.tennants.co.uk

TGM Ⓐ
THE GLASS MERCHANT
8 Soxon Close, Caterham, Surrey
CR3 5SY
Tel: 07775 683 961

VEC Ⓐ
VECTIS AUCTIONS
Fleck Way, Thornaby, Stockton on
Tees, County Durham TS17 9JZ
Tel: 01642 750 616
www.vectis.co.uk

VZ Ⓐ
VON ZEZSCHWITZ
Friedrichstrasse 1a, 80801 Munich,
Germany
Tel: 0049 89 38 98 930
www.von-zezschwitz.de

W&W Ⓐ
WALLIS AND WALLIS
West Street Auction Galleries,
Lewes, East Sussex BN7 2NJ
Tel: 01273 480 208
www.wallisandwallis.co.uk

WAD Ⓐ
WADDINGTON'S
111 Bathurst St., Toronto,
Ontario M5V 2R1, Canada
Tel: 001 416 504 9100
www.waddingtons.ca

WDL Ⓐ
MARTIN WENDL
August-Bebel-Straße 4, 07407
Rudolstadt, Germany
Tel: 00 49 3672 4243 50
www.auktionshaus-wendl.de

WW Ⓐ
WOOLLEY & WALLIS
51-61 Castle Street, Salisbury,
Wiltshire SP13SU
Tel: 01722 424 500
www.woolleyandwallis.co.uk

NOTE

For valuations, it is advisable to contact the dealer or auction house in advance to confirm that they will perform this service and whether any charge is involved. Telephone valuations are not possible, so it will be necessary to send details, including a photograph, of the object to the dealer or auction house, along with a stamped addressed envelope for response. While most dealers will be happy to help you, do remember that they are busy people. Please mention Miller's Antiques Price Guide 2009 when making an enquiry.

This is a list of auctioneers that conduct regular sales. Auction houses that would like to be included in the next edition should contact us by 1 February 2009.

ALABAMA
Flomaton Antique Auction
PO Box 1017,
320 Palafox Street,
Flomaton 36441
Tel: 251 296 3059
Fax: 251 296 1974
info@flomatonantiqueauction.com
www.flomatonantiqueauction.com

Jim Norman Auctions
201 East Main St,
Hartselle, 35640
Tel: 205 773 6878

Vintage Auctions
Star Rte Box 650,
Blountsville, 35031
Tel: 205 429 2457
Fax: 205 429 2457

ARIZONA
Dan May & Associates
4110 North Scottsdale Road,
Scottsdale, 85251
Tel: 480 941 4200

Old World Mail Auctions
PO Box 2224,
Sedona, 86339
Tel: 928 282 3944
marti@oldworldauctions.com
www.oldworldauctions.com

Star Auction Inc
PO Box 1232,
Dolan Springs, 86441-1232
Tel: 602 767 4774
Fax: 602 767 3900

ARKANSAS
Hanna-Whysel Auctioneers
3403 Bella Vista Way,
Bella Vista, 72714
Tel: 501 855 9600

Ponders Auctions
1203 South College,
Stuttgart, 72160
Tel: 501 673 6551

CALIFORNIA
Bonhams & Butterfields
7601 Sunset Blvd,
Los Angeles, 90046-2714
Tel: 323 850 7500
Fax: 323 850 5843
info@butterfields.com
www.butterfields.com

220 San Bruno Ave,
San Francisco, 94103
Tel: 415 861 7500
Fax: 415 861 8951
info@butterfields.com
www.butterfields.com

I.M. Chait Gallery
9330 Civic Center Drive,
Beverly Hills, 90210
Tel: 310 285 0182
www.chait.com

Cuschieri's Auctioneers & Appraisers
863 Main Street,
Redwood City, 94063
Tel: 650 556 1793
info@cuschieris.com
www.cuschieris.com

eBay, Inc
2005 Hamilton Ave, Ste 350,
San Jose, 95125
staff@ebay.com
www.ebay.com

San Rafael Auction Gallery
634 Fifth Avenue,
San Rafael, 94901
Tel: 415 457 4488
sanrafaelauction@aol.com
www.sanrafael-auction.com

L.H. Selman Ltd
123 Locust St,
Santa Cruz, 95060
Tel: 800 538 0766
lselman@got.net
www.paperweight.com

Slawinski Auction Co
PO Box 67059
Scotts Valley, 95067
antiques@slawinski.com
www.slawinski.com

Sotheby's
9665 Wilshire Boulevard,
Beverly Hills, 90212
Tel: 310 274 0340
info.sothebys.com
www.sothebys.com

NORTH CAROLINA
Robert S. Brunk Auction Services, Inc
PO Box 2135,
Asheville, 28802
Tel: 828 254 6846
auction@brunkauctions.com
www.brunkauctions.com

Historical Collectible Auctions
24 NW Court Square, Suite 201,
Graham, 27253
Tel: 336 570 2803
auctions@hcaauctions.com
www.hcaauctions.com

SOUTH CAROLINA
Charlton Hall Galleries, Inc
912 Gervais St,
Columbia, 29201
Tel: 803 799 5678
info@charltonhallauctions.com
www.charltonhallauctions.com

COLORADO
Pacific Auction
1270 Boston Ave,
Longmont, 80501
Tel: 303 772 9401
ojpratt@pacificauction.com
www.pacificauction.com

Pettigrew Auction Company
1645 South Tejon Street,
Colorado Springs, 80906
Tel: 719 633 7963

Priddy's Auction Galleries
5411 Leetsdale Drive,
Denver, 80222
Tel: 800 380 4411

Stanley & Co
Auction Room,
395 Corona Street,
Denver, 80218
Tel: 303 355 0506
Fax: 303 321 6986

CONNECTICUT
Braswell Galleries
125 West Avenue,
Norwalk, 06854
Tel: 203 899 7420

The Great Atlantic Auction Company
2 Harris & Main Street,
Putnam, 06260
Tel: 860 963 2234
www.thegreatatlanticauction.com

Norman C. Heckler & Company
79 Bradford Corner Road,
Woodstock Valley, 06282-2002
Tel: 860 974 1634
info@hecklerauction.com
www.hecklerauctin.com

Lloyd Ralston Toys
350 Long Beach Blvd,
Stratford, 06615
Tel: 203 386 9399
lrgallery@sbcglobal.net
www.lloydralstontoys.com

Winter Associates, Inc
21 Cooke Street,
PO Box 823,
Plainville, 06062
Tel: 860 793 0288

NORTH DAKOTA
Curt D. Johnson Auction Company
4216 Gateway Drive,
Grand Forks, 58203
Tel: 701 746 1378
merfeld@rrv.net
www.curtdjohnson.com

SOUTH DAKOTA
Fischer Auction Company
238 Haywire Ave,
P. O. Box 667,
Long Lake, 57457-0667
Tel: 800 888 1766/
605 577 6600
figleo@hotmail.com
www.fischerauction.com

DELAWARE
Remember When Auctions, Inc
42 Sea Gull Road,
Swann Estates,
Selbyville, 19975
Tel: 302-436-4979
sales@history-attic.com
www.history-attic.com

FLORIDA
Auctions Neapolitan
1100 1st Ave South,
Naples 34102
Tel: 239 262 7333
info@auctionsneapolitan.com
www.auctionsneapolitan.com

Burchard Galleries/Auctioneers
2528 30th Ave North,
St Petersburg, 33713
Tel: 727 821 1167
mail@burchardgalleries
www.burchardgalleries.com

Arthur James Galleries
615 East Atlantic Avenue,
Delray Beach, 33483
Tel: 561 278 2373
arjames@bellsouth.net
www.arthurjames.com

Kincaid Auction Company
3809 East Hwy 42,
Lakeland 33801
Tel: 800 970 1977
kincaid@kincaid.com
www.kincaid.com

Albert Post Galleries
809 Lucerne Ave,
Lake Worth, 33460
Tel: 561 582 4477
a.postgallery@juno.com
www.albertpostgallery.com

TreasureQuest Auction Galleries, Inc.
8447 S.E. Retreat Drive,
Hobe Sound, 33455
Tel: 772 781 8600
www.TQAG.com

GEORGIA
Arwood Auctions
26 Ayers Ave,
Marietta, 30060
Tel: 770 423 0110

Great Gatsby's
5070 Peachtree Industrial Blvd,
Atlanta, 30341
Tel: 770 457 1903
internet@greatgatsbys.com
www.greatgatsbys.com

My Hart Auctions Inc
PO Box 2511,
Cumming, 30028
Tel: 770 888 9006
myhart@antiquefurniture.us

Red Baron's Auction Gallery
6450 Roswell Rd,
Atlanta, 30328
Tel: 404 252 3770
rbarons@onramp.net

Southland Auction Inc
3350 Riverwood Parkway,
Atlanta, 30339
Tel: 770 818 2418

IDAHO
The Coeur d'Alene Art Auction
PO Box 310,
Hayden, 83835
Tel: 208 772 9009
cdaartauction@cdaartaution.com
www.cdaartauction.com

INDIANA
Kruse International
PO Box 190,
Auburn, 46706
Tel: 219 925 5600/
800 968 4444

Lawson Auction Service
923 Fourth Street,
Columbus, 47265
Tel: 812 372 2571
dlawson@lawsonauction.com
www.lawsonauction.com

Curran Miller Auction & Realty, Inc
4424 Vogel Road, Ste. 400,
Evansville, 47715
Tel: 800 264 0601
email@curranmiller.com
www.curranmiller.com

Schrader Auction
209 West Van Buren Street,
Columbia City, 46725
Tel: 219 244 7606

Slater's Americana
5335 North Tacoma Ave,
Suite 24,
Indianapolis, 46220
Tel: 317 257 0863

Stout Auctions
529 State Road East,
Williamsport, 47993
Tel: 765 764 6901
info@stoutauctions.com
www.stoutauctions.com

Strawser Auctions
200 North Main,
PO Box 332,
Wolcotville, 46795
Tel: 260 854 2859
info@strawserauctions.com
www.strawserauctions.com

ILLINOIS
Bloomington Auction Gallery
300 East Grove Street,
Bloomington, 61701
Tel: 309 828 5533
joyluke@verizon.net
www.joyluke.com

Butterfield & Dunning
755 Church Rd,
Elgin, 60123
Tel: 847 741 3483
info@butterfields.com
www.butterfields.com

The Chicago Wine Company
5663 West Howard Street,
Niles, 60714
Tel: 847 647 8789
info@tcwc.com
www.tcwc.com

Hack's Auction Center
Box 296,
Pecatonica, 61063
Tel: 815 239 1436

Hanzel Galleries
1120 South Michigan Ave,
Chicago, 60605-2301
Tel: 312 922 6247

Joy Luke Auction Gallery
300 East Grove Street,
Bloomington, 61701-5232
Tel: 309 828 5533
robert@joyluke.com
www.joyluke.com

Leslie Hindman, Inc.
122 North Aberdeen Street,
Chicago, 60607
Tel: 312 280 1212
www.lesliehindman.com

Mastro Auctions
7900 South Madison Street,
Burr Ridge, 60527
Tel: 630 472 1200
www.mastroauctions.com

Sotheby's
215 West Ohi Street,
Chicago, 60610
Tel: 312 670 0010

Susanin's Auction
228 Merchandise Mart,
Chicago, 60654
Tel: 888 787 2646/
312 832 9800
info@susanins.com
www.susanins.com

John Toomey Gallery
818 North Boulevard,
Oak Park, 60301
Tel: 708 383 5234
info@johntoomeygallery.com
www.johntoomeygallery.com

IOWA
Gene Harris Antique Auction Center
203 S. 18th Avenue,
PO Box 476,
Marshalltown, 50158
Tel: 641 752 0600
geneharris@geneharrisauctions.com
geneharrisauctions.com

Jackson's Auctioneers & Appraisers
2229 Lincoln Street,
PO Box 50613,
Cedar Falls, 50613
Tel: 319 277 2256
jacksons@jacksonsauction.com
www.jacksonsauction.com

Tubaugh Auctions
1702 8th Ave,
Belle Plaine, 52208
Tel: 319 444 2413
www.tubaughauctions.com

KANSAS
AAA Historical Auction Service
PO. Box 12214,
Kansas City, 66112
www.manions.com,

CC Auction Gallery
416 Court Street,
Clay Center, KS 67432
Tel: 785 632 6062

Spielman Auction
2259 Homestead Road,
Lebo, 66856
Tel: 316 256 6558

KENTUCKY
Hays & Associates, Inc
120 South Spring Street,
Louisville, 40206-1953
Tel: 502 584 4297

Steffen's Historical Militaria
PO Box 280,
Newport, 41072
Tel: 859 431 4499
www.steffensmilitaria.com

LOUISIANA
Estate Auction Gallery
3374 Government Street,
Baton Rouge, 70806
Tel: 504 383 7706

Neal Auction Company
4038 Magazine Street,
New Orleans, 70115
Tel: 504 899 5329
Fax: 504 897 3808

New Orleans Auction Galleries
801 Magazine Street,
New Orleans, 70130
Tel: 504 566 1849
info@neworleansauction.com
www.neworleansauction.com

MAINE
Cyr Auctions
P.O. Box 1238,
Gray, 04039
Tel: 207 657 5253
info@cyrauctions.com
www.cyrauction.com

James D. Julia Auctioneers Inc
Rte 201, Skowhegan Road,
PO Box 830,
Fairfield, 04937
Tel: 207 453 7125
jjulia@juliaauctions.com
www.juliaauctions.com

Randy Inman Auctions Inc.
PO Box 726,
Waterville, 04903-0726
Tel: 207 872 6900
inman@inmanauctions.com
www.inmanauctions.com

Thomaston Place Auction Galleries
PO Box 300,
Business Rt 1,
Thomaston, 04861
Tel: 207 354 8141
auction@kajav.com
www.thomastonauction.com

MARYLAND
Hantman's Auctioneers & Appraisers
PO Box 59366,
Potomac, 20859-9366
Tel: 301 770 3720
hantman@hantmans.com
www.hantmans.com

Isennock Auctions & Appraisals, Inc
4106B Norrisville Road,
White Hall, 21161-9306,
Tel: 410 557 8052
isennock@starix.net
www.isennockauction.com

Richard Opfer Auctioneering, Inc
1919 Greenspring Drive,
Lutherville,
Timonium, 21093-4113
Tel: 410 252 5035
info@opferauction.com
www.opferauction.com

Sloans & Kenyon
4605 Bradley Boulevard
Bethesda, 20815
Tel: 301 634-2330
Fax: 301 656-7074
www.sloansandkenyon.com

Theriault's
PO Box 151,
Annapolis, 21404
Tel: 410 224 3655
info@theriaults.com
www.theriaults.com

MASSACHUSETTS

Douglas Auctioneers
Route 5,
South Deerfield, 01373
Tel: 413 665 2877
www.douglasauctioneers.com
info@douglasauctioneers.com

Eldred's
PO Box 796,
East Dennis, 02641-0796
Tel: 508 385 3116
info@eldreds.com
www.eldreds.com

Grogan & Company Auctioneers
22 Harris Street,
Dedham, 02026
Tel: 781 461 9500
grogans@groganco.com
www.groganco.com

Shute Auction Gallery
850 West Chestnut St,
Brockton, 02401
Tel: 508 588 0022

Skinner Inc.
63 Park Plaza,
Boston, 02116
Tel: 617 350 5400
info@skinnerinc.com
www.skinnerinc.com

357 Main Street,
Bolton, 01740
Tel: 978 779 6241
info@skinnerinc.com
www.skinnerinc.com

Willis Henry Auctions, Inc
22 Main Street,
Marshfield, 02050
Tel: 781 834 7774
wha@willishenry.com
www.willishenry.com

MICHIGAN

Frank H. Boos Gallery
420 Enterprise Court,
Bloomfield Hills, 48302
Tel: 248 332 1500
artandauctio@boosgallery.com
www.boosgallery.com

DuMouchelle Art Galleries Co.
409 East Jefferson Ave,
Detroit, 48226
Tel: 313 963 6255
info@dumouchelles.com
www.dumouchelles.com

Ivey-Selkirk Auctioneers
7447 Forsyth Boulevard
Saint Louis, Missouri 63105
Tel: 314 726 5515
Toll: 800 728 8002
Fax: 314 726 9908
iveyselkirk@iveyselkirk.com
www.iveyselkirk.com

MINNESOTA

Buffalo Bay Auction Co.
5244 Quam Circle,
Rogers, 55374
Tel: 612 428 8480
buffalobay@aol.com

Tracy Luther Auctions
2548 East 7th Ave,
St. Paul, 55109
Tel: 612 770 6175

Rose Auction Galleries
3180 Country Drive,
Little Canada, 55117
Tel: 612 484 1415
auctions@rosegalleries.com
www.rosegalleries.com

MISSOURI

Ivey Selkirk Auctioneers
7447 Forsyth Blvd,
Saint Louis, 63105
Tel: 314 726 5515
www.iveyselkirk.com

Simmons & Company Auctioneers
40706 East 144th Street,
Richmond, 64085
Tel: 816 776 2936 / 800 646 2936
www.simmonsauction.com

MONTANA

Allard Auctions
PO Box 1030,
St. Ignatius, 59865
Tel: 460 745 0500
www.allardauctions.com

Stan Howe & Associates
4433 Red Fox Drive,
Helena, 59601
Tel: 406 443 5658 / 800 443 5658

NEW HAMPSHIRE

Paul McInnis Inc Auction Gallery
One Juniper Road
North Hampton, 03862,
Tel: 603 964 1301
www.paulmcinnis.com

Northeast Auctions
694 Lafayette Rd,
PO Box 363,
Hampton, 03483
Tel: 603 926 9800

R.O. Schmitt Fine Art
PO Box 162,
Windham, 03087
Tel: 603 432 2237
www.antiqueclockauction.com

NEW JERSEY

Bertoia Auctions
2141 Dearco Dr,
Vineland, 08360
Tel: 856 692 1881
toys@bertoiaauctions.com
www.bertoiaauctions.com

Craftsman Auctions
333 North Main Street,
Lambertville, 08530
Tel: 609 397 9374
info@ragoarts.com
www.ragoarts.com

David Rago Auctions
333 North Main Street,
Lambertville, 08530
Tel: 609 397 9374
info@ragoarts.com
www.ragoarts.com

Dawson & Nye
128 American Road,
Morris Plains, 07950
Tel: 973 984 8900
info@dawsonandnye.com
www.dawsonandnye.com

Greg Manning Auctions, Inc
775 Passaic Ave,
West Caldwell, 07006
Tel: 973 882 0004 / 800 221 0243
info@gregmanning.com
www.gregmanning.com

Rago/Dawes Lalique Auctions
333 North Main Street,
Lambertville, 08530
Tel: 609 397 9374
info@ragoarts.com
www.ragoarts.com

Sollo:Rago Modern Auctions
333 North Main Street,
Lambertville, 08530
Tel: 609 397 9374
info@ragoarts.com
www.ragoarts.com

Time & Again Auction Gallery
1080 Edward Street,
Linden, 07036
Tel: 800 290 5401 / 908 862 0200
tandagain@aol.com
www.timeandagainantiques.com

NEW MEXICO

Altermann Galleries
Santa Fe Galleries,
203 Canyon Road,
Santa Fe, 87501
info@altermann.com
www.altermann.com

NEW YORK

Christie's
502 Park Ave,
New York, 10022
Tel: 212 546 1000
info@christies.com
www.christies.com

Christie's East
219 East 67th St,
New York, 10021
Tel: 212 606 0400
info@christies.com
www.christies.com

Copake Auction, Inc
266 RT. 7A,
Copake, 12516
Tel: 518 329 1142
info@copakeauction.com
www.copakeauction.com

Samuel Cottone Auctions
15 Genesee Street,
Mount Morris, 14510
Tel: 716 658 3180

William Doyle Galleries
175 East 87th Street,
New York, 10128-2205
Tel: 212 427 2730
info@doylegalleries.com
www.doylegalleries.com

Framefinders
454 East 84th Street,
New York, 10028
Tel: 212 396 3896
framefinders@aol.com
www.framefinders.com

Guernsey's Auction
108 East 73rd St,
New York, 10021
Tel: 212 794 2280
auctions@guernseys.com
www.guernseys.com

William J. Jenack Auctioneers
62 Kings Highway Bypass,
Chester, 10918
Tel: 845 469 9095 / 845 469 8445
info@jenack.com
www.jenack.com

Mapes Auction Gallery
1729 Vestal Parkway,
West Vestal, 13850-1156
Tel: 607 754 9193
info@mapesauction.com
www.mapesauction.com

North River Auction Gallery
1293 Route 212
Saugerties, 12477
Tel: 845 247 9130
Fax: 845 247 9134

Phillips de Pury & Company
450 West 15 Street,
New York, 10011
Tel: 212 940 1200
info@phillipsdepury.com
www.phillipsdepury.com

Sotheby's
1334 York Ave,
New York, 10021
Tel: 212 606 7000
info@sothebys.com
www.sothebys.com

Stair Galleries
549 Warren Street
Hudson, 12534
Tel: 518 751 1000
Fax: 518 751 1010
www.stairgalleries.com

Sterling Auction House
40 Railroad Ave
Montgomery, 12549
Tel: 845 457 7550
www.sterlingauctionhouse.com

Swann Galleries, Inc
104 East 25th Street,
New York, 10010-2977
Tel: 212 254 4710
swann@swanngalleries.com
www.swanngalleries.com

OHIO
Belhorn Auction Services
PO Box 20211,
Columbus, 43220
Tel: 614 921 9441
www.belhorn.com

Cincinnati Art Galleries, LLC
225 East 6th Street,
Cincinnati, 45202
Tel: 513 381 2128
www.cincinnatiartgalleries.com

The Cobbs Auctioneers LLC
Noone Falls Mill,
50 Jaffrey Road,
Petersborough, 03458
Tel: 603 924 6361
info@thecobbs.com
www.thecobbs.com

Cowan's Historic Americana Auctions
673 Wilmer Avenue,
Cincinnati, 45226
Tel: 513 871 1670
info@historicamericana.com
www.historicamericana.com

DeFina Auctions
1591 State Route 45,
Austinburg, 44010
Tel: 440 275 6674
info@definaauctions.com
www.definaauctions.com

Garth's Auction, Inc
2690 Stratford Rd,
PO Box 369,
Delaware, 43015
Tel: 740 362 4771
info@garths.com
www.garths.com

Treadway Gallery, Inc
2029 Maidson Road,
Cincinnati, 45208
Tel: 513 321 6742
info@treadwaygallery.com
www.treadwaygallery.com

Wolf's Auction Gallery
1239 West 6th Street,
Cleveland, 44113
Tel: 216 575 9653

OREGON
O'Gallery
228 Northeast Seventh Ave,
Portland, 97232
Tel: 503 238 0202
Fax: 503 236 8211
www.ogallerie.com

PENNSYLVANIA
Noel Barrett
PO Box 300,
Carversville, 18913
Tel: 215 297 5109
toys@noelbarrett.com
www.noelbarrett.com

William Bunch Auctions
1 Hillman Drive,
Chadds Ford,
Philadelphia 19317
Tel: 610 558 1800
info@williambunchauctions.com
www.williambunchauctions.com

Concept Art Gallery
1031 South Braddock Avenue,
Pittsburgh, 15218
Tel: 412 242 9200
info@conceptgallery.com
www.conceptgallery.com

Dargate Auction Galleries
5607 Baum Blvd,
Pittsburgh, 15206
Tel: 412 362 3558
dargate@dargate.com
www.dargate.com

Freeman's
1808 Chestnut St,
Philadelphia, 19103
Tel: 610 563 9275 / 610 563 9453
info@freemansauction.com
www.freemansauction.com

Hunt Auctions
75E. Uwchlan Ave, Suite 130,
Exton, 19341
Tel: 610 524 0822
Fax: 610 524 0826
info@huntauctions.com
www.huntauctions.com

Pook & Pook, Inc
PO Box 268,
Downington, 19335-0268
Tel: 610 269 0695 / 610 269 4040
info@pookandpook.com
www.pookandpook.com

Sanford Alderfer Auction Co.
501 Fairgrounds Road, PO Box 640,
Hatfield, 19440-0640
Tel: 215 393 3000
info@alderfercompany.com
www.alderfercompany.com

Charles A. Whitaker Auction Co.,
1002 West Cliveden St,
Philadelphia, 19119
Tel: 215 817 4600
caw@whitakerauction.com
www.whitakerauction.com

RHODE ISLAND
Gustave White Auctioneers
37 Bellevue,
Newport, 02840-3207
Tel: 401 841 5780

TENNESSEE
Kimball M Sterling Inc
125 West Market Street,
Johnson City, 37601,
Tel: 423 928 1471
kimsold@tricon.net
www.sterlingsold.com

TEXAS
Austin Auctions
8414 Anderson Mill Road,
Austin, 78729-5479
Tel: 512 258 5479
austinauction@cs.com
www.austinauction.com

Dallas Auction Gallery
1518 Slocum Street,
Dallas, 75207
Tel: 214 653 3900
Fax: 214 653 3912
info@dallasauctiongallery.com
www.dallasauctiongallery.com

Heritage Auction Galleries,
3500 Maple Ave, 17th Floor,
Dallas, 75219-3941
Tel: 214 528 3500 / 800 872 6467
bid@heritageauctions.com
www.heritageauctions.com

UTAH
America West Archives
PO Box 100,
Cedar City, 84721
Tel: 435 586 9497
info@americawestarchives.com
www.americawestarchives.com

VERMONT
Eaton Auction Service
RR 1, Box 333,
Fairlee, 05045
Tel: 802 333 9717
eas@sover.com
www.eatonauctionservice.com

Sprague Auctions, Inc
Route 5,
Dummerston, 05301
www.spragueauctions.com

VIRGINIA
Green Valley Auctions, Inc.
2259 Green Valley Lane,
Mount Crawford, 22841
Tel: 540 343 4260
gvai@shentel.net
www.greenvalleyauctions.com

The Auction Gallery
225 Gun Club Road,
Richmond, 23221
Tel: 804 358 0500
www.estate-services.com

Ken Farmer Auctions & Estates
105 Harrison Street,
Radford, 24141
Tel: 540 639 0939
info@kfauctions.com
www.kenfarmer.com

Phoebus Auction Gallery
14-16 East Mellen Street,
Hampton, 23663
Tel: 757 722 9210
bwelch@phoebusauction.com
www.phoebusauction.com

WASHINGTON DC
Seattle Auction House,
5931 4th Avenue South,
Seattle, 98108
Tel: 206 764 4444
Fax: 206 764 0556
www.seattleauctionhouse.com

Weschler's
909 East Street NW,
Washington, 20004-2006
Tel: 202 628 1281 / 800 331 1430
www.weschlers.com

WISCONSIN
Milwaukee Auction Galleries
1919 North Summit Ave,
Milwaukee, 53202
Tel: 414 271 1105

Schrager Auction Galleries, Ltd
PO Box 10390,
2915 North Sherman Blvd,
Milwaukee, 53210
Tel: 414 873 3738
www.schragerauctions.com

CANADA
Bailey's Auctioneers & Appraisers
Tel: 519 823 1107
www.BaileyAuctions.com

ALBERTA
Arthur Clausen & Sons, Auctioneers
11802 - 145 Street,
Edmonton, Alberta,
Canada T5L 2H3
Tel: 780 451 4549
arthur.clausen@telus.net
www.clausenauction.com

Hall's Auction Services Ltd.
5240 1A Street S.E.,
Calgary, Alberta,
Canada T2H 1J1
Tel: 403 640 1244
info@hallsauction.com
www.hodginshalls.com

Hodgins Art Auctions Ltd
5240 1A Street S.E.,
Calgary, Alberta,
Canada T2H 1J1
Tel: 403 640 1244
info@hallsauction.com
www.hodginshalls.com

Lando Art Auctions
11130-105 Avenue N.W.,
Edmonton, Alberta,
Canada T5H 0L5
Tel: 780 990 1161
mail@landoartauctions.com
www.landoartauctions.com

BRITISH COLUMBIA
All Nations Stamp & Coin
Hudson's Bay Company
4th Floor, 674 Granville Street,
PO Box 54023, Vancouver,
British Columbia,
Canada V6C 3P4
Tel: 604 689 2230
collect@direct.ca
www.allnationsstampandcoin.com

Maynards Fine Art Auction House
415 West 2nd Avenue,
Vancouver, British Columbia,
Canada V5Y 1E3
Tel: 604 876 6787
www.maynards.com

Robert Derot Associates
P.O. Box 52205, Vancouver,
British Columbia,
Canada V7J 3V5
Tel: 604 649 6302
robert@robertderot.com
www.robertderot.com

Waddington's West
3286 Bellevue Road, Victoria,
British Columbia,
Canada V8X 1C1
Tel: 250 384 3737
www.waddingtonsauctions.com

Heffel Fine Art Auction House
2247 Granville Street,
Vancouver, British Columbia
Canada V6H 3G1
Tel: 604 732 6505
Fax: 604 732 4245
mail@heffel.com
www.heffel.com

ONTARIO
Empire Auctions
165 Tycos Drive,
Toronto, Ontario,
Canada M6B 1W6
Tel: 416 784 4261
www.empireauctions.com
Grand Valley Auctions
154 King Street East,
Cambridge, Ontario,
Canada
Tel: 519 653 6811
www.grandvalleyauctions.ca

A Touch of Class
92 College Crescent,
Barrie, Ontario,
Canada L4M 5C8
Tel: 888 891 6591
info@atouchofclassauctions.com
www.atouchofclassauctions.com

Estate and Antiques Sales
2030 Eglinton Avenue West,
Toronto, Ontario,
Canada,M6E 3S4
Tel: 416 780 9101
www.estateandantiquesales.com

Gordon's Auction Center
1473 Princess Street,
Kingston Ontario,
Canada K7M 3E9
Tel: 613 542 0963
mail@gordonsauction.com
www.gordonsauction.com

Ritchies
288 King Street East,
Toronto, Ontario,
Canada M5A 1K4
Tel: 416 364 1864
www.ritchies.com

Waddington's
111 Bathurst Street,
Toronto, Ontario,
Canada M5V 2R1
Tel: 416 504 9100
www.waddingtonsauctions.com

Walkers
81 Auriga Drive, Suite 18
Ottawa, Ontario,
Canada K2E 7Y5
Tel: 613 224 5814
www.walkersauctions.com

Deveau Galleries,
Robert Fine Art Auctioneers,
297-299 Queen Street, Toronto,
Ontario, M5A 157
Tel: 416 364 6271

Heffel Fine Art Auction House,
13 Hazelton Avenue,
Toronto, Ontario,
Canada M5R 2E1
Tel: 416 961 6505
Fax: 416 961-4245
mail@heffel.com
www.heffel.com

Sotheby's
9 Hazelton Avenue,
Toronto, Ontario,
Canada M5R 2EI
Tel: 416 926 1774
www.sotheby's.com

When The Hammer Goes Down
440 Douglas Avenue,
Toronto, Ontario, Canada M5M 1H4
Tel: 416 787 1700
Toll: 866 243 2257
BIDCALR@rogers.com
www.bidcalr.com

QUEBEC
Empire Auctions
5500, rue Paré,
Montréal, Québec,
Canada H4P 2M1
Tel: 514 737 6586

Iegor - Hôtel des Encans
872, rue Du Couvent,
Angle Saint-Antoine Ouest,
Montréal, Quebec,
Canada H4C 2R6
Tel: 514 842 7447
information@iegor.net
www.iegor.net

Montreal Auction House
5778 St. Lawrent Blvd.,
Montreal, Quebec,
Canada H2T 1S8
Tel: 514 278 0827
maison.des.encans@videotron.ca
www.pages.videotron.com

Pinneys Auctions
2435 Duncan Road (T.M.R.),
Montreal, Quebec,
Cananda, H4P 2A2
Tel: 514 345 0571
pinneys@ca.inter.net
www.pinneys.ca

Ritchies
1980, rue Sherbrooke O.
Suite 100 (Ground Floor),
Quebec, Canada H3H 1E8
Tel: 514 934 1864
www.ritchies.com

Specialists who would like to be included in the next edition, or have a change of address or telephone number, should contact us by 1 February 2009.

Readers should contact dealers by telephone before visiting them to avoid a wasted journey.

AMERICAN PAINTINGS

James R Bakker Antiques Inc
248 Bradford Street,
Provincetown, MA 02657
Tel: 508 487 9081

Jeffrey W. Cooley
The Cooley Gallery Inc, 25 Lyme
Street, Old Lyme, CT 06371
Tel: 860 434 8807
info@cooleygallery. com
www.cooleygallery. com

AMERICANA & FOLK ART

**American West Indies Trading
Co. Antiques & Art**
Tel: 305 872 3948
awindies@att.net
www.goantiques.com/members/awin
diestrading

Augustus Decorative Arts Ltd.
Tel: 215 587 0000
elle@portraitminatures.com

Axtell Antiques
1 River Street, Deposit, NY 13754
Tel: 607 467-2353
Fax: 607 467-4316
www.axtellantiques.com

Thomas & Julia Barringer
26 South Main Street,
Stockton, NJ, 08559
Tel: 609 397 4474
Fax: 609 397 4474
tandjb@voicenet.com

Bucks County Antique Center
Route 202, Lahaska, PA 18931
Tel: 215 794 9180

J.M. Flanigan American Antiques
1607 Park Ave, Baltimore, MD 21217
Tel: 410 225 3463
jmf745i@aol.com

Frank Gaglio, Inc
56 Market St., Suite B,
Rhinebeck NY 12572
Tel: 845 876 0616

Sidney Gecker
226 West 21st Street,
New York, NY 10011
Tel: 212 929 8769

**Pat & Rich Garthoeffner
Antiques**
122 East Main Street,
Lititz, PA 17543
Tel: 717 627 7998
Fax: 717 627 3259
patgarth@voicenet.com

Allan Katz Americana
25 Old Still Road,
Woodbridge, CT 06525
Tel: 203 393 9356
folkkatz@optonline.net

Nathan Liverant & Son
168 South Main Street, P.O. Box
103, Colchester, CT 06415
Tel: 860 537 2409
www.liverantantiques.com
mail@liverantantiques.com

Judith & James Milne Inc
506 East 74th Street,
New York, NY 10021
Tel: 212 472 0107
www.milneantiques.com
milneinc@aol.com

Olde Hope Antiques Inc
P.O. Box 718, New Hope, PA 18938
Tel: 215 297 0200
Fax: 215 297 0300
info@oldehopeantiques.com
www.oldehopeantiques.com

Pantry & Hearth,
994 Main Street South,
Woodbury, CT 06798
Tel: 203 263 8555
gail.lettick@prodigy.net

Sharon Platt
1347 Rustic View,
Manchester, MO 63011
Tel: 636 227 5304
sharonplatt@postnet.com

Raccoon Creek Antiques
Box 276, 208 Spangsville Road,
Oley, PA 19547
www.raccoonantiques.com

J.B. Richardson
6 Partrick Lane,
Westport, CT 06880
Tel: 203 226 0358

Marion Robertshaw Antiques
P.O. Box 435, Route 202,
Lahaska, PA 18931
Tel: 215 295 0648

Cheryl & Paul Scott
P.O. Box 835, 232 Bear Hill Road,
Hillsborough, NH 03244
Tel: 603 464 3617
rivrebend@mctttelecom.com

The Splendid Peasant
Route 23 & Sheffield Rd, PO Box
536, South Egremont, MA 01258
Tel: 413 528 5755
folkart@splendidpeasant.com
www.splendidpeasant.com

The Stradlings
1225 Park Avenue,
New York, NY 10028
Tel: 212 534 8135

Patricia Stauble Antiques
180 Main Street, PO Box 265,
Wiscasset, ME 04578
Tel: 207 882 6341
pstauble@midcoast.com

Throckmorton Fine Art
145 East 57th Street, 3rd Floor,
New York, NY 10022
Tel: 001 212 223 1059
Fax: 001 212 223 1937
www.throckmorton-nyc.com

Jeffrey Tillou Antiques
33 West Street & 7 East Street,
PO Box 1609, Litchfield, CT 06759
Tel: 860 567 9693
webmaster@tillouantiques.com

Paul and Karen Wendhiser
P.O. Box 155, Ellington, CT 06029

ANTIQUITIES

Frank & Barbara Pollack
1214 Green Bay Road,
Highland Park, IL 60035
Tel: 847 433 2213
FPollack@compuserve.com

ARCHITECTURAL ANTIQUES

Garden Antiques
Katonah, NY 10536
Tel: 212 744 6281
gardenantiques@pipeline.com
www.bigardenantiques.com

Cecilia B. Williams
12 West Main Street,
New Market, MD 21774
Tel: 301 865 0777

Hurst Gallery
53 Mt. Auburn Street,
Cambridge, MA 02138
Tel: 617 491 6888
manager@hurstgallery.com
www.hurstgallery.com

ARMS & MILITARIA

Faganarms
Box 425, Fraser, MI 48026
Tel: 586 465 4637
info@faganarms.com
www.faganarms.com

BAROMETERS

Barometer Fair
PO Box 25502,
Sarasota, FL 34277
Tel: 941 400 7044
john@barometerfair.com
www.barometerfair.com

BOOKS

Bauman Rare Books
535 Madison Avenue,
New York, NY 10022
Tel: 212 751 0011
www.baumanrarebooks.com

CARPETS & RUGS

John J. Collins Jr. Gallery,
PO Box 958, 11 Market Square,
Newburyport, MA 01950
Tel: 978 462 7276
www.bijar.com
bijar@telcity.com

Karen & Ralph Disaia
Oriental Rugs Ltd, 23 Lyme Street,
Old Lyme, CT 06371
Tel: 860 434 1167
www.orientalrugsltd.com
info@orientalrugsltd.com

D.B. Stock Antique Carpets
464 Washington Street,
Wellesley, MA 02482
Tel: 781 237 5859
www.dbstock.com
douglas@dbstock.com

CERAMICS

Charles & Barbara Adams
289 Old Main Street,
South Yarmouth, MA 02664
Tel: 508 760 3290
adams_2430@msn.com

Jill Fenichell
By appointment only
Tel: 212 980 9346
jfenichell@yahoo.com

Mark & Marjorie Allen
6 Highland Drive,
Amherst, NH 03031
Tel: 603 672 8989
mandmallen@antiquedelft.com
www.antiquedelft.com

Mellin's Antiques
PO Box 1115, Redding, CT 06875
Tel: 203 938 9538
rich@mellin.us

Philip Suval, Inc
1501 Caroline Street, Fredericksburg,
VA 22401
Tel: 540 373 9851
jphilipsuval@aol.com

COSTUME JEWELRY

Aurora Bijoux
Tel: 215 872 7808
www.aurorabijoux.com

Deco Jewels Inc
131 Thompson Street, NY
Tel: 212 253 1222
decojewels@earthlink.net

Junkyard Jeweler
www.tias.com/stores/thejunkyard-
jeweler

Million Dollar Babies
Tel: 518 885 7397

Terry Rodgers & Melody
1050 2nd Ave, New York, NY 10022
Tel: 212 758 3164
melodyjewelnyc@aol.com

Roxanne Stuart
Pennsylvania
Tel: 215 750 8868
gemfairy@aol.com

Bonny Yankauer
bonnyy@aol.com

CLOCKS
Kirtland H. Crump
387 Boston Post Road,
Madison, CT 06443
Tel: 203 245 7573
kirtland@sbaglobal.net
www.crumpclocks.com

RO Schmitt Fine Art
PO Box 162, Windham, NH 03087
Tel: 603 432 2237
www.antiqueclockauction.com

DECORATIVE ARTS
Sumpter Priddy Inc
323 South Washington Street,
Alexandria, VA 22314
Tel: 703 299 0800
info@sumpterpriddy.com

Leah Gordon Antiques
Gallery 18, Manhattan Art &
Antiques Center, 1050 Second
Avenue, New York, NY 10022
Tel: 212 872 1422

Lillian Nassau
220 East 57th Street,
New York, NY 10022
Tel: 212 759 6062
lilnassau@aol.com
www.lilliannassau.com

Susie Burmann
23 Burpee Lane,
New London, NH 03257
Tel: 603 526 5934
rsburmann@tds.net

H.L. Chalfant Antiques
1352 Paoli Pike,
West Chester, PA 19380
Tel: 610 696 1862
chalfant@gateway.net

Brian Cullity
18 Pleasant Street, PO Box 595,
Sagamore, MA 02561
Tel: 508 888 8409
info@briancullity.com
www.briancullity.com

Gordon & Marjorie Davenport
4250 Manitou Way,
Madison, WI 53711
Tel: 608 271 2348
GMDaven@aol.com

Ron & Penny Dionne
55 Fisher Hill Road,
Willington, CT 06279
Tel: 860 487 0741

Peter H. Eaton Antiques
24 Parker St, Newbury, MA 01951
Tel: 978 465 2754
peter@petereaton.com
www.petereaton.com

Gallery 532
142 Duane St, New York, NY 10013
Tel: 212 964 1282
www.gallery532.com

Stephen H Garner Antiques
PO Box 136,
Yarmouth Port, MA 02675
Tel: 508 362 8424

Samuel Herrup Antiques
35 Sheffield Plain Road (Route 7),
Sheffield, MA 01257
Tel: 413 229 0424
ssher@ben.net

High Style Deco
224 West 18th Street,
New York, NY 10011
Tel: 001 212 647 0035
Fax: 001 212 647 0031
www.highstyledeco.com

R Jorgensen Antiques
502 Post Road (US Route 1),
Wells, ME 04090
Tel: 207 646 9444
info@rjorgensen.com
www.rjorgensen.com

Leigh Keno American Antiques
127 East 69th Street,
New York, NY 10021
Tel: 212 734 2381
leigh@leighkeno.com
www.leighkeno.com

Bettina Krainin
289 Main St, Woodbury, CT 06798
Tel: 203 263 7669

William E. Lohrman
248 Rte 208, New Paltz, NY 12561
Tel: 845 255 6762

Lorraine's
23 Battery Park Avenue
Asheville, NC 28801
Tel: 828 251 1771
Fax: 828 254 9490
lorrainesantiques@cs.com

Gary & Martha Ludlow Inc
5284 Golfway Lane,
Lyndhurst, OH 44124,
Tel: 440 449 3475
ludlowantiques@aol.com

Macklowe Gallery
667 Madison Ave,
New York, NY 10021
Tel: 212 644 6400
www.macklowegallery.com

Milly McGehee
PO. Box 666, Riderwood, MD 21139
Tel: 410 653 3977
millymcgehee@comcast.com

Jackson Mitchell Inc
5718 Kennett Pike,
Wilmington, DE 19807
Tel: 302 656 0110
JacMitch@aol.com

Perrault-Rago Gallery
333 North Main Street,
Lambertville, NJ 08530
Tel: 609 397 9374
info@ragoarts.com
www.ragoarts.com

James L. Price Antiques
831 Alexander Spring Road,
Carlisle, PA 17013
Tel: 717 243 0501
jlpantiques@earthlink.net

RJG Antiques
P.O. Box 60, Rye, NH 03870
Tel: 603 433 1770
antiques@rjgantiques.com
www.rjgantiques.com

John Keith Russell Antiques Inc
110 Spring Street, PO Box 414,
South Salem, NY 10590
Tel: 914 763 8144
info@jkrantiques.com
www.jkrantiques.com

Israel Sack
730 Fifth Avenue, Suite 605,
New York, NY 10029
Tel: 212 399 6562

Lincoln & Jean Sander
235 Redding Road,
Redding, CT 06896
Tel: 203 938 2981
sanderlr@aol.com

Kathy Schoemer American Antiques
PO Box 429, 12 McMorrow Lane,
North Salem, NY 10560
Tel: 603 835 2105

Thomas Schwenke Inc
50 Main Street North,
Woodbury, CT0 6798
Tel: 203 266 0303
schwenke@schwenke.com
www.schwenke.com

Jack & Ray Van Gelder
Conway House, 468 Ashfield Road,
Conway, MA 01341
Tel: 413 369 4660

Van Tassel / Baumann American Antiques
690 Sugartown Road,
Malvern, PA 19355
Tel: 610 647 3339

Anne Weston & Associates, LLC
43 Pray St, Portsmouth, NH 03801
Tel: 603 431 0385
Cell: 603 521 4001
Anne-weston@comcast.net
www.anne-weston.com

DOLLS
Sara Bernstein Antique Dolls & Bears
Englishtown, NJ 07726
Tel: 732 536 4101
santiqbebe@aol.com

Theriault's
PO Box 151, Annapolis, MD 21404
Tel: 410 224 3655
info@theriaults.com
www.theriaults.com

FURNITURE
American Antiques
161 Main Street, PO Box 368,
Thomaston, ME 04861
Tel: 207 354 6033
acm@midcoast.com

American Art Display
514 14th West Palm Beach, FL 33401
Tel: 561 379 9367
americanartdisplay@msn.com

American Spirit Antiques
P.O. Box 11152,
Shawnee Mission, KS 66207
Tel: 913 345 9494
Tedatiii@aol.com

Antique Associates
PO Box 129W, 473 Main Street,
West Townsend, MA 01474
Tel: 978 597 8084
drh@aaawt.com

Antiquebug
Frank & Cathy Sykes,
85 Center St, Wolfeboro, NH 03894
Tel: 603 569 0000
dragonfly@antiquebug.com
www.antiquebug.com

Barbara Ardizone Antiques
P.O. Box 433, 62 Main Street,
Salisbury, CT 06068
Tel: 860 435 3057

Artemis Gallery
Wallace Rd, North Salem, NY 10560
Tel: 914 669 5971
artemis@optonline.net
www.artemisantiques.com

Axe Antiques
275 Alt, A1A (SR811) Jupiter,
Palm Beach County, Florida 33477,
Tel: 561 743 7888 / 877 689 1730
www.axeantiques.com

Carswell Rush Berlin, Inc
PO Box 0210, Planetarium Station,
New York, NY 0024-0210
Tel: 212 721 0330
carswellberlin@msn.com
www.americanantiques.net

Douglas Hamel Antiques
56 Staniels Road,
Chichester, NH 03234
Tel: 603 798 5912
doughamel@shakerantiques.com
www.shakerantiques.com

Joanne & Jack Boardman
522 Joanne Lane, DeKalb, IL 06115
Tel: 815 756 359
boardmanantiques@aol.com

Boym Partners Inc
131 Varick Street, Ste. 915,
New York, NY 10013
Tel: 212 807 8210
www.boym.com

Joan R. Brownstein
24 Parker St, Newbury, MA 01951
Tel: 978 465-1089
Fax: 978 465-2155
www.joanrbrownstein.com

Evergreen Antiques
1249 Third Ave,
New York, NY 10021
Tel: 212 744 5664
www.evergreenantiques.com

Eileen Lane Antiques
150 Thompson Street,
New York, NY 10012
Tel: 212 475 2988
www.eileenlaneantiques.com

Lost City Arts
18 Cooper Square,
New York, NY 10003
Tel: 212 375 0500
www.lostcityarts.com

Lili Marleen
www.lilimarleen.net

Alan Moss
436 Lafayette Street,
New York, NY 10003
Tel: 212 473 1310
Fax: 212 387 9493

Warehouse Provence
1120 Massachusetts Ave, (Rte. 111),
Boxborough, Maine, MA 01719
Tel: 978 266 0200
warehouseprovence@aics.net
www.warehouseprovence.com

GENERAL
Bucks County Antiques Center
Route 202, 8 Skyline Drive,
Lahaska, PA 18914
Tel: 215 794 9180

Camelot Antiques
7871 Ocean Gateway
Easton, MD 21601
Tel: 410 820 4396
camelot@goeastern.net
www.about-antiques.com

**Manhatten Arts
& Antiques Center**
1050 Second Avenue, 55th-56th
Street, New York, NY 10022
Tel: 212 355 4400
Fax: 212 355 4403
info@the-maac.com
www.the-maac.com

Showcase Antiques Center
Route 20, Sturbridge, MA 01566
Tel: 508 347-7190
Fax: 508 347-5420
www.showcaseantiques.com

South Street Antique Markets
600 Bainbridge Street,
Philadelphia, PA 1914

GLASS
Brookside Art Glass
44 North Water Street,
New Bedford, MA 02740
Tel: 508 993 4944
www.brooksideartglass.com

Holsten Galleries
Elm Street, Stockbridge, MA 01262
Tel: 413 298 3044
www.holstengalleries.com

Antiques by Joyce Knutsen
Tel: 315 637 8238 (Summer)
Tel: 352 567 1699 (Winter)

Paul Reichwein
2321 Hershey Ave,
East Petersburg, PA 17520
Tel: 717 569 7637

JEWELRY
Ark Antiques
PO Box 3133,
New Haven, CT 06515
Tel: 203 498 8572
www.ark-antiques.com

Arthur Guy Kaplan
PO Box 1942, Baltimore, MD 21203
Tel: 410 752 2090

LIGHTING
Chameleon Fine Lighting
223 East 59th Street,
New York NY 10022
Tel: 212 355 6300
mail@chameleon59.com
www.chameleon59.com

MARINE ANTIQUES
Hyland Granby Antiques
P.O. Box 457,
Hyannis Port, MA 02647
Tel: 508 771 3070
alan@hylandgranby.com
www.hylandgranby.com

METALWARE
Wayne & Phyllis Hilt
176 Injun Hollow Road,
Haddam Neck, CT 06424
Tel: 860 267 2146
philt@snet.net
www.hiltpewter.com

MODERN
Mix Gallery
17 South Main Street,
Lambertville, NJ 08530
Tel: 609 773 0777
www.mixgallery.com

Moderne Gallery
111 North 3rd Street,
Philadelphia, PA 19106
Tel: 215 923 8536
www.modernegallery.com

Modernism Gallery
800 Douglas Road, Suite 101,
Coral Gables, FL 33134
Tel: 305 442 8743 / 305 632 4725
www.modernism.com

ORIENTAL
Marc Matz Antiques
By appointment only
Tel: 617 460 6200
www.marcmatz.com

Mimi's Antiques
Peter Stitz
Tel: 443 250 0930

PAPERWEIGHTS
The Dunlop Collection
PO Box 6269, Statesville, NC 28687
Tel: 704 871 2626 or
(800) 227 1996

SCIENTIFIC INSTRUMENTS
Edison Gallery
Susanin's, 900 South Clinton Street,
Chicago, IL 60607
Tel: 617 359 4678
www.edisongallery.com

SILVER
Alter Silver Gallery Corp,
Gallery 49A & 50, 1050 Second Ave,
New York, NY 10022
Tel: 212 750 1928 or
917 848 1713
aftersilvergallery@mac.com

Antique Elegance
Tel: 617 484 7556

Argentum
The Leopard's Head, 472 Jackson St,
San Francisco, CA 94111
Tel: 415 296 7757
info@argentumtheleopard.com
www.arguentumtheleopard.com

Chicago Silver
www.chicagosilver.com

Jonathan Trace
PO Box 418, 31 Church Hill Road,
Rifton, NY 12471
Tel: 914 658 7336

Imperial Half Bushel
831 North Howard Street,
Baltimore, MD 21201
Tel: 410 462 1192
www.imperialhalfbushel.com

TEXTILES
Pandora de Balthazar,
Timeles Down and Textiles,
106 North Washington Street,
Round Top, TX 78954
Tel: 979 249 2070
roundtop@antiqueeuropean.com
www.pandoradebalthazar.com

Stephanie's Antiques
28 West 25th Street,
New York, NY 10010
Tel: 212 633 6563

Colette Donovan
98 River Road,
Merrimacport, MA 01860
Tel: 978 346 0614
colettedonovan@adelphia.net

M. Finkel & Daughter
936 Pine Street,
Philadelphia, PA 19107
Tel: 215 627 7797
mailbox@finkelantiques.com
www.samplings.com

Cora Ginsburg
19 East 74th Street,
New York, NY 10021
Tel: 212 744 1352
coraginsburg@rcn.com
www.coraginsburg.com

Nancy Goldsmith
New York, NY
Tel: 212 696 0831

Andrea Hall Levy
PO Box 1243, Riverdale, NY 10471
Tel: 646 441 1726
barangrill@aol.com

Stephen & Carol Huber
40 Ferry Road,
Old Saybrook, CT 06475
Tel: 860 388 6809
hubers@antiquesamplers.com
www.antiquesamplers.com

Fayne Landes Antiques
593 Hansell Road,
Wynnewood, PA 19096
Tel: 610 658 0566

Charlotte Marler
Booth 14, 1528 West 25th Street,
New York, NY 10010
Tel: 212 367 8808
char_marler@hotmail.com

TRIBAL ART
Arte Primitivo
Howard S. Rose Gallery,
3 East 65th Street, Suite 2,
New York, NY 10021
Tel.: 212.570.6999
www.arteprimitivo.com

Marcy Burns American Indian Arts
525 East 72nd Sreet,
New York, NY 10021
Tel: 212 439 9257
marcy@marcyburns.com
www.marcyburns.com

Domas & Gray Gallery
Tel: 228 467 5294
www.domasandgraygallery.com

Elliot & Grace Snyder
PO Box 598,
South Egremont, MA 01258
Tel: 413 528 3581

Hurst Gallery
53 Mount Auburn Street,
Cambridge, MA 02138
Tel: 617 491 6888
manager@hurstgallery.com
www.hurstgallery.com

Morning Star Gallery
513 Canyon Road,
Santa Fe, NM 87501
Tel: 505 982 8187
www.morningstargallery.com

Myers & Duncan
12 East 86th Street, Suite 239,
New York, NY 10028
Tel: 212 472 0115
jmyersprimitives@aol.com

Trotta-Bono American Indian Art
PO Box 34, Shrub Oak, NY 10588
Tel: 914 528 6604
tb788183@aol.com

CANADIAN SPECIALISTS

The Canadian Antique Dealers Association
PO Box 131, Bloor Street West,
Toronto, Ontario, Canada M5S 3L7
Tel: 416 483 1481
cada@bellnet.ca
www.cadinfo.com

CANADIANA

Antiquites Gerard Funkenberg & Jean Drapeau
900 Massawippi, North Hatley,
Quebec, Canada J0B 2C0
Tel: 819 842 2725

The Blue Pump
178 Davenport Road, Toronto,
Ontario, Canada M5R 172
Tel: 416 944 1673
john@thebluepump.com
www.thebluepump.com

Ingram Antiques & Collectibles
669 Mt. Pleasant Road, Toronto,
Ontario, Canada M4S 2N2
Tel: 416 484 4601

Old Canada Country Antiques
#407-17765 65a Ave, Surrey, British
Columbia, Canada V3S 5N4
Tel: 604 575 2577
Fax: 604 575 2573

2227 Granville St,
Vancouver, Canada V6H 3G1
Tel: 604 731 2576
www.oldcanadacountry.com

CERAMICS

Cynthia Findlay
Toronto Antiques Centre,
276 King Street West, Toronto,
Ontario, Canada M5V 1J2
Tel: 416 260 9057
call@cynthiafindlay.com
www.cynthiafindlay.com

Pam Ferrazzutti Antiques
Toronto Antiques Centre,
276 King Street West, Toronto,
Ontario, Canada M5V 1J2
Tel: 416 260 0325
pam@pamferrazzuttiantiques.com
www.pamferrazzuttiantiques.com

Staffordshire House
1 Chestnut Park Road, Toronto,
Ontario, Canada M4W 1W4
Tel: 416 929 3258
jjd@aol.com
www.staffordshirehouse.com

FINE ART

Barbara M. Mitchell
Tel: 416 699 5582
fineartsbarbara@hotmail.com

FURNITURE

Croix-Crest Antiques
49 Mary Street, St. Andrews, New
Brunswick, Canada E5B 1S5
Tel: 506 529 4693
Fax: 506 529 8734

Faith Grant
The Connoisseur's Shop Ltd.
1156 Fort Street, Victoria, British
Columbia, Canada V8V 3K8
Tel: 250 383 0121
Fax: 250 383 0121
info@faithgrantantiques.com
www.faithgrantantiques.com

Howard & Co.
158 Davenport Road, Toronto,
Ontario, Canada M5R 1J2
Tel: 416 922 7966
bhoward@on.aibn.com

Jonny's Antiques
Four Season's Hotel, 21 Avenue Rd,
Toronto, Ontario, Canada M5R 2G1
Tel: 416 928 0205
jonnysantiques@rogers.com

Lorenz Antiques Ltd.
701 Mount Pleasant Rd, Toronto,
Ontario, Canada M4S 2N4
Tel: 416 487 2066
info@lorenzantiques.com
www.lorenzantiques.com

Maus Park Antiques
176 Cumberland Street, Toronto,
Ontario, Canada M5R 1A8
Tel: 416 944 9781
mauspark@bellnet.ca
www.mausparkantiques

Milord Antiques
1870 Notre-Dame St W., Montreal,
Quebec, Canada H3L 1M6
Tel: 514 933 2433
Fax: 514 933 2539
www.milordantiques.com
showroom@milordantiques.com

The Paisley Shop
77 Yorkville Avenue, Toronto,
Ontario, Canada M5R 1C1
Tel: 416 923 5830
Fax: 416 923 2694
www.paisleyshop.com

Richard Rumi & Co. Antiques
55 Woodlawn Ave, Mississauga,
Ontario, Canada L5G 3K7
Tel: 905 274 3616
Fax: 905 274 3617
www.rumiantiques.com

Shand Galleries
Toronto Antiques Centre, 276 King
Street West, Toronto, Ontario,
Canada M5V 1J2
Tel: 416 260 9056
Fax: 416 260 9056

R.H.V. Tee & Son (England) Ltd.
7963 Granville Street, Vancouver,
British Columbia, Canada V6P 4Z3
Tel: 604 263 2791
Fax: 604 263 2339
info@teeantiques.com
www.teeantiques.com

GENERAL

Floyd & Rita's Antiques
Toronto Antiques Centre,
276 King Street West, Toronto,
Ontario, Canada M5V 1J2
Tel: 416 260 9066
antiques@floydrita.com
www.floydrita.com

Toronto Antiques Centre
276 King Street West, Toronto,
Ontario, Canada M5V 1J2
Tel: 416 345 9941
www.torontoantiquectr.com

Can/Am Antiques
760 Golf Club Road, Fredericton,
New Brunswick, Canada E3B 756
Tel: 506 455 2005
jon@theoldriverlodge.net
www.rubylane.com/shops/can-
tiquesnb

JEWELRY

Fraleigh Jewellers
1977 Yonge Street, Toronto, Ontario,
Canada M4S 1Z6
Tel: 416 483 1481
rfraleigh@sympatico.ca

Fiona Kenny Antiques
Tel: 905 682 0090
merday@cogeco.ca
www.fionakennyantiques.com

LIGHTING

Andrew W. Zegers Antiques
25 Rodman Street, St Catherines,
Ontario, Canada L2R 5C9
Tel: 905 685 4643

ORIENTAL

Pao & Molkte Ltd.
Four Seasons Hotel, 21 Avenue
Road, Toronto, Ontario,
Canada M5R 2G1
Tel: 416 925 6197
paomoltke@mail.com

Topper Gallery
1111 Finch Avenue West,
Toronto, Ontario, Canada M3J 2E5
Tel: 416 663 7554

TRIBAL

Jamieson Tribal Art
Golden Chariot Productions,
468 Wellington West Street,
Suite 201, Toronto, Ontario, Canada
M5V 1E3
Tel: 416 569 1396
www.jamiesontribalart.com

SILVER

Richard Flensted-Holder
By appointment only
Tel: 416 961 3414

Louis Wine Ltd.
140 Yorkville Avenue, Toronto,
Ontario, Canada M5R 1C2
Tel: 416 929 9333
louiswine@rogers.com
www.louiswine.com

INDEX TO ADVERTISERS

INDEX